JAMES JOYCE

James Joyce

A POLITICAL LIFE

FRANK CALLANAN

PRINCETON UNIVERSITY PRESS
PRINCETON & OXFORD

Published by Princeton University Press
41 William Street, Princeton, New Jersey 08540
99 Banbury Road, Oxford OX2 6JX

press.princeton.edu

GPSR Authorized Representative: Easy Access System Europe - Mustamäe tee 50, 10621 Tallinn, Estonia, gpsr.requests@easproject.com

ISBN 9780691227979
ISBN (epub) 9780691287478
ISBN (PDF) 9780691228099
Library of Congress Control Number: 2025944248

British Library Cataloging-in-Publication Data is available

Editorial: Ben Tate, Josh Drake
Production Editorial: Jenny Wolkowicki
Jacket design: Hunter Finch
Production: Danielle Amatucci
Publicity: Alyssa Sanford (US), Carmen Jimenez (UK)
Copyeditor: Ashley Moore

Jacket image: Courtesy of the Poetry Collection of the University Libraries, University at Buffalo, The State University of New York

This book has been composed in Arno

Printed in the United States of America

10 9 8 7 6 5 4 3 2 1

—O, don't ask me such questions, Madden. You can use these phrases of the platform but I can't.

—But surely you have some political opinions, man!

—I am going to think them out. I am an artist, don't you see? . . . How the devil can you expect me to settle everything all at once? Give me time.

JAMES JOYCE, *STEPHEN HERO*

CONTENTS

List of Illustrations ix

Foreword xi

Editors' Preface xxiii

Acknowledgements xxix

Abbreviations xxxi

PART I. IRELAND 1

Introduction 3

1 The Shade of Parnell 17

2 John Stanislaus Joyce 44

3 Four Friends of the Father 113

4 The 'Dead King' 152

5 'Christ and Caesar': The Origins of Joyce's Thesis of the 'Two Masters' 195

6 Joyce in University College, Dublin 256

7 Four Friends from University College 287

8 'The Language of the Outlaw' 354

9 Moving towards Exile: Encountering Literary and Radical Dublin, 1902–4 399

PART II. EXILE 473

Introduction 475

10 The Politics of *Stephen Hero* 483

11 'Professing to be a Socialist' 510

12 Writing *Dubliners* in Exile 542

13 Reading Ireland from Exile 590

14 The Triestine Joyce 630

15 Joyce's Triestine Lectures and Articles, 1907–10 662

16 Exile Affirmed 712

17 'The Society of Jewses': Gestating Bloom 766

18 Passing into Silence 810

Coda 849

Bibliography of Secondary Sources 853

Index 871

ILLUSTRATIONS

1.1. Charles Stewart Parnell 19

1.2. Timothy Michael Healy 25

2.1. John Stanislaus Joyce, May Joyce, her father John Murray, and James Joyce, aged six 73

2.2. Joyce coat of arms 78

2.3. Portrait of John Stanislaus Joyce by Patrick Tuohy 110

6.1. University College, Dublin graduation class 1902 260

7.1. Francis and Hanna Sheehy-Skeffington 291

7.2. Thomas Michael Kettle 311

7.3. James Joyce and college friends George Clancy and John Francis Byrne, 1900–1901 336

7.4. John Francis Byrne 352

8.1. Sketch of John Francis Taylor by James Walker 370

9.1. Arthur Griffith 425

11.1. Guglielmo Ferrero 529

14.1. Ettore Schmitz (Italo Svevo) 637

14.2. Silvio Benco 660

15.1. Myles Joyce 696

16.1. Giorgio and Lucia Joyce, with kitten, in Trieste, about 1910 724

16.2. 'The Shade of Parnell', *Sinn Féin*, 15 January 1910 732

17.1. Synagogue of Trieste 797

17.2. James Joyce's sketch of Leopold Bloom 800

18.1. Joyce with guitar in Zurich 824

FOREWORD

Robert Spoo

'. . . but hunt me the journeyon, iteritinerant, the kal his course, amid the semitary of Somnionia.'[1]

THESE STRANGE, reverberant words from Book IV of James Joyce's last work, *Finnegans Wake,* haunt and hunt through the pages of Frank Callanan's *James Joyce: A Political Life* as a knelling doom and a recurring promise. The doom relates to the tragedy that befell the leader of the Irish Parliamentary Party, Charles Stewart Parnell (1846–1891), when, on what had seemed the verge of a consummated Irish Home Rule bill, revelations of his years-long affair with a married woman, Katharine O'Shea, split the Irish party and unleashed a remorseless political hunting that hastened the deposed leader's death (one meaning of 'hunt me . . . amid the semitary'). The promise relates to Callanan's intention to probe fully the Parnellian themes and motifs of *Finnegans Wake* and thereby link up the birth of Joyce's political consciousness in 1890s Ireland with its full maturation in the war-menaced Europe of the late 1930s. Though tantalising elucidations of the *Wake* appear throughout this volume, and there is a moving analysis of the 'hunt me' passage in its Coda, Callanan's own untimely death prevented him from completing Joyce's political biography as he had envisioned it. Yet he left behind this large, luminous work, which takes the story from Joyce's early Dublin years up to his departure from Trieste in 1915. And unfinished though

1. *FW* 594.7–8.

it is, this book is quite simply the most penetrating and eloquent account of Joyce's politics that has ever been published.[2]

I first met Frank Callanan when his friend, the Irish Supreme Court Justice Adrian Hardiman, put together a lunch for the three of us at the Lord Edward in Christchurch Place, Dublin, in 2007. I had met Justice Hardiman a few days earlier, aware of his reputation as an eminent judge and barrister, but I was surprised to learn that he was also a Joyce scholar; he in his turn knew that I was a Joyce scholar but was surprised to discover that I was also a lawyer. Hardiman and Callanan had both taken degrees in history at University College Dublin before preparing for the law. When I met him, Callanan, a barrister and senior counsel, had already written a much-admired history of the hounding of Parnell by political and religious forces (*The Parnell Split, 1890–91*) and a provocative biography of Timothy Michael Healy (1855–1931), the supporter of Parnell who turned against him in the party Split and became one of the masters of the hunt that brought him down.[3] Our triangulated lunch in 2007 was a leisurely, talk-filled affair, spirited in all senses, in that large upper room of the Lord Edward with its great bay windows. Law, politics, history, Joyce—these and other themes wound in and out. Justice Hardiman's bright baritone cut through the dim air, learned, witty, with cadenzas of mimicry of politicians and lawyers. Callanan's lower, slower voice parried with carefully chosen ironies and unhurried judgements. It was a three-hour lunch to remember.

This was shortly before Callanan began publishing his articles on Joyce that would grow into the present volume, so I was not fully aware at the time of the depth of his Joycean engagement. I knew that Justice Hardiman was assembling a volume that would become *Joyce in Court: James Joyce and the Law*, published posthumously as an uncompleted project with the assistance of Luca Crispi, who is also among the

2. Among studies addressing this subject, Dominic Manganiello's *Joyce's Politics* (London: Routledge and Kegan Paul, 2016), first published in 1980, is a valuable thematic account, particularly regarding Joyce's reading of socialist and anarchist writers and other post-exile influences.

3. Frank Callanan, *The Parnell Split, 1890–91* (Cork: Cork University Press, 1992); Frank Callanan, *T. M. Healy* (Cork: Cork University Press, 1996).

preparers of the present volume. Hardiman's book follows law in its various forms through Joyce's life and writings—thus both Joyce in court and the court in Joyce—and argues that history, law, and the evidentiary problems that attend both as truth-seeking apparatuses are critical for understanding him. *Joyce in Court* contends that the Irish author was profoundly 'sceptical about the motives and practices of society's enforcers, uniformed or otherwise', and that this scepticism was 'rooted in his concrete experiences as a very young man and in his heritage of historical memory'.[4] Among the events that Hardiman identifies as shaking the young Joyce's confidence in a solid world of fact and fairness was the persecution of Parnell and the subsequent failure of parliamentary politics as a conduit of Irish independence. The long political futility that followed the 1890 Split gave 'past events', Hardiman argues, 'a personal, social and political resonance in Ireland which time would have eroded anywhere else'.[5] Both Callanan and Hardiman locate in the Parnell calamity a formative disturbance that contributed to Joyce's later sceptical, anti-teleological engrossment with themes of incompleteness, betrayal, doubt, and political and social injustice.

No one was better qualified than Callanan to write of the political wounding and awakening that Joyce experienced as a boy of eight or nine years when Parnell was toppled from power. Callanan asks a question that is rarely asked about writers in quite this way: What was the primal scene that hurt Joyce into politics? His answer, richly unfolding through the pages of this book, is that the young Joyce's intellectual precocity, his unusual alertness to injustice, and the complex patterns of his home life made him peculiarly receptive to the Parnell Split and its precipitated result. This is no simplistically assigned cause but rather a careful tracing of a rare political sensibility in the shaping contexts of biography, history, and literary self-representation. Yet, for all the details

4. Adrian Hardiman, *Joyce in Court: James Joyce and the Law* (London: Head of Zeus, 2017), 18, 19, 38. Observations in this paragraph and the previous one are developed more fully in 'Joyce at the Bar', my review of Hardiman's book in the *James Joyce Literary Supplement* 33 (Spring 2019): 11–13.

5. Hardiman, *Joyce in Court*, 28.

he assembles, Callanan never loses sight of the unique trauma inflicted by Parnell's fall. The effect of the Dreyfus Affair on Marcel Proust is not comparable, because Proust was in his twenties when Alfred Dreyfus was wrongfully convicted and sentenced to imprisonment on Devil's Island. In 1890–91, Joyce was closer to the age of the young protagonist of *À la recherche du temps perdu*, for whom a mother's withheld goodnight kiss has 'staggering consequences',[6] not unlike the aftershocks Callanan locates (though in a political register) in Joyce's personal and textual revisitations of the Parnell Affair.

There is something Proustian in the opulent architecture of Callanan's account of Joyce, as well as in his story of the young Irishman's search for lost political time. 'The depth and directness of the impact of the Split on Joyce as a child', writes Callanan, 'was unusual and left him with a sense of temporality different from that of his contemporaries'.[7] Yet it was not a mother's withheld affection but a father's uninhibited political passion that figured in Joyce's Parnellian initiation. Dissenting from other scholars, Callanan argues that John Stanislaus Joyce had not been an active supporter of Parnell until the Split stimulated his ardent sympathy for the embattled leader. This impulsive political gallantry affected his young son deeply, Callanan contends, and is registered directly in the Christmas dinner feud over the recently deceased Parnell in *A Portrait of the Artist as a Young Man* and, less directly, in *Finnegans Wake*'s themes of fall and redemption that pay distant homage to John Stanislaus's brief rise to political heroism. Callanan offers a startlingly original interpretation of Joyce's father that is attentive to that figure's remarkable composition: Fenian anticlericalism, humorous sentimentality, restless sociability, a faintly archaic remoteness from the Irish nationalism of his moment. The political eccentricity of John Stanislaus reasserted itself in his son's untimely political temporality, his 'recusant Parnellism'.[8] Yet the father's sudden Parnellite intensity burned less visibly in the son's brooding allegiance.

6. Michael Wood, *Marcel Proust* (Oxford: Oxford University Press, 2023), 23.

7. See 'introduction', 5.

8. See chapter 1, 35.

Callanan is too theoretically restrained to invoke concepts such as primal scene, family romance, or any overt Freudianism in describing the young Joyce's exposure to the fall of Parnell. Yet we may accept Callanan's subtle invitation to consider the psychological impact of politics, as well as his careful rehabilitation of a practice—perhaps too hastily discredited by Hugh Kenner and other critics[9]—of looking to Joyce's fictions as qualified resources for recovering elements of his life. The core transgressions of which Parnell was vociferously accused were adultery, debauchery, and theft of public funds; his opponents—especially Healy—were savage in their taunting denunciations and their threats to repeat them wherever Parnell showed himself in public.[10] In *A Portrait*, the young Stephen Dedalus is exposed to this scandal talk during the political detonations of his home life; and when he returns to school after the Christmas holiday, he hears more scandal when rumours circulate that the misdeeds of certain boys—homosexual petting and theft of cash are hinted—are causing the priests of the school to impose a harsh, punitive discipline on the entire student body.[11] When Stephen himself is unfairly punished by one of the Jesuit masters, he takes his complaint to the school's rector and obtains a measure of justice. Though his victory is a personal one, it is also, in its way, a heroic blow struck for all his schoolfellows, who cheer him when he comes from the rector's office.[12] The cluster of motifs—charges of sexual indiscretion and theft, priestly interference, generalised injustice—suggests that Stephen has been unconsciously emulating his father's anticlerical Parnellism and avenging the dead leader's victimisation, perhaps even becoming a local Parnell leading his fellows out of the priest-ridden house of bondage. Such a reading is consonant with

9. See, for example, Hugh Kenner, 'The *Portrait* in Perspective', in *Dublin's Joyce* (1955; repr., New York: Columbia University Press, 1987), 109–33.

10. For Healy's pursuit of the politically wounded Parnell, see Callanan, *Parnell Split*, 110–38.

11. For sustained discussion of scandal in Joyce's culture and writings, see Margot Gayle Backus, *Scandal Work: James Joyce, the New Journalism, and the Home Rule Newspaper Wars* (Notre Dame, IN: University of Notre Dame Press, 2013).

12. *P* 1.1456–848.

Callanan's tracing of the familial and psychological roots of Joyce's own early Parnellism.

Callanan notices something that has escaped many scholars: the slow, patient intentness with which Joyce absorbed the Irish political scene as a young man. This was Joyce's 'induction into the Irish political.'[13] The word 'induction', appearing several times in this book, suggests something formal, almost ceremonial, in the political development of Joyce, a candidacy for which he carefully prepared himself. Callanan offers other formulations for this process: Joyce's 'acquisition of a fealty to Parnell as a boy'; his 'early engagement with the Split'; his 'slow filtration of the political.'[14] Joyce's self-conscious political formation contributed to his enigmatic manner at University College Dublin and to the silence and cunning of his voluntary exile on the Continent a few years later. This political incrementalism contrasted with the spasmodic commitments of others. 'I distrust all enthusiasms', the young Joyce remarked of Irish nationalist fervour.[15] Politics should be compared and correlated before being internalised. 'By thinking of things you could understand them', concludes the young Stephen Dedalus.[16] Years later, working as a temporary and reluctant teacher, Stephen calls himself a 'learner rather' who distrusts 'those big words . . . which make us so unhappy.'[17]

Parnell remained a potent though latent idea for the young Joyce: 'His Parnellism as an active principle was in abeyance', Callanan notes, 'and he veiled the intensity of his imaginative engagement with Parnell.'[18] So we might add 'incubation' to 'induction' in describing Joyce's acquired political thought. His scrutiny of Italian politics from his vantage in Trieste—socialism, revolutionary syndicalism, anarchism, irredentism—exhibited an almost Thomistic fastidiousness of

13. See chapter 1, 30.

14. See chapter 1, 30; chapter 4, 161; chapter 7, 308.

15. Mary Colum and Padraic Colum, *Our Friend James Joyce* (New York: Doubleday, 1958), 20.

16. *P* 1.1269.

17. *U* 2.264, 403.

18. See chapter 4, 194.

purpose and organisation. He was never apolitical, according to Callanan, even when he seemed to have removed himself to regions of artistic independence. After his politically charged journalism and lecturing of 1907–12, Joyce's political reticence was the 'codification of a principle of authorial extra-textual silence'.[19] 'Extratextual' is the key word here, for the texts from *A Portrait* to *Finnegans Wake* engage and contest the political again and again, even as they render Parnell more and more obliquely, as an inhabitant of popular imagination rather than a historical figure.

This obliqueness was critical for Joyce's return to Parnell in his fictions. He had 'resolved', Callanan writes, 'not to portray Parnell directly but to catch him in the mirror of his myth in contemporary Ireland', 'taking his cue from public invocations of Parnell's memory'.[20] Thus, the Parnell that Joyce rendered was a residue in the devout popular mind, a figure both cultic and Celtic. This strategic indirection, this avoidance of a frontal presentation, curiously allowed Joyce to rediscover an intimacy with a figure that had long been submerged in the latency of his political novitiate. Parnell could now be approached in the sunlight, but it would be his long shadow that Joyce would depict, a shadow in the double sense of ghost and trace. ('L'ombra di Parnell', translated as 'The Shade of Parnell', is the title of a 1912 article that Joyce wrote for a Triestine newspaper.)[21] Though he was suspicious of features of the Parnell cult that were 'funerary' and 'morbidly exorbitant',[22] he rendered these, too, in his fictions: in the poignant doggerel of Joe Hynes's poem 'The Death of Parnell' in 'Ivy Day in the Committee Room'; and in the myth of Parnell's empty grave and expected return, as glimpsed in the 'Hades' and 'Eumaeus' episodes of *Ulysses*. These lugubrious imaginings were part of the received Parnell and so were entitled to inclusion among Joyce's textual voices.

Frank Callanan's gifts as a literary critic are on full display in this volume. His enviable mastery of history and modern politics, his alert

19. See chapter 18, 832.

20. See chapter 1, 36.

21. *OCPW* 191–96, 240–43.

22. The first quote ('funerary') is from chapter 15, 682; the second is from the Coda, 851.

eye for the telling image or metaphor, and his sure sense of narrative make for fresh readings of texts that have been scrutinised for decades. His analyses of Joyce's 1904 essay 'A Portrait of the Artist', *Stephen Hero,* 'Ivy Day in the Committee Room', the Christmas dinner scene in *A Portrait,* the Moses-Parnell correspondence in the 'Aeolus' episode of *Ulysses,* and the series of political articles and lectures that Joyce produced in Trieste are unrivalled for their penetration and fidelity to detail. Callanan is ever alert to historical effects and political dislocations. He argues convincingly, for example, that the lengthy delay in the publication of *Dubliners,* nearly ten years from the writing of many of the stories, muffled the political resonance of 'Ivy Day' and 'The Dead'. In 1907–8, 'Parnell's memory just about retained some lingering political currency', but by 1914 when the volume finally appeared, 'the generational cycle had turned, and Irish politics was in a markedly different phase with the Home Rule crisis'. With the lapse of years and memories, 'Ivy Day' had lost 'its sharply accusatory contemporary edge'.[23] Joyce's bitterness over the long delay was thus political as much as artistic. Acute observations such as these abound in the present book, rendered in an elegant prose that is often complex but always accessible, musical in its diction and rhythms, and fearless in its conceptual rigor and pursuit.

Callanan sets himself the task of isolating Joyce's essential politics, or his political essence. Beginning with what he takes to be a uniquely perceptive insight—Constantine Curran's characterisation of the youthful Joyce as 'a completely unpolitical Parnellite'[24]—Callanan meticulously compares Joyce with the student minds around him, as if holding slides up to the light to discriminate varying hues of Irish politics. Notably, among Joyce's university fellows, Francis Skeffington (the McCann/MacCann of *Stephen Hero* and *A Portrait*) was dogmatic, pedantic, anti-Parnellite, 'a confused left-utilitarian' who believed—delusionally, Joyce thought—in an alliance of Irish nationalism, post-

23. All quotes are from chapter 12, 565–66.

24. Cited in chapter 1, 32; and chapter 6, 232.

Gladstone Liberalism, and British left politics.[25] Thomas Kettle (a model for Robert Hand in *Exiles*) was pro-Parnell, advocated a European Catholicism, and, in the years after university, sought to reconcile Sinn Féin with the Irish Parliamentary Party. Callanan notes succinctly that Kettle's pro-clerical Parnellism and Skeffington's anticlerical anti-Parnellism exemplified for Joyce the incoherence of Irish politics after the Split.[26] The observant Joyce was taking in the ideological postures and posturings of his comrades, quietly measuring them against his own reserved Parnellite faith, his suspended commitment as a political learner.

Can Joyce, then, be described as an Irish nationalist? Callanan is unequivocal: yes, he declares, 'objectively' so.[27] Joyce believed that Ireland had claims to nationhood and an important literary culture, that it had suffered through conquest but had never ceased to protest it, and that 'the rhetorical power of nationalism [had engendered] a sense of a common political identity, even if his rendering of that power tends to be most discernible when he is resisting or parodying it'.[28] As a 'dissentient' thinker, Joyce's nationalism may also be defined by what it was not, by what he rejected in the culture around him: teleological narratives of predestined political salvation, self-exculpating victimhood and denial of any responsibility for Ireland's humiliated condition, chauvinistic exhibitions and religious bigotries, an over-zealous Irish language revivalism, insular anti-Europeanism, and resistance to modernity. These deficiencies were all part of what Joyce referred to in different contexts and at different times as the 'paralysis' of Irish life, a symptom of the abrupt defeat of political hope in the dead space after 1891, what Callanan evocatively calls the period of 'acrid backwash: the years of disillusionment in the dismal aftermath of the overthrow and death of Parnell'.[29]

25. From chapter 7, 300.

26. From chapter 7.

27. From the introduction, 10n9.

28. From the introduction, 11.

29. From chapter 1, 33.

One of the difficulties of classifying Joyce's nationalism is that the Ireland of his youth cannot properly be thought of as a nation. In a brilliant insight, Callanan argues that 'the statal inchoateness of Ireland' both constrained and liberated Joyce as a writer. On the one hand, Ireland's unsettled pre-statal condition blocked Joyce from completing *Stephen Hero,* a novel conceived of in a bildungsroman tradition dependent on the institutional structures of an established state. On the other hand, the memory of Ireland's political incompleteness and imaginative plasticity made *Finnegans Wake* possible: the 'tractability of the narrative of Ireland became the breach through which coursed all of Joyce's conception of historical and cultural cycles of change and continuity'.[30] Ireland's inchoateness before 1922 is one of the chief justifications for Callanan's immersive approach to Joyce's specifically Irish political initiation, and a source of his disagreements with other scholars who have written on Joyce's politics. If he rejects Richard Ellmann's claim that Joyce moved 'beyond Parnell' to a qualified embrace of Arthur Griffith and thence to a kind of modernist aloofness from politics ('There is in Joyce no "beyond Parnell" in Ellmann's sense'),[31] he also dissents from postcolonial theory's positing of a 'generic anti-imperialism' in Joyce's writing that both relativises his political particularity and lifts it away from its Irish contexts to what Callanan sees as a rather bleakly notional terrain of textual contestation and political retort. Notwithstanding the influences of socialism and anarchism, and his parodic assaults on empire and political authoritarianism in *Ulysses* and *Finnegans Wake,* Joyce's 'relationship to the Irish political', Callanan insists, was and remained 'his intellectual point of departure'.[32]

It is a consoling paradox that Frank Callanan's never-completed volume does so much to complete our understanding of Joyce's political life. This book might also be seen as extending the truncated political life of Parnell in that it shows how deeply that life reached into Joyce's own and animated his efforts to write 'the moral history of

30. See introduction, 14.

31. See chapter 1, 39.

32. See introduction, 13.

[his] country' and 'to forge the uncreated conscience of [his] race'.[33] Writing moral history and forging a racial conscience are grandiose ambitions for a youthful writer to declare, yet when we see, with Callanan's guidance, what Joyce lived through politically during his first thirty years, both in Ireland and in exile abroad, we are more likely to accept these declarations as affidavits of experience.

The spectacle of the unspeakable hunt—from Parnell to Oscar Wilde—was something the young Joyce witnessed, and it is never absent from his idea of the possible fate of any benefactor of Ireland. It is not absent from Callanan's assessments of Joyce either; and *Finnegans Wake*'s 'hunt me the journeyon', with its startling inclusion of 'me' as a quarry of the 'hunt', points beyond its immediate referent in the tracked, weary Parnell to a personal, emotional stake in Irish politics and history that Joyce keenly felt and that Callanan powerfully shared. That feeling is evident in the care and cogency of the present volume and in its tendresse (a favourite word of Callanan's) for its subject. The idea that political aspiration can be more than a brutal hunt grows as the book turns in its final pages to *Finnegans Wake* and its 'bleak social anthropology of hope . . . [for] the potential for human consciousness to translate into political agency'.[34] Joyce's slow induction into the political—a temporal and temperamental exile to match the geographical one—brought him to this bleak, precarious hope. With this book, we can see much more clearly how he got there, and why it matters.

Robert Spoo, Leonard L. Milberg '53 Professor in Irish Letters
Department of English
Princeton University
12 August 2025

33. *Letters II* 134; *P* 5.2789–90.
34. See chapter 18, 841.

EDITORS' PREFACE

IN A LECTURE HE gave about 2006 titled 'Joyce and the Historian of Modern Ireland', Frank Callanan explained how he came to write on Joyce:

> I am an historian of modern Ireland. I have worked and written on Parnell, his enemy Timothy Michael Healy, and on the Irish Parliamentary Party.
>
> I do not profess to be dispassionate. I am drawn to what it is that public men and women do.
>
> When I was writing the Healy book I was increasingly conscious of the potency of Joyce's rendering of Parnell and his myth, particularly in the article 'L'ombra di Parnell' that he published in *Il Piccolo della Sera* in Trieste in May 1912, and in *Finnegans Wake*. I had at the start of the long vacation in 1993 bought a copy of *Finnegans Wake* in Dublin airport on my way to Greece. I read it on the beach; a procedure I strongly recommend. On the last page I inscribed 'Petra, Patmos, 17 August 1993'. I was greatly affected by Joyce's valedictory evocation of the harried Parnell of the Split as the river returns to the sea at the end: 'but hunt me the journeyon, iteritinerant, the kal his course, amid the semitary of Somnionia. Even unto Heliotropolis, the castellated, the enchanting'. This provided the epigraph for the Healy biography.
>
> An interval of some years supervened before, subtly goaded by my friend Patrick Healy, a considerable scholar of Joyce, I began to peck around the relation of Joyce to Parnell with the intention of writing a short monograph. That must be ten years ago. I am now caught up in something that fluctuatingly resembles a politico-historical biography of Joyce.

My interest in Joyce is in some respects deviant. What I most enjoy in Joyce is his treatment of the Irish political, and of Irish history. I believe the acuity of Joyce's political sensibility, especially in relation to the Ireland of his lifetime, has remained weirdly underestimated and under-analysed.

The relationship of Joyce and the Irish historian is a curious one. In the first place, there is a sense in which Joyce has only in relatively recent times come to belong to Irish history. That is the sense described by Conor Cruise O'Brien in the magnificent opening of his essay 'The Parnellism of Seán O'Faoláin':

'There is for all of us a twilight zone of time, stretching back for a generation or two before we were born, which never quite belong to the rest of history. Our elders have talked their memories into our memories until we have come to possess some sense of continuity exceeding and traversing our own individual being.'

It is not merely that Joyce can now be set in historical context. The passage of time, and the cycle of Irish politics since independence, have been quite extraordinarily flattering to Joyce's political judgement and his espousal of a critical Irish nationalism. Joyce moreover is not merely a subject of history. He has become, both biographically and imaginatively through his works, a type of historical source which informs the contemporary historical perception in Ireland of the country in the era in which he lived and of which he wrote.

Historians of modern Ireland have for the most part given Joyce a wide berth. The grudging assessment of Joyce and axiomatic preference for Yeats enunciated in F.S.L. Lyons' uncharacteristically obtuse 1970 essay 'James Joyce's Dublin' is in some respects representative.

One does not of course have to be a historian to write on historical subjects. Richard Ellmann's biography of Joyce is marked by a high historical sensibility. He doesn't get Joyce's politics wrong, although he fails fully to apprehend its significance.

There has been something of a disciplinary stand-off. Irish historians have tended to seize the high ground, and what they have written on modern Ireland has not always been Joyce-friendly, in the sense of addressing the interests of Joyceans. On the other hand, some writers on Joyce's politics have been prepared to make remarkably sweeping historical generalisations as if there was no such thing as, or not a lot to, historical scholarship.

I don't for a moment suggest that writing about Joyce is confined by the world that is contemporary to him, nor by his subjective intentionality where that can be established. I am merely saying that in relation to Irish politics and history, on issues where Joyce has expressed himself, that expression has to be acknowledged and taken account of.

I say this because one does sometimes read things dogmatically imputing views to Joyce that one knows he would—justifiably on the basis of what he had written—have responded to with a thin smile, a dismissive gleam of his spectacles, or perhaps a light tenor snort. One should not in positing an argument about a person need to be fortified by the reflection that she or he is no longer around to scorn it.

One should not fit up a writer with convictions or intentions of a semi-ideological character without acknowledging the intelligence, and pertinacious elegance of his own negotiation of the ideological that is the glittering intellectual legacy of his schooling in Irish nationalism.

There is a matter in the end of intellectual good faith for a historian or biographer. It could be considered a disciplinary predisposition. Perhaps it is a prejudice of sorts. It is also a lot more fun.

Frank would go on to work for another fifteen years on his 'politico-historical biography' of Joyce. To Ruán Magan, his collaborator on their distinguished documentary, *100 Years of 'Ulysses'* (broadcast RTE, 2 February 2022), he explained 'that one typically works on Joyce for years before being able to formulate any valid propositions. . . . My own early scribblings were pretty much worthless.' In 2019, with the end of his book finally in sight, he signed a contract with Princeton University Press. On 12 December 2021, Frank died suddenly and unexpectedly at home in Dublin.

In mourning, it became imperative to us to honour his life's work and prepare his book for publication. The editorial team suggested itself: With

Margaret O'Callaghan, professor of modern Irish history and politics in Queen's University Belfast, Frank had carried on an unbroken dialogue on Irish history since they were students in University College Dublin, particularly around the period 1880–1920, in which they both specialised. Frank always credited meeting Luca Crispi, associate professor of James Joyce studies and modernism at University College Dublin, with professionalising his approach to Joyce studies. Through Peter Kennealy, deputy director and politics specialist at the European University Institute Library in Florence and senior commissioning editor at ECPR (European Consortium for Political Research) Press, and another close friend since college, Frank was kept on top of current movements in political science research. Bridget Hourican, Frank's partner for a decade, and wife for eighteen months, was working on her own book on James Clarence Mangan throughout their time together. Mangan was Joyce's favourite Irish poet and a significant influence on him.

Over the years, Frank had shared multiple drafts of his work in progress with all of us, as well as publishing articles in the *Dublin James Joyce Journal*, edited by Luca. We knew that Frank's working method was chronological and comprehensive, so we were unsurprised, if greatly relieved, to find that while the text that he left was inevitably truncated—it lacks Joyce's later years—it was not fragmentary or partial; the chapters were completed and sequential. This simplified our task: There was no question of having to rewrite or finish sections (fortunately, since Frank's cadence is inimitable) and little need for deletion. Our role has been to rearrange certain sections, reorganise some chapters, check for consistency, tidy up the footnotes, and clarify the working titles and subtitles that Frank left.

The book as published is as Frank wrote and intended, up until the point that it breaks off. It is a complete account of Joyce's life and political thought up until 1915, with a final chapter that covers his move to Zurich in the First World War and his subsequent move to Paris. Had he lived, Frank would have had more to say on Joyce's politics in the 1920s and 1930s, but the book was always intended to be very heavily weighted to Joyce's formative years in Dublin and early exile in Trieste and Rome, the years when, in Frank's telling, Joyce was working out his political position.

Until 1912, Joyce wrote and lectured on political matters in articles and discourses as well as reading very widely in politics, including whatever Irish newspapers he could get sent to him in Trieste and Rome. He made his last public political statement in his article 'L'ombra di Parnell' for *Il Piccola della Sera*, published on 16 May 1912, three months before his final visit to Ireland. He lived on through the dramas of the early twentieth century, but he did not comment publicly—and in private only rarely and obliquely—on the First World War, Easter 1916, Irish independence or the Irish Civil War, the rise of fascism, or the outbreak of the Second World War.

Joyce famously ended *A Portrait*, completed in 1914 and published in 1916, with the avowal that Stephen Dedalus should pass into 'silence, exile and cunning'. This dictum could be said to apply to Joyce himself. 'Silence' refers to his public silence on politics, and 'exile' to the exile affirmed by his final departure from Dublin on 11 September 1912, the day of the destruction of the print run of *Dubliners*. Frank characterises the period 1904–12 as Joyce's 'years of demi-exile, without foreclosure of return'.[1] Frank's intention was to write an intellectual and political biography of Joyce till 1941, but we see a strange symmetry to his book ending as Joyce passes into full exile and extratextual silence on politics.

Bridget Hourican *Margaret O'Callaghan*
Luca Crispi *Peter Kennealy*

1. See introduction to Part II, 475.

ACKNOWLEDGEMENTS

IN THE NORMAL COURSE OF EVENTS, an author keeps a list, if only a mental one, of all the institutions, libraries and archives, colleagues, and friends to whom he or she remains indebted for their material help, moral support, intellectual stimulus, or simply good company at the end of the day. The author of this work did not live to compile such a list, but the acknowledgements in his previous books were both extensive and fulsome. Frank never forgot that even the best endeavours of a scholar depend for their success on networks of support both personal and professional, and he was always meticulous in expressing his gratitude to all those who helped, whether their contribution was large or small.

This book was more than twenty years in the making, and the editors will not attempt to guess at such a list. Many scholars and institutions are already acknowledged in the notes, and Frank's extensive circle of friends, colleagues, fellow scholars, acquaintances, and sparring partners will know of their own involvement, as will his immediate family. Frank's literary agent and friend, Ivan Mulcahy, deserves a special mention not only for placing the original project with an outstanding publisher but also for his role in keeping the project on the road after Frank's sudden death in December 2021. Richard Bourke was exceptionally helpful with support and advice, both to Frank and the editors.

Frank's editor at Princeton University Press, Ben Tate, is to be thanked for his sustained involvement and consistent support. The anonymous reviewers of the Press gave time to reading the lengthy typescript and made many invaluable suggestions for improvement. Warm acknowledgement is due to Dr. James McGeachie for his wise and witty editing; to Patrick Gaffey for his tireless work on the scholarly apparatus of footnotes, references, and bibliography; to Niels Caul for his excellent work in sourcing images; to Eoin MacNally for his indispensable help with the index; and to the eagle-eyed copy editors of the Press for their relentless pursuit of precision. The online textual resources provided for free by the Internet Archive and JSTOR proved invaluable in answering their queries.

ABBREVIATIONS

Joyce's Works

CW *The Critical Writings of James Joyce*, ed. Ellsworth Mason and Richard Ellmann (New York: Viking, 1959)

D *Dubliners: Authoritative Text, Contexts, Criticism*, ed. Margot Norris, text edited by Hans Walter Gabler with Walter Hettche (New York: Norton, 2006)

E *Exiles: A Play in Three Acts* (New York: Viking, 1951)

FW *Finnegans Wake* (London: Faber, 1975); cited by page and line number

GJ *Giacomo Joyce*, ed. Richard Ellmann (New York: Viking, 1968)

LETTERS I *Letters of James Joyce*, vol. 1, ed. Stuart Gilbert (New York: Viking, 1957)

LETTERS II *Letters of James Joyce*, vol. 2, ed. Richard Ellmann (New York: Viking, 1966)

LETTERS III *Letters of James Joyce*, vol. 3, ed. Richard Ellmann (New York: Viking, 1966)

OCPW *Occasional, Critical, and Political Writing*, ed. Kevin Barry (Oxford: Oxford University Press, 2008)

P *A Portrait of the Artist as a Young Man: Authoritative Text, Contexts, Criticism*, ed. John Paul Riquelme, text edited by Hans Walter Gabler with Walter Hettche (New York: Norton, 2007); cited by chapter and line number

PSW *Poems and Shorter Writings* (London: Faber and Faber, 2001)

SH *Stephen Hero*, ed. Theodore Spencer, John J. Slocum, and Herbert Cahoon (New York: New Directions, 1963)

SL *Selected Letters of James Joyce*, ed. Richard Ellmann (New York: Viking, 1975)

U *Ulysses*, ed. Hans Walter Gabler (New York: Garland, 1986); cited by episode and line number

Secondary Sources

DIB *Dictionary of Irish Biography: From the Earliest Times to the Year 2002* (Cambridge: Cambridge University Press, 2009)

ODNB *Oxford Dictionary of National Biography: From the Earliest Times to the Year 2000* (Oxford: Oxford University Press, 2004)

Archival Sources

BL British Library

BM British Museum

NAI National Archives of Ireland

NLI National Library of Ireland

TCD Trinity College Dublin

UCD University College Dublin

JAMES JOYCE

PART I

Ireland

Introduction

> I'm not at all impressed by the expression that he was not interested in politics, that he was interested in style: I have the impression of somebody who had walked so much faster than the others, that he got there first, and he had to sit down and wait for a long, long time for the others to come along.
>
> —MARIA JOLAS, 1975[1]

THIS IS A POLITICAL AND INTELLECTUAL biographical treatment of James Joyce before he left Ireland in 1904, and in the first phase of what he characterised as exile in Trieste, and afterwards in Zurich.

Little has been written directly on Joyce's political formation. Dominic Manganiello's excellent *Joyce's Politics* (1980)[2] is a thematic analysis of Joyce's politics in its Irish and European aspects. I have taken an approach that is closer to that of political biography. Joyce was not of course a politician, nor was he politically engaged, but he was observant of politics and had an acute sense of the significance of the political, and his oeuvre stands in a defined relationship to the politics of Irish independence. The exercise of mapping Joyce as exactly as possible to

1. J. Aubert and M. Jolas, eds., *Joyce and Paris, 1902 . . . 1920–1940 . . . 1975: Papers from the Fifth International James Joyce Symposium, Paris, 16–20 June 1975* (Paris: Editions du CNRS, 1979), 14. Jolas was participating in a *colloque* on 'political perspectives on Joyce's work'.

2. Dominic Manganiello, *Joyce's Politics* (London: Routledge and Kegan Paul, 1980).

contemporary issues, movements, and personalities reconfigures the political understanding of Joyce. The warrant for that approach is principally in relation to the Joyce of Ireland and the Joyce of early exile, the focus of this book, but it also affords the most fecund approach to his political thinking in his middle and late periods of exile, when he wrote *Ulysses* and *Finnegans Wake*, and shows how his political thinking contributed to his literary modernism and set that modernism apart, and how those works which had Irish settings were as European in conception as they were 'Irish'. It is an approach that does something to retrieve the originality and coherence of Joyce's apprehension of the political in Ireland and in Europe, as he negotiated the vicissitudes of his era, from the late nineteenth into the first half of the twentieth century.

This narrative of Joyce's intellectual development in Ireland and early exile seeks to frame his life, thought, and writings in their political and cultural settings in Ireland and Europe. Its subject is Joyce's revolt against the post–Parnell Split Catholic Ireland in which he grew up, and the origins of his endeavour to understand and render imaginatively the political culture of Ireland. What Joyce observed and experienced before he left Ireland in 1904 informed his treatment of his country in his writings through his career; most obviously it fills the pages of *Ulysses*, which he set on a date some four months before his leaving. This coincided with the moment, immediately precipitated by his relationship with Nora Barnacle, when his mind had begun to turn towards imminent exile.

Joyce left Dublin with Nora from the North Wall on 8 October 1904 on a journey that took them through London, Paris, Zurich, and then Trieste to Pola, which they reached on 30 October. At the start of March 1905, they found their way back to Trieste. This was the commencement of Joyce's long exilic odyssey. He was to make three return visits to Ireland between 1909 and 1912. The third visit ended catastrophically with the aborting of an Irish publication of *Dubliners*. On

11 October 1912, he left Dublin with Nora and their children, Giorgio and Lucia. He would never again return to Ireland.

The span of Joyce's twenty-two and a half years in Ireland, while cut short—he was to live twice as long on the continent of Europe as he had in Ireland—encompassed an immensely significant period of Irish history. At the date of Joyce's birth, 2 February 1882, Charles Stewart Parnell was establishing his leadership of Irish nationalism. Parnell's fall in the Split of 1890–91 imposed itself on Joyce's political consciousness as a child. His adolescence was passed in the years of disenchantment that followed Parnell's death, but which saw the first stirrings of what would become the successor movements to the Irish Parliamentary Party that Parnell had led.

Joyce entered into elective political consciousness with the death of Parnell. He had some vague awareness of the inception of the Parnell Split in December 1890 (when he was eight) and an exposure—albeit at second hand, in school and at home—to the death of Parnell on 6 October 1891 (when he was nine) and its immediate aftermath. The Split had a searing effect on Joyce, deeper than that on other members of his age cohort. The reasons for the Split's peculiar impact on him are hard to calibrate with precision: some combination of extreme intellectual precocity, the refusal of a child to acquiesce to an unjust outcome, and the manner in which the Split and Parnell's death—which were his induction into the political—were communicated to him; the uninhibitedness of his father's expression of his Parnellite sympathies; and the bitter grief of John Kelly, the friend of the family who had been the most selfless of Parnell's close supporters. The depth and directness of the impact of the Split on Joyce as a child was unusual and left him with a sense of temporality different from that of his contemporaries. In University College, Dublin, he observed the politics of the immediate post-Parnell generation and became familiar with the thinking of the Irish writers he read, most of whom he had contrived to meet by the time of his departure. He was steeped in the political print culture of Dublin, its contemporary newspapers and weeklies. He observed the stirring of new nationalist modes of expression and incipient movements.

Joyce had in his curtailed but formative years in Ireland a wide exposure to the Irish political that enabled him to comprehend the Ireland that had just passed, and the Ireland that was beginning to emerge. The distanced clarity of his apprehension of post-Split Irish politics set him apart. His experience of the Irish political scene would, in turn, mark him out from contemporary internationalist modernist writers. Joyce never ceased to draw on the deep well of his years in Ireland both in his political construction and imaginative treatment of the country he had left and in his larger conception of politics.

A 'political life' of one who was not a politician, professional controversialist, or proponent of political ideas might seem an anomalous undertaking. Averse to intellectual proselytisation or Tractarianism, Joyce came after 1912 to profess the principle of 'silence' outside his fiction. That reticence came to condition in some degree how his work was read, and to be misconstrued as an avowal on Joyce's part that he was personally and authorially apolitical, without politics, as an exile from Ireland and a modernist writer.

The idea that Joyce was in any significant sense a political writer would have been disputed in his lifetime and was negated in most of the early critical readings of his work. In Ireland this was due principally to the fact that he had left the Catholic Church and his country, as well as to the perceived exoticism of his art. It was also because in Ireland the term 'politics' was understood in partisan and overtly patriotic terms. Beyond Ireland, Joyce's consecration as an international modernist writer who had in exemplary fashion transcended the political divisions and controversies of the country of his birth—a transcendence that seemed to have much to commend it in the aftermath of the Second World War—negated the idea that he was political, either personally or in his work. The establishment of a conception of Joyce as political was strangely retarded for these reasons. It is true that Joyce had renounced all forms of conventional political engagement in Ireland, but his opinions while he was in Ireland were neither actively concealed nor deeply buried. It is almost as if he was waiting for some of the more astute of his contemporaries to divine what his Irish political beliefs actually were, but his contemporaries were post-Parnellite, and so preoccupied with the politico-cultural themes of the turn of the century in Ireland, and so accepting of Joyce's mask as an aloof 'literary artist', that few queried his reticence.

A writer's political convictions and the political import of his or her writing are, it will be said, quite different things. But they are connected, and in the case of Joyce the connection is close.

To comprehend Joyce's political convictions in Ireland, it is necessary to elucidate what they meant in their contemporary setting. It is a doubtful proceeding to banish the fierce particularity of his responses to Irish nationalism and its controversies, or to render those responses in an unhistorically selective way and thereby forfeit any sense of their integrity. Joyce's political reticence is a considered protest that is intended to be intelligible; it is not to be treated as open ground that can be filled by critical or ideological conjecture.

The exercise of tracking Joyce through childhood to early exile yields an outcome at odds with the once regnant idea of Joyce as austerely politically disengaged through rigid and unyielding artistic conviction. The portrait of the young Joyce that emerges is of someone far more intimately familiar with contemporary Irish controversies than had been suspected; and of a writer in the making—'a literary artist'[3]—of highly sophisticated political sensibility who observed an heroic intellectual discipline in a patient striving for understanding. It is that exigent discipline which gave Joyce—however protean his art and his self-conception as a writer would become—his remarkable political and intellectual consistency. His approach to the political was highly considered and intellectually scrupled. It was also in significant respects consciously strategic. His thinking was guarded, sometimes to the point of diffidence. From early on, he knew that there were aspects of the Irish political he could not afford to get wrong, notably the emergence of the revival of the Irish language as a political issue. As it transpired, he was never to find himself obliged to recant or to significantly modify the stances he had adopted. For all his disregard, occasionally verging on the staggering, for political and historical exactitude, no contemporary

3. In *Stephen Hero* we read, 'Stephen had begun to think of himself as a literary artist' (*SH* 122).

Irish writer or commentator—or politician—came close to rivalling Joyce's strategically distanced political acuity. In the now somewhat petrified contest between the canonisation of Joyce as a modernist and its more recent postcolonial rebuttal, what is lost is an appreciation of the extraordinary intelligence of Joyce's close treatment of the political. The recognition of Joyce's high political intellectuality—and shrewd intuitiveness—has been too long deferred.

Was Joyce an Irish nationalist? It is a question of some importance. My assertion that he plainly was is not part of a project for an Irish re-appropriation of Joyce. It is not necessary to that belated repossession: Joyce was born and grew up in Ireland, and his writings in exile pertained to Ireland, and his contemporary reception in Ireland has not been premised on the belief that he was an Irish nationalist insofar as it has ever been considered. The question is of importance in elucidating Joyce's Irish politics and his relationship to Ireland, and for an understanding of his broader politics.

In the critical writing touching on Joyce's politics in the last three decades or so, there has been a reluctance to acknowledge his Irish nationalism, which is central to how one construes his treatment of the Irish political.[4] If anything, there has been something of a regression. In his 1939 biography, Herbert Gorman wrote that 'Joyce, if anything, was an Irish nationalist at heart'.[5] Richard Ellmann observed more elliptically in 1982 that 'if he was not a nationalist of anyone else's school he was his own nationalist'.[6] That same year, shortly before the publication of the revised edition of his biography, Ellmann commented in an interview, 'Joyce undoubtedly disapproved of the excessive nationalism that he saw so popular in Ireland at the time. On the other hand, he was

4. For further discussion of critical writing on Joyce's nationalism, see chapter 1, 'The Shade of Parnell', 38–43.

5. Herbert Gorman, *James Joyce* (New York: Farrar and Rinehart, 1939), 186.

6. Richard Ellmann, *James Joyce's Hundredth Birthday: Side and Front Views* (Washington, DC: Library of Congress, 1982), 16.

a nationalist in his fashion'.[7] Robert Scholes, one of the few Joyce scholars to confront squarely the issue of Joyce's politics, observed in 1986 that the Joyce of 1906–7 was 'antibourgeois, anticlerical, antiparliamentary, antimilitaristic, antibureaucratic, an Irish nationalist', though he contends—I believe wrongly—that Joyce abandoned 'all political commitment' some time before the outbreak of the First World War.[8]

Postcolonial critics have been notably wary of characterising Joyce as an Irish nationalist. An acceptance that Joyce was an Irish nationalist ought not to be controversial and is only rendered so by a strange coalescence of postcolonial theory and the residues of what was once the prevalent view of him in Ireland and of the early critical reception of his work.

For Irish nationalists, the idea that Joyce could have been retrospectively a supporter of the cause of the dead leader without having nationalist sympathies is a contradiction in terms. To argue that Joyce was Parnellite but not an Irish nationalist one is driven back on two possible arguments. The first is that Joyce's Parnellism was a boyhood infatuation that was not carried forward into his convictions and thinking in adulthood but endured as a fond relic of his Dublin boyhood—a proposition that is not maintainable on any considered reading of Joyce's fictional and non-fictional writing. The second is that his nationalism waned, but his identification with Parnell endured, so that Joyce came to sever his Parnellism from Irish nationalism, an act of some conceptual violence which would need clear attestation in what Joyce wrote.

Joyce, famously, never avowed himself a nationalist. Defending Sinn Féin against the criticisms of his brother Stanislaus, he wrote from Rome in late 1906, 'If the Irish programme did not insist on the Irish language I suppose I could call myself a nationalist. As it is, I am content

7. Richard Ellmann, interview by Craig Raine, broadcast on BBC Radio 3 on 5 February 1982, published in *Times Literary Supplement*, 5 February 1982, and republished in John Gross, ed., *The Modern Movement* (London: Harvill, 1992), 66.

8. Robert Scholes, 'Joyce and Modernist Ideology', in *Coping with Joyce: Essays from the Copenhagen Symposium*, ed. Morris Beja and Shari Benstock (Columbus: Ohio State University Press, 1989), 95, 102. Scholes is writing about Joyce's 'turn away from politics' (97) principally in relation to socialism.

to recognise myself an exile, and, prophetically, a repudiated one.'[9] That was as close as he ever got, in his extant correspondence or what is known of his conversations on the subject. In that letter he put forward the most convenient and straightforward of the many reasons why he declined to proclaim himself a nationalist when it became possible for him to consider doing so: it was an exorbitance for an exile to do so. It was an early instance of Joyce's invocation of the contingencies of absence which derived from the strategising of his exile. The following year he gave his lecture in Trieste entitled 'L'Irlanda: Isola dei santi e dei savi' ('Ireland: Island of Saints and Sages'). Having characterised with extravagant inaccuracy Irish complicity in the Norman invasion and the Act of Union, he said, 'In my opinion, these two facts must be perfectly explained before the country in which they took place has even the most elementary right to expect one of its sons to change his position from that of detached observer to convinced nationalist.'[10] The idea that Joyce could not avow himself a nationalist until these two facts were accounted for was a thin contrivance and at odds with the reason he had advanced to Stanislaus the previous year, though it had a certain rhetorical force. Joyce's inferential self-characterisation as a 'detached observer' was tactical rather than substantive, part of the long game he had played of seeking out and maintaining 'his ground of vantage' in relation to Ireland and its controversies.[11]

It may be objected that being opposed to British dominion in Ireland and sympathetic to Irish independence is not enough to establish whether a writer was a nationalist. One might also expect a receptiveness to some version of an Irish national narrative, and an identification with a significant strain or strains of the political heritage or tradition of Irish nationalism. Both are present in Joyce in his recognition that Ireland had historic claims to nationhood; that it had a literary culture of

9. Joyce to Stanislaus Joyce, 6 November 1906, *Letters II* 187. The first sentence suggests that Joyce is referring to the nationalism of Sinn Féin rather than of the post-Parnell Irish Parliamentary Party. That, however, is secondary to the argument advanced here that objectively Joyce has to be considered a nationalist.

10. *OCPW* 116.

11. *PSW* 218.

some importance that reached back in time; that it had endured conquest which it had not overthrown but had never ceased to protest against; and that the aspiration to self-determination had found expression in periodic rebellions and acts of socio-political resistance. There is something else that speaks to Joyce's nationalism: the way he wrote of the Irish people and their beliefs, taken with his sense of the rhetorical power of nationalism in engendering a sense of a common political identity, even if his rendering of that power tends to be most discernible when he is resisting or parodying it. It is difficult to conceive of someone inhabiting the communicative space of nationalism with the connoisseurship that Joyce did without being a nationalist, however dissentient.

He disdained, and sought to move beyond, the Irish preoccupation with England. In Irish politics he was intellectually revolutionary in refusing to treat the English subjugation of Ireland in isolation from the Irish response. Joyce was both provocative and rigorous in his refusal to subscribe to a narrative of Irish history as British conquest in which the Irish were passive victims. If he did not forgive the iniquities of English conquest and governance, he was unsparing on the subject of Irish disunion, enfeeblement, passivity, or objective complicity in the depredations of the conquering power. The English conquest and the Irish response had to be set side by side and understood integrally. This was an aggressively revisionist model of Irish history. Rather than a flat Irish saga of oppression, it was dialectical. What this came down to was Joyce's disdain for a political and historical narrative in which the subjugated Irish were acquitted of all responsibility for their fate and self-beatified as victims of history. For many of his contemporaries that was an anti-nationalist posture, but it was for Joyce a translation of the axiom that Ireland had responsibility for its own destiny. He was an Irish nationalist who refused to think in conventionally nationalistic terms.

One finally comes back to the strategically chosen vantage from which Joyce wrote. His fiercely Parnellian critique of Ireland and Irish nationalism is only politically intelligible as written from *within* Irish nationalism, if on an outer refractory edge. It is an argument addressed to Irish nationalists. The paradox of Joyce's nationalism is that it is in his critique of nationalism that his nationalism is most evident.

Joyce's non-avowal of nationalism was a strategic ploy which he sedulously pursued with adroitness and pertinacity. His proclaimed refusals to avow himself an Irish nationalist tended to be formulated in a way that was strangely redolent of the high vein of Irish patriotic rhetoric. Whether Joyce was an Irish nationalist cannot be determined by whether he accepted the designation.

Joyce's strategic position was one that he maintained across the contingencies of political time, which included the achievement of Irish independence, the central preoccupation of Irish nationalists, something which Joyce foresaw—not especially controversially—would be achieved in his lifetime, whether through Home Rule or otherwise. That he held aloof from the independent Irish state did not signify that he was, or became retrospectively, opposed to the achievement of Irish independence. Irish nationalism did not entail acceptance of the policies an independent state might pursue. In withholding acceptance, Joyce remained within the logic of Irish nationalism, and of democratic statehood. In considering Joyce's nationalism, it is important to appreciate that what he did *not* do was engage in the vain (in both senses) and incoherent intellectual exercise of conditioning his support of the idea of Irish independence. His realism, and his understanding of nationalism, ran too deep for that. Joyce instead embarked on an elaborate nominalist game in which he refused to avow himself an Irish nationalist. This has its origins in *Stephen Hero* as applied to Stephen Daedalus, when Home Rule seemed a distant prospect, and it is maintained almost playfully in the exegetics of exile of Shem the Penman in *Finnegans Wake,* written after the establishment of the Irish state.

Why is a recognition of Joyce's Irish nationalism of consequence? A number of reasons might be advanced. The first is that it reveals just how political Joyce was. If the idea that Joyce was apolitical from artistic principle no longer has much currency, there remains a lingering suggestion of detached unconcern: in 1969 the Joyce scholar Phillip Herring astonishingly imputed to Joyce an 'inherent lack of interest in the human condition'.[12] It is not simply that Joyce had and retained political convictions; his Irish nationalism attested to a belief in democratic self-determination. The second is that Joyce's Irish nationalism affects how one situates his broader politics and has filiations to other strains of political thought. A defining characteristic of Irish nationalism in its mainstream expressions (subtracting its vicious manifestations such as that of the Citizen in the 'Cyclops' episode of *Ulysses* or the Provisional Irish Republican Army) is its sceptical resistance to the claims of ideology and ethnicity, and a pragmatism that seems unbounded. Irish nationalism mediated or tempered Joyce's response to contemporary politics.

The virtuosity of his observation of and analysis of Irish nationalism—rarely if ever acknowledged as a discrete attribute—informed his apprehension of the political beyond Ireland. His sceptical interrogation of ideologies originates in his experience of Ireland. The core premise of this book is that the analysis of Joyce's politics is best approached through his relationship to the Irish political, his intellectual point of departure.

The Irish nationalism that Joyce came to espouse was one that was pared to its conceptual core of independent statehood, shorn of the incidental chauvinistic and religious excrescences that many of his contemporaries had come to regard as defining features of nationalism.

The principal change wrought by exile—or at least that was coincident with exile—is that Joyce ceased to perceive Ireland as having nothing to impart to continental Europe by reason of its economic backwardness and political stagnation. He continued to think comparatively of Ireland in relation to European states and nations, but the terms of comparison shifted. Ireland might after all have something to impart, as an island in the Atlantic with a historical rhythm of its own that had set it apart from the Continent, and as a country whose independence had been denied by conquest but which had as a corollary been spared entrapment in the rigidities of statehood or empire other than

12. Phillip F. Herring, 'Joyce's Politics', in *New Light on Joyce from the Dublin Symposium*, ed. Fritz Senn (Bloomington: Indiana University Press, 1972), 11, 10.

involuntarily as a constituent of the United Kingdom of Great Britain and Ireland. Ireland has escaped the imposition of rectilinearity. Joyce seized on the idea of Ireland having a strange exemplarity or imaginative plasticity, even if only in the abstract, deriving from the statal inchoateness of Ireland. That sense of the tractability of the narrative of Ireland became the breach through which coursed all of Joyce's conception of historical and cultural cycles of change and continuity. It permitted him to move beyond his straitened analysis of Ireland as it stood in 1904, and to negotiate the bleakness of his assessment of contemporary Irish politics. It found expression in his 1907 Trieste lecture 'L'Irlanda: Isola dei santi e dei savi' and came lastingly to inform how he rendered Ireland in his art:[13] it would be hard to conceive of *Finnegans Wake* had the country whose history provided its principal political subject been an established nineteenth-century European state or empire with a settled narrative of statal advance or colonial aggrandisement.

Philosophically, Joyce's Irish nationalism derives from a combination of political realism and European romantic nationalism. He was not an ideological nationalist. He was hostile to ethnocentrism and scornful of ideas of cultural purity. He was intrigued by, and not disapproving of, articulations of national cultures and narratives and could be scathingly funny about them. He was accepting of the historically sanctioned arrangement of human societies as nation-states. He conspicuously did not look to a dissolution of the state or nation-state, an idea that had a considerable currency in nineteenth- and twentieth-century Europe. Edmund Epstein in 1971 wrote that both Joyce and the Stephen of *A Portrait of the Artist as a Young Man* 'really believed in the existences of national races: neither of them was a modern internationalist. Joyce was an old-fashioned nationalist, of the school of Herder and Matthew Arnold and Mazzini. . . . His nationalism was the nineteenth century liberal variety which was prevalent in the Ireland of his time'.[14] This relates

13. *OCPW* 108–26.

14. Edmund L. Epstein, *The Ordeal of Stephen Dedalus* (Carbondale: Southern Illinois University Press, 1971), 90–91. The judgement of Leslie Fiedler four years later, at the Paris symposium, conveys the depth of the misapprehension created by the early readings of Joyce as divorced from Irish nationalism and an internationalist critic of the nation-state: 'There is one

to Joyce's acceptance of the nation-state; one has nonetheless to allow for the imaginative fluidity of Joyce's conception of national identity, while his consciousness of the unceasing cultural interpenetration particularly of European nations made 'national races' a relative concept.

The development over time of his views on the role of the nation-state in contemporary Europe is harder to elucidate, and open to debate, in part because while Ireland became a state in 1922, it was never a great power. It is certainly possible to read *Finnegans Wake*, written across the terrible interval between two world wars and completed three months after the outbreak of the second, as a critique of the idea of the European nation-state, though the stronger argument is that he remained bleakly realistic in relation to the institution of the nation-state.

To say that Joyce was an Irish nationalist is not to suggest that Irish nationalism exhaustively defined his political thinking. He believed in Irish independence and was sympathetic to Ireland's nationalist tradition. His Irish nationalism was not a politically exclusive belief. It is true that Joyce's expressions of sympathy with Sinn Féin had an approximate synchrony with his loss of interest in Italian socialism, but he did not posit any linkage between those developments of affinity. He did not conceive them as alternatives.

His Irish nationalism had nothing in common with and was deeply antipathetic to the reactionary (and typically anti-Semitic) ideological nationalism that found contemporary expression, for example, in France in L'Action Française. Joyce's was a nationalism that was explicitly European. The early Joyce is the first thoroughgoing exponent of an Irish nationalism that was consciously European—a title conventionally

fundamental political error which Joyce made in his work in terms of political analysis of the world. . . . What Joyce did not understand is that nationalism would indeed remain the sole dynamic force in the world in the decades and centuries which lay ahead of him'. Having said that Joyce in *Ulysses* treats Zionism and Irish nationalism as dead, he continues, 'As a political prophet, Joyce is simply wrong, wrong, wrong. Since I myself grew up as a young man sharing Joyce's illusions and thought that internationalism would be the politics of the future, it's a shock to me to realize that it in fact is the politics of the past, and there is something essentially therefore nostalgic and reactionary in the art of James Joyce.' Fiedler in 'Political Perspectives on Joyce's Work', symposium chaired by Morris Beja, in Aubert and Jolas, *Joyce and Paris*, 112. Fiedler's misreading of Joyce is total.

conferred on his most politically prominent contemporary in University College, Thomas M. Kettle, whose Europeanism was, however, of a more aspirational order and was politically hemmed in by his commitment to the Irish Parliamentary Party and acquiescence in the established Irish social order and the role of the Catholic Church in particular.

It could, of course, be asserted that even if Joyce was an Irish nationalist in Ireland and early exile, he ceased to be such as he passed into extratextual political 'silence' during the First World War, and by the time of writing *Ulysses* was not an Irish nationalist. That argument is really a subset of the proposition that, in passing into 'silence' outside his work, Joyce became apolitical, which I believe is incorrect. The idea that Joyce could have chosen to excise nationalism from his Irish political sympathies—which would have been a highly problematic exercise—reflects a misreading of Joyce, connected to a reductive understanding of Irish nationalism.

Even if one were to continue to resist the idea of his Irish nationalism, Joyce took from his experience of the fierceness of political and historical controversy in the inchoate Irish polity a scarred wisdom that set him apart from contemporary modernist writers, who were scions of established states and empires. It framed all that he wrote. In the broadside 'The Holy Office', written some two months before he left Ireland, Joyce wrote of

> Those souls that hate the strength that mine has
> Steeled in the school of old Aquinas.[15]

He was steeled also by the fierceness, and the intermittent passion, of the Irish political.

15. *PSW* 99.

1

The Shade of Parnell

JOYCE'S RELATIONSHIP TO the Irish political begins with Charles Stewart Parnell, and the Parnell Split, and it is to Parnell that one is consistently driven back in considering Joyce's nationalism and his political relationship to Ireland. One has therefore to address how it was that Parnell, a politician who was never the leader of a state, whose career and political project ostensibly ended in conspicuous failure, whom Joyce never saw and who was dead when he was nine years old, came to be so central to Joyce's political imagination and to his treatment of Ireland in his writing.

The advent of Parnell (1846–91) came to be hailed as something like a meteor appearing in the bleak firmament of late nineteenth-century Irish politics. A minor Irish landlord in County Wicklow, whose Avondale estate was heavily encumbered, Parnell showed seemingly little interest in politics and lived the life of a young man of his class. The earliest indication that he was considering a parliamentary candidacy was in 1873. In the event, since he held the office of high sheriff of County Wicklow, he confined himself at the general election of February 1874 to supporting the impromptu candidacy of his brother John Howard Parnell, who finished at the bottom of the poll. Charles Stewart stood and was defeated for County Dublin in a by-election immediately after the general election. He had to wait until the following year to be returned for County Meath, in April 1875, at the age of twenty-eight.

He was regarded at the outset of his career in Parliament as the unprepossessing and falteringly articulate scion of a distinguished 'patriotic' Anglo-Irish family—Sir John Parnell had staunchly opposed the Act of Union of 1800. After a brief parliamentary apprenticeship, he steadily dispelled the low expectations that attended his election by placidly exhibiting a fearless strength of purpose. He joined the ranks of the handful of Irish 'obstructives' and made of Irish parliamentary obstructionism at Westminster a strategic weapon. What was distinctive about Parnell was that he realised that nationalism could not prevail as an exclusively parliamentary phenomenon. In 1878–79, shortly before the beginning of the land agitation in response to distress in the west of Ireland, he came to a distanced but effective understanding with John Devoy, a leading member of the Irish Republican Brotherhood in the United States. Three weeks after meeting Devoy in Irishtown, County Mayo, on 20 April 1879, Parnell assumed the mantle of agrarian agitator by speaking at a meeting at Westport, County Mayo, on 8 June. The establishment of the Land League of Mayo followed on 16 August in Castlebar, and the Irish National Land League was founded in Dublin on 21 October. Parnell thus seized the possibilities of fusing obstructionism with Irish agrarianism, with the sanction of the more pragmatic Fenians (though hard-line Fenians remained dogmatically opposed to parliamentarism). He had come to assume a pivotal position and wide public prominence during the Land War in Ireland.

The 1880 general election caught Parnell and his allies somewhat off guard, but he emerged, at first precariously, as the leader of an Irish Parliamentary Party divided between those who shared his purpose and temporising 'Whig' or 'nominal' Home Rulers. In the general election, Joyce's father, John Stanislaus Joyce, managed the campaigns of the two Liberal candidates in Dublin city, Maurice Brooks and Robert Spencer Dyer Lyons, who achieved the considerable feat of wresting the two seats from the Conservatives, in a constituency which was not contested by a Home Rule candidate. By 1882, the year Joyce was born, Parnell was already on course to achieving a remarkable ascendancy in Irish politics. He clashed with the Liberal Prime Minister William Ewart Gladstone over the government's Land Act and coercive legislation and

FIGURE 1.1. Charles Stewart Parnell (National Library of Ireland). Reproduced courtesy of the National Library of Ireland, CLON1152.

was incarcerated in Kilmainham Jail from October 1881 to May 1882. His release just preceded the Phoenix Park murders on 6 May 1882, when the Chief Secretary Lord Frederick Cavendish and his undersecretary T. H. Burke were ferociously stabbed to death by members of a secret society called the Invincibles. The cabman in whose shelter part of the 'Eumaeus' episode of *Ulysses* takes place was reputedly James Fitzharris,

'Skin the Goat',[1] the jarvey who drove the assassins to and from the murder scene in Phoenix Park, in sight of the Viceregal Lodge. Parnell was aghast and thought of resigning but finally resolved on seeking to contain the destabilising effects of the violence of the murders.

Parnell had contrived to create a disciplined Irish Parliamentary Party at Westminster that put the English party system under intense pressure. Gladstone's government was brought down in early June 1885 by combined Irish and Tory votes. At the general election of July 1885, Parnell threw the Irish vote in England against the Liberals. He emerged with eighty-six seats, holding very narrowly the balance of power. After a protracted standoff, Gladstone introduced the Government of Ireland Bill on 8 April 1886. The Liberals split. The bill was lost in the Commons in June 1886. The general election the following month returned a Conservative government.

The introduction of what became known as the First Home Rule Bill nevertheless transformed how the prospects for Irish legislative independence were perceived. It inaugurated what was to be called in Britain the 'union of hearts' between Gladstonian Liberals and the Irish Parliamentary Party that Parnell led. There was a political cost. The governing precept of the Irish Party was of 'independent opposition' to both the Conservative and Liberal parties. The strategic fiction was that either British party could be brought to concede Home Rule to avoid the traditional debilitating dependence on the Liberals, though it was never likely that a Conservative government would enact Home Rule. Once a Liberal government had introduced a Home Rule measure, the idea that the Conservatives would contemplate doing so became still more improbable. Ireland was now the principal line of division between the British parties.

By 1886 Parnell's hegemony in Ireland was unchallenged. He attained the status of a living legend as Ireland's 'uncrowned king'. That made Parnell a Unionist target, in his own right and perhaps still more because the Liberal party, in what the Conservatives confidently believed to be its

1. See Vivien Igoe, *The Real People of Joyce's 'Ulysses': A Biographical Guide* (Dublin: University College Dublin Press, 2016), 107–8.

Achilles' heel, had allied itself with the Home Rule party. The Conservative government of Lord Salisbury, which succeeded Gladstone's, set out to establish that Parnell was privy to the Phoenix Park murders, following the publication by *The Times* in 1887 of letters from Parnell that implicated him in the murders but had in fact been forged by Richard Pigott, a rogue Irish journalist down on his luck. The instrumentality by which the government sought to achieve this was the establishment of a Special Commission whose loaded remit was to enquire into Parnellite complicity in political violence in Ireland in general. Pigott gave evidence to the Special Commission and was exposed to searching cross-examination by Sir Charles Russell in one of the great set pieces of Victorian advocacy in which Russell held all the cards. It could only get worse, and over a weekend recess the hapless Pigott fled from London and finally shot himself in Madrid. Parnell stood at the zenith of his career in Britain and Ireland, extravagantly acclaimed by those in the Liberal party who had doubted him. Both the Pigott forgery and the inquisition feature in the accusatory matrix of *Finnegans Wake*. Parnell's visit to Gladstone at home in Hawarden on 18–19 December 1889 marked the acme of the Liberal-nationalist alliance, the 'union of hearts'.

Parnell's public image had been of Spartan self-abnegation and solitude, of unforgiving political commitment; almost of secular sanctity as an Irish Protestant in the service of a predominantly Catholic people. That aspect of selfless austerity was to render Parnell vulnerable. In the latter part of 1881, he had begun a relationship with Katharine O'Shea, the wife of Captain William Henry O'Shea, an Irish member of Parliament of unrequited political ambition and social aspiration, and devoid of discernible political convictions. The relationship came to be an open secret in the Victorian manner in political and journalistic circles but was unknown to the wider public in Ireland or Britain. After O'Shea stood for the Liberal party in 1885 and lost, Parnell's brutal imposition of O'Shea as the nationalist member of Parliament in the Galway by-election of February 1886 bewildered ordinary nationalists and brought Parnell's relationship with O'Shea's wife to the brink of public disclosure.

On 24 December 1889, Captain O'Shea instituted divorce proceedings naming Parnell as a co-respondent. The action came on for hearing a year later, on 15–17 November 1890. Parnell was absolutely resolved that there would be a divorce, which would enable him to marry Katharine. O'Shea's evidence, highly damaging to Parnell, was unchallenged, and he obtained a conditional decree of divorce. A decree nisi could be made absolute after six months if nothing emerged to establish collusion or acquiescence on the part of the petitioner that could elicit the intervention of the Queen's Proctor. Divorce proceedings were, at the time, heard in public. The O'Shea divorce case created an immense sensation in which politics and morality intersected. The career of the promising Liberal Sir Charles Dilke had been substantially destroyed when he was named, quite possibly falsely, as a co-respondent in divorce proceedings in 1885–86. Parnell was a different proposition to Dilke given his status as the leader of nationalist Ireland and his immense popularity in Ireland as the leader who had transformed the prospects for Irish nationalism. If anything, the political assumption was that Parnell's leadership would survive, but then no-one quite knew how a divorce scandal might play out in Catholic nationalist Ireland.

The immediate nationalist response was a closing of ranks in support of Parnell. On 20 November leading nationalist parliamentarians endorsed Parnell's leadership at a meeting in the Leinster Hall. Timothy Michael Healy's endorsement was the most ringing and became a principal taunt of Parnellites after he had changed sides to become Parnell's most ferocious and *décomplexé* opponent. The Irish party re-elected Parnell as sessional chairman on 25 November. The divorce exposed a fault line in the Home Rule alliance between Gladstone's Liberal party and the Irish Party led by Parnell. Liberal nonconformist sentiment was affronted almost as much by the initial condoning by Irish nationalists of Parnell's relationship with Katharine O'Shea as by the relationship itself. Gladstone responded to Parnell's re-election by publishing a letter to John Morley, his principal co-adjutor on Irish affairs, asserting that Parnell's continued leadership of the Irish Party would render his own leadership of the Liberal party 'almost a nullity'.[2]

2. Quoted in Morley, *Life of Gladstone*, 3:437.

This was the situation characterised by Joyce in his 1912 article 'L'ombra di Parnell' ('The Shade of Parnell'): 'The ministers Gladstone and Morley openly refused to legislate in favour of Ireland if the felon stayed on as leader of the Nationalist Party'.[3] It was of course an intervention that was difficult to reconcile philosophically with Liberal support of Home Rule, premised on the idea that the Irish people were entitled to make their own political choices, but reflected Gladstone's assessment of what Liberal voters in Britain would tolerate. Gladstone's intervention caused many moderate nationalists to conclude that for Parnell to remain as leader would undo what was seen as his greatest political achievement, the winning of the Liberal party to the cause of Home Rule; for Parnellites that was to confuse the means with the end.

Parnell retaliated on 29 November 1890 with an inflammatory 'Manifesto to the Irish People'. It contained a highly tendentious account of his negotiations with Gladstone at Hawarden, an account which he asserted 'will enable you [the Irish people] to understand the measure of the loss with which you are threatened unless you consent to throw me to the English wolves now baying for my destruction'.[4] While most contemporary observers considered Parnell's manifesto to be a catastrophically counter-productive misjudgement, what it revealed was that Parnell fully apprehended the scale of the challenge he was facing, and was pre-emptively framing the issue in anticipation of what was fast becoming its inevitable second phase on Irish terrain. He hoped to deploy his immense political stature to overwhelm on Irish ground the rapidly mounting opposition to his leadership.

3. *OCPW* 196. The Liberals were not in office in 1890. John Morley was an essayist, biographer, and member of Parliament for the radical constituency of Newcastle-on-Tyne, which had a significant Irish electorate in 1883–95, and Gladstone's pre-eminent co-adjutor on Irish politics. He was Chief Secretary for Ireland in Gladstone's last administration in 1892–95, which is presumably why Joyce erroneously thought he was in office in 1890. Morley was subsequently the member of Parliament for Montrose Burghs from 1896 to 1908. He published his canonical biography of Gladstone in 1903. Created a viscount in 1908, he resigned from the Liberal government on its decision to intervene in the Great War in 1914. In the article, Joyce was often inaccurate in historical and political detail while capturing the essence of things.

4. *Freeman's Journal*, 29 November 1890; F.S.L. Lyons, *The Fall of Parnell* (London: Routledge and Kegan Paul, 1960), 320–36.

The Irish Party met in Committee Room 15 of the Houses of Parliament at Westminster from 1 to 6 December 1890 to debate Parnell's continued leadership. In the course of that debate, the Irish Catholic hierarchy, which had theretofore held back, intervened through a denunciation of Parnell by their standing committee. The meetings of the party were intense and fraught across a very long week. The debates were carried more or less verbatim by the *Freeman's Journal*, whose reporters were in attendance. It was apparent from early on that Parnell was in a minority. He chaired the meetings without much pretence of impartiality but without quite abrogating democratic norms. In his interventions he demonstrated once more his commanding political ability, but the debates also disclosed the problem that was to dog him throughout the Split. That was that whatever he said could be dismissed as a cynically self-serving attempt to maintain his leadership, rather than a disinterested assertion of Irish independence in the face of an impermissible Liberal attempt to dictate who was to be the leader of the Irish Party. Parnell fiercely—and with some justification, given his strange clairvoyance and his estimate of the political capacity of his opponents—refused to recognise the distinction. That was Parnell's difficulty, and it was one that his most adroit and uninhibited adversary, Healy, exploited to the hilt in Committee Room 15 and in Ireland. Joyce fully shared the Parnellite loathing of Healy, which was almost a correlative of loyalty to Parnell.

The most notorious episode in Committee Room 15 came on the last day as the disintegration of the party set in. When John Redmond interjected to refer to Gladstone as 'the master of the party', Healy scornfully enquired, 'Who is to be the mistress of the party?' Infuriated, Parnell repeatedly rose and subsided and was poised to strike Healy, whom he characterised as 'that cowardly little scoundrel there who dares in an assembly of Irishmen to insult a woman'.[5] Joyce never mentions the episode, perhaps reflecting the Parnellite precept of disdaining to refer to Healy, consigning him to the realms of the unspeakable.

Joyce extracted something else from the debates in Committee Room 15. On the first day, Redmond made a supportive speech which

5. Frank Callanan, *The Parnell Split, 1890–91* (Cork: Cork University Press, 1992), 52.

FIGURE 1.2. Timothy Michael Healy (National Library of Ireland). Reproduced courtesy of the National Library of Ireland, NPA DOCF1.

elicited an interpellation from Parnell that, slightly paraphrased, was to become part of the Parnell myth:

> Redmond—In deciding a question of this kind, where we are asked to sell our leader (loud cheers) to preserve an alliance, it seems to me that we are bound to inquire what we are getting for the price that we are paying (renewed cheers).
>
> Parnell—Don't sell me for nothing. If you get my value you may change me tomorrow (renewed cheers).[6]

Redmond's speech and Parnell's intervention prefigured Parnell's tactic of seeking to extract assurances from the Liberal leadership on the points in relation to the Home Rule Bill raised in the manifesto, which were not to be forthcoming. Parnell's almost conversational interjection revealed a great deal of his character: his sardonic realpolitik, the ability sweetly to feign reasonableness, and his superb contempt for his opponents in the imputation that they were submitting to a squalid bargain with the Liberals, which they had neither the political means nor the capacity to hold them to. For Joyce, who was prone to drawing oblique parallels between Parnell and Christ, it also recalled the pieces of silver of Judas Iscariot. The phrase 'get my price' recurs as a drumbeat through *Finnegans Wake*.

The party in Committee Room 15 finally divided almost two to one against Parnell. That sundering was designated as 'the Split', though the term can also, depending on context, refer to the duration of the Split in Parnell's lifetime, 1890–91, or to what might be termed the long Split of 1890–1900, the period during which the Irish Party was divided before its reunification in 1900.

Forsaken by a majority in his party, Parnell came back to Ireland to reassert his leadership of the Irish people. His speech in the Rotunda in Dublin was perhaps his last truly great speech, his power in Ireland as yet unbroken. In the course of it he declaimed to loud cheers, 'I am too unworthy to walk with you within the sight of the promised land, which,

6. *Freeman's Journal*, 2 December 1890; R. Barry O'Brien, *The Life of Charles Stewart Parnell* (London: Smith Elder, 1898), 2:278.

please God, I will enter with you.'[7] There had already been, in the cult of Parnell, equations of the Irish leader with Moses leading the Jewish people out of servitude, both before and after the divorce crisis, which were not lost on Joyce, and would provide the subtext of the rendering of J. F. Taylor's speech in the 'Aeolus' episode of *Ulysses*.[8]

Early the following morning, before leaving Dublin for his Cork constituency, Parnell led the forcible ousting of the anti-Parnellite personnel who had taken over the offices of *United Ireland*. Joyce was to deploy the 'historic fracas' in the 'Eumaeus' episode of *Ulysses*—where Leopold Bloom, who 'enjoyed the distinction of being close to Erin's uncrowned king in the flesh', restores Parnell's hat—inserting Bloom into the narrative of the episode quoted by Richard Barry O'Brien.[9]

The general expectation was that Parnell would prevail in Ireland. In carefully marshalling his strengths, Parnell knew the outcome was uncertain and required him to maximise every advantage. The scale of adversity was to prove greater than he could have anticipated, and he found himself in a desperate losing struggle. He was confronted by a majority of Home Rule politicians who asserted that, in seeking to maintain his leadership, he was subverting the alliance with the Liberal party, sustained by the influence of the Catholic Church, which was more or less uninhibitedly deployed against him. He found himself the subject of a ferocious populistic Catholic onslaught, conceived by his principal adversary, Healy, on his relations with Katharine O'Shea. His myth of selfless Protestant patriotism was thrown into reverse: now he was assailed as a Protestant landlord of dictatorial disposition who, with the selfishness of his caste, was prepared to jeopardise the attainment of Home Rule for Ireland in the furtherance of a sexual passion.

The first of the three by-elections in Ireland in what remained of Parnell's life took place in North Kilkenny in December. It was a ferocious

7. Callanan, *Parnell Split*, 63. Parnell had also referred to entering the promised land in his first major speech in Committee Room 15. Callanan, *Parnell Split*, 41.

8. *U* 7.812–69.

9. 'His hat was off now, his hair dishevelled, the dust of the conflict begrimed his well-brushed coat'. R. B. O'Brien, *Charles Stewart Parnell*, 2:296; *U* 16.1495–528; Callanan, *Parnell Split*, 64.

affair. Joyce, perhaps in part because of his own problems with his eyesight, was fixated on the episode in Castlecomer in which Parnell was struck in the eye by a projectile which the Parnellites said was of prepared lime (not quicklime, as Joyce was to assert).[10] This led to Parnell somewhat melodramatically wearing a large bandage over the side of his head for the duration of the election. The defeat of Parnell's candidate by a near two-to-one margin shattered the myth of his invincibility in Ireland. The drift of his more opportunistic supporters to the anti-Parnellite side on one pretext or another set in.

Parnell pressed on, fiercely insisting on the principle of Irish independence and denouncing anti-Parnellite obeisance to the Liberal party and the Catholic Church. The Parnellite candidate lost by a closer margin in North Sligo in April. When the divorce decree was made absolute, Parnell refused to defer his marriage to Katharine O'Shea until after the third by-election in Carlow. They were married at the registry office in Steyning, near Brighton, on 25 June 1891. The election descended into a carnival of coarse ribaldry, and the Parnellite candidate Andrew Kettle, father of Joyce's University College contemporary Thomas M. Kettle, sustained a heavy defeat.

Parnell fought implacably on, still showing considerable political adroitness and fiercely awaiting a reversal of fortune. He crossed every weekend from Brighton, where he lived with Katharine, to Ireland to address meetings in Ireland. His health, always frail, did not withstand the savagely punishing rhythm of the Split. After a year of terrible and unremitting reversals, he died in Brighton at the age of forty-five on 6 October 1891. The abruptness of the end was strangely of a piece with the pace of his astonishingly crisis-charged career, without parallel in contemporary Irish or British politics. Suddenly it was all over.

The memory of Parnell outlasted his immense funeral in Dublin. He was bitterly mourned and continued to be extravagantly commemorated in Dublin by his supporters on the anniversaries of his death. The Parnellite party had lost its leader and were reduced to a rump at the general election of 1892; the anti-Parnellites could not replicate his

10. Callanan, *Parnell Split*, 67.

charismatic command of Irish nationalism. The recriminations of the 'long Split' between the divided factions of parliamentary nationalism lasted from 1890 through the defeat of Gladstone's Second Home Rule Bill in the House of Lords in 1893 until the reunification of the Irish Party in 1900. While his name was ceaselessly invoked by both sides, and the reunited Irish Party sought to draw on his allure, the political memory of what had been Parnell's vital force seeped away inexorably across the 1890s. Other controversies and divisions within Ireland did something to displace the recall of the events of 1890–91. Unquiet residues of the Split endured nonetheless. In time those residues engendered a literary myth fashioned quasi-collaboratively by James Joyce and W. B. Yeats.

Joyce's Identification with Parnell

It is not possible to fathom the depth of Joyce's allegiance to Parnell without an appreciation of the Split's cruel rhythm and of Parnell's perseverance and refusal—one might say absolute temperamental incapacity—to be unnerved by the scale of the reversals he sustained. Joyce dwelt all his life on Parnell's undaunted defiance of crushing adversity in the Split. He fiercely upheld the principles that Parnell stood for in the Split, and scorned Parnell's opponents, but it is important to appreciate that this reflected more than abstract conviction. It was sustained by the warmth and affection of his identification with Parnell.[11] Joyce certainly considered Parnell a heroic figure and intensely admired him as a leader, but his relationship to the dead leader had nothing of the nineteenth-century deference for the statesman or the 'great man'. It was without hierarchical deference and had a certain democratic equality to it. In his 1912 article for *Il Piccolo della Sera* in Trieste, Joyce took pains, and derived some joy, from distinguishing Parnell from the two emblematic 'great men' of the late Victorian era, Benjamin Disraeli

11. Phillip Herring could hardly be more wrong in writing that Joyce's 'bitterness at the fall of Parnell did not apparently result from any sympathy with the man personally or the cause he championed'. Herring, 'Joyce's Politics', 8.

and Gladstone: 'But time is more merciful towards the "uncrowned king" than towards the wag and the orator. The light of [Parnell's] mild, proud, silent and disconsolate sovereignty makes Disraeli look like an upstart diplomat dining whenever he can in rich people's houses, and Gladstone like a portly butler who has gone to night school. How little Disraeli's wit and Gladstone's culture weigh in the balance today! What trifles are Disraeli's studied witticisms, greasy hair and doltish novels, or Gladstone's high-sounding sentences, Homeric studies and speeches on Artemis or marmalade!'[12]

The overlap in the lives of Parnell and of Joyce was short and pertained to a period in which Joyce was a child. For Joyce, who was preternaturally, almost superstitiously, attentive to coincidences, his childhood induction into the politics of the Split marked a first intersection of his life with Parnell's seemingly doomed but unyielding campaign to re-establish his ascendancy in the Split, and his death. Their lives remained thereafter occultly connected in Joyce's perception, fortifying a certain collusiveness in his identification with Parnell.

The impact of the Parnell Split on Joyce as a boy is principally perceived through the explosive Christmas dinner scene in the Dedalus household three months after Parnell's death, as depicted in *A Portrait of the Artist as a Young Man*. It is a superbly epitomised rendering of the Split in a domestic setting. The scene is so graphic, so formative of how Joyce's relation to Parnell is perceived, and so central to how the Split is faintly understood in contemporary Ireland that it is disappointing—and disorientating—to have to accept that it is unlikely ever to have taken place. It stands as a hauntingly exact invocation of the temper of nationalist Ireland in the terrible Christmas that followed Parnell's death, and a stylised rendering of Joyce's sudden immersion in Irish politics and acquisition of a fealty to Parnell as a boy. It contains biographical prompts and clues through which Joyce's induction into the Irish political can be elucidated.

There is a prevalent mischaracterisation of the Parnellism of Joyce's father—entrenched by John Wyse Jackson and Peter Costello in their

12. *OCPW* 194.

John Stanislaus Joyce: The Voluminous Life and Genius of Joyce's Father (1998)—as a committed Parnellite sympathiser and activist from 1880. In fact, John Stanislaus Joyce only became an ardent supporter of Parnell from the divorce crisis on. This is crucial. His father's impulsive support of the embattled Parnell of 1890–91 came, across the passage of years, to represent for Joyce an uncharacteristically heroic gesture, a large mitigation of his father's multiple foibles. The theme of the fall and redemption in *Finnegans Wake* was to be deeply informed by this. A significant integrating motif of the *Wake* has been lost through a misunderstanding of the politics of Joyce's father.

The young Joyce did not take on faith his father's support of Parnell in the Split. He sought to inform himself, as far as a young boy could, of the controversy in which Parnell died in order to put himself in a position to make what he conceived as an independent election to support Parnell's cause. It marks a forced and precocious transition from boyhood to independent critical thinking under conditions that were unimaginable in a boyhood in England, or in any established European state. Parnell is an emblematic figure in Joyce's rendering of what it was to grow up in a nation that statehood had eluded.

This belies the simplistic idea that Joyce adoptively mimicked his father's Parnellism, and that this shallow and derivative Parnellism mellowed into a sentimental memory of a boyhood allegiance, albeit one edged with the contemporary bitterness of the Split of 1890–91. The idea that Joyce's conception of Parnell was fixed and static, an icon borne aloft from a late nineteenth-century Irish nationalist childhood, does not withstand scrutiny.

Joyce was loyal to Parnell and was a nationalist. If he can be referred to as a Parnellite nationalist, that is not to assert that his nationalism was simply an emanation of his Parnellism. While Parnell was central to Joyce's nationalism, and the Split crystallised his nationalism, it does not follow that Joyce would not have been nationalist but for Parnell. He was born into and raised within a nationalist tradition (or a tradition that was becoming nationalist). There is a subordinate Fenian strain in Joyce's nationalism that descends in the male line that does not derive from Parnell. He came to have a deep sense of the rhythm of Irish nationalism, as well as a fecund mastery of demotic nationalist sentiment and rhetorical imagery, and he was adept at introducing personal flourishes mainly through ballad and song. That alone says much.

Parnell became a role model for Joyce as a child in a way that presaged how the figure of Parnell was to be bound up with the development of his art. There is little direct evidence, but it seems clear from his writings that Joyce in late boyhood dwelt intensely on Parnell and on what had transpired in the Split to bring about his fall. His bitter critique of contemporary Ireland derived in a significant and discernible degree from the Split. By the time he reached University College, Dublin, his Parnellism was reticent, even veiled. He had come to believe that Parnell had become occluded in Irish politics, damned with faint praise of his early career by those who had opposed him in the Split—an occlusion which the extravagant and repetitive laudations of his admirers in their unsustainable cult of a dead leader strangely served to complement. The cult of Parnell was fading by the time Joyce entered University College. His friend C. P. Curran, the most perceptive memorialist of Joyce as a college student, was able retrospectively to label him 'a completely unpolitical Parnellite'.[13]

A Parnellian ethic of silence and hauteur constrained Joyce from vaunting a futile Parnellism. In University College he was regarded as someone whose preoccupations were artistic and certainly not political, even if that did not quite account for the fierceness of his dissentient apartness. He avowed himself a disciple of Henrik Ibsen rather than of Parnell. The shadow of Parnell nevertheless fell between Joyce and his most politically prominent contemporaries in University College, Thomas Michael Kettle and Francis Skeffington, both partisans of the Irish Parliamentary Party. In University College, Joyce began to map out his relationship to contemporary Irish nationalism, just about managing

13. C. P. Curran, *Under the Receding Wave* (Dublin: Gill and Macmillan, 1970), 116. I take Curran as meaning that, as well as not being politically active, Joyce's Parnellism was severed from contemporary politics, an assessment I challenge. However, in realising that Joyce had some intellectual relationship to Irish nationalism, though he was far from recognising him as a nationalist, Curran was much more astute than Joyce's other contemporaries in University College.

to keep in check his dread of the quasi-ideological tendencies of the Irish language revival. Joyce in time found himself driven back upon a rediscovered Parnellism. His understanding of Irish politics transpired to be deeper as well as less compromised than that of Kettle and Skeffington. His friendship with George Clancy, who was a partisan of the Revival, is perhaps the most moving of his college relations, rendered in both *Stephen Hero* and *A Portrait,* and does much to subvert received ideas of Joyce's unyielding resistance to the radical nationalism of his generation.

The Split and Joyce's 'Two Masters' Thesis

Exposed to the Split as a boy, Joyce as an adolescent and young man lived through its acrid backwash: the years of disillusionment in the dismal aftermath of the overthrow and death of Parnell. His critique of the Split was not merely historical and confined to the events of 1890–91; it was an indictment of the course of post-Parnellite nationalism, the chronicle of a calamity foretold by Parnell. For Joyce, as an exasperated proponent of Ireland's modernisation as a European polity, the political regression of Ireland after Parnell demanded a response. His 'two masters' thesis—that the Irish had chosen to submit to the conjoint domination of Britain and of the Catholic Church—which he articulated in his 1912 poem 'Gas from a Burner' ('Ireland, my first and only love / Where Christ and Caesar are hand in glove!') and in the 'Telemachus' episode of *Ulysses,* derives directly from the Split. The thesis propounds that nationalist Ireland had degraded itself in submitting to the co-dominion of the Catholic Church and of the British state in its Liberal manifestation. Ireland would not be worthy of independence, nor achieve it, until the country had overcome the abjection of the Split. Ireland had severely compromised, if not quite forfeited, its own claim to independence. The culpability of the Church had been a major theme of the Split during Parnell's lifetime, and drew on the long-standing Fenian objection to the Church's encroachment in nationalist politics, but where Joyce stood alone was in his insistence on the inter-equation of the Irish Church and the British state in his analysis of Irish vassalage, and his maintaining that position long after the passion of the Split had abated.

In his treatment of the Split, Joyce was unusual in the fastidiousness with which he observed the interaction of the Irish and British political spheres. Most significantly for Joyce, the Catholic Church in Ireland was in incongruous alliance with Gladstone's Liberal party, whose opposition to Parnell owed much to the 'nonconformist conscience', the emergence of which in Britain was crystallised by the O'Shea-Parnell divorce crisis. It was a strange moment of opportunistic ecumenism: the Irish Church was untroubled by the alliance, just as the nonconformists were happy to suspend their suspicions of Catholicism. The cross-contamination of politics and religious moralism was innately offensive to Joyce. Resistance to Liberal and clerical 'dictation' was a conventional Parnellite stance in the Split. But there is an important twist in Joyce's response. He was profoundly disturbed by what he saw as the transgressive fusion of Catholic and evangelical values in opposition to Parnell. That affront was experienced in equal measure by Joyce as an Irish nationalist and philosophically as a former Catholic. Not merely had the majority of the Irish Party succumbed in the Split to 'Liberal dictation', but the Irish Church had submitted to a process of moralistic evangelisation. He saw the response of the Catholic Church in Ireland to the Split as its unthinking quasi-Protestantisation. For Joyce the Split was a fathomless pit of religious as well as political confusion and incoherence. His abhorrence was as much philosophical, and even quasi-theological, as it was political.

For Joyce the alliance of Irish Catholicism and British nonconformity lay at the heart of the political and intellectual morass of the Split. The widespread deployment of a pretended moralism and religiosity to political ends, suffused with an edge of pseudo-ethnicity and confessional prejudice, affronted Joyce and gave the Split a paradigmatic status and force in his thinking and writing. The Catholic-nonconformist coalition against Parnell is an early instance of the coincidence of opposites. Thus it was that Joyce's observation and experience of the political across his lifetime persistently drove him back to the Split.

Joyce could never quite bring himself to forgive his countrymen the outcome of the Split. In insistently reverting to Parnell and to the issues of the Split, Joyce embarked on a calculated act of defiance of the Irish nationalist dispensation after Parnell's death. He stood more or less alone in continuing to hold as an intellectual tenet that the issues of the Split remained to be confronted. Most Parnellites had in varying degrees come to acquiesce in political defeat, embracing in consolation the public cult of Parnell as the lost leader or, among the Parnellite elite, mourning in semi-privacy the extraordinary politician and disarming person they had known. Joyce's recusant Parnellism, and his critique of Irish nationalist obsequiousness to the Catholic Church and to Gladstonian Liberalism, was thoroughly considered and philosophically cogent. It was a position that Joyce adopted as an intellectual ethic, rather than one which he overtly proselytised.

To the vast bulk of his countrymen, Parnellite and anti-Parnellite, Joyce's belief in continuing to confront the issues of the Split would have seemed hopelessly devoid of any sense of political reality. He was certainly aware that the position he espoused was conventionally impolitic. His refusal to acquiesce in forgetting was not simply bred of personal conviction but owed something to strategic considerations. He realised that an uncompromising argument from a Parnellite-of-the-Split perspective remained deeply troubling to Irish nationalists and still had the capacity to disturb the post-Parnellite nationalist consensus; he was adamant in the belief that the consensus had to be challenged.

Joyce was scrupulously if sceptically receptive to contemporary politics. While he more or less ruled out the Irish literary movement, on grounds that were as much political as literary, he did set out to see if there were contemporaries or contemporary movements with which he could align himself, from Skeffington and Kettle, to Irish socialism, to the freethinking editors of *Dana*. It is true that he did not really expect to find allies but, with characteristic empirical thoroughness, he undertook the search. We tend to think of the intellectual trajectory that carried Joyce into exile as defined by his semi-alienation from contemporary nationalist politics (including the politics of the Literary

Revival) and objection to the social hegemony of the Irish Church (both in itself and as a measure of the irremediable backwardness of Irish society). But what is defining and renders haunting the isolation of the Joyce who left Ireland is that he was unable to find among his own generation, and in radical or dissenting movements, any with whom he could make common cause. It could well be said that Joyce's requirements were exorbitantly exigent, but from his perspective the prospects of a change of direction in Irish politics and intellectual life seemed, at the point of his leaving, forbiddingly bleak.

Refashioning the Parnell Myth in Exile

The Parnellism of the Joyce who left Dublin had been marked by a certain reticence—he was unsure of how it related to contemporary Irish politics, and relating it to his writing, then at an early stage of its development, seemed even more challenging. The early parts of the semi-autobiographical *Stephen Hero* covering the period of the Split have not survived and Parnell's name is not mentioned in what remains, though the treatment of the Catholic Church bears the clear impress of the Split. Joyce did not work out how to treat the figure of Parnell until early exile.

In the early *Dubliners* stories, written in Dublin, Parnell featured as an unnamed absence in the invocation of post-Split Ireland. Then came 'Ivy Day in the Committee Room', written in Trieste in August 1905 (though *Dubliners* was to be denied publication until 1914). The story marked the realisation of the strategy that Joyce had at length devised to overcome what had seemed an indefeasible combination of artistic and political constraints: he had resolved not to portray Parnell directly but to catch him in the mirror of his myth in contemporary Ireland. He would write of the unfolding of Parnell's myth, working within that myth as he found it. In rendering Parnell as a spectral absence in the flickering light of the committee room, he had finally found a means of reconciling his identification with Parnell and his art. He would track the contemporary course of the Parnell myth, so that his treatment of Parnell and Parnell-related themes would have, at least as a point of departure, an objective realism.

Joyce observed what was an exigent self-inhibition. It committed him to tracking the course of the Parnell myth, and to taking his cue from public invocations of Parnell's memory. Thus Joyce's magnificent 1912 article 'L'ombra di Parnell' in the Triestine newspaper *Il Piccolo della Sera* was less prompted than enabled within the terms of Joyce's stringent protocol by an editorial article on Parnell by Arthur Griffith in *Sinn Féin*. Joyce elected to observe and to draw on public or popular manifestations of the myth, rather than to run ahead of the unfolding of the myth and to impose a Parnell that was purely of his own contriving. Joyce had found a way of rendering Parnell that was neither messianic nor merely elegiac.

Parnell and Split-inflected themes thereafter featured in all of Joyce's writing after 'Ivy Day'. They inform the aestheticised Parnellian hauteur of Stephen Dedalus in *A Portrait of the Artist as a Young Man*. Parnell's presence in *Ulysses*, if naggingly recurrent, is for the most part spectral and oblique. In the only direct portrayal of Parnell in his fictional writing, in the fracas at the office of *United Ireland* at the outset of the Split on Irish terrain, Leopold Bloom gives Parnell back his hat, which had been knocked off. Joyce thereby cunningly inserts Bloom into the narrative of Richard Barry O'Brien's classic 1898 biography. Parnell later haunts *Finnegans Wake*. He endures as a Promethean figure, still and forever pursued by an anti-Parnellite horde in the dreamworld of the *Wake*. The register of the *Wake* is nevertheless different. Joyce at last acquiesces in, but negotiates with Parnellite bravura, Parnell's passing into history.

The imaginative transformation lay in using the contemporary traces of Parnell's memory to refashion Parnell's myth in such a way as to render it faithful to his attributes in life and to his political purpose. That was what Parnell's official apologists had signally failed to do in the aftermath of his death. Joyce was consciously writing against the grain of the received myth in its political aspect and against the oblivion of the Split. In reconstituting the myth from the bottom up, Joyce gracefully shadowed the process by which Parnell had risen to prominence by winning the trust of the Irish people. It was much more than an exquisite miniature portrait by which Joyce requited a debt of allegiance acquired in youth. It is a consummate imaginative achievement. It sealed his compact with the dead leader, with whom his sense of complicity was neither passive nor unearned.

The limits of the influence of Parnell and of the Split cannot be exhaustively demarcated. The biography and posthumous myth to which Joyce was most attentive was Parnell's. Parnell's life became in some degree a vade mecum in Joyce's own. Through his dwelling on the ascent and fall of Parnell, Joyce became acutely conscious of the personal myths that attach to individuals and that affected not just his treatment of the great and famous historical figures of whom people continue to tell stories and enhance their legends after their demise. His conception of the public self was more far-reaching: an artist as well as a political leader, or someone who was neither, could have a public self.[14] In his work and extra-textually, Joyce, who had been so long denied publication and such fame as might attend publication, acquired an authorial mythos which he sought to advance and to inflect. The fictionalisation of the authorial self is a defining stratagem of his modernism. For Joyce it had its inception as much in the contemplation of Parnell's life as that of any writer.

The Critical Treatment of Joyce's Parnellism

That Parnell was the dominant political figure of Joyce's childhood and youth is widely acknowledged by biographers and critics, but the significance of this, and the development of the Parnell motif and of issues derived from the Split in Joyce's work and thought, has defied integral treatment. Richard Ellmann treats the Parnell theme well in his biography so far as it relates to the early Joyce,[15] but misses Parnell's persisting

14. The idea of a public self is antecedent to that of a scandal in which the public figure is brought down, the subject of Margot Gayle Backus, *Scandal Work: James Joyce, the New Journalism, and the Home Rule Newspaper Wars* (Notre Dame, IN: University of Notre Dame Press, 2013).

15. See Richard Ellmann, *James Joyce* (1959; rev. ed., Oxford: Oxford University Press, 1982), 32–34. Unless otherwise noted, citations refer to the revised edition. Ellmann wrote that 'Joyce has described the Christmas dinner in 1891, when his father and John Kelly raged and wept over

significance for his subject. Ellmann's bracketing of Parnell with Christ in Joyce's early thinking and writing as victims of betrayal, though not impercipient,[16] is self-delimiting in his treatment of what was Joyce's complex lifelong relationship to Parnell. In a section entitled 'Beyond Parnell' in *The Consciousness of Joyce*, this deficiency is underscored by Ellmann's assertion that Joyce moved beyond Parnell to Arthur Griffith, the driving force behind the original Sinn Féin.[17] Ellmann's belief that Joyce 'was not the man to worship the dead' mis-poses the issue of Joyce's Parnellism.[18] It is aggravated by the dismissive rendering of Joyce's relation to Parnell as 'worship', missing the dialogic character of Joyce's relationship to the dead leader. Joyce admired Griffith's journalism and had sympathy with the political project he doggedly pursued, but Griffith did not exert anything like Parnell's influence on Joyce. There is in Joyce no 'beyond Parnell' in Ellmann's sense. Ellmann was sufficiently wedded to this idea to reformulate it five years later, on the hundredth anniversary of Joyce's birth: 'Joyce is sometimes said to have been a lifelong Parnellite, but he was opposed to turning great dead men into stone effigies. In *Ulysses* he mocks the idea that Parnell is still alive and will return.'[19] This too is an aberrant misreading in which Ellmann failed to appreciate that Joyce's critique, in resisting the foreclosure of political

---

Parnell's betrayal and death' (34). This translation from fiction into autobiographical factuality is what Ellmann is most sternly criticised for, but he is certainly not the first or the last to have done so in the case of the Christmas dinner scene. That he should have limited his description of the scene itself to the single sentence quoted, *after* a detailed consideration of Joyce's Parnell poem, suggests that he may have had some scruples about its historical actuality. I conclude for reasons that are advanced later that the Christmas dinner scene never took place.

16. Ellmann, *James Joyce*, 149, 293.

17. Richard Ellmann, *The Consciousness of Joyce* (Oxford: Oxford University Press, 1977), 86–90. Ellmann, in his biography, writes of Joyce in his correspondence with Stanislaus from Rome 'rejecting parliamentarianism and supporting Arthur Griffith', which is much too simplistic. Ellmann glosses this thus: 'In this stand he was not inconsistent; Parnell had gone as far with Parliament as possible, and Kettle could scarcely accomplish what Parnell had failed in' (*James Joyce*, 237). That Parnell had gone as far 'with Parliament' as possible was Ellmann's judgement rather than one expressed by Joyce.

18. Ellmann, *The Consciousness of Joyce*, 86.

19. Richard Ellmann, 'Joyce's Religion and Politics', *Irish Times*, 2 February 1982 (special supplement).

defeat of the entombment of Parnell's memory, was the expression of a quest to re-open the potentialities that Parnell espoused and embodied. Seamus Deane provided a lucid and elegant introduction to *A Portrait* for Penguin Classics but also treats Joyce's Parnellism as a youthful preoccupation: 'It seems remarkable that the heterogeneity of Joyce's later texts coincides with a diminution of the Parnellism that had been so evident in the early books and in the Italian essays and lectures.'[20] Phillip F. Herring, a distinguished scholar of Joyce, in a strangely bitter address entitled 'Joyce's Politics', said Parnell was 'a sort of political projection of his own role as persecuted artist victimized by the traitorous people he sought to serve' and asserted that 'his bitterness at the fall of Parnell did not apparently result from any sympathy for the man personally or the cause he championed.'[21]

Historians of Ireland, typically drawn to Yeats over Joyce, have not fared much better on Joyce's relation to Parnell: F.S.L. Lyons discerned in Joyce a 'bad case of arrested Parnellism.'[22] The diagnosis is nevertheless superior to Ellmann's in the instinctive recognition of a major historian of the period of the centrality of Parnell to Joyce's Irish politics.

The argument of this book departs from that of many postcolonial readings of Joyce's politics, principally on the ground that his politics in the large sense cannot be understood unless one first considers the political views Joyce actually held and his incisive response to contemporary Irish politics in both his fiction and non-fiction. Imputing to Joyce a generic anti-imperialism achieves little beyond positing a plane of discussion in which Joyce's actual politics can be conveniently relativised, if not ignored.[23] The same applies to misconceived historicising quests to contextualise a writer of high attentiveness to the Irish political by reference to strains of contemporary Irish (or English) political writing and thought which have no demonstrable bearing on Joyce's actual

20. Seamus Deane, introduction to *A Portrait of the Artist as a Young Man*, by James Joyce (London: Penguin Classics, 1993), xl.

21. Herring, 'Joyce's Politics', 7–8.

22. F.S.L. Lyons, 'James Joyce's Dublin', *Twentieth Century Studies* 4 (November 1970): 20.

23. I am here thinking particularly, and respectively, of Emer Nolan, *James Joyce and Nationalism* (London: Routledge, 1995); and Andrew Gibson, *Joyce's Revenge: History, Politics and Aesthetics in 'Ulysses'* (Oxford: Oxford University Press, 2002).

beliefs and convictions.[24] It is on the subject of Joyce's nationalism that postcolonial criticism of Joyce falls into ideological blatancy. Emer Nolan's work, which has had considerable influence, is entitled *James Joyce and Nationalism*. The 'and' says much. In her account, Joyce renders nationalism in his work but it is not suggested that Joyce is a nationalist, which could be inconvenient for her argument.[25] She explains that 'Nationalism', for the first children of the Irish Free State and the new republic, signified the official ideology of the post-revolutionary state, designed to distract attention from economic failure 'about "a people coming out of captivity", told by the pusillanimous middle class revolutionaries to whom all the benefits of independence accrued'.[26] That definition of course puts paid to the idea that Joyce could have been an Irish nationalist. Andrew Gibson, in his *The Strong Spirit: History, Politics and Aesthetics in the Writings of James Joyce, 1898–1915*, exhibits the same inhibition in relating Joyce's non-fictional writings of 1907–12 to his 'sense of a battle to be fought alongside nationalists, against conservatism and unionism, over the public image of the Irish, and their right to a place in the modern world'.[27] That tortuous construct asserts that Joyce the anti-imperialist was showing solidarity with the Irish nationalist cause, but was not himself an Irish nationalist. How Joyce could have been a Parnellite, as Gibson repeatedly accepts, without being a nationalist is not explained. On the other edge of postcolonialism, Marjorie Howes and Derek Attridge write of Joyce that 'philosophically he could be said to have been both a separatist and a unionist, thinking constantly in terms of oppositions and that which dissolves (or reverses)

24. Andrew Gibson, *The Strong Spirit: History, Politics and Aesthetics in the Writings of James Joyce, 1898–1915* (Oxford: Oxford University Press, 2013).

25. Nolan suggests that Joyce's Italian lectures and articles from 1907–12 'have played a major part in the recruitment of the writer as "soft" Irish nationalist by Richard Ellmann and later commentators on Joyce's politics' (*Joyce and Nationalism*, 121).

26. Nolan, *Joyce and Nationalism*, 22. Elsewhere she has asserted sweepingly, 'Nationalists may talk about coming to national self-consciousness of their own nations, but historically, nationalism has served to consolidate a system of states, whose underlying logic is that of the development of international capitalism'. Emer Nolan, 'State of the Art: Joyce and Postcolonialism', in *Semicolonial Joyce*, ed. Derek Attridge and Marjorie Howes (Cambridge: Cambridge University Press, 2000), 91.

27. Gibson, *Strong Spirit*, 112.

oppositions.'[28] There is no sense in which, philosophically or politically, Joyce could be said to have been a Unionist.

It is not simply that Joyce's relation to Parnell and the Parnell Split is a neglected facet of Joyce's political biography. There is a false frontier interposed between literature and politics that finds expression in a persisting critical disposition to treat Parnell as exogenous to Joyce's art, as something 'out there' in a separate realm of Irish politics, rather than as an active element in his thought and writing. Critically unfashionable as it may be as a proposition, the Parnell theme is an integral part of Joyce's *parcours* as a writer.

The increased critical attention to the role of Parnell and of nationalism in Joyce's work reflects a wider attentiveness to the treatment of the social and political in Joyce's writing, which in an important aspect is interwoven with his own struggles as an artist. Joyce is frequently taken to have embraced, through the figure of Stephen Dedalus in *A Portrait*, a concept of transcendental authorial autonomy. The idea that Joyce was asserting the freedom of the artist from history and social determination has been devastatingly assailed by Margot Norris. She has identified Joyce's insistent rendering in his fictional writing of the inhibitions, material and political, which as a writer he had to overcome. Her 1992 *Joyce's Web* contested what had been the prevalent identification of Joyce with modernistic aestheticism, which had brought about the canonisation of Joyce for 'an ahistoricism and an apoliticism that appears to repeat Stephen's heroic *Non-Serviam* from *Portrait*'. She asserts cogently that Joyce historicises and subverts his own modernist aestheticism: 'Joyce's texts can be made . . . to yield their own negation of artistic autonomy by betraying their genesis in Irish colonialism and lower class poverty'. This argument is the source of her disagreement with Ellmann: 'Perhaps more than other literary biographies, the Ellmann biography reinforces the ideology of artistic autonomy by trivialising and denigrating what falls outside Joyce's art, including, as Robert Scholes has argued, Joyce's

28. Marjorie Howes and Derek Attridge, introduction to Attridge and Howes, *Semicolonial Joyce*, 2.

socialist and other political tendencies.'[29] Norris has hacked away at a cornerstone of the edifice that sustains the idea of Joyce as a politics-disdaining artist.

It is striking that Joyce's actual political convictions, to the extent to which they can be established (which is considerable), have not been systematically addressed since Dominic Manganiello's pioneering and exemplary *Joyce's Politics*, published in 1980, over four decades ago. That is because the subject of Joyce's political philosophy and convictions is not favoured in contemporary Joyce criticism. Perhaps because Manganiello had Ellmann as a supervisor, his work is considered to be tainted like Ellmann's own by liberal humanism, something that is anathema to certain schools of Joyce criticism. (That is not to posit an argument that Joyce was a liberal, which he was not).[30]

Joyce's politics and his modelling of history are of a brilliance, originality, and coherence that have passed mostly unrecognised. That owes much to the fact that his negotiation of the political is for the most part oblique, rendered as from an angle of vision. His politics and imaginative rendering of history warrant consideration in their own right for what they tell us about Irish history and politics, rather than merely as an elucidation of particular episodes in Joyce's life, or as an explanatory gloss to his work.

29. Margot Norris, *Joyce's Web: The Social Unraveling of Modernism* (Austin: University of Texas Press, 1992), 6–8. The reference is to the title essay of Robert Scholes's *In Search of James Joyce* (Urbana: University of Illinois Press, 1992), 129–43. Norris is acutely perceptive on what she terms 'the Ellmann biography's blatant patronization of the way Joyce negotiated his material circumstances' (8; also see 30–33).

30. It is a corollary of Joyce's Parnellism that he was not a Liberal; and of his Irish nationalism and his affinities with socialism and anarchism that he was not a liberal.

2

John Stanislaus Joyce

One night he wept in his cups when telling of his forefathers. His father had parented a large family, and his grandfathers before him had been parents of families of from twelve to eighteen children. Joyce would sigh, and then pull himself together and swear that by the grace of God he was still a young man, and he would have more children before the end.

—ROBERT MCALMON[1]

Throughout his many wanderings James Joyce carried his family portraits as *pius Aeneas* bore his household gods. These portraits were the icons of a family cult, an oral history which transcended genealogy and attained the status of a foundation myth or an epic. We may refer to it as *The Joycead* in order to emphasize the conventions which govern it and to distinguish it from more orthodox history. The full text was lost, as it were, with the last breath of John Joyce, who was the principal author of this epic.

—COLBERT KEARNEY, 'THE JOYCEAD'[2]

And the greater the patrarc the griefer the pinch

—*FINNEGANS WAKE*[3]

1. Robert McAlmon, *Being Geniuses Together, 1920–1930*, rev. ed. (San Francisco: North Point, 1984), 27.

2. Colbert Kearney, 'The Joycead', in *Coping with Joyce: Essays from the Copenhagen Symposium*, ed. Morris Beja and Shari Benstock (Columbus: Ohio State University Press, 1989), 58. In this biographical essay on John Stanislaus Joyce, which contrives to be both brilliantly innovative and elegant, Kearney argues that James Joyce did not actually believe 'the Joycead' but neither would he dismiss it with contempt: 'Rather with an extraordinary sane generosity, he would understand why and how human beings tell each other stories to pass the time outside paradise' (71).

3. *FW* 269.25–26.

JOHN STANISLAUS JOYCE DIED in Dublin on 29 December 1931. James Joyce had not seen him in almost twenty years. He wrote to his friend and benefactor Harriet Shaw Weaver three weeks later,

> My father had an extraordinary affection for me. He was the silliest man I ever knew and yet cruelly shrewd. He thought, and talked of me up to his last breath. I was very fond of him always, being a sinner myself, and even liked his faults. Hundreds of pages and scores of characters in my books came from him. His dry (or rather wet) wit and his expression of face convulsed me so often with laughter. . . . I got from him his portraits, a waistcoat, a good tenor voice, and an extravagant licentious disposition (out of which, however, the greater part of any talent I may have springs) but apart from these, something else I cannot define.[4]

He added in a later letter, 'It seems to me his voice has somehow got into my body or throat. Lately, more than ever, especially when I sigh.'[5] Joyce told Louis Gillet, who knew him well in Paris in the 1930s, 'The humour of *Ulysses* is his [John Stanislaus Joyce's]; its people are his friends. The book is his spittin' image'.[6] Gillet wrote that Joyce's father was certainly the person Joyce most admired in the world: 'This simple man, tramp and drunkard, was a sort of lord. It was from him that the great writer had inherited the haughty air, the prodigious faith in himself, the refusal of all compromise and concession which are the features of his work.'[7] Gillet ventured that 'this peculiar rapport with his father would appear, the more one thinks it over, as the central factor in Joyce's life, the basis, the axis of his work'.[8] A legendary Dublin persona, at

4. Joyce to Harriet Shaw Weaver, 17 January 1932, *Letters I* 312.

5. Joyce to Harriet Shaw Weaver, 22 July 1932, *Letters III* 250.

6. Ellmann, *James Joyce*, 23. The source is Ellmann's unpublished notes of an interview with Gillet.

7. Louis Gillet, *Claybook for James Joyce*, trans. Georges Markow-Totevey (London: Abelard-Schuman, 1958), 77.

8. Gillet, *Claybook for James Joyce*, 103. 'I have always thought that this heroicomic individual played a leading part in the imagination of Joyce; he was one of those magnificent failures having in them abundant material for poetic creation, one of those originals from whom the artist can reprint at will a hundred copies'. Gillet, *Claybook for James Joyce*, 101.

least in his prime, it is through the writings of his son, and visually by an arresting portrait by Patrick Tuohy, that the memory of John Stanislaus Joyce vividly endures.

Origins

The bearers of the name of Joyce were reputedly of Anglo-Welsh origin and came to the west of Ireland in the thirteenth century. They gave their name to the Joyce Country, which lay in the Maum Valley west of Lough Mask in north Galway, extending between the villages of Cong and Leenane. John Stanislaus Joyce descended from a severed southern branch which found its way in the late seventeenth century to Lixnaw in County Kerry, where Seán Mór Seoighe became steward to the Fitzmaurices, and on to Athlacca in County Limerick before seeping into County Cork. John Stanislaus's great-grandfather George Joyce took up residence in Rose Cottage outside Fermoy, where he worked limestone, following the traditional trade of that line of Joyces, and dealt in horses. His son James was reputed to have been a Whiteboy, a somewhat generic term for adherents of semi-insurrectionary agrarian protest that had a more specific actuality in east Cork.[9] It seems fair to infer, principally from family lore and from the politics passed on to his grandson, that 'this primal James Joyce' was an agrarian radical,[10] anticlerical small farmer. It also seems likely that John Stanislaus's hearty disrespect for the Catholic clergy owed a good deal to his grandfather. James Augustine Joyce, John Stanislaus's father, was born at Rose Cottage in

9. John Wyse Jackson and Peter Costello, *John Stanislaus Joyce: The Voluminous Life and Genius of James Joyce's Father* (London: Fourth Estate, 1998), 16. In *A Portrait*, Simon Dedalus, pointing to the portrait of his grandfather, asserts that he was condemned to death as a whiteboy (*P* 1.1085–86). The Doneraile area of County Cork to the northwest of Fermoy had the most affrays during the tithe war, as the resistance to the collection of tithes to support the clergy of the Church of Ireland was known. See Noreen Higgins McHugh, 'The 1830s Tithe Riots', in *Riotous Assemblies: Rebels, Riots and Revolts in Ireland*, ed. William Sheehan and Maura Cronin (Cork: Mercier Press, 2011), 89. The riots in the Doneraile area date from 1832, and so postdate the likely departure of James Joyce for the city of Cork.

10. Kearney, 'Joycead', 60.

1827: the date of birth of his father is the first definite date John Stanislaus knew of his family's history. Soon after his birth, the family moved to Cork city, purchasing first a property at White Street. Their prosperity, deriving from the business of lime burning and horse dealing, is attested to by the first of the family portraits, of James Joyce and his wife, Anne, considered to date from the 1840s.[11]

This was the ancestral journey that brought the Joyces to Cork. Following in the steps of Colbert Kearney in his seminal 1986 paper 'The Joycead', John Wyse Jackson and Peter Costello succeed in tracing that journey with some precision. They observe that it followed a thread of Irish history, 'in that culturally significant shift from the medieval Gaelic-speaking life of Seán Mór Seoighe in 1680 to the anglophone entrepreneurism fostered by the growth of commerce in Cork'.[12] The family made a startlingly abbreviated transition from agrarian disaffection to commercial prosperity and property ownership in Cork in one generation, which may account for some of John Stanislaus Joyce's social and political idiosyncrasies and contradictions.

James Augustine Joyce married Ellen O'Connell, who was ten years older, on 29 January 1847 in Cork. John Stanislaus Joyce believed that his maternal grandfather John O'Connell was a cousin of Daniel O'Connell: 'I used to hear my poor mother say that the Liberator would pull up at the door, come in to see my grandfather and the two of them would walk down the street together, arm in arm.'[13] The bloodline of

11. See Jackson and Costello, *John Stanislaus Joyce*, 5–20. The Joyce family portraits are listed in a letter from Paul Léon to Frank Budgen, in which Léon says they are by Comerford. John Comerford (ca. 1770–1832) was a well-regarded portrait painter and miniaturist. See Walter G. Strickland, *A Dictionary of Irish Artists* (Dublin: Maunsel, 1913), 2:194–202.

12. Jackson and Costello, *John Stanislaus Joyce*, 18. According to Kearney, the Joyces who settled around Fermoy remained conscious of their origins in the Joyce country: 'To this day the Joyces of East Cork preserve a tribal memory of their Galway ancestry and they believe, with justification, that they are descended from masons who came south in search of work. They prospered but at some stage they excited the envy or the disdain of their neighbours who composed a saying which still survives, *never trust a Joyce, or Rice, or a Quirke*' ('Joycead', 59).

13. Maria Jolas, 'Interview with Mr. John Stanislaus Joyce', in *A James Joyce Yearbook*, ed. Maria Jolas (Paris: Transition, 1949), 163. Eoin O'Mahony, in a 1955 lecture, stated there was no

the O'Connells was not a source of pride to John Stanislaus Joyce. His second son, Stanislaus, though suspicious of his father's account of anything, seemed convinced by his father's male-line prejudices, perhaps on account of the pseudo-science of physiognomy. Thus he lamented in the diary he kept in Dublin before he left that he had 'a typically large Irish head, not the baboon-faced type, but the large, square, low-fronted head of O'Connell and Curran'.[14] Later, discussing his father's manipulative use of money in the family when he had it ('Pappie is a balking little rat'), he observed, 'In his face this is featured in his O'Connell snout.'[15] The final reference in his Dublin diary is, 'I like the City at night, wide O'Connell Street (I have O'Connell blood in me and an O'Connell face. I would prefer I hadn't. The Joyce blood is better)'.[16]

Stanislaus offers a significant piece of information in relation to his grandparents' marriage that is likely to have some truth to it and casts a shaft of light on his father's psychological make-up. Stanislaus states that the marriage was arranged by priests, 'to steady the young man, as one imagines'. He continues, 'In Ireland "priests' marriages" have a bad name, and my grandfather's marriage proved worthy of that evil repute. As a result, though fervently Catholic, he became very anti-clerical. He handed on his antipathy to priests as a precept to his son, and found him apt.'[17] Ellen Joyce gave birth to John Stanislaus Joyce on 4 July 1849. He was the third only son in succession on the Joyce side.[18] It was with that

---

kinship with O'Connell (*Irish Times*, 6 May 1955). O'Mahony was pre-occupied with Joyce's Cork connections, it is said to the point of developing an elaborate theory according to which *Ulysses* was actually set in Cork, masked by references to Dublin locations which in fact related to the topography of Cork.

14. Stanislaus Joyce, entry for 29 March 1904, in *The Complete Dublin Diary of Stanislaus Joyce*, ed. George H. Healey (Ithaca, NY: Cornell University Press, 1971), 21. The 'baboon-face' is the elongated upper lip of the rural Irish as rendered by Victorian cartoonists. Stanislaus's reference to O'Connell in this context is a little odd, in that while he was ethnically caricatured, this was not a prominent feature of it. Curran's face fitted the stereotype even less.

15. S. Joyce, entry for 3 April 1904, in *Dublin Diary*, 37.

16. S. Joyce, entry for 31 August 1904, in *Dublin Diary*, 72.

17. Stanislaus Joyce, *My Brother's Keeper: James Joyce's Early Years* (New York: Viking, 1958), 44. Stanislaus's account admittedly bears some of the impress of 'The Joycead'.

18. S. Joyce, *My Brother's Keeper*, 43. In his *Dublin Diary*, Stanislaus had only gone one generation back: 'Pappie is the only child of an only child (his father) and therefore the

male line that John Stanislaus was preoccupied, to the point of remorselessness.[19] In his dissection of the annals of what he calls 'The Joycead', Kearney observes, 'The most farcical of the mythological episodes was that of the naming of the only son. According to *The Joycead* it was intended to christen the son James, but thanks to the bungling of a drunken parish clerk, the baby was named John. It is infinitely more likely that John was named after his maternal grandfather, the irreproachable John O'Connell. The story of a drunken clerk was a Joycean denial of the O'Connell heritage, a heritage which teemed with scheming clerics.'[20]

The Joyces, as Kearney renders the legend engendered by John Stanislaus Joyce and abetted by James, 'were men of spirit who had sported in paradise until they were trapped into marriage with the O'Connells, a dull priest-ridden family whose only achievement was the breeding of priests and nuns'.[21]

The insolvency in 1853 of the family business, James Joyce & Son, 'salt and lime manufacturers and chapmen',[22] did not represent a major setback: James Joyce was back as a builder by 1856 at the latest. John O'Connell, John Stanislaus Joyce's grandfather on his mother's side, was markedly more successful and enjoyed greater prominence in the commercial life of Cork. By 1850 he was the alderman for the St Patrick's ward. His nephew Peter Paul McSwiney moved to Dublin in 1852, where he achieved consummate success in commerce and in municipal politics. John O'Connell's grandson John Daly was also a merchant prince of Cork, elected ahead of Charles Stewart Parnell in the two-seat constituency of the Cork city election of 1880. John Stanislaus's father, James Augustine Joyce, lacked the acumen of his father and grandfather and did not maintain their trade and business

---

spoiled son of a spoiled son, the spendthrift son of a spendthrift' (entry for 26 September 1903, 5).

19. In 'The Joycead' (72n1), Kearney asserts that John Stanislaus Joyce treated James as an only child, reflected to the end in the fact that he made him the sole beneficiary of his will.

20. Kearney, 'Joycead', 62–63. Also see Gorman, *James Joyce*, 8.

21. Kearney, 'Joycead', 65.

22. Jackson and Costello, *John Stanislaus Joyce*, 25.

interests.[23] John O'Connell secured the appointment of his son-in-law as inspector of Hackney Coaches.[24]

There was thus in place an at least notionally roisterous Joyce male line. Louis Gillet would later write sharply of Joyce's drinking that 'he had behind him centuries of alcoholism. His father, the old joker, left him this heritage'.[25] After giving John Stanislaus a fleeting formal education at the South Presentation Convent in Douglas Street, and at St Colman's College in Fermoy, his father, concerned for his son's health, arranged for him to go out on the pilot ships which worked Cork Harbour.[26] From this John Stanislaus acquired a certain cosmopolitanism and a gift for improvisation which extended to what his son Stanislaus termed 'the varied and fluent vocabulary of abuse that in later years was the delight of his bar-room cronies'.[27] According to his grandson Stanislaus, James Augustine Joyce died of typhoid on 28 October 1866, not yet forty.[28] Simon Dedalus says of his father in *A Portrait of the Artist as a Young Man*, 'He was the handsomest man in Cork at that time, by God he was! The women used to stand to look after him in the street'.[29] Joycean paternal myths extended back to James Augustine Joyce the elder and not a whole lot further.

John Stanislaus Joyce attended Queen's College, Cork, as a medical student from 1867 to 1870. His foreshortened years in Queen's College were marked by athletic prowess, companionable drinking, and the display of some promise as an actor and singer: 'There is not a field in County Cork that I did not know, for I hunted all of them. . . . I used to

23. Kearney writes, 'Before his early death in 1866 he had lost the family interests in brickmaking, building, and the sale of salt and lime' ('Joycead', 63).

24. Jackson and Costello, *John Stanislaus Joyce*, 26–28.

25. Gillet, *Claybook for James Joyce*, 105. Joyce observed a certain propriety with Gillet, who professed not to have seen him drunk. The context for his comment was Joyce's torment over Lucia. The same propriety may account for the fact that Joyce did not, as Gillet notes (102), ask him, when he was embarking on a visit to Dublin, to see his father or entrust him with a message for his father.

26. Kearney ('Joycead', 63) suggests that John Stanislaus Joyce had suffered from the typhus that was to kill his father.

27. S. Joyce, *My Brother's Keeper*, 45.

28. S. Joyce, *My Brother's Keeper*, 45.

29. *P* 2.1136–37.

hunt with the Southern Harriers.'[30] Thereafter he offered his services as an accountant to shops and businesses in Cork. He secured a position as secretary to a distilling company to be based in Dublin promoted by Cork businessmen, principal among whom was Henry Joseph Alleyn, who acquired a former flax mill in the village of Chapelizod. As John Stanislaus Joyce later recalled, 'I applied for shares—I had money at the time—and I took £500 on condition that they appointed me as secretary.'[31] It was an odd and, as it transpired, ill-starred arrangement. His mother leased the house they lived in on Anglesea Street, to which the name Rose Cottage had been transferred from Fermoy, and mother and son left Cork for Dublin. He served as secretary to the Dublin and Chapelizod Distillery Company for some four or five years. While his son Stanislaus gave an account in which John Stanislaus discovered that the manager was embezzling the firm's money, confronted him, and alerted the shareholders,[32] the reality was more prosaic. Irish whiskey was losing out to Scotch in the English market, and Alleyn and the other shareholders became estranged. The shareholders resolved on 1 April 1876 that the company should be wound up. Matters dragged on into 1878, but John Stanislaus Joyce had lost his employment and what was for him the substantial sum he had invested in the business.[33] The fall had already begun.

30. Jolas, 'John Stanislaus Joyce', 169. The idea of Joyce commissioning an interview with his father admittedly seems somewhat strange, but it was a stratagem devised by Joyce to bridge the gap of exile. In June 1962 on the occasion of the opening of the Joyce tower, Flann O'Brien (writing as *Irish Times*' diarist 'Quidnunc'), in his 'Irishman's Diary', referred to the *Yearbook* that contained 'an interview with Mr. John Stanislaus Joyce which reads like the real McKay, but is known to be the work of a master-parodist' (*Irish Times*, 19 June 1962). As Ellmann points out (*James Joyce*, 747n19), the hoax lies in O'Brien's own claim. 'Cruiskeen Law', by Myles na gCopaleen (another Flann O'Brien pseudonym), curiously appeared side by side with the 'Irishman's Diary' (*Irish Times*, 19 June 1962). O'Brien was magnificently subversive of the emergent cult of Joyce and had written the previous year (under his real name Brian O'Nolan), 'If I hear the word "Joyce" again I will surely froth at the gob': O'Nolan to Timothy O'Keefe, 25 November 1961, in *The Collected Letters of Flann O'Brien*, ed. Maebh Long (Dallas: Dalkey Archive Press, 2018), 286.

31. Jolas, 'John Stanislaus Joyce', 159.

32. S. Joyce, *My Brother's Keeper*, 48–49; Ellmann, *James Joyce*, 16.

33. Jackson and Costello, *John Stanislaus Joyce*, 76–79; Peter Costello, *James Joyce: The Years of Growth, 1882–1915: A Biography* (London: Kyle Cathie, 1992), 45–46.

The Early Politics of John Stanislaus Joyce

A nimbus of myth surrounds the politics of John Stanislaus Joyce. The principal source of conventional biographical information in relation to his early manhood is his son Stanislaus. While deeply critical of his father to the point of hostility in *My Brother's Keeper,* Stanislaus was, in spite of himself, in some degree unimaginatively accepting of aspects of his father's heroic narrative of himself. There is little in the way of historically verifiable fact concerning the later political course of John Stanislaus Joyce, so that Stanislaus's account is to be assessed principally by reference to the matrix of contemporary politics and to its discordance with his brother's rendering of their father.

It might be considered debatable whether John Stanislaus Joyce 'had' any 'politics' in the Irish sense of the term, but that sense itself is anachronistic, deriving its definitive modern form from the course of post-1912 politics, and is not readily applicable to the more fluid era of the prelude to Irish independence, beyond the broad distinction between nationalists and Unionists. Yet John Stanislaus Joyce had a distinctive political complexion or temper of ample if splenetic humaneness that was bound up with the idea that his was a gentlemanly lineage. His socio-economic conception of himself was politically complex. It is not simply reducible to the fact that he had inherited property which might, properly marshalled, have sufficed to give him a reasonable livelihood. He conceived himself as an Irish gentleman of extroverted nature, certainly on the nationalist side, but the fusion of sociability and rebelliousness with which he identified in his lineage were those of an Ireland which was evanescent and which Parnellism would displace. He needed to fashion strong connections either politically or in the commercial life of Dublin, but proved to have little capacity to do either. Gallant confidence yielded over time to a baffled irascibility, though the force of his personality remained undiminished, as did his remarkable aptitude in social performance, as a reciter of ballads and singer, conversationalist, raconteur, and purveyor of humorous observations and sometimes devastating put-downs. It may even be that he was simply bored by and mostly indifferent to the ordinary course of contemporary politics up until the Parnell Split, even if constrained to hold forth on politics in a city and country where nothing was untouched by politics.[34] He did not lack imaginative sympathy with Parnell's friends and interlocutors, as his relationship with John Kelly attested. What can be confidently ruled out is the backward projection of his Parnellite ardour in the Split of 1890–91 to invest him with the status of a dedicated, never mind active, Parnellite in the 1880s. That false inference muffles the form of secular redemption he achieved by his espousal of Parnell in the course of the fall and is a significant element in the misunderstanding of the relationship of his son's Parnellism to his own.

There is a further indication. John Stanislaus Joyce negotiated with immense aplomb the transition from Cork to Dublin. Dublin, like any nineteenth-century capital, and perhaps a little more, drew much of its energy from internal migration from the other urban centres of Ireland and the countryside. It remains striking that John Stanislaus Joyce attained the status of a rootedly Dublin character, whose Cork origins came to seem a remote incident of biography that did not detract from his metropolitan status. His spatial translation to Dublin was consummately achieved. His range of acquaintanceship was prodigious, and his grasp of Dublin lore surpassed that of most Dublin-born natives.[35] His transition in time, in political and commercial epoch, was more fraught.

34. In *Stephen Hero* Mr Wilkinson, the friend of Mr Daedalus, 'very often brought this guest home after a day's carousel and the two would sit in the kitchen for the rest of the night talking politics loudly': Stephen often heard his father's voice shouting or his fist banging the table as he turned the corner of the avenue (*SH* 161). This matches Stanislaus's recollection of 'those political rancours that formed the theme of my father's nightly, half-drunken rantings to the accompaniment of vigorous table-thumpings'. S. Joyce, *My Brother's Keeper*, 65. These accounts relate to the John Stanislaus Joyce of the fall, and whether they attest to a settled passion for politics is open to doubt. The suggestion is rather that John Stanislaus, in decline and disappointment, began to indulge repeatedly in drunken political tirades which were at odds with his former character as it had been observed by his children and were a matter of embarrassment as well as distress to them. Though the traducing of Parnell's enemies doubtless featured in the table-thumping, his offspring learned to distinguish Parnellism from alcoholically enhanced degeneration.

35. S. Joyce, *My Brother's Keeper*, 81.

He was—as evidenced by the range of figures to whom Joyce parcelled out features of his character and voice—a protean figure, of multiple aspects. He was at once idiosyncratic and original, touched by history in ways he did not necessarily understand, and an emblematic Irish figure, which endowed his persona with the plasticity on which Joyce was able to draw in so many of his works, not least *Finnegans Wake*.

John Stanislaus Joyce's relationship to Parnellism has an importance because of the issue of its influence on his son's Parnellism. There are two defining themes in the conventional rendering of his biographical profile. The first is that he was an ardent Parnellite at least from 1880. The second and related proposition is that his own decline more or less coincided with that of Parnell, or that he at least nursed a subjective connection between his professional failure and Parnell's fall. Richard Ellmann wrote in his biography of James Joyce, 'For John Joyce the fall of Parnell, closely synchronised with a fall in his own fortunes, was the dividing line between the stale present and the good old days.'[36] This proposition has a superficial attractiveness—the living conditions of John Stanislaus and his household did indeed begin to plummet shortly after Parnell's death—but it ignores the fact that the unravelling of the fortunes of Joyce predated the fall of Parnell, and assumes that his idea of 'the good old days' related to the period of Parnell's hegemony. The times whose passing John Stanislaus Joyce mourned were those that coincided with Parnell's emergence as a leader, most notably the Dublin city election of 1880.

There is no evidence of political passion, never mind activism, on the part of John Stanislaus Joyce in Parnell's cause before the Split of 1890–91. While he is conventionally rendered as an ardent Parnellite and even a Parnellite apparatchik, the more plausible view in the absence of any evidence to the contrary is that he held somewhat aloof from Parnellism in the 1880s. In purely generational terms, he was ostensibly a reasonably good candidate for Parnellite allegiance, having been born in 1849, three

36. Ellmann, *James Joyce*, 33. The idea of the interconnectedness of Parnell's fall and the sharp descent in the fortunes of John Stanislaus Joyce was an attractive proposition that antedated Ellmann's biography and is more or less rehearsed in Marvin Magalaner and Richard Kain, *Joyce: The Man, the Work, the Reputation* (New York: New York University Press, 1956), 32–37.

years after Parnell. Yet he did not fit easily into the Ireland of Parnell, more because his conception of himself was rooted in an older Ireland than by reason of his ambiguous sociological status in the new dispensation as a rentier whose income derived principally from urban property in Cork. The mischaracterisation of John Stanislaus Joyce as a Parnellite whose own rise and fall were connected to those of Parnell superimposes a thesis that does not square with Joyce's fictional rendering of his father in its socio-political aspect. That portrayal comprises both the mild and recessive Simon Dedalus of *Ulysses* and *A Portrait of the Artist as a Young Man* and the more blistering Simon Daedalus of *Stephen Hero,* as well as the John Stanislaus Joyce whose voice is heard through other characters in his son's writings. In the former direct portrayal, his father is fictionally rendered as someone who was in some degree remote from the Ireland in which he lived. Joyce did not render his father simply as idiosyncratic, mild, or wildly extrovert in his various direct and indirect manifestations, but as someone who was tangential to if not out of joint with his political time. John Stanislaus Joyce was an exuberantly assertive figure, well captured in *Stephen Hero,* but whose potentially destabilising fictional impact Joyce had to rein in in his comparatively pallid renderings of Simon Dedalus in *A Portrait* and *Ulysses,* which he was to redress in various ways in *Finnegans Wake.*

One searches Joyce's fiction in vain for an affirmation of his brother Stanislaus's later (and fairly sarcastic) suggestion that their father was an earnest partisan of Parnell through the 1880s. In a famous passage in *A Portrait,* Joyce, with beautifully modulated objectivity and affection, in an early foray in his use of the catalogue, serialises his father's multiple lives. Stephen is being interrogated by Cranly: 'But was your father what is called well-to-do? I mean when you were growing up?' Stephen begins 'to enumerate glibly his father's attributes': 'A medical student, an oarsman, a tenor, an amateur actor, a shouting politician, a small landlord, a small investor, a drinker, a good fellow, a storyteller, somebody's secretary, something in a distillery, a taxgatherer, a bankrupt and at present a praiser of his own past.'[37]

37. *P* 1.716–1151.

The characterisation of his father as 'a shouting politician' in a sequence of aborted careers is plainly a reference to the Dublin city election of 1880, possibly coloured by his support of Parnell in the Split. The catalogue scarcely sustains the idea of his father as tirelessly politically active or ambitious. In a similar vein to the catalogue, Joyce told Eugene Sheehy that he had put down his father's occupation as 'entering for competitions' when applying for University College.[38]

Padraic Colum wrote a remarkably sharply recalled account of his first real encounter with James Joyce as they left the National Library. It was the post–University College Joyce, whom Colum had been introduced to at Lady Gregory's and had crossed several times thereafter. Colum candidly acknowledges that Joyce knew that Colum was fascinated by him, and played up to that. His characterisation of his father was significant: 'On that occasion he showed himself as the scion of an outstanding family. His father, who had come to Dublin from Cork, had had a sinecure; he had lost it and got through his capital in practises of good fellowship. Joyce permitted himself to be a little homilectic: "What I kept, I lost; what I gave, I have. If my father was able to say that he need not regret what he has come to"'.[39]

John Stanislaus Joyce's eccentricity encompassed the idea that he was ex-centric to the Ireland in which Parnell was becoming hegemonic, and some part of his own humour played on the fact. His imaginative affinities were with a more politically formless anterior Ireland which he imperfectly understood. His roots in that Ireland, pre-Parnellite if not quite post-Gaelic, were shallow and only glimpsed by him through the receding memories or fables of three anterior generations. He was stranded between the vague contours of the still not yet post-Gaelic Ireland of the late eighteenth century and the more sharply edged modern Ireland of Parnell.

Joyce neither forgot nor discounted his father's embrace of Parnell in the Split, which had opened his mind as a child to the cause of Parnell,

38. Ellmann, *James Joyce*, 69.

39. Mary Colum and Padraic Colum, *Our Friend James Joyce* (New York: Doubleday, 1958), 21.

but he apprehended that it was a turn that was steeped in irony, and he came in time to love his father more on account of it. Joyce understood that Parnell represented a modern nationalism, from which his father stood apart. What he took from John Stanislaus, as well as an opening to Parnellism in the Split, was an intimation of the cruelty of displacement in the cycles of history. The phrase Joyce wrote on the first page of *Finnegans Wake*, 'a kidscad buttended a bland old isaac',[40] referring to Parnell's eclipsing of his predecessor Isaac Butt, had a distant origin in his contemplation of the broken life of his father.

Relationships to two contemporary institutions cast some light on John Stanislaus Joyce's thinking. The first is the Catholic Church. He was openly contemptuous of the Catholic clergy. It was something he saw as the proper attitude of an independent gentleman. It was also pointedly male: deference to the priesthood was the province of female piety, and unmanly. This is traceable to his grandfather James Joyce and his father, and was to descend to his son, the second James Joyce. John Stanislaus was little disposed to recalibrate his attitude to the Catholic clergy to reflect the consolidation of the social power and influence of the Catholic Church in Ireland that had taken place since his grandfather's youth. The second institution is Fenianism. John Stanislaus's affective relation to Fenianism in his early life is nebulous, turning essentially on a few scraps of information provided by his son Stanislaus, by Herbert Gorman, Joyce's first biographer, and by what might be inferred from the course of his later life and friendships. James Joyce never suggested that his father had any involvement with Fenianism, though his own openness to older Fenian ideas is consistent with at least passive Fenian affinities on his father's part. Gorman wrote that John Stanislaus as a medical student made an impetuous dash to join the French army after the outbreak of the Franco-Prussian War; his mother caught up with him in London and brought him back to Cork.[41] Stanislaus provides a little more detail, and adds an account of his father having an involvement in a Fenian group in Cork:

40. *FW* 3.11–12.

41. Gorman, *James Joyce*, 9.

> After an abortive attempt to volunteer with three college friends for the French army in '70 (he was twenty-one then), including a flight to London with his mother in stern chase and a crest-fallen return, he got mixed up with a Fenian group in Rebel Cork so that his harassed mother decided to leave Cork for good. She was influenced in her decision by the fact that in view of the approaching O'Connell Centenary, her cousin, Peter Paul M'Swiney, a cousin of the Liberator's, had been elected Lord Mayor of Dublin. She hoped the Lord Mayor would make her son his secretary.[42]

The chronology is garbled in the manner of family memories. The Germans defeated the French at Sedan in 1870; Peter Paul McSwiney was Lord Mayor of Dublin in 1864–65 and 1875–76, and in his second term presided over the O'Connell centenary. John Stanislaus Joyce's Fenian involvement, such as it may have been, post-dated the feeble rising of 1867. What Stanislaus's rendering of his father's narrative of his life suggests is less Fenian ardour than a marked resentment of his female line, in the person of his mother, in constraining his self-expression. One imagines that John Stanislaus Joyce would have made a great deal more of his putative relationship to Daniel O'Connell if it derived from the male line. Something of this reserve was transmitted to his son. O'Connell is a somewhat marginal figure in James Joyce's rendering of Irish history in a way that is not wholly accounted for by his embrace of Parnell as the pre-eminent nationalist Irish leader of the nineteenth century. That McSwiney, who in 1875 had a leading role in the commemoration of the centenary of the birth of O'Connell, was the creature of the ultra-montane and implacably anti-Fenian Cardinal Cullen, Archbishop of Dublin, who more than any other prelate embodied the consolidation of Catholic power in nineteenth-century Ireland, was not calculated to endear Joyce to his female ancestral line, nor, however unfair it might be, to O'Connell. There is a certain rivalry in myth between Parnell and O'Connell, but the fact that Joyce never celebrated a

42. S. Joyce, *My Brother's Keeper*, 46–47. See also Stanislaus Joyce, *Recollections of James Joyce* (New York: James Joyce Society, 1950), 5–6.

familial connection to the Liberator suggests an adoption of his father's prejudices.

Stanislaus Joyce wrote of his father that 'a position was found for him as secretary of the National Liberal Club.'[43] The position was as secretary of the United Liberal Club, which had its offices at 53 Dawson Street. Gorman states that he was appointed through the influence of McSwiney, his mother's relative. By 1877 the antecedent Liberal Registration Association was, as the *Freeman's Journal* wrote after the election, 'practically defunct. There was neither means nor organization to work the Registries'. The Conservatives in Dublin city and county had in the Constitutional Club 'a vigorous, active and opulent association'. The initiative for the establishment of the United Liberal Club came from pro–Home Rule professionals and businessmen. The *Freeman's Journal* stated,

> A few men in face of great discouragements initiated the United Liberal Club. The bulk of the Whig Liberals of Dublin refused them any support or assistance because they were Home Rulers. Many of the Home Rulers who claimed a monopoly of patriotism denounced them as Whigs because they were willing to co-operate with the whole Liberal Party for the registration purposes. The men who alone would benefit pecuniarily by the change of Government—lawyers and the whole class of place honour seekers—held aloof from them. The bulk of men who owed their fortunes to Liberal Administration would not touch them or contribute a shilling towards the objects of the Club. The Club worked on, and did the work in spite of the discouraging sneers and opposition of those who should have helped.[44]

The United Liberal Club was established at a point in time when the contest between Parnell's supporters and those loyal to Isaac Butt was already advanced. It is likely that most of its members were Home Rule moderates, though by no means all were necessarily opposed to Parnell.

43. S. Joyce, *My Brother's Keeper*, 49.

44. *Freeman's Journal*, 7 April 1880.

Its purpose of seeking to secure the defeat of Conservative candidates in Dublin was shaped by the exigencies of Dublin electoral politics, where on the prevailing franchise there was little prospect of a Parnellite candidate being returned.

It was in his capacity as secretary of the United Liberal Club that John Stanislaus Joyce had his most substantial political involvement, in the Liberal triumph in winning both seats in the city of Dublin at the 1880 election. At the general election of 1874, Sir Arthur Edward Guinness had been returned at the head of the poll, followed by Maurice Brooks, a Liberal and nominal Home Ruler. Had the Conservatives run only Guinness, there would not have been a contest. However, in a colossal misjudgement a second Conservative candidate, James Stirling, was also nominated.[45] This was regarded by Liberals and Home Rulers as throwing down the gauntlet in an attempt to restore the 'Dublin Six', the return of Unionists for all the Dublin constituencies, comprising Dublin city and county, and Trinity College. The then–moderate Liberal *Freeman's Journal* declared that 'Sir Arthur Guinness has forfeited every claim to personal consideration by becoming a party to this most insolent attempt of his faction to force a second Conservative upon the people of Dublin and to thus re-establish the hated ascendancy of the Dublin Six.'[46] The paper continued to denounce the Stirling candidacy as 'an audacious attempt . . . to renew the old ascendancy of the "Dublin Six", and to add, moreover, a new shackle to the yoke and degradation of that ascendancy'.[47]

At a meeting at the Liberal Club on 27 March 1880, the Liberals in their turn adopted a second candidate, Robert Dyer Lyons, a Liberal Catholic professional, along with the incumbent Brooks. His candidacy was hailed by the *Evening Telegraph*: 'The war-cry of "Guinness and Stirling" has been answered by the Liberals of Dublin. They shout in reply, "Up for Lyons and Brooks!"' The paper was obliged to add that his election address was 'all that a Liberal and a Catholic could wish, though it falls

45. It was reported that Stirling had obtained the support of the Presbyterian body and of the Temperance party. *Daily Express*, 26 March 1880.

46. *Freeman's Journal*, 29 March 1880.

47. *Freeman's Journal*, 31 March 1880.

short of what a thorough Home Ruler would desire'.[48] The *Freeman's Journal* professed its confidence in their return: 'The foe has more money and better organization, but on our side is right and justice and that mighty force of enthusiasm. The foe may have more paid agents fighting under their plutocratic banner, but on our side volunteers will show how infinitely more valuable their unbought aid is.'[49] Endeavouring to close over the gap between Liberals and nationalists in Dublin, the paper thundered against the imperialist Tory prime minister, Lord Beaconsfield, the former Benjamin Disraeli.

The contest for the parliamentary representation of the Irish capital was charged with symbolism, not only because of the issue of the Dublin Six. The *Irishman* noted, 'Since O'Connell fought Dublin there has not been such interest in the contest for the city.'[50] O'Connell had won in 1837 but lost in 1841. Whatever its intelligence on the register of voters in Dublin city, the hubristic running of two candidates reflected a Conservative strategy at the 1880 election of inflicting maximum damage on the Irish Liberal party and exploiting the divisions in the Home Rule party between the partisans of the activist policies espoused by Parnell and moderate or nominal Home Rulers. Thus, the Unionist *Daily Express*, immediately before the poll, warned against an electoral outcome that would result in the formation of a Liberal government by a William Gladstone beholden to Parnell:

> To secure this support it is plain that Mr. Parnell will become the arbiter of all questions of both home and foreign politics, and that whatever he asks must be given to him. What the nature of those demands is we all know well. The property of a great class of the community is to be confiscated, and the Union is to be repealed. Anything that brings these nearer will be accepted, and in return for any such concessions a temporary support may be secured. But Mr. Parnell will make no final compromise, no binding settlement. He is one of those politicians who stride straight onwards to their goal. He has

48. *Evening Telegraph*, 29 March 1880. See also *Freeman's Journal*, 29 March 1880.

49. *Freeman's Journal*, 29 March 1880.

50. *The Irishman*, 3 April 1880.

> shown the House already what mischief he could do with half a dozen at his back. With thirty at his back, and with parties equally divided, he will render the transaction of all public business impossible unless the Liberal party submit to his dictation.[51]

The shadow of Parnell's gathering ascendancy thus fell across the Dublin city election, in which there was no Parnellite candidate. The venerable *Nation*, which was pro-Parnell, complained bitterly of the restricted Irish borough franchise that denied Ireland the benefit of the Reform Act of 1867 that applied in England and Scotland, and of the Irish system of voter registration that favoured 'the Tory plutocracy'. It conceded that 'the popular candidates for Dublin are not politicians with whom we are particularly in love'. Brooks, though he had honoured his pledges at the preceding election, 'is not by any means an ideal advocate of the national demand for self-government. Dr. Lyons is even less to our taste, for he is not even a "moderate" Home Ruler but only a Liberal'. The reality, however, was that, given the restricted electorate, 'we must . . . put up with less advanced candidates of the popular type than we would desire to see come into the field'. The Home Rule League had endorsed the Liberal candidates.[52]

Whatever the tepidity of one of the Liberal candidates about Home Rule, and the lack of commitment of the other, popular nationalist support of their candidacy in resistance to the Conservatives was visceral and unstinted. The general election of 1880 was transitional, the last election before the establishment of a clear nationalist predominance, outside the north-east of the island, at the general election of 1885. It was fiercely contested. The Dublin Tory *Evening Mail* exuberantly prophesied that 'the present general election will show this result in Ireland, that those parts of the country where wealth, commerce and education most abound will return Conservatives, while the strongholds of Parnellites and other varieties of "United Liberalism" will be found among the population that are quite ready to believe in the miracles of Knock.'[53]

51. *Daily Express*, 3 April 1880.
52. *Nation*, 3 April 1880.
53. *Dublin Evening Mail*, 31 March 1880.

The reported apparition of the Virgin Mary in the Mayo village had taken place six months previously, on 21 August 1879.

The nomination of candidates took place on 31 March at Green Street Courthouse, under conditions, lamented the *Irish Times*, 'which deprived the proceedings of every feature of that excitement which was inseparable from nominations previous to the passing of the Ballot Act.'[54] The poll and count took place on 5 April. At five o'clock the returning officers conveyed the ballot boxes to the Exhibition Palace, constructed on a part of what would later be converted to examination halls for the Royal University of Ireland, and would ultimately become the Iveagh Gardens. There the count got under way a couple of hours later. The nineteen tables were arranged in the small Alexandra Concert Hall. John Stanislaus Joyce had four men at each table, as he recalled to the journalist whom his son sent to interview him in the late 1920s:

> I didn't at all expect that we would get the two members in—I would have been satisfied if I got Brooks in but I didn't at all expect that Lyons would get in. In the end towards the end of the count I got the rough figures and I totted them up two or three times and by Gor what was but I knew the two were returned! This was the hell of a thing for me. Our solicitor, Stephen Sheehan, a tremendous big man, he was over at a table and says I, 'By Gor our men are in, Stephen—not one but the two of them'. Who should be sitting next to me but Sir Arthur Guinness and his cousin the Hon. David Plunkett, and the two were in evening dress. He lived at the time in Stephens Green; at the north side of it he had a house, his brother Lord Iveagh has it now. Sir Arthur asked me 'Have you got the figures?' 'I have, Sir Arthur', I replied, and he asked me how did it go. I then had the pleasure of telling Sir Arthur Guinness that he was no longer a member and I said that Maurice Brooks got so much and Lyons so much.[55]

54. *Irish Times*, 1 April 1880.

55. Jolas, 'John Stanislaus Joyce', 166–67.

Outside the count, a crowd had begun to assemble in the enclosure in front of the Exhibition Palace, 'and it gradually assumed enormous proportions, the entire space being filled with a surging mob. It was computed that between ten and eleven o'clock there could not have been less than thirty thousand persons assembled opposite the building. There was a great deal of rough horse-play, but on the whole the people behaved with commendable good humour, and amused themselves principally by cheering or groaning for the respective candidates.'[56] After he knew the result, but before the declaration of the poll, John Stanislaus Joyce left the building into the throng, sustained by his friend 'the Baby Policeman', who was six feet, five inches tall: 'When I found we had the election won, I was going out but there was a great crush at the door. When the people heard the news there was the devil's shouting and cheering. . . . Gallagher of the *Freeman's Journal* got hold of me, when I pushed my way through the door, to get the figures.'[57] This was the semi-legendary Ignatius (Fred) Gallaher who was to feature in 'A Little Cloud' in *Dubliners*, and in *Ulysses*. Gallaher wrote in his report for the *Freeman*,

> About twelve o'clock a double line of police was formed from the door of the concert room to the outer door, so as to secure the passage for the High Sheriff. The scene presented was unique and unlike any declaration of the poll witnessed in this city within the memory of the oldest inhabitant. Cheers were still given for the different candidates, and there were occasional bursts of Kentish fire, which were hissed. At the last the intelligence was brought out by a gentleman on whose statements dependence could be placed, that the poll was headed by Mr. Maurice Brooks and Dr. Lyons, and that Sir Arthur Guinness was no longer member for the city. As this rumour spread it gave rise to fresh bursts of cheering.[58]

The 'gentleman on whose statements dependence could be placed' was John Stanislaus Joyce. While he could not be named because of the

56. *Daily Express*, 6 April 1880.
57. Jolas, 'John Stanislaus Joyce', 167.
58. *Freeman's Journal*, 6 April 1880.

official secrecy of the count before the poll was declared, it was a winking acknowledgement of a source in the Dublin manner. This and a similar report in the Unionist *Daily Express* were the only, innominate references to John Stanislaus Joyce in the press coverage of the Dublin elections.[59] John Stanislaus was the bearer of the glad tidings of the Liberal triumph. Two hours were consumed in the consideration of the large number of objections to voting papers. The official declaration of the poll came at 3.25 in the morning:

> Brooks 5,763
> Lyons 5,647
> Guinness 5,446
> Stirling 5,039[60]

The Conservatives had contrived to lose both the Dublin city seats. The secretary of the United Liberal Club had departed long before, proceeding from the office of the *Freeman's Journal* to the Oval Bar on Abbey Street. As John Stanislaus Joyce recalled,

> I had not taken a drink of any kind during the election—a whole fortnight—and I would not have one for God Almighty if he had come down especially from the Heavens. A car drove up and all around about there was shouting and cheering for the victors at that hour of the morning. My God it was three o'clock in the morning and the excitement was great and I was the hero of it all because they said that it was I that won the election. . . . We all went in and by God Almighty such drinking of champagne I never saw in my life. We

59. The *Daily Express* reported,

> About half past 12 o'clock the small crowd which enjoyed the privilege of waiting around the door of the Alexandra Hall, which was most jealously guarded by five stalwart policemen, were informed by a gentleman who had just left the counting room, that the scrutiny was concluded, and that Brooks and Lyons were at the head of the poll, and Sir Arthur Guinness third. . . . The names of Mr. Brooks and Dr. Lyons were passed out to the crowd in front of the building, and the demonstrations were continued. Many were still incredulous as to the result, but when a few minutes later another gentleman passed out of the Alexandra Hall and confirmed the announcement . . . there was no longer any questioning its accuracy. *Daily Express*, 6 April 1880.

60. *Daily Express*, 6 April 1880.

> could not wait to draw the corks, we slapped them against the marble-topped counter. The result was we were there drinking for about three hours and when we came out the question was what were we going to do at that hour of the morning. The Turkish Baths came into my mind and there I went after having any God's quantity of champagne. Oh dear, dear, God, those were great times.[61]

It was exhilarating stuff. He remembered, 'I was the cock of the walk that day and I will never forget it; I was complimented by everybody. I got one hundred guineas from each of the members'.[62] In his account there was a telling slip. He said, 'I was only twenty-two years old at the time.'[63] He was thirty.

It was a famous triumph. The *Freeman's Journal*, still clinging to a Home Rule Liberalism—what it referred to as 'the patriotic union of the Liberal and Home Rule Party'[64]—but wary of challenging Parnell, exulted that 'for the first time in its history Dublin has been completely rescued from the octopus-like grasp of the Tories, and has risen to its natural place as leader of the Liberal Party in Ireland'.[65] The diehard Tory *Dublin Evening Mail* noted that the majority was small, but any majority at all was 'a lamentable disgrace to the city', and 'the lowering of the franchise has added some eleven or twelve hundred voters to the electoral roll—a vast preponderance of whom are semi-paupers—a proletariat class, who are as destitute of the sense of public obligation as they are of proprietary stake in its prosperity, and who entirely out-vote the respectable minority in Dublin and in Ireland generally.'[66]

'Nothing that ingenuity could devise or energy accomplish has been left undone by the Liberal party to secure a victory', the *Irish Times* wrote on the day of the poll. 'Their battalions advance to the conflict with high boast and hope. The canvass on behalf of Messrs Brooks and

61. Jolas, 'John Stanislaus Joyce', 167–68.
62. Jolas, 'John Stanislaus Joyce', 167.
63. Jolas, 'John Stanislaus Joyce', 162.
64. *Freeman's Journal*, 1 April 1880.
65. *Freeman's Journal*, 6 April 1880.
66. *Dublin Evening Mail*, 6 April 1880.

Lyons has been carried on by hundreds of willing volunteers'.[67] The *Freeman's Journal* credited the United Liberal Club with the Liberal triumph in the city of Dublin.[68] John Stanislaus Joyce was certainly entitled to a share of the credit, though his later boast that 'I won the election in Dublin and I was the man that put in Maurice Brooks and Lyons, and put out Arthur Guinness . . . and of course Stirling',[69] was a gross, if pardonable, exaggeration. His name was not once published in the reporting of the election. This was not surprising: however significant his contribution, he was a figure in the background, whose role lay in directing the canvass on the ground. He was moreover a paid employee; he would never be one of the urban grandees such as John O'Hagan or Sergeant Hemphill who assented to the nomination of the Liberal candidates. The gratuity of £100 paid by each of the elected members served to underscore his status as a transient functionary, of whose personal services the successful candidates showed monetarily their appreciation.

On the day of the poll, the conservative *Irish Times*, sensing the tightness of the contest, had sought ingeniously to sway nationalist voters against the candidacy of Lyons, who did not profess to be a supporter of Home Rule in evoking Parnell's attack on Nicholas Dan Murphy, the Liberal candidate in the Cork city constituency which Parnell was contesting. 'The leader of the Irish Parliamentary Party assails the Whig with great vehemence, and states in plain terms that he would prefer that the Tory in Cork was returned to the Whig-Liberal'. Parnell was presaging a more active policy against what was clearly going to be a Liberal administration. The paper could 'well understand the process of reasoning by which Mr. Parnell is influenced, and the game in its new form which requires that he should make the Liberals feel the strength of his hand'.[70]

67. *Irish Times*, 5 April 1880.

68. *Freeman's Journal*, 7 April 1880.

69. Jolas, 'John Stanislaus Joyce', 162.

70. *Irish Times*, 5 April 1880. At a Conservative meeting in the Royal Exchange Ward, Parnell's brother-in-law lent his support to the party candidates: 'Captain Dickinson said that he happened to be a relative of Mr. Parnell, and though he was a Home Ruler, he intended to vote

Parnell did not campaign in the city of Dublin election and gave no direction to his supporters. Had he wished to, he could not have appeared to oppose Maurice Brooks, who was a member of the Irish Party. There was no love lost between Parnell and Brooks. When the Irish Party met in City Hall on 17 May 1880, it was Brooks who proposed the election of the tepidly pro–Home Rule banker William Shaw, the incumbent, as chairman, who lost eighteen to twenty-three to Parnell.[71] Brooks was among the 'intransigent Whigs' who seceded with Shaw from the Irish Party in January 1881.[72] Neither Brooks nor Lyons contested the general election of 1885, in which the Parnellite candidates on an enlarged franchise swept the four seats of the reconfigured Dublin city constituencies. The United Liberal Club seems to have faded away.[73]

Joyce became increasingly proud of his father's role and prepared to take his father's claims at face value. Explaining to Harriet Shaw Weaver about the Guinnesses in early 1925, he wrote that 'Sir Benjamin Lee Guinness had two sons, lord Ardilaun and lord Iveagh. My father unseated the former for Dublin city. No conservative was ever returned after.'[74] Joyce made two identified allusions to the Dublin city election in *Finnegans Wake*. Both convey the incrementalism of the political advance that the election marked, and its transitoriness. They also play on the commercial affiliations of Guinness and Stirling. The first had an evocation of the turf: 'Though since then stirlings and guineas have

---

for Mr. Stirling and Sir Arthur Guinness (*applause*)'. *Evening Telegraph* and *Daily Express*, 29 March 1880.

71. Michael McDonagh, *The Home Rule Movement* (Dublin: Talbot, 1920), 143.

72. Conor Cruise O'Brien, *Parnell and His Party, 1880–90* (Oxford: Clarendon, 1957), 26.

73. The biographers of John Stanislaus Joyce refer to the AGM of the club on 4 January 1881, at which J. S. Joyce ceased to be its secretary; Jackson and Costello, *John Stanislaus Joyce*, 101. They suggest that it was eclipsed by the overtly confessional Catholic Commercial Club, which had premises on Sackville Street. It was not a direct displacement. Politically, the United Liberal Club, with the rise of Parnell, had had its brief day. The Catholic Commercial Club was not concerned with registration, but with a counter-Protestant commercial fideism; see the report of a lecture on 'civilization' by Fr Hayden, the first of a series, which was presided over by the Lord Mayor Charles Dawson and attended by Thomas Sexton, in the *Freeman's Journal*, 11 December 1883.

74. Joyce to Harriet Shaw Weaver, 13 January 1925, *Letters I* 225.

been replaced by brooks and lions and some progress has been made on stilts and the races have come and gone and Thyme, that chief of seasoners, has made his usual astewte use of endadjustables and whatnot willbe isnor was.'[75]

In the second, Joyce wrote, 'The grinning statesmen, Brock and Leon, have shunned the grumbling coundedouts, Sterlin and Sur Artur Ghinis', with the marginal note on the right side, 'PANOPTICAL PURVIEW OF POLITICAL PROGRESS AND THE FUTURE PRESENTATION OF THE PAST'.[76] In the imagery that tends towards the heraldic, there is perhaps a humorous suggestion of an added motif to adorn his father's escutcheon. The election prematurely belonged to an antique past.

The Fortunes of John Stanislaus Joyce

His role in the Dublin city election certainly did not in itself compromise John Stanislaus Joyce in the emerging Parnellite dispensation. The United Liberal Club was pro–Home Rule, and the result makes it certain that enfranchised supporters of Parnell in Dublin in 1880 voted for the Liberals, if only out of the deep-rooted hatred of Tory ascendancy in the city. If, however, John Stanislaus hoped for preferment from the Parnellites, he needed to take steps to align himself closely with the Parnellite organisation. This he did not do. Drifting into Parnellite allegiance with the vast majority of his Catholic fellow countrymen would not have sufficed. His position was formally constrained by the fact that he took up official employment within two years, but he did not seem driven by strong political conviction, or interest. Engagement in Irish politics required a steady commitment and a high boredom threshold in the long intervals between moments of political excitement, of which the Parnell Split was an instance of unusual duration. John Stanislaus was deficient in both capacities. It does not seem that he was constrained other than by decorum from political involvement by reason of his employment in the Collector-General's Office. He was not a civil

75. *FW* 236.24–28.
76. *FW* 272.25–27.

servant, though he and his colleagues liked to regard themselves as such rather than as collecting agents for Dublin Corporation and the other authorities striking rates for the county and city of Dublin.[77]

That he continued to boast of his role in the Liberal victory in Dublin in 1880 after the Parnellite sweep of the city in 1885 suggests a certain deafness to ambition. However vast and wide-ranging his conversational appetites, he seemed somehow disengaged from and impatient with modern Irish politics. He also lacked the substance and standing to have maintainable political ambitions. These he might conceivably have earned, but there is little to suggest that he had the capacity to do so in the cruelly efficient world of Parnellite politics. Stanislaus Joyce wrote in the wake of the Dublin city election, which took place almost four years before his birth, that 'there was even some talk of his standing for a constituency, for he had a glib tongue and had been among the first to greet the rising star of Parnell'.[78] There was little prospect of John Stanislaus having a parliamentary career, and he was tardy in greeting Parnell's rising star, if he ever actually did so with any particular conviction. The fierce professional discipline of the Parnellite machine was scarcely his thing. He had personal relations of varying intensity with prominent Parnellites, with John Kelly, Valentine Blake Dillon, Tim Harrington, and John Clancy, but those relations were primarily social. He had also some Fenian friends, and his circle of relations was gregariously wide. He almost certainly became, with Parnell's rise to electoral supremacy—which was not fully consummated until the general election of 1885—someone who sympathised with Parnell, but up until the Split he was passive in his support of the Irish leader. There is little to suggest that he had an active sense of political disappointment; yet somehow the coinciding of the rising fortunes of Parnell's adherents in Dublin with his own deteriorating finances—which remained masked through the 1880s—cast a light on a discrepancy of outcomes of which he could scarcely have been unconscious. There was a long descent from

77. John Garvin, *James Joyce's Disunited Kingdom* (Dublin: Gill and Macmillan, 1976), 38.

78. S. Joyce, *My Brother's Keeper*, 49. This is the slender reed on which the biographers of John Stanislaus Joyce rest their account of his pursuit of parliamentary ambitions.

the 'great times' of the Dublin city election of 1880 which, as his career fell apart, became the emblem of his vanished hopes of advancement. The idea that John Stanislaus's deteriorating finances and loss of office in 1893 rendered him 'now quite out of the running in the political life of the city'[79] is an absurdity: he was never, at any point, in the running.

In 1880 John Stanislaus met and began a relationship with Mary Jane (May) Murray. She was the daughter of John Murray, a wine and spirit agent from Longford and proprietor of the Eagle Tavern in Terenure, and Margaret Theresa Flynn, who came from a musical family.[80] Trained by her Flynn aunts, May was a fine pianist and had a good singing voice. John Murray opposed the match. John Stanislaus, an expert nurser of insults, never forgave him, and extended his anathema to John Murray's two sons. His hatred of May's line inspired his recurrent maledictions. In *Stephen Hero* Joyce wrote that Stephen's mother, for all her unstinted loyalty to her husband, 'had never been able to expiate the offence of her blood. . . . Mr. Daedalus hated his wife's maiden name with a medieval intensity: it stunk in his nostrils'[81]. Joyce, in 1934, wrote to his son Giorgio and daughter-in-law, Helen, on the subject of Irish fairies, more malignant than the English, 'The feminine of fairy is bean sidhe = banshee. She is a sinister spirit who follows further certain Irish families. My father said she followed his mother's family the O'Connells.'[82]

John Stanislaus's own mother, Ellen, also opposed the match, and when the marriage took place she went back to Cork. He never saw her again, and she died at Sunday's Wells the following year.[83] Her departure and demise marked a severance with his Cork past, even before the eventual loss of his Cork properties, and drove his identification with Cork further back in time.

May Joyce, for all the pious meekness frequently imputed to her, flouted her father's wishes by continuing her relationship with John

79. Jackson and Costello, *John Stanislaus Joyce*, 184–85.

80. Peter Costello, *James Joyce* (Dublin: Gill and Macmillan, 1980), 28–29.

81. *SH* 110.

82. Joyce to Giorgio and Helen Joyce, 28 December 1934, *Letters I* 355.

83. S. Joyce, *My Brother's Keeper*, 52; Jackson and Costello, *John Stanislaus Joyce*, 104.

Stanislaus. The marriage took place in the Church of Our Immaculate Lady of Refuge, Rathmines, on 5 May 1880. The first child of the marriage, named John Augustine, was born on 23 November 1880, but died after a few days. The second, James Augustine Joyce, was born on 2 February 1882, the feast of Candlemas, at 41 Brighton Square West, in Rathgar.

By the time of the birth of James Joyce, the financial prospects of John Stanislaus had picked up and fleetingly appeared quite promising. On his mother's death on 27 June 1881, he had become the owner of six properties in Cork.[84] By that time, in what was probably a pay-off for his work in the Dublin city election, if one that still involved a prodigious amount of lobbying, he was nominated by the Liberal Lord Lieutenant, Lord Cowper, to fill a position as one of twelve rate collectors ('apostles') in the Office of the Collector-General of Rates for Dublin city and council office in March 1881 at a salary of £500 a year. He nevertheless managed to fail the not especially demanding qualifying examination in April; re-nominated, he passed in July. He entered the Office of the Collector-General at 43 Fleet Street in January 1882,[85] a month before the birth of James. Emboldened by the prospect of a substantial official salary, on 2 December 1881 he made the first mortgage of his Cork properties. It was an ill-omened venture; other mortgages ensued, so that there were eleven in total, the pace of their creation picking up in the final years from 1892 to 1894.[86] He was incapable of living within his means, which between his quite substantial salary and his rental income ought to have sufficed to sustain him and his proliferating offspring, four boys and six girls, born between 1882 and 1893. His expansive conception of the role of a Dublin gentleman, which extended to the generous benefaction of others, and indulgent provider for his household was not proportioned to the resources that were

84. Jackson and Costello, *John Stanislaus Joyce*, 104.

85. Jackson and Costello, *John Stanislaus Joyce*, 101–7; John Garvin, 'James Joyce's Municipal Background', *Administration* 33, no. 4 (1985): 553. The office was destroyed in the course of the Civil War; Jackson and Costello, *John Stanislaus Joyce*, 383.

86. Ellmann, *James Joyce*, 21; Jackson and Costello, *John Stanislaus Joyce*, 106, 126.

FIGURE 2.1. John Stanislaus Joyce, May Joyce, her father John Murray, and James Joyce, aged six, 1888. *Source*: 1.13, LIB-PC004, James Joyce Collection, The Poetry Collection of the University Libraries, University at Buffalo, The State University of New York.

available to him. His drinking was both an effect of that disparity and an aggravation of it.

He had an extraordinarily wide circle of acquaintanceship in Dublin. If he was tragically burdened by his aspirations, and alert to social gradation, he was abidingly democratic in his social relations and beguilingly indifferent to the snobbery that attended the consolidation of the Dublin Catholic middle class in the 1880s. That paradox was an aspect of his nonconformity, and it would come to inform the social reach of *Ulysses*. His social life had two parts: the formal and semi-public social life he conducted with his wife, and his life roaming the commercial premises and bars of the city. James Joyce borrowed much of the social life of his parents to create the narrative of the marriage of Leopold and Marion Bloom in *Ulysses*.

What can be discounted is the thesis that John Stanislaus was a sedulous Parnellite, promoted by his biographers, who construct a biographical narrative that threads together the episodes of Parnell's life with that of John Stanislaus in the 1880s, connected to the idea that he had some prospect of joining Parnell's Irish Party at Westminster. This proposition, which is essentially a projection of Stanislaus Joyce's assertion that after the Dublin city election 'there was even some talk of his standing for a constituency', is untenable conceptually and factually.[87] His biographers assert, as they are more or less driven to, that John Stanislaus attended the banquet in the Round Room of the Rotunda on 11 December 1883 at which Parnell was presented with the proceeds of the 'national tribute' raised to spare him the loss of his heavily encumbered Avondale estate.[88] This was a great occasion, anticipated by the *Freeman's Journal*: 'Tonight in the historic Round Room as banqueting hall, amidst a scene of brilliant rejoicing and national festivity a scene which we will be set like a star in the black expanse of the annals of a gloomy year—this splendid tribute of a nation's gratitude to be presented to the

87. S. Joyce, *My Brother's Keeper*, 49.

88. Jackson and Costello, *John Stanislaus Joyce*, 124. They assert that Parnell's terse receipt of the cheque was 'for John a living example of the almost regal detachment that he so admired in The Chief' (*John Stanislaus Joyce*, 124). The banquet did not take place in Morrison's Hotel, which could not have accommodated an event on that scale.

Leader of the Irish Party and the Irish People, Mr. Parnell'.[89] *United Ireland* was even more extravagant, in the gruesome bastardly classical prose of which it was frequently capable: 'It was the national tribute, in flesh and blood. It was the gathering of the chief men of the nation grouped in fealty around a chief of kinglier power than if a golden bauble encircled his brow for it is a power that rests on a people's love and upon their leader's inborn genius for command'.[90]

It was also a historically famous occasion that contributed an episode to the myth of Parnell. Parnell was given a cheque for a very substantial sum which he put in his pocket. He did not utter a word of thanks. Barry O'Brien's account of the cheque was rendered a little oddly through the account of Lord Spencer: 'That little incident always made an immense impression on me, because it showed the immense power of the man.'[91] It also made an impression on James Joyce, who wrote in 'L'ombra di Parnell', incorrectly in relation to the date of the incident, 'When the Irish people presented him, in 1887, the national tribute of forty thousand pounds, he put the cheque in his wallet, and, during the speech he addressed to the immense crowd, he made not the slightest mention of gift that he had received.'[92]

It is highly unlikely that John Stanislaus Joyce was present at the banquet. The *Freeman's Journal* published an alphabetical 'official list' of those who attended on which his name does not appear.[93] It would be surprising if it had: those who attended were largely established figures in Parnell's movement, members of Parliament, members of county and town councils and corporations, prominent local activists, parish priests, and curates. John Stanislaus was not numbered among *United*

89. *Freeman's Journal*, 11 December 1883.

90. *United Ireland*, 13 December 1883.

91. R. B. O'Brien, *Charles Stewart Parnell*, 2:28.

92. *OCPW* 194. See also Ellmann, *James Joyce*, 32, although one has to maintain some scepticism in relation to the ever-convenient testimony of Arthur Power. The misdating suggests that Joyce had confused the Parnell national tribute with the raising of subscriptions to defray the legal costs incurred in the Special Commission. That in turn supports the probability that Joyce wrote his essay on Parnell entirely from what he remembered of what he had read, rather than on a consultation of Barry O'Brien's biography.

93. *Freeman's Journal*, 12 December 1883.

Ireland's expansive conception of 'the chief men of the nation'. The attendance was not confined to the list of people officially attending the dinner, and there was a larger audience. The galleries were intended primarily to accommodate female supporters of Parnell. The *Freeman's Journal* wrote in advance of the event, 'Three hundred and fifty ladies can be accommodated in the galleries, and about two hundred more in specially reserved seats in the body of the room'.[94] The *Daily Express* reported that 'the gallery was crowded with ladies, who watched the proceedings with considerable interest'.[95]

The notion that John Stanislaus was present is pure surmise and ignores the gulf in standing that separated him from Parnell and his party, and from the leadership of the Parnellite machine in Dublin, which encompassed, as well as the organisation of the county and city of Dublin, the headquarters of the National League. Likewise, the proposition of his enthusiastic biographers that, throwing into reverse his migration to Dublin, John Stanislaus had a prospect either of being adopted for the seat vacated by his relative John Daly in Cork city in the by-election of February 1884 or of being the second candidate at the 1885 election, when Maurice Healy, brother of Timothy Michael Healy, was returned for Cork with Parnell,[96] is wholly divorced from contemporary political reality.

This does not mean that John Stanislaus did not ruminate on where his career might have carried him, though such ruminations may have been painful. His friends may well have suggested that he could have a parliamentary career, but if they did it was in sentimental evocation of his role as the secretary of the United Liberal Club in the Dublin city election of 1880. It also does an injustice to John Stanislaus to suggest that he nursed what would have been wholly illusory political ambitions,

94. *Freeman's Journal*, 10 December 1883; *United Ireland*, 13 December 1883.

95. *Daily Express*, 12 December 1883. The same (Unionist) paper also reported, 'The approaches to the building were blocked by a dense crowd so that it was with the utmost difficulty that ticket-holders were enabled to obtain admission to the building. Several ladies, who were lightly clad in the usual evening costume, was obliged to wait in the falling rain for a long period, and many were severely crushed before they gained access to the building'.

96. Jackson and Costello, *John Stanislaus Joyce*, 133–34.

without actually doing anything to further them. However given to self-praise, in which the Dublin city election was a major set piece, John Stanislaus retained a splenetic and blistering realism in his view of the world. His sense of self was at once extravagant and defensively alert to being tested. He was indefatigably gregarious and strove to project a *bella figura*. He fondly cultivated his male ancestry and had a Joyce coat of arms engraved in what his biographers fairly characterise as a 'corrupt piece of Victorian heraldry' to hang along with the family portraits he had inherited.[97] These, as his son did not fail to recall, were borne like processional icons as the family later shifted residence to one house after another. One of his favourite books, of which there were few, was Sir Jonah Barrington's *Personal Sketches of His Own Time* of 1827, a boisterously entertaining account of politics and society in late Georgian Ireland.[98]

It is difficult to get a full sense of the finances of John Stanislaus Joyce in the 1880s. The records show only his borrowings, some to pay off earlier advances. His financial situation ought to have been reasonably strong, and it is unclear why he should have been in financial difficulty even before his loss of office. This is difficult to explain purely on the basis of personal and household expenditures. Perhaps there were advances made to others, or improvident investments, though there is no actual evidence of either. All one can conclude is that he had outgoings across a wide front which he could not continue to meet. Central to his false sense of financial security was his position in the Office of the Collector-General of Rates. By the late 1880s he had already compromised that position and was the subject of unfavourable attention by his superiors. He was re-assigned from the Rural Districts Division on the edge of the city to the Inns Quay and Rotunda Wards at the heart of the city. He was again reassigned by the Collector-General in late 1888 to the North Dock Ward.[99] Arising from complaints against him and a colleague, he was given a formal warning in January 1889 and placed on

97. Jackson and Costello, *John Stanislaus Joyce*, 129.

98. Jackson and Costello, *John Stanislaus Joyce*, 131–32. See also Garvin, *Joyce's Disunited Kingdom*, 43–44.

99. Jackson and Costello, *John Stanislaus Joyce*, 150.

FIGURE 2.2. Joyce coat of arms. *Source*: 16.19, James Joyce Collection, The Poetry Collection of the University Libraries, University at Buffalo, The State University of New York.

probation for a year.[100] Stanislaus referred to his father's 'borrowings from the bag.'[101] He could not afford many more black marks against him in the Office of the Collector-General.

The principal mystery in the life of John Stanislaus that bears on his son's writing is an episode in the Phoenix Park in Dublin, a bizarre anecdote narrated early in *Finnegans Wake*, that is a struggle to integrate into his biography. At some point during his time in the Collector-General's Office, something happened to John Stanislaus in the Park—an encounter with 'a cad with a pipe'. In *Finnegans Wake*, Earwicker, strolling across the Phoenix Park on an April day, is accosted by the cad, who greets him in Irish and asks the time.[102] The episode is invested with a quasi-terroristic menace in which Earwicker feels impelled to deliver a kind of apologia against accusations that the cad has not actually levelled. Joyce wrote in a letter to Frank Budgen in 1937, 'The encounter between my father and a tramp (the basis of my book) actually took place in that part of the park.'[103] It is an emblematic episode in the guilt-clogged realm of the *Wake*. The victim of a menacing encounter and threat of assault or robbery is himself haunted by the disclosure of some form of contingent or collateral guilt that may have nothing to do with the threatened violence he is negotiating. In the intricate web of human relations, the public, or potentially public, nature of criminal conduct is a source of fear for the victim as well as to the perpetrator. A crime threatens to disclose more than the crime itself. That is an aspect of the rippling effect engendered by violence or the threat of violence in human society and by the threat of investigation and the prosecution of crimes that are alleged to have been committed. In the *Wake*, Earwicker's encounter with the cad follows his own heinous offence against decency, the news of which has already been bruited about. There is a further topographical layer of human fear and guilt arising from the location, the Park being where the Phoenix Park

100. Costello, *Years of Growth*, 71; Jackson and Costello, *John Stanislaus Joyce*, 142–43, 154.

101. S. Joyce, *My Brother's Keeper*, 63. The full quotation is given later in this chapter.

102. The scene is introduced at *FW* 34–44. See Vincent Deane, 'Sewing a Dream Together: "Work in Progress" 1923–4', *Dublin James Joyce Journal*, nos. 14–15 (2021–22): 102–25.

103. Joyce to Frank Budgen, 9 September 1937, *Letters I* 396.

murders took place: the locus of the murders may indeed be 'that part of the park' to which Joyce refers in his letter to Budgen, though it was in open view on the main road through the Park within sight of the Vice-Regal Lodge.[104] Through the cad's un-enunciated menace, there courses a pandemonium of Irish political violence. In the iterative and probably variant account his father rendered to his family, the seemingly disproportionate fear or anxiety of the episode in the Park seems to have had some bearing on his office and the rates payments he was carrying, and something of that sense of unease communicated itself to Joyce as a child.[105] In the episode in the *Wake*, Earwicker's fear is for his life rather than his property. He is nonetheless accoutred, and encumbered, like an armoured car in 'billowing across the wide expanse of our greatest park in his caoutchouc kepi and great belt and hideinsacks and his blaufunx fustian and ironsides jackboots and Bhagafat gaiters and his rubberised inverness'.[106] What was it that Earwicker had been carrying in his 'hideinsacks'? The course in which he was interrupted involved something more than a stroll in the park on a spring day.

Biographically, one is left to reconcile the perfect nightmare of the episode in the Phoenix Park with what Stanislaus Joyce, who is unlikely to have ever read *Finnegans Wake*,[107] recalled: 'Nor was the brown leather

104. The Phoenix Park as an enclosed hunting ground emblematically steeped in Irish history is magisterially explored as a quasi-theme in Alison Lacivita, 'Trouble in Paradise: Violence and the Phoenix Park in *Finnegans Wake*', *James Joyce Quarterly* 51, no. 2–3 (Winter–Spring 2014): 317–31.

105. HCE's account is accepted for the purposes of re-narration in the *Wake* on the basis that he is 'guiltless of much laid to him' (*FW* 34.33).

106. *FW* 35.7–10. Nathan Halper points out that while the Cad is speaking Irish, Earwicker's clothes resemble those of the Royal Irish Constabulary; Sean Golden has assessed the panicked contradictions of Earwicker as he tries to profess Sinn Féin sympathies: Nathan Halper, 'The Narrative Thread in the Cad Episode', and Sean Golden, 'Parsing Rhetorics: The Cad as Prolegomena to the Readings of *Finnegans Wake*', in *The Seventh of Joyce*, ed. Bernard Benstock (Bloomington: Indiana University Press, 1982), 171–72, 173–77.

107. While Stanislaus would certainly not be alone in this, it is a point of some importance. In what he first committed to print, at the end of the year of his brother's death, he wrote, 'When *Finnegans' Wake* [*sic*: the apostrophe's migratory revenge] was published more than a year ago on the author's fifty-eighth birthday, my brother wrote to me offering me a copy in homage. I refused it. It is useless for me to say how much regret that refusal costs me now, when that regret

bag in which he carried the taxes he collected always inviolable, though he did defend it against two thieves who set upon him one night. He succeeded in beating them off with his blackthorn stick, and so had another story to tell over and over again in later years. His own borrowings from the bag, however became more and more frequent and made it necessary for him to have recourse to money-lenders for fairly large sums at short notice.'[108]

John Stanislaus Joyce in the Parnell Split

Whether the episode in the Phoenix Park took place before (which seems more likely) or after the Parnell Split, the security held by John Stanislaus Joyce's office was under threat, and his financial position increasingly strained by the time of the Parnell-O'Shea divorce crisis.

Most of what is known of the response of John Stanislaus Joyce derives from what is to be inferred from the Christmas dinner scene of *A Portrait*.[109] This is a fictional account, but one in a novel that involves a stylised rendering of its author's early life. It requires a politically intelligent reading. The interventions of Simon Dedalus are principally anticlerical in tenor. It is anticlericalism of an old-fashioned semi-Fenian hue but activated in response to a contemporary controversy. The Irish episcopacy had held back from a formal renunciation of Parnell until the declaration of the standing committee of the Irish hierarchy on 3 December, by which time the debate in Committee Room 15 was in progress.[110] While that delay was the subject of controversy in the Split,

---

is useless'. S. Joyce, *Recollections of James Joyce*, 30. There is an emphasis in the language. If Stanislaus had not accepted his brother's offer, it was not in his angular nature to buy and read the book. He did receive the preliminary instalment of what was to be *Finnegans Wake* published in the *Transatlantic Review* in April 1924. Writing to his brother in August 1924, he ignored the *Finnegans Wake* extract to complain about *Ulysses*. Ellmann, *James Joyce* 577–78. Virtually everything in *My Brother's Keeper* relates to Joyce before exile. This plainly reflects an editorial choice on his part, though Ellmann wrote that 'the finished section' was 'somewhat over half the book he intended to write'. S. Joyce, *My Brother's Keeper*, 24.

108. S. Joyce, *My Brother's Keeper*, 63.

109. *P* 1.716–1151.

110. *Freeman's Journal*, 4 December 1890; Lyons, *Fall of Parnell*, 139.

what informed the interventions of Simon Dedalus in the Christmas dinner scene in favour of the dead leader was the massive deployment of ecclesiastical influence against Parnell nationally, and most concertedly in the three by-elections of the Split in Parnell's lifetime. Yet Joyce conveys that the Parnellite sympathy of Simon Dedalus ran deeper than indignant ancestral defiance of the Church, and registers a note of surprise, as well as of upset and affinity, on the part of his son: 'Stephen, raising his terrorstricken face, saw that his father's eyes were full of tears.'[111] This relates to a fictional character, but one modelled on John Stanislaus Joyce. It is all that Joyce ever wrote directly about his father's Parnellism, and is what Joyce let stand on the subject of his own early Parnellism and that of his father.

The issue in relation to the Parnellism of John Stanislaus Joyce is not whether but when. There is nothing in what Joyce wrote to sustain the idea of his father as a sedulous adherent of Parnell through the 1880s. It is, moreover, highly significant that Herbert Gorman, Joyce's first biographer, in the writing of whose principal work Joyce had an active involvement, should have written that John Stanislaus Joyce 'had become exceedingly pro-Parnell during the last scenes of that Leader's debacle'. The import of this was underscored by what Gorman had written just before, of Parnell's vindication before the Special Commission in the matter of the letters forged by Richard Pigott: 'John Stanislaus Joyce, while not of Parnell's party, was nationally-conscious enough to rejoice as full-heartedly as the rest of his countrymen at the clean-cut victory of the Irish leader.'[112] That 'while not of Parnell's party' is unexpectedly definite. It is hard to believe that Gorman's characterisation of the Parnellite allegiance of Joyce père, for which he had no other possible source, was not something he had picked up from his conversations with Joyce, or that Joyce would have allowed Gorman to be less than accurate on the subject of his father's adherence to Parnell in the Split.

John Stanislaus Joyce became an ardent supporter of Parnell in the final crisis of his leadership. It is not possible to calibrate precisely his

111. *P* 1.1150–51.

112. Gorman, *James Joyce*, 36, 35.

reasons for doing so. If it owed something to an inherited Fenian-derived anticlericalism, it owed more to an instinctive identification with an assailed leader, and to political intelligence. The Parnell Split was a great national rending in which Irish people, for emotional reasons, on principle, or on grounds of political judgement, took different sides. The fact that John Stanislaus took Parnell's part itself says a great deal. The erroneous belief that he was equably Parnellite before and after the Split muffles what is truly significant, his visceral rallying to Parnell. John Stanislaus's course from being a passive but disengaged Parnellite to becoming an impassioned supporter of the beleaguered leader in the Split was rare to the point of being extraordinary. In the Split many who had previously supported Parnell renounced their allegiance at the outset, more on the grounds that the evidence in the O'Shea divorce case imperilled the Liberal-nationalist alliance and the prospects of Home Rule than on moral grounds, though the moral objection tended to reinforce or underwrite the political judgement in a confused and confusing circular motion. Their ranks swelled as Parnell's cause waned. Those who had supported Parnell at the Split's inception out of miscalculated opportunism were afforded a chance of reprieve by Parnell's marriage in June 1891 and not a few took it, including the proprietor of the *Freeman's Journal*, on the shameless pretext that the allegation in the divorce proceedings of a relationship between Parnell and Katharine O'Shea had transpired to be true. In the first of several great controversies out of which modern Ireland was created, John Stanislaus Joyce stood fast against the surging tide of anti-Parnellism.

He and John Kelly had opened his son's mind to Parnell's cause, but so far as he could, Joyce had struck out on an intellectual path of his own to comprehend Parnell's public life and fate. There is almost no evidence on how Joyce's views developed before University College beyond the fact of his consistent lifelong Parnellism, so that it is an inference that he cultivated an allegiance to Parnell from about the time of the leader's death. This rests on the premise that *A Portrait* renders a schematic representation of Joyce's acquisition of an allegiance to Parnell, as it was the only account that he ever offered. In *A Portrait*, Joyce maintains with unsparing honesty a slightly chilly distinction between his father's

Parnellism and his own. He negates a direct transmission of allegiance, insisting that even as a boy he took his own considered course, though his father's views naturally exerted a considerable influence. He interposes a thin but critical hiatus in time between the Christmas dinner and Stephen's espousal of the posthumous cause of Parnell in his writing of his poem on the dead leader. This is pointedly accentuated by the lengthy interval between the two events in the novel. Joyce thereby half breaks and attenuates the political trajectory of the Christmas dinner scene. Through the figure of Stephen, Joyce was conveying his own fiercely insistent and Parnell-inflected sense of independence. This is of exquisite political subtlety, and not merely about Stephen's or Joyce's own relationship to his father.

For Parnellites, the idea of independence in the Split had, or more accurately came to acquire, a dual aspect. It was primarily about support for Parnell's pursuit of legislative independence, in opposition to the Liberal party's condemnation of his leadership. As the Split progressed, it widened into opposition to the alliance of the emergently ascendant anti-Parnellites with the Catholic Church. It was not about a secular Ireland—which was not then a sayable proposition—but about holding independent judgement in defiance of the majoritarian anti-Parnellite sentiment which was aligned with the Catholic Church in Ireland and the Liberal party in England. It endured after Parnell's death as a major if atrophied Parnellite theme, emblematic of defeat. For Joyce the readiness to defy prevalent nationalist thinking was fundamental to the fashioning of a second-generation intellectual fealty to Parnell.

It was also about his relation to his father. In *A Portrait*, the Parnellism of Mr Dedalus is in some degree ennobled by association with Mr Casey, the fictional character based on John Kelly. The disparity between Kelly, who had dedicated his life to Parnell, and John Stanislaus Joyce, who had rallied to Parnell in the Split, was momentarily suspended. Without his brother's remorselessness, James Joyce was fully conscious of his father's foibles and, at least in the retrospect of late boyhood and adolescence, he came to be highly sceptical of his judgement. He avoided a breach but would not take his father's views on faith. Implicitly his own interiorised support of Parnell was of a higher order, reflecting a more exalted mode of self-identification than his father's spontaneously emotional affinity with Parnell. *A Portrait* affirms this in Stephen's refined, aestheticised, and oblique Parnellism. Joyce's austere assessment of his father's Parnellism had already softened by the time of writing *A Portrait*, but he sought to convey scrupulously the primness of an earlier phase of attitude, which he had scarcely fully developed at the time of Parnell's death but came to hold in the years that immediately followed. Joyce's negotiation of his father's Parnellism—or what is better characterised as his negotiation of his relationship to his father through Parnell, which only achieved its final resolution in *Finnegans Wake*—is one of the great neglected themes of his work.

That John Stanislaus Joyce was an ardent Parnellite in the Split is incontrovertible. It is attested to by Stanislaus Joyce and is a premise of Joyce's fictional renderings of his father. It is consistent with the father's friendship with John Kelly, renowned as the most disinterested of the grief-stricken adherents of the dead leader. It is also a matter of record in that John Stanislaus Joyce was admonished for having pleaded illness to campaign in the Parnellite interest in Cork at the general election of 1892.[113]

Ellmann includes an account of an intervention by John Stanislaus Joyce at the Leinster Hall meeting of 20 November 1890. The timing of the meeting is important. It occurred after the divorce decree and before Gladstone's repudiation of Parnell. The meeting was a famous occasion because it marked the initial rallying of the Irish Party to Parnell, and Timothy Michael Healy's ringing if almost imperceptibly qualified endorsement of the leader, which he was never to be permitted to forget. Ellmann refers to 'a meeting at the Leinster Hall' and does not quite appreciate the significance of the Leinster Hall meeting of 20 November 1890,[114] not least in its sequence in the chronology of the Split. According to Ellmann, John Stanislaus cried out in the course of Healy's

113. Jackson and Costello, *John Stanislaus Joyce*, 171.

114. Ellmann, *James Joyce*, 33. I am not aware of any other meeting in the Leinster Hall at which Healy spoke in 1890–91 after the divorce crisis.

speech, 'You're an imposter! You're only waiting for the moment to betray him',[115] and then had to be forcibly removed.

John Stanislaus's biographers go the lengths of identifying remarks made by Healy in his speech as a 'skilfully obtuse' riposte to John Stanislaus's intervention. In their account, Healy treated the intervention as a call for Parnell's retirement, thereby further infuriating John Stanislaus and prompting a further exchange before 'officials were forced to drag him from the auditorium, still protesting loudly'. Such elaboration is a travesty of history. Healy's supposed retort to John Stanislaus was addressed not to a heckler present in the hall but to the absent Michael Davitt, who had already, through his *Labour World*, called for Parnell's retirement,[116] and it was immediately understood as such. The account is a means of inserting John Stanislaus into the public narrative of the Split and a measure of the frustration of his biographers: the name of John Stanislaus Joyce features in the Irish press initially as a performer in concerts or dramatic recitals, and latterly principally as a person attending the funerals of politically prominent friends. They seek to bolster their narrative by stating that 'the dramatic interruption arguably marked the high point of his political impact—years later several people, including W. B. Yeats's painter brother Jack remembered witnessing the incident'.[117] The reference they cite is Richard Kain in *Dublin in the Age of William Butler Yeats and James Joyce*, who writes, 'The painter Jack Butler Yeats used to recall seeing Joyce's father at a Parnellite rally. It must have been the great meeting in the Rotunda'.[118] This refers to the meeting of 10 December 1890 in the Rotunda when Parnell returned to Dublin after the meeting in Committee Room 15; the Leinster Hall meeting was three weeks earlier.

The issue of the veracity of what Ellmann wrote remains. His citation is 'Noted by Thomas MacGreevy on March 29, 1934, from Joyce's

115. Ellmann, *James Joyce*, 33.

116. Callanan, *Parnell Split*, 10.

117. Jackson and Costello, *John Stanislaus Joyce*, 160.

118. Richard M. Kain, *Dublin in the Age of William Butler Yeats and James Joyce* (Newton Abbot, UK: David and Charles, 1972), 115.

conversation; miscellaneous biographical notes by Niall Sheridan.'[119] In the first edition of his biography, before he knew of MacGreevy's note, what Ellmann wrote reflected only Sheridan's notes: 'But his anger against Healy and "the Bantry gang" was greatest of all, and so uncontrolled that according to one tradition he went up to him at the Theatre Royal to shout in his face "You're a traitor!"'.[120] On the face of it, the claim made by Ellmann in his 1982 revised edition based on MacGreevy that John Stanislaus heckled Healy seems bizarre, putting John Stanislaus in the odd position of confronting Healy in the course of a speech in which Healy was resonantly endorsing Parnell.

Even though the Leinster Hall speech was pre-Split, and therefore antecedent to what Parnellites regarded as Healy's unforgivable betrayal of Parnell, Healy had long been an object of suspicion to Parnellite loyalists, especially to Fenian-leaning Parnellites who detested both Healy and his kinsmen the Sullivans. There was an underlying volatility to Healy's attitude to Parnell, not least because Parnell was never fully disposed to trust Healy. Their relations came to a head in what was a kind of unconsummated proto-Split in the Galway election of February 1886, in which Healy and Joe Biggar resisted Parnell's imposition of William Henry O'Shea as a parliamentary candidate on the constituency until Parnell descended on Galway to impose his will.[121] Many of Healy's Irish Party colleagues thereafter dreaded a recrudescence of open confrontation between Healy and Parnell, who with grim implacability in October 1887 withdrew Healy's brief to appear on behalf of the Irish Party at the Special Commission, an inexpressible affront to an advocate of Healy's prominence.[122] For many in the Irish Party, a fresh outbreak of hostilities seemed only a matter of time.

In Joyce's account, as rendered by MacGreevy, John Stanislaus Joyce becomes a kind of ur-Parnellite, one who anticipated Healy's betrayal

119. Ellmann, *James Joyce*, 749n47.

120. Ellmann, *James Joyce* (1959 ed.), 32, 761n47. Sheridan had visited John Stanislaus Joyce, but it appears that he was relying on his conversations with Joyce fils. Jackson and Costello, *John Stanislaus Joyce*, 411.

121. Frank Callanan, *T. M. Healy* (Cork: Cork University Press, 1996), 155–61.

122. Callanan, *T. M. Healy*, 195–98.

even before the Split was engaged. It is possible this was historically true: John Stanislaus was an exceptionally shrewd judge of character and capable even in sobriety of unconventional intuitive interventions. There is also a certain psychological plausibility in the idea of John Stanislaus, passively Parnellite when the leader was at the height of his popularity in Ireland, becoming galvanised in fury by the contemplation of Parnell's prospective betrayal by a politician whom he almost certainly already loathed. Joyce's source for what he told MacGreevy could only be his father himself, or his friends or cronies. It is not possible to rule out categorically the possibility, but it remains improbable that John Stanislaus Joyce interpellated Healy at the Leinster Hall. The most plausible conclusion may be that at some point John Stanislaus did confront Healy, perhaps in something like the rumoured manner that Niall Sheridan had recorded; and that Joyce, with artistic license,[123] but drawing on memories of opinions his father had expressed, re-situated and re-scripted the encounter. Joyce thereby gave an account of his father's visceral rallying to Parnell's side even before the consummation of the Split, which was strikingly congruent with what he himself had written of Parnell in 'L'ombra di Parnell' in 1912: 'The sadness that devastated his soul was, perhaps, the profound conviction that, in his hour of need, one of the disciples who had dipped his hand into the bowl with him was about to betray him. To have fought until the very end with this desolating certainty in his soul was his first and greatest claim to nobility.'[124]

Joyce was imputing to his father, in the build-up of days to the Split, something of Parnell's own presentiment of what was to come. The figure of Parnell was a significant element of Joyce's renegotiation and later rendering of his relation to his father. In what he told MacGreevy two

123. There is perhaps a parallel in the quasi-fictive manner by which Joyce promoted the career of the Irish opera singer John Sullivan; Ellmann, *James Joyce*, 620–27. Singers attracted a particular imaginative indulgence on Joyce's part. John Stanislaus Joyce was not disentitled to the dispensations from exigent factuality that Joyce readily accorded to those who could sing in performance.

124. *OCPW* 196.

years after his father's death, Joyce was subsuming his father's Parnellism into the intensity of his own.

Of Joyce's surviving contemporaries, Constantine Curran was the only one who appreciated the significance of establishing Joyce's contemporary Irish politics. As he worked on his memoir, *James Joyce Remembered*, which appeared in 1968, Curran was troubled by the simplistic characterisation of Joyce's father as a Parnellite *tout court*, sanctified in the first edition of Ellmann's biography, which referred to John Stanislaus's 'growing and outspoken devotion to Parnell which . . . was already forming the mind of his watchful son'.[125] On 27 January 1964, Curran met Joyce's sister May Monaghan:

> I asked her was John Stanislaus really a Parnellite. She said she often heard Parnell's name mentioned, and always with heat but not as if there was any difference of opinion or controversy in the family. I pressed my argument further, asking was he not a Parnellite only since the 'Split' and because he was anti-clerical. She said he was not so very anti-clerical. Not in general but against the bishops at the Split. I argued that people were called Parnellites not because they supported him during the Split but that no one could truly be called Parnellite who had not supported him in forming his independent Parliamentary party and supported him in the land agitation. I pointed out that his first objective was to oust Whigs and nominal Home Rulers from Irish constituencies; that John Stanislaus was an election [agent] for two of these placehunters . . . who were successfully returned; that such a backer [?] could not be called a Parnellite or his conduct squared with Parnell. She laughed and said he just took it as a job.[126]

Curran had correctly intuited that John Stanislaus Joyce was that unusual creature, a Parnellite only in the Split, though he ascribed it too narrowly to anticlericalism.

125. Ellmann, *James Joyce* (1959 ed.), 24. This passage survived unchanged in the second edition: Ellmann, *James Joyce*, 25.

126. C. P. Curran, Joyce notebook, UCD Special Collections, Constantine Curran Collection, CUR MS 6.

There is no record of John Stanislaus's involvement in the Split in 1890–91. As Richard Kain surmised, he may have been amid the packed throng in the Rotunda at Parnell's great meeting on 10 December 1890, the leader's zenith in his campaign in Ireland, or in the crowd on the quays on the emotionally charged occasion of Parnell's return to Dublin from Thurles on 2 August 1891 after his repudiation by John Dillon and William O'Brien, which marked Dublin's last rallying to the embattled leader.[127] There is nothing to suggest that he participated in any of the three by-elections of the Split, none of which were in Dublin. He had no known experience of campaigning since the elections of 1880. He did have a relationship with Tim Harrington, the member of Parliament for the Harbour Division of Dublin, and with John Clancy, the pre-eminent figure in the Parnellite organisation in Dublin, and it is possible, but unlikely, that he was asked to render some political service. The probabilities are that he was ardent in sympathy in his social life and volubly supportive in conversations on the street or at Parnellite meetings in Dublin. His was a conspicuous personal identification with Parnell, but one that was without wider political impact.

The only record of John Stanislaus's active involvement relates to the period of the 'long Split', the decade after Parnell's death. It is a curious involvement that is hard to reconcile with the idea that he was ever an effective political activist. The leader's death gave rise to a bitter and turbulent by-election in his Cork constituency on 6 November 1891, in which John Redmond, as the Parnellite candidate, was defeated. Stanislaus Joyce recalled in his memoir that 'my father quitted his office without leave during an election, and travelled down to Cork to persuade his tenants to vote for "the Chief"'. Stanislaus, bad about dates, seems to have situated this close to the inception of the Split in Parnell's lifetime.[128] That is clearly wrong. Richard Ellmann, in his biography of Joyce, assumed that this related to the Cork by-election.[129] It would have been understandable if John Stanislaus—who had lived in Cork

127. Callanan, *Parnell Split*, 124.
128. S. Joyce, *My Brother's Keeper*, 70.
129. Ellmann, *James Joyce*, 33.

until 1873—had joined his friends in the frenetic canvassing at the by-election that followed Parnell's death. But that was not the election in which John Stanislaus participated. It transpires from the records of the Collector-General's Office that he absented himself from his duties on grounds of illness to engage in the Cork election in the general election of June 1892, so that a temporary collector had to be assigned to carry out his duties. This is a significant difference. His participation in a campaign in the immediate aftermath of Parnell's death might have been viewed more indulgently by his superiors and might not have attracted official censure. What John Stanislaus hoped to achieve in the general election contest is unclear. The idea that he hoped to influence his tiny cohort of remaining tenants, which he evidently advanced to his family, is as unconvincing as it was politically archaic. Given the absence of any recorded involvement in the by-election, why he should have felt impelled to campaign in the same constituency in the general election eight months later is a mystery. One is left wondering whether his superiors concluded that he had embarked on a pleasurable excursion to his native city in the rollicking ambience of a general election campaign. That was formally irrelevant: he was found to have participated in the election while he was pleading illness. It was a black mark he could ill afford given a gathering perception of delinquency around him. Against the background of a deteriorating relationship with his superiors, the formal admonition he received was not a trivial matter.[130]

Significantly this was something of which his family was aware at the time or soon afterwards. Of his father's quitting his office without leave to persuade his tenants 'to vote for "the Chief"', Stanislaus wrote, 'It was one of the things held against him when the office was closed down.'[131]

Stanislaus, admittedly a pitiless critic of his father's fecklessness and what he portrayed not entirely convincingly as his generalised political ranting, was identifying a disciplinary infraction connected to the Split that would be held against his father, rather than positing a causal

130. See Jackson and Costello, *John Stanislaus Joyce*, 171.

131. S. Joyce, *My Brother's Keeper*, 70. Stanislaus was under the impression that the election was during the currency of the Split in Parnell's lifetime.

connection between his father's Parnellism and the decline of the family's fortunes. For Stanislaus to have known of it, assuming he knew at the time rather than much later, his father must have complained. It can only have provoked worry and alarm among his father's dependents. The unauthorised absence had the potential to contribute to the loss of office and to reduce the only secure source of income on which the Joyce family depended. In this and perhaps in other ways, the dread of immiseration affected the Joyce household before its realisation in the serial changes of residence which began with the move from Carysfort Avenue in Blackrock north across the Liffey in late 1892 or early 1893 to Hardwicke Street, and thence to Fitzgibbon Street—respectable if not fashionable addresses—and the sharp deterioration in living standards which brought about and attended the family's migrations in the city.[132] Even in what remained of its better days, the older children of the Joyce family were denied by their splenetically voluble father the security conventionally afforded by bourgeois parental discretion.

The fallacious idea that the fall of the Joyces is related to the fall of Parnell has a seeming irresistibility, and a venerable history in what has been written about Joyce. Marvin Magalaner and Kain, in their important 1956 work on Joyce, which preceded by three years the first edition of Ellmann's biography, advance a reductive psychological explanation for Joyce's Parnellism through the socio-economic descent of the family: 'The tangible results for Joyce and his family of Parnell's shifting fortunes blend into, and become identified with, the ebb and flow of Joyce's youthful patriotism. The outcome seems to be that Joyce finds it impossible to separate his attitude concerning his own fate from his feeling for Ireland and the symbol of Parnell.' They characterise Parnell's fall for Joyce as 'a childhood wound', from which recovery entailed Joyce's exile from Ireland.[133] The fallacious idea of an indissociable connection, at least subjectively, between the fall of Parnell and the subsidence of the fortunes of John Stanislaus Joyce received

132. Vivien Igoe, *James Joyce's Dublin Houses and Nora Barnacle's Galway* (Dublin: Wolfhound, 1997), 37–38.

133. Magalaner and Kain, *Joyce*, 32, 35, 37.

Ellmann's imprimatur: 'For John Joyce, the fall of Parnell, closely synchronised with a fall in his own fortunes, was the dividing line between the stale present and the good old days.'[134] Colbert Kearney wrote that 'John Joyce had begun to mortgage his property ten years before the fall of Parnell but according to *The Joycead* the fall of John Joyce was part of the greater fall of Parnell.'[135] There is, however, no evidence that John Stanislaus himself posited an association between the fall of Parnell and his own ruin, and Joyce gave the idea no sanction. All there is is an approximate synchrony, and the high probability that his father, in the nocturnal ranting described by Stanislaus, aligned Parnell's enemies with his own. The persistence and seeming irresistibility of a narrative in which John Stanislaus Joyce's sharply declining fortunes and Parnell's fall were intertwined remain striking, and the idea becomes in itself a curious late accretion to the Parnell myth. If Joyce was entirely without illusion about his father's defects of character, his filial clemency was collusively generous. It seems reasonable to infer that *Stephen Hero* is autobiographical in its rendering of its author's father. Mr Daedalus 'knew that his own ruin had been his own handiwork, but he had talked himself into believing it was the handiwork of others.'[136] He is tormented by the blasted opportunities of his life, which he somehow connects, not to the rise or fall of Parnell, but to his marriage: 'Now that he was making for the final decades of life with the painful consciousness of having diminished comfortable goods and of having accumulated uncomfortable habits he consoled and revenged himself by tirades so prolonged and so often repeated that he was in danger of becoming a monomaniac. The hearth at night was the sacred witness of these revenges, pondered, muttered, growled and execrated. . . . The great disappointment of his life was accentuated by a lesser and keener loss—the loss of a coveted fame.'[137]

134. Ellmann, *James Joyce*, 33.

135. Kearney, 'Joycead', 65. He adds, 'It was probably at this juncture, c. 1891, that the family myth assumed its final form, which I have called *The Joycead*, and which for John Joyce, provided an acceptably coherent account of the Joyce family'.

136. *SH* 110.

137. *SH* 110.

That fame had nothing to do with parliamentary honours. 'On account of a certain income and of certain sociable gifts Mr Daedalus had been accustomed to regard himself as the centre of a little world, the darling of a little society.'[138]

Joyce did not have his brother's resentment of their father and eschewed confrontation with him, reflecting the difference in his relationship to his father as the eldest surviving male child, as well as a sagacious fatalism where family relations were concerned. It seems clear, however, that a distance and coldness entered his relations with his father.[139] The relationship remained nonetheless unbroken, and only came to be threatened on John Stanislaus's side by Joyce's elopement with Nora Barnacle in 1904. If Joyce tacitly shared his brother's assessment of their father's improvidence, it was one that he had come to re-balance even by the time of writing *A Portrait*, and consigned to the margins in his re-estimation of his father in part through the medium of their shared if disparate Parnellisms, and in the dispersed ubiquity of his rendering of his father in *Finnegans Wake*.

Decline and Death in the Joyce Family

The course of the socio-economic descent of John Stanislaus was inscribed before the Split, which was the last occasion on which he could assume a social position in public affairs unembarrassed by his own deteriorating fortunes. His decline subsequently gathered pace: 1892 saw three judgements against him. The first was at the suit of a solicitor, Reuben J. Dodd, whose name James Joyce would not forget. He must have paid off or compromised the amounts of the two judgements, depleting further his Cork properties to pay off Dodd.[140] The judgement

138. *SH* 110.

139. A fleeting and cryptic reference in *Stephen Hero*, if intended to relate to Joyce's relationship to his father, coming after that just quoted in the text, suggests that this had chiefly to do with John Stanislaus Joyce's realisation that his son could not condone his treatment of his wife: 'His son's silence during the domestic battles no longer seemed to him a conveyed compliment' (*SH* 111).

140. Ellmann, *James Joyce*, 37–38.

with the most serious implications was the third, which the creditor registered on 2 November 1892. This had the consequence that the name of Joyce père appeared in *Stubbs' Gazette* and *Perry's Weekly*, whose business it was to publish details of judgements and insolvencies. That seriously compromised his position as a collector of rates, and the Collector-General immediately suspended him.[141]

For the family it portended disaster. Florence Elizabeth Joyce, the second to last of the surviving children of the marriage, came into the world on 8 November 1892. The family was obliged to make a precipitate departure from 'Leoville' in Blackrock, as the sheriff's men arrived, for rooms at 29 Hardwicke Street in the north city. John Stanislaus's situation was rendered effectively irretrievable by events in the Office of the Collector-General. After protracted negotiations, Dublin Corporation was to assume responsibility for the collection of rates from the end of 1892. John Stanislaus's colleagues were offered three-quarters of their annual remuneration as an annual pension. The provision for John Stanislaus, on account of his accumulated delinquencies, was markedly more frugal, less than half of that made for his peers, reducing his income to one-third of what it had been. Even that was stopped, pending investigation of further matters of complaint, and only reinstated in May 1893.[142] Though it has not been established with certainty, it appears that John Stanislaus was driven into further borrowing which he could not repay: his later course of non-payments was principally at the expense of landlords rather than financial institutions or moneylenders, as he no longer had his Cork properties to offer as security. The family migrated from Hardwicke Street to superior if spartan accommodation at what was then numbered as 14 Fitzgibbon Street, off Mountjoy Square. John Stanislaus was obliged to submit to what was for him the ignominy of the enrolment of his two eldest sons in the O'Connell

141. Jackson and Costello, *John Stanislaus Joyce*, 172–73. As the authors point out, John Stanislaus Joyce was never at any time adjudicated a bankrupt, as has occasionally been suggested. (At the time of researching this book, it was not possible to access in the National Archives most of the records consulted by the biographers of John Stanislaus Joyce, and I am in consequence reliant on what they write.)

142. Jackson and Costello, *John Stanislaus Joyce*, 172, 176–78.

School run by the Christian Brothers in North Richmond Street. Curiously neither Joyce nor Stanislaus makes any reference to this, though that could suggest that they shared their father's prejudice against the Christian Brothers. The interruption of Joyce's Jesuit education was of some fifteen months' duration. John Stanislaus ran into Father John Conmee, who had been rector of Clongowes through most of the period James Joyce was there.[143] Conmee had become prefect of studies in Belvedere College and would go on to become the provincial of the Jesuit Order in Ireland. He agreed to admit the exceptionally promising Joyce he had known in Clongowes, together with his brothers, to Belvedere without the payment of fees. Pertaining characteristically to the male line, the enrolment of John Stanislaus's sons in a Jesuit school, coupled with his social associations, averted the possibility of his professional and financial ruin conducing to a loss of caste by the family. John Stanislaus had contrived, in his final effective intervention on behalf of his family, to maintain the possibility of reversing in the next generation the plummeting decline of the dynastic prospects of the Joyces. James Joyce resumed his Jesuit schooling, entering Belvedere College on 6 April 1893.[144]

Mabel Joyce ('Baby'), the last surviving child of the marriage, was born on 27 November 1893. John Stanislaus, on the registration of her birth, described himself as an accountant.[145] On 14 December 1893 the last of the Joyce Cork properties were auctioned in three lots at the Property Sale Room on the South Mall.[146] The migrations of the household continued: in 1894 to 2 Millbourne Avenue, Drumcondra, and later that year to North Richmond Street, where the family lived until 1897.

143. Bruce Bradley, *James Joyce's Schooldays* (Dublin: Gill and Macmillan, 1982), 75–76.

144. Ellmann, *James Joyce*, 35; Jackson and Costello, *John Stanislaus Joyce*, 176–77. Bruce Bradley refers to the possibility of Conmee's relationship to or friendship with the Joyce family, but the length of the interval between Joyce's leaving Clongowes and entering Belvedere makes that open to question; Bradley, *James Joyce's Schooldays*, 84–87.

145. Jackson and Costello, *John Stanislaus Joyce*, 184.

146. Jackson and Costello, *John Stanislaus Joyce*, 182.

James Joyce was in the privileged position of the eldest (surviving) male child. Something of his standing in the household is captured in the recall of Eva Joyce, Joyce's mild and pious sister who was almost ten years his junior, in a radio programme broadcast in 1950. Her father 'thought the world of Jim, and there was no one else according to him':

> My father was the most outstanding man as regards his brains and intellect, and Jim got his intellect from him, and his love of music more from his mother. The two combined made him what he was. He was a very lonesome boy. He was the greatest favourite in the family. Father and Mother idolised him, and all his brothers and sisters seemed quite happy that he was the one that got the most attention. He was a very gentle child, indeed I never remember him getting into a temper about anything—in fact he always laughed everything off.[147]

After the closure of the Collector-General's Office, John Stanislaus Joyce never had anything resembling secure employment or remunerative self-employment again. He episodically rendered services as an accountant, though that seems to have yielded to a period as a self-employed canvasser of advertisements for the *Evening Telegraph*, the more Dublin-focussed sister paper of the *Freeman's Journal*, a role likely to have been secured through the good offices of his friend John Hooper, the paper's editor. The role of a canvasser of advertisements was one that his son would appropriate for Leopold Bloom in *Ulysses*. John Stanislaus Joyce placed a few advertisements from friends in 1896,[148] but it never took off as a business and was quietly abandoned. His political and local government connexions delivered him intermittent work in the revision of voting lists, and as a presiding officer at

147. W. R. Rodgers, *Irish Literary Portraits* (London: British Broadcasting Corporation, 1972), 35. Eva was unfailingly polite and benign, and perhaps a little naïve, but her impression of her mother's relationship to Joyce remains striking. According to Rodgers, 'He undoubtedly was her favourite. She absolutely lived for him, and when he went away it seemed to be the breaking up of her life. She didn't seem to last long after he went, in fact she seemed to fade out altogether' (*Irish Literary Portraits*, 36).

148. Jackson and Costello, *John Stanislaus Joyce*, 190–93.

municipal elections, and occasional clerical employment.[149] He frequented the City Hall, where he hung about the muniments room in the hope of picking up a job.[150]

Some of these meagre benefactions were owed, perhaps distantly, to Tim Harrington, member of Parliament for the Harbour Division of Dublin, and Henry Campbell, town clerk at City Hall, both of whom had been adjutants who had been exceptionally close to Parnell. John Stanislaus Joyce was incapable of playing the docile role of a receiver of favours. He became embroiled in conflict with Harrington and his own loyal friend D. J. Hishon, a Parnellite functionary who was also a close friend to John Kelly, over the balance of the remuneration he claimed was due to him for work on the revision of the register of parliamentary voters in the South Dock Ward of the Stephen's Green Division of the city of Dublin. He took this to the lunatic extreme of suing L. A. Waldron, the member of Parliament for the Stephen's Green Division, for the monies.[151] The case came on before the Recorder at the Dublin City Sessions in the courthouse in Green Street on 14 January 1907. It was reported in the three principal Dublin newspapers, in the *Freeman's Journal* under the headline 'Action against Mr. Waldron, M. P.: Election Agent's Claim'. John Stanislaus Joyce was described in all three reports, presumably reflecting what was pleaded, as an election agent, as if it were a role in life. He gave evidence that he had been employed by Hishon on Waldron's behalf, as on a previous occasion when he had been paid by a cheque from Waldron. On this occasion he was paid five pounds but claimed to be entitled to twenty pounds for what he said was twenty weeks' work. Hishon was sworn in and gave evidence that Waldron had not employed anybody to look after the registration work but merely subscribed a certain amount to each ward. The Recorder observed that that was the usual practice for members of Parliament, and he did not see how he could give a decree as there was no direct contract. Waldron's counsel had earlier stated that an amount of five

149. S. Joyce, *My Brother's Keeper*, 80; Jackson and Costello, *John Stanislaus Joyce*, 249, 285, 290–91.

150. Curran, Joyce notebook, 124. Patrick Meehan was his informant.

151. Jackson and Costello, *John Stanislaus Joyce*, 286–92.

pounds had been tendered and lodged in court, and that he was prepared to hand over that sum in settlement. The Recorder said he would advise the plaintiff to accept the money, which his counsel did on his behalf. He dismissed the case.[152] If he was let down lightly, it was an outcome which left John Stanislaus Joyce paying his own legal costs incurred in the hearing out of the sum he could have accepted when it was tendered. Suing Waldron was a measure of John Stanislaus's drink-fuelled fecklessness. If there was a falling out with Hishon, it was short-lived. Harrington was unlikely to have been so forgiving, but John Stanislaus was nonetheless numbered among the mourners at Harrington's funeral in March 1910.[153] John Stanislaus did find occasional employment, but none that lasted. The most continuous if intermittent engagement was with his friend George Lidwell, a solicitor whose office on Upper Ormond Quay served as a stable address in his semi-nomadic existence in Dublin.[154] Stanislaus wrote archly of his father, 'He was always looking for a job, one suitable, of course, for a man that does not want to work, and now during spells of sobriety, for it must not be imagined that he was not occasionally sober, he would make optimistic calculations of how much he could earn "between hopping and trotting".'[155]

In the new century, the failing fortunes of the family were dogged by tragedy. In April 1902, Joyce's last year in University College, his fourteen-year-old brother, Georgie, was taken ill. Much loved, Georgie was considered the most promising of the Joyce sons after James. He died of peritonitis on 3 May 1902. At the point when Joyce left University College, his long-suffering sister Poppie had left school: the remaining five sisters were attending the Convent National School attached to

152. *Daily Express*, 15 January 1907; *Freeman's Journal*, 15 January 1907; *Irish Times*, 15 January 1907. John Stanislaus Joyce's self-marginalisation was accentuated by the fact that, on the day of the hearing, polling was taking place in thirteen of the twenty municipal wards of Dublin. The biographers of John Stanislaus Joyce incorrectly and without providing a reference assert that the hearing took place 'in the first week of January 1907'. Jackson and Costello, *John Stanislaus Joyce*, 292.

153. *Freeman's Journal*, 16 March 1910 ('J. S. Joyce').

154. Jackson and Costello, *John Stanislaus Joyce*, 295, 307.

155. S. Joyce, *My Brother's Keeper*, 80–81.

St Mary's Industrial Training School and Orphanage, run by the Sisters of Charity.[156] Their third brother, Charlie, of weak and inconstant resolve, and who had been close to Georgie, left Belvedere to enrol in the Dublin diocesan seminary in Clonliffe, where he did not dally long.[157] In a letter to Joyce in 1907 complaining of the burdens imposed by his ungrateful offspring, his father tartly designated Charlie as 'the aforesaid ex-ecclesiastic'.[158] John Stanislaus Joyce's final initiative to arrest the decline in the family's fortunes was to purchase, in October 1892, a modest residence at 7 St Peter's Terrace in Cabra, secured on a life insurance policy financed by his attenuated pension.[159] However provident his intent, in practice it was another property against the security of which John Stanislaus Joyce could borrow.

The greatest catastrophe for the Joyce household was the fatal illness of May Joyce, who was stricken by liver cancer. She died on 18 August 1903. She was forty-four years old. On the afternoon of her interment, Stanislaus and James Joyce accompanied their father and May Joyce's brother William Murray on a walk in the country in dismal weather, ending in a visit to a public house which James Joyce cut short. They returned home and William Murray left. In the weirdly candid narrative of Stanislaus, 'I found my father sitting alone in the parlour whining. Uncontrollable anger seized me. I vented all my seething bitterness on him, forgetting very little. He listened in silence, and when I had done, said without resentment:—You don't understand, boy'.[160] The most inconsolable child was Mabel, the nine-year-old 'Baby', who continuously crept away to weep. James intervened 'with his arm around her, talking to her in a very matter-of-fact voice—Mother is in Heaven. She is far happier now than she has ever been on earth, but if she sees you crying it will spoil her happiness'. Stanislaus was prompted to comment, 'In the end he succeeded in imposing a calmer grief on the child's mind, for he always had an ascendancy over the girls of the family because of his cleverness, his talents, his good looks, and that even

156. Jackson and Costello, *John Stanislaus Joyce*, 239.
157. Jackson and Costello, *John Stanislaus Joyce*, 239–40, 249.
158. John Stanislaus Joyce to Joyce, 24 April 1907, *Letters II* 222.
159. Jackson and Costello, *John Stanislaus Joyce*, 240–41.
160. S. Joyce, *My Brother's Keeper*, 232.

temper which was in striking contrast to mine though we were always together.'[161]

The posthumous publication in 1958 of the account of Stanislaus, who had died in Trieste on Bloomsday 1955, offended May Monaghan, his sister and the keeper of the family flame in Dublin. It still rankled when Constantine Curran spoke to her in January 1964 as he prepared his own *James Joyce Remembered*. He noted, 'She was outraged by it and vehemently and clearly and with evident good sense maintains that it gives a false picture of the family and especially of the relations between John Stanislaus and his wife. She finds the only excuse for Stanislaus to be youth—he was 19 when he left Dublin—and ignorance. She says that genuine love and affection always existed between husband and wife however feckless the father was.'[162]

She recounted, as Stanislaus had, that after her mother's death, Stanislaus 'once accused his father of bad conduct towards her. For once in his life John S. was silent contenting himself with saying: "You are young, my boy, you don't understand".' May Monaghan 'showed an equal affection for father and mother, laughing [word illegible] at his incapacity to hold down a job, but she dwelt more on her mother's qualities.'[163] Of the recent stage performance of Hugh Leonard's *Stephen D.*,[164] 'she said her mother was in fact of slight build and elegant in dress and appearance', and continued, 'She was a fine pianist playing much Chopin and she had a good soprano voice. At the piano she would sing operatic duets with John S. who was a tenor. . . . Jim would listen attentively to her piano playing. With this exception Jim cared nothing for other music than singing. She kept stressing her mother's intellectual capacity, emphasising that her mother was highly intelligent and ready to discuss serious subjects with Jim. In comparison John S. she said was "superficial".'[165] Curran was plainly struck by what May Monaghan said

161. S. Joyce, *My Brother's Keeper*, 232–33.

162. Curran, Joyce notebook.

163. Curran, Joyce notebook.

164. Hugh Leonard, *Stephen D.: A Play in Two Acts, Adapted by Hugh Leonard from James Joyce's 'A Portrait of the Artist as a Young Man' and 'Stephen Hero'* (London: Evans Brothers, 1964).

165. Curran, Joyce notebook.

to him. If he knew there was some exaggeration in her insistence 'on the permanent good relations in the family',[166] he also realised that some corrective was required to Stanislaus Joyce's account, beyond Joyce's correspondence that had appeared in 1957 in the first volume of the *Letters*.

His Son in Exile

John Stanislaus Joyce took exception to Joyce's elopement with Nora Barnacle. The existence of their relations had been advisedly concealed from him before they had left Dublin, though he had accompanied his son to the North Wall to embark. Furious when he became aware of it, he never quite broke off communications, though his principal conduit to Trieste became in protest his letters to Stanislaus. In April 1907 he wrote to James, 'I need not tell *you* how your miserable mistake affected my already crushed feelings, but then mature thoughts took more the form of pity than anger, when I saw a life of promise crossed and a future that might have been brilliant blasted in one breath.'[167] His anger was long in abating, but he wrote in May 1909, 'My feelings have undergone a change towards you, hastened by the receipt of the photo of your son whose *strong likeness* to you at his age brought vividly back to my mind, memories which I try strenuously to avoid, as I need not tell you, their recollection is hardly calculated to assuage the torture I at present endure, associated as it is with all the happiest moments of my life.'[168]

Eight years separated Mabel's own death from that of her mother. The youngest child, she was vivacious and winning, and a favourite of the family especially after Georgie's death. She was close to her father after her mother's death. Something of the challenge of having as a parent John Stanislaus Joyce in decline is conveyed in the journal Charles Joyce briefly kept to relay to Stanislaus in Trieste. The entry for Sunday, 24

166. Curran, Joyce notebook.

167. John Stanislaus Joyce to Joyce, 24 April 1907, *Letters II* 221.

168. John Stanislaus Joyce to Joyce, 16 May 1909, *Letters II* 228. This was almost four years after the birth of Giorgio, on 27 July 1905.

June 1906, reads, 'Pappie home to dinner very drunk: shouting, swearing etc: Pappie has thrown his dinner about the floor. Baby white as a sheet: Pappie gone out again.'[169] Joyce had last seen Mabel in late 1909 on the second of his return trips to Ireland. He had wanted to rescue one of his sisters from Dublin. He had thought of bringing her with him, but Margaret had proposed that he bring Eva instead, apparently on the basis that her piety might exert a salutary influence on her ungodly brother.[170] Mabel in Dublin secured an apprenticeship with the printers Gerrards Brothers on 37 St Stephen's Green, who as it happened had published Joyce's 'The Day of the Rabblement' in 1901.[171] On 19 June 1911 she fell ill and was diagnosed with typhoid. She was taken to the Fever Hospital on Cork Street, where she was confined. Eva set out from Trieste for home, finding her father 'particularly dirty and shabby' when she reached Dublin. Mary Kathleen (May) Joyce had taken over the role of the eldest from Margaret ('Poppie'), who had become a Sister of Mercy and had left for New Zealand in November 1909, seen off by Joyce on his second return visit. Mary Kathleen wrote to Stanislaus of her last visit with her father a week before Mabel's death. Mabel was asleep, but finally awoke with a start and stared at her visitors for a minute: 'Then after a minute o[r] so she commenced to talk but all we could understand was "May, I am dying. I am dying, its a positive fact". . . . Stannie, have you ever seen an animal in pain, do you know the look they have in their eyes? Well it was with just a look that our little sister followed us out of the ward after we had said Goodbye to her.'[172]

Mabel died on 12 July 1911, aged seventeen. Mary Kathleen wrote to Stanislaus two weeks later that 'there is one thing I know, and that is that none of us will be as happy again as we were when we had her with us.' She recalled Mabel saying on their evening walks 'that she would go to

169. Charles Joyce, quoted in Jackson and Costello, *John Stanislaus Joyce*, 289.

170. Ellmann, *James Joyce*, 285. Ellmann's source was an interview with Eileen Joyce Schaurek.

171. Jackson and Costello, *John Stanislaus Joyce*, 317.

172. May Joyce to Stanislaus Joyce, quoted in Jackson and Costello, *John Stanislaus Joyce*, 319.

Trieste, that was the dream of her life. The poor child used to dance along the road at the very thought of going over there.'[173]

Mabel's death unleashed the fury of the children of John Stanislaus Joyce. Even James, who consistently held back from open confrontation with his father (the rift over his relationship with Nora was of his father's making), felt compelled to say something. He wrote his father a letter which has not survived. Mary Kathleen politely reported to Stanislaus that 'Pappie had a very nice letter from Jim of course rather strange and bitter, but still it showed that he felt her death very much.'[174] The response, one of John Stanislaus's scarce letters to his favoured son, suggests that the letter had expressed condolence mixed with oblique remonstrance. John Stanislaus's response reflected the grief of a bereaved father but was not without the determination to keep at least his eldest son on his side. He wrote from the Eblana Hotel, run by Nora Hishon, on Great Denmark Street:[175]

> She became unconscious the day before she died and remained so to the end. I was with her for over an hour the day she died and I think she knew *me*. She got her sickness in this accursed hole. But this perhaps for the best, as she was too sensitive and highly-strung to endure the troubles of this wretched world. She is with her Mother who idolized her, and has left me to linger on, a broken hearted old man, but only for a very short time now until I will follow my darling Maime and my 'doatie darlie' to where partings are known. I am now most anxious to die, having lost the only one (*except you*) who loved me.—I must thank you Jim, for your kind and sympathetic letter and remittance and the beautiful wreath. Everything was carried out as it should be and as *you* would wish. So much for the past—now the present has been made so unbearable to me by the callous, unnatural treatment I am receiving from my three daughters, that I am resolved to leave Dublin and them on the 1st prox. Since my

173. May Joyce to Stanislaus Joyce, quoted in Jackson and Costello, *John Stanislaus Joyce*, 320.
174. Ellmann, *James Joyce*, 310, 773, quoting May Joyce to Stanislaus Joyce, 25 July 1911.
175. Jackson and Costello, *John Stanislaus Joyce*, 313.

> poor baby died they have left me alone, and refuse to even take a walk with me. Everyone here, as in the last house we stayed in, crys [*sic*] shame on them for their cruel conduct towards their father.[176]

Stanislaus, in his memoir of his brother, wrote that Mabel was 'the last victim of our family life'.[177]

Father and son met for the last time on Joyce's final visit to Ireland in 1912. By that time John Stanislaus had forgiven Joyce his elopement with Nora. Years later in Paris, Joyce recounted to Louis Gillet that he and his father subsequently went for a walk in the country and went into a public house in Rathfarnham. John Joyce sat down at the piano and played and sang to Joyce 'Di Provenza il mar', the aria of Alfredo Germont's remorse-stricken father about the dying Violetta in *La Traviata*, to signify that he had repined of his objection to his son's elopement with Nora.[178] The sixty-year-old John Stanislaus had not lost the faculty of the redemptive gracious gesture. Nora had the quiet triumph of reporting back to Eileen in Trieste that 'I was delighted to have your Father every time he would look at Lucia wept copiously all about Jim with your father.'[179] John Stanislaus Joyce supported and counselled his son in the final crisis over *Dubliners* and introduced him to his solicitor George Lidwell, though Lidwell exhibited a lawyer's caution overlaid by personal conservatism of taste.

That they were never to see each other again had remarkably little impact on their relations. The memory of the father continued deeply to inform the writing of the son, and the father's intense affection for the

176. John Stanislaus Joyce to James Joyce, 20 July 1911, *Letters II* 290. Writing to Stanislaus, Eva Joyce claimed that Mabel's illness had been caused by 'the surage in Hishon's'; Jackson and Costello, *John Stanislaus Joyce*, 321.

177. S. Joyce, *My Brother's Keeper*, 233.

178. Gillet, *Claybook for James Joyce*, 102–3; Ellmann, *James Joyce*, 276–77. Joyce recounted this also to Colum, whose grasp of opera was less sure than Gillet's; see Ulick O'Connor, ed., *The Joyce We Knew*, rev. ed. (Dingle: Brandon, 2004), 69–70. The perfection of the scene, and the fact that anything to do with opera tended to inflame Joyce's imagination, engenders the faint suspicion that the episode might never have occurred. If it didn't, it stands as a magnificently conceived rendering of the reconciliation of the two male Joyces.

179. Nora Barnacle Joyce to Eileen Joyce, 14 August 1912, *Letters II* 303.

son never abated. Joyce wrote to Ezra Pound on his father's death, 'He loved me deeply, more and more as he grew older.'[180] John Stanislaus had not taken up his son's invitation in 1910 to visit Trieste.[181] Joyce had decided against a return visit to Dublin to see his father, and deployed the stratagems of exile in which he was expert to rationalise his decision.

Joyce's friend Constantine Curran left a portrait of the old man, which he wrote in the disconsolate setting of Joyce's exhausted possibilities in Dublin before his departure:

> He was a man of unparalleled vituperative power, a virtuoso in speech with unique control of the vernacular, his language often coarse and blasphemous to a degree of which, in the long run, he could hardly himself have been conscious. A notable singer, with a wide knowledge of Italian opera, he would hold the attention of any room all night if there was a piano at which he could sit, play and sing. He could fascinate indefinitely with stories told with consummate art, one neatly fitting into another. And these stories would be of a perfectly drawing-room character till suddenly, as if taken unawares, he would slip into the coarse vein and another side of his nature and vocabulary be revealed.[182]

John Stanislaus Joyce cut a faintly archaic figure, somehow at odds with the recently acquired gentility of nationalist Dublin in the Edwardian era. Piaras Béaslaí recalled someone identifying John Stanislaus Joyce to him. He was 'a familiar figure, a real "man about town" with his monocle, spats and airs of faded gentility, he seemed to be treated with respect by everyone who knew him.'[183] This was John Stanislaus Joyce as 'the swaggerest swell off Shackvulle Strutt' on the third page from the

180. Joyce to Ezra Pound, 1 January 1932, *Letters III* 240.

181. John Stanislaus Joyce to James Joyce, 23 July 1910, unpublished, Cornell University, noted in Robert Scholes, *The Cornell Joyce Collection: A Catalogue* (Ithaca, NY: Cornell University Press, 1961), 109, item 676.

182. C. P. Curran, *James Joyce Remembered* (Oxford: Oxford University Press, 1968), 69–70. Curran had drafted this passage in his Joyce notebook but omitted from what he published the concluding sentence: 'He must also have been a man of violent habits of whom his daughters stood in terror'.

183. *Irish Independent*, 4 July 1962.

end of *Finnegans Wake*,[184] managing a decline that contrived to be at once precipitous and extraordinarily protracted.

There was no longer an extant Joyce household, and John Stanislaus migrated from one cheap hotel or boarding house to another.[185] His health was deteriorating, and through the good offices of his loyal friend Alfred Bergan he found lodgings in 1920 with the Medcalfs, a Protestant family, at 25 Claude Road, between Whitworth Road and the railway line in Drumcondra, a suburb of northern Dublin. Mary Medcalf had been a nurse, and faithfully tended to her elderly lodgers. In his notes on Joyce, Curran wrote that Joyce's father was treated as one of the family 'and largely reformed. The day after his arrival they had to take out his clothes to the garden to burn them. They were infested with lice.'[186] He stayed for over a decade, until his death.[187] His room overlooking the back garden was a shrine to his favourite son. There he received a remarkable succession of visitors, mostly friends or disciples of Joyce.[188] Joyce even prevailed on John Sullivan, the Cork-born tenor established in France, favoured by Joyce over John McCormack, to call on his father while on his first engagement in Dublin in April 1930.[189] Joyce's most remarkable contrivance to overcome the distance that separated them without actually coming to Dublin was to despatch in 1924–25 a journalist to interview his father.[190] John Stanislaus was

184. *FW* 626.10–11.

185. Coincidently, according to his biographers, one of these was the Ivy Hotel on Temple Street, which had once been the Dublin residence of the Parnells; Jackson and Costello, *John Stanislaus Joyce*, 333, 366.

186. Curran, Joyce notebook.

187. Jackson and Costello, *John Stanislaus Joyce*, 369, 393, 400–401; Curran, *James Joyce Remembered*, 70.

188. Ellmann, *James Joyce*, 579, 610.

189. Jackson and Costello, *John Stanislaus Joyce*, 410.

190. Jackson and Costello, *John Stanislaus Joyce*, 391–92. This was the interview in the *James Joyce Yearbook*, edited by Maria Jolas and published in Paris in 1949, where it is described as an 'interview given to an unidentified journalist who called on Mr. Joyce *père* at the request of his son in Paris.' It seems a little surprising that Jolas did not know the identity of the journalist—there is a possibility that she was, for reasons unknown, concealing it. The interview is polished in format, confirming that it was conducted and written up by a journalist rather than a stenographer, as the biographers of John Stanislaus Joyce assert; Jackson and Costello, *John Stanislaus*

indulgent towards the progeny who had ignored his advice: 'I often told Jim to go for the Bar, for he had a great flow of language and he talks better than he writes. However he has done very well'.[191]

In 1923 James Joyce commissioned the Irish painter Patrick Tuohy to paint his father's portrait. Tuohy was the son of a distinguished doctor who had tended the Joyces, and the grandson of J. M. Tuohy, the parliamentary correspondent of the *Freeman's Journal* at the time of the Split.[192] It was a late supplement to the strikingly Parnellite matrix of associations of John Stanislaus Joyce. Tuohy had called on Joyce in 1922 with a letter of introduction from James Stephens. Joyce chose Tuohy to paint his father's portrait over others proposed by Arthur Power,

---

Joyce, 391. The journalistic emissary refers to having called on John Stanislaus previously, almost a year before; Jolas, 'John Stanislaus Joyce', 159. He had been briefed by Joyce on the questions to ask. Some of the questions or topics are stated; others are to be inferred from the responses. As Joyce knew, and the journalist must have been aware from his previous encounter, the questions were scarcely more than prompts to elicit conversational flow. The questions reflect the unsentimental set of purpose with which Joyce drew on his father as a resource for his work. They relate to the time John Stanislaus spent at Chapelizod, including his knowledge of the Broadbent family (the question that puts Joyce's involvement in the questions asked beyond doubt); the Guinness family; the quality of water in the Liffey; the Jamesons; Daniel O'Connell; the Kettle family; (Hester) Vanhomrigh—Swift's Vanessa ('Van Homrig, who the hell was he? my God I could not tell you. Why does he want to know these things, Jim must be getting mad'); Father Charles of Mount Argus ('What in the name of God does he want to know these things for? I am afraid that his head is not all right'); Barton McGuckin; John McCormack; the Dublin city election of 1880 (prompted by an enquiry about the 'Baby policeman' which can only have come from Joyce); and, curiously enough, Oscar Wilde. In a letter to Harriet Shaw Weaver in October 1925, Joyce, by way of 'advance press opinions' on the publication of the 'Anna Livia Plurabelle' extract that had just appeared in *Le Navire d'Argent*, drew on the interview to anticipate his father's response and seemed disappointed with the results of the interview, if not faintly irritated with his father. Joyce to Harriet Shaw Weaver, 22 October 1925, *Letters I* 235.

Ellmann points out that after the death in November 1924 of his favourite aunt, Josephine Murray, who was a constant source of information, Joyce was driven to elicit family and Dublin intelligence from his father. Joyce wrote, in his last letter to his aunt, having learned of her illness, 'Only yesterday morning I was going to write to you—as usual about some point in my childhood as you are one of the two persons in Ireland who could give me information about it'. Joyce to Mrs. William Murray, 2 November 1924, *Letters I* 221. Ellmann records that Patrick Tuohy, at Joyce's direction, twice sent a solicitor's clerk to John Stanislaus in July 1926 with enquiries but got no response until Tuohy himself called in person; Ellmann, *James Joyce*, 579, 798n8.

191. Jolas, 'John Stanislaus Joyce', 169.

192. Ellmann, *James Joyce*, 565; Jackson and Costello, *John Stanislaus Joyce*, 385–86.

saying something about having known his father.[193] Tuohy duly attended on his sitter in Drumcondra. His portrayal of an intense, quizzically staring John Stanislaus Joyce in old age is a minor masterpiece. Stanislaus Joyce wrote to his brother in Paris in 1924, 'His portrait of Pappie is a wonderful study of that little old Milesian. I am especially glad that Tuohy is not that irritating kind of painter that sees in his sitter only a type. The likeness is striking.'[194] Joyce's characterisation of the portrait as 'splendid' transcended filial indulgence,[195] if Thomas McGreevy's description of it as 'the greatest portrait painted since Cezanne' could hardly be stood over.[196] The portrait attracted a good deal of attention on its exhibition in the Royal Hibernian Academy in Dublin in 1924,[197] and Joyce was invested in its success in something like the way in which he was invested in the singing career of John Sullivan. A supplement to the family portraits, it doubles as the phantasmal *carte de visite* of an absent son who swiftly reclaimed it. It presided over the other portraits in Joyce's successive Paris apartments.[198] Gisèle Freund, who created a brilliant photographic chronicle of Joyce in Paris, later wrote, 'Joyce, who possessed an almost mystical belief in blood ties, in the father-son relationship that pulsated through all his creative work, derived a strange pleasure from posing beneath the portrait of his own father.'[199]

In 1926, Joyce commissioned Tuohy to do a pencil portrait of his mother from a photograph.[200] Tuohy proposed painting Joyce himself, and Joyce agreed. This proved strangely protracted and a little fraught,[201] and elicited this comment from Joyce: 'Never mind my soul. Just be sure

193. Patrick J. Murphy, *Patrick Tuohy* (Dublin: Townhouse, 2004), 75–76.

194. Stanislaus Joyce to James Joyce, 7 August 1924, *Letters III* 101.

195. Joyce to Alfred Bergan, 27 October 1932, *Letters III* 264.

196. *Irish Times*, 6 March 1941.

197. P. Murphy, *Patrick Tuohy*, 76–77; Jackson and Costello, *John Stanislaus Joyce*, 386–89.

198. Joyce had the family portraits sent to him in Trieste in the spring of 1913; see *Letters II* 332n1.

199. Gisèle Freund and V. B. Carleton, *James Joyce in Paris: His Final Years* (London: Cassell, 1965), 72. This is in reference to the famous portrait of four generations of male Joyces, in which Joyce, Giorgio, and Stephen are seated beneath the Tuohy portrait in 1938, reproduced on the facing page.

200. P. Murphy, *Patrick Tuohy*, 78, 105; Joyce to Stanislaus Joyce, 28 September 1925, *Letters III* 127.

201. Joyce to Harriet Shaw Weaver, 2 June 1924, *Letters III* 96; 13 June 1925, *Letters I* 228.

FIGURE 2.3. Portrait of John Stanislaus Joyce by Patrick Tuohy, 1924. *Source*: 16.6, James Joyce Collection, The Poetry Collection of the University Libraries, University at Buffalo, The State University of New York.

you have my tie right.'[202] Joyce wrote to Harriet Shaw Weaver in mid-1924 that he was glad she liked the portrait: 'I like the folds of the jacket and the tie.'[203] Tuohy's portrait of Joyce is a comparatively rare rendering

202. Ellmann, *James Joyce*, 566.

203. Joyce to Harriet Shaw Weaver, 27 June 1924, *Letters I* 216. He added, 'He did not tell you all about the ownership of the portrait because he is going to have a little game with a person

of the artist no longer young but still in his prime in his early forties, *entre deux* ages. There is something lacking, and Joyce did not like the portrait. It was not exhibited at the 1925 Paris Salon as had been intended.[204] Tuohy embarked on a second portrait which Joyce considered to be a failure.[205] Tuohy's fiercely austere artistic promise was to be cut short by his death by his own hand in New York in 1930 at the age of thirty-six.[206]

John Stanislaus always wrote to his son on Joyce's birthday. He ended his 1925 missive with the statement, 'I am still what is left of me, your fond and loving father'.[207] He died on 29 December 1931.[208]

The fact that Joyce had not returned to see his father across the span of almost two decades remains striking. He wrote to T. S. Eliot in a fleeting moment of seeming misgiving of his grief at his father's death: 'He had an intense love for me and it adds anew to my grief and remorse that I did not go to Dublin to see him for so many years. I kept him constantly under the illusion that I would come and was always in correspondence with him but an instinct I believed in held me back from going, much as I longed to.'[209]

Joyce's decision not to come to Dublin to see his father owed much to his strategising of exile. Joyce did not consider that what a return visit to Ireland would achieve warranted compromising the political *acquis* of his absence from Ireland since 1912. He may have reasoned that the

---

in Dublin first. As you may have seen by his eyes he is very malicious—in a good sense of the word if it has one. I can imagine the scene and it amuses me though I would not do it' (*Letters I* 216-17).

204. *Letters I* 216; P. Murphy, *Patrick Tuohy*, 79.

205. Joyce to Harriet Shaw Weaver, 22 July 1932, *Letters III* 250.

206. P. Murphy, *Patrick Tuohy*, 107–8; Joyce to Harriet Shaw Weaver, 6 September 1930, *Letters III* 202.

207. John Stanislaus Joyce to James Joyce, 31 January 1925, quoted in Patricia Hutchins, *James Joyce's World* (London: Methuen, 1957), 171.

208. See Ellmann, *James Joyce*, 642; Jackson and Costello, *John Stanislaus Joyce*, 415–18.

209. Joyce to T. S. Eliot, 1 January 1932, *Letters I* 311. In an appreciation of C. P. Curran, Niall Montgomery wrote that Curran was never heard to criticise Joyce, and then added, 'Recently, when conversation turned to the mystery of Mr. Joyce's failure to come to his dying father, Mr. Curran, smiling, and with a characteristic movement of the eyes, almost in a whisper: "there was nothing whatever to stop him coming home that time, you know"'. *Irish Times*, 3 January 1972.

benefits of a return visit did not bear sustained scrutiny. It would have gratified his father but, knowing his father, could have become messy, as well as engendering an expectation of further visits. They had, after all, managed to observe the protocols of Joyce's exile without impinging on their compact of affinity, if also without strengthening it. Louis Gillet wrote, 'Without writing to one another, neither being a great letter-writer, they always found a way to correspond and exchange news about themselves. Above all, they felt bound by a common complicity and a connivance of nature which dispensed with formulas and further explanations. They understood each other by hints, even without words.'[210] The conflict was resolved finally by Joyce's confidence in the unconditionality of his father's love. It was not misplaced.

210. Gillet, *Claybook for James Joyce*, 102.

3

Four Friends of the Father

JOYCE'S WRITING HAS A double indebtedness to his father. When he wrote to Harriet Shaw Weaver on his father's death that 'hundreds of pages and scores of characters in my books came from him',[1] Joyce had in mind principally John Stanislaus himself, who became a protean archetype in his son's fictional writing and the source of a repertoire of extraordinarily diverse voices, but the words can also be taken to encompass the personalities whom Joyce came to know through his father. John Stanislaus Joyce had, by virtue of an almost lunatic gregariousness, a remarkably broad and disparate range of friends and acquaintances in Dublin, who not merely contributed to the personae of *Ulysses* and other works but did much to inform Joyce's conception of the polis of Dublin.

To take one instance, Patrick Meehan, whom Constantine Curran consulted in writing *James Joyce Remembered*, recalled that Joyce's father habitually called in to the Capel Street Library to gossip with Grogan the librarian: 'Grogan was a limping, dwarfish, cross-grained man whom we avoided but John Stanislaus and he were buddies. Unlike Michael Cusack who would seek him out at the end of the room where the counter-railing ended and would deliberately provoke him. Once Mr. Cusack raised his mighty blackthorn on him but brought it down on the counter where its mark long remained until the counter was removed.'[2]

1. Joyce to Harriet Shaw Weaver, 17 January 1932, *Letters I* 312.
2. C. P. Curran, Joyce notebook, 124; Curran, *Under the Receding Wave*, 56.

James Joyce can thus, through his father, be taken to have known something of Michael Cusack, the remorseless proponent of Gaelic sports, before he heard of him again in University College as someone admired by his ardently nationalist contemporaries. Cusack would gain an early appearance in *Stephen Hero* as 'a very stout black-bearded citizen',[3] and in a passage of fantasia in the 'Cyclops' episode of *Ulysses*, the Citizen's blackthorn becomes 'a couched spear of acuminated granite'.[4] Joyce's sense of the interconnectedness of the inhabitants of his native city, and of the elaborate protocols through which that interconnectedness had to be negotiated, owed much to his father's almost morbid extroversion. Dublin was the city of John Stanislaus Joyce, conceived and invented by him as an immigrant from Cork, before it was the city of his son—and in a discernible degree remained so in his son's writing.

Four very different friendships, or acquaintances, of John Stanislaus Joyce provide a loose matrix of his political relations, as well as elucidating his character; all four feature significantly in Joyce's fiction. The closest and most endearing relationship was with John Kelly, who more than any single other individual lit the flame of Joyce's Parnellism. While Kelly was the archetype of the selfless Parnellite nationalist, John Clancy was a Parnellite of the more opportunistic kind, whose life was rooted in the municipal politics of Dublin. John Stanislaus's friendships with the Casey brothers, Patrick and Joe, attest to a degree of emotional affinity with Fenianism. Joyce's encounters with Joseph Casey in Paris informed his assessment of what seemed a spent movement.

John Kelly

John Kelly (1848–1896) was a political activist who acquired a quiet legend in the Parnell era without having held elected or organisational office. Born in Bantry in 1848, he started a business in Tralee and was frequently referred to as 'John Kelly of Tralee'. He became caught up in

3. *SH* 61.

4. *U* 12.199–200.

the Land League agitation, and according to the *Freeman's Journal*, 'he was one of the first in the South of Ireland to join the Land League and contributed largely to introduce and extend that organization in the county of Kerry.'[5]

The police witness at his speech in Tralee on 11 April 1881 recorded him as referring to Sandes of Listowel as a bad landlord, and to Captain Chute as 'worse, he was the damndest hound of a "rackrenter in Kerry."'[6] Speaking publicly with Timothy Harrington at Killarney the following month, Kelly declared with obscure menace, 'Do not be in dread of Lord Kenmare's writs (groans), I believe that his name is on more writs in Ireland as a plaintiff than any man in the known world (groans for Lord Kenmare, and cries of "Leonard") and I also believe that if he persists in this business he will have a writ in his pocket himself.'[7]

Kelly was convicted and imprisoned on the charge of holding (Land League) illegal courts and was again imprisoned as a suspect under the Chief Secretary, William Edward Forster's internment legislation of 1881. By the time he was released from incarceration as a 'suspect', his business had fallen away and he was appointed a Land League organiser, but refused to take a salary.[8] In fact, the *Irish Daily Independent* observed on his death, 'at different times he was imprisoned in connection with the Land League, National League and Plan of Campaign in almost every jail in Ireland. . . . Mr. Kelly never murmured, but bore his penalties in the most manly and uncomplaining manner, so much as to win the esteem and admiration of his jailers.'[9]

Kelly's activism was marked by a stoicism that was without self-consciousness. It spanned the phases of Parnellite agitation in the 1880s

5. *Freeman's Journal*, 14 April 1896.

6. NAI, CSB/Irish National League 1/112. [At the time of writing, the National Archives of Ireland held the Royal Irish Constabulary's Crime Special Branch files relating to their surveillance of the Irish National League.—Eds.] See also Margaret O'Callaghan, *British High Politics and a Nationalist Ireland: Criminality, Land and the Law under Forster and Balfour* (New York: St. Martin's, 1994).

7. NAI, CSB/Irish National League/183.

8. *Freeman's Journal*, 14 April 1896; *United Ireland*, 18 April 1896.

9. *Irish Daily Independent*, 14 April 1896.

across the country and resulted in sustained periods of incarceration that no other Parnellite agitator suffered. As his friend the journalist John McGrath wrote,

For man in all that time became
The patriot of a period, then dropped out—
But never was there roll-call that his name
Was not heard singing in the answering shout.[10]

United Ireland characterised him as 'altogether a unique type of Irishman. Associated for almost twenty years with one of the hottest agitations Ireland has ever known, and during all that time doing work of the very greatest importance, he never seemed to bother about his position in the movement. Other men who had not a tithe of his ability . . . became "leaders" and very great persons in the country. It never seemed to occur to John Kelly that he should become either a leader or a great person.'[11]

He was much respected and widely liked, and in the manner of Irish politics his conversation was well stocked with contemporary political anecdote: 'The English papers used to say, during the Land and National League days, that all humour had gone out of Ireland; but John Kelly could have filled a book with good stories of those two agitations.'[12]

In the wake of the divorce crisis, 'he stood firm by the Irish Leader to the end'.[13] It is in the Split that Kelly flares into fleeting historical visibility as the exemplary longtime adherent of Charles Stewart Parnell. Parnell had briefly considered running Kelly as his candidate in the North Kilkenny election, in between Barry O'Brien, who was first proposed, and Vincent Scully, the actual candidate.[14] The correspondent of the *Daily News* rendered Kelly as disappointed but did appreciate his utter lack of interest in self-advancement: 'Mr. Kelly has long been

10. John McGrath, 'John Kelly', *Evening Herald*, 15 April 1896; *United Ireland*, 18 April 1896.

11. *United Ireland*, 18 April 1896.

12. *United Ireland*, 18 April 1896.

13. *Evening Herald*, 14 April 1896.

14. R. B. O'Brien, *Charles Stewart Parnell*, 2:299.

known in Dublin as "The Conundrum". Last Thursday week Mr. John Kelly became "a conundrum" to his own patriotic self, for he suddenly learned that he had been superseded; after which Mr. John Kelly might be seen in tattered, squalid little crowds at street corners, waving his hat, and with a pensive air of resignation cheering feebly for his successor.'[15]

In January 1891, the anti-Parnellite *Insuppressible* published an editorial emphasising that Parnell's honest supporters would not be excluded from the nationalist ranks on Parnell's defeat. Among these it numbered 'the famous John Kelly' and John Fitzgibbon of Castlerea, who 'have repeatedly proved their devotion by imprisonment',[16] generously exempting Kelly from the anathema the paper pronounced against prominent Parnellites.

Kelly's support remained steadfast as Parnell's fortunes waned, and he was with him to the end. An account of his fateful last meeting with Parnell survives in interviews with Kelly and John Clancy in an article published by John McGrath on the anniversary of Parnell's death in 1893. Parnell had addressed a meeting in Creggs in the west of Ireland on 27 September 1891 and was in Dublin until 30 September, when he left the city to embark on his long journey back to Brighton. In his narrative of the Creggs meeting and of Parnell's last leaving of Ireland, published in *United Ireland* on the second anniversary of Parnell's death, McGrath wrote,

> This, however, is not the last glimpse we get of the Leader on Irish soil. When he arrived at Westland-row two of his comrades and followers, Mr. John Kelly and Mr. John Clancy were in the station. Noticing him at the ticket office they went over and spoke to him. 'Are you not coming down?' he asked; and said John Kelly with whom I

15. *Daily News*, 23 December 1890. Barry O'Brien, also under consideration as a candidate, gave in his biography of Parnell an account of his own role. Parnell had cabled to him to come to Ireland, which O'Brien understood to be a request that he stand in North Kilkenny. Parnell, having decided that Vincent Scully would be the candidate, refused to let Joseph Kenny wire O'Brien not to come. When O'Brien arrived, he asked Kenny, '"And what does Parnell expect me to do now?" - "He expects you", said the Doctor, "to come to Kilkenny to help Scully". And we both laughed.' R. B. O'Brien, *Charles Stewart Parnell*, 2:299–300.

16. *Insuppressible*, 3 January 1891.

> have had a talk on the subject, 'Of course we went'. Mr. Kelly was also one of Mr. Parnell's oldest colleagues in the Irish movement, and when the Split came he stood by him stoutly, though perhaps he had many inducements to go with Mr. Dillon and Mr. O'Brien, with whom he had been closely associated for several years. 'Of course we went', he said, and I thought to myself there was a world of loyalty to the Chief suggested in the expression.[17]

On the short train journey down, Parnell remarked that the pain had left his arm, but that he feared it had got into his body. When they got to Carlisle Pier, Kelly noted that Parnell, ill and nervous, shrank from pressing into the crowd hurrying across the gangway to secure places on board the ship for Holyhead. He asked Kelly and Clancy to find a berth for him, and they got Parnell a fore-cabin.

> Mr. Clancy then went away, and Mr. Kelly and the Chief came on deck, where they chatted until the steamer started. Mr. Parnell talked about the political work that was before him in Ireland, saying that his intention was for the future to remain and fight the battle on the spot. He was hardly ever known to appear on deck on the cross-channel steamers, but on this occasion he remained there till the whistle blew, the sailors as they passed noting to each other that 'there was Mr. Parnell'. Mr. Kelly spoke to him very seriously about his condition, advising him to keep himself very warm. When he had a week's rest and quiet, he replied, he believed he would be all right. Then, said Mr. Kelly, the whistle blew, and, as I made a motion to go to the gangway, 'well, old man', he said quite cheerily, and slapping me on the back, 'I will be back on Saturday week for the Macroom meeting'.
>
> That was the last of Parnell in the Ireland of his love. He was not back on Saturday week. It was Sunday week when he again rested on Irish soil—on his way not to Macroom, but to Glasnevin.[18]

17. John McGrath, 'His Last Campaign: Creggs, and the Final Departure (Two Interviews)', *United Ireland*, 7 October 1893; Callanan, *Parnell Split*, 180–81.

18. McGrath, 'His Last Campaign'.

It was apt that John Kelly became the last person to speak to Parnell in Ireland. Kelly was able, as John Stanislaus Joyce was not, to provide the young James Joyce with firsthand accounts of Parnell and his campaign in the Split. While other actively Parnellite friends of John Stanislaus had memories of 'the Chief' to impart, they are unlikely to have had quite the emotional and imaginative impact of Kelly's. In Joyce's own leave-taking of Parnell, in the closing movement of *Finnegans Wake*, as the river goes back to the sea, he evokes with striking emphasis the ravages of the restless plying back and forth from Brighton to Ireland on the fragile health of Parnell (mocked by Timothy Michael Healy's *National Press* as 'Brighton's weekly emigrant'):[19] 'but hunt me the journeyon, iteritinerant, the kal his course, amid the semitary of Somnionia.'[20] It is hard to resist the idea that this does not owe something to John Kelly's narrating of the Split, and of his last meeting with Parnell.

A police description of Kelly, with a photograph, dating from 1892, gave as his occupation 'Land League Organiser', which was of course anachronistic, but still had a certain existential cogency. It characterised him somewhat slyly also as an associate of the leading Irish Republican Brotherhood (IRB) men in Dublin, and someone who stayed occasionally at the National Club. What is striking about Kelly is that his political involvement appears to have been entirely with the Land League and the National League without a preceding phase of Fenian involvement.[21] As a Dublin Parnellite activist, he could hardly have avoided

19. Callanan, *Parnell Split*, 181.

20. *FW* 594.7–8.

21. Adaline Glasheen's misreading of the Christmas dinner scene as a purely Irish brawl between Dante and John Casey, emblems of 'perverted Catholicism and perverted Nationalism', is due in part to her belief that Casey was a Fenian, and her misconception of what that entailed: Adaline Glasheen, 'Joyce and the Three Ages of Charles Stewart Parnell', in *A James Joyce Miscellany*, 2nd ser., ed. Marvin Magalaner (Carbondale: Southern Illinois University Press, 1959), 155. Joyce in *A Portrait* does not render Mr Casey a Fenian. The fact that it is not explained why he was imprisoned leads some readers, including the editors of the Norton Critical Edition, to infer that 'his hand has been crippled by forced labour during imprisonment for revolutionary activities' (*P* 24n1). John Kelly's serial incarcerations were for what might now be described as acts of civil disobedience, and Mr Casey is clearly characterised throughout as a Parnellite and not

being in some sense an associate of the city's leading IRB men.[22] He was present with Clancy for the Fenian leader James Stephens's symbolically charged visit to Parnell's grave on 25 October 1891.[23]

Kelly's own health was broken, and his active involvement in politics did not long outlast Parnell's death. As the *Daily Express* noted on his death, 'Within the last few years he was little heard of in connexion with politics.'[24] He moved from living in the National Club on Rutland (later Parnell) Square to the home of D. J. (Dan) Hishon, a fellow Parnellite, at 16 Belvedere Place,[25] off Dorset Street.[26] After some weeks in the Mater hospital, Kelly died 'comforted by the consolations of religion' on 13 April 1896,[27] at the age of forty-eight. The obituaries spoke of Kelly dying, as well as having lived, for Ireland. The *Irish Daily Independent* wrote,

> It was almost impossible that he could have passed through those sufferings and sacrifices in and out of prison without their having left behind them in Mr. Kelly the traces of a ruined physical constitution; and it will be for many a long year a cause of burning indignation to all who knew him that a man of such high purpose and integrity should have been virtually murdered by the operation of British law in Ireland. . . . Mr. Kelly emerged from his last imprisonment the merest wreck of his former self, and he never recovered his strength, though even to the last he was ready for a renewal of the fight for Ireland in any field of effort.[28]

---

a Fenian. The distinction is subtly maintained in his attack on the patriotic record of the hierarchy, which begins, 'Didn't the bishops of Ireland betray us in the time of the union', where 'us' means the (admittedly pre-Fenian) Irish, and goes on to refer to the bishops and priests denouncing 'the fenian movement from the pulpit' (*P* 1.1101–7).

22. NAI, CSB/12730/s.

23. *Freeman's Journal*, 26 October 1891.

24. *Daily Express*, 14 April 1896.

25. *United Ireland*, 7 October 1893.

26. Costello, *Years of Growth*, 135–36.

27. *Evening Herald*, 14 April 1896; *Irish Daily Independent*, 14 April 1896.

28. *Irish Daily Independent*, 18 April 1896.

At his funeral, John O'Connor, ex–member of Parliament, saluted Kelly as 'a strong and powerful man. His friends knew him in later days as a broken man physically, and all knew the cause.' The reference in the *Evening Herald* to 'the insidious malady super-induced by the grievous hardships to which he was subjected during the various long and trying terms of imprisonment which he underwent'[29] suggests tuberculosis.[30] His cortège followed an extravagantly circuitous route from the Mater hospital to Glasnevin, where he was buried at a tangent to the circle of Parnell's grave on 16 April 1896.[31] The Dublin Metropolitan Police noted the funeral was 'not as large as expected. Almost all who attended were prominent Land Leaguers and sympathisers.'[32] It was one of those funerals of loyalists of the dead leader which were in themselves evanescent Parnellite *lieux de mémoire,* attended by the Dublin-based old guard of the Split. One member of Parliament (J. J. Clancy); a handful of ex–members of Parliament (Dr J. E. Kenny, Henry Harrison, and John O'Connor); apparatchiks and activists such as John Clancy, the sub-sheriff of Dublin, John Wyse Power, and Andrew Kettle; Parnellite journalists, most notably Edward Byrne, the former editor of the *Freeman's Journal,* who had been very close to Parnell and whose livelihood was destroyed by his cleaving to Parnell in the Split. Many were friends of John Stanislaus Joyce, including the solicitor J. H. Menton, who appears in *Ulysses*. John Stanislaus Joyce was almost certainly present, and it is possible that he brought with him his fourteen-year-old eldest son.[33] If Joyce was present, there is no extant mention of it. After the interment,

29. In *A Portrait,* Mr Casey, when talking to Mr Dedalus about an episode in which a hotel-keeper they knew had been 'manufacturing' champagne for some customers, succumbs to what is described as 'a fit of laughter and coughing' and 'his fit of coughing and laughter' (*P* 1.763, 772–73).

30. *Irish Daily Independent,* 17 April 1896.

31. *Evening Herald,* 14 April 1896.

32. NAI, CSB/1162/s.

33. *Evening Herald,* 16 April 1896; *Irish Daily Independent,* 17 April 1896. The newspaper reports listed among the attendance 'J J Joyce' or 'John G Joyce'. It is unclear which referred to John Stanislaus Joyce, and probably too much to think that the two names were misspellings of the names of Joyce *père et fils*. John Stanislaus Joyce's own grave lies close to that of Kelly.

there was a meeting in the cemetery of Kelly's friends to subscribe to the erection of a gravestone. On the first anniversary of his death, a Celtic cross was unveiled at the grave in a ceremony attended by John Stanislaus Joyce.[34]

John Kelly was not just a friend to John Stanislaus Joyce. Of all the latter's friends, he was the one closest to family, present less as a guest than as an occasional member of the household. A few weeks after his mother's death, driven to accept that his parents were not after all ill-matched, Stanislaus Joyce wrote, 'It is strange, too, that the true friendships Pappie made (with Mr. Kelly for instance) were confirmed at home and, I think, under Mother's influence, his friends being scarcely less friendly towards Mother than towards himself.'[35]

Stanislaus Joyce recalled John Kelly coming on convalescent stays at the Joyce house in Bray on three or four occasions. Of one of these he recounted a visit by a police sergeant named Joyce, who warned that a warrant had arrived for Kelly's arrest, to enable Kelly to leave that night. Stanislaus remembered a genial presence who, 'when pressed by my father to do so, would recite "The Auld Plaid Shawl" or "Shemus O'Brien"—and recite it so movingly that my father would get busy with the tumblers of punch to hide his emotion', or sing ballads, sometimes to May Joyce's accompaniment:

> John Kelly of Tralee must I think have been of peasant stock. He was pale and handsome, slow of speech and movement, with regular, clean-cut features and a mass of black hair. The fingers of his left hand were permanently cramped from making sacks and picking oakum in jail. He had an old-fashioned courtesy, a peasant eloquence—in later years more than once in exercise on my brother's birthday, a natural gift of friendship, and a passionate loyalty to his country and his Chief, Parnell. His great expectations for my brother were hardly outdone even by my father. . . . At any rate he never tried to influence

34. S. Joyce, entry for 26 September 1903, in *Dublin Diary*, 9; *Irish Daily Independent*, 17 April 1897.

35. S. Joyce, entry for 26 September 1903, in *Dublin Diary*, 9.

him as Dante did with her narrow, restless, partisan bigotry. If the boy liked to listen, let him. He did.[36]

Stanislaus characterised Kelly as 'the sincerest of the little group of my brother's well-wishers.' The sense of his brother as a favourite remained sharply etched on his memory. Remembering being taken on walks and given donkey rides by Kelly, he wrote, 'My brother cannot have been at home or I should not have been so preferred, so that I reckon it must have been after he had gone up to Clongowes at the time.'[37]

Irrespective of whether the Christmas dinner scene in *A Portrait* occurred, Joyce's characterisation of Kelly as John Casey fastidiously reproduces what is known about him,[38] and the effects of his serial incarcerations: 'Mr. Casey had told him that he had got those three cramped fingers making a birthday present for Queen Victoria',[39] and the tubercular coughing that merges with his laughter. Politically, Mr Casey is passionately Parnellite.[40] Mr Casey's recollection of spitting tobacco juice into the eye of a bitter old woman must relate to an event

36. S. Joyce, *My Brother's Keeper*, 34–37.

37. S. Joyce, *My Brother's Keeper*, 35–36. Stanislaus concludes he must have been four at the time of the incident, which would date it to the latter part of 1888.

38. Why did Joyce assign to John Kelly the surname Casey when Patrick Casey was a friend of his father, and he had come to know Joseph Casey in Paris? One would not pose the question were it not for the fact that Joyce was extremely attentive, to the point of intricate game playing, in his assignation of surnames in his fictional writings. While it could still be an odd coincidence, it is faintly possible that Joyce was ascribing to John Kelly, who was not a Fenian, the virtues of selfless perseverance in the cause of Parnellism, in which the Casey brothers in their Fenianism were notably deficient, so that the true revolutionary was the Parnellite John Kelly.

39. *P* 1.738–40.

40. We will never know whether Mr Casey's account of spitting tobacco into the eye of an anti-Parnellite harridan at the meeting in Arklow 'not long before the chief died' (*P* 1.1013–14), a meeting that did not take place if attended by Parnell, is based on an account of John Kelly of an incident of the Split or was invented by Joyce. It has a certain verisimilitude, which could reflect either historicity or Joyce's artistry. The fact that Mr Casey's much interrupted telling of the 'story about a very famous spit' is provoked by Dante Riordan's reference to her religion being 'insulted and spit upon by renegade Catholics' does not seem to advance the issue (*P* 1.958, 963).

during the Split in Parnell's lifetime ('not long before the chief died',[41] although historically there was no such Arklow meeting). There was also Mr Casey's nocturnal flight after the visit by a 'Sergeant O'Neill' warning of his impending arrest. Stephen's feelings for Mr Casey are affectionate: 'He liked to sit near him at the fire, looking up at his dark fierce face. But his dark eyes were never fierce and his slow voice was good to listen to.'[42] And Stephen listens, as Stanislaus said Joyce did. When Stephen laughs as his father and Mr Casey joke about Christy the hotelkeeper, Simon Dedalus says benignly, 'What are you laughing at, you little puppy, you?'[43] Stephen is eagerly drawn into his father's relationship to Mr Casey.

John Kelly had been dead for two and a half years when Joyce entered University College, but Joyce kept Mr Casey alive in *Stephen Hero*—in what remains of the novel he appears twice. When Stephen is learning Irish, 'Mr Casey taught him a few Southern songs in Irish and always raised his glass to Stephen saying "Sinn Féin" instead of "Good Health"'.[44] When Stephen is about to deliver his address on 'art and life' in University College, while the minutes of the last meeting are being read, 'he had time to observe his father's eyeglass glimmering high up near the window and he divined more than saw the burly form of Mr. Casey hard by that observant centre.'[45] In both references Casey is rendered as a supernumerary member of the Daedalus household. We do not know the role of Mr Casey in the lost earlier part of *Stephen Hero*, but the references that survive suggest a tutelary influence on Stephen Daedalus that informed his political judgement and, in the setting of his familiar experience and before his arrival in University College, rendered

41. *P* 1.1013–14.

42. *P* 1.990–94.

43. *P* 1.777.

44. *SH* 56. It is plain that in the novel Mr Casey is treated as more or less a member of the Daedalus household. The immediately preceding sentence is, 'People at home did not seem opposed to this new freak of his.'

45. *SH* 100. Mr Casey is again rendered as a supernumerary member of the Daedalus household.

him potentially resistant to the Gaelicising reinvention of nationalism by the 'patriots', as if all that had gone before was of little account.

The last mention of John Casey in Joyce's work is through the mind of Leopold Bloom in the 'Eumaeus' episode of *Ulysses*: 'And does anybody hereabouts remember Caoc O'Leary, a favourite and most trying declamation piece by the way of poor John Casey and a bit of perfect poetry in its own small way.'[46] The reference is to a favourite nineteenth-century poem, 'Caoch the Piper', by John Keegan. This is Joyce's valediction to John Kelly. The epithet 'poor' is deftly unobtrusive, but through it Joyce forges an association between his friendship as a child with Kelly and the relationship between the narrator of the poem, who is a boy in its opening, and the blind piper of the title. Returning after an interval of twenty years during which he was assumed to have died, the piper asks,

'Are you the silky-headed child
That loved poor Caoch O'Leary?'[47]

Given that the blind piper, who dies the next day, bequeaths his pipes (and his dog Pinch) to the by now young man, the last reference to Casey conveys the recognition that Kelly had been, as well as a friend of Joyce in boyhood and of the Joyce family, a source of creative inspiration for Joyce.[48]

46. *U* 16.426–28. The reference is noted in Glasheen, 'Joyce and the Three Ages', 178–79. Don Gifford gets this wrong, by introducing the confusing presence of John Keegan Casey: the poem was written by John Keegan. Gifford, *Ulysses Annotated: Notes for James Joyce's 'Ulysses'*, with Robert J. Sheridan (Berkeley: University of California Press, 1989), 540.

47. There is a second reference to the poem in the sentence in *Ulysses* which serves as a decoy: the sentence invokes the lines, 'Does anybody hereabouts / Remember Caoch the Piper'. Likewise, the fact that the reference to Casey and the poem comes from Bloom rather than Stephen—or Simon—Dedalus increases rather than diminishes the force of the proposition that Joyce is making a finely wrought association between his relation to Kelly and the boy of the poem's relationship to Caoch O'Leary.

48. There is also something not easily defined to do with the idea of return in the poem applied to Joyce's relationship to Kelly. When Joyce wrote the 'Eumaeus' episode, it was getting on for twenty years since he had drawn on the character of John Kelly for Mr Casey in *Stephen Hero*, from which derived Joyce's immortalisation of Kelly in *A Portrait*.

John Clancy

Among the friends of Joyce's father, John Clancy (1844–1915) was in many respects the antithesis of the undemonstrative and selfless John Kelly, his fellow Parnellite. Clancy and Kelly are the emblematically contrasting faces of the Parnellism of the Split. John Stanislaus Joyce was not close to Clancy but had a potentially serviceable acquaintanceship with him. His loyal friend Alfred Bergan worked under Clancy.[49] He was—after Harrington, who mistrusted him—the most politically prominent of the friends of John Stanislaus, and the greatest potential dispenser of patronage to him. If the association with Clancy enhanced the standing of John Stanislaus, Clancy's largesse towards him was at best frugal.

An adept of the rougher arts of Irish politics, Clancy had been Parnell's chief henchman in Dublin. He belonged to the type of commercially careerist Dublin nationalist, combining municipal office with business interests of his own. Inhabiting the interstices of the Parnellite movement and Fenianism, Clancy had a radical edge that managed to combine political conviction with a generous measure of self-interest. The multiplicity of his roles and interests, combined with his authority and his height, rendered him a conspicuous figure in the city, posthumously immortalised in the figure of 'Long John' Fanning in *Ulysses*.

John Clancy was born in Carricknagat, County Sligo, in 1844.[50] His father had been for a time a 'tide waiter' or outdoor officer of customs at Liverpool. He came to Dublin at a very young age and found

49. Ellmann, *James Joyce*, 43–44. Ellmann includes an anecdote from an interview with a David Charles. It was necessary to hang a convicted man. Clancy 'having no stomach for the job, betook himself to London, confiding all the preparations to Bergan's equally reluctant hands.' Ellmann, *James Joyce*, 43. Bergan received a letter from an English barber offering his services as a hangman, which described his skill in fastening and pulling nooses, which found its way into the 'Cyclops' episode of *Ulysses*.

50. My account draws on Chief Superintendent John Mallon's riveting 1892 biographical profile of John Clancy in the National Archives of Ireland and is also greatly indebted to Owen McGee's *The IRB: The Irish Republican Brotherhood from the Land League to Sinn Féin* (Dublin: Four Courts, 2005), which tracks the neglected career of Clancy. That neglect owes much to the fact that Clancy, who began as an adherent of the Irish Republican Brotherhood, ended his

employment, first, as a printer in the *Irish Times,* whose proprietor Major Knox had been fleetingly elected for Sligo, and then 'got in to the office' of a ship's broker from Sligo, H. W. Scott, on Eden Quay. By then he had joined the IRB. In an 1892 profile, Chief Superintendent John Mallon of the Dublin Metropolitan Police wrote that Clancy 'was ultimately posted to Kingstown for the purpose of meeting ships coming into the bay. At that period, 1864 and 1865, Kingstown was a very hot bed of Fenianism and Clancy was among the most demonstrative of the crowd.'[51] When habeas corpus was suspended in 1866, Clancy was arrested under warrant of the Lord Lieutenant for 'treasonable practices', the making of seditious speeches, and was imprisoned for several months in Mountjoy. He entered the service of Palgrave, Murphy & Company as an outdoor manager and, as Mallon noted, was 'now a greater man with the Fenians than before.'[52] His next employment was as inspector of agencies for a Dublin porter brewery, travelling mostly through the midlands and northern towns of England. According to Mallon, the brewery Dublin firm of Caffrey & Son failed, and the business was taken over by their principal creditors in England, who 'appointed Clancy one of their agents, and also manager of a public house in Green Street on which they held a mortgage. The business of the brewery was wound up in a chancery suit, and Clancy somehow managed to get possession of the Licensed House in Green Street.'[53] In the politically becalmed pre–Land League Dublin of the middle 1870s, Clancy was well placed, a publican of excellent 'advanced' nationalist credentials and connections.

Clancy had a sharp eye for his own commercial advantage but was also possessed of a certain doggedness of conviction. His Fenianism was tinged by opportunism, and he supported the Land League,

---

career as a supporter of John Redmond's Irish Party, and something also to an historiographical neglect of Dublin municipal politics.

51. John Mallon, biographical profile of John Clancy, 1 July 1892, NAI, CBS/5314S (actually numbered 5379S). For Mallon, see Donal P. McCracken, *Inspector Mallon* (Dublin: Irish Academic Press, 2009); and O'Callaghan, *British High Politics.*

52. Mallon, biographical profile of John Clancy.

53. Mallon, biographical profile of John Clancy.

which Fenians of stricter dispensation did not. He met Parnell when he was acting as secretary to the first meeting Parnell addressed, at which Isaac Butt presided, when Parnell contested County Dublin in March 1874.[54] He was arrested as a suspect under Forster's regime in early 1882 and incarcerated for some months in Kilmainham, where Parnell had been confined since the previous October. After his release, he was elected for the Inns Quay Ward to the city council. He was thus the only member of the IRB on the city council, although of course not elected as such. It was the beginning of a long career in municipal politics, chiefly as a councillor for the South Dock Ward. In 1884 Clancy made a one-man protest against a vote of condolence to the queen on the death of a member of the royal family, deprecating 'toadyism to any foreign prince.'[55] The precociousness of Clancy's isolated gesture served him well as opposition to the visit of the Prince of Wales mounted the following year. He was now, as a conspicuous figure of Fenian allegiance, of considerable interest to those directing the Parnellite movement. If the momentum of the Land League had brought with it the support of many Fenians in rural Ireland, Dublin was always a special case. Parnell's loyal lieutenant and editor of *United Ireland*, William O'Brien, enlisted in 1885 the support of John Clancy, who agreed to join the National League. In the same year he disposed of his Green Street public house and was appointed sub-sheriff of Dublin, a role that entailed responsibilities for the registration of voters and the listing of jurors, functions which he discharged in an efficient and uncontroversial manner.

Whatever Clancy's formal relationship to the Parnellite National League, his resourcefulness and his diverse network of contacts rendered him indispensable for certain purposes. This was exemplified by his role in organising the escape from Ireland to France of John Dillon and William O'Brien. In October 1890 they were being prosecuted arising out of the Plan of Campaign and needed to get to the United States to raise funds. As the *Freeman's Journal* wrote on Clancy's death, 'There

54. *Freeman's Journal*, 19 November 1890. 'From that day to this his respect and admiration for Mr Parnell had grown in direct ratio as time passed on.'

55. McGee, *IRB*, 117–18; see also 139.

is a flavour of old time romance in the story of that voyage of the Ringsend trawler, St Patrick, with the refugees aboard, and John Clancy who had worked out the scheme, in command from Dalkey Island to Cherbourg Harbour.'[56]

By that time Clancy had resigned from the National League. In 1887 he established and ran the National Club on 41 Rutland Square. Apparently funded largely from the resources of the IRB, this was a Fenian haunt, 'effectively the IRB headquarters during the later 1880s and it became a nucleus for various other republican activities.'[57] The activities of the National Club were looked on with suspicious disdain by the Catholic Commercial Club, which met in the National League offices in O'Connell Street, and from which Mallon claimed Clancy had been expelled.[58] The National Club became the metropolitan site of the confluence of Parnellites and Fenians in the Split, frequently visited by Parnell, who stayed in the nearby house of Dr J. E. Kenny at 15 Rutland (later Parnell) Square. From about 1893 the National Club was taken over by the Parnellites, before it was closed down by Clancy in June 1899.

In the late 1880s Clancy, as well as discharging his functions as subsheriff, busied himself with the affairs of the National Club and collaborated with P. N. Fitzgerald, a leading Fenian, in establishing various political clubs and societies that were conceived as Fenian satellites. He was also, with Michael Davitt and John O'Leary, a patron of the National Monuments Committee. According to Mallon, 'Although he ceased to be a member of the National League for some time before the split among the Nationalists, when the split did occur he bossed everything in the Parnellite interest.'[59] The *Freeman's Journal* wrote in its obituary, 'He supported Mr. Parnell with all the strength of his strong and loyal nature to the end, and there was no one in Ireland on whom the deposed Irish leader had as much reliance.'[60] Like many Fenians,

56. *Freeman's Journal*, 30 January 1915.
57. McGee, *IRB*, 176.
58. Mallon, biographical profile of John Clancy.
59. Mallon, biographical profile of John Clancy.
60. *Freeman's Journal*, 30 January 1915.

Clancy was more drawn to the embattled Parnell of the Split, fighting the Liberals and the Catholic Church, than to the ascendant Parnell of the previous years. Clancy was instrumental in setting up, at the National Club, the Parnell Leadership Committee. Parnell's relationship with Clancy emblematised to a degree that was embarrassing the extent of his dependence on the Fenians in the Split, and his need to get Clancy to marshal his henchmen as required, for example in the assault on the *United Ireland* office. Clancy also played a role in Parnell's appeal to the Dublin working class in the Split.[61] The Healyite papers played up what they portrayed as the desperate expediency that reduced Parnell to association with Clancy. Bourgeois Catholic nationalists regarded Clancy as disreputable, sharing Mallon's conclusion that 'his character commercially, morally and politically, is of a shady kind.'[62] Clancy was also instrumental in procuring, under Parnellian-Fenian auspices, the return to Ireland from Paris in late September 1891 of the old Fenian James Stephens, whom Clancy had visited annually during his exile, and who featured conspicuously in Parnell's cortège.[63]

Writing in January 1893, John Mallon, who that month was appointed assistant commissioner of the Dublin Metropolitan Police,[64] attributed an upsurge in low-level revolutionary activity to a continuation of the refractory Parnellism of 1890–91: 'I believe the persons engaged are of a very low stratum of men who have been particularly active since the Parnellite split. From November 1890, the IRB rowdy element in Dublin became very aggressive, and they seemed to be under the leadership of Mr. John Clancy, Sub-Sheriff.'[65]

When Gladstone's last administration took office in 1892, Clancy induced the city council to refuse to present an address of welcome to the incoming Lord Lieutenant and led a campaign against the Chief Secretary John Morley over his resistance to the amnesty of Fenian prisoners. Clancy aligned himself with the Dublin ultras of Parnellism and

61. McGee, *IRB*, 196–205.

62. Mallon, biographical profile of John Clancy.

63. *Irish Times*, 30 January 1915; Callanan, *Parnell Split*, 252–23; McGee, *IRB*, 210.

64. McCracken, *Inspector Mallon*, 170.

65. Cited in McCracken, *Inspector Mallon*, 166.

Fenianism, ostentatiously refusing deference to or amity with the Liberal government.[66]

By the mid-1890s, Clancy's standing in republican circles was ebbing, not least on account of his expansive deployment of patronage.[67] He remained, for all the rich diversity of his associations, Parnellite, without quite forfeiting an edge of ambiguity that his command of Dublin politics required of him. He joined Redmond's Irish Independent League, the new Parnellite organisation, on its establishment in 1897. In 1899 the newly elected Unionist Lord Mayor dismissed him as sub-sheriff. Clancy responded with a campaign against the Lord Mayor and characteristically veered left by seeking unsuccessfully to support the initiative of Arthur Griffith and Maud Gonne to get the city council to confer the freedom of the city on the president of the Boer Republic, and intimating opposition to the visit of Queen Victoria.[68] Deprived of his sinecure, Clancy sought once more election to the corporation, and was elected for Clontarf.[69] He and J. P. Nannetti lent support that was critical to the establishment in Dublin of the United Irish League, which originated in the west, ensuring that it took hold of the organisation of the reunited Irish Party.[70] He remained a loyal supporter of Redmond. With the outbreak of war, two of his sons enlisted. Assistant Commissioner Mallon, by then retired, who died some months after Clancy, may have been gratified, or perhaps exasperated.

On 23 January 1915, in a development that came as a surprise to the wider public, Clancy was elected Lord Mayor of Dublin at the age of seventy-four. Before taking office, he died at his home in Clontarf on 29 January. His death was sudden and unexpected, even to friends aware 'that recently some severe illness had tried his magnificent health and

66. McGee, *IRB*, 225–26.

67. Owen McGee, 'John Clancy', *DIB* 2:521.

68. McGee, *IRB*, 283, 287–88. The unique political position of Clancy, and what might be called his mastery of the transitional, is reflected also in his support for the appointment of Tom Clarke to a clerical post in the corporation. Owen McGee, *Arthur Griffith* (Dublin: Merrion, 2015), 48.

69. McGee, 'John Clancy', 521.

70. McGee, *Arthur Griffith*, 48. See Paul Bew, *Land and the National Question in Ireland, 1858–1882* (Dublin: Gill and Macmillan, 1978).

vigour'.[71] The *Irish Independent* wrote with the permitted extravagance on his demise,

> A towering personality, long years of service, a vigorous intellect, and a genial presence were his outstanding qualifications for the post of Chief Magistrate of the Irish capital. Trenchantly he disputed when controversy was called for, and in many a fight he gave and received hard blows. But his native kindness was the counterpoise of his fearlessness and determination in dispute. The friends he had held, and his opponents were amongst his sincerest admirers. The feeling was widespread amongst the citizens that the election of Alderman Clancy to the Mayoral chair heralded the inauguration of a new era in the municipal life of Dublin. It was recognised that a strong man, who was no pliant time-server or self-seeking intriguer, could do much to check the abuses which have made Dublin municipal politics contemptible.[72]

In the city council, Clancy's death prompted an effusion of semi-genuine grief of the kind that only the death of a hardened and fairly cynical practitioner of the arts of municipal politics could elicit. Lorcan Sherlock, the outgoing Lord Mayor, who had previously mourned the city's loss of 'probably its most remarkable personality and citizen', broke down reading aloud a letter of condolence from T. P. Gill to Clancy's son,[73] and handed the letter to the town clerk, Henry Campbell, who had been Parnell's secretary, to finish reading it out. Gill had written,

71. *Freeman's Journal*, editorial, 30 January 1915. Confronted by the deepening disaffection with the Irish Party, the embattled *Freeman's Journal*, recalling his youthful adherence to the IRB, sought a little desperately to draw the moral of Clancy's extraordinary *parcours* across his long political life: 'To him the principles and the practice of the little group of modern "hillsiders" who, in their most characteristic utterances, mingle abuse of the Leader of the Irish people and the Irish Party with their admiration of the German Emperor, must have been simply detestable. For pinchbeck revolutionaries he could have only entertained contempt. He was one of the genuine extremists, the men who stood by Ireland and her leaders now, because, having well-nigh spent themselves in the sowing of the field, they wish to see the harvest gathered in.' Clancy's intelligent deployment of his status as 'one of the genuine extremists' is the redemptive leitmotif of his mercurial career.

72. *Irish Independent*, 30 January 1915.

73. 'An Appreciation', *Freeman's Journal*, 30 January 1915.

The news of his having been chosen Lord Mayor of Dublin, and at this present time, seemed to strike a universal chord. With a sort of surprise everyone recognised the fittingness of the idea; and all, no matter what party they belonged to, began to picture with pleasure what it would mean for Dublin and for Ireland to have this big-hearted, rugged, fearless, chivalrous, fascinating, most typically Irish personality, mellowed too, as he was by age and experience, at the Mansion House in the historic crisis through which we are passing and are about to pass. There was something else. Your father had always been a hard hitter; his way through Dublin civic life and work had not been unattended, from time to time, with enmity and misunderstanding. That all that enmity and misunderstanding had passed away, and given place to respect and popularity in every quarter, culminating in the general feeling about his election to the Lord Mayoralty, is something important gained for public life. For it is a gain of sheer character. . . . We thought, with a glow, of this recognition at last which must be so dear to his heart, of this valiant and war-battered fighter, who linked in his person another generation with this, and typified a whole epoch of Irish history.

John Stanislaus Joyce was recorded among the large attendance at Clancy's interment in Glasnevin.[74] The *Freeman's Journal*'s posthumous characterisation of Clancy—'his tall figure, his genial presence, his bonhomie—none of his friends can ever forget it'—was not shared by Stanislaus Joyce, who was suspicious of two friends of his father in particular:

There is one Mr. James Brady, a police-court solicitor, a brother-in-law of Mr. Bergan, whom I dislike very much. He seems to me a rare type of the common, cute Irish fool. He is a friend of Pappie's.

There is one, too, Mr. John Clancy, Sub-Sheriff, whom I also dislike very thoroughly. He is regarded with mild awe, chiefly I fancy because of his height. His creatures—and practically all the people he knows are his creatures in the degree of their intimacy—agree that if he had gone to America in his youth he would be President now.

74. *Freeman's Journal*, 1 February 1915 ('J. Joyce').

I think he should have become a policeman. He has the appearance, the walk, the bossing manner, and the intellect of a policeman. He is elderly, and drink-seasoned. Pappie boasts when he is drunk 'O! John Clancy has a wish for me! He'd do a fellow a good turn!' but I think his real idea about him is something like mine.[75]

There is no recorded expression of James Joyce's view of John Clancy other than what is to be gleaned from his fictional renderings: in *Dubliners* merely as 'Fanning' or 'Mr Fanning', and in *Ulysses* as 'long John Fanning', the alter ego of John Clancy. He is a fleeting presence in Joyce's fiction, a figure of mysterious and terrible power in the polity of Dublin, defined principally by absence but whose name ran ahead of him. Judging by that fictional rendering, Joyce does not seem to have regarded Clancy with the same antipathy as Stanislaus, and at least came to have some appreciation of his political intelligence, however opportunistic its manifestations. The *Freeman's Journal* wrote of the dead Clancy, 'He was, indeed, one of the most prominent figures in many of the Irish historic episodes of his time.'[76] There was no other extra-parliamentary figure in Dublin politics so richly steeped in contemporary history. He had been on the quayside at Kingstown to greet Parnell when he returned to Ireland from Committee Room 15 and was back there with John Kelly when Parnell left for the last time.[77] He was a leading participant in both the first and the second taking of the offices of *United Ireland*. In the first, the paper was under the control of anti-Parnellite editor Mathias McDonnell Bodkin. Parnell took possession of the vacant editor's office and, looking 'pale and weary', dismissed Bodkin 'in a cold passionless tone' when he arrived back.[78] Barry O'Brien, in his

75. S. Joyce, entry for 31 August 1904, in *Dublin Diary*, 78.

76. *Freeman's Journal*, 30 January 1915.

77. McGrath, 'His Last Campaign'; Callanan, *Parnell Split*, 180–81. John Clancy is not to be confused (as he is in Jackson and Costello, *John Stanislaus Joyce*, 165) with his fellow Parnellite John Joseph Clancy, a King's Counsel and parliamentarian who held the seat of Dublin County North from 1885 to 1918, when he was swept out on a two-to-one margin by a virtually unknown Sinn Féin candidate.

78. M. McDonnell Bodkin, *Recollections of an Irish Judge* (London: Hurst and Blackett, 1914), 174–75.

biography of Parnell, relates the 'brief and pithy' account given him by 'one of Mr. Parnell's Fenian supporters', certainly the unnamed John Clancy: 'I went up to Matty Bodkin. "Matty", says I, "will you walk out, or would you like to be thrown out?" and Matty walked out.'[79] In the anti-Parnellite account of *Suppressed United Ireland*, however, this had a prelude. When Bodkin refused to accept his dismissal, Parnell was quoted as saying, 'Send for Mr. John Clancy': 'In a few moments Mr. John Clancy, who has been the most violent partisan of Mr. Parnell, and organised all the rowdyism on his behalf in Dublin, broke into the room at the head of an uproarious mob of about fifty persons, and advanced threateningly to the acting editor with cries of "Throw him out", "Pitch him out", "Pitch him downstairs; he has been left too long here". Which cries were echoed by his followers.'[80] When the anti-Parnellites retook the offices of *United Ireland* while Parnell was making his great speech in the Rotunda, Clancy was to the fore in the considerably more violent mob assault on the building early the next morning, though unmentioned in O'Brien's narrative, which relies on the account of a bystander 'wholly unconnected with politics'[81] who could recognise only Parnell: this is the narrative into which Joyce in the 'Eumaeus' episode of *Ulysses* inserts Bloom to restore Parnell's hat knocked off in the fracas.[82] Joyce did not learn of the two takings of *United Ireland* from O'Brien's biography; they and Clancy's role were the stuff of Dublin legend and Joyce would have known about them from his father and from John Kelly, who was present for the second taking of the offices; his father's friend D. J. Hishon was moreover actively involved in that onslaught.[83]

Clancy had for most of his political life inhabited the richly ambiguous interstices of Parnellism and Fenianism. In the 'Wandering Rocks'

79. R. B. O'Brien, *Charles Stewart Parnell*, 2:291.

80. *Suppressed United Ireland*, 13 December 1890. McDonnell Bodkin's account closely matched this (*Recollections of an Irish Judge*, 174–75).

81. R. B. O'Brien, *Charles Stewart Parnell*, 2:293–97.

82. *U* 16.1333–39.

83. *Insuppressible*, 15 December 1890; *Insuppressible*, 5 January 1891, letter of James O'Connor to the editor; Jackson and Costello, *John Stanislaus Joyce*, 162–63.

episode of *Ulysses*, Joyce conveys the aura of authority he had for his contemporaries: 'The tall long form of long John Fanning filled the doorway where he stood', of James Kavanagh's wine rooms on Parliament Street.

> Long John Fanning made no way for them. He removed his large Henry Clay decisively and his large fierce eyes scowled intelligently over all their faces.
>
> —Are the conscript fathers pursuing their peaceful deliberations? he said, with rich acrid utterance to the assistant town clerk.[84]

The assistant town clerk adds his somewhat windy complaints about the members of the council. 'Long John Fanning blew a plume of smoke from his lips.' The sardonic references to 'the conscript fathers' (the members of the city council) and to 'their peaceful deliberations' reflect the attentive consideration that Joyce had given to Clancy's character and career. He renders also long John Fanning's commanding physical presence; as they go upstairs he asks about the just-deceased Paddy Dignam. 'Decent little soul he was, Mr. Power said to the stalwart back of long John Fanning ascending towards long John Fanning in the mirror'. Long John Fanning could not remember Paddy Dignam.[85]

It might seem a small point, but a contemporary report in the Unionist *Daily Express*, in the course of the Split, attests to the accuracy with which Joyce evoked the physical aspect of Clancy and rendered how he was regarded in the city as a figure possessed of an effectiveness underpinned by a certain menace that was not without grace. The paper described the scene as the first wave of the invasion of the *United Ireland*

84. *U* 10.996–1005. In *Dubliners* the whiff of corruption is more marked. In 'Ivy Day in the Committee Room', Mr Henchy says of the candidate Tierney, 'He's not a bad sort . . . only Fanning has such a loan on him' (*D* 109). Whatever the expression comes from, which is uncertain, it is chosen to convey by its secondary meaning a financial relationship between Tierney and Fanning, hinted at elsewhere in the story but not quite explained. In 'Grace' Mr Cunningham draws Mr Kernan's attention in the Jesuit church to 'Mr. Fanning, the registration agent and mayormaker of the city, who was sitting under the pulpit beside one of the newly elected councillors' (*D* 149). Fanning only becomes 'long John' in *Ulysses*.

85. *U* 10.1006–30.

office—on the first taking of the office—ran into unexpectedly stern resistance: 'Mr. Clancy, who had been standing in the background smoking a very large cigar, and displaying a very large rose, then commanded a general advance of his forces, who charged impetuously on the two office assistants, disarmed them, and ejected them from the premises.'[86]

Patrick Casey and Joseph Casey

There is an intriguing political rift within the amities and acquaintanceships of John Stanislaus Joyce. He enjoyed cordial social relations, at least in the 1880s, with eminently respectable figures aligned to the new Parnellite order. These did not include parliamentarians, with the exception of Tim Harrington, though his relations with Harrington do not seem to have been particularly close—and for practical purposes are likely to have ended with his failed suit against L. A. Waldron in 1907. He was friendly with the expansively hospitable Matthew Dillon, with his 'bevy of daughters' who entertained the Joyce family at his house in Brighton Square.[87] In *Ulysses* that provides the mise-en-scène for Leopold Bloom's first glimpse of Molly: 'First night when first I saw her at Mat Dillon's in Terenure. Yellow, black lace she wore. Musical chairs. We too the last. Fate.'[88] Matthew Dillon was a cousin of the nationalist leader John Dillon. Through Matthew Dillon, John Stanislaus Joyce and his family had some acquaintanceship with Valentine Blake Dillon, a solicitor who was a prominent political figure and, taking the opposite side to his cousin, espoused Parnell's cause in the Split and was the Parnellite candidate in the second by-election of the Split in North Sligo in the spring of 1891. He was Lord Mayor of Dublin in 1894–95. That role unluckily earned him posthumously a place in Molly Bloom's soliloquy

86. *Daily Express*, 11 December 1890.

87. *U* 13.1106; Jackson and Costello, *John Stanislaus Joyce*, 146–47.

88. *U* 11.725–26. The Mat Dillon of *Ulysses* is not coextensive with Matthew Dillon; see Luca Crispi, *Joyce's Creative Process and the Construction of Characters in 'Ulysses': Becoming the Blooms* (Oxford: Oxford University Press, 2015), 140–50.

in *Ulysses*: 'the lord mayor looking at me with his dirty eyes Val Dillon that big heathen.'[89]

John Stanislaus Joyce's evident pride in his more respectable Dublin friends and acquaintances renders his relations with the Fenian Casey brothers, burnt-out cases though they were, all the more striking. Kilkenny born, the brothers were cousins of the IRB leader James Stephens. Joseph Theobald (Joe) Casey (1846–ca. 1907), the elder of the two, came almost incidentally to police attention and public notoriety in the fevered aftermath in Britain of the execution of the 'Manchester Martyrs' who on 23 November 1867 had killed a police sergeant during an armed endeavour to liberate Fenian prisoners being conveyed in a police van. When Ricard O'Sullivan Burke, the chief figure in the Fenian importation of arms into Britain, was arrested in Woburn Square, Bloomsbury, on 20 November 1867, he was in the company of Joseph Casey. Casey followed the arrested Burke to Bow Street police station, where he was sufficiently obstreperous to be arrested himself and charged with obstructing Burke's arrest. Both men were incarcerated in Clerkenwell prison.

On 13 December 1867 a botched attempt to liberate Burke along with Casey took place with an attempt to blow up the prison wall, in which Patrick Casey (Joseph's younger brother) participated, and in which eleven people on the terrace opposite the prison lost their lives. There was no more sensational event in the Victorian narrative of Irish terrorism in Britain. Convicted of the Clerkenwell bombing, Michael Barrett, a Glaswegian Fenian, was hanged in what was to be the last public execution in England. Tried for seeking to overthrow the monarchy, effectively the importation of arms to subvert the government, Burke was convicted and sentenced to fifteen years' penal servitude, while the charges against Casey were withdrawn in April 1868,[90] allowing him to slip away to Paris to join his brothers. There was a serious

89. *U* 18.428–29.

90. Brian Jenkins, *The Fenian Problem: Insurgency and Terrorism in a Liberal State, 1858–1874* (Liverpool: Liverpool University Press, 2008), 148–49, 206–7; K.R.M. Short, *The Dynamite War: Irish-American Bombers in Victorian Britain* (Dublin: Gill and Macmillan, 1979), 7–11.

terrorist threat from the just-established Irish American Fenian movement which prompted intense concern on the part of the British government and extensive and shrill press coverage, but the role of Joseph Casey remained unelucidated beyond his stroll with Ricard O'Sullivan Burke in Woburn Square.

While both Joseph and his younger brother Patrick (1843–1908) were at the time active and committed Fenians, Joseph's acquisition of an unearned notoriety was to provide them with a reputational capital which, as their finances deteriorated, they worked as best they could. Richard Ellmann's characterisation of Joe Casey as 'once a leading Fenian' grossly overstates even his past role.[91]

The nucleus of the Casey family had already taken up residence in Paris, and the French government refused requests to extradite Patrick Casey. There were four Casey brothers, all of whom fought in the Franco-Prussian War of 1870–71 (the war in which John Stanislaus Joyce had reputedly sought to enlist alongside them).[92] Three of them sustained injuries in the siege of Paris and both Andrew, who was conferred the Légion d'honneur, and James later died of their wounds.

After the war Joseph and Patrick worked as newspaper compositors on English-language newspapers in Paris, eventually for the European edition of the *New York Herald*.[93] Journalism was a trade classically practised by nineteenth-century European radicals and revolutionaries, and in Dublin it provided Arthur Griffith's initial vocation. They were in contact with their cousin James Stephens, the deposed Fenian leader, who also lived in Paris. Together with their friend Eugene Davis, a Clonakilty-born poet and nationalist journalist who had studied at the Irish Colleges of Louvain and Paris,[94] they organised a modest Patrick's Day commemoration in Paris from 1881.[95] They were believed to have sheltered fleeing members of the Invincible conspiracy after

91. Ellmann, *James Joyce*, 125.

92. S. Joyce, *My Brother's Keeper*, 47; already noted in relation to John Stanislaus Joyce.

93. Patrick Maume, 'Patrick Casey', *DIB* 2:413.

94. Owen McGee, 'Eugene Davis', *DIB* 3:80.

95. McGee, *IRB*, 126; *Irishman*, 26 March 1881.

the Phoenix Park murders and were thereafter attentively watched by British spies.[96]

The Paris of the 1880s was deemed by British journalists, spies, agents provocateurs, and their masters to be the cockpit of extravagantly terroristic Fenian schemes, and the brothers acquired a considerable notoriety. They became habitués of Reynold's bar, an Irish American establishment on the Rue Royale, which runs down from the church of La Madeleine to the Place de la Concorde. There, with the more entrepreneurial Patrick to the fore, the brothers entertained grateful British journalists with their improbable accounts of projected dynamite attacks in Britain. They did not want for listeners. In 1884–85 sections of the British press whipped up a baseless 'Fenian Fever' following that which originated in 1867–68, centred on the idea that Paris was teeming with Irish American terrorists on the verge of perpetrating an atrocity in succession to the Phoenix Park murders.[97] Davitt, in his autobiographical narrative *The Fall of Feudalism in Ireland*, provided a scathing profile of Patrick Casey and Eugene Davis:

> There resided in Paris in 1884–5 two 'refugees', one named Kasey [*sic*] and the other Eugene Davis. Kasey had been suspected, some twenty years previously, of having been connected with the Fenian movement in England, and on the strength of this 'achievement' became a resident of Paris. He was as free to live in Great Britain or Ireland as I was, but it pleased him to live in France. . . . He was, originally, a working-man, very intelligent, a casual journalist and a most accomplished *farceur*. When sober he talked sense; when in the other condition he led those who listened to him to believe that all the revolutionary bodies in Ireland, America, and France took their inspiration or plans from this *soi-disant* desperado. . . . Bombs, dynamite, daggers, poison were his revolutionary media whenever those who wanted this sort of talk 'stood' the necessary absinthe or cognac, for which it could be produced *ad libitum*.[98]

96. Owen McGee, 'Joseph Theobald Casey', *DIB* 2:412.

97. McGee, *IRB*, 126.

98. Michael Davitt, *The Fall of Feudalism in Ireland* (London: Harper and Brothers, 1904), 434.

Coupling Patrick Casey with Eugene Davis—of whom his characterisation by association was unfair[99]—Davitt wrote that 'this precious pair might be truly called revolutionary bummers or camp-followers'. They had been lured into various essentially bogus plots and schemes by informers and agents provocateurs such as 'Red Jim' McDermott.[100]

A sensationalistic pamphlet, *The Repeal of the Union Conspiracy*, which attained a rapid notoriety as the 'Black Pamphlet', appeared in 1886.[101] It sought to implicate the Parnellites in terrorism and drew on Patrick Casey's sanguinary boastfulness to represent him as a master terrorist.[102] The biographer of Davitt's later life identifies Captain William Henry O'Shea; Darnley Stewart Stephens, who had known the Caseys in Paris in 1885; and George Mulqueeny as the putative authors of the pamphlet. It is doubtful that a collective authorship can be assigned, as distinct from what materials were provided or drawn on, and who was aware of or assisted in the publication of the pamphlet.[103] It seems unlikely that

99. McGee, *IRB*, 216n26.

100. Davitt, *Fall of Feudalism*, 434–38. The most frequently quoted characterisation of Patrick Casey ('Kasey') is extracted from the index. It reads, 'a blatant "refugee", who lived in Paris, with a leaning towards dynamite and a decided taste for absinthe'. Davitt, *Fall of Feudalism*, 737.

101. *The Repeal of the Union Conspiracy; or, Mr Parnell M.P. and the IRB* (London: William Ridgway, 1886).

102. Christy Campbell, *Fenian Fire: The British Government Plot to Assassinate Queen Victoria* (London: HarperCollins, 2002), 192–93.

103. Carla King, *Michael Davitt after the Land League, 1882–1906* (Dublin: University College Dublin Press, 2016), 255. At the Special Commission, Parnell's counsel George Russell pressed O'Shea on his association with Mulqueeny; see Myles Dungan, *The Captain and the King: William O'Shea, Parnell and Late Victorian Ireland* (Dublin: New Island, 2009), 305–7. McGee (*IRB*, 126) identifies Stephens as the author of the pamphlet. The historical relevance of all of this is in rendering Parnell's obdurate belief that O'Shea lay behind the Pigott forgeries (Callanan, *T. M. Healy*, 199) less lunatic than it might otherwise seem. However, there was little in Russell's cross-examination of O'Shea, particularly on the subject of his relations with Mulqueeny, to suggest that Parnell had any definite basis for his suspicion. That is not to say that O'Shea was not prepared to dabble effetely in Parnell's destruction by fostering what he could to lay the ground for, and sustain the case of, *The Times* at the Special Commission. Perhaps it was in the nature of *The Times'* allegations that they would rouse the opposing suspicion that behind Pigott lurked O'Shea. Parnell's suspicion had its roots in O'Shea's connections to Joseph Chamberlain, allied to the Conservative government, and anything beyond that he gleaned from his diverse sources

the Caseys knew O'Shea, the husband of Parnell's lover Katharine, who whatever the role he played had good reason to screen himself behind his intermediary Mulqueeny.[104] The Caseys certainly knew Richard Pigott, with whom they had a shared interest in eking out an existence and extracting what they could from talking up imaginary terroristic threats and monetising the thesis of Parnell's complicity in terrorism, though they were never prepared to get into this quite as deeply as Pigott. The modern historian of the IRB writes that Patrick Casey and Eugene Davis 'knew nothing about Irish revolutionary affairs except rumours, but they freely told stories and these were subsequently redrafted, evidently without their knowing, into sensational articles in the British press' and featured in *The Repeal of the Union Conspiracy* pamphlet.[105] Pigott was to assert that he had acquired the letters implicating Parnell in the Phoenix Park murders from Patrick Casey, and even that Patrick Casey had collaborated in forging them.[106] He also asserted that Eugene Davis, whom he had visited in Lausanne, was central to his discovery of the 'black bag' in which the forged letters were found.[107]

The golden jubilee of Queen Victoria's reign fell in June 1887. There was fevered speculation of an Irish American 'jubilee plot' to mount an attack on the queen, who was ceremonially to re-enter Westminster Abbey on 21 June 1887 for the first time since her coronation on 28 June 1838. This was grist to Patrick Casey's mill. On 15 June 1887 the

---

of intelligence seems to have been inconclusive. So far as O'Shea himself was concerned, his casting as the Professor Moriarty of the Pigott forgeries reflects an overestimation of his ability and deficient energy. See Margaret O'Callaghan, 'New Ways of Looking at the State Apparatus and the State Archive in Nineteenth-Century Ireland "Curiosities from the Phonetic Museum"—Royal Irish Constabulary Reports and Their Political Uses, 1879–91', *Proceedings of the Royal Irish Academy* 104C, no. 2 (2004): 37–56. For the Special Commission, see O'Callaghan, *British High Politics.*

104. Dungan, *Captain and the King*, 317.

105. McGee, *IRB*, 126.

106. Maume, 'Patrick Casey', 413.

107. King, *Michael Davitt*, 238–39, 247. My narrative is indebted to King's exemplary reconstruction of Davitt's extraordinary return to the underground world of his youth (or something ostensibly resembling it) as, as he ironically described it, 'an Amateur Detective'; and to the slightly earlier treatment of the subject in Dungan's biography of O'Shea, *Captain and the King.*

Central News Agency reported that 'the movements of Patrick Casey and his associates have been closely followed by special detectives.' The *Morning Advertiser* even carried an interview with Casey. The reporter enquired on the question of dynamite whether there was anything coming off and received the response: 'In all probability there will be something coming off, and very soon.'[108]

In the prelude to the Special Commission—established in the wake of the publication by *The Times* of what turned out to be the Pigott forgeries to enquire into the complicity of Parnell and members of his party and the Land League in the Phoenix Park murders, and more generally Land League responsibility for agrarian violence—Michael Davitt assumed the role of principal investigator on the nationalist side. He arrived in Paris days before the Special Commission opened and learned from Joseph Casey something of the background to Pigott's handing over of the forged letters in the Hôtel des Deux Mondes to Edward Caulfield Houston and Thomas Maguire, both of the Irish Loyal and Patriotic Union, the latter curiously enough professor of moral philosophy at Trinity College Dublin.[109] An agent for *The Times* asserted that Patrick conveyed all that he learned to Joseph, who alerted Davitt.[110] Yet Davitt also obtained information in relation to Pigott's role directly from Patrick.[111] Davitt kept a notebook semi-humorously entitled 'Notes of an Amateur Detective' in which he jotted down a record of his interviews in London and Paris. Among his chief informants were Joseph and Patrick Casey, who provided intelligence on Pigott and on the various agents of Scotland Yard active in Paris in the preceding years.[112]

Pigott was called as a witness before the Special Commission on 20 February 1889. As he took the stand, Parnell observed, as Davitt recalled,

108. Campbell, *Fenian Fire*, 238–41.

109. King, *Michael Davitt*, 235, 246. Campbell suggests that Patrick and Joseph Casey played the roles of the clan agents who handed over the black bag containing the letters downstairs once Pigott had secured his money order for £500 upstairs.

110. Maume, 'Patrick Casey', 413.

111. King, *Michael Davitt*, 239.

112. King, *Michael Davitt*, 260; TCD, Davitt Papers, MS 9551/8; Margaret O'Callaghan, 'Richard Pigott', *DIB* 8:120–24.

'quite audibly: "The rat caught in the trap at last!"'.[113] The cross-examination of Pigott by Charles Russell, perhaps the greatest set piece of Victorian advocacy, began on the afternoon of Thursday, 21 February. Pigott's position was utterly hopeless, but he was afforded a respite by the adjournment of the commission on Friday, 22 February, for the weekend. He seemed to have no option but flight, and Davitt therefore crossed immediately to Paris, where he met the Casey brothers. They dined together in a restaurant that evening. Joe Casey gave Davitt six of Pigott's highly damaging letters. He had acted as an intermediary for Pigott in the purchasing of books. Davitt pressed him on whether these were indecent books—in which the ever financially pressed Pigott conducted a minor trade—and he sheepishly admitted that they were. Davitt, exhibiting, as well as thoroughness in his role as 'an amateur detective', the puritan zeal that was to inform in part his response to the O'Shea divorce crisis some two years later, sought out Parisian purveyors of erotica with whom Pigott had dealt and discovered that they too had been defrauded. Pigott, who had wanted only the 'most scandalous books', had claimed to represent a club of Tory connoisseurs of erotica and had magnificently proposed that the booksellers send their invoices to the Irish Loyal and Patriotic Union.[114] Pigott had, contrary to Davitt's expectation, lingered in London over the weekend; Davitt suspected that Patrick Casey had alerted Pigott to his presence in Paris.[115] When Pigott failed to appear at the Special Commission the following week, on 26 February, Davitt made contact with Casey, who claimed that he had searched Paris for him in vain.[116] Pigott's flight took him to Madrid, where he shot himself on 28 February 1889 as the English police, who were without jurisdiction over him, arrived at his hotel.

113. Davitt, *Fall of Feudalism*, 576.

114. Campbell, *Fenian Fire*, 334. In the history of the Pigott forgeries, it was Edward Caulfield Houston of the Irish Loyal and Patriotic Union who had risen to Pigott's bait and was crucially the link to the editor of *The Times*. The forged Parnell letters and illicit Victorian erotica thereby merged, some two years before the scandal of the O'Shea divorce.

115. Davitt, *Fall of Feudalism*, 585.

116. King, *Michael Davitt*, 262.

The Times had not quite given up, and sought Scotland Yard's assistance to contrive a desperate last hurrah to establish Parnell's complicity in terrorism after Pigott's flight and death. The evidence for this is limited to an account that appeared in the *New York Nationalist* the following year.[117] Henri Le Caron, the highly effective spy, whose identity had been disclosed at the Special Commission—not the least cost that the British state incurred in seeking to make out the case of *The Times*—and others sought out Patrick Casey in Paris. The spectacular discrediting of Pigott portended the end of Casey's prospects of alleviating his chronic impecuniosity by exploiting the conspiratorial murk that had gathered around the Special Commission. Casey was reported to have been offered £10,000 to give evidence to the Commission about Patrick Egan's relations with the IRB in Paris to establish a connection to the Phoenix Park murders. Casey cabled John Patrick Hayes, who was then living in New Hampshire. Hayes had already been involved in entrapment schemes in Paris in 1884 when he had won the trust of Casey in the Shamrock Bar, another exilic haunt, on the Rue Duras. According to the *New York Nationalist*, Hayes crossed to France, his expenses paid by *The Times*, and held a series of meetings with Patrick Casey in yet another bar, this time on the Rue Faubourg St. Honoré. When friends warned Hayes and Casey of the implications of what they were doing, they protested that they merely wanted 'to make money out of the enemy' and to engage in 'grand bluff' vis-à-vis *The Times*. Hayes crossed to Dublin to enlist the participation in the scheme of Eugene Davis, who honourably rebuffed him. Hayes eventually returned to the United States. Patrick Casey demanded £10,000 to testify before the Special Commission.[118] It is impossible to resist the conclusion that in setting a preposterous price for his attendance, Casey, remembering the experience of his quasi-friend Richard Pigott, who had got in too deep, was making sure that he would not find himself before the Special Commission. The setting of that price marked Patrick Casey's exit from the role

117. *New York Nationalist*, 5, 19 July 1890; TCD, Davitt Papers, MS 9442/318 and 19, cited in King, *Michael Davitt*, 269–70, 617n260.

118. King, *Michael Davitt*, 269–70.

he had assumed; it had become a semi-career in the 1880s, made possible by the eagerness of the British Unionist press to establish endemic Irish nationalist complicity in political violence. His exit was a tacit acknowledgement that the market for his testimony had collapsed. With Pigott's suicide, whatever thin vestiges of credibility his arch and undemanding terroristic spoof might have attracted in tenebrous Paris bars had evaporated and would not withstand translation across the channel to the Strand. James Stephens returned to Ireland in 1891 and was one of the most prominent mourners at Parnell's funeral; it seems that Patrick Casey followed his cousin back to Ireland. After initially returning to Kilkenny, he was living in Cabra by 1893 and working as a night watchman for the Dublin Corporation paving board. His social life was centred on public houses and on the Fenians' Old Guard Benevolent Union.

Joseph, the less politically enterprising brother, lived on in Paris. By the 1890s he was living, separated, in the Rue de la Goutte d'Or in the eighteenth arrondissement, where James Joyce met him in 1903. Joyce fictionalised this account in the 'Proteus' episode of *Ulysses*. Joseph died in obscurity around 1907, and Patrick, who had entered the north Dublin workhouse after his health deteriorated, died in January 1908 and was interred in the Fenian plot in Glasnevin.[119]

In his *Dublin Diary*, Stanislaus Joyce gives an account of meeting his father with Patrick Casey in October 1904, within a week of James Joyce leaving Dublin, on the Phibsborough Road outside a public house. His father had just borrowed two shillings from the proprietor and 'had stood drinks and had been talking old times for an hour'. In the account, which does not evince any particular attitude towards Casey other than as an old crony of his father, Stanislaus admits to acute irritation at being told by Casey, whose faltering speech 'in a thick brogue' he mimics, to take care of his father 'now that James has gone away', and that his father 'loves you all': 'Knowing the immediate cause of the advice—drinks and the stories, Pat Casey's own struggles with poverty—and the temper of mind in which it was given to me, I was acutely bored.'[120]

119. Maume, 'Patrick Casey', 412–14.

120. S. Joyce, entry for 13 October 1904, in *Dublin Diary*, 133–35.

How did John Stanislaus befriend Patrick Casey, and what does it say, if anything, about his politics? Their friendship came about in the period after Casey had returned to Ireland in 1891. Casey lived in St Peter's Terrace in Cabra when he arrived back in Dublin from Kilkenny,[121] but John Stanislaus only moved there in 1904 and by that time they were already friends. It may be inferred they met as they roamed the north city and its public houses. John Stanislaus knew only the diminished figure who had arrived back in Ireland, not the Fenian fabulist who had lived in Paris at the height of his notoriety. Their relations seem to have been primarily those of two old men down on their luck who had fond memories of better days in the 1880s and before. It is nevertheless likely that John Stanislaus's relations with Patrick Casey owed something to an identification with the Fenian cause. What his fondness for Casey certainly attests to is a breadth of human sympathy that took no heed of bourgeois Catholic nationalist notions of respectability.

As recounted of Stephen Dedalus in *Ulysses*, Joyce met Joseph Casey during his Parisian stay of 1902–3 and seems to have already known him,[122] presumably from an occasion when Casey was visiting his brother in Dublin. In Herbert Gorman's account, Joyce had lunch on several occasions with Casey in the bistro Aux Deux Ecus across the road from what was then the *New York Herald* office where Casey worked on the Rue du Louvre.[123] On St Patrick's Day Joyce wrote a somewhat wheedling letter to his mother: 'I thought someone would send me some shamrock. However Mr. Casey gave me a bit. It is a pity I have no dress suit as he had an invitation to an Irish Ball tonight at the Salle Hoche. I am always on the fringes of things.'[124] Casey had lent Joyce a modest sum, but Joyce complained that he had overstated what he was owed.[125] He also seems to have borrowed from Casey's son Patrice, a soldier in the French army who had sided with his mother, who was separated from his father.[126]

121. McGee, 'Joseph Theobald Casey', 412.
122. Ellmann, *James Joyce*, 107.
123. Gorman, *James Joyce*, 102.
124. Joyce to May Joyce, 17 March 1903, *Letters II* 363.
125. Joyce to May Joyce, 26 March, [27 March], 4 April 1903, *Letters II* 40.
126. Joyce to May Joyce, 26 March 1903, *Letters II* 39. See Ellmann, *James Joyce*, 125, 127.

The figures of Kevin Egan and his son Patrice in the 'Proteus' episode of *Ulysses* are strikingly direct portrayals of Joseph Casey and his estranged son, whose Christian name is left unchanged. Stephen Dedalus is storming across Sandymount Strand in a mood of melancholy sceptical reminiscence. It is Patrice he first remembers, prompted by the Pigeon House to recall Léo Taxil's scandalous joke on the Virgin Birth ('C'est le pigeon, Joseph', Mary explains) in *La Vie de Joseph*, a book which Patrice had extolled to him. Patrice too, though rabbit-like and milk-drinking, is the offspring of a bird: 'Son of the wild goose, Kevin Egan of Paris.'[127] This stirs in Stephen a memory of dining with Egan in Paris: 'Kevin Egan rolls gunpowder cigarettes through fingers smeared with printer's ink, sipping his green fairy as Patrice his white.' (The 'green fairy' is absinthe.) 'His breath hangs over our saucestained plates, the green fairy's fang thrusting between his lips. Of Ireland, the Dalcassians, of hopes, conspiracies, of Arthur Griffith now, AE. . . . To yoke me as his yokefellow, our crimes our common cause. You're your father's son.'[128] Stephen is resisting both the influence of his father and a retrospective enlistment in Egan's Fenianism, though constrained to acquiesce in its incidents as 'our crimes' in a formulation of extraordinary deftness on Joyce's part. 'Yokefellow' comes from *Henry V*, where Pistol proposes to join the king's expedition to France:

> Yokefellows in arms,
> Let us to France, like horseleeches, my boys,
> To suck, to suck, the very blood to suck![129]

The muted reference suggests Joyce knew more of the activities of Patrick Casey's institutionalisation of the role of Fenian, or Fenianesque, braggart in the Paris of the 1880s, in which Joseph was at least acquiescent, than he elected to include in his portrait of Joseph as Kevin Egan. Egan strives to keep up with Irish affairs, but it is the dissonance

127. *U* 3.158–68.

128. *U* 3.226–30.

129. William Shakespeare, *Henry V*, 2.2.56–58, cited in *Ulysses*, annotated by Sam Slote (London: Alma Classics, 2012), 573, hereinafter cited as Slote, *Ulysses*.

of the naivety of his monomaniacally Irish nationalist treatment of contemporary French politics that re-affirms Stephen's resistance. When he mentions the journalist and publisher Edouard Drumont—'M. Drumont, famous journalist, Drumont, know what he called queen Victoria? Old hag with the yellow teeth'—Kevin Egan seems untroubled by the fact that Drumont, author of *La France Juive* (1886) and founder in 1892 of *La Libre Parole*, had built his career on an anti-Semitism which, while blatantly opportunistic, was vicious.[130] Kevin Egan moves on to 'Maud Gonne. Beautiful woman, *la Patrie*, M. Millevoye, Felix Faure, know how he died?'[131] Lucien Millevoye, editor of *La Patrie* and the lover of Maud Gonne, was an extreme nationalist and anti-Dreyfusard. Casey, the erstwhile revolutionary, was blind to anti-Semitism (rather than consciously anti-Semitic) and thereby prey to the influence of French reactionary politics. The reference to Félix Faure, the French president who had died of apoplexy in the Elysée Palace in February 1899 while engaged in sexual activity with a much younger woman, signified the jeering moralism of the old Fenian who was of the conventional conservative Irish Catholic order.

In the alphabetical notebook Joyce compiled in Trieste, Joyce wrote of Joseph Casey as 'a grey ember'.[132] He developed the image in a different direction in *Ulysses* through Casey's smoking: 'The blue fuse burns deadly between hands and burns clear. Loose tobaccoshreds catch fire: a flame and acrid smoke light our corner. Raw facebones under his peep of day boys hat.'[133] It is the mundaneness of Kevin Egan in the post-Fenian era that strikes Stephen. Egan's conversation features the escape

130. Gregoire Kauffmann, *Edouard Drumont* (Paris: Perrin, 2008), 189–90. Joyce's earlier invocation of Léo Taxil suggests Joyce knew of the mutual hostility of Drumont and Taxil, who published a substantial pamphlet in 1890 entitled *Monsieur Drumont: Étude psychologique* (Paris: Letouzey and Ané, 1890). See also Slote, *Ulysses*, 573.

131. *U* 3.230–35.

132. Robert Scholes and Richard M. Kain, eds., *The Workshop of Daedalus: James Joyce and the Raw Materials for 'A Portrait of the Artist as a Young Man'* (Evanston, IL: Northwestern University Press, 1965), 94.

133. *U* 3.239–40. The Peep o' Day Boys were working-class Protestants who raided Catholic homes in the Armagh region in the late 1780s, bringing into existence the Defenders to resist them.

of James Stephens: 'How the head centre got away, authentic version.'[134] What Stephen strives to call to mind is the intense violence of the moment of the Fenian attack on Clerkenwell prison in the vain attempt to liberate Ricard O'Sullivan Burke and Casey, across the intervening waste of vanished time: 'He prowled with colonel Richard Burke, tanaist of his sept, under the walls of Clerkenwell and, crouching, saw a flame of vengeance hurl them upward in the fog. Shattered glass and toppling masonry. In gay Paree he hides, Egan of Paris, unsought by any save by me.'[135] When Joyce met Joe Casey, he seems to have been relatively historically incurious, though that owes something to his sense of Casey's unreliability as a witness. How much Joyce knew by repute of the career of either Joseph or Patrick Casey is uncertain, but he clearly had some general sense of their former notoriety.[136] Joyce, in Paris in 1902–3, was a young man who aspired to be a writer and had some of the prejudices that came with that, and his father's friend transpired to be a slightly pedantic exilic bore, whose Fenian activism belonged to a distant time. Joyce was not interested in garnering historical detail or anecdote, but he was shrewdly attentive to the characterisation of Joe Casey, on which he was to draw to magnificent effect in *Ulysses*. Joyce's knowledge of the Caseys continued to grow after the meeting in Paris. It is unlikely that he failed to recognise the old friend of his father Patrick Casey in the 'Kasey' of Davitt's *The Fall of Feudalism in Ireland* (1904), which he acquired in Trieste.[137]

If Joyce was far too sceptical to share his father's sentimental indulgence towards the Fenians, he approached Fenianism in a matter-of-fact way while considering its methods outmoded: in his non-fiction in his early Italian exile, he was starkly objective about Fenianism as a

134. *U* 3.240–43.

135. *U* 3.245–50.

136. Stanislaus Joyce was much less politically alert than his brother, but a manuscript note to his Dublin diary, if it can be taken to reflect the state of knowledge of the children of John Stanislaus Joyce of the anterior career of Patrick Casey, is notably deficient: 'Besides, Pat Casey (called "of Paris") is an old man of few settled ideas, in secret an unbeliever (I believe) like myself, and a man who has lived abroad for fenian complicity'. S. Joyce, *Dublin Diary*, 134n4.

137. See Michael Patrick Gillespie, *James Joyce's Trieste Library* (Austin: University of Texas at Austin Press, 1986), 81.

revolutionary force in nineteenth-century Ireland. He was impatiently bored—and perhaps a little disappointed—by the conventionality of Joseph Casey. Among the scores of characters that John Stanislaus Joyce had given to him, Joe Casey was certainly not the least significant. He was in his Parisian 'exile' the most ostensibly exotic. Joyce repatriated him into the mundane universe of *Ulysses*. Casey's exile was more in time than space: 'They have forgotten Kevin Egan, not he them. Remembering thee, O Sion.'[138]

138. *U* 3.263–64.

4

The 'Dead King'

ON ONE OF THE anniversaries of Parnell's death—'Ivy Day' proper as distinct from the day on which the annual processional commemoration took place—James Joyce turned up in Belvedere College, which he attended from 1893 to 1898, wearing an ivy leaf on his collar. This was an act of defiance, and a Jesuit priest made him remove it while inside school grounds. The episode was recalled by Joyce's schoolfriend Eugene Sheehy, a reliable witness who was close to Joyce in Belvedere and in University College and was able to recall the name of the Jesuit, Father Tierney.[1]

The biographical scrap is significant set against the dearth of other evidence of Joyce's Parnellism in the lost political years of his late boyhood and adolescence. The only other evidence of the immediate impact of the Split and the death of Parnell on the young Joyce, to set against the stylised account in *A Portrait*, is what his brother Stanislaus could recall; the fact that as a child he wrote a now-lost elegy for Parnell;

1. Ellmann, *James Joyce*, 55. Other mentions of Joyce's boyhood relationship to Parnell are more bland and the precise basis for what is asserted left unstated. Thus Louis Gillet, who knew Joyce in Paris in the late 1920s and 1930s, wrote, 'But Joyce could not forget the memory of Parnell. The figure of this tribune and powerful agitator, today three-quarters forgotten, was the first to impress his young years. He had been the hero of his childhood. Joyce used to hear about his exploits as about those of Napoleon: both had been giants who made England shudder. . . . When Parnell died, victim of intrigues and pharisaism, Joyce was ten—one never gets over one's first impressions' (*Claybook for James Joyce*, 98–99). Gillet seems to have an intimation, in referring to Parnell as the 'victim of intrigues and pharisaism', that his comparison with the childhood impact of Napoleonic lore on a French child does not quite work.

and what can be inferred from his adult life and other writings that attest to the constancy of his identification with Parnell.

Modelling Joyce's early Parnellism entails mapping his writings and what is known of his life in its political aspect against the course of Irish politics through the 1890s, the trajectory of the Parnell myth, and the sources of political intelligence available to the young Joyce (primarily newspapers). This spans an extended arc of time. Joyce dwelt all his life on Parnell, and his relationship to the Irish political, especially in his exile, was discernibly inflected by the issues of the Split. In setting Joyce within the grid of contemporary politics, in correlating his treatment of Parnell and the Split with the course of nationalist politics and Parnell commemoration, and in attending to those features of Parnell's myth and legacy that Joyce elects to appropriate and those features he discards or repudiates, it becomes possible to re-trace the deeply incised line of Joyce's recusant Parnellism.

Joyce's Parnellism in *My Brother's Keeper*

In his memoir, *My Brother's Keeper*, Stanislaus Joyce makes some comments and observations on his brother's Parnellism, but they are imprecise and marred by his inability to perceive that Joyce did not share his own persistent indifference to Irish nationalism.[2] He did recognise that Parnell was a significant figure for Joyce but was unable convincingly to account for it. Stanislaus, born on 17 December 1884, was almost three years younger than James, and would have been six at the time of the Split. The title of his memoir, which corresponds to how Stanislaus spoke of himself, is doubly apt.[3] His role as a memorialist of his brother

2. The oddity of Stanislaus's political and religious perspective was not readily picked up by non-Irish readers. T. S. Eliot twice read the text, which Faber and Faber published. He was dismayed, and in some degree distracted, by Stanislaus's dismissal of religious belief, but captured something of the dogged obtuseness of 'this positive, courageous, bitter man', who had died on Bloomsday 1955, three years before the publication of the memoir: 'Where James, in political and religious matters, was indifferent or merely mocking, Stanislaus manifests a sometimes appalling violence'. T. S. Eliot, preface to S. Joyce, *My Brother's Keeper*, 12.

3. Richard Ellmann, who edited the text, wrote in his introduction, 'The book's title, *My Brother's Keeper*, summed up his painful service and his sense of bondage, and something else

was a perpetuation of his loyalty to Joyce in Dublin, and the unstinted support he gave him in the years in Trieste. He was the keeper of the early narrative of James Joyce, an office he performed serviceably well, but his memoir bears the impress of some of his own idiosyncrasies and was retrospectively conceived on the basis of his brother's writing.

Of his father's support for Parnell, Stanislaus writes, 'It was a fanatical life-long devotion he handed on to his eldest son.'[4] He saw, over-reductively, his brother's poem on Parnell's death as 'an echo of those political rancours that formed the theme of my father's nightly, half-drunken rantings to the accompaniment of vigorous table-thumping.'[5] The setting in time was Parnell's fall, but there is a certain generic vagueness in his reference to his father's 'half-drunken rantings' which makes one wonder whether Stanislaus could recall much of the actual subject matter beyond the thumping of the table.

Stanislaus wrote of his brother, 'In his childhood, the vaguely understood drama of Parnell had not stirred any feelings of patriotism or nationalism in his heart; rather, under his father's influence, it had implanted there an early spirit of revolt against hypocrisy and clerical authority and popular servility to it.'[6] This was a de-politicising of the effect that the Split wrought on his brother. Stanislaus was unable to grasp that Joyce's acquisition of a nationalist allegiance was inextricably bound up with this revolt. He added that 'when Parnell's name became the symbol of a national struggle, he stood aloof from it for artistic reasons.'[7] The language is imprecise and does not inspire confidence in Stanislaus's grasp of Irish politics. The reference to Parnell's name becoming the symbol of a national struggle would ordinarily refer to Parnell's rise rather than fall, but Stanislaus evidently intends to refer to

---

as well. When he referred to it himself, he would give the title and then add, smiling wryly, "You know . . . Cain"'. Ellmann, introduction to S. Joyce, *My Brother's Keeper*, 15. After Cain has murdered his elder brother, Abel, God asks him where his brother was. Cain answers in the Tyndale Bible, 'I know not; am I my brother's keeper?' (Genesis 4:9).

4. S. Joyce, *My Brother's Keeper*, 49.

5. S. Joyce, *My Brother's Keeper*, 65.

6. S. Joyce, *My Brother's Keeper*, 172–73.

7. S. Joyce, *My Brother's Keeper*, 173.

the period of the long Parnell Split, 1890–1900. In his narrative, 'Parnell's story had become a memory of the dead'[8] by the time Joyce reached University College, which is correct. Stanislaus related his brother's admiration for Parnell to his betrayal-inflected conception of sacrifice: 'My brother was always of opinion that a dramatist could understand only one or two of life's tragedies. . . . One of the tragedies that obsessed my brother's imagination, beginning from the time he first understood the Mass as drama, was the tragedy of dedication and betrayal. In later life, the story of Parnell became for him another aspect of that tragedy.'[9] This is not without insight in capturing some of the strange intensity of Joyce's identification with Parnell, and Stanislaus's periodisation of his brother's Parnellism is of some interest. He is asserting that Joyce's identification with Parnell came in adulthood, as he developed his conception of betrayal, as if it were in response to Joyce's own experience of real or imagined treachery in his life in Dublin, or at least that this was what conserved Joyce's allegiance to Parnell in his later life. This conveys something of Stanislaus's struggle to comprehend his brother's nationalism. What he was unable to fathom was the nationalism that both informed his brother's Parnellism and in some degree derived from it. His playing down of the impact of the Split on Joyce as a boy suggests incidentally that he regarded the Christmas dinner scene in *A*

8. S. Joyce, *My Brother's Keeper*, 173

9. S. Joyce, *My Brother's Keeper*, 172–73. Stanislaus's own perspective on the Split was as unsparing as his brother's, but as a socio-cultural critique of his male countrymen: 'Their sudden revulsion of feeling and malignant outcry against their former idol, Parnell, when he became the protagonist of as genuine a love drama as modern history affords, could hardly have happened in any other country in Europe. Love gets a cold welcome in Ireland unless it is obedient to priestly control before marriage, and, through the confessional, after marriage too. Unmarried mothers had better be dead than alive in the greenest of isles'. S. Joyce, *My Brother's Keeper*, 163–64; see also 234. It was not that James Joyce did not share these views of Stanislaus, but they serve to highlight how determinedly *political* his treatment of Parnell and the Split was. Stanislaus's ruminations on this subject were an improvement, at least at the level of serviceable aphorism, on what he had written in the year of his brother's death: 'Joyce exhibited a character trait so common among Irishmen that it could be called the Irish paradox—faithfulness to one woman and at the same time a profound hostility towards women in general'. S. Joyce, *Recollections of James Joyce*, 26; see also 11. This was probably written before his book; S. Joyce, *My Brother's Keeper*, 24.

Portrait as fictional, even if he was too loyal to what had become a constitutive part of his brother's myth to say so explicitly.

If Stanislaus struggled to comprehend his brother's nationalism, he was not unsympathetic to Parnell. In his *Dublin Diary* he has a characterisation of Parnell avowedly written the month before his brother left Ireland that is of some intrinsic interest but is also likely to owe something to what he knew about Parnell from his brother, with the nationalism filtered out. It is a pure *esquisse* of biographical attributes in the high nineteenth-century manner, drawing a contrast with William Gladstone, as Joyce himself would do in 'L'ombra di Parnell', and as many had ventured before. Once again Stanislaus reveals most when his revelatory intent is least. Stanislaus had insights of his own, but his views did tend to be essays in the reining in of his brother's, so that what he wrote on Parnell can be read as a strange and fragile palimpsest of fraternity:

> Gladstone is my idea of a great imposter. Jim tells me that the great word in Dante for damning a man is the Italian for 'imposter'. William Ewart Gladstone seems to me to deserve that title thoroughly. The English, with that admiration of theirs in which it is hard to hold the balance between falsity and stupidity, used to call him the Grand Old Man, but Parnell's perversion of this is a perfect description of him—a Grand Old Imposter. Parnell must have had a lovely contempt for him. Parnell had, I think, not much ability, except perhaps financial ability; he was not as intimately acquainted with the disadvantages of his country, as say, [Michael] Davitt, nor knew as well how to remedy them, nor what was most desirable to replace them. He was unlettered, no patriot, and in my judgement the only genius Ireland has produced. He had the power of managing men and using their capabilities, and a great eye for capability. He must have had a very fine mind; he had great words of contempt, 'imposters', 'peddling'. His genius was probably more distinguished and finer than Napoleon's, but in ambition and ability he was much the lesser as his success was less than the Corsican's.[10]

10. S. Joyce, entry for 14 September 1904, in *Dublin Diary*, 94–95.

Beneath the conventional remarks and comparisons, something stirs that is likely to reflect Joyce's influence, most obviously the 'lovely contempt' (the 'lovely' being an epithet of Stanislaus rather than Joyce) Parnell must have had for Gladstone, and his 'great words of contempt'.

Joyce's Poem on the Death of Parnell

The first thing that we know directly about Joyce's relation to Parnell is that as a child he wrote a poem about the latter's death. The text of the poem is not extant, although Stanislaus recalled an emblematic fragment. The writing of the poem is adverted to in one line in *A Portrait* and, according to Stanislaus, received a fuller treatment in the now-lost early part of *Stephen Hero*. Joyce pointedly enumerated it as his first publication in a list to be conveyed to B. W. Huebsch, his American publisher, that he sent to his English publisher, Harriet Shaw Weaver, in November 1916: '"Parnell", a pamphlet written when I was nine years old (in 1891) on Parnell's death. It was printed and circulated in Dublin. I do not know if any copy is to be found today.'[11]

The description, or misdescription, is intriguing. Bulking up the poem to a pamphlet perhaps enhanced the justification for its inclusion among his 'early publications', but it also avoided characterising the work as a poem: the classification is tilted away from the literary towards the political. But if Joyce is demarcating the poem from his artistic writing, why is he including it at all? A sentimental gesture towards Parnell would scarcely have been intelligible to Huebsch. In placing it at the head of the lineage of his 'early publications', he was asserting a salience to his later literary oeuvre. There is also the matter of the title. While it could have been simply a convenient means of designating the subject matter, Joyce is likely to be correct in stating that the title of the poem was 'Parnell' rather than the punningly classicising title of 'Et Tu Healy'

11. Joyce to Harriet Shaw Weaver, 8 November 1916, *Letters I*, 99; see Ellmann, *James Joyce*, 749. Joyce seems both reasonably confident and relieved that there were no extant copies.

that came to be assigned to it. Joyce also brought the date of its composition into immediate proximity to the death of Parnell.

In *My Brother's Keeper*, Stanislaus Joyce recalled the poem—though not the title of 'Et Tu Healy'—as an attack on Timothy Michael Healy. He was adamant that it was written when the Joyce family was living in Leoville, Blackrock, which dates it to 1892–93; it was likely written within six months of the immediate mourning for Parnell, who died 6 October 1891, and could well have been written before Joyce's tenth birthday on 2 February 1892, and may even have been written in winter 1891 as Joyce later asserted.

Of the poem itself Stanislaus recalled,

> At the end of the piece the dead Chief is likened to an eagle, looking down on the grovelling mass of Irish politicians from
>
> His quaint-perched aerie on the crags of Time
> Where the rude din of this . . . century
> Can trouble him no more.[12]

In an article written in the year of his brother's death, Stanislaus characterised the poem as 'childlike in its imitation of Byron, the eternal idol of the young', and observed it was much admired by friends of the family 'who, at least in matters of literature, were of an equally childlike

12. S. Joyce, *My Brother's Keeper*, 64–65. These are the only lines that Stanislaus quotes of the Parnell poem and are all that survive. John J. Slocum and Herbert Cahoon, in *A Bibliography of James Joyce, 1882–1941* (New Haven, CT: Yale University Press, 1953), 3, claim to quote a further four lines, beginning, 'My cot alas that dear old shady home', that are taken from Joyce's letter to Harriet Shaw Weaver of 22 November 1930 (*Letters I*, 295). As Stanislaus makes clear, these lines—parodied in *Finnegans Wake* (231.5–9)—are from contemporaneous juvenile poetry by Joyce 'in the style of the drawing-room ballads to which he was accustomed' (S. Joyce, *My Brother's Keeper*, 65), and are not from the Parnell poem. Ellmann (*James Joyce*, 33) strangely adopts the Slocum and Cahoon error. The surviving fragment of the Parnell poem as recalled by Stanislaus is more vivid and suffers by the false accretion. Stanislaus, who was apparently unaware that 'dear old tumtum home' had found its way into the *Wake*, explained, 'The lines I have quoted have stuck in my memory because "the dear old shady home" and the blandly appropriated "quaint-perched aerie" were standing jokes between us as late as when we were living at Trieste'. S. Joyce, *My Brother's Keeper*, 65.

ingenuousness.'[13] Stanislaus, who could never quite fathom his brother's Parnellism, failed to discern the striking anticipation of Joyce's later treatment of Parnell. The last three lines of the poem, as recalled by Stanislaus, prefigured Joyce's identification with the impassive silence he imputed to Parnell in his mature writings. Some two decades later in his article 'L'ombra di Parnell', he would write of 'the forlorn serenity of his character' and of 'the light of his mild, proud, silent and disconsolate sovereignty.'[14] Joyce, aged ten, was already addressing how Parnell might be written about, setting his poem in an accusatory frame against those who betrayed him, in which Parnell stands dispassionately at a certain distance from the fierce controversy that raged around him. The poem is also, as Richard Ellmann points out, 'faintly premonitory of Joyce's description of himself in "The Holy Office" as a stag on the highest mountain ridges.'[15] The haughty tone matches Parnell's distance. The identification of Parnell's dispassionate fierceness with Joyce's own role as a writer was present from the outset.[16]

The writing of the poem is not quite the spontaneous and proudly isolated gesture depicted in *A Portrait*. It had a specific contemporary politico-literary setting in the ephemeral sub-genre of poems on the death of Parnell. Verses on the subject were prominently arrayed in issues of *United Ireland*, at that time the sole metropolitan organ of Parnellism. These accretions to the anthology of Irish 'dirges at the biers of dead leaders'[17] were supplemented on each anniversary of Parnell's death through the ensuing decade. Since they were for the most part

13. S. Joyce, *Recollections of James Joyce*, 6. The suggestion of Stanislaus Joyce that the Hynes poem in 'Ivy Day in the Committee Room' is 'more or less in the same style' is suspect. Succumbing to the temptation of reimagining the rest of the lost Parnell poem through that recited by Hynes in 'Ivy Day', he missed the subtlety of the story, and the fact that his brother's implacable critique of how Parnell was commemorated extended to his own first published work. [See chapter 12, 'Writing *Dubliners* in Exile'.]

14. *OCPW* 194.

15. Ellmann, *James Joyce*, 33.

16. Backus, *Scandal Work*, 18–19.

17. In a sub-leader entitled 'The Cry of the Banshee', *United Ireland* wrote, 'As one looks through Irish poetry it is impressive and mournful to see how much of the best of it consists of

execrably hackneyed, it might be said that the first death of the Parnell myth was poetical. If Joyce's Parnell poem seems on first reading conformist and conventional, the collusive aloofness with its subject, evidenced in the lines that survive, sets it somewhat apart. Nonetheless, the fact that he had written a poem within a patriotic nationalist convention, reinforced by the critique he developed of the way Parnell was commemorated, contributed to Joyce's diffidence about the contents of the poem (as distinct from the fact of having written it).

Joyce's Parnell poem does not appear to have been submitted to any of the Parnellite papers, although the standard for poems was not exacting and poems much inferior to the surviving lines of Joyce's were readily carried. Instead, John Stanislaus had the poem printed by Alley & O'Reilly in Ryder's Row and distributed to friends—Stanislaus had 'a distinct recollection of my father's bringing home a roll of thirty or forty of them.'[18] This may reflect a protective scruple on the part of John Stanislaus as his young son's impresario, and a consciousness that the poem's Parnellism owed something to his own inspiration. He may also have considered the private publication of the poem grander than its appearance in public sheets.

Joyce never resurrected the lost text (if he retained it), but as well as including it in the list to Harriet Shaw Weaver, he took care to ensure that his contemporary biographer Herbert Gorman recorded the fact that he had written it.[19] His reticence strangely matched W. B. Yeats's

---

dirges at the biers of dead leaders. . . . The wail of the banshee seems to be the inevitable close to every Irish period of hope; it is never silent for a generation' (24 October 1891).

18. S. Joyce, *My Brother's Keeper*, 65; Costello, *Years of Growth*, 109. John Stanislaus Joyce's claim, made many years later to the bookdealer Jacob Schwartz, to have paid for the poem's printing and despatched a copy to the pope (Ellmann, *James Joyce*, 33n) led to successive enquiries of the Vatican Library, one of which I recall making myself twenty years ago. The lost broadsheet is the holy grail of Irish bibliophiles. The solicitor Ciaran Mac An Aili told me that his friend and fellow book collector Captain Tadhg MacGlinchey, founding director and publisher of the Irish University Press, had a dream in which he found Joyce's Parnell poem among a cache of Victorian music sheets.

19. Gorman, *James Joyce*, 36. Gorman describes the poem as 'a violently written attack on Timothy Healy', which would partially account for the ascription of the title 'Et Tu Healy'. Joyce seems to have been aware of the title: the enigmatic phrase '(*Et Cur Heli*!)' appears in *Finnegans Wake* (73.19). Perhaps it was a punningly classicising title conferred by his father.

aversion to his own poem on Parnell's death, 'Mourn and Then Onwards'.[20]

Joyce's taciturnity is the principal reason for the absence of reliable biographical evidence about the unfolding of his reaction to the Split after the writing of his Parnell poem (though this has to be qualified by the fact that he presumably treated of it more directly in the now-lost part of *Stephen Hero*). His taciturnity is less a conventional evidentiary void than an enigma created—or more precisely an issue left open for critical interpretation—by Joyce himself. It is a challenge almost explicitly thrown down in *A Portrait*, and it is difficult to avoid the conclusion that Joyce intended the novel to stand as the principal account, however stylised, of the relation in which he stood as a boy to Parnell and the Split. One is left to negotiate Joyce's ethic of reticence by an evaluation of the politics of *A Portrait*.

The Split in *A Portrait of the Artist*

To start from *A Portrait* is not to treat it as an autobiographical text. The account in *A Portrait* of the impact of the Split on Stephen is highly stylised and subservient to the themes of the novel. Still, it would be extravagant to conclude that it was not intended to convey the main lines of Joyce's early engagement with the Split.

The establishment of dates and places in the years from 1890 to 1892 becomes important. Joyce began attending Clongowes as a pupil on 30 August 1888 when he was six years old.[21] At the date of the divorce decree and the breakup of the party in November–December 1890, Joyce was eight years old. He was nine when Parnell died in October 1891. While the dates are hard to establish with precision, it seems that Joyce was withdrawn from Clongowes in December 1891, one of the early markers of his father's sharply deteriorating financial position.[22] In early 1892 the Joyces moved from 1 Martello Terrace in Bray, where they had

20. R. F. Foster, *W. B. Yeats: A Life*, vol. 1, *The Apprentice Mage* (Oxford: Oxford University Press, 1997), 116.

21. Bradley, *James Joyce's Schooldays*, 9.

22. Bradley, *James Joyce's Schooldays*, 80; Igoe, *James Joyce's Dublin Houses*, 40.

lived from 1887, to a house called Leoville, 23 Carysfort Avenue, Blackrock,[23] which is where Stanislaus recalled the family was living when his brother wrote the poem on Parnell.

The events in the second and third parts of chapter 1 of *A Portrait* take place in the course of Stephen's single year in Clongowes (1890–91), which equated in time to Joyce's third year at the school. In the novel, Stephen enters Clongowes in September 1890, three months before the Parnell Split. The world of nationalism before the Split is evoked on the first page of the novel by Dante Conway's odd practice of keeping two brushes, when Stephen was six years old, one backed in maroon velvet for Davitt, and the other for Parnell in green, curious imaginary additions to the sparse material culture of Parnellism. The brushes introduce the Split in the second part of the chapter:

> He wondered which was right, to be for the green or for the maroon, because Dante had ripped the green velvet back off the brush that was for Parnell one day with her scissors and had told him that Parnell was a bad man. He wondered if they were arguing at home about that. That was called politics. There were two sides in it: Dante was on one side and his father and Mr Casey were on the other side but his mother and uncle Charles were on no side. Every day there was something in the paper about it.[24]

This, then, was politics: 'It pained him that he did not know well what politics meant and that he did not know where the universe ended.'[25] What politics actually meant in Ireland was not straightforward. 'Politics' was not neatly demarcated. This was part of Joyce's setting apart of Stephen Dedalus from the norms of the continental bildungsroman, and of the English boyhood school narrative. The sense of the nationalist political was encountered from an early age. Ireland was not a state; and the sense of the political as thwarted statehood was more diffusely pervasive than the regimentedly linear sense of state that

23. Ellmann, *James Joyce*, 34; S. Joyce, *My Brother's Keeper*, 40; Igoe, *James Joyce's Dublin Houses*, 19, 40.

24. *P* 1.336–44.

25. *P* 1.345–46.

came with sovereignty. Politics in that zone of incompleteness and contestation was substituted for the settled narrative of the foundation of a state or the acquisition of an empire.

As *A Portrait* superbly attests, the experience of the contemporary political preceded the acquisition of much knowledge of history, and perhaps of sexual morality (the O'Shea divorce is not mentioned until the Christmas dinner, and then only in veiled terms). With the sundering of Parnell's great movement, the prospect of statehood seemed to slip away, a crisis of such epic proportion that a child could get some dim sense of it.

The principal event in the second part of chapter 1 is that Stephen takes ill as a result of being shouldered into the murky waters of the square ditch in Clongowes. The next day, he is put under the care of Brother Michael in the infirmary. In a mood of morose exaltation, Stephen considers the effect his death would produce: 'He wondered if he would die. . . . He might die before his mother came. Then he would have a dead mass in the chapel, like the way fellows had told him it was when Little had died.'[26]

Peter Stanislaus Little, who is given his real name in *A Portrait*, had died at the age of sixteen, in the small hours of 10 December 1890, apparently of rheumatic fever, reportedly contracted after a drenching on the windswept Bog of Allen, and was buried in the Jesuit cemetery in Clongowes. His death occurred during Joyce's second year at Clongowes but in *A Portrait* Stephen knows of it only by hearsay,[27] which resituates the death in the time before Stephen arrives in Clongowes. Historically, Peter Little died on the evening of the same day that Parnell addressed the great meeting in the Rotunda on his return to Ireland after his defeat in Committee Room 15, and a triangular relationship subsists in *A Portrait* between Little's death, Stephen's illness, and the Split and Parnell's death. It is difficult not to consider this a reflection of Joyce's contemporary response to the death of an older school contemporary set against the backdrop, remote from Clongowes and imperfectly

26. *P* 1.591–94.

27. *P* 1.593–94; Bradley, *James Joyce's Schooldays*, 63–64.

apprehended, of the inception of the Split. Joyce had experienced a double incursion into his childhood of unfamiliar phenomena conventionally considered to belong to the adult world. If the actual date of Little's death and its synchrony with the shift of the Split to Ireland are strictly extratextual, they seem palpably to pulse through the infirmary scene of *A Portrait*. The association of the Split and death in the first chapter in this way predates and prefigures Parnell's demise.

In the dusk of the day of his admission to the infirmary, watching the fire rising and falling on the wall, Stephen lapses into reverie:

> How pale the light was at the window! But that was nice. The fire rose and fell on the wall. It was like waves. Someone had put coal on and he heard voices. They were talking. It was the noise of the waves. Or the waves were talking among themselves as they rose and fell.
>
> He saw the sea of waves, long dark waves rising and falling, dark under the moonless night. A tiny light twinkled at the pierhead where the ship was entering: and he saw a multitude of people gathered by the waters' edge to see the ship that was entering their harbour. A tall man stood on the deck, looking out towards the flat dark land: and by the light at the pierhead he saw his face, the sorrowful face of Brother Michael.
>
> He saw him lift his hand towards the people and heard him say in a loud voice of sorrow over the waters:
>
> —He is dead. We saw him lying upon the catafalque.
>
> A wail of sorrow went up from the people.
>
> —Parnell! Parnell! He is dead!
>
> They fell upon their knees, moaning in sorrow.
>
> And he saw Dante in a maroon velvet dress and with a green velvet mantle hanging from her shoulders walking proudly and silently past the people who knelt by the waters' edge.[28]

Joyce engenders a haunting image of popular desolation that renders Stephen's imaginative connection to a distantly apprehended Ireland beyond the Clongowes infirmary.

28. *P* 1.695–715.

Evincing his determination to bind the narrative tightly to the temporality of the Split, Joyce goes to some lengths to date what transpires in the infirmary. The day after he is shouldered into the ditch, Stephen changes the number of days before the Christmas holidays he kept pasted up inside his desk from seventy-seven to seventy-six.[29] He is admitted into the infirmary in the small hours of the next day. If one takes 21 December as the day the Christmas holidays started, then Stephen experiences his reverie of Parnell's death in the infirmary on the afternoon of 7 October.[30] Visiting Cork with his father, Stephen recalls his having 'dreamed of being dead' in the infirmary: 'But he had not died then. Parnell had died.'[31] The synchrony was affirmed in the concept of sacrificial displacement.

The news of Parnell's death would have reached the infirmary in Clongowes by word of mouth in the course of the afternoon of 7 October. It seems clear that, in his semi-feverish state, Stephen hears Brother Michael, who has already been identified as a bringer of news, talking of it to someone, and processes this intelligence as if in a dream. Brother Michael is a sympathetic figure, from a poorer background than that of

29. *P* 1.100–102, 1.281–83.

30. I owe to Edmund Epstein the idea of making the computation; see Epstein, *Ordeal of Stephen Dedalus*, 36. However, my calculation leads to a different result from his. He dates the reverie on Parnell's death to 9–10 October. If one co-relates the dating to the infirmary scene itself, Epstein's count, which suggests a relation to Parnell's funeral on 11 October rather than his death, has the problem that Stephen could scarcely have remained so long in ignorance of the fact of Parnell's death.

Hans Walter Gabler undertakes the same exercise in 'The Christmas Dinner Scene, Parnell's Death, and the Genesis of *A Portrait of the Artist as a Young Man*', *James Joyce Quarterly* 13, no. 1 (Fall 1975): 27–38. Gabler ('Christmas Dinner Scene', 33) errs in taking this number pasted inside the desk to relate to the days to Christmas, whereas Joyce makes clear it is the days to the start of the Christmas holidays ('Soon they would be going home for the holidays' (*P* 1.10); 'But the Christmas vacation was very far away': (*P* 1.15). In Gabler's account ('Christmas Dinner Scene', 33), the seventy-sixth day before Christmas is 9 October. He then situates Stephen's 'dream or vision' to the night of 10–11 October, so that 'Stephen's return to life from a sickness-to-death (as he imagines it) are synchronized to take place during the same morning [as the return to Ireland of Parnell's body] of 11 October 1891' ('Christmas Dinner Scene', 34). This is all unnecessarily contrived and wrong, primarily because the novel conveys that Stephen in the infirmary feverishly overhears the news of Parnell's death.

31. *P* 2.1167–68.

Jesuit priests, socially closer to the people of Clane, and more likely than ordained Jesuits to mourn the passing of Parnell, or at the very least more sensible to popular grief.[32] At the same time, the fact that he is a cleric serves to heighten the immoderateness of Dante in her role as the triumphant Catholic lay zealot in the Christmas dinner scene that follows. Stephen hears of Parnell's death rather than dreams it. The dream is charged with a proleptic intimation of the return of Parnell's body to Ireland in the early morning of 11 October 1891, rendered as one with his death, as the event that confirms the terrible rumour of his death to the crowd foregathered on the water's edge.[33] In the novel, the bearing of Parnell's body back across the sea comes to stand for Parnell's funeral, a national event from which the schoolboys in Clongowes were shut out. Through the device of Stephen's fevered dream, Joyce contrives to avoid a direct or frontal narrative of the return of Parnell's body to Ireland and the funeral, which accords with the oblique approach he persistently adopted in treating of the persona (and body) of Parnell.

The third part of chapter 1 of *A Portrait* cuts to the Christmas dinner, which also relates to a precise moment of the Split. For Parnellites this was a bitter Christmas, the first after Parnell's death. John Redmond's victory as the Parnellite candidate over Michael Davitt in the Waterford by-election, in which polling took place unseasonably on 23 December, seemed to come too late, and did nothing to assuage the grief and loss that those who had remained staunch to Parnell felt at his death.

32. Brother Michael is based on Brother John Hanly, who had charge of the Clongowes infirmary; see Bradley, *James Joyce's Schooldays*, 59–60. Bradley notes that Jesuit brothers did not wear clerical collars at the time, as did Jesuit priests and scholastics, and dressed effectively as laymen. This is why Brother Michael is referred to as having 'a queer look . . . a different kind of look' (*P* 1.568–60). Stephen registers that Brother Michael addresses the prefect—a senior pupil—as 'sir'. Joyce was attentive to the matter of clerical collars, as his treatment of the swathing of Fr Keon's collar in 'Ivy Day in the Committee Room' in *Dubliners* was to attest. Frank Callanan, 'The Parnellism of James Joyce: "Ivy Day in the Committee Room"', *Joyce Studies Annual* 2015 (2015): 78–79.

33. The deployment of prolepsis is cunningly presaged several pages earlier in the anticipatory narrative of the joyous departure from Clongowes at the end of term, albeit based on what 'the fellows had told him' (*P* 1.20).

The bitter dispute that breaks out on the occasion of Stephen's first Christmas dinner sitting with the adults is narrated from his perspective. It is also, at least at the outset, conditioned by his presence. The controversy is initially not entirely unrestrained. Mr Casey refuses to mention the name that the old woman in Arklow had called Katharine O'Shea that led him to spit his tobacco in her eye.[34] This was unsatisfactory from Stephen's point of view: 'It was not nice about the spit in the woman's eye. But what was the name the woman had called Kitty O'Shea that Mr Casey would not repeat?'[35] The old woman in Casey's narrative is twice quoted screaming the name 'Kitty O'Shea', but Stephen does not wonder to whom this referred, meaning that he—no doubt like any other Irish schoolboy of the time—was already aware of the pejorative name anti-Parnellites used to refer to Katharine O'Shea, without necessarily fully apprehending why her relations with Parnell attracted opprobrium.

The limited observance of propriety has the paradoxical effect of heightening the unbridled ferocity of what is said. When Mrs Dedalus objects to her husband referring to Michael Logue, Archbishop of Armagh, in front of Stephen, as 'a tub of guts', Dante, Mr Casey, and Simon Dedalus each in turn seize on her intervention to express themselves with renewed fierceness:

> —O, he'll remember all this when he grows up, said Dante hotly, the language he heard against God and religion and priests in his own home.
>
> —Let him remember too, cried Mr Casey to her from across the table, the language with which the priests and the priests' pawns broke Parnell's heart and hounded him into his grave. Let him remember that too when he grows up.

34. Mr Casey's account implies, without explicitly stating, that Parnell was present at the meeting. I have not been able to find a report of a Parnellite meeting in Arklow, attended by Parnell or not. It seems that Joyce invented the Arklow meeting in Parnell's native county of Wicklow.

35. *P* 1.1058–60.

> —Sons of bitches! cried Mr Dedalus. When he was down they turned on him to betray him and rend him like rats in a sewer. Low-lived dogs! And they look it! By Christ, they look it![36]

It is thus Simon Dedalus who provides the culminating fillip. Stephen tries to weigh all this up as it unfolds. 'He liked to sit near [Mr Casey] at the fire, looking up at his dark fierce face. . . . But why was he then against the priests? Because Dante must be right then. But he had heard his father say she that was a spoiled nun. . . . Who was right then? And he remembered the evening in the infirmary in Clongowes, the dark waters, the light at the pierhead and the moan of sorrow from the people when they had heard.'[37] The puzzle persists: '[Mr Casey] was for Ireland and Parnell and so was his father: and so was Dante too for one night at the band on the esplanade she had hit a gentleman on the head with her umbrella because he had taken off his hat when the band played *God Save the Queen* at the end.'[38] Mr Casey litanises the highly equivocal political record of the Catholic Church in Ireland through the nineteenth century. 'His face was glowing with anger and Stephen felt the glow rise to his own cheek as the spoken words thrilled him.'[39] Dante taunts, 'Right! Right! They were always right! God and morality and religion come first'. As she chants, 'God and religion before the world!',

> Mr Casey raised his clenched fist and brought it down on the table with a crash.
>
> —Very well then, he shouted hoarsely, if it comes to that, no God for Ireland![40]

36. *P* 1.936–45.

37. *P* 1.991–1007.

38. *P* 1.1069–73.

39. *P* 1.1107–8. This is one of the two occasions, both in a private setting, in Joyce's fiction where Stephen Dedalus finds himself almost embarrassedly moved by high rhetoric. In the 'Aeolus' episode of *Ulysses*, the older Stephen finds himself moved when J. J. O'Molloy (like Mr Casey, a stricken man) intones Seymour Bushe's invocation of Michelangelo's Moses in his peroration in the Childs case: 'Stephen, his blood wooed by grace of blood and gesture, blushed' (*U* 7.776).

40. *P* 1.1114–21.

Uncle Charles and Mr Dedalus pull him back into his chair as he stares before him 'out of his dark flaming eyes', repeating the sentiment. Dante emits a shriek of triumph as she storms out.

> Mr Casey, freeing his arms from his holders, suddenly bowed his head on his hands with a sob of pain.
>
> —Poor Parnell! He cried loudly. My dead king!
>
> He sobbed loudly and bitterly.
>
> Stephen, raising his terrorstricken face, saw that his father's eyes were full of tears.[41]

In the Irish manner, Stephen's apprehension of what politics was about coincided almost immediately with the acquisition of a definite political allegiance. A later reminiscence in the novel treats of his abortive attempt on St Stephen's Day to write a poem about Parnell: 'He saw himself sitting at his table in Bray the morning after the discussion at the Christmas dinnertable, trying to write a poem about Parnell on the back of one of his father's second moiety notices.'[42] This consigning of the poem to a single sentence differs markedly from what is known of the treatment of the poem in the now-lost early part of *Stephen Hero*, which is recalled by Stanislaus in his memoir: 'In the first draft of *A Portrait of the Artist*, now called *Stephen Hero*, the poem was assigned to the period I have indicated [early 1892], and, further, describing a hasty packing up and departure from Blackrock, my brother referred to the remaining broadsheets, of which the young Stephen Dedalus had been so proud, lying on the floor torn and muddied by the boots of the furniture removers.'[43]

This recollection indicates that Joyce wrote at greater length about the Parnell poem in *Stephen Hero* and emphasised Stephen's pride in it and the printing of the broadsheets by his father. In *A Portrait* Joyce

41. *P* 1.1138–51.

42. *P* 2.366–70. Of his attempting to write a poem to Parnell on the obverse of a rent demand, Margot Norris has written luminously, 'Stephen's art however much it strives to epiphanize itself and thereby transcend its material and social context, is literally inscribed in the textuality of Ireland's political economic life' (*Joyce's Web*, 19).

43. S. Joyce, *My Brother's Keeper*, 65–66.

distances Stephen from a narrative in which his first emergence as a writer is connected to the writing of the Parnell poem. The idea of the first fruits of Stephen's ambitions as a writer being a tribute to an Irish nationalist leader was incompatible with the conception of *A Portrait*. In *Stephen Hero* the prominence given to the Parnell poem must have been in some degree problematic in rendering Stephen, in University College, alienated from or disillusioned with a nationalism he had espoused in boyhood, rather than consistently holding himself distant from it. What Stanislaus's recollection of *Stephen Hero* discloses almost accidentally is Joyce's elaborate strategising of the Parnell theme in his work.

The exposure of a child to unrestrained adult controversy on the Parnell Split was scarcely the nationalist bourgeois norm. A child might have been aware of the Split, but discussion of the controversy, involving marital infidelity and divorce, tended to be avoided in the presence of children, as Stephen's mother unavailingly urged it should be. Joyce's contemporary and friend Constantine Curran wrote of his own parental household, 'At home, as in so many Irish families, my father and mother took different sides in the Parnell split, but their unbroken affection and good sense brought them to a quick compromise by which the politics of the "split" were no longer mentioned in the house, but each took in the newspaper of what each regarded as the appropriate colour.'[44] As far as we know, the Joyce household was unconstrained by such protocols of civility. A domestic detonation of the Split of the type described as taking place within the Dedalus household had an exhilarating aberrancy of its own.

The Historical Actuality of *A Portrait of the Artist*

Did the Christmas dinner scene actually take place? It would be more than a little disappointing if it had not. The scene has come to be central to how the Split is recalled in modern Ireland. The question is rarely

44. Curran, *Under the Receding Wave*, 25. There is remarkably little record on the subject of the gender divide, primarily on account of the restricted franchise. My late friend and colleague Gregory Murphy informed me that on the mention of Parnell's name, his grandmother went into a sulk, and his grandfather, a clerk in the Guinness brewery, raised his hat.

posed for reasons that in themselves bear some consideration. Much has been written to underscore the fact that *A Portrait* is a novel and cannot be taken as autobiographical. It became a major point of criticism of Richard Ellmann's biography that it did not always hold out against the temptation to avail of what seemed plausibly autobiographical in Joyce's fiction to fill out the daunting lacunae in the record of Joyce's early life.[45] That which pertains to contemporary politics, most dramatically in the Christmas dinner scene in *A Portrait,* is largely exempt from this scruple. Its historical actuality is rarely queried. This can be explained in part by a false paradigm in which that pertaining to the political (including the Christmas dinner scene) is seen as extraneous, a raw incursion of the external historical into his fictional narrative, rather than as something that is dynamically intrinsic to Joyce's identity, his political intellectuality, and the development of his art.

In *My Brother's Keeper,* Stanislaus Joyce delineates the diametrically opposed characters and views of John Kelly and Dante Conway without mentioning the Christmas dinner scene in *A Portrait.* He neither corroborates nor disputes its occurrence. Having just turned seven before the Christmas of 1891, he may have been too young to have been allowed to dine with the adults.[46] Still, if there had been a scene of intense drama, one might have expected Stanislaus to have learned of it at the time or been told of it by his brother at a later date. He does not say so.

45. In this instance Ellmann wrote, 'Joyce has described the Christmas dinner in 1891, when his father and John Kelly raged and wept over Parnell's betrayal and death, and Dante Conway, full of venomous piety, left the table. The argument was so acrimonious that the Vances heard it along the street. Probably the evidence of *Ulysses* can be trusted that Mrs. Conway left the house for good four days later' (*James Joyce,* 34). This referred to the fact that in *Ulysses* it is stated that 'Mrs. Riordan (Dante), a widow of independent means, had resided in the house of Stephen's parents from 1 September 1888 to 29 December 1891' (*U* 17.479–80). Ellmann cited a 1953 interview with Eileen Vance for the penultimate sentence. The final sentence disregards the recollection of Stanislaus which put her departure somewhat later in time and did not relate it to a political falling out: 'In Blackrock the disintegration of our family set in with gathering rapidity. Dante left us and went to live with other friends' (*My Brother's Keeper,* 66).

46. Joyce writes of Stephen in the novel, 'It was his first Christmas dinner and he thought of his little brothers and sisters who were waiting in the nursery, as he had often waited, until the pudding came' (*P* 1.30).

It is not merely the silence of Stanislaus in his principal memoir that suggests that the scene is fictional. Hans Walter Gabler convincingly deduces from the notes for *Stephen Hero* that in the earlier novel the 'Christmas party' was set in Dublin in 1892. He does so without querying the veracity of the scene, concluding that it did take place, but in 1891, and that Joyce, 'responding to the narrative logic of *Stephen Hero*', transposed it in the earlier novel to 1892.[47] Gabler refers to the letter to Stanislaus of 7 February 1905 in which Joyce wrote, 'Your criticism of my novel is always interesting. . . . Mrs. Riordan who has left the house in Bray returns you have forgotten, to the Xmas dinner table in Dublin.'[48] What is striking is that Joyce is writing to his brother of the Christmas dinner scene without seeming to suggest that Stanislaus would have had any knowledge of such an event beyond the manuscript of the novel.

One is driven, not without regret, to the conclusion that no event corresponding to the Christmas dinner scene actually took place. But even if there was not a climactic Christmas dinner scene of the kind Joyce described, it is more than likely that there were pronounced contrary opinions vented and caustic altercations in the house in Bray that marred the Christmas of 1891. Even between John Stanislaus and May Joyce, who was a believing Catholic and temperamentally averse to acrimony, the Christmas dinner can hardly have been festive. Had John Kelly visited or stayed with the Joyce household in Bray that Christmas—as, being without family of his own, he quite conceivably did—he could not have concealed the bitter inconsolability of his grief at the death of the leader he had loved.

Whatever the actual antecedents of the Christmas dinner scene, Joyce was confronted with a conflict of warring opinions in his extended household. Electing between different opinions involved the exercise of his independent judgement, something almost forced on him in what was an abrupt elevation into the world of adult political controversy. In *A Portrait*, Stephen does not find himself compelled to take sides until

47. Gabler, 'Christmas Dinner Scene', 28–31.

48. Joyce to Stanislaus Joyce, 7 February 1905, *Letters II* 79.

after Parnell has died. Joyce's conscious identification with Parnell is likely to have coincided with that of Stephen in the novel—that is, in the close aftermath of Parnell's death.

The Christmas dinner in *A Portrait* is perhaps the most consummately realised dramatic scene in Joyce's fictional writing. It is also, aptly for that set in the closest proximity to his death, his most harrowing evocation of the memory of Parnell. The epitomisation in a domestic setting of the Split marked a revolution in the treatment of the Irish political in literature; the wrenching into critical political consciousness of a child etched a sharp contrast with the passivity of conventional English literary renderings of boyhood within an established statal order.

Joyce sets the drama of the Christmas dinner at a precisely chosen political moment, brilliantly reimagined to catch the motion of controversy. The scene is a historical tour de force in its rendering of the escalatory rhythm of the Split, colliding with the bitter reflux from Parnell's death. The point in time close on his death takes in the intensifying onslaught of his fiercest opponents against him in the period from June to October 1891, when he had already suffered defeat in his initial purpose of reversing the decision in Committee Room 15 and was struggling to remain politically viable. Parnell had married Katharine O'Shea on 25 June 1891, refusing to defer doing so until after the Carlow election, which further amplified the vituperation to which he and his wife were subject. His death coincided with the nadir of his political fortunes. Joyce does not narrate the course of the Split, but renders it through the savage dialectic of its final phase. Joyce captures with great deftness the momentum of the anti-Parnellite campaign that ran up to and beyond Parnell's death, thereby ensuring that the Christmas dinner scene was something more than a static tableau of the mourning for Parnell some three months after his death.

The boy Stephen is confronted by a scene of terrifying and unsettling acrimony. He is deeply disturbed rather than traumatised or brutalised by it. Yet he realises that there was something that did not make sense, and something that was wrong in what had led to Parnell's overthrow and death. Stephen's response is impressive in its impassivity. He does not resort to the passive victimhood of a child. He swiftly overcomes his bewilderment at the violent confrontation of views of his elders. His disconcertedness is resolved by an almost immediately acquired allegiance to Parnell in defeat and death. His upset is transformed into conviction and an idea of grief. It is an electrifying account of the acquisition of a political allegiance in childhood. What is unusual is Stephen's self-consciousness and steely working it out for himself, deferring judgement until after the Christmas dinner. Joyce is at once saying something about the acquisition of identity and allegiance in a polity like Ireland and conveying something about his own early life. The experience engenders a resolve on Stephen's part to vindicate Parnell that found its first expression in a poem. At the moment of electively acquiring a definite nationalist allegiance, Stephen, without fully realising it, was pitting himself against the majority of the Irish nationalist electorate, against the grain of mainstream nationalist sentiment after Parnell's death. That was Joyce's own position. It required a degree of reticence and strategic cunning which he carried with him into exile. It was one that he enunciated with deepening acerbity, continuing to insist that the issues of the Split remained to be confronted. Parnell and the Split framed his relationship to Ireland and contribute to its striking linearity. Something of his insurgent boyhood identification with Parnell and of the ethic of the seemingly forlorn Parnellism of the Split remained with him. Politically catechised in the terrible school of the Split, he did not abnegate the possibility of transformative political change, but perfectly apprehended that the prospects of achieving such change were against the odds. That Parnellite scepticism gave Joyce's politics its edge.

Joyce and the Newspapers of the Split

In the very carefully mapped structure of *A Portrait*, there are two significant references to newspapers during the Split. The Split is first mentioned in relation to the differing views within the Dedalus household before Parnell's death, but critically Joyce adds, 'Every day there was something in the paper about it.'[49] Stephen's fellow inmate in the infirmary, the strangely named Athy, has a particular interest in newspapers because his father keeps racehorses. He tells Stephen that

> his father would give Brother Michael a good tip any time he wanted it because Brother Michael was very decent and always told him the news out of the paper they got every day up in the castle. There was every kind of news in the paper: accidents, shipwrecks, sports and politics.
>
> —Now it is all about politics in the paper, he said. Do your people talk about that too?
>
> —Yes, Stephen said.
>
> —Mine too, he said.[50]

The double reference to newspapers—hard to access, while not formally proscribed—serves to convey the character of Clongowes in its fastness in rural Kildare as an enclosed community. More importantly, it conveys the critical fact that Stephen, before his reverie in the infirmary, and before the Christmas dinner some three months later, is reading whatever newspapers he can get his hands on.

If the setting of the dinner is of enclosed domesticity, it is unsheltered from the external controversy. By contrast with English fiction, particularly relating to Christmas, there is in the Ireland of the Split no such thing as an intact and isolated domestic setting, one that is not violated by the political. Moreover, a notable feature of the Christmas dinner scene in *A Portrait* is Joyce's fastidious rendering of the extent to which the storm without is mediated through the Irish press, which gives Stephen's deriving of information from newspapers its wider setting.

The boy over whose head the acrimony breaks at the Christmas dinner is not so uninitiated in the politics of the Split as he might at first appear, nor was he dependent exclusively on what factual intelligence could be gleaned from the positions espoused by the adults. Aside from

49. *P* 1.344.
50. *P* 1.628–35.

whatever access Stephen had had to contemporary newspapers, this was the second Christmas in the household since the events that unfolded in Committee Room 15. The first had fallen immediately after Parnell's decisive defeat in North Kilkenny, in which the result had been declared two days before Christmas: the second Christmas in the shadow of Parnell's death was incomparably more sombre. Stephen is seeking to find, from the positions taken by the adults in his home, his own political bearings. How was a child to evaluate, to judge? He could not make a final personal decision from the contradictory accounts he had gleaned from the newspapers, or from what may have passed conversationally between the boys in Clongowes; and he could not resolve the issue simply by adopting his father's view. It was an extraordinary political induction. The coordinates of Stephen's inherited Catholic nationalist identity were violently unsettled before he could embrace that identity. The nationalist and Catholic elements were in conflict, and the Split was experienced as a political trauma.

It is hard to believe that the pointed references to the newspapers did not have an autobiographical import. The Christmas dinner scene reflects an acute awareness of how the Split was played out within a domestic setting, and how it might have affected an alert small boy. It also reflects a profound understanding of the course of the Split that goes beyond what John Stanislaus Joyce and John Kelly can have imparted and could only have come from some familiarity with the newspapers covering the controversy. There was no secondary source that rendered the escalatory rhythm of the Split on which Joyce could have drawn for the novel. While his access to newspapers was discontinuous, it seems an inescapable conclusion that he was reading some of the newspapers contemporaneously (in addition to whatever newspaper coverage his father and John Kelly may have drawn indignantly to his attention) and had probably done so more systematically at a later date in the National Library or in some other public library where back numbers of newspapers could be consulted.

The idea that Joyce read such newspapers as he could in 1890–91, as well as thereafter, is not startling. It conforms to his curiosity and precociously sceptical disposition as a boy, to his voracious reading of newspapers across his life, and the interest in newspapers to which his writing attests.

Joyce's relationship to Irish newspapers is central to an understanding of the development of his thinking on nationalism, and his mastery of its idiom. The 'Aeolus' episode in *Ulysses* alone, set in the offices of the *Freeman's Journal* and the *Evening Telegraph*, attests to the depth of his familiarity with the main nationalist daily newspaper and his consciousness of how its recent history was inextricably bound up with Parnell's rise and fall. A recurrent plaint of Joyce in exile in Trieste and Rome was that he was not being sent Irish newspapers, and it is clear that he read Arthur Griffith's papers *United Irishman* and *Sinn Féin* on a pretty consistent basis, to the point where they provided his main continuous newspaper source of intelligence on Ireland.[51]

Wherever he found himself, for most of his life Joyce was a compulsive reader of newspapers. Newspaper reading in what was a great newspaper age was not often the subject of comment, but Nino Franck, who knew Joyce in Paris from 1926, recalled that Joyce 'had the habit of reading each day four or five newspapers. He read *The Times*, *Le Temps*—also the *Neue Zürcher Zeitung*, the Swiss newspaper, and especially the *Osservatore Romano*.'[52] In his 'Modern Ireland' lecture of 1932–33, Yeats alluded shrewdly, if with some numerical exaggeration, to Joyce's exilic reading of Irish newspapers: 'He was to spend many years in Zurich and in Paris, reading half a dozen Irish newspapers a day, running his eye down the advertisement columns and the accounts of funerals and marriages that he might keep in mind the familiar streets and names.'[53] Joyce had also of course a thinly consummated shadow career as a journalist, his profession manqué.[54]

51. See chapter 13, 'Reading Ireland from Exile'; and Frank Callanan, 'James Joyce and the *United Irishman*, Paris 1902–3', *Dublin James Joyce Journal* 3 (2010): 51–103.

52. Rodgers, *Irish Literary Portraits*, 55.

53. W. B. Yeats, 'Modern Ireland', in *Irish Renaissance: A Gathering of Essays, Memoirs, Letters and Dramatic Poetry from the 'Massachusetts Review'*, ed. Robin Skelton and David R. Clark (Dublin: Dolmen, 1965), 20.

54. He wrote for newspapers, notably in his book reviews for the *Dublin Daily Express* in 1902–3, and his Irish pieces for *Il Piccolo della Sera* in Trieste in 1907–12. As a young man in Paris he had hoped to become the Paris correspondent of the *Irish Times*, but succeeded only in publishing a

The way in which Joyce read newspapers and his deployment of material derived from them in his work underwent several mutations over time, but his practice of reading newspapers and drawing on what he read was a continuous feature of his life. Scholarly work on Joyce's notebooks for *Finnegans Wake* has demonstrated how his writing and newspaper reading were interwoven.[55]

There is a dearth of direct evidence in relation to Joyce's pre-exilic reading of Irish newspapers, but his vivid apprehension of Irish politics in the Split and of the course of the Parnell myth could only have been attained through a regular perusal of the Irish nationalist newspapers through the 1890s and for the remainder of his time in Ireland. Three phases of his newspaper reading in Ireland might be posited. The first is an initiatory phase in 1890–92, when he sought to educate himself as best he could in Irish politics, and to enlarge on what he was being told by his father and John Kelly; the second is in 1893–98, when he was an increasingly disenchanted observer of the course of Parnellite politics after Parnell; the third ran from 1898 to 1902, when he was in University College. Joyce's thinking on Parnell and the Split had acquired definite form before he entered University College in 1898.

His writings are replete with references to the newspapers of the Split. In his article 'L'ombra di Parnell' in *Il Piccolo della Sera* in April 1912, he wrote of the beleaguered Irish leader, 'The Irish press poured the phials of their spitefulness over him and the woman he loved.'[56] To take one instance from his fictional work, in *Finnegans Wake* the word 'Instoppressible' features,[57] a cross-pun on *Insuppressible*, the paper Healy

single piece, an interview with a French competitor in the motor derby, the Gordon-Bennett race, published in the paper on 7 April 1903 (*OCPW* 77–79). Joyce wrote to his mother, 'It would be quite easy for me to send any kind of news to that intelligent organ-motor news, dead men's news, any news: for I have all the Paris newspapers at my disposal'. Joyce to May Joyce, 8 February 1903, *Letters II* 27. On his first return to Dublin in 1909, he was prepared to pose as a correspondent of *Il Piccolo della Sera* and paid a number of visits to the offices of the *Evening Telegraph* on which he would draw for the 'Aeolus' episode of *Ulysses*. Ellmann, *James Joyce*, 288–90.

55. Vincent Deane, Daniel Ferrer, and Geert Lernout, eds., *The 'Finnegans Wake' Notebooks at Buffalo* (Turnhout: Brepols, 2004).

56. *OCPW* 196.

57. *FW* 568.16.

brought into being after Parnell repossessed *United Ireland*, and his ‘Stop Thief’ (a phrase which was itself a Wakean refrain) editorial in the *National Press*. With this intricately succinct reference, the newspaper controversy of the Split in Parnell’s lifetime flickered once again into print forty years on.

Two instances strikingly attest to the extent to which Joyce was steeped in the newspaper controversies of the Split. At Castlecomer on 16 December 1890, in the course of the turbulent North Kilkenny by-election, Parnell was struck in the eye by a missile which he claimed was a preparation of lime, described as quicklime in some Parnell accounts.[58] Michael Davitt gave an interview to the Liberal *Pall Mall Gazette* that it carried in its edition of 1 January 1891 in which, seeking to play down the impact of the scenes of disorder in the Kilkenny election that had been prominently reported in the British papers, he declared that ‘this fight at Kilkenny was full of fun and Irish good humour throughout.’[59] This prompted a deferred retort from Joyce, in his magnificently splenetic ‘Gas from a Burner’, written in mid-September 1912 on the train journey back to Trieste after his last visit to Ireland:

> That lovely land that always sent
> Her writers and artists to banishment
> And in a spirit of Irish fun
> Betrayed her leaders, one by one.
> ’Twas Irish humour, wet and dry,
> Flung quicklime into Parnell’s eye.[60]

What is significant is Joyce’s deployment after an interval of twenty years of a comment Davitt made to the *Pall Mall Gazette* immediately after the episode. That comment had not been republished or adverted to in the interval. It was evidently a source of offence to well-informed

58. F.S.L. Lyons, *Fall of Parnell*, 167–68; Callanan, *Parnell Split*, 67–71.

59. *Pall Mall Gazette*, 1 January 1891. I have not succeeded in finding a citation of Davitt’s remark in an Irish newspaper. The interview is mentioned in the *Evening Telegraph* of 2 and 5 January 1891, but without the ‘Irish good humour’ quotation.

60. *PSW* 103.

Parnellites in 1891. They never forgave Davitt his attacks on Parnell in the Split: bitter oral memory and the newspaper source merged.[61]

Joyce did not forget Castlecomer. In 1939, two years before his own death and suffering from severely compromised eyesight, he pointedly added to the proofs of Gorman's biography at the point it dealt with his final departure from Ireland a note explaining his failure to return to Ireland thereafter: 'Having a vivid memory of the incident at Castlecomer when quicklime was flung into the eyes of their dying leader, Parnell, by a chivalrous Irish mob, he did not wish a similar unfortunate occurrence to interfere with the composition of the book [*Finnegans Wake*] he was trying to write.'[62]

The second reference takes its cue from the twinned editorials that appeared in the *National Press* the day after news of Parnell's death reached Dublin. The first article was pretty ferocious, but the second, entitled 'Let Dissension Cease', contained the most stinging provocation. Two sentences stood out: 'With the death of Mr. Parnell the last pretext for faction died. All honest lovers of their country may shake hands over his open grave.'[63] The *National Press* editorials had a much wider impact than Davitt's interview with the *Pall Mall Gazette*. They achieved an instant notoriety, but again were never republished or quoted beyond the contemporary newspaper controversy they engendered. Half a century later, Joyce incorporated in *Finnegans Wake* a plangent reworking of Healy's sentence: 'We strike hands over his bloodied warsheet but we are pledged entirely to his green mantle.'[64] Like Davitt's comment, Healy's phrase was seared in Joyce's memory.

61. When Francis Sheehy-Skeffington's biography of Davitt was reviewed in *Sinn Féin*, the reviewer (probably Griffith) took exception to the author's assertion that Davitt had put the issues of the Split 'without rancour': 'The references to the leader he had deserted as one of "Cromwell's breed", "the Cromwellian", and his allusions to the woman in the case, are, we presume unknown to the guileless writer of this book, or else he is ignorant of the meaning of the word "rancour"' (20 June 1908).

62. Gorman, *James Joyce*, 217; see Ellmann, *James Joyce*, 338. Whatever was thrown at Parnell, it was not quicklime.

63. *National Press*, 8 October 1891; *United Ireland*, 17 October 1891; Callanan, *T. M. Healy*, 409.

64. *FW* 131.20–21.

The issue of Joyce's access to newspapers in 1890–91 arises. Joyce did not have anything approaching continuous access to newspapers at this time. He may have had some limited chance access to newspapers in Clongowes. Curiously the Jesuit provincial Fr Timothy Kenny received complaints that the scholastics and others in Clongowes were discussing 'divorces and other indelicate subjects', and much given to reading the *Pall Mall Gazette*,[65] but Joyce certainly did not get the benefit of their indiscretion. His principal reading of the papers has to have taken place at home, in the vacations or after he was taken out of Clongowes at the end of 1891. It is the episodic nature of his access to newspapers that suggests that his knowledge of the newspapers of the Split was later supplemented by consulting the National Library or some other public library in which back numbers of newspapers were available. If Joyce was interested in establishing for himself what transpired in the course of the Split, the only source available to 1898 was the contemporary newspapers. There was nowhere else to go in the absence of a published narrative of the Split in Ireland. Richard Barry O'Brien's biography of Parnell, when it appeared in 1898, while important for Joyce's understanding of Parnell's personality, did not capture the terrible escalatory rhythm of the Split, nor did it address Joyce's need to apprehend with exactitude the anti-Parnellite onslaught. Joyce somehow felt the pulse of the Split ('hunt me the journeyon')[66] through a self-acquired knowledge that could only have come from newspapers. Consulting newspaper files was not at the time an uncommon practice in Dublin,[67] and the idea that Joyce read some of the newspapers in 1890–91, and did so more comprehensively thereafter, is not particularly controversial and is consistent with the curiosity and sceptical disposition of the youthful Joyce. The implications, however, are far reaching. Joyce's cross-referencing of what he had been told to a textual source is a significant

65. Kenny-Devitt correspondence, 18 October 1891, Clongowes Archives, quoted in Bradley, *James Joyce's Schooldays*, 61.

66. *FW* 594.7.

67. See, for example, T. M. Healy's *Why Ireland Is Not Free: A Study of Twenty Years in Irish Politics* (Dublin: *Nation* office, 1898), which is a ferocious polemical account of the political career of John Dillon put together largely from newspaper sources.

moment in his intellectual development. He may have been encouraged to read the newspapers by his father and John Kelly, but to the extent that his purpose in doing so was to substantiate what they had told him, it was an enquiry that he pursued in his own right. Joyce thereby became electively an adherent of Parnell from a precociously young age.

As already discussed, *A Portrait* presents a highly stylised fictional account of Joyce's acquisition of a Parnellite allegiance in boyhood that is consistent both with the subsequent development of his Parnellism and with his attitude to his father. In *A Portrait*, Mr Casey is the ardent Parnellite. Mr Dedalus takes his side, but his utterances are mainly boisterously anticlerical in the manner of John Stanislaus. Joyce's rendering of the stop-start rhythm of the argument is superb. Mr Dedalus detests Dante Riordan and administers a couple of calculated fillips to keep the controversy going. His detestation of Dante, and enjoyment of argument, prompts him to subvert the role of the Christmas paterfamilias that he had adopted at the outset for Stephen's benefit. The end of the Christmas dinner scene is so perfect that we do not fully register the note of incredulousness in Stephen's looking up to find that 'his father's eyes were full of tears'. It is as if, at least up to that point, Stephen is unsure how seriously to take his father's support of Parnell. Stephen remains through the dinner unsure which side is right. He is weighing what is said. He makes up his mind thereafter. It is only the next day when he makes an unsuccessful attempt to write a Parnell poem—signalling that his Parnellism has a bearing on his development as an artist—that we know Stephen has embraced the cause of the dead leader.

It is not merely that the idea that Joyce's youthful identification with Parnell is pious filial mimesis is wrong. What is rendered in *A Portrait* is a moving beyond the father. The refusal to take his father's siding with Parnell on faith and his insistence on exercising his own judgement on the basis of whatever information he could garner is a calculated gesture of independence that is itself Parnellian. From it derives the fierceness and tenacity of Joyce's Parnellism. The point of origin of Joyce's Parnellism is vividly if liberally fictionalised in *A Portrait*.

The setting in time of the Christmas dinner scene afforded a strategic vantage point. Joyce had not set eyes on, nor had he stood and cheered, the Irish leader, but his boyhood was directly touched by his passing. Joyce prized the sense that he stood in a generationally distinctive relation to the dead leader, and marshalled with characteristic remorselessness the imaginative perspective it gave him. He was to perfect a technique of writing about Parnell scrupulously co-related to the indirection of his own experience of the Split, in which he approached Parnell through his myth rather than hazard the frontal portrayal of the leader he had never seen. His retrieval of Parnell's persona through myth and the traces of memory merges biography with the elusive proximities of a ghost story.

The Christmas dinner scene gave explosive expression to Joyce's Parnellism. At the time of its publication (in serial form in 1914 in the *Egoist*, and as a book in 1916–17), Irish politics was finally changing phases. It might have been thought that Parnell was safely dead, entombed beneath alternating layers of recrimination and panegyric. With the publication of *A Portrait*, the Split, as if out of nowhere, flared into life in all its rawness. Joyce had been thwarted in the publication of 'Ivy Day in the Committee Room', which he had written in Rome in late 1905 and which is concerned with an election in Dublin when the Split still had faint, if fast-fading, traces in municipal politics. With the Christmas dinner scene, Joyce contrived in some degree to redress the loss of the contemporary impact of 'Ivy Day'. He redirected the course of the posthumous Parnell myth in taking it back almost to its origin, stripping out its bland post-1900 commemorative accretions. The Parnell chapter was not closed after all.

T. M. Healy and the Newspaper War of the Split

The issue of Joyce's relation to newspapers has a particular significance because historically the Split was a newspaper war of words. The instrumentality of Parnell's defeat was journalistic. In a way that was and remains unprecedented in Irish politics, the sound and fury of the Split was transmitted by newsprint. It is the role of newspapers that gives the Split its ambiguous modernity. In North Kilkenny the correspondent of the Liberal *Daily News* wrote,

> Nothing in this struggle has more forcibly struck me than the eagerness of the people to ascertain the truth. Electioneering literature is not wasted upon them. Neither wind, nor rain prevents them from coming out of their houses by the roadsides to pick up—or perhaps chase the circulars and copies of newspapers thrown to them by passing cars. You may see at every hamlet or wayside smithy, and at almost every shop door, a group of two or three or more in earnest debates over its leaflet or journal. The longer this goes on the fainter grows Mr. Parnell's prospects of victory.[68]

Entering the fray in Ballinakill, Dr Tanner, an anti-Parnellite parliamentarian of near-lunatic eccentricity, from his brake 'produced a great bundle of copies of *Suppressed United Ireland* which he scattered broadside amongst the assembled multitude'.[69] Newspapers were of the first importance in the Split, as Parnell's seizure of *United Ireland*, Healy and his associates' starting of *Suppressed United Ireland* (which became *Insuppressible*), and the later establishment of the *National Press* demonstrate.

The anti-Parnellites had the advantage in the newspaper war, and that advantage grew as the Split progressed. Parnell's campaign was somewhat archaic: it comprised his campaigning across the country, the reporting of his speeches in the *Freeman's Journal*, and the Parnellite press vaunting in extravagant and often stilted rhetoric his merits as the indispensable leader of Irish nationalism. It was, moreover, difficult to scale back the grandiose tenor of the campaign as Parnell encountered defeats in Ireland in succession to that in Committee Room 15.

Healy proved a remorselessly innovative master of the demotic in the newspaper war. He assailed what he depicted as Parnell's egotism, his disregard of the Liberal and clerical allies of nationalism. He created a savagely revisionist caricature of Parnell as a leader whom he accused

68. *Daily News*, 20 December 1890.

69. *Daily Chronicle*, 17 December 1890.

of a rapacious selfishness that reflected his Anglo-Irish landlord origins. His idiom had a supremacist 'nativist' edge that stopped just short of overt sectarianism and anticipated the chauvinism of D. P. Moran's *Leader* a decade later. His virulence had a terrible freshness to it. His attacks on Parnell's relations with Katharine O'Shea were savagely personalised; these he sought to justify as a proportionate retaliation for what he condemned as Parnell's persistence in preferring his personal interests over those of the Irish people. Healy's purpose was to destroy the lingering residue of deference towards Parnell and to embolden displays of open disrespect for him. His attacks culminated in his denunciation, in the controversy over the Paris funds that followed Parnell's death, of Katharine Parnell as 'a proved British prostitute', which elicited the oblique intervention of Gladstone to restrain him.[70]

Newspapers drove the Split and are the principal source for the course it took. They are central to the problem of interpreting nationalist public opinion. The evidence, such as it is, suggests a reflexive allegiance to Parnell on the part of the people until they were persuaded otherwise. It is not possible to identify a popular anti-Parnellism that existed independently of and was not mediated through the anti-Parnellite press. Seemingly spontaneous demonstrations of opposition to Parnell, such as occurred frequently in the Carlow election, faithfully adopted the motifs of the *National Press*. Healy's rhetoric shaped rather than shadowed the popular response to Parnell in the Split. His lethal phrasemaking entered public consciousness. It served as a primer for anti-Parnellite spokesmen; was adopted by parish orators, lay and clerical; and pervaded the anti-Parnellite provincial press. The consequences overran the Split. Healy had contrived to invest the repudiation of Parnell with a vehemence and a finality it did not possess. Those nationalist voters, probably numerous, who aligned themselves with the anti-Parnellite cause reluctantly, and on the pragmatic grounds that Healy also urged, were implicated in his rhetorical strategy.[71]

70. Callanan, *Parnell Split*, 187–91.

71. Callanan, *T. M. Healy*, 258–59.

Healy's journalism was touched by genius. His newspapers taunted the Parnellite press with the inferiority of their communication skills. The sub-editorials of *Insuppressible* and the *National Press* carried running critiques of the utterances of Parnellite spokesmen, editors, and journalists, setting their invariant grandiloquence of utterance against the slide in their champion's fortunes. These commentaries were stingingly acute and droll, and reflected an intimate knowledge of the business and personalities of Irish journalism. They intermittently erupted into comic full-blown editorial pastiches of the rhetoric of Parnellite nationalism. These were exuberantly developed. It is a curious irony that Joyce's most accomplished precursor as a parodist of Irish nationalist rhetoric was Timothy Michael Healy.

The convention among Parnellites was not to utter Healy's name, and Joyce's references to him before *Finnegans Wake* are sparse. One effect of Healy's idiom on Joyce was to tighten still further the laconic Parnellism of his aphorisms on Ireland and Irish nationalism, and to sharpen his emphasis on the spareness of Parnell's idiom. Healy's journalism further served to inoculate Joyce against the sullen humour of Moran's *Leader*, which so many of his contemporaries in University College were to find irresistible. By the time Joyce came to write *Finnegans Wake*, Healy had acquired a new persona as Governor-General of the Irish Free State from 1922 to 1928. That prompted a different approach. Healy's name appears with some frequency in the *Wake*, but—Joyce's revenge—it indelibly signified the negative of Parnell's. The recurrent nativist idiom in the *Wake* of accusation, hunting down, and persecution owes more than a little to Joyce's attentive reading of the *National Press*.

The Parnellism of John O'Leary

The ambience of Joyce's father's circle of friends was Parnellite, and Joyce learned from newspapers of Parnell's other prominent followers. Of these, the only supporter outside his father's circle who might be surmised to have influenced his Parnellism is the Fenian leader John O'Leary (1830–1907), the most forceful defender of Parnell who had not been an adherent before the Split. In his letters to the *Freeman's Journal*,

O'Leary sounded a scornfully individualistic, almost Carlylean, note that Parnell's partisans in the Irish Party aspired to but rarely attained.

When he returned to Dublin from exile in Paris in January 1885, O'Leary remained a member of the supreme council of the IRB and initially held aloof from Parnellism. He had always been opposed to the linking through the Land League of political nationalism with agrarianism, and following his return, his principal involvement in political controversy was his outspoken opposition to the Plan of Campaign (which his enemies ascribed to his ownership of property in the town of Tipperary).[72] When he met Parnell on his return to Ireland, the two disagreed.[73] O'Leary was not opposed to Home Rule but, as Yeats recalled, he 'had a particular hatred for the rush of emotion that followed the announcement of Gladstone's conversion, for what was called "The Union of Hearts" and derided its sentimentality. "Nations may respect one another", he would say, "they cannot love".'[74]

O'Leary was sixty at the time of the divorce crisis and broken by the death of his sister. Katharine Tynan wrote that 'the Parnell struggle was just the distraction the old Chief needed. It made him young again.'[75] O'Leary told Barry O'Brien, 'I did not trouble myself much about the matter, until the Grand Old Man [Gladstone] interfered.' The divorce case had been nothing to him: 'It was for the Grand Young Man [Parnell] to get out of his scrape as best he could. I was not going to trouble my head about him, but when the Grand Old Man interfered, that gave a new aspect to the affair. It then became a question of submitting to the dictation of an Englishman, and for the first time I resolved to support Parnell.'[76]

The Split brought O'Leary back into active politics.[77] He had a clear conception of Parnell's commanding ability, and he dismissed the

72. Marcus Bourke, *John O'Leary: A Study in Irish Separatism* (Tralee: Anvil, 1967), 195–99.

73. Katharine Tynan, *Twenty-Five Years: Reminiscences* (London: Smith, Elder, 1913).

74. W. B. Yeats, *Autobiographies* (London: Macmillan, 1955), 210–11.

75. Katharine Tynan, *The Middle Years* (London: Constable, 1916), 25.

76. R. B. O'Brien, *Charles Stewart Parnell*, 2:253–56; see also 336.

77. Katharine Tynan, *Memories* (London: E. Nash and Grayson, 1924), 105. See also R. B. O'Brien, *Charles Stewart Parnell*, 2:253.

political capacity of the collective anti-Parnellite leadership. Temperamentally averse to sanctimoniousness, he scorned what he regarded as Irish cringing in the face of British moralising. Tynan recalled him roaring, 'Good God in Heaven. . . . Did any sane country ever throw over a leader for gallantry?'[78] While his interventions were not many, they were direct, cutting, laconic, and superbly in character. His first letter was published in the *Freeman's Journal* on the morning the Irish Party assembled in Committee Room 15:

> I say as plainly as I can that Mr. Parnell is the only man who has shown the capacity to lead, to use his own phrase, 'within the Constitution'. To talk of putting the leadership in commission, with your Justin McCarthys, Arthur O'Connors, and the like, is simply silly. The people want a man and not a committee. Mr. Parnell is, in my opinion, no more immaculate as a politician than as a man, but he is not only the fittest man intellectually to lead, but, so far as we know the only fit man, and it would be simply stupid and cowardly to abandon him because Mr. Gladstone screeches and his followers howl. We have been breaking most of the Commandments for years in Ireland, with all the aid possible from Mr. Gladstone and many other Englishmen, but when it comes to a breach of the Sixth (seventh), English morality is at once up in arms. We must suffer because the English sin, but they must at least allow us to refuse 'to compound for sins we are not inclined to by damning those we have no mind to'.[79]

Two weeks later as the Kilkenny election got under way, O'Leary weighed in to support Parnell's candidate with an attack on the manifesto of the anti-Parnellites:

> The seceders, secessionists, kickers, backsliders, or whatever else a not grateful country may choose hereafter to call them, alleged, for what reason I could never make out, that their defection was based on Mr. Parnell's manifesto; but if they did not like it, they could deny

78. Tynan, *Memories*, 418.

79. O'Leary to editor, 30 November 1890, *Freeman's Journal*, 1 December 1890.

its force and fervour. There was a man—whether a good or a bad one is beside the question—behind it. But what is behind the manifesto of the now notorious forty-five? Simply an old woman, or possibly several, for a more nerveless, boneless, sapless production I never remember to have read. These gentlemen had apparently nothing to say, and they have said that nothing very ill.[80]

In March 1891 O'Leary wrote a public letter agreeing to become a member of the Parnell Leadership Committee: 'I have written more than once, since the commencement of the crisis, in words as strong as I could find, that I went straight for Parnell and dead against the Davitts, Healys, Tanners, and the like; and straight I mean to go with him as long as he goes for an Irish Parliament with independent powers, and that will be, I hope, for the rest of his life, if necessary'. He added, 'I condemned many things he said and did in the past, and I condemn them still, but I have ever held that in him, and in him alone, rested all our hopes from constitutional action. He made that Parliamentary Party which now stupidly and traitorously strives to unmake him.'[81]

Three weeks before Parnell's death, O'Leary defiantly asserted the consonance of support for Parnell with his Fenian convictions: 'If Mr. Parnell were dead tomorrow, I and men like me, who are above and before all things Irish nationalists, should never dream of following the party of clerical dictation and compromise with England. We go with Mr. Parnell so far as he goes, and insofar as he goes, for Irish freedom.'[82]

O'Leary's prominent presence, along with that of James Stephens, in the cortège at Parnell's funeral symbolised the Split's complex Parnellite-Fenian entente. With Parnell's death, the fractiousness of the Split entered a new phase and O'Leary drew back. His final intervention was a scathing riposte to an attack by John Dillon, which ended, 'I say no word upon the present political crisis, as I believe that the least said is soonest

80. O'Leary to editor, 12 December 1890, *Freeman's Journal*, 13 December 1890.

81. O'Leary to honorary secretaries of the Parnell Leadership Committee, *Freeman's Journal*, 10 March 1891.

82. O'Leary to editor, *Freeman's Journal*, 14 and 15 September 1891. See also Callanan, *Parnell Split*, 251–52.

mended just now. Need, more need, there is for thinking, and need for acting too; but for talking there seems to me little if any need, save for newspaper contributors or professional agitators, and I belong to neither of these classes.'[83]

O'Leary died fifteen years later on 16 March 1907, aged seventy-six. A week later, on 22 March, *Il Piccolo della Sera* in Trieste carried an article by Joyce, 'Il Fenianismo: L'ultimo Feniano'. In the piece, Joyce recalls the old man he had attentively observed on the Dublin quays: 'He could often be seen walking along the river, a venerable old man dressed mostly in light clothes, with a flowing head of white hair, almost bent double with age and suffering; he would halt before the darkened shops of the antiquarian book sellers and then, having made his purchase, he would return along the river.' In this, the first of his articles the Triestine paper carried, Joyce was concerned principally to describe the position of Fenianism in nineteenth-century Irish politics and its relationship to the contemporary Sinn Féin. To emphasise the obsoleteness of old-style Fenianism—the death 'perhaps marked the disappearance of the last actor in the turbulent drama that was Fenianism'—he overstated the isolation of O'Leary's later years and suppressed the rich coda to O'Leary's career which followed his return to Ireland from Paris. The only allusion to Parnell was indirect, veiled in the flourish with which the article ended: 'Now that he is dead, his compatriots escort him to his tomb with a great show of pomp, because the Irish, even when they break the hearts of those who sacrifice their lives for their country, never fail to show a great reverence for the dead.'[84]

The perspective on the Split that Joyce adopted was typically that of Parnell himself. He was largely indifferent to what members of Parnell's party had to add. There are, however, affinities to O'Leary's Parnellism. O'Leary's idiom resembled that of John Stanislaus without the profanity and, like John Stanislaus, it was only in the Split that he rallied to Parnell. His interventions were marked by an old-fashioned sense of

83. O'Leary to editor, 28 October 1891, *Freeman's Journal*, 29 October 1891. Dillon's speech, in Dundalk, is reported in *Freeman's Journal*, 26 October 1891.

84. Joyce, 'Il Fenianismo: L'ultimo Feniano', *Il Piccolo della Sera*, 22 March 1907, in *OCPW* 138–41.

honour and plain speaking, and a certain pride of bearing. He gave terse public expression to what Joyce was hearing from his father and John Kelly.

It is likely that O'Leary's proud, spare idiom had some effect on Joyce, and in one instance this may have a particular salience. A corollary of O'Leary's romantic individualism was that, in turning on Parnell, the majority of the Irish Party had shown an inconstancy and an emotional febrility that was unmanly, whence his characterisation of the anti-Parnellite manifesto as the product of 'simply an old woman, or possibly several'. The image was not unique to O'Leary—in Kilkenny during the by-election Parnell himself had referred to 'all the old women and humbugs in England who are taking this opportunity of airing their virtue all over the country'[85]—but it is characteristic of him. Whatever its origin, the image was carried over into Joyce's writing in the denigratory feminising of T. M. Healy. In the *Dubliners* story 'A Mother', it is the pointedly named Miss Healy who professes to support and then reneges on Kathleen Kearney in the concert. In *A Portrait* it is an old woman who mouths Healy's catchcries against Parnell, into whose eye the usually benign Mr Casey spits the tobacco he is chewing. In the 'Aeolus' episode of *Ulysses*, J. J. O'Molloy refers to Gerald Fitzgibbon, then a lord justice of appeal, sitting with T. M. Healy on the Trinity College Estates Commission. 'He is sitting with a sweet thing, Myles Crawford said, in a child's frock.'[86] Joyce's satiric transgendering and infantilisation of Healy harks back to a specific Parnellite idiom of the Split.[87]

The respect for O'Leary that Joyce's Trieste article attested to, and their common Parnellism in the Split, is significant in constituting a link between Joyce and Yeats through the medium of Parnell. Yeats was politically a disciple of O'Leary and publicly associated with him: they collaborated in the establishment of the Young Ireland League, a Parnellite front in all but name, in September 1891.

85. *Daily News*, 22 December 1890.

86. *U* 7.802.

87. Joyce's allegorical depiction of Ireland as a toothless old woman is better treated as a discrete image with a different line of descent.

The issue of O'Leary's possible colouring of Joyce's Parnellism also raises the question of whether the Split influenced Joyce's attitude to Fenianism. Parnell in the Split was accused by the anti-Parnellites and the clergy of engaging in an 'appeal to the hillsides'. Determined to reassert his leadership, Parnell had no intention of compromising his commitment to constitutional nationalism.[88] He was, however, heavily dependent on the support of Fenian activists and maintained close relations with leading Fenians through the course of the Split.[89] Some of Parnell's younger adherents were drawn to Fenianism after his death, but Joyce did not follow this trajectory. Though historically sympathetic to Fenianism—his receptiveness owed something to the influence of his father—he remained sceptical of physical force.

Joyce and the Posthumous Parnell Myth

Joyce's nationalism departed from the contemporary norm of a child's acceptance of an Irish nationalist family identity. It was an elective Parnellite nationalism engendered in the Split and its immediate aftermath. He embraced nationalism just as its prevailing form had sundered. His nationalism was not petrified at the moment of Parnell's death. It was informed by a fluid critique which owed much to the disillusionment wrought by the politics of the long Split from 1890 to 1900.

The fact that Joyce grew to adolescence and adulthood in an Ireland dominated by the memory of Parnell is often taken to suggest that it was unremarkable that he should have been touched by Parnellite allegiance. This ignores, as well as the electiveness of his identification with Parnell, the fact that the posthumous Parnell myth was a frail construct. Joyce was quick to realise that the means by which Parnell was remembered did him little justice. By about the mid-1890s Joyce came to disavow as futile and un-Parnellian (i.e., lacking fidelity to Parnell's character and political principles) the conventional modes by which Parnell's political legacy was fostered and his memory commemorated.

88. Callanan, *Parnell Split*, 238–59.

89. McGee, *IRB*, 195–211.

Joyce's was a critical, dissentient strain of Parnellism after Parnell. He stood virtually alone.

What tends to be missed is that for Joyce the Split was a lost opportunity for modernisation. The victory of the anti-Parnellites was for Joyce, as both a nationalist and a contemporary European, a reactionary reflux. In rejecting the opportunity to achieve the aspiration of an ancient nation, the Irish had also refused modern European statehood. It was these considerations rather than a fetishisation of the Parnell of the fall that inspired and maintained Joyce's unsparing indictment of his countrymen's repudiation of their leader.

F.S.L. Lyons diagnosed in Joyce 'a bad case of arrested Parnellism'.[90] This could be taken as an argument that Joyce's espousal of Parnellite allegiance was self-indulgent and lacking in realism in its refusal to accept both the political constraints created by the massive repudiation of Parnell in 1891 and the anti-Parnellite ascendancy that defined the configuration of Irish politics in the quarter century following. But it is consistent with the radicalism of Joyce's critique of the Split that he should have refused to accept a conventionally constricted conception of what was politically realistic in the wake of Parnell's defeat. Joyce did not have to conform to the constraints to which a politician was subject. He was unforgiving towards his countrymen in a way that no Parnellite politician could afford, and that few of Parnell's contemporary adherents who were not politicians had the stamina to be. That unforgivingness was Joyce's political and intellectual homage to Parnell.

It has also been suggested that the overthrow of Parnell afforded Joyce a lifelong opportunity to rail against the Irish proclivity for treachery and betrayal and a pretext to disengage from Irish politics. This reflects a failure to take seriously what Joyce wrote on political subjects and on Ireland.

If there is anything enigmatic in Joyce's relation to Parnell and to the Split, it is its persistence. Joyce had already interiorised aspects of Parnell's views and persona—as if defensively—and he could have left it at that. He could have left it as a childhood experience. Any purpose he

90. F.S.L. Lyons, 'James Joyce's Dublin', 20.

may have had as a boy to vindicate the dead leader did not last; it survived into his maturity only in a radically different form. Joyce's Parnellism is consistent across his life, but there is nothing inevitable or linear in his development of themes and motifs relating to Parnell or deriving from the Split.

What is certain is that Joyce did not set out to proselytise his contemporaries on behalf of Parnell or the Parnellite cause. As a student in University College, Dublin from 1898 to 1902, his Parnellism as an active principle was in abeyance and he veiled the intensity of his imaginative engagement with Parnell. The Parnellite cause seems to have slipped into the realm of the archaic, in the sense of being perceived to lack contemporary political salience, and to have had little bearing on Joyce's prospective future as an artist as he then conceived it.

This changed. Joyce's Parnellism regained traction. His experiences in his own life, and the course of contemporary Irish politics, reaffirmed his identification with Parnell. Joyce in exile became exaggeratedly receptive to even faint stirrings of Parnell's memory, as if easily persuaded that Parnell was not after all forgotten. Most of all, he subsumed his Parnellism into his fiction.

Politically the outcome of the long Split after almost a decade of recrimination was the reunion of Parnell's fractured party in 1900, premised on consigning the Split to history. The negotiation of the emotional and intellectual residues of the Split was finally extruded from the political domain into the imaginative. What was to endure was the radical recasting of the relationship between the literary and the political in Ireland. There was to be an extraordinary rendering of Parnell's myth and of the Split in the writings of W. B. Yeats and Joyce, but no political *relancement* of Parnell's cause and memory.

5

'Christ and Caesar'

THE ORIGINS OF JOYCE'S THESIS OF THE 'TWO MASTERS'

The National League is all at sixes and sevens; the Catholic Church alone remains erect in the midst of the Irish chaos. Its bishops in council are the nearest approach to an Irish Senate that is to be found in Ireland; its priesthood constitute a more intelligent, respectable, and public-spirited body than the retinue of nominees who were decorated with the affix M. P. at the good pleasure of Mr. Parnell.

—W. T. STEAD, JANUARY 1891[1]

But I cannot hide from myself the fear and danger lest the completeness of Mr. Parnell's overthrow may imperceptibly lead to the substitution of clerical supremacy for his personal supremacy. . . . The priests have done well and gloriously so far.

—JOHN FRANCIS TAYLOR, JULY 1891[2]

IN HIS 1912 article 'L'ombra di Parnell', published in Trieste, Joyce summarised the course of the Split from the Parnellite perspective: 'He was

1. W. T. Stead, 'North Kilkenny and Its Moral', *Paternoster Review* 1, no. 4 (January 1891): 339–40.

2. *Manchester Guardian*, 14 July 1891.

deposed by the Nationalists obeying Gladstone's orders. Of the eighty-three deputies, only eight remained faithful to him. The Irish press poured the phials of their spitefulness over him and the woman he loved. The peasants of Castlecomer threw quicklime in his eyes. He went from county to county, from city to city, "like a hunted hind", a spectral figure with the signs of death upon his brow. Within a year he died of a broken heart at the age of forty-five.'[3] The parliamentary arithmetic was wrong: twenty-six members of the party remained in the committee room; forty-five departed. Joyce was perhaps confusing the outcome with that of the 1892 general election, in which nine Parnellites were returned against seventy-two anti-Parnellites. What Joyce described as the 'elastic quality of Gladstone's liberalism' was what Parnell had concluded at the outset would 'only yield to force', in the socio-political sense. If he had a sceptically realistic understanding of what he called 'the history of Anglo-Saxon Liberalism',[4] Joyce regarded Gladstone's portentous moralising with amused contempt. His suspicion of Liberal professions of disinterested altruism would set him apart from his more credulous contemporaries in University College.

The locus classicus of Joyce's 'two masters' thesis of the twin subjection of Ireland to British government and to the Catholic Church—to secular empire and ecclesiastical imperium—is in the opening 'Telemachus' episode of *Ulysses*. The Englishman Haines, who professes Liberal sentiments, at least in relation to Ireland, is pressing Stephen on the subject of his religious belief, eager to establish that he is not a believer:

> —After all, I should think you are able to free yourself. You are your own master, it seems to me.
>
> —I am a servant of two masters, Stephen said, English and an Italian.
>
> —Italian? Haines said. . . .
>
> —The imperial British state, Stephen answered, his colour rising, and the holy Roman catholic and apostolic church.[5]

3. *OCPW* 195–96.
4. *OCPW* 158.
5. *U* 1.636–45.

In his response, Haines screens out the reference to the dominion of the Church, which he doesn't understand: 'I can quite understand that, he said calmly. An Irishman must think like that, I daresay. We feel in England that we have treated you rather unfairly. It seems history is to blame.'[6] Stephen, however, is now thinking of the Church, and of the words of the Nicene Creed: 'The proud potent titles clanged over Stephen's memory the triumph of their brazen bells: *et unam sanctam catholicam et apostolicam ecclesiam*.'[7]

Haines's statement that 'it seems history is to blame' is an exoneration of the British state, but it also offers a false exculpation of the Irish for their submission to the Catholic Church. Stephen will not exempt his countrymen from historical responsibility. The term 'masters', with the connotation of servitude, was intended to carry a charge of demeaning acquiescence by the Irish people in the masterdom of the Church. But what gives it its rhetorical force is Joyce's use of the first person. He is also a servant of two masters. It seems unlikely that here Stephen is assuming a sacrificial burden: rather he seems to be acknowledging that he comes out of an enfeebled Catholic nationalist tradition, but one that does bear on him personally ('his colour rising'). With the idea of servitude comes the imperative of revolt, connecting with William Blake's idea of the twin oppression of priest and king. In the 'Circe' episode later in the novel, Stephen, more heroically than he intends, in the presence of the two British soldiers taps his brow and says, 'But in here it is I must kill the priest and the king.'[8]

The origins of Joyce's 'two masters' thesis and its duality lie in Gladstone's intervention in the Split sustained by the Catholic Church. Though a once and future prime minister, Gladstone was not in office at the time of Parnell's fall in 1890–91 and so could not really be considered to represent 'the Imperial British State'. Irish deference to Gladstone's Liberal party was uncoerced and voluntary, as was Irish allegiance to the Catholic Church. While therefore the 'two masters' thesis related to the fact that the two standing structures of authority in Ireland were those of the

6. *U* 1.647–49.
7. *U* 1.650–51.
8. *U* 15.4436–37.

British state in Ireland and of the Catholic Church—an equation offensive in itself to most nationalists—it carries in Joyce's writing the resonance of the Split. In Joyce's abhorrence of the confluence of thought of the nonconformist conscience in Britain and the Catholic Church in Ireland during the Split, it is possible to discern the distant origins of Joyce's intimation of the *coincidentia oppositorum,* that opposing ideas may touch, which was of importance in his later thinking on politics and history.

Joyce at other points of writing comes close to the 'two masters' proposition. As he left Ireland in 1912 for the last time, he wrote in 'Gas from a Burner',

O Ireland my first and only love
Where Christ and Caesar are hand in glove![9]

But it is in 'Telemachus' that the proposition acquired the complete and definitive formulation that had theretofore seemed to elude Joyce.

'The Bishops and the Party': The Role of the Church in the Split

To understand the origins and political cogency of Joyce's 'two masters' thesis, one has to consider the role that the Church played in the overthrow of Parnell, and the co-mingling of Irish Catholicism and the 'nonconformist conscience' in Britain which had a lasting impact on Joyce.

The two most politically preponderant Irish Catholic bishops—William Walsh, Archbishop of Dublin, and Thomas Croke, Archbishop of Armagh—had held back from immediate intervention after the granting of the divorce decree nisi, hopeful (more so in Walsh's case than Croke's) that Parnell would resign, and persuaded that the Irish Party should act first.[10] It was a delay Parnell was to exploit.[11] On

9. *PSW* 103, lines 25–26.

10. Conor Cruise O'Brien took the subtly but significantly different view that 'the unity of Parnell's followers, in the face of the divorce-court decree, was so impressive that the Catholic bishops felt they had better "let events take their course"' (*Parnell and His Party*, 297). Cruise O'Brien's posing of the issue of what would have happened had the Irish Party's support of Parnell held firm is illuminating even if the premise is improbable.

11. Callanan, *Parnell Split*, 261–62.

3 December 1890, in the course of debates in Committee Room 15, the standing committee of the episcopacy issued an address condemning Parnell on moral grounds and 'as Irishmen devoted to our country.'[12] That condemnation was affirmed in the declaration of the hierarchy of 25 June 1891:

> We, the Archbishops and Bishops of Ireland, assembled in General Meeting for the first time since the issuing of the declaration of our Standing Committee last December, hereby record the solemn express of our judgement, as Pastors of the Irish people, that Mr. Parnell by his public misconduct, has utterly disqualified himself to be their political leader; that since the issuing of that declaration, Mr. Parnell's public action, and that of his recognised agents and organs in the Press, especially their open hostility to ecclesiastical authority, has supplied new and convincing proof that he is wholly unworthy of the confidence of Catholics; and we, therefore, feel bound, on his occasion, to call on our people to repudiate his leadership.[13]

The interventions of the Catholic Church were not confined to the two formal statements. Catholic clerics were vociferous in their opposition to Parnell. Bishops pronounced against Parnell in pastorals and in visitations of their dioceses. Priests delivered sermons, deployed their moral authority and social influence, and campaigned in elections against him.

Timothy Michael Healy, the dominant anti-Parnellite, exulted in the support of the bishops and clergy and sought to maximise its political impact, not least in demoralising the Parnellites. Of the inauguration of the National Federation in March, the *National Press*, established by Healy, boasted that 'every priest who has been prominent in the national movement was present at the meeting. Almost every bishop in Ireland concurred in its benediction.'[14] Healy exultantly asked at the meeting,

12. *Freeman's Journal*, 4 December 1890.

13. *National Press*, 4 July 1891.

14. *National Press*, 11 March 1891; Callanan, *Parnell Split*, 111–12. See also Emmet Larkin, *The Roman Catholic Church in Ireland and the Fall of Parnell, 1888–91* (Chapel Hill: University of North Carolina Press, 1979), 260.

'I wonder how many hillsiders Mr. Parnell would give for the four archbishops?'[15]

In late May, Archbishop Croke embarked on a visitation of his archdiocese thundering against Parnell. He denounced Parnell's weekly meetings, 'these Sunday excursions, so dishonouring to the Sabbath, which are meant to spread Parnellism over the length and breadth of the land, and to demolish the Irish Church.' He claimed that 'a most particular friend' of Parnell had told him that Parnell had said that 'the purpose' of the meetings was for 'knocking the bottom out of the priests.'[16] When Croke went on to demand at Kilteely an audit of national funds, Healy seized on the 'terrible indictment of Dr. Croke' to launch the 'Stop Thief' sequence of editorials in the *National Press*. 'He never suggested that Mr. Parnell was a thief. We say so.'[17]

The difficulty for the Parnellites was that any attack on the abuse of clerical influence was immediately seized on by Healy and ecclesiastical publicists as an attack on the Catholic faith and the Church itself. Parnell had always viewed the clergy with equanimity. On his death, an 'Old Disciple' wrote,

> It has been said that Mr. Parnell, being a Protestant, had a latent antipathy to the Irish priesthood. Even when they were against him in the early days of his land agitation, the contrary was the fact. 'They are the purest and most democratic priesthood in the world', he once said to the writer, 'when they are let alone. They have power and like to keep it'. Only two months ago he complained bitterly that they should pursue him so relentlessly—boycott his followers in every parish. 'They are good men', he added apologetically, 'but they were never safe in politics. They mean well, but they do not know anything about English parties. Gladstone will teach them a little', and he laughed cynically.[18]

15. Callanan, *Parnell Split*, 112.

16. *National Press*, 23 and 27 May 1891.

17. *National Press*, 1 June 1891; Callanan, *Parnell Split*, 121–23.

18. *Daily Chronicle*, 9 October 1891.

Barry O'Brien wrote that while Parnell 'felt the pressure of the priests at every turn' during the Split, he only saw him show anger once. When it was announced that priests were proposing to act as personation agents in North Kilkenny, Parnell was furious and demanded that a protest be prepared to go to the sheriff. The candidate pointed out that the priests had a legal right to act and asked him to dissuade Parnell from registering the protest. O'Brien pointed out to Parnell that if the priests had to be fought, it should be by Catholics, not by Protestants, and Parnell relented: 'A Protestant leader must not do this. But the system must be stopped. You Catholics must stop it. The priests themselves must be got to see that it is wrong.'[19]

Parnell as a Protestant was thus to a degree confessionally constrained in dealing with the issue. He did so in a way that was both measured and direct. He emphasised the demarcation of spheres of professional competence. He retorted to Croke's attacks during the visitation of the diocese, 'I will only say to his Grace that while I believe his Grace to be a most excellent archbishop, I don't believe him to be a good political leader. . . . If you want advice about politics or political service I advise you to go to men who have served their time at it, and who understand it.'[20]

Clerical dictation became a theme in its own right on the Parnellite side. Parnell declared in April, 'The struggle has been changed, and materially changed, in its character since its commencement. Influences have been used, intimidation has been exercised against the due exercise of the constitutional right of Irishmen, which will have to be met and defeated (cheers and cries of 'No Dictation'), and this battle will have to be fought out.'[21]

He made other like pronouncements thereafter and went a step further in emphasising the importance for Home Rule of 'tranquillising the alarm of the Protestants of Ireland.'[22]

19. R. B. O'Brien, *Charles Stewart Parnell,* 2:306–7.

20. *Freeman's Journal,* 1 June 1891; Callanan, *Parnell Split,* 261.

21. *Freeman's Journal,* 20 April 1891.

22. Callanan, *Parnell Split,* 263–64.

Parnell's Catholic lieutenants were more at large to address the theme of clerical dictation and bore the brunt of the furious anti-Parnellite and ecclesiastical retaliation. It began with Kilkenny. The Parnellites insisted that their defeat was the direct result of clerical intervention. The *Freeman's Journal* deprecated the 'wholesale intimidation that was practised upon the voters.'[23] Tim Harrington at the National League characterised the anti-Parnellite victory as 'a clerical success', through a political combination of which he as Catholic felt ashamed. Reflecting Parnell's own objection, he enumerated the priests who were the sole anti-Parnellite personation agents in the seven divisions of the constituency and hinted at an election petition.[24] This speech was immediately designated by the *Insuppressible,* in what was an excellent illustration of Healy's journalistic tactics, as 'Mr. Harrington's No Popery Oration.'[25]

The principal spokesmen of the hierarchy proved thin-skinned. Croke irately denounced Harrington's suggestion that the episcopal attack on Parnell reflected 'an innate love of Whiggery' by invoking his own record as a nationalist.[26] The more febrile Walsh, provoked by anodyne editorial criticism in the *Freeman's Journal* of an article that appeared in the *Revue Française,* despatched a furious protest against the *Freeman's Journal,* a paper with which he had had an active association, to the *Irish Catholic,* a journal which he had in the past openly disdained. He asserted that the *Freeman* article dealt with the question of Parnell's 'leadership' in 'a spirit not unworthy of the traditions of some leading organ of the atheistic Freemasonry of the continent':

> The mask, so clumsily worn for the last few weeks, has at length been thrown aside. There is no longer to be kept up even a semblance, even a pretence of respect for the religious teaching of the religious guides of Catholic people of Ireland. Morality, it is now openly proclaimed, is henceforth to take only a second place in public affairs. . . . At all

23. *Freeman's Journal,* 24–25 December 1891.
24. *Freeman's Journal,* 31 December 1890.
25. *Insuppressible,* 1 January 1891.
26. *Freeman's Journal,* 13 January 1891.

> events it is my duty, the duty of the Bishop of the diocese in which the *Freeman's Journal* is published to put the Catholics of Dublin upon their guard against its poisonous teaching.[27]

Walsh's disenchantment with the *Freeman's Journal* found expression in a further letter to the *Irish Catholic* in August, in which, to that paper's great satisfaction, he referred to the *Freeman* as 'the apostate journal'.[28]

A number of the bishop's Lenten pastorals were broadsides against Parnell and the Parnellites. Michael Logue, the Archbishop of Armagh, forcefully articulated his primitive conception of God's relation to Ireland in words lauded by the *Irish Catholic*.[29] He declared it was no longer possible when the people were being misled by partisan speakers and partisan journalists 'to ignore, despise, trample under foot principles that lie at the very foundation of religious life and social purity':

> The question which comes up for immediate solution is—are we to sacrifice these principles for some passing temporal advantage, even were that advantage real and placed within our reach? We know how our forefathers have answered that question. By an act of national apostasy they might have secured for themselves temporal prosperity, political influence, the goodwill of monarchs, the fostering care of an empire, rich, powerful, prosperous. Did our forefathers consent to the sacrifice? No; in defence of their grand old faith; in defence of that religious teaching which safeguarded the honour of their wives and the purity of their daughters; in defence of that spirit of piety which made Ireland the Island of Saints, and which makes her still, even amid her sorrows, a model to the nations, they doomed themselves and their posterity to three hundred years of persecution, confiscation, poverty, and political extinction. And are we, their

27. *Freeman's Journal*, 23 January 1891. The bewilderment of the *Freeman's Journal* seems genuine.

28. Walsh to editor, *Irish Catholic*, 8 August 1891.

29. *Irish Catholic*, 14 February 1891. The *Irish Catholic* wrote on 28 February, 'On us, Irishmen of today, is cast the dread responsibility of deciding not merely for ourselves but for many future generations whether God shall smile upon the path of our nation, or His frown cast darkness on its course'.

descendants, to abandon that inheritance of faith, piety, virtue for which they resisted even unto blood![30]

The Bishop of Galway deplored that 'we are called upon to still accept as the Moses of our race a man steeped to lips in moral turpitude.' The Bishop of Clogher wrote a letter to his clergy urging them to 'rally our people to the side of virtue and honour, teaching them that in union alone is our strength, that all our efforts were vain without the help of the Liberal party, in whom, under Mr. Gladstone, we have every ground of confidence, and that even Home Rule, under the dictatorship of a vile adulterer might be only a calamity and a curse.'[31]

The Parnellite retort was that the issue of Parnell's leadership was a political rather than a moral or religious issue. The Parnellites argued, insistently if tendentiously, that the assertion that it was a moral issue could not be squared with the fact that the bishops had waited sixteen days after the divorce verdict before pronouncing against Parnell,[32] and had only done so after Gladstone's intervention, nor with the somewhat conflicting pronouncements of the episcopacy on whether Catholics or priests in their diocese were entitled to support Parnell.[33] The argument from the timing of the episcopacy's formal intervention, furiously disputed by Walsh,[34] achieved particular prominence in the controversy of the Split. A subset of the wider Parnellite argument concerning Liberal dictation, it had something of the aspect of a retaliation against the bishops for entering the political domain to oppose Parnell. The independent-minded and plain-spoken Parnellite Andrew Kettle drew back from this argument: 'Although it may be fairly open to argument,

30. *Irish Catholic*, 14 February 1891.

31. *Freeman's Journal*, 9 February 1891.

32. Dermot Meleady, *Redmond: The Parnellite* (Cork: Cork University Press, 2008), 178.

33. This was a theme emphasised by *United Ireland* on 21 March, 28 March, and 11 July 1891. The *Freeman's Journal* asserted that the Archbishop of Cashel, 'sagacious and far-seeing, has never publicly committed himself to the extreme attitude of some of his brethren and it has placed it on record that his priests are free to take either side in the discussion, although he significantly added that he did not think it possible for them to espouse Mr. Parnell's side' (16 April 1891).

34. *Irish Catholic*, 28 February 1891 (interview). Walsh wrote letters on the subject to the *Daily Express* and to *The Times* (*National Press*, 27 May 1891).

yet I altogether disagree with those who contend that the Irish bishops were influenced in their action against Mr. Parnell by the Englishman's letter, or by other English influence. I believe the delay in issuing their manifesto was caused by the stunning effect of the crisis, by the disagreeableness of the task, and by consideration for the man, and I further believe that the mistake of mixing the moral and the political question arose from their intense and honest interest in the success of the National cause.'[35]

What was undeniable was the thoroughgoing confusion of political and moral considerations in the denunciations of Parnell and the Parnellites by the Catholic priests and bishops. Parnellite publicists retaliated by pointing to the deficient patriotic record of the episcopacy in Irish politics. This related chiefly to the episcopal support of the Act of Union of 1800, the failure to sustain the tenant right movement, and the episcopal support of John Sadleir and William Keogh, who took office in Aberdeen's government at the end of 1852. Both instances were frequently cited in Parnellite speeches and were the subject of some extended articles and letters in the Parnellite press, all pseudonymous or anonymous.[36] The record extended into the contemporary era. An analysis of the Parnell campaign in the 1880 general election stated of Parnell's contest with William Shaw for the leadership of the Irish Party,

35. Letter to editor, 28 February 1891, *Freeman's Journal*, 4 March 1891. John Dillon complained, not especially convincingly, to William O'Brien in June of 'the foolish, most unwise attacks made by Harrington and Joe Kenny against the priests and bishops, which have thrown them more into Healy's hands than would otherwise have been the case.' F.S.L. Lyons, *John Dillon* (London: Routledge and Kegan Paul, 1968), 137–38.

36. 'Nemo', 'The Lesson from History' [Sadleir and Keogh], *Freeman's Journal*, 7 March 1891; 'A Student of Irish History', 'The Catholic Bishops and the Act of Union', *Freeman's Journal*, 4 March 1891; 'A Student of Irish History', 'The Catholic Bishops: The Great Betrayal' [Sadleir and Keogh], *Freeman's Journal*, 27 March 1891. *United Ireland* carried similar material: 'Irish Loyalty to English "Friends"', 3 January 1891; 'The Veto in Irish Politics', 10 January 1891; 'A Parallel for Carlow', 27 June 1891. In nationalist and more particularly Fenian accounts, the ultramontane Cardinal Paul Cullen was cast as the principal ecclesiastical villain of the post-1848 era. The historian of the Independent Irish Party concluded, 'The defection of Keogh and Sadleir and the quarrel with Archbishop Cullen did not help the party, but equally certainly they did not decide its fate.' J. H. Whyte, *The Independent Irish Party, 1850–9* (Oxford: Oxford University Press, 1958), 124.

'This fighting minority, then as now, had to face of the opposition of the Bishops.'[37]

If the argument from history generally did not extend to the period before the Act of Union, there were exceptions. Croke incautiously asked when all the Irish bishops were wrong in their political opinions, at the same time, on the same question. 'A Leinster Priest' took up the gauntlet in a letter to the *Freeman's Journal*:

> We might reply, *more Hibernico*, when were the majority of the Irish bishops right at the same time on any political question? Not when they opposed the policy of the Nuncio and Owen Roe O'Neill. Not when they—notably the archbishops and Dr. Troy, then Bishop of Ossory—published pastorals ordering prayers for the success of his Majesty George III's arms against his revolted American subjects. Not at the time of the Union, or during the agitation for its repeal, when the bishops as a body were as much opposed to the Liberator and the *Nation* as they appear to be nowadays to the *Freeman* and Ireland's great benefactor C S Parnell. Will this sad history keep repeating itself until the extreme demand of 'no free choice for the laity in matters purely political' will be met by the other extreme and anti-Catholic cry of 'no priests in politics'?[38]

This spirited protest enlisted the support of a writer calling himself 'Historicus', the pseudonym of Barry O'Brien.[39] He impugned, as Joyce would do later, the record of the episcopacy from the time of the Norman invasion:

> Commencing with the Norman Invasion down to the time of James I—four hundred years nearly—we do not find a single one of that body (if we except St. Laurence O'Toole) who could be credited with

37. 'The Parnell Campaign of 1880, Part II', *Freeman's Journal*, 31 March 1891. Part 1 appeared in the *Freeman's Journal* on 24 March 1891.

38. *Freeman's Journal*, 7 March 1891. The *United Ireland* of 3 January 1891 carried an article entitled 'Irish Loyalty to English "Friends"' that encompassed a critique of the Church and went back to the 'Flight of the Earls' [the term given to the departure of the Gaelic aristocracy of Ulster at the beginning of the seventeenth century—Eds.].

39. Callanan, 'Joyce and the *United Irishman*', 53.

> any profession of patriotism. We find them all, on the contrary, acknowledging from the first moment Henry II arrived in Ireland, the authority of the English King to appoint, or at least to approve of the selection of, the occupants of their various sees. The several so-called insurrectionists of the native population, which were never really attempts to throw off the foreign yoke, never found an active supporter or warm sympathiser in the Irish bishops.[40]

He went on through the Confederation of Kilkenny in the 1640s, the Act of Union, Catholic emancipation, and the tenant right movement to the Split, and ended, 'The same episcopal class who in 1800 to a man, actively, openly and ably supported the Union, are, unconsciously, let us hope, proving themselves the traditional agents of the same perfidious policy. Dr. Croke has appealed to History, let History answer him.'[41]

The argument concerning the bishops—the clergy were specifically exempted from his strictures—was unhistorical without being altogether wrong in point of fact. It had a certain political force and was deeply disquieting to the bishops in tracing a fissure in the patriotic legitimacy of the Catholic Church in Ireland. The heroic phase of collaboration between the political leadership of nationalism under Parnell and the episcopacy had, it had been hoped, healed some of the wounds of controversy over the role of the Church in the Act of Union. The hostile chronicle of the role of the Irish bishops, certainly from the Act of Union, was not new. While it was not confined to the Fenians, it had in their long contest with the Church come to be identified primarily with them. If Parnell was badly worsted in the trial of strength with the Church, the historical indictment of the role of the episcopacy in modern Irish history acquired in the Split a new currency.

40. Letter to editor, *Freeman's Journal*, 12 March 1891.

41. Letter to editor, *Freeman's Journal*, 12 March 1891. Barry O'Brien mistakenly believed he was endorsing the sentiments of 'Sacerdos', but they were those of 'A Leinster Priest'. Both letters had appeared together in the *Freeman's Journal*, 7 March 1891. 'Sacerdos' had made a striking point: 'The clergy must not forget that we have educated the people; that they are no longer children, but intelligent men, able to think and act for themselves. We have only to turn to France or Italy to see the effects of trying to keep the clerical sucking-bottle in the mouths of men.'

John O'Leary's *Recollections of Fenians and Fenianism*, published in 1896 but partially written in the course of the Split of 1890–91, was replete with excerpts from the editorials in the *Irish People* of 1863–65, principally those of Charles Kickham impugning the legitimacy and political competence of ecclesiastical denunciations of Fenianism and of the paper. O'Leary observed, 'History is for ever repeating itself, and often with astonishing closeness.'[42] His strangely abridged memoir, which professes to eschew the immediately contemporary and ends with his own conviction for treason felony in 1865, derived its principal contemporary salience from the renewed political incursion of the bishops and clergy in the Parnell Split.

On the left, historical criticism of the political role of the Church was to find cogent expression in 1910 in the foreword to James Connolly's pamphlet *Labour, Nationality and Religion*,[43] written to rebut the arguments of Fr Robert Kane, S.J. in his Lenten Discourses against Socialism in Gardiner Street Church. Joyce did not need to read Connolly to apprise himself of the argument. He learnt it from the Split in Parnell's lifetime and in the aftermath of his death. The Parnellite critique of the political role of the Church found expression in 'L'Irlanda: Isola dei santi e dei savi', Joyce's lecture delivered at the Università Popolare in Trieste on 27 April 1907:

> Ireland prides itself on being in body and soul as faithful to her national traditions as to the Holy See. The majority of Irishmen consider loyalty to these two traditions as their cardinal article of faith. But the fact is that the English came to Ireland following the repeated requests of a native king, without, it seems, much wanting to and without the sanction of their monarch, but provided with a papal bull from Adrian IV and a papal letter from Alexander. They disembarked on the southern coast, numbering 700 men, a gang of adventurers

42. John O'Leary, *Recollections of Fenians and Fenianism* (London: Downey, 1896), 2:40.

43. James Connolly, *Labour, Nationality and Religion: Being a Discussion of the Lenten Discourses against Socialism Delivered by Father Kane in Gardiner Street Church, Dublin, 1910* (Dublin: n.p., [1910]), republished in James Connolly, *Selected Writings*, ed. P. Berresford Ellis (London: Penguin, 1973), 57–117. It is striking that Connolly—quite deliberately—makes no reference to the Parnell Split.

> against a people. They were met by certain native tribes and, less than a year later, the English King Henry II noisily celebrated Christmas in the city of Dublin. Moreover, the parliamentary union of the two countries was not passed in Westminster, but in Dublin, by a parliament elected by the people of Ireland—a corrupted parliament goaded by the huge sums from the English Prime Minister's agent—but an Irish parliament none the less. In my opinion, these two facts must be perfectly explained before the country in which they took place has even the most elementary right to expect one of its sons to change his position from that of detached observer to convinced nationalist.[44]

The argument regarding the implication of the papacy, through the bull *Laudabiliter* of Pope Adrian IV, affirmed by Alexander III, in the English conquest of Ireland was widely rehearsed in the Split. Joyce was not too concerned with historical accuracy before his Triestine audience. There is a characteristically Joycean swerve away from the Parnellite argument in the Split to blame the Act of Union on the Irish people. It was not correct to say that a parliament of the Irish people had carried the Act of Union, as the Irish Parliament was notoriously a body exclusively representative of the Protestant ascendancy.[45] Joyce certainly knew this but elected not to lose the polemical thrust of his argument before his Triestine audience. If he was far from exculpating the Church, he did not wish to acquit the Irish people of primary responsibility for the fallen condition of nationalism. He was importing into his account of the historical role of the Church his bitterly implacable assessment of the Split.

As earlier discussed, the patriotic record of the Irish Catholic Church features also in the Christmas dinner scene in *A Portrait*. When Dante Riordan proclaims that the priests were always the true friends of Ireland, Mr Casey retorts, 'Didn't the bishops of Ireland betray us in the

44. *OCPW* 115–16.

45. While Irish references to the Act of Union were generally to the Irish act, two identical measures were passed in 1800 by the Irish and British Parliaments which created, with effect from 1 January 1801, the United Kingdom of Great Britain and Ireland.

time of the union when Bishop Lanigan presented an address of loyalty to the Marquess Cornwallis? Didn't the bishops and priests sell the aspirations of their country in 1829 in return for catholic emancipation? Didn't they denounce the fenian movement from the pulpit and in the confession box? And didn't they dishonour the ashes of Terence Bellew MacManus?'[46]

Stephen is powerfully affected. Casey's 'face was glowing with anger and Stephen felt the glow rise to his own cheek as the spoken words thrilled him.'[47] The last two sentences uttered by Mr Casey invoke the memory above all of Paul Cullen, Archbishop of Dublin from 1852 to 1878, and identify why Cullen was a hated figure to Fenians: his determination to crush the Fenians, of whom he procured a papal condemnation in 1870, and his refusal to allow the coffin of Terence Bellew McManus to rest in the Pro-Cathedral before his massively attended, Fenian-organised funeral in 1861.[48] This is the cue for Mr Dedalus, 'who uttered a guffaw of coarse scorn' and concluded, 'O God he cried, I forgot little old Paul Cullen! Another apple of God's eye!'[49] This is the final escalatory movement of the Christmas dinner scene.

At the National League in late February 1891, John Redmond enunciated the Parnellite response to the bishops and priests:

> I am entitled, when the bishops, in a political question, advocate a course which my intelligence and my conscience tell me is a wrong one, to perfect freedom to dissent from them, and to recall how, time and time again in the history of our country, the prelates took action which has since been proved to be shortsighted and unpatriotic (*applause*).... But it is said that in supporting Mr. Parnell those of us who are Catholics are condoning sin (*no, no*). I deny it. I repudiate this as an insult to the intelligence and the virtue of the millions of our race, who detesting as heartily as it is possible for men and women

46. *P* 1.1101–7.

47. *P* 1.1101–7.

48. Colin Barr, 'Paul Cullen', *DIB* 2:1073–74. Larkin analyses Cullen's condemnation of Fenianism in his pastoral letter of 10 October 1865, reprinted in Emmet Larkin, *The Consolidation of the Roman Catholic Church in Ireland, 1860–70* (Dublin: Gill and Macmillan, 1987), 404–7.

49. *P* 1.1110–12.

to do the charge which is laid at Mr. Parnell's door, yet declare they will not consent to drive him from public life to satisfy the demands of an English statesman or party (*applause*).[50]

Redmond's extremely careful negotiation of the issue of Parnell's affair with Katharine O'Shea is a reminder of the fact that Parnellite spokesmen did not generally seek to defend or justify Parnell's affair with a married woman, of which most Parnellites personally disapproved. There was a degree of palliation on the grounds that Parnell was a Protestant, even if it was the case that such acceptance of divorce as there was in contemporary Anglican doctrine was highly qualified.[51]

Redmond went on to make an argument which came to feature more prominently in Parnellite rhetoric: that the perception engendered by the Split that Irish nationalism was in thrall to the Catholic Church had a potentially catastrophic impact on the prospects for Home Rule: 'The question of Mr. Parnell's leadership was a purely political question (*applause*), and for my part I don't hesitate to say that if in this purely political question the bishops and priests of Ireland are able to make their power paramount and to overbear the will of the country, they will thereby have created the most formidable obstacle to the granting of Home Rule by the English people that the wit of man could devise (*applause*).'[52]

Anti-Parnellite apologists scoffed at this argument as self-serving and smacking of desperation. In late April Parnell at Irishtown, speaking 'in these days, fellow-countrymen, when you are told that Ireland is to be a nation of one religion only, when sectarian considerations are sought to be imported into the national movement', re-asserted to cheers the principle that 'the Irish nation is to be a nation of the whole of our people'. The *National Press* retorted that 'Mr. Parnell posed as the persecuted Protestant'.[53]

50. *Freeman's Journal*, 25 February 1891.

51. This was the burden of Walsh's letter of 6 August 1891 to the editor of the *Irish Catholic*, in response to 'the theologians of the *Freeman's Journal*'.

52. *Freeman's Journal*, 25 February 1891. The editorial echoed the argument of Redmond's speech.

53. *Freeman's Journal*, 20 April 1891; *National Press*, 20 April 1891; Callanan, *T. M. Healy*, 374.

Andrew Kettle advanced a subtle variation of this aspect of the Parnellite case. Seeking to turn around the anti-Parnellite argument that the division in the nationalist vote in Ireland was detrimental to Home Rule, he asserted that 'the alliance between the Catholic hierarchy and Mr. Parnell was the great stumbling block' to Irish Protestant adherence to the cause of Home Rule, and had now been removed. He cogently added, 'No two men in the world know better than Dr. Croke and Mr. [Michael] Davitt that in the coming electoral struggle with Mr. Parnell they could very easily succeed far enough to defeat themselves. A big Catholic clerical party will never get Home Rule from Protestant England.'[54]

Some but not all Parnellites followed their leader's cue in his laconic assertions that as clerical influence had been brought into play, the issue that it raised would have to be fought out to the end. If this certainly commended itself to Fenians for their own reasons, it was not pressed by Parnell's mainstream adherents. A notable expression was the mild-mannered but clear-sighted politician and writer Edmund Leamy, who, like most of the Parnellite parliamentarians, would go down to defeat at the 1892 general election. He declared at the National League in March 1891,

> I believe in my heart and soul that it is the best thing for Ireland, and for the future of Ireland, and for the relations between the priests and the people of Ireland, that this struggle which they have forced upon us should come before Home Rule (*hear, hear*). I say that we are going to fight the battle like men. I say that we are going to take care that every man in this country shall understand that the Home Rule we are seeking for is not the Home Rule of a class, of a section of the nation, however great that section may be; that we are not going to forget that the Protestant Grattan declared that he would never accept a Parliament which would exclude the Catholic nation; we will never accept a Parliament which will exclude our Protestant fellow-countrymen (*applause*) and I say I believe in my heart and soul that the result of this struggle which the priests have forced upon us will be to develop all that is best in our country, and, while we will

54. *Freeman's Journal*, 4 March 1891.

> respect our Church and our priests, we shall teach them that they shall not be our masters (*applause*).[55]

Few Parnellites were so forthright. They were in an impossible situation which Healy and his confederates exploited to the hilt. When Parnellite spokesmen responded to ecclesiastical condemnations and disputed the authority of the Church in political matters, they were denounced as anticlericals or worse. The Parnellite position was far removed from that of the proponents of *laïcité* in France, with which it was frequently compared in anti-Parnellite and clerical invective. Redmond put it thus in his National League speech of late February 1891:

> Recent public utterances show more and more clearly every day that this is rapidly developing itself into a fight in which most of the Irish bishops, and many, thank God not all, of the Irish priests (*hear, hear*), will be arrayed against us. Now, I speak as a Catholic, and as a Catholic, say, for the sake alike of my country and my creed, I deeply deplore this. God forbid I should deny to the prelates of my Church the most plenary powers in matters of faith and morals. In such matters they shall command my obedience and my devotion. God forbid also that I should echo the false and hollow cry of no priests in politics. Priests and bishops cannot by reason of their sacred office lose their civil rights or evade their duties as patriotic Irishmen, but for my part I say the two things must be kept apart (*applause*).[56]

The Parnellites were contending, not altogether realistically, that the bishops and clergy should observe a self-denying ordinance and not throw their very considerable socio-political influence massively and quasi-corporately on the side of the anti-Parnellites.

The Effects of Ecclesiastical Intervention in the Split

After Parnell's death, the Parnellites were routed in the general election of July 1892, which returned nine Parnellites against seventy-two anti-Parnellites. Commenting on the success of the Parnellite electoral

55. *Freeman's Journal*, 11 March 1891.
56. *Freeman's Journal*, 25 February 1891.

petition in South Meath, soon to be followed by that in North Meath, John Redmond asserted that it 'shows conclusively that, but for the undue influence of the clergy, the Parnellite party in Ireland, at the last General Election, would have won a clear majority of the representation of the country'.[57] The electoral impact of ecclesiastical intervention in the three by-elections of the Split in Parnell's lifetime, in the bitterly contested Cork by-election on Parnell's death (Redmond won the Waterford city by-election of 23 December 1891), and at the general election, if palpable, remains hard to quantify.[58]

Analytically, the abstraction of 'clerical influence' in the Split is problematic. Redmond's argument was premised on the clergy refraining from 'undue influence', a narrow legal concept which captured only that part of the immense socio-political influence of the Catholic clergy in late nineteenth-century Ireland which found overt expression in an actual election.

The effect of clerical influence is not easily isolated. The opposition to Parnell in the Split was composite, woven seamlessly into anti-Parnellite rhetoric, and its elements are hard to disaggregate. The operative mechanism of the Split was that the anti-Parnellite press, the majority of the Irish Party, and the priests and bishops strove to impress on Irish voters that Parnell's affair with Katharine O'Shea was immoral and had jeopardised the Home Rule alliance. The clergy were the conduit of anti-Parnellite propaganda as well as of moral instruction.

One has also to allow for the unquantifiable impact of the nationalist desire for unity, which introduced a 'winner takes all' element that favoured the anti-Parnellites. It is true that the electorate, habituated to

57. J. E. Redmond, 'The Lesson of South Meath', *Fortnightly Review*, n.s., 53, no. 313 (1 January 1893): 2. Redmond adroitly strove to vaunt the outcome of the petition while asserting it established that Irish nationalists were capable of transcending clerical influence. The Parnellites lost the ensuing by-elections in both of the Meath constituencies.

58. The issue is considered in J. H. Whyte, 'The Influence of the Catholic Clergy on Elections in Nineteenth Century Ireland', *English Historical Review* 75 (April 1960): 239–59; C. J. Woods, 'The General Election of 1892: The Catholic Clergy and the Defeat of the Parnellites', in *Ireland under the Union: Essays in Honour of T. W. Moody*, ed. F.S.L. Lyons and R.A.J. Hawkins (Oxford: Oxford University Press, 1980), 289–319; and Frank Callanan, '"Clerical Dictation": Reflections on the Catholic Church and the Parnell Split', *Archivium Hibernicum* 45 (1980): 64–75.

the achievements of a united Irish Party in Westminster, tended to rally to the majority in a crisis, and this was particularly marked among Catholic nationalists in Ulster. However, there remains abundant evidence of the effectiveness of clerical intervention. In the by-elections of the Split, where individual clerics actively supported Parnell, the local pattern of support moved discernibly in his favour. Correspondents for English Liberal papers found themselves awkwardly saluting the wondrous vigour of Parnell's clerical adversaries. In the counter-positivistic realm of what Joyce called 'ousted possibilities',[59] any judgement is speculative and approximate. In the politically unrealistic scenario that the Catholic Church in Ireland had held back from concerted intervention, it is eminently possible that Parnell would have prevailed in the contest in Ireland and thrown the course of the Split into reverse. On the most conservative assessment of possibilities, the effect of clerical intervention was a matter of degree that significantly amplified the aggregate scale of the Parnellite defeat. Even that was of great moment. Had Parnell carried even one of the three by-elections fought between December 1890 and July 1891, the course of the Split would have shifted incalculably. Had he won North Kilkenny (something of a long shot, as the potent influence of Davitt was added to that of the Church, and the anti-Parnellite majority was two to one), it would have changed utterly. On a cautious and necessarily crude measure, the concerted opposition of the bishops and clergy at the very least stripped Parnell's support to its core and brought his campaign by the time of his death disquietingly close to, though not below, the level of support at which it would have ceased to be viable. From the time of the 1892 election, the issue of clerical influence presented the Parnellites with an intensifying dilemma. If emphasising the role of the priests and bishops was a means of accounting for the fact of Parnellite defeat, or its scale, it also threatened to entrench their minority status in locking them into fighting what appeared to be a lost cause.

United Ireland responded to the overwhelming Parnellite defeat at the 1892 general election, which left 'the Independent Party in a very

59. *U* 2.51.

small minority of the Irish representation', with a trenchant critique of the effects of clerical influence: 'The people have been badgered, bounced, intimidated, drugged. They have been threatened with the gravest penalties of the Church'. The paper's condemnation of clerical interference was plain spoken:

> We have said over and over again in these columns that there is no chance in the world of making an Irish Parliament a success unless under conditions by which the civil rights of every Irishman can be exercised unfettered by any influence, high or low. We say so again. Whatever Mr. Healy and his colleagues are working for, we are working for an independent Irish Parliament, independent not alone of English interference, but of any interference. We want a Parliament whose members will be representative of the people, not of the priests. We use the words deliberately—of the people, not of the priests.[60]

John Dillon might have believed that it would be possible for the majority, once it had secured its position, to suppress clerical influence, 'but we can tell him that these influences are sinking down day by day on the Irish mind and leaving a deep and ugly scar on the Irish character'. The paper professed itself concerned less with the effect that the political role of the Catholic clergy in Ireland would have on English opinion than with 'the demoralization which it is spreading among the peasant population of Ireland'. The action of the clergy had been 'inspired by a deliberate intention on the part of the Bishops to stamp out Parnellism, because Parnellism refused to recognise their right to be the political arbiters of the Irish nation.'[61]

Parnellites were averse to being aligned either with the far more radical exponents of continental anticlericalism or with Unionist critics of nationalism. Thus, when the Unionist publicist Philip H. Bagenal published his anti–Home Rule *The Priest in Politics* in 1893, *United Ireland* recoiled: 'This matter of the priest in politics, if we say it without disrespect to the author of this book, and all others who approach it from his standpoint,

60. *United Ireland*, 16 July 1892.

61. *United Ireland*, 16 July 1892.

is one to be dealt with by Catholics and by Catholics alone. No good is gained by Protestants meddling in it.'[62]

Across the decade, Parnellite attacks on clerical influence for the most part abated in frequency, prominence, and ferocity. From 1900 the Parnellites were subsumed into the reunited Irish Party, and attacks on clerical influence by nationalist parliamentarians ceased entirely. For Joyce this represented a seemingly inexorable drift backwards that sealed the defeat of Parnell. Politically unrealistic this may have been, but it was far from an irrational obsession. It was left to Joyce, and to W. B. Yeats, to keep to the fore the issue of the influence of the Church in the Split, from which Irish politicians shied away. It was forty-five years after Parnell's death that Yeats wrote the famous lines, 'The Bishop and the Party / That tragic story made'.[63]

The *Irish Catholic*

Anti-Parnellism comprised a diversity of strands. Healy defined the rhetoric of the anti-Parnellite case in a brilliantly demotic ad hominem rhetoric, denouncing Parnell as a monster of egotistical ambition and self-gratification, attacking him as member of the landlord class rather than explicitly as a Protestant, but in a language shot through with avowedly Catholic nationalist values. Healy's kinsmen the Sullivans; their paper, the historic but imperilled *Nation*; and their confederate William Martin Murphy denounced Parnell in a more traditionally moralistic vein—'Affected Mob Follows in Religious Sullivence',[64] as Joyce would write with superbly tart contempt four decades after the Split in *Finnegans Wake*. At the most right-wing clericalist end of this semi-dynastic continuum was the *Irish Catholic*, edited by W. F. Dennehy.

62. *United Ireland*, 6 May 1893.

63. W. B. Yeats, 'Come Gather Round Me, Parnellites', in *The Variorum Edition of the Poems of W. B. Yeats*, ed. Peter Allt and Russell K. Alspach (New York: Macmillan, 1957), 350, lines 25–26.

64. *FW* 602.25–26.

Close to the Sullivans, as he would later be to Healy and to William Martin Murphy, W. F. Dennehy (1853–1918) was the eldest of the seven children of Alderman Cornelius Dennehy. The family originated in Castleisland, County Kerry. The older Dennehy, a supporter of Daniel O'Connell, was a Dublin merchant who through the Encumbered Estates Court acquired extensive lands in Longford. His son wrote articles on Catholic and historical subjects for the Catholic magazines. He became the editor of the *Irish Catholic* almost immediately on its establishment in May 1888 and remained its editor for the remainder of his life. The paper of which he was part proprietor and later sole owner emerged from the Sullivan stable in succession to the *Weekly News* as 'a new journal more exclusively dedicated to the religious interests of the Irish people'.[65]

The *Irish Catholic* did not take long to get into its stride in the Split. Before the Kilkenny election it wrote, 'The fight which we have now to fight is a good, a holy, and a glorious one. It is a conflict into which, we believe, men might go as Christian soldiers did of yore, crucifix on breast and shield, into which our priests might well descend, crucifix in hand; for it is a struggle in which are ranked powers of light and darkness, of Heaven and of Hell, of Virtue and adultery!'[66]

It thus hailed the result: 'To Catholic Irishmen it seemed as if that Providence which watches over our country and its Faith had again, by an inscrutable decree, ordained that the gates of hell shall not prevail against them. To all, the great victory in Kilkenny conveyed that, whatever to other lands may befall, to Ireland the cause of patriotism and morality is placed by a faithful and virtuous race high beyond the reach of treason or corruption.'[67]

The paper proclaimed that 'finally and irretrievably [Parnell] has been banished from his once high place as leader of the Catholic people of this Catholic country.'[68] It declared that 'if the repudiation of Mr. Parnell's leadership meant civil war instead of merely the turmoil of electoral

65. *Irish Catholic*, 9 March 1918; Callanan, *T. M. Healy*, 227–28.

66. *Irish Catholic*, 13 December 1890.

67. *Irish Catholic*, 27 December 1890.

68. *Irish Catholic*, 31 January 1891.

contention, the present is one of those occasions upon which honest citizens should not shrink from responsibility.'[69]

The relevance for Joyce lies in the hybridity of the editorial position of the *Irish Catholic*. The paper invoked absolute Catholic moral prescriptions and timeless Irish fealty to the precepts of the Church but espoused in the same breath the imperatives of the Liberal-nationalist alliance. While championing Irish Catholic morality, its editorials enunciated an explicitly contemporary political argument that was aligned with that of the Liberal party and of the publicists of the 'nonconformist conscience'.

The way in which the editorials of the *Irish Catholic* became still more shrill from August 1891 reveals the vicious dialectic of the Split and of its gathering bitterness even before Parnell's death. This was after Parnell's marriage to Katharine O'Shea, and after his third defeat in the Carlow by-election, and is not explicable simply by reference to moral indignation at Parnell's marriage to a divorced woman. Its anathematisation of the defeated Parnellites was a calculated radicalisation of the Split. Its opportunistic Catholic supremacism complemented and was broadly synchronised with Healy's escalating rhetoric from June 1891 as he sought to entrench his predominance among the anti-Parnellites. The common premise was that Parnellism was not tolerable even as the allegiance of a minority. The persistence of Parnellism in defeat was an affront to a now hegemonic Catholic nationalism. It was less Parnell than Catholic Parnellites who were now the target.

Seizing on a letter received from the Archbishop of Dublin condemning the *Freeman's Journal*'s condonation of Parnell's marriage, the *Irish Catholic* characterised Parnellism as 'the very negation of Christianity in any form, a foul invention devised by designing men to entrap the unwary into fatal error, and calculated to develop into an anti-Christian revolt fraught with deplorable consequences. . . . Parnellism is not merely irreligious, it is infidel. . . . The renegades of old who tramped on the Cross were not more openly the enemy of Christian teaching than

69. *Irish Catholic*, 14 February 1891.

those who now deride the mandates and warnings of the Sacred Scriptures and assail the representatives of God.'[70]

Parnell was 'a convicted libertine', whose guilt was 'full of infinite abomination in the sight of God':

> When, then, we find championship of the claims of such a man, allied with the display towards him, of a grovelling servility and with an exhibition towards our priests and prelates of an aggravated hostility, we are surely provided with knowledge which should enable us to understand the phenomenon which we witness. We are today face to face with what, despite its disguises, is undoubtedly a revolt against God, against the authority of the Church, against the teachings of the Church, against the teachings of morality, and against the first principles of Divine and human legislation. This is a fact which can neither be denied nor suppressed. Parnellism is an anti-Christian movement, having for its object the apotheosis of immorality.[71]

A week later it proclaimed, 'Evil—evil unexpiable and unforgivable—enshrouds Parnellism, and is of the very essence of the movement.'[72] The following week it characterised the battle to be fought as 'a renewal of the ancient warfare between religion and irreligion, between the spiritual and the temporal, between Christ and Anti-Christ.' It warned darkly that 'those who protest that politicians owe no allegiance to morality and ethics forget, or pretend to forget, that politicians have souls to be saved, and that heaven is as glorious and hell as terrible a fact in their case as in that of other men.' It celebrated the vanquishing of Parnell: 'Our quarrel with Mr. Parnell is not a political one, nor one to be judged by political rules. We have repudiated him as a leader because he is unfit to be the chieftain of a Christian people. We have stricken down Parnellism, and mean to crush it under foot, because its tendency has been proven to be towards hostility to religion, and towards disregard of the teachings of morality.'[73]

70. *Irish Catholic*, 8 August 1891.
71. *Irish Catholic*, 8 August 1891.
72. *Irish Catholic*, 15 August 1891.
73. *Irish Catholic*, 22 August 1891.

The aggressive moralising of Dennehy's *Irish Catholic* found its most notorious expression in its editorial response to Parnell's death, which *United Ireland* characterised as 'blasphemous and indecent':

> To Catholics the close of the career of Mr. Parnell will present itself with a terrible significance. Death has come upon him in the home of sin; he has died and his last glimpse of the world has been unhallowed by the consolations of religion, his memory is linked for ever with that of her whose presence seems to forbid all thought of his repentance. And we know that he passed into eternity with never a sigh of sorrow for the insult he offered to morality, and for the revolt which he sought to create in his native land against the anointed prelates and ministers of God's Church. The darkness is pierced by the cry of sorrow, but the light of hope shines not, and there is nought but darkness, dread and horrid.[74]

Katharine Tynan wrote in response in *United Ireland,*

> . . . this man doth smite
> The dead man lying in the rain at night
> And having smitten the sad body
> Spares not to smite the trembling soul . . . [75]

Dennehy's editorial—like that of the *Evening Press* on the day that news of Parnell's death reached Dublin which proclaimed that Parnell 'lay dead in the house of a woman who was his betrayer'[76]—was never forgiven by those who had remained loyal to their leader. Coupled with the inflammatory riposte of *United Ireland* written by John McGrath, these editorials launched the cycle of unrelenting recrimination that followed Parnell's death.

Dennehy's onslaughts on Parnellism, with their distinctive Catholic nationalist eschatological edge, kept pace with Healy's more conventionally political attacks. The later course of Dennehy and the *Irish*

74. *United Ireland,* 10 October 1891.
75. *United Ireland,* 24 October 1891.
76. Callanan, *T. M. Healy,* 369.

Catholic affirmed the nexus with Healy. The paper was to be a principal vehicle of Healyism through the 1890s. Dennehy had assisted in the foundation of the *National Press* and edited the Healyite *Daily Nation* from 1897. He was briefly the editor of the formerly Parnellite *Irish Independent* when William Martin Murphy acquired the paper in 1900. He was the secretary to the Citizens' Committee appointed to arrange for the receptions of Edward VII and George V on their first visits to Dublin on their accessions.[77] In the lockout of 1913, the *Irish Catholic* discovered that socialism, like Parnellism before it, 'is essentially Satanic in its nature, origin, and purposes.'[78] Dennehy's 1905 articles 'Nationality within the Empire' confirmed the feebleness of his conception of nationalism.[79] An advocate of devolution, he believed that Home Rule would come from the Conservatives.[80]

Dennehy's obituarist in the *Irish Catholic* wrote that 'ever vigilant where the interests of religion and morality were concerned, courageous and outspoken in the expression of his views, he always bore in mind that the proper place of the Catholic lay journalist is one of the most docile subordination to the official authorities of the Church.'[81] The docility was highly debatable. Aside from the stubborn idiosyncrasies of his own opinions, Dennehy sought to bring the views of lay and clerical zealots to bear on the hierarchy. There is little that more strikingly exemplifies the disordering wrought by the Split than Archbishop Walsh's fleeting alignment with the *Irish Catholic*. It did not take long for Walsh's antipathy to the *Irish Catholic* to reassert itself. In 1894 he had sent his administrator to advise its editor that 'the publication of the paper as a *Catholic paper* was seriously injurious to religious interests.'[82] The natural order of the 1880s was restored, so that in the 'Aeolus' episode of *Ulysses*, under the heading 'The Crozier and the Pen', in the office of the

77. *Irish Times*, 4 March 1918.

78. Callanan, *T. M. Healy*, 487.

79. *New Irish Review*, March and May 1905.

80. W. F. Dennehy, 'The Irish Situation', *Catholic World* 84 (December 1906): 298.

81. *Irish Catholic*, 9 March 1918.

82. Callanan, *T. M. Healy*, 228.

Freeman's Journal and National Press, Red Murray states gravely that 'his Grace phoned down twice this morning'.[83] The comment subtly marries very considerable political awareness with artistic purpose. Forming part of an initially inaudible overture, it is the second in the suite of evocations of the era of Parnell that runs through the chapter, of which the first is giving the *Freeman's Journal* its full title, which records its amalgamation with Healy's *National Press* in 1892. The suggestion of episcopal dictation merges insensibly into a deft characterisation of the wearisome meticulousness of the Archbishop of Dublin.

The professed ancientness of Dennehy's Catholic piety belies its innovativeness. There is no real historical precedent for the *Irish Catholic.* The paper asserted itself to be at once unimpeachably nationalist in its politics and undeviatingly orthodox in its submission to the moral dictates of the Catholic Church applied to the political domain. It ignored the historically fraught relationship of the Church to nationalism and blandly asserted an immanent and timeless solidarity of bishops and clergy with a Catholic people. Its position could only be sustained through a radical reconceptualisation of Irish nationalism as an explicitly Catholic phenomenon. The paper stood on the far right of Catholic opposition to Parnell. As the most thoroughgoing exponent of a Catholic nationalism, the paper functioned as the eschatological outrider of Healyite anti-Parnellism. Its articulation of an overt Catholic supremacism and its anathemising of Catholic Parnellites, even though not shared by most anti-Parnellites, signify a shift in the disposition of power within the nationalist polity. Its rhetoric was an early indication that the Split had brought about not merely the fall of Parnell but an enfeeblement of the authority of any secular nationalist leadership that might succeed his.

Joyce apprehended the significance of the *Irish Catholic* in the Split. In *A Portrait* he brilliantly sets in motion the ferocious dialectic of militantly Catholic anti-Parnellism. The rhythm of the Split, and the *dérapage* of Irish politics by the time of Parnell's death, is rendered in

83. *U* 7.61–62.

microcosm in the Christmas dinner scene of *A Portrait*. The bitterly moralistic Dante Riordan treats Parnellism as the repudiation of Catholicism, goading Mr Casey into a rhetorical repudiation of God, which she receives with a cry of triumph. In the micro-politics of the Split, she can be taken as an assiduous reader of the *Irish Catholic*, whose absolutist anti-Parnellite argument her declamations faithfully reproduce. The alignment of Dante with the *Irish Catholic* rather than with the more mainstream—if still ferocious—anti-Parnellite *National Press* seems deliberate. The viciously personalised idiom of the Split, more typical of Healy and the *National Press*, is evoked, with the sly feminisation characteristic of Joyce's treatment of Healy, through the 'old harridan' at the Arklow meeting who chants, '*Priesthunter! The Paris Funds! Mr Fox! Kitty O'Shea!*', and into whose eye Casey spat the tobacco he was chewing.[84] Joyce's incorporation of the trajectory of the *Irish Catholic* in the Christmas dinner scene reflects his appreciation that a decisive eruption of assertively Catholic nationalism in a modern form had occurred in the Split and permitted him to present the crisis of Church and nation at its most philosophically stark.

In the Christmas dinner scene in *A Portrait*, Joyce realised a stylised model of the Split. The role of the Church, the merging of Catholic and nationalist values in Healyite rhetoric, the anathematisation of Catholic Parnellites that was such a marked feature of the Split, and the role of the *Irish Catholic* in overreaching Healy and his *National Press* combine to provide the Christmas dinner with an extratextual historicity that enhances its harrowing verisimilitude.

The conviction that Irish politics had frozen itself led Joyce to freeze-frame Irish politics in the Split, from the divorce decree to the immediate aftermath of Parnell's death, a period that ran from November 1890 to December 1891. It is only in this limited sense that it is valid to speak of what the historian and biographer of Parnell F.S.L. Lyons termed, a little patronisingly, Joyce's 'arrested Parnellism'.[85]

84. *P* 1.1027–28.

85. Lyons, 'James Joyce's Dublin', 20.

The *Lyceum*: The Jesuits and the Parnell Split

Jesuit thinking, or a form of it, finds expression in the *Lyceum* (1887–94). It was founded and first edited by Fr T. A. Finlay, though some of its religious content came from the pen of his more austerely hard-line younger brother, Fr Peter Finlay, a theologian.[86] The *Lyceum* was closely associated with University College.[87] In his memoir of his university life, which with characteristic diffidence followed his memoir of Joyce, Constantine Curran describes the journal as 'conservative without being reactionary . . . observant and critical of the new trends in literature, practical in analysis, cautious, and beyond measure reticent in domestic politics': 'From start to finish, that is to say from 1887 to 1894, over the period of the land agitation, the later Home Rule movement and throughout the Parnell "split", the name of Parnell or of the Land League or of the National League, so far as I can see, does not occur in the paper. It is true that during the "split" in 1892 and 1893 there are three articles of an expository character—I should think from the pen of Father Peter Finlay—on the relation of Church authority with politics. But that is all.'[88]

86. See Thomas J. Morrissey, 'Thomas Aloysius Finlay and Peter Finlay', *DIB* 3:789–91. T. A. Finlay edited *Lyceum* from September 1887 to October 1891; its editor for the remainder of its existence was William Magennis. Its mission was thus formulated in the Jesuit history of the college and was noted, curiously enough, to have attracted the attention of W. T. Stead: 'The *Lyceum* was endeavouring to pull the Irish Catholic out of his political rut, to give him a Catholic consciousness which would inform his life in other directions beyond the mere interests of party politics. Stead, with his flair for new movements, seems to have seen the *Lyceum* in a clearer light than its Irish readers, for again and again he noticed it in his *Review of Reviews*.' It was succeeded in 1894 by the better-known *New Ireland Review*. Fathers of the Society of Jesus, *A Page of Irish History: Story of University College, Dublin, 1883–1909* (Dublin: Talbot, 1930), 289–90, 298–99, 299–322.

87. 'Its staff were all connected with the College, and as such their interests were primarily scholastic.' Curran, *Under the Receding Wave*, 76.

88. Curran, *Under the Receding Wave*, 76–79. Curran (78) refers to an article on Giordano Bruno. It is in large part an attack on the cult of Bruno ('But heroes of some kind, the modern Continental democrat must have for worship') and on the government of Francesco Crispi, but contains an account, probably second hand, of the procession in Bruno's memory and the unveiling of the monument to Bruno in the Campo de' Fiori on 9 June 1889. 'Giordano Bruno and United Italy', *Lyceum* 3, no. 25 (September 1889): 7–10.

These 'three articles of an expository character' (actually four) prompted the comment in the Jesuit history of the college that 'these are in a sense strongly political articles, but the Parnell controversy brought politics into the sanctuary itself to religion's very great detriment'.[89] Probably, as Curran suggests, written by Peter Finlay, the articles are barren of historical argument—the Jesuits were determined to cut off the Fenian-Parnellite argument concerning the political role of the Irish Church from the Act of Union[90]—and essentially theologically exegetical. The Jesuits were perhaps more conscious than the diocesan clergy and hierarchy of the need to tread a fine line in warning of the pernicious consequences of anticlericalism while avoiding any suggestion that anticlericalism had any immediate prospect of taking hold in Ireland, seeking in that way to articulate not a vulgar triumphalism from the Split (such as that of the *Irish Catholic*) but rather the quiet confidence of Catholic order restored. It was in its own way just as galling. Joyce was always intrigued by the professed dispassionateness of Jesuit ratiocination and jousted with it with feigned urbanity in University College, but was to repudiate its intellectual abstractness in *Stephen Hero*. It is a dimension of Joyce's revolt that is inadequately acknowledged.

The first *Lyceum* editorial article was entitled 'The Anti-clerical Cry'. While acknowledging that bishops and priests could in theory err in the political domain, it concluded with what would be termed in contemporary electoral law, skewed as that was, a spiritual threat (or perhaps a reminder of a spiritual threat) to Catholic Parnellites who challenged the role of the clergy:

> To arouse angry feelings against the priesthood is to inflict grievous injury upon the church. . . . Teach the people to contemn or hate their clergy, the practice of religion will not long survive the change of feeling. Non-Catholics cannot of course be expected to rate this

89. Fathers of the Society of Jesus, *Page of Irish History*, 297.

90. 'We are not concerned even to deny that a number of our bishops were mistaken in their Union policy. As a matter of personal opinion, we are very far from thinking them mistaken.' *Lyceum* 5, no. 6 (August–September 1892): 267.

> consideration highly. In their eyes it might even be a move for encouraging an anti-clerical agitation. But with Catholics it must be otherwise. . . . It must be a very great and a very certain political good which can prove a set-off against the injury to souls; and be the good what it may, those Catholics will have a serious account to render, who, unauthorised, and heedless of the means provided for redress, seek to remedy their grievances by dividing priest from people, to win a passing temporal success at the cost of large eternal interests.[91]

The author, probably Peter Finlay, of this sequence in the *Lyceum* reflected in the second article the Catholic internationalism of the Jesuits, to which Joyce's socialism can be seen in one aspect as an adaptive riposte:

> In Ireland, our Bishops too have ventured to declare that the moral should not be unconsidered in the domain of politics, and that a certain line of public conduct is necessary to give effect to the principle; at once the French anti-Catholic cry: *l'ennemi c'est le clericalisme,* has been raised in Ireland, and the clergy have been denounced on the platform and in the newspaper as unmeasuredly and as unreasonably as by any French atheistic and Freemason officials. 'No Bishop, no Priest, in politics' was adopted as the watchword of a party, composed largely of men who were born in the Church and should not ignore its doctrines.[92]

It was not, of course, that Ireland was threatened by 'the anti-Catholic policy' of 'M. Gambetta, or Prince Bismarck, or Signor Crispi', in France, Germany, and Italy, respectively: 'We are dealing with a mere hypothesis.'[93]

The third, and most revealing, article followed the success of the Parnellite petition in the South Meath election which resulted in setting aside the anti-Parnellite victory at the general election. The outcome,

91. 'The Anti-clerical Cry', *Lyceum* 6, no. 60 (August–September 1892).
92. 'The Bishops and Political Morality', *Lyceum* 6, no. 62 (November 1892): 23–26
93. 'The Bishops and Political Morality'.

further discussed in this chapter, controversial as it was, represented a check in the progress of anti-Parnellism after Parnell's death. What put the *Lyceum* editorialist under greater pressure than in the preceding articles was the setting aside by a judge (even if a Catholic judge: 'We do not regard Mr. Justice O'Brien as an especially enlightened exponent of Catholic theology')[94] of an election on the grounds of improper ecclesiastical influence in the anti-Parnellite interest, which starkly posed the issue of the proper domain of ecclesiastical authority. The effect produced was extraordinary. It prompted Peter Finlay, the presumed editorialist, to engage in an unrelenting rehearsal of the ultramontanism of the first Vatican Council of 1869–70,[95] situating Ireland in response to the Parnell Split squarely in the great deferred wave of reaction to the French Revolution and its outfall that swept through continental Catholicism in the nineteenth century.[96] Finlay upheld the view of Church doctrine of Cardinal Henry Edward Manning, one of the most influential and politically unscrupulous advocates of ultramontanism at the Council and after, against Gladstone's then-famous and still-resented *The Vatican Decrees in Their Bearing on Civil Allegiance: A Political Expostulation* of 1874.[97] He cited with approbation Manning's statement that 'it is clear that the Civil Power cannot define how far the circumference

94. The author could not let go of the idea of addressing the judge at the level of his Catholicism. The article concluded, 'Incidentally, it has appeared that Mr. Justice O'Brien was singularly unfitted to deal with the facts and inferences of the South Meath Election, so far as their due appreciation involved a knowledge of the doctrines of his Church. But this is a matter of minor moment, and of interest mainly if not solely for the Judge himself.' 'The South Meath Judgement', *Lyceum* 6, no. 64 (January 1893): 71–78.

95. This followed the definition of the Immaculate Conception in 1884 and the publication of the *Syllabus Errorum* in 1864, all during the reign of Pius IX (Pio Nono).

96. This is brilliantly analysed in the first and second chapters of John W. O'Malley, *Vatican I: The Council and the Making of the Ultramontane Church* (Cambridge, MA: Belknap, 2018). The relevance of ultramontanism for Joyce's relation to and treatment of Catholicism is discussed in chapter 2 of Geert Lernout, *Help My Unbelief: James Joyce and Religion* (London: Continuum, 2010), 28–35.

97. As H.C.G. Matthew wrote, 'The success of ultramontanism seemed to Gladstone to mark a major crisis in the progress of "civic individuality" in Europe, as well as in its effect on Anglican-Roman relations in England and on the Irish situation.' Matthew, *Gladstone, 1809–1874* (Oxford: Clarendon, 1986), 183.

of faith and moral extends. If it could, it would be invested with one of the supernatural endowments of the Church'. Finlay put it plainly: 'The attitude of men who would claim to be Catholics, while questioning or rejecting the Church's rights to define her own jurisdiction, can only be paralleled by that of the Jansenists . . . and that of Dr. Dollinger's followers in more recent times'. Finlay's argument cast a penumbra of ecclesiastical authority beyond infallibility: the Church 'has unquestionably the right to determine, and that infallibly, what the limits of her jurisdiction in faith and morals are.' The bishops singly or in council had the right 'to determine—fallibly but authoritatively—all questions of faith and morals which are neither "greater causes" reserved to the Holy See nor the subjects of controversy among grave theologians'. Taking as his point of departure a somewhat inept observation of the High Court judge who heard the petition, Finlay epitomised the issue of the Split in its moral aspect:

> The battle had been raging around this one question: Did these frailties and shames, when proved judicially, disqualify a man from being the guide and leader of Catholic people? The Bishops had answered 'Yes'—and declared that the retention of such a man in the highest place of honour and of trust in the nation's gift would be gravely prejudicial to the interests of morality; and a party had arisen which flouted the Bishops' teaching, and roundly denied their right to address it to the faithful. The issue was far more vital than any connected with the unhappy personality who gave occasion to it. It was a principle, not a man, that was at stake—and, when the man was laid to rest, the parties to the struggle recognised logically and rightly that his withdrawal made no charge. Personal sin and personal shame were buried with him; but the question remained and had to be fought out, were the Bishops within their rights when they taught, and were the clergy and great majority of Irish Catholics fulfilling a plain duty when they accepted their teaching, that convicted sin and shame, such as his had been, are a bar to the leadership of the Catholics of Ireland?[98]

98. 'The South Meath Judgement'.

Finlay at the end quite deliberately restated as a theological proposition what Bishop Nulty of Meath had been condemned in the judgement for conveying to the Catholics of his diocese. He had established, he asserted, that 'the exercise of the franchise, in Meath as elsewhere, may involve grave moral obligation—obligation under sin, even mortal sin; that it may in certain cases be mortally sinful to vote for or against particular Parliamentary candidates; and that where such a case occurs, it may be the duty of a confessor to intimate his obligation to a penitent, and deny him sacramental absolution should he refuse to comply with it'.[99]

The relatively short life of the *Lyceum* antedated Joyce's arrival in University College but it still informed the ambience of the college. Curran, referring to what he called '*The Lyceum*'s air of curule authority', noted that 'enough of [its] traits survived in my early [student] days to mark a good deal of college teaching.'[100] This renders it unnecessary to establish whether Joyce read Finlay's articles, though he probably did.[101] Peter Finlay was unswayed by the commitment to social progress of his famously sociable elder brother. Most Irish Jesuits would have shied away from the right of encroachment on the civic terrain of the political that he asserted, but without challenging the correctness of his highly aggressive—professedly apolitical but actually antipolitical—theology. The articles in the *Lyceum* are of prime importance for an understanding of Joyce's attack on ecclesiastical influence in Ireland because they emblematise so exactly what he was attacking. He was determined to respond at the level at which the argument was pitched and to match its scope. There is something in the scale of Jesuit intellectuality that Joyce takes up as a challenge, to which he responds with Luciferian ambitiousness (even if he was Luciferian in nothing else). In a way that is not easy to define, a coldly furious argument with the Jesuits lies close to the heart of Joyce's revolt against Irish Catholicism. The attraction for Joyce

99. 'The South Meath Judgement'.

100. Curran, *Under the Receding Wave*, 77, 79.

101. The title itself would philosophically have elicited his curiosity as an Aristotelian. The Lyceum was the gymnasium and grove beside the Temple of Apollo in Athens, where Aristotle taught.

in early exile of Italian revolutionary syndicalism as an integrated political doctrine owes something to his striving for a reach to match that of Catholicism.[102] There is something apt in the fact that, even though the Split continued to rage on Parnell's death, the two people in Ireland who believed most unflinchingly that 'the question remained and had to be fought out' were Joyce and the writer of those words in the *Lyceum*.

A further article in the *Lyceum*, in June 1893, contained the journal's confident retrospect on the Split up to that point: 'The bitter struggle of these last few years has shown conclusively how firm a hold religious principles have taken of the hearts and minds of our people'. A Catholic order had been restored:

> The Catholicity of Ireland has passed through the crucible since the close of 1890; and it has not suffered in the process. No doubt wild things have been said, most anti-Catholic doctrines have been preached by men previously reputed Catholics. But they found little or no echo in the country. They were pitied or despised, and condemned by nearly every Catholic. Influence they had none, except with a few dupes, and others predisposed to quarrel with the clergy; what influence they had is waning rapidly.... Those who know the country best, and are best able to judge of its condition, appear to think that religious influences were never more actively at work, that people and clergy were never more cordially united, than they are throughout Ireland generally at present. And we can ask no better augury for a Home Rule future.[103]

The 'Nonconformist Conscience'

What became known as the 'nonconformist conscience' in Britain found definitive expression in the Parnell divorce crisis and is a central element in Joyce's assessment of the Split. The term 'the nonconformist

102. See chapter 11, '"Professing to Be a Socialist"'.

103. 'Religion in the Home Rule Controversy', *Lyceum* 6, no. 69 (June 1893): 193–94.

conscience' was formulated in the Split in a letter received by *The Times* from a Wesleyan minister condemning Parnell. The paper seized on the term, and it entered public currency. What it described was the political expression of the intertwining of moral and social concerns of the non-Anglican Protestant churches in late Victorian England. What rendered it politically potent was the preponderant influence of nonconformists in the Liberal party, taken in conjunction with the fact that Gladstone had presented Home Rule for Ireland as a moral crusade. Gladstone had written to Parnell in advance of Parnell's visit to Hawarden that 'the back-bone of the Liberal party lies in the Nonconformists of England and Wales, and the Presbyterians of Scotland. These men have a higher level and stiffer rule of action than the Tory party.'[104]

The Liberal leadership and its semi-official organ, the *Daily News*, initially responded to the divorce decree with silence. The first editorial demands for Parnell's resignation came in the *Pall Mall Gazette*, lately edited by W. T. Stead, in its issue of 18 November 1890, followed by the weekend organs of the 'nonconformist conscience' on 20 November, synchronically with Michael Davitt's English-based *Labour World*. Outraged by Irish expressions of support for Parnell, the extravagantly evangelical Wesleyan Methodist Hugh Price Hughes wrote in his *Methodist Times*,

> We do not hesitate to say that if the Irish race deliberately select as their recognised representative an adulterer of Mr. Parnell's type they are as incapable of self-government as their bitterest enemies have asserted. So obscene a race as in those circumstances they would prove themselves to be would obviously be unfit for anything except a military despotism. . . . We are quite certain that the religious nonconformists of England, Wales, and Scotland will not allow any political principle to outweigh the tremendous moral issue which is now at stake. We have fought for a quarter of a century in favour of social purity, and we are not going to abandon all the fruits of victory even for the sake of home rule.[105]

104. Gladstone to Parnell, 30 August 1889 (copy), cited in Richard Shannon, *Gladstone: Heroic Minister, 1865–1898* (London: Allan Lane, Penguin, 1999), 484, 497.

105. *Methodist Times*, 20 November 1890.

What Hughes said in his weekly Sunday afternoon conference in St James's Hall on 'the public moral aspect of the Parnell case' anticipated what the anti-Parnellite moralists would proclaim in Ireland: 'We stand immovably on this eternal rock; what is morally wrong can never be politically right; and we are certain that any politician who is the acknowledged enemy of God and social purity can, under no circumstances, be the true friend and rightful leader of men.' Hughes had led the Methodist campaign for the repeal of the Contagious Diseases Acts, asserted to condone prostitution, and invoked the lesson learnt in that campaign that 'the sacred cause of Social Purity would never be secured until all notoriously immoral men were expelled from the House of Commons.'[106] The championship of populistic moralism owed something to inter-confessional competitiveness. Hughes was shortly to boast in an editorial in the *Methodist Times*, 'The strength of British Nonconformity was emphasized by the fact that for reasons into which we need not now enter, the Anglican Church, and even the Roman Catholic Church in Ireland preserved an absolute silence. The great battle of public morality—one of the most serious that has ever affected the course of British history—has been fought and won by the Nonconformists and the Nonconformists alone.'[107]

The groundswell of general nonconformist opposition to Parnell, and not just that expressed by the more vociferous exponents of the nonconformist conscience, weighed heavily with Gladstone, even if he declined to condemn Parnell on directly moral grounds.[108] While Gladstone also had the prospect of Tory derision on English platforms to consider, its publicists asserted that it was only the nonconformist conscience that prompted him to despatch his letter to John Morley stating

106. *Methodist Times*, 27 November 1890; John F. Glaser, 'Parnell's Fall and the Nonconformist Conscience', *Irish Historical Studies* 12 (September 1960): 199–238; Christopher Oldstone-Moore, 'The Fall of Parnell: Hugh Price Hughes and the Nonconformist Conscience', *Eire-Ireland* 30, no. 4 (Winter 1996): 94–110.

107. *Methodist Times*, 11 December 1890, cited in Oldstone-Moore, 'Fall of Parnell', 102.

108. It is fitting in a biographical study of Joyce to add that the great and much lamented authority on Gladstone H.C.G. Matthew recorded that Gladstone, in a memorandum written on 29 December 1890, his birthday, 'recorded the full extent of the débâcle, triggered by what he called "the sin of Tristram with Isault"' (*Gladstone*, 315).

that Parnell's continued leadership of the Irish Party would negate his leadership of the Liberal Party, and the claim was widely credited.[109] In the aftermath of Gladstone's intervention, and Parnell's retaliatory manifesto, the *Daily News*, a little awkwardly and quite unnecessarily, furnished a script for the anti-Parnellite campaign in Ireland:

> Mr. Parnell seems to have resolved that if he falls he will drag the Home Rule cause and the cause of the people and the tenants of Ireland with him. It will be for the patriotic men who have been the mainstay of the Nationalist movement to stand like a priest of old 'between the living and the dead till the plague be stayed'. They must make the Irish masses fully acquainted with the sad revelations of the Divorce Court, and they must make it clear to them that the whole of the present difficulty arises from the moral revulsion of the English people against lawlessness which invades the family and destroys the sacredness of domestic life. The question before the Irish people is whether they will quarrel with their English friends on grounds like these, or whether they will go on to gain the freedom they desire under another leader.[110]

Closely aligned with the 'nonconformist conscience' properly so called were the effusions of the campaigning journalism of William T. Stead. Stead (1849–1912) was to be a figure of especial significance for Joyce, who was familiar with his journalism even before meeting Francis Skeffington, a University College contemporary who was a disciple of Stead. An avatar of the 'New Journalism' that Matthew Arnold had condemned in 1887,[111] Stead's appetite for popular moralising was already

109. W. T. Stead later wrote, 'It was not until the Nonconformist conscience had begun to move very vigorously in the country, and found expression in the press and especially in the Sheffield caucus, that Mr. Gladstone suddenly woke up to the fact that something ought to be done, and as a result we had the famous letter from Hawarden excommunicating Mr. Parnell.' Stead, 'Archbishop Croke', *Review of Reviews* 12 (14 September 1895): 213.

110. *Daily News*, 29 November 1890.

111. In his masterly analysis of the New Journalism, Stephen Koss cites the more temperate formulation of its purpose by T. P. O'Connor, 'another of the founding fathers of the New Journalism', in 1889. He notes the embrace of the techniques of the New Journalism by the more staid 'quality' dailies: '*The Times*'s reports of the Parnell scandal were worthy of Zola or Flaubert.' Stephen Koss, *The Rise and Fall of the Political Press in Britain* (1981; repr., London: Fontana 1990), 343–46.

demonstrated in the 'Maiden Tribute of Modern Babylon', a child-prostitution exposé of July 1885, and less defensibly in his remorseless assault on the prominent Liberal politician Sir Charles Dilke, whose career was broken as a result of contested allegations made in a society divorce case, and whose return to political life intersected with the Parnell Split. Dilke returned to the House of Commons at the 1892 general election, though his career thenceforth was shorn of its former high political prospects.

Stead's moralism and the enhanced populism of the British press were inseparably bound up. He declared at the century's end, 'The printing press has become the Pulpit of Civilisation in the Nineteenth Century.'[112] T. P. O'Connor observed, 'Stead would be a capital newspaper man if he were not so much of a fanatic, and a capital fanatic if he were not so much of a newspaperman.'[113] Stead was an opinion-former of unrestrained egotism who exerted an immense influence in late Victorian Britain. An exponent of 'Government by Journalism',[114] he was drawn compulsively to making active and typically inept interventions in contemporary politics. His vociferous support of Home Rule was that of both a radical Liberal and an imperialist. Stead's somewhat fitful interest in Ireland was as a theatre of British moral sentiment rather than in the Irish cause itself. He later confessed that his one-time journalistic mentor John Morley used 'to bore me to death on Ireland'.[115]

Stead wrote of O'Connor, 'T. P. was one of the old Pall Mallers who from Morley to Milner have left so deep a dent upon the history of our time. He and I may fairly claim to have revolutionised English journalism'. Stead, 'Character Sketch: T. P. O'Connor, M. P.', *Review of Reviews* 26 (15 November 1902): 478.

112. W. T. Stead, *Lest We Forget: A Keepsake from the Nineteenth Century* (London: *Review of Reviews* office, 1901), 51.

113. T. P. O'Connor quoted in William O'Brien, *An Olive Branch in Ireland* (London: Macmillan, 1910), 10n1.

114. W. T. Stead, 'Government by Journalism', *Contemporary Review* 49 (1886): 664; Koss, *Rise and Fall*, 14, 343; Backus, *Scandal Work*, 28, 234n3. Backus writes that in the 'Circe' episode of *Ulysses*, 'the New Journalism's keynote sex scandal, "The Maiden Tribute of Modern Babylon" flagrantly informs Bloom's surreal descent into Dublin's brothel district' and picks up Bloom's reference in 'Eumaeus' to 'our modern Babylon' (*Scandal Work*, 202–3).

115. *Review of Reviews* 2 (November 1890): 429, cited in W. Sydney Robinson, *Muckraker: The Scandalous Life and Times of W. T. Stead* (London: Robson, 2012), 49.

Stead first visited Ireland in the autumn of 1886. He inquired of a prominent official of the National League, whom he later identified as Tim Harrington, whether there was any truth in the rumours of Parnell's involvement with Katharine O'Shea, and said the reply was, 'For God's sake, never breathe that woman's name in Ireland. We hope there may be nothing in it, and there may be nothing in it. If (which God forbid) there were anything in it, then it would be all up with Parnell in Ireland. No power on earth could save Parnell then.'[116] Following the appearance of a paragraph in the *Pall Mall Gazette* (which Stead then edited) that asserted Parnell was staying at Eltham in the absence of Captain William O'Shea, O'Shea called to the paper in December 1886 and indignantly assured Stead that he was entirely satisfied that the relations between Parnell and his wife were quite correct. This, Stead was to claim, led him to deny credence to the rumours of the affair and contributed to his fury when the divorce court evidence apprised him of their truth. O'Shea's denials were reinforced by Michael Davitt's reassuring of Stead that Parnell, who he said had never deceived him, had assured him that the allegations in the divorce petition were untrue. The supposed deception of Davitt was to feature prominently in Stead's attack on Parnell.[117] Whether Parnell simply lied or, what is marginally more probable, assured the naïve and inexact Davitt that he would emerge vindicated from the divorce proceedings is a matter of controversy.

Stead was also excited by the fact that Edward Caulfield Houston, the secretary of the Irish Loyal and Patriotic Union, had originally offered him what transpired to be the Pigott forgeries. He referred Houston to *The Times*.[118] This gave him a certain entrée into the 'Parnellism and

116. W. T. Stead, 'The Story of an Incident in the Home Rule Cause: The Fall of Mr Parnell', *Review of Reviews* 2 (December 1890): 598–608. Harrington is identified as the National League official in Stead's character sketch of Archbishop Croke ('Archbishop Croke', 212).

117. 'As my action in this matter has been much commented on, I may say that, while I did not like the adultery, it was not the breach of the Seventh Commandment that convinced me that Mr. Parnell had become impossible. The damning thing was the deliberate perfidy with which he had deceived Davitt.' Stead, 'Story of an Incident', 602.

118. 'Mr. Charles S. Parnell', *Review of Reviews* 1 (February 1890): 104–6.

Crime' controversy and the proceedings of the Special Commission, which he assiduously attended.[119] An intended intervention by Stead in advance of the sittings of the commission which threatened to destabilise the carefully conceived strategy to discredit forensically *The Times* case, and must have pertained to Pigott's role, infuriated Parnell. In response to an abbreviated account published on Parnell's death by an emissary of Stead who had approached Parnell with 'certain information which it was fondly believed would be welcomed by him', J. M. Tuohy recalled vividly the response of the Irish leader:

> The only occasion on which I ever knew him to lose his temper with a journalist was indeed when the provocation offered was beyond all endurance. . . . It was when Mr. Parnell was engaged with the utmost labour, and in face of unimaginable difficulties, in unravelling the forgery conspiracy, and when a premature disclosure of what had been done might easily have caused irreparable injury to his case. It is not hard to picture to oneself, therefore, the chagrin and annoyance one evening on being informed in the lobby by a representative of the *Pall Mall* that the indefatigable Mr. Stead had also forced his finger into the pie, and was meditating some action which would give the whole case away, and enable the forgery and perjury party to acquire all the benefits. Mr. Parnell turned on the journalist—who was merely Mr. Stead's plenipotentiary in the matter—and cried, in a voice loud enough to be heard all round . . . 'In God's name why does not Mr. Stead occupy himself with his own affairs and cease intermeddling with those of other people who don't need his assistance?'[120]

Stead, who had relinquished the editorship of the *Pall Mall Gazette* to establish the *Review of Reviews*, seized exultantly on the divorce crisis. On 19 November 1890 he wrote to Gladstone, of whom he aspired to constitute himself the journalistic conscience, that if Parnell did not

119. W. T. Stead, 'Lord Russell of Killowen, Lord Chief Justice of England', *Review of Reviews* 22 (15 September 1900): 230–33.

120. *Pall Mall Gazette*, 8 October 1891; *Freeman's Journal*, 9 October 1891.

relinquish the leadership of the Irish Party then he would be unwillingly 'compelled to undertake a vigorous campaign on press and platform against having this convinced liar and thoroughfaced scoundrel foisted on us by virtue of our Home Rule Alliance.'[121] He wrote again the next day, 'I know my Nonconformists well, and no power on earth will induce them to follow that man to the poll, if you are arm in arm in him.'[122] Stead despatched to what he termed his 'Helpers' (active subscribers and correspondents) a leaflet entitled 'Home Rule or Mr. Parnell?', which concluded, 'If the rump of the Irish party, against the convictions of many of the best of their leaders, determine to have this man to represent them, then in the Home Rule host in this country will be heard the cry, "To your Tents, O Israel!"'[123]

He followed this with a penny pamphlet titled *The Discrowned King of Ireland*, a copy of which was despatched to 'every Helper in the three kingdoms, and to every Catholic priest in Ireland.' Stead wrote an extended article on the crisis for his *Review of Reviews* for December 1890.[124] His *Discrowned King* was characterised by a politically competitive moralism. Stead sought to set himself apart, and to achieve an ascendancy over both Gladstone and the Liberal leadership, and over rival champions of the nonconformist conscience, notably Hugh Price Hughes. In this politico-moral struggle, Ireland became a subordinate element, a province of Liberal moral providentialism. Home Rule, once at least notionally the subject of high political Liberal-Conservative contestation, was now the subject of the fluctuating moralism of Liberal sentiment. With the Split, an Ireland without Parnell was entrapped within the 'union of hearts', no longer an alliance but an inexorable regression into dependency.

121. Stead to Gladstone, 19 November 1890, Gladstone Papers, British Library BM Add MS 56448, quoted in Shannon, *Gladstone*, 497.

122. Stead to Gladstone, 20 November 1890, Gladstone Papers, British Library BM Add MS 56448, f. 30, quoted in Callanan, *Parnell Split*, 17–18; Shannon, *Gladstone*, 497.

123. *Daily Chronicle*, 21 November 1890. The 'manifesto' was by Stead and Dr H. T. Lunn. It elicited an impressive rejoinder from R. B. Cunninghame Graham in the *Star* (25 November 1890).

124. Stead, 'Story of an Incident', 606–7.

Much of the controversy in Ireland surrounding the role of the exponents of the nonconformist conscience and of Stead had to do with the fact that they, along with Michael Davitt's *Labour World*, were first in the field after the divorce court decree. As the *Pall Mall Gazette* boasted in its account of the Split, 'The Puritan section of the Liberal Party was the first to speak.'[125] This was at a time when it was widely believed in Britain that nationalist Ireland would cleave to the Irish leader. The almost reflexive manifestations of support for Parnell at the outset from the two nationalist meetings in Dublin, from the Irish Party emissaries in the United States, and from the *Freeman's Journal*, coupled with the erroneous inference drawn from the silence of the Irish hierarchy, seemed to affirm the idea of Parnell's invincibility on the terrain of Ireland. Apart from the intriguing prospect of a culture war between Irish Catholics and British nonconformists, the maintenance of support for Parnell in Ireland portended the sundering of the Liberal-nationalist alliance, certainly in its then-current form, which would have represented a true crisis for the Liberals. With the overthrow of Parnell and the election in North Kilkenny, the threat receded.

Stead's preface to *The Discrowned King* was written in two stages, the first before the opening of Parliament, and the second as the Irish Party met in Committee Room 15. In his preface, Stead lamented in his gratingly portentous manner,

> I am almost heartbroken over this sad, sad tragedy. Oh the pity of it! The pity of it! To see a nation's hopes blighted on the verge of fruition, the labour of twelve long years of toil and agony undone in a moment, and all because of one man's weakness and of one woman's sin. What a sacrifice to be exacted, how immense the disproportion between the incident that has provoked the catastrophe and the doom that impends. But of the fact there can unfortunately be no doubt at all. As it was one woman's faithlessness that led the Greeks to the Trojan war, and one man's crime that opened the gate of Europe to the Moorish invasion that submerged Spain, so it seems

125. 'The Story of the Parnell Crisis', *Pall Mall Gazette*, 'Extra' No. 54, January 1891, 37.

> possible that Ireland, just as she is on the verge of triumph, may be thrust into the outer darkness by the sinister figure of Mrs. O'Shea.[126]

In a strange, haunting prolepsis, Stead palliated Irish support for Parnell in extravagantly patronising terms that disclosed the shallowness of his Irish sympathies:

> That in the first moment of confusion and of bewilderment, the Irish, speaking by the voice of those who have followed Mr. Parnell into Parliament, should have failed to perceive that the Star of Avondale has set is but natural. The Irish are a passionate, enthusiastic race. Their personal loyalty to their chieftains has in every age been one of the most strongly marked characteristics of the nation. . . . Under the sway of emotion rather than under the guidance of calculation they have refused to admit that they are leaderless. They have rallied round the empty chair of their discrowned king, and cry aloud for him to lead them forth to battle as of yore. It is often so when a leader falls. His followers cannot believe that so small a wound should have slain so great a warrior. And sometimes, as in the case of Frederick Barbarossa and many another, this deep-seated illusion of the human heart gives rise to strange dreams of the coming of a day when the long-lost leader will return and give victory to his people. But as the fiercest protestations of undying loyalty never brought back the dead, so no amount of vehement asseverations of devotion to Mr. Parnell can put him back in his old position as leader of the Irish race, joint leader of the Home Rule Party with Mr. Gladstone. The dead come not back save in the visions of the night, and Mr. Parnell's leadership is as much the memory of the past as the dictatorship of Julius Caesar.

126. W. T. Stead, *The Discrowned King of Ireland* (London: Review of Reviews, 1890), 2. Stead had a strange fixation on the influence exerted by older women over the male politicians whose lovers they were: 'That weird legend of the Northern lands is not more tragic or more pitiful than the story of the part played by women of late years in the great tragedy of contemporary history. That Strange Woman has played the Werewolf with a vengeance among the foremost men of our time. . . . The Were-Wolf Woman of Irish politics cannot be shaken off.' Stead, 'Mrs. O'Shea', *Review of Reviews* 2 (December 1890): 529.

> We listen to the clamour of protestations of devotion to Mr. Parnell which reaches us from the other side of the Irish Channel, and we recognize it as another form of the wailing keen which the Irish are wont to raise over the bier of those they have loved.[127]

Stead then embarked on a vacuous calibration of sexual immorality. He characterised adultery as 'a vice which varies by infinite gradations from the border of virtue to the confines of the abyss of the blackest crime', so that 'no sane man would every seriously assert that no person guilty of adultery should ever take part in public life'. Parnell, however, 'stands officially branded by judge and jury with having accepted his friend's hospitality in order to debauch that friend's wife'. He was moreover impenitent: 'He stands with head erect and with a smile of well-bred amazement on his features that anyone should dream of condemning his relations with Mrs. O'Shea'. He could not be trusted. Referring to Gladstone's letter, Stead wrote, 'That which weighed most with political men in England was not Mr. Parnell's adultery, but the evidence which it afforded of Mr. Parnell's incurable duplicity'. Stead concluded, 'No power on earth will ever induce the British public to establish Home Rule in order that the Discrowned King may make Mrs. O'Shea the Uncrowned Queen of Ireland as Mrs. Parnell'.[128]

In the extended article he wrote on 2 December 1890 for his *Review of Reviews*, Stead celebrated the expression of a newly invigorated popular morality in Britain to which Gladstone, as the leader of the Liberal party, had been compelled to yield. This robust sentiment had been called into being in reaction to the endorsements of Parnell by Irish nationalist politicians in the immediate aftermath of the divorce court verdict:

> If they had remained silent it is possible that English opinion might not have been so intensely excited. But it was more than flesh and blood could stand to hear the manner in which a grave outrage on the family and on morality was treated by the spokesmen of a race

127. Stead, *The Discrowned King of Ireland*, 4.
128. Stead, *The Discrowned King of Ireland*, 8, 11, 14.

> which has a right to regard itself as occupying a higher standard of morality in regard to those matters than either England or Scotland. We heard with amazement that, in the opinion of men who spoke for Catholic Ireland, adultery, complicated with treachery and habitual falsehood, was a venial offence, of no more account in the opinion of the people than the eating of flesh on Friday or non-attendance at church on Sunday. . . . The declarations at Dublin, unqualified by any expression of regret, or any sense of humiliation and shame at the degradation which has befallen the country, provoked an outburst of indignation on the part of the English public.

All that could be said was that 'unless Mr. Parnell is effaced, and that speedily, the Home Rule cause becomes practically extinct.'[129]

The Coincidence of Opposites

The two theatres, or spheres of action—nationalist Ireland and Britain—did not quite merge in the Split, but the competitively emulatory moralism unleashed by the Split did something to reconfigure their relationship. For the first time since the Act of Union, it was possible to contend that the United Kingdom of Great Britain and Ireland was a united moral realm, once the anti-Parnellites were taken to represent Irish nationalist sentiment. It was a strange and startling phenomenon that excited Joyce's philosophical scorn and political dread.

The fact that the 'nonconformist conscience' had declared itself first did not pass unobserved in Ireland. At the outset of the Split, moralistic Irish nationalists were exercised by what they considered the shameful anomaly that British nonconformists had condemned Parnell at a time when Catholic nationalist Ireland remained silent. The *Irish Catholic* wrote on 29 November 1890,

> So far we have dealt with this matter solely as a political one, but we must most earnestly point out to our people that something much

129. Stead, 'Story of an Incident', 598–608.

> more noble and more holy is at stake. The safeguarding of the elementary standards of national morality is in question, the sanctity of rules of life and conduct which are as the very basis of society and the foundation of the family and the home is imperilled. Is then the shameful story to be proclaimed to the world that Protestant England has shown a scrupulosity and anxiety about these things which Catholic Ireland was too craven to display? To us such a suggestion is not only hateful, but intolerable.[130]

A striking consequence of the sequencing of the emergence of opposition to Parnell's retention of the leadership is that there had been little public articulation of the deep moral repugnance felt by many Catholics at the disclosures of the divorce court before Gladstone's intervention. In whatever way that silence is to be construed, it leaves a historiographical void. While some Parnellite apologists, most notably the editorialists of the *Freeman's Journal*, alluded to Catholic disapprobation of Parnell's relations with a married woman, it was for the purpose of palliation. Prompted by what he termed 'the growth of public feeling in England and in Ireland, and the conflict of opinion between the two democracies' at the outset of the Split, the nationalist journalist and barrister John Francis Taylor, Irish correspondent of the *Manchester Guardian* and still in the brief interval of his initial support for Parnell, tried to explain the Irish position to his Liberal English readership: 'Probably if Mr. Parnell were left to the unfettered judgement of the Irish conscience it would have fared very hardly with him.' The Irish, 'the Old Guard among the European nations in championing social purity', were constrained by the consciousness of the 'magnificent services' rendered by Parnell, by the attacks he had borne over the previous decades in defending their interests, and by the consciousness of his indispensability. 'National humiliation and sorrow is one thing; national ruin is another.'[131] Taylor's article two days later reflected the pressure of Liberal outrage in the face of Irish political complaisance:

130. *Irish Catholic*, 29 November 1890.
131. *Manchester Guardian*, 24 November 1890.

> From all the sources of knowledge open to me I can say that no event in my recollection has so saddened and pained the Irish people. The reckless declarations on platforms must not deceive outsiders. Ireland is deeply shocked and shamed. The only white virtue to which she clung, her one special robe of glory, is besmirched and blackened. Hundreds of thousands of virtuous firesides are depressed and crushed as if by a family grief. That one unforgiveable blot cannot be mitigated or argued against. It cannot plead any of the provocations which lessen the guilt of other offences. All this is felt and the feeling is one of intolerable anguish. But we must and shall go through with it.

Taylor asserted: 'This is no case of closing a career. It is a question of political revolution in Ireland. Mr. Hughes and Mr. Stead are not wounding Mr. Parnell, but they are stabbing Ireland through him.'[132] That was the expiring gasp of Taylor as a defender of Parnell. Two days later, in the wake of the Gladstone letter, he switched to the anti-Parnellite side.

Parnell's apologists continuously sought to frame the Split as originating in the journalism of Stead and the exponents of the nonconformist conscience, and in the intrigues of radical 'wirepullers'. The *Freeman's Journal* vainly protested that 'it was Mr. Stead and the Rev. Hugh Price Hughes who raised the storm in England, and it was Mr. Stead whom the Irish Party obeyed when they endeavoured to thrust Mr. Parnell from the Chair of the Irish Party into the retirement of private life'.[133]

With Parnell's defeat in North Kilkenny in mid-December, Stead changed gear. In an article entitled 'North Kilkenny and Its Moral', he celebrated in extravagant terms the affirmation of Irish Catholic purity, and the new moral solidarity of British nonconformity and Irish Catholicism. He thus defined the issue in Kilkenny: 'That question was, broadly speaking, whether or not the Irish had ceased to be religious? whether or not the Isle of Saints had become the isle of cynics? whether or not the Irish people, who stand in the very front of Christian civilization for

132. *Manchester Guardian*, 26 November 1890.

133. *Freeman's Journal*, 31 March 1891; also see 10 April 1891.

purity of life and the reverence paid to the sanctity of the domestic hearth, had abandoned its moral pre-eminence, and sunk to the moral level of the London clubs?'[134]

The question extended to whether the Irish 'had confidence in their Priest'. Kilkenny was also the testing ground in Rome between the men of the old school and those of the new: 'The Old School is conservative and dynastic; the New School popular and democratic. The Pope is committed to neither'. The dispute was set to be determined: 'A typical Irish constituency was asked to decide yea or nay, whether the democratic policy of the Irish Church had justified the hopes of its leaders, or brought forth the evils so freely predicted by its enemies'. Parnell fell to the Catholic Church, which on this occasion proved to be 'the worthy exponent of the universal sentiment of the Christian conscience'. He saluted the moral coalescence of British nonconformity and Irish Catholicism:

> There was a time, not so long ago, when such a dramatic demonstration of the power of the Catholic priesthood of Ireland would have filled many Englishmen with dismay. Today it is not too much to say that there is hardly a Liberal in the United Kingdom who does not feel a profound sense of gratitude to the Pope's 'Black Dragoons', whose decisive charge swept Mr. Parnell from the field. The cassocked brigade, for perhaps the first time in our history, have won the enthusiastic admiration of the most Protestant of English Protestants. We have begun to recognise, however dimly and intermittently, that in the great moral and social questions which this generation has to solve, we are at one with the Catholic Church on a dozen points for one on which we differ. Of this [the] Kilkenny election was a vivid and conspicuous object-lesson. We are learning every day that in the campaign against the actual Devils of our time, we can, in nine cases out of ten, count upon the health, even when we are denied the sympathy, of the Catholic Church. And the more earnest we are in contending against the Evil One in all his protean shapes, the less inclined do we become to refuse as comrades in the war, those who

134. Stead, 'North Kilkenny'.

differ from us as to the Immaculate Conception or the doctrine of transubstantiation. It was worth the sacrifice of Mr. Parnell ten times over to bring the Catholic Clergy of Ireland into line with the militant Nonconformists of England.[135]

Stead pressed the question of whether the time had not now come 'for a more frank and friendly union between the two bodies which have saved the three Kingdoms from the profound moral disaster involved in the continued leadership of Mr. Parnell.' Warming to his theme, he bizarrely asserted that the priests and curates of Ireland could be acknowledged as 'the nineteenth century counterparts of the Puritan preachers and Covenanting confessors of the reign of the Stuarts': 'Although Cromwell's hot gospellers theologically were far apart from the Irish parish priest of the Catholic Church, they were in politics nearly identical. . . . Why should not the sons of the Puritans rejoice to recognize their spiritual kinship with the Catholic Clergy of Ireland? There is no danger of their absorbing us, or of our absorbing them. The Irish Ecclesiastical party, like the Irish political party, will find no difficulty in preserving its complete independence. . . . North Kilkenny is the first fruit of the new alliance.'[136]

History itself was yielding to the Catholic-nonconformist concordat. What Stead was proclaiming was a moral consensus that overrode the political differences between Ireland and Britain, and the doctrinal differences between Catholicism and Protestantism. This was both different from and went further than what was conventionally meant by the pejorative term 'Whiggery' in Irish politics, the support of the Liberals to secure office.

135. Stead, 'North Kilkenny'.

136. Stead, 'North Kilkenny'. Some five years later in a 'character sketch' of Archbishop Croke, Stead asserted that Parnell, seeking to elicit Croke's support for the Land League, had fallen on his knees before the archbishop. Stead wrote without the least trace of irony, 'It was a great scene which Thurles Palace witnessed that day, and one which perhaps an Irish Nationalist painter will commemorate some day. Mr. Parnell, a politician and leader of the Irish race, falling, Protestant though he was, at the feet of the Archbishop of Cashel, would make a very effective subject for a fresco on the walls of the Parliament House on College Green in which the first Home Rule Parliament assembled' ('Archbishop Croke', 210).

The significance of Stead lies not merely in the views he propagated but in the mode in which he gave them expression. Hugh Price Hughes, in his championship of 'Social Christianity', observed that 'the Press and the Pulpit are beginning to realise the advantage of an honourable alliance in the interest of justice and humanity. The Press, consciously or unconsciously, has exerted a very beneficent influence over the Pulpit.'[137] Stead saw his journalism not merely as aligned with the nonconformist conscience but as a definitive articulation of the spirit of the age. With its populistic moralising prurience, his campaign against Parnell was an ominous essay in the degeneracy of the new journalism. It was infused with a sense of the events of the Split as a tremendous moral spectacle. The 'historic importance' of the Kilkenny election was matched by its 'dramatic interest'. Stead's attentive professional eye was caught by the news bill of the *Echo* on the evening of 23 December: 'The man in the street read in monster type the execution of a murderess [Mrs. Pearcey], while the lower part of the bill was devoted to proclaiming the result of the Kilkenny election.'[138] This inspired Stead to write a portentous meditation on the more edifying sensationalism afforded by the Kilkenny election. Given the significance of the result,

> it is indeed marvellous that the blindest of the sub-editors or the most careless man in the crowd could for a moment have allowed his attention to be drawn away from the poll even by the execution of the worst criminal who ever swung upon the gallows. Even to the superficial observer the struggle was intensely interesting. It had all the excitement of the race for the Derby with something of the cruel fascination of the gladiatorial shows thrown in. It was a great drama in which the irresistible drollery of Irish humour was mingled with something of the awe of Greek tragedy. The genius of Lever never depicted scenes more exquisitely ludicrous than those which the papers recorded from day to day, and yet the tragic muse has seldom dealt with a more pathetic theme than that which unfolded day by day in North Kilkenny. The spectacle of Mr. Parnell, smitten as by the

137. Hugh Price Hughes, 'The Science of Preaching', *New Review*, June 1891, 494.

138. Stead, 'North Kilkenny'.

doom of the Gods, compelled to pull down with frenzied hands the edifice which he had spent the best years of his life in rearing with patient toil, striking mad blows at those who in many a well-fought field had been his most trusted comrades in arms, is one which fills the mind with a profound sense of pity and awe. It is as if we saw a nineteenth century Orestes pursued by the Furies.[139]

Stead's voyeuristic perspective on the contest in Ireland is striking. As his pre-eminence was turned against Parnell, the Split was rendered as the trial by ordeal of the Irish leader: 'Pale and haggard, with what seemed the fierce light of incipient madness flashing in his eyes, he hurried from town to town, from village to village, from hamlet to hamlet, breathing out threatenings and vengeance against the men who dared to oppose him. He spoke as if he had been the heir of a hundred kings insulted by the treachery of a miscreant mob.'[140]

The pervasive sense in Britain of the contest in Ireland as a cruel public entertainment was not confined to Stead's journalism. In one aspect the Split was the great late Victorian set piece of political scandal, played out on a much broader arena than the possibly wholly invented scandal that engulfed the promising career of the Liberal Sir Charles Dilke in 1885, and foreshadowing the conviction and imprisonment of Oscar Wilde a decade later.[141]

139. Stead, 'North Kilkenny', 336–37.

140. Stead, 'North Kilkenny', 337; Callanan, *Parnell Split*, 72–73.

141. It does not follow that it is valid to treat scandal, which might be the subject of an allegorical renaissance or baroque engraving, as a free-standing theme of Joyce's writing. Joyce's treatment of the Parnell Split is pre-eminently political, and informed by a philosophical aversion to introducing issues of sexual morality into politics. While Margot Gayle Backus, in her *Scandal Work*, offers some perceptive insights into Joyce's rendering of how scandal takes effect, 'scandal' in the works of Joyce of which she writes (which do not include *Finnegans Wake*) is a by-product of political conflict rather than a subject in itself. It is not the most advantageous point of departure to refer to 'Victorian Ireland's greatest sex scandal, the so called "Fall of Parnell"', blurring its political setting, nor to assert that 'Wilde ranks with Parnell as an iconic figure for scandal and its ills in Joyce's work'; Backus, *Scandal Work*, 2–3. Wilde is not a commensurate figure with Parnell in Joyce's thought and work, while it is true that Joyce's mellowing treatment of Wilde in his 1909 article for *Il Piccolo della Sera*, in which he refers to the 'howl of puritanical joy' that greeted Wilde's 'fall', makes a tacit but important political equation of Wilde's fate with Parnell's (*OCPW* 148–51).

Stead's excited proselytising of British opinion abated with the Kilkenny result. With the double defeat of Parnell in Committee Room 15 and in Kilkenny, British newspaper coverage of the Split in Ireland contracted into a fitful if fascinated commentary on Parnell's struggle against oblivion. The radical disarrangement of the British party system that the Split threatened to bring about had receded as suddenly as it had manifested itself. The brief moment of inchoate crisis in British politics had passed, and the dimensions of the Irish question had sharply contracted with Parnell's reversals in Committee Room 15 and in North Kilkenny in the Split's opening phase. Stead wrote in 1901, 'Then the disappearance of Mr Parnell from the scene reduced the Irish Nationalists to an aggregate of jarring atoms—a state from which, at the close of the Century, they are only just beginning to emerge.'[142]

Conservative journals, most notably the *Saturday Review*, had also with much relief discerned in Kilkenny the reversion to the rollicking turbulence of an earlier era of Irish life and politics that Parnell's austere hegemony had banished.[143] An old stereotype was resurrected in a modern mode. Alternatively put, the Unionist caricatures of the Irishman in his political aspect and in his religious aspect, theretofore held apart from each other, were aligned. Behind the cartooned Irish peasant, the stout cleric displaced the moonlighter. Irish fecklessness endured but was now constrained by clerical regimentation.

Joyce declined to treat the grotesque denunciations of Parnell in the *National Press* and the *Irish Catholic* in facile isolation. He co-related the Irish treatment of Parnell with that of Stead in particular, as a populist champion of the nonconformist conscience. Parnellite publicists in the Split decried the Irish nationalist (and British Liberal) deference to evangelical moralism as the fleeting coincidence of opinion in which the opposition to Parnell had originated at the outset. Joyce was virtually alone in insistently drawing out the convergence in purpose of Irish Catholicism and British nonconformity as deep-rooted and persisting.

142. Stead, *Lest We Forget*, 23.

143. Callanan, *Parnell Split*, 71–73.

Joyce's 'Two Masters'

In Joyce's interpretation of the Split, 'clerical dictation' in the Parnellite sense was politically objectionable in the first instance as a manifestation of 'Liberal dictation'. While Joyce's attack on the historical role of the Catholic Church in Ireland intermittently harked back to the Norman invasion in the twelfth century, the Church for Joyce was primarily the Church triumphant of the Parnell Split and its aftermath. His hostility to the political role of the Church existed independently of (and preceded) his personal loss of faith.[144] His attitude to Catholicism was always complex. The contemplation of the Church brought out in Joyces in the male line a curious streak of aphoristic defiance. Stanislaus wrote of his brother in 1904 with an authoritative succinctness: 'Catholicism he has appreciated, rejected and opposed and liked again when it had lost its power over him.'[145]

Joyce eschewed anti-Catholicism. Though without belief, he retained a Catholic intellectual sensibility. He never ceased to be a student of ecclesiastical history and was alert to Catholic doctrines, rites, and popular beliefs. The patterns of his thought retained strong conceptual filiations to Catholicism. His opposition to clerical and episcopal intervention in Irish politics coexisted with a respect for the spiritual *acquis* of Catholicism. A central but neglected aspect of Joyce's response to the Split was the affront it presented to his philosophical conception of Catholicism.

Joyce had a fascinated abhorrence of what was for him the grotesque confluence in the Split of Irish Catholic and British Protestant moralism which he apprehended as inseparable from its contemporary journalistic expression. It was an early and formative instance of what he came

144. Joyce's 'own crisis of belief' is the subject of chapter 4 of Geert Lernout's magisterial *Help My Unbelief*, 94–110. My concern is narrower than Lernout's and relates to Joyce's critique of Catholic social power and political authority in Ireland and the deference it attracted. Lernout might well be sceptical of the idea that it is a subject that can be treated separately from Joyce's loss of faith.

145. S. Joyce, entry for 13 August 1904, in *Dublin Diary*, 55.

to conceptualise as the coincidence of opposites.[146] Joyce sensed a shift in the Church in the Split that was less doctrinal than in its relation to the contemporary world. There is a subsidiary theme in Joyce's treatment of the Church in the Split: quite apart from its adverse consequences for nationalist politics, ecclesiastical intervention wrought a significant change within Irish Catholicism. If this owed something to the crudely overt alignment of the Church with the majoritarian anti-Parnellite party and the Liberal party, it found expression in the politico-moral idiom of the Split that fused the promptings of the 'nonconformist conscience' and Gladstonian Liberal moralism with Catholic or avowedly traditional Irish values, a fusion effected through the medium of the contemporary press. This hybridisation of Catholic and nonconformist Protestant moralism was a strange merger of Joyce's two domains of masterdom. It was the manifestation in religious sentiment of the 'blending and fusion' that Parnell had accused Gladstone of seeking to bring about between the Liberal and Irish parties.[147] In the blindly enthusiastic participation of Irish bishops and particularly Irish priests in the turning of the 'union of hearts' against Parnell, Joyce discerned a hideous travesty of reformation, a pseudo-modernising evangelicisation of the Irish Catholic Church, or its quasi-Protestantisation. It was a subject that Joyce, in condemning the role of the Church in the Parnell Split, did not elaborate on as a thesis, perhaps to avoid over-complicating his argument, but his sense of the shift in Irish Catholicism in a worldly direction would inform his treatment of compromised Catholic spirituality in 'Grace' in *Dubliners*. It was something Joyce felt deeply. Padraic Colum recalled meeting Joyce on his second return to Dublin 1909: 'He was glad, he told me then, to be away from a place where "the reformed conscience" had left its fetter, and away from the fog of Anglo-Saxon civilisation.'[148]

146. Applied politically, the idea was distanced from its origins in the writings of Nicholas of Cusa and Giordano Bruno, discussed in Donald Philip Verene, *James Joyce and the Philosophers at Finnegans Wake* (Evanston, IL: Northwestern University Press, 2016), 55–72.

147. Callanan, *Parnell Split*, 208.

148. Padraic Colum, *The Road Round Ireland* (New York: Macmillan, 1937), 317.

Joyce's excoriation of the role of the Catholic Church in the Split was not free-standing but derived from a Parnellite conception of nationalism. If his repudiation of ecclesiastical interventionism was consistent with his political modernity, it was rooted in the Irish experience of the Split. It originated in the Parnellite conviction that the bishops and clergy had fundamentally misjudged the central issue of the Split and had overreached their spiritual capacities in imposing that misjudgement on the Irish Catholic laity, though, unlike most Parnellites, Joyce took pains to say nothing that would diminish the political responsibility of nationalist voters for their submission to ecclesiastical influence. (Joyce's fierce critique of the Catholic Church in the Split bore little relationship to continental anticlericalism and none at all to anti-Catholic sentiment in England.)

To understand Joyce's 'two masters' critique, it is highly instructive to consider the arguments that he did not advance. He could have simply rejected the project of Irish independence on grounds of modern secularist principles, which would have aligned him with Unionist opponents of Home Rule. He could have attached prescriptive conditions for his support of Irish nationalism or declared that Home Rule under anti-Parnellite and Catholic auspices would not be worth achieving: positions that were not intellectually consistent with the idea of logic of independent democratic statehood. He did not bother with the argument that the demonstration of Catholic ecclesiastical power in the Split would alienate opinion in England or make it more difficult to reconcile Irish Protestants and Unionists to a Home Rule settlement, though it was scarcely a proposition with which he disagreed. Repudiating the role of the protesting Irish intellectual, he did not espouse neutrality on the issue of Irish independence. However provocatively couched and refractory, Joyce's was squarely an intra-nationalist political argument that did not resile from the ambitions for his country that inspirited Parnell's career and his stance in the Split.

Joyce thesis of the 'two masters' as it is articulated in the opening episode of *Ulysses* is sometimes interpreted as a device through which he subordinated his nationalism to his opposition to the socio-political influence of the Catholic Church in Ireland; it can just as easily be seen, and is better understood, as something that enabled him to be a nationalist. His elevation of resistance to the political dictates of the Catholic Church to the same level as opposition to the British governance of Ireland, by which he sought to break the conservative nationalist identification of the Irish nation with the Catholic Church, was highly provocative to most nationalists, and ensured that his nationalism could never be taken to imply any compact with variants of nationalism that he disdained.

Joyce's Parnellite nationalism found dual expression in his writing: first, overtly in his rendering of Parnell's political persona through his myth, but second in the 'two masters' thesis, his intellectual rendering of the dialectic of the Split. The second, often treated as a theme that was more or less independent of the Split, or came to be so, tends to be overlooked in measuring the influence of Parnell and of the Split on Joyce's rendering of Ireland. The 'two masters' thesis is the 'J'accuse' by which, refusing to acquiesce in the fading of Parnell's memory, he kept in play the issues of the Split. It mapped out the field across which Joyce was to array his most scathing aphorisms about the Irish.

The Split and the Repudiation of the Modern

For Joyce the Split was not merely the occasion when the prospects for Irish statehood were aborted, but a repudiation of the modern. It was not merely that the Irish had turned their back on Parnell and squandered his achievement and promise: the anti-Parnellite ascendancy in Ireland was actively counter-modernising. It instilled a hegemonic ethos of conservative Catholic nationalism. The triumph of Parnell's opponents signalled for Joyce an elective embrace of vassalage, as the idiom of the 'two masters' scathingly conveyed.

Gallingly for Joyce, the anti-Parnellites cast themselves as the party of modernisation and progress. What gave this a thin veneer of plausibility was primarily the alliance with the Liberals. The Gladstonian Liberal party was seen as the party of progress and social amelioration, and the anti-Parnellites contrived to appropriate some of that allure. The adherence of Michael Davitt, a figure who had played a leading role in the Land League and was now aligned with the left wing of the Liberal party, was in this especially serviceable to the anti-Parnellite cause.

The idea that the anti-Parnellites were the modern, democratically progressive, nationalist party of the future featured prominently in Healy's rhetoric, if principally as a negative. He consistently derided Parnell and his supporters as archaic and out of touch with modern Ireland. Parnell was portrayed as an Anglo-Irish landlord ('Mr. Landlord Parnell')[149] wildly posturing as a Fenian chieftain,[150] as if seeking to exchange one defunct role for another. His more voluble supporters were mocked as a disparate coalition of apparatchiks, opportunists who had failed to realise that Parnell's time was up, malcontents, Fenians, and urban radicals. This coalition of démodé nationalists was in Healy's account cynically abetted by Irish Unionists and the Conservative government who sought to ensure that Irish nationalism was evenly and hopelessly divided (this at least was true). Parnell and his motley confederates had failed to appreciate that nationalist Ireland had moved on from when Parnell first entered politics. Irish farmers had grown in confidence and were no longer prepared to prostrate themselves before an Anglo-Irish leader, nor were they susceptible to being patronised and misled by the de haut en bas rhetoric of Parnellism. The heroic leadership to which Parnell pretended belonged to a happily vanished era in Ireland. In the newly confident Catholic nationalist Ireland, Parnell was treated in anti-Parnellite rhetoric as an almost comically redundant figure, though of sinister pretensions that remained unabated.

The early Joyce was haunted by the dread of Irish regression. In his boyhood Joyce had a premonitory sense, brilliantly rendered in the Christmas dinner scene of *A Portrait,* that in the Parnell crisis something momentous was happening that bore on the nature of politics. He came to see the Split as having not merely stalled but thrown into reverse Ireland's aspiration to the achievement of a European norm of secular statehood. What he was certain of was that the anti-Parnellite

149. Callanan, *T. M. Healy*, 386.

150. Callanan, *T. M. Healy*, 334–45.

triumph was in no sense a victory of the cause of progress. That intimation informed his unsparing philosophical critique of the Split and lay at the roots of his despair for the future of his country. Quite apart from his disappointed Parnellism, Joyce recoiled from the incoherence of the controversy of the Split, its intellectual chaos and ideological confusion, and was unconvinced that the disarrangement it wrought could be undone. His response was to persevere in a refined rehearsing of the issues of the Split.

Joyce did not break with nationalism. Instead, he entered into a ferocious struggle with its regnant orthodoxies and most of its contemporary proponents. He cleaved to the outermost inner edge, resisting the exclusionary logic of anti-Parnellite nationalism.

6

Joyce in University College, Dublin

In those early days, as since, Joyce was a figure apart. It would be easy to exaggerate his apparent arrogance and reserve. If he seemed arrogant and aloof it was in self-defence. Silently or with some abrupt, devastating phrase he stood in fierce defence of his own integrity—his liberty to think differently. He was far and away the most mature of our student group. We were all conscious of it; cheerfully and disrespectfully aware that he was in correspondence with Ibsen, Arthur Symons and William Archer, and that his verse was beginning to appear in the *Saturday Review*, and his prose in the *Fortnightly*. He was just past eighteen then.

—C. P. CURRAN, OBITUARY OF JAMES JOYCE[1]

Somebody said that Jim was very determined. Jim denied [this], saying that like a wise man he was determined by circumstances.

—STANISLAUS JOYCE, 1904[2]

JOYCE ATTENDED UNIVERSITY COLLEGE, Dublin from September 1898 to June 1902, from ages sixteen to twenty, receiving his certificate

1. C. P. Curran, obituary of James Joyce, *Irish Times*, 14 January 1941, republished in *Envoy* 5, no. 17 (1951): 74.

2. S. Joyce, entry for 23 July 1904, in *Dublin Diary*, 44.

of graduation on 30 September 1902. With John Henry Newman as its first rector, the Catholic University had opened at 86 St Stephen's Green in 1854.[3] Following the enactment of the University Education (Ireland) Act of 1879, and the constitution of the Royal University of Ireland as a degree-awarding institution, the college became in 1882 University College, generally designated as University College, Dublin. The following year the Irish hierarchy entrusted its administration to the Irish Jesuits. Its facilities were sparse. The modern University College Dublin was not constituted until the year after the Liberal government enacted the Irish Universities Act of 1908.[4]

The nationalism of the Jesuit authorities, such as it was, was muted. This was in part because of the order's dread of popular enthusiasm, in part to avoid unnecessary offence to the Conservative party, which was (incorrectly as it transpired) presumed to be more likely than the Liberals to constitute University College a full university on a statutory basis.[5]

At the heart of University College, Dublin was the debating society, the Literary and Historical Society (L&H), an extraordinary institution. It was an arena in which the assertion of political and barristerial ambition was typically confronted more characteristically by artistic scorn and intellectual scepticism than by left-wing dissent. William G. Fallon went so far as to say that 'Joyce had passed unnoticed at the college

3. The older No. 85, built by Richard Castle, also Palladian, passed to the university in 1865. The Aula Maxima was constructed as a memorial to Cardinal Paul Cullen in 1878. With the completion of the first stage of the building of Earlsfort Terrace, the two houses fell into serious disrepair, and the great ceiling of the saloon in No. 85 was on the verge of collapse, until a decision was made to restore the buildings and adapt them for the purposes of the Students' Union. C. P. Curran, *Nos 85 and 86 St. Stephen's Green* (Dublin: President and Governing Body of University College, Dublin, n.d.), 3–10.

4. Donal McCartney, *UCD, a National Idea: The History of University College, Dublin* (Dublin: Gill and Macmillan, 1999), 17–18, 27, 47.

5. There was a perception that the Jesuits were more interested in entrenching clerical influence than fostering Irish nationalism that was given cryptic expression by John Francis Taylor, who wrote shortly after Parnell's death, 'Some of the least likely of our public men to take up positions of ecclesiastical championship in Irish politics were alumni of the Stephen's Green institution'. 'The Home Rule Problem, III: The Police', *Manchester Guardian*, 27 October 1891. This was a somewhat arch reference to John Dillon.

until he began to take an active part in the Literary and Historical Society's debates.'[6] Joyce, at the end of his second year, contested the auditorship of the society for the session of 1900–1901, losing by nine votes to fifteen to Hugh Kennedy (1879–1936), who was to become the first attorney general of the Irish Free State. It was to the L&H that Joyce delivered his papers 'Drama and Life' on 20 January 1900 and on James Clarence Mangan on 15 February 1902.[7] University College, and within it the L&H, was to provide the principal arena of Joyce's public engagement in Ireland.

There was a hiatus in the L&H that extended from the spring of 1891 to 1897, the year before Joyce's arrival, which the historian of the society suggested owed something to the Parnell Split: 'It may have been thought that a student society could not operate with advantage to the College or its members in an atmosphere that was steadily filled with hate.'[8] By the time the society was reconstituted, the Jesuits had tacitly abandoned their never entirely successful attempt to confine the discussion of contemporary Irish politics to 'the university question' (that is, whether to allow women to attend university in Ireland). This was achieved less by overt censorship than through the subtle deprecation of political controversy. Fallon, a near contemporary of Joyce, recalled that 'the Society was repeatedly cautioned against excursions into the field of domestic politics, even after the closing of the "Parnellite Split" in 1900.'[9]

The L&H was also the principal point of intersection between the life of the college and the wider world of politics that lay beyond St Stephen's Green. Public figures were invited to reply to the annual inaugural addresses of the auditor, and frequently to chair meetings. During Joyce's four years there, the public figures to attend the society included Timothy Michael Healy (twice), John Dillon, Timothy Harrington, J. G. Swift MacNeill, William Field, Mathias McDonnell Bodkin, Richard

6. U. O'Connor, *Joyce We Knew*, 51.

7. *OCPW* 23–29, 53–60.

8. James Meenan, ed., *Centenary History of the Literary and Historical Society of University College Dublin, 1855–1955* (Tralee: Kerryman, [1955]), 41.

9. Meenan, *Centenary History*, 97.

Adams, John Francis Taylor, Eoin MacNeill, and Patrick Pearse.[10] Joyce thus had the opportunity to observe members of the Irish Party with whose names and careers he was familiar from the time of the Parnell Split, and figures of the contemporary Irish language revival.

Constantine Curran (1883–1972) is the most important biographical source for Joyce's politics in University College. His *James Joyce Remembered* (1968), published over a quarter century after Joyce's death, was followed by a graceful memoir, *Under the Receding Wave* (1970). A barrister who never practised and who became the registrar of the Supreme Court,[11] Curran was a politically and institutionally trusted and well-connected figure on the fringes of Sinn Féin and in the new Irish state.[12] He was an acutely perceptive observer of his contemporaries. With his actor wife, Helen Laird, in his private life he moved in artistic and theatrical circles. An observant Catholic, and discreet to a fault—he was nicknamed 'cautious Con'—Curran was learned, highly intelligent, and possessed of a fine prose style.[13] He was the author of the first major work on seventeenth- and eighteenth-century Irish stucco.[14] Curran lived happily a divided life. 'Though most of my life was spent in the Four Courts—at the Registrar's desk, between Bench and Bar—my free hours were passed on the fringes of the arts in the company of men who lived outside the Common Law—poets, painters, musicians, theatre men and a few scholars who made up a Dublin that Pericles might have commended.'[15] His relationship with Joyce, of which he only wrote on his retirement, was the fraught emblem of this duality. Without Curran's

10. Meenan, *Centenary History*, 70, 327, et passim; Minutes of the Literary and Historical Society, UCD Archives, IE UCDA Soc 2.

11. Curran's appointment as registrar of the Supreme Court was noted in the *Irish Times* of 14 August 1906, and his retirement in its issue of 4 November 1952. He had been appointed a registrar of the Court of King's Bench in 1921.

12. See C. P. Curran, 'Griffith, MacNeill and Pearse', *Studies* 55, no. 217 (Spring 1966): 21–28.

13. Pauric J. Dempsey and Bridget Hourican, 'Constantine Peter Curran', *DIB* 2:1102–3.

14. C. P. Curran, *Dublin Decorative Plasterwork of the Seventeenth and Eighteenth Centuries* (London: Alec Tiranti, 1967).

15. C. P. Curran, 'The Side Walks of Dublin: Self-Portrait', *Studies* 51, no. 201 (Spring 1962): 108. This article originated as a radio broadcast.

FIGURE 6.1. Graduation group, University College, Dublin, 1902. Joyce is standing second from left; C. P. Curran is front row, far right; George Clancy is seated second row, first left, in mortarboard. *Source*: 1.12, James Joyce Collection, The Poetry Collection of the University Libraries, University at Buffalo, The State University of New York.

memoirs, the political relationship in which Joyce stood to his peers would be largely a matter of surmise and inference drawn from his own writings and from the recollections of his brother Stanislaus.

The years Joyce spent at University College Dublin, from 1898 to 1902, were marked by ostensible political stability, if not stagnation, but there were underlying rifts which were to reconfigure Irish politics and have devastating consequences for the generation to which he belonged. In the Ireland of 1898–1902, the vast majority of nationalists believed Home Rule would be won once a Liberal government was returned to office, and were prepared to accept the sufficiency of Home Rule, not perhaps for all time, but certainly for a generation or more. The students of University College for the most part subscribed to this consensus. Curran wrote of the student body,

> They were eloquently divided between an orthodox majority, readers of the Home Rule *Freeman's Journal*, many of them sons of members of the Irish Parliamentary Party, and a small minority who read the insurgent *United Irishman* and preached the new doctrine of Arthur Griffith and William Rooney. A very few were members of the Celtic Literary Society, or the militant Dungannon Club, or the Confederates, but this handful of artsmen was fortified by a strong battalion of medicals from the Cecilia Street School ready to play an active part in any intra or extra commotion. The Gaelic League occupied a middle field of general respect.[16]

The students were swept by the contemporary vogue for the Gaelic League and the revival of the Irish language and were the first generation of University College students to be so affected. It was principally the extent of the sympathy with the aims of the Gaelic League that set the University College students in Joyce's era in some degree apart from general nationalist opinion in Ireland, which looked on the revival of the language as a worthy but distant national aspiration towards which some progress might be made after the attainment of Home Rule.

The Gaelic League professed to political neutrality—hence Curran's 'middle field'—and many students in University College who were loyal adherents of the Irish Party professed ardent support for the revival of the language, though their attempts to learn Irish, however enthusiastically embarked on, were rarely sustained. Their attitude was naïve: Douglas Hyde's much-acclaimed 1892 address 'The Necessity for De-Anglicising Ireland' breathed contempt for the agenda of constitutional nationalism.[17] Their ingenuousness found expression in their enthusiasm for the Gaelicising chauvinism of D. P. Moran's *Leader*, conceived in opposition to what Curran characterised as 'the insurgent *United Irishman*'. Written in Moran's distinctively pungent English, the *Leader* dismissed the idea

16. Curran, *Under the Receding Wave*, 79.

17. Douglas Hyde, 'The Necessity for De-Anglicising Ireland', delivered before the Irish National Literary Society in Dublin, 25 November 1892, republished in *The Politics of Language in Ireland, 1366–1922: A Sourcebook*, ed. Tony Crowley (London: Routledge, 1999).

that political nationalism could reflect Ireland's Gaelic essence. Joyce, a political nationalist whose thinking was honed in the Split, was undeceived.

There are no direct avowals of Joyce's political convictions while he was at University College. But the reconstitution of his attitudes is nonetheless possible. It entails mapping against the course of contemporary politics his early Parnellism, what is recorded of him in University College, what he wrote while still in Dublin after his graduation from late 1902 to late 1904 and in early exile, and what he wrote in *Stephen Hero* set against the considerably later and highly stylised *A Portrait of the Artist as a Young Man*. This yields a comprehensible account of Joyce's Irish politics, which is coherent and disposes of any lingering idea that Joyce was devoid of political conviction, or that he set out to render his thinking undecipherably opaque. His later rendering of his fictional characters attested to an acute sense that in Ireland politics was an integral part of personal identity: the idea that he set out to maintain a godlike authorial exemption for himself was never altogether credible.

In contrast to many of his contemporaries in University College, Joyce was not a supporter of either of the factions of the Irish Parliamentary Party after Parnell, which remained divided up to 1900. He also had reservations that led him to withhold assent from the opponents of the Irish Party. This marked not a midway position but a Parnell-inflected solitude. He grasped the enormous and novel potential implications, both political and cultural, of the Irish language revival. He was instinctively more suspicious than most of his peers of Gaelicising rhetoric, and of the sources of support for the Gaelic League. However, probably not without a struggle with his own instincts, he managed to remain open-minded about the project of a Gaelic revival.

The great paradox is that in the midst of his volubly political contemporaries, Joyce, while appearing disengaged from politics, was more politically incisive in his thinking than they were. His nationalism was politically intelligent, and he intuited what the political implications of a Gaelic revival might be. While he declined to flaunt his convictions, his Parnellite and Fenian-inflected nationalism was politically more radical than theirs. He thought traditional Fenian conceptions of revolution to be superseded. He was not opposed to Home Rule, but he did not see the paradigm of Home Rule nationalism as either sacrosanct or ineluctably predestined to succeed.

Parnellism was neither Joyce's major nor immediate preoccupation while in University College. Quite apart from his bitter intimation of the contemporary eclipse of the Parnellism of the Split, his Parnellite affiliations seemed to have no relevance to his exalted prospective vocation as 'a literary artist',[18] to use the phrase applied to Stephen Daedalus, as he then conceived it. His Parnellism, already interiorised, had not abated. He did not vaunt the depth of his prior intellectual engagement with the Parnellism of the Split. It endured as a touchstone—he was always attentive to attitudes to the Split—and as an inhibition, as something that held him back from engagement in the indiscriminate fluidity of undergraduate political discussion. The Split informed his reticence. His recusant Parnellism was a major element in his holding back from the matrix of contemporary political debate among his peers. He seems to have been reluctant to be drawn on political subjects by declarations of opinion. There was too much explaining to do, unless he was prepared to engage in arguments from premises he was unable to accept. Joyce's marked political reticence was a kind of economy that can be understood as expressive of a despairingly resigned rationality rather than intellectual pride, artistic hauteur, or contemptuous disaffection. He negotiated a terrible solitude with measured urbanity and a surprising readiness to be proved wrong.

'Constructing the Enigma of a Manner'

In *Stephen Hero*, Stephen, in his quest for imaginative emancipation, spurns not merely the 'stale maxims' of the Jesuits but also his university peers, 'the company of decrepit youth—and he swore an oath that never would they establish with him a compact of fraud'.[19] Later in the novel,

18. *SH* 122.

19. *SH* 38; see also *SH* 171, 187, 193.

the inaugural address of Moynihan, as auditor of the L&H, provides the occasion for Stephen's most sustained contemplation of his peers in the aggregate.

Moynihan is modelled on Robert Kinahan, who delivered his inaugural address 'The Social Problem' on 20 November 1901, in Joyce's fourth and final year. The address comprised a cursory history of socialism in modern Europe that culminated in a deferential consideration of recent papal encyclicals on social issues informed by a concern that the pope's utterances might be considered even faintly sympathetic to socialism in any form: 'Private property has in him a staunch champion.'[20] It was an expression of the doctrinal docility of students in University College that exasperated Joyce. The occasion was enlivened by John Francis Taylor's speech in reply. Joyce's aloof presence was noted in *St Stephen's*, which compared Taylor's style to that of 'our own Joyce at his best' but claimed it had 'a broadness of sympathy' that, it is implied, Joyce had yet to acquire. During Taylor's speech, 'Dreamy Jimmy and J.F. Byrne, standing on a window-sill, looked as if they could say things unutterable.'[21]

Stephen Hero reproduces the scene: 'From his post beside Cranly [modelled on John Francis Byrne] in an angle of the hall Stephen glanced along the ranks of students':

> The faces which were now composed to seriousness all bore the same stamp of Jesuit training. . . . They admired Gladstone, physical science and the tragedies of Shakespeare: and they believed in the adjustment of Catholic teaching to everyday needs, in the Church

20. *Freeman's Journal*, 21 November 1901. Understandably misremembering that Kinahan's address was on socialism, rather than 'the social order', Eugene Sheehy wrote, 'Kinahan was a clever and witty debater who affected a rather precious way of expressing his thoughts and loved to use a high-sounding and unusual word. In his address on Socialism, he introduced us to the word "proletariat" and I and many other students had to consult our dictionaries to find out what he meant' (in Meenan, *Centenary History*, 80–81). Robert Kinahan became a barrister who practised on the Leinster Circuit and died at the age of forty on 21 July 1921; *Freeman's Journal*, 22 July 1921. His L&H address was enlivened by John Francis Taylor's speech in reply, which is discussed in chapter 8, 'The Language of the Outlaw'.

21. *St Stephen's*, February 1902.

diplomatic. Without displaying an English desire for an aristocracy of substance they held violent measures to be unseemly and in their relations among themselves and towards their superiors they displayed a nervous and (whenever there was question of authority) a very English liberalism. They respected spiritual and temporal authorities, the spiritual authorities of Catholicism and of patriotism, and the temporal authorities of the hierarchy and the government. The memory of Terence Bellew MacManus was not less revered by them than the memory of Cardinal Cullen.[22]

Paul Cullen, Cardinal Archbishop of Dublin, had famously refused to let the body of McManus rest in the Pro-Cathedral before the extravagant Fenian-sponsored obsequies of the exiled Young Irelander in 1861. The admiration of Gladstone and physical science was also part of the incongruous mix of patriotic piety: 'They listened to all the speakers attentively and applauded whenever there was an allusion to the President [of the college, William Delany], to Ireland or to the faith.'[23] This was a reworking of a passage in Joyce's 'Portrait of the Artist' essay of 1904. In the earlier text, in his analysis of the thinking of 'the younglings', Joyce had written with scathing subtlety, 'The exercise of authority might be sometimes (rarely) questionable, its intention, never.'[24] Joyce's assessment of his student contemporaries in the aggregate was more unforgiving than of his Jesuit preceptors.

Joyce assumed a mask in University College, of which his political reticence was part. In his social relations he cultivated a certain aloofness. This was not reflected in striking bohemian attitudes (he was for long austerely sceptical of Oscar Wilde's social presentation of the self, though admiring of *The Soul of Man under Socialism*), but by a degree of reserve and a dialectical conversational style. His aphoristic provocations were intended in part as decoys. In *Stephen Hero*, referring to Stephen's weekly English essay, Joyce wrote, 'He gave himself no great trouble to sustain the boldnesses which were expressed or implied in his essays.

22. *SH* 172–73.
23. *SH* 173.
24. *PSW* 213.

He threw them out as sudden defence-works while he was busy constructing the enigma of a manner.'[25]

The 'enigma of a manner' phrase first occurs in his February 1904 essay, 'The Portrait of the Artist'.[26] Joyce was writing of the artist's adolescent crisis of religious sensibility. Up to the point where 'he' (the impersonal artist) entered the university, 'he was still soothed by devotional exercises': 'About this period the enigma of a manner was put up at all comers to protect the crisis. He was quick enough now to see that he must disentangle his affairs in secrecy and reserve had ever been a light penance.' His reserve was 'not without a satisfactory flavour of the heroic.'[27] He was untroubled by the unremitting Jesuit strictures against intellectual pride.

He carried over, with slight modification, a passage from the 'Portrait' essay into *Stephen Hero*:

> It was part of that ineradicable egoism which he was afterwards to call redeemer that he conceived converging to him the deeds and thoughts of microcosm. Is the mind of youth medieval that it is so divining of intrigue? Field-sports (or their equivalent in the world of mentality) are perhaps the most effective cure and Anglo-Saxon educators favour rather a system of hardy brutality. But for this fantastic idealist, eluding the grunting booted apparition with a bound, the mimic warfare was no less ludicrous than unequal in a ground chosen to his disadvantage. Behind the rapidly indurating shield the sensitive answered: Let the pack of enmities come tumbling and sniffing to my highlands after their game. There was his ground and he flung them disdain from flashing antlers.[28]

The awkward transition from the rugby field to that of the hunt is redeemed by the image of the stag. Joyce deployed the same self-image in his poem 'The Holy Office' some months after its first use in the 'Portrait' essay: 'Firm as the mountain ridges where / I flash my antlers

25. *SH* 27.
26. *PSW* 211–18.
27. *PSW* 212.
28. *SH* 34–35.

on the air'.[29] When a dog approaches the apprehensive Stephen in the 'Proteus' episode of *Ulysses*, Stephen thinks, 'Dog of my enemy. I just simply stood pale, silent, bayed about.'[30] The image of the chased deer had for Joyce a strong association with Parnell, whom Joyce describes in 'L'ombra di Parnell' traversing the country to plead his cause 'like a hunted deer'.[31] Joyce's cultivation of reserve owed something to Parnell.

Curran wrote in the first article in which he referred to Joyce, 'He liked, too, to wear a mask but essentially he was never other than a reserved strong-willed artist, austerely, even savagely self-centred, but not selfish.'[32] A little later, writing of 'Joyce's D'Annunzian mask', he dated the 'change over from normal companionship to an increasingly defiant, arrogant isolation' from 1899, lasting four or five years.[33]

The severity of Joyce's mask in University College, his first large socio-political arena, is not to be exaggerated. It was not altogether newly acquired. Eugene Sheehy emphasised in his memoirs the continuity between the Joyce he knew in Belvedere and the later Joyce of University College: 'Joyce, the schoolboy, was as aloof, icy and imperturbable as later in this book I present Joyce, the man. He took the same pleasure, too, in baiting his masters and the Rector that he afterwards revelled in at the expense of his University Professors.' Of the Joyce coming to the Sheehy household as a friend of his brother Richard and of himself, Eugene Sheehy wrote,

> As I remember him then, he was a tall stripling, with flashing teeth—white as a hound's—pale blue eyes that sometimes had an icy look,

29. *PSW* 99.

30. *U* 3.310–11.

31. The point is made in John Whittier Ferguson's annotation of the passage in *PSW* 277–78. He refers also to a misquotation of Goethe comparing the Irish to 'a pack of hounds, always dragging down some noble stag', which Yeats, in his *Autobiographies* (190), recalled being cited in the newspapers in the recriminations that followed Parnell's death. Richard Ellmann (*James Joyce*, 145n) refers to Joyce's predilection for the self-image of a deer without reference to the Parnell association.

32. Curran, 'Side Walks of Dublin', 115.

33. C. P. Curran, 'Joyce's D'Annunzian Mask', *Studies* 51, no. 202 (Summer 1962): 309. The essay is republished in Curran, *James Joyce Remembered*, 105–15.

and a mobile sensitive mouth. He was fond of throwing back his head as he walked, and his mood alternated between cold, slightly haughty, aloofness and sudden boisterous merriment.

Sometimes his abrupt manner was a cloak for shyness. He refers in an early manuscript to 'the induration of the shield', meaning that each of us has to forge in self-protection a shield to interpose between oneself and the hostile world.[34]

Another contemporary, Thomas F. Bacon, recalled of Joyce as a debater, 'Joyce, thin and pale, stood erect, scarcely moving, cold and undisturbed by interruptions (and he had many), and seemed in passionless tones to wither the opposition by his air of indifferent disdain.'[35]

To believe that Joyce arrived in University College possessed of the hauteur of an artist in the making is a misconception that underestimates Joyce's preternatural tentativeness, his waiting on things to take their shape. In *Stephen Hero* Joyce wrote, referring to the spring of Stephen's first academic year in University College, 'Stephen had begun to regard himself as a literary artist: he professed scorn for the rabblement and contempt for authority.'[36] This is as densely charged a sentence as any in Joyce's writing as it bears on his own biography. The semi-ironic phrase 'literary artist' as distinct from writer is striking. It negotiates the gap between Joyce's ambition and what he had written to that point but is characteristic in its self-confidence. The 'had begun to' introduces a further degree of tentativeness. The sentence serves as a reminder that even though Joyce would reconstitute the projected novel under the title *A Portrait of the Artist as a Young Man*, we know little of the stages by which he came to conceive of himself as a writer. It seems reasonable to assert that by the time he had resolved to recast his 'Portrait of the Artist' essay as a novel to be entitled *Stephen Hero*—a resolution which Stanislaus dates to 2 February 1904, Joyce's twenty-second birthday[37]—he

34. Eugene Sheehy, *May It Please the Court* (Dublin: CJ Fallon, 1951), 8, 21. The reference is to 'the rapidly indurating shield' in the 'Portrait' essay (*PSW* 212), carried over into the passage in *Stephen Hero* already quoted.

35. Meenan, *Centenary History*, 69–70.

36. *SH* 122–23.

37. S. Joyce, entry for 2 February 1904, in *Dublin Diary*, 11–12.

had accepted that he would be a writer, and showing what he had written to friends was a quasi-public embrace of this decision which postdates his years in University College. Joyce's seemingly dauntless self-confidence notwithstanding, one must observe a degree of scepticism towards the semi-predestinarianism of *A Portrait of the Artist as a Young Man* in which there is scarcely a moment where we see Stephen as other than an artist in the making, and the title forbids us from seeing him otherwise. That deliberately elides Joyce's uncertainty, an uncertainty that was less about his ambition to be a writer than about whether and how that could be reconciled with a professional life or at least a livelihood of some sort in Dublin. A rare glimpse of that more uncertain Joyce, bereft of the solace that their confident ambitions gave his peers, is afforded by William G. Fallon. He wrote of Joyce's graduation, 'His attendance at lectures had been irregular, probably because, unlike a majority of the student body who had programmed their futures, Joyce had no plans, although he toyed for a while with the College's Cecelia St. Medical School.' Later, 'still perplexed by his own indecision and hesitancy',[38] Joyce confided in Professor William Magennis. The vocational incertitude observed by Fallon was the principal target of the sarcasm of Stephen's father in *Stephen Hero*: 'Can't you go for something definite, some good appointment in a government office and then, by Christ, you can think as much as you like. Study for some first-class appointment, there are plenty of them, and you can write at your leisure. Unless, perhaps, you would prefer to be a loafer eating orange-peels and sleeping in the Park.'[39]

The primary model for Joyce's emergent self-conception as 'a literary artist' was the Norwegian dramatist Henrik Ibsen. The publication in the prestigious London *Fortnightly Review* on 1 April 1900 of Joyce's review of Ibsen's play *When We Dead Awaken*,[40] towards the close of his second year, enhanced Joyce's standing among his peers, and the perception that he was a writer in the making. It was the following year that

38. U. O'Connor, *Joyce We Knew*, 51.

39. *SH* 217. The sequence of 'think' and 'write' preserves the concept of the 'literary artist'.

40. *OCPW* 30.

Curran and Joyce became friends. He recalled Joyce talking of Ibsen: 'Ibsen, the truth-compeller, the heroic intransigent, was by this time above controversy. At no time did I hear Joyce discuss him as a social reformer—such propaganda was to him inadmissible—and he was first to direct me away from such journalistic criticism to the poetry and symbolism of *Peer Gynt, Brand,* and *The Master Builder*.'[41] Curran's account of the young Joyce, which remained remarkably consistent, portrayed him as primarily influenced by the writers whom he discussed openly: 'His literary idols at that time—never, I think, to be overthrown—were Dante and Ibsen, and I cannot help thinking that he saw himself in relation to the Ireland of his day as the disdainful Florentine or as Ibsen among the Norse nationalists'.[42]

Curran wrote, 'Joyce lived a withdrawn life. . . . He schooled himself to silence. . . . He easily assumed a mask—that common end-of-the-century stage property—and it was rarely dropped'. Of Joyce's relations to his peers, Curran recalled, 'He was self-centred and centripetal. They were gregarious.' They engaged in interminable discussions 'but Joyce stood aside from such debate; his conclusions were already arrived at, *in petto*. They recognised his distinction, accepted his aloofness from discussion, and retained his friendship or goodwill.'[43] Fallon's memory of a Joyce who was half-disengaged was not dissimilar to Curran's: 'I believe that Joyce was a little too distant to be a close friend. When he was with us he sometimes appeared to be peering into the future. But he always entered into the spirit of things.'[44] Of Joyce's distance, Curran wrote perceptively,

> A good deal has been written about Joyce's youthful arrogance. Some things that he admired and most things that he rejected were admired or rejected by him in the teeth of his fellows. He was curt or, if you wish, arrogant, in the defiant proclamation or defence of these opinions. He was not so in behaviour or social conduct. He was aloof,

41. Curran, *James Joyce Remembered*, 29.
42. Curran, obituary of James Joyce.
43. Curran, *James Joyce Remembered*, 21–22.
44. U. O'Connor, *Joyce We Knew*, 48.

wary, dogmatic in statement, and mistrustful. He was scornful of the opposition he anticipated, and he was peremptory in his reply. To that extent, and to that extent only, he was arrogant. Stephen Dedalus confesses to throwing up defence works in the busy construction of the enigma of a manner. That enigmatic manner was very evident in Joyce in these student years.[45]

Curran sounded a more critical note in writing of the Joyce he met in Dublin in 1912: 'The reserve which was second nature to him had become more marked. His self-possession had grown even greater, but there was nothing at all of the artificial aloofness of the early D'Annunzian *sovrouomo*.'[46]

In *Stephen Hero*, Joyce wrote with reference to Cranly (modelled on J. F. Byrne), 'It was in favour of this young man that Stephen decided to break his commandment of reticence'.[47] Curran recalled, 'At no time, then or in later years, do I remember him in company taking part in any general discussion. For anything approaching serious talk he preferred the company of one to many, and even then you had to meet him on his own ground. You were reduced to the docile recipient of his earlier meditation, sententiously delivered. Many found his trick of recondite allusion affected. He certainly used it to evade reply. He did not debate. Question was turned aside by dark or gnomic answer.'[48]

Although in the preface to his Joyce memoir, Curran wrote that he had 'touched only lightly on the politics of my day', he was nonetheless the only contemporary to make any attempt to situate Joyce politically. It is clear that Joyce, whatever his general reserve, did not eschew the discussion of contemporary issues. Curran was shocked by the rawness

45. Curran, *James Joyce Remembered*, 34. Curran was referring to a sentence in *Stephen Hero* the full sense of which derives from the preceding one already quoted earlier: 'He gave himself no trouble to sustain the boldnesses which were expressed or implied in his essays. He threw them out as sudden defence-works while he was busy constructing the enigma of a manner' (*SH* 27).

46. Curran, *James Joyce Remembered*, 82.

47. *SH* 124.

48. Curran, *James Joyce Remembered*, 35. Curran added, 'The cryptic answer, the reticence on deep issues, which always seemed to me his dominant characteristic, never disappeared'.

of *Stephen Hero*, what it disclosed of Joyce's personal circumstances, and by its rendering of University College. Reflecting that Joyce's loan of the 'bulky wad of manuscript' in June 1904, followed by further instalments before Joyce left Dublin, 'was almost as much by way of an *apologia pro vita sua* as an experiment in criticism', he added, 'He knew perfectly well that I was wholly removed from his standpoint on religious matters, and that we differed equally on other issues which were vehemently agitated in the Dublin of our day.'[49]

Joyce's Veiled Parnellism in University College

Curran's most penetrating and sustained observations in relation to Joyce's politics in University College come not in *James Joyce Remembered* but in his memoir *Under the Receding Wave*, which was published two years later in 1970. In describing the political beliefs of Francis Skeffington (who became, on his marriage, Sheehy-Skeffington), he drew a significant contrast with Joyce:

> [Skeffington] took the side of labour and democracy in college discussions and was feminist in everything. In our other domestic quarrels he was secularist in the Irish sense of the term and retrospectively anti-Parnellite. How opposed he was in this to his friend, James Joyce, who admiring Parnell for his proud self-containment also held him the victim of disloyalty. Skeffington judged Parnell cold, conservative, and, before and after Committee Room 15, disingenuous. He wrote him down as political opportunist and the merely eponymous hero of the movement. These anti-Parnellite views may seem at variance with Skeffington's anticlericalism but only to those who see the Parnell controversy simply as a clerical and anti-clerical faction fight. . . .
>
> Skeffington and Joyce were always good friends, however much the publicist deplored the artist's seclusion. [In *A Portrait*] Joyce made play with Skeffington-McCann college propaganda but it is worth noting that even though Joyce was a completely unpolitical Parnellite he makes no reference to Skeffington's anti-Parnellism nor

49. Curran, *James Joyce Remembered*, viii, 50.

to Skeffington's adherence to the students' protest on the occasion of the first performance of Yeats' *The Countess Cathleen.* For Joyce to introduce either detail into his writing would put his *Portrait* out of drawing.[50]

Curran captures something of the intensity of Joyce's identification with Parnell's 'proud self-containment', a trait Joyce cultivated, and a Parnell-inflected sensitivity to betrayal. He was astute in his treatment of the relations of, and differences between, Joyce and Skeffington by reference to the Parnell Split. He was drawn to do so in the attempt to define what held Joyce and Skeffington apart, notwithstanding the anticlericalism they had in common. Curran's portrayal of Joyce as 'a completely unpolitical Parnellite' stands as the most important characterisation by a contemporary of Joyce's politics in University College. It encompasses the idea that Joyce was not actively political or aligned with the Irish Party or any of the movements that opposed or stood apart from the Irish Party, and perhaps also that he did not set out to convert others to his views. He also meant that Joyce's Parnellism was severed from contemporary politics and, without quite saying so, that Joyce was more a Parnellite than he was a nationalist. Reflecting conceptions of nationalism of the time, he could not conceive of Joyce as a nationalist other than in a residual sense. In *James Joyce Remembered* he touched obliquely on what Joyce and Skeffington shared in their views: 'John Eglinton and Fred Ryan, in their conduct of *Dana,* were declared anti-clericals, but John Eglinton was an imperialist and Fred Ryan a socialist and nationalist of the same temper as Frank Skeffington, and in his outlook not very far removed from Joyce himself.'[51] What Curran could not apprehend was that it was Joyce's nationalism that separated him from Ryan, whose nationalism was derivative of his socialism and anticolonialism. By discounting his nationalism, Curran did not get Joyce's politics quite right.

50. Curran, *Under the Receding Wave,* 115–16.

51. Curran, *James Joyce Remembered,* 78. Referring to pages 15–16 of the *Recollections of James Joyce,* Curran was taking issue with what he paraphrased as Stanislaus Joyce's suggestion that his brother 'had all the little literary world of Dublin against him'.

The only other contemporary to comment on Joyce's Parnellism in University College was his brother Stanislaus, in *My Brother's Keeper*. Stanislaus had little imaginative comprehension of Irish nationalism and could be grudgingly obtuse where his brother's Parnellism was concerned. He did not attend University College, but was close to his brother, knew his brother's friends, and accompanied Joyce to debates in the L&H. He wrote of his brother's standing aloof from the politics of the 1890s, 'When he attended the University and listened to its groups of talkative students, Parnell's story had become a memory of the dead and, though rancours still remained, time had begun to mellow the harshness of opinions that had been so violently agitated.'[52] Stanislaus was correct in implying there was something of a lull in Joyce's expression of Parnellite allegiance in University College.

To most of his contemporaries, Joyce appeared apolitical or vestigially political. Fallon, an active supporter of the Irish Party, and later a barrister, was a friend and perceptive observer of Joyce in Belvedere and University College and resumed his relations with Joyce in Paris in the 1920s and 1930s through the improbable medium of rugby football. Fallon wrote of Joyce, 'the complete Dubliner', having attended University College rather than Trinity, 'where he would have been a misfit'. Fallon captured something significant about Joyce's attendance at University College: 'At University College, at least, he would realise how native traditions and culture, held in common, were the bonds that linked his Dublin with the provinces. That revelation was Joyce's simple conception of Irish nationalism, but in the awakening political enthusiasm of those years he was wholly disinterested!'[53] What was distinctive about University College was its site as a confluence of Dublin and rural Ireland, the significance of which for Joyce is emblematised in his relationship with George Clancy (discussed in chapter 7).

52. S. Joyce, *My Brother's Keeper*, 172–73. Stanislaus's own view (*My Brother's Keeper*, 163–64) of Parnell's overthrow, which he saw in terms of quasi-misogynistic social Puritanism, abstracts the nationalist element.

53. U. O'Connor, *Joyce We Knew*, 50. Fallon was a selector for the Irish team on the second occasion he met Joyce in Paris, and president of the Irish Rugby Football Union from 1949 to 1950.

Both political and artistic considerations underlay Joyce's reticence in University College on the subject of Parnell. He had lived the defeat of the Split twice over: as a child on the occasion of Parnell's death, and in observing what he saw as the forsaking of Parnell's memory in the years of his adolescence that followed. Joyce had brooded on Parnell, interiorised aspects of Parnell's persona, and adopted a dissentient stance which owed much to the stark precepts he drew from the Split. But by the time he got to University College, Parnellism as a political movement seemed played out. Moreover, he perceived that amid the ebbing sound and fury of the late Split, Parnell's memory had lost contemporary political traction and was slipping prematurely into oblivion; this was to inform his later responsiveness to stirrings of the Parnell myth. Whatever his personal fealty to Parnell, he was certainly not disposed to proselytise in an obsolete cause. Perhaps he also wanted to guard his anger: in his October 1901 pamphlet essay 'The Day of the Rabblement', he wrote that the conformist artist 'inherits . . . a soul that yields up all its hate.'[54] The final source of inhibition is perhaps counter-intuitive: Joyce was actually more nationalist than most of his contemporaries. He despised competitions in nationalist ardour, and he had his mask to keep up.

Joyce in University College was preoccupied primarily with the development of his thinking on art, and the cultivation of a literary sensibility. There was a radical disjuncture between his Parnellism and the exaltedly high conception of the artist he held at that time. He did not believe that his experience of the Split, his Parnellite sympathies and insights, had any relevance to his aspirations as an artist. He was nevertheless alert to the literary referencing of Parnell, making in 'The Day of the Rabblement' a dismissive reference to 'Mr. Moore and his island', an allusion to George Moore's *Parnell and His Island*.[55]

The influence of the Split lingered still in University College, but Joyce's position was anomalous. He was not considered to be political;

54. *OCPW* 52.

55. *OCPW* 51; George Moore, *Parnell and His Island* (London: Swan Sonnenschein, Lowrey, 1887). See the introduction by Carla King to the reissue of the novel (Dublin: University College Dublin Press, 2004), vii–viii.

some of his contemporaries—notably, Thomas Michael Kettle and William Dawson[56]—were the sons of prominent political figures. Yet none had experienced the Split with the intellectual intensity that Joyce had. His recusant Parnellism was part of the distance he kept from his peers.

The Rabblement against *The Countess Cathleen*

A defining moment of Joyce's dissent from his contemporaries came early in his college career, near the end of his first year, in the controversy surrounding the inaugural production of Yeats's play *The Countess Cathleen* on 8 May 1899.

In the play, which Yeats had revised since its first publication in 1892 and continued to revise, a starved peasantry are driven by famine to sell their souls to demon merchants; the Countess offers her soul in return for the salvation of her people. The production was preceded by salvos of condemnation from Frank Hugh O'Donnell, an early parliamentary obstructionist who was marginalised by the rise of Parnell—whom he hated—and who came to profess in the era of the Dreyfus Affair virulently reactionary and anti-Semitic views in the guise of a Hiberno-continental ultra-Catholicism. O'Donnell's opposition was taken up by William Martin Murphy's Healyite *Daily Nation* in its contest with the liberal nationalist *Freeman's Journal*. The *Daily Nation*'s proclamation that 'the fundamental idea of the play is inherently false, vicious, and repugnant to all correct recognition of the doctrines of Religion and of Faith' re-inscribed the idiom of the Parnell Split.[57]

On the occasion of the premiere of *The Countess Cathleen*, the Antient Concert Rooms in Great Brunswick Street were invested by a party of protesting students from University College, whom the diarist and

56. William Dawson (1877–1934) was five years older than Joyce and the son of Charles Dawson (1842–1917), Lord Mayor of Dublin from 1882 to 1883 and member of Parliament for Carlow from 1880 to 1885. Felix Hackett wrote, 'Callan, Kettle, the Dawsons, the Sheehys, belonged to families which had been in the midst of the struggles of the Parnell period and after' (in Meenan, *Centenary History*, 50).

57. *Daily Nation*, 12 May 1899. Its editorial of 8 May 1899 achieves a plangent lyricism.

theatre critic Joseph Holloway characterised as an 'organised claque of about twenty brainless, beardless, idiotic-looking youths'.[58] They were drawn principally from the Central Branch of the Gaelic League but included—in exactly the kind of anomalous conjuncture that attracted Joyce's sharpest scrutiny—the ardently anti–Gaelic League Francis Skeffington.[59] Joyce was in the audience, applauding resolutely.[60] He heard sung 'Who Will Go Drive with Fergus Now' and 'Impetuous Heart, Be Still, Be Still', which remained in his personal repertoire all his life. He set the latter to music of his own. Three years later he sang these songs on the piano to his fourteen-year-old brother George, who lay dying of typhoid fever in an adjoining room.[61] In Yeats's play, Oona says, 'I'll sing how Fergus drove his brazen cars':

Who will go drive with Fergus now,
And pierce the deep wood's woven shade,
And dance upon the level shore?
Young man, lift up your russet brow,
And lift your tender eyelids, maid,
And brood on hopes and fears no more.

She ends,

And no more turn aside and brood
Upon Love's bitter mystery;
For Fergus rules the brazen cars,
And rules the shadows of the wood,
And the white breast of the dim sea
And all the dishevelled wandering stars.[62]

58. Joseph Holloway, *Joseph Holloway's Abbey Theatre: A Selection from his Unpublished Journal 'Impressions of a Dublin Playgoer'*, ed. Robert Hogan and Michael J. O'Neill (Carbondale: Southern Illinois University Press, 1967), 6. Holloway noted, 'Thomas Davis seemed to be the particular "bee in their bonnets", as they frequently made reference to the poet.'

59. Fathers of the Society of Jesus, *Page of Irish History*, 481.

60. Seamus O'Sullivan, *The Rose and Bottle* (Dublin: Talbot, 1946), 119–20.

61. Curran, *James Joyce Remembered*, 41.

62. W. B. Yeats, *The Variorum Edition of the Plays of W. B. Yeats*, ed. Russell K. Alspach (New York: Macmillan, 1966), 52–56.

In a deliberately overt way, unusual for Joyce, 'Who Goes with Fergus' was to be threaded through *Ulysses*. It provides the first quoted lines of verse in *Ulysses*, intoned by Buck Mulligan in the Martello Tower, plunging Stephen into the desolate recall of his mother and of singing to her the 'Fergus' song when she was dying;[63] hours later the drunken Stephen of night-town in the 'Circe' episode murmurs fragments of the lines.[64]

Two days after the premiere of *The Countess Cathleen*, a pompous remonstrance of striking vacuity issued forth from some of Joyce's most prominent University College contemporaries, who felt it their 'duty, in the name and for the honour of Dublin Catholic students of the Royal University to protest against an art, even a dispassionate art, which offers as a type of our people a loathsome brood of apostate'. The letter, published in the *Freeman's Journal*, was a sorry affair:

> The subject is not Irish. It has been shown that the plot is founded on a German legend. The characters are ludicrous travesties of the Irish Catholic Celt. The purpose of Mr. Yeats's drama is apparently to show the sublimity of self-sacrifice. . . . He represents the Irish peasant as a crooning barbarian, crazed with morbid superstition, who, having added the Catholic faith to his store of superstition, sells that faith for gold or bread in the proving of famine. . . . Why, if this is a true portrait of Irish Catholic character, every effort of England to stamp our religion and incidentally our nationality is not merely to be justified, but to be applauded.[65]

In the Healyite *Daily Nation* this letter appeared beneath one from Cardinal Michael Logue, the Archbishop of Armagh, also condemning Yeats's play.[66] The *Daily Nation* unctuously lauded the action of the Catholic students: 'We venture to prophesy that there will be no period in the bright and prosperous future which we trust lies before each and every one of them, in which they will not be entitled to recall with pride

63. *U* 1.239–53. This is also recalled by the ghost of his mother (*U* 15.4189–90).

64. *U* 15.4931–50.

65. *Freeman's Journal*, 10 May 1899.

66. *Daily Nation*, 10 May 1899.

the part they have now taken in denouncing what can only be regarded as an unparalleled insult to the honour of our race'.[67]

The signatories included Tom Kettle, Francis Skeffington, Hugh Kennedy, William Fallon, and others to whom Joyce was personally close: John Francis Byrne, George Clancy, and Richard Sheehy. Joyce, in his first year in University College, refused to sign. It was in its small way a defining moment of dissent from his contemporaries, and identification with Yeats, of whom Joyce was otherwise ostentatiously critical in University College. The significance of the schism for Joyce is attested to by the fact that Herbert Gorman refers to it in his 1941 biography. Gorman exaggerates, writing that 'all the students were gently coerced into signing it. That is, all except one. Joyce, contemptuously, refused to add his signature to the rest'.[68] This reflected Joyce's assertion, 'I was the only student who refused his signature.'[69]

Constantine Curran, who in his memoir goes to inordinate lengths to mitigate the letter, and Thomas F. Bacon, in his contribution to the history of the L&H, indignantly disputed that Joyce had stood alone.[70] But if others also declined to sign the letter, it was Joyce's refusal that was noticed at the time. Two and a half years later, it was recalled against him by the college magazine *St Stephen's* on the publication of his essay 'The Day of the Rabblement': 'So it happened that when this rabblement protested against *Countess Cathleen*, our fellow-students approved and supported the protest. Mr. Joyce alone, to our knowledge, stood aloof. If Mr. Joyce thinks that the artist must stand aloof from the multitude, and means that he must also sever himself from the moral and

67. *Daily Nation*, 10 May 1899.

68. Gorman, *James Joyce*, 61.

69. The importance that Joyce attached to this assertion is reflected in the fact that it appears in the list containing 'some account of my books' which Joyce forwarded in 1916 to Harriet Shaw Weaver for forwarding to B. W. Huebsch, where it serves to introduce his relations with Yeats (Joyce to Harriet Shaw Weaver, *Letters I* 98). Ellmann's assertion (*James Joyce*, 67n) that the letter of protest was left on a table in the college for students to sign appears to be a pure transposition of the account of the mode of gathering signatures for MacCann's peace petition in *A Portrait*.

70. Curran, *Under the Receding Wave*, 101–2; Meenan, *Centenary History*, 57. Curran noted that neither Arthur Clery nor Dawson signed. Clery wrote a letter of much milder criticism of Yeats (*Daily Express*, 11 May 1899).

religious teachings which have, under Divine guidance, moulded its spiritual character, we join issue with him, and we prophesy but ill-success for any school which offers an Irish public art based upon such a principle.'[71]

The schism over *The Countess Cathleen* was neither insignificant nor transient. In 1907 during the controversy that surrounded John Millington Synge's *The Playboy of the Western World*, Skeffington blamed the contention over *The Countess Cathleen* on 'the wanton provocation of the public by Mr Yeats'.[72]

It was not simply that the issue set Joyce in defiance against his peers. It enlisted him in a famous nationalist artistic controversy from which he was, to his intense frustration, to be excluded in the case of the *Playboy* riots, which erupted in the course of his sojourn in Rome. Moreover, it brought him, almost in spite of himself, into alliance with Yeats. He would still publish 'The Day of the Rabblement', a broadside against Yeats, but their alignment on *The Countess Cathleen* was important to how he came later to conceptualise his relation to Yeats and to the Celtic Twilight. While they had yet to meet, the premiere of the play marks the inception of a relationship that was from the outset characterised by a marred and jagged reciprocity that verged on the weird. Speaking in advance of the play's production at the National Literary Society, Yeats invoked Ibsen, at the time Joyce's principal inspiration: 'The only European country, he thought, which had a drama at once intellectual and popular was Norway. The national literary movement in that country between 1840 and 1860 in almost everything resembled the national literary movement going on in this country today.'[73]

Yeats had already elided the more provocative aspects of the play as originally published. T. P. Gill's *Daily Express* celebrated the fact that 'for the first time in at least a hundred years of Irish History the people of

71. *St Stephen's*, December 1901.

72. *Evening Telegraph*, 25 March 1907. In a typescript article in his papers titled 'Irish Playwrights and the Irish Public', Skeffington wrote with alarming insouciance that 'the will of the artist may need to be sometimes curbed by the direct censorship of the people'. Sheehy-Skeffington Papers, NLI MS 40,474/5.

73. *Daily Express*, 8 May 1899.

Dublin are agitated by a question which has nothing to do with politics or sectarian theology. We have found something new to take sides upon—something intellectual and literary.' This was the note Yeats chose to sound. At the grand dinner in the Shelbourne Hotel that Gill gave four days after the play opened, Yeats 'rejoiced to see the country fierce at last upon a purely intellectual issue.'[74]

Joyce was still a student, at the start of his final year, when in October 1901 he assailed in 'The Day of the Rabblement' what he saw as a craven change of direction on the part of Yeats and the Irish Literary Theatre. Joyce intended his piece as an article for *St Stephen's*, but it was vetoed by the Jesuit authorities, reportedly on account of a reference to Gabriele D'Annunzio, who was on the Vatican's Index of Prohibited Books. Joyce had 'The Day of the Rabblement' published as an essay in a pamphlet in conjunction with Skeffington's article championing the equal status of women in the university, which had met a similar fate.[75] Joyce was writing in response to the assessment Yeats had published in *Samhain* at the start of the same month of the first two years of the Irish Literary Theatre, and its programme for the third. The theatre would produce Yeats and Moore's *Diarmuid and Grania* and Douglas Hyde's *Casadh an tSúgáin* (*The Twisting of the Rope*).[76] Joyce asserted that in

74. *Daily Express*, 12 May 1899.

75. See *OCPW* 50–52; Curran, *James Joyce Remembered*, 17–20; S. Joyce, *My Brother's Keeper*, 151–53; Meenan, *Centenary History*, 61–62; and Ellmann, *James Joyce*, 88–89. One would have thought that the two references to Giordano Bruno would have done more to disquiet the Jesuit authorities than the single reference to D'Annunzio and *Il Fuoco*, and were more intentionally defiant on Joyce's part: see Lernout, *Help My Unbelief*, 44, 80–81. Joyce may have first read of Bruno in a setting of Jesuit condemnation of contemporary Italian anticlericalism in an article entitled 'Giordano Bruno and United Italy', *Lyceum* 3, no. 25 (September 1889): 7–10.

76. Curran, *James Joyce Remembered*, 18; W. B. Yeats, ed. *Samhain* (Dublin: n.p., 1891), republished in W. B. Yeats, *Explorations* (New York: Macmillan, 1962), 73–84. Joyce's attack was more distantly informed by the controversy initiated by William Archer's response to an attack in George Moore's introduction to Edward Martyn's *The Heather Field and Maeve* (London: Duckworth, 1899), vii–xvii, in which Yeats as well as Moore had vigorously participated (*Daily Chronicle*, 20, 26, 27, and 30 January 1899; the issue of 30 January, containing Yeats's letter, is illustrated by a cartoon by Max Beerbohm depicting Moore as an Irish peasant trailing his coat before William Archer in a kilt; Yeats's letter is republished in *The Letters of W. B. Yeats*, ed. Allan Wade [London: Rupert Hart-Davis, 1954], 308–11). Joyce was in part concerned to salvage the honour of

surrendering to the popular will, 'the Irish Literary Theatre must now be considered the property of the rabblement of the most belated race in Europe'. Yeats had cloyingly written in *Samhain* of Fr Patrick Dinneen's *Creideamh agus Gorta* (*Faith and Famine*) that 'the reverence and simplicity of the verse makes one think of a medieval miracle play'. Joyce coldly retorted that 'a nation which has never advanced so far as the miracle play affords no literary model to the artist and he must look abroad.'[77] He extolled Yeats's *The Wind among the Reeds* and 'The Adoration of the Magi' as showing 'what Mr. Yeats can do when he breaks with the half-gods. But an esthete has a floating will, and Mr. Yeats's treacherous instinct of adaptability must be blamed for his recent association with a platform from which even self-respect should have urged him to refrain'.[78] Joyce's pamphlet exhibited the first flash of his distinctive artistic temper, defined in relation to his critique of Yeats and foreshadowing his treatment of Mangan in his paper to the L&H the following February. The 'true servitude' of the artist is 'that he inherits a will broken by doubt and a soul that yields up all its hate to a caress.'[79]

'Gas from a Burner'

Joyce sat his final exams in September 1902. While *St Stephens* had numbered Joyce among those who might carry off the Irish studentship in 1903,[80] Joyce's degree was undistinguished. The conferring was on

---

the much-invoked Ibsen as the Irish Literary Theatre took a regressive turn. Near the end of 'The Day of the Rabblement' Joyce invoked 'the old master who is dying in Christiana' (*OCPW* 52).

77. *OCPW* 50. The reference was evidently not lost on Fr Dinneen, who had left the Jesuit order the year before. Joyce's tract opened with an enigmatic reference to Giordano Bruno as 'the Nolan'. Stanislaus recalled an excursion with Fr Dinneen and a group of students in the Dublin mountains shortly after the publication of the pamphlet which included Joyce's essay: 'He was a little man with a pale, prematurely old face, like a pathetic leprechaun, but on this occasion to show the lightness and innocence of his heart, he kept jumping up on the low stone walls along the way and off again, and every time he landed on the grassy border, he exclaimed amid the merriment of the students: "Said the Nolan"' (*My Brother's Keeper*, 152).

78. *OCPW* 51. Curran notes that Joyce's attack 'coincided with the moment when Yeats stood closest to the Gaelic League', and that Lionel Johnson had written of Mangan's 'floating will' (*James Joyce Remembered*, 18–19).

79. *OCPW* 52.

80. *St Stephen's*, June 1902.

31 October 1902. In deference to the anxiously receding aspirations of his father, Joyce submitted to a photograph in cap and gown.[81] The conferring took place in the Aula Maxima of University College. The interminable proceedings included the singing of 'God Save the King' to the accompaniment of the organ. This elicited muted resistance by the student body, some of whom, according to *St Stephen's*, intoned 'A Nation Once Again', 'Dolly Grey', and the 'Marseillaise', though not so volubly as to attract press comment. The *Freeman's Journal* merely noted that the conferring was 'even less imposing than usual'.[82] The subdued dissent foreshadowed the flamboyant protest at the conferring of 1905, in which some of the students seized the organ to prevent the singing of 'God Save the King'. Patricia Hutchins's assertion that Joyce led a revolt at the conferring is a canard.[83] Unlike many of his contemporaries, Joyce was resolutely unsentimental about University College as an institution. Debate about the Irish university question rumbled on during Joyce's early exile. He wrote an exasperated and brilliantly funny letter to Stanislaus from Rome in 1906 responding to newspapers sent by his aunt Josephine Murray, observing of some of his contemporaries that 'they are all in the public eye and favour'. He caustically noted, 'What do these gentlemen in Ireland want a new University for? The one they have is quite good enough for them—both in "saince and in art"'.[84]

The Irish Universities Act was enacted in 1908. It provided for the dissolution of the Royal University, of which University College had been a constituent part, and the establishment of University College Dublin. As it happened, Joyce was in Ireland on his second return trip for the transition and the opening of University College Dublin on 2 November 1909.[85] It was the only significant institutional change to have occurred since Joyce had left Dublin five years earlier. In the *Leader*, Joyce's contemporary Arthur Clery wrote an article titled 'The Passing of University College': 'A hearse-like furniture van stands at the door to

81. S. Joyce, *My Brother's Keeper*, 189.

82. *St Stephen's*, November 1902; *Freeman's Journal*, 1 November 1902 (editorial).

83. Patricia Hutchins, *James Joyce's Dublin* (London: Grey Walls, 1950), 68–70. Joyce was not the only bearer of his surname.

84. Joyce to Stanislaus Joyce, 31 August 1906, *Letters II* 153–55.

85. McCartney, *UCD, a National Idea*, 47.

excite the curiosity of the chance passer-by'. Clery wrote of the era which began with the return of William Delany S.J. to the presidency of the college in 1897, the year before Joyce's arrival:

> If University College of old had any special defect, it was really that it was too true a University. . . . If outsiders had known the brilliant and varied college life that existed behind the shabby exterior of the Stephen's Green buildings, they might be more of my way of thinking. Some of the men of that time are already on the road to distinction, in science, in philosophy, in public life, in various paths of effort. Others may never fulfil their early promise. It is all but a memory now. But the college life, which had these men in the first promise of youth as its chief figures was indescribably brilliant and interesting.[86]

The following week Clery wrote a further piece, asserting that the students of the college had refused to follow the path of more assured advancement that Trinity College offered, culminating in the declaration that 'we, University College men, fought the battle of the Church'.[87]

It was after his third return visit to Ireland and the destruction by the printer of virtually the entire print run of *Dubliners* that Joyce on 14 November 1912, on the journey back to Trieste, wrote his magnificently splenetic 'Gas from a Burner' on the back of his contract with Maunsel

86. *Leader*, 30 October 1909. Clery's piece was published in the Jesuits' 1930 history of the college: Fathers of the Society of Jesus, *Page of Irish History*, 583–87. A footnote was appended to Clery's assertion that the revival movement, 'by giving students an ideal, raised the tone of our lives, and an exceptionally high moral standard prevailed among us': 'Readers of Mr. James Joyce will get a different impression, but this is the actual fact. Among the students of the college about this time were—P. H. Pearse, T. M. Kettle, F. Sheehy-Skeffington. Joyce is true as far as he goes, but confining himself to one small knot of medical students he gives a wrong impression of the whole' (586). Joyce can scarcely have missed this indexed reference in the copy Eugene Jolas gave him. Pearse was not a student of University College.

87. Chanel [Arthur Clery], 'Down among the Dead Men', *Leader*, 6 November 1909. Not everyone was persuaded of this. A contributor to the *Leader*, evidently a Gaelicising cleric, expressed the conviction that the values of Irish Ireland would bring about a reformation of the decadent colleges of the Royal University: 'And once it takes possession of the University, as I hope it will, there will be created there a public spirit against the fashionable vices hitherto so lamentably common amongst the gentlemen that came from our great Catholic Colleges'. 'Ireland or Infidelity, Which?', *Leader*, 9 January 1909.

& Company. Its subject relates to Joyce's artistic travails and seems to have nothing to do with University College. However, its title and concept suggest an acrid secondary allusion to University College, and specifically to the L&H.

The form of the poetic broadside is an apologia by what is to be taken as a printer rather than a publisher to an unidentified audience. Formally it is an attack on John Falconer, the printer who burned almost the entirety of the print run of *Dubliners*, rather than the pusillanimous publisher George Roberts, who had retained him. It is an obsequious apologia that recounts in the first person how the printer had spurned printing the text once he had discerned the 'foul intent' of the author. The title encompasses a pun on the ignition of a fart, obliquely developed towards the poem's end. The title of the first draft is entitled 'Falconer Addresses the Vigilance Committee'.[88] The setting is ostensibly formal ('Ladies and Gents, you are here assembled . . .').

Oliver St John Gogarty suggested that the title referred to the gas jet in the office of the manager of Maunsel's responsible for the burning of the print run, from which Joyce had removed a suitcase containing ladies' underwear (which the manager sold as a side line).[89] There is a more obvious source. The debates of the L&H were conducted in the Old Physics Theatre, as the handsome Georgian space was designated, badly illumined by the light from two gas jets. Joyce's contemporary Thomas F. Bacon recalled, 'The illumination at night was furnished by two gas-jets with mantle burners, which were so unsatisfactory that during Arthur Clery's auditorship the secretary was directed to "procure and have at each debate a pair of white wax candles for the convenience of the gentleman occupying the chair"'.[90] Indeed the *Centenary History of the Literary and Historical Society* suggests that the two gas jets were

88. Robert Scholes, 'The Broadsides of James Joyce', in *A James Joyce Miscellany, Third Series*, ed. Marvin Magalaner (Carbondale: Southern Illinois University Press, 1962), 8–18.

89. Oliver St John Gogarty, *It Isn't That Time of Year at All* (London: MacGibbon and Kee, 1954), 72–74, 79. 'Gas from a Burner' did include a reference to 'swag, / from Maunsel's manager's travelling bag', to which Stanislaus alludes (*My Brother's Keeper*, 249).

90. Meenan, *Centenary History*, 69.

features of the institutional memory of the society,[91] and remained so into the era of Flann O'Brien.[92] The Catholic nationalist audience of the L&H and the Vigilance Committee had insensibly merged, enlarging the scope of Joyce's verse philippic beyond its identifiable (and predominantly Anglo-Irish) targets. Joyce had with his habitual economy found an occasion to deploy an image of oratorical flatulence he had evidently played with in the protractedness of the imperfectly lit debates of the L&H.

91. Meenan, *Centenary History*, 136, 140.

92. Meenan, *Centenary History*, 242, 257. Flann O'Brien also mentions the gas-jet in *At Swim-Two-Birds* (London: Penguin, 1967), 48.

7

Four Friends from University College

JOYCE APPREHENDED THAT he attended University College at an extraordinary hiatus—after the deemed termination of the Parnell Split, and before Irish politics began to take a different direction away from parliamentarism. He rendered that long moment with fastidious imaginative exactitude in *A Portrait*. His portrayal of a generation did not depend on what happened next, but it transpired to be startlingly proleptic. Joyce's contemporaries struggled to contain their later accounts within a frame of nostalgic reminiscence. In 1930 Arthur Clery reviewed the Jesuit-compiled *A Page of Irish History: Story of University College, Dublin, 1883–1909*—while affirming, 'I still look on the age of Kettle as the great age', he characterised the book as 'a record of the golden glorious days of troubled lives.'[1]

Joyce's generation became caught up in the crisis of Irish politics from 1912 to 1921. The four people with whom Joyce was most involved personally or intellectually in University College—Francis Skeffington, Tom Kettle, George Clancy, and John Francis Byrne—were all politically

1. *National Student*, n.s., 1, no. 2 (June 1930): 100. All the histories of University College were written after the establishment of the Irish state and tended to emphasise continuities that connected the college to the new state. While there was to be a significant connexion between the college and the early Irish state under Cumann na nGaedheal, to the point of alienating Eamon de Valera, the narrative thrust tended to downplay, if not to elide, the devastating rupture that the defeat of the Irish Party represented for most of those who belonged to 'the age of Kettle'.

active after graduation, and three of them died violently in conflict (in the Easter Rising, the Somme, and the Irish War of Independence). This represents a freakishly high proportion by reference to Irish fatalities in the period, including those of the Great War. His relationship to these men meant that, at a personal level, Joyce in exile was not divorced from the trajectory towards Irish independence. Their importance to his intellectual development is attested by his deploying all four as characters in his fiction.

There were romantic, as well as social and political, entanglements—Skeffington and Kettle were brothers-in-law through their marriages to Hanna and Mary Sheehy, daughters of the nationalist member of Parliament David Sheehy, and Joyce had a 'small, rich passion' for Mary, unsuspected by her.[2] The theatre of their relations was the Sheehy household in Belvedere Place, to which Joyce was first introduced while at school in Belvedere College, where he was friendly with Richard and Eugene Sheehy.

David Sheehy was the nationalist member of Parliament for Galway South (1885–1900) and South Meath (1903–18) who had been an anti-Parnellite in the Split. In the South Meath by-election of October 1903, he had defeated Charles Stewart Parnell's brother John Howard Parnell as an independent nationalist.[3] An ally of John Dillon, he loathed Timothy Michael Healy. Sheehy and his wife, Elizabeth (Bessie), lived with their six children at No. 2 Belvedere Place. The household was marked by its gregarious hospitality and its support for Home Rule. Eugene Sheehy recalled often seeing Tom Kettle and Francis Skeffington in the house 'writing articles and leaderettes on large, loose-paged notebooks, whilst conversation raged all round or parlour games were in progress.'[4] Elaborate parlour and party games, charades, and theatrical improvisations were de rigueur in Belvedere Place, as if translating the parliamentary into the domestic sphere.

2. Ellmann, *James Joyce*, 51, 149–50.

3. Owen McGee, 'David Sheehy', *DIB* 8:886–87.

4. Sheehy, *May It Please the Court*, 34.

Joyce was a popular guest on the Sheehys' 'Sundays'. He participated in charades and theatricals, and sang, often songs he had picked up from his father. Sometimes May Joyce came with her son and accompanied him on the piano.[5] Hanna Sheehy-Skeffington in old age recalled 'Jim Joyce' coming with other University College students to 'our Sundays' in Belvedere Place: 'Joyce was then gay and boyish, flinging himself into topical charades. He loved to "dress up" and produce plays and parodies and to sing old folk ballads in his sweet tenor.'[6]

Francis Skeffington

Francis (Frank) Skeffington (1878–1916) was born on 23 December 1878 at Bailieborough, County Cavan, and grew up in Downpatrick, County Down. An initiating oddity of his career is that he was educated at home by his father, J. B. Skeffington, an inspector of schools with the board of national education. He 'was I imagine, a crank by inheritance', Curran wrote. Stanislaus Joyce recalled, 'He had been educated by his father on some system—so, at least, Jim told me—and was endowed with an enthusiasm that responded mechanically to all the more obvious appeals to justice, reason and humanity.'[7]

He entered University College in 1896, one year before Kettle, two years before Joyce. He did much to bring about the revival of the Literary and Historical Society (L&H), of which he was auditor in his second year. He graduated in 1900 and took an MA in 1902. Skeffington, bearded—he never used a razor—and in tweed plus-fours and oversize boots, was a conspicuous figure in the city.[8] D. P. Moran's *Leader* in 1909 derided his 'aggressive whiskers, his high-pitched querulous voice,

5. Sheehy, *May It Please the Court*, 21–24; Ellmann, *James Joyce*, 51–53.

6. Typescript of radio interview of Hanna Sheehy-Skeffington with Dr Dixon, [1946], incomplete, Sheehy-Skeffington Papers, NLI, MS 24164.

7. Patrick Maume, 'Francis Sheehy-Skeffington', *DIB* 8:981–83; Leah Levenson, 'Francis Sheehy-Skeffington', *ODNB* 50:820–22; S. Joyce, *My Brother's Keeper*, 152; Curran, *Under the Receding Wave*, 112.

8. Sheehy, *May It Please the Court*, 30–31.

and his invariable, we had almost said his immortal knickerbockers'.[9] The impression was indelible. Over a half century later Oliver St John Gogarty could still recall encountering 'Joyce's friend Sheehy-Skeffington, an opinionated, bearded little theorist in knickerbockers.'[10] The speed of his talk and motion added to the effect. As Curran noted, 'His behaviour seemed to be regulated in accordance with long-settled opinions privately arrived at. All his movements were rapid and decisive. He thought, talked and walked. . . . His briskness appeared to be dictated by either a hygienic or a missionary purpose.'[11] As well as a Home Ruler and fin-de-siècle radical, he was a vegetarian, anti-vivisectionist, teetotaller, non-smoker, pacifist, and feminist. In 1900 he became engaged to Hanna Sheehy. They married on 27 June 1903 and merged their surnames. Sheehy-Skeffington thereby became for the *Leader* the 'hyphened' or 'hyphenated' democrat,[12] among multiple other epithets. (In this chapter, concerned principally with the college years, I follow Joyce and Curran's practice of referring to him as Skeffington, but in all citations after his marriage he is Sheehy-Skeffington.)

He was eccentric in a manner that might suggest Shaw as a model (he 'wore Jaeger and homespuns like Bernard Shaw'),[13] but in fact the ascendant influence was William T. Stead. Skeffington was a vociferous rebel against authority and received opinion. He was anticlerical and, almost alone in University College, an open opponent of the Gaelic League. Curran wrote that his 'favourite assaults were on Gaelic Leaguers, bishops and conservatives'.[14] Like Joyce he was suspicious of clerical involvement in the Gaelic League, which he wrote in 1906 was for the most part 'in the hands of the Catholic clergy, who hope

9. *Leader*, 20 February 1909, quoted in J. B. Lyons, *The Enigma of Tom Kettle: Irish Patriot, Essayist, Poet, British Soldier, 1880–1916* (Dublin: Glendale, 1983), 151.

10. Gogarty, *It Isn't That Time*, 31.

11. Curran, *Under the Receding Wave*, 112.

12. Leah Levenson, *With Wooden Sword: A Portrait of Francis Sheehy-Skeffington, Militant Pacifist* (Boston: Northeastern University Press, 1983), 94. The *Leader*, in its issue of 9 December 1911, referred to Sheehy-Skeffington as 'a spook in whispers and knickerbockers', as well as 'a hyphened democrat'.

13. Curran, *Under the Receding Wave*, 112–13.

14. Curran, *Under the Receding Wave*, 114.

FIGURE 7.1. Francis Sheehy-Skeffington and his future wife, Hanna Sheehy-Skeffington. Reproduced with the kind permission of the National Museum of Ireland.

to profit by the return to medievalism and the reaction against modern cosmopolitan democracy which the revival of the Irish language represents.'[15]

15. Francis Sheehy-Skeffington, 'Michael Davitt's Unfinished Campaign', *Independent Review* 10 (July–September 1906): 308.

Joyce and Skeffington were, as Curran recalled, 'always good friends'. Skeffington, as Eugene Sheehy fairly pointed out, was 'one of the first persons to recognize and appreciate the genius of Joyce'.[16] Stanislaus attributed to his brother the comment that Skeffington was 'the most intelligent man in Stephen's College after myself'.[17] It was Skeffington who proposed Joyce for auditor of the L&H, while Kettle proposed Hugh Kennedy, who was victorious.[18]

They held some views in common, though typically more in their conclusions than in their premises. They were both opposed to the political influence of the Church in Ireland. In a 1906 article titled 'Michael Davitt's Unfinished Campaign', Skeffington identified himself as 'one who revolts against the twin tyrannies of the country—that of British Government and of the Catholic Episcopacy.'[19] His 'twin tyrannies' equated precisely to Joyce's 'two masters', though without quite linking the tyrannies, and found published expression first. On the final analysis, theirs was a tactical accord rather than a meeting of minds.

16. Sheehy, *May It Please the Court*, 35.

17. S. Joyce, *My Brother's Keeper*, 152.

18. Sheehy, *May It Please the Court*, 30. Kennedy received fifteen votes and Joyce nine; Meenan, *Centenary History*, 61. In 1937 Eugene Jolas left with the concierge of Joyce's apartment in the Rue Edmond Valentin a copy of *A Page of Irish History*, the history of the university published under Jesuit auspices. Joyce noted the incorrect statement on page 338 that he had in 1897 contested the auditorship against Skeffington. Joyce was there referred to 'James A. Joyce, popularly described as "Jimmy" or "The Hatter"', and it was stated that 'the Hatter never wore this particular crown'. Joyce scarcely failed to register the combination of incorrectness with slighting jocularity. He wrote to Curran of his contest with Kennedy, adding his own inaccuracy: 'He won by ca 22 to 16 all the U. C. Staff voting for him'. Joyce to C. P. Curran, 10 June 1937, *Letters III* 400.

19. Sheehy-Skeffington, 'Michael Davitt's Unfinished Campaign', 312. In his Davitt biography, he wrote likewise of the attainment with political freedom of erecting Ireland 'into a great modern and progressive State, free from tyrannies either material or spiritual'. Francis Sheehy-Skeffington, *Michael Davitt: Revolutionary, Agitator and Labour Leader* (London: T. Fisher Unwin, 1908; London: McGibbon and Kee, 1967), 242. The difference lies primarily in the much greater expressive force of Joyce's 'two masters' and related propositions. Joyce was dismissive of the effectiveness of the writing of Irish intellectuals; and specifically of Skeffington's proselytising mode, at least carried beyond university.

Joyce's refusal of accommodation did not mean he did not have the capacity to think politically. This capacity the briskly dogmatic Skeffington lacked. Politically, the shadow that fell between Joyce and Skeffington was that of the Parnell Split. Skeffington's two heroes were Michael Davitt and W. T. Stead, both of whom had played prominent roles in bringing about Parnell's fall. While many of Joyce's intellectual jousts with Skeffington related to the disparate contemporary causes that Skeffington championed, a cleavage ran between them going back to the Split. Skeffington was, as Curran wrote with exactitude, 'retrospectively anti-Parnellite' in the sense of favouring the side taken by Parnell's opponents when the Irish Party split in December 1890.[20] In Irish affairs he 'chiefly reverenced' Davitt, 'his single admiration',[21] whom he considered 'the greatest Irishman of the nineteenth century'.[22]

In 1908, as Sheehy-Skeffington (following his marriage) he published an unauthorised biography of Davitt, who had died in 1906, entitled *Michael Davitt: Revolutionary, Agitator and Labour Leader*.[23] It is not known if Joyce ever read this vapid work, published four years after he left Ireland, but it exemplified the incoherence of Skeffington's political thinking. Skeffington extolled Davitt over Parnell, whom he characterised as 'Conservative and opportunist',[24] using the latter term perhaps as it was applied to leading politicians of the Third Republic; he wrote

20. Curran, *Under the Receding Wave*, 116.

21. Sheehy, *May It Please the Court*, 36; Curran, *Under the Receding Wave*, 115.

22. Sheehy-Skeffington, *Michael Davitt*, 269.

23. Sheehy-Skeffington, *Michael Davitt*. Davitt's widow, Mary, was not in favour of Sheehy-Skeffington writing her husband's biography; King, *Michael Davitt*, 554–55. Sheehy-Skeffington wrote to a correspondent, 'As was to be expected, my book has not pleased any section of the Irish press. It is too "rebel" for one side, and too anticlerical for the other. I believe Mrs Davitt's objections to the publication were inspired by the Jesuits'; Sheehy-Skeffington to John M. Robertson, 25 July 1908, typescript copy, Skeffington Papers, NLI, MS 40,471/6. Of H. M. Hyndman's review in *Justice*, he wrote, 'I see that he agrees with me, as against Keir Hardie, that Davitt was not actually a Socialist, though close to Socialism in his later days'; Sheehy-Skeffington to Theodore Rothstein, 16 September 1908, typescript copy, Skeffington Papers, NLI, MS 40,471/6. In his biography, he had written, 'Davitt was not a Socialist'; Sheehy-Skeffington, *Michael Davitt*, 273.

24. Sheehy-Skeffington, *Michael Davitt*, 181.

of Parnell's 'cold, cautious, conservative mind', of his 'cold, conservative intellect'.[25] Skeffington showed little understanding of Fenianism, and was over-trusting in the historically 'close connection' between Irish nationalism and 'the democratic movement' in Britain, making the revealing statement that Davitt, 'with his simultaneous attack upon the English and upon the feudal power, was the type of this happy alliance between Nationalism and Democracy, an alliance the severance of which means the destruction for the whole National movement—for Democracy would not suffer by the breach.'[26]

What was most jarring was Skeffington's combining of opposition to the Parnell of the Split with an outspoken denunciation of the political role of the Church on more or less abstract Enlightenment lines without being rooted in any particular set of Irish nationalist values. Of the Split he wrote, 'All the machinery of ecclesiastical power was unscrupulously brought into play in the campaign against Parnell.'[27] He proclaimed that 'the Irish Nationalism of which Davitt is the type is necessarily anti-clerical.'[28] The relentless advertisement of his anticlericalism produced the extraordinary result that Justin McCarthy, who had led the anti-Parnellites in the immediate aftermath of the Split, felt bound at the end of the introduction he provided to Skeffington's book to state, 'I cannot identify myself with some of the opinions expressed very strongly in the book by its brilliant author', specifically that 'the views which Mr. F. Sheehy-Skeffington sets forth very emphatically as to the position taken up by most of the Irish Catholic and Prelates and Clergy against the great National movements are altogether at variance with my own.'[29] The studiously vague note on which his book ended suggested Skeffington was unsure of his own political course:

25. Sheehy-Skeffington, *Michael Davitt*, 73, 126. He thought Parnell's pre-eminence was 'due to temperament and not to intellect' (108).

26. Sheehy-Skeffington, *Michael Davitt*, 272.

27. Sheehy-Skeffington, *Michael Davitt*, 186–87. He was constrained to add that it was one of the strangest ironies of Davitt's career 'that he, the least clerically minded of Irish politicians, should have become the standard-bearer of an outrageously arrogant clericalism' in the North Meath election of 1892.

28. Sheehy-Skeffington, *Michael Davitt*, 277.

29. Justin McCarthy, introduction to Sheehy-Skeffington, *Michael Davitt*, xix.

'What is wanted is to proceed along Davitt's lines; not to stand still where he stood. For the moment, the programme of Davitt may adequately represent our highest aspirations.'[30]

It is hard to resist the thought that W. T. Stead was a much more formative, and certainly an earlier, influence on Skeffington than Davitt. Curran recalled that 'Skeffington at college was a devout reader of *The Review of Reviews*. He adopted to his own purpose some of W. T. Stead's exhibitionist tactics but without that editor's pomposity.'[31] The influence of Stead ran deeper than Curran knew. It was attested to in an effusively candid letter which Skeffington sent to Stead in February 1901:

> Why do you continue to use the words 'Empire' and 'Imperialism' with approbation & sympathy?
>
> I write with some feeling, for I was myself, to some degree, misled by your use of the terms—which indeed is my only excuse for writing at all. I will explain how, you will perhaps better understand why, agreeing with you thoroughly as to *principles*, I yet attach so much importance to *names*. I am twenty-two of age, and, during the past ten years, I have obtained much of my political education from you. From the *Review of Reviews* I have learned, amongst other things, to be enthusiastic for the cause of Woman and the cause of Peace. From its columns, too, I learned to appreciate the greatness of the responsibilities which lie upon the people of these kingdoms. But you were fond of summing up your doctrines of the duties of a 'ruling race' in the world 'Empire'; thus I was led to believe in the *word* 'Empire'. I followed the word in other columns where it was used with a widely different meaning; and through it began insensibly to imbibe some

30. Sheehy-Skeffington, *Michael Davitt*, 279. It is striking that Skeffington had never met Davitt, though he had heard him speak, and was part of a group which included Kettle and Fred Ryan, who called to see Davitt in connection with a proposal for a national democratic committee, but Davitt was too ill to see them and died on 30 May 1906; Levenson, *With Wooden Sword*, 54–55; King, *Michael Davitt*, 553–56. While he clearly already took Davitt's side in the Split when in University College, one wonders if his full self-conception as a 'true Davittite' (the term used in Sheehy-Skeffington, *Michael Davitt*, 44), whatever exactly he thought that to mean, post-dated Davitt's death.

31. Curran, *Under the Receding Wave*, 114.

> of the poison of the 'Imperialistic' spirit. I began to lose sight of the difference in the *thing*; I held to 'Imperialism' as an expression of talismanic value. My views grew gradually more and more warped; I half-approved the behaviour of [Major-General] Kitchener at [the Battle of] Omdurman; I wholly approved of the American conduct in the Philippines. I grew daily more imbued with that arrogant, one-sided view which looks forward to the subordination of all and sundry to the English speaking races, without consideration for the rights of other stocks. The Boer war has been for me an awakening. It revealed to me, as I believe to many others, for the first time, what 'Imperialism' really means, what is the spirit which gives birth to it, what is the frame of mind it engenders, and what are its material consequences. So now, penetrated with a hatred not only of Imperialism the thing, but of the word ordinarily used to express it, the word which brought me for a space within its grasp, I venture to point out to you the dangers which arise from your using the word as if in itself it were innocuous. Of course, I admit that I was led away through my own fault; that, in clinging to the word, and in neglecting the modification of sense in which you used it, I was guilty of culpable carelessness, and have myself to blame.[32]

This rather tragic remonstrance, by which he sought to bring himself to Stead's attention, discloses much about Skeffington. It articulates a weird nominalism, in which Skeffington protests Stead's having given a false set of progressive coordinates which he had faithfully observed but explains that this was down to the use on Stead's part of a language of imperialism that departed from ordinary usage. What it reveals is that Skeffington was devoid of any instinctive sense of politics or of nationalism and sought to derive his political convictions from first principles with pedantic scrupulosity. It explains why Joyce found Skeffington diverting and was unable to take him entirely seriously.

On Stead's death, Skeffington, in an unpublished article written for the *British Weekly*, wrote, 'I was just eleven years old when the *Review of*

32. Sheehy-Skeffington to W. T. Stead, manuscript draft, endorsed 'copied and sent 20/2/1 to W. T. Stead', Sheehy-Skeffington Papers, NLI, MS 40,470/13.

Reviews was started. I read it with avidity from the first number, and for years it was my bible.' The crudity of Stead's writing style only brought 'into clearer relief the soundness of his heart, the transcendent moral value of his courage and sincerity'. It was Stead who had 'first directed my attention to the importance of the woman question', in a character sketch of Gladstone: 'It struck me very forcibly that Stead, who also made a hero of Gladstone, should so soundly reprove him for his antifeminism. From the reading of that article, I date my interest in feminism.' Stead's opposition to the Boer War 'roused my enthusiasm for him to the highest pitch'. He was involved as one of the correspondents of Stead's ill-fated *Daily Paper*. It was after its collapse that Skeffington met Stead in London in 1902 for the first time. He found Stead 'keenly interested in all things Irish', with Michael Davitt 'one of his greatest friends'. They met again in Stead's new offices in Kingsway 'just before he published his famous interview with the spirit of Mr. Gladstone'.[33] A dialogue of unfathomable absurdity ensued:

> He was full of spiritualism at the time. 'Gladstone and Bright often come round', he said. 'They're tremendously interested in the struggle that is going on at Westminster!' This was at the time of the fight over the Lloyd George budget. Stead spoke of the spirits in a most matter of fact way, and it was impossible to doubt his perfect faith in the reality of the communications he received. The most curious thing he told me about them was that the spirit of Manning, from whom he often received messages, wanted him to become a Catholic. 'You know', said Stead, in answer to my look of astonishment, 'they keep their own religions on the other side'. I said I could not understand this; that the spirits, if genuine, should surely be able to say definitely which religion was the true one, and that a difference of religion between them was impossible. 'No, there is a continuity', said he; but he did not pursue the subject.[34]

33. Sheehy-Skeffington, unpublished typescript article on W. T. Stead, Sheehy-Skeffington Papers, NLI, MS 40,475/6.

34. Sheehy-Skeffington, unpublished typescript article.

The last time Skeffington saw 'this fascinating and noble-hearted man' was when Stead came over to Dublin to study the Irish situation and Skeffington had a couple of long talks with him, arguing over Joseph Devlin.[35] Stead perished on the *Titanic* in the early hours of 15 April 1912.

In an almost perfect exemplification of the problem Joyce experienced in identifying himself politically with any individual or movement in contemporary Ireland, Sheehy-Skeffington, in the same article in which he identified his 'twin tyrannies', allied himself with 'the active liberal elements by Davitt himself, with which the cold, aristocratic conservative mind of Parnell had little sympathy.'[36] This was not a purely historical issue. Skeffington continued to believe ardently in a transnational alliance between Irish nationalism, the post-Gladstonian Liberal party, and movements on the emergent left of British politics to advance progressive causes, of which Home Rule for Ireland was but one. This served to affirm Joyce's conviction that contemporary nationalism had forfeited its coherence in the original error of the Split. For Joyce, Skeffington's stance was delusional, a faddish Irish adaptation of the nonconformist conscience and of Stead's opinionated journalism. A gulf separated Skeffington's views from his own, notwithstanding what they seemed to hold in common. In his bitter experience of the Irish political, Joyce learnt to become an exegete of ostensible like-mindedness.

The reach of the Split in Joyce's thinking beyond its immediate political setting is attested to in the treatment, in both *Stephen Hero* and *A Portrait*, of the episode in which Stephen declines to sign MacCann's petition in favour of world peace. The Skeffington figure in *Stephen Hero* is 'McCann', and 'MacCann' in *A Portrait*.[37] In August 1898 the Russian Tsar Nicholas II issued a rescript directed to the 'maintenance of the general peace, and possible reduction in the excessive armaments which

35. Levenson, *With Wooden Sword*, 134–35.

36. Sheehy-Skeffington, 'Michael Davitt's Unfinished Campaign', 301.

37. There was no necessity for the change, and one wonders if this was not one of the mordant name games to which Joyce was so drawn. It is possible that he was at once giving the figure who represented the anti–Gaelic League Skeffington a slightly more 'Gaelicised' name and sardonically reflecting the name change that Skeffington had embraced on his marriage.

weigh upon all nations', and proposing an international conference. The tsar's proposal was taken up with gusto by Stead, who inaugurated an International Peace Crusade at a public meeting in London in December 1898. The crusade was promoted by a million copies of a broadsheet and the foundation by Stead of a weekly journal, *War against War*. The first international peace conference, by which the episode is to be dated, opened in the Hague on 18 May 1899 and published its final act on 20 July.[38]

The basic features of the encounter with Skeffington over the petition are unchanged in both works: on a table, a petition for peace is laid out, between photographs of the tsar and Stead, but there is one radical departure in *A Portrait*. In *Stephen Hero* Stephen and Cranly conceive a triptych: the tsar resembles Jesus ('a wirrasthrue Jaysus', as Stephen suggests) and Cranly adds, looking in McCann's direction, 'wirrasthrue Jaysus, and hairy Jaysus'.[39] The triptychal concept survives in *A Portrait*, with an important variation: MacCann is displaced by the spectral evocation of Parnell's photographic image.

In *A Portrait* the episode opens with the table near the door of the entrance hall in the college, around which a throng of students were gathered, among whom MacCann 'went briskly to and fro'. On the table were 'two photographs in frames and between them a long roll of paper bearing an irregular tail of signatures.'[40] One of the photographs is of Nicholas II. The second, identified by implication in *A Portrait*, was in *Stephen Hero* expressly identified as a photograph of 'the Editor of the

38. F. Whyte, *The Life of W. T. Stead*, 2 vols. (London: Jonathan Cape, 1925), 2:122–53; James Sheehan, *The Monopoly of Violence: Why Europeans Hate Going to War* (London: Faber and Faber, 2008), 23–26. Tolstoy, who influenced Joyce politically, was opposed to the conference proposed by the tsar, as the *Review of Reviews* later reported: R.E.C. Long, 'Count Tolstoy in Thought and Action', *Review of Reviews*, 15 January 1901, 438–39.

39. *SH* 112–13. The idea of a resemblance between Skeffington and the tsar is rehearsed in *Stephen Hero*: 'As McCann was standing sideways to the light Stephen amused himself in tracing a resemblance between him and the pacific Emperor whose photograph had been taken in profile' (112). It disappears in *A Portrait* and, combined with the non-identification of Stead as the person in the second photograph, leaves the focus fixed on the photograph of the tsar.

40. *P* 5.716–20.

Review of Reviews' (Stead).[41] In *A Portrait*, Cranly (the character based on J. F. Byrne) tells Stephen it is a petition for universal peace and confesses a little sheepishly that he has signed it.

> Stephen pointed to the Czar's photograph and said:
> —He has the face of a besotted Christ.[42]

There is 'scorn and anger' in Stephen's voice in *A Portrait*, though he denies being annoyed.[43] The summation of the oratory by which MacCann seeks to persuade Stephen to sign his petition is certainly intended as Joyce's characterisation of Skeffington's beliefs. It is of lethal political exactitude. Joyce, before he left Dublin and in early exile, was interested in socialism and read widely in anarchist writers and Italian revolutionary syndicalists, and it is significant that he quite correctly did not recognise the Skeffington he had known in college as a socialist. Skeffington was a confused left-utilitarian, with a Stead-like susceptibility to that which was supposedly novel: 'MacCann began to speak with fluent energy of the Czar's rescript, of Stead, of general disarmament, arbitration in cases of international disputes, of the signs of the times, of the new humanity and the new gospel of life which would make it the business of the community to secure as cheaply as possible the greatest possible happiness of the greatest possible number.'[44]

Stephen does not expressly refuse to sign, probably because Joyce did not want to dignify the petition by the assertion of an adamant resistance it scarcely warranted. MacCann accusatorially asks Stephen if he is 'a reactionary': 'Do you think you impress me, Stephen asked, when you flourish your wooden sword?'[45] 'Wooden sword' suggests a toy, signifying the ineffectuality of the tsar's rescript, and 'flourish' implies a hollow theatricality on MacCann/Skeffington's part. It also gives rise to a kind of duel in which MacCann 'stood his ground'. MacCann's response

41. *SH* 112.
42. *P* 5.737–38.
43. *P* 5.739–44.
44. *P* 5.802–7.
45. *P* 5.838–41.

is 'Metaphors! Come to facts.' Stephen will not be drawn, though that physically involves a retreat:[46]

> Stephen, moving away the bystanders, jerked his shoulder angrily in the direction of the Czar's image, saying:
>
> —Keep your icon. If we must have a Jesus, let us have a legitimate Jesus.[47]

As he is led away by Cranly, Stephen catches sight of 'MacCann's flushed blunt featured face':

> —My signature is of no account, he said politely. You are right to go your way. Leave me to go mine.
>
> —Dedalus, said MacCann crisply, I believe you're a good man but you have yet to learn the dignity of altruism and the responsibility of the human individual.[48]

The reasons for Stephen's refusal are not explained, but it is the juxtaposition of the two photographs that accounts for his anger. Through the two photographs the episode is rendered as a displaced template of the Parnell Split. It is a variation—and enhancement—of Joyce's 'two masters' thesis. Nicholas II was both the emperor of Russia and a dominant figure in the Russian Orthodox Church (whence 'icon'). Stead was the journalistic exponent of the nonconformist conscience.[49] The alliance of Nicholas II and Stead—in *Stephen Hero*, 'both of the photographs were signed by the happy couple'[50]—is incongruous. They are MacCann's false gods. The reference to 'a legitimate Jesus' is in the first instance a sharp objection to the confusion of the realms of politics and

46. *P* 5.842–43. The rendering of the incident and its end is significantly reworked from *Stephen Hero*, where Stephen states he has no intention of signing the petition: 'All right, said McCann promptly, as if he was accustomed to rebuffs, if you won't, you won't' (*SH* 115).

47. *P* 5.852–53.

48. *P* 5.879–84.

49. Sheehy-Skeffington wrote breezily in his Davitt biography, 'Davitt was almost as good a Russian as Mr. W. T. Stead. He had no patience with the English Tory who holds up hands in horror at tyranny in Russia, while maintaining a state of things in many respects worse in Ireland' (*Michael Davitt*, 231).

50. *SH* 114.

moralism. Stephen is also bitterly reflecting that the dead Parnell, to whom Nicholas II had a distinct photographic resemblance, was 'a legitimate Jesus'. The figure of Parnell, which emblematised the difference between Joyce and Skeffington, hangs over the encounter. It is a doubling of the conceit of 'Ivy Day in the Committee Room' of Parnell's absence in which Parnell's name is not mentioned. Stephen would never have signed MacCann's petition, but to sign it with those two photographs arrayed on either side would be an act of apostacy. He sees something that would not occur to any of his contemporaries milling around the entrance hall. But Stephen is himself surprised and disconcerted by his own non-volitional recoil, as if recalled to a fealty that he thought had little bearing on his life in the university—and connects back to the Christmas dinner scene earlier in the novel.

There is no other surviving passage of *Stephen Hero* where the relationship of what survives of the unfinished novel and *A Portrait* is quite so intricate. The idea of Parnell's absent photographic image and the fact of Stephen's anger and disconcertedness do not feature in *Stephen Hero*: there is no trace of Parnell in the rendering of the episode in the earlier, unfinished novel.

The handsomeness of Parnell is evident from photos and was widely attested to in his lifetime.[51] His striking good looks were finely captured in the mid-1880s (before a series of illnesses took their toll on his appearance) in a sequence of photographic portraits by the Dublin firm of William Lawrence. In Parnell's lifetime his visual image was rendered principally by crudely hagiographical cartoon images carried in *United Ireland* and the *Freeman's Journal*. It was after Parnell's death that the Lawrence photographic portraits became accessible to a larger public. The association between photography and the memory of the dead, identified most poignantly by Roland Barthes, gives way to a more specific shock of the posthumous in the history of the dissemination in Ireland of the photographic image of Parnell. It is thus emblematic that in Barry O'Brien's biography of Parnell, the Lawrence portrait should face the title page. Dwelling on the contemporary traces of Parnell's memory,

51. Callanan, *T. M. Healy*, 679n57.

Joyce had worked out that, in Irish political iconography, the photographic portrait of Parnell was supercharged with the political desolateness of his demise.

Did something like the encounter described in both *Stephen Hero* and *A Portrait* actually take place between Joyce and Skeffington, as Richard Ellmann more or less assumes it did?[52] Unlike the student protest at *The Countess Cathleen*, the petition did not attract public attention outside University College, although Skeffington did organise a petition and wrote with reference to the Hague conference, 'I remember trying, not very successfully, to induce my fellow students in University College to sign it, and being satirised therefor in one of Chanel's first contributions to the college magazine, *St. Stephens*. Mr. T. M. Kettle, I recall, was one of those who refused to sign it, because the Tsar's disarmament proposals would mean the stereotyping of England's naval supremacy.'[53]

Skeffington's assertion that his endeavours to elicit signatures was not very successful is at odds with the account in *Stephen Hero*, in which 'nearly all the young men in the College were signing their names to it',[54] and with the 'crowded' entrance hall in which MacCann leads his peers 'one after another to the table' of *A Portrait*.[55] Moreover, in *A Portrait* Joyce cleverly renders the idea that, far from MacCann's petition being defiantly radical, it enjoyed at least passive assent from the Jesuits. Throughout the episode, the dean of studies is engaged in conversation with a student in the inner hall beyond the entrance hall without the slightest hint that he disapproves of the petition.[56] In the middle of the inner hall the prefect of the college sodality, biting on 'a tiny bone pencil' is working on enlisting the maximum number of signatories.[57] The

52. Ellmann, *James Joyce*, 62.

53. Sheehy-Skeffington, typescript article on W. T. Stead, April 1912, Sheehy-Skeffington Papers, NLI, MS 40,475/6. In one particular, Skeffington's memory seems wrong. *St Stephen's* was not in existence in 1899, presuming that the petition episode coincided with the Hague conference or its immediate prelude; 'Chanel' (Arthur Clery) did contribute to the *Leader*, but its first issue was 1 September 1900.

54. *SH* 112.

55. *P* 5.716–19.

56. *P* 5.721–23, 897–98.

57. *P* 5.903–7.

idea of Catholic approbation of the tsar who resembles 'a besotted Christ', and whose photograph sits alongside that of Stead, affirms the co-relation of the episode to the Parnell Split.

In Skeffington's account, Joyce was not alone in refusing to sign; writing in 1912 for an intended English readership, it was understandable that Skeffington chose to identify Kettle, who had been a member of Parliament until 1910 and was a public figure, as the recusant and saw no reason to mention the objections of an obscure contemporary in exile in Trieste. The fact that an account of the incident appears in the more autobiographical *Stephen Hero*, and the scorn to which Joyce was moved by 'the Tsar's air of besotted Christ',[58] does favour the likelihood that Joyce was angered, declined to sign, and had an altercation with Skeffington over it. It is possible that the episodes, as recounted in *Stephen Hero* and in *A Portrait*, bear some of the weight transposed from Joyce's refusal to sign the *Countess Cathleen* letter, which does not feature in either work, and which Curran reasoned 'would put his *Portrait* out of drawing'.[59]

Something of Stephen's scorn for the tsar's rescript and the fleeting enthusiasm it attracted lingers in *Ulysses*, in the 'Circe' episode as Bloom seeks to extract Stephen from his altercation with two British soldiers in night-town. Stephen says, 'Struggle for life is the law of existence, but human philirenists, notably the tsar and the king of England have invented arbitration. (*he taps his brow*). But in here it is I must kill the priest and the king.'[60]

58. *SH* 112–13.

59. Curran, *Under the Receding Wave*, 116. It is possible also that Stephen's irritation at Cranly's signing of the petition is a transposition of Joyce's annoyance that J. F. Byrne (the Cranly figure) had signed the later letter from students of University College condemning *The Countess Cathleen*.

60. *U* 15.4434–37. The Anglo-French entente of 1904, which was of greater significance than the settling of colonial disputes with which it was initially concerned, was exaggeratedly credited to Edward VII's visit to Paris of May 1903. He also played some role in improving relations with Russia after the Russian defeat in the Russo-Japanese War of 1904, culminating in a meeting with Nicholas at what is now Tallin, on the Baltic Sea. Nicholas was Edward's nephew, as was the kaiser; Jane Ridley, *Bertie: A Life of Edward VII* (London: Chatto and Windus, 2012), 376–82, 398–400. In the 'Cyclops' episode, a reference to 'Edward the peacemaker' prompts the scorn of the Citizen, who observes 'there's a bloody sight more pox than pax about that boyo' (*U* 12.1399–1401).

This of course heightens the hostility of the soldiers. Edward VII is thus linked with Nicholas II. Stephen's citation of William Blake captures the viscerality of Joyce's scorn for Skeffington's embrace of the idea of international arbitration championed by the tsar of Russia. It is a retrospective measuring of the thinness of Skeffington's programmatic aspirations against Joyce's deeper revolt, even if reduced to an exchange with two soldiers in Dublin's red-light district.

While Joyce enjoyed Skeffington's casuistry and approved in a general way of his remorselessly contestatory political stances, their convictions diverged, even when ostensibly similar. To take the politics of gender, Skeffington was an ardent advocate of women's rights and an ally of the suffragettes, derided by D. P. Moran as 'England's screeching sisterhood in Ireland'.[61] Had Joyce disagreed with Skeffington's support for the removal of legal disabilities on women, it seems unlikely that he would have agreed to the joint private publication in 1901 of his 'Day of the Rabblement' along with Skeffington's *A Forgotten Aspect of the University Question*, which advocated the equal status of women as students of University College. While the pamphlet carried the caveat that 'each writer is responsible only for what appears under his own name', there is nothing to suggest that Joyce dissented from Skeffington's conclusions on the status of women, whatever issues he may have had with the process by which Skeffington came to them.[62] But Joyce came to be increasingly suspicious that what he understood as Skeffington's reduction of the position of women to a purely political or legal issue was the expression of a philosophical aversion to the corporeal. He was opposed to, and in his early exile ever more irritated by, Skeffington's sexual asceticism.[63]

61. *Leader*, 28 January 1911.

62. Margot Norris challenges Ellmann's assertion that 'neither agreed with the other's position' (*James Joyce*, 888–89), which she says 'creates the long-lived assumption that Joyce feared contamination of his work by Skeffington's feminist text' (*Joyce's Web*, 14–15). The difference in Joyce's approach, at least as an artist, is exemplified in his notes to *Exiles*, where he writes, 'Richard must not appear as a champion of woman's rights' (*E* 153).

63. Sheehy-Skeffington's eccentric views on sex are well summarised by Patrick Maume in his authoritative *DIB* entry: 'Francis Sheehy-Skeffington', 981.

Before leaving Ireland, Joyce sought a loan from Skeffington. Skeffington, whose previous advances to Joyce had not been repaid, and who considered the elopement unfair to Nora, declined. In a letter to Joyce of 6 October 1904 he declared, 'You have my best wishes for your welfare and for that of your companion, which is probably much more doubtful than your own.'[64] Joyce found it difficult to forgive Skeffington for a gross breach of the protocols of friendship in treating his request for a loan as if it were for a donation to a political cause he was unable to support. The reference to 'your companion' rankled and came to stand for all the predictions in Dublin that Joyce's relationship with Nora would end badly for her.[65] Joyce was not of a forgiving disposition, and their friendship in University College was swiftly relegated to history. Joyce wrote to Stanislaus in February 1905 referring to 'working in' 'Hairy Jaysus', the soubriquet for Skeffington that featured in *Stephen Hero*: 'Do you not think the search for heroics damn vulgar—and yet how are we to describe Ibsen? . . . I am sure however that the whole structure of heroism is, and always was, a damned lie and that there cannot be any substitute for the individual passions as the motive power of everything—art and philosophy included. For this reason Hairy Jaysus seems to be the bloodiest imposter of all I have met.'[66]

Joyce's term 'heroics' is of some importance. It is paraphrased by Richard Ellmann as 'selflessness and social purpose'.[67] It was the public espousal or embrace of an ethic of asceticism and altruism. The idea of 'heroics' bears the impress of Joyce's observation of Skeffington.[68]

No principle of economy governed Skeffington's opinions. Curran's intellectual characterisation of Skeffington was of superb incisiveness:

> In the teeth of Joseph de Maistre, Skeffington was at any time ready to die not merely for truth but for any truth. He translated every

64. Quoted in Ellmann, *James Joyce*, 179n109, from a letter at Cornell.

65. Joyce to Stanislaus Joyce, 12 July 1905, 18 September 1905, *Letters II* 96–97, 108.

66. Joyce to Stanislaus Joyce, 7 February 1905, *Letters II* 80–81; *SH* 113.

67. *Letters II* xliv.

68. Joyce was extremely sparing in his use of the term 'hero' and its cognates but was prepared to apply it to Henrik Ibsen, of whose 'inward heroism' Joyce had written to Ibsen himself: Joyce to Henrik Ibsen, March 1901, *Letters I* 52.

belief he had into action and lived at its indecorous extreme, forcing it to your attention by its evident incongruity with circumstances. If his view of justice was at odds with actual conditions so much the worse for things as they were. He narrowed his fighting front in the course of time to two issues: suffrage and labour, but without much change in his propagandist tactics. In student days, his principles, exercised over too wide a ground, quickly lost their novelty. His positions in debate were all automatically assumed; his lively offensives were relished but taken for granted and his logic, like most logic, shut out more wisdom than it unlocked. His favourite assaults were upon Gaelic Leagues, bishops and conservatives. The controversies he so stirred up were rarely without a grain of reason. That they lacked a sense of proportion and were, as often as not, trivial did not trouble him. Impervious to ridicule, never known to be angry, they were part of his system of provocative tactics which he believed opened the way to cool reason. Tactics were his invariable defence to what to the rest of us was plainly absurd. 'Tactics' was a word often on his lips and the sound of it as he pronounced it, staccato and challenging, still brings his personality before me.[69]

While Joyce shared many of Skeffington's conclusions, he was suspicious of dogmatic radical premises, for reasons that had much to do with the restraint and scrupulosity of Joyce's own intellectual method. He remained determined to work things out patiently for himself, to consider issues on their merits within a coherent schema, and abhorred even in private conversation the expression of premature conviction. Stanislaus Joyce wrote, 'Habitually when Jim was talking in earnest, he spoke slowly, not hesitatingly, but choosing his words with care, unless it was a matter he had thought out, in which case he spoke almost as he wrote.'[70]

Skeffington is the college contemporary from whom Joyce learned most, chiefly by negation. His attentive observation of Skeffington honed the dialectical edge of his critique of ideological nationalism, to

69. Curran, *Under the Receding Wave*, 112–14.

70. S. Joyce, *My Brother's Keeper*, 155.

which Skeffington was as opposed as was Joyce but without Joyce's depth of understanding. It was also an early point of embarkation for what was to be Joyce's ever more sophisticated detection of points of collusion in ostensibly opposed political doctrines. If a relationship with a single person influenced Joyce's idea of the *coincidentia oppositorum*—the coincidence of opposites which could become the circularity of extremes—it was surely that with Skeffington.

Joyce apprehended what Skeffington could not: the unwisdom of premature convictions. This was especially marked in the case of Skeffington because of the inherent rapid obsolescence of his progressivism in the highly contemporary form he espoused. Curran lamented, 'I never knew him in those days to modify any opinion. It was both his and our loss that for all their modernity his ideas and attitudes were stereotyped.'[71] Skeffington's views affirmed Joyce's instinct of reserve. Unlike Skeffington, Joyce had a sceptical restraint, a slow filtration of the political, that contributed to ensuring that his writing in relation to the political in Ireland was free from dogmatic premises that could harden into anachronism.

Joyce's dissentience was more coherent and more politically farsighted than Skeffington's doctrinaire radicalism, in part because it retained an anchorage in the Parnellite nationalism in the Split. Bereft of a sure sense of the relation in which the radicalism he espoused stood to nationalism, Skeffington was not capable of the exigent realism that marked Joyce's appraisal of Irish politics. While it is true that in University College, Joyce was cultivating an aesthetic mask and maintained a posture of aloofness towards the contemporary political, the politico-philosophical gulf that separated him from Skeffington, in spite of their agreement on a number of significant contemporary issues, showed how circumscribed Joyce's options for alignment in Irish politics were. There is no mention of Skeffington in *Finnegans Wake*, or at least none

71. Curran, *Under the Receding Wave*, 114. What cannot be established is the extent to which Skeffington contributed to Joyce's scrupulous disdain for and fictional exploitation of prophesy, the subject of Paul K. Saint-Amour's excellent essay '"The Imprevidibility of the Future": On Joycean Prophesy', in *Renascent Joyce*, ed. Daniel Ferrer, Sam Slote, and Andre Topia (Gainesville: University Press of Florida, 2013), 90–105.

that has been identified. That may reflect Joyce's sense of the finitude, and inconsequence, of Skeffington's time-bound assertiveness.

Skeffington moved increasingly to the left. He resigned in May 1912 from the United Irish League, the organisation of the Irish Party, in protest at the refusal of the party to insist on the inclusion of votes for women in the Home Rule bill. He opposed the war and John Redmond's advocacy of Irish enlistment.[72] Skeffington's opposition to the war drew him into increasing contact with those who were to be the leaders of the 1916 rising, and James Connolly in particular. He strove to remain constant to his pacifist principles, advocating somewhat nebulously a cohort of civic resistance over military insurgency.[73] It was as if he had at last found a means of negotiating an exit from the generational impasse in which his objection to the Gaelic League had placed him. He passed the first two days of the Easter Rising discouraging looting and seeking to organise a civic police force. Taken as a hostage on Portobello Bridge by a party under the command of Captain John Bowen Colthurst, he was taken to Portobello Barracks, where he was shot with two other civilians the following morning, 26 April 1916.[74]

Kettle gracefully seized the paradox of the death of his non-combatant brother-in-law and friend with whom latterly he had differed so much: 'This brave and honourable man died to the rattle of musketry; his name will be recalled to the ruffle of drums.'[75]

72. By this time Skeffington had abandoned his indulgent view of the tsar which had survived his suppression of the 1905 revolution. Patrick Maume writes, 'He feared that an allied victory would strengthen the autocratic tsarist empire at the expense of a relatively advanced Germany, and a triumphant Britain would become aggressively imperialist and repress Ireland' ('Francis Sheehy-Skeffington', 982). Executed along with his wife and children by the Bolsheviks at Ekaterinburg in July 1918, Nicholas II did not long outlive Skeffington.

73. Dorothy MacArdle, *The Irish Republic*, 4th ed. (Dublin: Irish Press, 1951), 82. Conor Cruise O'Brien perceptively assesses Skeffington's position, the outcome of his 'brooding over the parallel lives of Tom and Frank', his uncles by marriage, in his *Memoir: My Life and Themes* (Dublin: Poolbeg, 1988), 9–27. He wrote of Kettle, 'He may have been "wrong" politically, but as a human being he was all right. But there seemed, from what I heard from my mother, to be something wrong with Frank as a human being' (*Memoir*, 19).

74. Maume, 'Francis Sheehy-Skeffington', 982–93; J. B. Lyons, *Enigma of Tom Kettle*, 285; MacArdle, *Irish Republic*, 181–82.

75. T. M. Kettle, *An Irishman's Calendar: A Quotation from the Works of T. M. Kettle for Every Day of the Year*, ed. Mary Kettle (Dublin: Browne and Nolan, 1938), 115.

Thomas Michael Kettle

In marrying Mary Sheehy in 1909, Thomas Michael Kettle (1880–1916) became Skeffington's brother-in-law. He was the son of Andrew Kettle, a North County Dublin farmer of independent mind and formidable character and an early and clear-sighted agrarian reformer of high initiative, who advised Isaac Butt and Parnell.[76] While bluntly telling Parnell he disapproved of his relationship with Katharine O'Shea—he was probably unique among Parnellites in venturing a view on the subject to Parnell—he remained steadfast, and contested Carlow as the Parnellite candidate in the third and last by-election of the Split in Parnell's lifetime.

Tom Kettle entered University College in 1897, a year before Joyce, and was auditor of the revived L&H in succession to Skeffington for 1898–99. Kettle was the pre-eminent contemporary of Joyce in University College. William G. Fallon characterised him as the 'idol' of a generation he dominated.[77] Robert Lynd, though not a college contemporary, accurately described Kettle as 'having lived in a blaze of adoration as a student'[78] and elsewhere characterised him as 'the most brilliant Irishman of his generation.'[79] Arthur Clery, not quite as magnanimously as the statement might suggest, described the recently dead Kettle as 'probably the most brilliant mind of his generation, the generation that succeeded Parnell and Yeats.'[80] Padraic Colum, meeting Kettle when the latter, three years his senior, was twenty-six, referred to him as 'the best known man I met in those early years.'[81] Skeffington wrote in 1912, 'He

76. Desmond McCabe, 'Andrew Joseph Kettle', *DIB* 5:161–63. Margaret O'Callaghan emphasises the importance of 'his exceptional and powerful father' in understanding Kettle: O'Callaghan, 'Forgetting to Remember: Tom Kettle in Modern Ireland', in *Remembering Tom Kettle, 1880–1916*, ed. Gerald Barry (Dublin: University College Dublin Archives, 2006), 7–15.

77. W. G. Fallon, manuscript script of speech on Kettle [1930–32?], W. G. Fallon Papers, NLI, MS 22598.

78. Robert Lynd, *Old and New Masters* (London: T. Fisher Unwin, 1919), 201.

79. Robert Lynd, *Essays on Life and Literature* (London: J. M. Dent and Sons, 1951), 52.

80. Arthur Clery, 'Thomas Kettle', *Studies* 5, no. 20 (December 1916): 503, reprinted in Arthur Clery, *Dublin Essays* (Dublin: Maunsel, 1919), 1.

81. Padraic Colum, 'Tom Kettle: A Memory', *Dublin Magazine* 24 (1949): 28–29.

FIGURE 7.2. Thomas Michael Kettle. Image courtesy of UCD Digital Library from an original in the Curran/Laird Collection, UCD Library.

is the public Orator of Ireland—our nearest analogue to Lord Rosebery in the ability to frame in faultlessly-cut phrases the thoughts and emotions of the man in the street.'[82]

Kettle was the nationalist member of Parliament for Tyrone East from 1906 to 1910, and from 1909 professor of national economy in University College Dublin. A lieutenant in the Royal Irish Fusiliers,[83] he

82. *Irish Review* 2 (1912): 55.

83. Kettle felt taunted for his advocacy of recruitment and that he had to serve at the front. T. P. O'Connor wrote to John Redmond in late October 1914, 'Tom Kettle came to see me today and said he thought it essential in the interests of Ireland that we should have some representation of our Party at the front, and he says he is quite willing to go himself. I suggested he should go as an interpreter. Stephen Gwynn, as you know, has applied for the same job. Of course Kitchener may stand in the way'. T. P. O'Connor to Redmond, 26 October 1914, Redmond Papers, NLI, MS 15215 (2). Kettle sought a commission in November 1914 but was not accorded one straightaway, on grounds of poor health arising from his alcoholism. Colin Reid, *The Lost Ireland of Stephen Gwynn: Irish Constitutional Nationalism and Cultural Politics, 1864–1950* (Manchester: Manchester University Press, 2011), 65–66; Senia Pašeta, *Thomas Kettle* (Dublin: University College Dublin Press, 2008), 82.

died in battle at Ginchy on the Somme on 8 September 1916, four months after the murder of Skeffington in the course of the Easter Rising.[84]

Kettle's dazzling progress as an undergraduate was punctuated by the first manifestation of a depressive condition which prevented him from taking his BA examination, and he spent some time on the Continent, including a period at the University of Innsbruck. He graduated in 1902, the same year as Joyce.[85] Of Kettle after University College, Padraic Colum recalled, 'A pessimism which he thought was hereditary now showed in him. I imagine it was the result of nervous exhaustion and of the loss of people dear to him. He could be genial, but he was no longer sunny.'[86] Later, after he had left University College, in the course of his parliamentary career, his depressive streak was exacerbated by an alcoholism that he struggled to overcome.[87] He enrolled as a student in the King's Inns in 1903 and was called to the bar two years later. The bar did not hold his interest and he turned to political journalism as a preliminary to the parliamentary career for which he was considered destined.[88]

On 16 December 1904, the month after Joyce left Ireland, Kettle, with Skeffington and Francis Cruise O'Brien, established the Young Ireland

84. Margaret O'Callaghan has written, in her astute essay 'The Politics of the Lost Generation and the Cult of Tom Kettle', that 'the almost unbelievable peculiarity of the fact that Home Rule became imminent and finally due to pass in the year that the First World War broke out meant that Kettle, like so many of his generation, operated in a terrain without maps.' In *From Parnell to Paisley*, ed. Caoimhe Nic Dhaibhead and Colin Reid (Dublin: Irish Academic Press, 2010), 74. Sheehy-Skeffington had been outraged by Kettle's recruiting activities on Irish platforms, and his enlistment, to the point of condemning in his diary Kettle's 'contemptible selling of himself', and accepting that 'a bullet at the front [would be] the best end for him.' Sheehy-Skeffington diary, entry for 29 June 1915, Sheehy-Skeffington Papers, NLI, MS 22277, quoted in Pašeta, *Thomas Kettle*, 90.

85. Donal Lowry, 'Thomas Michael Kettle', *DIB* 5:164.

86. P. Colum, 'Tom Kettle', 32.

87. Pašeta, *Thomas Kettle*, 60, 70, 82–83, 85–88. Professor James Meenan told me, when I was a University College Dublin student writing on Kettle, that it was said that Kettle had not drunk alcohol until prevailed upon to do so at dinners in the terms he kept in the King's Inns (private communication, 1978).

88. Lowry, 'Thomas Michael Kettle', 164. Arthur Clery related that Kettle had acted for the defence in a few prosecutions for cattle driving, for which there had been a brief political vogue. Clery, 'Thomas Kettle' (1916), 510–11.

Branch of the United Irish League, the political organisation of the Irish Parliamentary Party. At the inaugural meeting, Kettle said that the politics of Dublin might be described as being 'for the last ten years one of discouragement and disappointment, gradually waning into cynicism and selfishness, sheltering itself behind the plea of taking no interest in politics.' While new movements had sprung up, 'everybody was coming to see the absolute necessity of a movement which devoted itself to the purely political side of affairs.' John Redmond, the leader of the reunited Irish Party, also spoke. He conceded that the party suffered from 'an absence of young men' in its ranks, as a result of the Parnell Split and of the advent of 'more attractive' movements such as the Gaelic League. He insisted the Irish Party and the Gaelic League were complementary. He expressed the hope that the new branch would revive the spirit of 'the remarkable episode of the coming together in Parnell's time in '80 and '81 and the years that followed of such a galaxy of young and brilliant Irishmen willing to devote themselves and sacrifice their interests in the political movement.'[89] This had given Redmond his own start in politics, but the Irish Party of 1904 was sluggishly gerontocratic, lacking the fluid dynamism and responsiveness to the currents of the time that had characterised Parnell's early parliamentary party.

The 'Yibs', as members of the Young Ireland Branch were often called, stood for a more resolute and single-minded pursuit of Home Rule, and for a guarded rapprochement with cultural nationalism. The club functioned, insofar as it was permitted to, as 'a loyal opposition within the movement'.[90] Its members encountered both the entrenched scepticism of the gerontocratic Irish Party and its apparatchiks and the scorn of advanced nationalists. Nobly well intentioned, Kettle found his capacity for

89. *Freeman's Journal*, 17 December 1904; Dermot Meleady, *John Redmond: The National Leader* (Dublin: Merrion, 2014), 98–99. The inaugural meeting was a remarkable affair, characterised in one of the *Freeman's Journal*'s headlines as a 'splendid gathering of young men' (though women were in attendance). After the speeches there was 'a most delightful smoking concert'. Cathal McGarvey sang two of his comic Irish songs. John McCormack sang 'The West's Awake' and 'The Irish Emigrant'. Redmond declared, 'I think an organization like this branch ought very largely partake of the nature of the best class of debating society', which sounded ominously like a carrying forward of the L&H.

90. Meleady, *John Redmond*, 99.

action paralysed in the face of the widening schism between support for the Irish Party and the advance of an ever more politicised cultural nationalism. He had little instinctive sympathy with what he termed, following L. Paul Dubois, 'the struggle of the Gaelic Renaissance for "psychological Home Rule"'.[91] Kettle had immediately apprehended—as had Joyce—the potency of the appeal of cultural nationalism for his generation, but unlike Joyce, Kettle was constrained by his commitment to the idea of a regimented consensus under the hegemony of the Irish Party.

In the *New Ireland Review* for February 1905, Kettle wrote a consideration of Arthur Griffith's recently published pamphlet, *The Resurrection of Hungary: A Parallel for Ireland*.[92] To pronounce Griffith's argument in his 'brilliant pamphlet' to be 'certainly the largest idea contributed to Irish politics for a generation' was one thing; to bridge the gap between it and the parliamentarism that Kettle cleaved to was quite another.[93] A devastating exchange remembered by Oliver St John Gogarty revealed how that gap could never be bridged. He recalled relaying to Kettle Griffith's advocacy of a withdrawal from Westminster: 'I will never forget [Kettle's] answer. "Ireland politically is an invalid and is not yet strong enough for freedom"'.[94]

In September 1905 Kettle and Skeffington launched a paper effetely entitled the *Nationist* into the crowded market occupied by D. P. Moran's *Leader* and Griffith's *United Irishman*. In its first issue Kettle sought with heavy-handed defensiveness to 'have done with the blind and disastrous notion that there is some vague sort of hostility between the language movement and the political movement, between the campaign for better poetry and that for healthier industries'. This made what was his main—and valid—point seem like a feeble cavil: 'We constantly hear

91. L. Paul Dubois, *Contemporary Ireland*, introduction by T. M. Kettle (Dublin: Maunsel, 1911), viii.

92. Arthur Griffith, *The Resurrection of Hungary: A Parallel for Ireland*, 2nd ed. (Dublin: James Duffy, 1904).

93. T. M. Kettle, 'Would the "Hungarian Policy" Work?', *New Ireland Review* 22, no. 6 (February 1905): 321–28.

94. Oliver St John Gogarty, *Tumbling in the Hay* (1939; Dublin: O'Brien, 1996), 92.

it said that a decade ago the universal tendency was to identify politics with nationality. . . . No one today imagines that politics are everything. There is indeed a sign here that the pendulum has swung back too far, and that there is a tendency to regard politics as counting for nothing at all. But this is a delusion quite as baneful as the other. All the movements going forward on the people's side are indispensable.'[95]

The *Nationist* returned to this theme a month later, as Kettle again struggled to reconcile the new nationalism epitomised by the Gaelic League with parliamentarism:

> When the National mind turned away from politics in the nausea of despair it discovered the language, and discovered that it had been shamefully neglected by what claimed to be a national movement. . . . General ideas were discussed on tram tops, in drawingrooms, in bars, and in journals with an absolute fury of intellect. The extreme wing of one party ended by convincing itself that the language was a distracting inessential; the extreme wing of the other came to the conclusion that politics was a mere gabble of stupid and selfish demagogues. Those few who remembered that in great controversies both sides are always right, saw that the truth lay in an idea that included both language and politics. They saw that the concept of nationality had been enriched by an element which could never again be discarded, but also that the forces set working by the Gaelic League on the hitherto inert masses of the people must in due time bring forth a political movement of a more complex strength than any hitherto known in Irish history.

He appealed to the adherents of Griffith: 'Ourselves products of the newer order, and we hope, sharers of its spirit . . . we would ask those who have accepted the "Hungarian" policy, from mere desire of more vigorous

95. *Nationist*, 21 September 1905. It justified its title as 'a necessary coinage': '"Nationalist" was inadequate; it has been narrowed and cheapened down almost to blank nothing.' The paper had a short life in the course of which Kettle and Skeffington lost control of it. Of a controversy with Michael Davitt which arose in February 1906, Sheehy-Skeffington wrote that the weekly was 'then expiring in the hands of "Irish Ireland" fantasts' (*Michael Davitt*, 245). Its last issue appeared on 5 April 1906.

action, to consider whether the timeliness of a policy is not its essential virtue or vice. With the country massing on the older lines, believing that in certain conditions they can give it what it demands, and preparing to supply these conditions, is it the highest patriotism to bewilder it with adverse counsels?'[96]

Kettle's project was unrealistic. As he knew, the strategy of the Irish Party at this point did not admit of a radical change of direction and its leadership was suspicious of the new nationalism. Griffith's core constituency, which Kettle defined as 'the Extreme Right of Nationalism—the Separatists,'[97] would scarcely have been receptive to any overture from the Irish Party. In the event, Kettle's attempt to reconcile Sinn Féin with the Irish Party was not merely a conspicuous failure but was counterproductive, in that it served to suggest that the Irish Party lacked any serious comprehension of the new nationalism, and to deepen the generational rift it sought to bridge.

The Yibs and Griffith became increasingly estranged. Provoked by Griffith, two years later Kettle was driven to assert that the conclusion of his 1905 article 'Would the "Hungarian Policy" Work?' (in which he had described Griffith's policy as 'the largest idea contributed to Irish politics for a generation') was 'definitely hostile', arguing somewhat feebly, 'Does it occur to you that an idea may be large without being true? Anarchism is a large idea; the cosmic suicide of German pessimism is a large idea; the super-mania of Nietzsche is a large idea, but all three are false.'[98] Griffith was more adroit than Kettle, whom he enjoyed goading. He did so, on financial subjects in particular, after Kettle had left Parliament 'having been in the unfitness of things created a Professor of National Politics'.[99] Kettle wrote that Sinn Féin 'has been created out of the will and mind of one man, Mr. Arthur Griffith, whose strength

96. 'Home Rule, or Else—!', *Nationist*, 26 October 1905.

97. Kettle, 'Would the "Hungarian Policy" Work?', 321.

98. *Sinn Féin*, 9 November 1907; Patrick Maume, *The Long Gestation: Irish Nationalist Life, 1891–1918* (Dublin: Gill and Macmillan, 1999), 89.

99. 'Home Rule Finance', *Sinn Féin*, 1 April 1911.

is only less conspicuous than his narrowness.'[100] Writing in the *Leader* in 1910, Francis Cruise O'Brien—another brother-in-law who had married Kathleen Sheehy—characterised Griffith as, 'in vulgar English, a cod'. He described Griffith as 'a reactionary quack': 'Such ideas as he has are rooted in the narrowest conservatism. He embodies the militarist-protectionist spirit. He writes in the worst vein of illiberal thought.'[101]

Kettle, stung by 'the polemical fluency of Sinn Féin', did nevertheless seek to argue out the issue, something few of the partisans of the Irish Party troubled to do, and did so sometimes with a degree of effectiveness. In 1908, writing in response to a Sinn Féin apologist in the *North American Review,* he complained that the Sinn Féin sympathiser, Seumus MacManus, 'claims for his little party all modern Ireland, from the ballads to the bacon factories. . . . The Sinn Féin Party, according to his testimony, invented the language-revival. They invented Fenianism. They invented temperance'. Sinn Féin shied away from electoral contests with the Irish Party. 'Some of us fear that Sinn Féin is less a revolt against English rule, than a revolt against the limitation of life in general.' Sinn Féin was 'at best a *gamin* of the cities', while 'the man of the Irish countryside' had 'lived through the land war and carries in his mind the historical sense and perspective of which Sinn Féin is devoid.' On the principle of 'eaten bread', appeals to historical gratitude were not the most potent, but Kettle did try to measure what had changed in Irish politics in three decades:

> The Irish Party of Mr. Parnell was both wider and narrower than that of Mr. Redmond. It was wider inasmuch as it was the sole national focus of the time, and contained in germ almost every talent and idea

100. T. M. Kettle, 'A Note on Sinn Féin in Ireland', *North American Review* 187, no. 626 (January 1908): 49. As his relations with Griffith deteriorated, Kettle advanced a not especially convincing argument that because of respect for 'the extremist ideal' among other reasons, 'there existed a relationship of friendliness and tolerance between Mr. Griffith's group and us until the General Election of 1900. Then there was a misunderstanding. It grew less and less bridgeable; and in a little while Mr. Griffith found himself committed to bitter hostility to the Parliamentary Party'. Kettle, 'Note on Sinn Féin', 49.

101. *Leader*, 18 June 1910.

that has since come to maturity in Ireland. It was narrower in so far as, having given its rich soul to the political movement, it was less keenly aware than we are of the limitations of politics. This is the root of almost every criticism which has since been passed upon it. With that deplorable absence of the historical sense already noticed, a certain group denounces Mr. Parnell's party because it did the work of its own generation and not that of the next. It failed to create the Gaelic League twenty years before the time of the Gaelic League had come.

Yet his assertion that 'the Irish Party will continue, not weakened, but distinctly strengthened by the new current of thought' did not convince and was not borne out by events.[102]

Kettle inherited his father's allegiance to Parnell. He had frequently contemplated writing a study of Parnell.[103] His admiration for the Irish leader found acerbic expression in the poem he wrote on the occasion of the unveiling of the Parnell monument in 1911, which ended,

Limned in his blood across your clearing
  skies
Look up and read; Parnell![104]

He maintained that the plinth at the back of Parnell's statue should have been, in the classical manner, broken to symbolise the wrecking of his career.[105]

His verses to mark the acclaim that greeted Herbert Henry Asquith on his visit to Dublin in 1912 at the zenith of the Liberal-Nationalist

102. Kettle, 'Note on Sinn Féin', 47, 51–52, 55–57. This was written in reply to Seumas MacManus, 'Sinn Féin: Its Genesis and Purpose', *North American Review*, 16 August 1907. Even in this, a piece of straightforward political advocacy, Kettle's perceptiveness breaks through: 'Mr. MacManus and his friends are much too fond of the catastrophic and sensational type of change. What reality presents in Ireland, as in most countries, is a continual, slight dissolution, and re-integration.' Kettle, 'Note on Sinn Féin', 57.

103. T. M. Kettle and Mary Kettle, *The Ways of War, with a Memoir by Mary Kettle* (London: Constable, 1917), 52.

104. T. M. Kettle, 'Parnell', in *Poems and Parodies* (Dublin: Talbot, 1916), 55–57.

105. Kettle and Kettle, *Ways of War*, 52.

alliance, when Home Rule seemed ensured, were of an unexpected vehemence addressed to his fellow Dubliners. Kettle did not mention Parnell by name.

You stepped your steps, and the music
marched, and the torches tossed
As you filled your streets with your
Comic Pentecost,
And the little English went by and the
  lights grew dim;
We, dumb in the shouting crowd, we
Thought of Him.[106]

Citing part of the poem, Katharine Tynan wrote in 1924, 'That is how an old Parnellite—there are not so many of us left now—thinks on Mr. Parnell; and indeed we have cause for bitterness.'[107]

Joyce's relations with Kettle in University College were amical without cordiality. If Kettle vaunted his Parnellism, he was also from Joyce's perspective an acquiescent figure in the post-Split dispensation in Irish politics. Where they were diametrically opposed was in their attitudes to the ramifications of the Split, not least in relation to the role of the Catholic Church in Irish politics. Joyce's issue was not with Kettle's Catholic faith. Stanislaus wrote that Kettle was 'a man whose opinion my brother respected because his Catholicism was an intellectual conviction, not just a phase of nationalism.'[108] Kettle's attempt to hold in balance an allegiance to Parnell and a defence of clericalism in Irish politics exemplified what Curran charitably characterised as Kettle's 'Hegelian game of reconciling opposites'[109] and, to use the less kind term Joyce applied to Robert Hand in *Exiles,* his 'decrepit prudence'.[110] For Joyce, the fact that the anticlerical Skeffington was anti-Parnellite while the pro-clerical

106. Kettle, 'Asquith in Dublin (August 1912)', in *Poems and Parodies*, 67–68.

107. Tynan, *Memories*, 20.

108. S. Joyce, *My Brother's Keeper*, 80.

109. Curran, *Under the Receding Wave*, 148.

110. *E* 165.

Kettle avowed himself a Parnellite attested to the disarrangement of Irish politics wrought by the Split.

Joyce did not have to submit to, or make pragmatic accommodations with, majoritarian sentiment; under his mask of reticence, he did not even have to argue his case. He had the luxury of being able to insist that the issues of the Split could not, as a matter of contemporary politics, be passed over or left unaddressed. That would have been exorbitant for those like Kettle and Skeffington who were actively engaged in politics. It remains striking how well chosen Joyce's ground was strategically. Kettle and Skeffington were the most politically prominent figures in college, both deemed likely by their contemporaries to play prominent roles in the politics of a Home Rule state. Joyce's political reservations concerning Kettle and Skeffington, 'retrospectively' Parnellite and anti-Parnellite, were of penetrating acuity.

Kettle's prominence and what became his increasingly acrimonious dispute with Griffith and Sinn Féin, relayed in the columns of the *United Irishman* and *Sinn Féin*, meant that Joyce in exile remained quite closely apprised of the course of Kettle's political career. In the disputes that ensued over the Hungarian policy, and the finance of Home Rule, Kettle, a fine essayist but not an adept polemicist, was to be worsted in the war of words with Griffith. As late as January 1927, Joyce was asking Stanislaus to forward to Paris the two books by Kettle he had left in Trieste.[111]

Joyce regarded Kettle with a guarded, distant, and qualified respect but without especial affection. Their moments of rapprochement were not sustained and had the effect of leaving them further apart than before. On Joyce's first return trip to Dublin, in 1909, he saw Kettle, who was friendly, and wanted him to apply for the lectureship in Italian at University College Dublin (it transpired to be a lectureship in commercial Italian, which Joyce did not think suitable).[112] On 5 September, three days before Kettle married Mary Sheehy, Joyce spent four hours

111. Joyce to Stanislaus Joyce, 8 January 1927, *Letters III* 149. Ellmann, in his editorial capacity, suggests these books were *The Day's Burden* and *Home Rule Finance* (*Letters III* 149n6).

112. Joyce to Stanislaus Joyce, 10 August, 21 August 1909, *Letters II* 234, 238.

with him. He reported to Nora, 'He is the best friend I have in Ireland, I think, and he has done me great services here.' Kettle and his bride were going to spend a day or two of their honeymoon in Trieste, and Joyce bid Nora to prepare for their arrival: 'He is a very good-hearted fellow and I am sure you will like his wife.'[113] The Kettles did not come and Joyce's last encounter with Kettle was not amicable, but it was forthright. On his final trip to Dublin, in 1912, he asked Kettle to intercede with George Roberts in relation to the publication of *Dubliners*. In Stanislaus Joyce's account, Kettle declined and told Joyce he would slate the book when it was published.[114]

Recalling an occasion shortly after the death of May Joyce in August 1903 when he visited Kettle in Sandymount and walked along the strand with Joyce and Gogarty, Colum wrote, 'I took it for granted that Joyce and Kettle were friends at the University and was greatly surprised when, long afterwards, Joyce told me they were never friends and that he had no liking for Kettle.'[115] In his 1958 memoir of Joyce, Colum elaborated that he had been surprised to learn from Joyce that he hardly knew Kettle and did not like him on the grounds that he considered him too demonstrative.[116] This is consistent with Joyce's reference to Kettle, in his short and graceful letter to Mary Kettle on her husband's death, as 'my old school fellow and fellow student', rather than his friend.[117]

Herbert Gorman, Joyce's first biographer, enumerating a series of cameos intended to invoke the Joyce of 1900, 'brief flashes of Joyce, pictures from the memories of those who knew at the time', wrote of 'Joyce, evasive, slightly withdrawn and coldly polite with Thomas E. [*sic*] Kettle, who had been magnified by university students into a second Parnell.'[118] In Gorman's telling, this did not emanate from Joyce.

113. Joyce to Nora Barnacle, 5 September 1909; Joyce to Stanislaus Joyce, 9 September 1909, *Letters II* 247, 252.

114. S. Joyce, *My Brother's Keeper*, 80.

115. P. Colum, 'Tom Kettle', 31.

116. M. Colum and P. Colum, *Our Friend James Joyce*, 43.

117. Joyce to Mary Kettle, 25 September 1916, *Letters I* 96. Joyce did have Kettle's posthumous *The Ways of War*, a collection of his war writings and journalism, published in 1917, in his Trieste library. Gillespie, *James Joyce's Trieste Library*, 136, no. 260.

118. Gorman, *James Joyce*, 63–64.

The hint of competitive resentment of Kettle on Joyce's part is misplaced. The shadow of Parnell did not fall between Joyce and Kettle in quite the manner Gorman imagined. The support they shared for the Parnell of the Split did not create a bond between them. Joyce's conception of the politics of the Split was remote from, and indeed incompatible with, Kettle's Parnellism, which coexisted with a complacently Catholic and pro-clerical nationalism.

Kettle's attempt to hold in balance an allegiance to the Parnell of the Split and a defence of clericalism in Irish politics was anathema to Joyce. It was Kettle's clericalism, even more than his unqualified adherence to a reunited Irish Party which was composed principally of anti-Parnellites, that was emblematic for Joyce of Kettle's conservatism and acquiescence in the outcome of the Split.

Kettle's widow, admittedly herself morbidly pious, wrote, 'He was intensely Catholic and always flaunted the banner of his religion.' She recalled that he 'greatly liked the society of Irish priests. He used to say they were gentlemen first, and priests after.'[119] Arthur Clery characterised Kettle as 'a believing and enthusiastic Catholic' and 'a man of the strictest purity. Indeed in the many years of my association with him I think I never heard him tell a doubtful story or make a doubtful remark.'[120]

Gogarty joked in a limerick commonly mis-ascribed to Joyce,

A holy Hegelian Kettle
Has faith which we cannot unsettle
If no one abused it
He might have reduced it
But now he is quite on his mettle.[121]

What is relevant is Kettle's view on Catholicism and politics in Ireland. In an article in 1906, entitled 'Religion and Politics in Ireland' (a

119. Kettle and Kettle, *Ways of War*, 49–50.

120. Clery, 'Thomas Kettle' (1916), 507, reprinted in Clery, *Dublin Essays*, 5.

121. This limerick, and another on Æ (George Russell), are given by Curran in *James Joyce Remembered* (76n1) and ascribed to Gogarty. They are erroneously ascribed to Joyce and included in *PSW* (110, 263). The lines are in any case more ingratiatingly like Gogarty than Joyce. Curran discusses the influence of G.W.F. Hegel on Kettle in *Under the Receding Wave*, 145.

riposte to Skeffington), Kettle opined, 'There is no such thing in Ireland as Clericalism. There are individual priests', and characterised Irish countrymen as capable of judging whether to accept the advice of the priesthood. He added an unhappily de haut en bas defence of the invigilator role of the priests in the Split: 'A great politico-moral issue like the Parnellite Split no doubt forms an exception, and carries the untrained masses into a waters in which they can hardly be expected to swim.'[122] While Kettle was writing in an English review, and seeking to allay Liberal and progressive concerns in relation to the political role of the Catholic Church in Ireland, these sentiments reflected his personal convictions. There is a fundamental discordance between his allegiance to Parnell in the Split and his pro-clericalism, which was not capable of being addressed and which he did not attempt to.[123] It corresponded to a diametrical opposition between Joyce and Kettle. Joyce's Parnellism-of-the-Split was intellectual and political as well as visceral; Kettle's was romantic, even passionate, but severed from contemporary political actuality, though he regularly invoked the achievements of Parnell's pre-Split career as a talisman against the challenge of Sinn Féin.

Joyce was not alone in objecting to Kettle's treatment of the political role of the Catholic Church in Ireland. Reviewing in 1912 Kettle's *The Open Secret of Ireland*,[124] Skeffington wrote bluntly, 'His treatment of Ulster is inadequate; but then to treat Ulster adequately would require a faithful handling of clericalism, and that Mr. Kettle has eschewed since the days of the *Nationist*.'[125] Skeffington was moreover correct in detecting a certain regression that was to grow more marked over time. In what was a tacit acknowledgement of the threat to the hold of the Irish Party on Irish opinion, Kettle was driven increasingly to accentuate the

122. T. M. Kettle, 'Religion and Politics in Ireland', *Independent Review* 11 (October–November 1906): 155–64.

123. One could venture an explanation based on his Parnellism being an emanation of his father's, but that prompts the reflection that Kettle was lacking in the political tough-mindedness and the exceptional capacity for originality in action of Andrew Kettle.

124. T. M. Kettle, *The Open Secret of Ireland* (London: W. J. Ham-Smith, 1912).

125. Francis Sheehy-Skeffington, review of *The Open Secret of Ireland*, *Irish Review* 2 (March 1912): 55; Levenson, *With Wooden Sword*, 123.

Catholic element in his rhetoric in defence of the Irish Party against Sinn Féin, and in support of the Allied war effort.

Joyce's differences with Kettle were not merely political or philosophical. On 12 November 1898, in Joyce's first term in University College, the eighteen-year-old Kettle delivered his precociously fluent inaugural paper to the L&H, 'The Celtic Revival'. Given the current state of Ireland, he proclaimed 'he would expect to find its literature narrowed down to its own people, to find its men of letters chartered in a regenerative movement, pointing out the lost path of progress':

> He looked in vain for these characteristics in the present literary revival. He found in it no love of home, nor confidence in kin. He found it telling its message not to the men of its own race and name, but to the drawingroom dilettante of London. He found it groping in the dust and shrouds of the past, not for the lost thread of the labyrinth, but for the sorry tinsel of folklore and legend to dress them up for the gaze of the stranger. Since the Anglo-Celtic renascence had in it no manly vigour, no spring of action, since it was retrospective, exclusive, and for them no fruit but Dead Sea fruit, they repudiated it as an instrument of National revival.[126]

For Joyce, Kettle's political instrumentalisation of the Celtic Twilight exemplified and even exacerbated what he himself objected to in the Twilight. Curran in his own memoir referred to Kettle's speech at some length as 'a convenient yardstick to measure the standards of his University College at an undergraduate level', towards which Curran always felt Joyce was unfair. He wrote that Joyce must have been present, or at least read the address. In an unconvincing piece of special pleading, Curran wrote that 'we may note a similar initial critical outlook and very similar language when Joyce approaches the literary side of Kettle's theme', as in his paper on James Clarence Mangan: 'The shrouds of the past and the tinsel of folklore are their common targets and glimmer through Joyce as through Kettle though each looks for a different mode

126. *Freeman's Journal*, 15 November 1898.

of redemption.'[127] While Joyce was still developing his own ferocious critique of the Literary Revival, he certainly did not assent to Kettle's subordination of Irish literature to highly conventional nationalist values. It can only have prompted a silent identification with Yeats, the unnamed target of Kettle's paper, and of many of Joyce's own strictures. Curran unintentionally highlights the recurring feature of Joyce's years in University College, of a dissent that was most acute where there was a semblance of accord.

As William Dawson, a student a little older than Joyce, later wrote, there were in Kettle's address 'indications of the coming attack on *The Countess Cathleen*',[128] in which Kettle led the fray. Curran recalled that the letter of protest against the play signed by the student body 'now reads to me as a composite and hurried performance with Tom Kettle as the most evidently single influence. Certain sentences and phrases bear his unmistakable stamp—I can hear his voice leavening in characteristic fashion on the vowel sounds of the "crooning barbarian".'[129]

Three years later Kettle crassly restated the case against the play in an article in the *United Irishman*: 'It will be well for Mr. Yeats when he comes off his rationalistic whimsies, and understands the sanctity and compulsion with which the Catholic religion has established itself in the imagination of Ireland.' The gulf which separated him from Joyce was exemplified in his proposition that 'drama is implicitly moral, for it deals with conduct, and conduct has for its very essence morality'.[130] Something of his early instrumentalising of the Celtic Twilight endured in Kettle's polite review of Joyce's *Chamber Music* in the *Freeman's Journal* in 1907: 'The inspiration of the book is almost entirely literary. There is no trace of the folklore, folk dialect, or even the national feeling that have coloured the work of practically every writer in contemporary Ireland.'[131]

127. Curran, *Under the Receding Wave*, 142–43.

128. Meenan, *Centenary History*, 54.

129. Curran, *Under the Receding Wave*, 104.

130. 'Mr Yeats and the Freedom of the Theatre', *United Irishman*, 15 November 1902.

131. *Freeman's Journal*, 1 June 1907, reprinted in Robert H. Deming, *Critical Heritage: James Joyce* (London: Routledge, 1970), 1:37.

At least at the level of aphorism, Joyce's and Kettle's views coincided on the relationship of Ireland to continental Europe. In October 1910, Kettle wrote in the introduction to his collection of essays, *The Day's Burden*,

> Ireland, a small nation, is, none the less, large enough to contain all the complexities of the twentieth century. . . . If this generation has, for its first task, the recovery of the old Ireland, it has, for its second, the discovery of the new Europe. Ireland awaits her Goethe—but in Ireland he must not be a Pagan—who will one day arise to teach her that while a strong people has its own self for centre, it has the universe for circumference. All cultures belong to a nation that has once taken sure hold of its own culture. A national literature that seeks to found itself in isolation from the general life of humanity can only produce the pale and waxen growths of a plant isolated from the sunlight. In gaining her own soul Ireland will gain the whole world. . . . My only counsel to Ireland is, that in order to become deeply Irish, she must become European.[132]

This passage enjoyed an instant and enduring réclame in Dublin. The book was published in late 1910. While this was in the lengthy interval between Joyce's second (1909–10) and third (1912) return expeditions to Ireland, he quickly became aware of what Kettle had written.

It is a measure of the increasingly fevered nature of cultural controversy in Dublin that Kettle's pronouncement was considered objectionable in some quarters. The *Catholic Bulletin* carried an article by the Franciscan T. A. Fitzgerald memorably entitled 'Is It Not Enough to Be Anglicised without Becoming European?'[133] This was not an altogether isolated view. On the death of Kettle, his friend Arthur Clery wrote with a certain acridity that reflected how riven Ireland had become in the years that had intervened since they were in University College, 'With everything that could be described as "Irish Ireland" though he sometimes gave

132. T. M. Kettle, *The Day's Burden* (1910; repr., Dublin: Browne and Nolan, 1937), xi–xii.

133. T. A. Fitzgerald, 'Is It Not Enough to Be Anglicised without Becoming European?', *Catholic Bulletin* 1 (1911): 84–85. The article is not as bad as the title might suggest.

it nominal support in words, he had a very *minimum* of agreement. He looked upon it as insular and un-European. He was quite alive to the fact that his own family was not one of Gaelic race. He was fond of playing cricket. He looked forward to that progress which should be borne to Ireland across the seas.'[134]

The thrust of the sentiments that Kettle had expressed in the introduction to *The Day's Burden* came very close to Joyce's own.[135] It is true that Joyce could be disputatiously possessive when an idea touched one of his own; what is more salient is that he had learned from his experience of Irish political controversies to be sceptical about superficial coincidences of sentiment that masked underlying philosophical or ideological oppositions. Joyce's own sense of the contribution of the Catholic Church to European culture, profound as that was, could never have led him to assent to Kettle's assertion that the Catholic Church was 'the true creator of the spiritual freedom of European intellect'.[136]

Joyce's most direct response came in his play, *Exiles*, which he finished before leaving Trieste for Zurich in 1915. Richard Rowan, a writer just returned from exile, is close to being an alter ego for Joyce. The biographical attributes, though not the character, of Robert Hand, a successful journalist, are modelled primarily on Kettle. In an early scene, Joyce invokes Kettle's introduction to *The Day's Burden*. Robert Hand asks for one of Richard Rowan's cigars and says as he lights it, 'These cigars Europeanize me. If Ireland is to become a new Ireland she must first become European. And that is what you are here for, Richard.

134. Clery, 'Thomas Kettle' (1916), 505–6, reprinted in Clery, *Dublin Essays*, 3–4.

135. Padraic Colum wrote, 'On one thing, but with a difference, Kettle and Joyce agreed: the necessity of getting Ireland back into Europe. Having lived in Paris, Joyce was not encouraging. "When you say you are *Irlandais* they think they have misunderstood you, that what you said was *Hollandais*."' M. Colum and P. Colum, *Our Friend James Joyce*, 44; see *U* 3.220–21.

136. *Freeman's Journal*, 9 September 1913. Margaret O'Callaghan's assessment of Kettle's Europeanism serves as a measure of the chasm that separated Kettle from Joyce: 'His Europeanism was essentially bound up with his Catholicism. European civilization was for him, I think, essentially Catholic—and much of his Catholicism runs in tandem with that of Belloc and Chesterton' ('Forgetting to Remember', 20).

Some day we will have to choose between England and Europe. I am a descendant of the dark foreigners: that is why I like to be here.'[137]

The smoking of the cigar imports a hint of bourgeois complacency, as well as—with some audacity on Joyce's part—suggestions of plagiarism, since the cigar is Richard's. Joyce is reduced to parodying because he could not compete with the aphorism of Kettle, who had got there first. The 'new Ireland' has a certain banality accentuated by Hand turning the proposition into a choice between England and Europe.[138] The 'dark foreigners' are an allusion to the Norse ancestry of which Kettle was proud, and affirm the character's identification with Kettle.[139] Joyce's playing with aphorism is a feature of his writing and conversation that has not attracted the attention it warrants. If there was an arena of direct competition between Joyce and Kettle, it was that of the aphorism. By the time he arrived in University College, Joyce had developed a remarkable faculty for the hard-edged epigram and found Kettle's aphoristic mode grating: 'I made epigrams new and old', boasts Robert Hand.[140]

In the third act, Beatrice Justice, the cousin of Robert Hand who has been in love with Richard Rowan across his exile, gives him in the early morning the newspaper in which Robert Hand has written a sub-leader about Richard, and asks him to read it. Richard declaims the opening sentences 'in a rather loud hard voice'. The piece, headed 'A Distinguished Irishman', is a pastiche of the *Freeman's Journal*'s portentous editorial manner with an infusion of Kettle's prose style:

> Not the least vital of the problems which confront our country is the problem of her attitude towards those of her children who, having

137. *E* 43.

138. A 'new Ireland' had been on the go for quite some time (and still is). A. M. Sullivan, a barrister and parliamentarian of scrupled conservative nationalist orientation, had published his well-known *New Ireland*, half memoir, half narrative of Ireland since the Famine, in 1877, and it had come itself to seem part of a distant era. In shifting 'new' from 'Europe' to 'Ireland' (Kettle's aphorism ran, 'If this generation has, for its first task, the recovery of the old Ireland, it has, for its second, the discovery of the new Europe'), Joyce widens the gap between Kettle's thinking and his own, and half-ruins the Kettle epigram.

139. On Kettle's pride in his Norse ancestry, see, for example, Gogarty, *It Isn't That Time*, 20.

140. *E* 107.

> left her in her hour of need, have been called back, to her now on the eve of her long-awaited victory, to her whom in loneliness and exile they have at last learned to love. In exile, we have said, but here we must distinguish. There is an economic exile and there is a spiritual exile. There are those who left her to seek the bread by which men live and there are others, nay her most favoured children, who left her to seek in other lands that food of the spirit by which a nation of human beings is sustained in life.[141]

The play is set in the suburbs of Dublin in the summer of 1912. 'The eve of her long-awaited victory' was heralded by the introduction of the Third Home Rule Bill on 11 April 1912. (Joyce's third and last visit to Ireland took place from July to September 1912.)

The fictional *Freeman's Journal* sub-leader has a deliberate resonance. Kettle had published in the *Freeman's Journal* in June 1907 a review of Joyce's *Chamber Music*. Kettle's praise was qualified by the caveat already quoted that attested to the crude nationalist aesthetic that informed his attitude to the Literary Revival. He wrote in his review that 'those who remember University College life of five year's back will have many memories of Mr. Joyce.'[142] This was scathingly rendered in Hand's sub-editorial in *Exiles*: 'Those who recall the intellectual life of Dublin of a decade since will have many memories of Mr. Rowan. Something of that fierce indignation that lacerated the heart'.[143] The hackneyed invocation of Swift's epitaph that trails off is Joyce's riposte to Kettle's faintly condescending review of *Chamber Music*.

Read biographically in relation to Joyce, the commendatory tenor of Hand's sub-leader is undercut by an almost unconsciously patronising magnanimity, and a failure to understand the nature of Joyce's exile. Richard Rowan's exile and return is seen exclusively in terms of the politics of Home Rule. When Beatrice says to Richard, 'You see that you have a warm friend in Robert, a friend who understands you', Richard responds, 'Did you notice the little phrase at the beginning: *those who*

141. *E* 99.

142. *Freeman's Journal*, 1 June 1907; Ellmann, *James Joyce*, 261.

143. *E* 99.

left her in her hour of need.'[144] In his notes to *Exiles*, Joyce wrote, 'Why the title *Exiles*? A nation exacts a penance from those who dared to leave her payable on their return.' Later he stated, 'Exiles—also because at the end either Robert or Richard must go into exile. Perhaps the new Ireland cannot contain both. Robert will go.'[145]

The second note is part of an elaborate ironic joke Joyce permits himself in playing with the idea of an exilic role reversal between Kettle and himself. In *Exiles*, it is Robert who, in the short term, is to leave. He explains to Richard, 'I am going away by the next train to my cousin, Jack Justice, in Surrey. Perhaps for a fortnight. Perhaps longer.'[146] Robert's projected sojourn in Surrey scarcely compares in duration or rigour with Joyce's Triestine exile or constitutes any form of exile. Joyce is wryly conceding the implausibility of the counterfactual scenario as it bears on his and Kettle's actual circumstances. Joyce further amuses himself by importing a veiled reference to Oscar Wilde's *Importance of Being Earnest* and the frivolous divagations of its principal male characters in the south of England. The name Jack Justice evokes that of Jack Worthing, whose full title in the dramatis personae is John Worthing, Justice of the Peace (who transpires, of course, to be Ernest John Moncrieff, brother to Algernon).[147] In this intricate play of names and identities

144. *E* 99.

145. *E* 114, 123.

146. *E* 155. His departure is prompted by a casual act of sexual indiscretion with 'the divorced wife of a barrister' whom he met in a nightclub: this at least is certainly not like Kettle. Earlier, seeking to seduce Bertha, he has mentioned the nightclub as part of 'a long wandering night' in which 'your image was always before my eyes' and stated that he is going 'to foreign parts. That is, to my cousin Jack Justice, *alias* Doggy, in Surrey. He has a nice country place there and the air is mild' (*E* 150). The semi-droll reference to England as 'foreign parts' underscores the limited confines of Robert's proposed excursion to the south of England.

147. Peter Costello points out that Dante Conway had a sister whose married name was Maria Elizabeth Justice of Mount Justice, Millstreet, County Cork, and surmises, speculatively and erroneously in this reading, that this was the inspiration for the surname of Beatrice Justice, 'which suggests some complicated family connection dating back to his father's early years, which carried for Joyce or his father some intense emotional burden' (*Years of Growth*, 62). The surname Justice matches the scrupled Protestant temperament of Beatrice. It seems clear that the assigning of the surname derives from Wilde's play and comes first; but it is quite possible that the surname of Maria Elizabeth Justice, unusual in Ireland, opened Joyce's mind to the

which was extraneous to the action (or inaction) of the play, Joyce was importing an allusion to Wilde in a play whose inspiration was Henrik Ibsen, and thereby contriving to link Kettle to Gogarty, who was close to Kettle, and whom Joyce saw as imitative of Wilde. This had a certain brittle exquisiteness as it was Gogarty who had intuited the danger of Joyce exacting a writer's revenge.

The conflict between the contrasted forms of absence and of voyaging away from Ireland gives the plural title *Exiles* its ironic salience. In his brilliant and melancholy short essay 'On Saying Goodbye', written in 1910, Kettle quoted the Breton poet Auguste Brizeux: 'Do not cry out against *la patrie*. Your native land after all will give you the two most exquisite pleasures of your life, that of leaving her and that of coming back.'[148] Kettle was writing as an Irish parliamentarian plying between Dublin and London. The already-mentioned note to the play seems a calculated retort: 'A nation exacts a penance from those who dared to leave her payable on their return.'[149]

Ellmann surmised of Joyce that 'as antagonist for the projection of himself in *Exiles*, Richard Rowan, he made Robert Hand out of Gogarty, Cosgrave, Kettle and Prezioso.'[150] But Robert Hand is not an indiscriminate compound. The superficial biographical attributes, as distinct from those character traits from which the action (or inaction) of the play springs, are based clearly and coherently on Kettle.[151] There is quite possibly an overlay of Gogarty, aphorist and close friend of Kettle.

possibility of its use as a surname. The idea of the compressed association within a single surname of the Protestant scruple of his invented character and a sister of the actual Dante Conway, distantly redolent of the alliance of the nonconformist conscience and Catholic moralism in the Split, would have appealed to Joyce in assigning to Beatrice the Wilde-derived surname of Justice.

148. Kettle, *Day's Burden*, 101. Auguste Brizeux (1893–1958) was a poet reputedly of Irish origin who wrote in French and Breton and wrote a verse comedy, *Racine*, early in his career.

149. *E* 114.

150. Ellmann, *James Joyce*, 356.

151. The mise-en-scène of *Exiles* itself suggests something of Joyce's relations with Kettle. Two of the three acts are set in Richard Rowan's house 'at Merrion, a suburb of Dublin.' Merrion is continuous with Sandymount. Richard in the third act comes in from walking on the strand in the early morning. After Kettle graduated, he lived for a time at Tritonville Cottage, Cranford Place, Sandymount. Colum recalls an afternoon spent with Kettle, Joyce, and Gogarty on the

Ellmann's basis for suggesting the presence of elements of Vincent Cosgrave and the Triestine Roberto Prezioso, editor of *Il Piccolo della Sera*, derives purely from Robert Hand's sexual interest in Bertha, Richard's wife. The Kettle aspect of Robert Hand is in this sense severable, standing outside the romantic triangulation of *Exiles*. The stylised portrait of Kettle—achieved essentially through the language of Robert Hand—is in its way as developed as those of Joyce's other contemporaries, Skeffington, Byrne, and Clancy, in *Stephen Hero* and *A Portrait*, in which no surrogate for Kettle features.

It is significant that Joyce should have drawn on the persona of Kettle to create a political and professional antithesis to Robert Hand, and that he should have chosen to represent the view of his contemporaries of his exile through the medium of a figure based on Kettle. On the occasions of Joyce's three return visits to Dublin from 1909 to 1912, as he struggled in vain to have *Dubliners* published, Kettle was at what transpired to be the zenith of his career, initially as a member of Parliament and then as a university professor, as progress towards a Home Rule settlement gathered pace. Kettle's career, which by 1912 was in academia and higher journalism, was emblematic of the path that Joyce had not taken or not been able to take, of his career's 'ousted possibilities' in Ireland.[152] It was the requirement to conform to the norms of what was taken as an emergent nationalist governing caste, which Kettle represented, that determined the elective element in Joyce's resolve to leave and to remain in exile, and thwarted his ability to have even his short stories published in Dublin. While Joyce remained a nationalist, *Exiles* marked the beginning of Joyce's complex treatment of the personal irony that the achievement of Irish legislative independence represented. When *Exiles* was written, legislative independence through Home Rule appeared imminent; in the event, it was only to be achieved a decade later under Sinn Féin auspices. It was in *Finnegans Wake* (and in relation to independent post-1922 Ireland) that Joyce was fully to

---

strand at Sandymount near where Kettle then lived. M. Colum and P. Colum, *Our Friend James Joyce*, 43; P. Colum, 'Tom Kettle', 31–32; J. B. Lyons, *Enigma of Tom Kettle*, 52.

152. See *U* 2.49–51.

realise this theme of the contrarieties of exile to magnificent comedic effect, and thereby to carry his contestatory nationalism to a plane of almost mathematical abstraction.

In *Finnegans Wake*, Kettle appears principally in a military guise, caught up in 'those ars all bellical, the highpriest's hieroglyph of kettletom and oddsbones'.[153] His most significant manifestation is as 'Galorius Kettle',[154] associated with Dagda's Cauldron of Plenty, and following immediately on Clive Sollis (*An Claidheamh Soluis*, edited by Patrick Pearse, objectively Kettle's greatest adversary) in an enumeration of patrons of the Feenichts Playhouse. 'Galorius' evokes ideas of abundance.[155] Children, even poor children, can gain admittance to the playhouse: 'Jampots, rinsed porters, taken in token'.[156] The great Joycean scholar Margot Norris correlates this in the first instance to the scene in *A Portrait* in which Stephen returns home to find some of his siblings assembled round the table: 'Tea was nearly over and only the last of the second watered tea remained in the bottoms of the small glassjars and jampots which did service for teacups.'[157] Norris suggests that the teapot world of the 'Mime' chapter takes its inspiration from an episode noted in Stanislaus Joyce's *Dublin Diary* in which Tom Kettle called to see John Stanislaus Joyce: 'He asked her was she little Miss Joyce, told [her] to tell her father that Mr. Kettle called. "You won't forget now—Mr. Kettle—what you boil water in". Baby [Mabel, the youngest Joyce, then aged ten] was telling this as a joke, and Eva, [who] was sitting at the fire boiling water, said, "Unfortunately he didn't know it's Mr. Teapot we boil the water in". We have no kettle.'[158]

This was the ne plus ultra of Kettle jokes. Parnell was supposed to have absent-mindedly introduced Andrew Kettle, his candidate in the

153. *FW* 122.7–8.

154. *FW* 219.12.

155. One wonders if a distant echo of the 'Ad Maiorem Dei Gloriam' with which generations of Jesuit boys were trained to commence their compositions is audible.

156. *FW* 219.6.

157. *P* 163.

158. Norris, *Joyce's Web*, 191–92; S. Joyce, entry for 29 March 1904, in *Dublin Diary*, 24–25. The family had just migrated south to 60 Shelbourne Road from St Peter's Terrace, Phibsborough.

Carlow by-election, by saying his name was a household word in Ireland.[159] Tim Healy had punned copiously on Kettle's name in the same election.[160] Years later Healy had with malign ingenuity inverted the initials of Tom Kettle's forenames to designate him 'M. T. Kettle', and D. P. Moran took up the joke.

Remembering Kettle in 1949, Padraic Colum was unusual in drawing a direct comparison with Joyce:

> He was one of that brilliant generation that included James Joyce, Francis Sheehy-Skeffington, Padraic Pearse, Thomas MacDonagh. Unlike Pearse, MacDonagh, Sheehy-Skeffington, Tom Kettle had a divided soul. Joyce, too, had a divided soul, but he integrated himself as Stephen Hero through a tremendous assertion that meant agony. Tom Kettle knew himself to be equipped for leadership, but in the middle of a spirited and sanguine conversation he would show self-distrust:-
>
> For a thing I never could find,
> Nor a broken thing could I mend.
>
> He would say them in a way that made me feel that Belloc's lines expressed a doubt of his ability to deal with the world's affairs.[161]

Tom Kettle was enmeshed by the nets that Stephen Dedalus had promised to fly by.

George Clancy

Joyce's close relations with his contemporaries were not confined to those who were active in the L&H. The third politically significant peer relationship (though of a very different order) that Joyce had in University College was with George Clancy, the Madden of *Stephen Hero* and Davin of *A Portrait*.

159. P. Colum, 'Tom Kettle', 29.
160. Callanan, *Parnell Split*, 130–31.
161. P. Colum, 'Tom Kettle', 35.

Recalling Clancy as a close companion of Joyce, Eugene Sheehy characterised him as 'a well-built and dark-haired son of Munster who was keen on Gaelic games and the restoration of our ancient language. He had a keen sense of humour and no guile. That simplicity and sincerity in his character appealed to Joyce.'[162] Stanislaus Joyce, who did not follow Joyce into University College, plaintively recalled that at university Joyce formed some friendships and found among the students some admirers 'who took over my job of listener and became the critics of his theories as well as the more congenial recipients of his confidences'. Significantly he numbered Clancy 'first among them', before J. F. Byrne.[163] Byrne himself wrote with blunt presumptuousness, 'George was the one other person besides myself in University College whose companionship Joyce courted.'[164]

Obtusely pedantic in that which pertained to the Irish political, Stanislaus struggled to comprehend his brother's relationship with Clancy. 'As a student, Clancy was an Irish language enthusiast and a sportsman, so that he and my brother had very little in common except the mutual attraction of brilliance on one side and of plain honest intelligence on the other, of city-bred and country-bred.'[165] The triteness elided the political depth of Joyce's relationship to Clancy, a relationship which challenged the perception of Joyce as a figure of narrowly metropolitan preoccupations, and which, as shadowed in *A Portrait*, counterbalances Stephen's aspiration to aestheticism.

Davin is the most developed figure in the novel apart from Stephen. He is an intriguing composite of rural nationalist and Irish language revivalist. That is what George Clancy was, and it defines the duality of Davin in *A Portrait*. Clancy's rural nationalism rendered his revivalism of greater fascination to Joyce than the ingenuous revivalism of middle-class Dublin converts to the Gaelic League. Stephen's relation to Davin in the novel renders Joyce's affection for Clancy and his deep and

162. Sheehy, *May It Please the Court*, 14–15.

163. S. Joyce, *My Brother's Keeper*, 175.

164. J. F. Byrne, *Silent Years: An Autobiography with Memoirs of James Joyce and Our Ireland* (New York: Farrar, Straus and Young, 1953), 154.

165. S. Joyce, *My Brother's Keeper*, 175.

FIGURE 7.3. George Clancy (left), James Joyce (right), and John Francis Byrne (center) in University College, 1900–1901. *Source*: 1.8, James Joyce Collection, The Poetry Collection of the University Libraries, University at Buffalo, The State University of New York.

sympathetic interest in Clancy's rural background. It is Davin rather than MacCann, the Skeffington figure, who is the contemporary political pivot of *A Portrait*. Davin bears the burden of Joyce's interest in the capacity of the Gaelic revival, ostensibly cultural rather than political, to reshape mainstream Irish nationalism. This reflects the acute prescience of Joyce in University College. While his own attitude to the Revival was markedly ambivalent, he avoided foreclosure. He carried this contemporary scruple through into the novel. He not merely eschewed anachronism, insofar as this was humanly possible, but fastidiously rendered a particular phase in Irish politics. Parnell's Ireland and Davin's, if overlapping, stood in an uncertain and unresolved relation to each other.

George Clancy was born on 18 March 1881 in Grange, County Limerick. He was one of the numerous children of Patrick Clancy, a carpenter, originally from Doneraile in County Cork. Clancy's widow wrote in her hagiographical reminiscences of her husband after his assassination that 'Seoirse [the Gaelicization of 'George'] drank in the tenets of militant Irish nationality with his mother's milk.' His maternal grandfather, like his father, had active Fenian affiliations. Clancy attended Grange National School, and St Patrick's seminary in Bruff. Intellectually gifted and studious, he went to University College, Dublin. His brother Patrick, who was four years his senior (later a committed trade unionist and member of the East Limerick brigade of the Irish Republican Army, and after George's death Labour Teachta Dála [MP] for Limerick from 1923 to 1932), became a carpenter like his father and grandfather before him.[166] Clancy's father became a publican in Grange, a business he was still carrying on at the time of George's death.[167] Something of the artisanal and small commercial sufficiency of the family is caught in the 'wellmade boots that flanked the wall pair by pair' in Davin's Grantham Street flat that unsettle Stephen's expectation of the indicia of rural Irish deprivation.[168]

166. Maire Clancy et al., 'The Limerick City Curfew Murder of March 7th 1921', in *Limerick's Fighting Story, 1916–21, Told by the Men Who Made It* (Tralee: Kerryman, n.d. [ca. 1948]), 115–39; William Murphy, 'George Clancy', *DIB* 2:518–90; Pauric J. Dempsey, 'Patrick Clancy', *DIB* 2:523.

167. *Limerick Leader*, 7 March 1921.

168. *P* 180.

Though a year older than Joyce, Clancy arrived in University College a year after him, in 1899. Clancy's subjects included Celtic studies under Fr Edmund Hogan S.J., a benignly eccentric *érudit* whom his most celebrated pupil, Eoin MacNeill, accurately characterised as 'a link between the old and new tradition of Irish scholarship.'[169] Clancy also developed popular revivalist connections outside University College which were to feature so prominently in his posthumous repute as to occlude his academic study of the Irish language as an undergraduate.

Clancy came to know Arthur Griffith and William Rooney through the Celtic Literary Society. He joined the Gaelic League and met Patrick Pearse. According to his widow's account, 'He knew and loved old Michael Cusack, founder of the Gaelic Athletic Association, whom he often met in An Stad, an Irish tobacco shop kept by the famous Irish humourist, Cathal McGarvey, in North Frederick Street, Dublin.'[170] While Joyce knew of and most likely had met Cusack or had him pointed out to him as a figure in his father's comedic gallery of Dublin characters, Clancy gave him a closer sense of Cusack's revivalism. In the Trieste notebook, Joyce wrote of Clancy, 'He sat at the feet of Michael Cusack the Gael who hailed him as citizen.'[171] It is probably principally through Clancy that Joyce became aware of McGarvey, a more benign figure than the irascibly ideological Cusack. In contemporary accounts it is difficult to get a definite sense of McGarvey, in part because he tends to be pulled gravitationally into a merged identity with the more overbearing Cusack: if the Citizen in the 'Cyclops' chapter of *Ulysses* is based primarily on Cusack, he is likely to owe a little also to the lost persona of Cathal McGarvey.

Clancy was a sympathetic figure, well liked in University College: 'He was a man of attractive personality, and his lovable character equally

169. Fathers of the Society of Jesus, *Page of Irish History*, 184, 188, 225. For Edmund Hogan, see Eoghan O'Raghallaigh, 'Edmund Ignatius Hogan', *DIB* 4:738.

170. Clancy et al., 'Limerick City Curfew Murder', 118–19; Fathers of the Society of Jesus, *Page of Irish History*, 477–78.

171. Robert Scholes and Richard M. Kain, eds., *The Workshop of Daedalus: James Joyce and the Raw Materials for 'A Portrait of the Artist as a Young Man'* (Evanstown, IL: Northwestern University Press, 1965), 93; see *P* 5.237–38.

with his athletic record and gift for organization gave him an exceptional influence over his contemporaries.'[172] He defied reductive ideological characterisation by his contemporaries: 'The gossip of his fellow students which strove to render the flat life of the college significant at any cost loved to think of him as a young fenian.'[173] By inheritance of conviction a nationalist, and a convert to revivalism, he was also by disposition someone driven to educate and a civic activist. It was as much the civic and educational aspects of his character as his ideological convictions that were to carry him in later life, as if ineluctably and against the grain of his diffidence, into electoral politics.

Clancy was the person chiefly credited with the establishment of the Gaelic League in University College.[174] Outside University College, he was prominently involved in the establishment of Cumann na bPáirtíde (the Confederates' Club), which organised weekly debates on national subjects as well as *céilithe* and excursions. He was the captain of its hurling club.[175] It was under Clancy's influence that Joyce fleetingly studied Irish and was lectured by Pearse.[176]

As Joyce recalled years later, Clancy alone of his associates addressed him by his Christian name.[177] He pronounced Joyce's Christian name with beguiling idiosyncrasy: 'He always called Joyce "Jebh" as if the "b" were aspirated'.[178] This is caught in some degree by Davin's use of the name Stevie in *A Portrait*: 'The homely version of his christian name on the lips of a friend had touched Stephen pleasantly when first heard for he was as formal in speech with others as they were with him.'[179]

172. Fathers of the Society of Jesus, *Page of Irish History*, 477.

173. *P* 5.278–82.

174. Fathers of the Society of Jesus, *Page of Irish History*, 477.

175. Clancy et al., 'Limerick City Curfew Murder', 116; Fathers of the Society of Jesus, *Page of Irish History*, 478–79. 'He refused to admit to his club, called "The Geraldines", anyone who was not a beginner, so that the first year was disastrous as to matches'. Fathers of the Society of Jesus, *Page of Irish History*, 479.

176. S. Joyce, *My Brother's Keeper*, 175.

177. Joyce to Giorgio and Helen Joyce, 5 February 1935, *Letters I* 357.

178. Byrne, *Silent Years*, 54.

179. *P* 5.227–29.

In *A Portrait* Davin is referred to as the 'peasant student' from the perspective of Stephen Dedalus, but it is softened by being a 'jesting name' between Stephen and himself, and the reference to the Firbolgs is presaged by Stephen's thinking that the statue of Thomas Moore was that of 'a Firbolg in the borrowed cloak of a Milesian': 'The rude Firbolg mind of his listener had drawn his mind towards it and flung it back again, drawing it by a quiet inbred courtesy of attention or by a quaint turn of old English speech or by the force of its delight in rude bodily skill . . . repelling swiftly and suddenly by a grossness of intelligence or by a bluntness of feeling or by a dull stare of terror in the eyes, the terror of soul of a starving Irish village in which the curfew was still a nightly fear.'[180]

This passage exemplifies the grace of Joyce's method of rendering relations from life, even if the person of Davin, like that of Stephen Dedalus, is a character in a novel. It stands as a brilliant, priggishly heightened account of what separated Joyce and Clancy, in which there is a strange reciprocity between Davin's atavistic dreads and Stephen's fear of a sensibility shaped by them. It also affords a haunting instance of anticipatory coincidence in Joyce's writing. Curfews were not, as Joyce seemed to imagine, a common phenomenon in the rural Ireland of the 1880s and 1890s. By 1921 in the War of Independence, however, curfews were frequent, and raids and political assassinations were carried out by Crown forces under their cover. Clancy was killed in a raid during a curfew on 7 March 1921, one of three victims of what were referred to as 'the Limerick City curfew murders'.[181]

If Davin was an athlete, he was as slow to action as he was reticent, engendering that 'reluctance of speech and deed in his friend which seemed so often to stand between Stephen's mind, eager of speculation, and the hidden ways of Irish life.'[182] Davin tells Stephen of how, returning from a hurling match in Buttevant, north-east of Cork, he was given milk by a young woman in the Ballyhoura hills who invited

180. *P* 5.234–42.

181. This is the title of the chapter of *Limerick's Fighting Story* dealing with Clancy's murder.

182. *P* 5.261–64.

him to share her bed.[183] J. F. Byrne recalled 'the little tale about Davin's midnight adventure' (more accurately non-adventure) as 'almost exactly as George told it himself'.[184]

Joyce knew that Clancy was not some kind of atavistic type of the Irish peasant, but a scion of a family of skilled artisans who had sustained the Fenians and (one presumes) later supported Parnellite agrarian nationalism, but he was acutely respectful of the fact that Clancy had access to and knowledge of an Ireland closed to Joyce. In *A Portrait*, if Stephen's debates on the Irish language are principally with Davin, it is made clear that Davin is not someone who is reducible to a narrow ideological commitment to the revival of the Irish language. Rather he is representative of a type of nationalist rural Ireland with familial links to the agrarian agitation that engendered the Land League, as well as to the Fenians.

Clancy was a convert to the Gaelic League who learned his Irish in Dublin. What was politically important for Joyce was that Clancy's commitment to the Irish language was superimposed on a familial commitment to radical nationalism, and a cultural rootedness in the place in which he had grown up. Clancy's background set him apart from the mostly urban Gaelicising arrivistes Joyce encountered in University College. Clancy's antecedents and sincerity invested his support for the Irish language with a certain weight that, for Joyce, affirmed that the issue required serious consideration. It posed a challenge to Joyce in relation to the future evolution of nationalist politics: Was it possible that, in terms of the broad thrust of nationalist politics, the espousal of Fenianism and Parnellite agrarian nationalism would in his time widely translate itself into a nationalism that was centrally defined by its support of the revival of the Irish language? Whatever Joyce's own scepticism on the subject, he had a sharp intimation of the revolutionary shift in political sensibility that a nationalism that had at its heart the aspirational revival of the Irish language portended.

183. *P* 5.265–326.

184. Byrne, *Silent Years*, 54–55.

Edmund Epstein, in his fine analysis of the persona of Stephen Dedalus, wrote that it is Davin whom Stephen came to identify as his rival 'for the love of their "sister" Ireland'.[185] That has to be qualified by Stephen's tentativeness in his conversations with Davin, which subverts the polarity and mitigates the force of Stephen's more cutting aphorisms on the subject of his country. Joyce's relationship to Clancy was the most creatively combative he had in University College, and cannot be reductively equated to Stephen's susceptibility to Davin's 'simplicity and innocence'.[186]

Clancy's health, unlike that of Davin's in *A Portrait*, was not robust. When he graduated from University College in 1905, he became a language teacher in Clongowes.[187] Falling ill, he was obliged to return to Grange. There he taught Irish classes and, as his widow put it, 'organised indoor and outdoor entertainments that were thoroughly Irish in character'. Once again Clancy's activism was not confined to the narrowly Gaelicising. According to Maire Clancy's narrative, 'In 1906 he was the person mainly responsible for the agitation to divide up untenanted land on the de Salle Estate, near his own home, which ended successfully with a monster meeting at Grange in September 1906.'[188] This rendering served to veil the extent of George Clancy's support for the Irish Party and his involvement with the United Irish League. On 23 September 1906 John Redmond, the leader of the party, attended what the *Freeman's Journal*, in its characteristic manner, hailed as 'one of the most numerously attended and most enthusiastic Nationalist demonstrations that had ever been held even in the historic Counties of Limerick and Tipperary' at Grange. As well as being the secretary of the United Irish League in Grange, George Clancy was the honorary secretary of the Grange Demonstration.

185. Epstein, *Ordeal of Stephen Dedalus*, 106, 109–10. I do not agree with Epstein's projection of Stephen's contest with Davin into the pages of *Ulysses*.

186. *P* 5.1939–40.

187. The account of Clancy's life that follows is based, save where otherwise indicated, on that given by Maire Clancy in 'Limerick City Curfew Murder', 115–25.

188. Clancy, 'Limerick City Curfew Murder', 116.

The address of the Grange Demonstration Committee of which Clancy was one of the signatories lauded the Irish Party and the leadership of Redmond. That on behalf of the Grange Branch of the United Irish League, which he also signed, was addressed to 'the illustrious Leader of the Irish National Party'. The only words in Irish were those that appeared in both addresses: 'céad míle fáilte'. The meeting was a representative well-attended occasion in the autumn of the year that had seen the election of a Liberal government, and Redmond's speech was lauded by the *Freeman's Journal* as 'a most important declaration of the National policy in view of the reported intentions of the Government on the Home Rule question.' The matter of the de Salle estate was referred to in the resolutions and the speeches, as was the action of Lord Fermoy in resiling from purchase agreements with tenants. T. M. Kettle, who had been elected for Tyrone East at a by-election two months earlier, also spoke at the meeting.[189]

According to Máire Clancy, Redmond was sufficiently impressed by George Clancy to offer him the secretaryship of the Irish Party (more probably it was that of the United Irish League), which Clancy refused. Máire Clancy had not known George at the time and was after his death little disposed to detract from what had become a narrative of advanced nationalist martyrdom. She asserted that he refused on the grounds that he had no faith in parliamentary action, thereby eliding his involvement in the United Irish League. Three years later, before the general election of January 1910, Clancy was invited to stand for the Irish Party in East Limerick, an offer he also declined. That a second approach was made renders it unlikely that Clancy had by that time broken with the Irish Party.

This precisely exemplified the facet of George Clancy's political persona that Joyce had picked up on. Clancy's immersion in the Irish language revival in Dublin came at a time when that did not necessarily entail opposition to the Irish Party. As Sarsfield Kerrigan, a contemporary who arrived in University College a little after Joyce, shrewdly wrote, 'From 1901 to 1903 the Irish Ireland movement in the College,

189. *Freeman's Journal*, 24 September 1906; *Limerick Leader*, 24, 26 September 1906.

conscious of its latent strength, had a wonderfully detached view towards current politics.'[190] In the event, Clancy was not to align himself with Sinn Féin in opposition to the Irish Party until a decade after he left University College, probably at some point between 1912 and 1914. In Joyce's University College, the borders of parliamentarianism and cultural nationalism remained fluid. If the progress to Home Rule was to founder, and a serious contest were to arise between the Irish Party and what became Sinn Féin, Clancy would be found on the side of Sinn Féin, and so it transpired.

In October 1908 Clancy had moved from Grange to the city of Limerick as a teacher of Irish in schools and the Gaelic League. He was, over the decade he taught in Limerick city, increasingly drawn into the vortex of republican politics. He was involved in the establishment of Fianna Éireann and was a member of the Limerick committee of the Irish national volunteers from 1913, in which connection he encountered Roger Casement and again met Patrick Pearse. On the outbreak of the First World War, when Redmond's supporters formed the National Volunteers, Clancy aligned himself with the radical minority splinter group, the Irish Volunteers. In July 1915 he married Máire (Moll) Ní Cillín, whom he had met at Coláiste na Mumhan in Ballingeary, and later in the Limerick Gaelic League. He was briefly imprisoned in the aftermath of the 1916 Easter Rising. He campaigned for de Valera in the East Clare election of 1917. He was again imprisoned in the tense aftermath of the death of Thomas Ashe and went on hunger strike with his fellow prisoners.

In 1918 the tempo of Sinn Féin activity sharply increased. Clancy was responsible for organising resistance to conscription in Limerick. The strain in the months before conscription was abandoned took its toll on his health and he fell victim to the post-war influenza epidemic. He recovered but was obliged to give up teaching and became legal superintendent of the Irish National Assurance Company.

In the local government elections of 1920, Clancy finally made his entry into formal politics. With a vote more than double his nearest rival's, he

190. Fathers of the Society of Jesus, *Page of Irish History*, 506.

was returned as the senior alderman. He declined the mayoralty on grounds of lack of municipal experience, and it passed to his more prominent Sinn Féin colleague, Michael O'Callaghan. He was charged with the raising in Limerick of the Dáil Éireann loan of 1919, and against all the efforts of the authorities was in a position to go to Dublin in June 1920 and present the monies raised in specie and intact to the finance minister of the first Dáil Éireann, Michael Collins.[191]

On 30 January 1921, Clancy was elected Lord Mayor of Limerick. He was a highly respected civic figure, rather than a republican ideologue. On his death the *Limerick Leader* wrote, 'He was identified with the Irish Ireland movement all his life and in recent years was a prominent figure in the Sinn Féin movement. He devoted the early years of his life to the Gaelic League, and did great work for the advancement of the native tongue in the city. He was a gentleman of unassuming manners, and was popular with all classes of the citizens, and especially with the school children, with whom he was a great favourite.'[192] He was likewise described on his death by the *Irish Independent* as 'of a very quiet and retiring disposition, and a man of peace.'[193]

From 1919 Clancy was a sufficiently prominent adherent of Sinn Féin to be the subject of a succession of military raids. On 6 March 1921 his father-in-law was buried. At midnight, his wife wished him goodnight, leaving him, as she carefully recorded, reading in Irish Geoffrey Keating's counter-reformation tract *Eochairsgiath an Aifrinn* (*Defence of the Mass*). By that time, a Black and Tan raiding party had already killed Joseph O'Donoghue and were en route to Clancy's house at Thomondgate via the nearby home of his predecessor in the mayoralty Michael O'Callaghan, whom they also murdered. Clancy was gunned down in the hall of his house, and his wife was shot in the wrist.[194] The killings recalled the shooting of Thomas MacCurtain, Lord Mayor of Cork and commandant of the Cork Brigade of the IRA, a year earlier, on

191. Clancy, 'Limerick City Curfew Murder', 120.

192. *Limerick Leader*, 7 March 1921.

193. *Irish Independent*, 8, 9 March 1921.

194. *Irish Independent*, 8, 9 March 1921; Clancy, 'Limerick City Curfew Murder', 123–24.

20 March 1920.[195] 'The two murdered mayors' remained a familiar Limerick designation of the killings for decades to come.[196]

After college, Joyce had lost touch with Clancy. After the first two of his three return visits to Dublin, in 1909–10, he wrote in his Trieste notebook of his old friend, 'Chance did not bring us face to face on either of my visits to Ireland. I wonder where he is at the present time. I don't know if he is alive still.'[197] The slight oddness of the comment by one man in his late twenties regarding another suggests Joyce's awareness of Clancy's fragile health.

Joyce had not ceased to remember his friend. He learned of Clancy's death and the circumstances in which it occurred. The detail he had retrieved of Clancy's intervening life is uncertain, but he was at the very least aware of its broad outline from newspaper accounts of his death, supplemented by the intelligence of Irish friends such as James Stephens and Constantine Curran. Joyce would have known that Clancy had been lifted by the flowing tide of the conflict in Ireland out of his role as a teacher and civic activist and carried into political life, where he had lost his life. If Kettle and Skeffington had cleaved to the path of parliamentary nationalism (though Skeffington had by the end deviated from it) and lost their lives in different theatres of the Irish tragedy in 1916, Clancy had, as an adherent of Sinn Féin, also met a violent death five years later. It was always the deep politico-cultural continuities in Clancy's life, his filiations with an *Irlande profonde* of Fenian agrarian and nationalist rurality, that had drawn Joyce to him. If the Davin of *A Portrait* was representative of a type in University College, Clancy's life some years after he had left University College caught the rhythm of those who had become embroiled in the crisis of Irish politics from 1912 to 1921.

Of his three friends who died violently in conflict, it was Clancy who had meant most to Joyce. Writing to his son and daughter-in-law in 1935, he referred to 'my poor friend George Clancy', using the term 'friend'

195. MacArdle, *Irish Republic*, 333–34, 430–32.

196. Jim Kemmy, 'George Clancy—Murdered Mayor', in *Remembering Limerick: Historical Essays Celebrating the 800th Anniversary of Limerick's First Charter Granted in 1197*, ed. David Lee (Limerick: Limerick Civil Trust, 1997), 251–60.

197. 'The Trieste Notebook', in Scholes and Kain, *Workshop of Daedalus*, 93.

he had contrived to withhold in writing to Mary Kettle on the death of her husband.[198]

John Francis Byrne

The person with whom Joyce spent most time in University College was John Francis Byrne, the Cranly of *Stephen Hero* and *A Portrait*.

Byrne was two years older than Joyce, born on 11 February 1880 at 25 East Essex Street, Dublin, a house which he calculated stood on what had been three centuries previously part of the bed of the river. His father, who had farmed in County Wicklow, died in December 1883, when he was three, his mother ten years later in January 1893.[199] The further rearing of John Francis was undertaken by two female cousins in Dublin, though he continued to make trips back to Wicklow.[200]

Byrne was already a student in University College when Joyce, with whom he had maintained an acquaintanceship since Belvedere, arrived in 1898. On account of the physical disparity between Byrne's muscular strength and the slightness of build of the sixteen-year-old Joyce, Byrne recalled, 'my attitude towards him became, and to a great degree remained, protective'.[201]

Characterised by Stanislaus Joyce as 'a rather idle but very solemn-looking student', Byrne was extremely pale, of middle height and muscular: 'He is low-sized, square, and powerful looking, and has a strong walk. He dresses in light grey and wears square-toed boots. Jim calls him the Grand Byrne; he has the grand manner, the manner of a Grand Inquisitor'. He excelled at handball. He was the best chess player in University College. Clever and well-read, he was a brilliant conversationalist who was taciturn when in a group. He and Joyce carried on conversations in dog Latin.[202]

198. Joyce to Giorgio and Helen Joyce, 5 February 1935, *Letters I* 357.

199. Byrne, *Silent Years*, 1, 21; Lawrence William White and Lindsey Earner-Byrne, 'John Francis Byrne', *DIB* 2:215–16.

200. Byrne, *Silent Years*, 16, 93.

201. Byrne, *Silent Years*, 27, 40.

202. S. Joyce, *My Brother's Keeper*, 176–77; S. Joyce, entry for 14 September 1904, in *Dublin Diary*, 96; Sheehy, *May It Please the Court*, 16–17.

While Byrne was a well-known figure in the university, his only recorded formal intervention in college societies was a paper late in his prolonged career as an undergraduate on Thomas à Kempis given to the Library Conference in the same period as Joyce delivered his Mangan paper to the L&H. He claimed to regard it as a flop, though Stanislaus Joyce, while surprised at its subject matter, thought otherwise. James Joyce ambled in just before Byrne concluded, with a quotation from one of his poems.[203]

Joyce saw a great deal of Byrne, walking through the city, and frequently sitting beside him in the National Library. Contemporary characterisations of Byrne—and not only those by Joyce, who was to develop the perception for his own purposes—turned on the paradox of a person of sacerdotal aspect and manner being a non-believer and a phlegmatic materialist. 'Jeffbyrne', as some of his contemporaries called him, had also a curious dialogic mode. William G. Fallon recalled, 'Parading the four sides of St Stephen's Green, or Mountjoy Square, at times long after nightfall, I on more than one occasion, "listened in" to "Jeffbyrne". His deliberate procedure was not to monopolise, but to provide what he facetiously termed Platonics. But Joyce seemed to prefer Byrne, unaccompanied, for those leisurely walks. . . . Byrne was his trustworthy keeper'.[204]

The soubriquet bestowed on Byrne in University College of the 'White Bishop'[205] had a supplement of commentary beyond chess and the pallor of his complexion. In Byrne's account, Joyce translated this into 'Cranly', a name he liked that belonged to Thomas Cranly, an English Carmelite who was Archbishop of Dublin from 1397 to 1417. Joyce told Byrne in October 1898, just after he had entered University College, 'I'll go on calling you J. F., but I'll think of you as Cranly'.[206] Thomas Cranly being the model was disputed by Stanislaus Joyce, who wrote to Curran in 1954, 'Jim chose the name because he thought B's family was from Wicklow and that Cranly was a Wicklow name. While

203. *St Stephen's*, March 1902, 101; S. Joyce, *My Brother's Keeper*, 177.

204. Quoted in U. O'Connor, *Joyce We Knew*, 52.

205. Byrne, *Silent Years*, 43–44; *St Stephen's*, March 1902, 101.

206. Byrne, *Silent Years*, 43–47.

we were children in Bray, we had a nurse whose name was Cranly. Her people were fisher people who lived at the foot of Bray Head.'[207] This was an early instance of the controversies of the names and identities of characters in Joyce's fictions that were to consume a great deal of strenuous attention in early critical writing on Joyce. Whatever the origin of the name, the odd mental divide involved in assigning a fictional surname to a contemporary leaves open the possibility that Joyce, while holding himself out as a poet and critic, was playing with the idea of an autobiographical roman à clef throughout his undergraduate career.

Byrne was characterised in the Jesuit history of the college as 'our most ascetic student',[208] and by Joyce in the Pola notebook in the idiom associated with Robespierre as 'His Intensity the Sea-green Incorruptible.'[209] In *A Portrait,* Joyce writes of Cranly's 'priestlike face, priestlike in its pallor, priestlike in the lips that were long and bloodless and faintly smiling.'[210] Stanislaus, who said that Byrne 'has the features of the Middle Ages', touched on the schism between appearance and utterance: 'He deliberates behind an impenetrable mask like a Cistercian bishop's face. . . . Having spoken, he pretends to infallibility. The more subtle the conversation becomes, the more brutally he speaks. He is fond of the words "bloody" and "flamin".'[211]

The relationship of Joyce and Byrne was played out against a background of tacitly shared nationalism, distanced from institutional political allegiance. Joyce of course contrived to maintain a sardonic posture. Conversing with friends on the proposition that twelve men with resolution and the courage to give their lives if necessary could save Ireland, Byrne had observed that he could find twelve such men in Wicklow. They were rendered in *Ulysses* as 'the Tinahely twelve', taking their name from the railway station where Byrne got off on his visits to Wicklow, and (docking one to make a soccer team) 'Cranly's eleven true

207. Stanislaus Joyce to Curran, 1 January 1954, UCD, Curran Papers, Correspondence.

208. Fathers of the Society of Jesus, *Page of Irish History,* 398.

209. 'Pola Notebook', in Gorman, *James Joyce,* 137. See also S. Joyce, entry for 31 July 1904, in *Dublin Diary,* 48.

210. *P* 5.150–55.

211. S. Joyce, entry for 14 September 1904, in *Dublin Diary,* 96; entry for 3 April 1904, 32.

Wicklowmen to free their sireland'.[212] Byrne's nationalism was undemonstrative but deeply felt. He was proud of his paternal grandfather, who was a younger friend of Robert Emmet and was present at Emmet's trial and execution.[213] Unlike Joyce, Byrne had 'many a vivid boyhood memory' of Parnell.[214]

Byrne, the best chess player in University College,[215] frequently joined the chess players in the smoke-room of the Dublin Bread Company café on Dame Street, where Joyce sometimes waited for him. One afternoon he was introduced to John Howard Parnell, the brother of the dead leader. He presented Parnell to Joyce. Asked if he was a chess enthusiast like Byrne, Joyce replied that he was afraid he was not, and feared he would never master the intricacies of the game. While Byrne 'could thrill to the recent memory of [John Howard Parnell's] great brother', he evidently did not think that the introduction meant much to Joyce. In his memoirs, he recalls that for some months in late 1898, Joyce sat waiting 'session after session' while he played chess with John Howard Parnell until, after one such session in October 1898, Joyce took him by the arm and intoned softly into his ear: '"*Ite missa est*", your Grace. Come on Cranly; as you say yourself "Let us eke go"'. According to Byrne, all the time Joyce waited for him to finish the game, 'he sat alone and remained aloof. And he did this not because of shyness, but because he did not want to mix with the company even to the extent of a "Good afternoon". . . . Every minute I gave to chess was a sheer waste to him, and he was frankly jealous of John Howard who was my partner in profligacy.'[216] By the time Byrne had begun to beat Parnell consistently, Joyce had prevailed on him to quit the Dame Street Dublin Bread Company.

Joyce was not so inattentive to Parnell's brother or to the chess matches as Byrne's account might suggest. In the 'Wandering Rocks'

212. *U* 9.36; Richard Ellmann, 'The Backgrounds of *Ulysses*', *Kenyon Review* 16, no. 3 (Summer 1954): 361.

213. Byrne, *Silent Years*, 170–71.

214. Byrne, *Silent Years*, 49, 195.

215. S. Joyce, *My Brother's Keeper*, 177.

216. Byrne, *Silent Years*, 40–44, 53.

episode of *Ulysses*, the City Marshall, a post occupied by John Howard Parnell from 1897, is missing from the council chamber. Buck Mulligan and Haines stray into the Dublin Bread Company. Mulligan 'whispered behind his Panama to Haines:—Parnell's brother. There in the corner.'[217] They sit opposite him: 'John Howard Parnell translated a white bishop quietly and his grey claw went up again to his forehead whereat it rested. An instant after, under its screen, his eyes looked quickly, ghostbright, at his foe and fell once more upon a working corner.'[218]

Byrne's last address in Dublin was 7 Eccles Street, where he lived from 1906 to 1910 with the two older female cousins who had brought him up, one of whom, an especially devout Catholic, disliked Joyce. Joyce visited him on the first two of his three return trips to Dublin, in 1909–10. It was there that he arrived distraught, having been led to believe that Nora Barnacle had been involved with Vincent Cosgrave when Joyce was seeing her. It was there also that, after a long walk through the city before his return to Trieste, Joyce watched as Byrne, who had left his latchkey in another pair of trousers, climbed over the railings and dropped down into the basement area to get in, as Bloom would do in the company of Stephen in the 'Ithaca' episode of *Ulysses*.[219]

Byrne himself emigrated to the United States in April 1910, three months after Joyce had left Dublin for Trieste at the end of his second return visit. There he worked as a journalist. As an émigré, he became more politically active than he had been in Ireland. He came to know the prominent figures of Irish American nationalism, including John Devoy and Patrick Ford.[220]

When Skeffington, to whom Byrne was close, went to the United States in the autumn of 1915, Byrne received him at his home in Queens and put his contacts at his disposal. Byrne then followed Skeffington back to Ireland, leaving in February 'in order to be there

217. *U* 10.1042–44.

218. *U* 10.1050–53.

219. Byrne, *Silent Years*, 88, 94, 154–59.

220. Byrne, *Silent Years*, 92, 98.

FIGURE 7.4. John Francis Byrne. Image courtesy of UCD Digital Library from an original in the Curran/Laird Collection, UCD Library.

for developments that were plainly coming to a head.'[221] In the immediate prelude to the Easter Rising, Byrne met some of the leaders, including James Connolly. The mutual friend who introduced him must have been Skeffington: Byrne recalled in his memoirs that of the five people in Connolly's office in Liberty Hall that day, 'four were shot within the

221. Byrne, *Silent Years*, 95–101.

next few weeks.' He himself contrived to miss the Rising, having crossed to London on 17 April. Though Byrne was to a degree ambivalent about the Rising, he was impressed by the 'spirit of reckless, magnificent daring' of its leaders and outraged by the murder of Skeffington.[222]

Byrne was financial editor of the New York *Daily News Record* from 1929 to 1933 and visited Joyce in Paris twice, in 1927 and 1933. His eccentrically pedantic *Silent Years: An Autobiography with Memoirs of James Joyce and Our Ireland* was published in New York in 1953. Ellmann provided it to Stanislaus Joyce, who concluded with characteristic defensiveness that it was hostile to his brother. Stanislaus recorded that Byrne had 'nothing to say about the wit and subtlety in conversation with which my brother's affectionate memory invested him' in *A Portrait*. 'On the whole I find him in his book as I remember him, secretive, suspicious, tortuous, countrified, conceited, and yet not bad-hearted.'[223] Stanislaus's observations on Byrne's memoir mirrored Byrne's warning to Ellmann not to rely on the narrative of Stanislaus, 'a bitter, confused and inaccurate man.'[224]

Easily the most long-lived of the four people who had most defined Joyce's years in University College, and the only one to outlive him, Byrne died in New York in 1960.

222. Byrne, *Silent Years*, 111–12, 127, 135. Byrne's account drew extensively on his 'The Irish Grievance: The Case for the Anti-English Party', *Century Illustrated Monthly*, n.s., 71 (January 1917): 465–73.

223. Stanislaus Joyce to Curran, 1 January 1954, UCD, Curran Papers, Correspondence.

224. Byrne to Ellmann, 26 May 1958, cited in Brenda Maddox, *Nora: A Biography of Nora Joyce* (London: Hamish Hamilton, 1988), 520.

8

'The Language of the Outlaw'

For the new nationalist movement, the Gaelic League, [Joyce] had no regard. 'I distrust all enthusiasms', he said. . . . It was not with any youthful bravado. It was rather like one giving a single veto after a tiring argument.

—PADRAIC COLUM[1]

THE FACT THAT JOYCE'S generation in University College was the first to be swept by the wave of the revivalism of the Irish language finds ubiquitous expression in *Stephen Hero* and features prominently in *A Portrait*. Revivalism was brought to the fore primarily by the highly effective activism and propaganda of the Gaelic League. It answered a felt need which the League itself did much to engender, to address what came to be felt as a deficit in traditional nationalism. The widespread sympathy with the Gaelic League fell short of impelling most nationalists to learn or speak Irish. The disparity between sympathy with the revivalist project of the Gaelic League and the practice of its precepts is crucial. It conduced to a pervasive intellectual confusion and prompted accusations of humbug from the critics of the Gaelic League. The language question was a fraught and complex issue of uncertain political

1. M. Colum and P. Colum, *Our Friend James Joyce*, 20–21. This was in the course of their first conversation, after they had left the National Library in 1902 or early 1903.

magnitude that was devoid of precedent, national or international. The impact of the Gaelic League in a university setting was more potently concentrated than in the country at large. Joyce's generation in University College had to find its own way.

The novelty of the issue was something of which Joyce was acutely conscious. In the 'Aeolus' episode of *Ulysses*, professor MacHugh describes the occasion of the speech of John Francis Taylor that took place on 24 October 1901, at the start of Joyce's final year in University College. The inaugural address to which Taylor was responding was entitled 'The Irish Revival',[2] and professor MacHugh twice explains that it was not then a familiar topic. He states that 'the paper under debate was an essay (new for those days), advocating the revival of the Irish tongue',[3] and repeats a little later, 'It was then a new movement.'[4] This conveys the historically accurate fact that by the date on which *Ulysses* is set, three years after Taylor's speech, the subject has become more familiar, which is not to say that the full political impact of revivalism was apparent by 1904.

The co-relation of the Gaelic League's revivalism to contemporary politics added a further layer of complication. The Gaelic League claimed to be politically neutral. Even if it was, the opponents of the Irish Party sought to exploit the language issue. Some ardent revivalists were drawn to Arthur Griffith and the inchoate Sinn Féin. Griffith, who was a political nationalist, was wary of compromising his political conception of independence by co-identification with revivalism, but the cultural content of his *United Irishman* and the revivalist aspirations of many of his sympathisers meant that his emergent movement was seen by the country at large as ardently revivalist, and that was not a perception that Griffith could afford to repudiate.

In University College the line between the Gaelic League and what was to become Sinn Féin was sharply drawn. Though the Jesuits were largely sceptical of revivalism, it was something they were prepared to

2. *Freeman's Journal*, 25 October 1901.

3. *U* 7.795–96.

4. *U* 7.807.

encourage on the basis that—unlike the Parnellism of the Split and the stirrings of Sinn Féin—it was in their view politically harmless. Even after the establishment of the state, the distinction lingered, and was highlighted in the 1930 Jesuit history of the college: 'The fundamental difference between the Gaelic League and Sinn Féin lay, chiefly, perhaps, in the fact that while the former concentrated on the language, the latter was frankly a political movement. . . . And, although in full sympathy with the language movement, the Sinn Féiners did not allow it the paramount importance demanded for the proper programme of the Gaels.'[5]

Joyce came to observe the same discrimination, at least after his period in University College, but the other way around as he moved into sympathy with Griffith's Sinn Féin.

In University College in Joyce's era, the espousal of revivalism was not seen as having anything to do with support for Griffith's nascent and highly minoritarian faction of nationalism. The Gaelic League's profession of political neutrality was critically important in permitting revivalism to take hold as a national aspiration. The sons of farmers and urban members of the Catholic middle class, staunchly supportive of the Irish Parliamentary Party, were thereby denied any reason not to endorse the project of the Gaelic League. It enjoyed a broad support it would not have done if it was perceived as a challenge to parliamentary nationalism.

Revivalism was to subsist in parallel to conventional politics as practised by the Irish Party. The notion that Irish language revivalism was apolitical was doubtful from the start: it was theoretically possible but was never going to remain so in an Irish setting at the turn of the century. The acceptance of the Revival's political innocence had a remarkably long run because reviving the Irish language seemed disarmingly noble and progressively novel. The Irish Party knew that overt querying of the project of the Gaelic League would be represented as an attack on the Irish language, and this gave the revivalists something of a free run. Irish language revivalism had a complex duality. It existed

5. Fathers of the Society of Jesus, *Page of Irish History*, 482.

both as a discrete project and one which was inherently prone to become a vehicle—and in some respects a catalyst—for associated political philosophies and values which at once went beyond and fell short of revivalism, without quite forfeiting what seemed the pristine purity of its purpose.

The idea that the Gaelic League was apolitical—other than in the narrow sense that it did not pit itself against the Irish Party—was belied by its own history. Douglas Hyde, in his seminal paper to the National Literary Society of 25 November 1892 titled 'The Necessity for De-Anglicising Ireland', sought to exploit the disillusionment wrought by the Parnell Split. He was speaking in the aftermath of the bitterly contested election petitions for the North and South Meath constituencies that followed the general election of 1892. The issue of the Irish language was 'of greater importance than whether Mr. Redmond or Mr. McCarthy lead the largest wing of the Irish party for the moment, or Mr. So-and-so succeed with his election petition. To a person taking a bird's-eye-view of the situation a hundred years hence, believe me, it will appear of greater importance than any mere temporary wrangle, but unhappily our countrymen cannot be brought to see this.'[6]

Hyde's speech is considered important in the inception of revivalism, but a large part of its significance lies in it being the first attempt to relativise parliamentarism and Home Rule in the wake of the Split by reference to the revival of the Irish language: 'Just at the moment when the Celtic race is presumably about to largely recover possession of its own country, it finds itself deprived and stript of its Celtic characteristic, cut off from the past, yet scarcely in touch with the present'.[7] That 'scarcely in touch with the present' reveals a highly astute publicist. Hyde's pitch was finely calculated. He did not expressly advocate the general popular adoption of the Irish language but rather the arresting of its decay and the reversal of the political disfavour in which he asserted it to be mired. 'I have no hesitation in saying that every Irish-feeling

6. Douglas Hyde, 'The Necessity for De-Anglicising Ireland', lecture delivered before the Irish National Literary Society in Dublin, 25 November 1892, in Crowley, *Politics of Language*, 187.

7. Hyde, 'Necessity for De-Anglicising Ireland', 185.

Irishman, who hates the reproach of West-Britonism, should set himself to encourage the efforts which are being made to keep alive our once great national tongue.' There was something cloying in Hyde's rendering of the process of historical assimilation: 'Dane and Norman drawn to the kindly Irish breast issued forth in a generation or two fully Irished, and more Hibernian than the Hibernians themselves.'[8] It was that homogenising 'Irished' that Joyce rejected, as he came increasingly to underscore the ethnic and cultural diversity of the inhabitants of Ireland. Whatever can be said about Hyde's potently influential speech, it was far from being politically innocent.

In University College Joyce was surrounded by contemporaries who had superficial though not inconsequential sympathies with the Revival, a constituency much larger than the narrow core of dedicated Irish revivalists who spoke Irish and were seriously invested in the prospect of an Irish-speaking Ireland. Joyce stood apart from the naivety of most of his University College peers. He grasped immediately the potentially far-reaching cultural (his more immediate concern) and political ramifications of revivalism. He was instinctively sceptical of the delusive simplicities of popular revivalism, but held back from adopting a general opposition to revivalism per se. His overt opposition was reserved for the xenophobic cultural nationalism which instrumentalised revivalism; he was also exorbitantly suspicious of what he had observed of clerical sponsorship of the Revival, which gave a Parnellite edge to his resistance to a Gaelicised nationalism. His reservations on the subject of revivalism were philosophical but were also those of a political nationalist. In a malign scenario, revivalism had the potential to copperfasten the outcome of the Parnell Split, to affirm the complacent insularity of post-Parnellite Ireland, and to thwart his conception of Ireland as a modern European nation-state.

What Joyce had to gauge was the nature and scale of the impact of revivalism in Irish politics. He knew that revivalism was more than the

8. Hyde, 'Necessity for De-Anglicising Ireland', 184. Joyce made few references to Hyde in his correspondence and writing. Joyce was strategic in his choice of targets of criticism. Augusta Gregory and to a lesser extent Yeats were the proxies for Joyce's suspicions of Hyde's proselytising the revival of the language.

pursuit of extra-curricular self-improvement; that it had political ramifications and was not simply a neutral or natural emanation of the Irish pursuit of statehood, nor a semi-antiquarian retrieval of the Irish past. More clear-sighted than his University College contemporaries, he was able to discriminate between revivalism and the historical Irish language. He recognised revivalism as a phenomenon of contemporary politics. He was characteristically alert to the possibility of diverse outcomes. In retrospect, revivalism would prove more significant in the shaping of the course of Irish politics than in its professed purpose of resuscitating the Irish language, but in the Ireland of the turn of the century the outcome was uncertain. Revivalism could yet have proved a passing fad. The attention that Joyce paid it makes plain that he did not think revivalism would prove evanescent; he saw its potency as arising from its affiliations to the neo-nationalist currents in Irish politics after the fall of Parnell.

Many revivalists were possessed of a zealotry, often semi-moralistic, which affirmed Joyce's suspicions of their project. What repelled Joyce is captured best in a piece written of the Gaelic revival in 1912 by his University College contemporary Arthur Clery, who appears in *Stephen Hero* as 'Whelan, the College orator'.[9] Austere, not unintelligent, and unbiddable, Clery had joined the Gaelic League in 1897 and was an admirer of D. P. Moran, to whose *Leader* he was a regular contributor. Indeed, he was prepared to credit Moran with the achievement that many attributed to the Gaelic League itself, reflecting his idiosyncratic politicisation of the Revival. Clery was in later life implacably opposed to the Anglo-Irish Treaty, to the extent of refusing to accept a pension as a member of the Dáil courts from a government he deemed illegitimate, and finally drifted into support of the reactionary Catholic An Ríoghacht.[10] His 1912 article entitled 'The Sect of the Gael' was published in Moran's weekly. Clery lauded Moran's *The Philosophy of Irish*

9. *SH* 89. Alongside the reference to Whelan there appears the note in the manuscript 'offering him the grapes. I never eat Muscatel grapes'. Curran noted that Clery was in the habit of carrying grapes home with him and had offered him grapes in the Gaiety 'gods'; C. P. Curran, Joyce notebook, UCD Special Collections, Constantine Curran Collection, Curran MS 6, 89.

10. Patrick Maume, 'Arthur Edward Clery', *DIB* 2:584–86.

Ireland (first published between 1898 and 1900 as a series of articles in the *New Ireland Review*), which he declared 'had become the philosophy, though not as yet the practice of Ireland as a whole'. Of the revival of Irish as an ordinary medium of communication, Clery wrote, 'It was a purpose extraordinarily high, extraordinarily difficult of attainment. . . . The enterprise might fitly be described as miraculous, and though the Irish movement has achieved many miracles, it has not wrought that one *yet*.' He continued,

> If Ireland is to become Irish-speaking it requires a further miracle, and such may yet occur, but what has happened up to this is of a quite different kind. In fact, if one might put it so, the Gaelic movement in Ireland has brought about a result something like John Wesley's movement in the Church of England. He set out to reform the church to which he belonged and only succeeded in creating a new sect of non-conformists. The Gaelic movement has in fact created a sect, a body of men of pure lives and high ideals, but leading a life quite apart from the general body of the population, who look upon them for the most part with benevolent wonder. As I heard a well-known Gaelic Leaguer put it at a meeting some weeks ago, Gaelic Leaguers are a body as much estranged from the general life of the people as are the Jews.

He repeated his caveat: 'But you will never in our time get the general public to live at the intense pressure of Irish Ireland morality.'[11] Clery was going beyond what had become by 1912 the blandly conventional argument that the revival movement had re-inspirited nationalism, to assert that while its revivalist purpose was unlikely to be attained, it had created a sect of high-minded *dévots*. That proved highly prescient.

In *Stephen Hero* Joyce uses the term 'the patriots' with a sarcastic edge to designate those of his contemporaries who were associates of Gaelic Athletic Association founder Michael Cusack, frequenters of Cathal McGarvey's tobacco shop An Stad on North Frederick Street, adherents of Arthur Griffith and what was to become Sinn Féin, and committed

11. Chanel [Arthur Clery], 'The Sect of the Gael', *Leader*, 10 February 1912.

partisans of Irish revivalism. After an account of an exchange between Stephen and Madden, based on Joyce's friend George Clancy, the narrative turns to Emma Clery, with the pivot, 'Stephen's conversations with the patriots were not all of this severe type.'[12] Joyce may have taken the term from his father. In *Stephen Hero* Simon Daedalus complains of the company his son was keeping: 'lousy-looking patriots and that football chap in the knickerbockers'[13] (a reference to Skeffington). Joyce retained all his life an aversion to the terms 'patriotism' and 'patriots'. The indiscriminate designation 'the patriots' was to vanish completely in *A Portrait*. If that reflects the greater refinement of *A Portrait*, it also reflects Joyce's realisation that the aggregation was not analytically sustainable, which in turn owes something to his reassessment of Griffith.

'The extinct and the revived, theoretical or practical?': Joyce's Knowledge of Irish

As part of the abbreviated and highly stylised autobiography he furnished in instalments to Harriet Shaw Weaver, Joyce wrote in 1921, 'My father wanted me to take Greek as third subject, my mother German and my friends Irish. Result, I took Italian.'[14]

Joyce did fleetingly enrol in a course to learn Irish. In *Stephen Hero* Stephen buys O'Growney's primers, published by the Gaelic League, but refuses to pay a subscription to the League or to wear the badge in his buttonhole. His purpose was to join the class attended by Emma Clery: 'People at home did not seem opposed to this new freak of his.'[15] It may have been a relief to his mother, who complained that he 'never went to church, mass or meeting'.[16]

12. *SH* 65.

13. *SH* 216.

14. Joyce to Harriet Shaw Weaver, 24 June 1921, *Letters I* 167.

15. *SH* 56.

16. Scholes and Kain, *Workshop of Daedalus*, 103 (from the notes headed 'Mother' in Joyce's 'Trieste notebook').

From 1899 on the initiative of William Delany, Patrick Pearse taught, under the auspices of the Gaelic League, extra-curricular classes in the Irish language at University College. The first course was attended by fewer than a dozen students, among whom was George Clancy. In 1901–2 Pearse taught a second and somewhat more formally organised course attended by, among others, Constantine Curran and Hugh Kennedy.[17] The slightly greater probability is that Joyce's attendance was at the first course offered by Pearse.

Joyce did not maintain his attendance. Davin, the Clancy figure in *A Portrait*, having earlier asked Stephen, 'Are you Irish at all?', follows this up with urging him to be 'one of us': 'Why don't you learn Irish? Why did you drop out of the league class after the first lesson?'[18] It is clear that Joyce dropped out, but perhaps not after the first lesson. Frank Budgen, who first met Joyce in Zurich in 1918, two years after Pearse's execution, wrote in his 1934 memoir of Joyce that 'Joyce studied Irish under Pearse, but Pearse's enthusiasm for Irish led him often to disparage the English language, and on this account he discontinued the Irish lessons and turned his attention to Norwegian, which he has studied ever since.' He added in his 'Further Recollections of James Joyce' in 1955 that 'Pearse's ridiculing of the English word "thunder" was probably the limit.'[19]

Joyce had scarcely intended to linger long on the course; if he was looking for affirmation of his suspicions of the Gaelic League as intolerant of the English language, Pearse was unlikely to have disappointed. Joyce had subscribed in some degree as an aspect of his relationship

17. Fathers of the Society of Jesus, *Page of Irish History*, 503; Ruth Dudley Edwards, *Patrick Pearse: The Triumph of Failure* (London: Faber and Faber, 1979), 29. Pearse was a fairly familiar figure in University College. He chaired a debate at the Literary and Historical Society in the 1901–2 session—Joyce's last year, in which he delivered his paper on James Clarence Mangan—on the motion 'That the Irish Language Movement is the Essential Element in Irish Nationality'; Meenan, *Centenary History*, 70.

18. *P* 5.999–1004.

19. Frank Budgen, *James Joyce and the Making of 'Ulysses' and Other Writings* (Oxford: Oxford University Press, 1972), 183, 359. It is quite possible that Joyce's account of Pearse deriding the word 'thunder' was a conceit as he worked on *Finnegans Wake*, in which a Vico-derived idea of thunder featured prominently. Budgen does not date Joyce's observation on the subject.

with Clancy. He needed some grasp of orally communicated Irish, however initiatory. The experience of attending one or more Gaelic League classes was potentially useful to Joyce, though it did little to inform the account in *Stephen Hero* of Stephen's attendance at Irish language classes transposed to a venue in O'Connell Street.[20] His leaving of Pearse's class did not portend a complete abandonment of his study of the Irish language. Stanislaus Joyce recalled that his brother, under the influence of Clancy, 'studied Irish for a year or two'.[21]

It was characteristic for Joyce to refuse to see attendance at a class of the Gaelic League as coextensive with learning Irish. However, although Joyce's grasp of Irish, unlike his comprehension of Norwegian, remained fairly rudimentary, he still believed that he had an abstract understanding of Irish as a linguistic system. A clue to the obduracy of this conviction may find fictional expression within the sardonic grace of the catechistic interrogation in the 'Ithaca' episode of *Ulysses*, after Bloom and Stephen have exchanged snatches, sacred or pedagogic, of Hebrew and Irish which may represent a very large portion of their respective knowledge of those languages.

> Was the knowledge possessed by both or each of these languages, the extinct and the revived, theoretical or practical?
>
> Theoretical, being confined to certain grammatical rules of accidence and syntax and practically excluding vocabulary.[22]

The Irish scholar Brendan O'Hehir, in his *Gaelic Lexicon for 'Finnegans Wake'*, addressed the issue of Joyce's knowledge of Irish. He wrote of the slow dissipation of the assumption that Joyce knew little or no Irish, not least by Stanislaus's significant qualification of what was inferred from Stephen's dropping of the Irish course in *A Portrait*. O'Hehir suggests that Joyce attained 'a modest competence in Irish',[23] itself possibly a polite overstatement. He refers to Joyce's exceptional flair for languages,

20. *SH* 59–61.

21. S. Joyce, *My Brother's Keeper*, 175.

22. *U* 17.741–44.

23. Brendan O'Hehir, *A Gaelic Lexicon for 'Finnegans Wake' and Glossary for Joyce's Other Works* (Berkeley: University of California Press, 1967), vii.

the brothers' penchant for etymologising the place-names where they lived, and the fact that in Paris Joyce had Patrick Dinneen's Irish-English dictionary and Edmund E. Fournier D'Albe's (earlier and less highly regarded) *English-Irish Dictionary*;[24] both authors lectured at University College in Joyce's time. O'Hehir's revisionism is scrupled: 'It should not be supposed that Joyce was a profound Gaelic scholar. With a number of sharp and surprising exceptions, the Gaelic displayed in *Finnegans Wake* is of an elementary and commonplace character.'[25]

John Francis Taylor and *The Language of the Outlaw*

Joyce's most formal treatment of the issue of the revival of the Irish language is his deployment of the speech of John Francis Taylor of 24 October 1901, in the 'Aeolus' episode of *Ulysses*. The debate in which Taylor spoke captures the contemporary state of the debate on the Irish language in its political aspect, and its use in *Ulysses*, after an interval of some two decades from its delivery, casts a great deal of light on Joyce's intellectual response to, and imaginative treatment of, the movement for the revival of the Irish language. Taylor made his speech at the inaugural meeting of the Law Students' Debating Society of the King's Inns. The auditor's address was entitled 'The Irish Revival'. Taylor moved the vote of thanks, and Lord Justice Gerald Fitzgibbon, who was the president of the society, wound up the debate. For reasons which will become apparent, the debate attracted copious press coverage and Taylor's speech acquired instant political celebrity on the streets of Dublin.

Richard Ellmann considered that Joyce 'appears to have attended the meeting'[26] or 'probably' did so.[27] It is highly improbable that he did, though this is not a matter of great consequence. He certainly came to hear about it and read the detailed account in the *Freeman's Journal* and

24. O'Hehir, *Gaelic Lexicon*, viii; Patrick Dinneen, *Fócloir Gaedhilge agus Béarla: An Irish-English Dictionary* (Dublin: Irish Texts Society, 1927); Edmund E. Fournier D'Albe, *An English-Irish Dictionary and Phrase Book* (Dublin: n.p., n.d. [1905]).

25. O'Hehir, *Gaelic Lexicon*, vii–ix.

26. Ellmann, *James Joyce*, 90.

27. Ellmann, *Consciousness of Joyce*, 34.

possibly in the other newspapers that covered it (the *Irish Daily Independent*, the *Daily Express*, and the *Irish Times*). Ellmann points out that Joyce had access to a four-page leaflet entitled *The Language of the Outlaw* which contained an outline of the speech.[28] That slim pamphlet (undated but published in the *United Irishman* on 17 February 1906) is a curious document: it incorporates a letter written by 'X' to the *Guardian* on 14 November 1902, shortly after Taylor's death, together with an ardently revivalist narrative which positions the displacement of the native language as a deliberate and decisive step in the English conquest ('The language of a people is the fortress which the enemy first assails; and once that fortress is captured, and its stones levelled with the ground, every other stronghold of nationality must inevitably fall.')[29] Though Joyce was unaware of the fact, the pamphlet was published by Roger Casement with a short commentary of his own on the speech and on X's letter to the *Guardian*.[30] The identity of X remains unknown.[31]

The account of the speech by X in the letter to the *Guardian* is significant because Joyce drew on it, together with the contemporary newspaper reports, to remind himself of Taylor's speech when writing 'Aeolus'. This is certain because Joyce replicates some of the errors of the

28. Ellmann, *Consciousness of Joyce*, 35–36. Ellmann quotes the bulk of the letter of 'X' to the *Guardian*.

29. [Roger Casement], *The Language of the Outlaw* (n.p., n.d.), 1. The text of the pamphlet was republished in the *United Irishman* of 17 February 1906.

30. The issue of authorship is discussed in Abby Bender, 'The Language of the Outlaw: A Clarification', *James Joyce Quarterly* 44, no. 4 (Summer 2007): 807–12. The pamphlet is attributed to Casement by P. S. O'Hegarty in his *Bibliography of Roger Casement* (Dublin: Alex Thom, 1949), 5–6. It is included in Herbert O. Mackey's collection of Casement's writings *The Crime against Europe* (Dublin: C. J. Fallon, 1958), 112–16.

31. The suggestion of O'Hegarty, who was less than clear about why he was ascribing the authorship of the pamphlet to Casement, that 'the letter itself was possibly written by Casement himself' (*Bibliography of Roger Casement*, 6) can be discounted. Casement had not read any of the contemporary accounts and only learned of it later. Casement had in fact departed the Congo Free State and reached England from Lisbon on 12 October 1901. It seems as if he was in Portrush when reports of Taylor's speech were carried in the Dublin papers on 25 October; Séamas Ó'Síocháin, *Roger Casement: Imperialist, Rebel, Revolutionary* (Dublin: Lilliput, 2008), 134–35. Ó'Síocháin refers to Casement's publication of *The Language of the Outlaw* at 223–24.

pamphlet's commentary on the speech. One of those errors is Casement's, who writes in his gloss on the letter that 'the only record available' of the speech of 'one of the most eloquent of modern Irishmen, the late Mr. J. F. Taylor QC', was contained in X's letter to the *Guardian*. Joyce knew that to be incorrect but seized on and archly accentuated it as an enhancement of the idea that the speech was unprepared and that it survived chiefly in oral memory. Professor MacHugh in 'Aeolus' asserts, 'That he had prepared his speech I do not believe for there was not even one shorthandwriter in the hall.'[32] This affords a slight but perfect example of Joyce's fictional method applied to subjects of historical factuality, extending to matters actually known to him. Joyce may have taken as correct other errors or uncertain interpolations in X's account, including the date (not 'last November'), the location (not Trinity's 'college historical society', as professor MacHugh asserts), and the order of speakers (professor MacHugh repeats X's error that Taylor spoke *after* Fitzgibbon: 'When Fitzgibbon's speech had ended John F Taylor rose to reply.')[33] What Joyce made most out of was X's assertion that the Taylor who rose to reply 'had been very ill, and had come straight from his bed, and without food' and so began his speech 'with some difficulty' before reaching his stride.[34] Professor MacHugh, 'in ferial tone' addressed to J. J. O'Molloy, says, 'Taylor had come there, you must know, from a sickbed. . . . His dark lean face had a growth of shaggy beard round it. He wore a loose white silk neckcloth and altogether he looked (though he was not) a dying man.'[35]

The account of X scarcely did justice to Taylor's speech but did capture its concept: '[Taylor] set out the arguments which a fashionable professor with an attachment to the Egyptian Court might have addressed to Moses.'[36] X's rendering of the substance of Taylor's speech was a flat and abbreviated paraphrase, but flares into life at its close: '"And", broke out the speaker, "if Moses had listened to these arguments,

32. *U* 7.815–16.

33. [Casement], *Language of the Outlaw*, 2, 3; *U* 7.823, 7.793.

34. [Casement], *Language of the Outlaw*, 3.

35. *U* 7.815–18.

36. [Casement], *Language of the Outlaw*, 3.

what would have been the end? Would he ever have come down from the Mount with the light of God shining on his face and carrying in his hands the Tables of the Law written in the language of the outlaw?"'[37]

The speech as rendered in *Ulysses* is closer to Taylor's original than the limp paraphrase of X, which confirms that Joyce was aware of Taylor's speech when it was delivered and had a remarkable recall of what Taylor was reported to have said, or at the very least a high familiarity with the moves in the contemporary debate for and against the revival of the Irish language. The letter of X that was republished in the pamphlet served as a prompt, but the principal source for 'Aeolus' was Joyce's recollection of what he had read, and perhaps been told, about the speech.

To appreciate the contemporary impact of Taylor's speech and why it had made an impression, it is necessary to go back to the debate itself, of which the four principal Dublin daily papers—the nationalist *Freeman's Journal* and *Irish Daily Independent*, and the Unionist *Daily Express* and *Irish Times*—carried extensive reports in their editions of 25 October 1901.[38] The extent of the press coverage owed as much to the prospect of the encounter of Taylor and Fitzgibbon as to the subject. The debate in the dining hall of the King's Inns was recognised as a remarkable political occasion in the city even before Taylor and Fitzgibbon had uttered a word, and this accounted for the large and unusually diverse audience. As well as many who might be expected professionally to attend, the audience in the dining hall included a complement of Gaelic League supporters. The *Freeman's Journal*, in its characteristic manner that was to be affectionately parodied in *Ulysses*, carried a list of many of those present, including William Walsh, the Catholic Archbishop of Dublin, 'Patrick H. Pearse BL', John (Eoin) MacNeill, and Maud Gonne; the Archbishop of Armagh, Cardinal Logue, sent apologies.

37. [Casement], *Language of the Outlaw*, 4.

38. The reports reflect a degree of editorial bias. I have taken Taylor's speech principally from the *Freeman's Journal*, and that of Fitzgibbon from the *Daily Express*. That the debate was very much a Dublin occasion is reflected in the fact that no report was carried in the liberal Unionist *Northern Whig*.

The debate was a rhetorical joust between champions of the two Irelands, a first set-piece confrontation on the still-new issue of the Irish Revival. Gerald Fitzgibbon (1837–1909) had been an advocate of high distinction who had served as Solicitor-General in Ireland from 1877 to 1878 and had not ceased, on his appointment as a Lord Chief Justice of Appeal in 1878, to be a figure of immense political influence. Undeviatingly Conservative and of legendary intelligence and political acumen, Fitzgibbon was considered the pre-eminent intellectual figure of Irish unionism. He had remained close to Lord Randolph Churchill, whom he had met when Churchill was in Ireland during his father the Duke of Marlborough's lord lieutenancy from 1876 to 1880, and he significantly influenced Churchill's policies and pronouncements on Ireland.[39] The shrewdest commentator on the Irish judiciary wrote in 1890 that Fitzgibbon had been a candidate for appointment to the judicial committee of the English privy council (and membership of the House of Lords) in 1889, but that a sufficient obstacle to his promotion was 'his friendship with Lord Randolph Churchill, whose friends are not admitted to as the friends of the present [Conservative] government. Lord Randolph has stayed more than once with the Lord Justice, in his pleasant red-brick house that overlooks the sea from the Hill of Howth.'[40]

John Francis Taylor (1853–1902) was a respected but not especially successful member of the Irish bar. Passionately nationalist and notoriously irascible, his principal fame was as an itinerant nationalist orator, if mostly in Dublin city centre, within the confines of the two canals. That geographical confinement was mitigated by sociological depth. Yeats wrote in the *Trembling of the Veil*, in an instalment of his brilliantly fraught characterisation of Taylor in his autobiographical writings, 'He spoke in the most obscure places, in little halls in back streets where the whitewashed walls are foul with grease from many heads, before some audience of medical students or of shop-assistants,

39. Patrick Maume, 'Gerald Fitzgibbon', *DIB* 3:928–31; R. F. Foster, *Lord Randolph Churchill* (Oxford: Clarendon, 1981), 40–42. Churchill continued to attend the annual Christmas party in Howth of Fitzgibbon, who characterised the serial occasion as 'the *haute école* of intelligent Toryism' (Foster, *Lord Randolph Churchill*, 56–57).

40. Rhadamanthus [pseud.], *Our Judges* (Dublin: Irish Society Office, 1890), 36–37.

for he was like a man under a curse, compelled to hide his genius, and compelled to show in conspicuous places his ill-judgement and his temper.'[41] He was 'a great orator, the greatest I have heard, doomed by the violence of his temper to speak before Law Students Debating Societies, obscure Young Ireland Societies, Workmen's Clubs'.[42] Taylor's status in Britain was more securely institutionalised as the Dublin correspondent of the *Manchester Guardian*. He was marginalised during Parnell's ascendancy chiefly by reason of his refractory independent-mindedness, to which the tier below Parnell of the party leadership were acutely alert. In the O'Shea divorce crisis, he initially rallied to Parnell before reversing into alignment with the Gladstonian Liberal Party. He became estranged from the anti-Parnellites, but neither repented of nor critically addressed his anti-Parnellism in the Split in the politically long interval between Parnell's death and his own. That was a bitter silence. It might be said that Taylor's political life was twice broken by Parnellism. By the time of the debate in the King's Inns, he was close to Arthur Griffith, and a contributor to the *United Irishman* whom Griffith greatly valued. He had one final moment which for once he did not miss.

The debate was defined by its moment in political time. Irish Unionists were gratified by the enfeeblement of nationalism occasioned by the Parnell Split. A Unionist government was in office in Westminster from 1895 and would continue until 1906. Ameliorative Conservative measures characterised as 'killing Home Rule with kindness', principally in the domains of land purchase and local government, achieved a degree of success. The advances of nationalism under Parnell had nonetheless deeply unsettled the confidence of Irish Unionists, so that their hegemony in Ireland was marked by persisting unease masked by the sedulously maintained posture of confidence of Irish Unionist politicians and publicists.

J. F. Taylor spoke after the auditor's paper. He invoked Thomas Davis and welcomed the auditor's address 'because of its reinforcement of personal and national dignity': 'Many distinguished Irishmen were fond

41. Yeats, *Autobiographies*, 215.

42. Yeats, *Autobiographies*, 422.

FIGURE 8.1. Sketch of John Francis Taylor by James Walker. Reproduced courtesy of the National Library of Ireland, PD 3099 TX 13.

of going about saying they were Irishmen. He did not know of anything more humiliating than to see intellectual Irishmen going from one country house to another in England with cap and bells and turning their poor country into ridicule (*applause*). If this new movement did nothing more than make these men ashamed it would be a gain.'[43]

Taylor passed to the issue of migration from Ireland and thence to the Irish language, in the brilliant rhetorical flight that drew on the book of Exodus and won the speech its renown:

> Now as regards the language, suppose a great message was to be given to the human race, in what language was it likely to be given? What was the greatest message ever given to man? Christian and non-Christian alike were agreed upon that matter. Was that message given in the language of Imperial Rome or the language of intellectual Greece? No, it was given in the rustic dialect of the far-off land 'out

43. *Freeman's Journal*, 25 October 1901.

> of which no good could come.' Had that fact any meaning for them there and now? He could very well understand an intellectual Egyptian speaking to Moses 'Why bother about these people of yours in Egypt? I know possibly we have not treated them very well, but all that is over now, and you may be chosen to rule over Egypt, and every public position is open to your people. I have no patience with you talking about your history and literature. Why, I asked one of the learned professors of your literature the other day what it was like, and he told me it was made up of superstitions and indecency' (*prolonged applause and laughter*). If Moses had listened to the counsels of that learned Professor he would never have come down from the mountain, his face glowing as a star, and bearing the Tablets of the Law (*applause*). Had these facts no meaning for them here and now. He did not mean that they should expect any great message from the Irish language in the future, but if there was such a great message, it would come, not from a language encrusted with commercialism and materialism, but it would come from some pure language that was kept aloof and unsullied with contamination with the world (*applause*).[44]

The passionate though habitually over-vehement orator had found a still point of vantage in the equation of the destiny of the Irish with the Jews. He attained a high cogency on a great occasion that required it. It was a famous triumph.

Quite apart from the invocation of Moses and the comparison of the Irish and the Jews, Taylor's speech was of supreme political intelligence. It was not only directed at Fitzgibbon. It was a masterclass in political nationalism, and almost imperceptibly a rebuke, to a younger generation infatuated with the revival of the Irish language, for which it was almost a creed in itself. With grizzled audacity he appropriated the idea of a revival of the Irish language to deliver a magnificent restatement of the *political* argument for Irish nationalism that owed little to revivalism. Taylor was never a committed revivalist of the Irish language, and his reservations as a political nationalist about revivalism matched those of

44. *Freeman's Journal*, 25 October 1901.

Arthur Griffith, though Griffith was to find himself constrained to embrace revivalist ideas. Taylor's view of revivalism was not far removed from Joyce's own: Joyce was suspicious of revivalism but held back from creating a rift with his own political generation by condemning it, thereby showing a capacity for calculated restraint not easily accommodated within the conventional understanding of Joyce. Though the debate in the King's Inns was a contest between nationalist and Unionist Ireland, it embraced a contest between two conceptions of Irish nationalism. The contest within nationalism was to shift almost beyond recognition in the two decades that ensued, when the Irish language became a defining ensign of a radical political nationalism, which it did something to inspirit, and was a prominent feature in the politics of the Irish Free State (in part because it was instrumentalised by Sinn Féin and its successor parties to distinguish it from the Irish Parliamentary Party). Yet if the line of demarcation between revivalism and political nationalism became confusingly blurred, it was never effaced.

Taylor was speaking in anticipation of Fitzgibbon's winding up of the debate. As in Taylor's speech, the issue of the Irish Revival was overlain by the contest of unionism with nationalism. It transpired to be the last occasion on which a *plaidoyer* for unionism in Ireland as it stood after the Conservative chief secretaryships of Arthur Balfour (1887–91) and of his brother Gerald (1895–1900), and during the currency of that of George Wyndham (1900–1905), was delivered to a politically mixed audience. It was an event that had already become uncommon in Dublin and was only made possible by the fact that the Irish Revival, heavily Anglo-Irish in its initiation, was not yet tribally polarised, and because the King's Inns was an integral institution, albeit (like the Irish bar itself, and the Irish judiciary) an institution in political flux.

Fitzgibbon lacked, or through his long occupancy of judicial office had lost, the cunning in a public meeting that Taylor had come to possess in abundance through long practice in dreary venues. With lawyerly exhaustiveness, Fitzgibbon complacently rehearsed all the cogent arguments against the revival of 'this old language . . . an object of intense interest and affection from his very earliest days (*applause*)'. He dismissed the idea of bilingualism ('no man could have two mother tongues. No man could think in two languages'). He placed much emphasis on the issue, provocative to nationalists, of what he called 'the voluntary giving up of the Irish language': 'He took the best proof that English was spoken in those remote parts of Ireland where the inhabitants possessed it as their native language—he took as the clearest proof the case of Daniel O'Connell himself, the greatest master of invective and the greatest advocate of his day. He was speaking no foreign tongue when he spoke in English, either in the courts of this country or in the Parliament across the water.'[45]

He asked 'what Irish they were going to revive', noting the difference between ancient and modern Greek. This was a subliminally racial theme of nineteenth-century scholarship in Britain and Germany, connected to the proposition that there was no bloodline connecting modern Greeks with the ancient inhabitants of their country. Fitzgibbon's most cogent argument was pragmatically Darwinian, that the Irish language had not survived as a viable medium of communication: 'No living language could stand still. The inevitable law of life was that they must either be growing or decaying applied to a language as it did to a tree or a living being, and in that respect the history of the Irish tongue was eminently melancholy, for, arrested in its progress beyond doubt or question for more than a hundred years, it [lacked?] for that long period the perpetuation which no living tongue could ever do without, the perpetuation of contemporaneous literature, which would recall it as it was spoken.'[46]

Fitzgibbon was bravely trying to make a difficult and important argument, but the sympathy that it might have attracted was lost in the barristerial exhaustiveness of his argument, and its overt pro-unionism.

Fitzgibbon stated that the Irish language was exceedingly difficult to learn, and there were considerable regional variations. In conclusion he addressed the auditor's assertion that the loss of the Irish language had been fatal to Ireland as a nation. Here his imperialism brought him eerily close to the idiom of the 'intellectual Egyptian' of Taylor's speech,

45. *Daily Express*, 25 October 1901.

46. *Daily Express*, 25 October 1901.

with the difference that he was asserting that Ireland was already, rather than prospectively, a partner in an imperial project of incomparable vastness:

> Their friends or neighbours across the water were very proud of what they called Great Britain. We heard perhaps too much of the Empire on which the sun never set, and so forth. But what was that Great Britain? New Zealand was as large as the United Kingdom; Australia was as large in solid land as the whole of Europe, together with the Black Sea and the Mediterranean thrown in. These two taken together could be laid on the vast colony and territories of Canada, and have patches all round them quite big enough to prevent them falling off. Through the whole of that vast aggregation English was the language, with a few scattered exceptions, of the inhabitants and in the winning and making, aye, and in the governing of that vast aggregation of land, the lion's share had not gone to the lion, but to the Gael (*applause*). Scotch and Irish had been the wings that had carried the body forward as it spread over the whole earth. Was there no greater Ireland?[47]

Beneath the imperial grandiloquence, Fitzgibbon was playing on the economic interest and career opportunities of Irish graduates. It prompts Stephen's otherwise enigmatic statement in *Stephen Hero* that 'English is the medium for the continent',[48] a wry hint at his own forthcoming exile.

Knowing he had no right of reply, J. F. Taylor had contrived devastatingly to pre-empt Fitzgibbon's argument. He also contrived a right of reply in an article that was published in the *Freeman's Journal* four days after the debate, also entitled 'The Irish Revival'. Taylor's article encompassed a riposte to Fitzgibbon but was in the main an elaboration of his own response to the Revival and of the relationship of the English and Irish languages. The article served, whether intentionally or not, to

47. *Daily Express*, 25 October 1901.

48. *SH* 54. A little later in the novel, pursuing the same theme, he asks Madden, 'And, tell me, how many of your Catholic Leaguers are studying for the Second Division and looking for advancement in the Civil Service?' (*SH* 64).

widen the distance, latent in his King's Inns speech, between what he himself approbated in the language movement and what the most ambitious of the revivalists sought.

Fitzgibbon in the King's Inns had taken the revivalist case literally as the thoroughgoing advocacy of an Irish-speaking Ireland. Taylor had done no such thing, confining himself to commending the efforts of a younger generation to familiarise themselves with the language under the auspices of the Gaelic League. He disposed of Fitzgibbon's argument by a tartly realistic assessment of what the prospects of a full-blooded revival of the Irish language were:

> We may all be supposed to know that English is the great language of commerce; that a hundred million of human beings speak it; that it is spoken by the official rulers of India; and that mastery of it opens up communications with a great part of the world. These considerations urge themselves. If there happened to be an imminent prospect of the supplanting of English by Gaelic as the language of business in Ireland, perhaps one might dwell upon these matters more seriously; but I am not myself aware that such thoughts cross the mind of the most sanguine Gaels, who do not think that knowledge of Irish expels the English already acquired by habit and conversation. Commerce, law, administration, and all the other alluring things will remain open as before to the young gentlemen of Ireland; and so that topic may be dismissed.[49]

Taylor's confining of the ambitions of the Irish Revival was an affront to its more ardent proponents. While the issue remained fluid, Taylor was too astute and well informed to be unconscious of this. With dogged deliberateness, he persevered in subsuming the Gaelic League into an older nationalist narrative, negating what its more zealous advocates considered to be its revolutionary novelty. He saw the Gaelic League as a continuation of the work of mid-nineteenth-century Irish scholars, though infused with a new nationalist ardour that he welcomed: 'The Gaelic League takes up the work interrupted by the death

49. J. F. Taylor, 'The Irish Revival', *Freeman's Journal*, 28 October 1901.

of Eugene O'Curry, whose achievements are one of the added glories of Newman's illustrious career. (The treatment of poor John O'Donovan, on the other hand, needs no retelling).' Of the purpose of the Gaelic League, he wrote, 'The Gaelic League, as I understand the matter, is trying to gather from living lips all that it can preserve of Irish as a modern spoken language, and to spread the knowledge of this spoken language over as wide an area as possible, while at the same time stirring an interest in the ancient language, literature, 'origins', and history of Ireland, such as one finds among the educated classes of every other country in the world except Ireland.'[50]

He continued, 'The serious objections to Celtic studies come from Trinity College, which has, indeed, a Celtic chair of its own to teach clergymen enough Irish to labour in the fields of proselytism.' While many 'saw with pleasure some sign of intellectual awakening among the young men and women of Ireland (whether that awakening was caused by National love or mental curiosity)', something he also characterised as 'this groping after something on which their affections could rest', Trinity College 'sent out its champions to wage war, as if for dear life, against the whole thing.' He then referred to three prominent Trinity academics who had evinced their hostility to the Irish language. The first was Professor Robert Atkinson and the second was John Pentland Mahaffy, classical scholar and later provost of Trinity College, whose flamboyant unionism extended to the dismissal of literature in the Irish language and made him the bête noire of advocates of the Literary Revival:[51] 'Dr. Mahaffy, who, like [William] Congreve, prefers to be regarded not as a scholar or as men of letters, but as a man of the world and a gentleman of fashion, told us that Irish was of no use whatever unless you happened to be fishing or shooting and wanted to talk to your man. That is hardly the evidence of an expert in Celtic scholarship.'[52]

50. Taylor, 'Irish Revival'.

51. Patrick Maume, 'John Pentland Mahaffy', *DIB* 6:285–87.

52. Taylor, 'Irish Revival'. Both Professor Robert Atkinson and John Pentland Mahaffy gave evidence in 1898 to the Viceregal Commission enquiring into the intermediate school curriculum. Philip O'Leary, *The Prose Literature of the Gaelic Revival, 1881–1921* (University Park:

The third was Edward Dowden, a literary critic of the highest repute and professor of English literature at Trinity College, of adamant Unionist convictions and markedly hostile to the Irish Revival.[53] Taylor treated Dowden more respectfully, declaring him to be 'a little bigoted in favour of the great literature of England', though he could not restrain himself from observing, 'It may be that Dr. Dowden, like most of the guides of Trinity College, looks upon himself as doing outpost duty for England, and so feels bound to discourage Gaelic as an evil thing per se.' Taylor was making it plain that the 'intellectual Egyptian speaking to Moses' of his speech in the King's Inns was a composite of Atkinson, Mahaffy, and Dowden.[54] Taylor was rendering overt the animus against the three Trinity academics that in part drove his speech. This was the narrower aspect of his King's Inns speech which Joyce in *Ulysses* was to edit out in substituting a numinous high priest of Egypt for Taylor's 'intellectual Egyptian'.

Taylor referred to contemporary continental scholarship on the Irish language. He went on to say something that was remarkable for a student truly steeped in the Irish rhetoric of the late eighteenth and nineteenth centuries: 'No one can study Burke and Grattan and compare their styles with the styles of Pitt and Fox and Bright without seeing that our great countrymen were speaking what, to them, was a learned language, of which they had become superb masters in everything save simplicity. So with the foolish, florid, diction of the political platform. The words have no definite meaning to speakers or hearers, and rant is the result. See an Irish witness giving evidence in his own tongue, and how quick, definite and intelligent he is!'[55]

Pennsylvania State University Press, 1994), 223; Tony Crowley, *War of Words: The Politics of Language in Ireland, 1537–2004* (Oxford: Oxford University Press, 2005), 143.

53. Linde Lunney and Pauric J. Dempsey, 'Edward Dowden', *DIB* 3:425–27.

54. Taylor, in his article, also criticised Maynooth, though less trenchantly. He observed in passing, 'The fine tones of any language are for the few, and of two languages, for no one, not even Gibbon.' Taylor, 'Irish Revival'.

55. Taylor, 'Irish Revival'. The opening references are to Edmund Burke, Henry Grattan, William Pitt, Charles James Fox and Henry Bright.

This, if it was not altogether unique, was an exceedingly rare rehearsal of the proposition that classic Irish political rhetoric was informed by the fact that English was a language that had been 'learned'. Taylor meant by this primarily a language that had not been acquired and nurtured within an established tradition of established statehood, rather than a language that was not 'native', though this was added as a secondary connotation. That absence of a continuous tradition of statehood was to be of high importance in Joyce's treatment of Irish history and culture generally, not particularly in relation to the Irish language (with the qualified exception of Stephen's reflection as he speaks to the dean of studies that 'the language in which we are speaking is his before it is mine' in *A Portrait*).[56] While Joyce was acutely conscious of the dispassionate ruthlessness of history, his anti-positivism made him resistant to the idea that anything was entirely lost, something that found expression in the historical and cultural cyclicism which he later espoused. The reference to the Irish-speaking witness was also oddly anticipatory of Joyce's treatment of the trial and conviction of Myles Joyce in his 1907 article in Trieste 'Ireland at the Bar'.[57]

The relationship of the style of Irish rhetoric to the loss of the Irish language hinted at by Taylor in the reference to the Irish-speaking witness was little more than a comparative allusion, but it was made in the setting of what was for Taylor, as a lifelong champion and exponent of Irish rhetoric, an extraordinary concession and compressed to the point of being cryptic. (There was no lost Irish-speaking background in Henry Grattan, though at a push one could argue that the loss of the Irish language affected the reception of his oratory outside the ascendancy class in the wider Ireland in which Irish was still commonly spoken, and that he was conscious of that audience. The case of Edmund Burke was somewhat different.)[58] What was startling in Taylor's highly considered

56. *P* 5.553–59.

57. *OCPW* 145–46. See chapter 15, 'Joyce's Triestine Lectures and Articles', for discussion of article 'Ireland at the Bar'.

58. Conor Cruise O'Brien has written, in a brilliant rendering of the early Burke that owes much to his wife, the poet and scholar Máire Mhac an tSaoi, 'To be brought up in Ballyduff [in County Cork], and to love his Nagle relatives, as Burke did, was to share directly in a considerable

critique of the comparative stylistic extravagance or complexity of classic Irish rhetoric was the bitter—and not altogether consistent, in an admirer of Irish classical rhetoric—connection he sought to make to the frequent vapidity of contemporary Irish platform oratory. Taylor was torn: if he was striving to encompass the Revival within the frame of a traditional nationalism, the Revival had done something to subvert some of his former certitudes. He still refused to see the Revival as effecting a revolutionary transformation, a qualitative change in Irish nationalism:

> My own belief is that the Gaelic League has given a purpose to many purposeless lives, has filled many an empty heart, and, as its increasing numbers show, has stirred healthy emulation when there might have been envious and bitter dislike. . . . The work will, in my opinion, go on. I had grave misgivings that it was one of our many fads. Even as a fad it would be a relief. But it is no fad. When I find Dublin young men and women, after a day's hard work, cheerfully, gleefully, taking up this study, I am full of admiration.[59]

Taylor remained a political nationalist, of advanced views but striving to overcome a fear that the language movement, still in its early stages, could diminish the force of political nationalism. His position on the Irish language was not markedly different from Griffith's at that time. The crude instrumentalisation of revivalism was exemplified in the commentary on Taylor's speech of Griffith's adversary D. P. Moran in the *Leader*. It was a perfect instance of Moran's sullen opportunism in advancing his particular conception of an 'Irish Ireland':

> There was something curious in the insistence of separate nationality on the part of English-speaking Irishmen [a category to which Moran himself belonged]. They had need to claim it, and claim it fiercely,

part of the experience of the Irish, Gaelic-speaking, Catholic people and to be at least somewhat affected by Irish Catholic interpretations of history, and aspirations for the future.' He noted that 'Burke all his life retained an interest in the Irish language and its literature'. Conor Cruise O'Brien, *The Great Melody* (London: Sinclair Stevenson, 1992), 23.

59. Taylor, 'Irish Revival'.

> because they had given up the very foundation of their distinct nationality. If they remained Irish they need not have claimed that they were of distinct nationality for no one could deny it. . . . The Anglicisation of Ireland gave birth to the Anglo-Irish screech and testiness, and made it necessary for us to be constantly proving that we were not of a piece with Britishers.[60]

The speech had a renown and breadth of reception that lingered after Taylor's death. W. B. Yeats wrote fifteen years later in his *Reveries over Childhood and Youth* (1916) of the King's Inns speech, striving for magnanimity towards Taylor, whose truculent nationalism drove him to distraction and whom he brilliantly and accurately described as 'an obscure great orator': 'The other day in Dublin I overheard a man murmuring to another one of his speeches as I might some Elizabethan lyric that is in my very bones. It was delivered at some Dublin debate, some College society perhaps. The Lord Chancellor had spoken with balanced unemotional sentences, now self-complacent, now derisive. Taylor began, hesitating and stopping for words, but after speaking very badly for a little, straightened his figure and spoke as out of a dream.'[61]

A principal source of Yeats's information on the debate was Maud Gonne, who had been in the audience. She wrote from Paris that she was 'very glad you wrote about Taylor & quoted his wonderful speech'.[62] Confusingly, Yeats gave an account in *The Trembling of the Veil* (1922) of another debate between Taylor and Fitzgibbon, the latter of whom Yeats disliked:

> I remember Taylor at some public debate, stiff of body and tense of voice; and the contrasting figure of Fitzgibbon, the Lord Justice of Appeal of the moment, with his calm, flowing sentences, satisfactory to hear and impossible to remember. Taylor speaks of a little nation of antiquity, which he does not name, 'set between the Great Empire of Persia and the great Empire of Rome'. Into the mouths of those great

60. *Leader*, 2 November 1901.

61. Yeats, *Autobiographies*, 96–97.

62. Maud Gonne to Yeats, Paris, early 1916, in *The Gonne-Yeats Letters, 1893–1938*, ed. Anna MacBride and A. Norman Jeffares (London: Hutchinson, 1992), 367.

Empires he puts the argument of Fitzgibbon and such as he: 'Join with us in our greatness! What in comparison to that is your little, beggarly nationality?' And then I recall the excitement, the shiver of the nerves, as his voice rose to an ecstatic cry, 'Out of that nation came the salvation of the world'.

He added a footnote referring to *Ulysses*, which had appeared earlier that year: 'In the attack upon Fitzgibbon quoted . . . Taylor made an even more imaginative use of Egypt, but I did not hear that speech.'[63]

Joyce's Knowledge of Taylor

If Joyce did not hear Taylor's speech at the King's Inns, he heard him speak the following month at the Literary and Historical Society in University College. On 20 November 1901 Taylor replied to the inaugural paper of the auditor, Robert Kinahan, on the 'social problem'.[64] The occasion was, in the recall of William Dawson, 'chiefly remarkable for a very brilliant speech by J. F. Taylor'.[65] *St Stephens* noted Joyce's presence and observed that Taylor's style compared with that 'of our own Joyce at his best', though possessed of 'a broadness of sympathy' (which, it is implied, Joyce had yet to acquire). During Taylor's speech, 'dreamy Jimmy and J. F. Byrne, standing on a window sill, looked as if they could say things unutterable.'[66] That is likely to have more to do with their response to Kinahan's crude and obsequiously Catholic treatment of the subject of European socialism than with Taylor's reply.

63. Yeats, *Autobiographies*, 234–35, 235n. With the publication of *Ulysses*, the persona of Taylor had become a site of friendly and faintly comical contestation between Joyce and Yeats. Up to that point, Taylor's memory had been principally maintained in Yeats's rolling sequence of autobiographical writing, which rendered, with a remarkable combination of candour and striving for fairness, his fraught relationship with Taylor.

64. The debate is reported in the *Irish Independent* and the *Daily Express* of 21 November 1901.

65. Meenan, *Centenary History*, 48.

66. *St Stephen's*, December 1901. The comparison of Taylor's speaking style to Joyce's perhaps gives a deepened significance to Joyce's recording of the speech as reworked in *Ulysses*.

Taylor spoke frequently at student societies, and this may not be the only occasion on which Joyce heard him. Taylor's réclame as a patriotic orator among the students of University College was such as to provide a kind of benchmark. Of an excoriating attack by Arthur Clery on Augustine Birrell when the Liberal Chief Secretary for Ireland was brave enough to appear at the L&H in 1907, Joyce's friend Constantine Curran wrote later, 'Arthur Clery spoke as no one since J. F. Taylor had spoken on a university platform.'[67]

Joyce also knew a great deal about Taylor. Unusually for an ardent adherent of the dead Parnell, Joyce was not oblivious to the fate of nationalist public figures who were displaced and excluded by Parnell's rise; this would inform his gathering interest in the remorselessness of politico-cultural cycles. He saw Parnellism as a modernising force and knew its advance was not without unequally distributed costs. Some of Parnell's lieutenants—Timothy Michael Healy in particular—detested Taylor and opposed his going forward as a parliamentary candidate. Whether because of Taylor's support of Isaac Butt ('a kidscad buttended a bland old isaac'),[68] his closeness to Michael Davitt, or his defects of temperament, or because he himself knew nothing about Taylor's interest, Parnell did not override those in the Irish Party opposed to Taylor's candidacy. Taylor was the best example known to Joyce of a casualty of Parnell's rise.

Taylor was a figure of interest to Joyce as someone who had begun as a disciple of Isaac Butt, been an anti-Parnellite in the Split, and ended as a collaborator of Arthur Griffith. The principal reason why it can be stated with confidence that Joyce knew much about Taylor is the extraordinary knowledge of the milieu of Dublin advanced nationalist politics displayed in his review of *The Poems and Ballads of William Rooney* published in the *Daily Express* of 11 December 1902.[69] Rooney, who had died on 6 May 1901, was the closest political intimate of Arthur Griffith, who looked to him as a potential leader of the cause they

67. Michael Tierney, ed., *Struggle with Fortune: A Miscellany for the Centenary of the Catholic University of Ireland, 1854–1954* (Dublin: Browne and Nolan, 1954), 229.

68. *FW* 3.9–10.

69. *OCPW* 61–63.

shared. In his review, Joyce's most provocative and knowing taunt, directed to Griffith, was that Rooney's lamely nationalistic verse owed something to T. W. Rolleston.[70] Joyce knew Griffith detested Rolleston on account of his drift away from nationalism that had found its starkest expression in his support of the British in the Boer War. That detestation was shared by Taylor, and it was Taylor who wrote the most eloquent denunciations of Rolleston, commencing with 'Mr. Rolleston's Recantation', published anonymously in the *United Irishman* of 12 May 1900. Taylor's last act, before his death on 7 November 1902, was to engage in a public exchange of letters with Rolleston about the role of Oliver Cromwell in Ireland that ran in the *Freeman's Journal* from 9 to 25 September 1902. In his obituary written for the *United Irishman*, Griffith identified Taylor as the author of 'Mr. Rolleston's Recantation' and referred to the Cromwell controversy:

> So he scourged the accommodator. At the man's name his eyes were wont to blaze, and when, lying stricken, they showed him the letters of Mr. T. W. Rolleston in the *Freeman's Journal* written to prove that Irish writers had lied about Cromwell, who, according to Mr. Rolleston, was an excellent, humane, and highly moral person, all his scorn blazed up, and with dying hand he penned a scathing letter to the *Freeman's Journal*. It was in keeping with Taylor's splendid character that his last act should have been to lash the barterer of principle.[71]

It seems therefore as if Taylor was not dying at the time of his King's Inns speech, though Joyce is careful in *Ulysses* to stop short of an explicit assertion that he was. There is, by reference to Griffith's obituary of Taylor, a certain retrospective and quasi-ghostly blurring on Joyce's part in transposing the image of the stricken Taylor from Griffith's obituary to the occasion of the King's Inns speech a year previously.

70. Callanan, 'Joyce and the *United Irishman*', 72–77. For an account of the life of Thomas William Rolleston (1857–1920), poet and writer, see W. B. Yeats, *The Collected Letters of W. B. Yeats*, ed. John Kelly (Oxford: Clarendon, 1986), 1:508–9.

71. *United Irishman*, 15 November 1902.

John Henry Newman's *Callista*

If Taylor's speech was within a tradition of Irish political rhetoric, it had also a literary inspiration. The clue lies in what Taylor wrote in excoriation of T. W. Rolleston in May 1900, which was quoted by Griffith on Taylor's death. Taylor had written,

> Cardinal Newman in *Callista* anticipated all Mr. Rolleston's glowing imperialistic outbursts. He makes the comfortable accommodator speak eloquently of Roman grandeur, Roman justice, and Roman power, and his theme was loftier than Mr. Rolleston's lyrical chant on the 'Anglo-Celtic Empire'. Indeed the accommodator has always had the best of the argument. Why be fools and starve when Egypt offers her fleshpots? And in dealing with weak, egoistic natures the enemy of man has one very subtle device. He whispers high moral precepts in their ears before he unfolds his bribes. It is only when the victim is aglow with conscious rectitude that Satan opens his stores and says: 'All these I will give unto thee'.[72]

In the course of his rectorship of the newly established Catholic University in Dublin (1854–58), John Henry Newman published (first in an anonymous edition in 1856) a novel entitled *Callista: A Tale of the Third Century*. It was about the gradual, almost accidental, conversion of Callista, a Greek living in Roman North Africa, whose execution took place in a persecution of Christians during the reign of Decius as Roman emperor (249–51 CE) in one of the refluxes that preceded the imperial adoption of Christianity. Sicca, the town in which the novel is set, is remote from the empire and imperial decrees, but what seals the fate of Callista is the interaction of a plague of locusts which devastates the economy and inflames the local population with the distant decrees of Decius. It is a strangely beautiful novel in which the martyrdom of Callista is the denouement rather than a pre-inscribed outcome. Newman's

72. *United Irishman*, 12 May 1900. The passage is cited by Griffith in instancing Taylor's 'magnificent scorn' in his obituary of Taylor (*United Irishman*, 15 November 1902); see Callanan, 'Joyce and the *United Irishman*', 73–74.

biographer observed that what gave the book much of its interest 'is the largely unexpressed analogy between the situation of those early Christians and that of English Catholics in nineteenth-century Protestant England. In both cases an esoteric faith found itself in involuntary collision with the established religion of an imperial power'.[73]

To judge by Taylor's response, it struck the imagination of its Irish readers from a different angle less to do with religious persecution than with the coercive suasions of an imperial power over subject peoples. That is not really what decides the fate of Callista, who (though not yet a Christian) will not make sacrifice to the Emperor and arises rather from Newman's dramatisation of the cultural religious and political dialogues of adherents of Rome and Christians, and of Romans and Greeks, against a background in which the pagan 'Punic deities' continue to hold a place.

Cornelius, the son of a Roman freedman of distinction, recently returned from Rome at a supper party, extols Rome itself as 'the greatest of all divinities. . . . Emperors rise and fall, Rome remains.'[74] Later in the novel, Callista's pragmatic brother Ariosto brings to Callista's cell a philosopher he esteems, the subtle and conceited Polemo of Rhodes, friend of Plotinus,[75] to persuade her to make the gesture of obeisance to the Emperor. Polemo is the 'comfortable accommodator' described by Taylor, and he addresses Callista in precisely the manner of Taylor's 'intellectual Egyptian'. Resistance is futile and misconceived—'The whole earth, through untold centuries, has at length grown into the imperial dominion of One. . . . The principle of dissolution is eliminated. We have reached the *apotolesma* of the world.' In the culmination of his address, Polemo lauds the tolerance of Rome confronted with the diversity of beliefs within its empire:

> All she said to the peoples, all she dared say to them, was: 'You bear with me, and I will bear with you'. Yet this you will not do; you Christians,

73. Ian Ker, *John Henry Newman* (1988; Oxford: Oxford University Press, 2009), 420.

74. John Henry Newman, *Callista: A Tale of the Third Century* (London: Longmans, Green, 1904), 43, 47.

75. Newman, *Callista*, 84.

> who have no pretence to any territory, who are not even the smallest of the peoples, who are not even a people at all, you have the fanaticism to denounce all other rites but your own, nay, the religion of great Rome. Who are you? upstarts and vagabonds of yesterday. Older religions than yours, more intellectual, more beautiful religions, which have had a position, and a history, and a political influence, have come to nought; and shall you prevail, you, a *congeries*, a hotch-potch of the leavings, and scraps, and broken meat of the great peoples of the East and West? Blush, blush, Grecian Callista, you with a glorious nationality of your own to go shares with some hundred peasants, slaves, thieves, beggars, hucksters, tinkers, cobblers and fishermen! A lady of high character, of brilliant accomplishments, to be the associate of the outcasts of society![76]

It is improbable that the supremely astute Newman, living in Dublin and intellectually alert to Irish nationalism, was entirely oblivious to the possibility of an Irish crossover in the contest of religion and statal allegiance that informed the novel. What is clear is that Taylor was captivated by *Callista* in a profound way, and that the imaginative conceit of his King's Inns speech is a brilliantly realised translation of the discourse of Newman's novel to Irish politics, in which the stunning culmination is Taylor's own. In the annals of Irish rhetoric, it is difficult to think of a significant speech that owed so much to a single (and, as it happened, non-Irish) literary source as Taylor's.

Joyce almost certainly knew of Taylor's invocation of Newman's novel in his denunciation of Rolleston, whether in the original article or in its invocation in Griffith's obituary of Taylor. The inspiration of Newman was in any event discernible in Taylor's King's Inns speech. Joyce was familiar with *Callista*—in his assault on Irish Jesuits in *Stephen Hero*, he sardonically borrows Newman's graphic description of the plague of locusts.[77] Whatever its defiant irreligiousness, that passage is an homage to Newman's prose, which Joyce never ceased to admire—Joyce's early biographer, Stuart Gilbert, recalled his habit in

76. Newman, *Callista*, 312–13.

77. Lernout, *Help My Unbelief*, 117–18.

his Parisian exile of reciting Newman 'to his friends in the mellow after-dinner hours at Les Trianons or Fouquet's (his favourite Parisian restaurants)'.[78] Joyce makes no reference to Newman's novel in *Ulysses*, but his elaborate reworking of Taylor's speech is informed by the novel, translated to an Irish politico-historical setting.

The multiplicity of diverse levels at which Taylor's speech moved Joyce and informed the reworking of the speech in *Ulysses* is remarkable: the triumphant rhetorical moment of a thwarted figure displaced in the rise of Parnell; the inspiration of Newman for a speech in Dublin on the then-novel issue of the Irish Revival; the parallel of the Irish and the Jews; the themes of the cultural collisions and interactions of East and West and the inexorable rise and fall of empires, civilisations, and religions; and the resistance to conquest of subject peoples across vast expanses of time and space of what was for Joyce history sub specie aeternitatis.

Taylor's Speech in 'Aeolus'

In *Ulysses* Joyce radically reworks Taylor's speech and sets it within an intricately geometric interpretative frame, through a diversification of perspectives. The sequence in 'Aeolus' in which Taylor's speech is discussed and purportedly re-narrated is set in the office of the *Evening Telegraph*, the sister paper of the *Freeman's Journal* which shared the same premises. The small office is a curiously crowded space because of the presence of habitués who have no professional reason to be there. Prominent among these are the two figures through whom the reception of Taylor's speech is principally mediated. The first figure, who delivers the central parts of Taylor's speech, is professor MacHugh.[79] He is learned, a purveyor of classicising chiefly Latinate allusion and

78. Stuart Gilbert, introduction to *Letters I* 30.

79. Extratextually, the character of professor MacHugh is considered to be based on Hugh MacNeill (1866–1935), brother of Eoin MacNeill, and of James MacNeill, the second Governor-General of the Irish Free State, after T. M. Healy. He was not a professor but until 1913 a tutor in University College. He was a familiar figure in the offices of the *Freeman's Journal* and the *Evening Telegraph* and later in the *Irish Times*. Journalists working on the papers bestowed on him the title of 'professor'. Igoe, *Real People of Joyce's 'Ulysses'*, 185–86.

cliché, and given to un-obstreperous declamation that does not violate the norms of urbanity that prevail in the office. His title is given in lower case and the accumulation of anomalies subverts the idea that he is in fact a professor. If he were a professor, what would he be doing at midday in a newspaper office, where he even answers the phone? Moreover, reflecting Joyce's social realism in rendering the Dublin of 1904, his 'frayed stained shirtcuffs' and his 'unglazed linen collar . . . soiled by his withering hair' do not suggest professorial status or income. None of these hints quite prepare the reader for the interposed comment, in the course of his rendering of Taylor's oration, that 'a dumb belch of hunger cleft his speech.'[80]

The second figure is J. J. O'Molloy, who is conceived by Joyce with exceeding imaginative subtlety. Unlike professor MacHugh, he has no shadow of a conjectural real-life correlative, nor could he have. He has been succinctly epitomised as 'a broken-down barrister.'[81] He is also mortally stricken, as is made plain from his entrance when he meets Simon Dedalus:

> —How are you, Dedalus?
> —Well. And yourself?
> J.J. O'Molloy shook his head.[82]

J. J. O'Molloy has a dual existence in the novel. He is both a character in his own right and, as if in a spectral mirror, a reflection of J. F. Taylor, whose death, aged forty-nine, had occurred two years before the date on which *Ulysses* is set. (The exorbitant topographical fetishisation of the Dublin of *Ulysses* distracts from the fact that it is also a city of ghosts in which the living and the recently dead fleetingly overlap.) This dual aspect enables Joyce to render O'Molloy as a figure whose character is quite at odds with the fractious persona of the real-life Taylor. J. J. O'Molloy is mild and intuitively perceptive, sympathetic to Stephen, and interested in his future as a writer. Joyce's exaltedness in his negotiation

80. *U* 7.487, *U* 7.820–21.

81. Adrian Hardiman, *Joyce in Court: James Joyce and the Law* (London: Head of Zeus, 2017), 106.

82. *U* 7.286–90.

of the living and the dead, of actuality and literary invention, goes so far as to allow him to include in Stephen's stream of consciousness on J. J. O'Molloy a disorienting reference to Joyce's own story 'The Dead': 'Believe he does some literary work for the *Express* with Gabriel Conroy.'[83] Thus O'Molloy is only incidentally a conventionally conceived fictional figure in the novel. He owes his existence to Joyce's elaborate strategising of how the Taylor speech, as rendered by professor MacHugh, is to be apprehended. The same strategising ensures what may at first reading seem odd—and disappointing at the level of sentimental expectation (which Joyce deliberately holds in check)—that it is professor MacHugh rather than the more sympathetic proxy for J. F. Taylor who delivers the version of the Taylor speech.

The bustling emergence of the editor Myles Crawford from his inner sanctum sharpens the exchanges in the outer office. Professor MacHugh opens his declamation on empire with the statement, 'We think of Rome, imperial, imperious, imperative.'[84] He proceeds to condemn the civilisation of Rome, reducible to a 'cloacal obsession' in which the construction of sewers and water closets anticipated the English who followed. He holds obdurately to his theme: 'We were always loyal to lost causes, the professor said. Success for us is the death of the intellect and of the imagination. We were never loyal to the successful.' He resumes, 'The closetmaker and the cloacamaker will never be lords of our spirit. We are liege subjects of the Catholic chivalry of Europe that foundered at Trafalgar and of the empire of the spirit, not an *imperium*, that went under with the Athenian fleets at Aegospotami. Yes, yes. They went under.'[85]

Myles Crawford vaunts the feat of Ignatius Gallaher in reporting the Phoenix Park murders, and lauds other successful members of his profession. He passes on to a lament for the decline of eloquence at the Irish bar in remarks directed to J. J. O'Molloy, who responds by referring to a speech of Seymour Bushe in the Childs murder trial (which Joyce

83. *U* 7.306–7.

84. *U* 7.484–85. In *Stephen Hero*, in the debate on Joyce's paper, Whelan, 'the orator of the College', declaims that Greek art stands aloof and alone for all time', and is 'imperial, imperious and imperative' (*SH* 101).

85. *U* 7.551–53, 7.564–68.

had attended as a student in October 1899),[86] reciting, under the headline 'A Polished Period', a rather extravagant evocation of Michelangelo's statue of Moses in Rome.

Stephen is embarrassed to find he is moved: 'Stephen, his blood wooed by grace of language and gesture, blushed.'[87] Part of the effect was achieved by J. J. O'Molloy's gestures: 'His slim hand with a wave graced echo and fall.'[88] Rhetoric and patriotism are linked in 'Aeolus', as are forensic oratory and journalism. Stephen is susceptible to both while willing himself to resist the temptation they represent. That resistance is a defining attribute of his conception of the artist he has not yet become. After professor MacHugh commences his rendition of Taylor's speech, Stephen thinks, 'Noble words coming. Look out. Could you try your hand at it yourself?'[89] Joyce is also pre-signalling the impact of the more powerful Taylor speech on Stephen (an impact which is not otherwise described).

Professor MacHugh delivers his version of Taylor's King's Inns speech. It is a redraft by Joyce of the idea of the speech which superbly maintains a fidelity to what gave Taylor's speech its contemporary renown, while also improving on it. The principal change wrought by Joyce to Taylor's rhetorical conceit is that Taylor's 'intellectual Egyptian' becomes a high priest of Egypt in whom the merged authority of religion and state were vested. Joyce thereby elided Taylor's subtext of an attack on the Trinity professors (subsequently elaborated on in his *Freeman's Journal* article): 'It seemed to me that I had been transported into a country far away from this country, into an age remote from this age, that I stood in ancient Egypt and that I was listening to the speech of some highpriest of that land addressed to the youthful Moses.'[90]

86. Hardiman, *Joyce in Court*, 162.

87. *U* 7.776.

88. *U* 7.772. The only other occasion on which a similar blush is elicited from Stephen is in *A Portrait*. In the Christmas dinner scene, Mr Casey denounces the sequence of betrayals of the Irish patriotic cause by the Catholic bishops: 'His face was glowing with anger and Stephen felt the glow rise to his own cheek as the spoken words thrilled him' (*P* 1.1108–9).

89. *U* 7.836–37.

90. *U* 8.830–34.

Professor MacHugh's rendering of Taylor's speech continues, 'Why will you jews not accept our culture, our religion and our language? You are a tribe of nomad herdsmen; we are a mighty people. You have no cities nor no wealth; our cities are hives of humanity and our galleys, trireme and quadrireme . . . furrow the waters of the known globe. You have but emerged from primitive conditions; we have a literature, a priesthood, an agelong history and a polity.'[91]

The reference to 'a polity' is striking. It is central to Joyce's comparative thinking about Ireland as he refined it in exile. Conquered by a neighbouring imperial power, it was denied self-constitution as a polity and the narratives and literature of independent statehood by which Great Britain defined itself. The closing peroration of Joyce's reworking of Taylor mingled with the book of Exodus runs,

> But, ladies and gentlemen, had the youthful Moses listened to and accepted that view of life, had he bowed his head and bowed his will and bowed his spirit before that arrogant admonition he would never have brought the chosen people out of their house of bondage, nor followed the pillar of the cloud by day. He would never have spoken with the Eternal amid lightnings on Sinai's mountaintop, nor would he ever have come down with the light of inspiration shining in his countenance and bearing in his arms the tables of the law, graven in the language of the outlaw.[92]

Afterwards professor MacHugh craves an acknowledgement of the effect created by his performance, which he is denied. In the silence, J. J. O'Molloy, 'not without regret', observes abstractedly, in his spectral aspect, 'And yet he died without having entered the land of promise.'[93]

With this, Parnell flares into memory. In his speech in the Rotunda on his return to Ireland, he had famously expressed the aspiration 'to walk with you within the sight of the promised land, which, please God, I will enter with you,'[94] lending personal identification to a pre-existing

91. *U* 7.845–50.

92. *U* 7.862–69.

93. *U* 7.871–72.

94. Callanan, *Parnell Split*, 63.

comparison with Moses. His supporters drew heavily on the parallel in the Split. While never far away, evocations of Parnell directly or at length are comparatively infrequent in *Ulysses*, reflecting Joyce's calculated obliquity in his treatment of the Irish leader. When professor MacHugh, still trying to drum up a compliment, says 'that is oratory', it is as if the spell of Taylor's speech is broken. Stephen's thought pivots away from Parnell to the Daniel O'Connell of two of the famous 'monster meetings' for repeal of the Union in 1843: 'Gone with the wind. Hosts at Mullaghmast and Tara of the kings. Miles of ears of porches. The tribune's words, howled and scattered to the four winds. A people sheltered within his voice. Dead noise. Akasic records of all that ever anywhere wherever was. Love and laud him: me no more.'[95]

Still trying to cadge a response, the professor nudges Stephen: 'That is fine, isn't it? It has the prophetic vision. *Fuit Ilium!* The sack of windy Troy. Kingdoms of this world. The masters of the Mediterranean are fellaheen today.'[96] Greeks and Trojans coalesce in their geostrategic obscurity. Troy scarcely equated to contemporary Turkey. The complacent dismissal of contemporary Greece (to whose achievement of a form of independence Joyce was greatly sympathetic) exemplifies professor MacHugh's inexorable drift from Latinate fatalism to passive imperialism.

Joyce's strategy of having professor MacHugh deliver Taylor's speech and framing it by reference to the professor's pronouncements before and after is of masterly intricacy. As Joyce worked it out, it required and called into being the figure of J. J. O'Molloy. The realisation of that strategy enlisted all his imaginative cunning to convey something that is central to his treatment of Irish politics and rhetoric. On a superficial reading, professor MacHugh's earlier declamations are consistent with the spirit of the speech of Taylor which he is shortly to deliver. But in a characteristic Joycean move, professor MacHugh's declamation is a negation of Taylor's argument. There is a fundamental disjuncture. For all his own immiseration, professor MacHugh's views are those of the

95. *U* 7.880–84.
96. *U* 7.909–11.

Catholic professional classes. The lowercase-*p* professor delivers as a party piece a speech whose force he apprehends at the level of pure rhetoric but to whose political and imaginative resonance he is deaf. His pedagogic classicism immunises him against any idea of revival. He does not quite 'get' the speech that he re-delivers. His conception of Ireland as a country whose native Catholic leadership went under the waves at Trafalgar like the Greeks at Aegospotami is as extravagant in its absurdity as any of the propositions of the Citizen in the 'Cyclops' episode later in the novel. Above all, professor MacHugh sentimentalises Irish defeat and abjection. After that lyrical outburst, O'Madden Burke chimes in, drawing on Matthew Arnold via Yeats, 'They went forth to battle but they always fell'.[97] Insofar as Taylor's speech had within its larger argument a specific target, Joyce redirects it through the persona of professor MacHugh away from Trinity professors to the Irish educated professional class, which largely identified itself with the Irish Parliamentary Party. That underscores the rendering of Taylor's speech on the revival of the Irish language delivered by a classicist pedagogue temperamentally impervious to the idea of *any* Irish revival, linguistic or political.

Authorially, Joyce in *Ulysses* leaves Taylor's speech to speak for itself within the intricate framing devices of the 'Aeolus' episode, which permits Joyce (and Stephen) to hold himself at a certain distance from it. Stephen Dedalus must hold out against the siren songs of patriotism and rhetoric. If Stephen responds, it is in rendering his own enigmatic 'Parable of the Plums'. Yet within the framing devices, the Taylor speech rendered by professor MacHugh is left, as it were, geometrically open. Joyce's own tendresse towards Taylor's speech as reworked in *Ulysses* is reflected in the fact that it is the only part of *Ulysses* that he recorded, with haunting rhythm and passion, on phonodisc in 1924.[98]

97. *U* 7.572–73; Gifford, *Ulysses Annotated*, 139.

98. Abby Bender, *Israelites in Erin: Exodus, Revolution, and the Irish Revival* (Syracuse, NY: Syracuse University Press, 2015), 144, 231n59. The only other recording Joyce made is of the gossip of the washerwomen by the banks of the Liffey in the twilight of flitting bats, from *Finnegans Wake*, Book I, Chapter 8. The two recordings are in different voices; something of the

When Sylvia Beach asked Joyce to record part of *Ulysses*, he chose the Taylor speech as the only passage that could be lifted out of *Ulysses* and the only one that was 'declamatory' and therefore suitable for recital. Beach intuited the depth of Joyce's affinity with Taylor's speech: 'I have an idea that it was not only for declamatory reasons alone that he chose this passage from Aeolus. I believe that it expressed something he wanted said and preserved in his own voice. As it rings out—"he lifted his voice above it boldly"—it is more, one feels, than mere oratory.'[99]

Beach's impression is consistent with Joyce's treatment of Taylor's speech in *Ulysses*. Stephen must sternly resist its lure, but Stephen's coldness towards professor MacHugh does not equate to the austerely purist objection on Joyce's part to Taylor's oratory in its nationalist aspect that some commentators have taken it to be. The motif of the 'Aeolus' episode is rhetoric. Stephen's ambivalent disquiet about rhetoric and Joyce's loathing of essentialist nationalism, which Taylor's speech transcends, are distinct. Joyce's treatment of the Irish political—and of politics beyond Ireland—consistently resists neat theoretical extrapolation, superficial equivalencies, and facile judgement.

'Meer marchant Taylor's fablings of a race': The Significance of Taylor's Speech for Joyce

Joyce apprehended more incisively than Taylor the buried nationalist resonances of Taylor's speech. Taylor had found in the subject of the Irish language the pulse for an emotionally powerful restatement of nationalism. The refractory Parnellite was almost involuntarily situating the contemporary revival within the paradigm of the high nationalist idiom of the late 1870s and the 1880s, the last period of political renascence now pushed back by the Parnell Split into imperfectly apprehended historical memory.

Cork of John Stanislaus Joyce endures acoustically in the whispering chatter of his son's *Finnegans Wake* recording.

99. Sylvia Beach, *Shakespeare and Company* (London: Faber and Faber, 1956), 177–78.

In his speech Taylor did, however, add something important that the urgent advances of the Land War and the swiftness of Parnell's rise lacked: a sense of Irish cultural destitution which itself, in a weird and complicated spiral, owed much to the Split and Parnell's death. The imaginative rift created by the desolation of the Split and the mourning of Parnell had suddenly opened up the Irish past, and not only that immediate past from which the land agitation and Parnell came forth, but the Ireland that was anterior to Parnell. This was a complex phenomenon that was not obvious to most Irish people and observers at the time, or was at best half grasped. The enumeration in Parnellite rhetoric of heroic precursors of Parnell, which excited the derision of T. M. Healy, was crudely instrumental, but emblematic of a deeper sense of loss that Parnell's sympathisers could not adequately articulate. Both the transformation and the perception of it were unfolding processes that lay outside conventional notions of political consequence and causality. It was in the domain of literary imagination rather than politics that the transformation was apprehended. This imaginative sequel to the Split and Parnell's death was fully appreciated by only two writers, Joyce and Yeats, though other writers such as Katharine Tynan and Standish O'Grady had an intimation of how the Split had reinstated in modern Ireland a sense of the desolation of historico-cultural loss.

When he was writing *Ulysses*, Joyce realised something which Taylor—who had to negotiate his unrepented anti-Parnellism in the Split—did not quite grasp: that the speech had as much to do with the fallout, imaginative and political, of the Split as it had to do with the Irish Revival. Joyce's rendering of Taylor's speech in *Ulysses* presents an oblique but persistent querying of the naivety of 'the Irish Revival' as a quasi-ideology, the idea that only an Irish-speaking Ireland could represent a true and legitimate consummation of Irish independence. This was the idea that Taylor had simply dismissed in his speech as beyond the bounds of feasibility, but it was an ideological aspiration that Joyce in his generation could not simply pass over. Joyce counters the espousal of a willed counter-historical revival of Irish as the only authentic language of the Irish people, by the evocation of time—that is, time as the cycle of civilisations, nations, and empires (brilliantly turning the central conceit of Taylor's speech in explicit opposition to revivalism in its ideologically 'hard' form), and the time of human mortality, of Taylor, of the dying J. J. O'Molloy and the dead Parnell, and even of the terrible 'dumb belch of hunger' emitted by professor MacHugh. The mortal condition is not only about death but about the limits of what is humanly achievable, of which the more zealous revivalists took little account. It is what informs the affable midday melancholy in the *Evening Telegraph* office.

The idea of cultural transience subsists within the impermanence of form of the speech itself. Taking a cue from X, Joyce exaggerates in 'Aeolus' the supposed spontaneity of the speech and absence of press coverage, so that all that survives of Taylor's speech is the recollection of professor MacHugh and whatever anyone else present might have happened to recall. Formally it has a double ephemerality: a speech recalling a speech. It is *Ulysses* itself that rescues the speech from prospective oblivion, two decades after its delivery.

What the rendering of Taylor's speech in *Ulysses* shows is that Joyce saw revivalism as a political phenomenon of the time. He rejected, as did Taylor, the transcendental meta-historical pretensions of revivalism. In this Joyce differed from many of his peers in University College, who readily assented to the idea that revivalism stood outside contemporary politics. He was not for a moment susceptible to the idea that the Gaelic League, and revivalism generally, was politically innocent or transcended the contemporary political.

Joyce was intrigued by the interrelationship of the treatment of the ancient past and at least implied prophecy of the future in Taylor's speech. This engenders the sardonic echo of Taylor's speech later in the 'Ithaca' episode, where Joyce completes the running saga of Throwaway, the horse that had that day won the Ascot Gold Cup which Bantam Lyons erroneously believed Bloom to have backed at twenty to one, prompting a resentment of Bloom for his failure either to impart his occult knowledge to his indigent and avidly betting fellow citizens or even to include them in the bounty of his good luck by standing drinks in Barney Kiernan's.[100] When Bloom had been given back his copy of that day's *Freeman's Journal and National Press* by Bantam Lyons, 'which he had been about to throw away (subsequently thrown away), he had proceeded towards the oriental edifice of the Turkish and Warm Baths of Leinster Street, with the light of inspiration shining in his countenance and bearing in his arms the secret of his race, graven in the language of prediction.'[101]

Both the rhetorical and time-transforming aspects of the Taylor speech in *Ulysses* inform Joyce's *Finnegans Wake* reference to Taylor. There Joyce wheels round what he terms 'meer marchant taylor's fablings of a race' in time and political perspective to become a retrospective observation on Irish independence,[102] emblematised by references to Eamon de Valera. The passage in its principal strain, as I read it, is a critique from a hostile English, or Irish Unionist, vantage of the destruction of the prospects for the independence of Ireland ('the wastobe land, a lottuse land, a luctuous land, Emerald-illium') wrought by the violent means by which it was achieved.[103]

What, then, did Taylor's speech mean for Joyce? It revealed the possibility of invoking politically the culture of ancient Ireland and Irish history, in a way that was distinct from that of the Gaelic League and essentialist cultural nationalism, without denying the impetus of the Gaelic League. The contemporary élan of the language revival could be captured and redirected, as Taylor had contrived to do in the King's Inns. Joyce was susceptible to the argument of the kind enunciated by Taylor that married Ireland's artistic and historical heritage with high nationalism. The argument, implicitly dismissive of revivalism, of Joyce's

100. A. Nicholas Fargnoli and Michael Patrick Gillespie, *James Joyce A to Z* (London: Bloomsbury, 1995), 216.

101. *U* 17.337–41.

102. This encompasses an allusion to the Merchant Tailors' Guild of St John the Baptist, established in Dublin in 1704; Gifford, *Ulysses Annotated*, 61. The 'meer' is likely to be a gentle dig at Yeats's unforgettable half-admiring, half-condemnatory characterisation of Taylor in his autobiographical writings.

103. *FW* 61.28–62.25.

magnificent 1907 Trieste lecture 'Ireland: Island of Saints and Sages' is in the line of Taylor's speech: 'Just as ancient Egypt is dead, so is ancient Ireland. Its dirge has been sung and the seal set upon its gravestone. The ancient national spirit that spoke through the centuries through the mouths of fabulous seers, wandering minstrels, and [Jacobite] poets has vanished from the world with the death of James Clarence Mangan. With his death the long tradition of the triple order of the ancient bards also died. Today other bards, inspired by other ideas, have their turn.'[104]

A few months after giving this lecture, Joyce, in his article 'L'Irlanda alla sbarra' ('Ireland at the Bar'), plangently described the wrongly executed Myles Joyce, who spoke only Irish, as 'left over from a culture which is not ours'.[105]

104. *OCPW* 125.
105. *OCPW* 146.

9

Moving towards Exile

ENCOUNTERING LITERARY AND RADICAL DUBLIN, 1902–4

I think that the tensions that gave [Yeats and Joyce] their magnitude came from tensions produced from a transition from the nation to the State. The same transition was made forty years before when Norway, with Ibsen as its dominating figure, passed from the consciousness of the community of a nation into the consciousness of the community as a State. Yeats and Joyce show, as Ibsen showed, their stressful involvement in the political and social drift of their country. . . . I should place the period of transition in Ireland between the Parnell epoch and the establishment of a national government.

—PADRAIC COLUM, JUNE 1967[1]

James writes quietly and without haste and seems to write not what he is thinking but what he has thought. He does not grasp at a thought when it is presented to him, but waits until it has settled in his mind's perspective and then arranges it with easy lucidity, writing clearly, minutely and consequently.

—STANISLAUS JOYCE, OCTOBER 1904[2]

1. Padraic Colum, foreword to Curran, *James Joyce Remembered*, ix.

2. S. Joyce, entry for 2 October 1904, in *Dublin Diary*, 124.

THE TWO YEARS FROM JOYCE leaving University College to his leaving Ireland teem with events that would feature in his writing. The change in ambience and tempo from the claustral setting of the university was marked. It was not merely that he now met the leading figures of the Irish Literary Revival; he set out to enlarge his exposure to the experience of Dublin life, which included the contemporary political. If it was not from the outset, it became a poignant quest to see if Dublin could hold him. The persona of Stephen Dedalus in *A Portrait of the Artist as a Young Man* is a misleading guide to the Joyce of 1902–4.

Joyce experimented with exile in Paris for most of December 1902, returning for Christmas, and leaving Paris again in April on receiving a telegram from his father that his mother was dying. The death of May Joyce on 4 August 1903 was followed by a plummeting deterioration in the circumstances of the Joyce household. Joyce wrote the essay 'A Portrait of the Artist', rejected by the editors of *Dana* in January 1904, and immediately commenced writing his novel *Stephen Hero*. He wrote a number of the poems that would make up *Chamber Music*, and in August 'The Sisters', the first of the stories that would comprise *Dubliners*, appeared in the *Irish Homestead*. In June he met Nora Barnacle. He resided in and abruptly departed from the Martello tower in Sandycove in September. He left Ireland with Nora on 8 October 1904. In these crowded months Joyce began to revise, on his own terms, his conception of the political, and of the relationship of the political to his nascent art.

Accosting the Twilight

I have met with you, bird, too late, or if not too worm and early.[3]

It was not difficult to meet the leading Irish writers in the Dublin of 1902, but Joyce set about doing so with a certain system, beginning naturally with George Russell in August 1902. Two months later, he accosted W. B. Yeats near the National Library, and they repaired to the smoking room of a restaurant on Sackville Street. Yeats wrote a long account of their

3. *FW* 37.13; see Richard Ellmann, *Yeats and Joyce* (Dublin: Dolmen, 1967), 456.

meeting, which he had intended for a preface to his *Ideas of Good and Evil* published the following year, on the proofs of which he had been working in the National Library. Joyce read him 'a beautiful though immature and eccentric harmony of little prose descriptions and meditations'. He professed himself indifferent to Yeats's opinion of them, before battle commenced:

> Then, putting down his book, he began to explain all his objections to everything I had ever done. Why had I concerned myself with politics, with folklore, with the historical setting of events, and so on? Above all, why had I written about ideas, why had I condescended to make generalizations? These things were all a sign of the cooling of the iron, of the fading out of inspiration. I had been puzzled, but now I was confident again. He is from the Royal University, I thought, and he thinks that everything has been settled by Thomas Aquinas, so we need not trouble about it. I have met so many like him. He would probably review my book in the newspapers if I sent it there. But the next moment he spoke of a friend of mine [Oscar Wilde] who after a wild life had turned Catholic on his deathbed. He said that he hoped his conversion was not sincere. He did not like to think that he had been untrue to himself at the end. No, I had not understood him yet.

A long apologia from Yeats on the artistic use of folklore was met by the retort,

> 'Generalizations aren't made by poets, they are made by men of letters. They are no use.'
>
> Presently he got up to go, and, as he was going out, he said, 'I am twenty. How old are you?' I told him, but I am afraid I said I was a year younger than I am. He said with a sigh, 'I thought as much. I have met you too late. You are too old.'
>
> And now I am still undecided as to whether I shall send this book to the Irish papers for review. The younger generation is knocking at my door as well as theirs.[4]

4. Richard Ellmann, *The Identity of Yeats* (London: Faber and Faber, 1954), 85–88; Ellmann, *James Joyce*, 100–103.

In Russell's perhaps more plausible if second-hand account, Joyce's parting shot was a role reversal: 'We have met too late. You are too old for me to have any effect on you.'[5] While no doubt pleased with the irruptive éclat, Joyce later disavowed any suggestion of disrespect towards Yeats. Reviewing the proofs of Herbert Gorman's biography, he noted, 'The story as constantly retailed in the press is another story of Dublin public house gossip. J.J. at this time had an immense admiration for Yeats as a poet and though he did say the words or something to the effect attributed to him they were never said in the tone of contempt which is implied in the story.'[6]

Yeats was somewhat more affronted than his gracefully self-deprecatory account might suggest. He complained to his friend William Kirkpatrick Magee, 'Never have I encountered so much pretension with so little to show for it.'[7] In *The Trembling of the Veil* (1923) he recalled the response to his counter-Victorian declamations at the Rhymers' Club, where Lionel Johnston and others met over the Cheshire Cheese off Fleet Street in London: 'I say this because I am ashamed to admit that I had these ideas and that whenever I began to speak of them a gloomy silence fell upon the room. A young Irish poet, who wrote excellently but had the worst manners, was to say a few years later, "You do not talk like a poet, you talk like a man of letters", and if all the Rhymers had not been polite, if most of them had not been to Oxford or Cambridge, the greater number would have said the same thing.'[8]

In his 'Modern Ireland' address in America in 1932–33, he wrote, 'I remember the young Joyce as he [was] when I first met him in Dublin,

5. Ellmann, *James Joyce*, 101–2n. Curran adopts Russell's account in *James Joyce Remembered*: 'I have come too late to influence you; you are too old' (33–34).

6. Ellmann, *James Joyce*, 101n. What Ellmann called 'Joyce's middle-aged disclaimer' to Gorman continued, 'The whole point of the remark so far as he can remember was that the elder poet had grown up in an earlier aesthetic atmosphere (William Morris etc.) in which the younger had no part'. This seems less convincing than the disclaimer around tone and conveys perhaps the faintest hint of remorse. (Ellmann, *Yeats and Joyce*, 456).

7. John Eglinton, *Irish Literary Portraits* (London: Macmillan, 1935), 137. He wrote of Joyce, 'With Yeats he amused himself by delivering the sentence of the new generation' (137).

8. Yeats, *Autobiographies*, 165–66.

and he will forgive me for saying, knowing how much I admire his work, that [he] seemed to me in those [days] possessed of an extreme irritation, mounting to almost ungovernable rage against all that [he] saw and heard, even against the mere bodies and faces that passed him in the street.'[9]

It was an extraordinary Dublin encounter in which Joyce had the advantage of surprise. Yeats was caught off guard by Joyce's aloof offensive. He was unprepared for a meeting that was a point in a trajectory that Joyce had already begun to chart with 'The Day of the Rabblement' and his James Clarence Mangan paper in University College, but it was impressive that he realised his encounter with the calm but insistently assertive graduate of University College was of some significance. From Joyce's perspective, the fact of their meeting was more important than what was said. It was a necessary event in the intersecting sequence of their careers that Joyce had already decided would be constitutive of a modern Irish literature, and which required a correlative of personal acquaintance. It achieved more than it needed to: Joyce had irruptively inscribed himself into Yeats's narrative, as Yeats was already inscribed in his own.

It was probably at a meeting some months later that Joyce conveyed his admiration of Yeats's stories 'The Tables of the Law' and 'The Adoration of the Magi'. Elkin Mathews republished the stories in 1904 with a prefatory note from Yeats: 'These two stories were privately printed some years ago. I do not think I should have reprinted them had I not met a young man in Ireland the other day, who liked them very much and nothing else I have written.'[10]

Yeats wrote Joyce, 'You have a very delicate talent but I cannot say whether for prose or verse.' He said, 'I will do anything for you I can but

9. Skelton and Clark, *Irish Renaissance*, 20.

10. W. B. Yeats, *'The Tables of the Law' and 'The Adoration of the Magi'* (London: Elkin Mathews, 1904). Ellmann's suggestion that the discussion of Yeats's stories occurred when Yeats and Joyce met in September 1903 seems preferable to Stanislaus Joyce's belief it took place at their first meeting: Ellmann, *James Joyce*, 129; Richard Ellmann, *Eminent Domain: Yeats among Wilde, Joyce, Pound, Eliot, and Auden* (New York: Oxford University Press, 1967), 42; S. Joyce, *My Brother's Keeper*, 183.

I am afraid it will not be a great deal.'[11] In fact he did much, through introductions in Dublin and London and counsel politely and fearlessly tendered.[12]

Yeats had Lady Gregory invite Joyce to dine at the Nassau Hotel on 4 November 1902 to meet Yeats's father,[13] who became in later years a perceptive admirer of Joyce's works. Two weeks later Joyce wrote Lady Gregory a letter of fierce importunacy. He was going 'alone and friendless' to Paris: 'And though I seem to have been driven out of my country here as a misbeliever I have found no man yet with a faith like mine.'[14] She was not unsympathetic: 'Poor boy, I am afraid he will knock his ribs against the earth, but he has grit and will succeed in the end', she wrote, urging Yeats to meet him in London on his way through. She wrote also to John Millington Synge and sent Joyce to E. V. Longworth, the editor of the *Daily Express*, who agreed to send him books to review.[15] She did not offer financial support, but Joyce responded appreciatively to her reply on 1 December, the day he left Dublin.[16] However, he was always harshly ungrateful to her thereafter. She unfairly bore the burden of his sense of having been shut out from the Literary Revival. Joyce was desperately short of money in Paris but unflinching; he was compelled to ask his mother to draw on her meagre resources, which she readily did.[17]

In his letter to Lady Gregory, Joyce said he had met Synge. During Joyce's second Paris sojourn, Synge came to Paris for a week to evacuate his room on the Rue d'Assas. He must have alerted Joyce, who on 8 March 1903 called and left a card.[18] Synge sent a note to Joyce at the

11. Ellmann, *James Joyce*, 104.

12. Foster, *W. B. Yeats*, 1:276–78.

13. S. Joyce, *My Brother's Keeper*, 155; Ellmann, *James Joyce*, 104.

14. Joyce to Lady Gregory, n.d. [November 1902], *Letters I* 53.

15. Ellmann, *James Joyce*, 107–8.

16. Joyce to Lady Gregory, 1 December 1902, *Letters II* 18.

17. Curran was convinced that Joyce's circumstances in Paris were so poor as to undermine his health. In his 1964 interview with May Monaghan, he noted that she 'agreed that the hard experience of his first visit to Paris before his mother's death probably affected his later health.' C. P. Curran, Joyce notebook, UCD Special Collections, Constantine Curran Collection, CUR MS 6.

18. Their awareness of each other's movements is attested to by a letter of Synge to his mother from London on 23 January 1903 in which he referred to visiting editors in London: 'This week

Hotel Corneille to meet 'under the Odeon cloisters in front of your door'.[19] They met on 9 March and saw a good deal of each other in the days that followed. Something of their encounters is captured, as if through a haze of wine, in Stephen's memory in *Ulysses*, prompted by Mulligan's suggestion that the 'the tramper Synge' was looking to murder him: 'Harsh gargoyle face that warred against me over our mess of hash of lights in rue Saint André des Arts. In words of words for words, palabras. Oisin with Patrick. Faunman he met in Clamart woods, brandishing a winebottle. *C'est vendredi saint!* Murthering Irish. His image, wandering, he met. I mine. I met a fool i' the forest.'[20]

Stanislaus, to whom Joyce had evidently talked a good deal about Synge, wrote, 'In Paris my brother met John Synge, who was living there almost as poor as my brother himself, and had many quarrelsome discussions with him about language, style, poetry, the drama, and literature in general. . . . When [Synge] was at a loss for an argument, [he] was inclined to lose his temper. When that happened Synge's angry face and wagging beard used to send my brother into kinks of laughter that made Synge still angrier.'[21]

Synge reported back to Lady Gregory,

> He seems to be pretty badly off, and is wandering around Paris rather unbrushed and rather indolent, spending his studious moments in the National Library reading Ben Jonson. French literature I understand is beneath him! Still he interested me a good deal and as he is

---

Joyce—on his way back to Paris—[is] going to them all so I will not go round for a few days as it is better not to have too many Irishmen turning up at once'. John Millington Synge, *The Collected Letters of John Millington Synge*, ed. Ann Saddlemyer (Oxford: Clarendon, 1983), 1:66–67; Ellmann, *James Joyce*, 120. This also suggests a greater degree of integration of Joyce into the nexus of the Literary Revival than he ever deigned to acknowledge.

19. Callanan, 'Joyce and the *United Irishman*', 84.

20. *U* 9.576–79. Padraic Colum recalled that Synge 'had a laugh that was half grim, half good-humoured' (*Road Round Ireland*, 363). The sense of a vinously mirrored exchange between Joyce and Synge is deepened by the later observation of John Butler Yeats, who drew and painted Synge, and had met Joyce, that Joyce's 'portrait published in this month's *Little Review* reminds me of Synge'. John Butler Yeats to Augusta Gregory, 14 August 1920, quoted in Joseph M. Hassett, *The 'Ulysses' Trials: Beauty and Truth Meet the Law* (Dublin: Lilliput, 2016), 83.

21. S. Joyce, *My Brother's Keeper*, 213.

being gradually won over by the charm of French life his time in Paris is not wasted. He talks of coming back to Dublin in the summer to live there on journalism while he does his serious work at his leisure. I cannot think that he will ever be a poet of importance, but his intellect is extraordinarily keen and if he keeps fairly sane he ought to do excellent essay writing.[22]

Joyce responded with implacable dogmatism to *Riders to the Sea,* which Synge showed him, and which Yeats had already told him was 'quite Greek'. Joyce reported to Stanislaus, 'I am glad to say that ever since I read it I have been riddling it mentally till it has [not] a sound spot. It is tragic about all the men that are drowned in the islands: but thanks be to God Synge isn't an Aristotelian. I told him part of my esthetic: he says I have a mind like Spinosa.'[23] Joyce relayed his criticism to Padraic Colum that the play was too short to sustain the tragic mood: 'You can't have a tragedy in a play that lasts for twenty minutes.'[24] Joyce told Stanislaus a good deal about his meetings with Synge. Stanislaus wrote, 'He called *Riders to the Sea* a tragic poem. Synge did not agree, but he listened and countered my brother's arguments calmly. Perhaps he was mollified by the fact that the rhythm of certain phrases had stuck in my brother's memory—he already knew Maurya's final speeches almost by heart—and he repeated them with such a keen sense of their beauty that it must have tempered his strictures.'[25] Later in Trieste, Joyce would collaborate with his pupil and friend Nicolò Vidacovich on a translation of Synge's play into Italian.[26]

What else was discussed between Synge and Joyce in Paris is a matter of conjecture.[27] Stanislaus recorded that 'Synge was inclined to take

22. J. M. Synge to Lady Gregory, 26 March 1903, in *Collected Letters of John Millington Synge,* 1:68.

23. Joyce to Stanislaus Joyce, 9 March 1903, *Letters II* 35. Some of this re-entered Joyce's mind as he read in Rome of the *Playboy* riots: Joyce to Stanislaus, 11 February 1907, *Letters II* 212.

24. P. Colum, *Road Round Ireland,* 365–66.

25. S. Joyce, *My Brother's Keeper,* 213–14.

26. Ellmann, *James Joyce,* 267.

27. There may be a partial clue in the perhaps *Playboy*-proleptic passage in *Ulysses* (9.850–58) which ends, 'In rue Monsieur le Prince I thought it'.

the Irish language revival seriously.'[28] This did not betoken sympathy. Synge was highly critical of the language revival, a subject on which he was more trenchant than Joyce. In a remarkable piece written in the form of a letter and never published in his lifetime, Synge wrote, 'I believe in Ireland. I believe the nation that has made a place in history by seventeen centuries of manhood, a nation that has begotten Grattan and Emmet and Parnell will not be brought to complete insanity in these last days by what is senile and slobbering in the doctrine of the Gaelic League.'[29] Joyce evidently told his brother a good deal about his extraordinary encounters with Synge in Paris. The 'many quarrelsome discussions' which Stanislaus related his brother had with Synge 'about language, style, poetry, the drama, and literature in general' had to have been coloured by contemporary politics. Synge's art, and his hostility to the language revival, can only have unsettled the certitudes of Joyce's previous Twilight-tinted perception of the politics of the Literary Revival and its relationship to the west of Ireland—though it is erroneous to construe Joyce's carefully articulated strictures on aspects of the Revival under the auspices of Yeats and Lady Gregory as evincing an urban or modernist prejudice against rural Ireland as a subject matter.

In the period of seven months between August 1902 and March 1903, Joyce had encountered all the leading figures of the Literary Revival, with the exception of George Moore, who by then knew of him. He had fulfilled the project ascribed to him with mild sarcasm by the critic and editor W. K. Magee: 'It was while walking homeward one night across Dublin that I was joined by this young man, whose appearance was already familiar to me; and although I cannot remember any of the strange sententious talk in which he instantly engaged, I have only to open the

28. S. Joyce, *My Brother's Keeper*, 213.

29. John Millington Synge, 'Can We Go Back into Our Mother's Womb? A Letter to the Gaelic League by a Hedge Schoolmaster', in *J. M. Synge: Collected Works*, vol. 2, *Prose*, ed. Alan Price (Buckinghamshire: Colin Smythe, 1982), 399–400. Synge made clear, 'I speak here not of the old and magnificent language of our manuscripts, or of the two or three dialects still spoken, though with many barbarisms, in the west and south, but by the incoherent twaddle that is passed off as Irish by the Gaelic League' (400). His views were in some respects very close to Joyce's, as in the premise that 'Ireland is a living language dying out year by year' (399).

Portrait of the Artist as a Young Man to hear it again.' Magee continued, 'He had made up his mind at this period, no doubt with vast undisclosed purposes of authorship, to make the personal acquaintance of everyone in Dublin of repute in literature.'[30]

In this period of busy encounters, Joyce met not only 'everyone of repute' in literary Dublin but those of future repute, who would play important roles in his life and work. It was probably on his return from Paris for the Christmas of 1902 that he first met Oliver St John Gogarty, at the counter of the National Library, according to what Joyce told Stanislaus.[31] Born in 1878, Gogarty was three and a half years older than Joyce. The son of a surgeon, he was educated under Jesuit auspices at Mungret, Stonyhurst, and Clongowes. He attended first-year lectures in University College but did his medical degree in Trinity, graduating in 1907. Emulating Oscar Wilde, he would spend two terms in Worcester College Oxford in 1904 in the hope of winning the Newdigate Prize.[32]

Stanislaus Joyce, whose agency as a member of Joyce's circle tends to be eclipsed by his capacity of brother and memoirist, had submitted with equanimity to his partial displacement by the succession of Joyce's university friends. Significantly, in his principal memoir, it was after his account of his brother's meeting with Gogarty that he registered his protest, caught up in his dislike of his father:

30. Eglinton, *Irish Literary Portraits*, 131, 137. William Kirkpatrick Magee was second assistant librarian in the National Library and a scrupled critic and essayist who wrote under the name John Eglinton. His was a dissenting voice within the Literary Revival, both politically and aesthetically. He declined to attorn to Irish nationalism which, Padraic Colum observed, 'as it seemed to him, would obviously eventuate in a Catholic state—and a Catholic state that would not have the internal opposition that had grown up along with the European Catholic states.' M. Colum and P. Colum, *Our Friend James Joyce*, 32; Nicholas Allen, 'William Kirkpatrick Magee', *DIB* 6:244–45. Magee was of haunting significance in Joyce's life and work; see this chapter's section 'The Politics of *Dana*'.

31. S. Joyce, *My Brother's Keeper*, 178. Gogarty recalled they were introduced by Vincent Cosgrave (Oliver St John Gogarty, 'The Joyce I Knew', *Saturday Review of Literature* 23 [25 January 1941]: 3–4) but also thought he had met Joyce on a tram in 1901 (Rodgers, *Irish Literary Portraits*, 24).

32. J. B. Lyons, 'Oliver St. John Gogarty', *ODNB* 22; Patrick Maume, 'Oliver St. John Gogarty', *DIB* 4:123–27.

For my part, I hung on the border of these friendships, dubiously accepted by the students as my brother's taciturn henchman. My father, Thersites-like, called me my brother's jackal, and when his tongue tired of that he would explain to me scientifically that I gave no light of my own, but that I shone with borrowed light like the moon. On this simile he harped lovingly, until I retorted that he had better do something about his nose, which was beginning to shine with its own light. He was still strangely vain and vulnerable to remarks on his personal appearance.[33]

The much put-upon Stanislaus, in a diary entry for March 1904, wrote that his brother 'has used me, I fancy, as a butcher uses his steel to sharpen his knife'.[34] Stephen in *Ulysses* refers to his brother as 'my whetstone'.[35] Stanislaus observed in an entry for August 1904, 'It is terrible to have a clever elder brother'.[36]

Padraic Colum was born in Longford in December 1881, three months before Joyce, and educated in Dublin.[37] As a writer he was promoted successively by Griffith, and by George Russell (Æ)[38] and Yeats; in a diary entry written days before his brother left Ireland, Stanislaus Joyce referred to Colum as 'the Irish messenger-boy genius, the beloved of Yeats and Russell and their clique'.[39] Joyce and Colum were each known to the other by repute when they first met, at one of Lady Gregory's

33. S. Joyce, *My Brother's Keeper*, 180.

34. S. Joyce, entry for 29 March 1904, in *Dublin Diary*, 20.

35. *U* 9.977.

36. S. Joyce, entry for 13 August 1904, in *Dublin Diary*, 50. This is quoted by Ellmann but misdated as September 1903 (*James Joyce*, 134). The diary, which Joyce read, and looked to as a novelistic resource (S. Joyce, *Dublin Diary*, 148–49), both enacts and narrates the terrifying candour within the Joyce household of the triad of John Stanislaus–Stanislaus–James.

37. Michael A. Kinsella, 'Padraic Colum', *DIB* 2:703–4. A conversation between Colum and Joyce in Paris years later belies the myth of Joyce's narrow metropolitanism: 'He noted that I have a Longford accent. I asked him how he was able to place it. "My grand-uncle", he said, "was parish-priest in Granard, and your accent is like his". It might have been thirty years back he had heard his grand-uncle speak; and the accent of that particular county is not very marked; it merges with the accent of adjoining counties' (P. Colum, *Road Round Ireland*, 327).

38. Russell's printers misunderstood his self-chosen but poorly written pseudonym 'Æon' as 'Æ'. He subsequently adopted it as his own.

39. S. Joyce, entry for 2 October 1904, in *Dublin Diary*, 117.

evenings. Colum was introduced to Joyce and Gogarty, each of whom, he recalled, was 'something of a celebrity'.[40] Thereafter they passed each other in the National Library, until Colum spoke to Joyce after they had passed through the turnstile on the way out: 'I think he took my approach as an act of homage (it was), and he was willing to go along with me conversationally.' As they walked to O'Connell Street, Colum was struck by Joyce's assuredness: 'What maturity he had then!' They touched on politics: 'For the new nationalist movement, the Gaelic League, he had no regard. "I distrust all enthusiasms", he said.'[41]

Politics came between them. Colum was a member of both the Gaelic League and the Irish Republican Brotherhood.[42] He wrote that, because of his involvement, he could not at that time have been a familiar of Joyce's.[43] When he next met Joyce, after the death of his mother, Joyce was somewhat aloof. Colum thought 'Joyce's attitude of ironic detachment towards me was not surprising. The nationalist group around *The United Irishman*, with which I was associated, was to him nothing more than "the rabblement". Æ, whose Hermeticism he despised, was promoting whatever stock I had.'[44]

Colum's later view was that while 'for Joyce the post-Parnell Irish nationalism was only a noise in the street, a movement of the crowd of which he would never consider himself a part, he desired the independence of his country and he honoured those who had striven disinterestedly for it'. He cited Joyce's article on John O'Leary: 'For Parnell himself, from his earliest to his latest days, he felt hero worship.'[45]

40. M. Colum and P. Colum, *Our Friend James Joyce*, 10–12. Colum noted, 'I do not remember that Joyce entered the conversation that evening. He and Gogarty sat apart, near the door, as if they did not quite belong to the gathering'. It is tempting to surmise that this, the only Lady Gregory evening he is recorded to have attended, was the event that Joyce crashed. However, that occurred after Joyce's return from Paris, and Colum is insistent on having met Joyce before he went to Paris (35–36). The most plausible conclusion is that Joyce had attended earlier evenings of Lady Gregory's.

41. M. Colum and P. Colum, *Our Friend James Joyce*, 20.

42. Sanford Sternlicht, 'Padraic Colum', *ODNB* 12:803.

43. M. Colum and P. Colum, *Our Friend James Joyce*, 43.

44. M. Colum and P. Colum, *Our Friend James Joyce*, 38.

45. M. Colum and P. Colum, *Our Friend James Joyce*, 44. Colum did not quite grasp the depth of Joyce's Parnellism, adding in parentheses, as if by way of qualification, 'Of course Joyce, like several other Irishmen of his and the generation before, identified himself with Parnell.'

In his *Irish Elegies,* Colum merged the two Joyces of the early years, crossing one of the Liffey bridges to sell his books on the quay:

> In odds of wearables, wittily worn,
> A yachtsman's cap to veer you to the seagulls . . . [46]

'His Role as Dissipated Genius'

After receiving late on the night of Good Friday a telegram at the Hotel de Corneille from his father that read 'mother dying',[47] Joyce reached Dublin from Paris on 12 April 1903. Shortly after his return, Joyce saw Yeats, who reported to Lady Gregory that 'he said his mother was still alive, and it was uncertain whether she would die or not. He added "but these things don't really matter".'[48]

May Joyce lingered for four months and died on 13 August 1903 at the age of forty-four.[49] When she lapsed into unconsciousness, her elder brother John Murray, a reformed alcoholic and atheist hated by John Stanislaus Joyce above all his in-laws, gestured imperiously to James and Stanislaus to join the others around their mother's deathbed in kneeling as he declaimed a prayer. Stanislaus recalled, 'Neither of us paid any attention to him; yet even so the scene seems to have burnt itself into my brother's soul. Not into mine.'[50] Stanislaus was assertively atheistic and considered that his mother ought to have rebelled against her circumstances but lacked the strength to do so. He saw his brother's response in this light, but in his diary the following month sounded a note which his brother approbated and adapted: 'When I saw her lying in her brown habit on the bed in the front room, her head a little wearily

46. Padraic Colum, *Irish Elegies,* 4th ed. (Dublin: Dolmen, 1976), 24.

47. Gorman, *James Joyce,* 108.

48. Yeats to Lady Gregory, [late April 1903], in *Letters of W. B. Yeats,* 399.

49. Ellmann, *James Joyce,* 135.

50. S. Joyce, *My Brother's Keeper,* 229–33; Ellmann, *James Joyce,* 135–36. Stanislaus recalled that the last time he met Joyce, in Zurich in September 1936, Joyce told him that he had come principally to persuade George Antheil to set to music a libretto he had made based on Lord Byron's *Cain*: 'He did not succeed; but I knew that the idea of conflict between the mother who lives in fear of God, and the outcast son, wandering cursed upon the hostile earth, was still milling about in his mind, and it saddened me.' S. Joyce, *Recollections of James Joyce,* 11; Ellmann, *James Joyce,* 626–27, 669, 689.

to one side, I seemed to be standing beside the death-bed of a victim.'[51] Joyce wrote in the extraordinary confessional manifesto he sent to Nora a little after the first anniversary of the death of May Joyce, 'My mother was slowly killed, I think, by my father's ill-treatment, by years of trouble, and by my cynical frankness of conduct. When I looked on her face as she still lay in her coffin—a face grey and wasted with cancer—I understood that I was looking on the face of a victim and I cursed the system which made her a victim.'[52]

Constantine Curran wrote of the death of May Joyce as 'a calamity, leading very shortly to the breaking up of the family'.[53] As Stanislaus put it, 'Within two years we were all scattered'.[54] The eldest daughter, Margaret ('Poppie'), struggled to hold the household together, deferring her plan to become a Sister of Mercy until 1909.[55] Joyce's aunt Josephine Murray, who was married to his mother's brother William, took up the role of older confidant on his mother's death: 'Jim tells her practically everything.'[56]

It was a miserable time. After his return from Paris, Joyce was beset by an uncharacteristic lack of purpose. In disregard of his mother's anxious and politely proffered advice that 'you cannot get on in your line without friends',[57] he had written a ferocious review of Lady Gregory's

51. S. Joyce, entry for 26 September 1903, in *Dublin Diary*, 8.

52. James Joyce to Nora Barnacle, 29 August 1904, *Letters II* 48; Ellmann, *James Joyce*, 169. This letter belies the theory through which Stanislaus strained to account for Joyce's exilic treatment of Ireland, in which their mother featured prominently: 'With the passing of time, Joyce's perspective on his native city faded, and father and country blended before the eyes of the exile into a powerful attraction. Above all, she became for him the Irish woman, the accomplice of the Irish Catholic Church, which Joyce called the scullery-maid of Christianity.' S. Joyce, *Recollections of James Joyce*, 11; see also S. Joyce, *My Brother's Keeper*, 234–35.

53. Curran, *James Joyce Remembered*, 38. The youngest surviving child, Mabel ('Baby'), whom Joyce had consoled on the death of their mother, died of typhoid in 1911 at the age of fourteen. The event prompted what his sister May described as 'a very nice letter from Jim of course rather strange and bitter' which has not survived. Stanislaus, in his memoir, described her as 'the last victim of our family life'; S. Joyce, *My Brother's Keeper*, 232–33; Ellmann, *James Joyce*, 310.

54. S. Joyce, *My Brother's Keeper*, 235.

55. Ellmann, *James Joyce*, 143–44.

56. S. Joyce, entry for 6 August 1904, in *Dublin Diary*, 66; Ellmann, *James Joyce*, 19–20.

57. May Joyce to James Joyce, 2 March 1903, *Letters II* 32.

Poets and Dreamers.[58] W. K. Magee recalled an episode in which Joyce had attended a literary movement party Lady Gregory held at the Nassau Hotel to which he had not been invited: 'We were all a little uneasy, and I can still see Joyce, with his air of half-timid effrontery, advancing toward his unwilling host and turning away from her to watch the company.'[59] It was as if he was reasserting his independence of the Celtic Twilight precisely at the moment when he could least afford to do so.

In his principal memoir of his brother, Stanislaus wrote, 'Shortly after my mother's death in August, my brother began to drink riotously.'[60] His contemporary diary discloses a somewhat different temporal rhythm to Joyce's drinking. In an entry six months after the death of their mother, Stanislaus wrote,

> The other day Yeats, [Fred] Ryan, Colum and Gogarty [were] talking and Yeats mentioned a fellow in London who was making three hundred a year writing short clever articles for some London paper. 'It is a pity Joyce couldn't get something like that', said Ryan. 'He could write the articles all right, but then he couldn't keep sober for three days together'. 'Why put it at three days?' corrected Gogarty. 'For one day'. As a matter of fact, Jim has a reputation altogether out of keeping with his merits. Within the last two months he has been only once drunk, and showed signs of drink not more than three times.[61]

It was as if the legend of Joyce's drinking ran slightly ahead of the fact. It rapidly became a source of despair to Stanislaus. He wrote in July 1904 that Joyce's 'dissipation has disimproved him greatly',[62] and complained

58. *OCPW* 74–76.

59. Eglinton, *Irish Literary Portraits*, 137–38. His later account somewhat differed: 'I remember Joyce coming in rather timidly but still with his usual audacity. He was received by Lady Gregory, and then he turned away'; Rodgers, *Irish Literary Portraits*, 25. Stanislaus Joyce doubted Magee's account on unconvincing grounds; S. Joyce, *My Brother's Keeper*, 184. Ellmann plausibly surmises that Lady Gregory forgave Joyce in the wake of the death of Joyce's mother, and notes that Joyce was never invited to George Moore's at-homes; Ellmann, *James Joyce*, 135.

60. S. Joyce, *My Brother's Keeper*, 240.

61. S. Joyce, entry for 10 April 1904, in *Dublin Diary*, 25.

62. S. Joyce, entry for 31 July 1904, in *Dublin Diary*, 48; S. Joyce, *My Brother's Keeper*, 241–42.

the following September, 'I hate to see Jim limp and pale, with shadows under his watery eyes, loose wet lips, and dank hair. I hate to see him sitting on the edge of a table grinning at his own state. . . . He likes the novelty of his role of dissipated genius.'[63]

In the small confines of the literary polis of Dublin, Joyce's dissolute drinking became for a time something close to a defining attribute. Gogarty reported to Stanislaus that W. K. Magee [in art John Eglinton] had heard that Joyce was 'going the way of [William] Maginn and [Robert] Burns to ruin.'[64] With restrained mordancy, Colum characterised the post-Paris Joyce by saying, 'The Joyce all of us knew best at this period was the shabbily dressed, penniless, lewd-spoken youth whose disreputability was striking because of the witticisms that rose out of it.'[65] He recalled (the vegetarian) James Cousins after a lunch, 'as we watched the slender, shabby figure with the ashplant go away from us', describing Joyce as a 'lost angel of a ruined paradise.'[66] Colum distinguished this as 'the Gogartian Joyce': 'It was solely as a "character", and that partly a Gogartian creation, that Joyce was known to Dubliners of that time.'[67] He retailed an account of Joyce's ignominious drunken collapse at a rehearsal of the National Theatre Society, having been forewarned by Gogarty, 'Joyce gets drunk in the legs, not the head.'[68]

In the narrative of Stanislaus, Gogarty features as a medical Iago. Stanislaus half suspected a scheme on the part of the more alcoholically robust Gogarty, who had literary ambitions of his own, to break his brother's spirit.[69] With an archness that is almost disarming in his principal memoir, Gogarty characterised the Joyce of this period as 'the best

63. S. Joyce, entry for 14 September 1904, in *Dublin Diary*, 101; see also S. Joyce, *My Brother's Keeper*, 241–44.

64. S. Joyce, *My Brother's Keeper*, 247. The implicit reference here is to a line from James Clarence Mangan's poem 'The Nameless One': 'And he fell far through that pit abysmal / The gulf and grave of Maginn and Burns.'

65. M. Colum and P. Colum, *Our Friend James Joyce*, 45.

66. M. Colum and P. Colum, *Our Friend James Joyce*, 42–43.

67. M. Colum and P. Colum, *Our Friend James Joyce*, 38.

68. M. Colum and P. Colum, *Our Friend James Joyce*, 45–46.

69. S. Joyce, *My Brother's Keeper*, 240–41; S. Joyce, *Recollections of James Joyce*, 17.

example of a medical student's pal Dublin produced'.[70] Gogarty's mother, in the manner of Dublin matriarchy, was persuaded that the 'bad Catholic' Joyce was corrupting her Oliver.[71] This was to inspire a gracefully poised line in *Ulysses*: 'Baddybad Stephen lead astray goody-good Malachi'.[72]

Of Joyce's contemporaries, it was Curran who, in defence of his friend, provided the surest assessment of this 'brief period of dissipation' in the months when Joyce's fortunes were at their lowest ebb: the 'picture of a twentieth century Dublin Villon or Verlaine is grossly exaggerated.' Joyce continued to write, not confined to his work (from February 1904) on 'the steadily accumulating mass of the *Stephen Hero* MS'. Curran concluded with penetrating astuteness, 'Reckless as he seemed, Joyce never threw down the reins of will. His whole nature was bent excessively in the contrary direction, being perpetually often preposterously given to method and to elaborate astuteness, much of it miraculously executed.'[73]

Dublin's Radical Politics

Joyce, in his final two years in Ireland (1902–4), was preoccupied with his future as 'a literary artist'. It is exceedingly difficult to connect him to contemporary events: the 'long' Parnell Split which remained in being until 1900 stretched too far back in time, and he held himself

70. Oliver St John Gogarty, *As I Was Going Down Sackville Street* (London: Sphere Books, 1968), 293.

71. Margaret Gogarty wrote to T. M. Kettle, 'You can do an inestimable service, by your companionship and advice to counteract the bad effects of others, one, especially a bad Catholic who spent a great deal of time with Oliver last winter before I discovered he was, or pretended to be, an agnostic, so I forbade him to call here any more.' J. B. Lyons, *Enigma of Tom Kettle*, 54; Ellmann, *James Joyce*, 173.

72. *U* 14.1487–88.

73. Curran, *James Joyce Remembered*, 66. The 'picture' is interesting in that it is contemporary rather than retrospective. Even though mitigated by his composed manner on his three returns to Dublin (1909–12), it continued to inflect the perception of Joyce in Dublin before his achieved success as a writer in exile.

studiously aloof from identification with contemporary manifestations of Parnellism. Joyce eschewed political involvement. However, he was far from politically indifferent or incurious. It was not simply that his acute observation of contemporary Ireland extended to politics. On his leaving University College, Joyce's scheme of encounters was not narrowly artistic. He embarked on an exploratory quest to see whether there was any political grouping or movement with which he could align himself. It was a sceptical search—he did not expect to find that there was—but it was scrupulously undertaken, as if on a heuristic principle he felt obliged to try. The decision to leave Ireland to which it contributed was not undertaken on a whim.

For constitutional nationalists the years 1898–1904 formed a period of immobilism which would be broken by the election of a Liberal government in 1906. These years saw the stirrings of a radical nationalism that would lead to the later establishment of Sinn Féin and the emergence of an Irish socialist movement. Both were perceived at the time as movements on the fringe of Irish nationalism. The Irish Party, preponderantly rural, was ill-equipped to enunciate the concerns of the urban poor. The period was not generally experienced nor contemporaneously assessed as a time of crisis; no nationalist could feel much nostalgia for the passing of the social actuality of the nineteenth century. Joyce's idea of paralysis was a critique of complacently impotent drift. There were major advances in the legislative scheme of land purchase, favoured by the Conservatives but habitually regarded with suspicion by the Liberals, culminating in the Wyndham Land Act of 1903. The unbroken succession of Unionist governments from 1895 had worked up a semi-plausible counter-strategy to Home Rule. It was a strategy of retarding the progress of Irish nationalism by the entrenchment of a nationalist property-owning class in rural Ireland. This strategy sowed deep alarm on the agrarian centre-left of the Irish Party, especially on the part of John Dillon.[74] This unease was fortified by the relatively favourable contemporary economic conditions that prevailed. Rural

74. Paul Bew, *Ireland: The Politics of Enmity, 1789–2006* (Oxford: Oxford University Press, 2007), 361–63.

Ireland was undergoing a quiet transformation and there was a commercial buoyancy in the cities and towns, attended by the beguiling novelties of the late-Victorian manifestations of a consumer society. Joyce apprehended the dialectic of Conservative Unionist and Liberal politics, and the unease Conservative reforms caused among nationalists nurtured from the 1880s on a belief in an inexorable advance to Home Rule. The intent of the Unionist government and its Irish administration in Dublin Castle to exploit a sense of present satiety and future betterment found ceremonial expression in the conspicuous but frugal benefactions of the Lord Lieutenant. This is enacted by the wheeling of Lord Aberdeen and his consort in their carriage through Dublin in the 'Wandering Rocks' episode in *Ulysses*. Radical nationalists—Griffith, doggedly secure in his nationalist conviction, was an exception—had a deep and exorbitant fear of the tranquillising effects of the superimposition on a sense of economic well-being engendered in a long interlude of Conservative governance of a propitiatory concession of Home Rule by a Liberal government. This revolutionary dread of satiation would do much to precipitate the Rising of 1916. Joyce, with his sceptical sense of history, believed things could go either way, bringing his thinking closer to that of radical nationalists than to adherents of the Irish Party. What is more important is that he rendered with oblique exactitude in the political backdrop to *Ulysses* the contemporary sense of a Conservative-Liberal stalemate regarding Ireland. The debilitating dependency on the play of British politics was a defining condition of the stasis in Ireland.

These years at the cusp of the twentieth century were a prelude, which came to appear more remote from the period of escalating crisis in Ireland from 1913. They had a distinctive ambience which Joyce rendered with brilliant exactitude in *Ulysses*. Two connected issues define Dublin radical politics in the period: Irish identification with the cause of the Boers, and opposition to the royal visits of 1900 and 1903. There is nothing to connect Joyce to specific occurrences in relation to either, but his fictional and non-fictional writings attest to a close attentiveness to both, at the level of the politics of the street rather than high politics at Westminster. He thereby chronicled without comment the waning of the hegemony of the Irish Party in what had been the Parnellite stronghold of 'the Hibernian metropolis'.

The second Anglo-Boer war (1899–1902) between Britain and the South African Boer republics elicited strong Irish sympathy for the Boers that was not confined to separatists. Even though the opposition Liberals were divided on the war, the uninhibited support of nationalist parliamentarians at Westminster for the Boers scandalised British public opinion and further weakened the commitment to Home Rule of the post-Gladstonian Liberal leadership. Though the Irish Transvaal Committee included some nationalist parliamentarians, it became a precursor of the anti-parliamentary Sinn Féin.[75]

Major John MacBride, who had fought as second in command of one of the Irish brigades fighting for the Boers, was nominated by Griffith and other members of the Transvaal Committee to contest South Mayo in February 1900 in an unsuccessful attempt to embarrass the Irish Party.[76] In the capital, the most dramatic event in Ireland relating to the war was occasioned by the visit on 18 December 1899 of the Colonial Secretary Joseph Chamberlain to receive an honorary degree from Trinity College. Chamberlain, who had played an instrumental role in the defeat of Gladstone's First Home Rule Bill and in the initiation of the Boer War, was a hated figure in Ireland.[77]

There is a pointed contrast. Bloom, who serves in *Ulysses* in his political aspect as a mildly left-of-centre nationalist everyman, had climbed a tree to welcome Lord Ripon and John Morley on the occasion of their entrance to Dublin in February 1888, a high-water mark of the Liberal-nationalist alliance (Gladstone himself did not come to Ireland after his embrace of Home Rule).[78] The transition from acclaim for visiting Liberal ministers in the gracious suburbs to riot in the inner city marked the evanescence of the Gladstonian 'union of hearts' before the century's end.

75. Maume, *Long Gestation*, 28–29.

76. Maume, *Long Gestation*, 29, 34–35, 234.

77. Donal P. McCracken, *The Irish Pro-Boers, 1877–1902* (Johannesburg: Perskor, 1989), 62.

78. *U* 17.651–56.

If Joyce hoped for a forward movement within nationalism, he was not drawn to the Boer cause. He had in February 1899 responded satirically to a paper read by Hugh Kennedy at the Literary and Historical Society titled 'The War Machine: A State Necessity' with a militaristic rendering of the eight beatitudes,[79] which would be echoed in *Ulysses*: 'Beer, beef, business, bibles, bulldogs, battleships, buggery and bishops.'[80] That was some six months before the outbreak of the Boer War. In his 'L'Irlanda: Isola dei santi e dei savi' lecture, he told his Triestine audience that it took 'the genius of two commanders, Lord Roberts and Lord Kitchener (both of them Irish, born in Ireland) to restore endangered prestige, just as, in 1815, it took another Irish soldier, the Duke of Wellington, to overturn the renewed might of Napoleon at Waterloo.'[81] The historian Stephen Koss wrote that 'the pro-Boers derived much of their inspiration and organization, and even more of their rhetoric, from a fervent Christianity. That, above all else, distinguishes them from the opponents of later wars who became progressively more secular in their aims and attitudes.'[82] The Bible was to be found on both sides, and Joyce, always fastidious in his choice of causes and allies, was never disposed to align himself with exponents of nonconformist moralism.

In the middle of the Boer War, a visit to Dublin by Queen Victoria was announced, prompting what Joyce described as the 'lively uproar' that always occurred 'when an English monarch wants to go to Ireland for political reasons.'[83] Griffith and others responded furiously to a vote of Dublin Corporation to present a loyal address. Yeats too condemned the visit.[84] As the leader of the Parnellite minority, John Redmond's qualified welcome of the visit alienated the radical nationalists whom he had recently sought to enlist. John Howard Parnell, who held the ceremonial position of City Marshall, participated in the event, writing

79. Ellmann, *James Joyce*, 70.

80. *U* 14.1459–60.

81. *OCPW* 117. Roberts was not in fact born in Ireland.

82. Stephen Koss, ed., *The Anatomy of an Antiwar Movement: The Pro-Boers* (Chicago: University of Chicago Press, 1973), xiv.

83. *OCPW* 116.

84. Foster, *W. B. Yeats*, 1:227–28.

to Redmond that 'he was in a social position different from other nationalists'. He added that 'we have no quarrel with the Queen's doings . . . my brother would have taken the same view'.[85] The visit took place from 3 to 26 April 1900.

The queen's visit provided the centrepiece for Joyce's lecture 'L'Irlanda: Isola dei santi e dei savi' that he gave at the Università Popolare in Trieste on 27 April 1907 to characterise the relation of Ireland to England: 'A moral separation already exists between the two countries . . . to be convinced of this separateness, you would have needed to have been in the streets of Dublin when the late Queen Victoria entered the capital as she did in the year before her death.' He gave a graphic description of the visit, the streets lined by English soldiers in front of crowds of tourists and officials, 'unionist clerks and their wives':

> The queen's carriage passed by, tightly protected on all sides by an impressive bodyguard with bared sabres, while inside a little woman, almost a dwarf could be seen, hunched and swaying in movement with the carriage, funereally dressed with horn-rimmed glasses on her ashen vacuous face. . . . The English soldiers stood respectfully at attention while their queen passed; behind them, the crowd watched the sumptuous procession and its sad central figure with eyes of curiosity, almost of pity. When the carriage passed by, they followed its wake with ambiguous glances. This time there were no bombs or cabbages, but the queen of England entered the capital of Ireland in the midst of a silent people.[86]

Joyce skilfully conveyed the sense that he was an eyewitness to a cavalcade that marked the passing of the Victorian age in Ireland. He could have been, but probably was not, unless by happenstance. He was not someone to frequent processions or official events. But he was certainly in Dublin, observing from a tangent, listening, and reading newspaper reports. His account bears some resemblance to that which appeared in

85. R. F. Foster, *Charles Stewart Parnell: The Man and His Family* (London: Harvester, 1976), 297.

86. *OCPW* 116–18.

Griffith's *United Irishman*. Though plainly hostile to the British monarchy, he struck a tone markedly different to the more Anglophobic opponents of the visit who fulminated against 'the Famine Queen', a designation promoted by Maud Gonne.[87]

The 1900 royal visit of Queen Victoria was followed by that of her successor Edward VII, which took place from 21 July to 1 August 1903. This time the 'lively uproar' against the visit was more politically structured. The temporising endeavour of Timothy C. Harrington, the most prominent parliamentarian in Dublin, to steer a middle course, even though John Dillon came out against the visit, once again allowed the Irish Party's adversaries to assert that it was complicit in the visit. The motion brought before the corporation for a loyal address was defeated.[88] The issue allowed Arthur Griffith, through the *United Irishman*, to engage in a masterly demonstration of his political *pointillisme*, his use of specific controversies to promote the ideas of what would become Sinn Féin, and thereby to produce small fissures in the facade of the hegemony of the Irish Party. Significantly for Joyce, and for the genesis of his story 'Ivy Day in the Committee Room', Griffith pitted against the Irish Party the precedent of Parnell's response to the 1885 visit by Edward, then Prince of Wales.[89] On that occasion, the Irish Party had resolved that 'it is in our view the duty of the Irish people and of their representatives in all public bodies, while avoiding any act of discourtesy to the Prince and Princess of Wales, to maintain an attitude of reserve which will sufficiently demonstrate their inalienable attachment to National principles, and their resolute resentment of the suppression of their constitutional liberties.'[90] If the contrast that Griffith sought to draw was to a degree tendentious, it astutely targeted an ambivalence

87. Senia Pašeta, 'Nationalist Responses to Two Royal Visits to Ireland', *Irish Historical Studies* 31, no. 124 (November 1999): 488–97.

88. Pašeta, 'Nationalist Responses', 497–504.

89. *United Irishman*, 30 May 1903. The paper reverted to the theme on 20 June and 4 July 1903.

90. *Freeman's Journal*, 14 March 1885. Parnell also wrote a spirited letter to *United Ireland* referring to the absence in Ireland of 'the usages of the constitution' that prevailed in England, and the promotion of the visit for political ends by the government; R. B. O'Brien, *Charles Stewart Parnell*, 2:41–42.

and lack of leadership on the part of the Irish Party on an issue that was not merely highly charged symbolically but was a staging post that had the capacity to redraw the boundaries between the old and new nationalisms.

The opposition ensured that the attitude of candidates seeking election to Dublin Corporation to the royal visit featured prominently in the municipal elections of 1903, before the visit, and of 1904. The sordid ethics of Dublin municipal governance and the royal visit became connected themes. Joyce was to fuse these in 'Ivy Day in the Committee Room'. Though the contemporary resonance was lost in its deferred publication, it was in a significant aspect a veiled literary counterpart to the journalism of Arthur Griffith.

The National Council, which mobilised opinion on the issue, was a precursor of the Sinn Féin party, which was not established until after Joyce had left Ireland. 'Ivy Day in the Committee Room' conveys its author's scornful indifference to the visit, subsumed in a plangent lament for Parnell. In exile Joyce expressed, in his correspondence with his brother, a qualified identification with Sinn Féin, which found expression in his Triestine journalism and lectures. This did not come out of the exilic blue but articulated a transcendent continuity. In his time in Ireland, Joyce experienced both the aftermath of Parnell's death and the proximate origins of Sinn Féin. The consequences were far-reaching. His development as a writer tracked the waning of the active myth of Parnell and the beginning of the emergence of what would become Sinn Féin. Joyce's sense of having been compelled to leave the country of his birth was counterbalanced by his sense that his allotted time there had been, for all its torpor, of high significance in Ireland's faltering progress to statehood. His conspicuous disengagement belied what was an extraordinary induction in the Irish political. His life in Ireland had a defining intersection with Irish politics, specifically with the faint beginnings of a turning away from Home Rule and the early stirrings of the movement through which independent statehood was achieved. While Joyce was for long to be perceived as divorced from Irish politics, this political thread was at least as important as the Literary Revival for Joyce's sense of his relationship to Ireland.

Exile brought a shift of perspective but did not lead Joyce to reconceptualise in any fundamental way the country he had left. The notion of a Joyce sentimentally chastened by exile, pining for faith and fatherland but too proud to confess it—a perception that long held sway in Ireland—is untenable. He had a clear sense of the national controversy which he carried with him to Trieste and Rome. Politics, imaginatively transfigured, threw a bridge across migratory rupture and geographical distance. Almost mystically sensitive to dates and coincidences, Joyce came to think of this as anything but fortuitous. It was a large part of what enabled him to continue to conceive himself from Trieste and Paris as a writer of modern Ireland and permitted him to respond to the seeming foreclosure of exile with an extraordinary suppleness to which his fierce and frequently hilarious exilic plaints were an aside.

Joyce and the *United Irishman*

In the years before leaving Ireland, Joyce was an attentive reader of Griffith's paper, the *United Irishman*—Stanislaus recalled that he said it was 'the only paper in Dublin worth reading' and read it every week.[91] Joyce caused great offence to Griffith by a review of a book of the poems of Griffith's dead friend William Rooney that revealed just how expert an observer of the politics of the *United Irishman* he was.

Born in 1871 on Dominick Street, Arthur Griffith was eleven years older than Joyce. He was the son and grandson of printers. From the age of seventeen he was running the Eblana Literary and Debating Society, which merged with the Leinster Literary Society. These were groups comprised predominantly of working-class young men interested in Irish historical and literary subjects, and philosophically drawn to republicanism. There he met William Rooney, who became his inseparable friend. With characteristic diffidence, Griffith saw Rooney as a future Irish leader. Whatever reservations he had had about the Irish Parliamentary Party, Griffith fiercely supported Parnell in the Split. After Parnell's defeat in the three successive by-elections of the Split, he

91. S. Joyce, *My Brother's Keeper*, 173.

paid a visit to Timothy Harrington to urge him to resign in order to enable Parnell to contest a by-election in Dublin.[92] He saw his beleaguered leader off from Broadstone station on his journey westwards to his last meeting, at Creggs. His Parnellism intensified rather than diminished on Parnell's death. When an anti-Parnellite from Cork, who asserted that 'you are Parnellites here in Dublin but you would be anti-Parnellites if you were down in Mallow [the hometown of William O'Brien]', was admitted to membership of the Leinster Literary Society, Griffith resigned from it. Griffith's Parnellite sympathies were not shared by Rooney, a rigid cultural nationalist and Irish language revivalist.[93] Griffith remained loyal to Parnell's memory, though his articulation of his old fealty became necessarily constrained. He knew it was not entirely consistent with his critique of parliamentarism, and that his support of Parnell in the Split was suspect to doctrinaire republicans.

The influence that Griffith's journalism and political views exerted on Joyce had at the outset nothing to do with the fact that Griffith had been a Parnellite in the Split, though Joyce was almost certainly aware of it. Joyce's interest in Sinn Féin was as an emanation of contemporary Irish politics. When the Irish Party came to hold the balance of power in Westminster from 1910, Griffith had the occasion to write more about Parnell. That was for Joyce an important source of affirmation and prompted his most sustained consideration of Parnell in his 1912 article 'L'ombra di Parnell'. As Parnell's political memory faded, some still mourned for him, but Griffith and Joyce were almost virtually alone in continuing to dwell on the dead leader's relevance to contemporary Ireland. For them, the myth of Parnell held yet an active intellectual force.

It was not simply that Griffith persisted doggedly in espousing views with which Joyce came to feel an affinity, and later elicited wider sympathy in Ireland. His journalistic advocacy was of a high order. James Stephens, to whom Joyce became close in his Paris exile, wrote with some extravagance of Griffith's merits as a writer: 'He was, in my opinion, the greatest journalist working in the English tongue, with an astonishing

92. Calton Younger, *Arthur Griffith* (Dublin: Gill and Macmillan, 1981), 1–7.
93. McGee, *Arthur Griffith*, 18.

FIGURE 9.1. Arthur Griffith. Reproduced courtesy of the National Library of Ireland, HOG229.

lucidity of expression, and with a command of all the modes of tender, or sarcastic, or epigrammatic expression, and always with that ample, untroubled simplicity of utterance which ranks him among the modern masters of the English language.'[94]

Some months after Griffith returned from a two-year sojourn in South Africa, the first issue of the *United Irishman* of Griffith and Rooney appeared on 4 March 1899, following a purge of the Fenian coterie around Fred Allan from the Parnellite *Irish Independent*.[95] It was a brilliantly innovative politico-cultural weekly, but it never had more than an exiguous circulation. Griffith became known to a somewhat wider public in Ireland with the publication in November 1904 of the pamphlet *The Resurrection of Hungary*, derived from a series of articles he had published in the *United Irishman* in the earlier months of that year.[96] The articles advanced a strained and tortuous constitutional argument based on the Renunciation Act of 1783, by which the British Parliament had ceded the right to legislate for Ireland, which the Act of Union had repealed, merged with a parallel with the Austro-Hungarian dual monarchy. His pamphlet had an unexpected impact on a nationalist public which evidently could not take much more on the subject of the comparative merits of the 1886 and 1893 Home Rule Bills, and what powers a new Home Rule bill at some future time might or might not confer on an Irish legislature.

Griffith's emergence as a journalist and pamphleteer preceded the establishment of Sinn Féin. The National Council, formed in 1903 in opposition to the visit to Ireland of Edward VII, was Griffith's principal vehicle.[97] It made significant progress in Dublin municipal politics. Griffith largely succeeded in appropriating the name Sinn Féin, which had a coveted contemporary vogue, and gave it to the more politically focussed weekly *Sinn Féin* that he established in 1906 in succession to

94. James Stephens, *Arthur Griffith: Journalist and Statesman* (Dublin: Wilson, Hartnell, 1924), 19.

95. McGee, *IRB*, 270.

96. The *United Irishman* published twenty-seven articles under the title 'The Resurrection of Hungary' from 21 January to 2 July 1904. These appeared while Joyce was still in Ireland.

97. McGee, *IRB*, 302–3.

the *United Irishman*. He seems to have left the Irish Republican Brotherhood at around the same time. On 5 September 1907, the political party named the Sinn Féin Organisation came into existence after the North Leitrim by-election as a result of the merger of the National Council and a separate body called the Sinn Féin League.[98] It adopted the name Sinn Féin a year later.[99] The relevance in relation to Joyce of the tortuous genesis of Sinn Féin is that while the name and the constellation of political ideas associated with it were in circulation while he was in Dublin, Sinn Féin did not come into being until some three years after he had left. Though he was writing to his brother sympathetically of Griffith's programme in the latter part of 1906, the metamorphosis of Griffith from a journalist and editor into the principal figure in a party, however minoritarian, with a defined programme, post-dated Joyce's departure from Ireland.

Much of the *United Irishman* was written by Griffith and Rooney, the latter of whom had a variety of noms de plume. Two series of articles, 'Gaelicism in Practice' and 'A Recent Irish Literature', both based on lectures he had given, were published under Rooney's name. Rooney, a sternly hard-line Irish language revivalist and cultural nationalist, was constrained to concede that 'for a generation or two yet we must have Irish writers in English, just as till we are independent we shall have to use English in our daily life'.[100] What he sought to achieve was the political radicalisation of the language revival in opposition to nineteenth-century constitutional nationalism, as if to fill the political void left by the official neutrality of the Gaelic League. He loathed Daniel O'Connell, had a seeming aversion to uttering Parnell's name, and regarded the Split as providential ('in the rending of the veil we saw at last what was before us, and paused').[101] To an alert reader of the paper,

98. McGee, *IRB*, 316–18.

99. Michael Laffan, *The Resurrection of Ireland: The Sinn Féin Party, 1916–1923* (Cambridge: Cambridge University Press, 1999), 26.

100. William Rooney, 'A Recent Irish Literature', *United Irishman*, 9 February 1901.

101. Callanan, 'Joyce and the *United Irishman*', 60–66. 'Gaelicism in Practice' was a lecture delivered before the Celtic Literary Society on 4 January 1901. It was published in the *United Irishman* of 12 and 19 January 1901, and republished in William Rooney, *Prose Writings* (Dublin:

such as Joyce, to whom Rooney's opinions were anathema, there was an evident tension between the rigid dogmatism of Rooney and the supple political intelligence of Griffith as the paper's editorialist. There was a secondary rift between Rooney's didactic revivalism and the scholarly articles on Irish mythical and antiquarian subjects which the paper also published. Griffith remained in thrall to his admiration of Rooney without embracing his radical revivalist ideology. Padraic Colum later mildly commented, 'Those who did not know him personally found it difficult to understand Griffith's idealization of [Rooney]'.[102]

William Rooney died aged twenty-eight, most likely of tuberculosis, on 6 May 1901. A shattered Griffith was admitted to hospital. In the introduction he contributed the following year to Rooney's *Poems and Ballads*, published by the *United Irishman*, he wrote, 'I came to build my hopes on him, and to regard him as the destined regenerator of his people', and professed his belief that his friend, had he lived, 'would have become, perhaps, the greatest leader that Ireland had known'.[103] It happened that (along with a critical work on George Meredith) the first book that Joyce was sent to review for the *Daily Express* was Rooney's *Poems and Ballads*. This was just before Joyce's first Paris expedition; he sent his review from Paris probably on 4 December 1902, for publication on 11 December. It was unsparing. Joyce was not prepared to engage in post-mortem pieties, nor to heed Griffith's hedging plea in his introduction that he did not claim Rooney, who 'wrote merely to rouse his countrymen, even as [Thomas] Davis did, not to gratify his or their literary appetites', to be 'the greatest of Ireland's living men of genius'.[104]

Joyce's review commenced with alacrity: 'These are the verses of a writer lately dead, whom many considered the Davis of the latest national movement. They are issued from headquarters.' In referring to

M. H. Gill, 1909), 105–53. 'A Recent Irish Literature' was based on a lecture Rooney gave at the Celtic Literary Society on 20 January 1899. It was published in five parts by the *United Irishman*, 9 February–9 March 1901. It was republished in Rooney's *Prose Writings*, 1–71.

102. Padraic Colum, *Arthur Griffith* (Dublin: Browne and Nolan, 1959), 54.

103. Arthur Griffith, introduction to *Poems and Ballads*, by William Rooney (Dublin: United Irishman, 1903), ix, x.

104. Griffith, introduction to Rooney, *Poems and Ballads*, x–xi.

Davis, whom Griffith had defensively invoked, he was enlarging the scope of his attack. While the thrust of that attack was on the subordination of the political to the literary from the era of Young Ireland onwards, it also suggested that Joyce at that time remained sceptical of the politics of the *United Irishman*, from whose offices the book emanated. Asserting with ruthless inexactitude that the authors of the two introductions (Griffith's and a biographical sketch by Patrick Bradley) did not hesitate to claim for Rooney's verses 'the highest honours', he retorted that the claim could not be allowed 'unless it is supported by certain evidences of literary sincerity. For a man who writes a book cannot be excused by his good intentions, or by his moral character; he enters a region where there is question of the written word.' This was especially so 'now that the region of literature is so fiercely assailed by the enthusiast and the doctrinaire.' Rooney's verses attained little, 'because the writing is so careless, and is yet so studiously mean'. He did, however, unstintingly praise one of Rooney's translations.[105]

Joyce's review was a searing exposition of what happened 'when patriotism has laid hold of the writer'. Rooney's verses

> bear witness to some desperate and weary energy. But they have no spiritual and living energy, because they come from one in whom the spirit is in a manner dead, or at least in its own hell, a weary and foolish spirit, speaking of redemption and revenge, blaspheming against tyrants, and going forth, full of tears and curses, upon its infernal labours. Religion and all that is allied thereto can manifestly persuade men to great evil, and by writing these verses, even though they should, as the writers of the prefaces think, enkindle the young men of Ireland to hope and activity, Mr Rooney has been persuaded to great evil. And yet he might have written well if he had not suffered from one of those big words which make us so unhappy.[106]

Joyce's argument, in one aspect a stern application of Wildean aesthetics to nationalistic rhetoric, suffered from the abbreviations required

105. 'An Irish Poet', *Daily Express* (Dublin), 11 December 1907, in *OCPW* 61–63.
106. *OCPW* 62.

in a short review. It says something about his changing relationship to the political after University College. The 'blaspheming against tyrants' echoes the proposition in his Mangan paper of the start of that year that 'the poet who hurls anger against tyrants would establish upon the future an intimate and far more cruel tyranny',[107] but the content of the review carried him beyond the realm of his ostensible political virginality in University College.

The review exhibited a close familiarity with nationalist politics and the patriotic canon. 'The theme is consistently national, so uncompromising, indeed, that the reader must lift an eyebrow and assure himself when he meets on page 114 the name of D'Arcy McGee.' Thomas D'Arcy McGee had been a Young Irelander who became a prominent Canadian politician; his assassination in Ottawa in 1868 was believed to have been perpetrated by Fenians. Re-reading the review after Joyce's death, Stanislaus was prompted to recall, 'My brother had a stronger stomach for patriotic poetry than I. He could read through the collected poems of those insignificant poets with high-sounding names, Denis Florence MacCarthy, with cold patient scorn, when a very few pages of them left me helpless and speechless with devastating boredom.'[108]

That would have surprised Joyce's contemporaries in University College. If Joyce's breadth of reference would not have been unusual for a well-read nationalist of the older generation, his statement that 'even Mr T. D. Sullivan and Mr Rolleston have done something in the making of this book' was of a different order and revealed a striking connoisseurship of contemporary nationalist politico-cultural controversy. The invocation of Sullivan, an anti-Parnellite politician and writer of popular songs and ballads, was faintly disparaging, but the reference to Rolleston was a barb thrust deep. Thomas William Hazen Rolleston was an Irish intellectual and poet who initially had nationalist sympathies: at one time he, Yeats, and John Francis Taylor vied as disciples of John

107. *OCPW* 59.

108. S. Joyce, *My Brother's Keeper*, 203–4; James Joyce, *The Early Joyce: The Book Reviews 1902–3*, ed., with an introduction, by Stanislaus Joyce and Ellsworth Mason (Colorado Springs: Mamalujo, 1955), 9n1.

O'Leary.[109] He was employed from 1900 by Horace Plunkett's Department of Agriculture and Technical Instruction. His drift towards imperialism accelerated during the South African War, culminating in the publication of his 1901 pamphlet *Ireland, the Empire and the War*. Griffith came to revile Rolleston as an apostate, and repeatedly assailed him in the *United Irishman*. The paper also carried a fierce attack on Rolleston by John Francis Taylor entitled 'Mr Rolleston's Recantation', which Griffith cited at length on the death of Taylor the following year, in an obituary that appeared less than a month before Joyce's review.[110] The mention of Rolleston was on Joyce's part a calculated provocation.

The publication in a Unionist newspaper of a devastating review of Rooney's poems by a reviewer who displayed an extraordinarily expert and intimate knowledge of contemporary nationalist controversy can only have excited Griffith's most suspicious loathing. He mastered his wrath in not responding editorially. The *United Irishman* of 20 December 1902 carried a publicity notice for the book that comprised an abridgement of Joyce's review. There was an interpolation of one word, in the last sentence cited from Joyce's review, thus: 'And yet he might have written well if he had not suffered from one of those big words [Patriotism] which makes us so unhappy.' The insertion, with a capitalised *P*, of the word Joyce was referring back to earlier in the review, but had chosen not to repeat, was an effective riposte. (In the 'Nestor' episode of *Ulysses*, Stephen tells Mr Deasy, 'I fear those words which make us so unhappy').[111]

The invocation of Rolleston was addressed to Griffith. In bringing its author to Griffith's attention, the review is continuous with the suite of introductions to literary figures in Dublin on which Joyce embarked from the autumn of 1902. A friendly relationship with Griffith could have been of considerable benefit to Joyce, as it had been to Padraic Colum; but, in the same breath that he drew himself to Griffith's attention,

109. Yeats, *Autobiographies*, 423.

110. This is comprehensively discussed in Callanan, 'Joyce and the *United Irishman*', 72–77.

111. *U* 2.264. Joyce's persistent practice of citing extreme comments from condemnatory notices of his own books—which arguably spills over into the characterisation of Shem in *Finnegans Wake*—is likely to owe something to Griffith's example.

he proclaimed an absolute refusal to be beholden to him. All the Joyce of 1902–4 is present in this: a furious sense of independence, an embrace of what there was to experience, intellectual lucidity, erudition, and preternaturally exact observation; and a cavalier playfulness. There was a heartbreaking fortitude which to most of his contemporaries seemed indistinguishable from improvident pride.

Joyce's review of Rooney's poems was something more than a virtuoso exercise in provocation. He seized the opportunity to articulate his critique of the conjuncture of hard-line cultural nationalism and revivalism of the Irish language. There was something flawed about Rooney as a political persona—the capacity in which Griffith principally esteemed him—that Joyce intuited. He was probably not aware that Rooney had been seen within the Gaelic League as a divisive figure. Eoin MacNeill blamed a speech of Rooney's for alienating the Irish Parliamentary Party, which he had been seeking to cultivate, from the Gaelic League. There was moreover a distinct chill of politesse in the scholarly MacNeill's characterisation of Rooney as 'well remembered for his poems and writings on national subjects'.[112] Joyce was not alone in his refusal to subscribe to Griffith's dream of his dead friend.

Writing long afterwards, Colum, who knew Griffith very well and was his first biographer, as well as a friend of Joyce's, in assessing Griffith's misjudgements of Yeats and Synge, wrote that Griffith was 'inimical to what he knew of young James Joyce's work'. Of the Rooney review, he wrote, 'The young man who had belittled his poems in a Unionist journal was, to Arthur Griffith, a man of sinister mind and intention.'[113] Yet Griffith was not implacably affronted. His *Sinn Féin* was the only paper to publish in full Joyce's open letter in 1911 relating to the objections to 'Ivy Day in the Committee Room', and the following year Joyce solicited Griffith's advice and help in his continuing difficulties with his Dublin publishers.[114] Griffith received him 'very kindly'.[115] Though they must

112. Michael Tierney, *Eoin MacNeill: Scholar and Man of Action, 1867–1945* (Oxford: Clarendon, 1980), 80–81.

113. P. Colum, *Road Round Ireland*, 302.

114. Ellmann, *James Joyce*, 315, 334–35.

115. Joyce to Stanislaus Joyce, postmark 30 August 1912, *Letters II* 315.

have often passed each other in the National Library from 1898 to 1904, their encounter on 30 August 1912, presumably at the offices of *Sinn Féin*, was their first and only meeting, two weeks before Joyce left Ireland for the last time.

Joyce's reading of the *United Irishman* persisted unabated after the publication of his Rooney review in the *Daily Express*. On 7 March and 4 April 1903, under the title 'An Irish Rural Library', the paper published two lists of Irish books (reworking an earlier list that Rooney had compiled), with the stated purpose of informing the selection of books by rural Irish libraries. The first list comprised works in English, the second in Irish. The lengthy catalogue of Irish books that appears in Joyce's Paris–Pola Commonplace Book is drawn directly from and cleaves closely to the 1903 *United Irishman* lists.[116] Joyce meticulously transcribed virtually the entirety of the first list of works in English, his only innovation being to constitute a separate category of 'Speeches', which included Jennie Wyse Power's collation of quotations from the speeches of Parnell, *Words of the Dead Chief*. From the second list of books in Irish, Joyce took only twenty works, principally in the category of 'Older Literature', excluding contemporary writing in Irish. This attests to his interest in older works in the Irish language, principally the Irish myths, lives of the saints, and poetry, along with Geoffrey Keating's *History of Ireland*, the *Annals of the Four Masters*, and *The Ancient Laws of Ireland*.[117]

If the original source for the works listed in the Paris–Pola Commonplace Book is clear, Joyce's purpose in making such a list is less certain. While distantly presaging *Ulysses* and *Finnegans Wake*, the exercise is hard to match to the preoccupations of the Stephen Dedalus of *A Portrait* and is at odds with Joyce's public profile in University College. I have suggested elsewhere that the lists are 'best conceived as a scoping exercise on Joyce's part, a sizing up and textual mapping of the subject of Ireland'.[118] There is an almost eerie purposefulness in the need he

116. James Joyce, Paris–Pola Commonplace Book, 1903–1912, NLI, MS 36,369/02/A.

117. Callanan, 'Joyce and the *United Irishman*', where the *United Irishman* lists are included in facsimile.

118. Callanan, 'Joyce and the *United Irishman*', 88.

felt to apprehend the corpus of Irish writing and writing on Ireland as a whole. Something in the lists presages the selectively encyclopaedic ambitions of Joyce in the rendering of Ireland that were to find expression in *Finnegans Wake*.

What may bring greater clarity to his purpose in transcribing the lists is the intersection of their publication with his encounters in Paris with Synge, on 9 March 1903 and over the week or so that followed. Joyce would have received the edition of the *United Irishman* of 7 March 1903. Though a month would expire before the publication of the second list on 4 April 1903, it is possible that Joyce's interest in the *United Irishman* lists owed something to the competitive stimulus of meeting Synge which, in destabilising his conception of the Irish Revival, forced him to reconsider his own strategy as an Irish writer, if only in inflecting and giving a degree of urgency to approaches he may have already had in consideration.

The selection from the second list suggests that Joyce, however sceptical about the revival of the Irish language, and hostile to the *völkisch* orientation of the Celtic Twilight, was alive to the significance of the older literature in the Irish language, of Irish myths and annals. That he was interested in the modernistic deployment of Irish myths was to become clear from his story 'The Dead', which he wrote in Trieste in the autumn of 1907. The story has a teeming spectral sub-level that derives from Gaelic literature, principally 'The Destruction of Dá Derga's Hostel', that was identified by John V. Kelleher in 1965 and hauntingly—even terrifyingly—developed by Paul Muldoon's 1998 Clarendon lectures.[119] That raises the issue of whether Joyce drew on what the *United Irishman* published on the Irish myths. The sources of Joyce's knowledge of the Irish myths remain to be established. The magnificent ambitiousness of Griffith's weekly paper was epitomised in the publication of a series titled 'Old Irish Bardic Tales', written by Richard Irvine Best, from 11 October 1902 to 25 April 1903, an envelope of time that also

119. John V. Kelleher, 'Irish History and Mythology in James Joyce's "The Dead"', *Review of Politics* 27, no. 3 (1965): 414–33; Paul Muldoon, *To Ireland, I: An Abecedary of Irish Literature* (Oxford: Oxford University Press, 2000), 51–52, 86–87; Maria Tymoczko, *The Irish Ulysses* (Berkeley: University of California Press, 1994), 185–88, 230–34.

encompassed the publication of the rural library lists used by Joyce. Best's rendering of 'The Destruction of Dá Derga's Hostel' was published in the *United Irishman* of 27 January and 7 February 1903: the story does not feature in P. W. Joyce's *Old Celtic Romances,* though it does appear in Lady Gregory's *Cuchulain of Muirthemne.*

Joyce's reading of the *United Irishman* from its inception did not equate to support for Griffith's politics. There was an interval of over five years from the inception of the paper before Joyce expressed a qualified endorsement of Griffith, though that has to have owed a great deal to his reading of the paper. He was slow to detach Griffith from the ranks of the 'patriots' of whom his suspicions found expression in *Stephen Hero*. In that unfinished novel, Griffith is placed in the circle frequented by Madden (the character based on George Clancy) that was centred on Cathal McGarvey's tobacco shop, An Stad, on North Frederick Street. Identified as 'the editor of the weekly journal of the irreconcilable party', Griffith reports to the circle 'any signs of Philocelticism which he had observed in the Paris newspapers': 'The cry of a solitary Frenchman ("A bas l'Angleterre") at a Celtic re-union in Paris would be made by these enthusiasts the subject of a leading article in which would be shown the imminence of aid for Ireland from the French Government. A glowing example was to be found for Ireland in the case of Hungary, an example, as these patriots imagined, of a long-suffering minority, entitled by every right of race and justice to a separate freedom, finally emancipating itself.'[120]

Joyce was dismissive of the Hungarian parallel that informed Griffith's *Resurrection of Hungary*. Joyce's somewhat exaggerated emphasis on Griffith's invocation of isolated manifestations of French support was due in part to his identification of Griffith with Maud Gonne, of whom Griffith was a friend and chivalric defender. Joyce had yet to separate Griffith as a political persona from Griffith the editor and journalist, and to appreciate that Griffith was a political nationalist rather than someone who saw politics as a means of reviving the Irish language (a subject on which Griffith's views were quite moderate).

120. *SH* 61–62.

Reviewer for the *Daily Express*

Well, I'm ashamed of you, said Miss Ivors frankly. To say you'd write for a rag like that. I didn't think you were a West Briton.

—JOYCE, 'THE DEAD'[121]

It was through the intercession of Lady Gregory that Joyce was commissioned to write reviews for the *Daily Express* by its editor E. V. Longworth. The paper was described at the time as 'the organ of the landed gentry, the clergy, the professional and commercial classes', whose principles were 'distinctly Protestant and constitutional'.[122] Joyce wrote a series of reviews for the paper from December 1902 to November 1903, starting with his incendiary review of William Rooney's poems. Two more of his reviews stand out as politically significant: those of Stephen Gwynn's *Today and Tomorrow in Ireland: Essays on Irish Subjects* and of Augusta Gregory's *Poets and Dreamers: Studies and Translations from the Irish*.[123]

Joyce wrote his review of Gwynn's *Today and Tomorrow in Ireland* shortly after he returned to Paris in January 1903, and it was published in the *Daily Express* of 29 January 1903. Stephen Gwynn (1864–1950) had been a writer and journalist in London from 1896. He was to return to Ireland in 1904, and in 1906 was elected as a nationalist for Galway City, which he represented until 1918. Unusually for a member of the Irish Party, he had a close association with the Literary Revival.[124] In the preface to his book, he identified his political position: 'I call myself a nationalist. But my nationalism has nothing irreconcilable about it. If

121. *D* 163.

122. *Newspaper Press Directory*, 58th ed. (London: Mitchell, 1903). The *Daily Express* is listed under 'Dublin' in the 'Irish Newspaper Press' section of the directory.

123. Rooney, *Poems and Ballads*; Stephen Gwynn, *Today and Tomorrow in Ireland: Essays on Irish Subjects* (Dublin: Hodges, Figgis, 1903); Augusta Gregory, *Poets and Dreamers: Studies and Translations from the Irish* (Dublin: Hodges, Figgis, 1903).

124. Maume, *Long Gestation*, 228–29; Carla King, 'Stephen Gwynn', *ODNB* 24:365–66. In his admirable biography, Colin Reid writes that Gwynn's Irish Ireland idealism 'slackened during his parliamentary years, a reaction to the increasingly myopic assertiveness of the Gaelic League in Irish life.' Reid, *Lost Ireland*, 65.

Ireland had the status of Canada, I should be as good an Imperialist as Sir Wilfrid Laurier.'[125] This enabled Joyce to situate Gwynn politically as 'a convert to the prevailing national movement' and to observe that he 'professes himself a Nationalist, though his nationalism, as he says, has nothing irreconcilable about it. Give Ireland the status of Canada, and he becomes an Imperialist at once. It is hard to say into what political party Mr Gwynn should go, for he is too consistently Gaelic for the Parliamentarians, and too mild for the true patriots, who are beginning to speak a little vaguely about their friends the French. Mr. Gwynn, however, is at least a member of that party which seeks to establish an Irish literature and Irish industries.'[126]

The reference to 'that party' which favoured a revivalism that did not encompass the revival of the Irish language was deliberate and quietly startling. There was no such party in the conventional political sense of that term that answered to the definition. Writing for a Unionist paper, Joyce was refusing to submit to the choice between the post-Parnell Irish Party and the 'patriots'. In deploying the term 'party' in its non-institutional sense, he was disarranging the rigid party allegiances of Irish politics.

Joyce was highly unusual as a nationalist commentator who was unsparing and sardonically minute in identifying the contradictions and divergencies within nationalism; it was an exercise that Unionist commentators largely disdained to undertake. The readiness to engage in a dispassionate critique of schools of nationalist thought marked out Joyce's review of Gwynn, as previously of Rooney's poems.

Joyce wrote that the essays in literary criticism were the least interesting of Gwynn's essays, and he took the opportunity to draw an unfavourable comparison between the modern Irish writers (Yeats excepted) and Mangan, 'that creature of lightning'. He praised 'those essays which are illustrative of the industrial work which has been set in movement at different points of Ireland. His account of the establishing of the fishing industry in the West of Ireland is extremely interesting, and so are

125. Gwynn, *Today and Tomorrow*, x.

126. *OCPW* 65.

his accounts of dairies, old-fashioned and new-fashioned, and of carpet making'. The work was 'full of anecdotes': 'Mr Gwynn has evidently a sense of the humorous, and it is pleasing to find this in a revivalist.' He ended the review by rendering one of those anecdotes, less satisfactorily than had Gwynn.[127] Joyce had skilfully dissembled a degree of impatient boredom on reading Gwynn's book. Writing to Stanislaus, he referred to 'my review of Everyman's book (damn Everyman anyhow!)'.[128] The studied poise of the review was disturbed by the intervention of the editor in inserting, to Joyce's intense irritation, a ponderous sentence to end the review on a more positive note: 'The volume, admirably bound and printed, is a credit to the Dublin firm to whose enterprise its publication is due.'[129]

Stanislaus Joyce wrote much later of the review that 'some phrases in it are interesting because they reflect my brother's almost neutral attitude to Irish politics.' He wrote that Joyce's own political thought 'ran more or less in the same direction as Gwynn's' and that his 'political attitude was equally indefinable'. Conceding in a striking understatement that 'my brother was not favourable to an English government in Ireland', he asserted that Joyce 'could not imagine any form of Irish government that would not be still more uncongenial to him than anything to be found in England or abroad. He did not try to solve the problem of nationality. He flouted it to save his soul.'[130] This commentary reflected Stanislaus's unmovable inability, captured in the almost tragic impercipience of the phrase 'my brother's almost neutral attitude to Irish politics', to comprehend his brother's Irish nationalism.

While Joyce was beginning to refine his indiscriminate suspicion of the 'patriots', he had not relinquished the position he had taken as a student. He was also in a characteristic way at once taking advantage of and satirising the role of a reviewer writing for a Unionist newspaper. The game was conducted at two levels. The first was to write a superbly poised review that read superficially as if its author shared the politics

127. Gwynn, *Today and Tomorrow*, 59–61.

128. Joyce to Stanislaus Joyce, 8 February 1903, *Letters II* 27.

129. *OCPW* 65–66.

130. S. Joyce, *My Brother's Keeper*, 214–15.

of the paper, but on a closer reading probably did not. The second was to challenge those who realised its unidentified author was probably of nationalist convictions by its sceptical dispassion. As in the Rooney review, it was the consummate familiarity with nationalist politics that rendered it improbable that the writer was a Unionist. Joyce had feared that his reference to the 'true patriots who are beginning to speak a little vaguely about their friends the French' might have been suppressed, writing from Paris to Stanislaus to enquire, 'Was that in it?'[131]

When Longworth sent Augusta Gregory's *Poets and Dreamers: Studies and Translations from the Irish* to Joyce in Paris in March 1903, he anticipated that, however temperamental Joyce was as a reviewer, ordinary gratitude would ensure that he treated at least politely a work by the woman who had recommended him to the *Daily Express*. He could not have been more wrong. Joyce's review, published in the *Daily Express* of 26 March 1903, was of unsparing ferocity. It was a critique of the Celtic Twilight in which, Joyce argued, the vigour—the primaeval youth—of Irish myth had been lost in Lady Gregory's reverence for aged living renderers of Irish folklore: 'Perhaps, in the future little boys with long beards will stand aside and applaud, while old men in short trousers play handball against the side of a house. This may even happen in Ireland, if Lady Gregory has truly set forth the old age of her country. In her new book she has left legends and heroic youth far behind, and has explored in a land almost fabulous in its sorrow and senility.'[132]

On this occasion, Joyce's habitual exemption of Yeats from his strictures on contemporary Irish writers seems to have been intended to drive a wedge into the Twilight: 'In fine, her book, wherever it treats of the "folk", sets forth in the fullness of its senility a class of mind which Mr Yeats has set forth with such delicate scepticism in his happiest book, *The Celtic Twilight*.' Gregory's book improved with the poet Raftery (Antoine Ó Raifteari), who, 'though he be the last of the great bardic procession, has much of the bardic tradition about him', an observation of some significance in suggesting Joyce's knowledge, if rudimentary, of where

131. Joyce to Stanislaus Joyce, 8 February 1903, *Letters II* 28.

132. *OCPW* 74.

Raftery stood. He characterised the four one-act plays by Douglas Hyde, translations of which were included in the book, as belonging to the genre of the 'dwarf-drama'.[133] In his final paragraph Joyce asserted, in the interplay between 'memories of beliefs' and 'the central belief of Ireland', the linkage of political enfeeblement and cultural atrophy:

> This book, like so many other books of our time, is in part picturesque and in part an indirect or direct utterance of the central belief of Ireland. Out of the material and spiritual battle which has gone so hardly with her Ireland has emerged with many memories of beliefs, and with one belief—a belief in the incurable ignobility of the forces that have overcome her—and Lady Gregory, whose old men and women seem to be almost their own judges when they tell their wandering stories, might add to the passage from Whitman which forms her dedication, Whitman's ambiguous word for the vanquished—'-Battles are lost in the spirit in which they are won.'[134]

The line—like the rather anodyne verse that Lady Gregory had chosen as an epigraph, 'Will you seek afar off' (from 'A Song for Occupations')—came from Walt Whitman's *Leaves of Grass*, from 'Song of Myself':

> With music strong I came, with my cornets and my drums,
> I play not marches for accepted victors only, I play marches for conquer'd and slain persons.
>
> Have you heard that it was good to gain the day?
> I also say it is good to fall, battles are lost in the same spirit in which they are won.
>
> I beat and pound for the dead,
> I blow through my embouchures my loudest and gayest for them,
> Vivas for those who have fail'd.[135]

133. *OCPW* 75.

134. *OCPW* 75–76.

135. Quoted in *OCPW* 305. As the editor of the *OCPW*, Kevin Barry, comments, both perspectives are dramatised in 'The Dead'.

This is significant as the first recorded expression—by citation—of the idea that became increasingly important for Joyce of the 'ousted possibilities' of history, of the retroactive blindsiding that attended positivistic accounts of history's victors and of movements or forces that prevailed or are deemed to have done so. Here it is an ambitious turn in his argument that could not be fully developed within the confines of the review; Joyce was decrying Gregory's treatment of Irish myths and emphasis on the contemporary folkloric, which he saw as an editing of the Irish past that was collusive with teleological narratives of Irish nationalism. It is an assertion of the ungovernability of the Irish past, of the impossibility of assimilating Irish history and culture to retrospective socio-political ordering. It is a viscerally instinctual response. So far as is known, there is nothing to suggest that Joyce as of the spring of 1903 had much knowledge of old Irish literature; it was as if he was throwing down a challenge to the Celtic Twilight, as he conceived it, that he would have to make good.

Joyce's argument was that revivalism, which professed to be a corrective redressing of imperialist narratives of Irish history and culture, displaced one ideological order with another. The Irish response to 'the material and spiritual battle which had gone so hardly with [Ireland]' was to don a defensive carapace. Irish nationalism and the Twilight imposed a categorisation of the victorious and the vanquished of their own that was as much a distortion as were Unionist accounts of Irish history. The rehearsing of that intimation in the review of Gregory's book makes plain that Joyce's concept of 'ousted possibilities' derived from his contemplation of Irish history and politics, which had as its point of departure his unsparing assessment of the Parnell Split.

The ferocity of the review overshadowed the incisiveness of his challenge to the premises of the Celtic Twilight which would inform the intricate allusiveness to Irish myth in his own work. Joyce wrote to his mother from Paris, 'I sent in my review of Lady Gregory's book a week ago. I do not know if Longworth put it in as I sent it: the review was very severe.' He added, in deference to May Joyce's anxious counsels of prudence, 'I shall write to Lady Gregory one of these days.'[136] The

136. Joyce to May Joyce, 20 March 1903, *Letters II* 37–38.

editor of the *Daily Express*, with evident hesitation, published the review as written, but over the initials 'J.J.' to disavow personal responsibility for a review by the writer whom Augusta Gregory had commended to him.[137] The episode was to inspire Buck Mulligan's baiting remonstrance to Stephen Dedalus in *Ulysses*: 'Longworth is awfully sick, he said, after what you wrote about that old hake Lady Gregory. O you inquisitional drunken jewjesuit! She gets you a job on the paper and then you go and slate her drivel to Jaysus. Couldn't you do the Yeats touch?'[138]

Stanislaus Joyce concluded that the fact that Joyce continued to be sent books for review signified that Longworth bore him no ill will.[139] It is clear, however, that the Gregory review brought about a change in the relationship of editor to reviewer. There was a hiatus of almost six months before Joyce was asked to write another review. The books were sent for review with diminished frequency and were such as to deny Joyce the opportunity to display his gift for controversy. There were signs of open revolt in Joyce's review in October 1903 of three popular novels by Alfred Edward Woodley Mason which ended with the sentence, 'Isn't *Miranda of the Balcony* a pretty name?'[140] Joyce was perhaps in some degree placated with the next commission, reviewing J. Lewis McIntyre's biography of the sixteenth-century Italian heretic Giordano Bruno, which he did with some flair.[141]

Joyce's valedictory flourish to the *Daily Express* came in the ending to his review, published on 19 November 1903, of T. Baron Russell's novel *Borlase and Son*. Derisively echoing Longworth's insertion to his review of Stephen Gwynn's book, Joyce wrote, 'For the rest, the binding of the book is as ugly as one could reasonably expect.'[142]

Joyce's *Daily Express* reviews were written with consummate poise. Curran later wrote, 'They have complete assurance with due sense of

137. In 'The Dead' it is the fact that a review in the *Daily Express* appeared over Gabriel Conroy's initials that enables Miss Ivors to launch into her assault over his writing reviews for a Unionist paper (*D* 162–63).

138. *U* 9.1158–61.

139. S. Joyce, *My Brother's Keeper*, 239.

140. *OCPW* 91–92.

141. *OCPW* 93–94.

142. *OCPW* 99.

responsibility, occasionally harsh but more usually written with courtesy or a politeness touched with irony.'[143] They were certainly not 'dully expressed', Joyce's play on the name of the paper in *Finnegans Wake*.[144] In one aspect they afford a glimpse of the Joyce who was not to be: a Dublin- or London-based writer who got by on literary journalism, though the unbiddable 'enigma of a manner' of Joyce's persona as a reviewer seems intended to convey that this was a career prospect he had ruled out.

The incisive prose style of the reviews had nothing in common with the sentimental style of Gabriel Conroy in 'The Dead', as exemplified in the speech he makes. Miss Ivors's attack on Conroy was wide of the mark in relation to Joyce: while the paper was Unionist, Joyce's reviews scarcely conformed to either the paper's politics or its house style. In a double move of the type he was to make his own in addressing the political, he declined to mitigate his criticisms of the inferior literature or propaganda of the cultural revival, defying what might have been expected of him as a Catholic and putatively nationalist contributor, while subtly challenging the politics of the paper, and more overtly the authority of its editor.

In 'The Dead', in considering his response to Miss Ivors's attack on his writing for the *Daily Express*, Gabriel Conroy 'wanted to say that literature was above politics' but felt it was too abrupt given their past associations and shrewdly guessed that 'he could not risk a grandiose phrase with her'. Instead he 'murmured lamely that he saw nothing political in writing reviews of books.'[145] It is doubtful that Joyce subscribed to the first proposition in that facile formulation; his reviews disproved the second.

The Politics of *Dana*

References to the journal *Dana: An Irish Magazine of Independent Thought* in biographical and critical writing on Joyce feature chiefly as an early episode in the chronicle of the thwarted publication of his

143. Curran, *James Joyce Remembered*, 65.
144. *FW* 500.15–16.
145. *D* 163.

works in Ireland. The editors' rejection in early 1904 of his 'A Portrait of the Artist' essay is of significance in itself, but it is Joyce's inability to subscribe to the editorial politics of *Dana* that is critically important to an understanding of his political solitariness in the Ireland that he was to leave later that year.

The first issue of *Dana*, started and edited by William Kirkpatrick Magee and Frederick Ryan, and supported by George Moore, appeared in May 1904. In the first issue, its editors wrote that 'the elemental freedom of the human mind' had been absent from the Irish literary movement, and Ryan wrote, 'We need in Ireland a spirit of intellectual freedom, and a recognition of the supremacy of humanity. . . . Intellectual freedom and political freedom are not opposites. Rightly understood, intellectual freedom and political freedom are one.'[146] Moore wrote to his friend Edouard Dujardin, referring to Magee, 'One of my friends has started a tiny review in Dublin, somewhat on lines of the *Revue des Idées*, that is it has an anticlerical bias.'[147] As Magee recalled, 'Yeats held aloof, talking cuttingly of "Fleet Street atheism".'[148]

The significance of the intellectual relationship of Joyce and Magee has not been recognised. They were complementary opposites. Born on either side of the Irish sectarian divide—Magee was the son of a Presbyterian minister and superintendent of the Dublin city mission—each was uncompromisingly independent. Joyce was of nationalist conviction, while Magee declined to embrace or enter into a compact of subservience with Irish nationalism (though 'Yeats, A. E. and Arthur Griffith got hold of me and tried to turn me into a nationalist').[149] Joyce was modernistic; Magee's literary values were more classical. Their relations were informed by a strained reciprocal sense, never fully articulated, of their mirroring each other, that shifted across time.

146. *Dana*, 1 May 1904. Æ's bolder suggestion of the *Heretic* as the title was rejected; Eglinton, *Irish Literary Portraits*, 134 (Magee wrote under the pen name of John Eglinton).

147. George Moore, *Letters from George Moore to Edouard Dujardin* (New York: Crosby Gaige, 1929), 49.

148. Eglinton, *Irish Literary Portraits*, 135.

149. Eglinton, *Irish Literary Portraits*, 10–11.

Yeats characterised Magee as 'our one philosophical critic'.[150] While Magee was personally close to the literary figures of the Revival, his refusal of political compromise set him apart. Reviewing Magee's *Pebbles from a Brook* for the *United Irishman* in 1901, Yeats criticised his aloofness from the political: 'I believe him right in thinking that the great movement of our time is a movement to destroy modern civilization, but I cannot but believe him wrong in thinking that it will be ended by "liberated individuals" who separate themselves from the great passions, from the great popular interests, from religion, from humanitarianism.'[151]

Joyce's relationship with Magee was in its way the most intellectually haunting of his Dublin relations, belying the frequent cruelty of Joyce's comments. Joyce and Gogarty traded jokes and limericks on the subject of Magee's Presbyterian rectitude, and of the virginity which he had inadvisedly confessed to Gogarty.[152] The lines on Magee in 'The Holy Office', which Joyce wrote before he left Dublin in October 1904, were comparatively measured:

Or him who will not his hat unfix
Neither to malt nor crucifix
But show to all that poor-dressed be
His high Castilian courtesy.[153]

In 1907 Stanislaus evidently relayed to Joyce a joke about Magee having his cake and not eating it. In dire financial straits in Rome, Joyce

150. Yeats, *Explorations*, 160. Yeats wrote elsewhere, 'Magee states everything in a slightly argumentative form. This means that the soul is starved by the absence of self-evident truth.' W. B. Yeats, *Memoirs*, ed. Denis Donoghue (London: Macmillan, 1972), 210–11 (5 April 1909); see also Curtis Bradford, *Yeats at Work* (Carbondale: Southern Illinois University Press, 1965), 341–42.

151. *United Irishman*, 9 November 1901; W. B. Yeats, *Uncollected Prose by W. B. Yeats*, ed. J. P. Frayne and Colton Johnson (London: Macmillan, 1975), 2:260.

152. S. Joyce, *My Brother's Keeper*, 247, 249. A squib in the manner of Robert Burns beginning 'John Eglinton, my Jo, John' seems to be one of their collaborations on the subject. It ends,

Your virtue is a fare, John,
Ye cardna if ye tried. (*PSW* 111, 263)

153. *PSW* 98.

responded, 'I laughed at Eglinton and his cake but I fear I have eaten nearly all mine; still his must be a trifle stale by this.'[154] Nevertheless, in the literary *colloque* in the National Library in the 'Scylla and Charybdis' episode of *Ulysses*, it is to John Eglinton (Magee's nom de plume) that Stephen directs his argument on Shakespeare. Magee makes a later fleeting appearance '*with carping accent*' in 'Circe'.[155]

Their ideas touched closely from opposite directions. In controversy with Yeats on the idea of a national literature in 1899, Magee objected, 'In all ages poets and thinkers have owed far less to their countries than their countries have owed to them.'[156] He returned to the idea four years later, writing in the *United Irishman*, 'It is meaningless to say that national literature is the conscious and deliberate expression of what are called "national ideas". The ideas of a nation are those it receives from its poets and thinkers. The nationality of a literature represents the homage of a nation to her poets far more than the loyalty of poets to the nation.'[157]

Magee's thesis is congruent with, if not a distant point of departure for, Joyce's more egotistical formulations of the comparative importance of Stephen Dedalus and his country.[158] Likewise there was much with which Joyce agreed in Magee's essay 'The De-Davization of Irish Literature' in his *Bards and Saints*, which Joyce had in his library in Trieste. Magee had written, 'Since Davis the true religion of the Irish Nationalist has been patriotism.'[159]

154. Joyce to Stanislaus Joyce, [?1 March 1907], *Letters II* 219.

155. *U* 15.2233–60.

156. John Eglinton et al., *Literary Ideals in Ireland* (London: T. Fisher Unwin, 1899), 13.

157. John Eglinton, 'On the Relation of Poets to Their Country', *United Irishman*, 21 February 1903.

158. 'I suspect, Stephen interrupted, that Ireland must be important because it belongs to me' (*U* 16.1166–67). Magee (writing as Eglinton), in his essay 'The Beginnings of Joyce', does not draw a connection; Eglinton, *Irish Literary Portraits*, 137, 141.

159. John Eglinton, 'The De-Davization of Irish Literature', in *Bards and Saints* (Dublin: Maunsel, 1906), 38. Joyce also possessed Eglinton's *Anglo-Irish Essays* (London: T. F. Unwin, 1917) according to Ellmann (*Consciousness of Joyce*, 107). Magee also wrote a strikingly perceptive piece in the March 1909 issue of *Dana* entitled 'The Weak Point of the Celtic Movement', in which he asserted the weak point to be the failure of contemporary Irish literature to address the issue of religion which loomed so large in Irish politics.

Magee found the pre-exilic Joyce acutely bewildering and later confessed with austere candour that he had regarded him 'with a certain amount of condescension'.[160] It was only in retrospect, in an essay published in 1935, that he wrote of the figure he had known: 'Religion had been with him a profound adolescent experience, torturing the sensitiveness which it awakened; all its floods had gone over him. He had now recovered, and had no objection to "Fleet Street atheism", but "independent thought" appeared to him an amusing disguise of the proselytising spirit, and one night as we walked across town he endeavoured, with a certain earnestness, to bring home to me the extreme futility of the ideals represented in *Dana*, by describing to me the solemn ceremonial of High Mass.'[161]

Both Joyce and Magee were alive to the salience of confessional background and frank in their treatment of it. When Joyce appeared in the National Library in the course of one of his last visits to Ireland, 'marvellously smartened up and with a short trim beard', Magee discerned the early stages of a transformation: 'Certain it is that when he decided to scrap the scholastic habiliments of his mind, the poor disguise of a seedy snobbishness, and in lieu thereof endued himself with the elemental diabolism of *Ulysses*, he was transfigured.'[162] Many years later, Magee, by then living in England, called on Joyce at the Paris hotel where Joyce was staying at the time.[163]

The reasons for which Joyce declined to identify himself with *Dana*, the most ambitious and sophisticated journal of liberal intellectuality to appear in his time in Dublin, bear scrutiny. They lie in his Parnellite nationalism. In the absence of an alignment with nationalism, or at the very least a clear political direction in relation to nationalism, *Dana* had no prospect of mounting a challenge to the politico-cultural hegemony of the Catholic Church, or of winning over even an exiguous body of nationalist opinion. Moreover, as Magee had shrewdly discerned, Joyce

160. Eglinton, *Irish Literary Portraits*, 153. Magee stands virtually alone among Joyce's Dublin contemporaries in admitting he had got Joyce wrong.

161. Eglinton, *Irish Literary Portraits*, 135.

162. Eglinton, *Irish Literary Portraits*, 140, 143–44.

163. Eglinton, *Irish Literary Portraits*, 153–55.

disliked the didacticism of *Dana*. Even though the ethos of the journal was essentially free-thinking, it carried for Joyce a whiff of the 'nonconformist conscience', his loathing of which derived from the Split.

In the bitterly comedic letter he wrote from Rome to Stanislaus after he had read about the *Playboy* riot, Joyce gave vent to the same considerations that led him to dismiss the 'extreme futility' of *Dana*: 'Synge will probably be condemned from the pulpit, as a heretic; which would be dreadful: so that Stiffbreeches [Skeffington] and Ryan really *ought* to start another paper in defence of free thought, just for a week or so.'[164]

Referring principally to Moore, Magee, and Ryan, Geert Lernout has written perceptively, 'Joyce only rarely paid his ideological debts, and while he must have had sympathy for the ideas of these local freethinkers, he never acknowledges them as precursors.'[165] However, in this instance there was no debt: the only ideological debt to the publishers of *Dana* was in a reactive sharpening of his thinking. What is striking is Joyce's capacity to think politically, and the incisiveness of his political judgement. Joyce's enigmatic statement in the 'Portrait' essay that 'he saw between camps his ground of vantage' comes to mind.[166] Sustained criticism of the public influence of the Catholic Church in Ireland confronted two formidable inhibitions: the first being the Catholicism of a large majority of the population, the second to do with the identification of Church and nation. The first was a given. The only possible point of attack was the second, and the only mode of attack was the adumbration of a secular, non–confessionally based nationalism. Joyce realised that to have the least possibility of being entertained, criticisms of the Church had to be shorn of ascendancy and of

164. Joyce to Stanislaus Joyce, [?1 February 1907], *Letters II* 208–9. Ellmann, in his editorial capacity, makes the erroneous assumption that 'Stiffbreeches', a soubriquet Joyce applied to Sheehy-Skeffington, was a reference to Magee. Joyce's joke had a greater actuality than he knew. Sheehy-Skeffington and Ryan in fact produced, from February to August 1907, a short-lived monthly entitled the *National Democrat*, but Joyce seems to have been unaware of its appearance when he wrote his letter to Stanislaus.

165. Lernout, *Help My Unbelief*, 89.

166. *PSW* 218.

anti-nationalist (or even neutral) connotation or association. Joyce's political thinking had a hard-edged realism which has remained unnoticed and unsuspected.

Joyce's thinking was not altogether impersonal: there was something politically arid in Magee's (and Moore's) relation to nationalism. Nor was his objection merely tactical. Joyce's seemingly haughty intellectual mode belied the fact that he drew politically on the anticlerical residues of Fenianism and of the Parnellism of the Split, rather than looking to an alliance with contemporary freethinkers. What is most salient is that Joyce was prepared (whatever his doubts) to take the chance that the best prospect of containing the power of the Church was in an independent Irish state. That seemed a better bet than a futile struggle for free thought under then-prevailing political arrangements. That judgement revealed the wager that Joyce as an Irish nationalist was prepared to make, which was less a personal gamble than a deeply inscribed premise of radical nationalism.

It is highly revelatory that in a work published as late as 1968, the most fastidious contemporary observer of his politics was still unable to discern that it was finally Joyce's nationalism that set him apart from Magee and Ryan. In *James Joyce Remembered,* Constantine Curran took exception to Stanislaus Joyce's admittedly overblown depiction of Joyce in 1904 as someone who had all the little literary world of Dublin against him. Curran wrote, 'John Eglinton and Fred Ryan, in their conduct of *Dana,* were declared anti-clericals, but John Eglinton was an imperialist and Fred Ryan a socialist and nationalist of the same temper as Frank Skeffington and in his outlook not very far removed from Joyce himself.'[167] Curran missed the political fissure that separated Joyce from Magee and Ryan. He had known Joyce in Dublin and thereafter known personalities who featured in the Rising such as Patrick Pearse and MacNeill[168] and had held a role in the judicial establishment of the Irish state—he didn't reject the idea that Joyce was politically an Irish

167. Curran, *James Joyce Remembered,* 78.

168. Curran, 'Griffith, MacNeill and Pearse'.

nationalist, but it simply never occurred to him. It was as if Joyce's enigmatic reticence in University College was sealed forever in the establishment of the independent Irish state. Joyce understood this, and it informs the conception of the self-parodic figure of Shem, the exilic pariah, in *Finnegans Wake*.

What remains is the intriguing issue of how Joyce's response to *Dana* and to Magee and Ryan influenced his conception and practice of quasi-autobiographical fiction. There is of course a direct relation in the case of his 'A Portrait of the Artist' essay, considered later in this chapter, written for *Dana* and rejected by Magee. The densely subjective and intellectually autobiographical text, contained not without a degree of violence within the genre of an essay, was written as a personal statement, and as such was already a subversion of the tractarian mode of *Dana*. In the essay Joyce had found the theme of the formation of the artist in an inchoate national polity. His reservations about *Dana* were both political and artistic and mark the beginning of what drove him towards what became the *Portrait* novel. In a dynamic counter-*Dana* inversion, Joyce conceived a novel that contained essayistic traces in the aphorisms of Stephen Dedalus. Stephen's refusal of the collusive tyrannies of Church and nation had a fierceness and a grace not to be found in Magee and Ryan's journal. The novel maintained a rapport with its distant origins in the 'Portrait' essay and Joyce's critique of the politics of *Dana*, in significant respects eliding the middle term of *Stephen Hero*.

Joyce's inability to align himself with *Dana* has an intense poignancy. His exilic rupture was primarily with his own generation and his intellectual kind. He was suspicious of cultural nationalism. He repudiated the right and was indifferent to the left (such as it was) of Irish parliamentarism, and declined to align himself with secularist intellectual dissent. His solitude had a sub-fatalistic logic. It was not an egotistic conceit, nor was it a predetermined outcome or an end that he had willed. In his leaving Ireland, socio-political dissentience and personal material circumstances merged inseparably; this renders preposterous the now-faded idea that Joyce could have been at any level apolitical.

Joyce's 'A Portrait of the Artist' Essay for *Dana*

Without immediate literary projects after his mother's death, Joyce, 'probably acting on Yeats's suggestion', asked Stanislaus to suggest some titles for essays. One of the titles Stanislaus proposed was 'A Portrait of the Artist'.[169] Nothing came of this until Joyce became aware in January 1904 of the proposed inception of *Dana*, four months before the appearance of its first number in May, which contained the general solicitation, 'We invite the thinkers, dreamers and observers dispersed throughout Ireland and elsewhere, who do not despair of humanity in Ireland, to communicate through our pages their thoughts, reveries and observations.'[170] If Stanislaus is correct in saying that Joyce 'tossed out' the essay of 'A Portrait of the Artist' in a single day,[171] it expressed views and enunciated a style which had evidently been long in development. The holograph draft in his sister Mabel's copybook is dated 7 January 1904. Joyce offered the essay in the National Library to Magee, who later wrote, 'He observed me silently as I read, and when I handed it back to him with the timid observation that I did not care to publish what was to myself incomprehensible, he replaced it silently in his pocket.'[172] Stanislaus recalled that Joyce believed the real reason for the rejection was 'because it seemed too arrogant for a youth scarcely twenty-one years old to write an article about himself', which Stanislaus saw as a spur to his brother's recasting of the essay as the novel *Stephen Hero*.[173]

Joyce's essay was brazenly autobiographical: a rendering of the stages of his development and of the masks he assumed. Its trenchant subjectivity was expressed, in the third person, in prose of cryptic density, and of an allusiveness that veered into obscurity: the unapologetic shorthand of an artistic self. It was written in the consciousness that Magee would be its first reader, and there is a heightening at some points of

169. S. Joyce, *My Brother's Keeper*, 238.

170. *Dana* 1 (May 1904): 3.

171. S. Joyce, *Recollections of James Joyce*, 22.

172. Eglinton, *Irish Literary Portraits*, 136.

173. S. Joyce, *Recollections of James Joyce*, 22.

what Magee was likely to find provocative. That, and the intimation that what he had written was the template for the novel it would become, informed the uncharacteristic mildness of Joyce's response to its rejection. In the essay's first publication in book form, more than a half century after Joyce had written it, Robert Scholes and Richard M. Kain wrote, 'This little essay represents not only Joyce's literary manifesto but the commencement of his serious work as a literary artist. Here he has found his subject matter in the first twenty years of his own life.'[174] The theme is the development of the artist. It also marks in its referencing of European politics a critical early stage in Joyce's political thinking. What it did not have was the connection between the formation of the artist and the condition of an inchoate Irish polity with a thwarted aspiration for some form of independence, which would be a structuring principle of the novel of the same name, and would inform the distant and ironic rendering of the synchrony of Joyce's own life as an artist and the course of Irish politics in all that he wrote thereafter.

This portrait was stated at the outset to be 'not an identicative paper but rather the curve of an emotion'. It described the artist's extravagant religious ardour. While assailed by 'continued shocks . . . he was still soothed by devotional exercises when he entered the University'. At about the time he did so, 'the enigma of a manner was put at all comers to protect the crisis. He was quick enough now to see that he must disentangle his affairs in secrecy and reserve had ever been a light penance'.[175] There, aggressive sporting masculinity was 'a ground chosen to his disadvantage'. But behind a 'rapidly indurating shield', the sensitive and seemingly effete artist elaborated his response: 'Let the pack of enmities come tumbling and sniffing to the highlands after their game; there was his ground; and he flung them disdain from flashing antlers.' This, tempered by the sardonic ('there was evident self-flattery in the image'), was a silent evocation of Parnell.[176] The Parnell of the Split had frequently been compared to a noble beast dragged down by

174. Scholes and Kain, *Workshop of Daedalus*, 58. This is the first articulation of an aperçu later developed by Ellmann (*James Joyce*, 144).

175. *PSW* 212. 'The enigma of a manner' recurs in *SH* 27.

176. *PSW* 212.

pursuing hounds,[177] and later, in 'L'ombra di Parnell', Joyce would compare the lost leader to 'a hunted deer'. The 'flashing antlers' was the earliest instance of Joyce's insistent turning of Parnell's myth from within its received imagery, purging the image of the deer of its passivity, of its fate as prey. 'Identification' is a better word to describe Joyce's relationship to Parnell than 'admiration'. That identification was as much existential as political. It was imaginatively sustaining, as if Joyce were carrying Parnell with him as a living force in his own struggle. This was still Parnell as a heroic role model, though Joyce's identification with him is marked by a certain sense of intimacy, and free from conventional deference.

In the essay, Joyce rendered a first account of the artist's years in University College, which is mordant on the incongruous conformities of his contemporaries. He broke with the Church. There followed a period of dissoluteness and quasi-mystical exaltation: 'He established himself in the maddest of companies', which included 'Bruno the Nolan'. 'All the hierarchs of initiation cast their spells upon him'. From this 'he came forth at last with a single purpose—to re-unite the children of the spirit, jealous and long-divided, to re-unite them against fraud and principality'.[178] Others, pusillanimous, did not follow. He seemed first to refer to his university contemporaries: 'They pleaded their natural pieties—social limitations, inherited apathy of race, an adoring mother, the Christian fable.' He then made an unheralded transition to attacking, through allusions to theosophy, Yeats, Æ, and Lady Gregory. 'He lumped the emancipates together—Venomous Butter—and set away from the sloppy neighbourhood.'[179] He was presumably invoking 'The Day of the Rabblement', and perhaps his Literary and Historical Society paper 'Drama and Life'. Yet Joyce's characterisation of the artist as almost a revolutionary marks a reconceptualisation of his own years in university and a revisionary break with 'the enigma of a manner'. It is perhaps intended to reflect the impact of Joyce's embrace of 'the maddest

177. *PSW* 277–78n12.
178. *PSW* 214.
179. *PSW* 214–15.

of companies' and to establish a connection between his recently acquired interest in socialism and his earlier life.

The artist discovered isolation, beauty, and sex ('the blood hurries to a galop in his veins') in a setting of 'yellow gaslamps'.[180] Then came a crisis in his confidence, brought about in part by an enlarged sense of humanity. The vision of death, 'the vision (far more pitiful) of congenital lives shuffling onwards between yawn and howl, starvelings in mind and body, visions of which came a temporary failure of his olden, sustained manner, darkly beset him. The cold of difficulties about him allowed only peeps of light; even his rhetoric proclaimed transition. He could convict himself at least of a natural inability to prove everything at once and certain random attempts suggested the need for regular campaigning. His faith increased.'[181]

The faith that 'increased' was no longer religious but had to do with his sense of socialism. In the closing movement of the essay, Joyce's aperçus on the subject of Ireland and Irish nationalism acquired the formulations, at once aphoristic and open-ended, that were to recur in rich and unbounded variation through all that he wrote: 'But he saw between camps his ground of vantage, opportunities for the mocking devil in an isle twice removed from the mainland, under joint government of Their Intensities and Their Bullockships.'[182] It was an avowal that Joyce's political thinking on Ireland was informed by strategic considerations: the 'ground' was no longer that of the hunt but of military engagement. The phrase 'Their Intensities and Their Bullockships' is perhaps intended to defy precise identification.[183] The Irish Party was predominantly rural and sustained by Irish farmers, a class that also provided the bulk of the Irish priesthood and episcopacy. Its objective enemies, the precursors of Sinn Féin and cultural nationalists—

180. *PSW* 216–17.

181. *PSW* 217.

182. *PSW* 218.

183. Stuart Gilbert's attempted gloss on the phrase, used in a letter of Joyce to Gogarty of 3 June 1904, misses its aspiration to comprehensiveness: 'Their Intensities: earnest Sinn Féiners. Their Bullockships: countrified louts, or perhaps as Stanislaus Joyce suggests, priests' (*Letters I* 54n4).

'Their Intensities'—romanticised an ancient and pristine Ireland. In the Irish Catholic nationalist polity, the ecclesiastical and the secular, the material and the avowedly spiritual, merge indiscriminately.

The artist's 'Nego . . . hurled against the obscene hells of our Holy Mother [the Catholic Church]' was in consequence a political act as much as a disavowal of faith. 'That outburst over, it was urbanity in warfare':[184] again, this was an artist who was prepared, if not compelled, to think politically.

In a dramatic and unexpected shift, the conclusion of the essay opens out to embrace contemporary European politics. But there is a significant transitional move: 'Perhaps his state would pension off old tyranny—a mercy no longer hopelessly remote—in virtue of that mature civilization to which (let all allow) it had in some way contributed.' This was a reference to the prospects for Home Rule. What is striking is the temperateness of Joyce's conception of Home Rule, and the recognition that Liberal support of Home Rule partook of 'that mature civilization' informed in part by Irish writers and politicians of which he wrote. This was in the setting of the progress he discerned in European politics, to which he immediately turned.

> Already the messages of citizens were flashed along the wires of the world, already the generous idea had emerged from a thirty years war in Germany, and was directing the councils of the Latins. To those multitudes, not as yet in the wombs of humanity but surely engenderable there, he would give the word: Man and woman, out of you comes the nation that is to come, the [lightening] of your masses in travail; the competitive order is employed against itself, the aristocracies are supplanted; and amid the general paralysis of an insane society, the confederate will issue in action.[185]

In the 'thirty years war in Germany', Joyce was referring to the emergence of the German Social Democrats from the three decades that followed the Gotha Programme of 1875; the reference to 'the councils

184. *PSW* 218.
185. *PSW* 218.

of the Latins' was to the reformist Giovanni Giolitti becoming prime minister of Italy two months before, though the socialists had declined to join his government.[186] Joyce's enigmatically elliptical idiom masked a certain disproportion: whatever about the emergence of German social democracy, it was hard to discern in Giolitti's premiership a new dawn of 'the generous idea'.

What the close of the essay does make clear is that Joyce strongly sympathised with socialism and paid close attention to contemporary European politics. He turned from the stasis of Irish politics to what he saw as the greater prospect of progress in continental European states, looking to European socialism to provide the impetus for reform in Britain and Ireland. For Joyce, the European connection was co-ordinate with Irish statehood; unlike Kettle, at this point he conceived the European connection in terms of actual contemporary politics, specifically the movement of progressive and social democratic politics in continental Europe.

What is striking is the combination of the archaic obliquity (and near impenetrability) of Joyce's reference to German and Italian politics, and the refusal to mention socialism ('the generous idea') by name. He was striving to hold the artist apart from actual politics, principally by expressing himself as a prophet. He was determined, especially in an essay submitted to *Dana*, to ensure the essay did not degenerate into a tract. The 'Portrait' essay, exasperating and strangely magnificent, belongs to a genre unto itself, the innovativeness of which is palliated by our awareness that it became the writer's point of departure for two novels. Its nearest precursor is Wilde's *The Soul of Man under Socialism*,[187] which

186. Denis Mack Smith, *Modern Italy: A Political History* (New Haven, CT: Yale University Press, 1997), 193–99. The reference confirms that Joyce, who had taken Italian in University College, had an exceptional degree of familiarity with Italian politics long before his exile to Trieste.

187. Joyce's copy of Wilde's *The Soul of Man under Socialism* in his Trieste library was privately printed in 1904 by Arthur L. Humphreys, who first published it in 1895: Gillespie, *James Joyce's Trieste Library*, 261; Ellmann, *Consciousness of Joyce*, 133. This was presumably acquired after Joyce had written his 'Portrait' essay, but Joyce could well have consulted in the National Library Wilde's essay as originally published in the *Fortnightly Review* in February 1891, or read one of the many earlier editions.

Joyce later wanted to translate.[188] Wilde's most original argument—that socialism was needed to release humanity from the burden of altruism—had an immediate salience for Joyce because of the poverty of his siblings in his father's household. Nothing in Joyce's essay specifically refers to Wilde's. What they have in common is their subject matter to some degree, and the theme of the exemplary individuality of the artist. Where Joyce's essay differs from Wilde's is in its urgent if nebulous emphasis on 'the necessity for action'.

Some weeks after the death of May Joyce in August 1903, Stanislaus Joyce began what was posthumously published as his *Dublin Diary*.[189] In it he noted with considerable scepticism his brother's expressions of socialist sympathies. His first undated entry is a portrayal of his brother—he notes that 'his literary talent seems to be very great indeed' and adds, 'He is not an artist he says. He is interesting himself in politics—in which he says [he has] original ideas.'[190] It is significant that Joyce should have at that time conceived his interest in politics as in some way antithetical to a vocation as an artist. The next reference which has a bearing on Joyce's interest in socialism is in April 1904. Commenting on Joyce's borrowing from friends, Stanislaus added, 'Jim says he should be supported at the expense of the State because he is capable of enjoying himself.'[191] This seems an acridly jocular reworking of the argument of *The Soul of Man under Socialism* to conform to Joyce's more provocative conception of the imperious individuality of the artist.

188. Ellmann, *James Joyce*, 274.

189. The manuscript of the diary is in Cornell. It was first published with some omissions in 1962, and in a complete edition in 1971: Stanislaus Joyce, *The Complete Dublin Diary of Stanislaus Joyce*, ed. George H. Healey (Ithaca, NY: Cornell University Press, 1971). The principal concern in relation to the diary is that it may have been rewritten over time by Stanislaus. Stanislaus also refers elsewhere to 1904 material from his diary that is not found in the manuscript (*Dublin Diary*, ix). It is nevertheless difficult to believe that Stanislaus did serious violence to the integrity of his own diary, which provides an extremely rich account of Joyce in 1903–4, as well as an intensely moving account of Stanislaus's own life in Dublin.

190. S. Joyce, *Dublin Diary*, 2.

191. S. Joyce, *Dublin Diary*, 26

In *My Brother's Keeper*, Stanislaus wrote that while Joyce in Dublin favoured the embryonic Sinn Féin over the Irish Parliamentary Party (which Stanislaus supported), 'his political leanings were towards socialism, and he had frequented meetings of socialist groups in back rooms in the manner ascribed to Mr Duffy in "A Painful Case", one of the stories in *Dubliners*'. Stanislaus had accompanied him to 'these dimly illuminated melancholy haunts'. In 'A Painful Case', the deeply alienated Mr Duffy is pressed by Mrs Sinico to reveal events in his life rather than theories:

> He told her that for some time he had assisted at the meetings of an Irish Socialist Party where he had felt himself a unique figure amid a score of sober workmen in a garret lit by an inefficient oillamp. When the party had divided into three sections, each under its own leader and in its own garret, he had discontinued his attendances. The workmen's discussions, he said, were too timorous; the interest they took in the question of wages was inordinate. He felt that they were hardfeatured realists and that they resented an exactitude which was the product of a leisure which was not within their reach. No social revolution, he told her, would be likely to strike Dublin for some centuries.[192]

Stanislaus does not date the period in which his brother attended socialist meetings in Dublin. From the broad chronological parameters of *My Brother's Keeper*, and the fact that they are not referred to (curiously, not even retrospectively in the references to his brother's socialism), the best guess is that his attendance was in the year that followed Joyce's graduation in October 1902, which is also consistent with the turn towards European socialism in the close of the 'Portrait' essay. The dating has a bearing on the meetings he attended.[193] Stanislaus's account refers to a plurality of 'groups'. The capitalised reference to 'an Irish Socialist Party', as well as the relative prominence of James Connolly's party in the minuscule universe of Irish socialism, suggests that

192. *D* 92.

193. Stanislaus's usage of the verb 'frequented' is scarcely intended to convey actual frequency, given his brother's low boredom threshold, general aversion to political meetings, and ability to form an exact, almost photographic impression of that which he observed.

these included the Irish Socialist Republican Party (the joke in Dublin ran that it had more initials than members). Connolly played a leading role in the establishment of the party in 1896, but the party collapsed in a dispute over funds after Connolly came back from the United States in January 1903. Connolly returned to the United States in September 1903, where he remained for seven years.[194]

Stanislaus wrote that Mr Duffy, as well as the type of the male celibate, was 'also intended to be a portrait of what my brother imagined I should become in middle age'.[195] Stanislaus was hostile to socialism, as he was to what became Sinn Féin, and Mr Duffy's disillusionment reflected Stanislaus's own rather than this brother's ideas: 'At Trieste he still called himself a socialist'.[196] Mr Duffy's observation that no social revolution was likely to strike Dublin for some centuries was unmistakeably Joyce's.

Joyce's socialist sympathies were European rather than Irish. As part of the exercise on which he embarked after University College of experiencing as much of Dublin life as he could, he acquainted himself with the radical fringe, nationalist and socialist, of Dublin politics. He already knew the Fenian or Fenianesque members of his father's circle who had some involvement in municipal politics or officialdom. Joyce was not admiring of most of his father's friends, but it is salient that Joyce's family background gave him an angle of approach to Dublin municipal life that was more Fenian and more lower-middle class than that of his most prominent Home Rule–supporting peers in University College.

Joyce's alienation from the Catholic nationalist middle class and from the personae of the Celtic Twilight had a symmetry, and it was natural that he should have explored the milieu of nascent radical nationalism and socialism in Dublin. This quest was also aligned with Parnellism. Dublin was the political centre to which post-Split Parnellism was largely reduced. Nationalist Dublin remained Parnellite but with a sharp

194. Fergus D'Arcy, 'James Connolly', *DIB* 2:756–61. There is not the remotest basis for the assertion that Joyce 'was involved in the affairs' of the Irish Socialist Republican Party; Costello, *Years of Growth*, 214–15.

195. S. Joyce, *My Brother's Keeper*, 165.

196. S. Joyce, *My Brother's Keeper*, 174.

diminution in the vibrant excitement present while the leader remained alive. Fenians shifted their support away, and radical nationalists and socialists, though mostly admiring of Parnell, were ideologically hostile to parliamentarism and suspicious even of Redmond's Parnellite party. The opening up of Dublin politics to radical nationalism and socialism nevertheless owed much more to the Split than partisans of either liked to admit, and residues of the Parnell of the Split endured, which Joyce would crystallise with imaginative brilliance and political intelligence in the fictional persona of Joe Hynes, who recites his poem 'The Death of Parnell' in the *Dubliners* story 'Ivy Day in the Committee Room', written in Trieste in September 1905.

In the years leading up to Joyce's exile, Dublin saw a confluence of socialism and proto–Sinn Féin radical nationalism that found expression in Griffith's support of labour municipal candidates including James Connolly, though Griffith was emphatically not a socialist. Attractive as the idea may be of Joyce treading the streets of Dublin as a politically curious *flâneur*, his reading of Griffith's *United Irishman* and of the mainstream press is more important for the development of his thinking than was standing at the back of 'dimly illuminated' meetings. Joyce's investigation of Dublin socialism apprised him of its limitations. He did not adhere to Connolly's Irish Socialist Republican Party, which was Marxist and separatist. He remained sympathetic to socialism, but his ardent exilic interest in Italian socialism reflected a conscious turning away from Irish socialism towards the continental European left.

There were four groups in Dublin with which Joyce might conceivably have aligned himself in the two years before he left Dublin: There was, first, the faction of his University College contemporaries who supported the Irish Party, with Kettle on the centre-right and Skeffington on the left, who formed themselves into the Young Ireland Branch of the United Irish League the month after Joyce left Dublin. There was, second, the coterie of Griffith and the *United Irishman*, which had not yet constituted itself as Sinn Féin, and to whose cultural nationalism Joyce remained averse. Third, the *Dana* alignment of Magee and Ryan, and fourth, the final possibility was proletarian socialism, principally represented by Connolly's Irish Socialist Republican Party. In the course of what is best seen as an exploratory quest over the two years after he left University College, Joyce came to the realisation he could not subscribe to any of them. The quest does not conform to the stereotype of disdainful artist in the making, determined to express himself with forbidding individuality and to hold himself aloof from assent or alliance. There is a tentativeness to Joyce in these years which is too easily lost sight of—something of it survives in Stephen's exchange with Madden in *Stephen Hero*:

—But surely you have some political opinions, man!
—I am going to think them out. I am an artist, don't you see?[197]

'The Centre of Paralysis'

Politically, Joyce had not sought solitude as an end. To this period belongs Joyce's conception of Irish paralysis, which has been much overdetermined. The close of the 'Portrait' essay referred to 'the general paralysis of an insane society', which invokes the tertiary stage of syphilis, but does so in a European or universal setting. The history of Joyce's deployment of the image is important. In July 1904, Joyce's story 'The Sisters', written at the invitation of George Russell, and the first of the stories that would become *Dubliners*, was accepted by the *Irish Homestead*. It appeared the following month, the first publication of Joyce's fiction. He wrote to Constantine Curran, 'I have written one. I call the series "Dubliners" to betray the soul of that hemiplegia or paralysis which many consider a city.'[198] In 'The Sisters' Father James Flynn has died after his third stroke, his life 'crossed' by the episode of a broken chalice: his face is remembered as 'the heavy grey face of the paralytic'.[199] There is also a hint of madness when Father Flynn is found sitting in a confessional in a darkened church 'laughing—like softly to himself'.[200]

The following month, Stanislaus noted somewhat sceptically in his diary the drift of his brother's conversation on the subject of syphilis:

197. *SH* 56.
198. Joyce to Curran, 'Fri', n.d. [July 1904], *Letters I* 55; Curran, *James Joyce Remembered*, 49.
199. *D* 5.
200. *D* 11.

> He talks much of the syphilitic contagion in Europe, is at present writing a series of studies in it in Dublin, tracing practically everything to it. The drift of his talk seems to be that the contagion is congenital and incurable and responsible for all manias, and being so, that it is useless to try to avoid it. He even seems to invite you to delight in the manias and to humour each to the top of its bent. In this I do not follow him except to accept his theory of contagion, which he adduces on medical authority. Even this I do slowly for I have the idea that the influence of heredity is somewhat overstated.[201]

Stanislaus's reservations were well founded and came to be shared by his brother. Joyce was struggling to connect the idea of social stasis with the psychological pathology of individuals. The principal means of doing this was through a thinly punning invocation of the general paralysis of the insane, the tertiary stage of syphilis, which was rarely apposite. The paralysis-syphilis theme moreover is likely to reflect the influence of Gogarty,[202] which Joyce came to repudiate.

In relation to *Dubliners*, Joyce's playing with the clinical conception of paralysis was a means of proclaiming his intention to treat Dublin as a laboratory, and the stories as case studies informed by a sense of empirical rigour. It attests to the attraction for Joyce at that time of a quasi-scientific determinism, from which his interest in socialism also in part derives. While writing the stories that would make up *Dubliners*, Joyce quickly retreated from the idea of a pseudo-clinical diagnosis of paralysis. He instead invested the idea of paralysis with ethical and political connotations. This marked the reinstatement of a concept of political agency, however infirm, that permitted Joyce to reconcile his Parnellism and his art in 'Ivy Day in the Committee Room'. The shift is reflected in what he wrote to the publisher Grant Richards some two years later: 'My intention was to write a chapter in the moral history of my country and I chose Dublin for the scene because that city seemed to me the centre of paralysis.'[203]

201. S. Joyce, entry for 13 August 1904, in *Dublin Diary*, 51.

202. See *U* 1.127–29.

203. Joyce to Grant Richards, 5 May 1906, *Letters II* 134.

In *Stephen Hero* Joyce dropped the pseudo-clinical idea of paralysis and deployed the image of paralysis in relation to the influence of the Catholic Church. Stephen 'cursed the farce of Irish Catholicism' whereby the Irish entrust 'their wills and minds to others that they may ensure for themselves a life of spiritual paralysis.'[204] And later, 'The deadly chill of the atmosphere of the college paralysed Stephen's heart.' Stephen accused the Church of inculcating 'hemiplegia of the will.'[205] It was against this that Stephen resolved to rise up, in a passage that resembled the close of the 'Portrait' essay: 'The spectacle of the world in thrall filled him with the fire of courage. He, at least, though living at the farthest remove from the centre of European culture, marooned on an island in the ocean, though inheriting a will broken by doubt and a soul the steadfastness of whose hate became as weak as water in siren arms, would live his own life according to what he recognised as the voice of the new humanity, active, unafraid and unashamed.'[206]

The idea of Irish stasis—the political immobilism and suspicion of the modern in an island cut off from continental Europe and locked in on itself—remained central to Joyce's thinking. In the 'Aeolus' episode of *Ulysses*, Myles Crawford, the editor of the *Freeman's Journal*, declares, presaging heroic feats of drinking, 'We'll paralyse Europe, as Ignatius Gallaher used to say when he was on the shaughraun.'[207] If it is an expression of Irish incorrigibility, it is also a wry inversion permitted by Joyce of his and Stephen's theme of Ireland's insular paralysis.

'The Holy Office'

Joyce wrote his satirical broadside 'The Holy Office' some two months before he left Dublin. He mischievously offered it, or an early version, to Curran for *St Stephen's*.[208] Joyce commissioned its printing before he

204. *SH* 146.

205. *SH* 194, and 'The mortifying atmosphere of the college crept about Stephen's heart' (*SH* 193).

206. *SH* 194.

207. *U* 7.628–29.

208. Curran, *James Joyce Remembered*, 46–47, 107. Curran's amused letter of rejection is dated 8 August 1904.

left Dublin but failed to pay the printer. He had it reprinted in Trieste in mid-1905, and had Stanislaus distribute it in Dublin.[209] It is a scathing retort in Joyce's high, biting doggerel to Yeats (its true addressee, spared individual attack) and Russell and their circle. Writing it in adversity, as if repudiating the mode of Wilde's *De Profundis,* he does not cry from the depths unto the Lord; on the contrary, he calmly identifies himself with Leviathan, Satan in Isaiah, albeit against Mammon. It draws on his drunken dissolute phase in the wake of the death of his mother, to imply in a defiant retorsion of the negative image that was engendered that it had given them a certain imaginative license, as well as marked out his course as implacably opposed to theirs:

I, who dishevelled ways forsook,
To hold the poet's grammar-book,
Bringing to tavern and to brothel
The mind of witty Aristotle,

He contrived a defiant retorsion on his critics of their strictures.

But all these men of whom I speak
Make me the sewer of their clique.
That they may dream their dreamy dreams
I carry off their filthy streams[210]

'The Holy Office' was an insouciant raising of the wager on his own future as a writer. Joyce's local mythos as an author ran ahead of what he had written. He continued to insist that the mask he donned in University College ('the enigma of a manner') was defensive. The fact that he was perceived as someone who had avowed an ambition to be a writer before he had written much had objective consequences and corollaries. It introduced the persona, or surrogates for the persona, of the writer and his travails into the work, as a biographical fact before it became a creative stratagem. It also put Joyce under pressures which had

209. Joyce to Stanislaus Joyce, 19 November 1904, *Letters II* 70; 3 December 1904, *Letters II* 71, 73; 27 May and 3, 7, 11 June 1905, *Letters II* 90–91.

210. *PSW* 97–98.

the potential to destroy a writer of lesser genius and resolve. Joyce was closely observed, even in early exile. Skeffington recorded in his diary in September 1905, ten months after Joyce had left Dublin, '[John Francis] Byrne told me of Joyce's novel—Chapters up to 25 or 30 have recently been in Dublin with Stan. Curran and [Vincent] Cosgrave saw them. Byrne has appeared in it! Though Joyce always denied having Epiphanized him; [Michael] Lennon also; row with [William] Delany over paper. The child is a boy! Gogarty, says B[yrne], might easily go over to Trieste to horsewhip J. if he attacks G[ogarty]'s mother.'[211]

This was trivial, even flattering in a certain way, and in some degree intended by Joyce. Of greater concern to Joyce were the writers around Yeats. What 'The Holy Office' signified was that whether or not he had set out to create the challenge, he did not propose to resile from it and would make good on the promise of his status as a writer.

It was at this point, under intense pressure that was not only financial but as a writer, that Joyce re-found and brought into his writing, in however ephemeral a form, his identification with Parnell. He invoked the image of the stag at bay which he had already deployed in the 'Portrait' essay:

So distantly I turn to view
The shambling of that motley crew,
Those souls that hate the strength that mine has
Steeled in the school of old Aquinas.
Where they have crouched and crawled and prayed
I stand the self-doomed, unafraid,
Unfellowed, friendless and alone,
Indifferent as the herring-bone,
Firm as the mountain-ridges where
I flash my antlers on the air.[212]

211. Skeffington, diary entry for 12 September 1905, quoted in Levenson, *With Wooden Sword*, 42.

212. *PSW* 99.

The identification with Parnell is intense and apposite. Parnell was twice derided: at the outset of his career, and in the Split, which Parnell had insisted was a re-beginning. The Parnell of the Split is more salient; Joyce was only starting out but he, like Parnell in 1890–91, was already burdened by the expectations of a myth. Something else is breaking through. There is no record of the broadsheet having reached Yeats.[213] If it did, the specific invocation of Parnell was internal to Joyce's writing and scarcely obvious. But its import was plain. The Catholic idiom of Joyce's lines is incisively etched. In Joyce's repudiation of Catholicism, the stereotype of a submissive Irish Catholicism is deliberately reversed. It is the mainly Protestant figures of the Revival who 'have crouched and crawled and prayed'. Yeats would have to contend with the destabilising intervention of a writer of traditional Catholic nationalist provenance who had repudiated Catholicism. It is an outflanking move of Parnellian audacity that sought to shift the centre of gravity of modern Irish literature. It accounts for why Joyce in Pola should have gone to the bother of having 'The Holy Office' reprinted and distributed by Stanislaus in Dublin. Already, Joyce's relationship to Yeats has begun to be mediated through Parnell; and Joyce's relationship to Parnell is soldered at a time of personal crisis and creative flux which the writing of *Stephen Hero* could not register.

Meeting Nora and Leaving Ireland

On 10 June 1904 Joyce accosted a striking, tall, auburn-haired woman on Nassau Street. Nora Barnacle was two years younger than Joyce. She was born on 21 or 22 March 1884 in the maternity ward of the Galway workhouse which served as the hospital of the city of Galway, the second daughter of Thomas Barnacle, a journeyman baker who was illiterate, and his wife, Anne (née Healy). Her mother's people were hardworking and, as Joyce put it, 'toney';[214] her uncle Michael Healy, who became

213. Ellmann asserts that Joyce had 'enough discretion' not to distribute a copy to Yeats (*James Joyce*, 200).

214. Joyce to Stanislaus Joyce, 3 December 1904, *Letters II* 72.

H. M. inspector of customs and receiver of wrecks, at Galway and then at Dublin, was to be close to Joyce. Her father, a heavy drinker, drew apart from the family. She grew up with her grandmother in the centre of Galway, attending the Convent of Mercy National School. In 1897, at the age of thirteen, she attained the relatively elevated position of portress of the then-enclosed Convent of the Presentation Order, which she held for the remainder of her time in Galway. She had her first romance with Michael Bodkin, a handsome, dark-haired young man, a clerk with the Gas Company who had enrolled for a time as a student of University College, Galway. Stricken with tuberculosis, he died at the age of twenty on 11 February 1900. He was buried in Rahoon. Distraught, Nora confided in a Galway city curate who tried to take sexual advantage of her. She had a second romance with Will Mulvey, the son of a sergeant in the Royal Irish Constabulary. When her uncle caught her returning from an assignation with the Protestant Mulvey, he beat her. That experience led to her departure for Dublin in early 1904. She obtained employment as a waitress and chambermaid at Finn's Hotel on Leinster Street, at the end of Nassau Street on the southern perimeter of Trinity College.[215] It was close by Finn's Hotel that she was approached by the figure she recalled many years later: 'his expression strange and severe, an overcoat that hung down to his feet, shoes down at the heel, a big, white sombrero'.[216]

She stood Joyce up on 14 June. They met two days later, the day on which Joyce was to set *Ulysses*, and walked down the Liffey towards Ringsend. It was there that Nora brought Joyce to orgasm, 'all the time bending over me and gazing at me out of your quiet saintlike eyes'.[217] In *Ulysses* the initiation of Bloom's sexual relations with Molly takes place in Howth.[218]

215. The details of the early life of Nora Barnacle are taken from the exemplary account in Padraic O'Laoi, *Nora Barnacle Joyce* (Galway: Kenny's Bookshops and Art Galleries, 1982), 1–44.

216. Jacques Mercanton, 'The Hours of James Joyce', in *Portraits of the Artist in Exile: Recollections of James Joyce by Europeans*, ed. Willard Potts (Seattle: University of Washington Press, 1979), 238.

217. Joyce to Nora Barnacle, 3 December 1909, *SL* 182; Maddox, *Nora*, 41–42.

218. See Crispi, *Joyce's Creative Process*, 167–79.

On 29 August, Joyce despatched an extraordinary account of himself to her, as if to make sure she was under no illusions:

> Six years ago I left the Catholic Church, hating it most fervently. . . . I made secret war upon it when I was a student and declined to accept the positions it offered me. By doing this I made myself a beggar but I retained my pride. Now I make open war upon it by what I write and say and do. I cannot enter the social order except as a vagabond. I started to study medicine three times, law once, music once. A week ago I was planning to go away as a travelling actor.[219]

It was an oddly formal confession, given that he knew she had her own reasons to contest the sway of the Church and was aware of his lack of means. It was a way of conveying that their relationship had sociopolitical corollaries that incidentally dispelled any idea of a casual elopement: the informal solemnisation of their relationship lay in an accord that entailed her acceptance of all that his dissentience would entail. He knew the offer would not be repudiated, though Stanislaus ruminated a couple of days later, 'I never saw Jim manage any affair so badly as he has managed his affair with Miss Barnacle.'[220]

Joyce tried to stay away from the immiserated homestead in St Peter's Terrace in Cabra. After a series of other residential improvisations, Joyce on 9 September 1904 arrived in the Martello Tower in Sandycove, which Gogarty had leased from the secretary of state for war. He stayed for six days. The taking up of this highly volatile accommodation had the aspect on Joyce's part of a purposive exhausting of his narrowing options. As Curran later wrote, 'It was plain enough to me in that autumn that Joyce was at a dead end and that even with the prop of some auxiliary post he could not live in Dublin as the writer he meant to be.'[221] On the day before Joyce departed the tower, Stanislaus noted, 'At present he is staying on sufferance with Gogarty in the Tower at Sandycove. Gogarty wants to put Jim out, but he is afraid that if Jim

219. Joyce to Nora Barnacle, 29 August 1904, *Letters II* 48.

220. S. Joyce, entry for 31 August 1904, in *Dublin Diary*, 76.

221. Curran, *James Joyce Remembered*, 68.

made a name some day it would be remembered against him (Gogarty). . . . Jim is determined that if Gogarty puts him out it will be done publicly.'[222]

Also present in the tower was Samuel Chevenix Trench, of an old Anglo-Irish family, but a friend of Gogarty from Oxford who was an ardent convert to cultural nationalism and was to be the model for Haines in *Ulysses*. During the night of 15 September at two in the morning, Trench woke from a nightmare, screaming that a black panther was about to pounce, and shot his revolver at the fireplace. Gogarty confiscated the revolver, and when Trench woke again screaming and reached for his revolver, Gogarty fired the revolver at the fish kettle and tin cans hanging over Joyce's head. Gogarty recalled, '[Joyce] rose solemnly, dressed himself in his faded trousers, pulled on his shirt and his white yachting cap and shoes, took his ashplant and left the Tower and never came back'.[223] He walked from Sandycove into town. He presented himself at the National Library when it opened, where he was announced to W. K. Magee, to whom 'he related quite ingenuously how in the early hours of the morning he had been thrown out of the tower'.[224]

The episode in the Martello Tower brought forward, if it did not crystallise, Joyce's decision to leave Ireland, for which he had to enlist Nora Barnacle. He wrote to her on 16 September, 'When I was waiting for you last night I was even more restless. It seemed to me that I was fighting a battle with every religious and social force in Ireland for you and that I had nothing to rely on but myself.'[225] Two days later he received a letter from an agency purporting to have reserved a position for him in a Berlitz school.[226] The next day he wrote that 'your people cannot of course

222. S. Joyce, entry for 14 September 1904, in *Dublin Diary*, 85–86; Ellmann, *James Joyce*, 174.

223. Rodgers, *Irish Literary Portraits*, 33–34; Ellmann, *James Joyce*, 175.

224. Eglinton, *Irish Literary Portraits*, 139; Rodgers, *Irish Literary Portraits*, 34.

225. Joyce to Nora Barnacle, 16 September 1904, *Letters II* 53.

226. E. Gilford to Joyce, 17 September 1904, quoted in Ellmann, *James Joyce*, 176. He wrote to Nora, 'Just this moment I have received a letter that I was expecting but I shall not know definitely for a few days'; Joyce to Nora Barnacle, [?18 November 1904], *Letters II* 54. When Joyce wrote to the agency is unknown.

prevent you going if you wish but they can make things unpleasant for you', and that he would probably stay in his father's house 'until I leave Ireland'.[227] Joyce scraped together the financial means to get them just about as far as Zurich, to take up what transpired to be a phantom position in the Berlitz school.

The life in the Dublin Joyce was leaving behind went on in its accustomed way. A few days before Pigott and Company had advertised its *Familiar Irish Songs,* including Percy French's just-published 'Are You Right There Michael?',[228] Michael Davitt's *The Fall of Feudalism in Ireland* was selling well.[229] The Committee of the Anti-Emigration Society met on 4 October, planning its conference for later in the month.[230] The publication of Patrick Dinneen's Irish-English dictionary was hailed.[231] The first illustrations of the plaster models of St Gaudens' Parnell monument were published.[232] The *Freeman's Journal,* on the day of Joyce's departure, carried a report of the committee organising the annual Parnell commemoration to take place the next day.[233] Those coming from the country to participate were arriving by excursion trains, but the event was to be a disappointing affair, reflecting a continuing decline. Its most striking feature, according to the *Irish Daily Independent,* was 'the presence of such a large crowd to see such a small procession'.[234] That was also the last day of the rather more successful Iona Bazaar and Aonach in the Rotunda.[235]

Saturday, 8 October 1904, was a fine cold day, the clouds clearing towards the evening.[236] Joyce was accompanied to the boat by Stanislaus, his aunt Josephine Murray, and his father. Nora Barnacle boarded

227. Joyce to Nora Barnacle, 19 September 1904, *Letters II* 55.

228. *Freeman's Journal,* 28 September 1904.

229. *Irish Daily Independent,* 4 October 1904.

230. *Freeman's Journal,* 5 October 1904.

231. *Irish Daily Independent,* 5 October 1904.

232. *Irish Daily Independent,* 4 October 1904.

233. *Freeman's Journal,* 8 October 1904.

234. *Irish Daily Independent,* 10 October 1904. The paper disparaged the continuation of the procession.

235. *Freeman's Journal,* 10 October 1904.

236. *Daily Express,* 10 October 1904.

a little later, as John Stanislaus Joyce was to be kept unaware that his son was leaving with her.[237]

It did not escape Joyce's notice that the passenger steamer that bore him and Nora away from the North Wall at 9.20 p.m. for Holyhead was called the *Hibernia*.[238] Doubly occluded in the 'Sirens' episode of *Ulysses* by Bloom's memories of Molly and his desire for Martha Clifford, and brought forward to admit an invocation of the description of Cleopatra by Enobarbus in *Anthony and Cleopatra*, the passage recalls his thoughts as the *Hibernia* sails by Howth: 'Only the harp. Lovely. Gold glowering light. Girl touched it, Poop of a lovely. Gravy's rather good fit for a. Golden ship. Erin. The harp that once or twice. Cool hands. Ben Howth, the rhododendrons. We are their harps. I. He. Old. Young.'[239]

It fell to the bereft Stanislaus, who would follow his brother out to Trieste a year later, to write the most moving epitaph for the Joyce of Dublin: 'He seemed to me the person in Ireland who was most alive.'[240]

237. Ellmann, *James Joyce*, 179.

238. *Daily Express*, 8 October 1904. *The Anglia* left in the morning.

239. *U* 11.580–83. The ship is identified as the *Erin*. The connection is to the *Hibernia* on which Joyce and Nora sailed, rather than to the *Erin's King*—the excursion steamer around Dublin Bay on which Bloom took Milly—to which it is erroneously taken to be an abbreviated reference in Gifford, *Ulysses Annotated*, 79, 300.

240. S. Joyce, entry for December 1904, in *Dublin Diary*, 146.

PART II

Exile

Introduction

JOYCE AND NORA BARNACLE LIVED IN Pola from 20 October 1904 to 5 March 1905, when they moved to Trieste, where Giorgio was born on 27 July 1905. There was an interlude in Rome from 31 July 1906 to 7 March 1907. Lucia was born in Trieste on 26 July 1907. Joyce made three return visits to Ireland between 1909 and 1912. They left Trieste in the second year of the war and lived in Zurich from 30 June 1915 to 16 October 1919, then returned to Trieste, where they remained until they left for Paris on 3 July 1920.

The years 1904–12 can be characterised in relation to Ireland as the years of Joyce's first exile, which ran from his departure from the North Wall in October 1904 to his last visit to Ireland in 1912, which culminated in the destruction of the proofs of *Dubliners* in mid-September. These were years of demi-exile, without foreclosure of return, in which he continued to hope for an Irish publisher for his work and contrived to remain as well informed as he could be of the diurnal or at least weekly outfall of events in Ireland, principally through family members, newspapers, and reading what was published in Ireland. From Rome in October 1906 he complained to Stanislaus, 'Is there nobody in Ireland who will think it worth his or her while to make a bundle of any old papers that are lying about his or her house and send them to me?'[1]

He contrived to stretch out the period in which he maintained an active connexion to Ireland to 1912, the year of his last Triestine journalism on Irish affairs. It was only after the rupture of the aborted Irish publication of *Dubliners* in which his third return ended that exile became his default mode. The year 1912 is a more significant cut-off date in his intimate familiarity with Irish politics than 1904. In this first or

1. Joyce to Stanislaus Joyce, 18 October 1906, *Letters II* 182.

demi-exile, he did not see exile as irrevocable. In July 1905 he wrote to Stanislaus that his leaving of Ireland 'like everything else I have done in my life was an experiment' and, complaining of 'the very degrading and unsatisfactory nature of my exile', he went so far as to propose that he and Stanislaus should marshal their resources and 'take a small cottage outside Dublin in the suburbs',[2] an idea that had a rich afterlife in Joyce's writing. Three months later, on 16 October 1905, as if to convey that exile was not irrevocable, he wrote to Stanislaus, 'This day twelve months I was in Paris. . . . We drove from the Gare St. Lazare to the Gare de l'Est in an open carriage. I will be in Paris again I am sure and in Dublin too.'[3] The following week, on 24 October, Stanislaus left Dublin for Trieste to take up a post in the Scuola Berlitz; unlike his brother, he would never make a return visit to Ireland.

The periodisation of the first phase of Joyce's exile to 1912 has a political logic also. These years follow directly on Joyce's life in Dublin, and the controversies he had known in Dublin were continuous with those he watched closely from exile in Trieste and in Rome, and involved personalities he knew personally or knew much about. By the time he returned to Trieste from Dublin on 15 September 1912, Irish politics had entered a new and different phase: on 11 April 1912 the Liberal government had introduced its Home Rule Bill, and on 28 September, the Solemn League and Covenant was signed across Unionist Ulster—the 'Home Rule crisis' was engaged. In terms of Irish politics, the years 1890–1912 have a historical unity and are the prelude to the decade of crisis, 1912–21, which culminated in Ireland's fraught achievement of independence. Across that seminal period, from the Parnell Split to the Home Rule crisis, Joyce remained closely engaged with the course of Irish politics.

This period of his first or demi-exile is extremely important for the development of Joyce's politics. He was for a time immersed in the study of contemporary Italian socialism. His reflections on Irish nationalism in these eight years were fecund, carrying him far beyond the straitened

2. Joyce to Stanislaus Joyce, 12 July 1905, *Letters II* 92–98.

3. Joyce to Stanislaus Joyce, 16 October 1905, *Letters II* 124.

politics of his novel *Stephen Hero* (to which he continued to add chapters in the early months of exile) and found expression in the lectures he gave and the articles he wrote in Trieste, and in his correspondence. In this period also he succeeded in integrating his identification with Parnell into his literary work and his contemporary thinking about Ireland.

Socialism, Anarchism, and Sinn Féin

Joyce was drawn to socialism when in Dublin, but his strenuous self-education in Italian revolutionary syndicalism, largely from the columns of *Avanti!*, was a feature of his early exile. It reflects his belief that a school of Italian socialism could address the socio-political arrestation of post-Split Ireland. It was also a development of the socialist beliefs he had begun to profess while still in Ireland. While Joyce in Rome abandoned his auto-induction into revolutionary syndicalism, and revolutionary syndicalism itself ended badly, it does not follow that he renounced socialism. It is often silently assumed that Joyce's passing into 'silence' in this sense, coupled with his earlier loss of interest in embracing socialism as a political creed, reflects a retreat from the political or a shift to the right on his part. It is true that he never again identified himself with any institutional manifestation of socialism and became markedly sceptical of ideologically driven political teleology in any form, but it remains important in situating Joyce politically that he set out from the left and it is unwise to apply the *idée reçue* of a person becoming more conservative with age to Joyce. The extraordinary care and consideration that he had given to the opinions expressed in his early writing, combined with the insistently accretive mode of thought and method of writing, render problematic any sequencing of his career in which earlier phases are wholly superseded, never mind thrown into reverse. If his identification with socialism seems to have waned, it is anachronistic to impute to Joyce anything resembling the 'neo-conservative turn' that became irritatingly familiar among intellectual figures who ostentatiously renounced their former left-wing affiliations in the United States in the late twentieth century. The idea that Joyce repudiated socialism is negated by a politically astute reading of *Finnegans Wake.*

Part of what attracted Joyce to Italian revolutionary syndicalism was its anarchistic strain. Joyce was intellectually and perhaps politically drawn to anarchism, but it is hard to identify specific anarchist influences in his thinking beyond his habitual mistrust of statal authority, especially when it pertained to sexual morality and censorship. Assessments of Joyce's anarchism draw heavily on a single footnote in Herbert Gorman's biography—enumerating the anarchist writers who Joyce told Gorman had influenced him—and would be hard to identify from his correspondence or his fiction.[4] Anarchism was a movement of the left that was largely displaced by centralised parties of the left outside the Mediterranean regional fastnesses in which it held out. Joyce's interest in anarchism is consistent with his later suspiciousness of authoritarian or highly institutionalised left-wing movements which put him at odds with the mainstream of contemporary left-wing thought. While Joyce was philosophically sympathetic to anarchism, the altruistic libertarianism of Oscar Wilde's *The Soul of Man under Socialism* was closer to his heart.

Joyce's interest in Italian revolutionary syndicalism coincided with his developing sympathy with Arthur Griffith's Sinn Féin, which had come into institutional being after he left Ireland. He did not see affinities with socialism in Italy and Sinn Féin in Ireland as incompatible. In his correspondence from Rome with Stanislaus in 1906 and 1907, Joyce maintained a defence of Griffith, albeit qualified by his suspicion of Irish language revivalism. His sympathy with Sinn Féin found clear if comparatively moderate expression in his public pronouncements in Trieste. On the only occasion on which he met Griffith, in Dublin on 30 August 1912 during his last visit to Ireland, when he sought his advice on the publication of *Dubliners,* he told Griffith of the articles he had written, which Griffith asked him to send on to him. Their encounter was highly charged symbolically. Griffith remained still a minoritarian figure in Irish politics, though that was already beginning to change.

4. Gorman, *James Joyce,* 183n1; Manganiello, *Joyce's Politics,* 72.

In his journalism in Trieste, Joyce remained pragmatic rather than parti pris and had left open the possibility that the Irish Party might achieve Home Rule, a tightrope that Griffith himself had to walk in his journal *Sinn Féin*. Nonetheless, the significance of the fact that Joyce had through his journalism espoused in an Adriatic city a sympathy with the ideas of Sinn Féin, in connecting Joyce to the flowing tide of events that were to lead to Irish independence, cannot be overstated. The sense that his life in exile as well as in Ireland had intersected with the political course of the struggle for independence in the period from Parnell's fall was of critical importance to Joyce's sense of his political relationship to the emergent Ireland, and to his authorial politics. Joyce's sympathy with Sinn Féin in early exile, while important in itself, is also significant in belying the idea that in relation to Irish politics Joyce was an incorrigible nay-sayer, or an 'impossibilist' who posited expectations or imposed criteria he knew could not be met.

Rendering Parnell in Fiction

Rendering Parnell artistically was a problem. Outside biography and flashes of reminiscence, Parnell was artistically even more than politically an exceedingly challenging subject. He was a near-contemporary figure, laconic and of fabled inscrutability. His public career had brought unprecedented unity of purpose to nationalist Ireland but had ended in national acrimony. His myth in his lifetime had owed much to the extraordinary impact wrought by his fleeting physical presence, whether in Ireland or Westminster. His frequent and sometimes prolonged absences, or disappearances, from the political arena attracted lavish press commentaries and speculation, and were a commonplace of Westminster parliamentary conversation, as well as a source of continuing anxiety to the members of his own party. The subject became peculiarly corporeal: by the late 1880s the variations in his physical appearance as his health deteriorated were closely scrutinised, to the point that his physical aspect became almost a matter of state. His commanding personality and his heroic attributes, whether as displayed in his rise and ascendancy or in his fall, seemed to defy anything other than bland

and hackneyed literary rendering. Joyce was acutely conscious of the artistic problem. It was not so very far removed from the political dilemma encountered by Parnellites on his death, of upholding Parnellite principles after the death of the leader who not merely articulated but embodied them, which they sought to resolve by a cult of the dead leader the extravagance of which repelled Joyce as un-Parnellian.

In autumn 1905 Joyce wrote 'Ivy Day in the Committee Room', his rendering of the myth of Parnell through an account of a lull in canvassing in the late afternoon into evening in a committee room in a Dublin municipal election. The story reflected the contemporary atmosphere in Dublin: in anticipation of Home Rule, there had been a partial revival of Parnell's myth in the political domain in the form of a renewed contest for Parnell's legacy and myth. The Irish Party sought to enlist his prestige, while Arthur Griffith invoked Parnell's memory to assail what he asserted to be the pusillanimity of the Irish Party in its dealings with the Liberal party, raising again, if distantly and in a lower key, the issue of the Split. On 16 May 1912 *Il Piccolo della Sera* in Trieste published Joyce's magnificent article 'L'ombra di Parnell' (The shade of Parnell).

The Parnell myth now acquired a trajectory which half transcended, half challenged the course of contemporary nationalist politics and had a particular salience for Irish literary modernism. W. B. Yeats, outraged by Catholic middle-class philistinism over its opposition to John Millington Synge's *Playboy of the Western World* and its resistance to the project for a gallery to house Hugh Lane's collection of paintings, began to re-discover Parnell's heroic attributes. He increasingly saw the Split as the first of the defining controversies of contemporary Ireland, and the one from which the impetus for the modern Irish literary movement came. In 1913 he wrote the Parnell-invoking poems 'September 1913', which drew on the emotional residues of all that had happened since the Split, and 'To a Shade', which is addressed to Parnell. Yeats was identifying himself and the Irish literary movement with a leader who, despite the defeat in which his life ended, seemed to embody a modern Irish statehood and had not feared to confront his Irish enemies and to challenge majoritarian prejudices. The persona of Parnell, and not just the outfall of the Split, came to be central to Yeats's refiguration of the relationship of Irish literature to politics.

Yeats's insistence on the connection between the fall of Parnell and the Irish literary movement, while having as its historical point of departure the Split, was more pertinent to what was now being written and would be written than to what had previously been written in the 1890s. Yeats could not have had Joyce in mind when he first began to propound this argument, but it transpired to have remarkable prophetic force, and was sufficiently encompassing to frame the interrelationship of their separate work. Yeats's turn towards Parnell brought him into an alignment with Joyce, though there is no reason to believe that this was any part of his purpose (he could not in 1913 have been aware of the still-unpublished 'Ivy Day in the Committee Room' nor of 'L'ombra di Parnell', which was published only in *Il Piccolo della Sera*). The persona of Parnell came to mediate an enigmatic pattern of reciprocity in their work.

The significant, in some respects decisive, contribution of Joyce and Yeats in ensuring that Parnell was not relegated to a distant historical time is bound up with the fashioning of Irish literary modernism and its relation to Irish politics. Each, in treating Parnell as a tutelary figure of Irish politics, was acknowledging that their artistic lives were caught up in the pursuit of Irish independence from after his fall. Each recognised that the plasticity of Ireland's political form in the transition from political subordination to statehood had a correlation, not readily definable, in artistic and imaginative potentiality. It would, however, be entirely wrong to conclude that the myth of Parnell in the twentieth century is merely the creation of two writers and their successors, drawing on the romantic cult of the lost leader, scorning contemporary politics, and severed from what remained of the political inheritance of Parnell. The imposed invention of a literary myth of Parnell that stood outside history was utterly foreign to Joyce's purpose and method. Had it been a purely post hoc contrivance, rather than something that drew on actual sentiment, however sublimated, and on the reverberations of Parnell's political achievement that came to seem lingeringly faint but ran deeper than his fragile post-Split personal myth, it could never have attained the resonance that it did. Theirs was an imaginative recuperation of Parnell steeped in Irish politics in the wake not just of his fall but of the pursuit and attainment of independence that followed. The Parnell of Yeats and Joyce cohabited the realms of literature and politics, and in that he was the emblematic political figure of Irish modernism.

10

The Politics of *Stephen Hero*

> Joyce's impudicity had a fierceness behind it, the fierceness of a soul that demanded manumission, so that he could love, feel, assert, test for himself, create. Up and up under pressures insupportable, the jet of his violent nature mounted. In *Stephen Hero*, under sodden Dublin skies, he is accumulating this energy.
>
> —FRANCIS HACKETT, 1945[1]

JOYCE DECIDED AT THE START OF February 1904 to turn his rejected 'Portrait of the Artist' essay into a novel.[2] In June he entrusted Constantine Curran with a bulky wad of manuscript.[3] Progress on the novel then stalled but revived; by the time of his leaving Dublin, he had written at least eleven chapters.[4] These are lost. What survives of *Stephen Hero* are the final chapters, which find Stephen already in University College.

1. Francis Hackett, review of *Stephen Hero*, *New York Times*, 18 January 1945.

2. S. Joyce, entry for 2 February 1904, in *Dublin Diary*, 11–12. The dates of composition of the surviving chapters are usefully chronicled in Marc A. Mamigonian and John Noel Turner's pioneering 'Annotations for *Stephen Hero*', *James Joyce Quarterly* 40, no. 3 (Spring 2003): 347–518. They are also noted in Roger Norburn, *A James Joyce Chronology* (London: Palgrave Macmillan, 2004).

3. Curran, *James Joyce Remembered*, 48–49.

4. Mamigonian and Turner, 'Annotations for *Stephen Hero*', 348.

The extant chapters were written in the first nine months of exile, in Pola and Trieste, a fraught period during which he and Nora were enduring the dual strains of exile and their first experience of living together. The circumstances in which they were living strained their relationship, but it was sustained by Nora's fortitude and loyalty. On Christmas Eve 1904, Joyce wrote to his aunt Josephine Murray from Pola, which he described as 'a naval Siberia', 'I have been unable to discover any falsehood in this nature which had the courage to trust me. It was this night three months ago that we left the North Wall. Strange to say I have not yet left her on the street, as many wise men said I would. In conclusion—I spit upon the image of the Tenth Pius.'[5] Early in the new year, Joyce wrote to his brother, 'I admire her and I love her and I trust her—I cannot tell how much I trust her.'[6] When they moved to Trieste in March, Nora was already four months pregnant; she found the heat insufferable and Joyce's drinking difficult. The last reference to working on *Stephen Hero* is 7 June 1905, by which point Joyce had finished what became chapter 24.[7] Two more chapters were written shortly thereafter, and the text then simply breaks off. Their son Giorgio was born on 27 July 1905.

Stephen Hero is rightly considered more autobiographical than *A Portrait of the Artist as a Young Man* and is certainly closer to conveying the temperament of Joyce in University College. S. L. Goldberg observed that 'of all his novels, *Stephen Hero* gives the most accurate account of what the young Joyce's attitudes really were.'[8] That is so, but one must recall *Stephen Hero* is still formally a novel and what is extant of it was written during a time of almost constant upheaval when Joyce's 'attitudes'—his political thinking and his idea of himself as an artist—were not static.

Contrary to Joyce's normal artistic and political precepts, what survives of *Stephen Hero* manifests a great deal of raw anger that was

5. Joyce to Josephine Murray, 24 December 1904, *Letters I* 58.

6. Joyce to Stanislaus Joyce, [?2 or 3 May 1905], *Letters II* 89.

7. Joyce to Stanislaus Joyce, postmark 7 June 1905, *Letters II* 91.

8. S. L. Goldberg, *Joyce* (London: Oliver and Boyd, 1962), 16, 33.

informed in some degree by the conditions in which it was written: the travails of Joyce's final months in Dublin and the bitterness and exasperation of his early exile. Joyce chooses not to cloak Stephen's gathering disaffection. Politically it is not just that *Stephen Hero* lacks the subtle political poise that characterised Joyce's later writings; it also marks, at least at a formal level, an apparent regression from his more political reviews in the *Daily Express* and his 'Portrait' essay, and it lacks the acerbic bite of 'The Holy Office', written in autumn 1904.

Curran read and discussed with Joyce the earlier lost chapters as they were written. Though of conservative temper, Curran came to be aligned with Sinn Féin. Enlightened and perceptive, he was shocked by what he read in the manuscript. In his memoir of Joyce, he recounts his pain on reading the early chapters, due in part to realising the direness of Joyce's personal circumstances: 'I had little idea of the true extent and harshness of the situation which was hidden beneath his wry humour.'[9] He recalled a lost chapter ending with the words 'interminable wastes of bogland, interminable servitude of mind'.[10] He referred to 'the recurring tirades and railings against the Church, State and nation and the other "trolls" that spread their nets of convention about the feet of the aspiring artist. . . . As objective criticism of the Ireland of 1904 they seemed to me to have little validity.'[11] He deplored Joyce's depiction of his peers in University College: 'Confronted by this frieze of stooges against which Stephen plays his part as suffering protagonist, I find myself bewildered.'[12] When Joyce sent him a copy of *A Portrait* on its publication, he wrote in thanks,

> I admire, too, your courage in scrapping your first draft as I knew it. I think there were passages in that version which might well have

9. Curran, *James Joyce Remembered*, 49–50.

10. Curran, *James Joyce Remembered*, 51. This fragmentary quotation, which represents all that survives of the lost early chapters of *Stephen Hero*, suggests that the later chapters which survive are not discontinuous in tenor with the earlier ones. Stephen refers to 'the mental swamp of the Irish peasant' (*SH* 95).

11. Curran, *James Joyce Remembered*, 54.

12. Curran, *James Joyce Remembered*, 58.

> been retained but as the chapters were being added to it, it seemed to me that the writer's mood was changing too much from the reminiscent Dichtung of the opening to the literalness and finally to the harshness of the latest chapters I saw. This version is all of a piece and is much more skilfully and economically worked out. But all the same I regret some chapters in *Stephen Hero*.[13]

A Portrait was more sophisticated, not least in its politics. In *Stephen Hero* Catholicism seems to loom larger than nationalism. Much of the novel relates to Stephen's contest with the Catholic Church. That contest is less to do with a crisis of faith, as one might expect in a conventional bildungsroman—Stephen's loss of faith in what survives of the novel is essentially a fait accompli—than with Stephen's critique of the socio-political preponderance of the Catholic Church in Ireland, and his refusal to submit to it.

In this way *Stephen Hero* opens the issue of Joyce's relationship to the Catholic faith. The language is of Stephen losing his faith or leaving the Church. If Joyce was not a Catholic, it is difficult to conceive that he was any other kind of Christian believer or theist. It does not seem seriously disputable that Joyce was an atheist or just possibly, using the neologism first conceived by T. H. Huxley in 1869, an agnostic.[14] Joyce was not opposed to religious belief and despised proselytising, political or religious: if he was not a Catholic, he was certainly not viscerally anti-Catholic, in the mode of his brother. The paradox which Catholic apologists of Joyce, seeking to assert a residuum of faith, have baulked at accepting is that his profound interest in the intellectual, artistic, and imaginative heritage of Catholicism was plainly premised on a dissociative absence of belief.

13. Curran to Joyce, 26 February 1907, *James Joyce Remembered*, 63.

14. Lernout, *Help My Unbelief*, 61. Whether Huxley's brilliant coinage with its timeless-sounding bad Greek was an intellectual advance, given that it came to carve out an alternative within and to compromise the encompassing clarity of the idea of atheism, is debatable. Joyce was *a-theos*, without god, an atheist in the pre-Huxleyan dispensation. It is likewise unlikely that Joyce's self-characterisation to Lady Gregory as a 'misbeliever' goes any further than his being a non-believer. Joyce to Lady Gregory, n.d. [November 1902], *Letters I* 53; Lernout, *Help My Unbelief*, 102.

'The Farce of Irish Catholicism'

When his mother presses him to do his Easter duty—to confess and receive communion—Stephen responds with jokes about the Ascension:

> —Stephen, said his mother, I'm afraid you have lost your faith.
> —I'm afraid so too, said Stephen.[15]

Mrs Daedalus—whose objections, beautifully rendered by Joyce, include that 'none of your people, neither your father's nor mine, have a drop of anything but Catholic blood in their veins'—is in tears as Stephen departs.[16] He tells Cranly he has left the Church. Cranly proposes a sacrilegious communion. Stephen protests, 'At present I have a reluctance to commit a sacrilege. I am a product of Catholicism: I was sold to Rome before my birth. Now I have broken my slavery but I cannot in a moment destroy every feeling in my nature.' Cranly presses him to do his Easter duty, as it is only for him 'mockery, mummery'. Stephen refuses to simulate the practice of a faith he has repudiated: 'If I mum it is an act of submission, a public act of submission to the Church. I will not submit to the Church.'[17]

Stephen's most sustained denunciation of clerical influence is prompted by his walks through the Dublin slums:

> These wanderings filled him with deep-seated anger and whenever he encountered a burly black-vested priest taking a stroll of pleasant inspection through these warrens full of swarming and cringing believers he cursed the farce of Irish Catholicism: an island the inhabitants of which entrust their wills and minds to others that they may ensure for themselves a life of spiritual paralysis, an island in which all the power and riches are in the keeping of those whose kingdom is not of this world, an island in which Caesar confesses Christ and Christ confesses Caesar that together they may wax fat upon a starveling

15. *SH* 133.
16. *SH* 134.
17. *SH* 139.

> rabblement which is bidden ironically to take itself this consolation in hardship 'The Kingdom of God is within you'.[18]

The vehemence was connected to Stephen's repudiation of the Catholic faith: 'This mood of indignation which was not guiltless of a certain superficiality and was undoubtedly due to the excitement of release'. Stephen himself accepts that this verges on the demagogic: 'Though a taste for elegance and detail unfitted him for the part of demagogue, from his general attitude he might have been supposed not unjustly an ally of the collectivist politicians.'[19] The elliptical self-identification with socialism on the part of Stephen is significant. Joyce's was an intellectual European socialism which, applied with unavoidable crudity to Ireland, ratified his rebellion against the deference the Catholic Church commanded in Ireland.

In a related passage, Stephen ruminated on 'the plague of Catholicism. He seemed to see the vermin begotten in the catacombs in an age of sickness and cruelty issuing forth upon the plains and mountains of Europe'. The same passage contains a Jesuit-directed reference to 'black tyrannous lice'.[20] This outburst, as Geert Lernout has pointed out, reflects a strained endeavour on Joyce's part to retort upon John Henry Newman and the Jesuits the imagery of Newman's 1856 novel of martyrdom in the early Church, *Callista: A Tale of the Third Century*.[21]

This foreshadows an element of the 'two masters' thesis, discussed in chapter 5. Insisting that power was recognised for what it was, Joyce regarded 'the Roman supremacy' as imperial and geostrategic. Such a trenchantly secular treatment of the imperium of the Church was exceedingly rare in Irish nationalism. Joyce's approach permitted him a graceful consideration of the relationship of the imperial state to its periphery, viewed from an island on Europe's western perimeter, in the manner of Edward Gibbon and Thomas Babington Macaulay, and a

18. *SH* 146.

19. *SH* 146–47.

20. *SH* 194.

21. Lernout, *Help My Unbelief*, 117–18; Mamigonian and Turner, 'Annotations for *Stephen Hero*', 469–70.

contemplation of the rise and fall of empires, the perspective in which he situated the massive ascendancy of the Catholic Church in nationalist Ireland:

> He had been brought up in the belief of the Roman supremacy and to cease to be Catholic for him meant to cease to be a Christian. The idea that the power of an empire is weakest at its borders requires some modification for everyone knows that the Pope cannot govern Italy as he governs Ireland nor is the Tsar as terrible an engine to the tradesmen of St. Petersburg as he is to the little Russian of the Steppes. In fact in many cases the government of an empire is strongest at its borders and it is inevitably strongest there in the case when its power at the centre is on the wane. The waves of the rise and fall of empires do not travel with the rapidity of waves of light and it will be perhaps a considerable time before Ireland will be able to understand that the Papacy is no longer going through a period of anabolism. The bands of pilgrims who are shepherded safely across the continent by their Irish pastors must shame the jaded reactionaries of the eternal city by their stupefied intensity of worship in much the same way as the staring provincial newly arrived from Spain or Africa must have piqued the loyalty of some smiling Roman for whom the future way of his race was becoming uncertain as its past had already become obvious.[22]

Joyce was seeking at once intellectually to render in secular terms and to relativise, in time and space, the political ascendancy of Catholicism in Ireland. There is also his sense of the underlying irony that Ireland's principal geostrategic relationship to continental Europe was with papal Rome. The reference to the waning of the power of the papacy in Italy, like the reference to 'the councils of the Latins' at the end of his 'Portrait' essay, attests to the fact that Joyce was attentive to Italian politics. Joyce hearkened to 'the voice of a new humanity' that he could distantly

22. *SH* 147. The reference to Africa, as well as the subject of the passage, confirms that it owes something to Joyce's meditation on Newman's *Callista,* as discussed in chapter 8, '"The Language of the Outlaw"'.

hear from across the double marine divide of the Irish Sea and the English Channel. There was nothing from Spain to the south-west audible to him, though the Strait of Gibraltar was to become historically or prehistorically a pivotal locus in his conceptual geography, opening Ireland at least cartographically to the world of the Mediterranean. Even before exile, contemporary Italy occupied a special place in Joyce's thinking. He took it as axiomatic that the principal Irish connection to the Continent was that of Catholicism. Part of what drew Joyce in exile to Italian socialism was the idea, never fully articulated before he gave up on it, that it ought to be possible in some way for a secular Italo-Irish connection to undo 'the Roman supremacy' in Ireland.

Joyce's anticlericalism was moderate and confessionally tolerant by continental standards, but his opposition to the socio-political hegemony of the Catholic Church in Ireland was fiercely sustained. He was familiar with the history of the Church in the nineteenth century and well versed in contemporary European Catholicism. Apart from the 1798 rising, Ireland had been touched socially by the French Revolution and its doctrines only in strange and contrary ways, but it was subject to the profound post-revolutionary reflux that swept the post-1848 continental Catholic Church as it pitted itself implacably against socialism, liberalism, and modernism. This found expression in the reactionary ultramontanism of the First Vatican Council of 1869–70.[23] For Joyce, Ireland, beleaguered and benightedly backward, bore the burden of a quarrel which was not her own. In Joyce's critique, Catholic Ireland was perversely abject in a fealty to Rome which remained conspicuously unreciprocated. Irish backwardness was affirmed in papal servitude. Ireland was to the papacy 'the afterthought of Europe'.[24] It is true that the Catholic hierarchy had steadfastly defended Parnell against papal strictures in the 1880s, but this was negated by their role in Parnell's fall in the divorce crisis.

Stephen Hero lacks the retrieved Parnellism of *A Portrait*, which found its clearest expression in Joyce's equation of British and Catholic

23. O'Malley, *Vatican I*; Lernout, *Help My Unbelief*, 28–45.

24. *SH* 53.

political supremacy in his 'two masters' thesis in the 'Telemachus' episode of Ulysses. The Stephen of *Stephen Hero* is ostensibly still emerging from the crisis of his faith, though its author had already moved beyond his. The distillation of time alone ensures that *Stephen Hero* is not the raw and simplistic rendering of Joyce's contemporary opinions—the not-a-novel—that it is often seen as by contrast with *A Portrait*. In *Stephen Hero*, the Catholic Church and, to a lesser degree, nationalism threaten the individuality of Stephen Daedalus. *A Portrait* addresses how Irish politics, including the ecclesiastical, impinges on Stephen's formation as an artist.

In *Stephen Hero* it is the Catholic Church rather than British political dominion that is preponderant. Stephen's position is distinct from Madden's anti-English Irish nationalism: 'The Roman, not the Sassenach, was for him the tyrant of the islanders.' His contemporaries have cravenly interiorised the tyranny of the Church: 'The watchcry was Faith and Fatherland, a sacred word in that world of cleverly inflammable enthusiasms.'[25] Joyce in *Stephen Hero* approaches (but stops just short of) the idea of the two masters, the twin dominion of Church and nation or state: Stephen fulminates against 'an island in which Caesar confesses Christ and Christ confesses Caesar'.[26] Stephen's antipathy to the Church, if it is a central part of the novel's aspect of social realism, serves to destabilise the politics of *Stephen Hero*. While the Parnellite synthesis of British state and Catholic Church, that he was to achieve in *A Portrait*, still eluded Joyce, there remains in *Stephen Hero* a deep structural connection between Stephen's development and the atrophied condition of Irish politics and society.

'The Patriots'

In *Stephen Hero*, politics first appears in the household of the Daniels, which was based on that of the Sheehys in Belvedere Place. Stephen attends the Daniel family gatherings, and McCann, the character based

25. *SH* 53.
26. *SH* 146.

on Skeffington, is also a frequent visitor. The portrayal of Mr Daniel in *Stephen Hero*, while brief, is the most developed portrayal of an Irish parliamentarian (or sometime parliamentarian) in Joyce's fiction: 'Whenever the evening assumed the character of a serious affair Mr Daniel would be asked to recite something for the company. Mr Daniel had formerly been the manager of a theatre in Wexford and he had often spoken at public meetings through the country. He recited national pieces in a stern declamatory fashion amid attentive silence. The daughters also recited. During these recitations Stephen's eye never moved from the picture of the Sacred Heart which hung above the reciter's head.'[27] There were frequent parliamentary charades.

> Mr Daniel had sat for his county some years before and for this reason he was chosen to impersonate the Speaker of the House. McCann [Skeffington] always represented a member of the Opposition and he spoke point-blank. Then a member would protest and there would be a make-believe of parliamentary manners.
>
> —Mr. Speaker I must ask . . .
>
> —Order! Order!
>
> —You know it's a lie!
>
> —You must withdraw, Sir.[28]

Stephen 'imagined he had explored this region sufficiently' and would have ceased attending the Daniels' were it not for 'the unpleasant character of his home' and his romantic interest in the ardent Irish culture enthusiast Emma Clery.[29] She prompts him to return to the Daniels' after an interval of absence. Among the guests is an elder brother of Mrs Daniel's, Fr Healy, who has returned from the United States after seven years fundraising to build a chapel near Enniscorthy:[30]

27. *SH* 44.

28. *SH* 45.

29. *SH* 46.

30. It has been suggested that Fr Healy may be based on Fr Eugene Sheehy, a brother of David Sheehy, who later came to live for a period in the Sheehy household (Mamigonian and Turner, 'Annotations for *Stephen Hero*', 442). Fr Eugene Sheehy was famous as a firebrand nationalist cleric in the era of the Land League. It seems improbable that the somewhat

'He was greatly interested in the new Gaelic revival and in the new literary movement in Ireland. He paid particular attention to McCann and to Stephen, asking both of them many questions. He agreed with McCann that Gladstone was the greatest man of the nineteenth century and then Mr Daniel, who was glowing with pride at the honour he was paying so honourable a guest, told a dignified story of Gladstone and Sir Ashmead Bartlett and deepened his voice to reproduce the oratory of the grand old man.'[31]

These glimpses of the Daniel household in *Stephen Hero* permit Joyce to deal with parliamentarism in much shorter compass than his suspicions of the 'patriots' of which the novel treats at much greater length. Politically it serves to convey Stephen's amused indifference to Irish parliamentarism after Parnell.

Parnell's name is not mentioned in what survives of *Stephen Hero*. There is reference to a 'fierce argument about Tim Healy', which flares into a near brawl, in the billiard room of the Adelphi Hotel between Cranly's diminutive and drunken friend who was a clerk in the Agricultural Board Office and a 'thick set medical student'.[32] Joyce was at his least self-consciously Parnellite, and his resistance to nationalism was at its height, at the time of writing *Stephen Hero*. The rise of a nationalism defined by commitment to Irish language revivalism presented a fresh threat—a new regression—that was of more immediate concern to him.

It is revivalism—less the project of the revival of the Irish language in itself than the emergence of a neo-nationalism infused by the idea of revivalism—that provides the secondary political subject of *Stephen Hero*, after the hegemonic influence of Catholicism and the Catholic Church. *Stephen Hero* attests to the depth of Joyce's dread of an inexorable Gaelicising drift which, in a solipsistic spiral, would carry Ireland

---

ingratiating and Gladstone-reverencing figure of Fr Healy was modelled on Eugene Sheehy. It is possible that in giving Mrs Daniel the maiden name of Healy, Joyce was slyly emphasising the anti-Parnellism of David Sheehy (who hated Healy), anticipating a far more considered feminising of the surname of T. M. Healy in 'A Mother'.

31. *SH* 156–57.

32. *SH* 208–9.

still further than the Parnell Split already had from the paradigm of enlightened modern European statehood. In tracking Joyce's political thinking across time, what is most salient is the subsuming of 'advanced' nationalism within a category defined by him as 'the patriots' whose nationalism he characterised chiefly in terms of the advocacy of the revival of the Irish language. This was an exaggerated perception that attests to the degree of Joyce's alarm at the ideological direction of revivalism. The indiscriminate characterisation of 'the patriots' was not maintained in *A Portrait*.

As his review of William Rooney's *Poems and Ballads* discussed in chapter 9 makes clear, Joyce had a deep aversion to the term 'patriotism' and its cognates. His sarcastic designation of 'the patriots' is likely to derive from his father's sarcastic comments which affirmed his own reservations. His note on Oliver St John Gogarty that 'he called himself a patriot of the solar system' is not flatteringly conceived.[33]

In the novel, Stephen's position is starkly stated, if not quite in absolute terms. 'The programme of the patriots filled him with very reasonable doubts; its articles could obtain no intellectual assent from him.' In that programme as rendered in *Stephen Hero*, the revival of the Irish language was uppermost. Such assent 'would mean for him a submission of everything else in its interest and that he would thus be obliged to corrupt the springs of their speculation at their very source'.[34] Stephen's position is later restated: 'He himself was the greatest sceptic concerning the perfervid enthusiasms of the patriots.'[35]

There is a group portrait of the circle presided over by 'a very stout black-bearded citizen' (Michael Cusack) where 'reigned the irreconcilable temper'. Madden frequented that circle, which foregathered in Cooney's tobacco shop, inspired by the shop of Cathal McGarvey, An Stad, at 1A North Frederick Street. Griffith is indiscriminately included in the group. Though it attests to a certain intentness of observation on Joyce's part, the group portrait is scathingly reductive: 'By all this society

33. 'Trieste Notebook', in Scholes and Kain, *Workshop of Daedalus*, 98.

34. *SH* 76–77.

35. *SH* 204.

liberty was held to be the chief desirable; the members of it were fierce democrats. The liberty they desired for themselves was mainly a liberty of costume and vocabulary and Stephen could not understand how such a scarecrow of liberty could bring serious human beings to their knees in worship. As in the Daniels' household he had seen people playing at being important so here he saw people playing at being free.'[36] In the reference to their being 'fierce democrats', one can discern Joyce's despairing measuring of the Irish-language-driven patriots against continental European republicans, radicals, and revolutionaries.

Stephen fashions a connection between the proponents of an Irish revival and the Catholic Church. He propounds this in his principal exchange with Madden: 'Do you not see, said Stephen, that they [the priests] encourage the study of Irish that their flocks may be more safely protected from the wolves of disbelief; they consider it an opportunity to withdraw the people into a past of literal, implicit faith?'[37]

This was perhaps a debating point rather than a conspiracy theory, though it did not bear much scrutiny. If younger priests and postulants were adherents of the revival, they reflected the views of their class and generation. It did, at a secondary level, inform Stephen's suspicions of the revival and permitted a composite reference in the novel to 'the patriotic and religious enthusiasts'.[38]

The idea of a clerical-revivalist nexus lingers in the novel. It does not escape Stephen's notice that the weekly meetings of the League were 'largely patronised by priests'.[39] One of the objections that Stephen raises against the 'patriots' is what he sees as their deference to clerical authority. In the prelude to the last citation, Stephen objects to Madden (George Clancy) that the 'new movement' deferred to the Church (something that Fenianism certainly had not). Madden tells Stephen 'that the new movement was politic', and that 'if the least infidelity were hoisted on the standard the people would not flock to it'. Stephen replies by deploying against the 'new movement' an old Fenian tenet: 'Stephen

36. *SH* 61–62.

37. *SH* 54.

38. *SH* 159.

39. *SH* 61.

objected that this working hand in hand with the priests had over and over again ruined the chances of revolution. Madden agreed: but now at least the priests were on the side of the people.'[40] Stephen could not agree with this. It is striking that, in what survives of *Stephen Hero*, Stephen does not go any further in highlighting Fenian anticlericalism, though it was to come to the fore in the Christmas dinner scene in *A Portrait*.

There is a parallel, more personal sub-theme to do with the collaboration of the priesthood in one element of the 'new movement' and the Church. The relationship between Emma Clery and a young priest, Father Moran, is that between the Gaelic League and the Catholic Church made flesh. It is the person of Emma Clery who incarnates the link between the Irish Revival and the priesthood. Watching them together, Stephen was driven into 'a state of unsettled rage', partly from jealousy and partly because the spectacle seemed to him 'typical of Irish ineffectualness': 'Father Moran's eyes were so clear and tender-looking, Emma stood to his gaze in such a poise of bold careless pride of the flesh that Stephen longed to precipitate the two into each other's arms and shock the room even though he knew the pain this impersonal generosity would cause himself.'[41] Stephen is driven later to affront Emma's 'distressing pertness and middle class affectations'[42] by proposing 'just to live one night together'.[43]

The Mullingar Fragment

The bulk of what survives of *Stephen Hero* comprises what was in Joyce's library in Trieste. There was a further, earlier fragment that Stanislaus retained that closely and perhaps immediately precedes the principal surviving text.[44] It relates to a visit by Stephen to his godfather and

40. *SH* 53.

41. *SH* 66–67.

42. *SH* 67.

43. *SH* 197–99.

44. Mamigonian and Turner, 'Annotations for *Stephen Hero*', 487. It is published after the principal text in the Spencer edition of the novel.

benefactor, Mr Fulham, who lives outside Mullingar. The fragment is of importance in relation to what is lost because it is not set in University College or the city of Dublin.

Mr Fulham is a substantial farmer and patriarchal Catholic who 'saw in the pride of the Church the only refuge of men against a threatening democracy', and whose defence of the tenant farmers was enunciated on semi-feudal grounds. A neighbour, Mr Heffernan, who is of smaller holdings, comes to dine. It transpires that Mr Fulham is himself the beneficiary of land purchase legislation that had its inception in the Land League and Parnellism: Mr Heffernan points out to him that 'you enjoy the fruits of Nationalist agitation'.[45] This is affirmed during an argument in which Mr Fulham proclaims, 'I am a great enemy of disloyal movements. Our lot is thrown in with England.' Earlier, it is stated that Mr Fulham, 'like most of his countrymen, was a persuaded politician'.[46] This means that he possessed opinions on political subjects; while the issue of his voting allegiance is not addressed, his opinions would not have disqualified him from supporting the Irish Party.[47] Mr Heffernan has a different perspective to the grander Mr Fulham's. His son, who is studying for the priesthood in Clonliffe, is learning Irish 'because he believed that the Irish people should speak their own language and not the language of their conquerors . . . and he tells me all the young students there, those who are to be our priests afterwards, have these ideas'.[48] Declaring the Catholic Church would never incite

45. *SH* 247.

46. *SH* 241.

47. Leo Daly has pointed to the fact that Patrick Fulham had been elected for Meath South, which adjoined Westmeath, at the general election of 1892. The anti-Parnellites had won both Meath constituencies—Michael Davitt was the victor in North Meath—by fairly close margins. Following a bitterly contested and controversial election petition, both were unseated on grounds of clerical influence. The ensuing politico-legal controversy attracted considerable attention in Ireland and Britain and lingered into February 1893, when different anti-Parnellite candidates won both seats by similar margins, and beyond. It is perfectly possible that Joyce appropriated the surname of Patrick Fulham for the Mr Fulham of *Stephen Hero*; see Leo Daly, *James Joyce and the Mullingar Connection* (Dublin: Dolmen, 1975), 25; Mamigonian and Turner, 'Annotations for *Stephen Hero*', 489–90. Joyce's own godfather, Philip McCann, was a ship chandler who died on 12 January 1898; Ellmann, *James Joyce*, 748.

48. *SH* 246–47.

rebellion, Mr Fulham solicits the views of Stephen as 'one of the young generation'. Stephen provocatively declares, 'I care nothing for these principles of nationalism. . . . I have enough bodily liberty':

> —But do you feel no duty to your mother-country, no love for her? asked Mr Heffernan.
>
> —Honestly, I don't.
>
> —You live then like an animal without reason! exclaimed Mr Heffernan.
>
> —My own mind, answered Stephen, is more interesting to me than the entire country.
>
> —Perhaps you think your mind is more important than Ireland!
>
> —I do, certainly.[49]

This was Stephen at his most serenely provocative. 'Stephen had enjoyed this little skirmish: it had been a pastime for him to turn the guns of orthodoxy upon the orthodox ranks to see how they would stand the fire.'[50] Yet there is something more to it. At least on the Irish Revival, Stephen is aligned with Mr Fulham, who, pleased at the putting down of Mr Heffernan, is indulgently tolerant of his godson's opinions. After the passage of arms, Stephen considers, but thinks better of, making the observation that 'my godfather is the Papal ambassador to Westmeath'.[51]

The Mullingar fragment shows Joyce applying quasi-Marxist categories, if somewhat incoherently. Mr Fulham is possessed of 'the pride of the burgher' and 'had affection for the feudal machinery'.[52] In his characterisation of Mr Fulham, Joyce also adopts, though not harshly, the left-nationalist position that land purchase would create a sated conservative farmer class and should be postponed until the achievement of Home Rule. Joyce also awkwardly negotiates (or renders Stephen's awkward negotiation of) rural Ireland. Mr Fulham proclaims that 'our Irish peasantry' is the 'backbone of the nation'. The narrative continues, 'Backbone or not, it was in the constant observance of the peasantry

49. *SH* 247–48.
50. *SH* 249.
51. *SH* 250.
52. *SH* 249–50.

that Stephen chiefly delighted. Physically, they were almost Mongolian types, tall, angular, and oblique-eyed. Stephen whenever he walked behind a peasant always looked first for the prominent cheek-bones that seemed to cut the air and the peasants in their turn must have recognised metropolitan features for they stared very hard at the youth as if he were some rare animal.'[53] Even though the perceptions were rendered reciprocally, it came disquietingly close to hostile English stereotypes of Irish small farmers. Neither was the effect quite contained by the disarming statement later in the novel, 'He acknowledged to himself in honest egotism that he could not take to heart the distress of a nation, the soul of which was antipathetic to his own, so bitterly as the indignation at a bad line of verse.'[54] Stephen found himself in Mullingar still mired in a political impasse.

The Political Crux of *Stephen Hero*: Stephen's Nationalist Crisis

The crux of *Stephen Hero* is that, at the point at which it breaks off, Stephen continues to withhold assent from Irish nationalism, though conscious of his nationalist affiliations. It is a position so closely bound up with the argument of the novel that he is obliged to maintain it. The issue of who or what has claims on Stephen's allegiance is repeatedly put to the fore. The novel poses the issue of Stephen's relationship to Ireland and the Irish people. Stephen may refuse—perhaps somewhat formalistically—to embrace nationalism, but that relationship becomes the central preoccupation of the novel. Stephen's withholding of assent from nationalism means that the relationship cannot be axiomatic and yet Stephen's is plainly something more than a purely personal revolt. Central to Stephen's position is the conception of the role of an Irish writer, and a socialism which in application is informed by the outcome of the Parnell Split.

The issue of whether Stephen's revolt is personal or relates to his capacity as 'a literary artist' is blurred in the novel. Both are true at once.

53. *SH* 244.
54. *SH* 146.

When he remembers to do so, or when he has to, he stands on his role as an artist, but the fury of his protest seems to cut deeper, so that the accent seems to fall on a personal *non serviam* to nationalism and its shibboleths old and new.[55]

> He acknowledged to himself in honest egoism that he could not take to heart the distress of a nation, the soul of which was antipathetic to his own, so bitterly as the indignity of a bad line of verse; but at the same time he was nothing in the world so little as an amateur artist. He wished to express his nature freely and fully for the benefit of a society which he would enrich, and also for his own benefit, seeing that it was part of his life to do so. It was not part of his life to undertake an extensive alteration of society but he felt the need to express himself such an urgent need, such a real need, that he was determined no conventions of a society, however plausibly mingling pity with its tyranny should be allowed to stand in his way, and though a taste for elegance and detail unfitted him for the part of demagogue, [in] his general attitude he ought to have been supposed not unjustly an ally of the collectivist politicians.[56]

Stephen asserts an existential ethic of independence, but it is one that merges with the idea that a writer in a country like Ireland is compelled to assume a public burden in espousing an artistic and intellectual liberty which extends to the affronting of conventional pieties fervently sustained by his or her fellow countrymen. Such writers find themselves obliged to assume a quasi-exemplary role that is unsought, as if coerced into exemplarity.[57] This is implicit, if not always obviously so, in Stephen's thoughts and utterances.[58]

55. *SH* 56, 204.

56. *SH* 146–47.

57. This has a correlative in Wilde's idea of the burden of altruism in *The Soul of Man under Socialism*, which had a considerable influence on Joyce's thinking on socialism and the state, though it was never cited by Joyce and therefore is not readily identifiable with certainty in his writing.

58. An unexpectedly strong connection between his complex theory of art and contemporary Irish politics is disclosed at the start of chapter 19 of the novel. Stephen is working on the paper he is to give on 'art and life'. The paper was 'very consciously intended to define

Breaking with the Thomas Davis model of the writer as the publicist of nationalism, Joyce was revolutionary in redirecting the writer's role to the contestation of regnant nationalist sentiment and normative values. He was moreover implicitly asserting the potentially transformative role of the writer in the modernisation of Ireland. In relation to the role of the writer, Joyce's ambition surpassed the politic gradualism of the writers of the Celtic Twilight. He was measuring himself silently against Yeats: this was a maintenance of the guerrilla aspect of his role of 'literary artist' that related back to 'The Day of the Rabblement'. None of this is directly proclaimed in *Stephen Hero* in part because Stephen Daedalus is merely 'a literary artist' (or 'an amateur artist') rather than a consummated writer: it is nonetheless the public nexus of the agon of Stephen Daedalus without which the novel lacks meaning.

In general, Stephen does not assert a hegemonic role for the artist. The exception is in his thoughts for the paper that he is to give at the university titled 'Art and Life': 'In fine, the truth is that every age must look for its sanction to its poets and philosophers. The poet is the intense centre of the life of his age'. In the narrative this is treated with some scepticism: Stephen is characterised as 'this heaven-ascending essayist'.[59] But in the burden he assumes of fiercely contesting the condition of Ireland, there is an implicit assertion of a quasi-sacrificial co-identity with the Irish people, or with what the Irish people could yet become. Stephen conceives that connection as deriving from socialism rather than nationalism. His furious protests against what he discerns as a state of vassalage, while directed in considerable part and unsparingly at the passivity of his countrymen, are also pronounced on their behalf. His consciousness and defiance mean that he is not himself in a state of vassalage, so that it is predicated on a sense of being collectively demeaned and thereby diminished. Stephen refuses to accept

---

his own position for himself'. He was also 'persuaded that no-one served the generation into which he had been born so well as he who offered it, whether in his art or in his life, the gift of certitude'. Stephen dismisses the dogmas of the patriots. 'He refused therefore to set out for any task if he had first to prejudice his success by oaths to his patria, *and this refusal resulted* in a theory of art which was at once severe and liberal' (*SH* 76–78, my italics), which is then outlined.

59. *SH* 80.

the romantically abstract conception of Ireland as a noble ideal that is expounded in the novel primarily but not solely by Madden. He insists that Ireland must be understood to mean the people of Ireland; that much is socialist. He then has the problem that, on his analysis, the Irish people have been contemptibly acquiescent in the degraded state of Ireland, in both its submissive Catholicism and its political abjection. This derives from the defeated and receding Parnellism of the Split (though in what survives of the novel, that is not made explicit), reflecting Joyce's sense, at the time of writing, that the Split lacked contemporary traction and seemed for practical purposes a lost cause.

That is the political impasse that *Stephen Hero* describes. Joyce seeks to apply to Ireland a Marxist paradigm in the full consciousness that Ireland was in Marxist terms an anomaly, in a state of retardation that was anterior to the stages of development towards a socialist society. Ireland was a country, or an inhabited space, arrested in a pre-modern condition. Joyce seems to be positing the idea that Ireland was a country in which the possibility of political advance was forestalled; that the preconditions for the practice of politics in any enlightened or progressive sense of the term—and really in any sense at all—were absent; and that this was a condition of some significance and interest in comparative politics that could sustain his novel and the interest of a prospective readership in or outside Ireland. Aside from being a thin and dispiriting backdrop, it was critically dependent on the bleakness of Stephen's (and the novel's) conception of the possibilities for political advance in Ireland. Stephen seems to assert the imperative of political agency and the impossibility of it in the same breath. That conflict renders Joyce in some respects a figure of his generation in Ireland. Objectively he despaired of political progress in Ireland; at the same time, he shared in some degree the intimation of his generation that statehood was achievable, while making more allowance than most of his contemporaries for the possibility of it not being realised.

What is of significance is the novel's conception of the electiveness of adherence to nationalism. A significant part of Stephen's objection to conventional nationalism is what he sees as the self-exculpatory idea of victimhood arising from the fact of English conquest and dominion.

This he sees as a diminishing of the responsibility of the people of Ireland for the fate of Ireland, and an Irish refusal of agency which he sees as engendering a complacently passive collective conception of nationalist identity. What is original is Stephen's reconception of the idea of nationalist allegiance as an elective act rather than a passive acquiescence in an inherited or communal identity. That conception is dramatised in the novel by Stephen's withholding of assent from nationalism. It is an election of the same order as Stephen's repudiation of Catholicism, which in some respects it mirrors, with the difference that Stephen's refusal of assent to nationalism is contingent, a decision in response to a set of circumstances at a particular point in time, however improbable he may think it that either the circumstances or his own assessment could change. Part of what unsettles Stephen is that his ardently nationalist contemporaries, who share to some degree the idea of the embrace of nationalism as an elective act, turn out be deferential to the Church and acquiescent in the conventional pieties of nationalism. That is what lies at the heart of Stephen's solitude.

The Catholicism that Stephen opposes is Catholicism as a socio-political institution rather than Catholicism as a faith. His resistance to Catholicism is itself primarily political, and his rendering of Catholicism blurs into his treatment of nationalism reflected in his scorn for what he terms conjointly 'the patriotic and religious enthusiasts'.[60] His refusal of formal allegiance to nationalism and his criticism of the emergent new nationalism is, however, markedly less absolute than his repudiation of Catholicism. The characterisation of Stephen as 'the greatest sceptic concerning the perfervid enthusiasms of the patriots' falls short of imputing to him a complete repudiation of their stance.[61] The refusal of foreclosure is clearest in the significant exchange with Madden, the figure based on Joyce's friend George Clancy, who becomes the Davin of *A Portrait*. Stephen's exchanges with Madden represent the principal discussion of his relationship to Ireland and Irish nationalism in *Stephen Hero*, as do his exchanges with Davin in *A Portrait*.

60. *SH* 159.
61. *SH* 204.

—So you admit you are an Irishman, after all, and not one of the red garrison?

—Of course I do.

—And don't you think that every Irishman worthy of the name should be able to speak his native tongue?

—I really don't know.

—And don't you think that we as a race have a right to be free?

—O, don't ask me such questions, Madden. You can use these phrases of the platform, but I can't.

—But surely you have some political opinions, man!

—I am going to think them out. I am an artist, don't you see?[62]

Given that Stephen's objection to 'the patriots' largely relates to the language revival, the inference is that if that could somehow be negotiated, Stephen might be able to find common cause with them, however qualified.

Stephen's answers to Madden are open-ended rather than renunciatory and are a good deal more tentative than the statements in the body of the novel, such as, for instance, 'The programme of the patriots could obtain no intellectual assent from him'. It could be said that Madden's questions are pitched at a level that is more beguiling and general and less readily dismissed by Stephen than the policy prescriptions of the patriots.[63] There is also the fact that Stephen is close to Madden. Stephen was moreover drawn to the companionship of other 'patriots' in University College. His mediocre First Arts results lead to 'a domestic squabble'. Stephen's father 'ransacked his vocabulary in search of abusive terms' and threatens to write to Stephen's godfather in Mullingar to cut off his financial support. Stephen's mother pleads with him to be reasonable: 'Reasonable be damned. Don't I know the set he has got into—lousy-looking patriots and that football chap in the knickerbockers. To tell you the God's truth, Stephen, I thought you'd have more pride than to associate with such *canaille*.'[64] The depiction of McCann, the figure

62. *SH* 56.

63. *SH* 76.

64. *SH* 216. These sentiments are repeated at *SH* 231. In the 'Trieste Notebook', Joyce writes of his father, 'He quarrelled with my friends' (in Scholes and Kain, *Workshop of Daedalus*, 104).

in the novel who stands in an instantly recognisable way for Francis Skeffington, perhaps distracts from the significance of Stephen's companionship with the 'lousy-looking patriots' in the plural. Joyce permits the observations of the truth-telling Daedalus père to mitigate the distanced severity of Stephen's strictures on the patriots.

The novel remained unfinished. Joyce ceased working on it in the summer of 1905, within the first year of exile. While in principle he could have returned to it to incorporate some form of political resolution, it is unsurprising that there is nothing to suggest that he considered doing so. It would have entailed wheeling around the entire trajectory of the novel and forfeiting its suspense, such as it is, which consists of leaving Stephen on an indeterminate edge. His altered relationship to Ireland as subject is part of the reason Joyce could not go back to completing *Stephen Hero*.

Impasse

In March 1906 Grant Richards, the London publisher with whom Joyce was in touch about publishing *Dubliners*, suggested that Joyce should write a novel 'in some sense autobiographical'. Joyce replied from Trieste that he had already written 'nearly a thousand pages of such a novel', and that the twenty-five chapters written comprised about half the book, a remarkable statement that conveys how far he was from abandoning *Stephen Hero*. 'But it is quite impossible for me in present circumstances to think about the rest of the book, much less to write about it.'[65] Joyce continued to refer tenaciously to 'my novel' long after he had suspended work on it, but there was a note of doubt in what he wrote to Stanislaus from Rome in January 1907: 'The other day I was thinking about my novel. How long am I at it now? Is there any use in continuing it?'[66]

It was not easy to rework, as Joyce found when he returned to the text in late 1907. His revision of the first chapter became the inception of *A Portrait*. *Stephen Hero* remains a novel of some substance, distinct from

65. Joyce to Grant Richards, 13 March 1906, *Letters II* 131–32.

66. Joyce to Stanislaus Joyce, 10 January 1907, *Letters II* 206.

A Portrait, that reveals much of Joyce's thinking immediately before and after leaving Dublin. It is also a unique rendering of the Ireland that he left: what might be called the 'state of Ireland' element of the novel, which is substantial, was to be, if not absolutely abandoned, drastically curtailed by modernistic foreshortening in *A Portrait*. *Stephen Hero* retains a haunting incompleteness, and the idea that it is reducible to a discarded *esquisse* for *A Portrait* is to be resisted.[67] Joyce came to distance himself from it and did not wish it to be considered as part of his oeuvre. He had Paul Léon inform the editor Theodore Spencer in late 1938 that he called *Stephen Hero* 'a schoolboy's production written when he was 19 or 20' (in fact he was in his early twenties).[68] What survived of the manuscript was published in 1944, three years after Joyce's death.

Stephen Hero is a novel of impasse, the writing of which itself ended in impasse. It is not easy to see how it could ever have been finished. By its end Stephen is increasingly isolated. He has second thoughts about Cranly, sees little of Madden, and is thrown back on the company of his brother Maurice. There is a doubt about his return to University College for the second year of his arts degree, brought about by mediocre results that threaten his godfather's continued sponsorship, which in turn puts his relations with his father under further strain. Perhaps that portends a contemplated change in the novel's direction,[69] but it is the point at which the novel ends. Significantly, exile, towards which *A Portrait* turns at its close, does not feature in *Stephen Hero*, though that may reflect the point the novel had reached when Joyce put it aside. Stephen's predicament is unrelieved and seemingly irresolvable. That is perhaps what Joyce wanted to render with as much visceral

67. Margot Norris advances an ingenious argument to challenge the conventional conception of the relationship between *Stephen Hero* and *A Portrait*. She challenges the idea that the theoretical shift from the first to the second is 'a retrogressive manoeuvre on Joyce's part: a shift of attention away from art's social function to the self-display of individual genius' and asserts that 'Joyce had, I believe, a subtler and more critical end in view. By foregrounding *theory* itself in *Portrait*, Joyce has his text make a deliberate gesture of self-enclosure' (*Joyce's Web*, 57). One of the problems with this is the more refined treatment of political nationalism in *A Portrait*.

68. *SH* 8.

69. Stephen tells Cranly, 'I believe this will be an important season for me. I intend to come to some decision as to my course of action' (*SH* 219).

exactitude as he could achieve. One of the curious and beguiling subthemes of the novel is Stephen's persisting half-bemused, half-grateful cognisance of the kindnesses shown and the tolerance extended to him by some of his friends and family, including the solicitude of his father, though it finds expression chiefly in sarcasm, and even by the Jesuits. His estrangement is not the reciprocation of ill will that is shown towards him: his quarrel is structural, with Catholic Ireland.

What prevented Joyce from reworking *Stephen Hero* was that the novel was conceived over-programmatically as a bildungsroman of alienated youth, rendered contemporary by its socialistic hue and heightened allusions to science; there is a dissonance between its continental perspective and the opulence of the faintly archaic English in which it is written. The persona of Stephen is held captive by the construct. Joyce was precluded by the static depiction of Ireland, and by the conventions of the traditional bildungsroman—which pit a young person growing into adulthood within the fixed institutional confines of an established state—from developing what he would come to think was conceptually distinctive and interesting about Ireland: its pre-statal inchoateness.

Joyce wrote to Grant Richards in March 1906, 'This novel also has the defect of being about Ireland.'[70] That remark raises the issue of whether *Stephen Hero* was at any stage publishable. There is also the issue of readership and likely reception. In the unlikely event that it found a publisher, it risked achieving a meagre but damaging notoriety through being misconstrued as a fictional anti-Catholic or even anti-Irish tract. Joyce was quite conscious of this—it is one of the criticisms levelled at Stephen in the novel—but it is an inhibition he chose to defy.[71] The novel was unfinished, but Joyce made no attempts to secure an agreement for its publication other than mentioning its existence as

70. Joyce to Grant Richards, 13 March 1906, *Letters II* 131–32.

71. *SH* 64–65. It is an imbalance in the novel that Stephen's utterances are consistently milder than the thoughts that are imputed to him. Stephen is not without a sense of the politic. This gives rise to an intermittently distracting sense that the author is more strident than his creation. It is a dissonance that is rectified in *A Portrait*.

a half-written work in progress to Richards in terms that were scarcely calculated to inspire a wish to publish it when complete.

By the time he attempted to return to *Stephen Hero* in November–December 1907 (if not earlier), the paradigm of the novel had ceased to match Joyce's advances in technique, reflected in the *Dubliners* stories he was writing, and the shift in his political perspective that occurred in exile. In the summer of 1905, some few months after he had put *Stephen Hero* aside, Joyce would render Ireland in 'Ivy Day in the Committee Room' through the prism of the contemporary Parnell myth in the setting of a drab municipal election headquarters in Dublin. It was a stunning rendering of Irish political torpor, the more moving because Joyce could not suppress an affinity with its cast of struggling characters.[72] It would have been hard after 'Ivy Day' to return to piling up chapters of the projected unwritten half of *Stephen Hero*. Joyce's guarded expressions of alignment with Sinn Féin, which meant he no longer saw the 'patriots' as an indiscriminate bloc, were conveyed in his letters to Stanislaus in September–November 1906 and must have reflected long anterior consideration. This guarded alignment represented the resolution, extra-textual and post-exilic, of the impasse of Stephen Daedalus in *Stephen Hero*. It was scarcely a complete resolution, but it offered its author a way forward.

What gives *Stephen Hero* its not very effective edge of political drama, if not quite of uncertainty of outcome, is Stephen's slightly contrived withholding of assent to nationalism. Joyce never declared himself a nationalist—and it is part of the argument of this book that the issue of whether Joyce is an Irish nationalist cannot be determined by his refusal to avow himself to be such. His position is certainly not identical with Stephen's.[73] Stephen's opinions are more rigid and static than Joyce's, and he seems at times prepared to countenance a renunciation of nationalism without ever quite going that far. The device of not declaring

72. See Callanan, 'Parnellism of James Joyce'; and chapter 12, 'Writing *Dubliners* in Exile'.

73. It could be argued with some force that the actual biographical correlative of Stephen's refusal of assent to nationalism was Joyce's refusal to align himself with any group or movement in Ireland, before his qualified exilic identification with the early Sinn Féin of Arthur Griffith, which shortly preceded the beginning of his recasting of *Stephen Hero* as *A Portrait*.

himself a nationalist, applied with a degree of elasticity in response to changing circumstances, was one that Joyce nevertheless maintained. The fact that he was no longer living in Ireland came to be a feature of Joyce's apologetics. It was a stance that permitted him to observe a certain continuity from his initial critique of Irish nationalism right through to his aloofness from the independent Irish state, and it might be said to connect *Stephen Hero* to *Finnegans Wake,* written after the attainment of Irish independence. It was never likely that independence, or any other event, would cause a change in Joyce's posture; equally, the idea that independent Ireland's reactionary cultural politics and deference to the Catholic Church came as the least surprise to Joyce is naïve. That at least of *Stephen Hero* endured.

11

'Professing to be a Socialist'

> The other night, about ten days ago, we went into the wineshop over the way where I told you we dined once. . . . I was reading the *Avanti!* and between whiles casting about for a remark to make. Pace (the propr.) and his two nephews one of whom is a complete bowsy, a Roman Lenehan, were eating at a table hard by. . . . Finally, I said something about the congress. Pace nodded his head (his mouth being full). The bowsy watched me until he saw my head bend again on the paper: then he leaned over his plate and asked huskily 'Zio, è socialista il Signor Giacomo?' Pace, having eaten what was in his mouth, glanced at me and uncurled his lower lip and answered 'È un po' di tutto'.
>
> —JOYCE TO STANISLAUS JOYCE FROM ROME, OCTOBER 1906[1]

AT SOME POINT AFTER he graduated from University College, Joyce came to identify himself as a socialist. In a note to the first entry in his 'Dublin Diary' in late 1903, Stanislaus wrote, 'He is not an artist he says. He is interesting himself in politics—in which he says [he has] original ideas':[2] 'politics' pertains to socialism.

1. Joyce to Stanislaus Joyce, 18 October 1906, *Letters II* 183. The punch line of the proprietor to his nephew is, 'He's a little bit of everything'. Lenehan is the hanger-on in Joyce's story 'The Two Gallants'.

2. S. Joyce, *Dublin Diary*, 2n1. This entry is written before 26 September 1903, the date of the entry that follows.

In August 1904, Stanislaus logged in the diaries Joyce's first description of himself as a socialist, linked to Joyce's conception of the modern, but coexistent with a Nietzschean nihilism. Having noted that 'it will be obvious that whatever method there is in Jim's life is highly unscientific, yet in theory he approves only of the scientific method', he observed with a sigh, 'Jim boasts—for he often boasts now—of being modern. He calls himself a socialist but attaches himself to no school of socialism. He marks the uprooting of feudal principles. Besides this, and that subtle egotism which he calls the modern mind, he proclaims all kinds of anti-Christian ideals—selfishness, licentiousness, pitilessness.'[3]

That sigh 'for he often boasts now' is to do with Joyce's drinking, a subject of contemporary reproach by Stanislaus. In a gloss on this in his *Recollections* (1941), Stanislaus makes the improbable assertion that in Joyce's relations with the other writers of the Celtic Twilight, 'there arose a latent hostility toward him', at first because 'he separated himself from any purely national movement, calling himself a "socialist"'.[4] This admittedly much later recollection remains of some significance in that it suggests Joyce's avowals of socialism were not limited to Stanislaus, even if no one else paid much attention to them. Perhaps they were deemed an incident of his bohemianism.

Herbert Gorman's treatment in his 1939 biography of Joyce's early left-wing political reading reflects a combination of what he had read of Joyce's correspondence, what Joyce had told him, and his own opinions. Gorman downplays Joyce's Italian socialism, suggesting that the disputes at the congress of the Italian Socialist Party in Rome in October 1906 (whose proceedings Joyce followed in *Avanti!*) had 'caused to flicker up anew, but fitfully, that speculative curiosity that had moved him since the days he had first read the anarchist and socialist writers', on whom the accent is thus thrown. That statement is accompanied by a footnote: 'Among the many whose works he had read may be mentioned Most, Malatesta, Stirner, Bakunin, Kropotkin, Élisée Reclus,

3. S. Joyce, entry for 13 August 1904, in *Dublin Diary*, 53–54. Elsewhere, however, Stanislaus records Joyce dismissing science as 'another kind of false religion' (*My Brother's Keeper*, 147).

4. S. Joyce, *Recollections of James Joyce*, 15.

Spencer and Benjamin Tucker, whose *Instead of a Book* proclaimed the liberty of the non-invasive individual. He never read anything by Karl Marx except the first sentence of *Das Kapital* and he found it so absurd that he immediately returned the book to the lender.'[5] What is striking about this inventory is that all the authors were anarchists, with the exception of Herbert Spencer, whose philosophy was individualist. The heavy tilt towards anarchism was accentuated by the comment about *Das Kapital* which Joyce had strategically directed at his biographer. It is clear that Joyce did read widely among the leading anarchist authors of his day, and that this reading significantly informed the libertarian component of his thought, in particular his mistrust of public intervention in the sphere of sexual morality, and his perennially hostile attitude to officialdom and a certain residual resistance to the presumptions of statal authority. While his anarchist reading appreciably coloured Joyce's thinking, the fact that it is difficult to identify specific instances of indebtedness to anarchism and anarchist writers in his work ensured it has attracted less consideration than his engagement with socialism.

Joyce's socialism had first found written expression in his 'Portrait of the Artist' essay written in January 1904, in which he referred to socialism, without naming it, as 'the generous idea'. *Stephen Hero* shows the influence of his reading in socialism and anarchism, especially the American, Benjamin Tucker, and the German, Max Stirner.[6] Tucker was an adept and lucid popular exponent of pacific anarchist principles:

> Aggression is simply another name for government. Aggression, invasion, government are interconvertible terms. . . . He who attempts to control another is a governor, an aggressor, an invader; and the nature of such invasion is not changed, whether it is made by one man upon another man, after the manner of the ordinary criminal, or by one man upon all other men, after the manner of an absolute monarch, or by all other men upon one man, after the manner of a modern democracy. . . . This then is the Anarchistic definition of

5. Gorman, *James Joyce*, 183. There is nothing to suggest that Gorman had any source other than Joyce for this short catalogue.

6. Manganiello, *Joyce's Politics*, 72–79.

government: the subjection of the non-invasive individual to an external will.[7]

The once neglected but now resurgent Élisée Reclus (1830–1905), a geographer of French Protestant provenance, was perhaps the most persuasive advocate of anarchism.

In *Stephen Hero*, Stephen Daedalus struggles to find an idiom: 'Though a taste for elegance and detail unfitted him for the part of demagogue, he might have been supposed not unjustly an ally of the collectivist politicians.'[8] Suggestions of socialist sympathy in *Stephen Hero* are intertwined with an insistence on the necessary egotism of the artist: Joyce was certainly not proposing to renounce 'that ineradicable egotism which he was afterwards to call redeemer'.[9]

In the interplay of the public and the private, Joyce remained determinedly heterodox. Stanislaus noted in his diary in April 1904 in the context of his brother's borrowings, 'Jim says he should be supported at the expense of the State because he is capable of enjoying life.'[10]

Joyce's first extant written self-characterisation as a socialist occurs in October 1904, shortly after his arrival in Trieste. After finding that there was no job for him, Joyce met Almidano Artifoni, the proprietor of the Berlitz schools in Trieste and Pola, who offered him a post in Pola. Joyce reported to Stanislaus, 'By good luck he is a socialist like myself'.[11] The next month he told Stanislaus he was reading Italian translations of the German socialist Ferdinand Lassalle. He added a perceptive comment that reveals the extent to which he was seeking to master an intellectual understanding of modern politics as much as to subscribe to the principles of socialism: 'It is difficult to get to the bottom of a science like political science through pamphlets of too vivid

7. Benjamin Tucker, *Instead of a Book, by a Man Too Busy to Write One: A Fragmentary Exposition of Philosophical Anarchism* (New York: n.p., 1893), 23. Tucker, rather missing the point, had in 1881 hailed the Land League in Ireland as 'the nearest approach on a large scale, to perfect Anarchistic organization the world has yet seen' (*Instead of a Book*, 414–15).

8. *SH* 147.

9. *SH* 34.

10. S. Joyce, entry for 10 April 1904, in *Dublin Diary*, 26.

11. Joyce to Stanislaus Joyce, 31 October 1904, *Letters II* 68.

actuality'.[12] In March 1905 he complained of reading two books of Anatole France, 'perhaps his worst', and added sarcastically, 'He is an intellectual socialist, I understand.' At the same time, he was striving to reconcile his conception of art and politics, declaring at the end of the letter, 'I believe that [Henrik] Ibsen and [Gerhart] Hauptmann separate from the herd of writers because of their political aptitude—eh?'[13] Joyce's admiration for Ibsen had always had a significant political element, but in University College it had seemed cloaked in a theory of artistic transcendence. What was new was his readiness to characterise the affinity with Ibsen in expressly political terms.

Stanislaus remained highly sceptical of his brother's professed socialism. Joyce wrote in response to his criticisms in May 1905, 'It is a mistake for you to imagine that my political opinions are those of a universal lover: but they are those of a socialistic artist.'[14] The fact that Joyce goes on to discuss the attitude of others to his 'professing to be a socialist' serves to underscore the significance of the addition of the *-ic* in his self-description. Even in his private correspondence his self-characterisation as a socialist remained tentative. A tension between the terms 'socialist' and 'artist' was observed. He declined to embrace the identity of a 'socialist artist' *tout court*. For Joyce it was possible to be a socialist and an artist. Precisely because the categories belonged to different spheres, that did not render him syllogistically a socialist artist.

In the same letter, Joyce referred to his own financial circumstances and appeared to reiterate at least obliquely one of the more urgent precepts of his complex of socialist beliefs, that the artist should be subvented by the state: 'Some people would answer that while professing to be a socialist I am trying to make money: but this is not quite true at least as they mean it. If I made a fortune it is by no means certain that I would keep it. What I wish to do is to secure a competence on which I can rely, and why I expect to have this is because I cannot believe that any State requires my energy for the work I am at present engaged

12. Joyce to Stanislaus Joyce, 19 November 1904, *Letters II* 71.

13. Joyce to Stanislaus Joyce, 15 March 1905, *Letters II* 85–86.

14. Joyce to Stanislaus Joyce, [?2 or 3 May 1905], *Letters II* 89.

in.'[15] Given Joyce's extreme guardedness in political self-categorisation, his identification as a 'socialistic artist' remains highly significant. It is made on the cusp between the socialism to which he gave expression in the 'Portrait' essay and in *Stephen Hero,* and his plunge into the theory of Italian revolutionary syndicalism. Because of the ostensible dogmatic ardour of Joyce's embrace of the tenets of Italian syndicalism, there has been a tendency on the left to privilege his fleeting espousal of the principles of revolutionary syndicalism over other strains of socialist sympathy, and to treat Joyce's socialism and his adherence to syndicalism as synonymous. The equation is fallacious. His political identification as a socialist which was expressed in terms of sympathy with continental social democracy—and owed more to Oscar Wilde than he was ever prepared to concede—preceded the phase of his subscription to the principles of Italian syndicalism. It likewise had the potential to endure beyond the abrupt abandonment of his autodidactic tutorial in Italian syndicalist socialism. Joyce's socialism is not reducible to his sympathy with syndicalist left-wing socialism in his early Triestine and Roman exile.

Joyce's sympathetic interest in anarchism ran in parallel to that in revolutionary syndicalism, though the rigour with which he tried to express the principles of revolutionary syndicalism suggests that it was unrelated to his anarchism. Thus, he was delighted to learn of Leo Tolstoy's extended letter to *The Times* on 29 August 1905 denouncing the tsar and all governments, and was contemptuous of the pusillanimous response of the English press: 'The English liberals are shocked: they would call him vulgar but that they know he is a prince.'[16]

Stanislaus's scepticism endured. In the *Recollections of James Joyce,* written just after his brother's death, he situated Joyce's socialism in the life his brother was leading when Stanislaus arrived in Trieste in late October 1905: 'Often I had to seek him out in the bars around the dock area, where I would find him arguing socialism with the dock hands for

15. This is discussed in *SL* xv.

16. Joyce to Stanislaus Joyce, 18 [September] 1905, *Letters II* 106–7; Manganiello, *Joyce's Politics,* 155–56.

whom he was buying drinks. They addressed him as "Sir", and he called them "Sir" in turn. This was evidently a socialism of polite rather than familiar terms. I would sit at the table with them, and after a little while, with one excuse or another, I would get him to leave the bar. Then I would drag him home with as much force as was necessary.'[17]

Italian Revolutionary Syndicalism

The course of pre–First World War socialism in Italy was inflected by the ascendancy of the Piedmontese Giovanni Giolitti, five times prime minister. Giolitti was an enlightened liberal of high adroitness who was particularly expert in the tactical accommodation of socialism.

In the era of Giolitti's dominance, a more pragmatic school of socialism emerged, reflected in the editorial direction of the party paper *Avanti!*, of which the moderate Leonida Bissolati was editor from 1896. At the Rome party congress in 1900, Filippo Turati—whose reformism was influenced by the revisionism of the German social democrat Edouard Bernstein—procured the adoption of a minimum and maximum programme to avoid a split, with the minimum as the precursor of the maximum. The central figure in the resistance of the syndicalist ultras at the Rome congress was the Neapolitan professor Arturo Labriola, to whose views Joyce was drawn. Labriola was then in alliance with Enrico Ferri, professor of penal law at Rome and a distinguished disciple of Cesare Lombroso. Labriola made up for the lateness of his embrace of socialism by the extremism of the sentiments he was prepared to avow. The revolutionary syndicalists aspired to win control of the party but ultimately failed and seceded in 1908.[18]

Joyce's earnest self-education in and sympathy with the tenets of revolutionary syndicalism coincided with the zenith of its political influence. The reformists again prevailed at the 1902 congress at Imola, but their control of the party was slipping. In 1903 Ferri displaced Bissolati from the editorship of *Avanti!* and held the position till 1908. At the 1904

17. S. Joyce, *Recollections of James Joyce*, 24–25.

18. Smith, *Modern Italy*, 193–96; Manganiello, *Joyce's Politics*, 58–59.

Bologna congress, Ferri became in effect the leader of the party. Joyce wanted to attain an immersive understanding of Italian socialism; there is nothing to suggest that he specifically chose revolutionary syndicalism, which he came to through his reading of *Avanti!*, from a considered understanding of the variant strands of Italian socialism. He was touched by its intellectual excitement, without being in a position fully to appreciate what made it distinctive in the history of the Italian left. Norberto Bobbio wrote of the fleeting ascendancy of revolutionary syndicalism,

> In spite of the negative judgement of the syndicalists that hindsight provides, the syndicalists of the Giolitti era were, intellectually speaking, the liveliest wing of socialism, and they made a significant and memorable contribution—even on a theoretical level—to the debate about Marxism and the essence and future of socialism. Their rise was swift, but with their strong penchant for polemics and their aggressive political stance, they burned out in only a few years. They produced a tumultuous explosion without lasting effect either in theory (some of their works, especially those of Arturo Labriola and the early works of Enrico Leone, had merit but never enjoyed any broad resonance) or in politics (risen to prominence with the general strike in Parma in 1904, they were declared heretical and for all practical purposes were rendered ineffective as early as the Socialist Party Congress held in Florence in 1908).[19]

Revolutionary syndicalism shared the same critique of parliamentary reformism as Vladimir Lenin but not his theory of a centralised revolutionary party driven by intellectuals, which he had been promoting since 1902. The revolutionary syndicalists, as Bobbio pointed out, 'preferred the trade union over the party as an instrument for social transformation. . . . To replace the parliamentary system, which they saw as both an indirect form of action and inefficient, at best capable of correcting the system but not of changing it, they proposed the method of

19. Norberto Bobbio, *Ideological Profile of Twentieth-Century Italy*, trans. Lydia G. Cochrane (Princeton, NJ: Princeton University Press, 1995), 59.

the general strike, which, because it was carried out by the workers themselves rather than being delegated to party intellectuals or the political operators in Parliament, they termed "direct action". Assimilating the reformists to the conservative parties, Arturo Labriola asserted, 'The working class cannot emancipate itself if it does not both take possession of production and absorb political power.'[20]

The ideological instability of Italian revolutionary syndicalism is discernible in the political thought of its chief inspiration, the French intellectual Georges Sorel. Sorel's hostility to democracy and exaltation of proletarian violence derived from a volatile combination of conservatism and zeal for revolution. In Italian politics Sorel became a tutelary figure both of revolutionary syndicalism on the left and of the extreme nationalist right, which was to emerge as a political force from the first congress of the new Nationalist Party at Florence in 1910. Enrico Corradini, the theoretician of conservative extremism, proclaimed nationalism to be the true consummation of socialism.[21]

The revolutionary syndicalist acceptance of revolutionary violence had its own trajectory. Joyce's abandonment of revolutionary syndicalism spared him the embarrassment of Arturo Labriola's support of the Italian invasion of Libya in 1911–12 on the pretext that it provided a school of revolution. ('O my companions! Do you know why the proletariat of Italy is no good for making a revolution? Precisely because it is not even good for making war.') The signatories of the manifesto of the Fascio Rivoluzionario di Azione Internazionalista of 5 October 1914, advocating Italian intervention in the First World War, were largely revolutionary syndicalists.[22] If Joyce ever gave thought to the later course of revolutionary syndicalism, the crossover from revolutionary syndicalism on the left to nationalism on the right afforded a rich illustration of the contrariety of opposites.

The Italian edition of Sorel's work on syndicalism gained wide circulation from 1903, and his ideas were well entrenched in Italy by 1906

20. Bobbio, *Ideological Profile*, 60.

21. Smith, *Modern Italy*, 239; Bobbio, *Ideological Profile*, 50–56.

22. Bobbio, *Ideological Profile*, 62–63; Smith, *Modern Italy*, 245.

when he published his *Réflexions sur la violence*, which was swiftly translated into Italian.[23] Arturo Labriola and Enrico Leone were the principal disciples of Sorel on the Italian left. In Sorel's writings, some of what were to become the dominant themes of twentieth-century European history emerge. In 1926 Joyce's *frère-ennemi* Wyndham Lewis wrote of Sorel as 'a highly unstable and equivocal figure' and also 'the key to all contemporary thought'. Daniel Halévy wrote in 1940, 'Those who listened to him forty years ago owe it to him that they have not been surprised at the changes in the world.'[24]

Italian Socialism and Irish Nationalism

Joyce's letters to Stanislaus do not register the commencement of Joyce's study of Italian socialism, or when he became an attentive reader of the socialist paper *Avanti!*, his principal source of intelligence on Italian socialism. Nor does his correspondence reflect the early course of his engagement with socialism in Italy. Not the least reason for this is that Joyce was conscious of Stanislaus's highly sceptical attitude to his professions of socialist belief. In relation to the later phase, while it is hazardous to draw inferences from an incomplete trajectory, Joyce's correspondence taken by itself suggests that his active interest in Italian socialism may have peaked in the latter part of 1906 and ceased in March 1907. Joyce was in Rome during this period, and this is also when he began seriously to address his relationship to Sinn Féin and contemporary Irish nationalism in his correspondence. Though Joyce did not consider Italian socialism and Irish nationalism irreconcilable, his willed enthusiasm for revolutionary syndicalism yielded to a renewed interest in Irish nationalism, though now marked by his induction into Italian socialism.

Referring to what he considered Oliver St John Gogarty's deviousness in his communications about his forthcoming marriage, Joyce wrote to Stanislaus in mid-August 1906,

23. Smith, *Modern Italy*, 198.

24. Wyndham Lewis, *The Art of Being Ruled* (London: Chatto and Windus, 1926), 128; and Daniel Halévy, *Peguy et les Cahiers de la Quinzaine* (Paris: Grasset, 1941), 108; both quoted in James Joll, *The Anarchists*, 2nd ed. (London: Routledge, 1979), 194–95.

> You have often shown opposition to my socialistic tendencies. But can you not see plainly from facts like these that a deferment of the emancipation of the proletariat, a reaction to clericalism or aristocracy or bourgeoism would mean revulsion to tyrannies of all kinds. Gogarty would jump in the Liffey to save a man's life but he seems to have little hesitation in condemning generations to servitude. Perhaps it is a case which the piping poets should solemnise. For my part I believe that to establish the church in full power again would mean a renewal of the Inquisition—though, of course, the Jesuits tell us that the Dominicans never broke men on the wheel or tortured them on the rack.[25]

On 6 September 1906 Joyce wrote an affectionate letter to Stanislaus in which he said, 'On all subjects—except socialism (for which you care nothing) and painting (of which I know nothing)—we have the same or like opinions.' Joyce's argument with Stanislaus made clear that his interest in Italian socialism owed something to his belief that the Italian people had a greater capacity than the Irish to take decisive political action: 'You seem unable to share my detestation of the stupid, dishonest, tyrannical and cowardly burgher class. The people are brutalised and cunning. But at least they are capable of some honesty in these countries; or, at least, they will move because it is in their interest to do so. I am a stranger to them, and a prey for them often; but in the sense of the word in which I use it now, I am not an enemy of the people'.[26]

From 7 to 10 October 1906, the congress of the Italian Socialist Party took place while Joyce was in Rome, and Joyce followed its proceedings attentively in the columns of *Avanti!* Arturo Labriola was now pitted against Enrico Ferri. Ferri had drifted from the left of the party and was by this time at the head of the doctrinally ecumenical integralists, and in alliance with the reformists he had formerly condemned, he prevailed over Labriola's syndicalists.[27] Attentively scrutinising the internal politics of the party, Joyce noted the replacement by Ferri of two sub-editors

25. Joyce to Stanislaus Joyce, [?12 August 1906], *Letters II* 148.
26. Joyce to Stanislaus Joyce, 6 September 1906, *Letters II* 158.
27. Manganiello, *Joyce's Politics*, 58–59.

loyal to Labriola, who was to become the paper's German correspondent: 'Labriola is a person who interests me very much.'[28] Joyce's presence in Rome during the congress provided him with a platform from which to educate Stanislaus in the tenets of revolutionary syndicalism which he lucidly expounded:

> I am following with interest the struggle between the various socialist parties here at the Congress. Labriola spoke yesterday, the paper says, with extraordinarily rapid eloquence for two hours and a half. He reminds me somewhat of Griffith. He attacked the intellectuals and the parliamentary socialists. He belongs or is the leader of the sindicalists. They are trades-unionists or rather trade-unionists with a definite anti-social programme. Their weapons are unions and strikes. They decline to interfere in politics or religion or legal questions. They do not desire the conquest of public powers which, they say, only serve in the end to support the middle-class government. They assert that they are the true socialists because they wish the future social order to proceed equally from the overthrow of the entire present social organisation and from the automatic emergence of the proletariat in trades-unions and guilds and the like.[29]

Labriola had emphasised the efficacy of the instrument of the general strike and downplayed any necessity for recourse to revolutionary violence. Joyce disagreed and lucidly saw a general strike as inexorably entailing a confrontation with the Italian army:

> Their objection to parliamentarianism seems to me well-founded but if, as all classes of socialists agree, a general European war, an international war, has become an impossibility I do not see how a general international strike or even a general national strike is a possibility. The Italian army is not directed against the Austrian army so much as against the Italian people. Of course, the sindicalists are antimilitarists but I don't see how that saves them from the logical conclusion of revolution in a conscriptive country like this. It is strange

28. Joyce to Stanislaus Joyce, 18 October 1906, *Letters II* 183.

29. Joyce to Stanislaus Joyce, 9 October 1906, *Letters II* 173–74.

> that Italian socialism in its latest stage should approach so closely the English variety.[30]

Joyce's characterisation of the contemporary European socialist belief that there could not be a European war (largely because of the presumed influence of socialism itself on the working class) was slightly distanced, as if he was not altogether convinced of it.

An Irish nationalist subtext runs through Joyce's analysis. The extremely heterodox if qualified comparison of Arturo Labriola to Arthur Griffith, who was emphatically not a socialist, serves to invest the term 'parliamentarianism' with an Irish as well as an Italian signification, so that it is difficult to believe that Joyce was not at some level deploying the term 'intellectuals' to include his Irish contemporaries. Even the critique of the advocacy of a general strike that does not address the reality of statal military force comes to seem, in the context of the Irish nationalist subtext, as much Fenian as ultra-socialistic. The final reference to the timidity of English socialism discloses part of what Joyce was striving to escape from in his transient embrace of the tenets of revolutionary syndicalism. His antagonism to English socialism is charged with his unforgivingness towards Gladstonian progressive Liberalism in its role in the overthrow of Parnell.

On 6 November Joyce responded to Stanislaus, whose letters to Joyce have not survived:

> Of course you find my socialism thin. It is so and unsteady and ill-informed. You are wrong however in supposing that the intellectuals taught Labriola socialism. Intellectualism, instead, is a partial development, an alloy of sociological liberalism, of the original socialism which was really nothing but the manifesto of a class. Ferri, for example, seems a more intellectual and capable person than Labriola. But the latter contends that interest in psychiatry and criminology and literature and religion are beside the point. He wishes to hasten *directly*

30. Joyce to Stanislaus Joyce, 9 October 1906, *Letters II* 173–74. Joyce, with cheerful candour, proceeded from his socialist excursus to the matter of his own impecuniosity: 'After the preceding exordium I approach the question of my finances'. A Micawberesque disquisition on his personal budget followed.

the emergence of the proletariat. And to do this he would include in his ranks Catholics and Jews, liberals and conservatives.[31]

Joyce was certainly drawn to Labriola's dismissal of intellectuals and was much exercised about the inadequacies of Irish intellectuals in particular. In his next letter to Stanislaus, having objected to a criticism by Griffith in the journal *Sinn Féin* of the British army as mercenary, he continued, 'Italy, at least, has two things to balance its miserable poverty and mismanagement: a lively intellectual movement and a good climate. Ireland is Italy without these two.'[32] The desire to demarcate his thought from the conventional preoccupations of the socialist intellectual rendered him more susceptible than he would otherwise have been to the delusive revolutionary syndicalist concept of a transformative rupture whereby a pluralist society would be constituted by proletarian syndicalist action.

Joyce's ventures into syndicalist theory in his correspondence are few, but evidently reflect attentive reading, at least of *Avanti!*, and a fairly strenuous endeavour to educate himself in the principles of revolutionary syndicalism. His engagement was serious and sustained for quite some time and shaped his political self-conception in the early period of his exile. It raises delicate interpretative issues of some complexity that do not admit of a definitive conclusion. Some critics have seized on this phase of Joyce's life, as reflected in his correspondence with Stanislaus, to claim Joyce for the left without convincingly addressing his subsequent abandonment of interest in Italian left-wing socialism. The implications of the break-off become yet more far-reaching if Joyce's socialism is reduced exclusively to its most engagé (if still private) manifestation, that with revolutionary syndicalism, as it tends to be in the argument that seeks to classify Joyce as possessed of definite socialist convictions beyond 1907. What is most striking about Joyce's sympathy with revolutionary syndicalism is the radicalism of his disaffection with European (including Irish) political institutions in the age of transition

31. Joyce to Stanislaus Joyce, 6 November 1906, *Letters II* 187. This passage follows immediately on Joyce's characterisation of his relationship to Griffith and the *Sinn Féin* paper.

32. Joyce to Stanislaus Joyce, 13 November 1906, *Letters II* 189.

to mass democracy, even if the general tenor of his correspondence does not sustain a conception of him as socially or politically alienated.

Joyce's exploration of Italian socialism was obliquely Hiberno-centric. The *problematique* which Joyce seeks to address through Italian socialism is at least as much Irish as Italian. He was certainly striving to address the issues of Italian politics, but the correlation to the Irish political exists in parallel. A hostility to parliamentarianism, a term which meant very different things in Italy and Ireland, was nominally common to revolutionary syndicalism and Sinn Féin, and this is the only politically intelligible context for Joyce's comparison of Labriola to Griffith. The equation of the Italian and Irish expressions of anti-parliamentarianism was not, however, glibly superficial on Joyce's part. Joyce was asserting an analogy between the revolutionary syndicalist doctrine of 'direct action' and Griffith's conception of Irish economic self-organisation, which was not dependent on the fiat of the Westminster Parliament. This was the element of Griffith's programme to which Joyce was highly sympathetic. Joyce saw the disparate means—the civil insurgency of the general strike and pacific national economic organisation—as partaking of a common approach, the bypassing of the conventional parliamentary arena of political struggle by concerted socio-economic action, albeit with very different ends in view.

In one respect, Joyce was driven to make the far-fetched comparison of Griffith and Labriola. Joyce's analyses of Italy and of Ireland were separately conducted, with interposed points of comparison. He conspicuously did not seek to assert that a revolutionary transformation in Ireland by syndicalist or any other means was achievable: there is absolutely nothing to suggest that Joyce had the least illusion about the prospects for a socialist revolution in Ireland. The comparison of Griffith and Labriola was necessary to enable him to establish some sort of linkage, however improbable, between his thinking on Italy and on Ireland.

If Joyce's hostility to parliamentarism was particularly implacable in these years, 1905–7, the more deeply rooted and ideologically elusive suspicion of statal (or any) authority that informed his sympathetic interest in anarchism, of which his temporarily strident anti-parliamentarism can be seen as a derivation, never left him. For an orthodox Marxist, revolutionary syndicalism was an anarchist deviation from socialism, and Joyce's engagement with Italian socialism reflects a compound of socialist and anarchist affinities.

Joyce's antagonism towards the bourgeoisie was common to his Italian and his Irish political perspectives, but it is hard to resist the conclusion that his condemnation of intellectuals—which in revolutionary syndicalism was less a hostility to intellectuals than a refusal to concede them a hegemonic role—had a discernibly Irish twist. He had little basis in personal acquaintance for a dislike of Italian intellectuals. The intellectuals for whom he did have contempt were, first, Tom Kettle and Frank Sheehy-Skeffington, Catholic and rationalist exponents of Irish parliamentarism respectively, about whom his letters at this time were replete with unflattering references; and second, the intellectual adherents of the dominant English school of socialism, which he regarded as timidly parliamentary and as owing as much to Gladstonian Liberalism as to Marxism. To these might be added the freethinking that W. K. Magee and Fred Ryan espoused in *Dana*.

It is scarcely surprising that part of what propelled Joyce into immersive scrutiny of the internal controversies of the Italian left was the impulse to extricate himself from the constraining paradigm of Irish politics, to escape what was for him the dismal solipsism of Irish controversy. Joyce's embrace of the Italian left was in this respect a measure of the depth of the exasperation, not untinged by bitterness, towards Ireland which attended the initial phase of his exile. It was a following through of the logic of exile, a spirited elective embrace of what had been forced on him. That trajectory had its own ineluctable circularity, and an Irish colouration seeped into his austerely monochrome rendering of Italian socialism.

It is striking that, for the most part, Joyce's observations on contemporary socialism in his correspondence cleaved ostensibly to Italy. If he read Lassalle (in Italian) and was conscious of Marx, he did not essay a wider analysis of continental socialism. His focus was unsocialistically national: Italian, with an Irish subtext.

Socialism was, as Norberto Bobbio wrote, 'the first major nonreligious—and often provocatively irreligious—popular movement in Italian history'.[33] However dispiriting Joyce found the annual procession in honour of Giordano Bruno in Rome ('The spectacle of the procession in honour of the Nolan left me quite cold'),[34] the existence of an overt and politically formidable resistance to the political hegemony of Catholicism in Italian political culture meant Joyce could breathe more freely. In Rome he enjoyed the anticlerical *L'Asino*, a welcome respite from the more turgid *Avanti!*, and despatched a copy to Stanislaus.[35] Anticlericalism was certainly part of the appeal of socialism to Joyce. He despised the political authority of the Catholic Church as reactionary and believed that clerical domination was an aspect of the servitude to which the states of Europe would revert if they did not advance to socialism.

Joyce was almost embarrassedly conscious of the irony that Catholic obedience and orthodoxy in Ireland surpassed that in Italy. In *Stephen Hero* Stephen muses, 'The idea that the power of an empire is weakest at its borders requires some modification for everyone knows that the Pope cannot govern Italy as he governs Ireland'.[36] Addressing his Triestine audience in his lecture 'L'Irlanda: Isola dei santi e dei savi' in April 1907, Joyce referred to 'that religious fervour that still flourishes in Ireland of which you, fed over the past years on a diet of scepticism can only form an idea with difficulty'.[37] Joyce's socialism was in this aspect geostrategic from an Irish perspective: socialism was a new continental political nexus which had the potential to supplant Ireland's predominantly Catholic linkage to the European mainland.

Anticlericalism in Italy was not confined to socialists, but Joyce did not even mention liberal anticlericalism. For Joyce, anticlericalism required a popular political basis if it was to prevail. This correlates to his

33. Bobbio, *Ideological Profile*, 15.

34. Joyce to Stanislaus Joyce, [1] March 1907, *Letters II* 217. A statue to the condemned heretic Giordano Bruno, burned at the stake on 17 February 1600, had been erected amid much controversy in 1889 on the site of his execution in Campo de' Fiori in Rome. The annual commemorative procession held on 17 February was considered a celebration of free thinking and anticlericalism. Bruno was born in Nola. See chapter 6, footnote 77 for Joyce's use of 'the Nolan' to refer to Bruno.

35. Joyce to Stanislaus Joyce, 19 August, 6 September 1906, *Letters II* 151, 157.

36. *SH* 147.

37. *OCPW* 108–9.

dismissal in Dublin of the freethinking of the *Dana* editors, W. K. Magee and Fred Ryan. In the absence of a strong socialist movement in Ireland, their equivocal relationship to popular nationalism rendered their anticlericalism elitist and politically futile. The corollary was that Joyce did not regard nationalist Ireland as irretrievably submissive to the Catholic Church (in spite of the many magnificently tart aphorisms on the subject that suggest a more fatalistic view).

Joyce furiously repudiated the Church's claim to spiritual dominion over him as an Irish Catholic by origin, and he had a Parnellite's bitter opposition to clerical intervention in secular politics, but his opposition to the Church was mild by continental standards. His Irish Catholic background, and his sense of the spiritual and historical *acquis* of Catholicism, ensured that his anticlericalism was not marked by the intolerance that frequently characterised continental anticlericalism. He was not greatly exercised by the Church's entrenched philosophical antagonism to contemporary socialism, though he considered it doctrinally gratuitous and ascribed it to the Church's defence of its wealth. He wrote to Stanislaus of his visit to the Basilica of San Clemente, to where he had repaired to recuperate from the exhaustion of a visit to the Roman Forum,

> Then there was a sermon. The gentleman who delivered this addressed most of his remarks to me—God knows why. I suppose I looked pious. I didn't wait for benediction. While listening to the service a most keen regret seized me that I could not gain for myself from historical study an accurate appreciation of an order like the Dominicans. I think my policy of subtracting oneself and one's progeny from the church is too slow. I don't believe the church has suffered vitally from the number of her apostates. An order like this couldn't support their immense church with rent &c on the obolos of the religious but parsimonious Italian. And the same, I expect, in France. They must have vast landed estates under various names, and invested monies. This is one reason why they oppose the quite unheretical theory of socialism because they know that one of its items is expropriation.[38]

38. Joyce to Stanislaus Joyce, 25 September 1906, *Letters II* 165–66.

The extent to which Joyce's interest in socialism, or at least his reading of *Avanti!*, was bound up with his anticlerical convictions is reflected in what he wrote to Stanislaus from Rome on the election of a new general of the Jesuits ('the black lice') to whose headquarters he had called seeking news of the outcome: 'Unfortunately I have not bought the *Avanti!* these few nights. I would like to read an article on the subject.'[39]

Gradualist Socialism: The Influence of Guglielmo Ferrero

Joyce's engagement with Italian socialism was not confined to revolutionary syndicalism. He was also reading the journalism and works of Guglielmo Ferrero, which were to have a significant impact on his writing and thought.

Born in Portici, near Naples, in 1871, Ferrero studied law in Pisa, Bologna, and Turin and was in his youth a representative adherent of positivism.[40] Ferrero, still in his mid-thirties when Joyce began to read him, was already a writer of sociological and historical works, and a commentator on current affairs of considerable contemporary renown. He was the author of *L'Europa giovane* (1897) and *Il militarismo* (1898) and was completing his five-volume *Grandezza e decadenza di Roma* (1902–6). He also wrote intelligent and influential articles for papers including the Triestine *Il Piccolo della Sera*. Writing to Stanislaus from Rome in mid-August 1906, Joyce added, 'If there is anything interesting (Ferrero etc.) in *Il Piccolo della Sera* you might send it to me.'[41]

Ferrero was not an academic but a transitional figure who was both a savant in the manner of the nineteenth century and a precursor of the twentieth-century public intellectual. His cast of mind was sociological and anthropological and had immense attractions for Joyce. Ferrero emerged from positivism and took a benign view of the Industrial

39. Joyce to Stanislaus Joyce, [?12 September 1906], *Letters II* 158.

40. Bobbio, *Ideological Profile*, 7.

41. Joyce to Stanislaus Joyce, 19 August 1906, *Letters II* 152.

FIGURE 11.1. Guglielmo Ferrero (Wikimedia).

Revolution. He looked to a shift from militarily to economically organised society, and the displacement of feudal class stratification and religious authority by a competitive society regulated by scientific knowledge. The positivists were divided into proponents of aggressive economic liberalism and gradualist socialism; Ferrero was closer to the second. At a philosophical level, responses and reactions to the late arrival of positivism in the economically backward Italy of the late nineteenth century provided a defining line of cleavage. The adversaries of positivism were diverse: conservatives, nationalists, philosophical idealists (such as Benedetto Croce), and those of the radical left, including revolutionary syndicalists.[42] While positivism was philosophically meagre, and already in eclipse in the countries in which it had its origins, its

42. Bobbio, *Ideological Profile*, 1–14 et passim.

analytic force in Italian socio-economic conditions in positing a modernising intellectual rupture with pre-industrial hierarchies was considerable. Joyce was strongly drawn to Ferrero's admittedly not over-rigorous positivism. Applied to Ireland, his interest in Ferrero discloses an aspect of Joyce's politics in the first phase of exile, from 1904 to 1915, that is rarely recognised: that of Joyce as an exasperated but undeluded moderniser.

Ferrero was the disciple, collaborator and son-in-law of Cesare Lombroso (1835–1909), a psychiatrist and anthropologist, whose work on criminology was one of the most influential, if dubious, applications of Italian positivism. Lombroso was the founder of criminal anthropology, emphasising both environmental and putatively biological factors in criminal activity. Ferrero collaborated with Lombroso in the writing of *La donna delinquente, la prostituta e la donna normale* (1893) on female offenders. When, in *Stephen Hero*, Stephen declaims to Cranly that 'the modern spirit is vivisective' and says that 'Italy has added a science to civilisation by putting out the lantern of justice and considering the criminal in production and in action', he is referring to Lombroso.[43]

Joyce's first extant reference to Ferrero appears in response to Grant Richards's advising him in April 1906 that his English printers refused to print 'The Two Gallants'—the *Dubliners* story that Joyce acknowledged was inspired by Ferrero. In his reply to Richards, Joyce referred contemptuously to the printer: 'I would strongly recommend to him the chapters wherein Ferrero examines the moral code of the soldier and (incidentally) of the gallant. But it would be useless for I am sure that in his heart of hearts he is a militarist.'[44] The reference is likely to *Il militarismo*, which is also the probable inspiration for 'Two Gallants' itself.[45] Robert Scholes has pointed out that Joyce's statement that he had written his *Dubliners* stories 'for the most part in a style of scrupulous meanness' derives from Ferrero's attribution of a 'scrupulosa

43. *SH* 186; Manganiello, *Joyce's Politics*, 81–82.

44. Joyce to Grant Richards, 3 May 1906, *Letters II* 132–33.

45. Susan L. Humphreys, 'Ferrero Etc: James Joyce's Debt to Guglielmo Ferrero', *James Joyce Quarterly* 16, no. 3 (Spring 1979): 240, 243.

esatezza di analista' to nineteenth-century French novelists.[46] In mid-August Joyce reported to Stanislaus an episode involving his hated fellow clerks in the bank in the Rome: 'I absorbed the attention of the three clerks in my office a few days ago by a socialistic outburst. One of them is a German and he was ridiculing Lombrosianismo and anti-militarism. He said when children cried they "should be caned", favoured corporal punishment in schools, conscription, religion &c. I think he was surprised not to find an ally in an Inglese.'[47] The characterisation of his retort as 'socialistic' is of significance. Joyce conceived his approval of Lombroso, and by extension Ferrero, as partaking of his socialist outlook, which was thus not confined to revolutionary syndicalism. Joyce was intrigued by Ferrero and identified with him, promising four weeks later to send Stanislaus a postcard of Ferrero: 'By the way, talking of faces I will send you a picture postcard of Guglielmo Ferrero and you will admit that there is some hope for me. You would think he was a terrified Y. M. C. A. with an inaudible voice. He wears spectacles, is delicate looking and, altogether, is the type you would expect to find in some quiet nook in the Coffee-Palace nibbling a bun hastily and apologetically between the hours of half past twelve and one.'[48]

Ferrero's interests matched Joyce's quite closely, and it was in the period when he was reading Ferrero that Joyce first had the idea for a short story that was the genesis of *Ulysses*. He wrote from Rome to Stanislaus in a post-postscriptum to a letter of 30 September 1906, 'I have a new story for Dubliners in my head. It deals with Mr Hunter',[49] and two weeks later, on 13 November, he reported, 'I thought of beginning my story *Ulysses*: but I have too many cares at present.' He proceeded immediately to his most extended discussion of Ferrero, referring specifically both to *L'Europa giovane* and to *Grandezza e decadenza di Roma*. Of the latter, he wrote, 'Ferrero devotes a chapter in his history of Rome to

46. Scholes, 'Joyce and Modernist Ideology', 169. Scholes's (171) relating of Joyce's 'the conscience of my race' to Ferrero seems less cogent.

47. Joyce to Stanislaus Joyce, 19 August 1906, *Letters II* 151.

48. Joyce to Stanislaus Joyce, [?12 September 1906], *Letters II* 159.

49. Joyce to Stanislaus Joyce, 30 September 1906, *Letters II* 168.

the Odes of Horace: so, perhaps, poets should be let live.' In the fourth chapter, Ferrero had written that the poetry of Horace 'marks in literature the moral change proceeding in society. No one realised more profoundly than Horace the immense moral vacuum upon which the vast edifice of the empire rested'. Joyce continued, 'In his book *Young Europe* which I have just read he says there are three great classes of emigrants: the (I forget the word [*plasmativa*]: it means conquering, imposing their own language, &c), the English: the adhesive (forming a little group with national traditions and sympathies) the Chinese and the Irish!!!!: the diffusive (entering into the new society and forming part of it) the Germans.' Joyce then proceeded to refer to two chapters of *L'Europa giovane*, one concerned with the Jews, and the other with Germany and socialism: 'He has a fine chapter on Antisemitism. By the way, Brandes is a Jew. He [Ferrero] says that Karl Marx has the apocalyptic imagination and makes Armageddon a war between capital and labour. The most arrogant statement made by Israel so far, he says, not excluding the gospel of Jesus is Marx's proclamation that socialism is the fulfilment of a natural law. In considering Jews he slips in Jesus between Lassalle and Lombroso: the latter too (Ferrero's father-in-law) is a Jew.'[50] While Ferrero eccentrically discerned the Jewish 'barbaric passion' for proselytising as engendering anti-Semitism in the classical world and was suspicious of what he saw as the Jewish conviction that they possessed the secret of human redemption, he was sympathetic to modern Jewry and critical of anti-Semitism.[51] He wrote that 'a national disposition of the Jews is the ethical spirit, the passion for moral criticism of society and for the vivisection of its lies, the aggressive instinct against social prejudices'. Susan L. Humphreys has surmised suggestively, if a little too confidently, that Ferrero's characterisation of modern Jews prompted Joyce to give Leopold Bloom his vocation: 'Why is Bloom a canvasser of advertisements who haunts newspaper offices? "The Jew", says Ferrero, "possesses a genius for proselytism; it

50. Joyce to Stanislaus Joyce, 13 November 1906, *Letters II* 190; Humphreys, 'Ferrero Etc', 245.

51. Manganiello, *Joyce's Politics*, 52–53.

can even be said that propaganda is a creation, perhaps the greatest of the Jewish genius". In Italian, however, the word *propaganda* also means commercial advertising. And Ferrero believes that the messianic spirit is akin to the journalistic one: "Every great Jewish talent is always a bit of journalist", he says. Probably Joyce was ironically remembering Ferrero's theories when he chose Bloom's profession.'[52]

The vast profusion of contemporary commentary on Jews and anti-Semitism which was available to Joyce—his library in Trieste included Carlo Cattaneo's *Saggi di filosofia civile* (Essays in civil philosophy) and *Ricerche economiche sulle interdizioni imposte dalla legge civile agli Israeliti* (Economic research on the interdictions imposed by civil law on the Israelites) in a 1911 edition[53]—makes it problematic to assign to any one quarter a preponderant influence in the shaping of the Jewishness of Leopold Bloom, even in the case of so attractively plausible a hypothesis.

It was not merely that Ferrero was immensely clever and engaging. Just as importantly for Joyce, he was devoid of dogmatism or intellectual pretension. His critique of national sexual mores, and of martially derived codes of gallantry, was brilliant and innovative. His resolutely sardonic treatment of the Caesars and Caesarism caused a scandal in the world of contemporary classical scholarship and was to be invoked by Joyce in the lecture 'L'Irlanda: Isola dei santi e dei savi' which he gave in Trieste in April 1907. Ferrero saw Latin societies as caught up in a motion towards 'the agony of Caesarism', characterised by government by classes who did not engage in productive labour.[54] Ferrero's consideration of national characteristics in *L'Europa giovane* extended to Ireland. He asserted that Parnell's greatness was due to the fact that he was devoid of the emotive plasticity of the Irish and was possessed of the English characteristic of 'calculating fanaticism'.[55] This reflected, as well as an admiration of Parnell, Ferrero's Anglophilia. The emphasis

52. Humphreys, 'Ferrero Etc', 247–48.

53. Ellmann, *Consciousness of Joyce*, 104; Manganiello, *Joyce's Politics*, 53–56. Carlo Cattaneo (1801–1869) was an immensely distinguished figure of the Risorgimento movement, a democrat and European federalist of positivist orientation. See Bobbio, *Ideological Profile*, 3, 154–55, 205.

54. Manganiello, *Joyce's Politics*, 52.

55. Manganiello, *Joyce's Politics*, 49–50.

on Parnell's supposed 'Englishness', if somewhat trite, was a frequently encountered theme in obituaries and other analyses of Parnell's political authority and suggests a degree of familiarity with the rise and fall of Parnell that was uncommon among continental commentators. The references to Parnell perhaps provided Joyce with some reassurance in the incorporation of the figure of Parnell in 'Ivy Day in the Committee Room' in August 1905.

When it comes to elucidating Joyce's socio-political thought, what is at least as important as Ferrero's influence on Joyce is what drew Joyce to Ferrero. What attracted Joyce was Ferrero's facility for subjecting contemporary topics to a form of historical and sociological analysis that was not overly abstract or theoretical and did not stray too far from its subject matter. Ferrero continued to work with concepts of national types, partly aggregated into broader groupings (north/south, industrial/pre-industrial, Catholic/Protestant/Jewish), correlated to stages of economic development which he then sought to subject to reasoned scrutiny devoid of atavism or ethnic animus. This was congenial to, and anticipatory of, Joyce, whose instinct and intellectual method was to destabilise and subvert, without dispensing with, ideas of national type. Ferrero ran the risk that his writing on contemporary society would be (unfairly) discounted as ephemeral and obsolete, and as ideologically démodé and lacking in scientific rigour as the twentieth century progressed. Initially refusing to leave Italy, Ferrero was placed under house arrest by the Fascists, and later took a professorship at the Graduate Institute of International Studies in Geneva. He continued to write, but his works did not attract anything like the renown of his earlier books. Joyce heard Ferrero address the English PEN Club in London in April 1927, when he spoke of the burning of his books by the Fascists—Joyce was more exercised over the piracy of *Ulysses* in the United States at the time.[56] Ferrero died in Geneva during the Second World War, eighteen months after Joyce's death in Zurich.

Ferrero was more positivist than socialist, but Joyce's coming upon Ferrero can be seen as a by-product of his socialist reading on Italian

56. Jan Parandowski, 'Meeting with Joyce', in Potts, *Portraits of the Artist*, 155–56.

society. Ferrero answered Joyce's need to find a modern comparative European perspective on Ireland. While it is not valid to see Joyce as abandoning Italian socialism for Irish nationalism, it was important for Joyce that he had, through a process of parallel reading, validated a qualified sympathy with Sinn Féin by a comparative European route. He had come to Sinn Féin through Europe, as well as by the trajectory of his Irish political experience before exile. In a precociously modern way, Joyce's nationalism was soldered in the furnace of contemporary Europe. His nationalism is international. His interest in the Jews of Europe, which coincides with—if it does not originate in—his reading of Ferrero, and his creation of the Jewish and vaguely pro-Griffith Leopold Bloom, stands as an emblem of the political quest that marked Joyce's period in Trieste. The Jewishness of Bloom is hard-won and bears the traces of Joyce's political formation in exile.

'Do you believe in the sun of the future?'

Joyce's intellectual adventure in the realms of Italian socialism ended abruptly towards the end of his stay in Rome. He declared on 6 February 1907, 'I have given up reading *Avanti!*'[57] On 1 March 1907 he wrote in a disconsolate vein, 'It is months since I have written a line and even reading tires me. The interest I took in socialism and the rest has left me. I have gradually slid down until I have ceased to take any interest in any subject. I look at God and his theatre through the eyes of my fellow-clerks so that nothing surprises, moves, excites or disgusts me. . . . I have no wish to codify myself as anarchist or socialist or reactionary.'[58] William Empson spiritedly sought to diminish the significance of Joyce's statement that the interest in socialism had left him: 'But this is only to prove that he has been reduced to the hoggish mental condition of his fellow clerks—he has even been left cold by a procession in favour of the Nolan, so he had obviously better leave Rome at once.'[59] It is true

57. Joyce to Stanislaus Joyce, 6 February 1907, *Letters II* 210.

58. Joyce to Stanislaus Joyce, [?1 March 1907], *Letters II* 217.

59. William Empson, 'Joyce's Intentions', in *Using Biography* (1984), reprinted in *Modern Critical Views: James Joyce*, ed. Harold Bloom (New York: Chelsea House, 1986), 216.

that this was written when Joyce was at a low point, but his language has a certain resolute finality. Even if Joyce's articulation of his loss of interest could be considered somewhat impetuous, it was affirmed by the enduring silence that followed. He did not thereafter describe himself as a socialist, nor was there any renewal of his tortuous exegeses of the internal controversies of Italian socialism.

The least (and possibly the most) that can be said is that Joyce's socialism became radically de-institutionalised, bereft of any necessary alignment to party. In doctrinal terms this was profoundly heterodox. Conservatives professed allegiance to institutions that were at least notionally historical. The left—and the continental left in particular—looked to contemporary institutions (the party and the movement) as vanguards of the proletariat, and on occasion the proletariat itself. It was these that would ensure the triumph of socialism, and the nature of the fealty owed to them was a primary subject of disputation among contending schools of socialism. For much of the twentieth century, Joyce's renunciation of institutional allegiance to socialism would remain unintelligible if not unforgivable to critics on the left who recognised it as such.

This institutional rupture did not involve anything in the nature of a direct translation of Joyce's interest or allegiance from Italian socialism to Irish nationalism. While Joyce's engagement with nationalism antedated and far outlasted his strenuous interest in socialism, he did engage, at least for the period 1902–7, simultaneously with socialism and nationalism. For Joyce, socialism and nationalism were not incompatible but existed on different planes. While Joyce can properly be characterised for the period from 1905 to 1907 as a socialist and a nationalist (albeit a socialist chiefly in relation to Italy, and a nationalist exclusively in relation to Ireland), his sense of the incommensurateness of socialism and nationalism is attested to by the fact that he fastidiously eschewed any endeavour to construct a philosophical composite of nationalism and socialism. That project, which Sheehy-Skeffington and Fred Ryan undertook, was disdained by Joyce. It is also noteworthy that his sympathy for Sinn Féin was unaffected by Arthur Griffith's increasingly trenchant insistence that a nationalist could not validly hold a coequal allegiance to socialism.[60]

What can be said is that by early 1907 the belief in the paradigmatic contrast between progressive politics on the Continent and the inconsequentiality of contemporary Irish politics, which was part of the initial stimulus for his interest in Italian left-wing controversy, had left him. That he could characterise the Irish in his *Il Piccolo della Sera* article of May 1907 as 'a people which, poor in everything else, is rich in political ideas'[61] owed something to the sense of disenchanted ennui in which his laborious self-instruction in Italian socialism had ended.

Joyce did call himself a socialist for the period from 1904 to 1907, though this finds no obvious reflection in his creative writing. He conceded to Stanislaus that his socialism was 'thin . . . unsteady and ill-informed',[62] but as reflected in the correspondence it may be better seen as incomplete, inchoate, and unfinished, belonging to an initiatory phase that went no further. If Joyce had the desire to believe, that belief did not achieve final consummation.

Alessandro Francini Bruni, a close Triestine friend, recalled of the Joyce who no longer espoused a commitment to socialism, 'His attitude is as enigmatical towards politics as towards the Church. He told me one day, "My political faith can be expressed in a few words. Monarchies, constitutional or not, repel me. Republics, bourgeois or democratic, also repel me. Kings are clowns. Republics are worn out slippers that fit every foot. The Pope's temporal power is gone and good riddance. What is left? Do we want monarchy by divine right? Do you believe in the sun of the future?"'[63] The 'sun of the future' featured in

60. While Joyce had passed into silence on contemporary events in Ireland by the time of the 1913 lockout, Griffith's position had been pungently articulated in the immediately preceding years.

61. *OCPW* 143.

62. Joyce to Stanislaus Joyce, 6 November 1906, *Letters II* 187.

63. Alessandro Francini Bruni, 'Joyce Stripped Naked in the Piazza', *James Joyce Quarterly* 14, no. 2 (Winter 1977): 156; also quoted in Silvio benco, 'James Joyce in Trieste', in *Portraits of the*

the anthem of the Italian Socialist Party. Joyce had reverted to his instinctive mistrust of all forms of governance.

The 'problem' of Joyce's espousal of revolutionary syndicalism is one created by his yearning to espouse a sternly ideological form of socialism, seen through the prism of twentieth-century Marxist revolutionary dogma. When reclassified as a left-aligned anarchism, mysteriously touched by Wilde's ethical socialism rather than pertaining to an ideologically rigorous socialism, it fits into the sequence of Joyce's political thought. He did not renounce what might be characterised as the hard-left socialism of the revolutionary syndicalists, but he passed on from it. Two principal reasons suggest themselves. The first is that 'self-codification' as a socialist was an inhibition on his creativity as an artist and (presciently) a gratuitous impediment to the reception of his work. The second is that Joyce was, even at this stage, growing ever more implacably opposed to any teleological vision of human society or politics, and of periodisings of history that described an ineluctable progression. The hermeneutic scruple that prompted his refusal of the enchantments of ideology merged with Joyce's acute sense of the frailty of individual and collective memory of past events to become a theme of *Ulysses* and a driving artistic principle of *Finnegans Wake*.

What, then, was the legacy of Joyce's engagement with Italian socialism? His revolutionary syndicalist phase left him with a mistrust of institutional socialism and of doctrinaire Marxism. He retained enough interest in socialism to acquire in Trieste a Fabian pamphlet with the significant title *Socialism and Individualism*, published in 1909.[64] His socialist titles were outnumbered, however, by works on anarchism, which included a 1910 edition of Mikhail Bakunin's *God and the State* and a 1908 translation of a book by Paul Eltzbacher, *Anarchism*,

---

Artist in Exile: Recollections of James Joyce by Europeans, ed. Willard Potts (Seattle: University of Washington Press, 1979), 53.

64. This turgid tract, no. 3 in the Fabian Socialist Series, can scarcely have lived up to what Joyce must have thought to have been the promise of its title. One of its four essays, and the one that most likely prompted Joyce to order it, is George Bernard Shaw's sternly dogmatic 'The Impossibilities of Anarchism'.

purchased in 1913 or 1914, which was a source for Joyce's knowledge of Tolstoy's anarchistic views.[65] Joyce had never characterised himself as an anarchist, but an active, if more elusive, intellectual interest in anarchism outlasted his interest in contemporary socialism. He was drawn to anarchism by his resistance to the gratuitous interventions of statal authority in private and civic life, most pronounced in the sphere of religion, sexual morality, and censorship. An intellectual sympathy with anarchism survived Joyce's engagement with Italian socialism and would inform his sustained assault on conceptions of patriarchal authority in *Finnegans Wake*.

Joyce's socio-political thinking, at the point where his revolutionary syndicalist sympathies ceased, already showed an increasing historically inflected anthropological or sociological orientation, reflected in his interest in Guglielmo Ferrero. This was a shift from a personal belief in revolution to a fascinated attention to what drew men and women to revolution. By the time he came to write *Finnegans Wake*, Joyce saw the cycles of human life and society as driven by a recurrent and unreasoning but indefeasible human impulse of resurgence. That impulse was resistant to the experience of past disappointment. Man was by nature a hopeful creature, one destined or doomed to hope. Hope, the impulse of renewal, manifested itself cyclically, or rather in a complex of cycles. It was sustained by an intricate and shifting matrix of mythologies religious and secular. Joyce's interest in socialism and his identification with Easter or spring and their rites of renewal, and in *Finnegans Wake* the break of dawn, were at one. This was Joyce at his most unflinching, refusing the consolations of a divinity or of secular ideologies. It was Joyce godless and humane. Where socialism and anarchism came to rest in the oeuvre of Joyce was as manifestations of an (objective) anthropology of (subjective) hope.

The immediate significance of Joyce's engagement with Italian socialism is twofold. In the first instance, it discloses that Joyce was coming

65. Ellmann, *James Joyce*, 779, 786; Ellmann, *Consciousness of Joyce*, 100, 107, 132; Manganiello, *Joyce's Politics*, 155. Eltzbacher cannot, however, have been a source of Joyce's knowledge of Tolstoy's politics as early as 1905.

from the left, that his belief in the supremacy of the artist was constrained by an anchorage on the left. If Joyce was defined exclusively in terms of the doctrines of artistic egotism enunciated in *Stephen Hero* and in some degree reflected in his correspondence, one would expect to find him among the ranks of contemporary writers on the ideological right, with, for example, Gabriele D'Annunzio, whose literary writings had already had a marked effect on him.[66] Instead, at what was still a very early moment in the history of literary modernism, and before he had published any of his books, Joyce stood apart from the exalted romantic literary right. His identification with socialism was the gestural complement to the stories he was writing at the time which would be included in *Dubliners*.

Second, the fact that Joyce's disengagement with the Italian left occurred as early as spring 1907 meant that his disillusionment with the institutional left had antedated both the First World War, which exploded the confident pacifism of European socialism, and the unfolding of the sequelae of the Russian Revolution of 1917. Both events changed the face of European socialism. Quite apart from the fact that Joyce no longer avowed himself a socialist, he was radically out of sync with the sequence of controversy on the European left in the twentieth century. For the two generations in Europe that succeeded Joyce's, this was to render more difficult the imaginative understanding of a political stance that seemed to lack the urgency of contemporary engagement. It enabled left-wing critics of Joyce such as the eminent Hungarian Marxist György Lukács to suggest (on the basis of his works, and *Ulysses* in particular) that Joyce was not really a figure of the twentieth century at all, but of the nineteenth: a figure from a conquered Ireland, a petty bourgeois stranded in an arrested moment of European history.

All of this, the attacks from the left (as well as from the right), lay in the remote future, but Joyce was aware of what was at stake in the already ferociously contested theatre of twentieth-century European politics. In *Stephen Hero*, stung by his mother's disclosure that she has discussed his recalcitrance with her confessor, Stephen suggests that she

66. Curran, *James Joyce Remembered*, 105–15.

tell him that 'he was making a torpedo'.[67] In *Finnegans Wake*, HCE rejects Yaun's charge of conservatism as 'Ibscenest nansense'.[68] The unapparent reference is to a poem of Henrik Ibsen, which makes the fiercely 'Ibscenest' argument that compared with what he seeks to achieve as an artist, even the most completely realised revolution he can think of—the Flood—is a failure from the perspective of the Devil, because Noah survives. The poem is entitled 'Til min Ven Revolutions-Taleren' (To My Friend the Revolutionary Orator).

> They say I'm becoming conservative
> No; still in my life-long creed I live.
>
> Your changing pawns is a futile plan;
> Make a sweep of the chess-board, and I'm your man.
>
> Was never but one revolution unfaltering
> That was not marred by half-hearted paltering.
>
> To that, all since were but idle menaces.
> I allude, of course, to the Deluge in Genesis.
>
> Yet Lucifer tripped, even then; by a later ship
> Came Noah, you remember, and seized the dictatorship.
>
> Let us go, next time, to the root of the matter.
> It needs men to act as well as to chatter.
>
> You deluge the world to its topmost mark;
> With pleasure I will torpedo the ark.[69]

Joyce wrote to Stanislaus of Ibsen in October 1906, 'I fancy [Ibsen's] attitude towards litherature [*sic*] and socialism somewhat resembled my own.'[70]

67. *SH* 21.

68. *FW* 535.16–19. See B. J. Tysdahl, *Joyce and Ibsen: A Study in Literary Influence* (Oslo: Norwegian Universities Press, 1968), 16–19.

69. In Tysdahl, *Joyce and Ibsen*, 140–42 (trans. F. E. Garret).

70. Joyce to Stanislaus Joyce, 18 October 1906, *Letters II* 183.

12

Writing *Dubliners* in Exile

Whenever Joyce spoke of Parnell, he did so with a smile.

—LOUIS GILLET[1]

THROUGH HIS TRAVAILS IN EARLY EXILE, Joyce continued to write. After completing further chapters of *Stephen Hero* during the summer of 1905, he turned back to adding to the stories that were to make up *Dubliners*. On 1 September 1905 he sent Stanislaus by post 'the eighth story, Ivy Day in the Committee Room',[2] and in the following month he wrote 'An Encounter' and 'A Mother'. Between late October and late November 1905, he wrote 'Grace', which he conceived of at the time as the twelfth and last story of *Dubliners*. By late January 1906 he had nevertheless added 'Two Gallants', which became the sixth story sequentially. He signed a contract with the London publisher Grant Richards in March and was preparing to send another story, 'A Little Cloud', in April when Richards told him that the printer objected to passages in 'Two Gallants' and was refusing to set it. The final story in *Dubliners*, 'The Dead', was written in Trieste in August–September 1907.

1. Gillet, *Claybook for James Joyce*, 99.

2. Joyce to Stanislaus Joyce, 1 September 1905, *Letters II* 105.

'Ivy Day in the Committee Room'

'Ivy Day in the Committee Room' was a revolutionary departure within the canon of *Dubliners* as it then stood, and an extraordinary treatment of contemporary Irish politics in Parnell's wake, written before the sustained consideration of the emergence of Sinn Féin that was to feature prominently in Joyce correspondence the following year.[3] The story enlarges the scope of *Dubliners* to embrace the political and initiates a conceptual shift in the collection as a whole. It is also Joyce's first major treatment of the Parnell theme and the politics of the Split. Alone among the stories in *Dubliners,* 'Ivy Day' has a specific political setting familiar to its potential contemporary readership in Ireland and—at least as it related to the death of Parnell—in Britain.

The perspective that frames 'Ivy Day in the Committee Room' is the *débâcle* of 1890–91, retrospectively perceived from the eleventh anniversary of Parnell's death on Ivy Day, the term that came to designate the date of his death: 6 October 1891. The Split had endured in Irish politics for almost a decade, until the Irish Parliamentary Party was reunited in January 1900. The prolongation of the Split beyond Parnell's death was marked by bitter recriminations between the adherents of Parnell and the overwhelmingly ascendant anti-Parnellite party, itself rancorously divided. Popular mourning for Parnell found expression in a mass commemorative procession in Dublin on the Sunday after Ivy Day, a kind of re-enactment of Parnell's immense funeral. The quiet mourning of Ivy Day stood in contrast with the more exuberant commemoration on the Sunday following. By the latter half of the 1890s, the Parnell commemoration had begun to seem an extravagant exercise in futility. The reunification of the party, under John Redmond, the leader of the Parnellites, was intended to mark the drawing of a line under the controversies of the Split.

3. An earlier version of this section was published as Frank Callanan, 'The Parnellism of James Joyce: "Ivy Day in the Committee Room"', *James Joyce Studies Annual* 2015 (2015): 73–97.

The reunification of the party served to formalise Joyce's isolation. He had little affinity with the Irish Party without Parnell. He had some sympathy with Fenianism, the physical force movement, but considered it superseded. He was not drawn to the new schools of cultural nationalism. The political high ground of the Split, the issues of the relationship of parliamentary nationalism to the British Liberal party, and to the Catholic Church of Liberal and clerical 'dictation', had been ceded. Those issues, which had for Joyce a deadly seriousness, were left unresolved. As if in homage to Parnell's own quasi-solitary perseverance, Joyce's recusant Parnellism subsisted beyond the formal termination of the 'long Split' of 1890–1900.

The titles of all the stories in *Dubliners* are carefully chosen, but 'Ivy Day in the Committee Room', poised between a fractured aphorism and a Joycean epiphany, stands apart. The title is a brilliant Parnellite conceit that inflicts a shock through its deliberate and unsettling disarrangement of time. Whereas the 'committee room' in the Split was universally understood to designate Committee Room 15 of the Houses of Parliament at Westminster, where on 6 December 1890 the Irish Party had fractured after a week of debate on the subject of Parnell's leadership, the committee room in the story is in Dublin, that of a candidate in a municipal election on 6 October 1902. The effect wrought by the disorienting juxtaposition of Ivy Day and what would at first be taken to be the parliamentary committee room re-creates the shock of the initial disbelief that the news of Parnell's death elicited and prompts a momentary resurgence of the terrible sense of loss experienced by Parnellites on the death of their leader. The startling impact of the title challenges the official orthodoxy that the bitterness of the Split was spent, and that the issues of the Split were, with the passage of time and the reunification of the Irish Party, safely consigned to history. The story itself could scarcely be further removed from the high political drama, on which the attention of the world was fixed, that was acted out in Committee Room 15, high over the Thames, in early December 1890. Apart from Parnell, no prominent nationalist parliamentarian is so much as mentioned in Joyce's story, nor is the reunification of the Irish Party alluded to. Yet in the grim sparseness of Joyce's committee room, emblematic of the fallen condition of Irish nationalism, the memory of Parnell stirs yet.

The Dublin Corporation ward where the election is taking place is the Royal Exchange Ward, an actual municipal ward, comprising the centre of Dublin city south of the river and encompassing both Dublin Castle, the seat of British power in Ireland, and the City Hall itself on Cork Hill. Its name, Royal Exchange, is symbolically charged: the theme of exchanging fealty to Parnell for allegiance to Edward VII, whose planned visit to Ireland the following year provides the principal subject of discussion in the committee room, gradually displacing the election itself. The committee room of the nationalist candidate Richard J. Tierney is on Wicklow Street, which bears the name of the county in which Parnell's home was situated, a rare allusion to Avondale on the part of Joyce, whose Parnellism was pointedly centred on Dublin. Tierney, representing at a municipal level the recently reunited Irish Party, is contesting the seat against a workingman, identified only by his surname, Colgan.

Quite apart from the fact that the Irish Party's raison d'être was specifically as a parliamentary party, Tierney's political allegiance is artfully subdued. His canvassing card does not proclaim him to be the nationalist candidate. The decoding of the card is a matter of acronyms and initials: 'Richard J. Tierney, P. L. G.' As a Poor Law Guardian, he is a respectable personage likely to be of a socially conservative disposition. The portentous middle initial 'J', coupled with the Irish surname, proclaims him a socially aspirant Catholic. The formality of the canvassing card admits of a cunning obsequiousness intended to convey to Unionist voters that they can safely vote for Tierney in the absence of a candidate of their own. Within the narrative, it is left to Mr O'Connor to declare without much conviction that 'our man . . . goes in on the nationalist ticket'.[4]

There are two people continuously present in the committee room throughout the story: Old Jack, the caretaker, and Mr O'Connor, 'a grey-haired young man, whose face was disfigured by many blotches and pimples', and who has been retained by Tierney's election agent as a canvasser.[5] The first to enter the committee room is Joe Hynes, a supporter of Colgan. The next to push in the door is Mr Henchy, 'a bustling

4. *D* 103.

5. *D* 99.

little man with a snuffling nose and very cold ears', one of Tierney's more vigorous supporters. Hynes leaves.[6] There is a fleeting appearance by a Fr Keon. An errand boy from the Black Eagle, a public house, brings a basket of bottles of stout, a frugal benefaction from Tierney, and is despatched to get a corkscrew. On his return, he is rewarded on Mr Henchy's initiative with one of the bottles, which he drinks, before departing with the bottle-opener. Crofton, a Conservative supporting Tierney, enters with another canvasser for Tierney, Bantam Lyons, who wears a 'very high double collar and a widebrimmed bowler hat'.[7] Hynes reappears in the doorway and, summoned by Mr Henchy, re-enters the committee room, whose population has grown since he left from two to five, understandably 'slowly.'

The description of the day—'It was the sixth of October, dismal and cold out of doors'—recalls less the atrocious rain and wind that marked the day of Parnell's funeral than the bleakness of the anniversary. Because his shoes 'let in the wet', Mr O'Connor had passed most of the day in the committee room.[8] The poem that Hynes later declaims refers to Erin's 'monarch's pyre' and to the spirit of Parnell rising 'like the Phoenix from the flames'.[9] The fire in the grate is almost as important as the figurative one in Hynes's poem. The symbolism of the fire is sustained and made retrospectively explicit but, in what is a rupture with the method of the earlier stories in *Dubliners*, is subordinated to, or at the very least held in counterbalance with, the physical need for the fire's heat and light.

As the story opens, Old Jack is raking the embers of the dying fire. Mr O'Connor needs to light his cigarette and tears a strip from one of the Tierney canvassing cards, which he lights from the fire: 'As he did

6. *D* 103.

7. *D* 110. By the time Bantam Lyons reappears in *Ulysses*, he is less dapper, and down on his luck. In the 'Lotus Eaters' episode, he accosts Leopold Bloom outside Sweny's chemist shop and consults Bloom's copy of the *Freeman's Journal* for the racing: 'He rustled the pleated pages, jerking his chin on his high collar. Barber's itch. Tight collar he'll lose his hair. Better leave him the paper and get shut of him'. Bloom tries to give him the paper, saying, 'I was just going to throw it away' (*U* 5.528–34). Lyons believes this is a veiled tip on Throwaway in the Gold Cup but fails to back the horse.

8. *D* 100.

9. *D* 114–15.

so, the flame lit up a leaf of dark glossy ivy on the lapel of his coat.'[10] When Hynes enters, he asks, 'What are you doing in the dark?'[11] Old Jack stumbles about the room and returns with two candlesticks, which he successively thrusts into the fire. The candles have an emblematic funerary aspect: 'A denuded room came into view and the fire lost all its cheerful colour.'[12] Mr Henchy demands coal, and Jack shuffles off once more and finds a few lumps to put on the fire. Mr Henchy later seizes one of the candlesticks to light Fr Keon's descent of the dark stairs.

When Lyons and Crofton come in, Mr Henchy tells Jack to open two bottles of stout. Jack points out there is no corkscrew. The resourceful Mr Henchy deploys what he calls 'this little trick' which involves putting the bottles on the hob of the fire so that the heat expels the cork. A few minutes later there is 'an apologetic *Pok!*' as the cork flies out of Mr Lyons's bottle, followed later by a further '*Pok!*' as the cork departs from the bottle destined for Mr Crofton. When Mr Hynes re-enters the room, Mr Henchy puts a third bottle on the hob for him. A little later, after Hynes has finished declaiming his poem, the cork shoots from the bottle: '*Pok!* The cork flew out of Mr Hynes's bottle but Mr Hynes remained sitting, flushed and bareheaded on the table. He did not seem to have heard the invitation.'[13] As Frank O'Connor was the first to point out, or at least to record, the three '*Poks*' parodically enact the volleys over the grave of the dead patriot.[14]

Across the salvoes of the popping corks, the dialogue has moved on. Mr Henchy begins to express himself in support of the royal visit. He

10. *D* 100.

11. *D* 101.

12. *D* 101. Thomas B. O'Grady, in his perceptive 1986 piece on the story, which is in its central aspect a counter-reading to mine, writes, 'Throughout the story, the darkness is obviously symbolic of the condition of Irish politics without Parnell; the brief glimpses of light reflect only the past glory of Parnell.' This, however, poses a challenge to his contention that the theme of 'Ivy Day' is Joyce's condemnation of the passive thraldom of the Irish to the historical past, on the lines of Nietzsche's 1874 essay *The Use and Abuse of History*. Thomas B. O'Grady, '"Ivy Day in the Committee Room": The Use and Abuse of Parnell', *Éire-Ireland* 21 (1986): 31–42.

13. *D* 116.

14. Frank O'Connor, 'Work in Progress', in *Twentieth Century Interpretations of Dubliners*, ed. Peter K Garrett (Englewood Cliffs, NJ: Prentice-Hall, 1968), 22.

brutally cuts off Mr O'Connor, who wants to do no more than explain the position of Parnell on royal visits. 'Parnell, said Mr Henchy, is dead.'[15] Lauding Edward VII as 'an ordinary knockabout like you and me', Henchy adds, 'He's fond of his glass of grog, and he's a bit of rake, perhaps, perhaps and he's a good sportsman. Damn it, can't we Irish play fair?'[16] With this exquisite display of humbug, Henchy has overreached himself in an almost insultingly jaded conversational move. It prompts Bantam Lyons, to Henchy's intense exasperation, 'to raise the case of Parnell'.[17] However, this is not to defend Parnell. Rather, Lyons is opposed to the royal visit on the same moral grounds on which he has recently come to be hostile to Parnell: 'Do you think he was a man I'd like the lady who is now Mrs Lyons to know?'[18]

Lyons's intervention, the import of which is generally lost as the Parnell theme achieves its deferred surge, is a brilliant Joycean device that rivals Mr Henchy's 'little trick' with the bottles of stout. It casts light back on the preceding narrative in a way that is characteristic of the story's insistently intricate recurving structure. Fr Keon's entry earlier in the story is described this way: 'A person resembling a poor clergyman or a poor actor appeared in the doorway. His black clothes were tightly buttoned on his short body and it was impossible to say whether he wore a clergyman's collar or a layman's because the collar of his shabby frock coat, the uncovered buttons of which reflected the candlelight, was turned up about his neck.'[19]

Stanislaus Joyce took this passage to mean that Fr Keon was an 'unfrocked priest',[20] and he is clearly correct in this.[21] The symbolic

15. *D* 112.

16. *D* 112–13.

17. *D* 113.

18. *D* 112–13.

19. *D* 106.

20. S. Joyce, *My Brother's Keeper*, 206.

21. An exchange between Mr O'Connor and Mr Henchy, leading up to Mr Henchy's description of Fr Keon as 'travelling on his own account', makes this clear:

> —What is he exactly?
>
> —Ask me an easier one, said Mr Hinchy.

significance of Bantam Lyons's primly fashionable 'very high double collar', in contrast to Fr Keon's apparent lack of a priest's collar, is suddenly illumined by his vapidly uxorious condemnation of Parnell. Lyons has unwittingly assumed the role of the preacher left vacant by the de-collared cleric. He is the only person in the story to express disrespect for Parnell on the anniversary of his death. However, he does so on prudish secular grounds that do not derive, at least directly, from either Irish Catholicism or Irish nationalism. The point is not simply that opposition to Parnell, or the espousal of a puritanical respectability, was confined to Irish ecclesiastics or ardent Catholics. Irish Catholics, English nonconformists, and others had united to oppose Parnell and had found a common moral idiom. In the figure of Mr Lyons, the impact in Ireland of the nonconformist conscience merges with Irish social aspiration. This is suggested by the fact that Mr Lyons condemns the morals of both Parnell and Edward VII; while this might at first seem to work against the grain of the story's placing of the two 'kings' in opposition to each other, it is deliberate and reflects Joyce's acute sense of the ugly hybridisation of British and Irish moral sentiment that had brought about Parnell's fall.[22] It is not an accident that Fr Keon is a fallen priest.

The conversation has thus turned back to Parnell just as Mr Hynes re-enters the room. Mr O'Connor, supported by Henchy, calls on Hynes to recite what, suppressing his emotion, he describes in the downbeat Dublin manner as 'that thing you wrote':

> Mr Hynes did not seem to remember at once the piece to which they were alluding, but, after reflecting a while, he said:
>
> —O, that thing is it . . . Sure, that's old now.[23]

> —Fanning and himself seem to me very thick. They're often in Kavanagh's together. Is he a priest at all?
>
> —'Mmmyes, I believe so . . . I think he's what you call a black sheep. (*D* 107)

The issue is posed almost by way of a riddle. Fr Keon is defrocked but remains a priest and still uses the title 'Fr Keon' on the principle of *sacerdos in aeternum*. A priest cannot cease to be such.

22. See chapter 5, '"Christ and Caesar": The Origins of Joyce's Thesis of the "Two Masters"'.

23. *D* 114.

Hynes recites his poem 'The Death of Parnell, 6th October 1891', which evidently had achieved a certain local fame, and is to be taken as having been written on or immediately after that date. On the surface, the poem is Joyce's exquisite pastiche of the kind of verse that had appeared in the Parnellite press on the death of Parnell and bloomed seasonally on the anniversary of his death throughout the 1890s—a genre to which Joyce's lost boyhood poem that came to be assigned the title 'Et Tu Healy' belonged. While the poems treating Parnell's death were, for the most part, hackneyed and maladroit, they conveyed perhaps better than speeches or newspaper editorials the sense of personal and political loss engendered by Parnell's death. In Hynes's poem, Joyce recapitulates all the conventional themes and tropes of the laments, and fastidiously reproduces their literary deficiencies. Hynes's verse is haunting in the setting of the committee room precisely because it is not, as Mr Crofton politely describes it, with benevolent Unionist politesse in the last line of the story, 'a very fine piece of writing'.[24]

If the poem is representative of what had become a minor politico-literary sub-genre, it owes much to the distinctive political persona of Hynes. Evidently a youthful Parnellite in 1890–91, he is now a radical urban nationalist. Mr Henchy charges Hynes in absentia with being 'a spy of Colgan's', but this is casually almost negated by his further accusation of 'sponging' and the question, 'Couldn't he have some spark of manhood about him?'[25] He also slyly imputes to Hynes Fenian allegiances, but as this is by way of generic anti-Parnellite abuse of 'these lousy hillsiders and fenians', we are not to believe that Hynes actually is a Fenian.[26] Though Colgan, the candidate Hynes supports, is not explicitly described as a socialist, but as a workingman and Labour candidate, he can be taken as a socialist in a Dublin setting.[27]

Colgan and Hynes are figures from the post-Parnell radical ferment in Dublin municipal politics who challenged the ascendancy of what

24. *D* 116.

25. *D* 105.

26. *D* 106.

27. In relation to the difficulties of the labour or trade union candidates actually elected maintaining a distinctive political identity, see Mary E. Daly, *Dublin: The Deposed Capital* (Cork: Cork University Press, 1985), 216–18.

amounted to the municipal machine of the Irish Parliamentary Party (although operating semi-independently). For a time, this municipal resistance brought into alignment radical Parnellites, electorally active Fenians, and socialists and included some who would become adherents of Sinn Féin. Arthur Griffith, though emphatically not a socialist, in his *United Irishman* endorsed James Connolly and other Labour candidates in the municipal elections of 1902 and 1903.[28] Some of the social topics touched on in 'Ivy Day' plainly derive from Joyce's attentive reading of the *United Irishman*, notably the influence of publicans and the housing issue in municipal politics. Tierney has 'extensive house property in the city', as Henchy had been at pains to impress on a Conservative voter.[29]

Endorsing Connolly's candidacy in 1903, the *United Irishman* described the city's poor as 'festering in the fever-dens of Dublin owned largely by members of the Dublin Corporation'. Of the candidates in the election, it noted that 'thirteen are publicans or ex-publicans; ten are tenement-house owners or jerry-builders; nine are loyal-address flunkeys or supporters of Dublin Castle detectives for Corporation jobs; and one is a music-hall singer.' The 'able and honest men who are going forward' could be counted on one hand, and Connolly was foremost among them. His candidacy in the Wood Quay Ward was 'opposed by the shoneens, the tenement-house rackrenters of the poor, the publicans, and we regret to say the priests. . . . We are not Socialists, but we would be intensely gratified to see a man of Mr Connolly's character returned to the Dublin Corporation, to let the light in on the corruption that reigns on Cork Hill.'[30]

Hynes is, like Joyce, unregenerately anticlerical. The clearest expression of Joyce's own sentiments occurs in the comparison of those who betrayed Parnell to Judas in the sixth stanza of Hynes's poem. A casual

28. Manganiello, *Joyce's Politics*, 126.

29. *D* 112.

30. *United Irishman*, 10 January 1903. James Fairhall uses the congruence between some of the social issues raised by Connolly and those the story touches on to underpin his claim that 'beyond doubt, Connolly's solid historical reality underlies the vague, absent figure of the Labour candidate in 'Ivy Day'. Fairhall, *James Joyce and the Question of History* (Cambridge: Cambridge University Press, 1993), 103–4. He does so without reference to the fact that the *United Irishman*, which Joyce read assiduously, raised most of the same issues. In Joyce's play with surnames, Colgan and Connolly are temptingly close, but not quite close enough to admit a confident equation.

blasphemy in the comparison of Parnell to Christ was not uncommon in the poems on Parnell's death. Joyce was himself drawn to the identification of Parnell with Christ, in part because it carried the taunt that the Irish hierarchy and clergy had so dislocated the relations of Catholicism and secular politics as to forfeit any entitlement to complain of it. The superb contemptuousness of Hynes's characterisation of the obsequious deference of the anti-Parnellites to the Catholic clergy in the Split prevails over the technical deficiencies of his verse:

Shame on the coward caitiff hands
That smote their Lord or with a kiss
Betrayed him to the rabble-rout
Of fawning priests—no friends of his![31]

By 1902, such sentiments were jarring in their radicalism, but their expression is sanctioned by the politically diverse audience in the committee room because the poem had been written in the immediate aftermath of Parnell's death when such views were expressed by many Parnellites. If strictly extra-textual, this is part of the intricate temporal sequencing of the story that its title proclaims. Hynes's lines serve as a benchmark for the regression of Irish politics from the Split of 1890–91, the years immediately following the death of Parnell, when the issue of clerical influence at least had been openly addressed.

The ninth verse rehearses the sentiments Joyce had expressed in the fragment of his youthful poem on Parnell that survived in his brother's memory. At the end of that piece, the dead Chief is likened to an eagle, looking down on the grovelling mass of Irish politicians from

His quaint-perched aerie on the rages of Time
Where the rude din of this . . . century
Can trouble him no more.[32]

Hynes's lines are:

No sound of strife disturb his sleep!
Calmly he rests; no human pain

31. *D* 115.

32. S. Joyce, *My Brother's Keeper*, 65.

Or high ambition spurs him now
The peaks of glory to attain.[33]

It is easy to miss the brilliance with which Joyce deploys Hynes's poetic voice. The initially inept-seeming but powerfully affecting phrase 'no human pain / or high ambition' is poised ambiguously. The 'human pain' could allude to the suffering of the Irish poor that Parnell strove to alleviate but is also, and chiefly, intended to refer to the physical pain and attendant intimation of death that drove Parnell onwards in the Split: a puissant leader who believed against all the odds that he would overmaster his adversaries, and who feared only the frailty of his own body. This is the Parnell who, as Joyce was to write in 'L'ombra di Parnell' (1912), in 1890–91 'went from county to county, from city to city, "like a hunted hind", a spectral figure with the signs of death upon his brow'.[34]

In the final two verses of Hynes's poem, Joyce brings the Parnellite poem back within mainstream nationalist rhetoric in an uplifting anticipation of Irish independence, but with a bitterly elegiac twist. For Hynes and those who shared his convictions, national freedom would be tinged inconsolably by the memory of Parnell.

They had their way: they laid him low.
But Erin, list, his spirit may
Rise, like the Phoenix from the flames,
When breaks the dawning of the day,

The day that brings us Freedom's reign,
And on that day may Erin well
Pledge in the cup she lifts to Joy
One grief—the memory of Parnell.[35]

From Joyce's perspective, these lines are politically highly considered. The idiom is somewhat Fenianesque, but the 'dawning of the day' was generally a trope for Home Rule. Hynes's lines capture both the Parnell

33. *D* 115.
34. *OCPW* 196.
35. *D* 115.

myth of the Parnellite Home Rulers and that of Fenians drawn to Parnell's cause, which merged more or less indistinguishably in 1890–91 and in the years that immediately followed Parnell's death. That common idiom was obsolete by 1902 but was evidently not altogether so for Hynes, nor was it for Joyce.

Commentaries on 'Ivy Day' tend to elide the traces of tendresse on Joyce's part, inherent in the exactitude of its observation of the political life of Dublin, and to discount the force of the homage to Parnell in Hynes's poem. This critical inattention applied to even so sensitive (if irritable) a reader of Joyce as Frank O'Connor, who thought that the death of Parnell was treated in the story 'with an icy, clinical touch.'[36] He comments,

> Three corks, removed by the old-fashioned method of heating the bottles, pop one after another, and Joe recites his reach-me-down lament for the dead Chief. . . . The three corks represent the three volleys over the hero's grave and the lament is the pinchbeck substitute for a Dead March. This is the mock-heroic at its poker-faced deadliest. . . . In 'Ivy Day' the greatest tribute a degenerate nation can pay to a dead leader is the popping of corks from a few bottles of stout, earned by the betrayal of everything for which that leader had stood.[37]

O'Connor complained that Joyce had in *Dubliners* 'deprived his submerged population of autonomy' and complexity.[38] One might counter this claim by noting Margot Norris's approach to Henchy in her gracefully intelligent *Suspicious Readings of Joyce's 'Dubliners'*. In many critical accounts, Henchy is the villain of the piece; Seamus Deane characterises him as 'vicious and slithery'.[39] Henchy is the most unflinching

36. Frank O'Connor, *The Backward Look* (London: Macmillan, 1967), 198.

37. Frank O'Connor, *The Lonely Voice* (London, Macmillan, 1963), 120. He had made the point about the popping corks earlier, in *The Mirror in the Roadway* (London: Hamish Hamilton, 1957), 298.

38. F. O'Connor, *Lonely Voice*, 121.

39. Seamus Deane, 'Dead Ends: Joyce's Finest Moments', in Attridge and Howes, *Semicolonial Joyce*, 29. Remarkably, these epithets are applied by Deane in castigating Henchy as the story's 'most prolific name-caller'.

and effective supporter of Tierney's candidacy. Yet the politically facile vilification of Henchy runs against the grain of Joyce's story. It is Henchy who ensures that the errand boy and Hynes are provided with bottles of stout, though this could, of course, reflect his arrogation of a dominant role: when he enters the room, he twice says to Old Jack 'don't stir' before assuming his seat. The most searing comments on Tierney are Henchy's. It is Henchy who, after Hynes's departure, repeats and damningly elaborates on Hynes's characterisation of the candidate he supports as 'Tricky Dicky Tierney', whom Henchy describes as 'a mean little shoeboy of hell!'[40] In ideologically driven readings of the story, this is taken to render Henchy's support of Tierney all the more iniquitous. But as Norris rightly emphasises, when O'Connor complains to him of Tierney's failure to 'stump up' payment for his canvassers, Mr Henchy responds, 'I can't help it . . . I expect to find the bailiffs in the hall when I go home'.[41] This lament cuts across the ostensible political polarisations of the dramatis personae of a story in which Joyce lays a carefully crafted (and, as it has transpired, pretty effective) trap for critics determined to impose on it a sternly doctrinaire resolution.

That Joyce's imaginative comprehension of the predicament of his largely impecunious characters extends even to Henchy—Mr O'Connor defends Hynes to Mr Henchy as 'hard up like the rest of us'—does not mean that the story isn't hard-edged in its delineation of contemporary Irish politics. The characterisation of 'Tricky Dicky Tierney' and of the

40. Margot Norris, in her annotation of the story in the Norton critical edition (*D* 104), loses a little of the force of Henchy's splenetic characterisation of the operation of 'the hand-me-down shop' in Mary's Lane by Tierney's father. In the rendering of 'moya!' as 'an Irish expression of ironic sympathy', Henchy's 'moya!' is surely '*mar dhea*', a heavily sarcastic Gaelic taunt of phoniness that has endured in Irish conversation in English. It means, in feeble translation, 'as if'. The import of the passage is that patrons of the shop, on the pretext of seeking to purchase a second-hand garment, could on Sunday mornings obtain drink from the 'tricky little black bottle' that 'Tricky Dicky's little old father' kept up in a corner of the shop. Joyce's enjoyment of the idiom of Mr Henchy prefigures his relishing of the discourse of the Citizen in the 'Cyclops' episode of *Ulysses*, who is at once a more comedic and much darker figure than Mr Henchy, and whose characterisation is divorced from the persona of John Stanislaus Joyce even if a certain commonality of idiom survives.

41. *D* 105; Margot Norris, *Suspicious Readings of Joyce's 'Dubliners'* (Philadelphia: University of Pennsylvania Press, 2003), 183.

municipal political machine into which he has been enlisted is unsparing. At the centre of the web of Dublin municipal politics sits Mr Fanning. He is first mentioned when Henchy complains of Tierney: 'Couldn't he pay up like a man instead of: *O, now, Mr Henchy, I must speak to Mr Fanning . . . I've spent a lot of money*.'[42] Fr Keon enters the committee room 'just looking for Mr Fanning.' O'Connor interrogates Mr Henchy after Fr Keon leaves: 'Fanning and himself seem to me very thick. They're often in Kavanagh's together. Is he a priest at all?'[43] Henchy refers to the last of his three requests to Tierney to send over a dozen bottles of stout. Tierney had been talking to Alderman Cowley.

> There's some deal on in that quarter, said Mr O'Connor. I saw the three of them hard at it yesterday at Suffolk Street corner.
>
> —I think I know the little game they're at, said Mr Henchy. You must owe the City Fathers money nowadays if you want to be made Lord Mayor. Then they'll make you Lord Mayor. By God I'm thinking seriously of becoming a City Father myself.[44]

Mr Henchy's opinion of the candidate is considerably assuaged by the arrival of the stout: 'He's not a bad sort, said Mr Henchy, only Fanning has such a loan of him.'[45]

Mr Fanning, 'the registration agent and mayormaker of the city', reappears in 'Grace' in the Jesuit church in Gardiner Street, 'sitting immediately under the pulpit beside one of the newly elected councillors of the ward', and he also turns up in *Ulysses* as Long John Fanning.[46] He would have been readily identifiable to contemporary Irish readers of *Dubliners* as John Clancy, a prominent figure in Dublin municipal politics and one of the four notable friends of John Stanislaus Joyce whom Joyce deploys in his fiction. A Fenian opportunist who supported the Land League, Clancy was appointed sub-sheriff of Dublin in 1885, a position that involved responsibilities for the registration of voters. He

42. *D* 104.
43. *D* 107.
44. *D* 108.
45. *D* 109.
46. *D* 149.

established and ran the National Club on Rutland Square, itself a licensed premises, which became a Fenian haunt. In old age, he was elected Lord Mayor in early 1915, but died before taking office.[47]

Joyce uses the familiar figure of the formidable and faintly disreputable Clancy, whom he evidently disliked as much as did his brother,[48] to portray the stasis of Dublin municipal politics after Parnell, and after the reunification of the Irish Party. It is significant that Clancy had been a prominent supporter of Parnell in the Split. If Joyce extravagantly exaggerates Clancy's personal influence, it is emblematic of the ascendancy of the Parnellites as the predominant nationalist faction in Dublin municipal politics through the 1890s.[49] Joyce is conveying the debasement of municipal Parnellism in what had been the Parnellite citadel in Parnell's lifetime and continued to be such after his death. In the wake of the reunification of the Irish Party, the distinction of Parnellite and anti-Parnellite has been abrogated. There was even an element of ad hoc collaboration between nationalists and Unionists that features in the politics of the story. Mr Crofton had been a canvasser for the Conservative candidate, but 'the conservatives had withdrawn their man and, choosing the lesser of two evils, given their support to the nationalist candidate'.[50] That Fanning, the erstwhile Parnellite apparatchik, is in communion with the shady cleric of ambiguous status, Fr Keon, is emblematic of the fallen world of Dublin municipal politics a decade out from the death of Parnell.

47. See chapter 3, 'Four Friends of the Father'.

48. S. Joyce, entry for 31 August 1904, in *Dublin Diary*, 78.

49. The municipal franchise in Dublin was limited. It was enlarged by the Local Government Act of 1898 from some eight thousand to just short of thirty-eight thousand: M. Daly, *Dublin*, 216. Daly's account conveys the extent to which Dublin municipal politics in the 1890s was a world unto itself, in which national trends were filtered by the narrow franchise, commercial interests, and what might be termed corporate particularity. David Dickson puts the franchise as of January 1899 somewhat higher, at forty-nine thousand. 'Parnellites vanquished anti-Parnellites in 1899, and then after 1900 the re-united Irish party completely dominated representation in City Hall for the next two decades, with the retail trade, especially publicans, still pre-eminent'. David Dickson, *Dublin: The Making of a Capital City* (Dublin: Profile Books, 2014), 414–15.

50. *D* 111.

The critical tendency to read the story as an unrelieved and unforgiving repudiation of the public life of Dublin is in part attributable to the treatment of the stories in *Dubliners*, with the exception of 'The Dead', as univocal in tone, and to a reduction of Joyce's Parnellism to a magnificently contrived and forbiddingly bleak stage set. The claustrophobic ambience of the committee room provides a deceptive semblance of continuity within the corpus of the stories that make up the book. Joyce's radical departure in *Dubliners* lies, in part, in the multiplicity of its cast and richness of dialogue, but chiefly in the opening out of the collection of stories to Irish politics. It might be suggested that the gathering in the committee room is merely an aggregation of isolated, anomic individuals, but the familiar, weary civility of the exchanges makes that hard to sustain.

The political sensibility that informs the story is a composite of the Parnellite and the socialist. What is socialist in perspective is the rendering of the debilitating economic dependency of the dramatis personae, and the foreboding that Tierney, however lethargic his canvassers may be, will easily prevail over Colgan and fortify the ascendancy in municipal politics of rentiers and publicans, who are promoters of their own commercial interests and not really politicians at all.

Some months before writing 'Ivy Day', Joyce had written to Stanislaus that his political opinions were 'those of a socialistic artist'.[51] Politically the story is the site of a confluence of Joyce's socialism and his Parnellism. It is also possible to discern a distant and oblique stirring of the identification with Sinn Féin that Joyce would express to Stanislaus a year and a half later in November 1906. By permitting Arthur Griffith's treatment of social issues in Dublin politics in *United Irishman* to inform the story, he was for the first time drawing on the political content of the paper (significantly, at this point, on social rather than 'national' issues), moving beyond using it to keep himself informed about current political and literary controversies in Dublin, the progress of his contemporaries, and cultural events in Ireland.[52]

51. Joyce to Stanislaus Joyce, [?2 or 3 May 1905], *Letters II* 89.

52. For more context, see Callanan, 'Joyce and the *United Irishman*'. Griffith and the *United Irishman* were prominent opponents of the visit of Edward VII in 1903, and Griffith's organisation, the National Council, a precursor of Sinn Féin, originated in the protest against the visit.

To impose a postcolonial *marxisant* reading on 'Ivy Day' involves a denial or at least heavy discounting of the reflexive consciousness of its actors. The characters in the committee room may be in varying degrees passive or ineffectual, but with the exception of Mr Lyons, they are by no means stupid. They are conscious of their fallen state, and the exchanges in the committee room are an intricate negotiation of their common predicament. The downbeat male heartiness of the committee room is predicated on an awareness of what they hold in common. However adverse the circumstances, and however unlikely it is they will act, the prospect of redemptive collective action subsists. This hope is muted almost to the point of inaudibility, which is perhaps the aim of 'Ivy Day'. Why else would Joyce continue to care about Parnell quite as interestingly as he did?

Of Joyce's contemporaries who wrote about 'Ivy Day', the most receptive was Padraic Colum. Of Hynes's poem, he wrote in 1926 in his frequently republished introduction to *Dubliners*, 'It is an amateurish and conventional piece of rhetoric, and yet, amazingly enough, a real grief and a real loyalty break through the hand-me-down verse.' Joyce 'must have entered into Hynes's mind before he could re-create the verses that have just the exact heat, just the exact flourishes that a passionate and semi-literate man would give to his subject writing according to the literary convention which he knew.'[53]

'Ivy Day' is Joyce's first mature deployment of the Parnell myth, and it marks the point of the integration of his Parnellism and his art. Joyce's retrieval of Parnell was engendered by his own thoughts and imaginative processes. It was not prompted by any immediately contemporary

---

It would, however, be erroneous to see the foregrounding of the anticipated royal visit in 'Ivy Day' as a gesturing forward to, or a coded avowal of, the sympathy with Griffith's Sinn Féin that Joyce later professed. The story is specific to the time in which it is set, and at which it was written. The relation of municipal politics in 1902 to Parnell's death is itself delicate in its complexity. Joyce moreover abhorred teleological anachronism, which he considered a besetting intellectual vice of nationalism. The story is a brilliant rendering of the time of its setting, and its prescience is objective.

53. Padraic Colum, introduction to *Dubliners*, by James Joyce (New York: Modern Library, 1926), x. Colum's introduction is referred to approvingly by Stanislaus Joyce in both S. Joyce, *Recollections of James Joyce*, 6; and S. Joyce, *My Brother's Keeper*, 206.

external political event or significant occurrence in the unfolding of the Parnell myth—the year 1905 saw only the publication of an eccentric and unreliable memoir by Parnell's sister Emily Monroe Dickinson entitled *A Patriot's Mistake*, of which the *Irish Times* commented, 'It does not appear to be a book that should have been published'.[54] What is more relevant is that the memory of Parnell had by 1905 reached a nadir of political oblivion, from which it was to recover only slightly after the Liberal landslide the following year.

In the story, Parnell is ubiquitous in his absence. His name is not uttered until toward the close of the story—a sequencing thrown into reverse in Hynes's poem, boldly entitled 'The Death of Parnell'—but there are ghostly traces from the outset: in the title, in the date, in the ivy leaves of Messrs O'Connor and Hynes, and in the discussion of the English king. Through the gathering accentuation of Parnell's absence, a desolating sense of political loss seeps into the story.

Joyce later wrote to Stanislaus that Anatole France—whom he had been reading since early 1905, initially without enthusiasm—had given him the idea for 'Ivy Day' and for 'The Dead'.[55] Parnell and Michael Furey (the youthful lover remembered by Gretta Conroy in 'The Dead') are both absent from the action of the *Dubliners* stories in which, in different ways, they exercise a preponderant influence. If 'The Dead' is, as John V. Kelleher pointed out fifty years ago, a ghost story,[56] so also is 'Ivy Day'.

Richard Ellmann suggested, very probably correctly, that the inspiration for the two stories may have come from France's story 'Le procurateur de Judée'.[57] In France's story, Laelius Lama, a Roman cast out

54. Emily Monroe Dickinson, *A Patriot's Mistake: Being Personal Recollections of the Parnell Family by a Daughter of the House* (Dublin: Hodges, Figgis, 1905); *Irish Times*, 4 December 1905.

55. Joyce to Stanislaus Joyce, 15 March 1905 and 11 February 1907, *Letters II* 85, 212.

56. Kelleher, 'Irish History and Mythology', 455–56. Kelleher develops a suggestion of Stanislaus Joyce in his *Recollections of James Joyce*. Paul Muldoon's brilliant *To Ireland, I* draws, in turn, on Kelleher to terrifying effect.

57. *Letters II* 212n8, annotation to Joyce's letter to Stanislaus of 6 February 1907. It is worthy of note that in a passage of a letter of Joyce's of September 1905, shortly after he had written 'Ivy Day', Anatole France, Ernest Renan, and Christ ('the Galilean') mingle: Joyce to Stanislaus

by the emperor Tiberius, passes his exile in the Near East, and after his return meets Pontius Pilate in Campania, whom he had known when Pilate was procurator of Judea. Pilate ruminates bitterly on his relations with the Jews. Laelius Lama recalls an infatuation with a beautiful Jewish dancer who disappeared one day, and whom he was unable to find in the demi-monde of Jerusalem. He later learned that she had joined a small group of men and women who followed 'un jeune thaumaturge galilean' who called himself Jésus of Nazareth. Pilate furrows his brow and strains to remember, and then murmurs, 'Jésus? . . . Jésus le Nazaréen? Je ne me rappelle pas.'[58]

Jesus's absence from France's story helped Joyce find a way out of an impasse. Joyce's resolution was far-reaching, and extended beyond the two short stories to inform the obliqueness of Joyce's treatment of Parnell in his literary work. In this a multiplicity of artistic and political considerations coalesced. Joyce was angrily conscious of the failure of institutional Parnellism to transmit his legacy after his death, a failure that Joyce judged to be as much imaginative as political. For Joyce there was a grotesque discordance between Parnell and the rhetoric in which he was championed after his death. Parnellite platform bombast was an un-Parnellian travesty of the defining characteristics of Parnell personally and of his political manner and method. Parnell was absent from Parnellite panegyrics, as if renewing his solitude in life. What had been lost was what Joyce was to characterise as 'the forlorn serenity of his character'.[59] This taciturn elusiveness within his own myth was to become a defining feature of Parnell's spectral presence in Joyce's writing.

The strategic choice to render Parnell through his myth resolved an artistic problem that extended beyond Joyce's austere critique of Parnellite rhetoric. Parnell's persona was hard to render, and direct depictions

---

Joyce, 24 September 1905, *Letters II* 110. In the letter that Ellmann annotates, Joyce expresses his admiration for France's story 'Crainquebille', which concerns a miscarriage of justice visited on a vegetable seller who plied his trade by cart in Montmartre, at one level an allegory on the Dreyfus Affair in which Alfred Dreyfus is not once mentioned, but it is clear from the letter that the story could not have been the inspiration for either 'Ivy Day' or 'The Dead'.

58. Anatole France, 'Le Procurateur de Judée,' in *L'Étui de nacre*, ed. C. Lévy (Paris, 1892).

59. 'L'ombra di Parnell', in *OCPW*, 194.

of him in life or death as a heroic leader were, as Joyce realised, all too prone to falling flat. Affronted directly, the Moses-like image of Parnell leading the Irish people from servitude was numbingly bland, and it was harder to sustain in the wake of the Split. Approaching Parnell through his myth avoided the grandiosely heroic and permitted an integral treatment of the cycle of his years: the emergent Parnell, the unchallenged leader, and the Parnell of the fall.

What is rendered is an oral myth. In conveying Parnell's memory through the conversation of Dublin men in a drab committee room and the declamation of an unpublished poem, Joyce delicately captures the ephemerality of the legend of Parnell. In this aspect, the story achieves something of the effect of a plangent prose ballad. The treatment of Parnell through his myth had also a fidelity to Joyce's own biography. An epistemological scrupulousness informed his approach: he would write only of that which he knew, and within the context of his knowledge. He belonged to a generational cohort affected in childhood by Parnell's fall. He was of an age in which he could not have participated in the Split and had never set eyes on the Irish leader he came so intently to admire. He was drawn into a highly informed reimagining of the Split, which as a child he had perceived distantly through flashes of immediate apprehension at Clongowes and within his domestic environment. Joyce knew that he belonged to a post-Parnell generation. His perspective was necessarily different from that of the generation of Yeats and Katharine Tynan, who had been young adults at the time of the Split, and who had known or could have known Parnell, and played some part in the events of the Split while Parnell was still alive. Making a virtue of this was part of Joyce's complex and refractory self-individualising in relation to the Irish Literary Revival. Whether he was also subverting Standish O'Grady's portrayals of Irish mythological heroes is perhaps an open question.

With great deftness, Joyce contrives to use Hynes's poem both to illustrate the extravagance of Parnellite panegyrics and to redeem Hynes from the taint of hackneyed insincerity through the dogged passion of the Dubliner's allegiance to his dead chief and his undiminished contempt for the anti-Parnellites and the clergy. Hynes's poem at the end of the story complements and recalls the title, disarranging time and revivifying the bitter shock of Parnell's death. It is a reproach to the tepid post-Parnellism of the reunited Irish Party.

In his later fictional writing, Joyce did not depart from, but unceasingly refined and elaborated, the oblique approach to Parnell of 'Ivy Day'. He did not seek to render Parnell in life but approached him through his myth. He worked the myth imaginatively with great ingenuity to make it conform to Parnell's attributes in life. One of the results of the skill and intimateness of Joyce's deployment of the Parnell myth is that one is scarcely conscious that virtually all that Joyce wrote fictionally on Parnell is written through the medium of the myth. The extraordinary richness and subtlety of the evocation of 'the shade of Parnell' in Joyce's writing derives from his electing to work within this creative constraint.

Eschewing a direct narrative of Parnell was a radical and formally confining manoeuvre. In its modernism it required a classical severity, and Joyce can hardly have come to it without a protracted struggle with himself. One of the stories for *Dubliners* that Joyce contemplated writing was entitled 'At Bay'.[60] Robert Spoo has perceptively suggested that this could have been a story about Parnell, and I believe it was.[61] The climactic chapter 23 of R. Barry O'Brien's biography of Parnell, which deals with Parnell's composition of his manifesto 'To the People of Ireland' in response to William Gladstone's intervention after the divorce hearing, the marshalling of the two camps, and the confrontation in Committee Room 15 that ensued, bears this title.[62] Parnell, moreover, enjoyed something approaching a monopoly of the idiom and imagery of the hunt in Joyce's writing. It was a story Joyce never wrote.

He did, however, invoke Parnell in the 'Eumaeus' episode of *Ulysses*, where we learn that Leopold Bloom returned Parnell's hat in the course of the siege of the offices of *United Ireland* in December 1890.[63] By inserting Bloom into O'Brien's canonical Parnellite narrative of the

60. Joyce to Stanislaus Joyce, 6 February 1907, *Letters II* 209.

61. In conversation with the author.

62. R. B. O'Brien, *Charles Stewart Parnell*, 2:257–88.

63. *U* 16.1495–528.

Split,[64] Joyce does for a moment write in the present tense of the hero in a virtuoso flourish that violates his own earlier practice. While this is a gesture of confidence in the approach to fiction he had taken since 'Ivy Day', the anecdote of Parnell's hat is also the exception that discreetly advertises Joyce's rule.

Joyce conceived Parnell as neither outside history nor consigned to history. He continued to situate the Parnell myth in the domain of the popular imagination. The Parnell myth in Joyce thereby remained a national and democratic emanation. The cause endured as it had commenced, in the first election Parnell contested, in Meath in April 1875, in which he went down to defeat. Even though the Irish people had at the beginning and the end repudiated Parnell, his and their destinies remained intertwined. Joyce's Parnellism is remote from the febrile rejectionism of contemporary Irish nationalism to which it is all too often reduced.

'Ivy Day' marks the inception of an extraordinary imaginative endeavour that runs through Joyce's writings in which he selects and edits the expressions of the Parnell myth to bring out Parnell's characteristics in life and to render his spare political style. Joyce conceived the myth as continuous with, and maintaining the rhythm of, Parnell's public life and mode of utterance. This conception informs and shapes his beautifully crafted evocations of Parnell and gives them their politically haunting force. Joyce's treatment of the Parnell myth was, at once, an extraordinary exercise in literary modernism and one that belies the suggestion that he was apolitical or anti-political, or other than politically a nationalist.

Stanislaus Joyce, the first, and for a long time the only, reader of the story apart from publishers, wrote to his brother in late 1905, 'It seems to me that your book "Dubliners" is becoming almost as important as your novel. "Ivy Day in the Committee Rooms" [*sic*] is accurate, just and satisfactory. It is original too. I don't think that this which forms so great a part of Dublin, of Irish life has been done before by an artist. . . . And the poem—the "turn" in this case—is entirely Irish.'[65]

64. R. Barry O'Brien, *Charles Stewart Parnell*, 2:296: 'His [Parnell's] hat was off now, his hair dishevelled, the dust of the conflict begrimed his well-brushed coat.'

65. Stanislaus Joyce to Joyce, 10 October 1905, *Letters II* 115

Stanislaus appreciates how Hynes's lament is the 'turn' that ripples back through the narrative. Generally purblind where his brother's politics was concerned, Stanislaus understood perfectly the instant enlargement of the scope of Irish literature that 'Ivy Day' effected, or would have effected if published. He wrote later with candour of the personae of 'Ivy Day' as those Dubliners he had thought 'below literary interest'.[66] Joyce's incorporation at the end of a poem that is deficient in literary merit, along with the text of Tierney's canvassing card at the start, underscored his disrupting of literary convention. The setting of an ostensibly uneventful scene in the transiently commandeered committee room of a candidate in a Dublin municipal election was an infraction of the prevailing boundaries of Irish fiction. In a characteristically Joycean double move, this was directed against both contemporary English writing and the avoidance of the contemporary socio-political in the Celtic Twilight.

It was almost a decade after 'Ivy Day' was written that *Dubliners* struggled at last into print in June 1914. When Joyce sent the text of the story to Stanislaus in September 1905, he was still hopeful *Dubliners* might be published in the spring of 1906.[67] The publication of *Dubliners* within a year or two after Joyce had written it would have, whatever its reception, transformed Joyce's reception as a writer in Ireland. A significant and generally overlooked element in Joyce's exasperation at the deferral is that the reception of 'Ivy Day' was inevitably going to be radically different in 1914, almost a full quarter century after Parnell's death, from what it would have been had it appeared, say, in 1908, or in *Dubliners* as it then stood minus 'The Dead' in mid-1907, when Parnell's memory just about retained some lingering political currency. By 1914, the generational cycle had turned, and Irish politics was in a markedly different phase with the Home Rule crisis, and as the Great War crept up on the unsuspecting peoples of Europe, Parnell had slipped into history. Bloom muses in *Ulysses*, 'Ivy Day dying out.'[68] Politically, 'Ivy Day' was rendered

66. S. Joyce, *My Brother's Keeper*, 206.

67. Joyce to Stanislaus Joyce, 1 September 1905, *Letters II* 105.

68. *U* 6.856.

a period piece for readers in 1914 when the story appeared, shorn of its sharply accusatory contemporary edge. No other story in *Dubliners* was so susceptible in its political salience to the attrition of time. Joyce, who had shatteringly disarranged temporal relations in contemporary history in the title of 'Ivy Day', found the project of his story itself brutally disarranged by time.[69] That this mattered to Joyce as much as it evidently did negates any lingering notion of a haughty disregard of Irish politics on Joyce's part.

The story remains utterly bound up with the unfolding of Joyce's art: the writing of it is not to be taken as an occasion contrived by Joyce to advertise his pro-Parnell convictions. 'Ivy Day' was a bridgehead that signalled Joyce's reconfiguration of *Dubliners*. In the published sequence, it was the first of the stories that Joyce conceived as relating to the 'public life' of Dublin. (The term 'public life' is noteworthy, and something more than a convenient rubric under which to group several stories: it attested to Joyce's project of enlarging the conventionally straitened conception of what constituted 'politics' in Ireland, or anywhere else.) 'Ivy Day' was the hinge on which the broadening out of the stories of *Dubliners* turned. Sequentially, Joyce wrote 'A Mother' and 'Grace' in quick succession to 'Ivy Day', and 'The Dead' in September 1907. It was the opening out effected by 'Ivy Day' that enabled Joyce to posit a quadripartite schema for *Dubliners*: stories of 'my childhood', of adolescence, of mature life, and 'of the public life of Dublin'.[70] With 'Ivy Day', Joyce not merely sensibly widened the scope of what was deemed the subject matter of Irish literature; he also mitigated the naturalistic bleakness of *Dubliners* through his treatment of the abandonment of Parnell by introducing an idea, however heavily qualified, of political agency.

The fall of Parnell is not the biographical episode in the life of the young James Joyce or of his father to which it is commonly reduced. It is not merely that Joyce's allegiance to Parnell is at the heart of his

69. In the intricate sequence of Joyce's work, the Parnell-saturated opening chapter of *A Portrait of the Artist as a Young Man* appeared before 'Ivy Day' in the serial publication in the *Egoist* from early 1914, though not in book form until 1917.

70. Joyce to Stanislaus Joyce, [ca. 24 September 1905], *Letters II* 111. Joyce repeated the quadripartite scheme in a letter to Grant Richards: 5 May 1906, *Letters II* 134.

conception of the political and his relationship to Ireland. The Parnell motif is not extraneous, but an insistently recurring theme that threads through Joyce's development as an artist. Across the course of his life, he maintained a form of dialogue with Parnell, and his sense of complicit identification with the dead Irish leader, enlarged by the web of Parnell-related complementarities in his own *parcours* as a writer, gathered strength rather than fell away.

In Joyce's life and oeuvre, there is no 'beyond Parnell' in Ellmann's sense.[71] There is a leave-taking, at the end of *Finnegans Wake*, published almost half a century after Parnell's death and two years before Joyce's. As the river flows back to the sea, Parnell's shade finds a first-person voice. An arc flashes from the travails of 1890–91 to the modern Irish state, in which Parnell's most ferocious enemy in the Split, Timothy Michael Healy, had been installed as Governor-General: 'But hunt me the journeyon, iteritinerant, the kal his course, amid the semitary of Somnionia. Even unto Heliotropolis, the castellated, the enchanting.'[72]

'A Mother'

'Ivy Day' does not stand alone in Joyce's evocation of his Parnellism. Immediately after completing it, Joyce wrote 'An Encounter' and 'A Mother' in September 1905. In the sequence of *Dubliners*, 'An Encounter' is the second story and 'A Mother' follows 'Ivy Day'. In the story Mrs Kearney is ambitious for her daughter Kathleen, who had been taught music at her convent school and at the Royal Academy of Music in Dublin: 'When the Irish Revival began to be appreciable Mrs Kearney determined to take advantage of her daughter's name and brought an Irish teacher to the house.'[73] At least in her mother's imagination, 'Kathleen' stands for Ireland, and more specifically the Ireland of Gaelic League nationalism. Mr Holohan is the assistant secretary of the fabulously named Eire Abu Society. He contracts with Mrs Kearney for her daughter's

71. See chapter 1, 'The Shade of Parnell', 39.

72. *FW* 594.7–9.

73. *D* 117.

engagement as a piano accompanist at a series of four concerts which the society was organising to take place in the Antient Concert Rooms. The concerts are scaled back from four to three. In the interval of the 'grand concert' on the final night, Mrs Kearney, calculating that the finale cannot conclude without her daughter, insists that she is to be paid in cash the eight guineas for the four concerts contracted for. The concert resumes after the intermission without Kathleen. Mrs Kearney, who has been 'haggard with rage, arguing with her husband and daughter, gesticulating with them', finds herself compelled to head their exit.[74]

If Mrs Kearney drives the action of the story, its outcome is determined by a less prominent character. One of Kathleen Kearney's 'nationalist friends', meaning a creature of the language revival, is the flirtatious Miss Healy, the contralto.[75] In the caucus in the intermission in the dressing room, the infuriated organisers and most of the artistes gather in one corner. In the revivalist corner are the Kearneys, Mr Bell, 'the second tenor . . . a fairheaded little man who competed every year for prizes at the Feis Ceoil', the young lady who had delivered the 'stirring patriotic recitation' with which the first part of the concert had concluded, and Miss Healy. Miss Healy 'wanted to join the other group but she did not like to do so because she was a great friend of Kathleen's and the Kearneys had often invited her to their house'. It is Miss Healy's agreement at the end of the intermission to substitute for her friend that allows the concert to proceed: 'Miss Healy had kindly consented to play one or two accompaniments. Mrs Kearney had to allow the baritone and his accompanist to pass up to the platform.'[76]

Who is Miss Healy, or rather why does she bear that surname? The answer lies in the speech of T. M. Healy at the nationalist meeting in Dublin on 20 November 1890 that became a rally in support for Parnell in the immediate aftermath of the divorce decree. In a speech for which he was to be taunted for the duration of the Split and for the rest of his life, Healy brought the house down with his ringing endorsement of Parnell's leadership. He made the first invocation in the Split of the

74. *D* 127.

75. *D* 122.

76. *D* 126–27.

comparison of Parnell with Moses ('in this moment within sight of the promised land') and famously enjoined his audience 'not to speak to the man at the wheel'. By the time he reached London a week later, after Gladstone's repudiation of Parnell, he was the Irish leader's most deadly enemy.[77] Joyce gave Healy's surname to the friend of Kathleen Kearney who forsook her after an initial show of support.[78]

The meeting at which Healy spoke was held in the Leinster Hall. The Antient Concert Rooms, situated on Great Brunswick (now Pearse) Street, where the concerts take place in 'A Mother', were a political as well as a musical venue and, like the Leinster Hall, host to nationalist meetings in the Parnell era and afterwards.[79] Neither was an exclusively political venue. It is highly unlikely that Joyce erred in his recollection of where Healy had spoken: Healy's 'Leinster Hall speech' was a fixed point of Parnellite reference in the Split. Joyce opted for another south city centre locale which, as its name proclaimed, was a habitual concert venue, in the consciousness that underscoring the invocation of Healy's name by setting the story in the Leinster Hall would compromise the slyness of his Parnellite allusion and render the story too crudely

77. Callanan, *Parnell Split*, 11, 22–23.

78. Joyce was, as ever, attentive to surnames. There is a heartily Gladstonian Father Healy, a brother-in-law of Mr Daniels, in *Stephen Hero* (*SH* 156–58), and a Father Healy is mentioned in 'The Dead' (*D* 177), but neither has attributes that would identify him specifically with T. M. Healy, which does not eliminate the possibility of a private joke.

There was a celebrated Fr Healy, James Healy (1824–1894) whom Joyce had met as a boy. Fr Healy's celebrity as a wit and raconteur was such that he had been introduced at Coolatin in County Wicklow to Gladstone on the latter's first visit to Ireland in 1877. He was a member of the Howth circle of the high Unionist Lord Justice Gerald Fitzgibbon. He was parish priest of Little Bray from 1868 to 1893, and finally of Ballybrack, Killiney, and Cabinteely; Andrew O'Brien and Linde Lunney, 'James Healy', *DIB* 4:559–60. Joyce wrote to Lucia when she was on her ill-fated visit to Bray in 1935 that if she was going to the library, she should look for his life (the *Memories of Father Healy* published in 1898 anonymously but in fact by W. J. Fitzpatrick). Joyce had known him and believed that he had baptised someone in the family. He had been parish priest of Little Bray and 'used to visit very frequently the Viceregal Court and was a very witty man'. Joyce to Lucia Joyce, 27 April 1935, letter and card (in Italian), with typescript translation, NLI, MS 5754.

79. In the Cornell alphabetical notebook, Joyce wrote of his mother, 'She was taken sometimes to a performance of Christy Minstrels in the Leinster Hall'. In Scholes and Kain, *Workshop of Daedalus*, 103.

political. The price of his restraint was that the evocation of T. M. Healy's conduct at the outset of the Split was to pass unnoticed.

A story that had as its secondary theme the social ambitions of the language revival had as a tertiary layer the politics of the Parnell Split. In the perspective of Joyce's story, a predisposition to unabashed hypocrisy and disloyalty prevailed as much in Irish society as in Irish politics, mitigated in some degree by perceived economic necessity, and particularly in situations of high patriotic ardour. Complicity in betrayal was ubiquitous and quotidian. It did not have to be a grand exhibition of political villainy, as Healy's Leinster Hall endorsement of his leader was to Parnellites. Petty treachery was pervasively alive and active, placidly tolerated in Irish social mores. Miss Healy attracts none of the obloquy that Mrs Kearney draws on herself. 'A Mother' was in this aspect a transcription of the ethics of the Parnell Split. 'Ivy Day' had opened a rift in what had been Joyce's Parnellite reticence.

'Two Gallants'

> *Silent, O Moyle.* Of course I know it, IT. You must have heard me sing it often. The best setting is by Sir Henry Bishop. It goes very well with a harp accompaniment.[80]

Joyce wrote 'Two Gallants' between December 1905 and January 1906, immediately after writing 'Grace'. Sequentially it is placed as the sixth story in *Dubliners* and belongs to the stories of mature life rather than those of public life, but like 'Ivy Day', it is inflected by Joyce's reading in socialism, and the subtle deployment of the weary harpist and his weary harp as allegorical images of Ireland is on a continuum with—and in the published book it foreshadows—the treatment of the absent figure of Parnell in 'Ivy Day'.

The story opens on a warm Sunday evening in August when the 'gaily coloured' crowds have not yet dispersed and the 'two gallants' walk across to the south city centre from the north. Corley, son of a police

80. Joyce to Giorgio and Helen Joyce, 26 February 1935, *Letters III* 348.

inspector and familiar of plainclothes men, has an assignation with a girl he has met. He describes her to his sidekick Lenehan, from whose perspective the narrative unfolds, as 'a slavey in a house on Baggot Street', who 'thinks I'm a bit of class, you know'. As they turn up Kildare Street, near the Kildare Street Club,

> a harpist stood in the roadway playing to a little ring of listeners. He plucked at the wires heedlessly, glancing quickly from time to time at the face of each newcomer and from time to time, wearily also, at the sky. His harp too, heedless that her coverings had fallen about her knees, seemed weary alike of the eyes of strangers and of her master's hands. One hand played the bass the melody of *Silent, O Moyle* while the other hand careered in the treble after each group of notes. The notes of the air throbbed deep and full.[81]

The 'mournful music'—one of the most famous of Thomas Moore's Irish melodies, 'Silent, O'Moyle', also called 'The Song of Fionnuala'—follows them as they progress silently up the street towards Stephen's Green. Corley meets his lady friend, with whom he disappears up the stairs of the Donnybrook tram. Lenehan resumes his torpid wandering about the city centre, awaiting Corley's return. When he comes to the railings of the Duke's Lawn at the back of Leinster House, 'he allowed his hand to run along them. The air which the harpist played began to control his movements. His softly padded feet played the melody while his fingers swept a scale of variations idly along the railings after each group of notes'.[82] Lenehan is complicit in Corley's purpose but doubts that Corley will 'pull it off'. Corley, however, prevails, but what he extracts are not sexual favours but a gold sovereign or half sovereign, either of which was a multiple of a housemaid's weekly wage.

When Grant Richards's printer refused to print 'Two Gallants', Joyce wrote to Richards, 'I would strongly recommend to him the chapters wherein [Guglielmo] Ferrero examines the moral code of the soldier

81. *D* 43.
82. *D* 45.

and (incidentally) of the gallant. But it would be useless for I am sure that in his heart of hearts he is a militarist.'[83] Joyce wrote later to Stanislaus that Ferrero 'gave me' the story.[84]

Ferrero had already contributed the title of one of the stories in *Dubliners*, 'A Little Cloud'. Susan L. Humphreys and Dominic Manganiello have independently established that Joyce's specific point of reference for the Ferrero element in 'Two Gallants' is Ferrero's *Il militarismo*.[85] Taking as his point of departure the memoirs of D'Artagnan (whom Alexandre Dumas was to adopt as his hero in *The Three Musketeers*), Ferrero scrutinises the lives of the younger sons of the lesser gentry drawn to Paris to serve as minor officers in the king's army. Ferrero wrote, 'These officers, being short of money to pay for the dissolute lives they were leading, tried, nearly all of them, to become the lovers of rich middle-class ladies, getting money out of them for the honour they conferred on these ladies by condescending to make them their mistresses.'[86]

Joyce transposes Ferrero and the class structure of which he was writing to contemporary Dublin, where the idea of gallantry makes a further steep descent from somewhat predatory romance to venality, shorn of the least redemptive vestige of aristocratic grace or of jouissance. On the edge of the foreground sit harp and harpist, ambiguously poised on the cusp of the same fallen world as the gallant, emblematic of Ireland's lost possibilities.

The immediate inspiration for the image of the harp in 'Two Gallants' comes from a book review in Arthur Griffith's *United Irishman*. In late 1905 the exuberantly named William Henry Grattan Flood published *The Story of the Harp*. Flood (1859–1928) was characterised on his death

83. Joyce to Grant Richards, 3 May 1906, *Letters II* 132–33.

84. Joyce to Stanislaus Joyce, 11 February 1907, *Letters II* 212.

85. Manganiello, *Joyce's Politics*, 46–57; Humphreys, 'Ferrero Etc'. See also Robert Spoo, '"Una Piccola Nuvoletta": Ferrero's Young Europe and Joyce's Mature *Dubliners* Stories', *James Joyce Quarterly* 24, no. 4 (Summer 1987): 401–10; and chapter 11, '"Professing to Be a Socialist"'.

86. Ferrero, *Il militarismo*, 129–30, quoted in Giorgio Melchiori, 'The Genesis of *Ulysses*', in *Joyce in Rome: The Genesis of Ulysses*, ed. Giorgio Melchiori (Rome: Bulzoni, 1984), 42; John McCourt, *The Years of Bloom: James Joyce in Trieste, 1904–1920* (Dublin: Lilliput, 2000), 68–69.

as 'the author of several important works and an incessant contributor to musical, ecclesiastical, and antiquarian journals and to other periodicals and frequently to the newspaper press—notably on Irish Music and Song and on Irish Catholic History'. Ardently Hiberno-centric, and claiming relationship to both Henry Grattan and Henry Flood, he was an organist and music teacher, and had taught in Clongowes. In 1922 he was appointed a knight of St Gregory by Pope Benedict XV.[87]

Flood's 1905 work was not a history of the Irish harp, but he declared in his preface that no apology was required for 'the prominence given to the Irish harp in the following pages. Ireland has been for centuries associated with "The harp that once thro' Tara's Halls", and the instrument figures in the arms and coinage of the kingdom'.[88] In Flaubertian mode, one could not refer to the Irish harp without mentioning Tom Moore in the next breath.

The *United Irishman*—the Irish newspaper Joyce received most regularly in Trieste—in its editions of 11 and 18 November 1905 carried an extended review in two parts of Flood's book by 'Sean-Ghall'. This was the nom de plume of Henry Egan Kenny, a childhood friend and early collaborator of Arthur Griffith.[89] Egan Kenny's review, a supplement to Flood's scholarship, was at once nationalist and erudite, and representative of the popularisation—without intellectual compromise, unless conceptions of the patriotic dictated otherwise—of historical and antiquarian subjects by the *United Irishman*. Egan Kenny noted approvingly Flood's acknowledgement of the role of the *United Irishman* and William Rooney in reviving interest in the study of the harp as 'the National instrument of Ireland'. Egan Kenny opened the first part of his review in a traditional vein, but one that was infused with an overt intimation of the contemporary political:

87. 'W. H. Grattan Flood', *Irish Book Lover* 17 (March–April 1929): 26; obituary, *Irish Times*, 7 August 1928; Patrick M. Geoghegan, 'William Henry Grattan Flood', *DIB* 3:1030–31.

88. W. H. Grattan Flood, *The Story of the Harp* (London: Scott, 1905), viii–x. The harp features prominently in Flood's important *History of Irish Music*, 3rd ed. (Dublin: Browne and Nolan, 1913).

89. Richard P. Davis, *Arthur Griffith and Non-violent Sinn Féin* (Dublin: Anvil Books, 1974), 16, 122; P. Colum, *Arthur Griffith*, 17.

> Into the texture of the fabric of Irish history the harp is woven with colours at once bright and dun. It symbolises Erin's power, it typifies her misery. Its proud music echoed exultingly and majestically in the halls of Aileach and Tara, its hearse-like strains told in saddest numbers the ruin of castle and cabin, of chieftain and clansman, of country and prosperity. Whenever the senile arteries of our nation were quickened into new life, after the destruction of Independent Ireland, the harp was crowned with a measure of public favour, when Irish Ireland slept the sleep of indifference, the harp's sweet voice was all but mute. Indeed the fluctuation of national endeavour may be read in the story of the harp of Erin.[90]

Egan Kenny wrote in his review of the diasporic aspect of the history of the Irish harp: 'The Irish harp was known throughout broad Europe from the sixth century far into the heart of Mediaeval days, for wherever the Gaelic scholars, teachers, monks, and warriors went, there also went their harps and harpers.' The harp had also a romantic aspect: 'The most famous story of Mediaeval Europe, "Tristram and Iseult", was often chanted to the strains of the harp.' It was to the political that Egan Kenny reverted at the end of the first part of the review: 'So potent was the harpers' power in rousing the patriotism of the clan that England massacred them without mercy. Irish music has its head roll of martyrs as well as the national religion.'[91]

It is the account of an episode in the second part of Egan Kenny's review that provided the immediate imaginative stimulus for the harp and harpist (a term Joyce preferred over 'harper') in 'Two Gallants.' The account is taken from what was professedly a diary kept in Ireland by Henry Harvey, secretary to Robert Devereux, the second Earl of Essex, in 1599, the year of his fraught lord lieutenancy in Ireland. The campaign in Ireland from April to September 1599 against Hugh O'Neill, Earl of Tyrone, indirectly precipitated the downfall of Essex, who was executed in the Tower of London on 25 February 1601.

90. *United Irishman,* 11 November 1905.

91. *United Irishman,* 11 November 1905.

The episode concerned an ancient bearded harpist with an immense and ornately wrought harp. Egan Kenny cited the 'very graphic description' of the harper. 'For his face, it was well writ over with the map of his age, only the eyes still dark and fiery, and the look of them very strange, being both fierce and timorous at once.' Egan Kenny quoted also the description of the harp and its ornamentation. Time had lent a patina of decay to the harp, described in the cited account as 'all much bleached and defaced, doubtless by rough weather and the evil usage it had met with.' There follows an interpellation by Egan Kenny by way of descriptive summary: 'The harper played by request; but the lament he struck up seemed to come from his fingers rather than his soul.'[92]

Egan Kenny explained that Delahide, an Irishman of the Pale with Essex, intervened to ask the harper in Irish to play the 'Dirge of Rory Oge O'More', lord of Laois, a rebel against Elizabethan government in Ireland, who had been killed in 1578,[93] whose name Essex vaguely recalled, and whose *seanchaí* (here reciter of ancient lore) the harper had been. Egan Kenny's quotation from the account ascribed to Harvey is as follows (the omissions are Egan Kenny's):

> Mr. Delahide spake a few words again in Irish to the harper; who thereat straightened himself, flinging suddenly off that bowed and dejected aspect he had hitherto worn, and looking a full score of years younger, so brightly did his eyes flash and his whole face alter. And he looked about him now, no longer scared and timorous, but with a fierce, defiant air. . . . So, having turned his harp about, he lifted it a little, and set it upon a stool or trestle that stood there; and placing himself beside it, struck his hands across the strings with a careless gesture. Then having played awhile, he suddenly broke out into a sort of singing which yet was hardly singing, but rather a chant or crooning noise which swelled and swelled so that it seemed to rise to the very rafters, rolling and beating about like thunder in our ears, and again to sink till it was no louder than the whisper of a summer stream over grass and small stones, his harp the while seeming to follow and

92. *United Irishman*, 18 November 1905.

93. Emmett O'Byrne, 'Rory (Ruaidhrí Óg) O'More (Ó'Mórdha)', *DIB* 7:717–19.

> take part, more like a thing of separate life, joining in at its own pleasure, than an instrument played by the hands. . . .
>
> It chanced that, being next to the window, I saw what was not I think seen of others, in the company. For when that strange song or chant began all the kernes, galloglasses, and other wild Irish mustered without salary started and stared, seeming to prick their ears, as a horse does at the sound of the trumpet. Presently, as it went on, they began to draw nearer and nearer . . . they began to grip at one another with their hands, and to move to and fro with their feet, as if they fain would have broken into wild dancing and leaping . . . their very souls fed upon what they heard![94]

There is a twist. What Egan Kenny took to be a historical source was in fact a recent literary fiction. In 1890 a book was published entitled *With Essex in Ireland*, with the descriptive subtitle *Being Extracts from a Diary Kept in Ireland during the Year 1599 by Mr. Henry Harvey, Sometime Secretary to Robert Devereux, Earl of Essex, with a Preface by John Oliver Maddox, M.A., Introduced and Edited by Hon. Emily Lawless*. Published by Smith, Elder & Company in London, it enjoyed sufficient success to be republished in 1902.

Emily Lawless (1845–1913) was an Irish novelist, historian, and poet, the eldest daughter of Edward Lawless, a Kildare landlord who succeeded in 1853 as the third Baron Cloncurry. A Unionist in politics, Emily Lawless had an apprehensive fascination with the Irish peasant class. Her *Hurrish* (1886), which was set in the west of Ireland, published in the immediate prelude to Gladstone's First Home Rule Bill, enjoyed a considerable réclame in England. Her *History of Ireland* followed in 1887. In 1890 she published *With Essex in Ireland*, which has been accurately characterised as 'a documentary-style novel . . . a fictionalised first-hand account of Essex's 1599 expedition to Ireland'. Egan Kenny

94. *United Irishman*, 18 November 1905. As if to exemplify the phenomenon of Joycean coincidence, Tom Moore's harp was exhibited (along with the death mask of Robert Emmet) at the Irish Industrial Exposition in Madison Square Garden in New York for three weeks from 18 September 1905; *Gaelic American*, 16 September 1905. This does not seem to have been noted in the Irish papers.

was not alone in the belief that this was based on a genuine historical source: the misapprehension was shared by Gladstone, among others.[95]

The eagerness to accept the text as a historical source goes beyond casual credulousness and reflects the preoccupation of the era with the historical conceptualisation of contemporary Ireland. The nationalist demand for Home Rule was an argument from history, and Liberal support for Home Rule was underpinned by an elaborate narrative of English errors of policy in relation to Ireland. Gladstone's prodigious labours were historical as well as legislative. Unionist opponents of Home Rule had their own, more brusque historical account, which spoke of Irish violence, sectarian excess, socio-economic retardation, and political incapacity.

Lawless had made her authorship as plain as she could without imperilling the aesthetic verisimilitude of the book as an edition of a historical source. The promised introduction by Lawless, prominently described as the author of the fictional *Hurrish*, was lacking, nor were there many of the conventional indicia of editorship. Her authorship was not a secret: Yeats in 1895 included *With Essex in Ireland* in a list of thirty Irish books to be read in the category of 'Novels and Romances'.[96] By 1905, Egan Kenny had less excuse than Gladstone a decade and a half earlier for taking *With Essex in Ireland* at face value as an edition of a historical document.

The episode with the harper on which Egan Kenny, in his *United Irishman* review, drew is based on what purports to be an entry in Harvey's diary for 12 July 1599 that comprises thirteen pages of Lawless's book. The scenes that make up the entry are as it happens brilliantly conceived by Lawless. In her narrative, Delahide gives Harvey a scroll on which he had written his own translation into English of the lament just sung by the harper. At the request of Essex, Harvey reads out the lament, which he considers 'a confused and bombastical invention, setting forth with many savage illustrations the greatness and glory of this

95. Frances Clarke and Patrick Maume, 'Emily Lawless', *DIB* 5:351–53.

96. Yeats to the editor of the *Daily Express* (Dublin), 27 February 1895, in *Collected Letters*, 1:440–42.

Rory Oge O'More, and the treachery by which his end had been accomplished'. Essex, musing after the reading is finished, reacts differently. He asks Harvey whether he ever thought that it was better that 'these Irish, such as are given to the composing of similar songs and dirges—should not be acquainted with the English tongue, or indeed with any civilised and current language'. Harvey replies that 'the best hope of their ceasing from their savagery lies in the learning of them our own tongue'. Essex asks him whether if the tale of O'More were 'put into some language current among men of letters 'twould produce no effect upon those that heard it'. Harvey says that in his judgement it would be 'a wild and heathenish sort of composition, not pertaining to any recognised progression of words, whether or prose or poetry'. Essex again differs. He suggests that it would be impolitic to equip the Irish to argue their cause in English. However cynical his argument, the English Lord Lieutenant discloses an imaginative insight into what the native Irish might be able to make of their cause in which his interlocutor, Delahide, an Irish supporter of the English conquest, is completely lacking:

> It seemed to me as I listened, and especially as I recalled the looks and gestures of yonder harper in the hall, that 'twere as well for our credit that we alone had the exposition of our quarrel with this people, and not they theirs also. And of this I am sure, that were I born an Irishman, and given to the poetic craft, I could tell such a tale as would send every maid that heard it weeping to her bed; aye, and might chance to leave behind it not a few of those Tragedies by which our London stage has of late been held.[97]

Lawless's intricate interweaving of the historical with themes of contemporary political controversy is of great brilliance. The reciprocal gaze of harper and Lord Lieutenant initiates at the inception of modern history what was to be the unceasing clash and interpenetration of their nations and cultures: the harper is rightly wary of Essex, and Essex appraises the harper's aspect and performance with high sensibility subordinated to placidly ironic strategic calculation. Before the onset of the

97. Lawless, *With Essex in Ireland*, 162.

Irish language revival, Lawless has an acute intimation of the paradox across historical time of the fate of the Irish language. In her account it is Essex who, for reasons of political calculation, contemplates the merits of maintaining an Irish-speaking Ireland.

The retro-prescient argument Lawless gives to Essex anticipates the highly effective propaganda offensive of Parnellite nationalism in England in the early 1880s that did much to bring about Gladstone's introduction of the First Home Rule Bill, as well as what was to be the creative achievement of Irish writers in the English language. The contest between the turbulence of Irish creativity and the graceful Machiavellianism of the Lord Lieutenant subtly advantages the imperial perspective. The Essex whom Lawless creates is an avatar of that high Tory imperial sardonicism which found its Irish apogee in the chief secretaryship of Arthur Balfour (1887–91) and the second premiership of the Marquess of Salisbury (1886–92), during which the sophisticated and sustained Unionist strategy to thwart Home Rule and to break the élan of the Liberal-nationalist alliance was conceived and initiated. The characterisation of Essex in this way incarnates the political moment at which *With Essex in Ireland* was written and first published.

It is unlikely that Joyce was familiar with *With Essex in Ireland,* and he almost certainly took the account in Egan Kenny's *United Irishman* review as it was presented, as emanating from an authentic Elizabethan historical source. It is intriguing that the immediate inspiration for Joyce's superbly modernist rendering of the harp and harper in 'Two Gallants' was not the historical source he took it to be, transmitted to him in exile through the medium of Griffith's paper, but a novel by an Irish author who was a Unionist in politics and more rooted in the fiction of nineteenth-century Ireland than she was affiliated to the Celtic Twilight. Joyce's use of the stimulus of what he did not know to have been written by Emily Lawless is more sharply suggestive than most instances of what passes for intertextuality.

In the marriage of inspiration from Guglielmo Ferrero and the *United Irishman,* 'Two Gallants' is an emblematic text of Joyce's early Triestine exile. Joyce took from Egan Kenny's review in the *United Irishman* of Flood's *Story of the Harp* the image of the semi-autonomy of harp and harper, and of the harp as a register of the cyclical rise and fall in Irish hopes, and probably the effect the harper's playing had on the kernes, transposed to Lenehan's indolent passage by the railings of Leinster House. His refashioning of these affords a striking example of his transfigurative utilisation of Irish literary, historical, and cultural material. There is a double effect which was to become characteristic of Joyce's deployment of allegorical images of Ireland, already presaged in the absent figure of Parnell in 'Ivy Day': the image of an older, mythic, or historical Ireland, modernistically rendered, is countered by the tawdry reality of modern Dublin. That contrast works, however, as Joyce intended it to, in an unexpected way to purge the motif of the harp of the stale ideological accretions by which it had become overlain. The pristine associations of the image of the harp are hauntingly reinstated.

It is the use of 'traditional' motifs and the evocation of Dublin that admitted of Joyce's striking characterisation of the story as a landscape. In the same letter from Rome to Stanislaus in September 1906 in which he confessed that he had not reproduced Dublin's 'ingenuous insularity and its hospitality', he wrote, 'After all 'Two Gallants'—with the Sunday crowds and the harp in Kildare Street and Lenehan—is an Irish landscape'.[98] Even as landscape, it has a political colouration. The Kildare Street Club, outside which the harper plays, was a bastion of ascendancy, and Richard Castle's Leinster House, built for James FitzGerald, the Earl of Kildare, later created Duke of Leinster, was the largest and finest townhouse of eighteenth-century Dublin.[99]

Whether the wider *parcours* of Lenehan and Corley through the south city centre in particular is intended to invoke sites associated with Dublin's eighteenth-century aristocratic gallants, as Donald Torchiana has suggested with scrupulous tentativeness, is doubtful: the very most that could be ventured is that such an association was left deliberately unresolved.[100] When Lenehan regains alone the corner of Rutland

98. Joyce to Stanislaus Joyce, 25 September 1906, *Letters II* 166.

99. Christine Casey, *The Buildings of Ireland: Dublin* (New Haven, CT: Yale University Press, 2005), 498.

100. Donald T. Torchiana, *Backgrounds for Joyce's 'Dubliners'* (Boston: Allen and Unwin, 1986), 91–98.

(now Parnell) Square on the north side, he feels 'more at ease in the dark quiet street, the sombre look of which suited his mood'.[101] Rutland Square was of course itself a fine eighteenth-century square, though inexorably less glamorous over time as the aristocracy followed the Duke of Leinster south, and less rich in the former habitats of rakes and bucks.

Constantine Curran was discountenanced by his friend's indifference to the intrinsic architectural merits of Georgian Dublin. He noted that Joyce's interest in buildings was 'for their associations'.[102] Whatever Curran took to be the aesthetic deficit in Joyce's appreciation of the splendours of eighteenth-century Dublin, then still largely intact, Joyce's sociological and political cartography of his native city was unsparingly lucid.

In relation to harper and harp in Joyce's story, the transfigurative modernist effect prevails over the idea that they, in their listlessness, partake of the same decadence as the two gallants. Some readings of 'Two Gallants' posit a moral equivalence between harper and harp and Corley and his servant girl in a generalised colonial demoralisation, or come close to doing so. That is to miss the appropriately suppressed political argument of 'Two Gallants'. Harp and harper are not a poignantly archaic decorative embellishment of the story. They are integral to its plot and suggest the only possibility of egress from the almost unbearable claustrophobic stasis of the narrative of Corley's pursuit of his servant girl as observed by Lenehan. The egress—the thwarted possibility of extra-textual resolution—is blocked, but it is there. The misreading of the text is not ideologically innocent in its fatalism and derives a superficial plausibility from treating the story as if it were one of the austerely minimalistic early stories in *Dubliners*, and by a coarsened conceptualisation of Joyce's idea of the paralysis of Dublin. Joyce's accusatory Parnellism never ceases to admit of, if not quite tacitly to invite, redemptive action.

It is easy, in the disenchantment of the story's dénouement, to miss the subtle radicalism of Joyce's feminisation of the harp as an allegorical

101. *D* 45.

102. Curran, *James Joyce Remembered*, 39–40.

figure of Ireland, and the eroticisation of 'Erin's misery' and of the exilic languishing of 'Lir's lonely daughter' in the occluded lyrics of Moore's 'Song of Fionnuala'. Part of the effect is wrought by the severance of harp and harper. The ignominy of the harper, an artist in a city of vassals, is of a different order to that of Corley. The harp, a feminised instrument that is not permitted to control its fate, stands at a still-further remove.

Joyce contrived to pack a great deal into the feminisation of the harp besides doubling the allegorising of Ireland. He posited an equation of the subjugation of the country with the oppression of women. He went still further and presented that oppression as a thwarting, or a prostitution, of female sexuality. This was a highly transgressive move within the nationalist rhetorical canon, and a considered insult to moralising Conservative nationalists who had a particular fondness for the trope of Ireland as a captive maiden whom they were to liberate with heroic laboriousness. He was also, through the slackened voluptuousness of the image, aiming a side kick at the sexual puritanism of Francis Sheehy-Skeffington's advocacy of the emancipation of women. Joyce was greatly irritated at the time, as his correspondence with Stanislaus attests, by Sheehy-Skeffington's altruistically abstracted and sexually abnegatory 'heroics'. The grace of that exquisitely conceived double move, simultaneously affronting the right and the left of nationalism, was deeply characteristic, and expressive of Joyce's contempt for the solipsistic nature of contemporary Irish political controversy.

'The Dead'

The controversy around John Millington Synge's *The Playboy of the Western World* in early 1907 rendered Joyce's absence particularly exasperating to him. It was as if what had been the Celtic Twilight had suddenly, through Synge, reinvented itself—a startling though not entirely unexpected development for Joyce given his consistent admiration for Yeats and the impression left on him by his encounters with Synge in Paris. The Literary Revival was no longer a static target. Joyce was caught off guard and deeply disoriented. In his correspondence with his brother Stanislaus, he momentarily forfeited his poise (the only recorded occasion he did so). The *Playboy* controversy radically affected what he proposed to write, though he put it negatively in the first instance, complaining that it 'has put me off the story I was "going to write"—to wit, "The Dead"'.[103] He left Rome for Trieste in March 1907 a little over a month after he had first learned of the *Playboy* affair. He wrote 'The Dead' in August–September 1907.

'The Dead' encompasses a response to the Irish literary movement first by its naturalistic rendering of the social life of Dublin, and second in its subtext drawn from the ancient Irish saga of 'The Destruction of Dá Derga's Hostel', which was an incursion deep into the terrain of the Celtic Twilight and the Irish literary movement. It cost Joyce a great deal of effort. To Stanislaus he made the rare admission immediately after finishing it that 'he had put more work in one story than any of the Irish put into two or three plays.'[104]

Joyce's knowledge of Irish mythology is apparent in *Finnegans Wake,* but the depth of his apprehension of old Irish literature and myths in his earlier writing, notably in 'The Dead', passed unnoticed and unsuspected for a long time. His encryption of 'The Destruction of Dá Derga's Hostel' remained unbroken in 'The Dead' until John V. Kelleher published in 1965, almost a quarter of a century after Joyce's death, his 'Irish History and Mythology in James Joyce's "The Dead"'.[105] Kelleher identified the tale of Dá Derga's hostel as a spectral subtext of Joyce's story.

103. Joyce to Stanislaus Joyce, 11 February 1907, *Letters II* 212. The first reference to 'The Dead' that has survived was five days earlier, the second letter written after Joyce had read of the *Playboy* affair, when he listed 'The Dead' among five titles of stories he could write 'if circumstances were favourable'. Joyce to Stanislaus Joyce, 6 February 1907, *Letters II* 209.

104. Stanislaus Joyce, Triestine diary, entry for 7 September 1907, quoted in McCourt, *Years of Bloom*, 127.

105. Kelleher, 'Irish History and Mythology'. Kelleher does not say so, but it seems possible, if not likely, that his paper on the 'The Dead' (read to the Conference of Irish Studies at the University of Illinois on 25 April 1964, subsequently published as his 1965 article) arose from his reading of *Finnegans Wake,* in which as he writes Joyce makes 'large use of the saga' ('Irish History and Mythology', 419). That a reading of *Finnegans Wake* could have prompted a major re-reading of 'The Dead' is a reflection of the encircling integrity of Joyce's oeuvre. That Joyce could have anticipated this in invoking Dá Derga's hostel in the *Wake* invests Kelleher's paper with yet another level of the presence of the dead: he might have thought the identification of the subtext was a long time coming.

That discovery was greatly amplified and enriched in Paul Muldoon's Clarendon Lectures at Oxford in 1998, published in 2000 as *To Ireland, I: An Abecedary of Irish Literature*.[106] In the interval between Kelleher and Muldoon, Maria Tymoczko published *The Irish Ulysses*,[107] which had Joyce's use of older Irish sources as a central theme.

'Togail Bruidhne Dá Derga' is a strange and sanguinary tale from a culture as remote from the modern as could be conceived but which retains its haunting propensities. Conaire Mór (Conary in the poem of Samuel Ferguson, Gabriel Conroy in 'The Dead') is the beleaguered king of Tara. His fate is sealed by his breaking of a number of *geasa*, or taboos. One such is not to go round Tara in the right-hand direction; another relates to hunting birds. His kingdom is the subject of an invading raid by a coalition of three foster brothers he had exiled and a Saxon pirate. Conaire is forced to take refuge in Dá Derga's hostel somewhere along the Dodder outside Dublin.[108] The hostel is set on fire, and the water runs out. Conaire dies of thirst or is slain, and is decapitated. Dá

106. Muldoon, *To Ireland, I*. While Muldoon does not betray its promise, the title is a brilliant conceit: it is a meditation on 'The Dead' primarily by reference to Dá Derga's hostel, taking 'The Dead' as a pivotal text, drawing on antecedent Irish literature or literatures, and providing a primary point of departure for Irish literature after its belated publication in *Dubliners* in 1914. Muldoon, it might be thought defensively to minimise the extent that he adopts and carries further Kelleher's thesis, refers to Kelleher's essay as 'magnificently provocative' (*To Ireland, I*, 51). He does much to build on Kelleher's argument and to put it beyond dispute. When Muldoon makes a point that is possibly subjective or debatable, he scrupulously flags that he is doing so. Frank Shovlin, writing post-Muldoon, characterises Kelleher's Dá Derga's hostel thesis as 'brilliant, and still controversial'. Shovlin, *Journey Westward: Joyce, Dubliners and the Literary Revival* (Liverpool: Liverpool University Press, 2014), 53.

107. Tymoczko, *The Irish Ulysses*. O'Hehir's *Gaelic Lexicon for Finnegans Wake* (1967), published two years after Kelleher's article, seemed to promise a dawn that did not quite break, at least at that time. Perhaps due to a lag in the publication of the submitted text, O'Hehir does not refer to, and his short bibliography does not include, Kelleher's article.

108. Kelleher notes parenthetically a small but intriguing detail. Joyce was far too imaginatively cunning to equate the Morkan house on Usher's Island with Dá Derga's hostel. On the journey that he is forced to take to find refuge in Dá Derga's hostel, Conaire crosses the Liffey by the hurdle ford from which the Irish name of Dublin derives, which was very close to the Morkan house, which stood at the dead centre of the old city; Kelleher, 'Irish History and Mythology', 420. It might be added, for what it is worth, that the house was situated in the tightly circumscribed locale in which Joyce's close friend in University College, John Francis Byrne, born on East Essex Street, which was once submerged in and intermittently flooded by the river, grew up. Byrne, in his memoir, narrated a ghost story concerning a house on Cork Hill almost

Derga's hostel provides an intricate subtext for 'The Dead', in which Gabriel Conroy, like his near namesake, violates some of the *geasa* that bound Conaire Mór. Kelleher emphasises Miss Ivors's faintly menacing, 'I have a crow to pluck with you'.[109] Muldoon observes, 'The "crow" is surely a manifestation of the Morrigu, or Morrigan, the bird of battle whose name finds its way directly into "The Dead" as "Morkan", the family name that presides over all.'[110]

In Kelleher's compelling account, Gabriel's infringement of the *geasa* is connected to a second level of historical reference, which he describes as that of 'old Catholic Dublin'. Gabriel, whose tastes Kelleher characterises as 'palely European', speaks slightingly of his grandfather. Patrick Morkan kept a starch mill on the historically charged Back Lane, where Tailor's Hall stands. Gabriel characterises his grandfather, to whom he owes much of his own social status and means, as 'a glue boiler' and 'a very pompous old gentleman'.[111] He recounts the story of his grandfather's horse bringing him round and round the equestrian statue of William III which stood on College Green.[112] Gabriel has thereby displayed impiety to his ancestry and political antecedents.[113]

The interest here is in Joyce's grounding in Irish mythology. Kelleher asserts that the main source for Joyce's knowledge of 'The Destruction of Dá Derga's Hostel' is the edition and translation of Whitley Stokes,[114] lawyer and prolific Irish Celtic scholar, which was published in the *Revue Celtique* in 1901–2 (vol. 22). This is likely to be correct.[115] The edition was published when Joyce was still in Dublin, a

opposite the City Hall, which, since he devoted a chapter to it, he can scarcely have failed to recount to Joyce; Byrne, *Silent Years*, ix, 27–28, 67–73.

109. Kelleher, 'Irish History and Mythology', 423.

110. Muldoon, *To Ireland, I*, 52.

111. *D* 180–81.

112. Kelleher, 'Irish History and Mythology', 418, 424–27.

113. Kelleher's article disrupts and transcends Ellmann's bland if dutifully informative chapter 'The Backgrounds of "The Dead"' (*James Joyce*, 243–53). Ellmann's second edition of his biography (1982) did not pretend to be a comprehensive revision of the first (1959).

114. Subsequently published as Whitley Stokes, ed. and trans., *Togail bruidne Dá Derga / The Destruction of Dá Derga's Hostel* (Paris: Émile Bouillon, 1902).

115. If Stokes's translation is Joyce's principal source, the issue remains of when Joyce read it. One presumes that he first read it in Dublin, the most likely proposition. He was at least aware

couple of years after his induction to Irish through the Gaelic League classes he had fleetingly attended. Joyce was alert at least to the fact of advances in the modern scholarship on older Irish-language literature.[116] That Joyce relied on a scholarly translation rather than a summary retelling is not merely more consistent with the precision of his incorporation of the story into his own. It subserved his collateral purposes of outflanking the promoters of the Celtic Twilight, and in a lesser degree the revivalists of modern spoken Irish of the Gaelic League. Muldoon does not so much dispute that Stokes's translation was a source as assert—convincingly—that Joyce's 'sense of this tale' drew as much from Samuel Ferguson's *Conary* and *Lays of the Western Gael.*[117] Muldoon also identifies traces in 'The Dead' of the 'Toraigheacht Dhiarmada agus Ghrainne', the great Irish tale of the proscribed love of Diarmuid and Grainne that parallels the story of Tristan and Isolde that meant so much to Joyce.[118]

What is significant in terms of Joyce's politics is what this discloses of Joyce's knowledge of and interest in early Irish literature while he was still in Dublin. Muldoon picks up what he suggests is an overt challenge to Yeats. The poet had written in his introduction to Augusta Gregory's 1904 *Gods and Fighting Men,* 'Lady Gregory's book of tales is full of fellowship like theirs, and made noble by a courtesy that has gone perhaps out of the world.'[119] This is echoed by Gabriel Conroy in his speech after

---

of and struck by the story, and presumably had access to the *Revue Celtique* in Trieste, where he wrote 'The Dead' in August–September 1907.

116. In 'L'Irlanda: Isola dei santi e dei savi', his 1907 Trieste lecture, he principally credited German scholars with the advances that had been achieved (*OCPW* 109). Stokes was himself greatly influenced by the work of Johann Kaspar Zeuss and collaborated with Kuno Meyer, Ernst Windisch, and Adalbert Bezzenberger; Georgina Clinton and Sinead Sturgeon, 'Whitley Stokes', *DIB* 9:105–7.

117. Muldoon, *To Ireland, I,* 53–54.

118. Muldoon, *To Ireland, I,* 109–11. This is a kind of *post scriptum,* wittily encompassed in Muldoon's entry in his abecedary for Laurence Sterne.

119. Muldoon, *To Ireland, I,* 44, 59. Ellmann, in his treatment of the story, cites Joyce's statement in a letter to Stanislaus of 25 September 1906 that there were some elements of Dublin he had not rendered in the stories written up to that point, specifically 'its ingenuous insularity and its hospitality'. Ellmann, *James Joyce,* 245. That reference to 'hospitality' does not negate Muldoon's proposition.

dinner extolling 'the true spirit of *camaraderie*'. This new generation, he fears, will 'lack those qualities of humanity, of hospitality, of kindly humour which belonged to an older day.'[120]

The mythological subtext was unknown and unsuspected until Kelleher's 1965 article. Perhaps if the story had been published shortly after it was written, the subtext might have been recognised, perhaps backwards through the invocations of Ferguson; perhaps Yeats would have had some intimation of what Joyce was doing. As it was, too much had happened—and was yet to happen in short order—by the time of the publication of *Dubliners* in June 1914 in an edition of only 1,250 copies. After 'Ivy Day', 'The Dead' was the story in *Dubliners* whose public and critical reception was most adversely affected by the stalled publication.

The story—what Kelleher called 'the surface story'[121]—worked beautifully without a sense of its subtext, and after Joyce's death, 'The Dead' became, for Irish readers, the best-loved thing he wrote. Yet the subtext was far from a literary game directed to the cognoscenti—who transpired not to be—of the Irish Literary Revival. Story and subtext are intricately connected, culturally and politically. The occasion is 'the Misses Morkan's annual dance' in 'the dark gaunt house on Usher's Island' along the quays of the Liffey,[122] on the upper floors of which they live. It is in the new year of 1904, Joyce's last Dublin Christmas, perhaps 6 January, 'twelfth night', the feast of the Epiphany, and the last day of Christmas.[123] The characters of the story are middle class by comparison with the figures in 'Ivy Day', but they are neither grand nor particularly well-off and maintain their position by holding stubbornly to educational attainments, chiefly musical in the case of the Morkan women. With the exception of the Gaelicising Miss Ivors and the Protestant Mr Browne, their sympathies—certainly Gabriel's—were likely to have lain with the Irish Party.

120. *D* 177.

121. Kelleher, 'Irish History and Mythology', 418.

122. *D* 152.

123. Don Gifford, *Joyce Annotated: Notes for 'Dubliners' and 'A Portrait of the Artist as a Young Man'*, 2nd ed. (Berkeley: University of California Press, 1982), 110.

The story does not seriously admit of a Marxist reading in which the stratum of society depicted was archaic and vulnerable, even though Gabriel's indulgently nostalgic speech could be given a strained interpretation to support such a reading. It may or may not be relevant that Joyce had written exasperatedly to Stanislaus from Rome some months earlier saying that his interest in socialism had left him.[124] There is in fact considerable continuity in the extension to a higher subclass or stratum of the sense that people in Dublin had to get on with their lives as best they could in absolutely or relatively straitened circumstances which informed all of the stories in *Dubliners*. (This was to contribute to Joyce's protest that no one in his stories had any money.) But beneath the beguiling geniality of the Morkans' party, and the touches of celebratory plushness unique in *Dubliners*, there is a continuous seepage of unease that is not confined to Gabriel's relations with Gretta. There is something that is not quite right. It is that sense that is completed by the subtext, in the idea that beneath the fragile crust of a Dublin Christmas celebration in the Edwardian era, nationalist in the broad sense, there was a deep and turbulent past which both constituted in itself and stood for contemporary forces that those present at the Misses Morkan's party (not excluding the early-departing Miss Ivors) could not control, and scarcely apprehended. Though there was enough in the surface text to justify the title, 'The Dead' has a terrible and restless secondary level of meaning which merges with it in the hard definiteness of the phrase with which Gabriel's snowy swoon, and the story, ends: the uneasy conjuncture of 'all the living and the dead'.[125]

The mythological excavation of 'The Dead' by Kelleher and Muldoon is transformative of our understanding of the Joyce who left Dublin, but the advances that have been made in the exegesis of 'The Dead' have remained strangely unintegrated in the corpus of biographical treatments of Joyce and in studies of his relationship to Ireland. Perceptions of the early Joyce are disproportionately shaped by *Stephen Hero* and *A Portrait*; Joyce must have been aware of the influence that *A Portrait*

124. Joyce to Stanislaus Joyce, 1 March 1907, *Letters II* 217.

125. *D* 194.

would exert. Both novels are notable in not identifying what Stephen Dedalus, Joyce's semi–alter ego, was writing or contemplated writing. While they deal with Stephen's attempted learning of Irish, neither hinted at a study of older Irish literature. In that deliberate omission resides their primary incompleteness. It becomes in that way Joyce's second mask, directed not this time to how he was perceived by his contemporaries but to how he was understood biographically as a writer. That is an aspect of the *décalage* between Joyce the 'literary artist' and Joyce the writer. Before he left Dublin he had written some juvenilia, poems and the earliest stories of *Dubliners*, and had embarked on *Stephen Hero*. His boldly enunciated literary precepts and critique of the Irish Literary Revival ran ahead of his own writing. What might seem a presumptuous inversion of sequence reflected Joyce's magnificently unflinching (and as it transpired well-founded) confidence that he could make good on his strictures on the Revival in his own fictional writing.

'The Dead' was a maximal development of what could be achieved within the short story, and Joyce turned the circumscription of the genre to haunting advantage. In addition to a remarkable feat of the characterisation of the major and minor dramatis personae, Joyce completed the integration of the public rhetorical idiom of Dublin, in its formal social manifestation, into *Dubliners*. In a story which relied on severe authorial distance from the figure of Gabriel Conroy, Joyce contrived to be most complicit with his creation in his performative aspect, epitomised in Conroy's old-fashioned but strangely affecting after-dinner speech. The effect which he had invented in Joe Hynes's Parnell poem in 'Ivy Day' was carried forward, and Joyce thereby contrived to reinstate the hospitable urbanity of Dublin, in which he had come to feel the original *Dubliners* might have been deficient.

13

Reading Ireland from Exile

JOYCE'S LETTERS TO Stanislaus from Trieste and Rome in 1905–7 convey the experience of exile. They contain, as well as statements on Joyce's attitude to Sinn Féin, extensive observations on his University College contemporaries, and on Oliver St John Gogarty. As a biographical source they are unique in containing a semi-continuous contemporary record of Joyce's response to Irish events and politics.

It is superficially tempting to see in Joyce's comments on Ireland an exilic turn, a revisionist softening towards 'the old country' from afar. It is unwise to impute to Joyce, the supreme ironist of exile, conventional expatriate sentimentality. Moreover, hypotheses of radical change in Joyce's political thinking about Ireland are to be treated guardedly, not least on account of the depth of the consideration he had given to Irish politics even before he arrived at University College. Joyce was exasperated by his exile and the hardship that attended it, but what is striking is the adamantine purpose with which he set out to master the constraints of exile as it bore on his thinking and writing. In the period of his first exile, 1904–12, he managed to maintain a remarkable continuity of engagement with the subjects and themes which had exercised him when he was in Ireland, and to finish out at least the phase of Irish controversy that existed when he left. Joyce's hermeneutic scrupulosity prevailed over any sentimental sense of separation from Ireland: he would only write of that which he had experienced or thoroughly understood. He was consistently vexed at being cut off from what was happening in Ireland, and his most irate exilic protests were at breakdowns in the meagre flow of intelligence from Ireland on which his apprehension of Irish affairs was dependent. He strove to remain astringently objective. He rendered his exile as virtual as it could be.

Joyce's contemplation of Irish politics led him to a qualified identification with the early Sinn Féin of Arthur Griffith. He conveyed this privately in his correspondence with his brother, who was hostile to Sinn Féin, and it found clear if oblique public expression in what he wrote and said on Irish affairs in Trieste. The importance of Joyce's support of Sinn Féin, however guarded, can scarcely be overstated: like his Parnellism, it was an aspect of his fashioning of a political self, and it provided him with a bridgehead into the politics of Ireland after the introduction of the Third Home Rule Bill. Joyce's sympathy with the early Sinn Féin arose from his contemplation of contemporary Irish politics. He did not see Sinn Féin as a projection of Parnellism. His Parnellism and his identification with Sinn Féin were discrete, though he and Griffith were both Parnellites of the Split, and his essay 'The Shade of Parnell' ('L'ombra di Parnell') owed something to the prompting of what Griffith had written on Parnell in his journal *Sinn Féin*.

Sinn Féin, the advanced national political movement founded by Griffith in 1905, was in Joyce's early exile a tiny movement which achieved a disproportionate but still limited public profile through Griffith's trenchant journalism. For many of Griffith's readers, the role of *Sinn Féin*, the weekly paper, and of Sinn Féin, the exiguous political entity, was to stiffen the resolve of the Irish Parliamentary Party rather than to displace the party. Nationalist politics remained, in the absence of a serious challenge to the Irish Party, highly fluid until late in the Home Rule crisis from 1912. Joyce's favouring of Sinn Féin was tentative and contingent, and did not reflect an ideological opposition to parliamentarism, as distinct from a sceptical indifference to the activities of the Irish Party at Westminster. If his acerbic comments in his correspondence on Sheehy-Skeffington and Kettle may have been fortified by Kettle's election to Parliament, it was because Joyce saw it as representing an avenue of Catholic nationalist social advancement rather than by reason of anti-parliamentary conviction.

Joyce's first reference in the correspondence to Griffith is in a letter to Stanislaus of 15 March 1905. He had read in *Le Figaro* of the judicial separation of Maud Gonne and John MacBride, and added the comment, referring to Griffith's close friendship with both and to his paper, *United Irishman*, 'Poor little U. I.: indignant little chap'.[1] Joyce was not an admirer of Gonne, 'the Irish Joan of Arc', and disliked the extravagant Francophile republicanism for which the *United Irishman* unflaggingly lauded her. The characterisation of Griffith at that stage suggested an attitude of mingled sympathy and political scepticism.

While Joyce continued to read copies of the *United Irishman* and of Griffith's next paper, *Sinn Féin*, which launched 4 May 1906,[2] a long silence supervened in the correspondence. The Liberal landslide at the general election of January 1906 passed without comment from Joyce. It had brought to an end over a decade of Conservative-Unionist governance in Ireland and was psychologically transformative in raising popular expectations, but it wrought little in the way of immediate change in Ireland: the Liberals had an overall majority and were not reliant on the support of the Irish Party. Joyce's silence on Irish politics was broken by Kettle's election to Parliament in a by-election in East Tyrone on 25 July 1906, which Joyce learnt of after the fact. From Rome he sent to Stanislaus a copy of *Sinn Féin* for 4 August 1906, which contained a parody by Arthur Griffith (writing as 'Shanganash') of Sheehy-Skeffington's series of articles entitled 'Dialogues of the Day' and serialised in the *Nationist*. Griffith situated his little drama in the office of Sir Antony MacDonnell, the influential Under-Secretary for Ireland, who had served in India, and whose office Griffith depicted as populated with flunkeys from Trinity College as well as his officials:

> 'I see', said the Private Secretary, 'that Kettle has won East Tyrone'.
>
> 'To the truly Irish and National tune of "We're off to Bom-bom-bay"', remarked the Future Provost.
>
> 'What is the difference between an Irishman going off to Bom-bom-bay to work out the salvation of his country and going off to Lon-don-don?' asked the Present Provost.

1. Joyce to Stanislaus Joyce, 15 March 1905, *Letters II* 185.

2. The *United Irishman* ceased publication in the wake of a libel action with its issue of 14 April 1906. Two weeks later, its successor *Sinn Féin* appeared: it ran from 4 May 1906 to 28 November 1914.

'He might make trouble for us in Bombay', said Sir Antony reflectively.[3]

It was thus that Joyce received the news of Kettle's election. He had overlooked Stanislaus having marked the news of this in a copy of the *Irish Independent* sent from Trieste. Always superbly recriminatory in relation to delays in receiving intelligence from Ireland, Joyce protested to Stanislaus, 'I suppose it is by the merest chance that I learn this. Who knows what else has taken place in Dublin?' In the same letter, he referred to the news of Gogarty's marriage, of which Nora had found a newspaper announcement: 'I fancy when he emerged from the church door his agile eye went right and left a little anxiously in search of a certain lean myopic face in the crowd but he will rapidly grow out of that remaining sensibility.'[4]

'A bundle of any old papers': *Sinn Féin*, the *Nationist*, and the *Irish Catholic*

Joyce's seven-month sojourn in Rome with Nora and Giorgio from 31 July 1906 to 7 March 1907 proved extremely difficult. He liked neither Rome nor his employment with the Nast-Kolb and Schumacher bank. Exhausted by a visit in September to the desolate and tourist-thronged expanse of the Forum, he superbly pronounced, 'Rome reminds me of a man who lives by exhibiting to travellers his grandmother's corpse.'[5] Early in his Rome sojourn, he declared himself to Stanislaus 'damnably sick of Italy, Italian and Italians, outrageously, illogically sick.'[6] Early in 1907 he wrote, 'My hatred of Italy and Italians is on the increase.'[7]

Joyce's Roman crisis was not attributable to conventional nostalgia, but to a concern that he needed, for artistic reasons, to be in Dublin: he

3. 'A "Dialogue of the Day" [with acknowledgements to Mr Sheehy-Skeffington]', *Sinn Féin*, 4 August 1906.

4. Joyce to Stanislaus Joyce, [ca. 12 August 1906], *Letters II* 147.

5. Joyce to Stanislaus Joyce, 25 September 1906, *Letters II* 165. The church to which Joyce retreated is evidently San Clemente.

6. Joyce to Stanislaus Joyce, 7 December 1906, *Letters II* 201.

7. Joyce to Stanislaus Joyce, postmark 10 January 1907, *Letters II* 205.

was still adding stories to *Dubliners*. Joyce's anxiety of absence from Dublin when in Rome derived from an acute intimation of flux in the city that was his subject matter, if not quite of the 'sparkling excitement over art and politics in the air above the Liffey' of which his first biographer wrote.[8] That intimation antedated the *Playboy* riots.

For Irish news in Rome, he was reliant on what his aunt, Josephine Murray, could send from Dublin. At his request she sent him copies of Griffith's paper *Sinn Féin*; Sheehy-Skeffington's short-lived weekly, the *Nationist*; and the *Irish Catholic*. Stanislaus occasionally forwarded Irish newspapers from Trieste, including the *Irish Independent*, and Joyce got some Irish news from English papers in Rome, chiefly the *Daily Mail*. But the difficulty of getting news from Ireland was a constant refrain throughout his time in Rome. On 25 September 1906, he complained to Stanislaus that their aunt 'has left off sending me Skeffington's paper or writing at all',[9] and three weeks later, lamenting that 'my imagination is starved at present', he protested, 'Does Aunt Josephine write to you? She never writes to me and sends me *Sinn Féin* at long intervals. Is there nobody in Ireland who will think it worth his or her while to make a bundle of any old papers that are lying about his or her house and send them to me?'[10]

The political weeklies were valuable to Joyce for their political intelligence and as found objects. This was not the common exilic demand for 'news from home'. Joyce craved text, newsprint, the thing itself. In November his request to his aunt for material extended to a collage of the cultural detritus of contemporary Dublin—he reported to Stanislaus that he had written to his aunt to send him some Irish books 'and to send me a Xmas present made up of tram-tickets, advts, handbills, posters, papers, programmes & c. I would like to have a map of Dublin on my wall. I suppose I am becoming something of a maniac'.[11] In February 1907, he reported happily to Stanislaus, 'Baby, Poppie, Pappie and Charlie sent me picture postcards on my birthday!! The postcards

8. Gorman, *James Joyce*, 184.

9. Joyce to Stanislaus Joyce, 25 September 1906, *Letters II* 165.

10. Joyce to Stanislaus Joyce, 18 October 1906, *Letters II* 182.

11. Joyce to Stanislaus Joyce, 6 November 1906, *Letters II* 186.

are all coloured green, dark sea, sage, emerald, cabbage etc.'[12] But days later, he was back complaining: 'Of course just the very week I wanted it most Aunt J did not send *Sinn Féin*.'[13]

The politics of his contemporaries and the emergence of Sinn Féin as a political force dominated Joyce's correspondence with Stanislaus throughout his time in Rome. On these, he sought constantly to wrong-foot his brother. Evidently prompted by Joyce's reaction to Kettle's election, Stanislaus despatched some further news of the newly elected member of Parliament, to which Joyce ferociously retorted, 'How the devil did you think the news about Kettle would interest me? But I would like to see a copy of *Dialogues of the Day*.'[14] (In his correspondence Joyce frequently misnames the *Nationist*, of which Sheehy-Skeffington was assistant editor, as *Dialogues of the Day*—in fact the title of a series of articles, written by Sheehy-Skeffington, which appeared in the *Nationist*.) The wounded Stanislaus, in his lost response, evidently attacked Joyce's failure to forge alliances with any of his male contemporaries. Joyce's assuaging reply began with an adroit deflection:

> You seem to be annoyed about Kettle. The reason I was not interested is because I take no interest in parliamentarianism as I suppose you know. However, I have asked Aunt J. to send me a copy of *The Nationist*—if it still exists. As for a possible friendship with Kettle it seems to me my influence on male friends is provocative. They find it hard to understand me, and difficult to get on with me even when they seem well-equipped for these tasks. On the other hand two ill-equipped women, to wit, Aunt Josephine and Nora, seem to be able to get at my point of view, and if they do not get on with me as well as they might they certainly manage to preserve a certain loyalty. . . . Of course I am not speaking of you.[15]

Joyce, in the same letter, defended Arthur Griffith's *United Irishman* (which had ceased publication on 14 April 1906): 'I don't quite agree

12. Joyce to Stanislaus Joyce, 6 February 1907, *Letters II* 210.

13. Joyce to Stanislaus Joyce, 11 February 1907, *Letters II* 211.

14. Joyce to Stanislaus Joyce, postmark 19 August 1906, *Letters II* 151.

15. Joyce to Stanislaus Joyce, 6 September 1906, *Letters II* 157.

with you about the U. I. In my opinion, it is the only newspaper with any pretensions in Ireland. I believe that its policy would benefit Ireland very much. Of course so far as any intellectual interest is concerned it is hopelessly deaf. But even that deafness is preferable to the alertness of *Dialogues of the Day*.'[16]

This is a striking election. Having held aloof not just from Sheehy-Skeffington's various political projects but from other intellectual coteries in Dublin, to the point of looking as if he might be incapable of aligning himself with any movement in Ireland, Joyce was not inhibited in expressing support for the 'policy' advocated by Griffith's papers. It marks a clear departure from his cultivated political aloofness in Dublin. But it is not a sudden turn towards radical nationalism engendered by the experience and perspective of exile. With Griffith's 'policy', nationalism found an institutional, albeit journalistic, expression with which Joyce could identify. The ease and readiness of Joyce's expression of sympathy for the views Griffith enunciated in the now-defunct *United Irishman* retrospectively illumine the extent to which his repudiation of William Kirkpatrick Magee, Frederick Ryan, and *Dana* before he left Ireland had derived from his convictions as an Irish nationalist and his sensible and realistic reservations about the viability of an intellectual journal or grouping that did not have a clear conception of political nationalism.

The *United Irishman* had been in existence since 1899, and Joyce read it attentively without it eliciting from him any statement of sympathy with Griffith's radical nationalism. What had changed was that Griffith was now hammering his views into a more programmatic form, and that Sinn Féin, though not formally constituted as an organisation until September 1907, was emerging as a movement in Irish politics. Sinn Féin's prospects of ending the hegemony of the Irish Party seemed exceedingly remote, but its emergence did mark a change in Irish politics and represented in some limited degree an answer to Joyce's denunciations of the passivity and ineffectuality of nationalist politics.

Deeply frustrated in Rome by the continuing impasse over the publication of *Dubliners*, he observed the progress of his contemporaries in

16. Joyce to Stanislaus Joyce, 6 September 1906, *Letters II* 157–58.

Dublin. He conveyed his exasperation to Stanislaus in a report at the end of his first month in the city, with impressive humour:

> Aunt J. sent me papers: no letter. *The Irish Catholic* and *Dialogues of the Day*. Unluckily I lost the latter in the street. I shall send you the next copy: it was very 'brilliant'. Three pages of puff by F.S.S. at the end: full of thick typed catch phrases such as 'this novelty of Irish journalism' 'order at once' 'absolutely unique'. An advt appears for some booklet by (very big letters) Thomas Kettle, M.P. A column of the Irish Catholic is devoted to a series of letters between Dr Delany and J. M. O'Sullivan M.A.: philosophical student at Bonn. They are all in the public eye and favour: even Dr O. S. Jesus Gogarty. And here am I (whom their writings and lives nauseate to the point of vomiting) writing away letters for ten hours a day like the blue devil on the offchance of pleasing three bad-tempered bankers and inducing them to let me retain my position while (as a luxury) I am allowed to haggle for two years with the same publisher, trying to induce him to publish a book for which he has an intense admiration. Orco Dio![17]

Joyce's description of Sheehy-Skeffington's paper was comically exact: a disproportionate amount of space was taken up with advertisements for, or notices of, or correspondence about itself. The eighth issue, that of 25 August 1906, evidently the first Joyce had seen, did not disappoint. As if to exemplify the circularity of Dublin social controversy, the rambling 'Dialogue' ('A Holiday Miscellany') extended to the university question, with J. M. O'Sullivan's views on the 'Bonn scheme' respectfully invoked. Most satisfying from Joyce's point of view was a letter from William J. Maloney, who criticised the fact that the female gender was represented by a solitary lady, with the ironic appellation of the 'Mere Woman'. As if frantic to fill his columns, Sheehy-Skeffington responded, 'I should be glad to publish comments, approving or otherwise, on Mr. Maloney's letter. Are women's interests adequately represented in "Dialogues of the Day"? Or should the "Mere Woman" be reinforced or superseded by a number of other types? These are questions

17. Joyce to Stanislaus Joyce, 31 August 1906, *Letters II* 153–54.

again upon which I should like to receive, in particular, the opinion of the women who read the "Dialogues"'.[18]

The issue carried an advertisement for a penny pamphlet, *The Philosophy of Politics*, by 'T. M. Kettle, B.A., B.L. (M.P. for East Tyrone)'. It had also an advertisement for another penny pamphlet, by Sheehy-Skeffington himself, *A Forgotten Aspect of the University Question*, now severed from Joyce's 'The Day of the Rabblement', with which it had first been published in 1901.

If Kettle and Sheehy-Skeffington were politically active contemporaries of Joyce, supporters of the dominant Irish Party of whom much was expected, John Marcus O'Sullivan was in a somewhat different category. Ardently Catholic, O'Sullivan (1881–1948) was a brilliant politically conservative philosopher who studied in Bonn, Berlin, and Heidelberg. He had a prominent political career in the independent Irish state: elected as Cumann na nGaedheal Teachta Dála [MP] for Kerry in 1923, he served as minister for education from 1926 to 1932.[19]

The relevant issue of the *Irish Catholic*, that of 25 August 1906, carried a letter from William Delany S.J., the president of University College, along with a letter from O'Sullivan to Delany. Delany commended an article written by O'Sullivan the previous year in the *New Ireland Review*,[20] the purpose of which was to deny that the attendance of Rhineland Catholics at the University of Bonn afforded a valid precedent for Irish Catholics accepting Trinity College as a solution to the Irish university question. Having learned that O'Sullivan had returned to Ireland, Delany had written asking him 'if his longer stay had modified his views expressed in the article'. O'Sullivan replied at length in the negative, duly rebutting the claims of 'the supporters of the Bonn scheme'.[21]

Delany's determined promotion of his protégé, and the uncoerced conformity of O'Sullivan's response, served to confirm the tight confines of professional advancement in Catholic nationalist society. For

18. *Nationist*, 25 August 1906.

19. Patrick Maume, 'John Marcus O'Sullivan', *DIB* 7:971–73.

20. J. M. O'Sullivan 'Bonn University and Trinity College: A Parallel', *New Ireland Review* 23 (March 1905): 1–9.

21. *Irish Catholic*, 25 August 1906.

Joyce, O'Sullivan's academic progress was a paradigm of the career of an Irish contemporary under ecclesiastical patronage. Neither a career aligned to the fortunes of the Irish Party nor one under clerical auspices was an option that Joyce could have entertained, and he closed off the subject with ebullient sarcasm: 'What do those gentlemen in Ireland want a new University for? The one they have is quite good enough for them—both in "saince and in art". But you must read "Dialogues of the Day".'[22]

Joyce's observation of his ambitious contemporaries had a political edge but did not of itself predispose him to sympathy with Griffith. That Joyce's receptiveness to Griffith arose from a purposive and strategic nationalism is clear from his uncharacteristic readiness to overlook Griffith's occasional moralising and to tolerate his revivalism, and his refusal to be put off by some of the contributions to *Sinn Féin* which were deeply objectionable to him.

Assessing Griffith's Economic Programme

Griffith's speech in the Rotunda on 6 September at the second annual convention of the National Council (a group co-founded by Griffith and Maud Gonne in 1903, and the precursor to Sinn Féin) was reported in *Sinn Féin* 8 September 1906. The speech, and the assessment of it that Joyce despatched to Stanislaus, reveals much of what drew Joyce to Griffith and Sinn Féin. Griffith's speech displayed a dogged adroitness which would have struck most contemporaries as interesting but forlorn. Two features were striking: the advocacy of an ethic of active civic responsibility, and the endowing of an economic programme to what would become Sinn Féin. These were in fact inseparably connected. While Joyce in his response dwelt chiefly on the economic programme, the ethic that underpinned it had a particular significance for him in relation both to his critique of Irish paralysis and political ineffectuality and to the Parnellism that informed it.

Griffith proposed four resolutions chosen for their symbolism, the first of which enjoined members of the National Council to reduce their

22. Joyce to Stanislaus Joyce, 31 August 1906, *Letters II* 155.

consumption of commodities on which excise was payable by a set amount which, if taken up by the rest of the country, would reduce the revenue of the British government annually by £2.5 million:

> The proposer said construction was the essence of Sinn Féin policy. It could not fail, for it builds as it goes, and recognises in the individual not a pawn but an individual force. In this it was the antithesis of the Parliamentarian policy—a policy which taught by precept and example that there was only one position for the fighting forces of Ireland to occupy—the British House of Commons—a position wherein Ireland was placed in a permanent minority of 1 to 7. . . . So long as Ireland did this thing England was left free to occupy the strong places of Ireland, and she occupied them every one. It was in the school, the college, and the university, in the playground, and the athletic field, in the social circle, in the theatre and the learned society, in the counting house and the commercial chamber, in the bank, in the railway office, in the insurance society and in the harbour board England was entrenched in Ireland, and the policy of Sinn Féin was to drive her from these entrenchments whence she dominated the people of Ireland, and to plant the flag of a self-conscious and an united Ireland over each and all. Parliamentarianism treated the unit as a pawn—Sinn Féin treats him as a living force and preaches the doctrine of personal responsibility to and for the nation. . . . Ireland will be 'ripe for freedom' and will seize freedom for herself when her men and women have realised that there is work for each to do—and do it. That work is there for each to do while the strong places in the land are in the hands of the enemy. Where is Ireland's national bank, where is Ireland's national university, where is Ireland's foreign trade, where is Ireland's railway control, where is Ireland's waterway control, where are Ireland's schools, institutions, commerce? They are still where they were thirty-five years ago when Irish Parliamentarianism was born—under the thumb of the British Government in Ireland.[23]

The second resolution looked to the devising of a scheme of primary and secondary education 'on Irish lines', for which it was proposed to

23. *Sinn Féin*, 8 September 1906.

enlist the assistance of the Christian Brothers. The third advocated a scheme for the filling of appointments to county councils by competitive examination. This might seem a modest and uncontentious idea, but it was boomed by Griffith as 'aiming at creating a National Civil Service in Ireland', and marked an early expression of the idea of requirement of a competence in the Irish language for public employment in Ireland:

> We have heard a good deal to the effect that the Irish language has no commercial value—which is supposed to be the last and triumphant word, for other values than commercial values are inconceivable to the Britishised mind in Ireland. But when you make all public employment under the public authorities in Ireland dependent, besides other qualifications for the position itself, upon the knowledge of Ireland's history, Ireland's literature, Ireland['s] potentialities, and Ireland's language, you will have given the Irish language in Ireland a commercial value which will force its teaching in the places where it is now ignored, and its study and use in quarters where it is now regarded with indifference or hostility. When no man can hope to secure position under the Irish local authorities unless he possesses a fair knowledge of Ireland and her language, you will have the schools qualifying the pupils in that knowledge even as they now qualify them for the British Civil Service.[24]

The fourth resolution advocated a scheme for the foundation of a national banking system in Ireland. Griffith declared that 'the banking system in Ireland is rotten to the core' and broadened out his theme: 'We aim at securing the commerce, the banking, the transit of Ireland for Ireland—we aim at the National control of all departments of Irish life.' He bemoaned the decline in Irish foreign trade, and the overtaxation of Ireland.[25] There was a resolution advocating the promotion of Irish consuls in the chief foreign ports, and Griffith took up this theme as a coda to his National Council speech in *Sinn Féin* a week later.

24. *Sinn Féin*, 8 September 1906.

25. *Sinn Féin*, 8 September 1906.

> If there was in place a commonsense policy of establishing Irish Consuls in the chief ports and centres of the world, direct trading relations between Ireland and other countries could with ease be revived, and Irish products find a market in every country whose experts now come to her from England, laded with a string of middlemen's profits. . . . The mere existence of direct communication with the Continent might do much to encourage Irish industries. Irish lace, linens, poplin, serges, tweeds, homespuns, hides and sheepskins, if better known, might look for a respectable market in the Latin countries; while it is a matter for wonder that the famous Irish gingerale should not be a popular beverage abroad instead of, as at present, comparatively unknown.[26]

Whatever about the ginger ale, this was of evident interest to Joyce, who the previous year had conceived the idea of obtaining a concession to sell Irish Foxford tweeds in Trieste and later made arrangements to act as an agent for the Dublin Woollen Company. This was something he took quite seriously. When Herbert Gorman, in the proofs of his *James Joyce*, wrote that nothing had come of Joyce's seeking an agency, Joyce wrote a corrective footnote: 'He got the agency and did, in fact, succeed in clothing several of his Triestine male pupils in Irish homespun ordered by them.'[27]

Some of the cultural aspects of Griffith's speech, in relation to the presaging of compulsory Irish and the promotion of a Christian Brothers–inspired education system 'on Irish lines', scarcely appealed to Joyce. Griffith's broadening out of the promotion of the Irish language to include a knowledge of Irish historical and cultural subjects was astute and owed something to his own reservations. His economic proposals were aspirational and unrealistic, but they were politically well judged in venturing onto a terrain that the Irish Party austerely insisted should await the establishment of a Home Rule Parliament. William G. Fallon observed that 'the one clever thing the "Hungarians" did was to steal the social and industrial programme of the orthodox

26. *Sinn Féin*, 15 September 1906.

27. Ellmann, *James Joyce*, 199, 303, 772n19; Gorman, *James Joyce*, 200.

Irish-Ireland movement',[28] which was a shrewd if not quite accurate assessment. At best, it was the canvassing of a programme of the kind that Sinn Féin could hope to promote if it ever came to power in an independent Ireland, something that did not seem even remotely in prospect in 1906.

There was another facet of Griffith's speech which would not have escaped Joyce. Aside from challenging the overwhelming ascendancy of the Irish Party, Griffith was seeking to define a platform distinct from that of D. P. Moran and the *Leader*. Particularly in his economic proposals, he was deliberately articulating something more politically ambitious than Moran's meagre and chauvinistic Irish Irelandism, with its preponderant emphasis on buying Irish goods (which the *Leader* had made a proprietary theme), and the appointment of Catholic nationalists to corporate roles.

In his letter of 25 September 1906, Joyce sent to Stanislaus, who had evidently argued back against his previous letter, a carefully reasoned assessment of Griffith's address:

> In my opinion Griffith's speech at the meeting of the National Council justifies the existence of his paper. He, probably, has to lease out his columns to scribblers like Gogarty and [Padraic] Colum, and virgin martyrs like his sub-editor. But, so far as my knowledge of Irish affairs goes, he was the first person in Ireland to revive the separatist idea on modern lines nine years ago. He wants the creation of an Irish consular service abroad, and of an Irish bank at home. What I don't understand is that while apparently he does the talking and the thinking two or three fatheads like [Edward] Martyn and [John] Sweetman don't begin either of the schemes. He said in one of his articles that it cost a Danish merchant less to send butter to Christiania and then by sea to London than it costs an Irish merchant to send his from Mullingar to Dublin. A great deal of his programme perhaps is absurd but at least it tries to inaugurate some commercial life for Ireland and to tell you the truth once or twice in Trieste I felt myself humiliated when I heard the little Galatti girl sneering at my impoverished country. You

28. *Leader*, 24 April 1910.

> may remember that on my arrival in Trieste I actually 'took some steps' to secure an agency for Foxford tweeds there. What I object to most of all in his paper is that it is educating the people of Ireland on the old pap of racial hatred whereas anyone can see that if the Irish question exists, it exists for the Irish proletariat chiefly. I have expressed myself badly, I fear, but perhaps you will be able to see what I mean. A Belfast linen company does a great deal of business in Rome through this bank. On the whole I don't think it fair to compare him with a stupid mountebank like Knickerbockers.[29]

Joyce's letter discloses a knowledge of the personae and politics of what would become Sinn Féin. His identification of the significance of Griffith was prescient. Griffith was the first contemporary active Irish political figure of whom Joyce was prepared to express a favourable opinion. It was to Griffith and not anyone else that he was drawn, distinguishing Griffith from Edward Martyn, the president of the National Council, and the former member of the Irish Party, John Sweetman, who served with Griffith as vice president. It was moreover striking that Joyce was prepared to overlook aspects of Griffith's project he disapproved of. He showed himself sensible and realistic about the need for Griffith to publish material from contributors whom Joyce did not rate or whose opinions he disagreed with. One could quibble with Joyce's tentatively couched view that Griffith 'was the first person in Ireland to revive the separatist idea on modern lines nine years ago'. Members of the Irish Republican Brotherhood would deny that the separatist idea ever had to be revived and dispute that Griffith was a separatist, and indeed that hostile view of Griffith provided an undercurrent of dissent at the convention.[30] While Joyce saw the proto–Sinn Féin movement as a continuation of Fenianism, it was with Griffith rather than the adherents of the Irish Republican Brotherhood that he identified. Joyce's point—and it was cogent—was that separatism had been moribund at least since the rise of Parnell, and that Griffith had articulated a modern and viable alternative to parliamentarianism. Joyce's 'nine years ago'

29. Joyce to Stanislaus Joyce, 25 September 1906, *Letters II* 167.

30. Davis, *Arthur Griffith*, 29.

would bring one back to 1897, the year of Queen Victoria's jubilee, during which Griffith was in South Africa, having immigrated there at the end of 1896, returning to Ireland in October 1898. Joyce can only have been referring to 1899, the year in which Griffith started the *United Irishman* (also the year of the foundation of the pro-Boer Transvaal Committee and of the protests that attended Joseph Chamberlain's visit to Dublin, in both of which Griffith played a prominent role).[31]

What Joyce expressed was a broad measure of sympathy for Griffith's programme, rather than one hedged about with dissents and reservations. This attests to both the strength of his nationalist convictions and his realism, and negates the idea that he was too fastidious or disdainful to engage with Irish politics. He did protest at 'educating the Irish people on the old pap of racial hatred', followed by a socialistic gesture of obeisance to the betterment of the proletariat. This did not preclude his support for Griffith, suggesting that he sensibly accepted that no Irish nationalist movement was going to be devoid of animus against England.

Joyce placed disproportionate weight on Griffith's advocacy of measures to promote Irish commerce and economic development, which was a subsidiary aspect of what would become the Sinn Féin programme. Joyce's sympathy for the idea attests to Griffith's astuteness in exploiting the dispiriting impact of the Irish Party's insistence that positive economic measures had to await the concession of Home Rule, and in recognising that something less meagre was called for than the remorseless promotion of the purchase of Irish goods by his rival D. P. Moran. Joyce's receptiveness to this aspect of Griffith's programme reflects the frustration of a generation at Irish socio-economic retardation, which Joyce, living in exile, experienced as a sense of national shame.

The final sentence of the passage quoted was evidently prompted by a comparison by Stanislaus of Griffith with Sheehy-Skeffington. Joyce's response ('a stupid mountebank like Knickerbockers') reaches beyond Sheehy-Skeffington, for whom nationalism was one item in a cornucopia

31. Davis, *Arthur Griffith*, 12; Calton Younger, *Arthur Griffith* (Dublin: Gill and Macmillan, 1981), 10–15.

of progressive politics. Griffith stood apart from other figures in the political and civic space of contemporary Ireland because he articulated an intelligent modern nationalism.

Joyce's emphasis on Griffith's economic programme did reflect surprisingly strong convictions of his own on the subject of Irish trade, perhaps in some degree reinforced by the anarcho-socialistic ideas of direct socio-economic action to which he was briefly attracted in Italian politics. It was, however, striking that Joyce made little reference to Sinn Féin's core policy of abstentionism (declining to take up elected seats at Westminster), about which he may have been sceptical without caring too much either way. It is difficult to resist the conclusion that Joyce's emphasis on Sinn Féin's economic programme was a displacement of aspects of Sinn Féin about which he was uncertain or had active reservations.

Joyce was in some degree fashioning an idea of Griffith's politics that conformed to his own convictions. But what is most important in understanding the nature of Joyce's sympathy with what was to become Sinn Féin is its distanced realism. Philosophically parsing every aspect of what would become the programme of Sinn Féin was an activity he associated with the world of his college contemporaries and Dublin intellectuals, and which he disdained. While he was in broad political sympathy with Griffith, he did not believe it was necessary for him to assent to the full range of Griffith's opinions, some of which he certainly did not share. Joyce's relationship to what became Sinn Féin was dual, existing at two related but distinguishable levels: that of personal affinity with Griffith's nationalism and that of an objectively conceived assessment of Sinn Féin as a phenomenon in contemporary Irish history. He had a large measure of sympathy with the tenor of Griffith's nationalism and evidently believed that it had the potential to attract considerable support in Ireland. Sinn Féin's future depended on its political and electoral fortunes, which were inversely related to the fortunes of Home Rule, and Joyce did not seek unrealistically to condition his support for Sinn Féin by reference to features of its policy he disagreed with. This permitted him to express a restrained and politically intelligent sympathy with Sinn Féin that created a continuity of connection with the Irish political that outlasted his first exile and informed his response to the independent Irish state when it came into being in 1922.

The latitude he afforded Griffith attested to a readiness on Joyce's part to take a relatively pragmatic view of Irish politics. The exaggerated political deference to the Catholic Church was deep-rooted and pervasive in Ireland, as was the linkage of nationalism and moralism. Sinn Féin, like any other party, was never going to be immune from this—though Griffith was certainly not pro-clerical and was viewed with suspicion by most ecclesiastics—and it had the potential to become fervently moralistic, if in a nationalist rather than Catholic mode. Joyce's readiness to discount this risk, which might at first seem surprising, can be explained by his Parnellite-Fenian convictions. For Fenians and Parnellites of the Split, the model of modern Irish history to which they adhered was one in which the political aggrandisement of the Catholic Church occurred in periods of political immobility and was held in check by the emergence of assertive secular nationalist movements, and would be constrained by independence. Whether a fervent moralism deriving from cultural nationalism and the revival of the Irish language would be similarly constrained was more uncertain, but Joyce was enough of a radical nationalist to be prepared to take the chance that it would. This is consistent with Joyce's view of the attainment of Irish independence as a necessary event in the modernisation of Ireland, something more than a concession to the historical grievances and sentimental aspirations of Irish nationalists.

There is a further aspect to Joyce's readiness to suspend his misgivings and to give Griffith the benefit of the doubt. His fear that his Parnellite nationalism was politically archaic, fortified by his dread of the anachronistic, had been in some degree a silent inhibition for Joyce in University College when it came to engaging with contemporary national politics. Appreciative that there was an Irish movement in gestation which articulated a nationalism that was not dissimilar to his own, he was not disposed to hold back from a qualified expression of sympathy, or to hedge that sympathy with conditions he knew to be unrealistic.

There is a striking dearth of references in Joyce's correspondence to the activities of the Irish Party, the speeches of its members in the House of Commons and Ireland that filled the columns of the *Freeman's Journal* (a paper he rarely saw in exile but with whose political style he had been very familiar). That sparsity would be carried over into *Ulysses*. His disesteem for the Irish Party is reflected in his comment on an incident in the 1906 Galway by-election in which the Irish Party nominee, Stephen Gwynn, was challenged by Captain John Shawe-Taylor, a nephew of Lady Gregory who was an advocate of conciliation between landlords and tenants and of administrative devolution. Joyce wrote Stanislaus, 'I see that John Dillon at the Galway election alluded to Capt. Shawe Taylor as a bastard and a blackguard. Note the discrimination.'[32]

'Venereal Excess': Gogarty's Articles in *Sinn Féin*

Of the articles published in *Sinn Féin*, most distasteful to Joyce were the three written by Oliver St John Gogarty, published in late 1906. From a chance acquaintance, Gogarty had become friendly with Griffith,[33] and spoke at the first annual convention in November 1905 of the National Council, a precursor of Sinn Féin.

Gogarty's first 'Ugly England' piece appeared in *Sinn Féin* 15 September 1906. This was a daintily written diatribe on the decline of England after Oliver Cromwell. His thoughts were prompted by the incursion of day-trippers on a brake into the English pastoral setting in which Gogarty was staying on his honeymoon: 'These are the English middle-class, the common men than whom the world cannot show more ugly or more animal human beings. . . . For them the choicest spots of Europe must become sties and lazar houses. For them the sea must receive their shapeless skeleton pier with its bands, promenades, and side-shows; the nigger minstrel must shout and grin, and the slattern comedienne must dance and smile.'[34]

32. Joyce to Stanislaus Joyce, 13 November 1906, *Letters II* 190. It is unlikely that the austere Dillon, though fiercely opposed to 'conciliation', made such a remark.

33. Terence de Vere White, 'Oliver Joseph St. John Gogarty', in *Dictionary of National Biography, 1951–60* (Oxford: Oxford University Press, 1971), 415.

34. O. G. [Oliver St John Gogarty], 'Ugly England', pt. 1, *Sinn Féin*, 15 September 1906.

Gogarty insisted on treating the English middle class and 'the common man' as one and proposed substituting the term 'Sludge' for John Bull. His piece was replete with the snobbish fatuities of the Dublin Catholic professional classes. What Joyce fastened on was the latter part of the article—that by which Gogarty intended to ingratiate himself politically with the readers of *Sinn Féin*. Gogarty complained that it was in deference to Sludge that 'the best of our peasantry have become renegades, and, by selling their strength and manhood as a woman might her beauty enter the ranks of the R.I.C.' This transpired to be a prelude for a theme by which Gogarty was much exercised and which enabled him to deploy his professional expertise to align himself with Griffith's type of nationalism: the high incidence of venereal disease in the British army.

> [Sludge] cries out again at the godlessness of the foreign Governments regarding their treatment of how those women who associate with their soldiers, and he points to his own virtuous forbearance, when all the time, for anyone who cares to buy it, he has published a book—too sordid and too lost to see his own hypocrisy—wherein are statistics to prove, if any proof were needed, that his own army is rottener and more immoral than any or all of the armies in Europe put together. And also as he remains with his eyes devoutly lifted he cannot perceive that at his very feet in India are slave-compounds, where women are incarcerated with more than the horrors of a harem to be debauched at the good pleasure of the Army, a body of men who, as their own statistics show, are already more than half leprous from venereal excess. So concentrated are Sludge's thoughts on prayer that he never has time to realise the fact, however he may denounce it in others, that his Army at home is in a condition so immoral as not to leave even room for such hesitation as that which preceded the destruction of Sodom.[35]

35. *Sinn Féin*, 15 September 1906. The sexual morality of the British army was a favourite theme of *Sinn Féin* in its anti-recruitment campaign. Its issue of 4 August 1906, for example, which Joyce read, contained alongside Griffith's parody of 'Dialogues of the Day' an article

Joyce, whose loathing of nationalist moralising postures extended to a sensibly realistic view of military behaviour, sent on from Rome to Stanislaus in Trieste this edition of what he persisted in designating 'U. I.' 'with an article by Gogarty of which I hope you will appreciate the full flavour. The part about the chummies is particularly rich. I am delighted to see it is only an instalment. . . . Isn't it strange that O.G. should be anathematising ugly England just when I wanted to be in an English watering place. . . . Mrs G mustn't have been very entertaining while in England since O.G. found time to write those two columns.'[36] A week later, Joyce wrote to Stanislaus referring to *Sinn Féin* of 22 September:

> I regret he has not continued his Ugly England yet. I would fain hear more about the slattern comediennes—renegade artist that I am. Starkey [Seamus O'Sullivan] writes two little immortal things in *Sinn Féin* about a fiddler and (damme if I can think of the other), a Piper I think . . . I wish some unkind person would publish a book about the venereal condition of the Irish; since they pride themselves so much on their immunity. It must be rather worse than England, I think. I know very little on the subject but it seems to me to be a disease like any other disease, caused by anti-hygienic conditions. I don't see where the judgement of God comes into it nor do I see what the word 'excess' means in this connection. Perhaps Gogarty has some meaning of his own for this word. I would prefer the unscientific expression 'venereal ill-luck'. Am I the only honest person that has come out of Ireland in our time? How dusty their phrases are![37]

Gogarty's second article appeared in the issue of *Sinn Féin* of 24 November 1906. His pseudo-patrician disdain for modern England now

---

entitled 'Anti-enlistment' by 'Sinn Féin'. It stated, 'The medical reports and revelations tell a terrible tale of the morality of soldiering', and complained of prostitution in India.

36. Joyce to Stanislaus Joyce, 25 September 1906, *Letters II* 164–65. Joyce had written to Stanislaus from the torpor of the Roman summer two weeks previously, 'Lately I found myself wishing myself at a seaside place in England or Ireland: rashers and eggs in the morning, the English variety of sunshine, a beefsteak with boiled potatoes and onions, a pier at night or a beach and cigarettes.' Joyce to Stanislaus Joyce, 6 September 1906, *Letters II* 157.

37. Joyce to Stanislaus Joyce, 4 October 1906, *Letters II* 170–71.

found expression in virulent anti-Semitism, a meditation on 'the Jew mastery of England . . . England becoming Jewry'.[38] Writing to Stanislaus, Joyce tartly conveyed his contempt, adding a sarcastic comment to the effect that Gogarty's bad French was presumably acquired in Oxford: 'I send you S.F. with a column of O.G.'s stupid drivel. I see he has advanced from "le petty mere" as far as "le bête noir". This he learned I suppose from the stolidly one-languaged Sludge.'[39]

Gogarty's third piece appeared in the issue of *Sinn Féin* of 1 December 1906. Dire, inane, and vicious, it introduced the Anglo-Irish 'Snudge' ('the Irish for Sludge'). This characterisation was again steeped in anti-Semitism: 'Strange it is that if his descent is Norman his manner is a Jew's. See the Jew breaking out in Snudge!' Gogarty brought his series to an end with the statement, 'I can smell a Jew though, and in Ireland there's something rotten.'[40] It is unclear whether Joyce saw this, but if he did, it did not elicit further comment from him to Stanislaus.

William Bulfin ('Che Buono') was another contributor to *Sinn Féin* who expressed anti-Semitic sentiments and whose Irish Irelandism had an overtly racist edge. Joyce did not advert to the anti-Semitism but commented to Stanislaus, 'By the way, one of the little illusions which gladden the heart of the staff of *Sinn Féin* is that the English don't know how to pronounce their own language. When an English tourist meets Che Buono, the latter sneers at him because he says 'Haw, I cawn't heawh wot youah saying . . .'. Joyce later derided in similar vein a letter in *Sinn Féin* by Bulfin 'ridiculing a Union Jack regatta in Galway. Two columns are consumed by his account of the talk of the classes'.[41]

On 9 October 1906 Joyce had made his abstractly conceived comparison of Arturo Labriola, who inveighed at the socialist congress

38. *Sinn Féin*, 24 November 1906.

39. Joyce to Stanislaus Joyce, postmark 3 December 1906, *Letters II* 200. In the same letter Joyce wrote, 'O.G., I understand, writes in Sinn Féin under the name of "Mettus Curtius", the gent who leaped into the chasm in the forum, I think' (198).

40. *Sinn Féin*, 1 December 1906.

41. Joyce to Stanislaus Joyce, 13 November 1906, *Letters II* 191; Joyce to Stanislaus Joyce, [?1 February 1907], *Letters II* 209. Bulfin was an emigrant who returned from Argentina to whom Griffith was close, and whose *Rambles in Eirinn*, first published in book form in 1907, had been serialised in *Sinn Féin*. C. J. Woods, 'William Bulfin', *DIB*, 1:977–78.

against the intellectuals and the parliamentary socialists, to Arthur Griffith.[42] In a lengthy missive to Stanislaus in November 1906, Joyce noted a report of a protest of David Sheehy and Francis Sheehy-Skeffington at the playing of 'God Save the King' at the conferring of degrees at University College. He struggled to reconcile his support for Sinn Féin to the socialism that he was still at this stage professing:

> You ask me what I would substitute for parliamentary agitation in Ireland. I think the Sinn Féin policy would be more effective. Of course I see that its success would be to substitute Irish for English capital but no-one, I suppose, denies that capitalism is a stage of progress. The Irish proletariat has yet to be created. A feudal peasantry exists scraping the soil but this would with a national revival or with a definite preponderance of England surely disappear. I quite agree with you that Griffith is afraid of the priests—and he has every reason to be so. But, possibly, they are also a little afraid of him too. After all, he is holding out some secular liberty to the people and the Church doesn't approve of that. I quite see, of course, that the church is still, as it was in the time of Adrian IV, the enemy of Ireland: but I think her time is almost up. For either Sinn Féin or Imperialism will conquer the present Ireland.[43]

Joyce's sense of a defining generational crisis in Ireland owes something to his immersion in Italian socialism. It is striking that he was sufficiently dispassionate, and sceptical of the notion that Irish nationalism would inevitably prevail, to be prepared twice in this passage to allow for the possibility of what he called in the first statement 'a definite preponderance of England'. For most nationalists, weaned on the idea that the eventual prevailing of Irish nationhood was ordained by providence, this was anathema. Joyce followed this with one of his most oft-quoted political self-characterisations: 'If the Irish programme did not insist on the Irish language I suppose I would call myself a nationalist.

42. Joyce to Stanislaus Joyce, 9 October 1906, *Letters II* 173–74.

43. Joyce to Stanislaus Joyce, 6 November 1906, *Letters II* 186–87.

As it is, I am content to recognise myself an exile: and, prophetically, a repudiated one.'[44]

It is Joyce's clearest statement of his objection to Sinn Féin's promotion of the language revival as something that forbade his unqualified personal identification with what was to become Sinn Féin, but did not preclude sympathy with its broader policy. Joyce's use of the term 'nationalist' is predicated on his equation of contemporary nationalism with Sinn Féin, and on having defined the policies enunciated by Sinn Féin as 'the Irish programme'. His ostensible refusal to avow himself a nationalist is subtly but inextricably bound up with his exiled state. The strategic deployment of the political uses of exile is graceful, and opens up a mode of trenchantly aphoristic self-characterisation that would feature in all that he was to write, reaching a brilliant culmination that is quasi-parodic in the creation of Shem the Penman in *Finnegans Wake*. There is a terrible consistency in the fact that he first gave expression to his most extended commentary on Irish politics in his correspondence while he was in exile, from Rome in November 1906.

In the final part of this extended letter, Joyce underscored the fact that the political content of *Sinn Féin* of which he approved was that provided by Griffith as editor or contributor. His condemned Gogarty by reference to two notorious Irish informers, Leonard MacNally and Thomas Reynolds:

> You complain of Griffith's using Gogarty & Co. How do you expect him to fill his paper: he can't write it all himself. The part he does write, at least, has some intelligence and directness about it. As for O. G I am waiting for the S.F. policy to make some headway in the hope that he will join it for no doubt whatever exists in my mind but that, if he gets the chance, and the moment comes, he will play the part of MacNally and Reynolds. I do not say this out of spleen. It is my final view of his character, and if I begin to write my novel again it is in this way that I shall treat them. If it is not far-fetched to say that my action, and that of men like Ibsen &c, is a virtual strike I would

44. Joyce to Stanislaus Joyce, 6 November 1906, *Letters II* 187.

call such people as Gogarty and Yeats and Colum the blacklegs of literature. Because they have tried to substitute us, to serve the old idols at a lower rate when we refused to do so for a higher.[45]

The bracketing of Yeats and Colum with Gogarty was unjustifiable and marked by a raw anger uncharacteristic of Joyce, which owed something to his unhappiness during his Roman sojourn, which the outbreak of the *Playboy* controversy in Dublin some three months later was to exacerbate greatly.

Joyce remained deeply irritated by the sanctimoniousness of Sinn Féin's anti-recruitment campaign, which culminated in an ebullition of lucid fury directed at Gogarty's conception of 'venereal excess' in a letter to Stanislaus from Rome of 13 November 1906. What provoked Joyce was a competition of national moralities which recalled the dialectic of the Parnell Split. On 31 October 1906 Lieutenant Colonel E. Macartney Filgate, commanding the Fourth Battalion of the Royal Irish Rifles, the County Antrim and Belfast Territorial Battalion, inspected the recruits of the battalion at the Victoria Barracks in Belfast. He addressed the recruits on the subject of moral character. This was a carefully rehearsed retort to an attack on him in *Sinn Féin*. He asked the men who were teetotallers to hold up their hands, and a majority were reported to have done so. He then launched into an attack on *Sinn Féin*: 'There is published in Dublin a newspaper which loses no opportunity of pouring contempt upon those who wear the King's uniform. It is a newspaper which openly boasts of its sympathy and alliance with what is known as the anti-recruiting movement—a movement which was responsible for the posting in this city recently of many placards, some of them, to put it in the plainest language, of a peculiarly filthy character.' The *Belfast Newsletter* reported these utterances in full and endorsed them in an editorial which pronounced it scandalous that the law should tolerate the continued publication of *Sinn Féin*.[46] *Sinn Féin* responded on 10 November 1906. Griffith, almost certainly prompted by Gogarty, his principal adviser on sexually transmitted disease, cited the *Report of*

45. Joyce to Stanislaus Joyce, 6 November 1906, *Letters II* 187.

46. *Belfast Newsletter*, 1 November 1906.

Venereal Disease in the British Army, an official publication, and asserted that statistically, 'if Russia be excluded, the immorality of the British Army is almost as great as that of the other combined Great Powers of Europe':

> The appendix to the Official Report shows by diagrams that the immorality of the British Army has been on the increase since 1900. It presents a picture of the British Army in India, which shows that army to be simply riddled through and through with disease. Finally it may be said that the Report shows about one-fourth of the British Army to be annually incapacitated through immorality, and it holds out no hope of raising the army's moral standard.
>
> In the publication 'War with Disease', written by Dr. MacCabe, a British Army doctor, and commended to officers by General Rimington, and published within the last few months, Dr. MacCabe proposes that the British Army should be preserved by having the soldiers disinfected every night. He proposes dealing with the appalling state of affairs that exist by erecting a disinfecting room in every barracks in which the soldier is to be disinfected nightly, under the direction of a sergeant. Such is the state to which the British Army is reduced.
>
> It is in such an army, the only mercenary and the most diseased army in civilisation, Lieutenant-Colonel Macartney-Filgate assures the young men of Ulster their 'moral' welfare is looked after.[47]

In a remarkable letter to Stanislaus of 13 November 1906 from Rome, Joyce's first passing comments were mordantly oblique: 'The editor of S.F. alludes to the British army as the only mercenary army in Europe. I suppose he prefers the conscription system because it is French. Irish intellectuals are very tiresome.'[48]

Joyce returns to the moral argument of the *Sinn Féin* article later, suggesting the letter may have been written in more than one sitting. His magnificently scornful repudiation of the rhetoric of sexual purity embraces not only Griffith but Sheehy-Skeffington and Fr Bernard

47. *Sinn Féin*, 10 November 1906.

48. Joyce to Stanislaus Joyce, 13 November 1906, *Letters II* 189.

Vaughan,[49] an English Jesuit whose sermons were fashionable in Dublin.

> By the way, they are still at the 'venereal excess' cry in Sinn Féin. Why does nobody compile statistics of 'venereal excess' from Dublin hospitals. What is 'venereal excess'? Perhaps Mr Skeffington-Sheehy could write something on the subject, being as [John Francis] Byrne puts it 'a pure man.' 'Infant Jesus, meek and mild, Pity me a little child. Make me humble as thou art, And with Thy love inflame my heart.' Anyway my opinion is that if I put down a bucket into my own soul's well, sexual department, I draw up Griffith's and Ibsen's and Skeffington's and Bernard Vaughan's and St Aloysius' and Shelley's and Renan's water along with my own. And I am going to do that in my novel (inter alia) and plank the bucket down before the shades and substances above mentioned to see how they like it, and if they don't like it I can't help them. I am nauseated by their lying drivel about pure men and pure women and love for ever: blatant lying in the face of the truth. I don't know much about the 'saince' of the subject but I presume there are very few mortals in Europe who are not in danger of waking some morning and finding themselves syphilitic. The Irish consider England a sink: but, if cleanliness be important in this matter, what is Ireland?[50]

There are few comments about Sinn Féin in Joyce's correspondence after 1906. The period where Joyce engaged closely with Sinn Féin transpires to be remarkably short: the major statements in the correspondence run from 6 September to 13 November 1906. Joyce had ceased his commentary to Stanislaus before Sinn Féin was formally constituted, by the amalgamation of the National Council and the Sinn Féin League in August 1907, and before its trial of strength with the Irish Party in the North Leitrim by-election of February 1908. It is a significant phase in

49. In the 'Wandering Rocks' episode of *Ulysses*, Fr Conmee thinks, 'Yes, it was very probable that Father Bernard Vaughan would come again to preach. O, yes: a very great success. A wonderful man really' (*U* 10.24–25).

50. Joyce to Stanislaus Joyce, 13 November 1906, *Letters II* 191–92. That Joyce could commence his response to *Sinn Féin*'s issue of 10 November on 13 November attests to the efficiency of the European postal system, even though it is likely *Sinn Féin* went on sale in Dublin a day earlier than the published date.

the history of Sinn Féin, and in the emergence of Griffith as a (still-minor) political figure in Ireland. Sinn Féin was taking institutional form, and Griffith's role was no longer merely that of a newspaper publisher and editor. Joyce had been an attentive reader of the *United Irishman* for a variety of reasons that were not exclusively political, and neither the political content of the *United Irishman* nor Griffith's pamphlet *The Resurrection of Hungary* prompted a profession of sympathy from Joyce. It took the passage to political action to win something close to endorsement from him. Joyce had made the high, almost abstract election to align himself with Griffith's challenge to the hegemony of the Irish Party. That election derived from Joyce's Parnellite-Fenian political principles, affirmed by the application to Ireland of a conception of political action he had derived from his contemporaneous exploration of Italian socialism.

Joyce's correspondence with Stanislaus in late 1906 made clear where he stood, and there was not much to be added. Joyce had no intention of maintaining a running commentary on the course of Sinn Féin or the prospects for Home Rule in the manner of Dublin intellectuals and political activists which he disdained. Significantly, the frequency of Joyce's references to Sheehy-Skeffington and Kettle sharply diminish, suggesting that his attentive observation of their careers was as much political as personal. The political issue between them was by now clearly defined: *les jeux sont faits*.

The silence in his correspondence did not signal a change of mind on Joyce's part. The debate between Stanislaus and Joyce continued, at least for a time, after it ceased to feature in the correspondence, as episodic comments recorded in Stanislaus's Trieste diary attests.[51]

The *Daily Mail*

Joyce's sense of isolation in Rome was exacerbated by his restricted access to English newspapers, which still tended to give extensive coverage to Ireland. He frequented the Caffè Greco on the Via Condotti,

51. Stanislaus Joyce's 'Triestine Book of Days 1907–09' remains unpublished, but extracts are cited in McCourt, *Years of Bloom*; and in Laura Pelaschiar, 'Stanislaus Joyce's "Book of Days": The Triestine Diary', *James Joyce Quarterly* 36, no. 2 (Winter 1999): 61–71.

which ran parallel to the Via Frattina, where the Joyce family lived for the first four months. Rome was deficient especially by comparison with Trieste in the grand cafés for which Joyce had a predilection ('the first thing I look for in a city is the café'). He referred to the Caffè Greco as 'a little Greek restaurant', though he did not fail to mention that former patrons included Byron and Ibsen. His principal complaint, apart from the prices, was that the only English newspaper it provided was the *Daily Mail*.[52]

The innovatively populistic halfpenny newspaper Alfred Harmsworth (later Lord Northcliffe) established in 1896, the *Daily Mail* was circulated through Paris as well as London and Manchester.[53] It was editorially hostile to Irish nationalism, and its Irish coverage was notably sparse. Its most sustained treatment of Irish affairs during the period of Joyce's sojourn in Rome was a series of twelve articles titled 'The New Ireland' by the writer Sydney Brooks which ran from 12 December 1906 to 16 January 1907.[54] While Joyce often mentioned in his correspondence literary items and notices from the *Daily Mail* as an index of English middle-class taste, he did not refer to Brooks's articles. He was scarcely going to defer to the opinions of an English journalist visiting Ireland, but the view from outside was of value to him. There is little doubt he read them. They strikingly confirmed his sense that a shift was taking place in Irish politics and—what was of intense interest to Joyce—that this shift was capable of bringing about a rapid and radical transformation of how Ireland was perceived in Britain and in continental Europe. Brooks's articles perhaps also suggested to Joyce what he might himself be able to achieve in writing of Irish affairs in Italy. Brooks, an intelligent observer if slightly too impressionable—faintly in the manner of the character Haines in the opening episode of *Ulysses*—was

52. Joyce to Stanislaus Joyce, 7 August 1906, *Letters II* 146. For an indication that the *Daily Mail* was the English paper that Joyce principally read in Rome, see *Letters II* 146, 159, 189, 190, 198, 208. He also, of course, read the Italian press, in part in search of advertisements for private English lessons. Carlo Bigazzi, 'Joyce and the Italian Press', in Melchiori, *Joyce in Rome*, 52–62.

53. Koss, *The Rise and Fall of the Political Press in England*, 358, 368–69.

54. Sydney Brooks (1872–1937) was a British author and critic. Brooks's series was later published in book form as *The New Ireland* (Dublin: Maunsel, 1907).

greatly taken with the idea of an Irish renaissance, political, literary, and cultural, and the emergence of Sinn Féin. He devoted his first two articles to Sinn Féin: 'I bring back from a two months' tour through Ireland no stronger impression than this—that Ireland is becoming Irish. A movement is on foot, broader, grander, and more revolutionary than any even she has ever known. It is a movement of national resurrection, of national self-realisation and self-dependence. . . . There is no modern miracle more stupendous and more fascinating than the rebirth of an ancient nation.' He noted the existence of 'a group of young writers giving expression in prose and verse, passionate and full of a wild charm and tenderness, to the fervour of the Celtic Renaissance'. There was also 'the tentative beginnings of a national drama'. Sinn Féin was the spearhead of the new Ireland, and he was persuaded that 'for winning Irish independence the Sinn Féin policy is by far the most efficient instrument that has yet been devised, easy and flexible to wield, most bafflingly difficult to counter or to beat down, and that if Ireland were to adopt it and stand by it, all effective British rule would disappear from the country in less than twenty years.'[55]

To understand 'the Ireland of today, and still more the Ireland of tomorrow . . . one had to make a weekly study' of the 'vivid, catholic and outspoken columns' of the *Sinn Féin* weekly.[56] It can only have sharpened Joyce's exasperation to find himself reading in Rome a chronicle of the current state of Ireland after he had left it by an English journalist in a Conservative newspaper.

Joyce's concerns remained primarily artistic. Art and politics touched in his preoccupation with the Irish transition to modernity. This was most hauntingly expressed in a passage in Joyce's correspondence referring to the recently dead Ibsen and Christiania (now Oslo). He had mentioned Christiania a year previously, writing to Stanislaus from Trieste, 'Is it not possible for a few persons of character and culture to make Dublin a capital such as Christiania has become?'[57] In his

55. 'The New Ireland, No. 1', *Daily Mail*, 12 December 1906.

56. 'The New Ireland, No. 2', *Daily Mail*, 13 December 1906.

57. Joyce to Stanislaus Joyce, 1 September 1905, *Letters II* 105.

lengthy letter to Stanislaus of 23 September 1906, he famously commented, 'Sometimes thinking of Ireland it seems to me that I have been unnecessarily harsh. I have reproduced in *Dubliners* at least none of the attraction of the city for I have never felt at my ease in any since I left it except Paris. I have reproduced its ingenuous insularity and its hospitality.' He then went on to write, 'Ibsen ibself [*sic*] seems to have disclaimed some of the rumorosity attaching to *A Doll's House*. He said testily to one Italian interviewer, if you can believe the I.I. [*Irish Independent*]. "But you people can't understand it properly. You should have been in Norway when the Paris fashion journals first began to be on sale in Christiania". This is really my reason for constantly plaguing reluctant relatives at home to send me papers or cuttings from them.'[58]

The sharp anguish of his sense of distance from Dublin in its bearing on his art came on Joyce quite suddenly. It followed swiftly on the deepened artistic identification with Dublin that attended the widening of his subject matter from 'Ivy Day in the Committee Room' onwards. How could he from afar render change in Dublin? This was reinforced by his fear of the fading of memory and the waning of his imagination. He wrote to Stanislaus a couple of months after, late in the evening, 'It is a very dark, cloudy day, drizzling rain. I wish some power would lift me as far as, say, Talbot Street and let me walk about for an hour or so and then lift me back again. My imagination is so weak that I am afraid all the things I was going to write about have become uncapturable images.'[59]

He wrote the following month, after reading Rudyard Kipling's *Plain Tales from the Hills*, 'If I knew Ireland as well as R.K. seems to know India I fancy I could write something good. But it is becoming a mist in my brain rapidly. I have the idea for three or four little immortal stories in my head but I am *too cold* to write them.'[60]

Yet Joyce's clarity and tenacity of purpose remained intact. He had maintained in Rome the trajectory of the later stories he wrote in Trieste

58. Joyce to Stanislaus Joyce, 25 September 1906, *Letters II* 166–67. I have been unsuccessful in locating the quotation of what was written on Ibsen's death in the *Irish Independent* or the *Daily Mail*.

59. Joyce to Stanislaus Joyce, 7 December 1906, *Letters II* 202.

60. Joyce to Stanislaus Joyce, postmark 10 January 1907, *Letters II* 205.

of the historical and political widening of the scope of *Dubliners*. In mid-November he researched the First Vatican Council in the Biblioteca Vittorio Emanuele, to enable him to rewrite part of 'Grace'. 'I want now an account of the unveiling of Smith O'Brien's statue to see if MacHale was there. . . . What a pity I am so handicapped'. He recalled a conversation with Stanislaus: 'You remember the book I spoke to you of one day in the Park into which I was going to put William Dara and Lady Belvedere. Even then I was on the track of writing a chapter of Irish history. I wish I had a map of Dublin and views and Gilbert's history [of Dublin].'[61]

Joyce's absence from Dublin was thus a source of acute anxiety before what remained of his equanimity was shattered by the news that reached Rome of the opening of John Millington Synge's *The Playboy of the Western World* in the Abbey Theatre in Dublin in late January 1907 and of the controversy that attended it.

The *Playboy* Riots Perceived from Rome

On Saturday, 26 January 1907, Synge's *The Playboy of the Western World* opened at the Abbey Theatre in Dublin, performed after *Riders to the Sea*. By the second act there were hostile interjections from indignant nationalists. The *Freeman's Journal* denounced an 'unmitigated, protracted libel upon Irish peasant men and, worse still, upon Irish peasant girlhood'.[62] Their opposition was more organised on the second night, 28 January. At the end of the first act, the police were sent for, but they were dispensed with at the end of the second. Synge looked on with impassivity, and according to Walter Starkie, 'his face was pale and shrunken'. Starkie recounted, 'I watched him closely as he sat motionless through the dumb-show of his play, amidst the rioting and insults of the mob, but not a trace of emotion could I discern in the pale mask-like face that gazed unseeing at the raging auditorium'.[63] Yeats arrived in

61. Joyce to Stanislaus Joyce, 13 November 1906, *Letters II* 192–94.

62. *Freeman's Journal*, 28 January 1907.

63. Walter Starkie, *Scholars and Gypsies: An Autobiography* (London: John Murray, 1963), 37–39.

Dublin the next morning and recruited his own claque from the ranks of the undergraduates of Trinity College. During the performance of the second act that evening, the police arrested protesting members of the audience identified by Yeats and Hugh Lane. The Abbey was attended by the police on the succeeding four nights.[64]

Joyce in Rome first learnt of the *Playboy* riots from an account in the *Daily Mail* for 31 January 1907 under the heading 'Riot in a Theatre: Irish "Patriots" Try to Stop a Play'. This reported the conviction for disorderly behaviour of 'a clerk named Patrick Columb'—whom Joyce incorrectly assumed was Padraic Colum but was in fact Colum's father—and Piaras Béaslaí, an Irish journalist, in the Dublin Police Court the previous day.[65]

It was on the *Daily Mail* that Joyce had to rely for the account he sent to Stanislaus in Trieste. Joyce's marshalling of the limited information he had to hand revealed his excitement and exasperation. The *Daily Mail* had reported that 'one of the characters in the play is a self-accused parricide, with whom several Irish peasant girls are in love'.[66] Joyce reported to Stanislaus that 'the story, I believe, is of a self-accused parricide with whom all the girls of a district FALL IN LOVE'.[67]

The *Daily Mail* quoted Yeats's evidence that the play was 'no more a caricature of the people of Ireland than "Macbeth" was a caricature of the people of Scotland, or Falstaff of the gentlemen of England. It was an example of the exaggeration of art'. Relaying the last remark, Joyce added in parenthesis, 'I am glad he has got a phrase to add to that priceless one of Saint Boooooof [Saint-Beuve] about style'. He referred to the schism in the Abbey of which he had known, and to the hostility of the *United Irishman* to the Abbey's productions. He believed Colum and the Theatre of Ireland would prevail over the Abbey of Yeats and Gregory sponsored by Horniman,

64. Hilary Berrow, 'Eight Nights in the Abbey', in *J. M. Synge: Centenary Papers 1971*, ed. Maurice Harmon (Dublin: Dolmen, 1972), 75–83.

65. *Daily Mail*, 31 January 1907.

66. *Daily Mail*, 31 January 1907.

67. Joyce to Stanislaus Joyce, [?1 February 1907], *Letters II* 208.

> which will please me greatly, as Yeats cannot well hawk his theatre over to London. . . . Synge will probably be condemned from the pulpit, as a heretic; which would be dreadful: so that Stiffbreeches [Skeffington] and Ryan really *ought* to start another paper in defence of free thought, just for a week or so. I'm sure Ryan is the man for it. . . . I suppose *Sinn Féin* and *The Leader* will find out *all* about Synge's life in Paris: which will be nice for Lady G and Miss H. And as for pore old A.E. I suppose he is nibbling cabbages up in Rathgar in quite an excited frame of mind at the amount of heresy which is rife in Dublin.[68]

Joyce's objective self-alignment with the nationalist and populist enemies of Yeats and Synge owed much to his exasperation at his remoteness from the scene of the controversy. He somehow contrived to obtain some editions of the *Freeman's Journal* dealing with the controversy, though he complained, 'Of course just the very week I wanted it most Aunt J did not send *Sinn Féin*.'[69]

Among the editions of the *Freeman's Journal* which Joyce secured, and sent on to Stanislaus in Trieste, was that of 5 February containing the account of the debate in the Abbey, which provided the basis for what he wrote to Stanislaus on 11 February. Yeats was lucid and uncompromisingly defiant, though he did a little unwisely declare during his second intervention of the evening, 'The author of "Kathleen Ni Houlihan" appeals to you'. He pointed out that he had called in the police during the production of *The Countess Cathleen* in 1899 'when he was still President of the Wolfe Tone Commemoration of Great Britain (*cheers and groans*)'. Of the interventions by Joyce's contemporaries, Skeffington's afforded an extreme example of unwitting self-parody:

68. Joyce to Stanislaus Joyce, [?1 February 1907], *Letters II* 207–9. He had written earlier in the letter, 'I suspect Synge's naggin is on the increase'.

69. Joyce to Stanislaus Joyce, 11 February 1907, *Letters II* 211. *Sinn Féin* declared, 'Mr. Synge's play as a play is one of the worst constructed we have ever witnessed. As a presentation on the public stage it is a vile and inhuman story told in the foulest language we have ever listened to from a public platform.' It continued in the same vein, and complained that the directors of the Abbey Theatre 'have now got hopelessly away from life' (2 February 1907). Griffith attended the third performance, which was also the first which Yeats saw.

'Mr. Sheehy-Skeffington said he was both for and against (*laughter*). The play was bad (*hear, hear*), the organised disturbance was worse (*hear, hear*), the methods employed to quell that disturbance were worst of all (*cheers and dissent*)'. Francis Cruise O'Brien condemned Yeats's 'coercion'. Joyce's old friend Richard Sheehy declared that 'the play was rightly condemned as a slander on Irishmen and Irishwomen. An audience of self-respecting Irishmen had a perfect right to proceed to any extremes.' The surprise for Joyce came in the defiant intervention of Daniel T. Sheehan, whom Joyce had known in University College.[70] He defended the play 'as a peasant who knew peasants, and also as a medical student (*loud laughter and groans*)' and continued,

> Mr. Synge had drawn a type of character that ever since he studied any science he had paid strong attention to (*laughter*), and that was the sexual melancholic (*hisses and disorder*). He said that in any country town in Ireland they would get types of men like Christy Mahon. He would refer them to the lunacy reports of Ireland (*disorder*) and to Dr. Connolly Norman's lecture at the Richmond Lunatic Asylum (*some laughter and great disturbance*). He came that night to object to the pulpit Irishman just as they objected to the stage Irishman (*renewed noise*). A type of life had been brought on and held up to their praise lately in Ireland utterly unproductive altogether (*cries of 'Order'*).

Sheehan persevered through booing and hissing. He referred to the frequent occurrence in Ireland of a marriage between 'a fine woman like Pegeen Mike' and a tubercular male such as Shaun Keogh, and then stated that the issue 'was not the murder at all (*hisses*), but when an artist appears in Ireland who was not afraid of life (*laughter*) and his nature

70. One wonders whether Daniel Sheehan might not be the doctor referred to in a passage of 'J. M. Synge and the Ireland of His Time' in which Yeats discussed his response to the third night of *The Playboy*, the first he attended: 'As I stood there watching, knowing well that I saw the dissolution of a school of patriotism that had held sway over my youth, Synge came and stood beside me, and said, "A young doctor has just told me that he can hardly keep himself from jumping on to a seat, and pointing out in that howling mob those whom he is treating for venereal disease".' W. B. Yeats, *Essays and Introductions* (New York: Macmillan, 1961), 312.

(*boos*), the women of Ireland would receive him (*cries of "Shame" and great disorder*)'. At this point 'many ladies whose countenances indicated intense feelings of astonishment and pain, rose and left the place. Many men also retired.'[71]

Joyce's letter to Stanislaus of 11 February on the Abbey debate contained a couple of errors, the most notable in suggesting that Yeats had appealed to the audience as the playwright of *The Countess Cathleen* rather than *Cathleen Ní Houlihan*. He had not retained the newspaper itself, which he had sent on to Stanislaus the previous day.

> The debate must have been very funny. Our old Friends Skeff. and Dick Sheehy seem to have just been taking a walk round themselves since October 1904. I read Sheehan's with pleasure and surprise. I would like, however to hear the phrases which drove out the ladies with expressions of pain on their faces. The pulpit Irishman is a good fellow to the stage Irishman. I see Synge uses the word 'bloody' frequently, and the great phrase was 'if all the girls in Mayo were standing before me in their shifts', wonderful vision. Yeats is a tiresome idiot: he is quite out of touch with the Irish people, to whom he appeals as the author of the 'Countess Cathleen'.[72]

In his views on the politics of Irish theatre, Joyce was still working from what had become an out-of-date script: 'As I told you before I think the Abbey Theatre is ruined. It is supported by the stalls, that is to say, Stephen Gwynn, Lord X, Lady Gregory etc who are dying to relieve the monotony of Dublin life.' On Synge he was more measured than in his earlier letter: 'Synge is better at least he can set them by their ears. One writer speaks of Synge and his master Zola (!) so I suppose when *Dubliners* appears they will speak of me and my master Synge.' He recalled his criticism in Paris in 1902 of *Riders to the Sea* to which Synge had paid no heed. His flaccid

71. *Freeman's Journal*, 5 February 1907. A typescript by Sheehy-Skeffington, entitled 'Irish Playwrights and the Irish Public', contains the statements quoted. It includes the Jacobin proposition that 'the will of the artist may need to be sometimes curbed by the direct censorship of the people' (Sheehy-Skeffington Papers, NLI, MS 40, 474/5).

72. Joyce to Stanislaus Joyce, 11 February 1907, *Letters II* 211. Joyce's use of the word 'bloody', though sparing, was a recurrent difficulty in having *Dubliners* published.

observation that 'if Synge really knows and understands the Irish peasant, the backbone of the nation, he might make a duodecimo Björnsen' [*sic*], referring to the Norwegian writer eclipsed by Ibsen, equates the Western people of Synge's play with the peasantry of nationalist rhetoric. Of Sheehan's courageous intervention, he wrote, 'Sheehan seems to be a little different from the other young men with ideas in Ireland. I suspect he must have got a high place in all his exams and so can afford to treat the church on equal terms.' Joyce's anxiety of absence and sense of confinement in Rome then broke plangently through: 'I feel like a man in a house who hears a row in the street and voices he knows shouting but can't get out to see what the hell is going on. It has put me off the story I was "going to write"—to wit, *The Dead*.'[73]

The controversy from which Joyce was shut out rattled on in Dublin. Sheehy-Skeffington had already, in a letter to the *Irish Times*, while professing himself 'for over three years an enthusiastic admirer of Mr. Synge's work', pronounced that, given 'Mr. Synge's bad taste', 'the hostile demonstration, manifestly spontaneous and sincere, was thoroughly justified and distinctly healthy'. He stated sanctimoniously that he himself had participated neither in the groaning nor in the counter-cheering that broke out towards the close of the third act in response to what he delicately termed 'one particularly objectionable phrase'.[74] In March, Sheehy-Skeffington, at a large public meeting under the auspices of the Literary and Historical Society in the Oak Room of the Mansion House, gave a paper entitled 'Stray Thoughts about the Modern Dramatic Movement in Ireland'. He asserted that Synge 'has lately given rein to what Mr. Yeats has justly called his singularly harsh imagination, and has lost himself and wasted his talents in repellent studies of the morbid'. If a dramatist 'wishes his plays to be stage-plays, and if he further wishes to see them staged in his own lifetime, amid applause, he is practically compelled to choose between the applause of the masses of his own countrymen and the applause of a clique'. Kettle, in putting the vote

73. Joyce to Stanislaus Joyce, 11 February 1907, *Letters II* 211–12.

74. 'F. S. S.' to the editor, *Irish Times*, 29 January 1907.

of thanks, vented his Catholic nationalist animus against Yeats: 'He had always thought that Mr. Yeats despised his fellow-man a little too openly to be a good dramatist.'[75] Both thus replicated their response to *The Countess Cathleen.*

In his fulminations against Yeats and Synge, Joyce abrogated the exemplary artistic intellectual patience he had observed in exile. They were also a departure from his consistent artistic resistance to the demands of Catholic nationalist opinion. Joyce's refusal to call to mind his dissociation from the denunciation of *The Countess Cathleen* in University College affords the most striking measure of his psychological disorientation. His reaction attested to the depth of his exasperation at his absence from the fray and—which touched off his resentment—at what he felt to be his exclusion when he was in Dublin from the circle dominated by Yeats, which he habitually directed with remorseless unfairness and lack of gallantry at the person of Augusta Gregory. Above all, the *Playboy* controversy sharpened his exacerbation at the thwarting of the publication of *Dubliners.*

Joyce's reaction was especially ill judged in its timing in relation to Yeats. This was a critical moment in the redirection of their politico-artistic relation towards convergence. Joyce had reoriented his own relationship towards his Irish subject matter, and Yeats's position had for the first time begun to move sensibly closer to his own.[76] The perverseness of Joyce's immediate response to the *Playboy* 'riots' is most apparent in what Yeats said at the end of his third intervention in the debate at the Abbey, reported in the *Daily Express* but omitted in the *Freeman's Journal,* every word of which echoed Joyce's own deeply held sentiments: 'He refused to give up the work of a man of genius because the mob cried out against it. Some novelists represented the Irish peasant as a cherub with wings and no body. Mr. Synge represented him with a body, but without wings, and he was sure that even "the man who killed his father" was a more acceptable figure in a woman's eyes than the

75. *Evening Telegraph,* 25 March 1907.

76. Yeats's role is excellently discussed in Foster, *W. B. Yeats,* 1:359–67.

timid, cowering creature who was afraid to stay in the house with his lover for fear of "what Father O'Reilly would say" (*great groaning and hissing*).'[77]

What Joyce, in the bitterness of his Roman captivity, and with very limited intelligence about the controversy in Dublin and no knowledge of the play itself beyond what was thrown up in that controversy, did not apprehend was the significance of *The Playboy* in the modernistic recasting of the Celtic Twilight. The perfect alignment of the critics of Synge's plays with what he had identified as the political and cultural opposition to his own artistic project should have led him to hold back. That it did not is a measure of the temporary disorientation wrought by his understandably deep sense of frustration at not being in Dublin at a critical moment, as if to affirm the artistic anxieties he had expressed to Stanislaus over the previous months about his absence.

The *Playboy* controversy marked Joyce's exilic nadir, and the only point in his life at which adversity overbore, albeit briefly and in private correspondence, his poise. He quickly reasserted his self-control and reassessed the significance of *The Playboy* for the Irish literary movement. The controversy over the play became for him the obverse of the non-publication of *Dubliners*. He wrote to Stanislaus in mid-February, 'Synge is a storm centre: but I have done nothing.'[78] He wrote to Nora from Dublin in September 1909, during the crisis in their relations brought about by the allegations of Vincent Cosgrave, 'When is this cursed thing going to end? When am I going to start?'[79] When, in August 1912, the hope of Maunsel actually publishing *Dubliners* flickered for the last time, Joyce wrote to Nora in Galway urging her to come to

77. *Daily Express*, 5 February 1907. The report in the *Daily Express*, which Joyce did not see, went to greater lengths to describe the ambience of the debate. It identified two mutually antagonistic younger groups, aesthetes and nationalists: '[A] portion of the audience looked grimly in earnest, the group of long-haired young men, between whom and other little knots of serious youths who affect broad-leafed hats, there appeared to be no love lost.' The proceedings had commenced late, but the early arrivals, who were predominantly hostile to the play, 'amused themselves with whistling, and a song of many verses, having pungent reference to "The man who killed his Da", was sung and applauded with great gusto'.

78. Joyce to Stanislaus Joyce, 16 February 1907, *Letters II* 215.

79. Joyce to Nora Barnacle, 2 September 1909, *Letters II* 243.

Dublin: 'The *Abbey Theatre* will be open and they will give plays of Yeats and Synge. You have a right to be there because you are my bride: and I am one of the writers of this generation who are perhaps creating at last a conscience in the soul of this wretched race. Addio!'[80]

Joyce brought his unhappy sojourn in Rome to an end, returning to Trieste via Florence on 7 March 1907.

80. Joyce to Nora Barnacle, postmark 22 August 1912, *Letters II* 311.

14

The Triestine Joyce

It is a great title of honour for my city that in *Ulysses* some of the streets of Dublin stretch on and on into the windings of our old Trieste. Recently Joyce wrote to me: 'If Anna Livia (the Liffey) were not swallowed up by the Ocean, she would certainly debouch into the Canal Grande of Trieste'.

—ITALO SVEVO, 1927[1]

Trieste is strange. The most wonderful landscape. . . . But it is not a town. One has a sense of being nowhere at all. I had the feeling of being suspended in unreality. Here, the state has caused the city to withhold its character. Naturally this cannot work because it is an Italian town. But it is not allowed to be so. Hence the vexation that one feels everywhere. It is a town that pursues an unwilling existence. What she is, she is not allowed to be.

—HERMANN BAHR,
ON A VISIT TO TRIESTE IN 1909[2]

1. Italo Svevo, 'James Joyce', trans. Stanislaus Joyce, rev. John Gatt-Rutter, in *Memoir of Italo Svevo*, by Livia Veneziani Svevo, trans. Isabel Quigley (London: Libris, 1989), 149.

2. Quoted in N. Powell, *Travellers to Trieste* (London: Faber and Faber, 1977), 137; and in Elizabeth Schachter, *Origin and Identity: Essays on Svevo and Trieste* (Leeds: Northern Universities Press, 2000), 5. Bahr was a playwright and director of the Vienna Burgtheater. Bahr provides the inspiration for the title of Jan Morris, *Trieste and the Meaning of Nowhere* (London: Faber and Faber, 2001), 4.

'THE STAY IN ROME had seemed purposeless, but during it Joyce became aware of the change in his attitude towards Ireland so towards the world. He embodied his new perceptions in "The Dead"', wrote Richard Ellmann.[3] There is a change in Joyce in 1906–7, but it is not to be seen as entailing a belated yearning for Ireland. That is to underestimate both the ferocious emotional discipline Joyce maintained in exile and his intellectual constancy. What exile did entail was a shift in perspective. Ireland and the choices facing Ireland did not look quite the same from outside. What occurs is a major shift within what Joyce conceived as his exilic project that led him to semi-invert the relationship of Ireland to continental Europe he had perceived as he headed into exile. It was where his experiment in exile took him. His initial, somewhat callow belief that exile would yield universal political truths that could remedy Irish backwardness yielded to the realisation that Ireland after all had something to offer Europe. Ireland's relation to Europe was more reciprocal and dynamic than he had originally conceived it to be.

Something else takes place. Joyce's early Parnellite nationalism was abstractly conceived, with the high-minded political disinterestedness of the Irish Catholic elite of which he was precariously a member. Exile was in its material aspect a humiliation, and he and his household had experienced its privations.[4] He was prepared, objectively and without self-pity, to acknowledge a correlation between his own circumstances and Ireland's colonial status, even if he remained extremely wary of the sense of victimhood. With that, something more humane enters his nationalism and his relation to Ireland which had a profound influence on his development as an artist. Margot Norris has magisterially chronicled the process by which Joyce over time came to revise his early aestheticism and to make the material, religious, and political constraints that he encountered part of his art.[5] That shift derives from

3. Ellmann, *James Joyce*, 243; Robert Spoo, *James Joyce and the Language of History: Dedalus's Nightmare* (Oxford: Oxford University Press, 1994), 16.

4. Joyce wrote in his Trieste notebook of the birth of Giorgio on 27 July 1905, 'Before he was born I had no fear of fortune' (in Scholes and Kain, *Workshop of Daedalus*, 99).

5. Norris, *Joyce's Web*.

the adversity of his final two years in Dublin as well as his early exile, but principally bears the impress of exile.

Stanislaus was ill prepared for the apparition of Joyce, Nora, and Giorgio, grubby and 'almost as thin and poverty stricken as Italian immigrants', arriving back in Trieste from Rome on 7 March 1907. Joyce, clad 'in a manky shapeless capecoat', was pallid, gaunt, and unshaven.[6] He had no money. When Stanislaus asked what he would do, he said he would give lessons. When Stanislaus pointed out it was the end of the season, Joyce laughed and replied, 'Well, then, I have you'.[7] In the hard five years to follow, Joyce's impositions on Stanislaus were to strain their relations to breaking point. Stanislaus was acutely conscious that their pupils thought him and his brother, on account of their culture and educational attainments, to be reasonably well off.[8] The perpetuation in Trieste of the anomalous socio-economic state of the Joyces in Dublin, coupled with the persisting non-publication of Joyce's fiction, created the oppressive sense of stasis that hung like a curse over Joyce's household and his relations with his brother.

The publication by Elkin Mathews of Joyce's collection of poems *Chamber Music* in London in May 1907 served only to deepen Joyce's frustration at his failure to secure the publication of *Dubliners*. Stanislaus had walked up and down outside the Trieste post office to dissuade Joyce from his professed intention to countermand publication. Joyce asserted of his poems 'all that kind of thing is false'. The publication was out of phase, and it was *Dubliners* that informed Stanislaus's reservations: 'It seemed to me that the strength of his mind and his moral courage had not gone into [the poems]'.[9] Arthur Symons reviewed *Chamber Music* favourably in the London *Nation*,[10] as did Kettle in the *Freeman's Journal*[11] and Arthur Clery two years later in

6. Stanislaus Joyce, Triestine diary, 7 March 1907, in McCourt, *Years of Bloom*, 85.

7. Stanislaus Joyce to John Stanislaus Joyce, not sent, cited in Ellmann, *James Joyce*, 255.

8. Pelaschiar, 'Stanislaus Joyce's "Book of Days"', 68.

9. Stanislaus Joyce, Triestine diary, 3 March 1907, in McCourt, *Years of Bloom*, 125; Ellmann, *James Joyce*, 260.

10. *Nation*, 25 June 1907, in Deming, *Critical Heritage*, 1:38–39.

11. *Freeman's Journal*, 1 June 1907, in Deming, *Critical Heritage*, 1:37.

the *Leader* (22 June 1909). Joyce later told his first biographer, Herbert Gorman, that Kettle's review was the first and last mention of him in any Dublin newspaper.[12] This was incorrect, but a less wild exaggeration than it might appear. Joyce's concern was characteristically with the mainstream popular Irish media, and he was referring specifically to Irish newspapers. No Dublin newspaper reviewed *Dubliners*. The next extended Irish newspaper mention of Joyce or his work was the mildly horrified anonymous review of *A Portrait of the Artist as a Young Man* that appeared in the *Freeman's Journal* in 1917.[13]

Around mid-May, Joyce's health collapsed. He was laid up for an extended period into the autumn, with a combination of inflammation of his eyes and rheumatic fever.[14] It was an ill omen for a young man of twenty-five. Stanislaus took over his teaching and read to him in the evening: Joyce favoured Arthur Conan Doyle's Sherlock Holmes stories.[15] On 26 July Nora gave birth in the Ospedale Civico di Trieste to a daughter. Before the onset of his ocular problems, Joyce had resolved on the name Lucia, patron saint of eyesight.[16]

Joyce's debility coincided with a recuperation of the imaginative powers and of the acuity of memory of Dublin that he had feared in Rome were waning. By the end of September he had finished 'The Dead', completing the transformation of the cycle of his *Dubliners* stories which he had begun with 'Ivy Day in the Committee Room' without knowing quite how far it would take him. Joyce, his own most unsparing critic, knew the story was a tour de force. He told Stanislaus that he 'had put more work in one story than any of the Irish put into two or three plays'. Stanislaus too considered the story 'magnificent . . . worthy of any of the Russians I have read'.[17] Psychologically the effect was to deepen

12. Ellmann, *James Joyce*, 260–61.

13. *Freeman's Journal*, 7 April 1917; 'A Dyspeptic Portrait', in Deming, *Critical Heritage*, 1:98–99.

14. McCourt, *Years of Bloom*, 122; Norburn, *James Joyce Chronology*, 36–37; Ellmann, *James Joyce*, 262; Stanislaus Joyce to Elkin Mathews, 19 July 1907, *Letters II* 223.

15. McCourt, *Years of Bloom*, 125.

16. McCourt, *Years of Bloom*, 123; Ellmann, *James Joyce*, 262.

17. Stanislaus Joyce, Triestine diary, 7 and 20 September 1907, in McCourt, *Years of Bloom*, 127.

Joyce's frustration at his persisting inability to find a publisher for *Dubliners*, doubtless aggravated by the awareness that the publishers he had canvassed since 1905 had seen *Dubliners* without its climactic story.

'Professor Zois': Joyce's Triestine Pupils

The major change in Joyce's standing as a teacher of English came when he left the Berlitz school in September 1907 and began relying on giving private lessons. While Nora and Stanislaus were apprehensive about the move, it was a success.[18] 'Professor Zois'[19]—he appeared in the General Guide to Trieste of 1909 as 'Joyce Giac. Prof. d'ingl'[20]—took with him some of his former pupils and added numerous others from the Triestine upper-middle class. It meant that Joyce went 'from house to house',[21] at least until he took an apartment on the Via della Barriera Vecchia in August 1910. It probably conduced to a greater degree of self-discipline on Joyce's part and liberated him from rigid adherence to the Berlitz method; his preferred method of teaching English was highly improvisational.

One of his pupils, Mario Nordio, a young journalist, recalled, 'He continually skipped from one topic to the other, embellishing his words with anecdotes told in his favourite form, that of the fable.'[22] With Paolo Cuzzi, who would become a distinguished lawyer in Trieste, he liked to discuss Thomism; when Cuzzi was reading Sigmund Freud, whose works were all the rage in Trieste, and discussed slips of the tongue, Joyce listened politely but said that Freud had been anticipated by Giambattista Vico.[23] Boris Furlan, from a Triestine Slovenian family, who was to be a distinguished jurist who came to play a prominent role

18. Renzo S. Crivelli, *James Joyce: Triestine Itineraries* (Trieste: MGS, 1996), 78.

19. In a letter to Francini Bruni, Joyce complained about the lack of Triestine subscribers, other than Baron Ralli, to 'un libro di Zois', meaning *Ulysses*. Joyce to Alessandro Francini Bruni, 30 December 1921, *Letters III* 56.

20. Renzo S. Crivelli, *A Rose for Joyce* (Trieste: MGS, 2004), 64.

21. L. Svevo, *Memoir of Italo Svevo*, 66.

22. Mario Nordio, 'Gli anni triestini di James Joyce', *Il Gazzettino*, 15 April 1960, cited in Crivelli, *James Joyce*, 144.

23. Ellmann, *James Joyce*, 340.

in Yugoslavian politics in resistance to Josip Broz Tito, was enthused by Arthur Schopenhauer and Friedrich Nietzsche; Joyce told him that Thomas Aquinas, whose reasoning was 'like a sharp sword', was the greatest philosopher.[24] Not all of Joyce's teaching was at this elevated level of discourse. Adriano Sturli, a highly distinguished and innovative Triestine surgeon, took lessons from Joyce. Sixteen pages of Sturli's notes from the lessons survive; three pages were removed by Sturli and apparently relate to the vocabulary of the brothel in advance of a trip he was making to attend a medical conference in London. What survives includes what seems to be an exercise in the pronunciation of the word 'whore'.[25]

Among Joyce's students was Ettore Schmitz, who had written two neglected novels under the pen name Italo Svevo. He had married in 1896 Livia Veneziani, whose father had set up a factory manufacturing underwater paint in Chiarbola Superiore, a suburb of Trieste, beside which stood the Villa Veneziani. The product had military application, and the business was international, with a branch office in Charlton outside London. Schmitz had commercial as well as literary reasons for improving his English.[26] His wife recalled, 'Ettore wanted not only to learn the language but to find an expert guide to modern English. He turned to Joyce, who at that time was a fashionable teacher to Trieste's rich bourgeoisie, and that was how they met. The lessons had nothing to do with grammar; the pair of them talked of literature, and touched on a hundred other subjects. Even I took part in them. The expressions Joyce used were extremely amusing, and he spoke like us in Trieste dialect'[27]—a remark that might suggest that as much Italian as English was spoken. Schmitz's appraisal of Joyce's physical aspect, recalled in 1927 after he had re-met Joyce in Paris, reflects their closeness: 'In appearance Joyce has not changed much from what he was when he arrived in Trieste. He is over forty. Lean, lithe, tall, he might almost seem

24. Ellmann, *James Joyce*, 341–42.

25. Crivelli, *Rose for Joyce*, 28–38; Crivelli, *James Joyce*, 140–42. A list of sweets and jams concludes, 'James eats jams'.

26. Crivelli, *James Joyce*, 78–79; L. Svevo, *Memoir of Italo Svevo*, 31–32.

27. L. Svevo, *Memoir of Italo Svevo*, 66.

a sportsman if he had not the negligent gait of a person who does not care what he does with his limbs. . . . He is very short-sighted and wears strong glasses that make his eyes look enlarged. The eyes are blue and very notable even without the glasses, and they gaze with a look of ceaseless curiosity matched with supreme coldness.'[28]

In autumn 1907 Joyce brought his just-completed story 'The Dead' to Schmitz and read it: Livia went down to the garden to present a bouquet to Joyce.[29] A curious reciprocity underpinned their relations. Schmitz was prompted to give Joyce copies of his two overlooked novels. Returning them, Joyce told Schmitz, 'Do you know that you are a neglected writer. There are passages in *Senilità* that even Anatole France could not have improved?'[30] Livia wrote, 'These words were a balm to Ettore's heart. He gazed wide-eyed at Joyce, delighted and amazed. That day he could not leave Joyce, he accompanied him all the way back to his home in Piazza Vico, telling him of his literary disappointments. It was the first time he had opened his heart to anyone and showed his profound bitterness.'[31]

It was in Trieste that Joyce's interest in Christian liturgy found overt expression. What seems to have been his first attendance at the Greek Orthodox mass in the Chiesa della Santissima Trinità e San Nicolo in the spring of 1905 was a moment of high significance. It gave the Catholicism in which he had grown up, and which he had repudiated, a comparative referent. Intrigued by the ritual, he wrote to Stanislaus describing how the Greek Orthodox mass differed from the Catholic. Joyce's refusal to miss anything, coupled with his poor eyesight, drove him towards the front of the congregation: 'The Greek priest has been taking a great eyeful out of me: two haruspices'. It made him think of his story 'The Sisters',[32] and led him to revise it.[33] It was likewise in Trieste that Joyce's lifelong practice of attending Easter ceremonies, by which

28. I. Svevo, 'James Joyce', 151–52.

29. L. Svevo, *Memoir of Italo Svevo*, 66.

30. Stanislaus Joyce, 'L'incontro di Svevo e Joyce', reprinted in *Joyce nel giardino di Svevo / Joyce in Svevo's Garden*, ed. Renzo S. Crivelli and John McCourt (Trieste: MGS, 1995), 79.

31. L. Svevo, *Memoir of Italo Svevo*, 67.

32. Joyce to Stanislaus Joyce, 4 April 1905, *Letters II* 86–87.

33. McCourt, *Years of Bloom*, 58–59.

FIGURE 14.1. Ettore Schmitz (Italo Svevo) (Wikimedia).

he was fascinated, began. Alessandro Francini Bruni, who lived with the Joyces for six months after they left Pola for Trieste, recalled, 'On the morning of Palm Sunday, then during the four days that follow the Wednesday of Holy Week, and especially during all the hours of those great symbolic rituals at the early morning service, Joyce is at church.'[34] Joyce's sister Eileen Schaurek, who moved to Trieste in 1910, recalled, 'He used to go to the Greek Orthodox Church because he said he liked the ceremonies better there. But in Holy Week he always went to the Catholic Church. He said that Catholics were the only people who knew how to keep Holy Week.'[35] He reported to Stanislaus that the English teacher in the Berlitz school said to him that Joyce would 'die a Catholic because I am always moping in and out of the Greek Churches and am a believer at heart: whereas in my opinion I am incapable of belief of any kind.'[36] Stanislaus recorded his brother as observing that every man was religious and had in his heart some faith in a deity.[37]

34. Alessandro Francini Bruni, 'Joyce Stripped Naked in the Piazza', in Potts, *Portraits of the Artist*, 35–36.

35. E. H. Mikhail, ed., *James Joyce: Interviews and Recollections* (London: Macmillan, 1990), 65.

36. Joyce to Stanislaus Joyce, [?2 or 3 May 1905], *Letters II* 89. The plural reference presumably encompasses the Serbo-Orthodox church of San Spiridione: Crivelli, *James Joyce*, 38.

37. Stanislaus Joyce, Triestine diary, 18 September 1907, in McCourt, *Years of Bloom*, 59.

Joyce was not in the process of becoming a *borghese*. If the pattern of out-of-control drinking, that spanned roughly the summer of 1905 through his Roman sojourn and return to Trieste, seemed to abate after the birth of Lucia in July 1907, his drinking continued to be on a significant scale.[38] His nocturnal descents into the *cità vecia*, the 'old city' in the *triestino* dialect, where he drank in cheap dives, were frequent.[39] He would often dine in the open air in front of what Stanislaus characterised as 'a workman's Trattoria', where Stanislaus was rigid with anxiety that he would be observed by some of his grander students.[40] His young student Mario Nordio recalled that 'during the hours of his

38. The principal source on this is Alessandro Francini Bruni, who lived with the Joyces for six months after they left Pola for Trieste and remained close to Joyce. While his dating of events is often inaccurate, the pattern that emerges is clear. He refers to the summer of 1905 as 'the most tormented period of our communal life together' and to the anger of Stanislaus at his brother's drinking ('it was a comic scene, these Irishmen exchanging insults in Italian'), though Stanislaus only came out to Trieste in late October 1905. He wrote that 'later on [Joyce's] exuberance was broken by periods of moderation, but that summer he reached the summit of his Bacchic indulgence'. He said that Joyce 'resumed his senseless wine drinking' in Rome. Alessandro Francini Bruni, 'Recollections of Joyce' (1947), reprinted in Potts, *Portraits of the Artist*, 40–41, 43. In his earlier 'Joyce Stripped Naked in the Piazza', he refers to his trying to dissuade Joyce from 'a fury of alcoholism and madness' in the year of the publication of *Dubliners*, 1914. Francini Bruni added, 'He stinks of the gentleman a mile away, even when he is stinking drunk'. Alessandro Francini Bruni, 'Joyce intimo spogliato in piazza' (Trieste, 1922), trans. as 'Joyce Stripped Naked in the Piazza', *James Joyce Quarterly* 14, no. 2 (Winter 1977): 127–59, and reprinted in Potts, *Portraits of the Artist*, 33. One wonders if Francini Bruni did not overstate at least the frequency of Joyce's drunken nocturnal bouts post-1907. Dario de Tuoni, who was friendly with Joyce in 1913–15, having been introduced by Francini Bruni, recalled walking with Joyce from the Via Bramante apartment, 'very often stopping to drink a glass of *Opollo*': 'In the early years of his Triestine sojourn he appears to have drunk too much of that wine with serious consequences for his eyesight. When I knew him he was being careful to be moderate and I never saw him lift his elbow too much.' Dario de Tuoni, *Ricordo di Joyce a Trieste / A Recollection of Joyce in Trieste* (Trieste: MGS, 2002), 127. While it could be objected that de Tuoni's relations with Joyce were simply less bibulous than Francini Bruni's, he is a memoirist less given to effect.

39. In his biography of Svevo in which keeps an astute half eye on Joyce, John Gatt-Rutter writes that Joyce, 'in the taverns of the working-class areas around his frequently shifting lodgings, Città Vecchia, Barriera Vecchia and San Giacomo, made a magnificent contribution to Triestine alcoholism'. John Gatt-Rutter, *Italo Svevo: A Double Life* (Oxford: Clarendon, 1988), 229.

40. McCourt, *Years of Bloom*, 62–63, 261n85. The source is a typescript by Ellmann of an unsent letter from Stanislaus to his father ca. 1910 in the Ellmann papers (Richard Ellmann Collection, Box 77).

nightly escapes, it was easy to find him in some of the wine shops in the old part of town, where he carefully emptied glasses of a generous Dalmatian wine and sang in chorus with the wharf porters.'[41] The wine was Opollo, the wine of the island of Lissa on the Dalmatian coast (now Vis in southern Croatia),[42] characterised by Dario de Tuoni as 'a treacherous white wine which, without going to your head, cuts the legs from under you.'[43]

The brothels of Trieste were concentrated in the *cità vecia*. While there is no direct evidence, it seems unlikely that Joyce, having availed himself of the services of prostitutes in Dublin, did not patronise these institutions of a maritime port city. The brothels are the feature of Trieste most starkly carried over into *Finnegans Wake*. The old ghetto of Trieste was within the *cità vecia,* whence 'jerumsalemdo', close to the fruit markets: 'Not to wandly be woking around jerumsalemdo at small hours about the murketplots, smelling okey boney, this little figgy and arraky belloky this little pink into porker.'[44] Stanislaus, in his Triestine diary, makes a point of the fact that he would not patronise brothels, invoking 'my prejudice against availing myself of whores, because they are the scapegoat class of humanity.'[45] In the *Wake,* the Rainbow Girls worship their sun god, Shaun, hailed as 'dear sweet Stainusless', the antithesis of his brother, the Joyce surrogate Shem. Their incantation includes the lines, 'You are pure. You are pure. You are in your puerity. You have not brought stinking members into the house of Amanti. Elleb Inam, Titep Notep, we name them to the Hall of Honour.'[46] As John McCourt points out in breaking Joyce's pseudo-Egyptianising code, 'Elleb Inam' is 'belli mani' backwards, and 'Tipet Notep' is 'petit peton',

41. Mario Nordio, 'My First English Teacher', *James Joyce Quarterly* 9, no. 3 (Spring 1972): 324.

42. Niny Rocco-Bergera, 'James Joyce and Trieste', *James Joyce Quarterly* 9, no. 3 (Spring 1972): 343.

43. De Tuoni, *Ricordo di Joyce,* 127.

44. *FW* 368.8–11, quoted in McCourt, *Years of Bloom,* 54.

45. Quoted in McCourt, *Years of Bloom,* 56.

46. *FW* 237.24–27. This is part of a passage characterised by Bernard Benstock as Joyce's 'most succinct statement' in the *Wake* concerning his brother. Benstock notes John Henry Raleigh's identification of the 'loving irony' of 'the guilty forgiving the innocent'. Bernard Benstock, *Joyce's Again Wake* (Seattle: University of Washington Press, 1965), 219.

French for 'little feet', and more significantly (beyond high fetishism) Triestine for 'ample breasts',[47] either the attributes or real or invented noms de guerre of women professionally providing sexual services.

If Joyce became respected in Trieste, his remuneration remained frugal, and there was an issue of class. Lina Galli, who helped Livia Schmitz (Svevo's widow) in writing her memoir of her husband, bluntly observed, 'In the eyes of the Triestine merchant class, Joyce was a member of the lower class. He lived in a modest flat, and his wife had to work. He was not considered worthy of being invited to parties'.[48] Joyce wrote of the dead Schmitz to Stanislaus in 1932, 'My relations with S were quite formal. I never crossed the *soglia* [threshold] except as a paid teacher and his wife became longsighted when she met Nora in the street'.[49] It is easy to make too much of this. There were issues of cultural as well as social difference: the Joyce household was short of money and conspicuously failed to meet the Triestine bourgeois norms of cleanliness, hygiene, and economy, deviations that were held more against Nora than Joyce.[50] Joyce was not too preoccupied with the social conventions of the Triestine *haute bourgeoisie*, perhaps in part because he himself enjoyed a certain bohemian licence.

Issues of class did impinge on Joyce's erotic, or at least amorous, interests in his female pupils. They are reflected in the set of fragments published posthumously as *Giacomo Joyce*, about his distant infatuation with a 'young person of quality', 'a lady of letters', Jewish, whom he at one point observes throughout a performance from the *loggione*, the gods, whose 'sodden walls ooze a steamy damp'.[51] Ellmann identifies the figure of the woman as Amalia Popper, daughter of Leopoldo Popper, a Jewish businessman.[52] The Triestine scholar Stelio Crise identified

47. McCourt, *Years of Bloom*, 54–56.

48. Lina Galli, 'Livia Veneziani Svevo and James Joyce', *James Joyce Quarterly* 9, no. 3 (Spring 1972): 334. Nora was paid to do the ironing for Livia Schmitz; Maddox, *Nora*, 151.

49. Joyce to Stanislaus Joyce, 29 March 1932, *Letters III* 241.

50. Crivelli, *James Joyce*, 144; Letizia Svevo, 'Joyce si ispirò a mio padre' (intervista di Elvira Dolores), *Il Punto*, 6.

51. *GJ* 1, 12.

52. Ellmann, *James Joyce*, 342–48. John McCourt considers that Amalia Popper remains the most plausible candidate, principally because she 'alone of the three girls has a clear Jewish

a second candidate, Anna Maria (Annie) Schleimer. According to Crise, Joyce had kissed Annie and suggested she marry him, a project which foundered on the objections of her father, Andrea, a prosperous merchant, who was aghast at the involvement of his daughter with a language teacher.[53] A further possible model, more nebulously, is the young Emma Cuzzi, daughter of the Triestine lawyer Giuseppe Cuzzi whom he taught along with two of her friends, all of Jewish or Catholic-Jewish origin.[54] Renzo Crivelli concludes, 'It is not about "one" woman, but the fusion of two (or three if we include Emma Cuzzi)', representing the projection of several women, including Nora, 'united by the common anomalous relationship between a seducer who ends up being seduced (Joyce himself) and a pupil who gives lessons rather than receive them (lessons in desire naturally)'.[55]

The Politics of Trieste

In spring 1907 Joyce was invited by a student, Attilio Tamaro, secretary of the irredentist Università Popolare, to lecture at the university, and by a former student, Roberto Prezioso, political editor of the irredentist newspaper *Il Piccolo*, to contribute articles on Irish politics and literature to its evening paper. These invitations from prominent irredentists attest to Joyce's standing as an expatriate Irish writer in Trieste and came on the basis that he was an Irish nationalist, and that his Irish nationalism struck a chord with Triestine irredentism. It is therefore necessary to assess the impact of the politics of Trieste on the political thinking of Joyce, as well as Triestine perceptions of Joyce's Irish politics.

In the decade that preceded the entry of Italy into the Great War, Trieste—the 'docile Trieste' of which Joyce wrote in *Giacomo Joyce*—enjoyed a certain tranquillity, but one riven by sharply escalating

identity' (*Years of Bloom*, 202–3).

53. Stelio Crise, 'Il Triestino James Joyce', in *Il ritorno di Joyce* (Trieste: Comitato per l'anno joyciano, 1982), 94–95; Crivelli, *Rose for Joyce*, 86–92.

54. Crivelli, *Rose for Joyce*, 40–41; Ellmann, *James Joyce*, 340–41; McCourt, *Years of Bloom*, 200–201.

55. Crivelli, *Rose for Joyce*, 92–94.

tension between its dominant population of those who were culturally Italian, and identified politically with Italy, and its Slav (Slovene) minority. Much of the First World War in Italy would be fought in close proximity to Trieste, with the city a principal strategic target of the Italian army. In the peace settlement, the region of which Trieste was part, known to Italians as Venezia Giulia, along with Venezia Triestina—the Alto Adige (South Tyrol) in the north-west—were the 'New Provinces' wrested by Italy from the collapse of the Austro-Hungarian Empire. The Italian nationalists of the New Provinces were to play a significant role in the triumph of Italian fascism.[56] The fulfilment of the aspiration of the Italian population of Trieste to union with Italy exacted a very high price, and left the city economically diminished and its *triestinità*—the attributes of distinctiveness and politico-cultural hybridity that had defined it—severely compromised. 'Docile Trieste' had become a cockpit of the bellicose nationalism of the First World War and one that, through the ascent to power of Benito Mussolini, was to feed directly into the second.

The central concept during Joyce's time in Trieste was of irredentism, the idea of *Italia irredenta*, the incorporation within the newly united Italy of the 'unredeemed' Trentino to the north-west and, to the south-east, Trieste, Gorizia, and the lower Isonzo: the irredentist cry was for 'Trento and Trieste'. For Italian nationalists, and for the Italian inhabitants of the regions, this was the unfinished business of the Risorgimento that had brought the modern Italian state into being. Yet there was an inherent tension between irredentism and the precepts of the liberal nationalism of Giuseppe Mazzini predicated on the idea of national self-determination, which logically involved accommodating the right to self-determination of the Slovenes also living in the region Venezia Giulia. The politico-geographical issue of Italy's 'just frontiers' was fraught, dividing, as well as European opinion, irredentists from more scrupulously liberal Italian nationalists. The historian Dennison Rusinow finely characterised Italian irredentism as the 'eldest child of *Risorgimento* nationalism and half-brother of Italian imperialism'.[57] If irredentism

56. Dennison I. Rusinow, *Italy's Austrian Heritage, 1919–1946* (Oxford: Clarendon, 1969), 1–5.

57. Rusinow, *Italy's Austrian Heritage*, 15–20. Rusinow notes that 'of all the claims advanced by Italian Irredentism, that to the Trentino always seemed the most reasonable' (31).

seemed mostly benign, the extravagant cult of its pre-eminent martyr Guglielmo Oberdan made clear that it had the capacity to become seized with fanatical zealotry. In 1882, on the occasion of the five hundredth anniversary of Trieste's submission to Austria, Franz Joseph I came to Trieste. Oberdan, an extreme nationalist, resolved to assassinate him but was arrested en route. The emperor most unwisely declined to pardon him, and Oberdan was hanged in a barracks cell in Trieste.[58]

Trieste commands a broad bay in the north-east Adriatic. Behind the city rises the great barren limestone plateau of the Carso that extends as far as the Isonzo River to the north-west, where the Triestines sought refuge from the summer heat. Established by the Romans as Tergeste, the city of Trieste belonged to Austria for more than five hundred years, from 1382 to 1918. From the late eighteenth century, it was the principal seaport of Austria-Hungary. It acquired an impressive merchant fleet, busy shipyards, and a thriving insurance and banking sector.[59] In 1857 the Sudbahn reached Trieste from Vienna, and the railway link tightened the integration of Trieste into the Austro-Hungarian Empire.[60] The city was transformed with the construction from the second half of the nineteenth century of handsome neoclassical and neo-historicist buildings in the Viennese manner,[61] the imperial superimposition of an assertively confident second city on the creaking seaport that Trieste had once been.

The dominant culture in Trieste was Italian, and the Italian population tenaciously upheld the idea of the *italianità* of the city. Its younger writers and intellectuals looked to Florence. Cosmopolitan Trieste was at once hyper-modern and provincial. Freud and Ibsen were read with avidity, and the music of Richard Wagner and Richard Strauss appreciated, but as the young writer Scipio Slataper impatiently proclaimed in the first of his 'Lettere Triestine' for the Florentine journal

58. Mark Thompson, *The White War: Life and Death on the Italian Front, 1915–1919* (London: Faber and Faber, 2008), 15–16. There are obvious parallels with the execution of the leaders of the 1916 rising in Ireland, though given that the Irish rebels had achieved an insurrection against Britain in a time of war, the hanging of Oberdan was more gratuitous.

59. Schachter, *Origin and Identity*, 6–7.

60. Rusinow, *Italy's Austrian Heritage*, 26–27.

61. Schachter, *Origin and Identity*, 7.

La Voce, 'Trieste non ha tradizioni di cultura'.[62] Something of the provincial ennui of Trieste is captured in its characterisation by its most important poet, Umberto Saba, as a city of 'peevish grace' (una scontrosa grazia).[63] That property may have led Joyce to relativise his critical conception of the city of his birth.

If an older generation of Italian nationalists had sympathy and fellow feeling with the Slavs, irredentism in Trieste came to be intertwined with a fear of the Slavs. As Rusinow has written, 'The Slovenes of the Kustenland were one of the nations traditionally considered "unhistorical"', with little consciousness of their own heritage. Slovenes, or Croats, who migrated from working the land to become officials or enter the professions or go into business would once typically have shed their Slavic identities in favour of an Italian identity. That changed with the rapid development of Slav national self-consciousness that followed from the 'Slav awakening' of the mid-nineteenth century. Trieste's hinterland was overwhelmingly Slovene (southern Slav), so that urbanisation as a force came to represent of itself a threat to *italianità* and was given a fillip of active encouragement by the Austrian authorities.[64] The Triestine socialist Angelo Vivante appreciated but sought to inculcate resistance to the fear of 'slavificazione . . . non piu gli slavi assorbiti dagli italiani, ma vice versa',[65] the livid and paranoid spectre of reverse assimilation. These developments prompted a shift from purely cultural irredentism or one that was suffused by a Mazzinian breadth of sympathy with other nations to a more radical annexationist irredentism. Slav resentment was also fostered by the fact that, in Istria and in the rural surrounds of Gorizia, the dominant mode of cultivation was sharecropping; while the owners, frequently absentee landlords, were invariably Italian, the peasants were typically Slav.[66]

62. Schachter, *Origin and Identity*, 16.

63. Quoted in Thomas F. Staley, 'Italo Svevo and the Ambience of Trieste', *Modern Fiction Studies* 18, no. 1 (Spring 1972): 10.

64. Rusinow, *Italy's Austrian Heritage*, 22–23.

65. 'Slavification—no longer Slavs absorbed by Italians but the contrary'. Vivante, *Irredentismo adriatico* (1912), quoted in Schachter, *Origin and Identity*, 30.

66. Rusinow, *Italy's Austrian Heritage*, 24. Rusinow comments, 'The addition of a national to a social conflict, here as in Ireland, proved incendiary'.

Camillo Cavour's proclamation of a united independent kingdom of Italy, of which he became the first head of government, in March 1861 was a culminating moment not just for Italy but for the liberal European nationalism to which Joyce subscribed. The problem was that for most Italians the kingdom was territorially incomplete. In the wake of the creation of the Italian state, the irredentist National Liberal Party was established in Trieste in 1868. Its leader, until his death in 1908, was Felice Venezian, who was related to Ettore Schmitz's wife, Livia. *L'Indipendente*, established in 1877, was the principal irredentist organ, harried by the Austrian authorities, for which Ettore Schmitz wrote a large number of articles in the 1880s, his 'most active commitment to the Irredentist cause',[67] though Schmitz also had some socialist sympathies.[68]

Trieste was politically splintered. According to Gatt-Rutter, 'Piemontese describes how Trieste in the first decade of the century was uniquely gripped by fiercely exclusive political passions and allegiances. A Socialist would never step into an Irredentist café or hotel, while no Irredentist (National Liberal) would show himself in a Socialist, Slav or Austrian milieu. People lived in almost watertight social compartments, signalling their allegiance by their matchbox labels. "Tell me what matches you use, and I will tell you who you are"'.[69]

The political divisions of Trieste owed much to class. While the working classes were socialist, irredentists typically belonged to the upper and middle classes, a division that recalls Joseph Roth's tart observation that in the Austrian empire 'national self-determination' was 'an intellectual luxury for a group that has nothing else to worry about'.[70] The intellectuals and writers hovered between ethnic pluralism and irredentism but, whenever it came to the point, veered in a nationalist direction. Thus in 1915 when the socialists still resisted Italy's entry into the war, Scipio Slataper and the brothers Giani and Carlo Stuparich enlisted

67. Schachter, *Origin and Identity*, 21–24.

68. Gatt-Rutter, *Italo Svevo*, 92–93, 117, 151.

69. Gatt-Rutter, *Italo Svevo*, 184. Giuseppe Piemontese was the historian of the working-class movement in Trieste.

70. Joseph Roth, *The Wandering Jews* (London: Granta, 2001), 51–52. Mark Thompson plausibly comments, 'Of nobody was this more true than Trieste's irredentists' (*White War*, 101).

in the Italian army.[71] The charismatic Slataper, born in Trieste in 1888, who wrote a haunted memoir of place titled *Il mio carso,* espoused the idea of a multi-cultural Trieste but could never shake off the idea of the intrinsic superiority of Italian over Slav culture. He favoured the Italian entry into the war in 1915, candidly with a view to Italy sharing the spoils with Serbia, but with a touch of exaltation. He died by an enemy bullet, fighting on his beloved Karst, at Podgora, a hill above Gorizia that the soldiers renamed Calvary, in November 1915. His female admirer Elody Oblath wrote of his circle that his death 'shattered our fanaticism for ever'.[72]

Joyce's pupil Attilio Tamaro, who had asked him to lecture in the Università Popolare, was an uncompromising hard-line irredentist and historian of Trieste. He was not merely an enemy of Austria-Hungary but a critic of the cosmopolitanism of Trieste which he saw as more or less an Austrian plot. In his polemical *L'Adriatico—golfo d'Italia: L'italianità di Trieste* (1915), he denounced the 'scheming and lawless Germans, Illyrians, Greeks and Jews', whose arrival threatened to deprive Trieste of its national (Italian) character. He rehearsed the well-worn line of the uncompromising irredentists that the Slavs in Venezia Giulia had no national claim: 'The Slavs who immigrated into Julian Venetia have not succeeded in forming even an elementary civilization of their own . . . they have no civilization as they have no history'.[73]

The socialists challenged the irredentist National Liberals and won a great if ultimately not consequential victory in the parliamentary elections of 14 May 1907, held across Austria on universal male suffrage, itself an achievement of the Austrian Social Democrats.[74] In Trieste the socialists took the four town seats, and the Slavs both the country

71. Gatt-Rutter, *Italo Svevo,* 242.

72. Thompson, *White War,* 105, 116–23. Slataper had written in December 1914, 'Oberdan is a duty. He is war.' Joyce must have read Slataper and heard of him through their mutual friend Dario de Tuoni (*Ricordo di Joyce,* 78). He gets a mention in *Finnegans Wake*: 'my slataper's slate' (*FW* 542.32).

73. McCourt, *Years of Bloom,* 98–102.

74. Peter M. Judson, *The Habsburg Empire: A New History* (Cambridge, MA: Belknap, 2016), 374–75.

seats.[75] It was the high-water mark of Triestine socialism. Joyce had suffered a collapse in his health the day before; a couple of months earlier from Rome, he had pronounced, 'The interest I took in socialism and the rest has left me'.[76] It is nonetheless striking that there is nothing to suggest that Joyce took any notice of the event, though that is consistent with the absence of any recorded observation of the quotidian politics of Trieste. When his interest in socialism was at its height, it seemed to bypass Trieste and was mediated through the columns of *Avanti!*, which was published in Rome, and his letters to Stanislaus made no mention of issues peculiar to Trieste and its environs.[77] All of this attests to Joyce's distanced attitude towards Triestine politics in general.

But the socialists are important for an understanding of Joyce's attitude to irredentism. The leadership of the Triestine socialists was Italian, but their socialism was aligned with the Austro-Marxism of Karl Renner, Friedrich Adler, Max Adler, and Otto Bauer. Confronted with the daunting challenge of promoting socialism across a multi-ethnic political space, the Austro-Marxists did not uphold the Marxist shibboleth that nationalist identifications were only superstructural. They subscribed to what was termed a 'personality principle' of nationhood against the idea of nationhood prescribed by territory or history. At its conference in Brno in 1899, the Social Democratic Party espoused a programme under which Austria would be federalised as a nationally egalitarian, politically democratic state.[78] The Triestine party leadership under Valentino Pittoni and the editor of the party's Trieste daily newspaper *Il Lavoratore*, Angelo Vivante, were clear and reasoned in their opposition to irredentism, adamant that the interests of the working class were best served by a democratised Austria. The socialist programme, deriving from the Brno Congress of the Second International of 1906, was an autonomous Trieste: what that meant was a Trieste that

75. Gatt-Rutter, *Italo Svevo*, 226–27.

76. Joyce to Stanislaus Joyce, [?1 March 1907], *Letters II* 217.

77. John McCourt's surmise that 'Joyce's socialist views may have owed more to Trieste than has previously been recognised' (*Years of Bloom*, 72) is hard to accept without qualification and explanation.

78. Judson, *Habsburg Empire*, 373–74.

was not ceded to Italy.[79] Joyce said nothing or is not recorded as saying anything explicit on Triestine socialism or on irredentism. If Joyce post-Rome no longer identified himself as a socialist, he had not renounced socialist tenets or social analysis. There is nothing in what survives of Joyce's observation of Triestine politics that relates to Triestine socialism. Yet Joyce's holding back from irredentism was consistent with the principles of Triestine socialism that were largely supported by the city's working class. In the end the revolutionary fervour unleashed by the Russian Revolution destabilised the Triestine Socialist Party, and the socialist conception of an autonomous Trieste was lost in the ceding of Trieste to Italy,[80] even before Mussolini's accession to power in Rome.

Joyce and Triestine Irredentism

Joyce's social circles in Trieste were heavily tilted towards moderate irredentism. Presumably through Francini Bruni, whom he knew first as a fellow language teacher in Pola and Trieste, but who joined *Il Piccolo* in June 1906, he met Roberto Prezioso, political director of *Il Piccolo* and acting editor of its evening paper *Il Piccolo della Sera*, who asked him to contribute articles.[81] That led to his meeting the writer and journalist Silvio Benco. The owner of *Il Piccolo* was Teodoro Mayer, a co-eval of Ettore Schmitz and, like Schmitz, a Jew of Hungarian antecedents. Mayer, a moderate irredentist drawn also to socialism, rapidly became 'a member of the caucus of grey eminences who managed Trieste's national and political life from the behind the scenes.'[82] He collaborated closely with Felice Venezian, leader of the National Liberals, with whom he founded a Masonic lodge, Alpi Giulie.[83] Mayer is mentioned by Ellmann, in a footnote, as a possible model for Leopold Bloom, though, if one wishes to engage in that indeterminate quest, then Ettore Schmitz (Italo Svevo) is a far more plausible candidate, as Ellmann himself

79. Rusinow, *Italy's Austrian Heritage*, 87–89; Thompson, *White War*, 105.

80. Rusinow, *Italy's Austrian Heritage*, 89–91.

81. Ellmann, *James Joyce*, 255.

82. Judson, *Habsburg Empire*, 55.

83. Gatt-Rutter, *Italo Svevo*, 54–55, 110. See also McCourt, *Years of Bloom*, 106.

believed.[84] Joyce and Stanislaus taught members of the family of Felice Venezian,[85] who also was a relative of Schmitz's wife, Livia. Joyce's friend and pupil Nicolò Vidacovich, lawyer, translator, and essayist, also an irredentist, provided a nexus to a younger generation of Triestine writers and intellectuals. He was president of the irredentist La Giovane Trieste (Young Trieste) and of the Società di Minerva.[86] Triestines of all persuasions were much given to societies.

Joyce could not be said to have been a member of an irredentist circle. He did not frequent meetings of Triestine writers and intellectuals in the grander cafés of Trieste. His professional and personal acquaintances were not confined to Italians. He taught pro-Austrian Triestines, including the wife and children of the governor, Prince Konrad Hohenlohe-Schillingsfürst.[87] The assimilated Slovenes he taught included Count Mario Tripcovich, son of a Triestine shipbuilder, and he had closer relations with Nicolò Vidacovich, with whom he translated Synge's *Riders to the Sea* in 1908, and the first version of Yeats's *Countess Cathleen* in 1911.[88] It was through Vidacovich that he found the four businessmen, also Slovenes, whom he enlisted in the project to establish a cinema in Dublin.[89] Joyce taught Josip Wilfan, a leading figure among the Slovenes of Trieste and a post-war member of the Italian parliament;[90] Boris Furlan, already

84. Gatt-Rutter, *Italo Svevo*, 234–35; Ellmann, *James Joyce*, 374–75. Ellmann observes that there is no evidence that Joyce and Mayer were closely acquainted. Joyce did know Mayer; McCourt, *Years of Bloom*, 106. A footnote in Gorman's biography to Joyce's first mention in 1906 of a new story for *Dubliners* which 'deals with Mr. Hunter' seems designed to spike the quest for an original for Bloom: 'It may be mentioned here that this Mr. Hunter of Dublin was only one of the two living models for the character of Leopold Bloom in *Ulysses*. There were two others, one in Trieste and the other in Zurich, the former a Greek and the latter a Hungarian'. Gorman, *James Joyce*, 176.

85. McCourt, *Years of Bloom*, 106.

86. McCourt, *Years of Bloom*, 105–6; Gatt-Rutter, *Italo Svevo*, 231.

87. McCourt, *Years of Joyce*, 102–3, 242–43.

88. Ellmann, *James Joyce*, 266–67.

89. Ellmann, *James Joyce*, 300–301; Ivo Vidan, 'Joyce and the South Slavs', in *Atti del Third International James Joyce Symposium*, ed. Niny Rocco-Bergera (Trieste: Università degli studi, Facoltà di magistero, 1974), 121, published also in *Studia Romanica et Anglica Zagrabiensia* 33–36 (1972/73): 272. The citations are from the journal.

90. Vidan, 'Joyce and the South Slavs', 274.

mentioned, was an employee in Wilfan's office and became a pupil and friend.[91] Another pupil, Alois Skrivanich, was a Croatian gallant who was 'a source of information about the corruptions and distortions of Slovene and Croatian words in the Triestine melting pot'[92] (the *triestino* dialect). Skrivanich was killed early in the war in the Carpathians. He is honourably mentioned in *Finnegans Wake*, contributing to a surname for Shem as he is denounced by his sanctimonious brother Shaun, who accuses him of plagiarism: 'Shem skrivenitch, always cutting my prhose to please his phrase'.[93]

If Joyce's engagement with Slav culture was slight, as Ivo Vidan points out with measured acerbity in his authoritative treatment of the subject,[94] it would be a mistake to conclude that his somewhat sceptical assessment of Triestine irredentism was not informed by a consciousness of its having pushed the Slovene population to the margins.

Was Joyce an irredentist, or rather, as a non-Triestine, was he pro-irredentist? It was an issue on which he contrived to remain adroitly non-committal. Some weight is to be given to his silence. It seems clear that he had significant reservations about irredentism,[95] but as an Irishman living in Trieste he did not feel obliged to give expression to them, and thereby cause offence to his Triestine irredentist friends. He was conspicuously non-irredentist rather than anti-irredentist. Silvio Benco was almost alone in posing the issue of whether Joyce was pro-irredentist. Having discussed Joyce's Irish political concerns as manifested in his Triestine journalism, Benco concluded with astuteness and tact, 'He could not suffer in the same way over Trieste's dogged effort towards national freedom. But precisely because he was not

91. Vidan, 'Joyce and the South Slavs', 272.

92. Vidan, 'Joyce and the South Slavs', 274.

93. *FW* 423.15–16; Vidan, 'Joyce and the South Slavs', 274. In Slovene and Croatian, *skriven* means 'hidden'.

94. Vidan, 'Joyce and the South Slavs', 274–77.

95. Richard Robinson's judgement that Joyce 'retained a certain detachment from the Triestine Irredentist enterprise' is perhaps an understatement. Richard Robinson, 'A Stranger in the House of Habsburg: Joyce's Ramshackle Empire', *James Joyce Quarterly* 38, no. 3/4 (Spring/Summer 2001): 332.

passionately and painfully involved, he could consider it with intelligent sympathy.'[96]

One might approach a consideration of Joyce and irredentism from two perspectives, the first to do with Joyce's status in Trieste, and the second at the level of political judgement. On the first, exile defined a relationship to the place of exile, as well as to the country of departure. There was an issue about the appropriateness of intervention in a country where Joyce was present for some years but in which he might not remain, an issue of exilic protocol. There was Joyce's characteristic epistemological scruple: he knew he could not know Trieste or Triestine politics as intimately as he comprehended the sullen polity that was Dublin and Ireland. To pronounce on the politics of a place implied something greater than transient presence. Somewhere at the back of Joyce's mind was perhaps the recollection of Skeffington's unbounded espousal of radical causes.[97] There were therefore several considerations to warrant what was Joyce's first (and consummately successful) sustained experiment in more or less complete political silence.

From the second perspective, that of the substantive politics of irredentism, there was much to demarcate the position of Trieste from the situation of Ireland: Joyce's inner measuring of Trieste was significantly against Ireland rather than against Dublin, so that they could never be quite commensurate. Objectively there were major differences. The most obvious is that between Trieste as a city denied inclusion in the newly united Italian state and Ireland as a nation denied freedom. Moreover, not merely was the yoke of Vienna comparatively light,[98] but the connection to the empire was undeniably the motor that

96. Potts, *Portraits of the Artist*, 53–54.

97. Eugene Sheehy recounted in his memoir that the editor of the *Freeman's Journal* had asked Skeffington to submit a sub-leader on rats. The editor read the piece submitted. '"Mr. Skeffington", he said plaintively, "I really do not know what I can do with you. You have written about rats as if they were an oppressed nationality"'. Eugene Sheehy, *May It Please the Court*, 34.

98. Richard Robinson, in his article 'Stranger in the House' (324–25, 334), has reasonably (and with some courage) ventured the proposition that the Austro-Hungarian monarchy was not an empire in its modern sense, meaning mainly in the sense favoured in post-colonial studies.

propelled the economy of Trieste, while it was a tenet of Griffith's Sinn Féin and of the wider Irish nationalism, fully subscribed to by Joyce, that the union with Britain had retarded Ireland's economic development. Two entries in Stanislaus's Triestine diary in April 1907, in the immediate prelude to Joyce's transformative lecture 'L'Irlanda: Isola dei santi e dei savi', which he delivered on 27 April, suggest that Joyce was fully alert to and had discussed with Stanislaus the economic difference. Stanislaus recorded on 20 April that in relation to Ireland his brother believed that 'no intellectual or artistic revival is possible until an economic one has already completed because people haven't the time or the stomach to think.'[99] This was almost two months after Joyce's admission to Stanislaus in a letter that socialism had ceased to interest him; it suggests that if he was no longer studying socialism, he had not renounced its precepts. In the second entry two days later, on 22 April 1907, Stanislaus wrote, '[The irredentists] don't count of course that now Venice is under Italian government, and is poor, that Trieste was under Italian government and was poor, but Trieste is under Austrian government and is rich.'[100] This admittedly is a comment of Stanislaus only, who evidently believed—in what was a pretty significant error, reflecting the struggle to apprehend the history of Trieste while living there and perhaps a false Irish assumption translated to Trieste from conversations with irredentists—that there was a time when Trieste had been Italian. It is hard to resist the suspicion that for Joyce there was something complacent and facile about irredentism, and perhaps somewhat passive (irredentism was less a liberationist than an annexationist concept, in which irredentists, if they sought to hasten the hour, awaited deliverance by Italy), that left him not so much cold as somewhat bored.

In holding out against irredentism, Joyce maintained a fastidious consistency with his pluralistic conception of Irish nationalism. His academic formation was Italian, and his social and intellectual ambience in Trieste overwhelmingly irredentist, but he assumed a position of reticence which aligned him with the Slavs of Trieste and its hinterland, and

99. Stanislaus Joyce, Triestine diary, 20 April 1907, in McCourt, *Years of Bloom*, 120.
100. Stanislaus Joyce, Triestine diary, 22 April 1907, in McCourt, *Years of Bloom*, 102.

the politics of the working class of Trieste. It was an enriching, a deepening and broadening out, rather than a redirecting of his Irish political thinking.[101] That is the coherence that allowed him to merge his political experience of Trieste with that of Dublin in *Ulysses*.

Not merely did Joyce decline to take a position on the irredentist issue, he conspicuously refuses to make comparisons between Ireland and Trieste in his journalism, his lecture, or even in recorded comments. This is a radical departure from the tortuous comparisons of Ireland and Italy that characterised Joyce's meditations on Italian revolutionary syndicalism in 1906–7 which only ceased some two months before Joyce gave his lecture 'L'Irlanda: Isola dei santi e dei savi' to the Università Popolare. His lecture was about what Ireland (an Ireland defined by its ethnic heterogeneity) might have to impart to Europe rather than to learn from the more advanced states of Europe, but more than that it was, or at least initiated, a breaking of the mould of static comparisons of polities and economies, which pitted one state or political culture against another, in favour of a more fluid conception of ethnic and cultural migrations and influences bearing on the ordinary life of humanity. That Joyce was at the time living in a city that exemplified multi-ethnicity, which Stanislaus compared to a European 'salad',[102] is of importance.

If Joyce avoided direct comparison between Trieste and Ireland in his lecture, he deftly co-mingles the two through their ethnic and cultural hybridity, thereby taking up the challenge of demonstrating that the historical heterogeneity of the Irish was not so different from the more obvious diversity of the contemporary population of Trieste. Discussing the difference between the Irish and the English, he wrote of the Irish, 'Our civilization is an immense woven fabric in which very different elements are mixed, in which Nordic rapacity is reconciled to Roman law, and the new bourgeois conventions to the remains of a Syriac religion [Christianity]. In such a fabric, it is pointless searching for a thread that has remained pure, virgin and uninfluenced

101. Rocco-Bergera, 'James Joyce and Trieste'. (The nearest contemporary Irish comparator of Triestine irredentism is Catalan independence, which attracts blithe nationalist or *bien-pensant* sympathies from Ireland.)

102. Stanislaus Joyce, Triestine diary, 16 January 1907, in McCourt, *Years of Bloom*, 50.

by other threads nearby. What race or language can nowadays claim to be pure?'[103]

This is not a passing observation, but the hinge on which Joyce's reasoning pivots. That Joyce, in addition to sustaining the weight of the tacit equation—or rather co-universalisation—of Ireland and Trieste, is straining to endow Ireland with the credentials of nationhood (the 'immense' fabric of 'our civilization') confirms Kevin Barry's proposition that Joyce is at once expressing agreement with the argument of Ernest Renan that 'there is no pure race' and 'the most noble countries, England, France, Italy are those where blood is most mingled' and challenging Renan's exclusion of Ireland ('the only country in Europe where the native can produce the titles of his descent').[104] The lecture is also pivotal in Joyce's oeuvre and political thinking, holding in perfect balance an overt and traditional nationalism and his ambition to reconceptualise Ireland.

The lecture moreover contains Joyce's only public comment that bears on irredentism—his likening of the Celtic spirit to the Slavic one[105]—and is his only actually recorded statement on the subject. This swerve is the single most important indication of Joyce's attitude to irredentism. Accepting the premise of nationalism, he is preparing to consider the issue of minorities in nation-states and does so integrally. The implication that the Slavs provide a better parallel to Ireland than the Italians of Trieste is highly calculated since the idea that the Italians were oppressed was central to the rhetoric and mythology of irredentism. It is an oblique criticism of the irredentist hostility to the Slovenes and denial of their claim to nationhood, which was aligned with the critique of irredentism by socialists and even by some of the enlightened and more moderate irredentists, such as Scipio Slataper. Joyce did not like the bullying of the Slovenes. His veiled criticism of irredentism echoed his deprecation of the Hungarian oppression of ethnic minorities within its frontiers in *Stephen Hero*. Joyce had there scorned Griffith's

103. *OCPW* 118.

104. *OCPW* 318n58. The quotations are taken from William G. Hutchinson's translation of Ernest Renan's *The Poetry of the Celtic Races, and Other Studies* (London: Walter Scott, 1896).

105. *OCPW* 124. Richard Robinson also makes this point ('Stranger in the House', 329).

'Hungarian policy', which advocated the emulation of the dual monarchy of Austro-Hungary, by reference to 'the capable aggressions of the Magyars upon the Latin and Slav and Teutonic populations, greater than themselves in number'.[106]

It is true that Joyce was giving the lecture at the invitation of Attilio Tamaro, who was a hard-line irredentist publicist, to whom Joyce was determined not to be politically beholden. It is perhaps also possible that Joyce was sending a polite signal to his more moderate irredentist friends not to push him too far towards supporting the irredentist cause or equating it with Irish nationalism.

Giacomo Joyce, a set of connected epiphanies centred on a Jewish woman with whom the narrator is enamoured, gives an idea of Joyce's personal thinking. The fragments were written between 1911 and 1914; Joyce never sought to publish them, and probably had not written them for publication. They include the sentence, 'Trieste is waking rawly: raw sunlight over its huddled browntiled roofs, testudoform; a multitude of prostrate bugs await a national deliverance.'[107] The odd but strangely effective image of bugs awaiting a national deliverance can only be a moderately sarcastic reference to the irredentism of the city. In another passage the irredentist sympathies of the woman are rendered coldly: 'She thinks the Italian gentlemen were right to haul Ettore Albini, the critic of the *Secolo*, from the stalls because he did not stand up when the band played the Royal March. She heard that at supper. Ay. They love their country when they are sure which country it is.'[108]

This refers to the episode when the pacifist and anti-imperialist Albini, a music critic for *Avanti!* (Joyce in Trieste was much interested in at least some music critics), had heroically refused to stand for the

106. *SH* 62. Of the *Ausgleich* of 1867, Judson has written, 'Many federalist nationalists accused the Settlement of enshrining Hungarian and German national domination over the other nationalities in each half of the empire' (*Habsburg Empire*, 262–63).

107. *GJ* 8. Richard Robinson's exegesis of this sentence, if brilliant, does not convince ('Stranger in the House', 330). In 'prostrate' there is a suggestion of ineffectuality or passivity, which matches the more benign 'docile Trieste' (*GJ* 10).

108. *GJ* 9. In *Ulysses*, John Wyse asks why a Jew can't love his country like the next fellow: 'Why not? says J. J., when he's quite sure which country it is' (*U* 12.1628–30).

'Marcia Reale', the anthem of the Kingdom of Italy, at a concert in La Scala in support of the Italian Red Cross and the families of soldiers killed or wounded in Libya,[109] where Italy was at war with the Turks and indigenous Arabs in 1911–12.

In March 1922 Joyce wrote to Stanislaus from Paris that the 'Dail Eirann [*sic*] Minister of Publicity' Desmond FitzGerald (who was director of publicity for Dáil Éireann from April 1919 until he was appointed minister for external affairs in the provisional government in August 1922) had visited him 'and asked me if I intended to return to Ireland at present. I told him not for the present. One redeemed city (and inhabitants thereof) will last me for a few years more.'[110] Directed equally at Trieste and Dublin as the capital of the newly independent Ireland, it was a pretty good joke, but it attests also to Joyce's lack of affinity with irredentism. Joyce's affective compact with his Triestine irredentist friends was sternly unilateral: it rendered them sympathetic to, and understanding of, his Irish nationalism. There was no reciprocating gesture.

There is a strange crossover in the fraternity of Joyce and Stanislaus. They had taken different views on Sinn Féin in Ireland, with Stanislaus favouring the more moderate Irish Parliamentary Party. If Joyce was at best reticent on the subject of irredentism, Stanislaus was an ardent irredentist.[111] It is even possible that Stanislaus, grotesquely imposed on by Joyce in Trieste, was taking the opportunity to demonstrate his independence of judgement; his Triestine diaries give the impression that they had previously discussed the curious politics of *italianità* in Trieste. Stanislaus was no match in political acuity for his brother. The consequences were significant, if indirect. While Joyce left for Zurich when Italy entered the First World War, Stanislaus was interned by the Austrian authorities for the duration of the war. Admittedly the brothers' relations had by then cooled, or at least they had seen less of each other in the preceding years; but their divergent approaches to irredentism contributed to the growing apart of the two brothers.

109. *GJ* xiv.

110. Joyce to Stanislaus Joyce, 20 March 1922, *Letters III* 61.

111. Their circumstances were not identical. There was always a high possibility that Joyce would move on from Trieste, whereas Stanislaus was a resident of Trieste until his death.

Triestine Perceptions of Joyce's Politics

Of the assessments by Triestines of Joyce's Irish politics, the most important is that of Ettore Schmitz (Italo Svevo) in a lecture given in Milan in 1927, five years after the publication of *Ulysses*. Some twenty years older than Joyce, Schmitz was wry, temperate, and phlegmatic. He understood Joyce very well, so that he could write with magisterial understatement of Joyce's litany of grievances, 'I was always much amused by Joyce's indignation at the misadventures that befell him.' His analysis of a Joyce 'driven by his fate into many rebellions in order to succeed in being himself' is penetrating. 'Whenever you read a biographical notice of Joyce, you find definitely stated that he never took any share in his country's struggles; and that in his *Ulysses* the part of Telemachus (far from the struggle) is appropriately given to the character who most resembles him. On the contrary, Joyce took part in those struggles from afar, from Trieste, with two articles in *Il Piccolo della Sera*.'[112]

Schmitz presumably had in mind Joyce's articles 'Ireland at the Bar' ('L'Irlanda alla sbarra') and 'The Shade of Parnell' ('L'ombra di Parnell'), the latter of which was 'magnificent in its indignation and irony'. He quotes the close of the second, in which Joyce states that Parnell's countrymen 'did not throw him to the English wolves: they tore him to pieces themselves':

> Here you see Joyce walking through the world with one sole comrade in faith, Parnell. And Parnell is dead. Our poet here, it seems, is Zarathustra carrying the great man's corpse on his back.
>
> He is twice a rebel, against England and against Ireland. He hates England and would like to transform Ireland.[113]

Schmitz returns to the Parnell theme in considering the character of Stephen Dedalus in *A Portrait*: 'As a child he is entrusted to the care of the Jesuits. Already he is marked out to be an artist and no education can obliterate that hallmark. See how his whole soul responds to the

112. I. Svevo, 'James Joyce', 157.
113. I. Svevo, 'James Joyce', 154.

news of Parnell's death. He is ten years of age, just the age Joyce was at the time.'[114] Schmitz realised that Joyce's relationship to Trieste and to Italy was complicated, perhaps enriched, by his Irish sympathies: 'In Joyce's culture there is a marked Italian bias, accentuated by the desire, which was very lively at some periods of his life, to feel less English.'[115]

In his eccentric and self-indulgent lecture of 1922, entitled 'Joyce intimo spogliato in piazza' (later translated and published as 'Joyce Stripped Naked in the Piazza'), Joyce's teaching colleague and drinking companion Alessandro Francini Bruni related some of the mordant fables of Ireland that Joyce invented to keep boredom at bay in his teaching. Francini Bruni otherwise characterised Joyce's patriotism as being of the drunken Irish type. He recounts Joyce frequenting a bar on the Via Belvedere kept by a Sicilian called Storky: 'Although already drunk and glassy-eyed, he enjoyed stuffing poor Storky's head with extraordinary stories about the Emerald Isle.'[116] He portrayed the Irish nationalist in his cups, alternately scornful and sentimental: 'In those moments if you asked him, for example, about Ireland, you would have heard a man discoursing on the heartrending state of his land, all the while showering it with scorn, his moist eyes gazing at some point in the void. In an outburst of weeping he would speak of the tears cried from thousands of eyes by thousands of tormented souls over the course of the centuries, trying himself to drown those tears in a river of eloquence. Here was the sorrow of the laughing Pagliacci.'[117]

Francini Bruni returned to this theme in his 1947 'Ricordi su James Joyce', adding that, 'however ironically he may have treated it, Ireland was his agony. His spirit, particularly when he was depressed, would always return to Ireland.'[118]

It is Francini Bruni who advanced the idea of Joyce's suspicions of governments. In the provocative, invented vignettes, there is one in

114. I. Svevo, 'James Joyce', 159.

115. I. Svevo, 'James Joyce', 150. Svevo was astute in recognising that his friend's nationalism was variant in intensity.

116. Potts, *Portraits of the Artist*, 31.

117. Potts, *Portraits of the Artist*, 33.

118. Potts, *Portraits of the Artist*, 41.

relation to the tax collector, in which he has Joyce referring Venezia Guilia to 'that swindler, his master. Today, the swindler is the government in Vienna. Tomorrow it could be the one in Rome. But whether Vienna or Rome or London, to me governments are all the same, pirates'.[119] If there is some licence in a vignette, Joyce gave a more elaborate statement of his thinking to Francini Bruni when he voiced his disillusion, already quoted, with politics, and with Italian socialism in particular: 'His attitude is as enigmatical towards politics as towards the Church. He told me one day. "My political faith can be expressed in a few words. Monarchies, constitutional or not, repel me. Republics, bourgeois or democratic, also repel me. Kings are clowns. Republics are worn out slippers that fit every foot. The Pope's temporal power is gone and good riddance. What is left? Do we want monarchy by divine right? Do you believe in the sun of the future?"'[120]

The question 'What is left?' relating to the Socialist Party and its anthem 'The Sun of the Future' conveys a sense of exhausted options, at least at the level of Joyce's 'political faith'. It was a loud sigh of boredom and exasperation; it did not signal a repudiation of socialism but an irritated dissociation from its institutional manifestations.

Of those whom Joyce came to know in Trieste, the most perceptive apart from Ettore Schmitz was Silvio Benco, who had been a notably moderate and intelligent irredentist, sympathetic to and respected by Joyce. His 'James Joyce a Trieste' was published in an Italian periodical in 1930 and might be characterised as a meditation on the inter-relationship of Joyce's Irish nationalism and irredentism, but one that raises the neglected issue of Joyce's relationship to modern Italy, the kingdom that came into being in 1861. While Benco had known Joyce quite well in Trieste, and had access to the articles that Joyce had written for *Il Piccolo della Sera*, his memoir both drew on and was provoked by Francini Bruni's lecture, which Benco politely referred to as 'a delightful, but today rather rare, book with the ugly title, *Joyce intimo spogliato in piazza*'.[121] What

119. Potts, *Portraits of the Artist*, 26.

120. Potts, *Portraits of the Artist*, 38.

121. Silvio Benco, 'James Joyce a Trieste', reprinted in Potts, *Portraits of the Artist*, 52.

FIGURE 14.2. Silvio Benco (Wikimedia Commons).

most affronted Benco was the assertion attributed to Joyce by Francini Bruni that 'Italian literature begins and ends with Dante' and that the rest was 'ballast'. This was probably accurately rendered by Francini Bruni—Stanislaus recorded his brother's dislike of the 'vain pompous bombast' of Giosuè Carducci,[122] recipient of the Nobel Prize in 1906 and often considered the national poet of modern Italy.

Benco, who was sympathetic to Joyce, was driven by Francini Bruni's assertion to suggest that Joyce held cliché-driven—even semi-touristic—views on modern Italian literature, and on the Renaissance papacy: '[Joyce] had instinctively found his point of affinity [with Dante], and he was right; but his hasty judgement of the rest was only one of those opinions which one hears on any literature from superficial intellects. Nor did he like Rome. Only the Roman Church seemed great to him; but great with a sort of mixed grandeur, composed of good and evil—the idea which most foreigners draw from their hyper-romantic concept of the Renaissance papacy. Concerning Italy we have nothing to learn from Joyce.'[123] Besides querying the strength of Joyce's relationship

122. Stanislaus Joyce, Triestine diary, 8 March 1907, in McCourt, *Years of Bloom*, 105.
123. Potts, *Portraits of the Artist*, 54.

to and understanding of Italy, Benco was raising, with great astuteness, the issue of the relationship in Joyce's thought between 'modern' nineteenth-century nationalism and the pre-modern: the anterior literatures, histories, and cultures of European empires, states, races, and polities. That was precisely the relationship, or fracture, that Joyce was negotiating in *Ulysses* and *Finnegans Wake*. Benco was also, of course, gently querying the strength of Joyce's interest in, and understanding of, contemporary Italy. In his letter to his aunt Josephine on New Year's Eve 1904, Joyce had expressed his impatience with Pola—'I am trying to move on to Italy as soon as possible'[124]—but something of that belief in Italy as an exilic abode waned, and not only because of the disillusionment wrought by his Roman sojourn. Joyce's ambivalent attitude towards contemporary Italy was not likely to have particularly predisposed him in favour of irredentism, and perhaps contributed something to his apparent boredom with the subject.

Benco called on Joyce in Paris sometime after the death of Ettore Schmitz in a car accident in 1928, and recorded a conversation in which Joyce repudiated politics: 'The only thing, he says, which no longer interests him at all is politics. "No one bothers with politics anyway," he adds. "It's no longer in style".' This was not something Benco, whom Roberto Prezioso had asked to look over the Italian of Joyce's articles for *Il Piccolo della Sera*, had heard before from Joyce, and he was somewhat shocked by it. Referring to those articles written between 1907 and 1912, Benco observed, 'At that time Joyce did not believe that politics were out of style. He had brought with him from Ireland a passionate interest in the subject: indeed he had the bitterness of disillusion, the intolerance of a persecuted man and the bravado of a sceptic.'[125]

124. Joyce to Josephine Murray, New Year's Eve 1904, *Letters I* 57.

125. Potts, *Portraits of the Artist*, 49, 53.

15

Joyce's Triestine Lectures and Articles, 1907–10

Joyce is twice a rebel, against England and against Ireland.

—ITALO SVEVO[1]

ATTILIO TAMARO, a student of Joyce's who was a prominent publicist of the idea of the *italianità* of Trieste, and secretary of the irredentist Università Popolare, invited him to give three lectures at Università Popolare in April and May 1907, only the first of which, 'L'Irlanda: Isola dei santi e dei savi', Joyce was to deliver. In the same period Roberto Prezioso, political editor of the irredentist *Il Piccolo* and acting editor of its evening paper, asked him to contribute articles on Ireland; Joyce would write a total of nine articles for *Il Piccolo della Sera* between 1907 and 1912.

Joyce considered, or came to consider, his journalism as having more than ephemeral interest and aspired to give it a wider circulation. On his last fraught visit to Dublin in 1912, he discussed his Triestine articles with Arthur Griffith, who asked him to send on copies.[2] On 25 March 1914,

1. Quoted in L. Veneziani Svevo, *Memoir of Italo Svevo*, 154. Svevo delivered his lecture at the literary circle of the periodical *Il Convegno* in Milan on 26 March 1927.

2. Joyce to Stanislaus Joyce, postcard postmark 30 August 1912, *Letters II* 315.

at the time of the Curragh 'mutiny' in Ireland, Joyce wrote to a socialist publisher in Genoa, Angelo Fortunato Formiggini, proposing a book on Ireland for Italian readers which would include his articles in *Il Piccolo della Sera*. He wrote, 'This year the Irish problem has reached an acute phase, and indeed according to the latest news, England, owing to the Home Rule question, is on the brink of civil war. . . . I am an Irishman (from Dublin); and though these articles have absolutely no literary value, I believe they set out the problem sincerely and objectively.'[3] The project failed to entice Formiggini. The survival of typescripts of the Italian originals and some typescript translations has led Giorgio Melchiori plausibly to infer that Joyce, having failed with Formiggini, switched to thinking of an English publication.[4]

'L'Irlanda: Isola dei santi e dei savi'

Whatever the intellectual impact on the audience gathered in Trieste's Sala della Borsa on 27 April 1907 of Joyce's overlong address, it was a remarkable feat of exilic self-dramatisation. It was not an apologetic plea on behalf of a remote and obscure western island, but one which posited as axiomatic Ireland's place in the world and its historical role in Europe. It was the voice of a new Ireland: 'The Irish nation's desire to create its own civilization is not so much the desire of a young nation wishing to link itself to Europe's concert, but the desire by an ancient nation to renew in a modern form the glories of a past civilization.'[5] That new Ireland might after all have something to bring to 'old Europe.'[6]

The lecture's considerable factual weight was borne aloft by Joyce's grace and wit, and by its method which owed something to Guglielmo Ferrero. It was not merely historical or antiquarian because it was sustained

3. Giorgio Melchiori, 'The Language of Politics and the Politics of Language', *James Joyce Broadsheet* 4 (February 1981): 1; *OCPW* x–xi. Joyce in 1913 attempted to have his essay on Daniel Defoe published in a journal in Florence, *Il Marzocco*. Corinna del Greco Lobner, 'A *Giornalista Triestino*: James Joyce's Letter to *Il Marzocco*', *Joyce Studies Annual* 4 (Summer 1993): 184–91.

4. *OCPW* xi–xii, quoting letter of Melchiori to the editor.

5. *OCPW* 111.

6. *OCPW* 125.

by sociological intelligence. It opened with the statement that 'nations, like individuals, have their egos'.[7] Deprecating conceptions of racial purity, Joyce wrote, 'Nationality [*la nazionalità*] (if this is not really a useful fiction like many others which the scalpels of the present-day scientists have put paid to) must find its basic reason for being in something that surpasses, that transcends and that informs changeable entities such as blood or human speech.'[8] National temperament is not static: as in 'another national temperament grew up'.[9] The historical narrative was sustained by boldly etched themes that owed much to his meditations on the Parnell Split: of Irish schisms and disunion, of English conquest, of the complete elimination of the old Gaelic order, of imperturbable Irish Catholic submissiveness to Rome.

W. J. McCormack has written that 'Joyce's notions of Irish history . . . were little more than commonplace'.[10] That misses Joyce's patches of detailed knowledge, but most of all the ordering of the material, and his sense of the occult rhythms of time. As in all of Joyce's Triestine nonfiction, he made errors, not a few of which were egregious. He engaged in some research for his lecture. That related probably exclusively to the subject that gave him the point of departure for his argument, and his title, the missionaries to the Continent from Ireland, 'then an enormous seminary'.[11] Joyce rolled out an exhausting catalogue of Irish missionary saints, of exuberant onomastic pedantry: the first of his great lists. Joyce drew chiefly on two works. The first was Abbé James MacGeoghegan's *The History of Ireland, Ancient and Modern*, published in Paris in 1758–63,[12] which came to have a new lease of life when John Mitchel entitled his own work which took up the narrative *A Continuation of the History of Abbé MacGeoghegan from the Treaty of Limerick to the Year 1868*.[13] Joyce's second source was John Healy's *Insula Sanctorum et*

7. *OCPW* 108.

8. *OCPW* 118.

9. *OCPW* 114.

10. W. J. McCormack, *From Burke to Beckett* (Cork: Cork University Press, 1994), 264.

11. *OCPW* 108.

12. Turlough O'Riordain, 'James MacGeoghegan', *DIB* 5:1022–23.

13. James MacGeoghegan, *The History of Ireland Ancient and Modern, with a Continuation from the Treaty of Limerick to the Present Time by John Mitchel* (New York: D. and J. Sadlier, 1868), 186–213.

Doctorum; or, Ireland's Ancient Schools and Scholars,[14] whose author was by that time the Archbishop of Tuam.[15] Joyce's embrace of this subject is less strange than it might seem. It was central to his argument that Ireland had made a significant contribution to European culture before it was shut out from continental Europe by English invasion and conquest.[16]

Joyce assured his audience that he did not intend to detain them with an account of Irish affairs over the eight centuries 'under foreign occupation',[17] but proceeded to do just that, at least in impressionistic fashion. The English conquest was the dominant theme, addressed in various and subtle ways. 'A moral separation already exists between the two countries'. He did not remember 'God Save the King' being sung in Ireland 'without a storm of whistles, yells and shushes' that rendered it inaudible.[18] He illustrated 'the gulf that still separates the two countries' by an account of the entry of Queen Victoria into Dublin on her 1900 visit to Ireland which ended, 'The English soldiers stood respectfully at attention while their queen passed; behind them, the crowd watched the sumptuous procession and its sad central figure with eyes

14. John Healy, *Insula Sanctorum et Doctorum; or, Ireland's Ancient Schools and Scholars* (Dublin: Sealy Bryers and Walker and M. H. Gill and Son, 1890). Healy states (at 468–69) of this work that Alfred, later king of the Northumbrian Saxons, had studied in Ireland, and quotes the first two verses of James Clarence Mangan's translation of a poem attributed to Alfred. Joyce, in his lecture, translates into Italian the first verse of Mangan's translation (*OCPW* 112–13). Joyce did not have access to what Henry R. Montgomery referred to as O'Donovan's 'admirable literal translation'. Henry R. Montgomery, *Specimens of the Early Native Poetry of Ireland*, (Dublin: James McGlashan, 1846); James Clarence Mangan, *The Collected Works of James Clarence Mangan: Poems, 1845–1847*, ed. Jacques Chuto (Dublin: Irish Academic Press, 1996), 437. He would scarcely have preferred O'Donovan's over Mangan's translation if he had. Joyce affectionately parodies the poem in the 'Cyclops' episode of *Ulysses* (*U* 12.68–86). There are declared translations of two verses of 'O'Hussey's Ode to the Maguire' in Joyce's Mangan lecture (*OCPW* 266).

15. Patrick Maume, 'John Healy', *DIB* 4:561–64.

16. Len Platt's insistence that Joyce set out to displace the historiographical model of Anglo-Irish cultural revivalism, and specifically its emphasis on pre-Christian Ireland, seems for this reason misconceived. Len H. Platt, 'Joyce and the Anglo-Irish Revival: The Triestine Lectures', *James Joyce Quarterly* 29, no. 2 (Winter 1992): 259–66; Len H. Platt, *James Joyce: Texts and Contexts* (London: Continuum, 2011), 23–24.

17. *OCPW* 114.

18. *OCPW* 116.

of curiosity, almost pity. When the carriage passed by, they followed its wake with ambiguous glances. This time there were no bombs or cabbages, but the queen of England entered the capital of Ireland in the midst of a silent people.'[19]

The account was so graphic as to suggest Joyce actually witnessed it, but there is nothing to indicate that he did. What Joyce has done is to deploy with brilliance the established conventions of nationalist newspaper coverage of royal arrivals in the city of Dublin. While Joyce was clearly not sympathetic to the visit, he cultivates a more measured tone than, for example, Arthur Griffith in the *United Irishman*.[20]

Joyce's nationalism in its relation to England is tart rather than strident. Joyce twice decried extravagant Irish denunciations of the English: 'I find it a bit naive to heap insults on the Englishman for his misdeeds in Ireland. A conqueror cannot be amateurish, and what England did in Ireland over the centuries is no different from what the Belgians are doing today in the Congo Free State'.[21] He did not 'see the use in bitter invective against England, the despoiler, or in contempt for the vast Anglo-Saxon civilization—even if it is almost entirely a materialist civilization'.[22] The two propositions perfectly exemplify Joyce's Parnellite nationalism. The critique of extravagant nationalist rhetoric against England is not eirenically Anglophile but a Parnellian refusal to take up a position that could not be made good.

He observed, 'If a victorious country tyrannizes over another, it cannot logically take it amiss if the latter reacts. Men are made that way'. Neither was it logical for British historians to praise George Washington or to salute the constitutional progress of Australia 'while they treat Irish separatists as madcaps'. The ending of the Penal Laws was 'thanks partly to the never-ending discussions and in part to Fenian violence'.[23]

19. *OCPW* 118.

20. *United Irishman*, 24 March, 31 March, 7 April 1900. Griffith, as Joyce knew, was being egged on by Maud Gonne, whose article 'The Famine Queen' appeared in the edition of 7 April 1900.

21. *OCPW* 119.

22. *OCPW* 125.

23. *OCPW* 121.

Joyce, nonetheless, determined to maintain the integrity of his ideas of modernisation, made the countermove, typical of the flow and counterflow of his lecture, of conceding historic English advances towards democracy ahead of any in Ireland.[24]

What is pivotal in the lecture is its exploitation of its form—the delivery of a lecture by an Irishman in Trieste—to recast the Irish relation to Britain in a continental setting. There was a strategic advantage in Joyce's position which he was determined to make the most of. Europe for Joyce was continental Europe (he excises the Irish missionaries who went to England, Wales, and Scotland)[25] and the address to his audience a conversation from which the English were excluded. The central idea was what Ireland had contributed and could again contribute to continental Europe. The Irish contribution to English life and culture, which was more obvious than that to continental life, was not part of that argument. It did feature at some length in the lecture; there is something almost comical in Joyce's insistence on smuggling it in as a very bulky stowaway, to demonstrate what the Irish were capable of achieving outside Ireland, or might be capable of achieving if liberated from British dominion. It was in that way a performative exercise in independence, but underpinned by Joyce's determination to bypass the Irish preoccupation with England, which he considered anomalous on the part of cultural nationalists, and to recast the Irish relation to Britain against a continental backdrop, notionally broadcasting back to Ireland a nationalism honed in Europe.

In presenting the new Ireland, Joyce placed some emphasis on the revival of the Irish language through the Gaelic League. He noted that in Dublin the street names were written in both languages. This was a perpetual source of sarcastic amusement to Joyce. He wrote in 1924 to Valéry Larbaud that a citizen of the Irish Free State by now 'can probably read (when sober enough) ten street names'.[26] It was not just that Joyce in performance in Trieste was on his best expatriate behaviour.

24. *OCPW* 120.

25. These are discussed in P. W. Joyce, *A Short History of Ireland*, 3rd ed. (London: Longmans Green, 1904), 166; though it does not appear that Joyce used this work for his lecture.

26. Joyce to Valéry Larbaud, 28 July 1924, *Letters I* 217.

He was prepared to draw on the revival of the Irish language to make his argument. He tempered his personal scepticism with mild humour: 'Often on the streets groups of young people may be seen speaking Irish perhaps a little more emphatically than is really necessary.'[27] The real qualification was contained in what was an insistent theme of the lecture, that the old Irish order had gone, so that the revival of the language could not engender the resuscitation of Gaelic civilisation: 'Just as ancient Egypt is dead, so is ancient Ireland. Its dirge has been sung and the seal set upon its gravestone. The ancient national spirit that spoke throughout the centuries through the mouths of fabulous seers, wandering minstrels and Jacobite poets has vanished from the world with the death of James Clarence Mangan. With his death the long tradition of the triple order of the ancient bards also died. Today other bards, inspired by other ideals, have their turn.'[28]

This cuts deeper than an assault on the naivety of the ideology of the revival of the Irish language. The seeming severity of Joyce's judgement is a gesture of respect to an anterior civilisation that was now in its integrity irretrievably lost. It was through that recognition that it was possible to pick up its lingering cadences. It was the first articulation of Joyce's extraordinary sensitivity to the processes of human defeat, displacement, and supersession in history.

A striking corollary to Joyce's argument on the irretrievable collapse of the old order is the attention he pays, albeit with mordant sarcasm, to the fallen state of the descendants of the kings of the old Gaelic order ('poor fallen kings') at the expense of the contemporary Anglo-Irish aristocracy of whom he makes no comment: 'So Ireland (a country destined by God to be an eternal caricature of the serious world) is now an aristocratic country with no aristocracy. The descendants of the ancient kings (who call themselves by their surnames alone, without using a first name) can be seen with their wigs and notarial deeds in the palaces of justice where they go to defend some accused man or other by invoking the very laws that suppressed their royal titles.'[29]

27. *OCPW* 109.
28. *OCPW* 125.
29. *OCPW* 120.

Already in the narrative of Irish history—wonderfully rendered in *Finnegans Wake* as 'decades of longsuffering and decennia of brief glory'[30]—Joyce was turning to ideas of the cyclical. Just when the 'past glories of Ireland' were fading, 'there arose a new Celtic race [*una nuova razza celtica*] which was made up of the old Celtic stock and the Scandinavian, Anglo-Saxon and Norman races. On the foundation of its ancient predecessor, another national temperament grew up, in which the various elements intermingled and renovated the ancient body. The ancient enemies made a common cause against the aggression of the English.'[31]

'To deny the name of patriot to all those not of Irish stock', he wrote, 'would be to deny to it almost all the heroes of the modern movement'. That line ran from Lord Edward FitzGerald to Charles Stewart Parnell, 'perhaps the most formidable man ever to lead the Irish, but in whose veins not a single drop of Celtic blood ran.'[32] He had earlier referred sarcastically to an Irish member of Parliament attacking a rival at a recent election as a descendant of a Cromwellian settler, a mode of denigration which had featured prominently in T. M. Healy's attack on Parnell in the Split.[33] Joyce's 'new Celtic race' was a racial hybrid. He had a predilection for the term 'race', perhaps for its historical resonance, at the expense of

30. *FW* 472.36–473.1.

31. *OCPW* 114–15.

32. *OCPW* 115. Joyce also rendered an account of a horrific story Parnell had been told as a boy by the old lodge keeper at Avondale of the killing of a 1798 rebel by the lashing of his stomach (*OCPW* 119). This was a story Parnell often recounted. It appears in R. Barry O'Brien's biography: *Charles Stewart Parnell*, 1:53–54. However, it also appears in T. P. O'Connor's earlier *Charles Stewart Parnell: A Memory* (London: Ward, Lock, Bowden, 1891), 12–13. For what it is worth, O'Connor states, as O'Brien does not, that the man was to be flogged to death at the end of a cart, and Joyce refers to the victim being tied to a carriage. The relevance is as to whether Joyce in Trieste owned or had access to a copy of O'Brien's biography before he acquired the 1910 Nelson Library edition that was in his library in Trieste. Katharine Tynan later gave a further account of the story that Parnell retold that concludes, 'In this story told by old Gaffney, the gatekeeper at Avondale, to the growing boy—Mr. Parnell used to tell it without apparent emotion—lay the genesis of a great Irish rebel' (*Twenty-Five Years*, 88). Joyce presumably, for the sake of simplicity, characterised the victim as 'a peasant who had infringed against the penal laws' and asserted that it was this story that rendered Parnell 'a thorn in the side of the English' (*OCPW* 119). Joyce's somewhat heightened rendering ('his intestines spilling out on the road') served as the lecture's set piece of gruesome English cruelty for his Triestine audience.

33. Callanan, *T. M. Healy*, 321–33.

the term 'nationality', which he used more sparingly. In Joyce's terms, 'race' equated to national narratives and myths (old and new) and to the mould of geography. His lecture both conformed to and departed from the traditional model of the 'story of Ireland', and the idea of Ireland as an island gave it its title and deeply shaped its substance. Joyce moreover is careful to institute a dialogue with modern thought and scholarship—with Ferrero, Ernest Renan ('himself a Breton Celt'),[34] and Herbert Spencer—and with contemporary philology.

There is a certain insistence in Joyce's heterodox use of the term 'race' and its cognates. He deployed the term with a calculated looseness and liberality that defied ideological conceptions of race. He was quite happy to discuss ideas of national temperament and did so in the semi-analytic mode of the time that Ferrero practised. He was fiercely dismissive of claims to racial purity in modern Europe and in Ireland.

> Our civilization is an immense woven fabric in which very different elements are mixed. . . . What race or language (if we except those few which a humorous will seems to have preserved in ice, such as Iceland) can nowadays claim to be pure? No race has less right to make such a boast than the one presently inhabiting Ireland. . . . In Ireland we can see how the Danes, the Firbolgs, the Milesians from Spain, the Norman invaders, the Anglo-Saxon colonists and the Huguenots came together to form a new entity, under the influence of a local god, one might say. And although the present race in Ireland is second-rate and backwards, it merits some consideration as it is the only one in the entire Celtic family that refused to sell its birthright for a plate of lentils.[35]

In posing the question, Joyce plays on the connotations of the word 'pure', reacting to the Conservative nationalist association of the idea of racial purity with that of moral purity. His abhorrence of the idiom of sexual purity had found expression in his outburst to Stanislaus six months earlier, prompted by Oliver St John Gogarty's denunciation of 'venereal excess' in the British army ('I am nauseated by their lying

34. *OCPW* 113.
35. *OCPW* 118–19.

drivel about pure men and pure women and spiritual love and love for ever: blatant lying in the face of truth').[36]

Somewhat in the manner of an eighteenth-century pamphlet, Joyce's lecture encompasses a compendium of the Irish political vices and foibles that made Ireland incapable of casting off English dominion. The Irish had an invincible aptitude for disunion (he did not give full vent to his ideas on the Irish proclivity for betrayal) and were their own worst enemies. A disaffected Irish king had invited the Normans to invade, and the Irish Parliament in 1800 (which Joyce wildly mischaracterised as one 'elected by the people of Ireland') had voted for union with Britain in 1800. 'In my opinion, these two facts must be perfectly explained before the country in which they took place has even the most elementary right to expect one of its sons to change his position from that of detached observer to convinced nationalist.'[37] However crude or deficient Joyce's rendering of the historical facts, the examples are intelligible as a retrospective projection of the disloyalty, opportunism, and pandering to English opinion in the Split.

Also pertinent to the Split was Ireland's unreciprocated loyalty to the Holy See, to which Irish Catholics showed themselves 'so accommodatingly affable': 'Ireland prides herself on being body and soul as faithful to her national traditions as to the Holy See. The majority of Irishmen consider loyalty to these two traditions as their cardinal article of faith.'[38] Irish allegiance to Catholicism had been ill rewarded, from the time when the papal bull 'Laudabiliter' of Adrian IV conferred the sovereignty of Ireland on Henry II. Throughout the lecture, the English government and the Catholic Church were depicted as interconnected and mutually reinforcing: 'The truth is that the English government increased the moral value of Catholicism by banning it.'[39] This was part

36. Joyce to Stanislaus Joyce, 15 November 1906, *Letters II* 191–92. The two passages are juxtaposed by Colin MacCabe, who writes, 'If we reflect on these quotations, I think that it becomes clear why the hero of *Ulysses* is a Protestant Jew and that of *Finnegans Wake* is a Scandinavian Protestant. The notion of miscegenation at the level of biology, culture and language is crucial to Joyce.' Colin MacCabe, *James Joyce and the Revolution of the Word*, 2nd ed. (London: Palgrave Macmillan, 2003), xxii–xxiv.

37. *OCPW* 115–16.

38. *OCPW* 115.

39. *OCPW* 121.

of the counterflow that ran through Joyce's lecture: 'I confess I do not see what good it does to fulminate against English tyranny while the tyranny of Rome still holds the dwelling place of the soul.'[40]

The success of many who left Ireland for other countries contrasted with the fallen state of the country they left. Joyce did not shrink from including the contributions to British military success of the Duke of Wellington, Lord Kitchener, and Lord Roberts (whom Joyce strangely believed to have been born in Ireland). He added the writers from those 'who adopted the English language in the seventeenth century and almost forgot their native country' to 'the over-rated Oscar Wilde, son of a revolutionary poetess', a line that stopped short of Yeats.[41] 'In the field of practical affairs', Irishmen often excelled outside Ireland: 'The economic and intellectual conditions of his homeland do not permit the individual to develop.'[42] The flight of the Wild Geese had not ceased. Varying Charles Gavan Duffy's celebrated comparison of Ireland to a corpse on the dissecting table by transposing it to that of a person in extremis, he characterised the condition of contemporary Ireland: 'Standing around the death-bed where the poor bloodless and almost lifeless body lies are agitating patriots, proscribing governments, and priests administering the last rites.'[43]

Joyce passed on to address the possibility of a 'resurgence' (risorgimento) of the Irish. It is Joyce's preferred term, used four times, the first as 'the Irish dream of resurgence',[44] straddling art and politics, possibly with a bit more politics in its Italian connotation. Though guarded ('Alas, we amateur sociologists are only second-rate soothsayers. . . . Only our supermen can write the history of the future') and hypothetically framed, what he said was striking:

40. *OCPW* 125.

41. The translation is harsher than the Italian. He spoke merely of 'il troppo celebre Oscar Wilde' (*OCPW* 257). At the end of the lecture, he quoted what Wilde had said about the Irish being 'the greatest talkers since the days of the ancient Greeks' to 'a friend of mine'. The friend was Yeats (*OCPW* 126).

42. *OCPW* 122–23.

43. *OCPW* 124.

44. *OCPW* 124.

> It would be interesting, but beyond the aims I have set myself this evening, to see what the probable consequences would be of a resurgence of this people; to see the consequences of a rival, republican, self-centred and enterprising island next to England, with its own commercial fleet and its ambassadors in every port throughout the world; to see the moral consequences of the appearance in old Europe of Irish artists and thinkers, those strange souls, cold enthusiasts, artistically and sexually uninstructed, full of idealism and incapable of sticking to it, childish spirits, unfaithful, ingenuous and satirical, the 'loveless Irishmen' as they are called.[45]

This extraordinary passage defies reductive analysis, but it does posit a connexion between an independent Irish state and the advent as of old of 'Irish artists and thinkers'. It is a rare explicit reference on Joyce's part to the interconnectedness of an Irish literary movement and Irish statehood. In the exordium with which he concluded, he said,

> One thing alone seems clear to me. It is high time Ireland finished once and for all with failures. If it is truly capable of resurgence, then let it do so or else let it cover its head and decently descend into the grave forever. . . . Though the Irish are eloquent, a revolution is not made from human breath, and Ireland has already had enough of compromises, misunderstandings and misapprehensions. If it wants finally to put on a show for which we have waited so long, this time, let it be complete, full and definitive. But telling these Irish actors to hurry up, as our fathers before us told them not so long ago, is useless. I, for one, am certain not to see the curtain rise, as I shall have already taken the last train home.[46]

The reference to 'our fathers before us' is plainly to the Fenian revolutionary tradition. The concluding sentence is deft and quite moving. Joyce is having a small Parnellite joke with himself. It is almost imperceptibly a meditation on Parnell's request in his Rotunda speech of 10 December 1890 to be permitted to 'walk with you within the sight of the

45. *OCPW* 125.
46. *OCPW* 125–26.

promised land'.[47] It is a measure of Joyce's collusive identification with Parnell across his lifetime that some of his invocations of Parnell slip into a semi-private register in which he is indifferent as to whether they are picked up. The issue of whether the last train that would take him home would be in Trieste or Dublin, or another city altogether, was left gracefully indeterminate.

It was a remarkable if idiosyncratic performance, judged by Stanislaus as 'too long and somewhat braggart'.[48] It was not unstructured, but succeeded through the rhythm of its inner dialectic. The relationship of the old and new Irelands was incisively rendered: the deployment of the old Ireland that was gone achieved an almost incantatory effect. What was most extraordinary was Joyce's capacity at once to express and to hold himself critically distant from the élan of the new Ireland.

Joyce was in some degree liberated by the fact that it was spoken, albeit from a script written in longhand (it was never included in the projects for republication of his journalism). It had, once he had got his roll call of missionary saints over with, a certain conversational playfulness. It does not quite attain the fantasia by which he sought to enliven (chiefly for himself) his teaching of English in Trieste. Alessandro Francini Bruni recalled one of the pseudo-pedagogic 'vignettes' that Joyce improvised: 'Ireland is a great country. They call it the Emerald Isle. The Metropolitan Government, after so many centuries of having it by the throat, has reduced it to a spectre. Now it is a briar patch. They sowed it with famine, syphilis, superstition, and alcoholism. Up sprouted Puritans, Jesuits and bigots.'[49]

It has been suggested that Joyce was going to some lengths to play to the liberal irredentism of his Triestine audience. This is not especially convincing. *Il Piccolo della Sera* championed the cause of oppressed nationalities, and attacks on the British Empire were readily equated to attacks on the Austro-Hungarian. Joyce needed little stimulus to condemn the iniquities of the British Empire. If Joyce had been stiffly

47. Callanan, *Parnell Split*, 63.

48. Stanislaus Joyce, Triestine diary, 20 April 1907, quoted in McCourt, *Years of Bloom*, 117.

49. Potts, *Portraits of the Artist*, 27.

unbiddable in Dublin, he is unlikely to have been otherwise in Trieste. It is striking that in the lecture, Joyce should have thrown in a reference to the Celtic spirit resembling in many respects the Slavic[50]—a view that Joyce held, though not one especially relevant to his lecture—in the knowledge that Attilio Tamaro, who had asked him to give the lecture, was stridently anti-Slav.[51] What Joyce was acutely conscious and proud of was pleading Ireland's cause in Italian in a distant Mediterranean city.

He was certainly conscious he was addressing a Triestine audience: he referred at the outset to 'the religious fervour that still flourishes in Ireland of which you, fed over the past years on a diet of scepticism, can only form an idea with difficulty'.[52] Joyce in Trieste and Rome was always vaguely mortified by the fact that Irish Catholics were more submissive to the Church than were their Italian co-religionists. At the Università Popolare venue, Joyce was unsparing. His audience was subjected to a fierce and unremitting blast of dissentient nationalism from a distant Atlantic island. What is salient is the perspective of exile. More than his sedulous reading of Italian newspapers, the perception or non-perception of Ireland in casual conversation left a deep impression on Joyce. He realised that the idea of an Irish *relancement* framed by the political ideas of Griffith and Sinn Féin had an imaginative potency internationally which surpassed that of the Home Rule project of the post-Parnellite Irish Party that remained stalled even though a Liberal government was in office (with an overall majority which meant it was not dependent on the votes of the Irish nationalists).

Joyce, by his lecture, impressed a sharply etched exilic persona on his exhausted Triestine audience. He had delivered a lecture of great élan in an Italian that was still slightly idiosyncratic to an Italian audience in a city of the northern Adriatic that was part of the Austro-Hungarian Empire. Joyce is consciously negotiating the distance between Ireland, as an Atlantic island on the edge of Europe, and Trieste, and fiercely

50. *OCPW* 124.

51. Tamaro's anti-Slavism, as expressed in subsequently published works, is discussed in John McCourt, 'Joyce on National Deliverance: The View from 1907 Trieste', *Prospero: Rivista di culture anglo-germaniche* 5 (1998): 27–48.

52. *OCPW* 109.

contesting the reactionary Catholic nationalist conception of that island as geographically ordained by providence to be a self-enclosed politico-cultural space.

Giving the lecture left Joyce elated. He boasted to Stanislaus that his own mind 'was of a type superior to and more civilised than any he had met up to the present'. The Irish were 'the most intelligent, most spiritual, and most civilized people in Europe' and would, if given the chance, contribute 'a new force to civilization, not less than that contributed in our time by the Slavs'. Stanislaus responded that, on the contrary, Ireland, once free, would be intolerable, and was upbraided by his brother: 'What the devil are your politics? Do you not think Ireland has a right to govern itself and is capable of doing so?'[53] Stanislaus's irritable response had something to do with his thankless role in his brother's household. Joyce had set out to deliver the lecture elegantly attired, wearing Stanislaus's overcoat over a frock coat borrowed from Almidano Artifoni. Stanislaus noticed Nora and Giorgio at the corner of the Sala della Borsa and feared that Nora, who was poorly dressed, would attend the lecture. He waited for Joyce and Artifoni to arrive and then went over to Nora, who explained she would not dream of appearing among the 'well-dressed people' and had only wanted to see Joyce arrive. Stanislaus gave her a crown to go to the cinema.[54]

'James Clarence Mangan' and 'The Irish Literary Renaissance'

The original arrangement with Tamaro was that Joyce would deliver three lectures. This was then cut back to two at a reduced fee, whereupon Joyce, emulating the tenacity of Mrs Kearney in 'A Mother',

53. Ellmann, *James Joyce*, 259, 769n27. This is taken from the Triestine diary of Stanislaus Joyce, 27–28 April 1907.

54. Pelaschiar, 'Stanislaus Joyce's "Book of Days"', 68–69. Pelaschiar points out that Ellmann (*James Joyce*, 258), who used the diary for his account of the lecture, did not comment on Nora's presence outside the hall. She is critical of Ellmann's scant use of the Triestine diary, to which he had access. The Triestine diary remains unpublished.

decided not to give a further lecture, asserting he could not achieve his purpose in two lectures. He had almost completed the text of what was intended to be his second lecture, on Mangan, and only a tantalising fragment of the third, on the Irish literary renaissance, survives.[55]

Most of the script of Joyce's intended lecture on Mangan is extant.[56] While it is in large part a reworking of his 1902 lecture on Mangan to the college Literary and Historical Society, the political background is more strongly etched. As in the earlier lecture, Joyce unexpectedly insists on the relationship of Irish literature to the contemporary political, this time on the reception of Mangan: 'Mangan will be accepted by the Irish as their national poet the day the conflict between Ireland and the foreign powers, the Anglo-Saxon and the Roman Catholic, reaches a settlement that will give rise to a new civilization, either indigenous or purely foreign.' As he does elsewhere, Joyce explicitly acknowledges the possibility that the Irish nationalist project could fail. The thing could go either way. He shares the sense of crisis of radical nationalists of his generation, but with a marked difference: they regarded Home Rule as something that would petrify Irish subordination to Britain, whereas Joyce was addressing the possibility that even Home Rule would not be achieved, and that Ireland would be permanently stabilised as a Catholic province of empire. While there is a degree of provocation to this, it has to be emphasised how rarely such a stark alternative outcome was posited by contemporary nationalists. He ventured a comparison he had not made in 1902 between the moral obloquy that attached to Mangan (because he took opium) and that which later fastened itself on Parnell: 'Until that time, either he will be forgotten or just barely remembered on holidays, like many other poets and heroes, all the more so because, like Parnell, he sinned against that incorruptible chastity that Ireland would demand of any John who would baptise her or of any Joan who would liberate her, as being the first essential and divine test of their worthiness for such lofty offices.'[57]

55. McCourt, *Years of Bloom*, 117; Ellmann, *James Joyce*, 259.

56. *OCPW* 127–36.

57. *OCPW* 130.

Only one sheet survives of what is thought to be the script for what was to be the third lecture, 'The Irish Literary Renaissance'. Joyce had already flagged this lecture in his Mangan script, stating that 'the literary movement of the present day' about which he was to speak in a later lecture belonged, like the literary movement of Young Ireland, to the nineteenth century.[58] What survives is part of an attempt by Joyce to model the relationship of radical nationalist movements to literary revivals. He identifies in the time period since the rebellion of 1798 'no less than three decisive clashes between the two nationalist tendencies'. The first was 1848, the second 1867: 'The third belongs to the present day, as the youth of Ireland, disillusioned by the ineffectiveness of parliamentary tactics after the moral assassination of Parnell aligns itself increasingly with a nationalism that is broader and, at the same time, more severe; a nationalism that involves a daily economic battle, a moral and material boycott, the creation and development of independent industries, the propagation of the Irish language, a ban on English culture and a revival in another guise of the ancient civilization of the Celt.'[59]

This is the only occasion on which Joyce draws an explicit link between the fall of Parnell and the rise of the new nationalism. In doing so, he adopts what was a fairly common view. He imputes to the new nationalism a greater rigour than it possessed. What is striking is that Joyce stands outside what he describes: it does not encompass his own relation to the Parnell Split, and his identification with the new nationalism is qualified. If he is acknowledging some generational relationship to what he describes, he is conscious of standing apart. He continues, 'Each of these uncompromising political movements has been accompanied by a literary one.'[60] While what survives is a fragment, it is significant that he sees the current literary movement as having a connection to Parnell's fall. This represented a shift in his critique of the naïve politics of the Literary Revival, and brought him closer to Yeats, who had begun from the late 1890s to elaborate his resonant thesis on

58. *OCPW* 128.

59. *OCPW* 137.

60. *OCPW* 137.

the modern Irish literary movement having its proximate origins in the fall of Parnell.

The Politics of Home Rule in *Il Piccolo della Sera*

Three of Joyce's articles for *Il Piccolo della Sera* run together: ''Il Fenianismo, L'ultimo Feniano' (Fenianism: The Last Fenian; 22 March 1907) on the death of John O'Leary, 'Home Rule Maggiorenne' (Home Rule Comes of Age; 19 May 1907), and 'La Cometa dell "Home Rule"' (The Home Rule Comet; 22 December 1910). His final and most significant article on contemporary Irish politics, 'L'ombra di Parnell', is discussed in chapter 16.

The occasion for the publication of 'Fenianism: The Last Fenian'[61] was the death in Dublin of John O'Leary on 16 March 1907. Its commissioning came about quite casually. Joyce was complaining to Roberto Prezioso, the editor of *Il Piccolo della Sera,* about the ignorance on Ireland that prevailed in Europe. He illustrated the point by taking up that evening's edition of the paper to point out that O'Leary's name was mangled even in the report of his death. Prezioso asked him to write the article which became Joyce's most sustained non-fictional consideration of Fenianism.[62]

His thesis is succinctly stated: 'Whoever studies the history of the Irish revolution during the nineteenth century will find himself confronted by a dual struggle, that is, of the Irish nation against the English government, and the struggle, perhaps no less fierce, between the moderate nationalists and the so-called physical force party.'[63] This is a lucid proposition with which it is difficult to quarrel, save in the reference to a physical force 'party', which gives an exaggerated sense of coherence to disparate movements and events. He characterises Robert Emmet's rebellion as 'ridiculous' and the Young Ireland movement as 'fervent', but considers the 1867 Fenian rebellion to have been well organised and to have had a prospect of success: 'The Fenianism of '67 was not one of

61. Stanislaus Joyce records that the article was 'sensibly changed in some points' by the editorial staff. Triestine diary, 9–31 April 1907, quoted in McCourt, *Years of Bloom,* 109.

62. Stanislaus Joyce, Triestine diary, quoted in McCourt, 'Joyce on National Deliverance', 36–37.

63. *OCPW* 138.

those usual outbursts of Celtic temperament that burn brightly for a moment in the darkness, leaving a deeper darkness than before in their wake'.[64] Joyce extravagantly overstated both the planning and the prospects of the event, enabling him to pose the question, 'Why this collapse of such a well-organized movement? Simply because in Ireland, just at the crucial moment, an informer appears'. Thereafter 'the traditional doctrine of the physical force sporadically appears in violent acts'. Perhaps to avoid overcomplicating his account, he attributed to the Invincibles, who did not exist in 1867, the episode for which the 'Manchester martyrs' were executed and the blowing up of Clerkenwell prison in 1867, as well as the Phoenix Park murders. His analysis shifted from betrayal to disunion: 'After each of these crimes, when the general outrage had died down a bit, an English minister would table some motion for reform in Ireland before the Commons, and the Fenians and the parliamentarians would strenuously vilify one another, the former attributing the measure to the success of their parliamentary tactics, the latter attributing it to the hidden persuasiveness of the dagger or the bomb. Meanwhile, as a backdrop to this sad comedy, the spectacle unfolded of a population decreasing with mathematical regularity year by year'.[65]

Ireland had submitted to exploitation by England and Rome. 'It is impossible now that an extremist and bloody doctrine such as Fenianism can continue to survive in such an environment'. Fenianism 'has once again changed its name and form. The new Fenians have regrouped in a party called "ourselves alone". They aim to make Ireland a bilingual republic'. He detailed some of the features of Griffith's programme and added, 'From many points of view, this latest form of Fenianism may be the most formidable. Its influence has certainly once again remoulded the character of the Irish.'[66]

This was Joyce's clearest published profession of sympathy with Sinn Féin, which had still not been formally constituted. The reference to its having 'remoulded the character of the Irish' was no doubt an exaggeration

64. *OCPW* 138.
65. *OCPW* 139.
66. *OCPW* 140.

before his Italian audience, but it nonetheless suggests that, whatever his suspicions of the 'patriots', he was impressed by the seriousness of purpose of its adherents.

Characterising Sinn Féin as 'the new Fenians' was historically incorrect. While Griffith might not have objected, most members of the Irish Republican Brotherhood considered that Griffith had deviated from Fenianism in his refusal to accept recourse to physical force. Sinn Féin and Fenianism nevertheless had in common their opposition to parliamentarism. Joyce's attitude to Fenianism is subtle. He considered that physical force could in principle bring about change and inclined to the view that it had done so in the past. He was not disposed to condemn Fenianism on account of its principled belief in modalities of insurrection. He understood the ambivalent sympathy that those who undertook political acts of violence were capable of eliciting from his more pacific fellow countrymen, as when Leopold Bloom, in the cabman's shelter in the 'Eumaeus' episode of *Ulysses,* experiences 'a certain kind of admiration for a man who had actually brandished a knife, cold steel, with the courage of his political convictions (though personally he would not be a party to any such thing)'.[67] He knew perfectly well that the perpetration of the Phoenix Park murders was not a Fenian act. His imaginative affinity was with what he conceived as the historical temper of Fenianism, its consistency of revolutionary purpose, however theoretical. The Fenians were moreover pitted against clericalism and had individually rallied to support Parnell in the Split. He was not altogether immune to its conspiratorial glamour, though that found expression principally in his disappointed observation of the tawdriness of the Fenians he actually encountered. His delineation of the contest between constitutional and 'physical force' nationalists had a perennial quality, and Joyce was far too historically acute to exclude the possibility, theoretical as it might seem, that a change in circumstances might render viable a resort to force.

What was clear was his agreement with the view he imputed to Griffith (whose *Sinn Féin* he grandly designated 'the intransigent press')

67. *U* 16.1057–60.

that, 'owing to the enormous might of England, armed revolt has become an impossible dream.'[68] That indeed was the whole premise of the article. O'Leary's death 'perhaps marked the disappearance of the last actor in the turbulent drama that was Fenianism.'[69] The 'venerable old man' Joyce had seen browsing the bookshops of the quays was 'a figure from a vanished world.'[70] His funeral would be marked by great pomp 'because the Irish, even when they break the hearts of those who sacrifice their lives for their country, never fail to show a great reverence for the dead.'[71] That graceful final sentence of Joyce's article redirects attention to Parnell, to whom O'Leary had, heroically overriding his prior misgivings, rallied in the Split. It is the only explicit statement in Joyce's non-fictional writing which conveys his opposition to the funerary cult of Parnell, an opposition which informs all of Joyce's jealously Parnellian refashioning of the Parnell myth and finds fictional expression in the 'Cyclops' episode of *Ulysses*.

The edition of *Il Piccolo della Sera* of 19 May 1907 carried an article by Joyce entitled 'Home Rule Maggiorenne' (Home Rule Comes of Age). It is significant as a response to a specific political event, and as the article in which Joyce most closely imbricated the journalism of Arthur Griffith. The 1906 general election resulted in a Liberal landslide. The scale of the Liberal victory meant that the Liberals were not dependent on the votes of the Irish Party, and starkly posed the issue of the Liberal commitment to Home Rule. William Gladstone's Irish legacy was silently resisted rather than openly disavowed. On 7 May 1907 the government introduced its Irish Council Bill, which was to provide for a council of 107 members which would be given control of some of the existing Irish departments. The bill was a supreme disappointment to a country nurtured on the Liberal promise of Home Rule. John Redmond temporised but, at the convention of the United Irish League at the Mansion House in Dublin on 21 May 1907, proposed a resolution rejecting the bill which was overwhelmingly carried. The bill was withdrawn on 3 June 1907.[72]

68. *OCPW* 138.
69. *OCPW* 138.
70. *OCPW* 140.
71. *OCPW* 140–41.
72. Meleady, *John Redmond*, 100–108.

The month before, Arthur Griffith had published in *Sinn Féin* an editorial to mark the twenty-first anniversary of the introduction of the First Home Rule Bill on 8 April 1886. Twenty-one years might seem a curious choice for an anniversary, but Griffith knew what he was about. It opened with an extensive quotation from the *Freeman's Journal* of the following day, 9 April 1886, that recorded the excitement around the *Freeman* offices and the offices of the *Evening Telegraph* when news came through of Gladstone's speech, first on the bulletin board of the evening paper and then in the paper itself. 'The infant born on the [eve] of its publication has come of age. He is a man—he demands his birthright'. Griffith professed to have been sceptical at the time:

> We believed then what we know now that the British Liberal Party—or the British Tory Party—will keep its pledges to Ireland so long as Ireland makes it unprofitable for it to do otherwise. It is a truth many Irishmen assent to, but few realise and act upon it. Parnell realised and acted upon it, and therefore British Liberalism contrived to get rid of Parnell when it had swindled the Irish people into believing it honest. Since then it has broken every pledge it made to Ireland and publicly hauled down its Home Rule flag without a voice being cast against it or a voice raised in protest by the Irish Parliamentary Party.[73]

Griffith set out what he asserted to be the salient facts of what he characterised as the Liberal abandonment of Home Rule and Irish economic decline over the supervening twenty-one years. 'From these facts we conclude that the policy of Parliamentarianism is a policy of national suicide, diverting the efforts of the Irish people from their own resources and leaving them prey to their enemies.'[74]

With the introduction of the Irish Council Bill the following month, *Sinn Féin* resumed its twenty-one-year refrain, dwelling on the failure of the Second Home Rule Bill in 1893, seven years after the failure of first bill. The Irish Council Bill was 'the thing which British Liberalism offers

73. *Sinn Féin*, 13 April 1907.

74. *Sinn Féin*, 13 April 1907.

Ireland in return for the twenty-one years service of the Irish Parliamentary Party as tail to the British Liberal Party'. Griffith pronounced, 'This is the fruition of Parliamentarianism. For twenty-one years it has lived and thrived by shouting in the ear of Ireland that it would bring about Home Rule. Where is Home Rule now?'[75]

Joyce's article 'Home Rule Comes of Age' in *Il Piccolo della Sera* took from Griffith the framing devices of the street scene in Dublin as news of Gladstone's speech on the First Home Rule Bill came through, and the twenty-one-year interval connected to the idea of achieving adulthood. Joyce was sternly critical of 'a devolutionary measure that does not go beyond the proposals made in 1885 by the imperialist Chamberlain'. Joyce's article was published two days before the convention that repudiated the bill met in Dublin. At that point Joyce saw the House of Lords as the principal obstacle: 'The Lords will probably kill the measure, as this is their job, but, if they are wise, they will hesitate before they alienate Irish sympathies for constitutional agitation, especially now that India and Egypt are in turmoil and the overseas colonies are demanding an imperial federation. From their own point of view, it would be inadvisable to let a stubborn veto provoke a reaction from a people which, poor in everything else, is rich solely in political ideas, has perfected the tactics of obstructionism and has made the word "Boycott" an international battle-cry.'[76]

Joyce did not have the advantage of being in Dublin, and he knew that *Sinn Féin*, his principal source of intelligence, was not representative of mainstream nationalist opinion. He did not anticipate that a convention of the United Irish League would reject the bill, and his own view seemed to be that it would be better that the bill, paltry as it was, passed. What is of greater significance for the politics of Joyce's exile is the remarkable reference to the Irish as 'rich solely in political

75. *Sinn Féin*, 11 May 1907. Deeming the bill 'an insult to the Irish nation', the national executive of the recently constituted Sinn Féin called on 'the Irishmen who have attended the British Parliament during the last 21 years in support of the British Liberal Party, to withdraw from parliament and return to Ireland to devise in conjunction with others means of advancing the international recognition of Ireland's political rights' (*Sinn Féin*, 18 May 1907).

76. *OCPW* 143.

ideas'. It is inconceivable that Joyce would have made this observation at the outset of his exile, though it does represent a carrying forward, into the realm of the modern political, of the theme of Irish influence in his lecture delivered the previous month. It was not so long since Joyce had immersed himself in Italian socialism to see what lessons it had to impart to the backward Irish.

'Even from a cursory study of the history of Home Rule', two lessons could be drawn. The first was that 'the most powerful weapons that England may use against Ireland are no longer those of Conservatism, but of Liberalism and the Vatican'. 'Conservatism, for all that it may be tyrannical, is a frank and openly hostile doctrine.' It did not want 'a rival island to grow up beside Great Britain'. Joyce's scathing conclusion was that 'it takes little intelligence to see that Gladstone inflicted greater damage on Ireland than Disraeli did, and that the fiercest enemy of the Catholic Irish is the leader of English Vaticanism, the Duke of Norfolk.' The second lesson was that 'the Irish Parliamentary Party is bankrupt'.[77] While the country continued its decline, the parliamentarians had improved their own lot.

Contemplating the twenty-one years, Joyce brooded on what he saw as the betrayal of Parnell. He had earlier in the article referred to Gladstone between his two Home Rule bills as 'having in the interim effected the moral assassination of Parnell with the help of the Irish bishops'.[78] He now argued that while the country had continued its decline, the parliamentarians had improved their own lot. This left him poised for attack: 'Only in 1891 did they give proof of their altruism when they sold Parnell, their master, to the pharisaical conscience of the English nonconformists, without exacting the thirty pieces of silver.'[79] The recall of Parnell's placidly contemptuous urging of his followers in Committee Room 15 not to sell him for nothing merges into the thirty pieces of silver paid to Judas Iscariot to betray Christ. It was superbly cutting.

77. *OCPW* 144.
78. *OCPW* 142.
79. *OCPW* 144.

Joyce's third Home Rule article was 'La Cometa dell "Home Rule"' (The Home Rule Comet) which was published on 22 December 1910. Two and a half years had supervened since the publication of 'Home Rule Comes of Age', and there is a new assuredness of tone. While Kevin Barry is likely correct to claim that the image of its title derived from a cartoon in *Sinn Féin* of 11 June 1910,[80] its text discloses little that takes its inspiration from Griffith's journalism, and suggests Joyce was not as reliant on *Sinn Féin* for news of Ireland as he had been. This reflects the fact that the two elections of 1910 had left the Irish Party with the balance of power, and the controversy over the removal of the veto of the House of Lords meant that the question of Home Rule featured prominently in the English newspapers. The level of political detail suggests that Joyce had greater access to, and was quite extensively reading, English newspapers.[81] The election in January 1910 which left Redmond's Irish Party with the balance of power precipitated a deep schism within Herbert Henry Asquith's Liberal government, and a new and not entirely scrupulous aggressiveness on the part of the Conservatives.[82] The results of the December election closely mirrored those of January. An article of John Redmond, though published early in the new year, after Joyce's article had appeared, succinctly expressed the Irish Party's interpretation of the result against which Joyce's article was largely set: 'The result of the General Election of December, 1910, may fairly be claimed as a great and an unprecedented triumph for the Progressive and Democratic forces of Great Britain and Ireland. It has sealed the doom of the Veto power of the House of Lords, and it has given a clear and unequivocal mandate to the Premier to settle the Irish question finally'.[83]

80. *OCPW* 328.

81. Aside from the familiarity displayed with English politics and politicians, Joyce refers to the frequency with which parliamentary sketch writers picked up on Arthur Balfour's 'absorbed and quibbling manner' (*OCPW* 157).

82. Ronan Fanning, *Fatal Path: British Government and Irish Revolution, 1910–22* (London: Faber and Faber, 2013), 30–52.

83. *Freeman's Journal*, 6 January 1911, quoted in Meleady, *John Redmond*, 186–87.

Joyce in fact attributes strikingly similar sentiments to Redmond, who 'announced the happy news to a crowd of fishermen' the previous week, and immediately comments, 'Now, it would take a voracious nationalist to swallow that mouthful.'[84]

Joyce's article was written in the hiatus between the general election and the meeting of the new Parliament on 31 January 1911. The prospects for Home Rule remained far from clear, which engendered Joyce's conceit that the Home Rule comet on its most recent appearance was barely visible due to a thickening of 'the fogginess that usually envelops the shores of Britain'. Joyce negotiated the void of uncertainty with considerable grace, revealing in the process a close familiarity with the personalities of British and Irish politics and a high adeptness in characterising them.

He observed that while the three leaders, Asquith, Arthur Balfour, and Redmond, 'until now had managed to maintain a certain dignity of conduct that does not ill-become vacuous men, the recent election campaign marks a considerable lowering of tone in English public life'. Joyce continued, the jibes of David Lloyd George 'pale before the vulgar invective of Conservatives' such as F. E. Smith, Edward Carson, and the editor of the *National Review* (Leopold James Maxse, a committed imperialist), who were to be prominent in promoting Ulster resistance to Home Rule. Meanwhile 'the two Irish factions' (by which he meant Redmond's Irish Party and William O'Brien's All-for-Ireland League, which held seven seats in Cork city and county) were 'oblivious of their common enemy, have been waging an [undeclared] war in an attempt to exhaust the lexicon of contempt'.[85]

In charting the confusion of politics, Joyce noted that 'it is the clerical and intractable [*intransigente*] Irish party that forms the majority within an anticlerical and Liberal government'.[86] The secularism of the Liberal party was a concern of dissentient conservative nationalists in Ireland.

84. *OCPW* 157–58.

85. *OCPW* 155. The Italian phrase '*guerra sorda*' (*OCPW* 223) is open to more than one rendering, but that of 'a secret war' makes little sense (*OCPW* 155).

86. *OCPW* 157.

Joyce turned the point round the other way, to stress the clericalism of the Irish Party.

A further source of confusion was that 'the English parties no longer answer to their names . . . a paradoxical situation reflected in the persons who are the party leaders'. He wrote of Joseph Chamberlain[87] and Lord Rosebery, 'who, the one from extreme radicalism and the other from Gladstonian liberalism, have both crossed over to the ranks of imperialism (while the young minister [Winston] Churchill has made his imaginary journey in the opposite direction)'. Yet more remarkably 'we find the cause of Anglican Protestantism and conciliatory Nationalism under the guidance of a religious renegade and a converted Fenian'. The 'religious renegade' who espoused the 'cause of Anglican Protestantism' was Arthur James Balfour, nephew of the third Marquess of Salisbury, and prime minister from 1902 to 1905, who retained the leadership of the Conservative party till 1911. He had no institutional role whatever in relation to Anglicanism, so that one is driven back upon the adage of the Anglican Church being the Conservative party at prayer. Joyce was fascinated by the fact that Balfour, whom he elsewhere claimed as a Celt, was a philosopher and the author of *A Defence of Philosophic Doubt* (1879), before he was pressed into politics by the third Marquess of Salisbury. He wrote that Balfour's biographer 'will be able to say of him that in his philosophical essays he skilfully dissected and stripped bare the secret fibres of the religious and psychological principles whose champion he became by a turn of the parliamentary wheel of fortune.'[88]

The 'converted Fenian' who became an exponent of 'conciliatory nationalism' was the agrarian agitator and member of Parliament William O'Brien. O'Brien had become persuaded of the merits of conciliation as a result of the conference that led to the enactment of the Wyndham Land Act of 1903 and was thereafter mostly at odds with the leadership of the Irish Party. He grew again close to T. M. Healy, with whom he had bitterly fallen out in the course of the Parnell Split. He established the

87. Chamberlain had from 1906 withdrawn from public life and died in 1914.

88. *OCPW* 157.

All-for-Ireland League on 31 March 1910. O'Brien was prone to sudden political lurches. Joyce wrote, 'O'Brien, the leader of the Irish dissidents, who calls his handful of ten deputies the All-for-Ireland League, has become what all fanatics become when their fanaticism dies before they do. Now he fights along with Unionist magistrates who, twenty years ago, would probably have issued a warrant for his arrest; nothing remains of his fiery youth apart from those violent outbursts that make him look like an epileptic.'[89] Joyce's assessment of O'Brien was not far from that of John O'Leary, who described him as 'a historic lunatic'.[90]

Joyce's bracketing of Balfour and O'Brien is intriguing. It is not merely his amusement in yoking together two entirely disparate individuals who had nothing in common but the oddness of their political *parcours*. While Joyce makes no reference to the fact, which might have been too much for his Triestine readership, O'Brien had been pitted against Balfour during Balfour's Chief Secretaryship of Ireland from 1887 to 1891. Balfour's prosecution of O'Brien under the Crimes Act led to a confrontation between the Royal Irish Constabulary and demonstrators at Mitchelstown in September 1887 at which the police shot three people. Balfour became hated in Ireland as 'Bloody Balfour'.[91] It is as if Joyce, in a kind of geometric exercise, were trying to work out whether one could apply the idea of the 'coincidence of opposites', conceptualised in his 'Two Masters' thesis, to individuals.

Joyce countered the sanguine expectations of John Redmond with the lessons of 'the history of Anglo-Saxon Liberalism'. The Irish question would divide the cabinet, 'following which it will be amply demonstrated that the English electorate had not really authorized its government to legislate to such an end'. If the government took the alternative route of palliative measures with the intention of undermining the strength of nationalist feeling, and if they introduced a reform or a pretence of reform that Ireland rejected, that would be an opportune moment for the Conservatives to intervene: 'Faithful to its long tradition of cynical

89. *OCPW* 157.

90. Callanan, *T. M. Healy*, 703n65.

91. James Quinn, 'Arthur James Balfour', *DIB* 1:239–42.

faithlessness', it would take the opportunity 'to declare that the Irish dictatorship is intolerable' and seek to have reduced the number of Irish seats. Joyce's reply to Redmond was plain: 'The link, therefore, between the abolition of the veto of the Lords and Irish autonomy is not as immediate as some might have us believe'. 'In the final reckoning', he wrote, the abolition of the veto of the House of Lords 'is the business of the English themselves'.[92] He thought the English would probably proceed, slowly and cautiously, with the abolition of the Lords' veto. Joyce did not actually oppose the Irish Party's support of the Liberals in ending the veto, as *Sinn Féin* did. With the somewhat casuistic and disingenuous logic to which he frequently resorted in his critique of Redmond's political strategy, Griffith objected to linking the fortunes of Home Rule with the success of the attack on the House of Lords, partly on the grounds that 'Mr. Parnell always refused to permit the Irish party to take part in the agitation for the curtailment of the power of the English House of Lords', as to do so would align the Irish Party with the Liberals and undermine the playing off of the British parties against each other.[93] In the event the Parliament Act was enacted on 18 August 1911, though the substitution of a suspensive veto for two years for an absolute veto was to have unanticipated consequences.[94] The looming abolition of the House of Lords did have the effect of prompting the beginnings of the mobilisation of loyalist resistance to Home Rule, the idea of which scarcely impinged on nationalist thinking in 1909–11.

Nationalist divergences over Irish enlistment in the abolition of the veto of the House of Lords were nonetheless significant and went back to the divergent attitudes of Parnell and Michael Davitt to the relationship in which Irish nationalism stood to the British 'democracy'. The concluding part of Joyce's article was honed by the politics of the Split, and was bitingly Parnellite:

> The fact that Ireland wishes to make common cause with British democracy should be neither surprising nor persuasive. For seven cen-

92. *OCPW* 158.

93. 'The Irish Liberal Party', *Sinn Féin*, 24 December 1909.

94. Fanning, *Fatal Path*, 50–57.

turies it has never been a faithful subject of England. Nor, on the other hand, has it been faithful to itself. It entered the British dominion without forming an integral part of it. It almost entirely abandoned its language and accepted the language of the conqueror without being able to assimilate its culture. It always betrayed its heroes in their hour of need without even earning the bounty payment. It has driven its spiritual creators into exile and then boasted of them. It has only ever served one mistress faithfully, the Roman Catholic Church, which is, however, accustomed to paying her faithful in long-term drafts.

What durable alliance could exist between this strange people and the new Anglo-Saxon democracy? The rhetoricians who now speak so warmly about this alliance will soon become aware (if they have not done so already) that there exists a mysterious communion of blood between the English nobles and workers.[95]

It was not that long since Joyce had been drawn to Italian revolutionary syndicalism, but he was harshly suspicious of the British Labour Party and movement, perhaps because of Fabian influence and a tendency to think of the Labour Party as an annex of the Liberal party.[96]

Maamtrasna: 'Who Killed Myles Joyce?'

Joyce published in *Il Piccolo della Sera* of 16 September 1907 an article entitled 'L'Irlanda alla sbarra', translated by Conor Deane as 'Ireland at the Bar' and perhaps better by Adrian Hardiman as 'Ireland in the Dock.'[97] It is an account of the Maamtrasna murder trials of 1882, which Joyce uses as an image for the denial to Ireland of a hearing of its protests against English injustice.

On 19 October 1902, the Lord Lieutenant of Ireland, the Earl of Dudley, accompanied by the Countess, left Dublin in an entourage for a tour

95. *OCPW* 159.

96. Griffith, in a similar vein, accused the United Irish League of seeking to merge the Irish in 'the English Liberal-Labour Party' (*Sinn Féin*, 24 December 1909).

97. *OCPW* 145; A. Hardiman, *Joyce in Court*, 52.

of the west of Ireland. It was not a cavalcade by carriage as in the 'Wandering Rocks' episode in *Ulysses*, but a journey by train to Galway, and thence by motor car: two Panhards and a Mors. The Unionist press deferentially chronicled the progress of viceroy and vicereine. They reached what was known as Joyce country, which lay between the villages of Leenane and Cong in north-west County Galway bordering Mayo (Maamtrasna itself became part of Mayo in 1898). On the morning of 21 October, the motorcade set off from Leenane through steep mountain roads: 'The route followed had, for the greater part, never previously been traversed by motor cars, and the appearance of these vehicles naturally excited great curiosity on the part of the peasants'.[98] The *Irish Times* reported that the 'wild mountain road' led to Maamtrasna, 'a name famous some twenty years back by reason of one of the most shocking murders of the Land League days. The scene of the tragedy was pointed out to their Excellencies as they drove past. The whole environment was now of surpassing loneliness. Gloomy mountains loomed up on all sides, and vast expanses of boggy land extended on each side of the road'.[99] At Derrypark, the viceregal party visited a lace school carried on by the parish priest under the auspices of the Congested Districts Board:

> When their Excellencies left the school one of the most affecting incidents of the tour occurred. Amongst the crowd of peasants who had assembled on the roadside were three women, the wives of three men who were sentenced to penal servitude in connection with the Maamtrasna murders. Approaching their Excellencies the women pleaded for the release of their husbands. One of them, sobbing bitterly, seized Lady Dudley's hands and poured out the story of a lonely life since her husband had been sent to prison. The other women were also demonstrative in their appeal, and their Excellencies were much affected by the scene. Lord Dudley assured the poor creatures that their petition would be carefully considered when he returned to Dublin.[100]

98. *Daily Express*, 22 October 1902.
99. *Irish Times*, 22 October 1902.
100. *Daily Express*, 22 October 1902.

The *Irish Times* reported, 'The bleak region charged with bleaker memory was then left behind, and the motor cars made rapid progress towards Cong.'[101] What the accounts in the *Daily Express* and the *Irish Times* omitted was the fact that the women's pleas were 'in expressive Gaelic', and an interpreter was quickly found.[102]

Three days later, having served all but one month of the twenty years to which a sentence of penal servitude equated, Martin Joyce, Patrick Joyce (John), and Thomas Joyce (Pat) were released from Maryborough Jail.[103] They were taken by train to Dublin, and thence to Ballinrobe. Terrified of the crowd that waited to greet them, they asked to be taken in a covered wagon to the Cavalry Barracks. After midnight they headed off in the rain, making the eighteen-mile half circuit of Lough Mask that took them back at last to their homes in Cappanacreha, three miles beyond which lay Maamtrasna.[104]

With their release the bitterly contested events of 1882—the murders, the trials, and the sentences—flared back into public controversy for a final time. Unionist and nationalist papers carried opposing characterisations of Maamtrasna and its sequel. The *Daily Express* referred to the murders as 'perhaps the most horrible occurrence in connection with the Irish land agitation'. The *Freeman's Journal*, whose coverage carried full reports of the major speeches on the amendment to the address moved by Timothy C. Harrington on 23 October 1884, insisted that the murders were 'unconnected with any agrarian or public question.'[105]

The one incontrovertible fact was the killings. On the night of 17–18 August 1882, five members of the family of John Joyce were slaughtered in their Maamtrasna habitation: Joyce, his mother, his wife, his daughter, and a son who lived for a while; a second son survived his injuries. The Maamtrasna murders created an immediate sensation. The killing of the Joyce family occurred in the enervated aftermath of the Phoenix Park

101. *Irish Times*, 22 October 1902.

102. *Ballinrobe Chronicle*, 30 October 1902, quoted in Jarlath Waldron, *Maamtrasna: The Murders and the Mystery* (Dublin: Edmund Burke, 1992), 307.

103. *Freeman's Journal*, 25 October 1902.

104. Waldron, *Maamtrasna*, 307–11.

105. *Freeman's Journal*, 25 October 1902.

murders on 6 May. Maamtrasna was investigated by the police and by newspapermen. On that was superimposed the disjuncture between the savagery of the murders and the beauty and remoteness of the setting.

Maamtrasna was inaccessible. The reporter for the *Daily Express*, given conflicting information on how best to reach it, went by the longer route through Oughterard and took fourteen hours to reach his destination: 'The journey as regards time and distance was the longest I could have taken, and though I passed through scenery almost unsurpassed for wild majestic splendour, it was at the moment scarcely a compensation for the physical exhaustion and the risk of travelling unescorted through the most dangerous fastnesses of the Joyce country.'[106]

He rendered it a journey into the ever-deepening unknown: 'Little as I knew of the goal to which I was tending when I left Dublin, my knowledge grew less and more perplexing as I approached.' Maamtrasna 'seems shut out from all other life by mountain chains and ranges, high, bleak, and strangely impressive, confusedly huddled, the fragments of an earlier world.' The house of John Joyce was 'a hovel, his land a patch of potatoes and cabbage': 'There was nothing in the shape of furniture in the house, than which it is impossible to conceive anything meaner or more horrible as the habitation of human beings. No window threw light into the domicile. A hole in the wall of the second chamber gave it all the ventilation and illumination it possessed, and fire was simply made by burning peat on the floor, the smoke finding an exit by the little door.'[107]

Anthony Joyce and his brother John, sons of Maolra Joyce, were tenants of Lord Leitrim and regarded as interlopers by their neighbours: Anthony Joyce had previously feuded with his cousin Myles Joyce, one of the 'Shaun' Joyces whom the Maolra Joyces hated. They came forward, with John's son Patrick claiming to have followed the murder gang over the mountainside to the house of John Joyce, to have witnessed the murders, and to be able to identify the murderers. All except two of the ten men they named were neighbours, and three were their own first cousins.[108]

106. *Daily Express*, 21 August 1882.
107. *Daily Express*, 21 August 1882.
108. Waldron, *Maamtrasna*, 29, 35–36, 40–42.

George Bolton, then Crown Solicitor for Tipperary, was put in charge of the case. Notorious for his aggressive techniques and absence of scruple, Bolton was already deeply involved in the investigation into the Phoenix Park murders.

In Dublin's Kilmainham Jail, two of the Maamtrasna prisoners, Anthony Philbin and Thomas Casey, turned 'approvers', meaning that they had agreed to inculpate their co-accused. Eight men, five bearing the surname Joyce, were tried for the murders.

Under the provisions of the Prevention of Crimes Act of 1882—for nationalists 'the Coercion Act'—the prosecution could transfer a case out of the local area. The ten Maamtrasna prisoners were transferred from Galway to be tried by a special commission sitting in Green Street in Dublin comprising a judge and a jury made up of 'Special Jurors', who were propertied but by no means exclusively Protestant.[109]

By the time Myles Joyce stood trial, Patrick Joyce and Pat Casey had already been convicted and sentenced to death. Myles Joyce did not speak or understand English, and he had the benefit of an interpreter only at the beginning and end of the trial. He was convicted and sentenced to death at the end of the second day of his trial. When the interpreter explained the verdict to him, according to the report of the *Daily Express*, 'the facility with which he spake, the easy, rapidly-changing and not ungraceful motion of his hands as he accentuated his declaration, combined with the strange, unusual, but sonorous sounds of the mountain Gaelic in which he apostrophised, as it were, heaven to bear testimony to his freedom from guilt, made a remarkable impression on the court.'[110]

The remaining prisoners, encouraged by Fr Michael McHugh, the curate of Clonbur, pleaded guilty in an equivocal plea bargain. Their

109. Waldron, *Maamtrasna*, 54, 132.

110. Waldron, *Maamtrasna*, 108–23; *Daily Express*, 20 November 1882. Myles Joyce and his co-accused were not the only Irish speakers sentenced to death in Green Street Courthouse in this period, but there appears to have been something striking in his protests. Katharine Tynan, then a member of the Ladies Land League, recalled, 'I saw more than one murder trial in Green Street. I suppose it was the psychology of the crowd that carried me thither and kept me there. I remember those Irish-speaking prisoners who stood in the dock, their arms outstretched in the form of a cross, while the sentence was passed in a tongue of which they did not understand a word, after a trial in the same strange speech' (*Twenty-Five Years*, 81).

FIGURE 15.1. Myles Joyce. Reproduced courtesy of the National Library of Ireland, ALB40.

death sentences were commuted to penal servitude for life. 'At the last moment', the Liberal viceroy, Lord Spencer, received 'a memorial or quasi-memorial through the *Freeman's Journal* to say Myles Joyce was not guilty and that the other two would state that on the scaffold'. Spencer, who had granted the reprieve to the prisoners who had pleaded guilty in the face of considerable pressure, declined the memorial on behalf of Myles Joyce.[111]

Three days before the date set for the executions in Galway Jail, Patrick Joyce and Patrick Casey made statements exculpating Myles Joyce. The three men were hanged in the exercise yard of Galway Jail on 15 December 1882. Myles Joyce, who paused at the base of the scaffold to say, 'Ara, tá mé ag imeacht' (I am going), continued volubly to protest his innocence, whether to the functionaries carrying out the execution or to the reporters who were present. Perhaps because he persisted in his protests, the execution was botched. Marwood, the executioner, struggled for a minute or two to disengage the rope, which had slipped down Myles Joyce's pinioned arm, and the prisoner died of strangulation.[112]

T. P. O'Connor wrote, in his somewhat facile manner, 'That scene will live in Irish memory to the end of time', but its impact was anything but immediate. There was a marked revulsion within mainstream nationalism against atrocities. O'Connor wrote, 'The outbursts of bloody passion which had followed the arrest of Mr. Parnell had left behind feelings of profound horror, and these feelings were transformed into a sense of sickened loathing by the Maamtrasna massacre.'[113] Horror over the Phoenix Park murders conditioned the initial response to the Maamtrasna convictions, which the nationalist press largely welcomed.[114] While there was a certain unease from the moment of his

111. Waldron, *Maamtrasna*, 126–31, 140.

112. Waldron, *Maamtrasna*, 149–51.

113. T. P. O'Connor, *The Parnell Movement*, 2nd ed. (London: Kegan Paul, Trench, 1886), 473–74.

114. Waldron, *Maamtrasna*, 132. *United Ireland* redeemed itself with a famous editorial of 23 December 1882 entitled 'Accusing Spirits'; Waldron, *Maamtrasna*, 156–57.

conviction,[115] two years supervened before a general public outrage at the fate of Myles Joyce took hold. His death became the subject of a time-lagged retro-politicisation. This came about because of the sequence of disclosures from 1884 about the trial which merged with the unsettling narrative of Myles Joyce being taken to execution.

On 8 August 1884 Thomas Casey, one of the approvers, made a public confession of his perjury in the church in Tourmakeady to a congregation assembled for a confirmation during the annual visitation of the Archbishop of Tuam. He gave an interview to Edward Byrne of the *Freeman's Journal*, as did Anthony Philbin. Both elaborated on the role of George Bolton, who was at that time the subject of unsavoury disclosures concerning his personal life.[116] Spencer stood over the convictions. He became the object of increasing public opprobrium in Ireland. Timothy Harrington was the politician principally responsible for pressing the issue of Maamtrasna. He attacked the trials in a series of letters to the *Freeman's Journal* from August to October 1884,[117] subsequently published in book form.

Edward Ennis, a nationalist barrister, came upon the discarded brief of one of the prosecuting counsel in Green Street Courthouse. It contained the undisclosed statements of Patsy Joyce, the boy who had survived, and Michael Joyce, the boy who had lingered before dying, that the murderers wore bright clothes and had their faces blackened, which undermined the concerted prosecution evidence that the attackers had worn dark clothes and were not disguised. Ennis gave the brief to T. M. Healy, who already had concerns—when he was imprisoned in Richmond Jail in early 1883, he had heard an account from the warder, who had been in Kilmainham when the Maamtrasna prisoners were there. He was now converted to the cause.[118] On 24 October 1884 Harrington moved an amendment of the queen's speech on the subject of Maamtrasna. The debate took place over four days. Parnell spoke, and Gladstone

115. Tynan, *Twenty-Five Years*, 79.

116. Waldron, *Maamtrasna*, 167–69, 172–75, 179.

117. Waldron, *Maamtrasna*, 197.

118. Waldron, *Maamtrasna*, 179; T. M. Healy, *Letters and Leaders of My Day* (London: Thornton Butterworth, 1928), 1:186–89.

was drawn in to defend Spencer. What was most significant was the interventions of Tories such as Randolph Churchill and Edward Clarke criticising the conduct of the cases.[119]

The controversy over Maamtrasna engulfed Lord Spencer. The state of Irish opinion is illustrated by the bemused account of Sir Charles Dilke, a leading Liberal who visited Ireland in May 1885. On Whit Sunday, Dilke and Spencer, under discreet but heavy police protection, walked by the site of the Phoenix Park murders on to the Strawberry Beds, past thousands of Dubliners. 'In the course of the whole long walk but one man lifted his hat to Spencer, who was universally recognised, but assailed by the majority of those we met with shouts of "Who killed Myles Joyce?", while some varied the proceedings by calling "Murderer!" after him. A few days later, when I was driving with Lady Spencer in an open carriage, a well-dressed bicyclist came riding through the cavalry escort, and in a quiet, conversational tone observed to us, "Who killed Myles Joyce?"'[120]

A year after Dilke's visit, in a division on the budget in the early hours of 9 June 1885, the Conservatives and the Irish Party brought down Gladstone's government. T. P. O'Connor described the scene as it became apparent the government had lost:

> Lord Randolph Churchill was the leader of the uproar. . . . The Parnellites, meantime, kept silence, having delivered so many blows that had just stopped short. But when the paper was handed to Mr. Winn, the Parnellites felt secure, and burst into a deep, wild note of triumph. 'Coercion!' 'Buckshot!' 'Spencer!' and in one solitary instance 'Myles Joyce!' rose from their thick and excited ranks; their self-controlled leader did not join in the cries, but his pale face was a trifle paler, and there was a happy smile upon it. Throughout all this mad tumult—one of the maddest ever seen in the House of Commons—Mr. Gladstone remained outwardly untroubled, unheeding, even unhearing.[121]

119. J. L. Hammond, *Gladstone and the Irish Nation* (London: Longmans, Green), 319–21.

120. Stephen Gwynn and Gertrude Tuckwell, *The Life of the Rt. Hon Sir Charles W. Dilke* (London: John Murray, 1917), 2:138–39.

121. T. P. O'Connor, *Gladstone's House of Commons* (London: Ward and Downey, 1885), 553–54. This originally appeared as a parliamentary sketch in the *Pall Mall Gazette*.

Sir William Harcourt, the outgoing Liberal home secretary, notable for a candid impatience on all matters that pertained to Ireland, referred to the combining of the Tories and the Irish Party as 'the Maamtrasna alliance'.[122]

The new Conservative government of Lord Salisbury decided not to concede Parnell's demand for an inquiry into Maamtrasna. On 15 July 1885 Parnell moved for an inquiry. The vehemence of the Irish onslaught on Spencer miscarried, and the debate did little more than open a rift between the Irish and the government, so undermining the prospects for the negotiations that Parnell was to conduct with Carnarvon, the Lord Lieutenant.[123] The debate was barren of results for the four prisoners. Carnarvon subsequently rejected the memorials of appeal submitted on their behalf. One of the prisoners, Michael Casey, died in Maryborough prison a month after the debate. He was believed to have been guilty. The remaining prisoners were believed innocent by Harrington and others.[124] So ended the belated and improbable elevation of Maamtrasna into late Victorian high politics. If something of the trial lingered in the public mind, the releases of the last three Maamtrasna prisoners in the Edwardian Ireland of late October 1902 had the aspect of a historical and topographical curiosity.

The Maamtrasna murders were not political in any meaningful sense of the term. The horror of the slaughter of the household of John Joyce was such that it would inevitably create a public sensation. Its timing months after the Phoenix Park murders ensured that it acquired a political colouration. In a contemporary political *imaginaire* steeped in ideas of incorrigible Irish criminality, it was perceived as complementary to the assassinations perpetrated by the Invincibles in the Phoenix Park. Nationalist opinion was itself shaken by the Phoenix Park assassinations and the Maamtrasna murders. In their calculated atrociousness, neither was compatible with the nationalist and post-1886 Liberal narrative of a degree of low-level rural crime in Ireland attributable to

122. T. M. Healy, *Letters and Leaders*, 1:188. Harcourt could not pronounce the name Maamtrasna, which he pronounced as 'Mantrasma'.

123. Hammond, *Gladstone and the Irish Nation*, 380–82. The piously Gladstonian Hammond commented, 'Thus the ghost of Maamtrasna still worked mischief' (382).

124. Waldron, *Maamtrasna*, 297–300; T. Harrington, *The Maamtrasna Massacre* (Dublin: Nation Office, 1884), ix.

the underlying injustices of Irish land law. Maamtrasna was in an area of Galway/Mayo that had eluded the control of the Land League. There were rumours that the murders had something to do with a secret society, a survival of 'Ribbonism', 'the name given to the sporadic, ineffective, and usually violent agrarian combinations which had preceded the Land League'.[125] In October 1881 Parnell, dining with two Irish members, was asked who was to take his place if he was arrested, and replied, 'Ah, if I am arrested, Captain Moonlight will take my place'.[126] What he meant was that a recrudescence of localised agrarian intimidation and violence would be the result of his arrest and the suppression of the Land League. Parnell later asserted that the Maamtrasna murders involved a secret society dispute.[127] His purpose was to reinforce his own narrative on the subject of crime in rural Ireland, and to suggest the existence of a structure of agrarian violence which the Land League had held in check. What prompted the murders was probably what George Bolton claimed when he briefed the press at the time and later asserted. On 3 January 1882 Joseph Huddy and his grandson, who were serving ejectments for the non-payment of rent, were murdered at Clonbrack, County Galway. Their bodies were thrown in weighted sacks into the middle of Lough Mask. According to Bolton, a paragraph in a Dublin paper said that the authorities had been aided in finding the bodies later in the month by an old woman residing on the mountain overlooking Lough Mask who had seen the bodies being thrown in when she was gathering firewood. The perpetrators believed this woman to be Margaret Joyce, the mother of John Joyce, who had shortly before the murders gone to live with her son. Bolton believed this led to her murder and to that of her son, and that the rest of the household were killed to ensure the perpetrators were not identified.[128] Bolton's account has the merit of explaining how the entire Joyce household came to be slaughtered.

125. C. C. O'Brien, *Parnell and His Party*, 3.

126. R. B. O'Brien, *Charles Stewart Parnell*, 1:311–12. O'Brien notes that threatening notices to landlords or refractory tenants were signed 'Captain Moonlight'.

127. Waldron, *Maamtrasna*, 249.

128. George Bolton, *A Short Account of the Discovery and Conviction of the 'Invincibles'* (Dublin: Hodges, Figgis, 1887), 34–35. Michael Davitt largely adopted Bolton's account (*Fall of Feudalism*, 384). For the dissemination of Bolton's hypothesis at the time, see Waldron,

Jarlath Waldron, the well-informed and attentive modern chronicler of the murders, has characterised John Joyce as 'unquestionably the champion sheep-stealer in the Valley'. Big John Casey of Bunachrick was 'easily the wealthiest man in the Valley',[129] where wealth was measured in sheep. Harrington, in his pamphlet, identified Casey as the 'supposed leader' of the attack on the Joyce household,[130] and *United Ireland* repeatedly charged that the murders were carried out at Casey's instigation.[131] What is plain is that the murders took place on a plane that was utterly remote from the contemporary political and had nothing to do with Parnell, with the Land League, with the Fenians, or indeed with the Invincibles.

The story of Maamtrasna retained a certain currency in Ireland, though marked by a tendency to fade into vaguely remembered anecdote that contrasted with the more deeply incised recall of the Phoenix Park murders, which fitted into the binary narrative of physical force versus constitutional nationalism. Joyce perhaps heard of the murders and the execution of Myles Joyce first from his father, who was friendly with Harrington.[132] He may have heard it again from Nora.[133] The newspaper accounts of the release of the last three prisoners in 1902 certainly called it back to mind, across the span of the two decades that had supervened. Joyce had no materials on Maamtrasna in Trieste, and it seems unlikely that he had ever read Harrington's *The Maamtrasna Massacre*. Many of the details of Joyce's narrative were wrong. Those arrested and put on trial were not 'four or five peasants', nor were all the prisoners 'members of the ancient tribe of the Joyces', as he proudly stated. Myles Joyce had not given evidence, but Joyce invented a couple

---

Maamtrasna, 20; and the reports collated under the heading 'Crime and Law in Ireland', *Irish Times*, 21 August 1882.

129. Waldron, *Maamtrasna*, 30.

130. Harrington, *Maamtrasna Massacre*, ix. Big John Casey headed a list remarkably entitled 'The Actual Murderers (Now Alleged)'.

131. Waldron, *Maamtrasna*, 180.

132. Jackson and Costello, *John Stanislaus Joyce*, 121–22.

133. The possibility that Joyce had reheard of Maamtrasna from Nora does not warrant Kevin Barry's statement that 'his version of the Maamtrasna murders is the shreds of a story told by his wife Nora' (*OCPW* xxi).

of exchanges of Myles Joyce with the bench, in which the voluble answers of 'the patriarch of the miserable tribe' were translated with economic paraphrase by 'the officious interpreter'. He characterised Myles Joyce as 'protesting, shouting, almost beside himself with the distress of not making himself understood, weeping with rage and terror'.[134] As it happens, Joyce had not done justice to the scene that took place when, after Myles Joyce was convicted, the judge asked him if he had anything to say. The *Freeman's Journal* reported, 'The hitherto silent and placid Myles suddenly broke into a tirade of rapid and fluent Gaelic, all of which was accompanied by the most violent but expressive gestures and bodily movements. His eyes blazed, his face reddened and yet, withal, there was no anger or resentment there but surprise, total incomprehension, a passionate desire to communicate to God, to the court, to the world, his solemn affirmation of innocence.'[135]

Joyce even missed Myles Joyce's protestations of innocence on the scaffold, substituting a narrative in which the square in front of the prison was 'packed with people who were kneeling and calling out prayers in Irish for the repose of the soul of Myles Joyce'. Struggling to recall what he had been told about the execution, he wrote that 'legend has it that even the hangman could not make himself understood by the victim and angrily kicked the unhappy man in the head to force him into the noose.'[136] In Joyce's account, Myles Joyce was convicted because his lack of English denied him the ability to defend himself, rather than by reason of the false testimony of kinsmen and neighbours. Joyce's account unintentionally exemplifies what came to be his conviction that historically nothing was properly remembered but neither was it entirely lost.

Joyce's narrative pivots into a magnificent metaphor: 'The figure of this bewildered old man, left over from a culture which is not ours, a deaf-mute before his judge, is a symbol of the Irish nation at the bar of public opinion.'[137] The characterisation of Myles Joyce as 'left over

134. *OCPW* 145.

135. *Freeman's Journal*, 20 November 1902; Waldron, *Maamtrasna*, 121–22.

136. *OCPW* 145.

137. *OCPW* 146.

from a culture which is not ours' (avanzo di una civiltà non nostra) is strangely affecting. It matches the pronouncement in 'L'Irlanda: Isola dei santi e dei savi' that 'just as ancient Egypt is dead, so is ancient Ireland'.[138] The evocative resonance of the phrase is not limited to the dying out of the Irish language, though it is that which principally gives it its haunting force. It is also about the fading out of pre-Parnellite Ireland, even the remorseless effacement of that anterior Ireland by Parnellism as a modernising nationalist movement, as well as by socio-economic advances. The new Ireland rudely displaced all the old Irelands, but in Joyce's strange way the brutality of the moment of passing briefly revives that which has seemingly vanished and flickeringly reinstates the potentialities that are lost. The statement that the culture to which Myles Joyce belonged was 'not ours' by reference to that of Joyce's audience in Trieste as well as that of Ireland accentuates the distance in epoch from the Maamtrasna of 1882.

That reverberating phrase 'left over from a culture which is not ours' opens an imaginative rift of consummate complexity that cuts through the complacently nationalist narrative to restore the terrible solitude of Myles Joyce as he met his fate. If the judicial authority could not understand Myles Joyce (nor he its procedures), analogously to the way England denied Ireland a political hearing, the world of Myles Joyce was also lost to comprehension in the Ireland and Europe of the early twentieth century. There was in that way a subtle filiation between how Myles Joyce was perceived at his trial in 1882 and how he was perceived in 1907 that prevented Joyce's account being read simplistically as merely an account of a gross miscarriage of justice perpetrated under British rule in Ireland. That filiation had a more powerful salience for the contemporary Irish audience Joyce's article never reached than it had for his Triestine readership. It is the first articulation of Joyce's anti-positivistic imaginative sympathy with individuals and cultures defeated and displaced in the process of history.

Two-thirds of the article is devoted to the subject for which the story of Myles Joyce provides the overture: 'Like him, Ireland cannot appeal to the modern conscience of England or abroad. The English

138. *OCPW* 126.

newspapers act as interpreters between Ireland and the English electorate which, though it lends an ear every so often is finally irritated by the eternal complaints of the Nationalist deputies who, it believes, have come to their House with the aim of upsetting the order and extorting money.'[139]

Abroad, Ireland did not feature unless there were some violent episodes such as those that had recently received coverage. These were riots in Belfast, and episodes of cattle-driving, where cattle was driven off graziers' lands in an attempt to force the graziers' lands to be divided into smallholdings.[140] 'The public skims through the dispatches received from London, which, while they may be lacking in acrimony, have some of the laconic aspect of the interpreter mentioned above.'[141] The Irish were thus rendered in continental Europe as murderous criminals.

England's misgovernment of Ireland contrasted with the decisive judgement it deployed on imperial matters. There was no question more entangled than that of Ireland: 'The Irish themselves understand little of it, the English even less, and for other peoples it is complete darkness.' The Irish did know that it was the cause of all their suffering, 'and this is why they employ extremely violent methods to resolve it'.[142] This was an odd overstatement, as cattle-driving, to which Joyce was referring, was scarcely 'extremely violent', as indeed he went on to make clear.

Having started with Maamtrasna, Joyce ended by referring to a miscarriage of justice in England in the Great Wyrley case. This related to a series of vicious attacks on cattle and horses in an area of the West Midlands that resulted in the conviction and imprisonment of George Edalji, a solicitor of half-Indian descent, who was released in October 1906 after three years in prison and was later pardoned:[143] 'Last week two horses were found dead with the usual cuts to the base of the stomach and their guts spilled out over the grass.'[144]

139. *OCPW* 146.

140. James Joyce, *The Critical Writings of James Joyce*, ed. Ellsworth Mason and Richard Ellmann (New York: Viking, 1959), 198n2; Maume, *Long Gestation*, 80.

141. *OCPW* 146.

142. *OCPW* 146–47.

143. Hardiman, *Joyce in Court*, 68–75.

144. *OCPW* 147.

There is immense subtlety to what Joyce was doing in this article. Maamtrasna had already generated an extraordinary and intense controversy that had deep political repercussions. His article elided this, beyond the opening reference to 'a sensational trial' that had taken place in Ireland several years before, and the statement that 'public opinion considered [Myles Joyce] innocent then, and he is now thought of as a martyr.'[145] That controversy could be looked at in two ways: Ireland had been *alla sbarra* in 1882, when the Maamtrasna murders were set on a continuum with the Phoenix Park murders; and at least for nationalist Ireland, the responsibility of the English government in Ireland for the hanging of Myles Joyce had long before been exposed. The controversy was long spent. Joyce's Triestine readership knew very little of Ireland and had certainly never heard of Maamtrasna or of Myles Joyce. That gave Joyce the occasion to present a modernistically pared-back account of the trial of Myles Joyce, as a man from a remote western region speaking only Irish convicted in criminal proceedings he could not understand, and hanged. However uncertain Joyce's grasp of the detail, it was an extremely poised artistic reworking of the subject of Maamtrasna. As if stripping back the accretions of controversy that instrumentalised the trials, it reinstated the terrible solitude of the conviction and death of Myles Joyce. In Joyce's high rendering, the fate of Myles Joyce became an emblematic argument for Irish statehood.

In all of Joyce's Triestine journalism, it is the treatment of Maamtrasna that is closest to his fictional writing. The depiction of Myles Joyce as an image of a conquered Ireland has a correspondence with the harpist in the 'Two Gallants', which Joyce had written the previous year. Joyce contrived to fashion a symbol of Ireland out of events in the 1880s rather than out of conventionally sanctioned literary or mythic materials. In its para-literary treatment of an agrarian crime and its sequel in Ireland in the Parnell era, it enunciates Joyce's critique of the deemed subject matter of the Ireland of the Celtic Twilight.

'L'Irlanda alla sbarra' has a privileged place in Joyce's Triestine journalism. When in 1914 he proposed to Angelo Fortunato Formiggini

145. *OCPW* 145.

publishing the journalism as a collection, he intended this article to be placed first and to provide the title for the whole.[146] The prioritising of the essay reflected the fact that it advanced a justification for Joyce's journalism, the breaking through the wall of English newspaper coverage of Ireland. This was a long-standing subject of Irish nationalist complaint but had an enhanced urgency in an age of increased democratic participation and intensified mass communication, and it was a frequently expressed concern of Arthur Griffith. Joyce had a particular concern with how Irish affairs went unreported or misreported on the Continent. In contemporary notes that survive, he referred to the 'Celtophobia of French and Italian papers.'[147] Joyce's misplaced belief in the viability of publication in book form derived from the fact that he had actually published articles abroad. Asked in Dublin in 1912 why he did not use his talents 'for the betterment of his country and people', Joyce retorted that 'he was probably the only Irishman who wrote leading articles for the Italian press, and that all his articles in "Il Piccolo" were about Ireland and the Irish people'.[148]

The memory of Maamtrasna stayed with Joyce. In the trial of Festy King in *Finnegans Wake*, there are traces of Maamtrasna mixed up with the Special Commission, the O'Shea divorce case, and the trial of Oscar Wilde. Festy King, 'a child of Maam', on trial in relation to the unauthorised possession of a pig and firing a stone, is acquitted, 'having murdered all the English he knew'.[149]

146. *OCPW*, x–xiii.

147. Quoted in McCourt, *Years of Bloom*, 113. These 'Notes on Ireland' are in the Cornell Joyce Collection archives.

148. Charles Joyce to Stanislaus Joyce, 5 September 1912, *Letters II* 316.

149. *FW* 85.22–23, 93.2. The references that point towards Maamtrasna are enumerated in Christine O'Neill-Bernhard, 'Symbol of the Irish Nation, or of a Foulfamed Potheen District: James Joyce on Myles Joyce', *James Joyce Quarterly* 32, nos. 3–4 (Spring and Summer 1995): 712–21. One of those references, 'the one fellow's fetch being the other follow's person' (*FW* 85.28–29), if it relates to Maamtrasna as seems likely, suggests that Joyce had read more on Maamtrasna than he had before the 1907 article. O'Neill-Bernhard's complaint that Joyce's sympathy for the plight of Myles Joyce in 1907 'gives way in the *Wake* to a pig-in-the-parlor style burlesque' is unwarranted (721).

The republication, and even the knowledge, of Joyce's lectures and journalism in Trieste was extraordinarily lagged, even in the history of stalled publication of Joyce's works. The consciousness was posthumous. When Joyce died on 13 January 1941, the canonical myth of him as a modernist was established and there was almost no critical consciousness of his journalism. The Triestine journalism, when disclosed, seemed an affront to the post-war internationalist perception of Joyce as a modernist who had transcended the dismal politics of national origin. That shock is registered in Ellsworth Mason's introduction to a republication of some of the journalism in 1956. While in many respects his comments were astute, he was driven to protest: 'But when he turns to Ireland's oppressor, the trumpets and the drums let loose together, and Joyce is at one with the Citizen in Barney Kiernan's pub.' The entry into public consciousness of Joyce's non-fictional articles and his Trieste lectures came with the publication in 1959 of *The Critical Writings of James Joyce*, edited by Mason and Richard Ellmann. Joyce's *Occasional, Critical, and Political Writing*, edited by Kevin Barry, appeared in 2000.[150]

Joyce's Triestine non-fiction has more recently become a major source of citation but continues to elude comprehensive treatment and integration into the critical and biographical treatment of Joyce's life and oeuvre.[151] What Joyce wrote in Trieste, to deliver or to be read, is a rebuttal of the views of the now vanished constituency of high modernist critics who deemed Joyce loftily transcendent of the particularism of the Irish political. Post-colonial or neo-nationalist critics have drawn on Joyce's Triestine pronouncements to indict the fleetingly prevalent high modernist idea of an apolitical Joyce, but those same pronouncements

150. Both collections include an unsigned sub-editorial in the *Freeman's Journal* of 10 September 1912, 'Politics and Cattle Disease'. The idea of Joyce's authorship of this was always extremely unlikely, and has been comprehensively demolished by Terence Matthews in his 'An Emendation to the Joycean Canon: The Last Hurrah for "Politics and Cattle Disease"', *James Joyce Quarterly* 44, no. 3 (Spring 2007): 441–53.

151. For a start, see Katherine Ebury and James Alexander Fraser, eds., *Joyce's Non-fiction Writings: 'Outside His Jurisfiction'* (Cham, Switzerland: Palgrave Macmillan, 2018).

subvert the idea that Joyce held such radically abstracted anti-imperialist views as to renounce engagement with Irish politics in its actual or realisable contemporary forms. The subtle trenchancy of Joyce's Parnellite nationalism is lost, and the coincidence of opposites strangely endures.

If Joyce's Triestine non-fiction has tended latterly to attract somewhat joyless readings, Francini Bruni, who worked on *Il Piccolo della Sera,* recalled in 1947 of Joyce's articles, 'Though veiled in a steely coldness, they are intense pieces treating various burning issues relating to his native land.'[152]

That Joyce, in what he publicly wrote and lectured on in Trieste, was sympathetic to Sinn Féin is important. He contrived to be so by endorsing subsidiary but significant aspects of Griffith's programme without avowing himself an adherent of Sinn Féin or committing himself to its central tenet of parliamentary abstentionism. What he wrote or said in public was more guarded than what he wrote to Stanislaus. His journalism disclosed that, as well as favouring its policy of national assertiveness, he saw Sinn Féin as having a legitimacy that derived historically from the Fenian separatist tradition, though it did not espouse a recourse to revolutionary violence. Politically his was a soft sympathy with Sinn Féin. He was certainly not an 'out and out' Sinn Féiner, if indeed it is accurate to term him a 'Sinn Féiner' *tout court,* which it is not. His articles are Sinn Féin aligned rather than Sinn Féin, and he understood the difference. He continued to decry Irish political divisions and was prepared to accept the Home Rule bill of 1912 as introduced. While he pronounced the Irish Party politically 'bankrupt' in 1910, he had no doctrinaire antipathy to parliamentarism.[153] What was significant was that in the broad division of allegiances that opened up in his generation, Joyce was drawn to and aligned with Sinn Féin rather than the Irish Party. That is attested to in the extent to which he drew on *Sinn Féin,* his main continuous source of intelligence on Ireland, for his Tri-

152. Potts, *Portraits of the Artist,* 43.
153. *OCPW* 144.

estine journalism.[154] He read Griffith's journalism critically, and had other sources, but it is through *Sinn Féin* that he principally sought to feel the pulse of Dublin from Trieste.

There is a limit to how far one can go in precisely calibrating Joyce's attitude to Sinn Féin, largely because of the dearth of evidence on Joyce's actual thinking after the publication in May 1912 of his article 'The Shade of Parnell' (discussed in chapter 16). His position was well judged and trenchantly expressed. One could argue that he found a strategic position, though that is not what he set out to achieve: it was certainly a pivotal position for Joyce himself in permitting him to articulate his critique of nation and empire. He was acutely conscious of a shift in opinion in Ireland, at least in his generation. Largely because of his own ambivalence in relation to cultural nationalism, he was prepared to afford a degree of latitude to those in his own generation such as George Clancy who were more ardently nationalist than he was. Parnell's adage about not setting bounds to the march of a nation had a particular, and in some ways cruel, salience for Joyce's age cohort in University College. Joyce had a certain presentiment of this.

Whatever Joyce's later attitude to Sinn Féin, the fact that he had—both privately and in what he said and wrote publicly—identified himself with Sinn Féin affirmed a nexus to contemporary Ireland that was to be of some importance. Aside from what could be gleaned of his Parnellism from *A Portrait of the Artist as a Young Man*, Joyce's political views were to remain for long unknown in Ireland. The views that he expressed served to add at least a private irony to, and complicate, his laceratingly funny self-caricature as Shem the Penman in *Finnegans Wake*, who stood accused of cowardly and egotistical flight from Ireland.

In Joyce's Triestine lectures and writing, Parnell is a ubiquitous presence, as much where he is mentioned as where he is not. In this relatively short interval of Joyce's Triestine articles and lectures, 1907–12, Joyce for the first and only time speaks publicly and writes directly of Parnell and of the Split and seeks to situate Parnell in Irish history and in contemporary politics. Joyce's account of Irish history from the Nor-

154. This was first identified by Kevin Barry in his edition of *OCPW*.

man invasion of 1169 in 'L'Irlanda: Isola dei santi e dei savi' approximates to a projection of the Parnell Split backwards in time. Looked at the other way out, Irish disunion, treachery, and pusillanimity in relation to England, and deference to the Catholic Church, culminated in the overthrow of Parnell in 1890–91. The repudiation of Parnell by the Irish Party, and by the voting Irish public, was as if inscribed in the history of Ireland since the Norman invasion. This is of course an invalid exercise by the standards of historical scholarship, of which Joyce was never particularly respectful. The conventional fable of Irish history did not meet those standards either, and Joyce re-rendered that mournful and flaccid nationalist narrative of oppression with a strongly incised theme that, without detracting from the iniquities of British conquest and dominion, imputed to the Irish a large measure of responsibility for their own fate. It was an ambitious undertaking on Joyce's part that, in venturing a Split-themed history of modern Ireland, went beyond the episodic historical controversies that were canvassed in the course of the Split.

Parnell's shade suffuses the treatment of the contemporary political. Joyce resisted the temptation to make a facile equation between Sinn Féin and the dead leader. While Griffith's resuscitation of his own admiration for Parnell did much to release Joyce from his inhibition that his Parnellism was archaic and devoid of contemporary political traction, he was acutely conscious that Griffith's and Parnell's nationalism were disparate and related to different phases of political time. Joyce was sufficiently scrupulous to venture an argument to the contrary, that Griffith's Sinn Féin was the inheritor of the Fenian rather than the Parnellite tradition. If Joyce was far too politically fastidious to see Sinn Féin as blurredly continuous with Parnellism, his readiness to countenance support for Sinn Féin did not signify an abandonment of his Parnellite critique of Irish society. If anything, the significant act of expressing even qualified sympathy with Sinn Féin, initially in private correspondence but carried over into his Triestine pronouncements as a lecturer and journalist, served to sharpen his self-conception as a Parnellite nationalist.

16

Exile Affirmed

'But don't you remember', said Joyce to me, 'how the prodigal son was received by his brother in his father's house. It is dangerous to leave one's country, but still more dangerous to go back to it, for then your fellow-countrymen, if they can, will drive a knife into your heart'.

—ITALO SVEVO[1]

JOYCE HAD WRITTEN THREE CHAPTERS OF *A Portrait of the Artist as a Young Man* by early April 1908, when he put it aside,[2] having earlier protested to Stanislaus, 'Why would I bother my head writing when nobody will publish what I write?' Over the next five years he would work on the book only sporadically. If his suspension of fiction writing was in some degree a form of protest, it reflected what he experienced as the futility, or impossibility, of writing when what he had written was unpublished. In late August 1912, as his hopes for the publication of *Dubliners* by Maunsel and Company flickered still, he wrote to Nora,

1. Italo Svevo, 'James Joyce', trans. Stanislaus Joyce, rev. John Gatt-Rutter, in L. Veneziani Svevo, *Memoir of Italo Svevo*, 150. The third person in the conversation when Joyce made this observation, at a performance of *Exiles* in London, was Padraic Colum, who seems to have adopted Svevo's account of what Joyce said. U. O'Connor, *Joyce We Knew*, 72–73.

2. Stanislaus Joyce, Triestine diary, 5 February 1908, quoted in McCourt, *Years of Bloom*, 127–28; Ellmann, *James Joyce*, 264.

'I hope I shall have good news tomorrow. If only my book is published then I will plunge into my novel and finish it.'[3]

In 1908, having suspended his novel, he cast around for non-writing projects or went through the motions of doing so. Among those he conceived was to become a commission agent for Irish tweeds.[4] He was sufficiently taken with the idea of an interim role as a journalist on Irish affairs that he proposed to *Il Corriere della Sera* in Milan to travel to cover the Dublin exposition, and to *La Stampa* in Turin and *Il Mattino* in Naples to cover Irish affairs, all to no avail.[5] He also turned his hand to translation projects. As if in atonement for his response to the *Playboy* riots, he had commented to Stanislaus in May 1907 that Synge's art 'is more original than my own'.[6] In March 1908 he re-read *Riders to the Sea* and enlisted his friend and pupil Nicolò Vidacovich (another sophisticated Triestine irridentist) to collaborate on its translation into Italian. The following year, after Synge's death, he unsuccessfully sought the consent of Synge's estate for a production of the play in their translation by the actor-manager Alfredo Sainati.[7] On 24 March 1909 *Il Piccolo della Sera* published Joyce's essay 'Oscar Wilde: Il poeta di "Salome"', written to coincide with the production in Trieste of the Richard Strauss opera based on Wilde's play. However critical Joyce had been of Wilde, he wrote to Fratelli Treves Editori in Milan proposing an Italian translation of *The Picture of Dorian Gray*. The negative reply invoked 'the difficulties in introducing this name and of recommending his works in catalogues and newspapers which had family readerships'.[8] Joyce also sought the permission of Robert Ross to translate *The Soul of Man under Socialism*, the work of Wilde that had most influenced him.

3. Joyce to Nora Barnacle, postmark 22 August 1912, *Letters II* 310.

4. Ellmann, *James Joyce*, 269.

5. McCourt, *Years of Bloom*, 121; Ellmann, *James Joyce*, 260.

6. Ellmann, *James Joyce*, 267.

7. Ellmann, *James Joyce*, 267; McCourt, *Years of Bloom*, 133–35, 195; S. Joyce, *My Brother's Keeper*, 214. A less successful exercise in collaborative translation related to Joyce's own work: 'Vidacovich also tried his hand with me on a version of my story "Ivy Day in the Committee Room" for the *Nuova Antologia* but the attempt was a dismal failure'. Joyce to W. B. Yeats, 14 September 1916, *Letters II* 95.

8. McCourt, *Years of Bloom*, 133.

While Joyce received permission, he did not proceed with the translation.[9]

Joyce's relations with Nora remained difficult. Their finances were parlous, dependent on episodic bailouts by Stanislaus. Joyce was sufficiently alarmed by an attack of iritis in May 1908 to adhere for some months to a renunciation of alcohol. Nora had a miscarriage at about three months on 4 August 1908.[10] In the autumn, Joyce enrolled for singing lessons with Romeo Bartoli in the Conservatorio Musicale di Trieste. His casting about for other destinies was too much for Stanislaus, who protested that his brother had 'too many futures'.[11] On 5 October 1908, the eve of the anniversary of Parnell's death, Joyce, elongated on a sofa, declared that he had 'retired from public life'.[12] This of course was precisely what Parnell had not done, and what Joyce so greatly admired him for. Stanislaus wrote sarcastically of 'the budding tenorino' and characterised Joyce's serial careers with unprecedented trenchancy: Joyce had failed 'as a poet in Paris, as a journalist in Dublin, as a lover and novelist in Trieste, as a bank clerk in Rome, and again in Trieste as a Sinnféiner, teacher and University Professor'.[13] In fact Joyce was to achieve the modest but not trivial feat of singing in the 'extremely difficult quintet' from Richard Wagner's *Die Meistersinger von Nürnberg* at the Sala della Società Filarmonico-Drammatica, directed by Bartoli.[14]

9. Ellmann, *James Joyce*, 274. Ross took particular pride in the dissemination of *The Soul of Man under Socialism*, which Arthur Humphreys had kept in print from 1895 when he published a private edition; Oscar Wilde, *The Letters of Oscar Wilde*, ed. Rupert Hart-Davis (London: Hart-Davis, 1962), 364; Robert Ross, introduction to *The Soul of Man under Socialism*, by Oscar Wilde (London: Arthur L. Humphreys, 1912), vi. At the dinner in the Ritz in London on 1 December 1908 to mark the winding up of the Wilde estate, Ross declared that 'Chinese and Russian translations of *The Soul of Man under Socialism* are sold in the bazaars of Ninji Novgorod'. Margery Ross, *Robert Ross, Friend of Friends: Letters to Robert Ross, Art Critic and Writer, Together with Extracts from His Published Articles* (London: Jonathan Cape, 1952), 56, 104–5.

10. Ellmann, *James Joyce*, 268–69.

11. Ellmann, *James Joyce*, 269.

12. Ellmann, *James Joyce*, 269.

13. Stanislaus Joyce, Triestine diary, 12 October 1908, quoted in McCourt, *Years of Bloom*, 131–32.

14. Erik Schneider, 'Joyce in Concert: The *Meistersinger* Performance in Trieste', *James Joyce Quarterly* 38, nos. 3 and 4 (Spring and Summer 2001): 495–97. '*Die Meistersinger* was his

In December 1908 Joyce had written to his sister Margaret (Poppie) proposing to send Giorgio in the charge of Stanislaus on a visit to Dublin the following year.[15] At the last moment he substituted himself for Stanislaus, thereby depriving his brother of what transpired to be his last scheduled revisiting of his native city. Aside from the need to address the publication of *Dubliners*, in the impasse that he seemed to have reached in Trieste, Joyce appeared amenable, at least in principle, to the idea of resuming a life and career in Ireland.

Joyce's First Return Trip to Ireland, 1909

Joyce reached Dublin with Giorgio on 29 July 1909 and went to his family's then home at 44 Fontenoy Street. 'All are delighted with Georgie', he reported to Nora, 'specially Pappie'.[16]

In the manner of the Dublin of those years, Joyce ran into almost everyone he knew. William Kirkpatrick Magee, who, like George Russell, was friendly, thought Joyce was 'looking very ecclesiastical'[17]. With Oliver St John Gogarty, whose 'fat back'[18] he had espied on reaching the pier at Kingstown, Joyce was unyielding: 'You and I of 6 years ago are both dead. But I must write as I have felt.'[19] He opened negotiations with George Roberts of the publishers Maunsel & Company, a young firm founded in 1905 but already the leading publishers for writers of the Revival.

Joyce was hardly in Dublin a week when, on the afternoon of 6 August, Vincent Cosgrave asserted that Nora had gone out with him on alternate nights when she was not with Joyce. Distraught, Joyce despatched two accusatory letters to Nora[20] and was planning to return

favourite opera, and he borrowed its quintet for the "Sirens" episode of *Ulysses*'. Ira B. Nadel, *Joyce and the Jews: Culture and Texts* (Gainesville: University Press of Florida, 1996), 52.

15. Joyce to Margaret Joyce, 8 December 1908, *Letters II* 225–26.

16. Joyce to Nora Barnacle, 29 July 1909, *SL* 156.

17. Joyce to Stanislaus Joyce, 4 August 1909, *SL* 156.

18. Joyce to Nora Barnacle, postmark 29 July 1909, *SL* 156.

19. Joyce to Stanislaus Joyce, 4 August 1909, *Letters II* 231.

20. Joyce to Nora Barnacle, 6, 7 August 1909, *Letters II* 231–23.

to Trieste when John Francis Byrne convinced him, as he wrote to her on 19 August, that it was all 'a blasted lie' by Cosgrave.[21] When Nora broke her silence to reply, she did so with restraint and 'great shrewdness',[22] attesting to how well matched they were in strength and suppleness of character. This crisis had the incidental effect of setting Joyce's correspondence with Nora at a high level of drama and imprecatory tendresse, and to intensify its eroticism.

Thomas Michael Kettle was 'extremely friendly' and urged Joyce to apply for the lectureship in Italian at the reconstituted University College Dublin under the Universities Act of 1908.[23] There was no professorship, only a lectureship for evening classes in commercial Italian. Joyce decided to apply for an examinership which did not require residence in Dublin,[24] but then concluded he would be ill advised to take it.[25] On 19 August he signed the contract with Maunsel for the publication the following March of *Dubliners*,[26] on which George Roberts almost immediately had second thoughts.

The possibility of a parallel career as a journalist mediating between Ireland and Italy was of greater interest to Joyce than that as a university examiner in Italian. Enrico Caruso was singing in Dublin, but the *Irish Times*, *Daily Express*, and *Daily Mail* did not take up Joyce's proposal to interview the singer. Joyce had cards printed with his name and 'Il Piccolo della Sera, Trieste', and prevailed on the manager of the Midland Railway to give him a press pass for Galway.[27] On 25 August, the last night of Horse Show week, he attended, in the capacity as a journalist-critic of *Il Piccolo della Sera*, the premiere of George Bernard Shaw's *The Shewing-Up of Blanco Posnet* at the Abbey Theatre. Joyce's piece, written

21. Joyce to Nora Barnacle, 19 August 1909, *Letters II* 235–36.

22. Maddox, *Nora*, 130.

23. Joyce to Stanislaus Joyce, 10 August 1909, *Letters II* 234.

24. Joyce to Stanislaus Joyce, 16 August 1909, *Letters II* 235; Ellmann, *James Joyce*, 282.

25. Joyce to Stanislaus Joyce, 21 August 1909, *Letters II* 238.

26. Joyce to Nora Barnacle, 19 August 1909, *Letters II* 235.

27. Joyce to Stanislaus Joyce, 21, 25 August 1909, *Letters II* 238, 240. Joyce had evidently concluded that in Dublin the Unionist press was more likely to be receptive to external contributors.

in Dublin on 31 August, was carried in Trieste on 5 September. It opened with a characterisation of the Horse Show that was a recension of his view of Dublin as a centre of paralysis, mellowed by humour: 'For a few days the tired and cynical city dresses itself up like a newly wed bride and its senile sleep is broken by an unaccustomed uproar.' Of the controversy that attended the production of the play (the authority of the Lord Chamberlain who had banned the play in England did not extend to Ireland), Joyce, no doubt recalling the production of Synge's *Playboy of the Western World*, wrote that 'Dubliners, who couldn't care less for art, but have an immoderate love of arguments, were rubbing their hands in glee.' The play he dismissed as 'a sermon' and the playwright as 'a born preacher'.[28]

Joyce's pose as a Triestine journalist gained a certain amount of traction. At the Shaw premiere, he met Piaras Béaslaí, who worked on the *Evening Telegraph*. Béaslaí was much later a Dáil Éireann deputy, and a close associate and later the biographer of Michael Collins.[29] Through Béaslaí, Joyce paid several visits to the offices of the *Evening Telegraph*—sister evening paper of the *Freeman's Journal* in Prince's Street—then edited by Patrick J. Mead, who introduced him to the staff. Mead inspired the figure of Myles Crawford in *Ulysses*.[30] Of the institutional sites of Dublin, it was these offices, rather than University College, the National Library, and the Abbey, that were for Joyce most congenial. The offices of the most important newspapers in Ireland were also a *lieu de memoire* of Parnellism. Joyce's visits were to inform the 'Aeolus' episode of *Ulysses* and represent the principal projection backwards in time of episodes of Joyce's life that post-dated 1904. Joyce was enthralled by the offices that the *Evening Telegraph* shared with the *Freeman's Journal*. In relation to Joyce's presence in the offices, one incident in 'Aeolus' is particularly striking. It comprises two seemingly minor references that

28. *OCPW* 152–54. When Joyce returned to Trieste in September 1909, he sent Richard Irvine Best the Wilde article as he had promised, 'and throw in another (very poor) on GBS', hoping Best could succeed in puzzling out their Italian. Joyce to Richard Irvine Best, NLI, MS 11, 001.

29. Patrick Maume, 'Piaras Béaslaí', *DIB*, 1:386–89.

30. Ellmann, *James Joyce*, 289. Ellmann's account is based on what Béaslaí told him. The actual editor of the *Freeman's Journal* at the time was Morris Cosgrave.

are elevated to cunning comic effect by Joyce's headings, which replicate the idiom of contemporary Irish newspapers. The first reference is, 'His grace phoned down twice this morning, Red Murray said gravely'. This appears in the section headed 'THE CROZIER AND THE PEN'.[31] The second is a statement of the print foreman: 'Wait. Where's the archbishop's letter? It's to be repeated in the *Telegraph*.' The heading under which this appears is 'NOTED CHURCHMAN AN OCCASIONAL CONTRIBUTOR'.[32] The two references relate to a letter the Archbishop of Dublin, William Walsh, had sent for publication. Ellmann's treatment of this is based on what he was told by Béaslaí.[33] In Béaslaí's narrative, the publisher of the *Freeman's Journal*, Thomas Sexton, a leading nationalist politician out of Parliament since 1896, was at odds with the Archbishop of Dublin, with the effect that the paper tended to enlarge the coverage it afforded to the Archbishop of Armagh, Michael Logue (even though Logue was a conservative right-wing prelate who was a protector of Timothy Michael Healy, while the *Freeman's Journal* was closely aligned to John Dillon, Healy's most implacable adversary in nationalist politics). Béaslaí's explication to Ellmann overlooks what is more salient for Joyce's sardonic headlines: that the pedantic and officious Archbishop of Dublin was indefatigable in his interventions on what were often marginal points of public controversy, and that the publication of his letters were wearisomely routine for the staff of the newspapers. The personae invoked by Béaslaí are relevant. Sexton, Walsh, and Logue were all prominent in their opposition to Parnell. The offices were steeped in the institutional memory of the Split.

The *Evening Telegraph* published an evidently Joyce-inspired brief account of his Shaw article, characterising Joyce as a 'fellow-citizen of Mr. Shaw's and one of the few Irishmen on the Italian Press'.[34] While Joyce was to be bitterly critical of his neglect by the Irish press, his criticism was not directed at journalists, whose profession had been most receptive to him, and whose bustling urbanity is commemorated in *Ulysses*.

31. *U* 7.41–42.

32. *U* 7.178–81.

33. Ellmann, *James Joyce*, 288–29.

34. *Evening Telegraph*, 8 September 1909; *Letters II* 242n1.

The breakup of the Joyce family in Ireland continued. On 20 August Joyce was present for the leave-taking of his sister Margaret, on whom the burden of running the impoverished household had devolved since her mother's death, to become a Sister of Mercy. She left for Kilkenny 'and will not be seen again until she goes to New Zealand', though in fact Joyce was to be present in Fontenoy Street on 11 November when she passed through on her way out of the country; she would never return, dying in New Zealand in 1964.[35] Doing what he could, Joyce had decided to extricate one of his sisters from Fontenoy Street. Margaret had determined that, rather than Mabel, it would be the more religiously observant Eva, who had a better prospect of winning her brother from impiety.[36]

Joyce went by train with Giorgio to Galway, where they stayed with Nora's uncle Michael Healy, a port official of reasonable means with whom Joyce got on well.[37] Back in Dublin, he spent four hours on 5 September talking to Kettle, attending a reception at the Gresham Hotel to mark Kettle's forthcoming wedding to Mary Sheehy, which took place on 8 September and which he did not attend. He referred to Kettle as 'the best friend I have in Ireland, I think'.[38] The evening of the day he met Kettle, he wrote to Nora, 'O take me into your soul of souls and I will then become indeed the poet of my race.'[39]

On one of these last evenings, Joyce had supper with J. F. Byrne and two female cousins of Byrne who resided from 1908 to 1910 at 7 Eccles Street, to which Joyce had already repaired in distress on the evening that followed Cosgrave's false statement about his relations with Nora. After supper, Joyce asked Byrne to go for a walk with him. Joyce had wanted to renew his acquaintance with familiar scenes of Dublin; as Byrne recalled, 'we walked Dublin that night and early morning', returning to Eccles Street at three in the morning. Byrne had forgotten his key but let himself down into the basement, where there was an unlocked

35. Joyce to Stanislaus Joyce, 21 August, 10 November 1909, *Letters II* 238, 261.

36. Ellmann, *James Joyce*, 285.

37. Ellmann, *James Joyce*, 266–67.

38. Joyce to Nora Barnacle, 5 September 1909, *Letters II* 247–48; Ellmann, *James Joyce*, 287.

39. Joyce to Nora Barnacle, 5 September 1909, *Letters II* 247; Norburn, *James Joyce Chronology*, 44.

side door through which Byrne got into the house.[40] In *Ulysses*, 7 Eccles Street became Bloom's home, and his return home with Stephen Dedalus in the 'Ithaca' episode was inspired by Joyce's night with Byrne.

On the eve of his departure, Joyce met Joseph Holloway, the obsessive diarist of the Abbey Theatre. Holloway that afternoon discussed Joyce with a kindred spirit, D. J. O'Donoghue, who had also run into Joyce. In an exemplary Dublin valediction, Holloway concluded, 'He was a precocious youth and learned to sneer young.'[41] On 9 September Joyce left Dublin for Trieste with Giorgio and Eva.

Joyce's Second Return Visit, 1909–10

Joyce's second return visit was really a continuation of his first and, at two and a half months, was his most extended trip. After spending just over a month in Trieste, Joyce arrived back in Dublin on his own on 21 October 1909. His principal business was the opening of Dublin's first cinema, financed by four Triestine businessmen. Two of them followed Joyce a month later and also went with him to Belfast and Cork, where it was proposed to open other cinemas.[42] Joyce worked, as the *Evening Telegraph* approvingly noted, 'apparently indefatigably' on the project,[43] identifying and securing a premises for the cinema at 45 Mary Street, supervising the work, and even designing the posters. The Volta Cinema opened on 20 December: Joyce reported to Stanislaus that just before the opening an electrician, 'a Sinn Féiner' whom O'Leary Curtis had recommended, had left them in the lurch 'and I had to scour Dublin' for a replacement.[44] The cinema, however, failed to meet the expectations of the partners and was sold the following June.[45] Joyce, pursuing the scheme conceived in 1908 to become an agent for Irish tweeds, also

40. Byrne, *Silent Years*, 154, 156–59.

41. Holloway, *Joseph Holloway's Abbey Theatre*, 130–31.

42. McCourt, *Years of Bloom*, 144.

43. *Evening Telegraph*, 21 December 1909.

44. Joyce to Stanislaus Joyce, 20 December 1909, *Letters II* 277; Ellmann, *James Joyce*, 302–3.

45. McCourt, *Years of Bloom*, 147.

arranged to represent the Dublin Woollen Company in Trieste.[46] He actually sold tweeds on its behalf in Trieste in 1910 and 1911.[47]

Absence in strained circumstances—Nora was threatened with eviction in Trieste—took its toll on Joyce's equanimity. He wrote in late October after a visit to the theatre with his father and sister—'a wretched play, a disgusting audience'—that 'I felt (as I always feel) a stranger in my own country'. Nora was evidently by this stage practised in the demanding art of managing Joyce's fulminations against his countrymen. She felt scepticism towards respectable Catholic nationalism in her own right, but her sympathetic acquiescence in his views on his countrymen was evidently highly important to him. This is one of few instances when the surviving correspondence registers a little of what was a sustained duet on the subject of Ireland. It was as if he were amorously proclaiming his relationship to her to be the inverse of his relation to Ireland:

> Yet if you had been beside you [*sic*] I could have spoken into your ears the hatred and scorn I felt burning in my heart. Perhaps you would have rebuked me but you would also have understood me. I felt proud to think that my son—mine and yours, that handsome dear little boy you gave me, Nora—will always be a foreigner in Ireland, a man speaking another language and bred in a different tradition.
>
> I loathe Ireland and the Irish. They themselves stare at me in the street though I was born among them. Perhaps they read my hatred in their eye. I see nothing on every side of me but the image of the adulterous priest and his servants and of sly deceitful women. It is not good for me to come here or be here.[48]

Joyce put up his two Triestine visitors in Finn's Hotel. On 19 November he wrote to Nora an emotional rhapsody to her in the third person. He had that evening dined with the Triestines at Finn's Hotel, where 'a pale-faced girl waited at table, perhaps her successor':

46. Ellmann, *James Joyce*, 303.

47. McCourt, *Years of Bloom*, 176.

48. Joyce to Nora Barnacle, 27 October 1909, *Letters II* 255.

> The place is very Irish. I have lived so long abroad and in so many countries that I can feel at once the voice of Ireland in anything. The disorder of the table was Irish, the wonder on the faces also, the curious-looking eyes of the woman herself and her waitress. A strange land this is to me though I was born in it and bear one of its old names.
>
> I have been in the room where she passed so often, with a strange dream of love in her young heart. My God, my eyes are full of tears! . . .
>
> A strange land, a strange house, strange eyes and the shadow of a strange, strange girl standing silently by the fire, or gazing out of the window across the misty College park. What a mysterious beauty clothes every place where she has lived![49]

Aside from his cinema business, Joyce had had to deal with the continuing subsidence of the fortunes of his family in Dublin. He had resolved to take back with him his sister Eileen to join Eva, who was already in Trieste. He wrote from Fontenoy Street to Stanislaus, who suspected with reason that Joyce's altruism would be charged to his account, on 23 December, 'This is such a dreadful house that it is a God's act to rescue Eileen from it. Let us try to manage it.'[50] On 2 January 1910, Joyce left Dublin with Eileen, travelling back through Paris and Milan to Trieste, which they reached on 6 January.

Trieste 1910–12

Joyce's relations with Stanislaus, already strained by the eviction crisis in his absence, continued to deteriorate with Joyce's continuing demands on his brother, and reached a culmination in July when Stanislaus briefly broke off relations.[51] Joyce resumed giving private lessons a month after his return, and in the autumn was appointed to teach an evening English course in the Scuola Commerciale di Perfezionamento.[52]

49. Joyce to Nora Barnacle, 19 November 1909, *Letters II* 266.
50. Joyce to Stanislaus Joyce, 23 December 1909, *Letters II* 280.
51. Ellmann, *James Joyce*, 311; McCourt, *Years of Bloom*, 151.
52. McCourt, *Years of Bloom*, 172.

There was a modest but steady improvement in the living conditions of the family. In August 1910 they moved to an apartment at 32 Via della Barriera Vecchia. The household now comprised James, Nora, Giorgio, Lucia, and Joyce's sisters Eva and Eileen. The young Maria Kirn from St Peter's Station, a small village outside Trieste, answered an advertisement for a maid. Her monthly income from Joyce was supplemented by tips from the students of Joyce whom she would lead up the three flights of stairs to the apartment. She was there when Joyce tried to burn an earlier manuscript version of *A Portrait*. She noticed that Joyce would not permit his sisters to take Giorgio and Lucia to mass with them on Sunday. He remained nonetheless a culinary Irish traditionalist: his favourite food was lean bacon, cabbage, and potatoes. Some of Kirn's memories had faded by the time the Joyce scholar Thomas Staley spoke to her about Joyce: 'She remembers Nora's pleasant Irish smile, and a slender head, silhouetted against the bright light in the kitchen, bent over a book or paper.'[53]

On 12 January 1911 Joyce despatched a letter to Stanislaus stating that he was about to leave Trieste. The occasion for this particular démarche is not clear, but it seems to relate to pupils of theirs. Joyce accused Stanislaus of in some way betraying him to 'your friend Miss O'Brien (of London)', whom he characterised as 'the aforesaid Cockney virgin and comfortress of the afflicted', and to an unnamed person referred to as 'the preoccupied Christographer of the Via dell Olmo'. Whatever was involved, it seemed that Stanislaus was in the wrong and that Joyce was determined to press a temporary advantage that he rarely enjoyed: 'I intend to do what Parnell was advised to do on a similar occasion: clear out, the conflict being beneath my dignity, and leave you and the *cattolicissime* to make what you can of the city discovered by my courage (and Nora's) seven years ago, whither you and they came in obedience to my summons, from your ignorant and famine-stricken and treacherous country. My irregularities can easily be made the excuse of your conduct.'[54]

53. Thomas F. Staley, 'James Joyce in Trieste', *Georgia Review* 16, no. 4 (Winter 1962): 446–49.

54. Joyce to Stanislaus Joyce, 12 January 1911, *Letters II* 288–89; Ellmann, *James Joyce*, 313; McCourt, *Years of Bloom*, 176–77.

FIGURE 16.1. Giorgio and Lucia Joyce, with kitten, in Trieste, about 1910. *Source*: 2.1, James Joyce Collection, The Poetry Collection of the University Libraries, University at Buffalo, The State University of New York.

Joyce's remonstrance suggests how infuriating (if in the end suasive) he must have been as a controversialist in financial and domestic affairs from the perspective of Stanislaus. The bracketing of the sternly atheistic Stanislaus with the 'ultra-Catholic' Eileen and Eva, and with the country of his birth that Stanislaus had repudiated with a remorselessness of which Joyce was incapable, was magnificent in its preposterousness. Joyce's high rhetorical identification with the Parnell of the Split, who had disregarded the advice to 'clear out', is strikingly characteristic. The only Joyce to leave Trieste was Eva, who returned to Dublin six months later.[55] Joyce's situation did not, however, improve, and by the winter of 1910–11 he intensified his efforts to find a more stable teaching post in Italy by applying to sit the examination for a teaching diploma held in Padua.[56]

55. McCourt, *Years of Bloom*, 177.
56. McCourt, *Years of Bloom*, 178.

The publication of *Dubliners* had become once more bogged down, this time as a result of objections first raised by George Roberts in December 1909 to a passage in 'Ivy Day in the Committee Room' in which Edward VII is discussed in relation to Victoria. Mr Henchy says, 'Here's this chap come to the throne after his bloody old bitch of a mother keeping him out of it till the man was grey. He's just a jolly decent fellow if you ask me. . . . He's fond of his glass of grog and he's a bit of a rake, perhaps.' Joyce agreed to some alterations. On 10 June 1910, Roberts objected that Joyce's deletion of the terms 'bloody' and 'bitch' in reference to Victoria was not 'effective' and asked him to rewrite or delete the passage, which Joyce declined to do.[57]

Joyce wrote to Maunsel on 10 July 1911 threatening, in the absence of a response, to 'communicate the whole matter of the dispute in a circular letter to the Irish press' and to sue Maunsel.[58] To put himself in a better position to carry out the first threat, Joyce had the idea of writing to George V, which he did on 1 August, enclosing a printed proof of the story with the disputed passage marked and begging the king 'to inform me whether in his view the passage (certain allusions made by a person of the story in the idiom of his social class) should be withheld from publication as offensive to the memory of his father'. The king's private secretary responded on 11 August that 'it was inconsistent with rule for His Majesty to express his opinion in such cases'.[59]

Armed with the royal non-response, Joyce on 17 August 1911 despatched a letter to the press, setting out the history of his dealings over the previous six years in relation to his two contracts for *Dubliners*, with Grant Richards, 'publisher of London', and with Maunsel. He carefully crafted his letter as one 'which throws some light on the present conditions of authorship in England and Ireland'; in his only nationalist flourish, he wrote of Maunsel that their 'attitude as an Irish publishing firm may be judged by Irish public opinion'. The passage to which Maunsel objected was set forth. The letter concluded, 'I, as a writer, protest

57. Ellmann, *James Joyce*, 310–11; *Letters II* 291. Ellmann points out that the passage was a slightly fortified version of that which had been submitted to Grant Richards.

58. Joyce to Maunsel & Company, 10 July 1911, *Letters II* 289.

59. Ellmann, *James Joyce*, 314–15; *Letters II* 291–93.

against the systems (legal, social and ceremonious) which have brought me to this pass.'[60] Only two papers published Joyce's letter: Arthur Griffith's *Sinn Féin* published it in full,[61] while the Belfast liberal Unionist *Northern Whig* primly omitted the passage in dispute.[62]

In November 1911 Joyce applied for a position in the Istituto Tecnico in Como but was told there was none available, and that in any case he would need a teaching diploma to be eligible to be considered.[63] That led him to write to the Ministry of Education in Rome asking to sit the examination for the teaching diploma in Padua. He duly made his way there for the examination set for 24–26 April 1912. He wrote an essay in Italian titled 'The Universal Literary Influence of the Renaissance'. It was of consummate brilliance but poorly marked. The next day he sent a postcard to Stanislaus saying he had to write his essay in English on Charles Dickens, 'and saw my English examiner, an old, ugly, spinster from the tight little island—a most dreadful *fRump* (reformed spelling)'.[64] The lady was the exotically named Margherita de Renoche, who, as well as supervising the essays of the first two days, administered the section of the examination on the final day, dictation from Sir Edward Bulwer-Lytton's grandiosely convoluted novel of 1834, *The Last Days of Pompeii*.[65] She was also a member of the examination commission.[66] His essay 'The Centenary of Charles Dickens' got full marks but Joyce characteristically took a grudge which migrated to his ruminations

60. Joyce's letter appears both in his published correspondence (*Letters II* 291–93) and as 'A Curious History' in *OCPW* 160–62. Grant Richards, to whom Joyce sent a copy, replied amicably (*Letters II* 291n2) and did ultimately publish *Dubliners* in 1914.

61. *Sinn Féin*, 2 September 1911. This does not mean that Griffith had forgiven Joyce for his review of the poems of William Rooney in 1903. Griffith was not the forgiving type.

62. *Northern Whig*, 26 August 1911.

63. McCourt, *Years of Bloom*, 178.

64. Joyce to Stanislaus Joyce, postmark 25 April 1912, *Letters II* 294–95.

65. The inflated cult of Bulwer-Lytton (1803–1873), a writer, and alternately Whig and Conservative politician, who fleetingly held cabinet office and declined the crown of Greece on the abdication of King Otto in 1862, was already more or less exploded in England. His survival in Italy is presumably down to the fact that his 1843 *Harold, the Last of the Saxons* inspired Verdi's opera *Arnaldo* of 1857, which itself seems to have gone the way of all Bulwer-Lytton. His *Rienzi* of 1835 also inspired the Wagner opera of 1842.

66. Louis Berrone, ed., *James Joyce in Padua* (New York: Random House, 1977), xxi.

on national character to Frank Budgen in Zurich. Budgen renders their conversation: '[Joyce] liked Italy and the Italians, but he could never forgive the Italian university (it was Padua I think) that failed him in an examination in English. The examining professor was an old woman looking like Sairey Gamp, black bag and all complete, and no knowledge of English at all.'[67] In fact the judging committee deemed him to have passed the examination but on 1 August 1912, the rector of Padua wrote to Joyce to convey that the Ministry of Education had advised that its higher council, meeting on 14 June 1912, had not recognised the equivalence of Joyce's 1902 Dublin degree with that of an Italian university.[68] This intelligence could not have come at a worse time for Joyce, who was then in Galway as the crisis over the publication of *Dubliners* in Ireland entered its final stages. He concluded he was jinxed, writing in exasperation to Stanislaus, 'Of Padua I understand nothing. The sooner you convince yourself that I am pursued by *scalogna* the better.'[69]

Joyce continued to give lectures in the Università Popolare and to contribute articles to *Il Piccolo della Sera*. In February 1912 he delivered two lectures on 'verismo e idealismo nella letteratura inglese (Daniele Defoe e William Blake)'. The first, on 9 February, was on Defoe, followed a few weeks later by a better-attended lecture on Blake.[70] Only the text of the Defoe lecture survives in full, with a substantial fragment of that on Blake.

The Defoe lecture is an arresting example of Joyce's rare capacity to assess a writer both in terms of the history of literature and by intelligent reference to the writer's national politics. Defoe is both 'the great precursor of the Realist movement' and 'the first English writer to write

67. Frank Budgen, 'James Joyce' (1941), reprinted in *Making of 'Ulysses'*, 345. The shift in the story serves as a reminder that we only have Joyce's word for the Englishness of Margherita de Renoche, though his postcard to Stanislaus is clear and presumably based on her accent. In enmity Joyce took imaginative licence. He mentions Sara Gamp in his essay as one of the characters of Dickens who inhabit 'the borderland of the . . . human fantastic', along with, among others, Micawber and Peggoty (*OCPW* 185).

68. Berrone, *James Joyce in Padua*, xxii.

69. Joyce to Stanislaus Joyce, 10 August 1912, *Letters II* 301.

70. McCourt, *Years of Bloom*, 178–79; Ellmann, *James Joyce*, 318–19.

without copying or adapting foreign works, to create without literary models, to instil a truly national spirit into the creations of his pen . . . the father of the English novel'. Of Defoe he writes with admiration, transposing his restrained sarcasm to Defoe's countrymen. He dismisses the caricature of John Bull:

> The true symbol of the British conquest is Robinson Crusoe who, shipwrecked on a lonely island, with a knife and a pipe in his pocket, becomes an architect, carpenter, knifegrinder, astronomer, baker, shipwright, potter, saddler, farmer, tailor, umbrella-maker and cleric. He is the true prototype of the British colonist just as Friday (the faithful savage who arrives one ill-starred day) is the symbol of the subject race. All the Anglo-Saxon soul is in Crusoe: virile independence, unthinking cruelty, persistence, slow yet effective intelligence, sexual apathy, practical and well-balanced religiosity, calculating dourness. Whoever rereads this simple and moving book in the light of subsequent history cannot but be taken by its prophetic spell.[71]

What Joyce writes implies that there was an innate impulse to conquest, rather than an instinct acquired with empire. Joyce was not averse to the idea of national types, treated with historical intelligence. If Joyce had come to the realisation quite independently of his own nationalism that England was aberrant within Europe, he was not prepared to dispense with English empiricist realism. The conclusion he drew was open-ended: 'Saint John the Evangelist saw on the island of Patmos the apocalyptic collapse of the universe and the raising up of the walls of the eternal city splendid with beryl and emerald, onyx and jasper, sapphire and rubies. Crusoe saw but one marvel in all the fertile creation that surrounded him, a naked footprint in the virgin sand: and who knows if the latter does not matter more than the former?'[72]

Of Defoe's *Duncan Campbell*, which he characterised as 'a spiritualistic study, as we would put it, of an interesting case of clairvoyance in Scotland', Joyce wrote, 'Seated at the bedside of a boy visionary, gazing

71. *OCPW* 174.
72. *OCPW* 174–75.

at his raised eyelids, examining the position of his head, noting his fresh complexion, Defoe is the realist in the presence of the unknown; it is the experience of the man who struggles and conquers in the presence of a dream which he fears may fool him; he is, finally, the Anglo-Saxon in the presence of the Celt.'[73]

In his draft, beyond the point of conclusion of the lecture, Joyce wrote, 'The narrative that pivots upon this simple marvel is a whole, harmonious, and consistent national epic.'[74] Joyce was beginning to turn to a national epic of his own, what he had originally conceived in 1906 as 'a new story for *Dubliners*', that of Mr Hunter, which became *Ulysses*.[75]

'The Shade of Parnell'

'The Shade of Parnell' ('L'ombra di Parnell') was published in *Il Piccolo della Sera* on 16 May 1912. The immediate occasion was the introduction of the Third Home Rule Bill on 11 April 1912. A great deal had occurred in the year and a half that had elapsed since the second election of 1910, when Joyce had written 'The Home Rule Comet' for the Triestine paper.

The fact that the Irish Party again held the balance of power at Westminster had drawn attention to Parnell's masterly fashioning of the circumstances in which Gladstone had introduced the First Home Rule Bill in 1886. At the unveiling of the Parnell monument in Dublin on 1 October 1911, John Redmond had declared, 'We have got back at long last, to the point to which Parnell had led us, before he and our cause were submerged in that catastrophe of twenty years ago.'[76] Equally Redmond's critics would use the Parnell precedent to criticise his every move. At the very least, the memory of Parnell was brought out from

73. *OCPW* 171.

74. *OCPW* 332.

75. Joyce to Stanislaus Joyce, 30 September 1906, *Letters II* 168. A year later Stanislaus noted in his diary that 'Jim is going to expand his story "Ulysses" into a short book and make a Dublin *Peer Gynt* of it.' Stanislaus Joyce, Triestine diary, 10 November 1907, quoted in Ellmann, *James Joyce*, 265.

76. Callanan, *T. M. Healy*, 461.

the shadow of the divorce court and the recriminations that ensued in the Split. This had a particular salience for Joyce. He did not require the legitimation of some degree of rehabilitation of Parnell to write his article, but he observed an artistic principle in writing of Parnell of tracking the contemporary course of the Parnell myth that owed much to his aloof critique of the futile—and un-Parnellian—bombastic mode of the Parnellite remembering of the dead leader. In its Irish political setting, Joyce's dread of anachronism in writing of Parnell was complicated: it meant not moving too far ahead in writing of the past. He craved something exogenous, something objective, that arose independently of his volitional early identification with Parnell. He needed the traction of some contemporary synchrony in the public remembering of Parnell and in the course of contemporary Irish politics to unveil his thinking. He was now free to use the occasion of the introduction of the Home Rule bill to publish a masterly, politically astringent characterisation of Parnell.

In the prelude to the introduction of the Home Rule bill, Arthur Griffith, in what was a discernible shift, had begun to write more fully and freely of Parnell in *Sinn Féin*. The Parnell issue posed difficulties for Griffith from the right and the left. T. M. Kettle wrote to *Sinn Féin* in November 1907, 'Sinn Féin says that it is a violation of national principle to enter the Westminster Parliament. Now, was Parnell likely to join in a violation of national principle? But he entered the Westminster Parliament, and what was good enough for him is good enough for me. Will you kindly point out the flaw in the argument? Parnell is to you a problem, so far unsolved; to us he is the great precedent. If you would print the Parliamentary oath with his name on it, you would help your readers to appreciate your arguments better.'[77]

Griffith's support of Parnell in the Split had made him the object of suspicion of doctrinaire republicans and cultural nationalists, but he could now politically justify lauding Parnell as a means of assailing Redmond. Identifying with Parnell was also a means by which Griffith could reassure potential sympathisers that he was not predisposed for ideological reasons to thwart the achievement of Home Rule. Sinn Féin

77. *Sinn Féin*, 9 November 1907.

was beleaguered. Griffith had to allow for the possibility that Home Rule would be achieved,[78] and to seek to win over nationalists who were not hardened opponents of the Irish Party. His constrained political position meant that he had to advance arguments that were somewhat opportunistic, sometimes crudely so. In this instance the constraints worked positively to provide political cover to rehearse his old admiration for Parnell. It was strangely complementary to Joyce's purpose of tracking the actual course of the Parnell myth.

Two of Griffith's articles in *Sinn Féin* which express views that were for Joyce gratifyingly axiomatic have a bearing on his piece. The first was written just before the election of January 1910 and was accompanied by a cartoon in which Herbert Henry Asquith stood with his foot on the neck of a recumbent representative of the Irish Party, with a spectral Parnell standing with clenched fists by his side. It was entitled in part 'The Shade of Parnell', which may well have given Joyce his title.[79]

The point of departure of Griffith's article was a statement by the obstructionist Joseph Biggar that the Irish parliamentarians were sent to Westminster not to promote legislation but to block it. He wildly charged that the Liberals had connived in the Conservatives' attempt to destroy Parnell at the Special Commission. He celebrated in Carlylean terms Parnell's vindication:

> Where the strength of England had failed, the cowardice of Ireland played out the game, and delivered her from the man she hated and feared. Parnell went, and Ireland no longer blocked the way. Nineteen years have passed since the greatest political leader Ireland has possessed since Shane O'Neill died, deserted, but like the man he was, unconquered to the last. It is just twenty years since his proud

78. Making a virtue of necessity, Griffith had Sinn Féin take the position that it would impose upon itself a cessation of political activity so as to enable Redmond to make good his pledge that, if not hampered by opposition in Ireland, he would secure the enactment of a satisfactory measure of Home Rule: see Griffith's speech at the Central Branch of Sinn Féin, *Sinn Féin*, 14 October 1911. Redmond would thus not be able to blame others if the measure was unsatisfactory: 'He has the freest field an Irish Parliamentary leader has ever been given. If he fails, his policy fails with him' (*Sinn Féin*, 7 October 1911).

79. *OCPW* 336.

THE SHADE OF PARNELL—"AND THIS IS HOW THEY BLOCK THE WAY WHEN I AM GONE."

FIGURE 16.2. 'The Shade of Parnell', *Sinn Féin*, 15 January 1910. With thanks to Irish Newspaper Archives.

voice was heard in appeal to his infatuated countrymen—believers in English promises, credulous dupes of English diplomacy—'Before you throw me to the English wolves get my price'.

The price of Mr. Parnell's blood has not been paid.[80]

For Joyce this was almost eerily vindicatory. Ten years after the formal closing over of the Parnell Split, an Irish political figure of substance was trenchantly enunciating the view that Joyce had always held but had feared was without contemporary salience. Griffith returned to the subject following the unveiling of the Parnell monument:

> On Sunday last Mr. John Redmond unveiled the Parnell statue, and in the course of his eloquent address inquired where were the libellers of Parnell's greatness that day. Some were beside him on the platform, amongst them Mr. William Abraham, who moved Parnell's deposition in Committee Room 15. A dozen public men stood on that platform cheering Parnell's name, who during the last years of Parnell's life held him up to the deluded people of Ireland as another Dermott MacMurrough and pledged their faith that if Ireland got rid of Parnell, Ireland would be immediately given Home Rule by those English Liberals who planned his destruction and used the Irish Parliamentary Party as its tool. . . . Twenty years after Parnell is laid in Glasnevin, the men who failed him appear in the white sheet in the centre of Dublin city. Let us leave it at that.[81]

Griffith described the scene as Parnell left the terminus of the Midland Great Western Railway at Broadstone in Dublin on 26 September 1891 for his last meeting, playing on the fact that none of the Parnellite parliamentarians accompanied him. Parnell was 'wretchedly ill': 'His face was livid and haggard, one of his arms bandaged, and the hand I shook no longer had the firm grip I had felt previously. His eye was still keen and his mouth firm, but it was evident it was a case of Parnell using his iron will to surmount his physical pain.'[82]

80. *Sinn Féin*, 15 January 1910.

81. 'Parnell', *Sinn Féin*, 7 October 1911.

82. 'Parnell', *Sinn Féin*, 7 October 1911.

Griffith wrote something that certainly caught Joyce's attention: 'Even still there are many in Ireland who do not believe him dead. I heard of a group of men at ten o'clock on Sunday night at the base of his memorial reiterating their belief that he was not dead and that he would come back again.' Griffith discounted this: the Parnell he had met in Broadstone station was dying, although Griffith had not realised this at the time. What Griffith wrote has some importance for Joyce, as there is relatively little to document the existence of the belief that features in *Ulysses* that Parnell was not dead. Griffith made the connection to Parnell's first return to Dublin in the Split: 'When Parnell came to Dublin after his followers betrayed him to the English Liberals, he told those who rallied round him on the raw winter's morning that he would fight to the death and he did. That he knew when he was going to Creggs that the railway journey sealed his doom, I now believe, but the pledge he had given that British Liberalism would never conquer him while he lived he kept.'[83]

Griffith concluded his assessment of Parnell's attributes: 'Parnell has passed into the region of history and his place is determined. He stands beside Shane O'Neill—the Irish leader whom England could neither bend nor trick. Parnell outmatched all her statesmen, outgeneralled all her diplomatists.'[84]

Joyce's piece appeared some six months after Griffith's, and it was not prompted by Griffith alone. In 'The Shade of Parnell', he referred to 'recent criticism' that had sought 'to minimise the greatness of this strange spirit'. This was a reference to Frank Hugh O'Donnell's *History of the Irish Parliamentary Party*, published the previous year. O'Donnell's two volumes had a single refrain: everything Parnell did originated with, and was largely achieved by, others. Principal among these was of course O'Donnell himself: 'I founded the [obstructionist] policy. I trained its first exponents. When Mr. Parnell became my runaway apprentice, I had taught him every detail of the trade he spoiled. *Pauvre ingrat! Pauvre Roi de Carton!*' He adopted the argument that Healy had plied

83. Parnell', *Sinn Féin*, 7 October 1911.

84. 'Parnell', *Sinn Féin*, 7 October 1911.

remorselessly in the Split, that from the early 1880s it was Parnell's lieutenants who did the work for which the credit accrued to the increasingly absent Irish leader: 'They were Parnell's men, *and they were Parnell*, the ubiquitous, untiring, inexhaustible, ever-ready, non-existent Parnell'.[85] The impossibly narcissistic and affected, inconstant, and disloyal O'Donnell was to resurface in *Finnegans Wake*, brilliantly dubbed 'Hyacinth O'Donnell B. A.'[86]

Joyce's article drew significantly on Richard Barry O'Brien's *Life of Charles Stewart Parnell*. It is quite likely that Joyce looked at or read the biography in the National Library on its first publication in 1898. He had in his library in Trieste the cheaper Nelson Library edition of 1910, and he may have first read or read thoroughly the book in that edition.[87] It does not, of course, necessarily follow that Joyce acquired his 1910 edition immediately on its publication. What is clear is that he had access to O'Brien's biography of Parnell when he was writing his article on the Irish leader. It was to become the most important published source for Joyce's understanding of Parnell's character.

O'Brien's biography of Parnell is an extraordinary work which had a significant impact on how Parnell was perceived a decade after his death and historically. Much has been written in one way or another of Parnell's elusiveness: this extended to the comparative ephemerality of the historical record as it related to Parnell personally. Parnell was not an avid correspondent and did not keep letters. Aside from his quasi-conspiratorial dealings with extreme nationalists, and his negotiations with English political leaders, his life was acted out on the public stage. The major parliamentary and public episodes had been identified in the myth while he lived. O'Brien knew Parnell reasonably well and collated the views of Parnell's Irish collaborators and others. His two volumes are replete with anecdote. O'Brien honed the Parnell anecdotes, those

85. O'Donnell, *Irish Parliamentary Party*, 1:289. Healy had said in the interview he gave the *Pall Mall Gazette* at the outset of the Split, 'We created Parnell, and Parnell created us—the Irish party'. Callanan, *T. M. Healy*, 268–69.

86. *FW* 87.12.

87. R. Barry O'Brien, *The Life of Charles Stewart Parnell* (London: Nelson Library, 1910); Gillespie, *James Joyce's Trieste Library*, 178.

that were already known or were new to his book. These are not the anecdotes of the conventional Victorian biography of the political great man, which were often tales of reassuring humanity, not always free from condescension or from pomposity in the retelling. Instead, they were moments on the edge of great events when Parnell delivered himself of judgements that were shrewd, tart, and often wry. They were as much as was known, at least before the appearance of Katharine Parnell's memoir in 1913 (O'Brien refused to be drawn into Parnell's relations with her), of the personality and character of the public man. Those personal glimpses of Parnell,[88] supplemented by the columns of Hansard and of the press reports of speeches, a couple of family memoirs or reminiscences, and over time the memoirs and biographies of Parnell's contemporaries and their correspondence when it became accessible, were all there was. The account O'Brien rendered permitted contemporaries to form an estimate of Parnell's character and thinking. This was especially important for Joyce, as it enabled him to flesh out what had been an understanding of Parnell gleaned from newspapers beyond what he had heard as a boy from John Kelly. It is difficult to conceive of Joyce's collusive identification with Parnell in Trieste without O'Brien. The biography conformed to, and did something to shape, Joyce's exigent criterion that what was written or said about Parnell should be Parnellian—which is to say that it should maintain some consonance with the attributes of Parnell himself.

Joyce proceeds on the premise that the Home Rule bill would be enacted: 'The House of Commons has resolved the Irish question.' This had occurred after the long century from the Act of Union: 'It was a century adorned by seven Irish revolutionary movements that, with dynamite, eloquence, boycotts, obstructionism, armed revolt and political assassination, managed to keep awake the slow, apprehensive conscience of English Liberalism.'[89] It is uncertain how Joyce computed his seven, but it is clear from the sentence that they encompassed movements that were constitutional, agrarian, and insurrectionary. It is an idea with a

88. These are discussed well in F.S.L. Lyons, *Charles Stewart Parnell* (London: Collins, 1977), 612.

89. *OCPW* 191.

Parnellite ring to it. His subject matter and the introduction of the bill shift Joyce back towards Parnell and render him less close to Sinn Féin than in the earlier articles. He instinctively anticipates that independence will have a fusionary effect on the disparate Irish movements.

Joyce criticises the reduction in the Irish representation at Westminster under the bill and surmises that it would lead to the alignment of the nationalists with the small Labour Party 'so that from this incestuous embrace a coalition will probably arise and function as the far left', under Liberal auspices.[90] If this owes a little to Griffith,[91] it reflects Joyce's dismissive view of British socialism. He criticises also the financial provisions. He makes clear, however, that he did not adopt the stance of Sinn Féin, which at a convention on 13 April had adopted a resolution refusing to accept 'as a final settlement . . . any arrangement which leaves a single vestige of British rule in Ireland'.[92] Joyce wrote somewhat dismissively, 'The Irish separatist party would like to reject this Greek gift,' and continued, 'No matter: the appearance of autonomy is there'. Joyce referred to the national convention which had taken place in Dublin on 23 April, where 'the denunciations and protests of the nationalists belonging to the bitterly sceptical school of John Mitchel did not greatly disturb the popular jubilation'.[93] The delusive promise of the Home Rule bill brought Joyce into fleeting agreement with Kettle, who spoke at the convention.[94]

For Joyce, an important aspect of the seeming ineluctability of the passage of the bill, now that the veto of the House of Lords was to become suspensory in nature, was that it did something to close the controversy of the Split in a way that Joyce considered would be a bitter vindication of Parnell. This reflected how the diminishing numbers of Parnell's remaining ardent loyalists felt, though Joyce retained a certain edge of

90. *OCPW* 191.

91. See, for example, *Sinn Féin*, 1 January 1910.

92. *Sinn Féin*, 20 April 1912.

93. *OCPW* 191, 193.

94. *Freeman's Journal*, 24 April 1912; Meleady, *John Redmond*, 215. This event was only fleetingly alluded to in *Sinn Féin* 27 April, so Joyce evidently had some other newspaper source. The nephew of Gladstone to whom Joyce referred as a speaker at the convention was in fact his grandson W.C.G. Gladstone, who spoke briefly immediately after John Redmond.

implacability and restrained sarcasm: 'In two years' time at the latest, with or without the assent of the House of Lords, the doors of the old parliament in Dublin will re-open, and Ireland, freed from her century-long imprisonment, will set out towards the palace like a new bride accompanied by music and nuptial torches. A grand-nephew of Gladstone (if there is one) will scatter flowers beneath the feet of the sovereign, but there will be a shade at the feast: the shade of Charles Parnell.'[95]

The historical outcome was to be vastly more protracted and fraught, but the prevailing belief that the bill would lead to the realisation of Home Rule permitted Joyce to render his assessment of Parnell. This setting is important because the circumstances in which Irish independence was actually achieved made it virtually impossible to trace any direct lineage to Parnell. Joyce began by addressing F. H. O'Donnell's critique. Even if it was to be conceded that independent opposition, obstructionism, and the Land League were devised by others, such 'concessions evince all the more the extraordinary personality of a leader who, with no forensic gift or original political talent, forced the English politicians to follow his orders. He, like another Moses, led a turbulent and volatile people out of the house of shame to the edge of the Promised Land.'[96] This, apart from the reference to 'a turbulent and volatile people', was consistent with the received perception of Parnell. Joyce moreover was happy to adopt the comparison of Parnell to Moses that was frequent in the Split.

Joyce continued, addressing Parnell's true enigma, his mesmeric command of the Irish nationalist populace: 'The influence that Parnell exercised over the Irish people defies the critic's analysis. Lisping, of delicate build, he was ignorant of the history of his country. His short, broken speeches lacked all eloquence, poetry or humour. His cold, polite behaviour divided him from his own colleagues. He was Protestant, a descendant of an aristocratic family, and (to complete the affliction) he spoke with a distinctly English accent.'[97]

95. *OCPW* 193.
96. *OCPW* 193.
97. *OCPW* 193.

Joyce again was prepared to accept the tropes of the Parnell myth, even those that were negative. He was wedded to the idea that Parnell had a slight impediment of speech, which is probably an inference he drew from Parnell's notoriously halting utterance on his first entry into public life. He accepted and even accentuated the idea already inherent in the received myth of Parnell that political leadership did not require conventional eloquence or erudition. It did require purpose, resolve, and depth of personality: 'Neither the applause nor the anger of the crowd, neither the invectives nor the praises of the press, neither the denunciations nor the defences of the British ministers ever perturbed the forlorn serenity of his character.'[98] It was this characterisation of Parnell as having an intimation of the tragic gracefully borne, developed in the article, that went beyond O'Brien, and indeed Griffith.[99]

Joyce rehearsed some of the set pieces of the Parnell legend before picking up on Gladstone's description in an interview with O'Brien included in the biography of Parnell as 'an intellectual phenomenon':[100] 'Nothing more singular can be imagined than this appearance of this intellectual phenomenon in the midst of the stifling morals of Westminster. Now, looking back over the scenes of the drama and listening again to the speeches that caused his listeners' souls to tremble, it is useless to deny that all the eloquence and all those strategic triumphs begin to taste stale.'[101]

98. *OCPW* 194.

99. Griffith, for reasons of his own, imputed to Parnell a presentiment that was more crudely political: 'He never achieved victory, but the Parliamentarianism he hoped to win with slew him in the end, and the day it slew Parnell Parliamentarianism avowed its own worthlessness. Parnell was too great a man not to have foreseen the possibility of his end. He knew he could not hope to keep an Irish Party in the British Parliament uncorrupted for more than a few years, but he hoped that within that period he could succeed, and the failure of his hopes was not his fault' (*Sinn Féin*, 5 February 1910).

100. O'Brien asked Gladstone what it was that first drew his attention to Parnell. '*Mr. Gladstone* (with much energy): "Parnell was the most remarkable man I ever met. I do not say ablest man; I say the most remarkable and the most interesting. He was an intellectual phenomenon."' R. B. O'Brien, *Charles Stewart Parnell*, 2:357. The interview took place on 28 January 1897. Gladstone died the following year at the age of eighty-eight.

101. *OCPW* 194.

Joyce was searching for the persona that lay behind the frozen tableau of the myth. It is in this article that he makes the devastating comparison of the character of Parnell with those of Benjamin Disraeli and Gladstone, the Conservative and Liberal leaders whose rivalry had seemed to define British party politics in the latter half of the nineteenth century: 'But time is more merciful towards the "uncrowned king" than towards the wag and the orator. The light of his mild, proud, silent and disconsolate sovereignty makes Disraeli look like an upstart diplomat dining whenever he can in rich people's houses, and Gladstone like a portly butler who has gone to night school. How little Disraeli's wit and Gladstone's culture weigh in the balance today!'[102]

Aside from renewing his attack on Gladstone, who in 1858 had published his *Studies on Homer and the Homeric Age*, Joyce was subverting the conventional adversarial twinning of Gladstone and Disraeli to mark Parnell apart from the conventional conception of the Victorian statesman.

Joyce noted that 'although Parnell's tactic was to avail himself of any one of the English parties, Liberal or Conservative, according to his pleasure, a set of circumstances involved him in the Liberal movement.'[103] Joyce understood the asymmetry of 'independent opposition' in practice: the Conservatives set their face against Home Rule, which became a defining difference between them and the Liberals in British politics:[104] 'The elastic quality of Gladstone's Liberalism must be borne in mind if we are to appreciate the extent and degree of Parnell's task', and 'Parnell, convinced that such a liberalism would only yield to force, united every element of national life behind him, and set out on a march along the borders of insurrection.'[105] Gladstone was driven to introduce the First Home Rule Bill.

Joyce charted Parnell's abrupt fall: 'He fell helplessly in love with a married woman'; in fact, Parnell's relationship with Katharine O'Shea dated back to 1882. In the wake of the O'Shea divorce proceedings,

102. *OCPW* 194.

103. *OCPW* 194–95.

104. For wider discussion of this, see Margaret O'Callaghan, *British High Politics*.

105. *OCPW* 195.

Gladstone and John Morley refused to commit to legislating for Home Rule if, as Joyce nicely rendered it, 'the felon stayed on as leader of the Nationalist Party'. Parnell denied the right of a minister (Gladstone was in fact out of office) 'to exercise a veto over the affairs of Ireland, and refused to resign. He was deposed by the Nationalists obeying Gladstone's orders. Of the eighty-three deputies, only eight remained faithful to him.'[106] This was a substantial underestimate: the final division was forty-five to twenty-seven, excluding Parnell.[107] It is possible Joyce was confusing the outcome with that of the 1892 general election which left the Parnellites with nine seats.

Joyce now turned implacably to the course of the Split in Ireland: 'The Irish press poured the phials of their spitefulness over him and the woman he loved. The peasants of Castlecomer threw quicklime in his eyes. He went from county to county, from city to city, "like a hunted hind", a spectral figure with the signs of death upon his brow. Within a year he died of a broken heart at the age of forty-five.'[108]

What was thrown at Parnell in Castlecomer was not quicklime, but Joyce succeeds in rendering the terrible motion of the Split. He is careful to emphasise that the press attacks on Parnell encompassed Katharine, a thrust at Healy's *National Press*. The comparison to 'a hunted hind' occurs in O'Brien: J. J. Horgan, Parnell's election agent in Cork, remembered seeing Parnell after his speech there at the outset of the Split: 'He looked like a hunted hind; his hair was dishevelled, his beard unkempt, his eyes were wild and restless.'[109] The 'signs of death upon his brow' may owe something to Griffith, who had written that he had not realised at the time of seeing Parnell in Broadstone station that 'it was death and not wasting illness that was written in his face'.[110]

Joyce continued, in the closing paragraph, 'The shade of the "uncrowned king" will weigh upon the hearts of those who remember him, when the new Ireland soon enters into the palace *fimbris aureis*

106. *OCPW* 196.

107. C. C. O'Brien, *Parnell and His Party*, 326.

108. *OCPW* 196.

109. R. B. O'Brien, *Charles Stewart Parnell* (1898), 2:298, cited in *OCPW* 339n29.

110. *Sinn Féin*, 7 October 1911.

circumamicta varietatibus: but it will not be a vindictive shade.'[111] The Latin is from Psalms 44:14–15 in the Vulgate translation: 'girded with golden fringes, in varied colours.'[112] This was the prelude to Joyce's brilliantly wrought denunciation of those who betrayed Parnell. The first was on the leading anti-Parnellite nationalist, whom as a matter of taste and Parnellite principle he did not name: 'The sadness that devastated his soul was, perhaps, the profound conviction that, in his hour of need, one of the disciples who had dipped his hand into the bowl with him was about to betray him.' The depiction of T. M. Healy as Judas permitted Joyce to insinuate the identification of Parnell with Christ. The casually blasphemous equation had been made in Parnellite rhetoric in the year or two after the death of Parnell but had long since ceased to be heard in the anti-Parnellite and clerical ascendancy that followed Parnell's death. The second was on the Irish nationalist people, or at least on the enfranchised portion of that people. That also had some precedent in the bitter anguish of Parnell's death but had never found expression as incisive as Joyce's: 'In his last proud appeal to his people, he implored his fellow-countrymen not to throw him to the English wolves howling around him. It rebounds to the honour of his fellow-countrymen that they did not fail that desperate appeal. They did not throw him to the English wolves: they tore him apart themselves.'[113]

The 'English wolves' originated in Parnell's manifesto 'to the people of Ireland.' The stated purpose of the manifesto was in response to Gladstone's letter to Morley 'to put before you [the Irish people, to which it was addressed] information . . . which will enable you to understand the measure of the loss with which you are threatened unless you consent to throw me to the English wolves now howling for my destruction.'[114] The phrase, widely considered at the time to represent a misjudgement on Parnell's part, was validated as a trope by Joyce, who calculatedly redirected it against the people to whom it was addressed.

111. *OCPW* 196.

112. Joyce, *Critical Writings*, 228n1.

113. *OCPW* 196.

114. *Freeman's Journal*, 29 November 1890, reprinted in F.S.L. Lyons, *Fall of Parnell*, 321.

Lest the violence of Joyce's concluding image should seem extravagant, it is worth citing an exchange that later appeared in the memoirs of Sir Edward Clarke, published in 1918. Clarke was a prominent English barrister and Conservative parliamentarian who held the office of Solicitor-General when he appeared for Captain O'Shea in the divorce proceedings. He recalled a conversation with David Plunkett, an Irish Unionist advocate and parliamentarian: 'I once said to David Plunkett, "I knew I was throwing a bombshell into the Irish camp, but I did not know it would be quite so much mischief". "Ah", said he, "you didn't know that when it burst they would pick up the pieces and cut each other's throats with them"'.[115] 'The Irish camp' was the Irish Party. Joyce widened his attack to the Irish people.

In his lecture on Joyce in Milan in 1927, Ettore Schmitz referred to Joyce's article as 'magnificent in its indignation and irony'. He quoted the conclusion and said, 'Here you see Joyce walking through the world with his one comrade in faith, Parnell. Parnell is dead. Our poet, here, it seems, is Zarathustra carrying the great man's corpse on his back.'[116]

It is important to recall the temporal political setting of Joyce's conclusion. He was persuaded, as were the majority of his nationalist fellow countrymen, that the Home Rule bill would be enacted. He had held out implacably against what he saw as a course of forgetting from the moment of Parnell's death, but tacitly acknowledged that the enactment of Home Rule would for practical purposes relegate the controversy of the Split to the past. There was something to be said before that happened and Joyce said it, even if in an evening newspaper published in faraway Trieste. If Home Rule was imminent, it was the last occasion for the flame of Parnell to flare before he was subsumed into history. This is the highly specific setting for the ferocity of Joyce's conclusion. It was no small thing for Joyce to countenance, even tentatively, drawing a line under the Split.

115. Edward Clarke, *The Story of My Life* (London: Ohn Murray, 1918), 293; Callanan, *T. M. Healy*, 241.

116. I. Svevo, 'James Joyce', 154.

Joyce's views were closer to the Parnellite response to the Second Home Rule Bill of 1893 than to the nationalist response to the Third Home Rule Bill of 1912. His views were certainly not representative, but neither were they divorced from the rhythm of Irish nationalist politics. The outcome widely anticipated in nationalist Ireland in 1912 did not come about. The Home Rule bill would be enacted, after a fashion, in 1914, but would never come into effect. The Parnell myth did not achieve the relative quietus that Home Rule might have brought. 'Do not flingamejig to the twolves'.[117]

Joyce had written an article on Oscar Wilde for *Il Piccolo della Sera* on 24 March 1909, three years previously. He drew no direct comparison with Parnell. He still maintained the view that Wilde had exposed himself to fate by assuming the role (in a distinguished line of Irish dramatists) of 'court jester to the English'. This owed something to a Parnellite nationalist calibration of Victorian scandal, as well as to Joyce's reservations about Wilde. He did address the process of unfolding scandal whereby 'the fantastic myth of the apostle of beauty' that had formed around Wilde was thrown into reverse.[118] What is striking is not just Joyce's alertness to scandal but his Parnell-inflected sensitivity to Wilde's personal myth. It was not simply that the plummeting depths of their falls were to be measured by the fact that both Parnell and Wilde were contemporary celebrities. Both had strong myths which became part of their fall, and their fall became part of their posthumous myths. Of Wilde he wrote, 'His fall was greeted by a howl of puritanical joy'. When he came out of prison, 'he was driven, like a hare hunted by dogs, from hotel to hotel'. Innocent or guilty, 'he was undoubtedly a scapegoat. His greatest crime was to have caused in England a scandal.'[119] There had been three attempts to criminalise Parnell's political actions—the Dublin state prosecution of 1881–82, his imprisonment in Kilmainham 1882–83, and the Special Commission of 1888–90 (which almost exclusively held Joyce's attention)—but Parnell fell in the political

117. *FW* 479.14.
118. *OCPW* 149.
119. *OCPW* 149–50.

backwash of a sexual scandal.[120] Wilde fell as a result of sexual conduct deemed criminal of which he was convicted. The sympathy Joyce evinced for Wilde itself presaged a certain softening. His schema of the victimhood of scandal was to become less rigid. Held apart in Joyce's article, Parnell's and Wilde's falls would intersect and intermittently coalesce in the fantasia of *Finnegans Wake*.

Joyce's Third Return Visit to Ireland, July–September 1912

Nora had been away from Ireland for eight years when Joyce decided that she should go with Lucia to Galway. He may have calculated that a visit would have the incidental benefit of sapping the force and diminishing the frequency of the rhetorical threats of returning to her family to which she resorted when they rowed. Nora was also charged to intercede with George Roberts of Maunsel & Company in relation to the stalled publication of *Dubliners*.[121]

Nora and Lucia arrived in Dublin on 8 July 1912. At Westland Row, as she reported later to Eileen Joyce, 'all the family of Joyces were there to meet me'. They went round to Finn's Hotel, where Nora was to stay for two nights: 'Your father every time he would look at Lucia wept copiously all about Jim with your Father'.[122] If Joyce had conceived of her visit to Roberts as that of a Madonna with or without child, Roberts was confronted the day after her arrival by a deputation comprising Nora, John Stanislaus Joyce, and Charles Joyce, who together, as Nora reported, 'just pinned that charming gentleman'. Roberts said to call again, but 'kept out of our way' when she and Charles called twice the next day. Nora went on to Galway, from where she reported to Joyce.[123]

This letter crossed with an indignant remonstrance from Joyce, who complained of having received from her only a collectively signed

120. For the Special Commission, see O'Callaghan, *British High Politics*.

121. Ellmann, *James Joyce*, 322.

122. Nora Barnacle to Eileen Joyce, 14 August 1912, *Letters II* 302–3.

123. Nora Barnacle to Joyce, 11 July 1912, *Letters II* 296–97.

postcard: 'Not one word of the places in Dublin where I met you and which have so many memories for us both!' He was going to leave Trieste for Dublin that evening.[124] Joyce then set out from Trieste with Giorgio. In London he saw Yeats and commented petulantly, 'For a wonder he was polite',[125] and Joseph Hone of Maunsel & Co, whom he had earlier deemed 'an Oxford insipid'[126] but now hoped to play off against Roberts. He declared to Hone that he had 'crossed Europe' to see him.[127] In Dublin, where Joyce arrived on 15 July, he saw Roberts: 'He says the Giant's Causeway is putty compared to me'. Roberts now offered him the option of publication by Maunsel with the offending paragraphs of 'Ivy Day' and 'An Encounter' deleted and replaced by asterisks, with a preface by Joyce, or that Joyce would himself take over the publication, bringing the book bound and printed over to London to be issued by Simpkin Marshall on commission.[128] Roberts wrote shortly afterwards varying the latter proposal, suggesting that 'the best way out of the deadlock would be for you to offer the printed sheets to Grant Richards'.[129]

Of Joyce's arrival in Galway, Nora later reported proudly to Eileen in Trieste,

> I suppose it was a great surprise to you when you received my postcard saying I was leaving for Ireland. What must it have been like when you heard Jim was coming. well what have you to say to Jim now after all our little squabbles he could not live without me for a month can you imagine my joy when I received a telegram a week after Jim and georgie on their way it seems to me that he can do wonders. he sent me a wire from the boat and it out on the deep sea at midnight, but to make a long story short he arrived in Galway on a Tuesday night with Georgie all the people here were talking about him for running after me.[130]

124. Joyce to Nora Barnacle, 12 July 1912, *Letters II* 297.
125. Joyce to Stanislaus Joyce, postmark 17 July 1912, *Letters II* 298.
126. Joyce to Stanislaus Joyce, 4 August 1909, *Letters II* 230.
127. Joseph Hone, 'A Recollection of James Joyce', *Envoy* 5, no. 17 (1951): 45.
128. Joyce to Stanislaus Joyce, postmark 17 July 1912, *Letters II* 298; Ellmann, *James Joyce*, 324.
129. Joyce to Stanislaus Joyce, postmark 10 August 1912, *Letters II* 301.
130. Nora Barnacle to Eileen Joyce, 14 August 1912, *Letters II* 302.

In Galway Joyce cycled out to Oughterard and visited the graveyard which is the fictional burial place of Michael Furey in 'The Dead', though Nora's old love, Michael Bodkin, was buried in Rahoon.[131] He went with Nora to the Galway races.[132] He pondered the history of Galway, through a perusal of James Hardiman's *History of the Town and County of Galway* (1820), considering the interface of the new and old Galways, and the street names which 'recall the connections of the city with Latin Europe'. He interested himself in what was an old political chestnut, the prospects for Galway as a transatlantic port. They travelled by steamboat to Aranmor, 'the holy island that sleeps like a large shark under the grey waters of the Atlantic Ocean which the islanders call the old sea.' The fruits of his travels, historical research, and ethnographic reveries were two articles that appeared in *Il Piccolo della Sera*: 'The City of the Tribes: Italian Memories of an Irish Port' (published 11 August 1912) and 'The Mirage of the Fisherman of Aran: England's Safety Valve in Case of War' (published 5 September 1912), which dwelt once more on Irish saints. On Inishmore he and Nora had the encounter that gives the title to the latter piece, in which he affirms his counter-revivalist perception of the antecedent Gaelic culture as vanished:

> We halt, uncertain, in one of the steep laneways. An islander, who speaks an English all of his own, bids us good day, adding that it had been a horrible summer, thanks be to God. The phrase which at first seems to be one of the usual Irish blunders comes, rather, from the inmost heart of human resignation. The man who said it bears a princely name, O'Flaherty, the name which the young Oscar Wilde proudly had printed on the cover of his first book. But time and the wind have razed to the ground the civilization to which he belongs—the sacred oaken groves of the island, the principality of his forefathers, his language and perhaps the name of that Aran hermit [Columba] who used to be called the dove of the church. Around the shrubs growing with difficulty on the hillocks of the island, his

131. Joyce to Stanislaus Joyce, postmark 7 August 1912, *Letters II* 300; Ellmann, *James Joyce*, 324–25.

132. Joyce to Nora Barnacle, [21 August 1912], *Letters II* 309.

imagination has woven legends and fables that reveal the hereditary taint of his psyche. Under his apparent simplicity there is something sceptical, humorous, spectral. He looks away when he has spoken and lets the enthusiastic scholar note down in his pocket-book, the amazing fact that it was under yonder whitethorn bush that Joseph of Arimathea cut his walking stick.[133]

As the steamboat plies back to Galway, Joyce, perhaps remembering the climate of Trieste that turned men to butter, described a moment of serenity on this fraught final visit to Ireland: 'The rain is falling on the islands and on the sea. It is raining as it can rain only in Ireland.' A girl was noisily flirting with a deckhand, 'holding him on her knees'.[134]

Joyce was also involved in a comical journalistic errand which would find its way into *Ulysses*. Joyce in Trieste was friendly with, and intrigued as much as he was bored by, Henry N. Blackwood Price, an Ulster Protestant and assistant manager of the Eastern Telegraph Company. An outbreak of foot-and-mouth disease in Ireland in July led to an embargo on the export of Irish cattle to Britain. Blackwood Price was much exercised over a treatment for foot-and-mouth disease which had been applied in the Austrian province of Styria. He wanted Joyce to publicise this in Ireland and wrote repeatedly on the subject to him. Joyce wrote to William Field, the nationalist member of Parliament for the St Patrick's Division of Dublin and the president of the Irish Cattle Trader's Society. Field, as it happened, was the Irish parliamentarian who remained most closely involved in the commemorations of Parnell. Joyce forwarded to Field a letter from Blackwood Price which opened with a reference to 'my friend, Professor Joyce'. Field had the letter published in the *Evening Telegraph* of 19 August 1912.[135] Ellsworth Mason and Ellmann included in *The Critical Writings of James Joyce* (1959) a lengthy sub-leader in the *Freeman's Journal* of 10 September 1912 headed 'Politics

133. *OCPW* 204. This contrasts starkly with Stephen's reaction at the end of *A Portrait* to the old man whom John Alphonsus Mulrennan told him he had met in a mountain cabin in the west of Ireland: 'I fear him. I fear his redrimmed horny eyes' (*P* 223).

134. *OCPW* 205.

135. Joyce to Stanislaus Joyce, postmark 7 August 1912, *Letters II* 300; Ellmann, *James Joyce*, 325–27; McCourt, *Years of Bloom*, 175, 185.

and Cattle Disease'.[136] The false attribution of its authorship to Joyce, repeated in Ellmann's biography,[137] arose from Charles Joyce's incorrect report to Stanislaus in a letter of 6 September 1912 that 'Jim wrote a sub-editorial today for the *Freeman* about the Styrian cure for the foot-and-mouth disease.'[138] Joyce's authorship of what was a weary defence of the Irish Party on the subject of foot-and-mouth disease was textually never even faintly plausible and it is odd that it remained unchallenged for so long.[139]

In Trieste there was a further rent crisis, as the landlord demanded possession of the Joyces' apartment where Eileen was staying. Stanislaus had ultimately to rent an apartment at 4 Via Donato Bramante—where Joyce and Nora were to live on their return until they left Trieste—and had to move across their possessions. Joyce's response from Galway was grandiosely insouciant.[140] The crisis which actively engaged Joyce's attention was that of his negotiations with Roberts over the publication of *Dubliners*, which now entered their final phase. Roberts wrote to Joyce in Galway. He now gallingly claimed to have come to the realisation that the drift of the book was anti-Irish, and therefore not in keeping with his aims as an Irish publisher. Joyce arrived back in Dublin from Galway alone on the evening of 16 August. There followed an

136. Joyce, *Critical Writings*, 238–41. 'Politics and Cattle Disease' is also included in *OCPW* 206–8.

137. Ellmann, *James Joyce*, 325–27.

138. Charles Joyce to Stanislaus Joyce, 6 September 1912, *Letters II* 318.

139. The idea of Joyce's authorship of 'Politics and Cattle Disease' was finally debunked by Terence Matthews in his excellent 'Emendation to the Joycean Canon'. Matthews points out that a sub-leader in the *Freeman's Journal* of 6 September 1912 does refer to Blackwood Price and to the Styrian cure, which explains the error of Charles Joyce. In the 'Nestor' episode of *Ulysses*, Mr Deasy wants Stephen to secure the publication in the press of his letter on foot-and-mouth disease. Stephen skims over Deasy's letter: 'May I trespass on your valuable space. . . . Our cattle trade. The way of all our old industries. Liverpool ring which jockeyed the Galway harbour scheme' (*U* 2.324–27). Ellmann was further misled by this conflating on Joyce's part of the issue of foot-and-mouth disease and the Galway harbour scheme to which he had referred in his 'Fisherman of Aran' article. Ellmann, *James Joyce*, 327.

140. Joyce to Stanislaus Joyce, postmark 7 August 1912, *Letters II* 298–301; Ellmann, *James Joyce*, 326–28; McCourt, *Years of Bloom*, 186–87.

extraordinary three weeks of negotiations with Roberts, whose grounds of objections were constantly shifting and demands increasing.

Joyce had retained a solicitor, George Lidwell, who had some connection with his father. Lidwell, in his initial advice to Joyce, was concerned that 'An Encounter' could attract prosecution:

> It would be well to remember that although these paragraphs in your book might possibly escape notice that there is at present in existence in this city a Vigilance Committee whose object is to seek out and suppress all writings of immoral tendencies and I am of opinion that if the attention of the Authorities be drawn to these paragraphs it is likely they would yield to the pressure of this body and prosecute. Whether a conviction could be obtained is another matter altogether. But I would advise you to take no risks and under the circumstances either delete or entirely alter the paragraphs in question.[141]

One wonders if this was not a play by a weary solicitor who felt the best he could do for his client was to urge him to compromise. Hone recalled somewhat vaguely that Maunsel published tracts on behalf of Lady Aberdeen, the wife of the Lord Lieutenant, in her campaign against tuberculosis, and thought this may have been a consideration, though Roberts denied to Ellmann, possibly truthfully for once, that this was an influence.[142] The account Stanislaus sent to Constantine Curran almost half a century later is suggestive in its portrayal of the 'two masters' in operation, the objective collusion of the British government in Ireland and the Catholic Church or its lay zealots, as it bore on the publication of *Dubliners*:

> Roberts told Jim that he had no end of trouble with a certain Vigilance Committee and though he was as shifty as they make 'em that fits in with the rest of the story. He mentioned people who were supposed to be on the Committee. I vaguely remember Lady Aberdeen, some priests and priests's creatures . . . who all got in on the good cause. Why should Roberts himself have broken his contract to

141. J. G. Lidwell to Joyce, n.d., enclosed with Joyce to Stanislaus Joyce, [21 August 1912], *Letters II* 306.

142. Hone, 'Recollection of James Joyce', 44; Ellmann, *James Joyce*, 328.

> publish a book that promised to be at least as successful as the others he had published unless he too had yielded to pressure? Falconer, besides his official work for the Crown, did a lot of printing for Catholic Societies.[143]

It was Joyce's solicitor who, in the correspondence that survives, had raised the spectre of the Vigilance Committee. It is a curious circumstance that the Lord Lieutenant of Ireland from 1905 to 1915, Lord Aberdeen, presided with his wife, Lady Aberdeen, over the National Vigilance Association, the largest group promoting social purity in Britain, which had a branch in Dublin, the Dublin White Cross Vigilance Association. The Irish Vigilance Association, composed predominantly of Catholics, was established in 1911, to which Aberdeen lent his patronage,[144] but it lacked influence until the establishment of the Irish state, when it was aligned with the Legion of Mary. Katherine Mullin has written, 'The Irish Catholic purity movement was, then, oddly belated. . . . Only when a Catholic Free State was established did a Catholic purity movement thrive in Ireland; conversely, before 1922, purity work was in the main carried out by a Protestant evangelical satellite of a British organisation.'[145] From the perspective of the Joyce brothers, it was hard not to make something of the cross-contamination of Protestant and Catholic moralism and institutional crystallisation of the 'two masters'. Joyce expressed himself with lofty tentativeness on the subject, subsuming it into his own myth, in an account of his publication history ('the story of my books is very strange') he sent to Carlo Linati in 1919. He wrote of the 'burning' in Dublin of 'the whole first edition of 1000 copies' of *Dubliners*: 'Some say it was the doing of priests, some of enemies, others of the then Viceroy or his consort, Countess Aberdeen. Altogether it is a mystery.'[146]

143. Stanislaus Joyce to Constantine Curran, 2 March 1955, quoted in McCourt, *Years of Bloom*, 189. Curran did not deal with the debacle of *Dubliners* in *James Joyce Remembered*.

144. Patrick Maume, 'John Campbell Aberdeen', *DIB* 4:147. Aberdeen had the longest term of office of any Irish viceroy.

145. Katherine Mullin, *James Joyce, Sexuality and Social Purity* (Cambridge: Cambridge University Press, 2003), 21.

146. Joyce to Carlo Linati, 19 December 1919 (in Italian), *Letters I* 132. Herbert Gorman wrote in his 1939 biography, 'There has never been any valid explanation for this crude sacrifice and

Whatever the matrix of specific influences to which he was subject, Roberts saw trouble in a book that potentially affronted Irish middle-class susceptibilities, as well as a more unpredictably volatile maverick fringe. The attitude of Kettle was in this respect emblematic. Stanislaus Joyce recalled in his principal memoir of his brother, 'Tom Kettle . . . declared against the book. He kept saying, "Oh, I'll slate that book when it comes out, I'll slate it!" That was a fair fight that my brother accepted, and that Kettle, by the by, would have lost had the First World War not claimed him as one of its wasted victims. My brother pointed out that was an actual experience, but Kettle waved the reply aside. "I know", he said, "we have all met him."'[147]

Joyce did not refer in his correspondence to Kettle's comments. There is no reason, however, to doubt Stanislaus's account, which is consistent with an entry in Joseph Holloway's diary recording that Kettle considered 'An Encounter' to be 'beyond anything in its outspokenness he had ever read'.[148] In his much later account to Curran, Stanislaus also stated that when Joyce was thinking of publishing *Dubliners* in Trieste, he went around the principal booksellers of Dublin to ask if they would retail the book. Their response was friendly, but 'they all hesitated when they heard the facts'.[149]

On 21 August, Roberts demanded third-party indemnities to publish the book which Joyce could not provide. He then said he would act on his legal advice and not publish the book. Joyce agreed to omit 'An Encounter' from the book subject to four conditions, of which the last was 'that the book be published by you not later than 6th October 1912.'[150]

---

wanton destruction on the part of the printer. It may be pointed out here that the printers were Falconer and Company who did a lot of work for various Roman Catholic societies and were in a small way official printers to the Crown' (*James Joyce*, 216–17).

147. S. Joyce, *My Brother's Keeper*, 80.

148. Quoted in Ellmann, *James Joyce*, 329.

149. Stanislaus Joyce to C. P. Curran, 2 March 1955, quoted in McCourt, *Years of Bloom*, 189. The manager of one bookshop told Joyce that a couple of weeks previously two young men had presented themselves who insisted that he take a particular French novel out of the window. When asked, they declined to state their authority for giving such an order other than to say he would otherwise have his windows broken.

150. Joyce to Nora Barnacle, [21 August 1912]; Joyce to George Roberts, 21 August 1912, *Letters II* 308–10.

The final date of publication Joyce had nominated was that of the anniversary of Parnell's death. This was a characteristic Parnellite flourish on Joyce's part that in its political irony mitigated the concession he was making. Pointedly asserting the political correlation between the content of *Dubliners* and the history of its thwarted publication, it reflected the prominent part that objections to 'Ivy Day' had played in the first phase of the resistance he had encountered to the publication of *Dubliners*. The *hommage* to Parnell was, in the highly charged circumstances in which it was rendered, a striking expression of the depth of Joyce's personal and political identification with the dead Irish leader.

On 22 August 1912, Joyce saw Roberts. They got as far as discussing the binding, paper, and advertisement of the book.[151] The following day Joyce called to see Roberts as arranged, and received a letter left for him. Roberts now asserted that, on the basis of his legal advice, 'the publication of the book by Maunsel & Co. is out of the question'. His advice was that Joyce was in breach of contract in submitting a book that he ought to have known was libellous. 'I should be extremely sorry to take proceedings against you to protect the interests of Maunsel & Co., but as it appears that the chance of selling the sheets is very remote, I must ask you to make a substantial offer towards covering our loss.'[152] Joyce read it and walked down the street, as he wrote to Nora, 'feeling the whole future of my life slipping out of my grasp'. Parnell was still on his mind: 'I don't know what I will or can do. I will think. I will fight to the last.'[153] To Stanislaus he wrote, 'I will fight to the last inch with every weapon in my power.'[154]

Lidwell, Joyce's solicitor, advised him that Maunsel were in the right. As Joyce told his brother, 'Then I went to Pappie who told me to put the

151. Joyce to Nora Barnacle, postmark 22 August 1912; Joyce to Stanislaus Joyce, 23 August 1912, *Letters II* 310–12.

152. George Roberts to Joyce, 23 August 1912, *Letters II* 313–14.

153. Joyce to Nora Barnacle, postmark 23 August 1912, *Letters II* 311.

154. Joyce to Stanislaus Joyce, 23 August 1912, *Letters II* 313. Joyce retained in his family circle a certain equanimity. When Curran interviewed May Monaghan in 1964, he noted, 'She returned more than once to Jim's gentleness and good humour. Even at the time he was distressed over the failure to publish *Dubliners* he was no more than gloomy and would sit down to piano and improvise and yet out of his moodiness evoked comic street ballads and opera' (UCD, Curran Collection, MS 6).

letter in my pocket, buck up, take back the MSS and find another publisher'. He passed two hours in the afternoon arguing with Roberts.[155] His negotiations with Roberts followed their doomed course as Roberts further radicalised his demands for changes. On 30 August Joyce went to see Arthur Griffith. Joyce must have frequently observed Griffith in the National Library when he was still living in Dublin. Griffith certainly knew of Joyce from Joyce's review of William Rooney's *Poems and Ballads*. Perhaps he too remembered Joyce by sight, but they had never met. Their conversation extended beyond *Dubliners*. Joyce reported to Stanislaus,

> I then went to Griffith who received me kindly and remembered my letter. He says I am not the first person from whom he has heard this story. He says Roberts has been playing that game for years. He says the idea of Maunsel suing me is simple bluff and believes that they will not come into court and that if I get a strong solicitor on my side they will yield. He gave me a note of a first class solicitor in Westmoreland Street. He asked me also to send him copies of my articles in [*Il Piccolo della Sera*] and to give him Price's address.[156]

The finale is recounted in three letters to Stanislaus from his brother Charles,[157] whom Joyce had got involved in the faint hope of bringing about an alleviation in his dire circumstances. Charles wrote, 'I have had to get outdoor relief here, but there is a possibility that this business of Jim's book may lead to something for me.'[158] Joyce had resolved to buy the sheets from Maunsel and to publish the book himself. Roberts said that the printer, John Falconer of Upper Sackville Street, refused to give them to him until he had read the whole book through. Griffith had referred Joyce to Henry Dixon, who was a chief clerk in a solicitor's office rather than a solicitor. Dixon regretted that he could not conscientiously see his way to assisting Joyce to recover the sheets 'as he

155. Joyce to Stanislaus Joyce, 23 August 1912, *Letters II* 312.

156. Joyce to Stanislaus Joyce, postmark 30 August 1912, *Letters II* 314. 'My letter' was Joyce's letter to the press about the thwarted publication history of *Dubliners* which Griffith had published in *Sinn Féin* on 2 September 1911.

157. Charles Joyce to Stanislaus Joyce, 5, 6, 11 September 1912, *Letters II* 314–19.

158. Charles Joyce to Stanislaus Joyce, 6 September 1912, *Letters II* 317.

considered the book objectionable and unworthy of publication'. Charles recounted the story to his brother Stanislaus:

> Dixon then said it was a pity that Jim did not use his 'undoubted' talent for a better purpose than writing a book like *Dubliners*. 'Why did he not use his talents for the betterment of the country and his people?' Jim replied that he was probably the only Irishman who wrote leading articles for the Italian press and that all his articles in 'Il Piccolo' were about Ireland and about the Irish people. He said also that he was the first to introduce Irish tweeds into Austria although that business was not in the least in his own line.[159]

Joyce agreed on a price for the sheets with Roberts. An elaborate scheme was devised for Joyce to take possession of the first 104 copies of the text. The last act came on 10 September 1912. Roberts told Joyce that the printer refused to hand over the sheets to him. Joyce went back to Dixon, and finally went to see Falconer, Roberts having declined to accompany him. Joyce said he would himself bring the book out in Dublin, London, Trieste, or elsewhere, relieving the printer of any responsibility. As Charles reported to Stanislaus,

> Faulkner [*sic*] said it made no difference where the book was published nor whose name was on it as printer they could not and would not allow it to go out of their hands to anyone. Jim then asked how they would destroy it and he said they would burn the sheets and break up the type. They cared nothing for the loss of the fifty-seven pounds they had learnt a lesson and would not easily be fooled again. There was nothing else to do and this is the end of *Dubliners* so far as Dublin is concerned.[160]

Charles's final letter to Stanislaus enclosed a short note from Joyce, the last sentence of which stated, 'The 1000 copies of Dubliners which are printed are to be destroyed by fire this morning.'[161] On the evening

159. Charles Joyce to Stanislaus Joyce, 5 September 1912, *Letters II* 316.

160. Charles Joyce to Stanislaus Joyce, 11 September 1912, *Letters II* 319.

161. Joyce to Stanislaus Joyce, [11 September 1912], *Letters II* 319. Roberts told Ellmann they were guillotined rather than burnt.

of the day of the destruction of the print run, 11 September 1912, Joyce left Dublin with Nora and the children, bringing with him the page proofs, one set of which he had extracted by a ruse from Roberts and which were used to set the book when published by Grant Richards in 1914.[162] Joyce never returned to Dublin.

'Gas from a Burner'

In the waiting room at the train station at Flushing in Holland, where he was changing trains, Joyce began to write 'Gas from a Burner' on the back of his contract with Maunsel and finished it on the journey from Flushing to Salzburg.[163] It was characterised by Joyce as a 'pasquinade' written after the 'malicious burning' by Falconer of what he tenaciously referred to as 'the 1st edition of Dubliners'.[164] He had it printed in Trieste and distributed in Dublin by his brother Charles.[165] This superb verse invective was in the form of a speech—its first line was, 'Ladies and gents you are here assembled'—delivered by George Roberts, who assumes Falconer's role of printer, and also appears in the third person as 'Maunsel's manager'. It is Roberts's sanctimonious *apologia pro vita sua* which alludes to the writers he had published, including Gregory, Synge, and Padraic Colum. In its final lines Joyce punctures the unctuousness of Roberts:

> Who was it said: Resist not evil?
> I'll burn that book, so help me devil.
> I'll sing a psalm as I watch it burn

162. Joyce to Stanislaus Joyce, postmark 11 September 1912, *Letters II* 320.

163. *PSW* 261; Gorman, *James Joyce*, 217; Slocum and Cahoon, *Bibliography of James Joyce*, 11–12. One might be tempted to see this as a reprise of Stephen writing his Parnell poem 'on the back of one of his father's second moiety notices' (*P* 61). That is to assume that Joyce did actually write the poem on a rent demand, but Stanislaus does not refer to his having done so; S. Joyce, *My Brother's Keeper*, 64–65. It is, on the other hand, perfectly possible that writing 'Gas from a Burner' on the back of the Maunsel contract inspired the description in *A Portrait* of Stephen using the second moiety notice.

164. Slocum and Cahoon, *Bibliography of James Joyce*, 12.

165. Ellmann, *James Joyce*, 335.

And the ashes I'll keep in a one handled urn.
I'll penance do with farts and groans
Kneeling upon my marrowbones.
This very next lent I will unbrace
My penitent buttock to the air
And sobbing beside my printing press
My awful sin I will confess.
My Irish foreman from Bannockburn
Shall dip his right hand in the turn
And sign crisscross with revert thumb
Memento homo upon my bum.[166]

While the content of the poem is itself sufficient to account for the title 'Gas from a Burner', Oliver St John Gogarty was to suggest that the title was a reference to the gas jet in the office of the Hermetic Society, where Joyce, accompanied by Gogarty, had found a suitcase containing ladies' underwear; the office was used also by Roberts, who had been a travelling salesman in ladies' underwear.[167] Gogarty's theory was prompted by the lines,

I printed the great John Milicent Synge
Who soars above on an angel's wing
In the playboy shift that he pinched as swag
From Maunsel's manager's travelling bag.[168]

Gogarty's theory is unpersuasive, but his intuition that the title had a secondary reference that went beyond the 'farts' of the 'burner' Roberts-Falconer should not be discounted. The more obvious source, as already discussed in chapter 6, 'Joyce in University College, Dublin', are the two gas burners that provided the notoriously feeble illumination in the Old Physics Theatre where the Literary and Historical Society debates were held in University College.

166. *PSW* 105.

167. Gogarty, *It Isn't That Time*, 72–74. The episode is recounted with some difference of detail in S. Joyce, *My Brother's Keeper*, 249.

168. *PSW* 104.

Not merely is the poem constituted as a formal speech, but the defining characteristic of the speaker is his obsequiousness towards the respectable audience he is addressing. The tenor of the speech is Protestant revivalist, reflecting Joyce's targeting of Roberts. Joyce's University College contemporaries are not mentioned in the verses, which feature the writers and critics of the Irish Revival. That it should have an admittedly somewhat faint secondary framing as a speech at the Literary and Historical Society is a balancing movement. In this oblique fashion, Kettle's ferociously conservative response to 'An Encounter' is present in 'Gas from a Burner' without being referred to. In a more general sense, 'Gas from a Burner' in this way is a formalisation of Joyce's rupture with his own peer group in University College, and with middle-class Dublin as well as with the Revival. Joyce's treatment by Roberts and the destruction of the print run of Dubliners exemplified Joyce's 'two masters' thesis, derived from the Split:

O Ireland my first and only love
Where Christ and Caesar are hand and glove![169]

It affirmed, and cast a quasi-objective basis for, Joyce's saturnine identification with Parnell, to which he gave biting expression in 'Gas from a Burner'. Ireland was

This lovely land that always sent
Her writers and artists to banishment
And in a spirit of Irish fun
Betrayed her own leaders, one by one.
'Twas Irish humour, wet and dry,
Flung quicklime into Parnell's eye . . . [170]

Joyce had shown himself unwontedly accommodating to Roberts's demand, almost to a fault, and had been repudiated. In a manner characteristic of Joyce's strangely proleptic life experience, his expatriation in 1904 was retrospectively invested with an expulsive force. Joyce's treatment of exile thenceforth had a high Parnellian edge. Herbert Gorman in his 1939 biography wrote of the *Dubliners* debacle that Joyce,

169. *PSW* 103.
170. *PSW* 103.

'defeated and alone, left Ireland about the middle of September and has not set foot in that country since'. What followed was written by Joyce:

> He was invited to Ireland twice by the late William Butler Yeats in connection with the Tailteann Games and then in connection with the foundation of the Irish Academy of Letters. These invitations (the first was personal) and this membership were declined by him. He has not even sought refuge there during the present calamitous events in Europe. Having a vivid memory of the incident at Castlecomer when quicklime was flung into the eyes of their dying leader, Parnell, by a chivalrous Irish mob, he did not wish a similar unfortunate occurrence to interfere with the book he was trying to write.[171]

Joyce thus, almost two decades later, re-etched 'Gas from a Burner' into his own biography.

Exile Affirmed

The experience of Dublin prompted Joyce to make a choice. His return to Trieste in September 1912—or rather the decisions he made following on his return—had a quality of contingent finality that his initial departure from Dublin eight years previously lacked. Perhaps the destruction of the Irish edition of *Dubliners* acted as a spur to his resolve. He realised he could not live on the basis of an equal possibility of exile or return. It was not a decision that he would never return to live permanently in Ireland, but he had to proceed on the premise that he would not. The extending of his exile itself diminished in some degree the prospect of his returning, but he had not resolved to stay away from Ireland. It was a calibrated strategy, in which the longer he was away from Ireland, the less likely he was to compromise the *acquis* of exile by returning. As exile became part of his authorial mythos, the idea of his returning to Ireland became virtually abstract.

It is true that Joyce had no immediate prospects in Ireland and now had a family outside Ireland, but it is important not to detract from the significance of Joyce's 'second' Triestine exile. Joyce's concept of exile is

171. Gorman, *James Joyce*, 216–17; Ellmann, *James Joyce*, 338, 775n68.

political and strategised. It was a revolutionary gesture, firm in its purpose of revolt against contemporary Ireland and embrace of Europe. It is arguable that the clarity of conception of Joyce as an exile from 1912 was at once imaginatively necessary and important for the reception of his work which was impressed with the authorial image of youthful revolt. The destruction of the Dublin edition of *Dubliners* was superseded by Joyce's definitive embrace of the role of an exiled Irish author writing for an international readership, a role that was already implicit in the writing of *A Portrait*, on which he had embarked from the end of 1907.

The irate Joyce who arrived back from Dublin on 15 September 1912 was thirty years old, and a semi-established figure in Trieste. His reputation was as a teacher and journalist; few knew him as a writer of fiction. *Il Piccolo della Sera* characterised him in 1912 as 'a thinker, man of culture, and freelance writer'.[172] 'Better', as Silvio Benco reasoned later, 'to be the conscientious and successful teacher who accepted exile'.[173] At the invitation of the Minerva Society, on the Via Carducci (the premises of the Università Popolare), he gave twelve lectures on *Hamlet*, in English, between 11 November 1912 and 10 February 1913: 'I expound Shakespeare to docile Trieste.'[174] All that survives of these is the commentary of *Il Piccolo della Sera* at the conclusion of the series, possibly by Roberto Prezioso, which noted that 'his original and slightly bizarre talent changed the nature of his commentary, which might otherwise have been dry, into attractive *causeries*'. The hall was crowded for all the lectures, notwithstanding that 'the English colony appeared to be thinly or not at all represented'.[175] That comment was a reminder of how immersive in Triestine life Joyce's exile was, and how little the members of *la colonia inglese* featured in it.

On 28 June 1913 Joyce was appointed to the chair of 'English Language and Correspondence' at the prestigious Scuola Superiore di

172. Peter Hartshorn, *James Joyce and Trieste* (Westport, CT: Greenwood, 1997), 58.

173. Silvio Benco, 'James Joyce in Trieste' (1930), reprinted in translation in Potts, *Portraits of the Artist*, 52.

174. *GJ* 10.

175. Ellmann, *James Joyce*, 345, 775–76; Crivelli, *James Joyce*, 136, 218–20; McCourt, *Years of Bloom*, 191–92.

Commercio 'Revoltella' and was subsequently cleared by the Austrian authorities after he had taken up the position on 26 September 1913 when he became a member of the Academic Council. Trieste did not have a university—a matter of imperial policy—and the 'Revoltella' was looked on as a prospective nucleus for an Italian, or even Slavic, university.[176] The teaching programme that Joyce prepared had as the subject of the second term of the second year 'conversation, business letters, dictated letters, the Army and Navy, the British Empire, London, business calculations'.[177]

After another of the crises with Joyce's landlords, which he had to manage since it occurred during Joyce's third return trip to Ireland, Stanislaus had arranged for Joyce to take an apartment at Via Donato Bramante 4, a building of recent construction below the castle and the Basilica di San Giusto.[178] It stood alongside a run of steps (now, as if inevitably, the Scala James Joyce) up to a little mediaevalesque turreted castle built the previous century by the admired architect Eugenio Geiringer.[179] The Joyce family took up residence there in mid-September 1912. Giorgio and Lucia went to school nearby. Dario de Tuoni remembered them speaking 'both English and the harshest version of Triestine: the dialect of San Giacomo, which was rougher than that of the old city'.[180]

De Tuoni, who saw a good deal of Joyce from late 1913 until the end of December 1914, when on leave from enlistment in the Austrian army he was planning to desert, was acutely conscious of the struggle that Joyce's life in Trieste had been, and in some degree continued to be, even if 'in the period when I knew them things did not appear to have been

176. Crivelli, *Rose for Joyce*, 179.

177. Crivelli, *Rose for Joyce*, 142–64; McCourt, *Years of Bloom*, 207.

178. Crivelli, *James Joyce*, 132.

179. De Tuoni, *Ricordo di Joyce*, 106.

180. De Tuoni, *Ricordo di Joyce*, 107. Francini Bruni, who visited Joyce at home in Paris, noted that Joyce would initiate discourses in Italian as he did not want his children to forget the language. In a house where many languages were spoken, the only words that were not permitted to be translated were the names of his children. 'He used to say that the language of family affection could only be Italian' (*Ricordo di Joyce*, 45). Benco observed, 'It's a strange thing, that luxurious Parisian apartment full of the speech of Trieste's slums' ('James Joyce in Trieste', 49).

going too badly'. That struggle he noted was conveyed in *Finnegans Wake*. On their walks, the poet whom Joyce quoted most was Paul Verlaine, including the poem 'O triste, triste était mon âme'. This resurfaced in the *Wake* as his great sigh of Trieste. 'And trieste, ah trieste ate I my liver!' That led into Joyce's melancholy riff on the days of the week excluding the Christian Sabbath: 'All moanday, tearsday, wailsday, thumpsday, frightday, shatterday till the fear of the Law'. The Triestine setting is affirmed (in what was a reworking of Ezekiel): 'How diesmal he was lying low on his rawside laying siege to goblin castle.'[181] De Tuoni thought that referred to the old castle of San Giusto up the hill, but the 'goblin castle' is surely Geiringer's folly which Joyce had earlier described. Loyal to his city, de Tuoni observed that this 'moment of bad humour' reflected the conflict between Joyce's ambitions as a writer and the need to provide for his family by giving English lessons: 'In those ten years, therefore, he would have eaten his liver no matter where he was, and not only in Trieste.'[182]

The war was to change everything. Joyce and his family returned briefly from Zurich to a Trieste that had become part of Italy in October 1919, before departing for Paris in July 1920. In assessing Joyce's principal period in Trieste, the decade from March 1905 to June 1915, it is necessary to exercise some wariness in relation to retrospective comments made by or credibly attributed to Joyce. Joyce certainly did not start out as an admirer of the Austro-Hungarian Empire. He wrote from Pola to his aunt Josephine Murray on the New Year's Eve of 1904, 'I am trying to move on to Italy as soon as possible'—meaning he did not wish to stop at Trieste on his way out—'as I hate this Catholic country with its hundred races and thousand languages, governed by a parliament which can transact no business and sits for a week at the most and by the most physically corrupt royal house in Europe.'[183] There is something faintly suspect in the alleged remark to a friend made many years post-Trieste that Herbert Gorman attributes to Joyce: 'I cannot begin to give you the flavour of the old Austrian Empire. It was a ramshackle affair

181. *FW* 301.16–27.

182. De Tuoni, *Ricordo di Joyce*, 109, 128–29.

183. Joyce to Josephine Murray, New Year's Eve 1904, *Letters I* 57.

but it was charming, gay, and I experienced more kindnesses in Trieste than ever before or since in my life. . . . Times past cannot return but I wish they were back'.[184] The sentimentality (reserved by Joyce, when not entirely sober, for his own country) applied to an empire—any empire—is not in character, and 'gay' sounds a false and hackneyed note. The more tartly elliptical observation recalled by Mary Colum, the most likely source of the earlier comment that Gorman attributes to Joyce,[185] is a lot more convincing: 'They called the Austrian Empire a ramshackle empire. . . . I wish to God there were more such empires.'[186] What is intriguing in relation to the comment to Mary Colum is that, reflecting the impact of the First World War and its aftermath, Joyce had begun—analytically and not sentimentally—to conceive his Triestine exile in the setting of the Austro-Hungarian Empire and its dissolution. The shift in Joyce's perspective was brought about primarily by the war and its outfall, but it was also informed by Joyce's intimation of the precariousness of European Jewry in a post-war continent mapped out on a principle of ethnic territoriality. The idea that Joyce succumbed to a nostalgic hankering for 'old Auster and Hungrig'[187] is unsustainable. Though only one reference to Giuseppe Mazzini has been identified in any of Joyce's writings[188]—the brilliantly sardonic 'conclamazzione' in *Finnegans Wake*[189]—Joyce was and did not cease to be a Mazzinian nationalist, an internationalist, Europe-federating nationalist.[190] Joyce as

184. Gorman, *James Joyce*, 143.

185. Gorman's acknowledgements include Mary and Padraic Colum.

186. Mary Colum, *Life and the Dream* (New York: Doubleday, 1947), 383.

187. *FW* 464.27–28.

188. Adaline Glasheen, *Third Census of 'Finnegans Wake': An Index of the Characters and Their Roles* (Berkeley: University of California Press, 1977), 190.

189. *FW* 173.15.

190. Mazzini did not actually favour Irish independence: he 'believed, as did Garibaldi and Cavour, that the Irish should not aim to become a separate nation state. Britain was greatly at fault in her treatment of Ireland, but he suspected reactionary motives in some Irish patriots who wanted to end the union, and when Fenians asked for his support he gave a discouraging answer. He believed unconvincingly that nations could sometimes be identified by their possession of a distinctive "mission" for the progress of humanity, and failed to find such a mission in Ireland, Denmark or Portugal'. Denis Mack Smith, *Mazzini* (New Haven, CT: Yale University Press, 1994), 156–57.

a Mazzinian was a realist rather than fervently apostolic as Mazzini had been. What Mazzini could not begin to address was the position of minorities within European nation-states. The honourable old-school Triestine Mazzinians, who made up the left wing of the National Liberals, were irredentist, but their nationalism was based on 'the old Mazzinian dream of a federation among European peoples, free, democratic, and republican'.[191]

Joyce was unsentimental about Trieste. The lines from his letter to Nora of 7 September 1909, two days before he left Dublin at the end of his first trip, during which Vincent Cosgrave had asserted that he had had a romantic involvement with Nora, are much quoted: '*La nostra bella Trieste!* I have often said that angrily but tonight I feel it true. I long to see the lights twinkling along the *riva* as the train passes Miramar. After all, Nora, it is in the city which has sheltered us. I came back to it jaded and moneyless after my folly in Rome and now again after this absence.'[192]

Aside from the frantically cloying prose, if his relationship to Trieste was based on a sense of gratitude, it was not in the case of Joyce the most secure foundation. Joyce's composite pun in referring in *Finnegans Wake* to Trieste as 'tarry easty, his città immediata'[193] is ingeniously calibrated. The rendering of Trieste as exotically a land of the East is less geographical than to do with the ethnic diversity of the population of the city and its hinterland. 'Tarry', as if to reinforce both the idea of colonial indolence and occidental conceptions of Eastern indolence, renders the frustration of Joyce's ambitions while he was in Trieste, while the idea of leavening ('easty' invoking yeast as well as the East)[194] conveys Joyce's sense that his writing was self-generated rather than engendered by any conventional sense of place.

What Joyce took from Trieste was not its *italianità* but its *triestinità,* its distinctive diversity and political geography, conveyed not as political grand theory but principally through the dialect of *triestino,* a flamboyant

191. Rusinow, *Italy's Austrian Heritage,* 87–88.

192. Joyce to Nora Barnacle, 7 September 1909, *Letters II* 249.

193. *FW* 228.22–23.

194. Brian Carraher, 'Semicolonial Cities and Triestine Joyce: The Cultural Politics of Reading Joyce's Homeplaces', *James Joyce Quarterly* 38, nos. 3 and 4 (Spring and Summer 2001): 509.

rendering into language of the ethnic and cultural heterogeneity of the city that for Joyce had the merit that it was the common invention of its inhabitants rather than an imposition of ideology or state. Language was successful in achieving what formal politics had failed to do. Onto a basic template of Italian was grafted a vocabulary drawn from Italian dialects, Slovenian, Croatian, Hungarian, German, Greek, Turkish, and Armenian, a list that is not exhaustive. Its variations were boundless. The infinite suppleness of the language matched Joyce's conception of cultural impurity and plasticity. Rosa Maria Bosinelli has established that Joyce's *triestino* was better than his unimpeachable Italian.[195] *Triestino,* and the non-Italian languages that contribute to its richly impure demotic, runs through *Ulysses,* and more particularly *Finnegans Wake,* where it is present both as vocabulary—to take one example noted by John McCourt, the Slovene word for God, *bog,* appears in *Finnegans Wake* as 'by the wrath of Bog'—and as an active source of polyglottal word compounding and creation ('Shem skrivenitch').[196]

Though what he wrote pertained to Ireland, it was in pushing out into the Mediterranean from the built-up port of Trieste that Joyce embarked on his own odyssey, his sustained meditation on European ethnicities, nation-states, national cultures, and nationalisms. Stanislaus was quite wrong in venturing, 'The cosmopolitan atmosphere of the Trieste of the early twentieth century did not inspire him at all. . . . No, Trieste did not give Jim anything.'[197] As a political construct, Trieste came, against Joyce's own expectations, to sustain the weight of his high rhetoric of exile.

195. McCourt, *Years of Bloom,* 53.

196. *FW* 76.31. See McCourt, *Years of Bloom,* 208.

197. Quoted in Stelio Crise, *Epiphanies & Phadographs: Joyce e Trieste* (Milan: All'insegna del pesce d'oro, 1994), 20, 22, cited in McCourt, *Years of Bloom,* 3. See also H. Leeming, 'James Joyce's Slavonic Optophones', *Slavonic and East European Review* 55, no. 3 (July 1977): 289–309.

17

'The Society of Jewses': Gestating Bloom

An old caftaned Jewish refugee, sitting in a train compartment, shows his ticket to the inspector. The inspector, suspicious, thinking that perhaps he is hiding a child in his caftan to save the price of a ticket, asks the Jew what he has in there. The Jew produces a framed portrait of Emperor Franz Joseph.

—A TALE JOSEPH ROTH LIKED TO TELL[1]

THERE IS IN THE 'Proteus' episode of *Ulysses* an account of Stephen Dedalus having lunch with Kevin Egan (the semi-accidental but sentimental Fenian Joseph Casey, friend of Joyce's father, whom Joyce had met in Paris). Postprandially, as the absinthe takes effect, Kevin Egan rolls 'gunpowder cigarettes' and reminisces. He talks 'of Ireland, the Dalcassians, of hopes, conspiracies, of Ireland now'. His conversation runs on: 'M. Drumont, famous journalist, Drumont, know what he called

1. From David Bronsen's biography of Roth, as rendered by Michael Hofmann in Roth, *Wandering Jews*, xix.

FW 423.36. Joyce liked the play on Jews and the Society of Jesus sufficiently to end a 1935 letter to his son Giorgio and Jewish daughter-in-law, 'My cordial salutations to you both not forgetting the Society of Jewses (quip borrowed from W.i.P)', meaning his *Work in Progress*. Joyce to Giorgio and Helen Joyce, 19 March 1935, *Letters III* 350.

Queen Victoria? Old hag, with the yellow teeth. *Vieille ogresse* with the *dents jaunes*. Maud Gonne, beautiful woman, *la Patrie*, M. Millevoye. Felix Faure, know how he died?'[2]

The old Fenian in whom Stephen had hoped to find some revolutionary glamour, if not inspiration, turns out to have unreflectively absorbed the conventional wisdom of the French anti-Semitic ultra-right, remote from the affiliation to the French Revolution which Fenians professed. This is beautifully layered. It is the conversation of Kevin Egan that is rendered. It is he who explains to Stephen that Edouard Drumont is a 'famous journalist', which, while not untrue, hardly characterises the notorious and virulently anti-Semitic French publicist; Egan cites Drumont in his Anglophobe rather than anti-Semitic aspect. But Stephen does not know enough about French politics or the anti-Jewish convulsions of French life to know who Drumont is. Joyce in Paris in 1902–3 knew very well who Drumont was, but he is conveying that Stephen (and perhaps Joyce himself) was not particularly responsive to manifestations of anti-Jewish prejudice at the time.[3] The episode poses the issue of the sources of Joyce's personal interest in the Jews, subsequently fortified by his reading.

Ettore Schmitz professed the hope that Joyce would write of Trieste. He did not do so, other than in the slight but significant *Giacomo Joyce* that remained unpublished in his lifetime. But Joyce did translate aspects of his experience of Trieste into *Ulysses*. Having chosen exile and having passed a decade of that exile in Trieste, Joyce had the challenge of making sense of, and rendering at least obliquely, his 'second country'.[4] Trieste was multi-ethnic and liminal: on the Dalmatian coast, with a predominantly Italian culture, on the edge of the Balkans, with a vast Slavic hinterland that

2. *U* 3.230–35. *La Patrie* was a paper edited by Lucien Millevoye, Maud Gonne's far-right lover. Reizbaum refers to this passage to assert that the text suggests an equation of Edouard Drumont and Arthur Griffith which cannot be sustained. Marilyn Reizbaum, *James Joyce's Judaic Other* (Stanford, CA: Stanford University Press, 1999), 41.

3. My reading corresponds with that of Neil R. Davison, *James Joyce, 'Ulysses', and the Construction of Jewish Identity* (Cambridge: Cambridge University Press, 1986), 93–94.

4. McCourt, *Years of Bloom*, 282n196, citing Ellmann's 1954 interview with Alessandro Francini Bruni, who ascribed the phrase to Joyce.

stretched to the Black Sea. The possible approaches were infinite, but it was through the Jews of the city that he strategised Trieste, and his own experience of early exile.

The purpose of a novel about Dublin with a Jewish central character was long nurtured by Joyce. If Jewishness was not quite a universal, there were Jews in every country in Europe. The subject of the Jews in Europe embraced polarities, whether real or supposed: East and West, Old Testament and New Testament, the ancient and the modern, the Semitic and the classical. Having declined to acknowledge crude affinities between the Irish and the Italian irredentists, Joyce was creative and resourceful in exploring more subtle affinities between the Irish and the Jews. But he was not privileging the narratives of two races or national cultures: they were co-emblematic of European history. The choice of Ireland was foreordained: Ireland was the country of Joyce's birth and early life, the culture with which he was most intimately familiar and which had shaped his early understanding of politics, and the country in which all his fictional writing was set. The Jews were dispersed across Europe. Theirs was an ancient history and culture, more closely interwoven with European history and more centrally constitutive of the idea of Europe. In *Ulysses* the Jewishness of Bloom bore the principal weight of the connection of Ireland to Europe.

From the hatred unleashed on Émile Zola, Joyce knew there was an idea, assiduously promoted in right-wing reactionary polemic, of the Jews as cynical promoters of a corrosive modernism. This was part of a rich stock of anti-Semitic narratives and images which were to become important for Joyce, but were not what initially drew him to Jewish themes.

Crucially, the Irish and the Jews stood outside the paradigm of established European statehood. Their common statelessness, for radically disparate reasons, provided a strategic perspective on a European state system shaped by the Congress of Vienna which more or less perdured until the First World War. Bloom embodied two stateless tribes, one an island people, the other dispersed. Their peripherality or marginality to the schema of constituted statehood and empire is as much a matter of providing an enabling perspective as it is of the prejudice and oppression to which the two races were (unequally) subject.

There were centuries of struggle and oppression remembered in both cultures with mournful pride. Both were minorities in imperial settings (though the Jews were minorities in every European country) with contested issues about assimilation and language. There was some correlation between Irish nationalism and Zionism (Joyce was borderline sceptical on the subject of Zionism, though understanding of its inspiration). Joyce was drawn to the richness and fluidity of associations between the Irish and the Jews, a great lurch forward from his doomed attempt to establish tortuous equivalences between the Irish working class and peasantry and the Italian proletariat in his revolutionary syndicalist phase at the start of his exile.

To all of this has to be added Joyce's sympathetic curiosity about the Jews, developing into a sense of affinity, and a prescient sense of unease at the pervasiveness of anti-Semitism elsewhere in the Austro-Hungarian Empire, and in Europe and Russia generally, beyond what seemed the comparatively tranquil enclave of pre-war Trieste. His identification with the Jews was affirmed in exile, especially post-1912, by the 'Hebraic theme of non-return' that runs through *Ulysses*[5] and by the idea of the Jews as People of the Book, leading to Ira Nadel's proposition that 'the essential Judaism of Joyce is textual'.[6]

Joyce knew what he could make in his novel of the progress of an Irish Jewish protagonist across a day through the semi-resistant medium of the Irish capital. He knew also that the foregrounding of a Dublin Jew would irritate most conservative Catholic Irish nationalists, those who were in sympathy with Healy's attacks on Parnell as an Irish Protestant, as well as xenophobic cultural nationalists. That might be thought within its limits as a perfectly judged—and rare—political deployment of literary modernism. But the annoyance the novel might provoke in those whom Joyce most despised politically in Ireland was a secondary consideration. His ambitions for his work were vaster in scope. He had read

5. Nadel, *Joyce and the Jews*, 3. Less convincing is Nadel's characterisation of Joyce's departure from and living outside Ireland as exodus rather than exile, arguing that 'exodus brings emancipation' (3, 18–19). 'Exile' better captures the solitariness, with Nora Barnacle, of his leaving of Ireland; and Joyce's edge of protestatory rancour.

6. Nadel, *Joyce and the Jews*, 6.

a great deal of contemporary writing as well as newspaper coverage on the subject of the Jews. He was writing not merely against overt anti-Semitism; he was also pitting his art against the dogmatic characterisation and objectification of Jews in contemporary 'informed' discourse, most typically in portentous meditations on the 'Jewish question', mainly in relation to Austro-Hungary and eastern Europe, in avowedly non-partisan or even philosemitic writing as well as in anti-Semitic texts. In this Joyce's placid Bloom of Dublin was conceived as a radically revisionist figure on a European scale.

The political course which led Joyce to write a novel which he characterised to Carlo Linati as 'l'epopea di due razze (Israele-Irlanda)' (an epic of two races [Israelite-Irish])[7] is highly intricate, not least because it intersects with almost every other sphere of Joyce's art, life, and thought. If the fictional Leopold Bloom is born in Dublin, he is a creation of Joyce's arc of exile.

Irish Jews in Joyce's Era

Joyce, like most of his Catholic Dublin contemporaries, knew very little about the Jews of Dublin before he left Ireland in 1904. In late 1903 Joyce had conceived an idea for a continental-style evening newspaper and asked Padraic Colum if he knew any Jewish people who might support and finance the project. Colum later commented, 'It is odd that the creator of the most outstanding Jew in modern literature did not at that time know any of the Jewish community in Dublin.'[8] Joyce in 1903 had a distant sense of Jews as part of the economic life of the city, and was aware of a degree of sullen prejudice against Jews, but he had not at that point come to think politically of the position of Jews, in Ireland or continental Europe.

The Irish Jewish community, concentrated in Dublin, was not large. Towards the end of the eighteenth century, the tiny community more or less broke up, some members returning to England, some making

7. Joyce to Carlo Linati, 21 September 1920 (in Italian), *Letters I* 146.

8. M. Colum and P. Colum, *Our Friend James Joyce*, 58. Colum introduced Joyce to what seem to have been his only two Jewish friends in Dublin—'intellectuals'—William Sinclair (Samuel Beckett's uncle by marriage) and his twin, Harry Sinclair.

their way back to the Continent, and a handful remaining. The synagogue in Marlborough Green, near where the Custom House stands, was shut. There was a modest recovery, but the Jewish population of Dublin in 1820–80 was fewer than 350 people.[9] What was transformative for the community in Dublin and in the provinces, though still on a very small scale, was the immigration of Jews from the Lithuanian provinces that were then part of Russia in the wake of pogroms that followed the assassination of Tsar Alexander II in 1881 and the promulgation of the May Laws in Russia in 1882; though, as Cormac Ó Gráda has convincingly suggested, 'Ireland's Litvaks should perhaps be seen less as victims of persecution than as individuals and families—many of them poverty stricken—bent on "bettering themselves".'[10] The Jewish population of Ireland rose from 472 in the 1881 census to 3,769 in 1901.[11] The new arrivals greatly outnumbered the older Irish community or 'English' community (English by virtue of linguistic proficiency) who had from 1836 worshipped in St Mary's Abbey Synagogue off Capel Street. The Dublin Jewish writer Edward Raphael Lipsett described in a 1906 article in the *Jewish Chronicle* the 'most singular feature' of Dublin Jewry: 'The entire Hebrew community of Dublin, excluding the few—very few—"Englische Yiudden" are as one family, coming from the same stock, and knowing each other from home down to many generations past. With a few isolated exceptions they all hail from the Government of Kovno, and some time ago it used to be said that the town of Okmyan[12] had emptied itself out into the arteries of the South Circular Road, Dublin.'[13] The recently arrived 'foreign' Jews lived in the compact area of the streets that radiated from the South Circular Road, on the south side of the city just north of the Grand Canal, sometimes designated Little

9. Louis Hyman, *The Jews of Ireland from Earliest Times to the Year 1910* (Shannon: Irish University Press, 1972), 89, 155.

10. Cormac Ó Gráda, *Jewish Ireland in the Age of Joyce: A Socioeconomic History* (Princeton, NJ: Princeton University Press, 2006), 14, 21.

11. Hyman, *Jews of Ireland*, 160.

12. Okmyan refers to the shtetl of Akmyan (Akmene in Lithuanian), near the border with Latvia to the north. Ó Gráda, *Jewish Ireland*, 23–24.

13. Halitvack [pseud.], 'The Dublin Hebrew Community: Historical Sketch and Character Study', *Jewish Chronicle*, 8 June 1906.

Jerusalem.[14] (Leopold Bloom is born in May 1866 at 52 Upper Clanbrassil Street, which is just outside Little Jerusalem proper, and where few Jews resided or ran businesses, unlike Lower Clanbrassil Street, 'the epicenter of Jewish Dublin for well over half a century.')[15]

The resistance to the influx of poor eastern European Jews by the established Jewish community in Dublin found expression in the 1881 resolution of the governing body of St Mary's Abbey to 'refuse to admit into Free Membership any person directly or indirectly engaged in the business of lending small sums on Bills of Sale to persons in the humbler ranks of society'.[16] A split came in 1883 when the newer members of the community broke away from St Mary's Abbey to establish a number of *hebroths*, or conventicles, of their own: St Kevin's Parade, Oakfield Place, Lennox Street, Heytesbury Street, Camden Street, and Lombard Street. With the sharp diminution of worshippers at the St Mary's Abbey Synagogue, its governing council set about obtaining a site for a synagogue where all the Jews of Dublin might worship. A circular dated 25 March 1890 'to our English co-religionists' stated that 'after much trouble (there having been exhibited by the owners, considerable unwillingness to sell or let for the purpose) a plot of ground was secured in a respectable, quiet, well circumstanced neighbourhood, near the streets in which most of the foreign Jews reside.'[17] On 3 December 1892, the Very Reverend Dr Hermann Adler, the Chief Rabbi of the British Empire, officiated at the last Sabbath service at St Mary's Abbey. The following afternoon Adler presided at the opening of the new synagogue, newly built in a vaguely Eastern Romanesque style on Adelaide Road, backing onto the Grand Canal. Adler declared, 'You have come here, my foreign brethren, on from a country like unto Egypt of old to a land which offers you hospitable shelter. It is said that Ireland is the only country in the world which cannot be charged with persecuting the Jews.'[18]

14. Ó Gráda, *Jewish Ireland*, 99–108.

15. Ó Gráda, *Jewish Ireland*, 206–7. Thus A. J. Leventhal was born in 1896 in Lower Clanbrassil Street, the son of Moses (Maurice), draper, and Rosa Leventhal: Frances Clarke, 'Abraham Jacob ("Con") Leventhal', *DIB* 5:474–75.

16. Ó Gráda, *Jewish Ireland*, 48.

17. Bernard Shillman, *A Short History of the Jews of Ireland* (Dublin: Cahill, 1941), 96–97.

18. Hyman, *Jews of Ireland*, 195–96; Shillman, *Short History*, 99–101.

In *Ulysses* Joyce was to show a sense of the shift of the centre of gravity of Dublin Jewry from the north to the south of the river Liffey, a topographical revolution that preoccupied the Jews of Dublin in the late nineteenth century.[19] The short scene in the 'Wandering Rocks' episode set in St Mary's Abbey encompasses what is for Joyce an unusually elaborate excursus in which its history is touched on at several points. A Benedictine monastery founded in 1139 that came almost immediately to adhere to the Cistercian branch of the Benedictines, St Mary's Abbey came to have a pivotal role in the medieval city. It was, for a time, where the Irish Privy Council met, and its lands stretched across what is the northern modern city into Meath. In the annals of Irish rebellion, it had enduring fame as the site of a meeting of the Irish Privy Council on 11 June 1534, at which 'Silken Thomas' FitzGerald surrendered the sword of state in defiance of Henry VIII, the first act in the failed rebellion that led to his execution at Tyburn three years later. After the dissolution of the Irish monasteries that began in the year of the execution of Silken Thomas, substantial elements of the external fabric survived into the late seventeenth century. The abbey was only restored to public attention through the enthusiastic amateur archaeological excavation of the chapter house in the mid-1880s,[20] by which time the abbey had served as the principal Jewish synagogue of Dublin for a half century. When it ceased in 1892 to serve as a synagogue, what remained of the chapter house became part of the premises of Alexander & Company, seed merchants.[21]

Within the general scheme of the novel, the St Mary's Abbey interlude in the 'Wandering Rocks' episode of *Ulysses* stands somewhat apart. Typically, historical topography in Joyce is fleeting. Here there is a certain pause, as Joyce dwells neither on the point of origin of the Viking city nor in the pre-union swagger of the Irish Parliament on College

19. Shillman, *Short History*, 93. Shillman writes of 'this change of the Jewish ghetto from the north to the south of the River Liffey'. The decline, in turn, of the Jewish community in the once vibrantly Jewish Little Jerusalem area as many of its members moved to the Rathgar-Rathmines area and Terenure (where a synagogue was opened in 1952) is symbolised in the deconsecration of Adelaide Road in 1999. Ó Gráda, *Jewish Ireland*, 207–8.

20. My account draws heavily on that of Christine Casey in her excellent *Buildings of Ireland*, 86–89.

21. Gifford, *Ulysses Annotated*, 168. Ned Lambert taps with his lath 'the piled seedbags' on the floor (*U* 10.424).

Green, but on its medieval node, which he situates in what the modern architectural historian Christine Casey describes as a 'fragmentary ruin' that remains 'the most evocative medieval building in the city of Dublin'.[22]

In the scene in 'Wandering Rocks', 'two pink faces turned in the flare of the tiny torch', specifically a match. Ned Lambert, who has an undefined curatorial role in a historical edifice that now serves as a storehouse of seeds, is showing around the chapter house the Reverend Hugh C. Love, of Rathcoffey in Kildare, a young clergyman of 'refined accent' and antiquarian interests who is writing a book about the FitzGeralds. It is he who holds the match that is extinguished in 'the mouldy air' of the half-submerged chapter house. Seeking Lambert, J. J. (Jack) Molloy enters the dark space that is as unfamiliar to him as to most of the city's inhabitants. Ned Lambert is in the course of invoking the Silken Thomas episode to explain that 'this is the most historic spot in all Dublin'. O'Madden Burke is 'going to write something about it one of these days. The old bank of Ireland was over the way till the time of the union and the original jews' temple was here before they built their synagogue over in Adelaide road'. The mise-en-scène was sufficiently steeped historically in rebellion for J. J. O'Molloy to venture, 'I thought you were at a new gunpowder plot'. Spatially the comparison relates to subterranean vaults. Temporally the gunpowder plot—that came to be identified with Guy Fawkes but was also designated as 'the Jesuit treason'—to blow up the House of Lords at the opening of Parliament and to assassinate James I and replace him with a Catholic monarch took place in 1605, well over half a century after the revolt of Silken Thomas. J. J. O'Molloy's jocose comparison is presaged by the striking of a match by the mild Reverend Love, as if to suggest that his innocently antiquarian interest in the FitzGeralds could lead him from the subterranean pit of the chapter house unwittingly in the direction of a betrayal of the political allegiances considered consonant with his Protestant faith.[23]

In the 'Ithaca' episode, Bloom is identified as one who had worshipped in St Mary's Abbey: in the enumeration of what Bloom and

22. Casey, *Buildings of Ireland*, 86.

23. *U* 10.380–429.

Stephen have in common is included 'the isolation of their synagogical and ecclesiastical rites in ghetto (S. Mary's Abbey) and masshouse (Adam and Eve's tavern)'.[24] That intricate reference includes an evocation of religious persecution: signboards for the tavern Adam and Eve's had supposedly in the time of the Tudors signalled the whereabouts of, and provided an alibi for, entering the Franciscan church that stood in Rosemary Lane beside where the church of St Francis of Assisi on Merchant's Quay now stands.[25]

In the era when St Mary's Abbey flourished, from the twelfth to the sixteenth century, the Jewish population was tiny; an established Jewish community only came into being around 1660, quickening in the aftermath of the Battle of the Boyne in 1690.[26] The deft designation of St Mary's Abbey as 'the original jews' temple'—'original' relative to Adelaide Road—cast a superficial pall of biblical *ancienneté* over what had been the principal synagogue of Dublin only for the late period of 1836–92. What remains central for Joyce's purpose is the image of the exiguous Dublin Jewish community worshipping in the half-submerged vaulted chapter house of a medieval monastery at the heart of the city north of the Liffey until just over a decade before 1904, the date when the novel is set.[27]

This seemingly minor episode is a perfect microcosm of Joyce's historical reconceptualising of the conventional topography of Dublin. The treatment of the chapter house of St Mary's Abbey as 'the original Jews' temple', in a scene in which Leopold Bloom plays no part, discloses Joyce's political strategising of the role of Irish Jews in the novel. The Jews are a complicating element, their history interwoven into that of Ireland, fracturing the conventional binary narrative in which native

24. *U* 17.756–58.

25. Weldon Thornton, *Allusions in Ulysses: An Annotated List* (Chapel Hill: University of North Carolina Press, 1968), 468–69.

26. Shillman, *Short History*, 13; Hyman, *Jews of Ireland*, 19.

27. The oldest, most evocative and continuous Jewish site in Dublin was actually the cemetery at Ballybough (*Baile bocht* in Irish, 'the town of the poor') to the north-east of the city; Shillman, *Short History*, 18–37. The cemetery lay outside the ambulatory circuit of the novel and was less congenial to Joyce's fictional purpose. That it is on or close to the site of the Battle of Clontarf, Nadel suggests, may inform references to Clontarf in the *Wake*; Nadel, *Joyce and the Jews*, 188.

Irish Catholics and conquering English Protestants are pitted against each other. He is also reminding the city of its own pluralism, of the diversity that made it, which is denied in assigning to its Jewish population a fixed and static marginality.

The closest non-fictional correlative to Joyce's rendering of the position of Jews in Ireland in *Ulysses* in the late nineteenth and early twentieth centuries is a single article by 'Halitvack' in the London *Jewish Chronicle* of 21 December 1906 entitled 'Jews in Ireland'. Edward Raphael Lipsett (1869–1921) was a Dublin Jew, writer, and journalist.[28] His assessment was bleakly lucid: 'There is undoubtedly a mutual estrangement between the Jews and the Irish. The Jews understand the Irish little; the Irish understand the Jews less. Each seems a peculiar race in the eyes of the other; and in a word the position of Jews in Ireland is peculiarly peculiar'.[29] He observed that 'religious intolerance, so far as Jews are concerned, is practically non-existent', adding that 'all the warfare of creed is carried on between the two native sections', meaning Catholic and Protestant. He immediately said that the 'sorrows and difficulties' besetting the Irish Jews were real and many, even if 'there is no official open hostility shown against Jews':

> We are seldom told directly what is wrong, where the wrong lies, or, indeed, whether there is any wrong; only we ourselves are made to feel that all is not right with us. The feeling is ever present with us that we are not wanted. There is an invisible but impassable barrier between Jew and Christian—a barrier which one party will not, and the other cannot, break through. You cannot get one native to remember

28. A native of Lithuania and the son of a rabbi, Lipsett, originally Lipschitz, immigrated to Ireland and, in a remarkable transition, within a single generation became a writer of lucid grace. He married out, but it is unclear why Hyman says he is said to have converted to proselytising Christianity before leaving for New York in 1908, which is not mentioned in the notice of his death in the *Jewish Chronicle* of 25 November 1921; Hyman, *Jews of Ireland*, 333n98. Leventhal referred to the *Jewish Chronicle* in which he read Theodor Herzl's speeches as 'a London weekly publication that arrived in time for the candles of the Sabbath eve'. A. J. Leventhal, 'What It Means to Be a Jew', *Bell* 10, no. 3 (June 1945): 211.

29. Halitvack's article was discussed and first cited in Hyman, *Jews of Ireland*, 176, 333–34; see also Nadel, *Joyce and the Jews*, 196.

> that a Jew may be an Irishman. The term 'Irish Jew' seems to have a contradictory ring upon the native ear; the very idea is wholly inconceivable to the native mind.

We have, he wrote, 'neither Irish Jews nor Jewish Irishmen. . . . Irish Jews feel that if they spoke of themselves as Jewish Irishmen, it would be met with a cutting cynicism from the natives that the two elements can ever merge into one, for any single purpose. Day by day, often many times a day, I can see this idea driven into the Jew's head with a sledgehammer by the natives.' He touched on an important class difference within the Christian population: 'The bulk of the lower orders do not know what the name "Jew" stands for; the better classes may not be so ignorant, but they do not want to know the man bearing that name.'

While the Jews of Dublin had contributed substantially to the prosperity of the city, 'the cry is that Jews are battening upon the poverty of the natives'. At this point the frustration that Lipsett diurnally experienced broke through:

> The cry may not be always directly uttered in so many words; but Jews feel it is there, everywhere, always. The air is full of it; and Jews are made to breathe it in. One cannot be a Jew in Ireland without being reminded of it ten times in the day. At every hand's turn, it is driven home to one that one is a Jew, and to be a Jew here means to be nothing else. A Jew—well, what is a Jew? Ah! well—don't you know—a Jew—a Jew, that's it. It is practically a mystery what the average Irish conception of a Jew might be.

Lipsett was extremely astute and measured. He picked up on the term used in Ireland of the 'Jewman': 'Nowhere else is the term "Jewman" known; here we hear nothing else, and not infrequently we see it too. It is a piece of vulgarity which has crept into print unconsciously; though instances may not be lacking where it has been pushed in on purpose. Often I have seen the "Jewman" staring up from the placards on the street'. The fact that Jews, who, 'in a sense, have no politics worth speaking of', voted Unionist out of gratitude for the protection the Union afforded them had some impact. He concluded that 'the Irish people have contracted a certain unaccountable prejudice against the Jews because they do not know them' and that the Jews should make themselves known to the Irish because the Irish would not come to the Jews, a proposition that brought Lipsett back to 'the Irish clannishness, the Irish exclusiveness', from which he had set out at the start of his magisterial protest. Lipsett breaks through the strained rhetorical protocol under which Irish nationalists celebrate their own inclusiveness, and Irish Jews hold back from putting it in question, in what was a meagre compact of coexistence.

There is no reason to believe Joyce had read Lipsett's piece in the London *Jewish Chronicle*, nor had he identifiable Dublin Jewish informants when he was writing *Ulysses*; one could add that Lipsett has the commanding merit of never having heard of Leopold Bloom, having died in the year before the publication of *Ulysses*. There is something pristine in how closely Lipsett's account matches Bloom's experience in *Ulysses* of a Dublin day, while the sceptical querying of the idea of a Jewish Irishman has, in a country as preoccupied with the politics of national identity as Ireland, an impugning of the civic status of Irish Jews. Lipsett closely anticipates Joyce in *Ulysses*. Lipsett does not discern atavistic Christian bigotry (he considered that many Dubliners did not actually realise Jews were not Christians); so far as the tension he identifies arises from Irish nationalism, the political prejudice Lipsett identifies is specifically modern. The Irish nationalists of whom he was writing did not conceive themselves to be anti-Semitic; but insofar as they considered that the Jew was incapable even of understanding why he or she could not partake of Irish patriotism or nationalism, they unthinkingly proffered a double insult to their Jewish fellow citizens. The relationship seemed for long frozen in this frame. Lipsett's perceptions are borne out by Samuel Beckett's friend and successor as lecturer in French in Trinity College, A. J. Leventhal (1896–1979), who in 1944 posed and starkly answered the question, 'What does it mean to be a Jew?' in the Ireland of the Second World War.[30]

The Joyce who left Ireland in 1904—if, like most born as Catholics in the city, knowing very little about the Jews of Dublin—was alive to the level of prejudice against and suspicion of the Jews that existed in

30. Leventhal, 'What It Means'; Nadel, *Joyce and the Jews*, 193.

Ireland, though that was something that imperfectly matched his political preoccupations at that time. His sense of that is gleaned primarily from the street, taking 'the street' to encompass what had been imparted to him socially, and to include whatever he might have been told or overheard in his Jesuit schools or in University College. In Dublin there is more evidence of middle-class professional resentment of Jews than among the working class. Neither anti-Semitism nor opposition to Jewish immigration was a significant theme in Irish politics, but there were periodic ebullitions of controversy that revealed the obdurate presence of prejudice against Jews that owed more to an entire lack of familiarity than to considered animosity.

Middle-Class Dublin Anti-Semitism: T. A. Finlay S.J. and Sir Frederick Falkiner

The highly respected Jesuit and University College professor Fr. T. A. Finlay published in 1893 three successive editorials in the monthly *Lyceum*, which he had founded and edited, the first entitled 'The Jew in Ireland' and the second and third 'The Jew amongst Us'. These articles are a response to the establishment of the Lithuanian Jews. Finlay registers some of the shock to Catholic nationalist conceptions of homogeneity by the establishment of their community. In Dublin, 'where they are settling in ever-increasing numbers', they did not gravitate to the working-class areas of the Coombe or the Liberties:

> They possess themselves rather of the quarter traversed by the South Circular Road. In this thoroughfare itself and in the streets opening off they have established a flourishing colony—so flourishing that for their religious needs a spacious synagogue has lately been built close by. In some of the streets that open off the South Circular Road one may walk along the pavement from end to end and hardly hear a word of English spoken by the children who are at play on the footpath. We are in as completely a Jewish quarter, as if we were wandering through some city of Poland or Southern Russia.[31]

31. T. A. Finlay, 'The Jew in Ireland', *Lyceum* 6, no. 70 (July 1893): 215–18.

Finlay posed the question, 'Should the Jew be made welcome in Ireland?' which he then answered in the negative. This was to protect the Irish poor from Jewish hawkers, 'weekly men', and moneylenders, and by implication to prevent the emergence of an anti-Semitic party in Ireland. If the Jew 'comes merely as a parasite . . . then let him not be more welcome here than he is among the peasants of Germany or among the labourers of France'. Disclaiming 'all hostility to the Jew on the score of race, religion or nationality', Finlay's intellectually dire articles were a compendium of objectively anti-Semitic received ideas. He did contrive to add one slur that was original, deriving from Irish land legislation: 'It is significant that the appearance of the Jew in Ireland as trader and money-lender on a large scale, coincides with the change in the law which gave the Irish tenant a saleable interest in his farm. We trust it is no more than a coincidence. But we fancy we see reason to doubt it.'[32]

The Jew, 'as he appears in modern European society, is, to a certain extent, an alien'. Finlay did not consider that the Jew could be a patriotic Irishman, a point rendered in the high elliptical Jesuit manner: 'We have no right to rebuke the Jew as a stranger or an alien amongst us, to make it a reproach that he does not share our national life or enter into sympathy with our national ambitions.'[33] The third article was the most intellectually incoherent. Having, as he wrote, 'already disclaimed all hostility to the Jew on the score of race, religion, or nationality', Finlay imperturbably pronounced, 'We find in the Jewish habit of mind, in the Jewish character, as it exhibits itself in the social life of other people, sufficient to make their presence in Ireland on any large scale obnoxious'. The flaccidity of Finlay's reasoning was disclosed in what he considered his clinching argument, that 'one of the most remarkable features of the Jewish character is its consistency under diverse circumstances and even widely separated intervals of time. What the Jews have

32. Finlay, 'The Jew in Ireland'. Strangely, Finlay's complaints about the Jewish promotion in Germany of what he called 'this system of gombeening' did not address the Irish provenance of the term *gombeen*, defined by P. W. Joyce as 'a usurer who lends money to small farmers and others of like means, at ruinous interest' (*English As We Speak It in Ireland* [Dublin: Gill, 1910], 264).

33. T. A. Finlay, 'The Jew amongst Us', *Lyceum* 6, no. 71 (August 1893): 235–38.

been in the thirteenth century they are found to have been in the nineteenth; what they have shown themselves to be in the Ukraine, they may be expected to be in Ireland.'[34] The constancy of prejudice was self-validating. Finlay is not to be taken as a spokesman for the Catholic Church, though his articles refracted aspects of the views of Irish bishops and priests, as well as of the 'informed' Catholic professional laity.

Finlay's mistake was that, as a result of his confident sense of the benign regard in which he was held as an intellectual and generally public-spirited Jesuit, he decided to write at considerable length on a subject that most Irish people—Jews and non-Jews—fastidiously avoided, and thereby revealed the depth of his ignorance and prejudice. Moneylending and the sale of goods on credit were matters of public concern, and not all condemnations of practices deemed to be usurious were anti-Semitic in nature. This was a distinction of which Joyce was conscious. In *Ulysses* he took his family's revenge on the non-Jewish but faintly Jewish-sounding possessor of the name Reuben J. Dodd, a moneylender from whom John Stanislaus Joyce had borrowed. John Stanislaus Joyce was unable to raise the money to pay back the loan, resulting in the sale of his remaining houses in Cork in 1893, which ended his connection to the city.[35] Dodd was never forgiven by Joyce, father or son; but Joyce was prepared, in a daringly black joke, to render him the object of the obloquy a Jewish moneylender might have attracted under the guise of demonstrating the arbitrariness and plain error of anti-Semitic prejudice. In *Ulysses* Dodd is twinned with Sir Frederick Falkiner, his judicial near nemesis. Finlay, attesting to Jesuit familiarity with the professional life of the city, in the third of his articles on the Jews, wrote, 'Not many of us realise that we have in our midst in Dublin a civil court whose chief function is to arrange disputes between Jewish creditors and the debtors who have been tempted into fatal bargains by their wily offers, a court where the part of Shylock is often rehearsed, and the pound of flesh not seldom paid.'[36]

34. T. A. Finlay, 'The Jew amongst Us', *Lyceum* 6, no. 72 (September 1893): 251–55.

35. Jackson and Costello, *John Stanislaus Joyce*, 176–82.

36. Finlay, 'Jew amongst Us' (September 1893), 254.

This was the court where Falkiner presided as the Recorder of Dublin from 1876 to 1905, a high municipal functionary rather than a judge proper. Two outbursts of judicial spleen towards the Jews marred his career in office. In the first, in October 1892, trying a case of debt against a Jew, he declared, 'These fellows would swear to anything. The Jews are here in this city and are evidently going to stay, but if they are they will have to obey the laws of this Court.' His remarks caused controversy, and he offered a convincing apology in open court. The second was worse. After sentencing a Jewish defendant to a year's imprisonment for window-breaking, an offence that had become gallingly frequent, he burst out, 'You are a specimen of your race and nation that cause you to be hunted out of every country.' This was too much, and elicited an immediate protest from Ernest Wormser Harris, president of the Dublin Hebrew Congregation, 'against anyone occupying a judicial position making use of the words that level the grossest insult upon every member of the Jewish Community in Dublin and throughout the United Kingdom'. Harris also had T. M. Healy and Stuart Samuel raise the comments in the House of Commons. Falkiner apologised in a letter to Sir Joseph Sebag Montefiore, president of the London Committee of Deputies of British Jews, and in open court in Dublin.[37]

In Dublin Falkiner had a popular renown as a compassionate 'poor man's judge'.[38] Falkiner characteristically sought to find ways to grind down the law's angularity. The anonymous Dublin barrister who wrote an astute weekly column titled 'Our Judges' in 1890 intriguingly invoked Bassanio, the suitor of Portia in *The Merchant of Venice*, whose loan his friend Antonio guarantees to Shylock with his own flesh as surety: 'I do think that Mr. Falkiner has some sympathy with Bassanio's view of the equitable duty of a court. "To do a great right do a little wrong". Certain it is that he has recourse to every kind of device in order to bring about what he conceives to be the fair and reasonable settlement of a dispute.

37. Hyman, *Jews of Ireland*, 163–64; Shillman, *Brief History*, 104. Bernard Shillman, an Irish senior counsel, is notably less forgiving of 'that ignominious pronouncement' than Hyman, but Shillman had come to the Irish bar in 1923, almost two decades after Falkiner had left office and so had no personal experience of the Recorder.

38. Igoe, *Real People*, 100.

He assumes, to begin with, in litigation one side is only a little better than the other, and he endeavours to strike an even balance between them.'[39] This pretty much corresponds to what Bloom muses: 'Has his own ideas of justice in the recorder's court. Well-meaning old man.'[40] In *Ulysses* Joyce's principal purpose is to render how Falkiner is perceived from the Dublin street. What is striking is that Bloom aligns himself with the generally favourable view of Falkiner. Bloom observes Falkiner in 'Lestrygonians' entering the Freemason's Hall in Molesworth Street for, he surmises, postprandial wine and judicial bavardage: 'Old legal cronies cracking a magnum.'[41] Bloom then elaborates: 'The devil on moneylenders. Gave Reuben J. a great strawcalling. Now he's really what they call a dirty jew. Power those judges have. Crusty old topers in wigs. Bear with a sore paw. And may the Lord have mercy on your soul.'[42]

This is magnificently done. The moneylender and the high judicial functionary are each assigned their place in the commedia dell'arte of Dublin litigation. There is a suggestion of the arbitrariness of legal authority; and Bloom is allowed to call Reuben Dodd, who isn't Jewish, 'a dirty jew'. As Robert Boyle S.J. noted, 'Bloom is adopting the phrase used by the anti-Semites, but he is using it to condemn a Catholic' and the anti-Semites who use the phrase.[43] It is the most prominent instance of Joyce enlarging the category of Jews to include those perceived as or accused of being Jewish, his complex and sophisticated retorsion on anti-Semites of the subjectivity and insubstantiality of their categorisations.[44]

Talk of Falkiner recurs in the 'Cyclops' episode. As they discuss the case of a Jewish swindler who offered cheap passages to Canada, Alf

39. Rhadamanthus, *Our Judges*, 124.

40. *U* 8.1155–56.

41. *U* 8.1152–53.

42. *U* 8.1158–61.

43. Robert Boyle, 'A Note on Reuben J. Dodd as "A Dirty Jew"', *James Joyce Quarterly* 3, no. 1 (Fall 1965): 64–66.

44. Claudia Rosenhan, '"Grace" and the Idea of "the Irish Jew"', *James Joyce Quarterly* 47, no. 1 (Fall 2009): 73.

Bergan's observations ('Poor old sir Frederick, says Alf, you can cod him up to the two eyes') and Ned Lambert's comment that 'you can cod him up to the two eyes' relate to Falkiner's likely sympathy for a Jewish victim of the swindle who attracts little fellow feeling in Barney Kiernan's.[45] Part of Joyce's point is that it is naïve to believe that the threads of commercial as of civic life can be separated out, and it is senseless to dwell on one single moment of a sequential transaction considered apart from its socio-economic setting. It transpires that the anti-Semitic narrator of 'Cyclops' has himself been reduced to the role of a collector of bad debts ('How are the mighty fallen!') and is retained by Moses Herzog of St Kevin's Parade (whom he refers to as 'the little jewy') to pursue monies owed to Herzog by a Stoneybatter plumber called Geraghty, whom, as the episode opens, he has called on. Geraghty insouciantly threatens to have Herzog prosecuted for trading without a moneylender's licence.[46] All are caught in the coils of the immiserated commerce and limited employments of Dublin, calling to mind the setting of 'Ivy Day in the Committee Room', where Joe Hynes makes his first entrance in Joyce's fiction.

The Limerick Boycott, 1904

An aggressively assertive young Limerick-born Redemptorist priest named John Creagh, who was the director of the Archconfraternity of the Holy Family, established by the Redemptorists in Limerick, preached on 11 January and 18 January 1904 viciously and inflammatory anti-Semitic sermons. His first sermon exemplified the transcontinental contagion of anti-Semitism reaching even into a highly insular culture with little sense of European politics, to which Joyce was acutely alert. Proceeding from the blood libel ('Nowadays they dare not kidnap and slay Christian children'), Creagh declaimed, 'They were sucking the blood of other nations, but those nations rose up and turned them out and they came to our land to fasten themselves on us like leeches, and

45. *U* 12.1084–110.

46. *U* 12.13–51.

to draw our blood when they had been forced away from other countries.' There were moreover 'no greater enemies of the Catholic church than the Jews'.[47] Creagh urged his congregation to have no commercial dealings with Jews. His sermons gave rise to manifestations of anti-Semitism in the city, causing great terror in the small Jewish community, and to a boycotting of the city's Jewish traders, leading not only to a loss of new business but opportunistic defaulting on existing debts, which in turn led to several households leaving the city over the months that followed.[48] The attack on the Jews of Limerick was condemned by Michael Davitt and deprecated by John Redmond.[49] The Bishop of Limerick, whose intervention was solicited, did not disavow Creagh's sermons, of which he is unlikely to have approved.[50] Creagh's views, so far as they related to the exploitation of the poor of Limerick, continued to be defended in a characteristic tone of defiance by Arthur Griffith in the *United Irishman*: 'We are glad Fr. Creagh has given the advice he did. We trust he will continue to give it. We have no quarrel with the Jews' religion, but all the howling of journalistic hacks and the balderdash of uninformed sentimentalists will not make us, nor should it make any honest man, cease to expose knavery, because the knavery is carried on by Jews.'[51] Creagh continued to fulminate against the perils of alcohol, evil literature, and obscenity in the theatre. When the thrusting young populist was appointed to the Redemptorists' new mission in the Philippines, there was a large crowd to see him off when he left the railway station in Limerick in May 1906.[52]

The Limerick boycott, while far short of a pogrom, was disquieting. It is duly noted, though a little perfunctorily, in the 'Eumaeus' episode of *Ulysses*, as Bloom, having escaped Barney Kiernan's in the 'Cyclops' episode, talks to Stephen about the Jews and says, referring to the invocation

47. Dermot Keogh, *Jews in Twentieth-Century Ireland: Refugees, Anti-Semitism and the Holocaust* (Cork: Cork University Press, 1998), 28, 32; Hyman, *Jews of Ireland*, 212–17.

48. Ó Gráda, *Jewish Ireland*, 191–92.

49. Keogh, *Jews in Twentieth-Century Ireland*, 32.

50. Ó Gráda, *Jewish Ireland*, 193; Keogh, *Jews in Twentieth-Century Ireland*, 37–39.

51. *United Irishman*, 23 April 1904, quoted in Keogh, *Jews in Twentieth-Century Ireland*, 42.

52. Keogh, *Jews in Twentieth-Century Ireland*, 51, 53.

of prejudice by Irish parish priests, 'That's the juggle on which the p.p.'s raise the wind on false pretences'.[53]

Intercommunal occasions were sparse. One such was when, on 13 February 1909, John Wyse Power lectured on 'the Jews in Ireland in the Middle Ages' to the Jewish Literary and Social Club at 57 Lombard Street West, chaired by Maurice Solomons, honorary consul for the Austro-Hungarian Empire.[54] Power (1859–1926) was a journalist and a Parnellite who, when the *Freeman's Journal* forsook Parnell, left its employment for the *Irish Independent*. He thereafter edited the *Evening Herald* for several years,[55] and Joyce knew him. The 1909 lecture, of which Joyce must have somehow become aware, is likely to have inspired the fact that in 'Cyclops' it is John Wyse Nolan, who is inspired by Power, who patiently advises the Citizen that it was said that Bloom had given Griffith the idea for many of the issues for which Sinn Féin agitated.[56] 'And after all, says John Wyse, why can't a Jew love his country like the next fellow?'[57]

Joyce did not carry with him from Dublin in 1904 any strongly marked sense of the Jews of Dublin. There is a period of overlap between Dublin and Trieste that is a prelude to Joyce's active curiosity about Jews. Some of the *Dubliners* stories showed an orientalising sense of Eastern exoticism. From Rome in September 1906 he wrote to Stanislaus, 'I have a new story for Dubliners in my head. It deals with Mr. Hunter'.[58] Since he did not describe who Alfred H. Hunter was to Stanislaus, they must have discussed him previously. Joyce may at some point have thought, as Stanislaus told Richard Ellmann for the first edition of the biography,[59] that Hunter was Jewish; he may have had an

53. *U* 16.1130–31. This was first picked up by Marvin Magalaner in 'The Anti-Semitic Limerick Incidents and Joyce's "Bloomsday"', *PMLA* 67, no. 5 (September 1953): 1219–23.

54. Hyman, *Jews of Ireland*, 183. The speech was reported in the *Evening Telegraph*, 15 February 1909. See also *Jews of Ireland*, 336n132.

55. Igoe, *Real People*, 224–26. Joyce also knew and had in Trieste a copy of Power's wife Jennie's *Words of the Dead Chief*. Gillespie, *James Joyce's Trieste Library*, 182.

56. *U* 12.1573–77, 1623–24.

57. *U* 12.1628–29.

58. Joyce to Stanislaus Joyce, 30 September 1906, *Letters II* 168.

59. Ellmann, *James Joyce* (1959), 238, 778n38.

unfaithful wife, and he seems to have extricated Joyce from an altercation in Dublin in 1904.[60] Though it would not have prevented him from being an inspiration for Leopold Bloom, Hunter was not in fact Jewish.[61]

'Kicking Up a Bloody Murder about Bloody Nothing'

What is striking is the rarity of public expression of anti-Semitic sentiments in Ireland. These relatively meagre episodes are rehearsed in all the treatments of Joyce and the Jews, and in the history of Irish Jewry in which they merge. But they are various and disparate and do not cohere in the expression of a continuous anti-Semitic theme in Irish public life. It is open to debate what that owes in nationalist Ireland to the thin if much-vaunted Irish immunity to sectarian prejudice, to the extent to which English parliamentary norms—however formalistic—informed Irish political discourse, or to pure demographics: the fact that the size of the Jewish population prevented it becoming a political issue. European Jews were, for very good reason, highly sensitive to manifestations of anti-Semitism, which were capable of having a sharply dissuasive effect on Jewish immigration to Ireland. The socio-political reception of Jews in Ireland, as well as economic prospects, constrained the size of the Jewish population.

In Ireland anti-Semitism, or the potential for it, lay for the most part submerged beneath the surface of formal public discourse. Part of the political conception of *Ulysses* was the universality of arbitrary prejudices in Europe against Jews, even in a country where the Jewish population was slight. This is a rich and challenging theme, which involved addressing demotic prejudices that had scant political articulation and proportionately sparse political rebuttal. It became a critical point of entry into Joyce's critique of nationalist chauvinism and insularity, but one that necessitated discerning measure.

60. Ellmann, *James Joyce*, 161–62.

61. Hyman, *Jews of Ireland*, 175.

In relation to anti-Semitism in Ireland, what Joyce does with consummate brilliance is to abrogate the protocols of discourse which avoided the subject, and to render prejudice against Jews in the Dublin middle class or lower-middle class foregathered in a public house in a commercial part of the north city. The continuities with 'Ivy Day' are strong. Joyce has a certain human tolerance of Dublin people of the lower-middle-class living in perpetual financial insecurity, watching the fortunes of their urban neighbours with desperate covetousness. Elsewhere in the novel, Joyce deals with Protestant prejudice against Jews, and what Joyce correctly discerns as the peculiar proclivity of the professional classes to anti-Semitism, rendered in the figure of Buck Mulligan.

In renderings of anti-Semitism, Joyce is a pivotal figure in European literature and culture. *Ulysses* is a strategically conceived indictment of anti-Semitism that did much at a crucial time to make anti-Semitism unacceptable, and to render the opinions of anti-Semites on non-Jewish issues inherently suspect and at odds with the modern. It could be said that in this aspect Joyce maximised what could be achieved politically by a novel. In *Ulysses*, at the same moment at which he fixes anti-Semitism as a pernicious political and intellectual evil, he recognises that not every anti-Semitic comment establishes that its maker is to be considered an anti-Semite, and perhaps that there are gradations as well as types of anti-Semitism. These, of course, are propositions that could now, in the rigid identitarian usages of the twenty-first century, in which any manifestation of prejudice is equated with an anti-'ism', be considered highly objectionable. But identitarian categorisations, insofar as they may be valid—and it is hard to forget that Joyce has always managed to outlive ideological and quasi-ideological fashions—cannot usefully be applied to Joyce's writings, even in their relation to anti-Semitism. It is not simply that they are anachronistic, that Joyce, for all his modernism, is a child of the nineteenth century and its (not universally) less constrained protocols of discourse, but he is a writer, a weigher of words and of what prompts their expression, and of the people by whom and of the settings in which they are uttered.

There is an ambivalence in the Citizen as a figure of anti-Semitism. He is a developed character of some complexity with a genuine if splenetic sense of humour that is not always thuggishly applied, rather than a flat archetype of anti-Semitism.[62] His anti-Semitism is an aspect of a larger xenophobic racism. He is a thoroughly, it might be said extravagantly, bigoted Irish nationalist. The Citizen certainly does not like Jews, but his antipathy to Bloom is a corollary of his blind nationalism rather than the expression of a free-standing anti-Semitism. His race hatred is securely fixed on the English; the Jews are marginal to the binarism that characterises the politics of the Citizen. That does not render the Citizen not an anti-Semite, but it is relevant to characterising his anti-Semitism. It could hardly be said that the political worldview of the Citizen was significantly informed by a prejudice against Jews: he is not that type of anti-Semite. It is more that his anti-Semitism is a marker of the fallacy of his rabidly anti-modern Irish nationalism. Bloom has interposed what is to the Citizen his extremely irritating presence in the Citizen's obsessional quarrel with the English. When Bloom defies him, which is to say when he refuses to efface himself, the Citizen explodes.

The Citizen is not the only person of anti-Semitic disposition in Barney Kiernan's. There is also the narrator, and the Citizen's cynical and sullenly complicit public house admirers who serve as a kind of chorus. Anti-Semitic sentiment in the episode is portioned out among them.

The Citizen is exquisitely conceived in the balance struck between his prejudices and a choler sharpened by the impairments of his physique: against the pseudo-heroical interludes of the chapter, in the scene which precedes that in which the Citizen throws the biscuit-tin at Bloom as he departs in the jarvey's carriage, the narrator observes 'the citizen getting up to waddle to the door, puffing and blowing with the dropsy'.[63] His compromised lumbering mobility is contrasted with the mock-heroical pageants that break up the episode, and invests the

62. The easy ideological villainisation of both the Citizen and Mr Henchy in 'Ivy Day' is mitigated by a closer reading of the texts. The utterances of both owe something to Joyce's father, though the views of John Stanislaus Joyce had nothing in common with those of the Citizen.

63. *U* 12.1783–85.

efforts to restrain him from violence towards Leopold Bloom with pantomimic effect.

Joyce's creation of the Citizen amply fulfils the episode's promise of gigantism. The Citizen is as sharply etched and memorable a figure as any in Dickens, with the difference that the Citizen lacked Dickensian frozenness across time and was destined, as Joyce intended, to attract conflicting political interpretation. The colossus of impaired mobility that is the Citizen casts a corpulent shadow over the intricate passage of the episode in which Joyce's analysis of anti-Semitism finds its most explicit, if almost abstruse, expression in his fictional writing, which is independent of how the figure of the Citizen is politically interpreted. This occurs in the same prelude of the culminating moment of 'Cyclops', as the Citizen lurches towards the door in pursuit of Bloom, who is about to depart in the jaunting car summoned by Martin Cunningham. In the narrator's account, which throws the reader on a first reading, it is the Citizen who says sarcastically, 'Three cheers for Israel!'[64] That prompts an unexpected scornful commentary on the Citizen's interjection by the narrator, who is himself prejudiced against Jews and hostile to Bloom: 'Arrah, sit down on the parliamentary side of your arse for Christ' sake and don't be making a public exhibition of yourself. Jesus, there is always some bloody clown or other kicking up a bloody murder about bloody nothing. Gob, it'd turn the porter sour in your guts, so it would.'[65] That observation—'kicking up a bloody murder about bloody nothing'—is the defining characterisation of anti-Semitism in Joyce's fictional writing. It is moreover uttered by an invisible character—the narrator of the episode—who is of an anti-Semitic disposition, and in language that is close to that of the Citizen. Its effect is scarcely diminished by his description in the paragraph that follows of Bloom 'on his high horse about the jews',[66] which the narrator takes to be a reaction to the Citizen's mocking salute to Israel. The confusion of the scene (it is not always clear to whom the pronoun 'he' refers) serves to underscore

64. *U* 12.1791.
65. *U* 12.1792–95.
66. *U* 12.1798.

the proposition that the altercation between the Citizen and Leopold Bloom—that anti-Semitism itself—is 'about bloody nothing'. It is the vortex of a void. That is Joyce's final analysis of the intellectual finitude of anti-Semitism.

The Jews of Trieste

The Jews of Trieste made an extraordinary contribution, fostered by Austrian policy, to the city's commercial success in banking and insurance. The nucleus of the Jewish community in Trieste consisted of a handful of families who were mainly of Venetian, Piedmontese, and Ferrarese origin. The Italian provenance did much to explain why Triestine Jews such as Felice Venezian and Teodoro Mayer were leading figures in *irredentisimo*.[67] It was not only that most of the Triestine Jews had come from Italy: Arnoldo Momigliano wrote that 'the Italian character of Trieste was and is owing to a great extent to Jews who were often of German and Eastern origins but chose Italy—the Italy beyond the border, which seemed to offer an equality for Jews that did not exist in the Austrian Empire'.[68] The Jewish community of Trieste was highly assimilated, reflected in a high degree of intermarriage with non-Jews. Jewish support for, and the role of Jewish leaders in, Italian irridentism was a measure of Jewish integration in Trieste. Support for Zionism was conversely limited among the Jews of Trieste. As Neil Davison has pointed out, Zionism was nevertheless strenuously promoted and publicised by the only Jewish paper in Trieste, the slim weekly *Il Corriere Israelitico*, 'one of the only vehicles for an open discussion of both ancient and modern Zionism in the whole of Jewish Italy' in Joyce's time.[69] Some of the Jews whom Joyce knew in Trieste belonged to what was very much the minority of ardent Zionists, most notably Moses Dlugacz, born in Galicia, a rabbi and Zionist intellectual who

67. Schachter, *Origin and Identity*, 45.

68. Arnoldo Momigliano, 'The Jews of Italy', *New York Review of Books*, 24 October 1985, quoted in Nadel, *Joyce and the Jews*, 201.

69. Neil R. Davison, '"Still an Idea behind It": Trieste, Jewishness and Zionism in *Ulysses*', *James Joyce Quarterly* 38, no. 3/4 (Spring–Summer 2001): 375–80.

worked as chief cashier on the Cunard line in Trieste and who was a student of Joyce,[70] and who appears in the 'Calypso' episode as a 'ferreteyed porkbutcher' on Upper Dorset Street.[71] Louis Hyman, the Dublin Jew who had emigrated to British Mandate Palestine and wrote the invaluable *The Jews of Ireland* (1972), was preoccupied with the idea of Dlugacz as the inspiration for the Zionism he imputed to Bloom, and even for the character of Bloom himself, from which Ellmann patiently sought to dissuade him.[72]

Joyce was sufficiently interested in Zionism to purchase in Zurich Theodor Herzl's *Der Judenstaat*.[73] There is, however, little to suggest that Joyce was sympathetic to Zionism. Davison refers to 'Joyce's recognition of the Zionist argument that Jews would never be fully accepted into most European societies even after radical assimilation.'[74] Joyce's consciousness of the ubiquity and persistence of anti-Semitism cannot be rendered as an acceptance of a specifically Zionist premise. Joyce's sceptical self-distancing from Zionism is important for an understanding of his Irish-derived conception of nationalism in establishing that his was not an ideological or indiscriminate espousal of nationalism, but one that was contingent on claims to statehood being validated historically, culturally, and geographically and being politically conceivable and achievable even in the face of resistance by a conquering power. One might add that that nationalist realism was held in check by his rooted suspicion of positivistic dogma. While—or possibly even because—he was imaginatively haunted by the concept of exodus, he was markedly sceptical of ideas of return. The subject closest to Zionism which Joyce addressed was the revival of the Irish language. As with his

70. McCourt, *Years of Bloom*, 235–36.

71. *U* 4.152. The basis for assigning Dlugacz's name to a pork butcher seems to have been that, aside from Joyce's general love of any form of anomalousness, Dlugacz stayed on in the city during the war and traded as a provisions merchant who provided meat, presumably including pork, to the Austrian army fighting on the Isonzo front. McCourt, *Years of Bloom*, 235.

72. Neil R. Davison, '"Not a Propagandist for the Better Treatment of Minorities": The Richard Ellmann-Louis Hyman Correspondence', *James Joyce Quarterly* 50, no. 3 (Spring 2013): 741–65.

73. Davison, '"Still an Idea"', 377.

74. Davison, '"Still an Idea"', 379.

attitude to the language revival, he is himself unsympathetic to the Zionist idea but does not discount the intelligence or conviction of those like Moses Dlugacz who espoused it. Joyce died just over a year before the Nazis' Lake Wannsee conference of 20 January 1942, and so we cannot know whether knowledge of the Shoah would have altered his attitude to Zionism.

In the 'Calypso' episode of *Ulysses*, Bloom is introduced after the opening three episodes of the novel, the 'Telemachiad', which concern Stephen Dedalus. Bloom breakfasts and ventures forth, telling his slumbering wife—as yet unnamed—that he will be back in a minute. The warmth of the sun prompts a reverie of an oriental city that establishes that his view of the East is conventional and acquired, but he is perfectly aware of the fact: 'Probably not a bit like it really. Kind of stuff you read: in the track of the sun.'[75] He goes into Dlugacz's. Waiting to buy kidneys, he is preoccupied principally by the body of the girl ahead of him but picks up one of the cut sheets from the stack that Dlugacz keeps to wrap meat in, which contains two advertisements of Zionist inspiration. The first is for the model farm at Kinnereth in the city of Tiberias on the Sea of Galilee. The second is for the Zionist colony in Palestine of Agendath Netaim (properly Agudath Netaim, 'Company of Plantations', set up to purchase land in Palestine from the Turkish government, and not established till 1905).[76] Reading the advertisements, Bloom thinks to himself, 'Nothing doing. Still an idea behind it'.[77] The idea is Zionism. He is moved to a reverie not unlike that of the oriental city by the photographs, rendered as if they were photographic prints and not newspaper reproductions: 'He looked at the cattle, blurred in silver heat. Silverpowdered olivetrees.'[78] He thinks of his Jewish friends in Dublin, and of the Mediterranean trade in citrus fruits and olives. As the sun clouds over and he heads back in the direction of his home on Eccles Street—the imminent shadow over his relationship to his wife is only faintly hinted at—Bloom's mood abruptly darkens, in relation to both Palestine

75. *U* 4.99–100.

76. Hyman, *Jews of Ireland*, 339n194.

77. *U* 4.200.

78. *U* 4.201–2.

and the prospect of return. He ruminates on the barren land, the Dead Sea, and the biblically cursed cities of the plain: 'It bore the oldest, the first race. A bent hag crossed from Cassidy's, clutching a naggin bottle by the neck. The oldest people. Wandered far away over all the earth, captivity to captivity, multiplying, dying, being born everywhere. It lay there now. Now it could bear no more. Dead: an old woman's: the grey sunken cunt of the world.'[79]

This is Bloom in uncharacteristically grim, almost apocalyptic, vein, stabbed with the pain of the prospective infidelity of his wife which he is to struggle pretty successfully to master in the course of the day. The idea of Zionism recurs towards the novel's end, in the mellow nocturnal setting of the 'Ithaca' episode. With masterly obliquity, the 'points of contact' are enumerated, not actually between Bloom and Stephen, but between the Irish and Hebrew languages and those who speak them, as Stephen and Bloom have just done in the most perfunctory way, though respectively they cannot speak Irish or Hebrew. The last point of equivalence is 'the restoration in Chanah David of Zion and the possibility of Irish political autonomy or devolution.'[80] It is an acknowledgement of the place occupied in the Jewish sensibility by the idea of return. 'Chanah David' is from Isaiah 29:10[81] and represents an acknowledgement of the power and ancientness of the sentiment on which modern Zionism drew. In his notesheets for 'Cyclops', Joyce had written, 'Jews & Irish remember past.'[82]

Joyce's discounting of Zionism owed much to his inability to conceive the coming into existence of a Jewish state, an ability unaffected by the Balfour declaration of 1917. It was a view widely shared among Jews and non-Jews. When his friend Ottocaro Weiss in Zurich mentioned the possibility of a Jewish state, Joyce responded with an inelegant joke: 'That's all very well, but believe me, a warship with a captain

79. *U* 4.223–28.

80. *U* 17.759–60.

81. Davison, '"Still an Idea"', 390.

82. Phillip F. Herring, ed., *Joyce's 'Ulysses' Notesheets in the British Museum* (Charlottesville: University of Virginia Press, 1972), 82, line 53.

named Kanalgitter and his aide named Captain Afterduft would be the funniest thing the old Mediterranean has ever seen.'[83]

If Joyce was not personally sympathetic to Zionism, he fully apprehended its intellectual significance. He recognised that Zionism attracted the allegiance of an ardent minority of European Jews and entered into the consciousness of even the highly assimilated Jews he knew who were dismissive of the idea itself but found themselves forced to address the issue of their Jewish identity by anti-Semitic prejudice, by the external imposition of a sense of apartness. Hostile to ideological conceptions of racial (or confessional) exceptionalism, Joyce recognised the distinctiveness of the Jews as a race without a country dispersed across the continent of Europe. The situation and experience of the Jews entered into his modelling of nationalism, and of the scheme of nation-states and their relations, and refined his Irish-derived nationalism. The most discernible political legacy of his continental exile, this found expression in the creation of the Irish Jewish or Jewish Irish Leopold Bloom.

While it is possible to track the broad trajectory of Joyce's interest in and sympathy with Jews, it is difficult to establish dates with precision. The principal early expression of his interest in the subject of the Jews is in his letter to Stanislaus from Rome on 13 November 1906 when he refers to having just read Guglielmo Ferrero's *L'Europa giovane* and comments that Ferrero has 'a fine chapter on Antisemitism.'[84] That is anti-Semitism in the abstract, but in the journal Stanislaus kept in Trieste there are two accounts dated close together of the stirring of Joyce's curiosity on the subject of the Jews of Trieste.

On 15 September 1907, Joyce for the first time went to one of the Jewish synagogues of Trieste, having almost certainly attended Catholic and Greek Orthodox ceremonies. He was surprised to find many of his students present: 'He asked had the Jews any theology in the sense that Catholics have one, and was the priesthood with them a caste or a profession. Also he wanted to know whether they had a school of theology

83. Ellmann, *James Joyce*, 395–96.

84. Joyce to Stanislaus Joyce, 13 November 1906, *Letters II* 190.

in which it was necessary to study, and lamented that none of his pupils seemed to know anything about the religion to which they were supposed to belong.'[85]

There is of course high comedy in the disappointment of the apostate Irish Catholic on his interrogation of his young Jewish students in Trieste. Yet something stayed with Joyce. Stanislaus wrote in an entry three days later, 'Today until sundown was a Jewish holiday. Jim and I walked through the principal streets to see how many shops were shut. It was astonishing, a good third of the principal firms in the city are Jewish. Besides many names I knew to be Jewish, Steiner, Levi, Mendel, I found many I had never suspected before, such as Morpurgo and Bolaffio whom I thought thoroughly Italian.'[86]

It might be thought odd that Stanislaus was surprised that a third of the city's businesses were Jewish owned, or that the name Morpurgo is that of one of the great Italo-Jewish families of Trieste, but these might be thought characteristic gaps in immigrant comprehension of the cultures they have entered. The narrative of a joint crossing of the city tentatively suggests a shared level of knowledge with his brother. Joyce was almost certainly more alert to the Jewish presence in Trieste than Stanislaus. The fact that Stanislaus frequently reflected his brother's thinking means that it is likely that a shift occurred in relation to Joyce's interest in the Jews of Trieste in or around, if not before, September 1907, and that Joyce then set out to fill the void of his ignorance. This was four years into Joyce's exile, and six months after he came back to Trieste from Rome, suggesting a deepened patience in discovering what Trieste had to offer. Yet taking the two entries together, it can be concluded that Joyce was until September 1907 not especially interested in or curious about the Jews of Trieste, at least as a writer. In late 1906 Joyce had begun to think distantly of the idea for *Ulysses*. In the spring of 1907 he gave his lecture 'L'Irlanda: Isola dei santi e dei savi', in which he reconceptualised his relationship to Ireland, its pasts and its futures. What is

85. Stanislaus Joyce, Triestine diary, 15 September 1907, quoted in McCourt, *Years of Bloom*, 219.

86. Stanislaus Joyce, Triestine diary, 18 September 1907, quoted in McCourt, *Years of Bloom*, 219.

FIGURE 17.1. Synagogue of Trieste. Image courtesy of the Photo Library of the Civic Museums of History and Art, Trieste.

clear, and what the entries in Stanislaus's journal portend, is that from September 1907 the Jews of Trieste as a body and individual Jews as Jews attracted Joyce's observation for the duration of his time in the city. This is a time of rich fecundity in Joyce's political thinking, on which the contemporary sources are sparse. Joyce had been, from the outset in Ireland, scornful of the obsessionally and perversely Anglocentric axis of Irish nationalism, but had given little thought to a conception of Europe. As Joyce began to think in comparative terms of European nations, and of Europe, he became increasingly interested in the Jews. The situation of Trieste, torn between Austro-Hungary, Italy, and its Slavic hinterland to the east, forced Joyce to think beyond Irish nationalism about the system of continental states and empires. His consideration of a statal Europe set against a backdrop of confessional diversity and conflict from the early modern era is bound up with his finding of the Jews. The issue of the relationship of his discovery of the Jews of Trieste to

Joyce's Irish nationalism is hard to unravel, but it is clear that something more was involved than the inventing of Leopold Bloom as a central figure, a Jewish Dubliner who mediates Irish nationalism in *Ulysses*.

This is a complex sequence of movements rather than a unitary exilic shift. It is triadic: Ireland, Europe, and the Jews (shading on occasion into semi-orientalist Jew Greeks or Greek Jews). Joyce reconceptualises his relationship to Ireland from the perspective of exile; however, he would have had to reconceptualise that relationship even had he remained in Ireland, though remaining in Ireland would have left him with a highly constricted space within which to do so. His experience of Trieste pushed Joyce beyond a blurredly romantic radical conception of a Europe that was the aspirational locus of selective and fragmentary conceptions of French *laïcité* or Italian revolutionary syndicalism. Joyce's particular route to an affirmation and elaboration of the European identity he had asserted from the start was not unique; there were others in pre–World War Two Europe who followed a similar path to Joyce, in finding in the idea of Europe a means of overcoming the exorbitantly anti-modernistic or aberrantly anomalous politics or policies of the statal entities of which they were members. Joyce was nevertheless exceptionally early, and lucid, in this. His experience and intellectual formation made him a precursor of modern conceptions of a more integrated Europe, as much through the process by which he became (or in exile became again) a European as through the consummation of a willed telos of European belonging.

Joyce in exile in Trieste tests and validates his Irish nationalism through European pathways, so that his nationalism becomes part of his European birthright. In that *parcours* he encounters for the first time the Jews of Trieste. The Jews of continental Europe are an emblematic part of Joyce's Europeanisation of his relationship to Ireland in exile and are so rendered in *Ulysses*. There is a connection between Joyce's reconceptualisation of Ireland and the development of his interest in the Jews of Trieste that is more than a coincidence in time, and which animates *Ulysses*.

Yet Joyce's observation of the practices and thinking of observant members of the Triestine Jewish community was limited. His Triestine

Jewish friends were highly assimilated, and often irredentist. Livia Schmitz's father came from a Jewish family in Ferrara but had turned Catholic, unlike his cousin Felice Venezian, the leader of the Italian nationalist party in Trieste who kept his name and religious identity unchanged. Ettore Schmitz (Italo Svevo) was a non-observant Jew who had, after his marriage to the Catholic Livia in a civil marriage, agreed to convert to Catholicism and underwent a second marriage in the church of San Giacomo.[87] Schmitz had been in the 1890s, in the words of his biographer, 'a curious Schopenhauerian Socialist', the qualification reflecting Schmitz's sceptical pessimism.[88] His socialist leanings tempered his irridentist sympathies. To Schmitz was ascribed the remark, 'It isn't race that makes a Jew, it's life.'[89] While some doubt has been cast on whether Schmitz actually said this, it seems perfectly to convey his assessment of his own Jewishness, and something of his phlegmatic temperament. Stanislaus recalled an occasion where, because his brother was having eye trouble, he himself went out to Servola to give the English lesson to Schmitz. Schmitz asked him wryly, 'Tell me something about Irishmen—something intimate, something not generally known. You know your brother has been asking me so many questions about Jews that I want to get even with him.'[90] Richard Ellmann believed that the 'prototype' (as if there had to be one) for Leopold Bloom was 'almost certainly Ettore Schmitz, whose grandfather came from Hungary'.[91] This is overconfident, but it seems unquestionable that the character of Schmitz did contribute to the making of Bloom, while a sketch done by Joyce suggests that in his physical aspect, Bloom was modelled on Schmitz.

Joyce's relationship with Schmitz was unique, and each influenced the other's writing. It is at the same time representative of how Joyce's understanding of the Jews of Trieste was achieved principally through his relations with assimilated Jewish bourgeois whom he met primarily

87. Gatt-Rutter, *Italo Svevo*, 128, 138–44.

88. Gatt-Rutter, *Italo Svevo*, 117; Nadel, *Joyce and the Jews*, 205.

89. Nadel, *Joyce and the Jews*, 205; Gatt-Rutter, *Italo Svevo*, 342.

90. Stanislaus Joyce, 'The Meeting of Svevo and Joyce', in *Joyce nel giardino di Svevo*, 93.

91. Ellmann, *James Joyce*, 374.

FIGURE 17.2. James Joyce's sketch of Leopold Bloom, Paris, ca. 1923 (Wikimedia).

through his professional role as the prestigious teacher of English in Trieste that he became. To that has to be added what he gleaned from his scanning of Triestine newspapers, which is untraceable but certainly significant: he was, quite apart from his voracious appetite for newsprint, a contributor to *Il Piccolo della Sera*, and many of his Triestine friends had journalistic involvements.[92] Some of the Jews of Trieste he knew were observant, such as Moses Dlugacz. There is a fleeting glimpse of Joyce's engagement with the community of observant Jews, from an anonymous source which there is no particular reason to discount. Louis Hyman relayed to Richard Ellmann an interview he had conducted in Haifa with a woman who had been a former student of Joyce in Trieste and who did not wish to be named. She told Hyman, 'Joyce seemed to like the company of Jews and often frequented their parties at homes and the Hanukkah and Purim parties at the Zionist society of Trieste and danced once or twice upright as a rod in perfect rhythm.'[93]

92. Schmitz, for example, had been a regular contributor to the irridentist *L'Indipendente*, which came to be challenged by Teodoro Mayer's more populist *Il Piccolo della Sera*. Gatt-Rutter, *Italo Svevo*, 36, 54, 58–59.

93. Louis Hyman to Richard Ellmann, 3 December 1966 (University of Tulsa), quoted in Davison, '"Still an Idea"', 379–80.

'Jewgreek is Greekjew': Archetypes and Stereotypes

While Joyce's interest in Jews, Jewishness, and the political predicament of Jews in Europe derives from his life in Trieste, his thinking was informed by what he read before and after his Triestine exile. The discrimination with which he drew on what he read, and how he refined his conception of what he was writing against, reveals much about his fastidious political judgement and imaginative discernment.

It begins with Matthew Arnold, whom Joyce read in Dublin. Arnold's younger brother Thomas, a convert to Catholicism, taught English in University College, Dublin until his death in 1900.[94] Joyce was highly sceptical of Matthew Arnold's conception of Celticism, but Arnold is important for Joyce also in his promulgation of the highly influential idea of the conflict in British culture between the rigidity of Hebraism (by which Arnold meant Judeo-Christianity) and the spontaneity and crystalline purity of Hellenism, which he believed had to be reconciled. It was the idea of a contest between Judaism and Hellenism, rather than its fatuous elaboration by Arnold, that caught Joyce's attention. More important for Joyce was Friedrich Nietzsche, whose writings attracted considerable interest in Dublin.[95] Among Joyce's contemporaries, Thomas Michael Kettle was an admirer but ceased to be at the outbreak of the First World War. Joyce began to read Nietzsche from around 1903 while still in Dublin,[96] and Mr Duffy in 'A Painful Case', which Joyce wrote in Trieste in 1905, is a portrait of a thwarted and unreflective aspirant Nietzschean.[97] The Promethean will to power of the Greeks had been corrupted by Judeo-Christianity, originating weirdly enough in Nietzsche's argument of the 'slave mentality' of the Jews in their revolt against the Egyptians, in Nietzschean ressentiment, the merging of resentment against the ruler with the self-hatred engendered by subjugation. Nietzsche was, however, admiring of the 'resourcefulness in soul and intellect of our modern Jews', and his rendering of the

94. Patrick Maume, 'Thomas Arnold', *DIB* 1:164–66.

95. Davison, *James Joyce*, 112–13.

96. Ellmann, *James Joyce*, 42.

97. Manganiello, *Joyce's Politics*, 204.

Jews of modernity informed or was at least a stage in Joyce's own thinking and distantly contributed to the formation of Leopold Bloom, as Davison has convincingly argued.[98] While Joyce played endlessly with and subverted the idea of the polarity of Hellenism and Hebraism, Greek and Jew, it retained at least a superficial valency for him in his sense of contemporary ethnicities. While he was walking with his Jewish friend Ottocaro Weiss in Zurich, they met and conversed a long while with a Greek acquaintance. Joyce remarked afterwards, 'It's strange—you spoke like a Greek and he spoke like a Jew.'[99]

Joyce's reading on the Jews continued in a less abstract vein. The treatment by the then highly influential Guglielmo Ferrero in *L'Europa giovane* (1897) of the 'Messianic conscience' of the Jews, of which he cited Karl Marx as a modern exponent, had a significant if transient effect on Joyce when he read it in November 1906.[100] If this was in part because it helped him break free of the impasse of his espousal of Italian revolutionary syndicalism, it also prompted him to begin to conceptualise the intellectual role of the Jews in the modern era, starting with Cesare Lombroso, Ferrero's father-in-law.[101] He also discovered an affinity: Ferrero characterised German Jews such as Heinrich Heine and Karl Marx as 'esuli voluntari';[102] Joyce had the previous year described his situation to Stanislaus as that of 'a voluntary exile'.[103] Joyce read also an 1836 tract of Carlo Cattaneo, a Milanese liberal economist, which pointed to the effect the curtailment of the economic activities of Jews had in retarding the economic and cultural development of the countries which imposed them.[104]

Joyce's reading carried him further, into psychological works on real or supposed Jewish character traits. He acquired some familiarity with the works of Otto Weininger, though when and by what means is

98. Davison, *James Joyce*, 114–21.

99. Ellmann, *James Joyce*, 295.

100. Manganiello, *Joyce's Politics*, 52–57.

101. Joyce to Stanislaus Joyce, 13 November 1906, *Letters II* 190.

102. Manganiello, *Joyce's Politics*, 56.

103. Joyce to Stanislaus Joyce, 28 February 1905, *Letters II* 84.

104. Manganiello, *Joyce's Politics*, 54–55.

uncertain. Weininger (1880–1903) was a precocious philosopher who achieved fame after his suicide in the house in Vienna where Beethoven had died. He wrote that 'by Judaism I mean neither a race nor a people nor a recognised creed. I think of it as a tendency of the mind, as a psychological constitution which is possible for all mankind, but which has become actual in the most conspicuous fashion only amongst the Jews. Antisemitism itself will confirm my point of view.' This explained the fact that 'the bitterest Antisemites are to be found amongst the Jews themselves.'[105] This was an instance of the circularity in treatments of Jewish traits (not only among anti-Semites, which objectively Weininger, a Jewish convert, was) which Joyce seems to have come to find exasperating. Weininger believed that there were transitional states between male and female. More misogynistic than anti-Semitic, Weininger saw the Jew or the Jewish type (whatever that might have been) as sharing what were for him the negative attributes of the feminine. It seems likely that Weininger is a principal source for the idea of Bloom as 'a finished example of the new womanly man',[106] as Dr Punch Costello, in the 'Circe' episode of *Ulysses*, characterises him.[107] The 'Subject Notebook' now in the National Library of Ireland which Joyce began compiling in October 1917 establishes definitively that Joyce read Weininger—the notes relate to *Über die letzten Dinge*, a collection of aphorisms and essays published not long after Weininger's death—but suggests that at least by that stage Joyce's interest in Weininger's work ranged beyond his treatment of the Jews.[108]

Joyce owned in Trieste Maurice Fishberg's *The Jews: A Study of Race and Environment* (1911).[109] Fishberg, an American sociologist, noted

105. Otto Weininger, *Sex and Character* (London: William Heinemann, 1906), 310–11, quoted in part in Davison, *James Joyce*, 143.

106. *U* 15.1798–99.

107. Davison, *James Joyce*, 141–45. The proposition that the idea credited to Weininger of the 'self-hating Jew' influenced the creation of Bloom seems, however, far-fetched. Bloom did not hate himself—as a Jew or otherwise—nor did he hate anyone else.

108. Wim Van Mierlo, 'The Subject Notebook: A Nexus in the Composition History of *Ulysses*—a Preliminary Analysis', *Genetic Joyce Studies*, no. 7 (Spring 2007): 1–4, 33–40. Stephen's meditation on time and space in the first two paragraphs of 'Nestor'—'the ineluctable modality of the visible'—transpires to be a dialogue with Weininger.

109. Nadel, *Joyce and the Jews*, 49–51.

that there was no book in English treating of 'the race traits of the Jews. . . . It appears that the prevailing opinion is that the Jews, alleged to have maintained themselves in absolute racial purity for three or four thousand years, may prove hard to assimilate.' Fishberg's lengthy treatise is an essay on assimilation: 'The fact that the differences between Jews and Christians are not everywhere racial, due to anatomical or physiological peculiarities, but are solely the result of the social and political environment, explains our optimism as regards the ultimate obliteration of all distinctions between Jews and Christians in Europe and America.'[110] That was a bit too positivistic for Joyce, even if he agreed with the discounting of the idea of racial purity. Fishberg did discuss the supposed Jewish proclivity to suicide, concluding after somewhat exhaustive analysis that 'the rates of self-destruction among the Jews are not at all influenced by ethnic factors.'[111] In *Ulysses*, Bloom's father, Rudolph Bloom, formerly Rudolf Virag, a Hungarian Jewish immigrant, ends his own life in a hotel in Ennis. Ettore Schmitz died on 13 September 1928 from injuries sustained the previous day when the car in which he was a passenger slid off the bridge over the Livenza River outside Treviso and collided with a tree.[112] Awaiting further intelligence, Joyce relayed his 'bad news' to Harriet Shaw Weaver, to whom he avowed, 'Somehow in the case of Jews I always suspect suicide though there was no reason in his case especially since he came into fame, unless his health had taken a very bad turn.'[113]

It is futile to try to capture the range of Joyce's reading on the subject of the Jews. In Trieste, he purchased in the year of its publication and read at least in part Henry Wickham Steed's *The Habsburg Monarchy*, published in 1913.[114] Joyce was certainly aware of the author before making his purchase. Henry Wickham Steed (1872–1956) joined *The Times* in 1895 and was successively its correspondent in Berlin, Rome, and Vienna from 1902 to 1913. He was considered the pre-eminent English

110. Maurice Fishberg, *The Jews: A Study of Race and Environment* (London: Walter Scott, 1911), v, vii.

111. Fishberg, *Jews*, 350–55.

112. Gatt-Rutter, *Italo Svevo*, 356–58.

113. Joyce to H. S. Weaver, 30 September 1928, *Letters I* 268.

114. Gillespie, *Joyce's Trieste Library*, 222.

authority on the Austro-Hungarian Empire and was also an expert on Italian affairs. Suspicious of the intentions of Austria-Hungary (which banned his book) and Germany, he was correctly to predict the Austrian annexation of Bosnia-Herzegovina and the attack on Serbia, and was principally responsible for the editorial policy of *The Times* in the prelude to the First World War and was the paper's editor from 1919 to 1922.[115] His considerable expertise and astuteness were marred by a gross vein of anti-Semitism to which his *Habsburg Monarchy* amply attested. He was obsessed by the twin influences in Austria of 'Jesuitism and Clericalism' and of 'anti-Clerical Liberalism' in which he discerned, as in the press (which he characterised as 'almost entirely Jewish'), the preponderant influence of 'the "Liberal" Jew'. Jews were also behind '"Revolutionary" Socialism and Social Democracy'.[116] This was explicable by the 'distinguishing characteristic' of the Jew: 'This characteristic is superabundant intellectualism or power of abstract ratiocination. His faculty of concentration, his intense inner life, his freedom from the trammels of place and country, his practical rationalism and workaday purposefulness would fit him in a peculiar degree to rule a world organised on some intellectual, symmetrical plan.'[117] He proclaimed 'the superiority of the Sephardim type' over 'the degraded, bow-legged repulsive type often to be found among the Ashkenism', whose influx he considered to be at the root of anti-Semitism in the empire. He was sympathetic to and acutely prophetic on the subject of Zionism.[118] Steed provided a reminder to Joyce of English imperial anti-Semitism, and may have contributed something to the anti-Semitic sentiments expressed by the Irish Unionist Garrett Deasy in *Ulysses*: 'England is in the hands of the Jews. In all the highest places: her finance, her press. And they are the signs of a nation's decay.'[119]

115. A. P. Robbins, 'Henry Wickham Steed', In *The Dictionary of National Biography, Supplement 1951–60* (Oxford: Oxford University Press, 1971), 921–23; A.J.A. Morris, 'Henry Wickham Steed', *ODNB* 52:346–48.

116. Henry Wickham Steed, *The Habsburg Monarchy* (London: Constable, 1913), xxiv–xxv, 155.

117. Steed, *Habsburg Monarchy*, 157, 181–82.

118. Steed, *Habsburg Monarchy*, 147–49, 175–81.

119. *U* 2.344–47.

Joyce in Trieste also encountered members of the Greek minority which played a significant role in the city's mercantile economy. Baron Ambrogio di Stefano Ralli, whose great wealth derived from his family's trans-European insurance interests centred on Trieste, and Count Francesco Sordina, whose lineage was Corfiot and whose wealth also derived from insurance, were among his most illustrious students.[120] Joyce never studied ancient Greek, a fact of which he was faintly self-conscious, and which Oliver St John Gogarty overtly sought to exploit in their contest of wits. Joyce wrote to Harriet Shaw Weaver in mid-1921 in a carefully crafted confessional letter, 'I don't even know Greek though I am spoken of as erudite': 'I spoke or used to speak modern Greek not too badly (I speak four or five languages fluently enough) and have spent a great deal of time with Greeks of all kinds from noblemen down to onionsellers, chiefly the latter. I am superstitious about them. They bring me luck.'[121]

He was intrigued by the rites of the Greek Orthodox Church. He reported to Stanislaus in April 1905, 'The Greek mass is strange. The altar is not visible but at times the priest opens the gates and shows himself.' He concluded, 'Damn droll! The Greek priest has been taking a great eyeful out of me: Two haruspices.'[122] That informed his revision of his story 'The Sisters',[123] and Bloom's bemused perspective on the Catholic mass when he strays into St Andrew's Church (then All Hallows) in Westland Row: 'Queer the whole atmosphere', and 'more interesting if you understood what it was all about'.[124]

In Zurich in 1917 Joyce read Victor Bérard's *Les Phéniciens et l'Odyssée.* In Bérard's scholarly analysis, the *Odyssey* is an account by a Greek narrator of the journeying of a Phoenician merchant-adventurer; and the Phoenicians were a Semitic people. The importance of the discovery of Bérard for Joyce can scarcely be overstated. In his 1907 lecture 'Ireland: Island of Saints and Sages', Joyce had already asserted that the Irish

120. McCourt, *Years of Bloom*, 37–38.

121. Joyce to H. S. Weaver, 24 June 1921, *Letters II* 167.

122. Joyce to Stanislaus Joyce, 4 April 1905, *Letters II* 86–87.

123. McCourt, *Years of Bloom*, 58–59.

124. *U* 5.392–93, 423–24; McCourt, *Years of Bloom*, 60–62.

language had been identified by philologists with the ancient language of the Phoenicians, and that the Phoenicians had established a colony in Ireland 'which was in decline and had almost disappeared before the first Greek historian took up his quill'.[125] Joyce was drawing on the eccentric works of the English eighteenth-century antiquarian and military engineer Charles Vallencey, who lived in Ireland from the mid-eighteenth century and whose tendentious arguments on the Phoenician-Irish nexus were based largely on the Irish *Book of Invasions*.[126] With Bérard, he could now add a Phoenician-Jewish nexus to the *Odyssey*. Bérard was a means of achieving two purposes that were close to Joyce's heart: the imaginative reintegration of the world of the eastern Mediterranean, always for Joyce the originary site of Europe, and the connecting of Ireland to that world. Joyce in Zurich enthusiastically discussed the Greek-Hebrew cognates strewn through Bérard's work with Dr Isaiah Sonne, a rabbi.[127]

If Joyce's often-cited phrase 'Jewgreek is Greekjew' derives from Bérard, it brings together many of the themes of Joyce's life and work. The phrase occurs in the 'Circe' episode, as part of a parodic retort by Lynch's cap to some highfalutin and obscure utterances of the drunken Stephen: 'Woman's reason. Jewgreek is Greekjew. Extremes meet. Death is the highest form of life. Ba!'[128]

Bérard's work also assisted Joyce in escaping from what had become something of an impasse. He had read all he needed, or perhaps could take, on the subject of supposed Jewish racial traits (the common topic of much of the philo-semitic and anti-Semitic tracts of the era) and of disquisitions on the 'Jewish question' as then understood. He had not read so intensively on any contemporary political subject since his self-induction into the principles of Italian revolutionary syndicalism. He was moreover wary of exceptionalism. There is a trace in *Ulysses* of Joyce's sense of the exhaustion for his own fictional purposes of his reading, and of a certain weariness, in a passage in the 'Eumaeus' episode of

125. *OCPW* 110.

126. Tymoczko, *Irish Ulysses*, 25–41; Monica Nevin, 'Charles Vallencey', *DIB* 9:635–36.

127. Ellmann, *James Joyce*, 498; Nadel, *Joyce and the Jews*, 27.

128. *U* 15.2097–98.

consummate subtlety. Bloom is striving to impart to Stephen the standard Jewish and liberal historical arguments in relation to the economic contribution of the Jews in Europe that he assumes, probably correctly, are unknown to Stephen: Spain decayed with the expulsion of the Jews, and England flourished in the wake of the fostering of Jewish immigration by Oliver Cromwell, whom he characterises as 'an uncommonly able ruffian who in other respects has much to answer for'.[129] The condemnation 'in other respects' of Cromwell, an execrated figure in Ireland, is precautionary. It is made not to vaunt his own Irishness but for fear of offending Stephen, the possibility of whose ardent nationalism he is habituated by painful experience to allow for: he does not really know Stephen, whom he has only met that day. It is a perfect exemplification of the exigent prudence that Bloom as an Irish Jew had learned the necessity of observing. He strives also to avoid being heavy-handedly pedagogical. He adds that 'you know the standard works on the subject,'[130] which, if true, would render the argument he has just imparted altogether unnecessary. This is hardly a typical 'Bloomism'; the doubly jarring reference to 'the standard works on the subject' in such an elaborately literary novel is a sigh of authorial weariness of 'the standard works on the subject' that is carefully pitched to be only faintly audible. It shows Joyce's moving beyond 'the standard works' and political arguments to render imaginatively the position and predicament of the Jewish people in Europe and in Ireland. That strikingly attests to Joyce's innate sense of what could be achieved politically by his art that could not be attained by engaging directly in political or intellectual controversy.

By the time he read Victor Bérard in 1917, Joyce was turning to the writing of *Ulysses*. There was an asymmetry. He was left knowing a great deal about anti-Semitism as a prejudice and as a quasi-ideology, its inexhaustible tropes, and the political proclivities which engendered it. His acquired knowledge of Judaism and Jewish culture was imperfect, though much greater than that of most non-Jews. His deployment of

129. *U* 16.1119–25.

130. *U* 16.1126.

what he had read in the characterisation of Leopold Bloom was extraordinarily assured. Born in Ireland, severed from his father's past as a Jew in Hungary,[131] the assimilated Bloom was at once alive to his Jewishness and daily forced to negotiate or confront the suspicious or overtly hostile characterisation to which he was subject as a Jew in Ireland. Joyce's admiration for and sense of personal affinity with the Jews, born in Trieste and affirmed in Zurich, stayed with him.

131. See F. K. Stanzel, 'All Europe Contributed to the Making of Bloom: New Light on Leopold Bloom's Ancestors', *James Joyce Quarterly* 32, nos. 3 and 4 (Spring and Summer 1995): 619–30.

18

Passing into Silence

ON 28 JUNE 1914 Archduke Franz Ferdinand, the heir to the Habsburg throne, and his wife were assassinated in the Bosnian capital, Sarajevo. The bodies of the imperial couple were brought to Trieste, without eliciting any recorded comment from Joyce, and thence to Vienna.[1] While Italy was a member of the Triple Alliance with Austria and Germany, the level of Italian patriotic resentment of Austria as the occupier of Trento and Trieste made fighting alongside Austria out of the question. Italy remained neutral for the first nine months of the Great War before the politically incongruous advocates of intervention prevailed.[2]

In Trieste, males sympathetic to Italy found themselves enlisted in the Austrian army. More and more soldiers drawn from the Italian middle class planned to desert from the Austrian army, including Joyce's friend Dario de Tuoni, who visited Joyce on his Christmas leave. After initial German advances, the war in the west had become bogged down on the Marne and became a war of position. De Tuoni remembered Joyce's prescient words as they parted: 'Whoever has the last sack of flour will win the war.'[3]

It was only with the conclusion of the secret Treaty of London on 26 April 1915 that Italy's government, persuaded that the tide of war was imminently turning, and anxious not to be denied the spoils of a peace

1. McCourt, *Years of Bloom*, 241–43; Ellmann, *James Joyce*, 383.

2. Thompson, *White War*, 37.

3. De Tuoni, *Ricordo di Joyce*, 119–21.

settlement and covertly aspiring to control the eastern Adriatic coast and to become a power in the Balkans,[4] agreed to fight against Germany and Austria. In a heavily manipulated atmosphere of febrile patriotism in Rome that came close to being a parliamentary putsch, Italy declared war on 23 May 1915.[5] The consequences for liberal democracy in Italy were to be far-reaching. The great contemporary idealist philosopher and political figure Benedetto Croce, with whose writings Joyce seems to have declined to engage, though several of his students were ardent Croceans, astutely concluded that the gratuitous Italian intervention in the war was intended to displace the liberal order with 'a modern plutocracy, unencumbered with ideologies and scruples'.[6]

Though Joyce had convinced Tullio Silvestri in late 1914 that Italy would enter the war, the event seems to have taken him by surprise.[7] It provoked chaos and confusion in Trieste.[8] Joyce made his way with Giorgio to the British consulate, where he was told there was no reason for concern on the part of British subjects. He went on to the house of his friend Boris Furlan, who had a less sanguine view, which was affirmed as a pro-Austrian mob laid siege to the nearby Italian consulate.[9] For Joyce the most immediate impact of the war was financial. On 17 September he was suspended without pay from the Scuola Superiore di Commercio 'Revoltella', because approval from the Ministry of Public Instruction in Vienna had not come through. The office of the Trieste lieutenancy was well disposed. Prince Konrad von Hohenlohe, the lieutenant, whose wife and children were taught by Joyce, added to the

4. Thompson, *White War*, 4.

5. Smith, *Modern Italy*, 255–67. In an attempt to keep Italy in the Triple Alliance, Austria offered to cede Trieste. Smith, *Modern Italy*, 264.

6. Quoted in Thompson, *White War*, 36. Joyce's seeming indifference to Croce may have resulted quite arbitrarily from Croce being characterised as a liberal, which triggered Joyce's loathing of William Gladstone and hostility to English liberalism in general.

7. De Tuoni, *Ricordo di Joyce*, 119. Joyce's view may not have been constant over time as circumstances changed. According to Gatt-Rutter (*Italo Svevo*, 276), Joyce bet a case of wine against it with the bookseller Eugenio Borsati, and scrupulously repaid the wager when they were both back in Trieste in 1919. The source is unidentified.

8. Thompson, *White War*, 121–22.

9. Ellmann, *James Joyce*, 380.

recommendation of the chief education inspector the words, 'Joyce is known as a quiet young man who is worried only about making a living.' It was five months before Joyce was able to resume teaching, though the respite was to be of short duration. The loss of income was alleviated by his part-time position in the naval paint business of Ettore Schmitz's father-in-law, Gioacchino Veneziani, but the shortfall in salary meant he struggled once again to support his family in a city afflicted by food shortages and had to borrow money.

Hohenlohe's reference to Joyce's repute as that of a 'quiet young man' unfortunately did not apply to his brother. Stanislaus's convictions, which married fervent irredentism to anticlerical resistance to the Holy Roman Empire, remained unmuted after the outbreak of war. He thereby attracted the attention of the Austrian authorities; Stanislaus also wondered whether a tour with a friend of the fortifications of Trieste had not precipitated his arrest on 9 January 1915, before Italy's entry into the war. He was interned and passed the remainder of the war in Austrian detention centres.[10] It was a savage twist of fate. Stanislaus's political temperament was rigidly linear. His Irish nationalism had been tepid, largely in reaction to the cruelties of Irish society and the hegemonic role of the Catholic Church, in which he might be thought to have been ahead of his time. He favoured the Irish Parliamentary Party as the exponent of a residual moderate nationalism, and refused to subscribe to his brother's qualified identification with Sinn Féin. He found himself interned for the war's duration on account of his irredentism, a cause from which his brother had kept a sceptical distance. It was as if the harsh and implacable logic of fraternity was working itself out politically. Their easy if unequal relations in Dublin and Trieste were never quite restored.

When Italy did join the Allies, Joyce expressed himself sceptically: 'If the Italians think it will be a cakewalk to Vienna . . .'[11] The extended Joyce household, bereft of Stanislaus, strove to maintain a semblance of normality. On 12 May 1915 Joyce's sister Eileen married Frantisek

10. Ellmann, *James Joyce*, 380; McCourt, *Years of Bloom*, 249.

11. Ellmann, *James Joyce*, 383.

Schaurek, a bank official of Czech ethnicity, in the cathedral of San Giusto, with Joyce as the best man in an oversized dress suit borrowed for the occasion.[12] Within a fortnight Italy was at war. The irredentists now owed their allegiance to a country at war with Austria. Immediately on the declaration of war, pro-Austrian mobs burned down institutions identified with Italy, including the offices of *Il Piccolo*, along with Italian-owned shops; cafés favoured by the irridentists, such as the Café Polare, which Joyce liked, were devastated before the Austrian authorities tardily declared a state of siege on 29 May and restored order. Italian nationalists were rounded up, and public meetings banned.[13] On 16 June, what would become Bloomsday, Joyce wrote a postcard to Stanislaus in German reassuring him they were being well treated, but principally to announce that 'the first chapter of my new novel *Ulysses* is written'.[14]

Altogether, apart from the physical threat to his household presented by Trieste's sudden instability, Joyce's financial situation was untenable. The Scuola 'Revoltella' had closed, and Joyce's income from private lessons had dried up.[15] He had to get his family out of Trieste, and to borrow to fund the exodus. The departure involved first applying to the American consul Ralph C. Busser, who had charge of British interests. Encounters with diplomatic personnel never failed to excite Joyce's latent sense of the Hibernian grandeur of the Joyces. In Herbert Gorman's account, when the consul became nonplussed by Joyce's offhand responses, he informed Joyce that he was proud to act as the British consul, 'the representative of the King of England', and Joyce retorted, 'The British consul is not the representative of the King of England. He is an official paid by my father for the protection of my person.'[16] He had also to obtain permission to leave from the Austrian authorities, secured by the intercession of his 'Greek' protectors Baron Ralli and Count Sordina (to whom

12. Ellmann, *James Joyce*, 385.

13. Gatt-Rutter, *Italo Svevo*, 277–78.

14. Joyce to Stanislaus Joyce, 16 June 1915, *SL* 209.

15. Joyce to A. Llewelyn Roberts, secretary of the Royal Literary Fund, 30 July 1915, *Letters II* 356.

16. Gorman, *James Joyce*, 234; Ellmann, *James Joyce*, 385–86. See also Budgen, *Making of 'Ulysses'*, 202.

he paid homage in a footnote to Gorman's biography as 'one of the greatest swordsmen in Europe');[17] and by giving an undertaking that he would not participate in belligerent activity against the emperor.[18] The Joyces left Trieste for Zurich on 27 or 28 June 1915; the train was detained in Innsbruck, but it was only to allow the emperor's train to pass.[19]

Zurich during the First World War

Zurich in neutral Switzerland in the First World War was an extraordinary place, a city filled with a large influx of recent immigrants and refugees—Joyce's first biographer, Herbert Gorman, noted that the city's Bahnhofstrasse was nicknamed Balkanstrasse[20]—which included spies or imagined spies and the security services of the powers in diplomatic or consular guise watching them. The course of the war was an intense preoccupation of the immigrants of conflicting ethnic and ideological allegiances who now made up a significant part of its population, and a source of incessant concern to the *bürgerlich* natives of the Swiss city. Joyce's friend Frank Budgen observed that Switzerland is 'a small country with a long frontier and a long memory. At every point of the compass stands a powerful and dangerous neighbour. During the war all Swiss talked war strategy and politics, and in general all were pacifists.'[21] Joyce and his circle in Zurich were no exception in their discussions of the war and its politics.[22]

Joyce was not, as he is routinely characterised, a pacifist, but he was certainly opposed to the war from its inception as a transcontinental

17. Gorman, *James Joyce*, 229n1; Ellmann, *James Joyce*, 386. Joyce's abiding gratitude to Sordina and to Ralli, and to Ralph Busser, attests to just how fraught the departure from Trieste actually was, even if masked by Joyce's sangfroid. Ellmann, *James Joyce*, 385–86.

18. Ellmann, *James Joyce*, 386.

19. Ellmann, *James Joyce*, 386.

20. Gorman, *James Joyce*, 231.

21. Budgen, *Making of 'Ulysses'*, 32.

22. Georges Borach recalled of the evening gatherings in the Pfauen restaurant drinking Fendant wine, where Joyce would often read from the manuscript of *Ulysses*, that 'war news, art, and music' were discussed. Georges Borach, 'Conversations with James Joyce', in Potts, *Portraits of the Artist*, 67, 69.

manifestation of human folly, a view that was underscored by the inept opportunism that prompted Italy's belated entry into the war against its former allies in the Triple Alliance. In his exuberantly sardonic self-portrayal and rendering in *Finnegans Wake* of how he was or might be perceived, Shem the Penman, 'swobbing broguen eeriesh myth brock-endootsch', is a 'zurichschicken',[23] a chicken sitting out in Zurich both the European war and the Irish rebellion of 1916. The Irish and the British were preoccupied, aside from Gallipoli, with the war on the western front—the strategic semi-indifference of the Allies to the war on the Italian front was a matter of immense resentment to the Italians[24]—and Joyce had a mutually reinforcing double perspective on the cataclysm, from both the western and Italian fronts. He knew all about the western front, from the war-watching of his Zurich friends and from the Irish friends with whom he remained in contact. His by then semi-broken college contemporary Thomas Michael Kettle was slain in the assault on Ginchy in the Battle of the Somme in September 1916; the murder of Francis Sheehy-Skeffington on the margins of the 1916 rising in Dublin the previous April was attributable to the unbridled militarism unleashed by the Great War. Joyce and Kettle were both, if divergently, enlightened prophets of a European Ireland; that Kettle and his brother-in-law would lose their lives in a European war recast in a sombre light the undergraduate controversies and disagreements they and Joyce had in University College, though Joyce had always had a deeper intimation of political consequence than his slain peers.

The Italian front extended across the length of the Italian-Austrian border; but while the western end, Trent and the South Tyrol, heavily fortified by the Austrians, was notionally in play, the fighting was massively concentrated on the eastern front, along the Isonzo River, which ran between eastern Friuli and the Carso plateau above Trieste, the unredeemed city the taking of which would consummate the Italian risorgimento. The mountainous and barren limestone terrain of the Carso, which had been a place of excursion for Joyce like all the inhabitants of

23. *FW* 70.8.

24. Thompson, *White War*, 5.

Trieste, as a site of war was even more harshly unforgiving than the Flanders of the trenches as the Italians struggled uphill against fortified Austrian positions.[25] 'In Italy, the names Isonzo and Carso still resonate like the Somme, Passchendaele, Gallipoli or Stalingrad.'[26]

The Italian war, observed by Joyce from Zurich, followed its peculiarly atrocious course. The Italians sustained massive losses, and it was not until the sixth battle of the Isonzo that they took Gorizia, and the Austrians withdrew from the western Carso. Military discipline was enforced with unstinted ferocity by Luigi Cadorna, the Italian commander. Italian morale was shattered in the twelfth battle of the Isonzo, centred on the town of Caporetto in the northern Isonzo, where a well-planned Austro-German offensive commencing on 24 October 1917, in which the twenty-five-year-old Lieutenant Erwin Rommel distinguished himself, routed the Italians. The only mitigating consideration was the failure of the Austro-Germans to press their advantage. The new front was 150 kilometres west of the Isonzo, running in its southern sector along the river Piave.[27] There was a grim coda that revealed how the extent of militaristic hegemony, abetted by the civil power, had coarsened Italian life. Three hundred thousand Italian prisoners were taken during the twelfth battle, joining two hundred thousand already in Austrian camps. The Central Powers had declared early in the conflict that, due to the Allied blockade, they would no longer be responsible for feeding and clothing Allied prisoners. Britain and France subsidised food and aid to their imprisoned soldiers. The Italian government refused to do so, fearing it would incentivise defections, and this undeclared policy was bolstered by an atrocious propaganda campaign against prisoners of war, whom Gabriele D'Annunzio grotesquely characterised as 'sinners against the Fatherland, the Spirit and heaven'. One hundred thousand Italian prisoners died in captivity.[28] Italian martial honour after Caporetto was salved in part by the failure of the Austrian offensive ('the starvation offensive') on the Piave in June 1918; and by the final

25. Thompson, *White War*, 66–68, 108–9.

26. Thompson, *White War*, 5.

27. Thompson, *White War*, 296–327.

28. Thompson, *White War*, 324, 351–52.

drive eastwards of the Italians in October 1918, hastened by the imminence of an armistice, culminating in victory at Vittorio Veneto in the closing days of the war.[29]

On the evening of 31 October, the last Habsburg governor of Trieste received a cable from Vienna that announced the end of Austrian rule in the Adriatic. He left the next day as the Italian army began its general advance the length of the front.[30] On 3 November 1918 the destroyer *Audace* entered the bay of Trieste and was greeted by a roaring throng, which, as well as 'Viva l'Italia!', cried 'At last!'; among the crowd was a benignly quizzical Ettore Schmitz smoking the inevitable cigarette.[31] On board was General Carlo Petitti di Roreto, who would be the city's first Italian governor, and who declared, 'From today our dead are dead no longer!'[32] Trieste, viewed from Zurich, was ceasing to be the city Joyce had known. The catastrophic consequences of Italian participation in the war, whether measured in the slaughter of its soldiery on the Isonzo or in the undermining of Italian democracy and civil society, affirmed Joyce's deep hostility to the war and reinforced his marked disillusionment with contemporary Italy which had its proximate origins in his miserable Roman sojourn of 1906–7.

Throughout the war Joyce was working on *Ulysses*, the writing of which gathered pace in Zurich. His friends there were the first to become inured to his practice of writing rapid notes in the small notebook he carried in his waistcoat pocket when he read or heard a comment, phrase, or word that he might use.[33] In his conversations on the subject of his work, he asserted the unchallengeable greatness of the *Odyssey* and his admiration for Odysseus, which suggest how much his sense of the character of Odysseus was sharpened by the contemporary European war. Odysseus became for Joyce a salvific presence in a time of continental military cataclysm.

29. Thompson, *White War*, 342–47, 355–61.

30. Thompson, *White War*, 362.

31. Gatt-Rutter, *Italo Svevo*, 290 (see plate 15).

32. Thompson, *White War*, 366.

33. Budgen, *Making of 'Ulysses'*, 176–77; Gorman, *James Joyce*, 238.

Georges Borach, a Zurich businessman who had been an English-language student of Joyce and became a close friend, recalled a conversation with Joyce in August 1917 which he seems to have noted down. Joyce said that 'the most beautiful, all-embracing theme is that of the *Odyssey*', eclipsing in greatness and humanity even the Shakespeare of *Hamlet* and Dante ('Dante tires one quickly; it is as if one were to look at the sun'):

> Why was I always returning to this theme? Now *al mezzo del' camin* I find the subject of Odysseus the most human in world literature. Odysseus didn't want to go off to Troy; he knew that the official reason for the war, the dissemination of the culture of Hellas, was only a pretext for the Greek merchants, who were seeking new markets. When the recruiting officers arrived, he happened to be plowing. He pretended to be mad. Thereupon they place his little two-year-old son in the furrow. In front of the child he halts the plow. Observe the beauty of the motifs: the only man in Hellas who is against the war, and the father. Before Troy the heroes shed their lifeblood in vain. They wish to end the siege. Odysseus opposes the idea. The stratagem of the wooden horse. After Troy there is no further talk of Achilles, Menelaus, Agamemnon. Only one man is not done with; his heroic career has hardly begun: Odysseus. Then the motif of wandering.[34]

Through his assessment of the character of Odysseus, Joyce's attitude to the Great War can be discerned. Joyce had conceived the idea of a novel based on the *Odyssey* in Rome long before the Great War, but the war at once affirmed and deepened his conception of the character of Odysseus/Ulysses. The Great War served to underscore the humanity and shrewd intelligence of Odysseus, opposed to the Trojan War but whose intervention was decisive once he was compelled to enlist, after which he embarked on the 'wandering' that took him back at last to his island home of Ithaca.

To his friend Frank Budgen, Joyce also vaunted the merits of the 'all-round' character of Odysseus, on their second meeting, in the summer of

34. Borach, 'Conversations with James Joyce', 70 (1 August 1917), in Potts, *Portraits of the Artist*, 70.

1918. 'Hamlet is a human being, but he is a son only. Ulysses is son to Laertes, but he is father to Telemachus, husband to Penelope, lover of Calypso, companion in arm of the Greek warriors around Troy and King of Ithaca.' He was at the outset 'a war-dodger': 'But once at the war the conscientious objector became a *jusqu'au boutiste*', the contemporary French term for an advocate of war to the very end. 'When the others wanted to abandon the siege he insisted on staying till Troy should fall.' Joyce was closing the vast expanse of time that separated the Trojan from the Great War: 'He was an inventor too. The tank is his creation. Wooden horse or iron box—it doesn't matter. They are both shells containing armed warriors.'[35]

Joyce's *Ulysses* is set in 1904, ten years before the outbreak of the Great War, and Joyce was fastidious in avoiding anachronism, but his conception of Odysseus, whose role the mild Leopold Bloom assumes in the loose Homeric structuring of the novel,

> . . . my Ulysses born anew
> In Dublin as an Irish jew . . . [36]

is honed in the Great War. If Zurich was a haven of neutrality, the war remained the constant preoccupation of its inhabitants. It affected even Joyce's meagre teaching. To the Blitznakoff sisters, to whom he taught English, he riffed on the word 'battlefield': 'A battlefield is a field where the battle is raging. When the battle is over and the field is covered in blood it is no longer a *battlefield*, but a *bloodfield*.'[37]

Out of Obscurity

By the time Joyce had left Trieste for Zurich, the transformation of his authorial fortunes had already begun. The intervention of Ezra Pound, the driving arbitrageur of literary modernism, was decisive in this. On 15 December 1913 Pound had introduced himself to Joyce by a letter which began, 'Mr. Yeats has been speaking to me of your writing', in

35. Budgen, *Making of 'Ulysses'*, 15–18; Ellmann, *James Joyce*, 426–27.
36. *PSW* 118; Ellmann, *James Joyce*, 416.
37. Ellmann, *James Joyce*, 397.

which he canvassed the possibility of publishing Joyce's work in a number of literary magazines with which he was 'informally connected', principally the *Egoist*.[38] The following month Grant Richards agreed at last to publish *Dubliners*; it was published in June 1914. The *Egoist* began the serial publication of *A Portrait of the Artist as a Young Man* on 2 February 1914, Joyce's thirty-second birthday, and it ran interruptedly until 1 September 1915. Through the *Egoist* connection, Harriet Shaw Weaver, discerning and steadfast, in scrupled revolt against a puritanical English upbringing, and one of the remarkable women who made possible the publication of Joyce's work, came into his life, corresponding with him from October 1914.[39]

As if to emphasise the uncertainties of exile, he wrote on the day of his arrival in Zurich to Weaver, 'I stopped here as it is the first big city after the frontier. I do not [know] where I shall live in Switzerland. Possibly here.'[40] If he was not enamoured of the topography of Zurich with its girding mountains, he did not take up the suggestion of H. G. Wells and Ford Maddox Ford, relayed by Pound, that he move to England.[41] The election to continue living in continental Europe was in part a political choice that was informed also by the exilic status that was even by that stage an integral part of his mythos as a writer.

In the manner of the modernist avant-garde, Joyce's image as a writer began to crystallise in advance of any wide publication of his work. His repute or infamy as an author ran far ahead of the reading of his work. It was an inversion of sequence that proved of long duration. Joyce, possessed through all his travails of a steely confidence in his own art, was strikingly unaffected by his gathering celebrity, but was conscious that it bore on the reception and readership of his past work and on the novel he was writing, a subject on which he was meticulously parsimonious. Pound played a critical role, not merely in facilitating the publication of Joyce's work but in informing how his works were to be read. In promoting Joyce's work, Pound set out to claim Joyce for literary

38. Ezra Pound to Joyce, 15 December 1913, *Letters II* 326.

39. Joyce to Harriet Shaw Weaver, 11 November 1914, *Letters I* 75.

40. Joyce to Harriet Shaw Weaver, 30 June 1915, *Letters I* 82.

41. Ellmann, *James Joyce*, 390.

modernism as he conceived it, which entailed the proposition that Joyce transcended any form of national allegiance or relationship to contemporary Irish politics. Joyce's exilic status merged with and was emblematic of his modernism.

In his earliest salvo, on *Dubliners*, Pound wrote in the *Egoist* in July 1914, 'It is surprising that Mr. Joyce is Irish. One is so tired of the Irish or "Celtic" imagination (or "phantasy" as I think they now call it) flopping about. Mr. Joyce does not flop about. He defines. He is not an institution for the promotion of Irish peasant industries. He accepts an international standard of prose and lives up to it.'[42]

In February 1915, when Joyce was still in Trieste, Pound published in the influential *New Age* an article of brilliant tendentiousness entitled 'The Non-existence of Ireland'. Pound provocatively declared, 'I have seen no adequate proofs of the continued existence of Ireland.' Pound's Ireland was the construct of contemporary writers. He was advancing an argument that challenged Yeats and went further than Joyce had ever gone. The repudiation of Synge was pivotal: 'When Ireland turned against Synge's genius it [Ireland] ceased, quite simply to exist. . . . A nation's claim to a man depends not upon the locality of his birth, but upon their ability to receive him.' He continued, 'Coming down to the present, I can find only one man calling himself Irish who is in any sense part of the decade. I refer to the exile James Joyce. Synge fled to Paris, driven out presumably by the local stupidity. Joyce has fled to Trieste and into the modern world. And in the calm of that foreign city he has written books about Ireland.' Praising the 'hardness and gauntness' of Joyce's writing, Pound wrote that 'he writes as a European, not as a provincial.'[43] Pound's influence on how Joyce was understood was considerable, not least in negating the political content of his work—and was to be of long duration.

The impact was in some ways paradoxical: if Pound's analysis was concerned to identify what was distinctive in Joyce's writing, it had a

42. Ezra Pound, '*Dubliners* and Mr. James Joyce', *Egoist*, 15 July 1914, 267, reprinted in *Pound/Joyce*, ed. Forrest Read (London: Faber and Faber, 1965), 28–29.

43. Ezra Pound, 'The Non-existence of Ireland', *New Age*, 25 February 1915, 451–55. The reprinting of the article in Read, *Pound/Joyce* (32–33), is truncated and omits some of what is here quoted.

significant and somewhat petrifying effect on how the author was understood biographically, co-equating Joyce with the Stephen of *A Portrait* even as the character of a somewhat older Stephen was being developed by Joyce in *Ulysses*. Joyce's departure from Ireland in 1904, a gesture of defiance but one that was informed by contingency, had become an authorial *acquis*. That might be considered a triumphant vindication of Joyce's stratagem of exile, as in one aspect it certainly was, but it was not quite right, entailing as it did a simplification of Joyce's relationship to the Ireland he had left. Pound was certainly not alone, given the proximity of the belated publication of *A Portrait* to *Ulysses*, but he set the tone. Joyce's exilic status, and an over-harshly drawn rendering of his adversarial relationship to the Ireland in which he had lived, was heavily imbricated in the reception of his work. It was a phenomenon on which Joyce was to play with rich humour in his self-characterisation as Shem the Penman in *Finnegans Wake*. If that might seem to be, apart from *Stephen Hero*, his only true self-portrait, Shem the Penman transpires to be an autobiographically inflected portrait of his authorial image.

Ezra Pound's intervention was decisive not only in procuring the publication of Joyce's writing but in defining, with other modernist commentators, how it was to be received. Fortified by his own idiosyncratic modernistic prejudices, he realised that Joyce could not be permitted to be defined by his subject matter as an Irish author if his work was to have an international reception. Pound's impact was to carry over into a second phase, in the aftermath of the Second World War, where Joyce could be hailed as exemplary as a modernist writer who had risen sternly above the politics of his own ethnicity.

The ground for the reception of *A Portrait* was well furrowed in advance of the publication of the novel by Huebsch in December 1916, followed by the English edition by Harriet Shaw Weaver's Egoist Press in February 1917.

Joyce in Zurich

Joyce arrived in Zurich on 30 June 1915. The recent advance in his avant-garde fame did not provide him with an income. He continued to undertake teaching assignments. Yeats and Pound sought to put Joyce's finances on a sounder footing at least in the short term by seeking to procure through Edmund Gosse a grant from the Royal Literary Fund, which, while a private endowment, sought to live up to its name.[44] Gosse pointed out that Joyce had not affirmed allegiance to the Allied cause (neither had Yeats). Yeats parried this elliptically by saying that, 'as I have never known Joyce to agree with his neighbours', he had in Austrian Trieste 'probably made his sympathies as frank as you could wish': 'He has never had anything to do with Irish politics, extreme or otherwise, and I think disliked politics. He always seemed to me to have only literary and philosophic sympathies. To such men the Irish atmosphere brings isolation, not anti-English feeling.'[45] Joyce was awarded a grant of seventy-five pounds payable over nine months.

Joyce gathered a circle of largely expatriate friends, Italians and Austrians (many of them Jewish, some from Trieste) and Greeks.[46] He frequented the cafés of the city, including the Odeon, which was a favourite venue of Vladimir Lenin.[47] Joyce's circle finally centred on the Pfauen restaurant as the venue of the night, with Joyce seated 'before a carafe of Fendant de Sion, that pale greenish-amber wine which he called *Erzherzogin*, the Archduchess, and talking dryly of art and letters.'[48] He walked, up the Uitliberg and Zürichberg flanking the valley of the Limmat, and beside the lake at Küsnacht.[49] He enjoyed the city's rich cultural life, its opera concerts and theatre.[50]

In a city that was marked by a high level of espionage by the warring powers, and indiscriminate international political gossip, Joyce maintained, as a transient resident with his family, a level of alertness and was

44. Ellmann, *James Joyce*, 390–92.

45. Yeats to Edmund Gosse, 28 August 1915, in *Letters of W. B. Yeats*, 596.

46. Budgen, *Making of 'Ulysses'*, 173–75.

47. Gorman, *James Joyce*, 240; Ellmann, *James Joyce*, 409. One is reminded more of Joyce and Arthur Griffith coinciding in the National Library in Dublin than of brilliant Stoppardesque fantasias, of casual proximities in the public or commercial spaces of European cities.

48. Gorman, *James Joyce*, 233; Budgen, *Making of 'Ulysses'*, 171–73. Ellmann repeats the anecdote that a friend compared the pale greenish colour of the wine to urine, and Joyce agreed but insisted that it was 'di un'archiduchessa' (Ellmann, *James Joyce*, 455), presumably because of the delicacy of the flavour.

49. Ellmann, *James Joyce*, 394.

50. Ellmann, *James Joyce*, 393, 411–12.

FIGURE 18.1. Joyce with guitar in Zurich, 1915. *Source*: 2.13, James Joyce Collection, The Poetry Collection of the University Libraries, University at Buffalo, The State University of New York.

conscious of the commitment he had made to the Austro-Hungarian authorities that had secured his departure from Trieste. The ambience fell well short of the oppressive. It did not inhibit Joyce from engaging in his only quasi-political involvement in Zurich, as a translator from the end of 1915 for the short-lived *International Review*. This was the journal, published in English and German, of the humanitarian Viennese professor Siegmund Feilbogen. One of its pacific aims was to establish that atrocity stories on both sides were without foundations, a ludicrously benign view to which it is scarcely likely that Joyce subscribed. The German authorities permitted the review to circulate, but the English and American deemed it enemy propaganda, so that it ceased publication in 1916. Joyce remained friendly with Feilbogen, and with the Viennese poet Felix Beran, who was also associated with the review.[51] One of the

51. Ellmann, *James Joyce*, 397–98. Joyce told Budgen that the only poem of the war that interested him was by Felix Beran, which Joyce translated as 'Lament for the Yeoman'. Budgen, *Making of 'Ulysses'*, 12–13; Ellmann, *James Joyce*, 431–32.

notes sent by Joyce to inform Budgen's 1934 *James Joyce and the Making of 'Ulysses'* contained the observation, '*Sigmund Feilbogen*: Ear trumpet which he oriented and occidented night and day to catch rumours of peace anywhere at any hour'.[52]

The most sustained statement of Joyce's attitude to the war is in 'Dooleysprudence', six verses of admirable doggerel he wrote in 1916, inspired by the character Martin Dooley, who was created by the Chicago writer Finley Peter Dunne, syndicated in sketches published across the United States, and celebrated in a 1901 song by Billy Jerome. Joyce's appropriation of Dunne's figure is introduced in the opening lines, which reflect Joyce's scorn for the propaganda of the contesting powers:

Who is the man who when all the gallant nations run to war
Goes Home to have his dinner by the very first cablecar
And as he eats his cantaloup contorts himself in mirth,
To read the blatant bulletins of the rulers of the earth?

The penultimate stanza runs,

Who is the tranquil gentleman who won't salute the State
Or serve Nabuchodonosor or proletariat.
But thinks that every son of man has quite enough to do
To paddle down the stream of life his personal canoe?
It's Mr Dooley,
Mr Dooley,
The wisest wight our country ever knew
'Poor Europe ambles
Like sheep to shambles'
Sighs Mr Dooley-ooley-ooley-oo.[53]

The pre-chorus part of the final stanza goes,

52. Budgen, *Making of 'Ulysses'*, xiv–xv, 29.

53. *CW* 246–48; *PSW* 120–22; Ellmann, *James Joyce*, 424–25. Nothing is known of the contextual setting of 'Dooleysprudence', which exists in a typed copy in the Slocum collection of the Yale University Library (*CW* 246n1).

Who is the sunny sceptic who fights shy of Noah's arks
When they are made in Germany by Engels and by Marx
But when the social deluge comes and rain begins to pour
Takes off his coat and trousers and prepares to swim ashore.[54]

The reference to the proletariat as against the Babylonian king Nebuchadnezzar—semi-Italianised presumably in reference to Verdi's 1842 opera *Nabucco*, which includes 'Va, pensiero', the chorus of the Hebrew slaves which became the great Italian patriotic anthem of protest against the Austrian occupation—is striking. It is reinforced by arks 'made in Germany by Engels and by Marx'. This could conceivably encompass a reference to the German submarine and U-boat campaign, if one that does not quite come off.

While 'Dooleysprudence' is a casual piece, it is important in capturing the shift towards a bleak realism in Joyce's political thinking that the war brought about. The efforts of the socialist parties of Europe to prevent the war had been unavailing, largely because the German Social Democrats had voted to approve the grant of war credits to the government,[55] and they went their separate ways. Joyce was repudiating a strain of left-wing analysis of the war, which he seems to have associated with the German left, that continued to vaunt transnational working-class solidarity as something vital and capable of ending the war. To Joyce, this seemed absurd in the face of the overwhelming fact of the war, and he discerned in it an innate ideological authoritarianism of which he was as scornful as he was of the propagandistic bellicosity of the governments of the states participating in the conflict. The war had cracked the world apart, and Joyce was charting the rift that had opened between his own thinking and that of Marxists or *bien-pensant* progressives in lost conversations in the cafés and restaurants of Zurich before the Russian Revolution.

Joyce met Frank Budgen, who worked in the commercial department of the British consulate, in Zurich almost every day from mid-1918: 'On one subject he [Joyce] is more uncommunicative than any man I know:

54. The final stanza appears only in *PSW* 122.

55. Catherine Merridale, *Lenin on the Train* (London: Allen Lane, 2017), 81.

the subject of politics. . . . An occasional reference to the pacific American anarchist, Tucker, was the only indication I ever heard of a political outlook.'[56]

The Easter Rising broke out in Dublin on 24 April 1916. The rebels held out until 29 April, and the leaders of the insurrection were executed in early May. The full political significance of the Rising was not immediately apparent, and Joyce was dependent on what he could glean from the newspapers. Sheehy-Skeffington was shot on the orders of a commanding officer later found to be insane. Among the executed leaders of the Rising, Joyce had fleetingly been taught Irish by Patrick Pearse; knew a good deal about James Connolly as an Irish socialist leader and had likely heard him speak; and at least knew of Thomas MacDonagh as a writer. He came to know more from his Dublin friends: James Stephens, to whom he was close in Paris, was in Dublin through the Rising and wrote immediately one of its principal narratives, *The Insurrection in Dublin*. There is no record of Joyce's response to the Rising. Herbert Gorman divagates into Joyce's general attitude to Irish independence. Asked whether he did not look forward to Irish independence, Joyce was said to have retorted, 'So I might declare myself its first enemy?' Gorman was, however, quick to qualify this: 'There is reason to believe, however, that Joyce was convinced from the first that the cause of Irish independence would be eventually won. But he was very guarded in expressing his opinion except to his intimate friends.'[57] Asked by Gorman whether he would die for Ireland, he said, anticipating the response of Stephen Dedalus in *Ulysses*, 'I say . . . let Ireland die for me.'[58] The Rising was to shift the direction of Irish politics and became for ardent nationalists a culmination of heroic nationalist martyrdom and a foundational myth of Irish independence. The Rising and its cult rapidly became indistinguishable, and it was a cult to which Joyce was never likely to be sympathetic. The Rising would scarcely feature in the sweep

56. Budgen, *Making of 'Ulysses'*, 9–13, 353, 191–92.

57. Gorman, *James Joyce*, 234; Ellmann, *James Joyce*, 399.

58. Ellmann, *James Joyce*, 399. In 'Circe' in *Ulysses*, Stephen says, 'Let my country die for me' (*U* 15.4474).

of Joyce's modelling of the history of modern Ireland from Parnell to the establishment of Irish statehood in *Finnegans Wake*.

If anything in Joyce's life in Zurich seemed almost frivolously remote from the agon of Irish politics, it was his involvement with the English Players, which he and Claud Sykes started,[59] but even that was marked by sharply escalating tensions between the non-aligned Irish writer and the British consular representation, to whom he later referred as 'the English foulplayers'.[60] Joyce instituted two sets of proceedings in a feud with Henry Carr, who had played Algernon Moncrieff in Wilde's play *The Importance of Being Earnest*.[61] A. Percy Bennett, the British Consul General in Zurich, wrote in July 1918 asking Joyce to enlist. Joyce was incensed and deemed Bennett's letter a suborning of the pledge he had given on leaving Trieste not to take part in belligerent activity against the emperor. According to Sykes, Joyce was seized with anti-British fury: he praised the German offensive, changed his daily newspaper from the pro-Allied *Neue Zürcher Zeitung* to the pro-German *Zürcher Post*. He also (it would seem for the first time) expressed his pleasure at British setbacks in Ireland.[62]

The fog of espionage, actual and suspected, clouded the air of Zurich, and touched Joyce. His role as an intermediary between a Triestine pupil and his fiancée caught the attention of the Austrian authorities. The Trieste police report concluded that while none of the three were 'members of any subversive societies, Joyce was politically suspect although he never expressed his views openly.'[63]

Joyce's financial position in Zurich was considerably improved from mid-1917 by payments made through the medium of English solicitors on behalf of an anonymous benefactor, who revealed her identity three years later.[64] As a determinedly principled rebel against the values of the

59. Ellmann, *James Joyce*, 423.

60. Joyce to Frank Budgen, 3 January 1920, *SL* 245. If, as Budgen believed it to be, his involvement with the Players was conceived as a vaguely friendly gesture towards the English, which is doubtful, that can only have accentuated its souring. Budgen, *Making of 'Ulysses'*, 35, 200, 346.

61. Ellmann, *James Joyce*, 423–28, 440–52, 455–57.

62. Ellmann, *James Joyce*, 440–41.

63. McCourt, *Years of Bloom*, 248–49.

64. Ellmann, *James Joyce*, 413, 481.

wealthy Church of England family she was born into in Cheshire, Harriet Shaw Weaver turned to the promotion of literary modernism (principally Joyce), feminism, and communism. She had been editor of the *Egoist* since 1916 when it published portions of *A Portrait*. Later, the Egoist Press published the English edition of the novel.[65] She was to be a stalwart support to Joyce for the rest of his life. Joyce also received payments from the more inconstant Mrs Harold McCormick, née Edith Rockefeller, in 1918–19.[66]

Joyce lingered in Zurich for almost a year after the armistice, arriving back in Trieste on 16 October 1919. It was an altered city, its fragile equilibrium shattered by the collapse of the Austro-Hungarian Empire and the Italian occupation. The fate of Venezia-Gulia remained undetermined until the end of 1920, and the Slovene population of Trieste lived in the hope that Trieste and the surrounding region would be ceded to Yugoslavia.[67] In an atmosphere of gathering ethnic tension and industrial unrest, a Fascio di Combattimento was formed in Trieste in April 1919, while confederates of the Bolsheviks ousted the reformist leadership of the Trieste Socialist Party. Antonio Mosconi, the Italian civil commissioner, aligned himself with the Italian nationalists and Fascists. The right was enthused by the seizure in September 1919 of Fiume led by Gabriele D'Annunzio, of whose work Joyce had been a fervent admirer, turned rabid and violent Italian ultra-nationalist.[68] In July 1920, a fortnight before Joyce left, a Fascist rabble burned down the Balkan Hotel, the chief meeting place of Slav nationalists, and rampaged through the city destroying Slav premises.[69] Joyce had returned to a city that was a cockpit of the emergent Italian fascism, in which the immediate aftermath of the Great War was marked by ethnic violence.

65. Jane Lidderdale and Mary Nicholson, *Dear Miss Weaver* (London: Faber and Faber, 1970), 23, 108–31.

66. Ellmann, *James Joyce*, 442, 461.

67. Rusinow, *Italy's Austrian Heritage*, 92.

68. Asked in 1936 what he thought about D'Annunzio, he responded, 'Magnificent'; Ole Vinding, 'James Joyce in Copenhagen', in Potts, *Portraits of the Artist*, 149. He told David Fleischman in 1938, 'I believe the three great writers of the nineteenth century who had the greatest natural talents were D'Annunzio, Kipling, and Tolstoy—it's strange that all three had semi-fanatic ideas about religion or about patriotism'. Ellmann, *James Joyce*, 661.

69. Gatt-Rutter, *Italo Svevo*, 294–97.

Living conditions in Trieste were grim, accentuated by galloping inflation and food shortages. In the aftermath of the war, everyone seemed to find those from whom they had been separated strangely altered. Stanislaus had written in May complaining that Joyce would not let them know whether he intended to come back, and of having paid the rent on Joyce's apartment for eight years: 'I have just emerged from four years of hunger and squalor. . . . Do you think you can give me a rest?'[70] He was not enthused by the eventual arrival of his brother, not least because it involved accommodating him and his family in an already crowded apartment in which the Schaurek marriage was quietly falling apart. His relations with Joyce were not the same over the eight months of his brother's return, and were never fully restored.[71]

Joyce still seemed to cling to the idea of living in Trieste and tried to pick up the threads of his former life in the city. He resumed his position at the Scuola Superiore di Commercio 'Revoltella', about to become the Università di Trieste. Some of his old friends were gone and, desperate to have someone with whom to discuss *Ulysses*—'Not a soul to talk to about Bloom'[72]—he even tried to lure his friend from his Zurich days Frank Budgen to Trieste.[73] There were weekly evenings in Alessandro Francini Bruni's apartment. Silvio Benco recalled, 'Many times during that last year in Trieste he offered to take me with him to one of those old inns in the Città Vecchia which he loved so much, to spend the evening chatting, smoking and drinking—as indeed poets and philosophers have always enjoyed doing.'[74]

Finally, the sense that his time in Trieste had come to its term was borne in on him. Once again, the decisive intervention was from Ezra Pound, who in May 1920 proposed that Joyce visit him in Sirmione on Lake Garda. A train collision down the line prevented Joyce's first departure. He immediately despatched to Pound an exquisitely honed letter of oblique supplication, devised to prompt altruistic action as if by

70. Stanislaus Joyce to Joyce, 25 May 1919, *Letters II* 442–43.

71. Ellmann, *James Joyce*, 470–71, 482.

72. Joyce to Frank Budgen, 3 January 1920, *Letters I* 134.

73. Ellmann, *James Joyce*, 473–76.

74. Silvio Benco, 'Joyce in Trieste', in Potts, *Portraits of the Artist*, 57–58.

auto-suggestion on the part of its recipient: 'Without saying anything about this city (*de mortuis nil nisi bonum*), my own position for the past seven months has been very unpleasant.' He was confined in a flat with eleven (on Ellmann's calculation, eight) other people, which inhibited the completion of *Ulysses*. He proposed to pass three months in Ireland to write 'Circe'. He claimed, 'The disturbed state of Ireland is of course a reason for not going. There may be others. But I could not go to an English seaside town as it would be too dear.'[75] When Joyce got to Sirmione on 8 June 1920, meeting Pound for the first time, they agreed that Joyce would go to Paris for a few days, preceded by Pound. While he wrote to his aunt Josephine Murray that he was leaving Trieste but 'must remain a week or so between Paris and London',[76] one suspects that Paris was the destination on which he had settled some time previously and contrived patiently to attain. Joyce arrived with his family in Paris, where he would live for twenty years, on 8 July 1920.

Passing into Silence

In the famous exchange towards the end of *A Portrait*, just before the book briefly assumes the format of diary entries, Stephen, pressed by Cranly on his absence of belief, retorts, 'I will tell you what I will do and what I will not do. I will not serve that in which I no longer believe whether you call it home, my fatherland or my church: and I will try to express myself in some mode of life or art as freely as I can and as a wholly as I can, using for my defence the only arms I allow myself to use, silence, exile and cunning.'[77] The interrelationship of the terms of this triad, if not their individual signification, was fluid across Joyce's life.

Joyce never directly elaborated on 'silence' or the reasons for it, consistent, it might be said, with the idea of silence. Passing into silence is aligned with the development of the character of Stephen Dedalus in *A Portrait*, which Joyce wrote in 1907–14. Dedalus was of course a figure

75. Joyce to Ezra Pound, 5 June 1920, *SL* 252–55; Ellmann, *James Joyce*, 477–78.
76. Joyce to Josephine Murray, 17 June 1920, *Letters II* 471–72.
77. *P* 5.2574–80.

in a novel, but the autobiographical resonance is clear. It could be said that Joyce had been an adept of silence from much earlier and that his extra-authorial silence, which may have been contingent and gradual, is not susceptible to precise dating. His veiled Parnellism in University College, while plainly not the same as the silence into which he later passed, was an exercise in political reticence. The period in which he did not practise some form of silence, in his specialised sense of the term, is the relatively short interlude between 1902 and 1912, relating principally to his journalism for the *Daily Express* in Dublin and *Il Piccolo della Sera* in Trieste; but the deployment of the term in *A Portrait* does broadly coincide in time with Joyce's adoption of a more severe concept of silence, and the beginnings of a codification of a principle of authorial extra-textual silence.

It is hard to sustain the idea that Joyce's resort to silence was merely an election to devote himself to his fictional writing. It was a choice that was politically consequential and owed something to his alertness to future contingencies, authorial and political. His last Irish political article in *Il Piccolo della Sera*, 'L'ombra di Parnell', was published in May 1912. All his journalism predated his final departure from Dublin on 11 September 1912 after the projected publication of *Dubliners* by Maunsel had aborted. The non-publication of *Dubliners* closed out what had been the fluidity and open-endedness of Joyce's first phase of exile. The end date of Joyce's journalism might have been extended from 1912 to 1914 when he proposed the publication of his articles in book form to Angelo Fortunato Formiggini were it not for the fact that, remarkably, he did not propose to add anything to bring the collection up to date.

We do not know precisely why he wrote no more articles, but he ceased contributing articles as Irish politics changed phase. The Home Rule crisis that followed the introduction by the Liberal government in April 1912 of the Government of Ireland Bill continued to escalate: on 28 September ('Ulster Day') Unionists in the north-east of Ireland signed en masse a Solemn League and Covenant to resist Home Rule. Joyce could not write of Irish affairs with the same confidence as he had from 1904. Intellectually scrupulous, he was not disposed to comment on that which he could not observe and with which he could no longer claim an immediate familiarity. His journalism, conceived initially as a means of asserting and maintaining his closeness to Ireland, came to formalise his distancing. The journalistic nexus was spent. The Great War would shatter the paradigm of the politics of Home Rule after Parnell that Joyce understood intimately. By the time of the 1916 Rising, Joyce was in Zurich.

He strenuously maintained the position of silence in post-war Europe. Thereafter he did not allow himself to be drawn on the issue of politics and seems even privately to have observed a degree of political reticence, even if that reticence had an exasperated communicativeness of its own. As time went on, he found additional grounds to warrant his practice of silence. He did not give interviews or render autobiographical accounts of his life. He was concerned to safeguard the reception of *Ulysses* from distractions created by expressions of his political opinions. His Dublin journalism, and his journalism and lectures in Trieste, remained almost entirely unknown in his lifetime.

The onset of silence directly affects what can be established about Joyce's political thinking. For the period 1904–12, Joyce's correspondence with Stanislaus—frustratingly only Joyce's side of the correspondence survives—is politically rich for the year before Stanislaus arrived in Trieste, and for Joyce's period in Rome. His thinking can also be gauged by his Triestine journalism and lectures. For the rest of his life on the European continent, the sources are a good deal thinner. One is left to piece together occasional political comments in his correspondence with what contemporaries recalled of his conversation, and with other odd sources such as Joyce's observations on Herbert Gorman's biography, and to correlate these to his work.

Joyce and Irish Independence

A silence enshrouds Joyce's response to the Easter Rising in Dublin in 1916. Apart from contemporary newspaper reports, Joyce would have heard more of it in time from his friends James Stephens, whose *Insurrection in Dublin*, published immediately after the Rising, is an important commentary on the event, and Constantine Curran, as well as others.

Joyce was in Paris from July 1920. The month in Ireland was marked by serious rioting in Belfast and Catholics were expelled from the shipyards and engineering works. It was from Paris that Joyce, preoccupied with the completion of *Ulysses*, read the newspaper reports of the escalating course of the War of Independence. A truce was signed on 9 July, and negotiations for a settlement opened on 11 October 1921. The Anglo-Irish Treaty was signed on 6 December 1921. The next day a crowded gathering elaborately choreographed by Joyce took place in Sylvia Beach's bookshop, Shakespeare and Company, on the Rue de l'Odéon where extracts from the novel were read in English and French. The eminent French critic Valéry Larbaud made the famous utterance that with the novel that was about to appear, 'Ireland is making a sensational re-entrance into European high literature.'[78]

Larbaud did not expressly refer to the Treaty, but later said his lecture was delivered in that context. The making of the connection was almost certainly at Joyce's insistence. As he finished the writing of *Ulysses* and devised the publicity to attend its publication, Joyce was not avidly following the daily course of events in Ireland, but he both seized on and was caught off guard by the unanticipated synchrony of the Treaty with a long-planned event to promote the forthcoming publication of *Ulysses*.

Larbaud said, 'As an Irishman, James Joyce has not, in actual fact, taken sides in the conflict which, from 1914 to recent times, has pitted Ireland against England. He does not serve any party, and it is possible that his books do not please anyone and that he is equally repudiated by the Nationalists and Unionists.'[79] Such a temporally limited statement raised more questions than it professed to answer. It fell far short of the ascription to Joyce of political neutrality that it was taken to mean, as it came to cast a long shadow on how his relationship to Ireland and Irish nationalism was understood internationally.

What Joyce wanted to convey through Larbaud was that he was not a *patriotic* writer. On the eve of the triumph of the publication of *Ulysses*, he prompted Larbaud to renew the attacks he had made on the Irish

78. Valéry Larbaud, 'James Joyce', *Nouvelle Revue Française* 103 (April 1922): 385–409.

79. Larbaud, 'James Joyce', 388.

Literary Revival when in University College: '[Joyce] does not cut a figure as a militant patriot, and has nothing in common with those writers of the Risorgimento [e.g., the Irish Literary Revival] who were, above all, the servants of a cause and who presented themselves as citizens of an oppressed nation for which they demand independence, and for which they asked the aid of patriots and revolutionaries of all countries. . . . In short he does not plead.'[80] That almost certainly came from Joyce. It was ungenerous: the discontinuity with the Irish literary renaissance, whatever about nineteenth-century Irish patriotic literature, was overstated to the point of travesty. The point Joyce was making was that he had broken with any conventional notion of patriotic writing, that what he wrote about Ireland was unbidden and unbiddable. 'He does not plead' is a perfect characterisation of Joyce's treatment of the Irish political in all that he wrote, and aptly recalled Parnell, for whom pleading was not in his nature.

Larbaud added that 'it should be mentioned that in writing *Dubliners*, *A Portrait of the Artist* and *Ulysses*, he did as much as all the heroes of Irish nationalism in gaining the respect of intellectuals from all countries towards Ireland'.[81] That is probably not a direct paraphrase of what Joyce said to Larbaud, but it perfectly captures the political ambitiousness of his writing in its Irish aspect. His writing subsisted in parallel to the pursuit of Irish independence, the achievement of which adventitiously coincided with the publication of his novel, but in Larbaud's address signalled something deeper than temporal coincidence.

What Larbaud declaimed encapsulates Joyce's contestatory, quasi-competitive relationship to the Irish political as it was conventionally understood. It was Larbaud, or Joyce-Larbaud, who identified the relationship of objective rivalry between Joyce and Irish politicians as well as more complaisant writers and intellectuals in Ireland. For what were they rivals? One could say they were rivals for the occupancy of a terrain of political imagination, but they were also rivals for the possession of a defined historical and cultural heritage. In that contest it could not

80. Larbaud, 'James Joyce', 388–89.

81. Larbaud, 'James Joyce', 389.

seriously be argued that Joyce was politically neutral on Irish nationalism or Irish independence (which Larbaud's carefully crafted formulation fell short of asserting).

Joyce held aloof from the Irish Free State and remained, as he had been born, a citizen of the United Kingdom. There is little to substantiate Richard Ellmann's assertion that he was 'briefly exhilarated at the foundation of the Irish Free State.'[82] His response to the establishment of the new state was a reprise of his old game of refusing to avow himself a nationalist. Over strenuous objections from Joyce, Nora decided to return to Ireland so that their children could see their grandparents, and set off on 1 April 1922. The Irish Republican Army (IRA) in Galway had split into pro- and anti-Treaty factions. Pro-Treaty forces entered the Caseys' boarding house on Nun's Island, where Nora and her teenage children were staying, to fire at the anti-Treaty IRA combatants, who had taken up position in a store across the street. Nora and her children got the train out of Galway for Dublin the next day. The train left under protection of the Free State army. The IRA were in occupation of the Renmore Barracks half a mile up the line and fired on the train. Nora and Lucia were terrified.[83] Joyce in Paris was outraged. While his concern for the safety of his wife and children was understandable, there was a disproportionateness and irascibility to his response, as if he took the shooting from the Renmore barracks as an affront to himself. When Nora in 1935 thought of returning to Galway to see her mother, Joyce wrote to Weaver, 'The last time, however, that she went there she left that blissful isle lying on the floor of a railway carriage with her two children (and mine) while the natives were firing at one another through the carriage windows.'[84] The violence of the Civil War became unreasoningly another justification for his holding aloof from the new state.

Joyce had reason to object to the politics of the new state. The conservative Catholic-nationalist values of post-Parnellite Ireland that he had strenuously contested all his life were largely maintained in

82. Ellmann, *James Joyce*, 533.

83. O'Laoi, *Nora Barnacle Joyce*, 98–112; Ellmann, *James Joyce*, 533–35.

84. Joyce to Harriet Shaw Weaver, 7 April 1935, *Letters I* 362.

independent Ireland, especially in the spheres of censorship and sexual morality, overlain with a thin sheen of Irish language revivalism. The socially hegemonic role of the Catholic Church was unchallenged. The continuities with the values of anti-Parnellite Ireland were symbolised by the appointment of T. M. Healy, Parnell's leading adversary in the Split, as the first Governor-General. There was a harshness to the Irish Free State that reflected the straitened circumstances of its birth, and the weight of the undertaking of building the institutions of the new state. Yet Joyce did not make these his grounds of objection. He refused to be drawn on the reasons why he declined to endorse or identify himself with the new state, standing on the established fact of his long absence from Ireland, and leaving his writing to speak for itself. That was consistent with his principle of silence, and the logic of exile he had wrought. This was not an evasion: what he had to say about the independent Irish state, which was considerable, he would say in *Finnegans Wake*.

Ulysses was of course set within the rigid temporal confines of 1904. With *Finnegans Wake*, which he began writing in 1923, Joyce consummated the conception of his oeuvre as coextensive with Irish statehood. It was to consume his creative energies until its publication in 1939. The first extract from his 'Work in Progress' (he carefully withheld the proposed title) was published in the *Transatlantic Review* in April 1924, and further instalments followed, principally from 1927 in *transition* in Paris. The response of reviewers and critics was comprehensively negative, if constrained by a certain deference towards the author of *Ulysses*. Even some of those close to Joyce, such as Weaver, could not conceal their misgivings. He added to the novel the sentence, 'You'll have loss of fame from Wimmegame's fake'.[85] Beset by woes, principally relating to his eyesight, for which he had repeated treatment, and the deteriorating psychiatric condition of Lucia, and not free from financial anxieties in spite of the success of *Ulysses*, Joyce persevered, sustained by Nora, who became his wife in 1931, and by a tight circle of friends.

85. *FW* 375.16–17.

Joyce's Political Outlook in the 1920s and 1930s

While the sources on Joyce's politics are thinner than for earlier periods, the contours of his political outlook in the last two decades of his life are reasonably clear. One has to distinguish his contemporary political outlook from his politics in the broader sense, which—beyond what traces remain of his contemporary opinions—are rendered in *Ulysses* and *Finnegans Wake*. Joyce's suspicion of political institutions, governments, and parties grew during and after the Great War. That ran counter to the direction of European left-wing thinking, with its emphasis on the party or the movement, and rendered Joyce's thinking suspect to doctrinaire Marxists. Broader schools of progressive politics in the 1930s expected affirmative pronouncements from writers which Joyce withheld.[86] His objection to teleological thinking, which saw politics in terms of predestined ends, always present in his treatment of Irish nationalism, was maintained if it was not deepened in his treatment of continental and universal politics and history.

Joyce wrote *Finnegans Wake* in the fraught interval of two world wars. The outfall of the Great War had extended long after the armistice of November 1918. The rise of fascism and Nazism posed the threat of another war. Benito Mussolini came to power in Italy in 1922, Adolf Hitler in Germany in 1933, and Francisco Franco prevailed in the Spanish Civil War in 1936. That provided the miserable political backdrop against which *Finnegans Wake* was written. Joyce abhorred fascism, and especially despised anti-Semitism. He saw fascism and Nazism as recrudescences of viciously ethnocentric nationalisms, of bellicosity and barbarism, and thus as part of an ancient human cycle to which he responded not quite fatalistically but with a degree of weariness. He did not quite grasp their grotesque novelty and modernity. That assessment was widely shared in the generation who had lived through the Great War. It might be added that the full bureaucratic fury of the Holocaust was not unleashed in Joyce's lifetime. The Lake Wannsee conference of senior Nazi officials to

86. Most famously, in 1937 Joyce declined to fill out a questionnaire on his views on the Spanish Civil War, objecting that 'politics are getting into everything'. Ellmann, *James Joyce*, 704.

give effect to the 'final solution' of the extermination of the Jewish people took place a year after Joyce's death. Nonetheless, Hitler had scarcely veiled his genocidal purpose, so that Joyce's reductive cyclicism, attuned to the war-weariness of his generation, reflects a degree of ideological deafness uncharacteristic of him. It does not invalidate the historical rhythm of *Finnegans Wake*, but it does prescribe the limits of the cyclical interpretation of human history which it advanced.

Finnegans Wake is a richly, in some ways an extravagantly, Irish text. Its title says as much. As well as invoking the ballad of that name—Tim Finnegan was not dead, and so returns to life at his own wake—the absence of an apostrophe permits it to convey that Finnegans (the Irish) are awake, or may awaken, making a connection to Irish independence. It is a work of multiple aspects, in one of which it is the book of Ireland and Irish independence, taking in a rich sweep of Irish mythology, literature, history, and politics. It is an Irish story or intersecting set of stories which relate to an Irish family. It is mostly written in English, with a particularly Irish quality about it. It is as densely intricate and challenging to most Irish readers as to readers who are not Irish nor steeped in Irish history and culture. Its complexity has a levelling effect between the Irish and non-Irish reader which itself subverts the idea that it is to be read as a work pertaining to Ireland alone.

Finnegans Wake is not—at any level—a merely Irish work. The interweaving of the Irish and the European is one of the imaginative feats of the *Wake* and is not susceptible to being unstitched. It is a summa, a vast integrative work which encompasses Joyce's cultural experience, his observations and his thinking, and his reading across the course of a life passed cumulatively far longer in Trieste, Zurich, and Paris than in Dublin, and fertile with cross-references to other histories, cultures, religions, and mythologies. Joyce's treatment of human beings in communities and states and his exuberant exploration of foundational national narratives are enfolded within an Irish story. He adamantly refused to explain or justify—any more than to instrumentalise—the *Wake*'s Irish narrative. He was not prepared to explain extra-textually that it aspired to being a universal work that had an Irish frame. He left the work to speak for itself. His strategy of silence had many aspects.

If there is a single piece of writing by Joyce in which the origins of the *Wake* are discernible, however distantly, it is his 1907 lecture in Trieste 'L'Irlanda: Isola dei santi e dei savi'.[87] There he began his shift from the confining idea of primitive Irish backwardness he had held when he left Ireland towards a reconceptualisation of the relationship of Ireland to continental Europe: Ireland, subjugated and politically formless but without the rigidities of statal institutions and a culture of state. Ireland still had a long-rehearsed claim to statehood, an island in the Atlantic with an ancient culture, which, while part of Europe, was in a significant degree bypassed by what were and are considered the constitutive movements of modern history and culture; an insular fragment of Europe that stood at a certain angle to the European mainland. That gave his lecture its point of vantage, but it also adumbrated what became one of the governing concepts of *Finnegans Wake*. Ireland and Europe stood in relation to each other as if presenting a mirror to the other so that they could observe what they had in common and their disparities; with a faint degree of Irish malice, Britain politically was treated primarily as a subset of its relationship to Ireland rather than as an integral part of Joyce's imagining of Europe.

Much of course had changed from Joyce's lecture in Trieste by the time he wrote *Finnegans Wake*. A world war had taken place, and a second was imminent. Ireland was an independent state. However distant Joyce held himself from the new state, Irish independence framed the *Wake*'s treatment of the Irish past and sustained the great Wakean theme of rebirth and renewal. Joyce had continued to read vastly in that long interval, much of it non-fictional, refining an imaginative framework of human society in history that could not find full expression within the tight formal constraints of *Ulysses* but would irradiate *Finnegans Wake*. Some of his reading was of and around his preferred thinkers, Giordano Bruno, Nicholas of Cusa, and Giambattista Vico,[88] all heterodox, and in their diverse ways on the cusp of the modern, each of whom in one way or another challenged conventional ideas of intellectual cause and

87. *OCPW* 108–26. Patrick Healy has made this point to me.

88. See Verene, *James Joyce*.

effect and of sequentiality. They are present in the *Wake* but are also emblematic of Joyce's wider reading of non-fiction.

The Political Vision of *Finnegans Wake*

It is certainly incautious to venture a paraphrase of what Joyce is saying about human society in political time in *Finnegans Wake*, but it is hard to avoid doing so in a work concerned with his politics. He is saying that men and women, in the cycle of the year and of the generations, find themselves existentially compelled—doomed—to hope. This is a compulsion integral to the human condition. It is not that there is philosophically any reason to hope, nor is there much empirical ground for doing so, given the experience of history. It is uncertain whether in Joyce's view humans are impelled to hope individually and pre-socially, in what was once called a state of nature, but it becomes a defining feature of their coming together in society, sanctified in religious rite and secular ceremony. In Joyce's conception, hope is pre-eminently a socio-political phenomenon, rather than an anterior spiritual state or disposition. The course of human society is marked by great resurgences of hope. These originated in politics, or in what was deemed successful propitiation of the gods, in the negotiation of internal or exogenous shocks or challenges. They acquired over time a cyclical pattern and were ritualised in secular heroic myths and ceremonials or in religious belief and practice (which is why Joyce was acutely Easter observant, drawn in whatever city he found himself to attend ceremonies irrespective of Christian denomination, ceremonies he correlated to non-Christian rites of spring). That is the godless but not god-proscribing theology of *Finnegans Wake*. Intellectually what deprived it of unrelieved bleakness was that Joyce did not exclude the possibility that religious or socio-political tradition properly apprehended could have a restraining effect on the descent into barbarous violence (which, on the positive side, he also saw as politico-social rather than an intrinsic human attribute). In Joyce's bleak social anthropology of hope, the potential for human consciousness to translate into political agency, if not altogether promising, endured. Through that, Joyce's own philosophical affinities with anarchism and early socialist sympathies survive into the *Wake*. What is more important is that what is philosophically the dispassionate austerity of Joyce's conception of communal hope is ceaselessly countered by the ebullience and tendresse of his prose, reflecting his belief in the potency of language as an active principle.

He disdained to take fascism seriously as a political philosophy. It is for that reason that his political critique has to be taken as primarily directed to the contemporary left. Socialism and communism have a dual significance in the political cosmogony of the *Wake*. On the one hand, they bore out Joyce's idea of the human proclivity to hope. On the other, he was increasingly disenchanted with their institutional manifestations, but his true quarrel was to do with what he saw as the false instrumentalisation of hope in the idea that progress was predestined. This lay at the heart of Joyce's dissent from the mainstream of contemporary socialism. It was not an indifference to or dismissal of the possibility of political advance and socio-economic progress, but a refusal to accept the premise that they were ineluctably fore-ordained, that the telos of human advancement was pre-inscribed in human history. That premise was, for Joyce, philosophically false and historically ignorant. This was not a mere intellectual quarrel: a misconception of that magnitude in human society was actively dangerous, part of the havoc that human folly and philosophical error could wreak. It was not the reasoning of someone who was or had become apolitical.

This stance was closely associated with Joyce's treatment of human community. If he shared to the full Aristotle's idea that people are political creatures, he developed it in unexpected directions, and had a profound and original intimation of its darker corollaries. Joyce's idea of political community is disruptively ambivalent. It is in his sense of why the individual member has to dread the constituting of human community that Joyce's affinity with anarchism is most pronounced. Political society, if it draws the human person to it, is also an object of profound dread. Just as political leaders apprehend scandal, members of human communities live in the fear of the intrusion of the suspicion of others and communal denunciation. That fear in Joyce's rendering is pre-statal, but capable of enlisting savage intrusions of statal authority.

All the figures in the *Wake* experience deep societal fears. In response to suspicions that are never fully articulated, they wonder anxiously what in their lives might be deployed against them to render them objects of obloquy, persecution, and exclusion. The dread of accusation intersects with the private sense of shame which for Joyce is close to a secularised conception of the idea of original sin. The standing persecutory horde of the *Wake* is never far away. The sense of prospective guilt is social, engendered by the real or apprehended deviation from whatever is deemed to be the communal purpose. What renders that sense menacingly ubiquitous is the almost lunatic volatility of what, at any given moment, a human society may consider the communal purpose to encompass. This is the nightmare of the *Wake*'s dreamworld.

Joyce thus has a semi-philosophical conception of human community (rather than of the state) that is fleshed out in history and in contemporary politics. If the narrative frame of the *Wake* is Irish, the subject of the *Wake* is European and indeed universal. Joyce did not conceive the *Wake* as a work in response to the rise of fascism, not least because he was sceptical of the idea that fascist movements and governments were novel phenomena, but it encompasses his response to fascism and Nazism. It is discernibly a work by a European modernist written in the ever-darkening shadow of the crisis of European society and civilisation in the 1920s and 1930s. It would be difficult to maintain that the heightened persecutory matrix of the *Wake*—even as nightmare—was conceived exclusively as an emanation of Irish historical experience.

Reconceiving the Political

Joyce was a highly political writer in a way that sets him apart from other modernist writers. His conception as a writer of what politics began to alter as he passed into silence from about 1912. *A Portrait* is a text of the transition. His sense of politics ceases to be defined by the preoccupations that had marked his life in Dublin and in early exile, though a good deal of the old passionate anger flares when he is addressing Irish political subjects. It is markedly more abstract, reflected in a shift towards a philosophical historicity and an approximation to comparative anthropology.

It is no longer concerned with programmatic expressions of politics but with the relationship of politics to the modern, how men and women informed and were touched by the political, how they came imaginatively to conceive their relationship to the history and culture of the statal communities in which they were born or found themselves. He recognised that how they did so was definitionally modern; it is a disjuncture in Joyce that he refused to see fascism and Nazism as distinctively modern phenomena. Yet Joyce's authorial reconception of politics is not renunciatory of his own antecedent politics. His concept of politics withdraws to a certain distance but retains a filiation to his own anterior convictions.

Joyce realised that the modern, itself a product of history, was not merely the contemporary. He recognised that through the fractures of the modern, the rubble of myth and of the human past, individual and collective, imperfectly apprehended, obtruded. The modern was the negotiation of fragmentation; and of transitory states, of that which was not quite finished and that which had not quite begun. It was not something Joyce deplored. He spontaneously accepted it as a defining aspect of the modern, which he sought to translate into an active principle in his writing.

Joyce defies conventional political characterisation, but one can attempt to situate him by reference to contemporary political affiliations. A liberal he certainly was not. The role of W. E. Gladstone, the commanding figure in late nineteenth-century Liberalism in Britain in the overthrow of Parnell, seemed to Joyce emblematic of something coldly calculating in Liberalism; its identification with the 'nonconformist conscience' left him ill disposed to British Liberalism, but he was in any event unsympathetic to the economic ideas that informed liberalism. Republicanism, which mitigated the individualism of liberal political thinking, came much closer to attracting Joyce's sympathy. He had admired the French republican idea of *laïcité* and lived with apparent political contentment in the France of the closing phase of the Third Republic. One nevertheless wonders whether republicanism as a political philosophy was not finally too severely statal, too exclusivist in its political mythology, to hold Joyce's allegiance. He had not maintained the early ardour of his identification with socialism and was alienated from its institutional manifestations. An elusive philosophical sympathy with anarchism endured, but it is hard to identify its impact on his political thinking.

Joyce's sympathy with Irish nationalism is vested in the particularities of Ireland rather than ideological, but it did render him more disposed to measure politics on a human scale and more sceptical of ideology. He had a political affinity with the strain of liberal romantic nationalism that was perhaps the dominant force in bringing about the 1848 revolutions in Europe, even if he was semi-hostile to its frail Irish manifestation in the Young Ireland of Thomas Davis. Liberal romantic nationalism connected Joyce at least to nineteenth-century contemporary history while permitting him to transcend the contesting claims of economic ideologies. Intellectually hostile to the rigidities of determinism and of historical periodisation, Joyce's politics in its final manifestation in the *Wake* maintained a rapport with the fluvial properties of the novel.

Joyce was one of the two major Irish modernist writers who dwelt most intensely on his relationship to the political, and on the intersection of the imaginative and the political, the other being W. B. Yeats. Joyce's life and work had two phases: the politically exercised Joyce of Dublin and early exile, and the politically distanced author of *Ulysses* and *Finnegans Wake*, both of which kept conspicuously alive the earlier Joyce/Daedalus/Dedalus. The later Joyce, in reconceiving his idea of the political, taken with his observance of the precept of silence, did not retreat from politics into a realm of monastic passivity. Political values—most obviously (but by no means only) a loathing of intellectual intolerance, religious or secular fanaticism, and political violence—were inscribed in *Ulysses* and *Finnegans Wake*. It is a corollary of the line Joyce insistently inscribed between the creative writer and active political engagement that neither work is reducible to the tracts in favour of tolerance, the celebration of human diversity and the renunciation of illicit political force which they have traditionally been commended for being. Politically they are vastly more ambitious. Both works render civic and statal processes and dialogue and draw the reader into the modernistic exercise of reconceptualising across time and space her or his relationship to the society and universe to which they belong.

Even if silence was a negative concept, it came to be something close to an active principle in Joyce's writing and thought. It certainly came to touch on the live controversies of the 1930s as many of the succeeding generation of writers and intellectuals became politically engaged. Joyce held out against what he knew to be the risk of being misconstrued as indifferent to or passive in the face of the rise of fascism and Nazism in Europe. That was not Joyce's position, but he was sceptical of thinking defined by its response to a single phenomenon, even one as momentous as the advent to power of Mussolini and Hitler. It was an argument for dispassionate clarity even in the shadow of the European dictatorships and the drift to a world war.

Joyce's precept of authorial silence was not anti-political. It was predicated on the existence of a parallel sphere of politics. From his time in Ireland, he was fastidiously averse to the confusion of categories and domains. If he never ceased to believe literature could inflect politics, he had become highly sceptical about direct interventions of writers in the political domain. At a personal level, what after all would be achieved by his making or subscribing to statements condemning fascism in Europe? This was something he had thought about long before the advent of European totalitarianism. He had in his strangely proleptic manner scorned in 1902 William Rooney's 'blaspheming against tyrants'.[89]

Joyce Now

This work is conceived as a contribution to a project proposed in 1991 by Ira Nadel, to provide 'a proper contextual life of Joyce, one that recognises that he lived during one of the most unsettling periods of European history, from agitation by the Irish Land League to the rise of Hitler. Such a biography would alter Joyce's pose of indifference to political and social changes around him, whether it was the socialist actions in Rome in 1907, the fascists in Trieste in 1920, or the Nazis in Paris in 1939.'[90]

89. *OCPW* 62.

90. Ira B. Nadel, 'The Incomplete Joyce', *Joyce Studies Annual* 2 (1991): 98.

The benignity of time towards Joyce's politics, obliquely rendered in his works, and his treatment of the political, is not adventitious. The first sentence of the introduction to Ellmann's biography is, famously, 'We are still learning to be James Joyce's contemporaries, to understand our interpreter.'[91] But how did Joyce contrive to make himself our contemporary? The feat is all the more remarkable when one considers that Ellmann's sentence was written sixty years ago. It is still not quite clear how, but Joyce strategised the relationship of the modernist writer to time: historico-political time rather than Marcel Proust's *temps perdu*. There is something astonishing—and exhilarating—in the idea that the work of an author preoccupied with the theme of renewal can still, eighty years after his death, catch the light of contemporary politics and shimmer.

His political judgement—and the encompassing span of his writing continued to require the constant exercise of political judgement—reflects the intelligence and intellectual discipline of his Irish-inflected rendering of historical processes. His disregard of the inessential, and gift for stripping out the contingent and ephemeral, his search for the rhythm of events, was honed across his exile from Irish beginnings.

In Ireland he is now hailed as an emblematic figure, the prophet of the Irish modern. Beyond Ireland his rendering of the political has since his death outlasted many of the once prevalent schools of thought to which he declined to attorn. Joyce's choice of what he opposed or resisted in the sphere of politics was strategic, and his strategic judgement in what was an uncharted field was of an exceptionally high order. The post-war hegemony of liberal democratic values casts a skein of celebratory complacency over how Joyce was read. As that hegemony is threatened, and the skein rent, we read Joyce anew, in political circumstances that are closer to those in which he was writing than we might wish. That renewal seems somehow pre-inscribed in Joyce's oeuvre.

Our current disenchantments, and the vogue in what was once conceived as a unitary West for aggressive nationalism and populist notions of ethnic exclusivity and the exaltation of false homogeneities, give

91. Ellmann, *James Joyce*, 3.

Joyce's ethically rigorous and unsparingly mordant democratic nationalism a contemporary relevance. He is without sanctimoniousness, and his humour defies the rigidities of ideology and the censoriousness of political correctness. The questions his work poses, and to which without foreclosure it offers tentative responses, are still our questions. Something abides of the distanced humaneness that pivots between joy, hilarity, and sardonic bleakness. Joyce has somehow weathered political time across the treacherously shifting course of the twentieth and twenty-first centuries. His strategically chosen 'ground of vantage' has not been yielded up. With this work I have intended to address how that was achieved by a writer who stayed aloof from the practice of politics and did not profess an aptitude for the political.

Coda

IT IS JUST BEFORE DAYBREAK, in the fourth and final part of *Finnegans Wake*. The coming of the dawn is attended by heightened expectations, of peace, of reconciliation and rebirth, and of a new Irish state. History and legend are astir.

The words proclaiming the dawn are given to Pu Nuseht ('the Sunup' backwards), as if an emanation of the Egyptian Book of the Dead, but another voice has broken through or the speaker has acquired a new character. In its directness of utterance, in the first person, it is as if it stands outside the dream that is the *Wake*: 'But hunt me the journeyon, iteritinerant, the kal his course, amid the semitary of Somnionia. Even unto Heliotropolis, the castellated, the enchanting.'[1]

Just before Anna Livia commences her final journey to the sea, James Joyce is making his last great tribute to Charles Stewart Parnell. Joyce, when he wrote of him, liked to emulate the spare clarity of Parnell's speech. In 'but hunt me the journeyon', he is rendering with searing conciseness Parnell's terrible last year, in which the once unassailable Irish leader plied a doomed course between England (Brighton, where he lived with Katharine O'Shea, and Westminster) and Ireland, where he rallied his forces in Dublin, fought three by-elections which he lost, and campaigned at the weekend in far-flung parts of the country, hunted at every step. His principal persecutor was Timothy Michael Healy, who became the first Governor-General of the Irish Free State:

1. *FW* 594.7–9.

whence 'Heliotropolis', which means also 'city of the sun'. 'Journey' is also 'jour né' (day born), but Parnell's journeying serves to bleaken for a moment the onset of the dawn. The words that so succinctly convey Parnell's embattled solitude are a culmination: by the *Wake*'s end, the idea of the hunt, of remorseless pursuit, is charged with the dreamed memory of the campaign that Parnell endured against him. Joyce had prefigured 'hunt me the journeyon' in epitomising Parnell in his 1912 essay 'The Shade of Parnell' as 'strong to the verge of weakness'. As his health failed and his appearance deteriorated, Parnell persevered because it was not in his nature not to do so.

The invocation of Parnell is of necessity brief—the new Ireland approaches. It is heralded by and it rebukes 'The Leader, the leader!' on the preceding page.[2] Yet it suffuses with a semi-faintness that is carefully calibrated to the passage of which it is part. The dawn breaks over the ancient standing stones ostensibly set in New Ireland in Melanesia: 'The spearspid of dawnfire totouches ain the tablestoane ath the centre of the great circle of the macroliths of Helusbelus in the boshiman brush on this our peneplain by Fangaluva Bight whence the horned cairns erge, stanserstanded, to floran frohn, idols of isthmians. Overwhere. Gaunt grey ghostly gossips growing grubber in the glow. Past now pulls.'[3]

It appears that in Brittany there are some menhirs that in Breton are known as 'the Gossips', but these gossips sound more like seagulls. They *are* seagulls. The *Wake* is full of them, but these gulls have a particular lineage. In 1913 William Butler Yeats, infuriated by the controversy over the construction of a municipal gallery in Dublin, wrote 'To a Shade'. In it he imagines Parnell's ghost returning to Dublin, and advises against it. Its first stanza runs,

> If you have revisited the town, thin Shade,
> Whether to look upon your monument
> (I wonder if the builder has been paid)
> Or happier-thoughted when the day is spent
> To drink of that salt breath out of the sea

2. *FW* 593.13.
3. *FW* 594.20–25.

When grey gulls flit about instead of men,
And the gaunt houses put on majesty:
Let these content you and be gone again;
For they are at their old tricks yet.[4]

While Joyce's gaunt, grey ghostly gossips explicitly invoke Yeats, the tenor of what he wrote differs from that of Yeats's poem, the last verse of which opens,

Go, unquiet wanderer,
And gather the Glasnevin coverlet
About your head till the dust stops your ear . . . [5]

Irish independence had supervened; Joyce also, in the great wheeling movement of the passage in *Finnegans Wake,* steers clear of Parnell's grave in Glasnevin, an artistic election but one that owes a little to Glasnevin's association with a morbidly exorbitant commemorative cult of Parnell which he disdained.

Joyce's valediction marks Parnell's passing into history and myth in the transition to an independent Irish state, but it is a passing touched by the diurnal pain and travail that Parnell endured in the final phase of his life. It is the preciseness of that recall that enables Joyce to transcend the tragic mode.

Joyce published *Finnegans Wake* in 1939. He died in 1941. This book is about what prompted Joyce to write with harrowing exactitude at the end of his last work of an event that had occurred a half century earlier, when he was not yet ten years old.

4. W. B. Yeats, 'To a Shade', in *The Variorum Edition of the Poems of W. B. Yeats,* ed. Peter Allt and Russell K. Alspach, 292–93.

5. Yeats, 'To a Shade'.

BIBLIOGRAPHY OF SECONDARY SOURCES

Newspapers (including dailies, weeklies, and monthlies)

Irish Newspapers

Daily Express
Daily Nation
Dana
Dublin Evening Mail
Evening Herald
Evening Telegraph
Freeman's Journal
Insuppressible
Irish Catholic
Irish Daily Independent
Irish Independent
Irishman
Irish Times
Leader
Limerick Leader
Lyceum
Nation
National Press
National Student
Nationist
Northern Whig
Sinn Féin
St Stephen's Review
Suppressed United Ireland
United Ireland
United Irishman

Non-Irish Newspapers (Great Britain, United States and Continental Europe)

Avanti! (Rome)
Catholic Bulletin
Catholic World
Daily Chronicle
Daily News

Fortnightly Review
Gaelic American
Il Piccolo della Sera (Trieste)
Jewish Chronicle
L'Asino (Rome)
Le Figaro (Paris)
L'Indipendente (Trieste)
Manchester Guardian
Methodist Times
National Press
New Age
North American Review
Pall Mall Gazette
Review of Reviews
Star
The Times (London)

Archives

Constantine Curran Collection, University College Dublin Special Collections
Davitt Papers, Trinity College Dublin
Gladstone Papers, British Library
James Joyce Papers, National Library of Ireland
Literary and Historical Society Records, Special Collections, University College Dublin
Redmond Papers, National Library of Ireland
Richard Ellmann Collection, University of Tulsa McFarlin Library, Tulsa, OK
Royal Irish Constabulary, Crime Branch Special Reports, National Archives of Ireland
Sheehy-Skeffington Papers, National Library of Ireland
W. G. Fallon Papers, National Library of Ireland

Secondary Sources

Allen, Nicholas. 'Frederick Michael Ryan'. *DIB* 8:690–91.

———. 'William Kirkpatrick Magee'. *DIB* 6:244–45.

Alspach, Russell K., ed. *The Variorum Edition of the Plays of W. B. Yeats*. New York: Macmillan, 1957.

Aubert, J., and M. Jolas, eds. *Joyce and Paris, 1902 . . . 1920–1940 . . . 1975: Papers from the Fifth International James Joyce Symposium, Paris, 16–20 June 1975*. Paris: Editions du CNRS, 1979.

Backus, Margot Gayle. *Scandal Work: James Joyce, the New Journalism, and the Home Rule Newspaper Wars*. Notre Dame, IN: University of Notre Dame Press, 2013.

Balfour, Arthur James. *A Defence of Philosophic Doubt*. London: Macmillan, 1879.

Barr, Colin. 'Paul Cullen'. *DIB* 2:1073–74.

Beach, Sylvia. *Shakespeare and Company*. London: Faber and Faber, 1956.

Benco, Silvio. 'James Joyce in Trieste'. In *Portraits of the Artist in Exile: Recollections of James Joyce by Europeans*, edited by Willard Potts, 49–58. Seattle: University of Washington Press, 1979.

Bender, Abby. *Israelites in Erin: Exodus, Revolution, and the Irish Revival*. Syracuse, NY: Syracuse University Press, 2015.

———. 'The Language of the Outlaw: A Clarification'. *James Joyce Quarterly* 44, no. 4 (Summer 2007): 807–12.

Benstock, Bernard. *Joyce's Again Wake*. Seattle: University of Washington Press, 1965.

Bérard, Victor. *Les Phéniciens et l'Odyssée*. Paris: Armand Colin, 1902/3.

Berrone, Louis, ed. *James Joyce in Padua*. New York: Random House, 1977.

Berrow, Hilary. 'Eight Nights in the Abbey'. In *J. M. Synge: Centenary Papers 1971*, edited by Maurice Harmon, 75–83. Dublin: Dolmen, 1972.

Bew, Paul. *Ireland: The Politics of Enmity, 1789–2006*. Oxford: Oxford University Press, 2007.

———. *Land and the National Question in Ireland, 1858–1882*. Dublin: Gill and Macmillan, 1978.

Bigazzi, Carlo. 'Joyce and the Italian Press'. In *Joyce in Rome: The Genesis of 'Ulysses'*, edited by Giorgio Melchiori, 52–62. Rome: Bulzoni, 1984.

Bobbio, Norberto. *Ideological Profile of Twentieth-Century Italy*. Translated by Lydia G. Cochrane. Princeton, NJ: Princeton University Press, 1995.

Bodkin, M. McDonnell. *Recollections of an Irish Judge*. London: Hurst and Blackett, 1914.

Bolton, George. *A Short Account of the Discovery and Conviction of the 'Invincibles'*. Dublin: Hodges, Figgis, 1887.

Bourke, Marcus. *John O'Leary: A Study in Irish Separatism*. Tralee: Anvil, 1967.

Boyle, Robert. 'A Note on Reuben J. Dodd as "A Dirty Jew"'. *James Joyce Quarterly* 3, no. 1 (Fall 1965): 64–66.

Bradford, Curtis. *Yeats at Work*. Carbondale: Southern Illinois University Press, 1965.

Bradley, Bruce. *James Joyce's Schooldays*. Dublin: Gill and Macmillan, 1982.

Budgen, Frank. *James Joyce and the Making of 'Ulysses' and Other Writings*. Oxford: Oxford University Press, 1972.

Bulwer-Lytton, Edward. *The Last Days of Pompeii*. London: G. Routledge and Sons, 1834.

Byrne, J. F. 'The Irish Grievance: The Case for the Anti-English Party'. *Century Illustrated Monthly*, n.s., 71 (January 1917): 465–73.

———. *Silent Years: An Autobiography with Memoirs of James Joyce and Our Ireland*. New York: Farrar, Straus and Young, 1953.

Callanan, Frank. '"Clerical Dictation": Reflections on the Catholic Church and the Parnell Split'. *Archivium Hibernicum* 45 (1980): 64–75.

———. 'James Joyce and the *United Irishman*, Paris 1902–3'. *Dublin James Joyce Journal* 3 (2010): 51–103.

———. 'The Parnellism of James Joyce: "Ivy Day in the Committee Room"'. *James Joyce Studies Annual* 2015 (2015): 73–97.

———. *The Parnell Split, 1890–91*. Cork: Cork University Press, 1992.

———. *T. M. Healy*. Cork: Cork University Press, 1996.

Campbell, Christy. *Fenian Fire: The British Government Plot to Assassinate Queen Victoria*. London: HarperCollins, 2002.

Carraher, Brian. 'Semicolonial Cities and Triestine Joyce: The Cultural Politics of Reading Joyce's Homeplaces'. *James Joyce Quarterly* 38, nos. 3 and 4 (Spring and Summer 2001): 505–18.

Casement, Roger. *The Crime against Europe*. Edited by Herbert O. Mackey. Dublin: C. J. Fallon, 1958.

[Casement, Roger.] *The Language of the Outlaw*. N.p., n.d.

Casey, Christine. *The Buildings of Ireland: Dublin*. New Haven, CT: Yale University Press, 2005.

Cattaneo, Carlo. *Ricerche economiche sulle interdizioni imposte dalla legge civile agli Israeliti*. Milan: Sonzogno, 1911.

———. *Saggi di filosofia civile*. Milan: Sonzogno, 1907.

Cheng, Vincent J. *Joyce, Race, and Empire*. Cambridge: Cambridge University Press, 1995.

Clancy, Mrs [Maire], et al. 'The Limerick City Curfew Murder of March 7th 1921'. In *Limerick's Fighting Story, 1916–21, Told by the Men Who Made It*, 115–39. Tralee: Kerryman, n.d. [ca. 1948].

Clarke, Edward. *The Story of My Life*. London: Ohn Murray, 1918.

Clarke, Frances. 'Abraham Jacob ("Con") Leventhal', *DIB* 5:474–75.

Clarke, Frances, and Patrick Maume. 'Emily Lawless', *DIB* 5:351–53.

Clery, Arthur. 'Thomas Kettle'. In *Dublin Essays*, 1–14. Dublin: Maunsel, 1919.

———. 'Thomas Kettle'. *Studies* 5, no. 20 (December 1916): 503–15.

Clinton, Georgina, and Sinead Sturgeon. 'Whitley Stokes'. *DIB* 9:105–7.

Colum, Mary. *Life and the Dream*. New York: Doubleday, 1947.

Colum, Mary, and Padraic Colum. *Our Friend James Joyce*. New York: Doubleday, 1958.

Colum, Padraic. *Arthur Griffith* (Dublin: Browne and Nolan, 1959).

———. Introduction to *Dubliners*, by James Joyce, v–xiii New York: Modern Library, 1926.

———. *Irish Elegies*. 4th ed. Dublin: Dolmen, 1976.

———. *The Road Round Ireland*. New York: Macmillan, 1937.

———. 'Tom Kettle: A Memory'. *Dublin Magazine* 24 (1949): 28–35.

Connolly, James. *Labour, Nationality and Religion: Being a Discussion of the Lenten Discourses against Socialism Delivered by Father Kane in Gardiner Street Church, Dublin, 1910*. Dublin: n.p., [1910].

———. *Selected Writings*. Edited by P. Berresford Ellis. London: Penguin, 1973.

Costello, Peter. *James Joyce*. Dublin: Gill and Macmillan, 1980.

———. *James Joyce: The Years of Growth, 1882–1915: A Biography*. London: Kyle Cathie, 1992.

Crise, Stelio. *Epiphanies & Phadographs: Joyce e Trieste*. Milan: All' Insegna del Pesce d'Oro, 1994.

———. 'Il triestino James Joyce'. In *Il ritorno di Joyce*, 85–99. Trieste: Comitato per l'anno joyciano, 1982.

Crispi, Luca. *Joyce's Creative Process and the Construction of Characters in* Ulysses*: Becoming the Blooms*. Oxford: Oxford University Press, 2015.

Crivelli, Renzo S. *James Joyce: Triestine Itineraries*. Trieste: MGS, 1996.

———. *A Rose for Joyce*. Trieste: MGS, 2004.

Crowley, Tony, ed. *The Politics of Language in Ireland, 1366–1922: A Sourcebook*. London: Routledge, 1999.

———. *War of Words: The Politics of Language in Ireland, 1537–2004*. Oxford: Oxford University Press, 2005.

Curran, C. P. *Dublin Decorative Plasterwork of the Seventeenth and Eighteenth Centuries*. London: Alec Tiranti, 1967.

———. 'Griffith, MacNeill and Pearse'. *Studies* 55, no. 217 (Spring 1966): 21–28.

———. *James Joyce Remembered*. Oxford: Oxford University Press, 1968.

———. 'Joyce's D'Annunzian Mask'. *Studies* 51, no. 202 (Summer 1962): 308–16.

———. *Nos 85 and 86 St. Stephens Green*. Dublin: President and Governing Body of University College, Dublin, n.d.

———. 'The Side Walks of Dublin: Self-Portrait'. *Studies* 51, no. 201 (Spring 1962): 108–16.

———. *Under the Receding Wave*. Dublin: Gill and Macmillan, 1970.

Daly, Leo. *James Joyce and the Mullingar Connection*. Dublin: Dolmen, 1975.

Daly, Mary E. *Dublin: The Deposed Capital*. Cork: Cork University Press, 1985.

D'Arcy, Fergus. 'James Connolly'. *DIB* 2:756–61.

Davis, Richard P. *Arthur Griffith and Non-violent Sinn Féin*. Dublin: Anvil Books, 1974.

Davison, Neil R. *James Joyce, 'Ulysses', and the Construction of Jewish Identity*. Cambridge: Cambridge University Press, 1986.

———. '"Not a Propagandist for the Better Treatment of Minorities": The Richard Ellmann-Louis Hyman Correspondence'. *James Joyce Quarterly* 50, no. 3 (Spring 2013): 741–65.

———. '"Still an Idea behind It": Trieste, Jewishness and Zionism in *Ulysses*'. *James Joyce Quarterly* 38, no. 3/4 (Spring–Summer 2001): 373–94.

Davitt, Michael. *The Fall of Feudalism in Ireland*. London: Harper and Brothers, 1904.

Deane, Seamus. 'Dead Ends: Joyce's Finest Moments'. In *Semicolonial Joyce*, edited by Derek Attridge and Marjorie Howes, 21–36. Cambridge: Cambridge University Press, 2000.

———. Introduction to *A Portrait of the Artist as a Young Man*, by James Joyce, vii–xliv. London: Penguin Classics, 1993.

Deane, Vincent. 'Sewing a Dream Together: "Work in Progress" 1923–4'. *Dublin James Joyce Journal*, nos. 14–15 (2021–22): 102–25.

Deane, Vincent, Daniel Ferrer, and Geert Lernout, eds. *The 'Finnegans Wake' Notebooks at Buffalo*. Turnhout: Brepols, 2004.

del Greco Lobner, Corinna. 'A *giornalista triestino*: James Joyce's Letter to *Il Marzocco*'. *Joyce Studies Annual* 4 (Summer 1993): 184–91.

Deming, Robert H. *Critical Heritage: James Joyce*. 2 vols. London: Routledge, 1970.

Dempsey, Pauric J. 'Patrick Clancy'. *DIB* 2:523.

Dempsey, Pauric J., and Bridget Hourican. 'Constantine Peter Curran'. *DIB* 2:1102–3.

Dennehy, W. F. 'The Irish Situation'. *Catholic World* 84 (December 1906): 298–313.

de Tuoni, Dario. *Ricordo di Joyce a Trieste / A Recollection of Joyce in Trieste*. Trieste: MGS, 2002.

de Vere White, Terence. 'Oliver Joseph St. John Gogarty'. In *Dictionary of National Biography, 1951–60*, 415. Oxford: Oxford University Press, 1971.

Dickinson, Emily Monroe. *A Patriot's Mistake: Being Personal Recollections of the Parnell Family by a Daughter of the House*. Dublin: Hodges, Figgis, 1905.

Dickson, David. *Dublin: The Making of a Capital City*. Dublin: Profile Books, 2014.

Dinneen, Patrick. *Foclóir Gaedhilge agus Béarla: An Irish-English Dictionary*. Dublin: Irish Texts Society, 1927.

Dubois, L. Paul. *Contemporary Ireland*. Introduction by T. M. Kettle. Dublin: Maunsel, 1911.

Dudley Edwards, Ruth. *Patrick Pearse: The Triumph of Failure*. London: Faber and Faber, 1979.

Dungan, Myles. *The Captain and the King: William O'Shea, Parnell and Late Victorian Ireland*. Dublin: New Island, 2009.

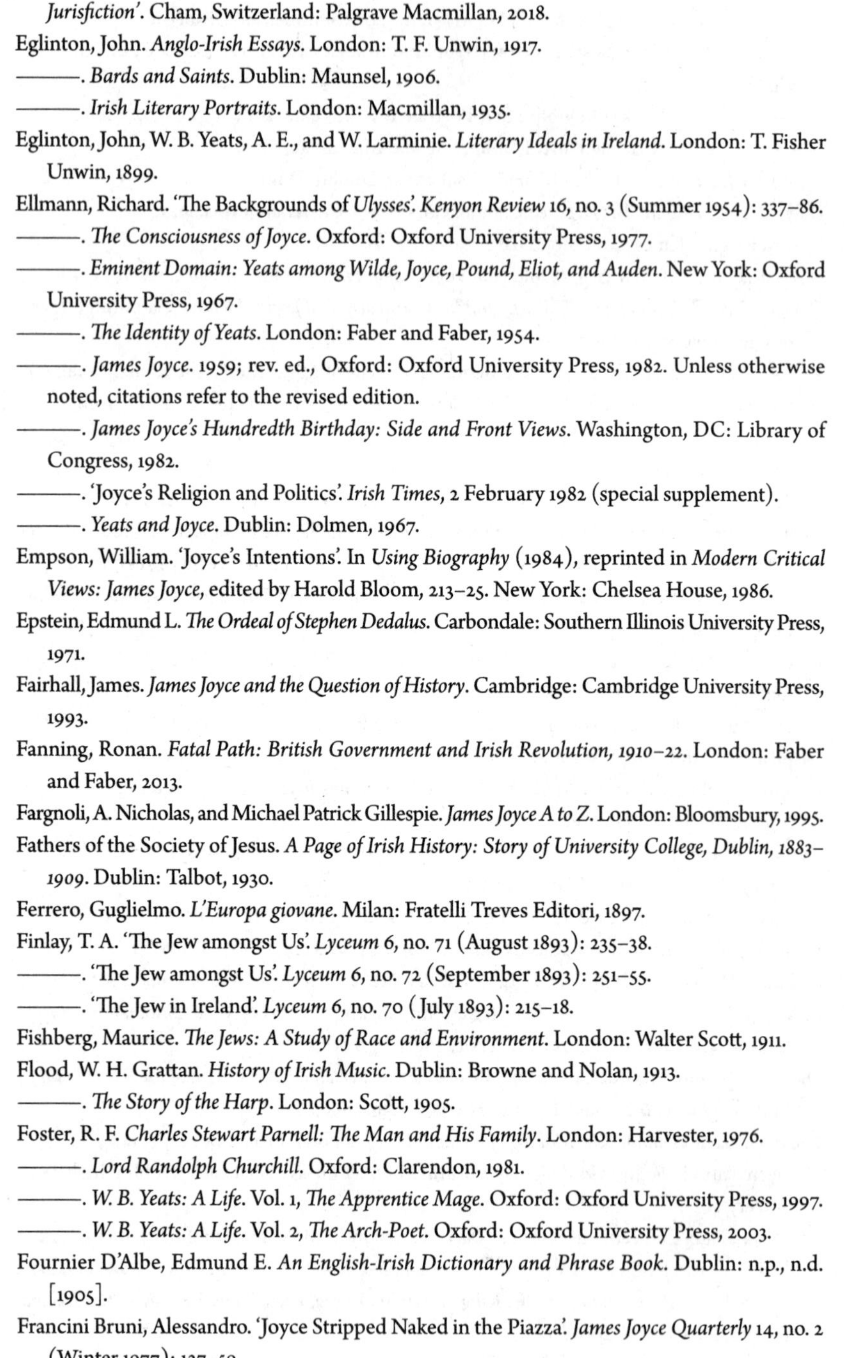

Ebury, Katherine, and James Alexander Fraser, eds. *Joyce's Non-fiction Writings: 'Outside His Jurisfiction'*. Cham, Switzerland: Palgrave Macmillan, 2018.

Eglinton, John. *Anglo-Irish Essays*. London: T. F. Unwin, 1917.

———. *Bards and Saints*. Dublin: Maunsel, 1906.

———. *Irish Literary Portraits*. London: Macmillan, 1935.

Eglinton, John, W. B. Yeats, A. E., and W. Larminie. *Literary Ideals in Ireland*. London: T. Fisher Unwin, 1899.

Ellmann, Richard. 'The Backgrounds of *Ulysses*.' *Kenyon Review* 16, no. 3 (Summer 1954): 337–86.

———. *The Consciousness of Joyce*. Oxford: Oxford University Press, 1977.

———. *Eminent Domain: Yeats among Wilde, Joyce, Pound, Eliot, and Auden*. New York: Oxford University Press, 1967.

———. *The Identity of Yeats*. London: Faber and Faber, 1954.

———. *James Joyce*. 1959; rev. ed., Oxford: Oxford University Press, 1982. Unless otherwise noted, citations refer to the revised edition.

———. *James Joyce's Hundredth Birthday: Side and Front Views*. Washington, DC: Library of Congress, 1982.

———. 'Joyce's Religion and Politics.' *Irish Times*, 2 February 1982 (special supplement).

———. *Yeats and Joyce*. Dublin: Dolmen, 1967.

Empson, William. 'Joyce's Intentions.' In *Using Biography* (1984), reprinted in *Modern Critical Views: James Joyce*, edited by Harold Bloom, 213–25. New York: Chelsea House, 1986.

Epstein, Edmund L. *The Ordeal of Stephen Dedalus*. Carbondale: Southern Illinois University Press, 1971.

Fairhall, James. *James Joyce and the Question of History*. Cambridge: Cambridge University Press, 1993.

Fanning, Ronan. *Fatal Path: British Government and Irish Revolution, 1910–22*. London: Faber and Faber, 2013.

Fargnoli, A. Nicholas, and Michael Patrick Gillespie. *James Joyce A to Z*. London: Bloomsbury, 1995.

Fathers of the Society of Jesus. *A Page of Irish History: Story of University College, Dublin, 1883–1909*. Dublin: Talbot, 1930.

Ferrero, Guglielmo. *L'Europa giovane*. Milan: Fratelli Treves Editori, 1897.

Finlay, T. A. 'The Jew amongst Us.' *Lyceum* 6, no. 71 (August 1893): 235–38.

———. 'The Jew amongst Us.' *Lyceum* 6, no. 72 (September 1893): 251–55.

———. 'The Jew in Ireland.' *Lyceum* 6, no. 70 (July 1893): 215–18.

Fishberg, Maurice. *The Jews: A Study of Race and Environment*. London: Walter Scott, 1911.

Flood, W. H. Grattan. *History of Irish Music*. Dublin: Browne and Nolan, 1913.

———. *The Story of the Harp*. London: Scott, 1905.

Foster, R. F. *Charles Stewart Parnell: The Man and His Family*. London: Harvester, 1976.

———. *Lord Randolph Churchill*. Oxford: Clarendon, 1981.

———. *W. B. Yeats: A Life*. Vol. 1, *The Apprentice Mage*. Oxford: Oxford University Press, 1997.

———. *W. B. Yeats: A Life*. Vol. 2, *The Arch-Poet*. Oxford: Oxford University Press, 2003.

Fournier D'Albe, Edmund E. *An English-Irish Dictionary and Phrase Book*. Dublin: n.p., n.d. [1905].

Francini Bruni, Alessandro. 'Joyce Stripped Naked in the Piazza.' *James Joyce Quarterly* 14, no. 2 (Winter 1977): 127–59.

Freund, Gisèle, and V. B. Carleton. *James Joyce in Paris: His Final Years*. London: Cassell, 1965.

Gabler, Hans Walter. 'The Christmas Dinner Scene, Parnell's Death, and the Genesis of *A Portrait of the Artist as a Young Man*'. *James Joyce Quarterly* 13, no. 1 (Fall 1975): 27–38.

Galli, Lina. 'Livia Veneziani Svevo and James Joyce'. *James Joyce Quarterly* 9, no. 3 (Spring 1972): 334–38.

Garvin, John. *James Joyce's Disunited Kingdom and the Irish Dimension*. Dublin: Gill and Macmillan, 1976.

———. 'James Joyce's Municipal Background'. *Administration* 33, no. 4 (1985): 551–72.

Gatt-Rutter, John. *Italo Svevo: A Double Life*. Oxford: Clarendon, 1988.

Geoghegan, Patrick M. 'William Henry Grattan Flood'. *DIB* 3:1030–31.

Gibson, Andrew. *Joyce's Revenge: History, Politics and Aesthetics in 'Ulysses'*. Oxford: Oxford University Press, 2002.

———. *The Strong Spirit: History, Politics and Aesthetics in the Writings of James Joyce, 1898–1915*. Oxford: Oxford University Press, 2013.

Gifford, Don. *Joyce Annotated: Notes for 'Dubliners' and 'A Portrait of the Artist as a Young Man'*. 2nd ed. Berkeley: University of California Press, 1982.

———. *Ulysses Annotated: Notes for James Joyce's 'Ulysses'*. With Robert J. Sheridan. Berkeley: University of California Press, 1989.

Gillespie, Michael Patrick. *James Joyce's Trieste Library*. Austin: University of Texas at Austin Press, 1986.

Gillet, Louis. *Claybook for James Joyce*. Translated by Georges Markow-Totevey. London: Abelard-Schuman, 1958.

Gladstone, William. *Studies on Homer and the Homeric Age*. 3 vols. Oxford: Oxford University Press, 1858.

Glaser, John F. 'Parnell's Fall and the Nonconformist Conscience'. *Irish Historical Studies* 12 (September 1960): 199–238.

Glasheen, Adaline. 'Joyce and the Three Ages of Charles Stewart Parnell'. In *A James Joyce Miscellany*, 2nd ser., edited by Marvin Magalaner, 151–78. Carbondale: Southern Illinois University Press, 1959.

———. *Third Census of 'Finnegans Wake': An Index of the Characters and Their Roles*. Berkeley: University of California Press, 1977.

Gogarty, Oliver St John. *As I Was Going Down Sackville Street*. London: Sphere Books, 1968.

———. *It Isn't That Time of Year at All*. London: MacGibbon and Kee, 1954.

———. 'The Joyce I Knew'. *Saturday Review of Literature* 23 (25 January 1941): 3–4.

———. *Tumbling in the Hay*. Dublin: O'Brien, 1996.

Goldberg, S. L. *Joyce*. London: Oliver and Boyd, 1962.

Golden, Sean. 'Parsing Rhetorics: The Cad as Prolegomena to the Readings of *Finnegans Wake*'. In *The Seventh of Joyce*, edited by Bernard Benstock, 173–77. Bloomington: Indiana University Press, 1982.

Gorman, Herbert. *James Joyce*. New York: Farrar and Rinehart, 1939.

Gregory, Augusta. *Poets and Dreamers: Studies and Translations from the Irish*. Dublin: Hodges, Figgis, 1903.

Griffith, Arthur. *The Resurrection of Hungary: A Parallel for Ireland*. 2nd ed. Dublin: James Duffy, 1904.

Gross, John, ed. *The Modern Movement*. London: Harvill, 1992.

Gwynn, Stephen. *Today and Tomorrow in Ireland: Essays on Irish Subjects*. Dublin: Hodges, Figgis, 1903.

Gwynn, Stephen, and Gertrude Tuckwell. *The Life of the Rt. Hon Sir Charles W. Dilke*. 2 vols. London: John Murray, 1917.

Halévy, Daniel. *Peguy et les Cahiers de la Quinzaine*. Paris: Grasset, 1941.

Halper, Nathan. 'The Narrative Thread in the Cad Episode'. In *The Seventh of Joyce*, edited by Bernard Benstock, 171–72. Bloomington: Indiana University Press, 1982.

Hammond, J. L. *Gladstone and the Irish Nation*. London: Longmans, Green, 1938.

Hardiman, Adrian. *Joyce in Court: James Joyce and the Law*. London: Head of Zeus, 2017.

Hardiman, James. *History of the Town and County of Galway*. Dublin: W. Folds and Sons, 1820.

Harrington, T. *The Maamtrasna Massacre*. Dublin: Nation Office, 1884.

Hartshorn, Peter. *James Joyce and Trieste*. Westport, CT: Greenwood, 1997.

Hassett, Joseph M. *The 'Ulysses' Trials: Beauty and Truth Meet the Law*. Dublin: Lilliput, 2016.

Healy, John. *Insula Sanctorum et Doctorum; or, Ireland's Ancient Schools and Scholars*. Dublin: Sealy Bryers and Walker and M. H. Gill and Son, 1890.

Healy, T. M. *Letters and Leaders of My Day*. 2 vols. London: Thornton Butterworth, 1928.

———. *Why Ireland Is Not Free: A Study of Twenty Years in Irish Politics*. Dublin: *Nation* office, 1898.

Herring, Phillip F. 'Joyce's Politics'. In *New Lights on Joyce from the Dublin Symposium*, edited by Fritz Senn, 3–14. Bloomington: Indiana University Press, 1972.

———, ed. *Joyce's 'Ulysses' Notesheets in the British Museum*. Charlottesville: University of Virginia Press, 1972.

Holloway, Joseph. *Joseph Holloway's Abbey Theatre: A Selection from His Unpublished Journal 'Impressions of a Dublin Playgoer'*. Edited by Robert Hogan and Michael J. O'Neill. Carbondale: Southern Illinois University Press, 1967.

Hone, Joseph. 'A Recollection of James Joyce'. *Envoy* 5, no. 17 (1951): 44–45.

Hughes, Hugh Price. 'The Science of Preaching'. *New Review*, June 1891.

Humphreys, Susan L. 'Ferrero Etc: James Joyce's Debt to Guglielmo Ferrero'. *James Joyce Quarterly* 16, no. 3 (Spring 1979): 239–51.

Hutchins, Patricia. *James Joyce's Dublin*. London: Grey Walls, 1950.

———. *James Joyce's World*. London: Methuen, 1957.

Hyde, Douglas. 'The Necessity for De-Anglicising Ireland'. Lecture delivered before the Irish National Literary Society in Dublin, 25 November 1892. In *The Politics of Language in Ireland 1366–1922: A Sourcebook*, edited by Tony Crowley, 182–88. London: Routledge, 1999.

Hyman, Louis. *The Jews of Ireland from Earliest Times to the Year 1910*. Shannon: Irish University Press, 1972.

Igoe, Vivien. *James Joyce's Dublin Houses and Nora Barnacle's Galway*. Dublin: Wolfhound, 1997.

———. *The Real People of Joyce's 'Ulysses': A Biographical Guide*. Dublin: University College Dublin Press, 2016.

Jackson, John Wyse, and Peter Costello. *John Stanislaus Joyce: The Voluminous Life and Genius of James Joyce's Father*. London: Fourth Estate, 1998.

Jenkins, Brian. *The Fenian Problem: Insurgency and Terrorism in a Liberal State, 1858–1874*. Liverpool: Liverpool University Press, 2008.

Jolas, Maria. 'Interview with Mr. John Stanislaus Joyce'. In *A James Joyce Yearbook*, edited by Maria Jolas, 159–69. Paris: Transition, 1949.

Joll, James. *The Anarchists*. 2nd ed. London: Routledge, 1979.

Joyce, James. *The Critical Writings of James Joyce*. Edited by Ellsworth Mason and Richard Ellman. New York: Viking, 1959.

———. *The Early Joyce: The Book Reviews, 1902–3*. Edited, with an introduction, by Stanislaus Joyce and Ellsworth Mason. Colorado Springs: Mamalujo, 1955.

———. *Ulysses*. Annotated by Sam Slote. London: Alma Classics, 2012.

Joyce, P. W. *A Short History of Ireland*. 3rd ed. London: Longmans Green, 1904.

Joyce, Stanislaus. *The Complete Dublin Diary of Stanislaus Joyce*. Edited by George H. Healey. Ithaca, NY: Cornell University Press, 1971.

———. *Joyce nel giardino di Svevo / Joyce in Svevo's Garden*. Edited by Renzo S. Crivelli and John McCourt. Trieste: MGS, 1995.

———. *My Brother's Keeper: James Joyce's Early Years*. New York: Viking, 1958.

———. *Recollections of James Joyce*. New York: James Joyce Society, 1950.

Judson, Peter M. *The Habsburg Empire: A New History*. Cambridge, MA: Belknap, 2016.

Kain, Richard M. *Dublin in the Age of William Butler Yeats and James Joyce*. Newton Abbott, UK: David and Charles, 1972.

Kauffmann, Gregoire. *Edouard Drumont*. Paris: Perrin, 2008.

Kearney, Colbert. 'The Joycead'. In *Coping with Joyce: Essays from the Copenhagen Symposium*, edited by Morris Beja and Shari Benstock, 55–72. Columbus: Ohio State University Press, 1989.

Kelleher, John V. 'Irish History and Mythology in James Joyce's "The Dead"'. *Review of Politics* 27, no. 3 (1965): 414–33.

Kemmy, Jim. 'George Clancy—Murdered Mayor'. In *Remembering Limerick: Historical Essays Celebrating the 800th Anniversary of Limerick's First Charter Granted in 1197*, edited by David Lee, 251–60. Limerick: Limerick Civil Trust, 1997.

Keogh, Dermot. *Jews in Twentieth-Century Ireland: Refugees, Anti-Semitism and the Holocaust*. Cork: Cork University Press, 1998.

Ker, Ian. *John Henry Newman*. 1988; Oxford: Oxford University Press, 2009.

Kettle, T. M. *The Day's Burden*. 1910; repr., Dublin: Browne and Nolan, 1937.

———. 'Independent Politics in Ireland'. *Independent Review* 11 (October–November 1906: 155–64.

———. *An Irishman's Calendar: A Quotation from the Works of T. M. Kettle for Every Day of the Year*. Edited by Mary Kettle. Dublin: Browne and Nolan, 1938.

———. 'A Note on Sinn Féin in Ireland'. *North American Review* 187, no. 626 (January 1908): 46–59, 49.

———. *The Open Secret of Ireland*. London: W. J. Ham-Smith, 1912.

———. *Poems and Parodies*. Dublin: Talbot, 1916.

———. 'Religion and Politics in Ireland'. *Independent Review* 11 (October–November 1906): 155–64.

———. 'Would the "Hungarian Policy" Work?' *New Ireland Review* 22, no. 6 (February 1905): 321–28.

Kettle, T. M., and Mary Kettle. *The Ways of War, with a Memoir by Mary Kettle*. London: Constable, 1917.

King, Carla. *Michael Davitt after the Land League, 1882–1906*. Dublin: University College Dublin Press, 2016.

———. 'Stephen Gwynn'. *ODNB* 24:365–66.

Kinsella, Michael A. 'Padraic Colum'. *DIB* 2:703–4.

Koss, Stephen, ed. *The Anatomy of an Antiwar Movement: The Pro-Boers*. Chicago: University of Chicago Press, 1973.

———. *The Rise and Fall of the Political Press in Britain*. 1981; London: Fontana, 1990.

Lacivita, Alison. 'Trouble in Paradise: Violence and the Phoenix Park in *Finnegans Wake*'. *James Joyce Quarterly* 51, no. 2–3 (Winter–Spring 2014): 317–31.

Laffan, Michael. *The Resurrection of Ireland: The Sinn Féin Party, 1916–1923*. Cambridge: Cambridge University Press, 1999.

Larbaud, Valéry. 'James Joyce'. *Nouvelle Revue Française* 103 n.s. (April 1922): 385–409. An extract appeared as 'The *Ulysses* of James Joyce', *Criterion* 1 (October 1922). Partially reprinted in 'Valéry Larbaud on Joyce: 1902–1927'. In *James Joyce: The Critical Heritage*, 2 vols., edited by Robert H. Deming, 252–261. London: Routledge and Kegan Paul, 1970.

Larkin, Emmet. *The Consolidation of the Roman Catholic Church in Ireland, 1860–70*. Dublin: Gill and Macmillan, 1987.

———. *The Roman Catholic Church in Ireland and the Fall of Parnell, 1888–91*. Chapel Hill, NC: University of North Carolina Press, 1979.

Lawless, Emily. *With Essex in Ireland*. London: Smith, Elder, 1890.

Leeming, H. 'James Joyce's Slavonic Optophones'. *Slavonic and East European Review* 55, no. 3 (July 1977): 289–309.

Leonard, Hugh. *Stephen D.: A Play in Two Acts*. Adapted by Hugh Leonard from James Joyce's *A Portrait of the Artist as a Young Man* and *Stephen Hero*. London: Evans Brothers, 1964.

Lernout, Geert. *Help My Unbelief: James Joyce and Religion*. London: Continuum, 2010.

Levenson, Leah. 'Francis Sheehy-Skeffington'. *ODNB* 50:820–22.

———. *With Wooden Sword: A Portrait of Francis Sheehy-Skeffington, Militant Pacifist*. Boston: Northeastern University Press, 1983.

Leventhal, A. J. 'What It Means to Be a Jew'. *Bell* 10, no. 3 (June 1945): 208–16.

Lewis, Wyndham. *The Art of Being Ruled*. London: Chatto and Windus, 1926.

Lidderdale, Jane, and Mary Nicholson. *Dear Miss Weaver*. London: Faber and Faber, 1970.

Lipsett, E. R. ['Halitvack']. 'Jews in Ireland'. *Jewish Chronicle*, 21 December 1906.

Long, R.E.C. 'Count Tolstoy in Thought and Action'. *Review of Reviews*, 15 January 1901, 438–39.

Lowry, Donal. 'Thomas Michael Kettle'. *DIB* 5:164.

Lunney, Linde, and Pauric J. Dempsey. 'Edward Dowden'. *DIB* 3:425–27.

Lynd, Robert. *Essays on Life and Literature*. London: J. M. Dent and Sons, 1951.

———. *Old and New Masters*. London: T. Fisher Unwin, 1919.

Lyons, F.S.L. *Charles Stewart Parnell*. London: Collins, 1977.

———. *The Fall of Parnell*. London: Routledge and Kegan Paul, 1960.

———. 'James Joyce's Dublin'. *Twentieth Century Studies* 4 (November 1970): 6–25.

———. *John Dillon*. London: Routledge and Kegan Paul, 1968.

Lyons, J. B. *The Enigma of Tom Kettle: Irish Patriot, Essayist, Poet, British Soldier, 1880–1916*. Dublin: Glendale, 1983.

———. 'Oliver Joseph St. John Gogarty'. *ODNB* 22. September 23, 2004. https://doi.org/10.1093/ref:odnb/33439.

MacBride, Anna, and A. Norman Jeffares, eds. *The Gonne-Yeats Letters, 1893–1938*. London: Hutchinson, 1992.

MacCabe, Colin. *James Joyce and the Revolution of the Word*. 2nd ed. London: Palgrave Macmillan, 2003.

MacGeoghegan, James. *The History of Ireland Ancient and Modern, with a Continuation from the Treaty of Limerick to the Present Time by John Mitchel*. New York: D. and J. Sadlier, 1868.

Maddox, Brenda. *Nora: A Biography of Nora Joyce*. London: Hamish Hamilton, 1988.

Magalaner, Marvin. 'The Anti-Semitic Limerick Incidents and Joyce's "Bloomsday"'. *PMLA* 68, no. 5 (December 1953): 1219–23.

Magalaner, Marvin, and Richard Kain. *Joyce: The Man, the Work, the Reputation*. New York: New York University Press, 1956.

Malatesta, Errico. *L'Anarchie*. Montreal: Lux Éditeur, 2004.

Mamigonian, Marc A., and John Noel Turner. 'Annotations for *Stephen Hero*'. *James Joyce Quarterly* 40, no. 3 (Spring 2003): 347–518.

Mangan, James Clarence. *The Collected Works of James Clarence Mangan: Poems, 1845–1847*. Edited by Jacques Chuto. Dublin: Irish Academic Press, 1996.

Manganiello, Dominic. *Joyce's Politics*. London: Routledge and Kegan Paul, 1980.

Matthew, H.C.G. *Gladstone, 1809–1874*. Oxford: Clarendon, 1986.

Matthews, Terence. 'An Emendation to the Joycean Canon: The Last Hurrah for "Politics and Cattle Disease"'. *James Joyce Quarterly* 44, no. 3 (Spring 2007): 441–53.

Maume, Patrick. 'Arthur Edward Clery'. *DIB* 2:584–86.

———. 'Francis Sheehy-Skeffington'. *DIB* 8:981–83.

———. 'Gerald Fitzgibbon'. *DIB* 3:928–31

———. 'John Campbell Aberdeen'. *DIB* 4:147.

———. 'John Healy'. *DIB* 4:561–64.

———. 'John Marcus O'Sullivan'. *DIB* 7:971–73.

———. 'John Pentland Mahaffy'. *DIB* 6:285–87.

———. *The Long Gestation: Irish Nationalist Life, 1891–1918*. Dublin: Gill and Macmillan, 1999.

———. 'Oliver St. John Gogarty'. *DIB* 4:123–27.

———. 'Patrick Casey'. *DIB* 2:412–14.

———. 'Piaras Béaslaí'. *DIB* 1:386–89.

———. 'Thomas Arnold'. *DIB* 1 :164–66.

McAlmon, Robert. *Being Geniuses Together, 1920–1930*. Rev. ed. San Francisco: North Point, 1984.

McArdle, Dorothy. *The Irish Republic*. 4th ed. Dublin: Irish Press, 1951.

McCabe, Desmond. 'Andrew Joseph Kettle'. *DIB* 5:161–63.

McCartney, Donal. *UCD, a National Idea: The History of University College, Dublin*. Dublin: Gill and Macmillan, 1999.

McCormack, W. J. *From Burke to Beckett*. Cork: Cork University Press, 1994.

McCourt, John. 'Joyce on National Deliverance: The View from 1907 Trieste'. *Prospero: Rivista di culture anglo-germaniche* 5 (1998): 27–48.

———. *The Years of Bloom: James Joyce in Trieste, 1904–1920*. Dublin: Lilliput, 2000.

McCracken, Donal P. *Inspector Mallon*. Dublin: Irish Academic Press, 2009.

———. *The Irish Pro-Boers, 1877–1902*. Johannesburg: Perskor, 1989.

McDonagh, Michael. *The Home Rule Movement*. Dublin: Talbot, 1920.

McGee, Owen. *Arthur Griffith*. Dublin: Merrion, 2015.

———. 'David Sheehy'. *DIB* 8:886–87.

———. 'Eugene Davis'. *DIB* 3:80.

———. *The IRB: The Irish Republican Brotherhood from the Land League to Sinn Féin*. Dublin: Four Courts, 2005.

———. 'John Clancy'. *DIB* 2:521.

———. 'Joseph Theobald Casey'. *DIB* 2:412.

McHugh, Noreen Higgins. 'The 1830s Tithe Riots'. In *Riotous Assemblies: Rebels, Riots and Revolts in Ireland*, edited by William Sheehan and Maura Cronin, 80–95. Cork: Mercier, 2011.

Meenan, James, ed. *Centenary History of the Literary and Historical Society of University College Dublin, 1855–1955*. Tralee: Kerryman, [1955].

Melchiori, Giorgio. 'The Genesis of *Ulysses*'. In *Joyce in Rome: The Genesis of Ulysses*, edited by Giorgio Melchiori, 37–50. Rome: Bulzoni, 1984.

———. 'The Language of Politics and the Politics of Language'. *James Joyce Broadsheet* 4 (February 1981): 1.

Meleady, Dermot. *John Redmond: The National Leader*. Dublin: Merrion, 2014.

———. *Redmond: The Parnellite*. Cork: Cork University Press, 2008.

Merridale, Catherine. *Lenin on the Train*. London: Allen Lane, 2017.

Mikhail, E. H., ed. *James Joyce: Interviews and Recollections*. London: Macmillan, 1990.

Mitchel, John. *Jail Journal*. Dublin: M. H. Gill and Son, 1913.

Montgomery, Henry R. *Specimens of the Early Native Poetry of Ireland*. Dublin: James McGlashan, 1846.

Moore, George. Introduction to *The Heather Field and Maeve*, by Edward Martyn, vii–xvii. London: Duckworth, 1899.

———. *Letters from George Moore to Edouard Dujardin*. New York: Crosby Gaige, 1929.

———. *Parnell and Ireland*. Dublin: University College Dublin Press, 2004.

Morley, John. *The Life of William Ewart Gladstone*. 3 vols. London: Macmillan, 1905.

Morris, A.J.A. 'Henry Wickham Steed'. *ODNB* 52:346–48.

Morris, Jan. *Trieste and the Meaning of Nowhere*. London: Faber and Faber, 2001.

Morrissey, Thomas J. 'Thomas Aloysius Finlay and Peter Finlay'. *DIB* 3:789–91.

Muldoon, Paul. *To Ireland, I: An Abecedary of Irish Literature*. Oxford: Oxford University Press, 2000.

Mullin, Katherine. *James Joyce, Sexuality and Social Purity*. Cambridge: Cambridge University Press, 2003.

Murphy, Patrick J. *Patrick Tuohy*. Dublin: Townhouse, 2004.

Murphy, William. 'George Clancy'. *DIB* 2:518–19.

Nadel, Ira B. 'The Incomplete Joyce'. *Joyce Studies Annual* 2 (1991): 86–100.

———. *Joyce and the Jews: Culture and Texts*. Gainesville: University Press of Florida, 1996.

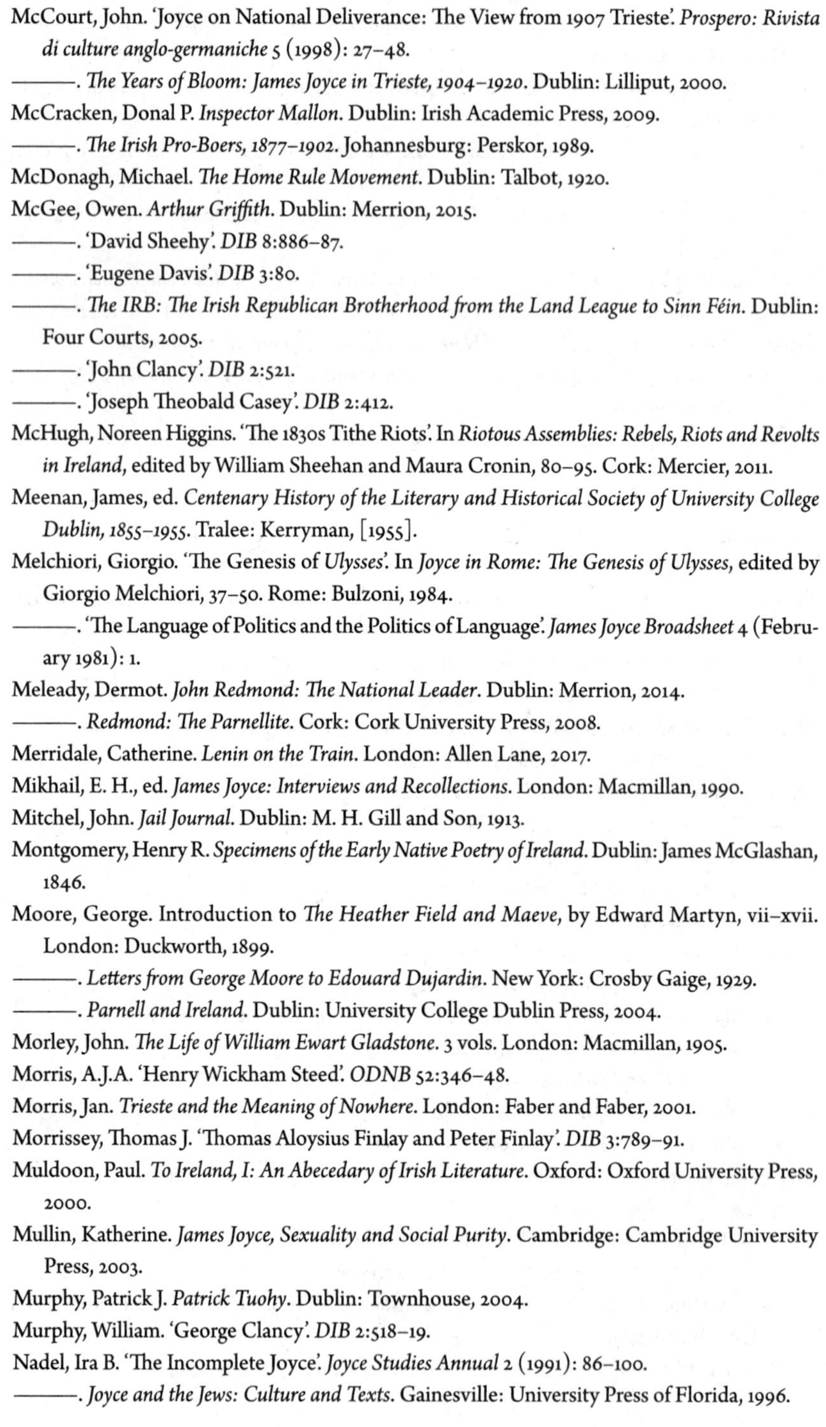

Nevin, Monica. 'Charles Vallencey'. *DIB* 9:635–36.

Newman, John Henry. *Callista: A Tale of the Third Century*. London: Longmans, Green, 1904.

Newspaper Press Directory. 58th ed. London: Mitchell, 1903.

Nolan, Emer. *James Joyce and Nationalism*. London: Routledge, 1995.

———. 'State of the Art: Joyce and Postcolonialism'. In *Semicolonial Joyce*, edited by Derek Attridge and Marjorie Howes, 78–95. Cambridge: Cambridge University Press, 2000.

Norburn, Roger. *A James Joyce Chronology*. London: Palgrave Macmillan, 2004.

Nordio, Mario. 'My First English Teacher'. *James Joyce Quarterly* 9, no. 3 (Spring 1972): 323–25.

Norris, Margot. *Joyce's Web: The Social Unraveling of Modernism*. Austin: University of Texas Press, 1992.

———. *Suspicious Readings of Joyce's 'Dubliners'*. Philadelphia: University of Pennsylvania Press, 2003.

O'Brien, Andrew, and Linde Lunney. 'James Healy'. *DIB* 4:559–60.

O'Brien, Conor Cruise. *The Great Melody*. London: Sinclair Stevenson, 1992.

———. *Memoir: My Life and Themes*. Dublin: Poolbeg, 1988.

———. *Parnell and His Party, 1880–90*. Oxford: Clarendon, 1957.

O'Brien, Flann. *At Swim-Two-Birds*. London: Penguin, 1967.

———. *The Collected Letters of Flann O'Brien*. Edited by Maebh Long. Dallas, TX: Dalkey Archive Press, 2018.

O'Brien, R. Barry. *Irish Memories*. London: T. Fisher Unwin, 1904.

———. *The Life of Charles Stewart Parnell*. 2 vols. London: Smith Elder, 1898.

O'Brien, William. *An Olive Branch in Ireland*. London: Macmillan, 1910.

O'Byrne, Emmett. 'Rory (Ruaidhrí Óg) O'More (Ó'Mórdha)'. *DIB* 7:717–19.

O'Callaghan, Margaret. *British High Politics and a Nationalist Ireland: Criminality, Land and the Law under Forster and Balfour*. New York: St. Martin's, 1994.

———. 'Forgetting to Remember: Tom Kettle in Modern Ireland'. In *Remembering Tom Kettle, 1880–1916*, 7–15. Dublin: University College Dublin Archives, 2006.

———. 'New Ways of Looking at the State Apparatus and the State Archive in Nineteenth-Century Ireland "Curiosities from the Phonetic Museum"—Royal Irish Constabulary Reports and Their Political Uses, 1879–91'. *Proceedings of the Royal Irish Academy* 104C, no. 2 (2004): 37–56.

———. 'The Politics of the Lost Generation and the Cult of Tom Kettle'. In *From Parnell to Paisley*, edited by Caoimhe Nic Dhaibhead and Colin Reid, 56–77. Dublin: Irish Academic Press, 2010.

———. 'Richard Pigott'. *DIB* 8:120–24.

O'Connor, Frank. *The Backward Look*. London: Macmillan, 1967.

———. *The Lonely Voice*. London: Macmillan, 1963.

———. *The Mirror in the Roadway*. London: Hamish Hamilton, 1957.

———. 'Work in Progress'. In *Twentieth Century Interpretations of Dubliners*, edited by Peter K Garrett, 18–26. Englewood Cliffs, NJ: Prentice-Hall, 1968.

O'Connor, T. P. *Charles Stewart Parnell: A Memory*. London: Ward, Lock, Bowden, 1891.

———. *Gladstone's House of Commons*. London: Ward and Downey, 1885.

———. *The Parnell Movement*. 2nd ed. London: Kegan Paul, Trench, 1886.

O'Connor, Ulick, ed. *The Joyce We Knew*. Dingle: Brandon, 2004.

O'Donnell, Frank Hugh. *A History of the Irish Parliamentary Party*. 2 vols. London: Longmans, Green, 1910.

Ó Gráda, Cormac. *Jewish Ireland in the Age of Joyce: A Socioeconomic History*. Princeton, NJ: Princeton University Press, 2006.

O'Grady, Thomas B. '"Ivy Day in the Committee Room": The Use and Abuse of Parnell'. *Éire-Ireland* 21 (1986): 31–42.

O'Hegarty, P. S. *Bibliography of Roger Casement*. Dublin: Alex Thom, 1949.

O'Hehir, Brendan. *A Gaelic Lexicon for 'Finnegans Wake' and Glossary for Joyce's Other Works*. Berkeley: University of California Press, 1967.

O'Laoi, Padraic. *Nora Barnacle Joyce*. Galway: Kenny's Bookshops and Art Galleries, 1982.

Oldstone-Moore, Christopher. 'The Fall of Parnell: Hugh Price Hughes and the Nonconformist Conscience'. *Éire-Ireland* 30, no. 4 (Winter 1996): 94–110.

O'Leary, John. *Recollections of Fenians and Fenianism*. 2 vols. London: Downey, 1896.

O'Leary, Philip. *The Prose Literature of the Gaelic Revival, 1881–1921*. University Park: Pennsylvania State University Press, 1994.

O'Malley, John W. *Vatican I: The Council and the Making of the Ultramontane Church*. Cambridge, MA: Belknap, 2018.

O'Neill-Bernhard, Christine. 'Symbol of the Irish Nation, or of a Foulfamed Potheen District: James Joyce on Myles Joyce'. *James Joyce Quarterly* 32, nos. 3–4 (Spring and Summer 1995): 712–21.

O'Raghallaigh, Eoghan. 'Edmund Ignatius Hogan'. *DIB* 4:738.

O'Riordain, Turlough. 'James MacGeoghegan'. *DIB* 5:1022–23.

O'Siochain, Seamus. *Roger Casement: Imperialist, Rebel, Revolutionary*. Dublin: Lilliput, 2008.

O'Sullivan, J. M. 'Bonn University and Trinity College: A Parallel'. *New Ireland Review* 23 (March 1905): 1–9.

O'Sullivan, Seamus. *The Rose and Bottle*. Dublin: Talbot, 1946.

Pašeta, Senia. 'Nationalist Responses to Two Royal Visits to Ireland'. *Irish Historical Studies* 31, no. 124 (November 1999): 488–504.

———. *Thomas Kettle*. Dublin: University College Dublin Press, 2008.

Pelaschiar, Laura. 'Stanislaus Joyce's "Book of Days": The Triestine Diary'. *James Joyce Quarterly* 36, no. 2 (Winter 1999): 61–71.

Pick, Daniel. *Faces of Degeneration: A European Disorder, c. 1848–c. 1918*. Cambridge: Cambridge University Press, 1989.

Platt, Len H. *James Joyce: Texts and Contexts*. London: Continuum, 2011.

———. 'Joyce and the Anglo-Irish Revival: The Triestine Lectures'. *James Joyce Quarterly* 29, no. 2 (Winter 1992): 259–66.

Potts, Willard, ed. *Portraits of the Artist in Exile: Recollections of James Joyce by Europeans*. Seattle: University of Washington Press, 1979.

Pound, Ezra. '*Dubliners* and Mr. James Joyce'. *Egotist*, 15 July 1914, 267.

———. 'The Non-existence of Ireland'. *New Age*, 25 February 1915, 451–55.

Powell, N. *Travellers to Trieste*. London: Faber and Faber, 1977.

Quinn, James. 'Arthur James Balfour'. *DIB* 1:239–42.

Read, Forrest, ed. *Pound/Joyce*. London: Faber and Faber, 1965.

Redmond, J. E. 'The Lesson of South Meath'. *Fortnightly Review*, n.s., 53, no. 313 (1 January 1893): 1–6.

Reid, Colin. *The Lost Ireland of Stephen Gwynn: Irish Constitutional Nationalism and Cultural Politics, 1864–1950*. Manchester: Manchester University Press, 2011.

Reizbaum, Marilyn. *James Joyce's Judaic Other*. Stanford, CA: Stanford University Press, 1999.

Renan, Ernest. *The Poetry of the Celtic Races, and Other Studies*. Translated by William G. Hutchinson. London: Walter Scott, 1896.

The Repeal of the Union Conspiracy; or, Mr Parnell M.P. and the IRB. London: William Ridgway, 1886.

Rhadamanthus [pseud.]. *Our Judges*. Dublin: Irish Society Office, 1890.

Ridley, Jane. *Bertie: A Life of Edward VII*. London: Chatto and Windus, 2012.

Robbins, A. P. 'Henry Wickham Steed'. In *The Dictionary of National Biography, Supplement, 1951–60*, 921–23. Oxford: Oxford University Press, 1971.

Robinson, Richard. 'A Stranger in the House of Habsburg: Joyce's Ramshackle Empire'. *James Joyce Quarterly* 38, no. 3/4 (Spring/Summer 2001): 321–39.

Robinson, W. Sydney. *Muckraker: The Scandalous Life and Times of W. T. Stead*. London: Robson, 2012.

Rocco-Bergera, Niny. 'James Joyce and Trieste'. *James Joyce Quarterly* 9, no. 3 (Spring 1972): 342–49.

Rodgers, W. R. *Irish Literary Portraits*. London: British Broadcasting Corporation, 1972.

Rooney, William. 'Gaelicism in Practice'. In *Prose Writings*, 105–53. Dublin: M. H. Gill, 1909.

———. *Poems and Ballads*. Dublin: M. H. Gill and Son, 1903.

Rosenhan, Claudia. '"Grace" and the Idea of "the Irish Jew"'. *James Joyce Quarterly* 47, no. 1 (Fall 2009): 71–86.

Ross, Margery, ed. *Robert Ross, Friend of Friends: Letters to Robert Ross, Art Critic and Writer, Together with Extracts from His Published Articles*. London: Jonathan Cape, 1952.

Roth, Joseph. *The Wandering Jews*. London: Granta, 2001.

Rusinow, Dennison I. *Italy's Austrian Heritage, 1919–1946*. Oxford: Clarendon, 1969.

Saint-Amour, Paul K. '"The Imprevidibility of the Future": On Joycean Prophesy'. In *Renascent Joyce*, edited by Daniel Ferrer, Sam Slote, and Andre Topia, 90–105. Gainesville: University Press of Florida, 2013.

Schachter, Elizabeth. *Origin and Identity: Essays on Svevo and Trieste*. Leeds: Northern Universities Press, 2000.

Schneider, Erik. 'Joyce in Concert: The *Meistersinger* Performance in Trieste'. *James Joyce Quarterly* 38, nos. 3 and 4 (Spring and Summer 2001): 495–97.

Scholes, Robert. 'The Broadsides of James Joyce'. In *A James Joyce Miscellany, Third Series*, edited by Marvin Magalaner, 8–18. Carbondale: Southern Illinois University Press, 1962.

———. *The Cornell Joyce Collection: A Catalogue*. Ithaca, NY: Cornell University Press, 1961.

———. *In Search of James Joyce*. Urbana: University of Illinois Press, 1992.

———. 'Joyce and Modernist Ideology'. In *Coping with Joyce: Essays from the Copenhagen Symposium*, edited by Morris Beja and Shari Benstock, 91–107. Columbus: Ohio State University Press, 1989.

Scholes, Robert, and Richard M. Kain, eds. *The Workshop of Daedalus: James Joyce and the Raw Materials for 'A Portrait of the Artist as a Young Man'*. Evanston, IL: Northwestern University Press, 1965.

Shakespeare, William. *The Works of William Shakespeare*. London: Frederick Warne, 1892.

Shannon, Richard. *Gladstone: Heroic Minister, 1865–1898*. London: Allen Lane, Penguin, 1999.

Sheehan, James. *The Monopoly of Violence: Why Europeans Hate Going to War*. London: Faber and Faber, 2008.

Sheehy, Eugene. *May It Please the Court*. Dublin: CJ Fallon, 1951.

Sheehy-Skeffington, Francis. 'The Collapse of Sinn Féin'. *New Age* 6, no. 9, 30 December 1909.

———. 'Frederick Ryan'. *Irish Review* 3 (May 1913): 113–19.

———. *Michael Davitt: Revolutionary, Agitator and Labour Leader*. London: T. Fisher Unwin, 1908; London: McGibbon and Kee, 1967.

———. 'Michael Davitt's Unfinished Campaign'. *Independent Review* 10 (July–September 1906): 298–312.

———. Review of *The Open Secret of Ireland*. *Irish Review* 2 (March 1912): 55.

Shillman, Bernard. *A Short History of the Jews of Ireland*. Dublin: Cahill, 1941.

Short, K.R.M. *The Dynamite War: Irish-American Bombers in Victorian Britain*. Dublin: Gill and Macmillan, 1979.

Shovlin, Frank. *Journey Westward: Joyce, Dubliners and the Literary Revival*. Liverpool: Liverpool University Press, 2014.

Skelton, Robin, and David R. Clark, eds. *Irish Renaissance: A Gathering of Essays, Memoirs, Letters and Dramatic Poetry from the 'Massachusetts Review'*. Dublin: Dolmen, 1965.

Slocum, John J., and Herbert Cahoon. *A Bibliography of James Joyce, 1882–1941*. New Haven, CT: Yale University Press, 1953.

Smith, Denis Mack. *Mazzini*. New Haven, CT: Yale University Press, 1994.

———. *Modern Italy: A Political History*. New Haven, CT: Yale University Press, 1997.

Spoo, Robert. *James Joyce and the Language of History: Dedalus's Nightmare*. Oxford: Oxford University Press, 1994.

———. '"Una Piccola Nuvoletta": Ferrero's Young Europe and Joyce's Mature *Dubliners* Stories'. *James Joyce Quarterly* 24, no. 4 (Summer 1987): 401–10.

Staley, Thomas F. 'Italo Svevo and the Ambience of Trieste'. *Modern Fiction Studies* 18, no. 1 (Spring 1972): 7–16.

———. 'James Joyce in Trieste'. *Georgia Review* 16, no. 4 (Winter 1962): 446–49.

Stanzel, F. K. 'All Europe Contributed to the Making of Bloom: New Light on Leopold Bloom's Ancestors'. *James Joyce Quarterly* 32, nos. 3 and 4 (Spring and Summer 1995): 619–30.

Starkie, Walter. *Scholars and Gypsies: An Autobiography*. London: John Murray, 1963.

Stead, W. T. 'Archbishop Croke'. *Review of Reviews* 12 (14 September 1895): 204–16.

———. 'Character Sketch: T. P. O'Connor, M. P.'. *Review of Reviews* 26 (15 November 1902): 478.

———. *The Discrowned King of Ireland: Manifestoes to the Irish People*. London: Review of Reviews, 1890.

———. 'Government by Journalism'. *Contemporary Review* 49 (1886): 653–74.

———. *Lest We Forget: A Keepsake from the Nineteenth Century*. London: *Review of Reviews* office, 1901.

———. 'Lord Russell of Killowen, Lord Chief Justice of England'. *Review of Reviews* 22 (15 September 1900): 230–33.

———. 'Mrs. O'Shea'. *Review of Reviews* 2 (December 1890): 529.

———. 'North Kilkenny and Its Moral'. *Paternoster Review* 1, no. 4 (January 1891): 332–41.

———. 'The Story of an Incident in the Home Rule Cause: The Fall of Mr Parnell'. *Review of Reviews* 2 (December 1890): 598–608.

Steed, Henry Wickham. *The Habsburg Monarchy*. London: Constable, 1913.

Stephens, James. *Arthur Griffith: Journalist and Statesman*. Dublin: Wilson, Hartnell, 1924.

———. *The Insurrection in Dublin*. London: Macmillan, 1916.

Sternlicht, Sanford. 'Padraic Colum'. *ODNB* 12:803.

Stokes, Whitley, ed. and trans. *Togail bruidne Dá Derga / The Destruction of Dá Derga's Hostel*. Paris: Émile Bouillon, 1902.

Strickland, Walter G. *A Dictionary of Irish Artists*. 2 vols. Dublin: Maunsel, 1913.

Svevo, Italo. 'James Joyce'. Translated by Stanislaus Joyce, revised by John Gatt-Rutter. Appendix in Svevo, *Memoir of Italo Svevo*, 147–72.

Svevo, Livia Veneziani. *Memoir of Italo Svevo*. Translated by Isabel Quigley. London: Libris, 1989.

Synge, John Millington. 'Can We Go Back into Our Mother's Womb? A Letter to the Gaelic League by a Hedge Schoolmaster'. In *J. M. Synge: Collected Works*, vol. 2, *Prose*, edited by Alan Price, 399–400. Buckinghamshire: Colin Smythe, 1982.

———. *The Collected Letters of John Millington Synge*. Vol. 1. Edited by Ann Saddlemyer. Oxford: Clarendon, 1983.

Taxil, Léo. *Monsieur Drumont: Étude psychologique*. Paris: Letouzey and Ané, 1890.

Thompson, Mark. *The White War: Life and Death on the Italian Front, 1915–1919*. London: Faber and Faber, 2008.

Thornton, Weldon. *Allusions in Ulysses: An Annotated List*. Chapel Hill: University of North Carolina Press, 1968.

Tierney, Michael. *Eoin MacNeill: Scholar and Man of Action, 1867–1945*. Oxford: Clarendon, 1980.

———, ed. *Struggle with Fortune: A Miscellany for the Centenary of the Catholic University of Ireland, 1854–1954*. Dublin: Browne and Nolan, 1954.

Tóibín, Colm. *Mad, Bad, Dangerous to Know: The Fathers of Wilde, Yeats, and Joyce*. London: Viking, 2018.

Torchiana, Donald T. *Backgrounds for Joyce's 'Dubliners'*. Boston: Allen and Unwin, 1986.

Tucker, Benjamin. *Instead of a Book, by a Man Too Busy to Write One: A Fragmentary Exposition of Philosophical Anarchism*. New York: n.p., 1893.

Tymoczko, Maria. *The Irish Ulysses*. Berkeley: University of California Press, 1994.

Tynan, Katharine. *Memories*. London: E. Nash and Grayson, 1924.

———. *The Middle Years*. London: Constable, 1916.

———. *Twenty-Five Years: Reminiscences*. London: Smith, Elder, 1913.

Tysdahl, B. J. *Joyce and Ibsen: A Study in Literary Influence*. Oslo: Norwegian Universities Press, 1968.

Valente, Joseph, ed. *Quare Joyce*. Ann Arbor: University of Michigan Press, 2000.

Van Mierlo, Wim. 'The Subject Notebook: A Nexus in the Composition History of *Ulysses*—a Preliminary Analysis'. *Genetic Joyce Studies*, no. 7 (Spring 2007): 1–46.

Verene, Donald Philip. *James Joyce and the Philosophers at Finnegans Wake*. Evanston, IL: Northwestern University Press, 2016.

Vidan, Ivo. 'Joyce and the South Slavs'. *Studia Romanica et Anglica Zagrabiensia* 33–36 (1972/73): 265–77.

Waldron, Jarlath. *Maamtrasna: The Murders and the Mystery*. Dublin: Edmund Burke, 1992.

Weininger, Otto. *Sex and Character*. London: William Heinemann, 1906.

White, Lawrence William, and Lindsey Earner-Byrne. 'John Francis Byrne'. *DIB* 2:215–16.

Whyte, F. *The Life of W. T. Stead*. 2 vols. London: Jonathan Cape, 1925.

Whyte, J. H. *The Independent Irish Party, 1850–9*. Oxford: Oxford University Press, 1958.

———. 'The Influence of the Catholic Clergy on Elections in Nineteenth Century Ireland'. *English Historical Review* 75 (April 1960): 239–59.

Wilde, Oscar. *The Letters of Oscar Wilde*. Edited by Rupert Hart-Davis. London: Hart-Davis, 1962.

———. *The Soul of Man under Socialism*. London: Arthur L. Humphreys, 1912.

Woods, C. J. 'The General Election of 1892: The Catholic Clergy and the Defeat of the Parnellites'. In *Ireland under the Union: Essays in Honour of T. W. Moody*, edited by F.S.L. Lyons and R.A.J. Hawkins, 289–319. Oxford: Oxford University Press, 1980.

———. 'William Bulfin'. *DIB* 1:977–78.

Yeats, W. B. *Autobiographies*. London: Macmillan, 1955.

———. *The Collected Letters of W. B. Yeats*. Vol. 1. Edited by John Kelly. Oxford: Clarendon, 1986.

———. *Essays and Introductions*. New York: Macmillan, 1961.

———. *Explorations*. New York: Macmillan, 1962.

———. *The Letters of W. B. Yeats*. Edited by Allan Wade. London: Rupert Hart-Davis, 1954.

———. *Memoirs*. Edited by Denis Donoghue. London: Macmillan, 1972.

———. 'Reveries over Childhood and Youth'. In *Autobiographies: Memories and Reflections*, 1–106. London: Macmillan, 1995.

———, ed. *Samhain*. Dublin: n.p., 1891.

———. *'The Tables of the Law' and 'The Adoration of the Magi'*. London: Elkin Mathews, 1904.

———. 'The Trembling of the Veil'. In *Autobiographies: Memories and Reflections*, 107–381. London: Macmillan, 1995.

———. *Uncollected Prose by W. B. Yeats*. 2 vols. Edited by J. P. Frayne and Colton Johnson. London: Macmillan, 1975.

———. *The Variorum Edition of the Plays of W. B. Yeats*. Edited by Russell K. Alspach. New York: Macmillan, 1966.

———. *The Variorum Edition of the Poems of W. B. Yeats*. Edited by Peter Allt and Russell K. Alspach. New York: Macmillan, 1957.

Younger, Calt on. *Arthur Griffith*. Dublin: Gill and Macmillan, 1981.

INDEX

Abbey Theatre, 277n58, 717; Joseph Holloway and, 720; Joyce attends, 716; *Playboy* riots and, 621–23, 625, 629

Aberdeen, John Campbell (Lord) (lord lieutenant of Ireland), 205, 751, 751n144; in *Ulysses*, 417; and wife, Lady Aberdeen, 750–51

L'Action Française (French Royalist and Nationalist movement), 15

Act of Union (1800), 10, 18, 205–6, 209n45, 242, 426, 736; Catholic Church and, 207, 226; the Split and, 209

Adler, Hermann (Chief Rabbi of the British Empire), 772

Adrian IV (Pope), 612; *Laudabiliter* bull and, 208–9, 671

'Aeolus' episode, *Ulysses*, 168n39, 191, 717; 'Crozier and the Pen' in, 222–23, 718; *Evening Telegraph* and *Freeman's Journal* in, 177, 177n54, 387, 396, 463; Joyce records reading of, 394; *National Press* in, 223; Taylor's King's Inns speech and, 27, 355, 364–67, 377, 387–98; transgendering of T. M. Healy in, 191. *See also* Taylor, John Francis

Africa, 384, 426, 489, 489n22

agrarian protests, 46; agrarian violence, 143, 701, 706, 736; Captain Moonlight and, 701; Whiteboys and, 46

Albini, Ettore (music critic for *Avanti!*), 655–56

Alexander II (Tsar of Russia), 771

Alexander III (Pope), 208–9

Allan, Fred (Fenian and journalist), 426

Alleyn, Henry Joseph (Cork businessman), 51

All-for-Ireland League, 687–89

altruism, 685, 722; Joyce's suspicion of, 196; in *Portrait*, 301; Skeffington and, 306; Wilde and, 457, 500n57

anarchism, xvi, 316, 513n7, 827; censorship and, 478, 539; Joyce and, 478, 512–13, 515, 524–25, 535, 538–39, 842, 845; socialism and, xx, 43n30, 512, 525, 538, 539, 606, 842

Anglo-Irish Treaty (1921), 359, 834

anticlericalism, 89, 216, 272–73, 281n75, 294; Fenianism and, xiv, 81, 83, 495–96; Joyce and, 490, 526–28

anti-Semitism, 149, 276; 'The Citizen' and, 789–91; Ferrero and, 532, 533, 795; Gogarty and, 611; Holocaust and, 793, 838–39; Irish and, 769, 776–78; Jews of Trieste and, 792, 795; Joyce and, 769, 792, 838; Limerick Boycott and, 784–85; middle-class Dublin and, 779–84; H. W. Steed and, 805; in *Ulysses*, 767, 781, 783–91, 805, 808

Aquinas, Thomas, 16, 401, 465, 635

Archer, William (theatre critic), 256, 281n76

Aristotle, 230n101, 464, 842

Arnold, Matthew, 801

Artifoni, Almidano (proprietor of Berlitz Schools in Trieste and Pola), 513, 676

Ashe, Thomas (Irish republican), 344

L'Asino (newspaper), 526

Asquith, Herbert Henry (British prime minister), 318, 686, 687, 731; in cartoon 'Shade of Parnell', 732
Atkinson, Robert (professor at Trinity College Dublin), 376, 376n52, 377
Australia, 374, 666
Austria-Hungary, 543, 643, 646–47, 651n98, 655, 674, 748, 762–63, 766, 805; First World War and, 810, 811, 811n5, 816–17; military of, 521, 761, 792n71, 810
Avanti! (newspaper), 526, 647, 655; editors of, 516, 520–21; Joyce and, 510, 517, 519, 520, 523, 528, 535; socialism and, 477, 516–17, 519–20

Bacon, Thomas F. (Joyce's contemporary at University College), 268, 279, 285
Bagenal, Philip H. (Unionist publicist), *The Priest in Politics*, 216–17
Bakunin, Mikhail, 511; *God and the State*, 538
Balfour, Arthur James, 372, 579, 686n81, 687–89; brother Gerald Balfour and, 372; *A Defence of Philosophic Doubt*, 688
Barnacle, Nora, 713, 723; Vincent Cosgrave and, 351, 628, 715–16, 719, 764; early years, 466–67, 467n215; John Stanislaus Joyce, and, 94, 102, 104, 105, 471; Joyce and, 4, 5, 306, 400, 466–71, 475, 484, 641, 702, 714, 745, 769n5, 837; letters from Joyce, 321, 412, 469–70, 628–29, 712–13, 715, 719, 721–22, 745–46, 753, 764; letter to Eileen Joyce Schaurek, 745, 746; marriage of, 837; parents, Thomas and Anne Barnacle, 466, 467; in Rome, 593, 595; in Trieste, 484, 632, 633, 640, 676, 721–23; visits to Ireland, 745–49, 753, 756, 836
Barrington, Jonah (Sir), 77
Barry, Kevin (Irish republican), 440n135, 654, 686, 702n133, 708
Barthes, Roland, and association between photography and memory, 302
Beach, Sylvia, 394, 834
Béaslaí, Piaras, 106, 622; arranges Joyce's visits to *Evening Telegraph*, 717–18, 717n30
Beckett, Samuel, 778
Beerbohm, Max, and cartoon, 281n76
Belfast Newsletter (Irish newspaper), 614
Benco, Silvio, 648, 659–61, *660*, 760, 761n180, 830; and article 'James Joyce in Trieste', 537n63, 659; Joyce's irredentism and, 650
Benedict XV (Pope), 573
Benedictines, 773
Bennett, A. Percy (British Consul General, Zurich), 828
Beran, Felix (Viennese poet), Joyce translates 'Lament for the Yeoman', 824
Bérard, Victor (author of *Les Phéniciens et l'Odyssée*), importance to Joyce, 806–8
Bergan, Alfred (loyal friend of John Stanislaus Joyce), 107, 126, 126n49, 133; in *Ulysses* as 'Alf Bergan', 783–84
Berlitz schools, 469–70, 476, 513, 634, 637
Bernstein, Edouard (German social democrat), 516
Best, Richard Irvine (scholar of Celtic Studies), 434, 717n28. *See also* 'Destruction of Dá Derga's Hostel, The'
Bible, the, 153n3, 419; Exodus, 370, 391; Isaiah, 794; Psalms, 741–42
Biggar, Joseph (IPP member of parliament, obstructionist), 87, 731
Birrell, Augustine (chief secretary for Ireland), 382
Bissolati, Leonida (editor of *Avanti!*), 516
Bjørnson, Bjørnstjerne (Norwegian writer), 626
Blake, William, 197, 305, 727
Blitznakoff sisters, Olga and Vela (students of Joyce, Zurich), 819
Bloom, Leopold (fictional character, *Ulysses*), 27, 37, 418, 648, 770, 792, *800*; characterisation of, 803, 803n107, 809; Citizen and, 789, 790–91; father's suicide and, 804; Frederick Falkiner and, 783;

Freeman's Journal and, 546n7; Alfred H. Hunter and, 649n84, 787; as Jewish, 533, 535, 768, 778, 795, 798, 802, 808; models for, 649n84; Molly Bloom and, 74, 137, 467, 471; Odysseus and, 819; Parnell and, 563, 565; profession, 97, 532, 533; Ettore Schmitz and, 799; 7 Eccles Street and, 720, 793; Stephen Dedalus and, 774–75, 808; as 'womanly man', 803. *See also Ulysses*

Bloomsday (16 June), 101, 153n2, 813

Bobbio, Noberto (historian and political philosopher), 517–18, 525–26

Bodkin, Mathias McDonnell (anti-Parnellite editor of *United Ireland*), 134–35, 258

Bodkin, Michael, 467; buried Rahoon, 747; as model for Michael Furey in 'The Dead', 747

Boer Republic, 131, 418

Boer War (1899–1902), 296, 297, 383, 417, 418, 431; Joyce not drawn to Boer cause, 419

Bolton, George (crown solicitor, Tipperary), in charge of Maamtrasna case, 695, 698, 701

Bonaparte, Napoleon, 152n1, 156, 419

Borach, Georges (student and friend of Joyce in Zurich), 814n22, 818

Brady, James (friend of John Stanislaus Joyce, brother-in-law of Alfred Bergan), 133

Britain [including references to England and Great Britain], 14, 140, 374, 391, 685, 816; and Fenian violence in, 138–40; Gogarty's 'Ugly England' articles in *Sinn Féin*, 608–15; Joyce on relation of Ireland to England: in *Exiles*, 328–30; in 'The Home Rule Comet', 686; in 'L'Irlanda: Isola dei santi e dei savi', 420, 666, 667; military of, 614–15, 670, 672; Ettore Schmitz on Joyce as rebel against, 657, 662; in *Ulysses*, 197. *See also* Conservative Party; Liberals

British Weekly (journal), 296–97

Brizeux, Auguste (Breton poet), Kettle quotes, 331

Brooks, Maurice (Liberal candidate for Dublin city 1880), 18, 60, 63–66, 68

Brooks, Sydney, articles on 'New Ireland' in *Daily Mail*, 618–19, 618n54

brothels, in *Ulysses*, 235n114; Joyce teaches vocabulary of, 635; brothels of Trieste, 639; language of Triestine brothels in *Finnegans Wake*, 639

Bruno, Giordano, 225n88, 251n146, 281n75, 442, 840; annual commemorative procession of, 526, 526n34; article on, in *Lyceum*, 225n88, 281n75; as 'the Nolan,' 282n77, 453, 535

Budgen, Frank, 362n19, 814, 825; Joyce and, 362, 727, 727n67, 818–19, 824n51, 826–27, 828n60, 830; letter from Paul Léon, 47n11; letters from Joyce, 79, 80; works: 'Further Recollections of James Joyce', 362; *James Joyce and the Making of 'Ulysses' and Other Writings*, 362n19, 825

Bulfin, William ('Che Buono') (contributor to *Sinn Féin*), 611; *Rambles in Eirinn*, 611n41

Bulwer-Lytton, Edward (Sir) (author of *Last Days of Pompeii*), 726

Burke, Edmund, 377, 378

Burke, Ricard O'Sullivan (Fenian), 138–39, 150

Burke, T. H. (under-secretary for Ireland), 19

Burns, Robert, 414, 445n152

Bushe, Seymour, speech in Childs murder trial invoked in 'Aeolus', 168n39, 389

Busser, Ralph C. (American consul, Trieste), 813, 814n17

Butt, Isaac, 57, 59, 128, 310; name punned on in *Finnegans Wake*, 382

Byrne, Edward (Parnellite editor of *Freeman's Journal*), 121, 698

Byrne, John Francis 'Jeffbyrne', *336*, 341, 347–53, *352*, *370*, 584n108; *Countess Cathleen* letter and, 279; death, 353; Easter Rising and, 351–52; as model for Cranly in *Stephen Hero* and *Portrait*, 347; and 7 Eccles Street, 351, 719–20; Sheehy-Skeffington and, 351–52, 353, 465

Byron, George Gordon (Lord), 158, 411n50, 618

Cadorna, Luigi (General), 816
Campbell, Henry (town clerk, Parnell's secretary), 98, 132
Carnarvon (Lord Lieutenant), 700
Carr, Henry, feuds with Joyce in Zurich, 828
Carson, Edward, mentioned in Joyce's 'Home Rule Comet' article, 687
Caruso, Enrico, 716
Casement, Roger, 344; as author of 'The Language of the Outlaw' pamphlet, 30, 31, 365–66
Casey, Joseph Theobald (Fenian), 143n109, 766; brothers Andrew and James and, 139; Clerkenwell prison bombing and, 138, 150, 680; Fenians and, 138–39, 148–50; John Stanislaus Joyce and, 114, 123n38, 137–51; Joyce and, 146–51; in Paris, 138–44, 146–48, 150–51
Casey, Patrice (son of Joseph Casey), as character in *Ulysses*, 147, 148
Casey, Patrick (Fenian), 143n109; Fenians and, 138–40, 146–48, 150n136; John Stanislaus Joyce and, 114, 123n38, 137–51; in Paris, 138–48, 141n100, 150
Castle, Richard (architect of Leinster House), 257n3, 580
Catholic Bulletin (newspaper), 326, 326n133
Catholic Church, 24, 28, 327n136, 691, 776, 778, 781, 812; Bloom's perspective on mass, 806; Gaelic League and, 290–91, 496; Gladstonian Liberals, alliance with, 33–36, 84, 244–46, 544, 750; the Irish Revival and, 495–96; 'Ivy Day' and, 549; Jews and, 784–85, 795–96; John Stanislaus Joyce, disrespect for, 46, 57; Joyce and, 6, 57, 250, 448–49, 453, 466, 468, 486, 489–90, 527, 636, 637, 660, 837; in Joyce lecture, 'L'Irlanda: Isola dei santi e dei savi', 208–9, 671–72; Kettle, and, 319, 322–23; the Split and, 84, 197, 198–217, 238–39, 242–44, 249–53, 294, 549, 552; *Stephen Hero* and, 463, 487–91, 495, 502, 503, 509, 526. *See also* 'two masters' thesis
Catholic Commercial Club, 68n73, 129
Catholic University, 257, 384. *See also* University College, Dublin
Cattaneo, Carlo, *Saggi di filosofia civile* (Essays in civil philosophy), 533; Joyce reads, 802
Cavendish, Frederick (Lord), 19
Cavour, Camillo, 645, 763n190
Celtic Literary Society (University College, Dublin), 261, 338, 427n101
Celtic Twilight, 325, 441, 579, 586; Joyce and, 280, 324, 413, 434, 439, 459, 565, 582–83, 706; *The Playboy of the Western World* and, 628; writers of, 501, 511
Chamberlain, Joseph, 141n103, 418, 605, 684, 688
Christian Brothers, 96, 601–2
Christianity, 219, 412n52, 419, 636, 653, 776n28, 801; Christians, 384–86, 777, 804
Churchill, Randolph (Lord), 368, 368n39, 699
Civil War, Irish, xxvii, 72n85, 836
Civil War, Spanish, 838, 838n86
Clancy, George, *260*, *336*, 710; biography of, 334–47; *Countess Cathleen* letter and, 279; imprisoned and hunger strike, 344; Irish Volunteers, aligns with, 344; Joyce, and, 33, 274, 287, 334–47; as Lord Mayor of Limerick, 345; as model for Davin in *Portrait*, 334–35; as model for Madden in *Stephen Hero*, 334; murdered, 345; at University College, Dublin, 337–39, 342, 362
Clancy, John, 70, 90, 126–37; incarceration, 127, 128; IRB and, 126n50; John Stanislaus Joyce and, 114, 126–37, 335; as model for Mr Fanning in 'Ivy Day' and 'Long John Fanning' in *Ulysses*, 126, 136n84; Parnell and, 117–18, 126, 128, 130, 134–35
Clancy, Máire (wife of George Clancy), 339n175, 342–45, 342n187
Clarke, Edward (Sir), 699, 743
Clery, Arthur, 279n70, 287, 303n53, 382; articles in *The Leader*, 283, 284, 360; on Kettle, 310, 312n88, 322, 326–27; review of

Chamber Music, 632–33; on University College, Dublin, 283–84; as 'Whelan, the College orator' in *Stephen Hero*, 359, 389n84
Clongowes (school), 342, 573; Oliver St John Gogarty at, 408; Joyce attends, 96, 123, 161–63, 181, 562; Stephen Dedalus at, 33, 162–66, 168, 175–76
Collins, Michael, 345, 717
Colthurst, John Bowen (Captain), orders shooting of Sheehy-Skeffington, 309
Colum, Mary (writer, wife of Padraic Colum), 327n135, 331n151, 354n1, 410n45, 763, 770n8
Colum, Padraic, 405n20, 428, 603, 614, 622, 756; *Dubliners* introduction, and, 559; father's conviction over *Playboy* riots and, 622; on Gogarty, 331n151, 410; Joyce and, 56, 251, 321, 334, 354, 399, 406, 409–11, 413–14, 770; on Kettle, 310, 312, 327n135, 334; on W. K. Magee, 408n30; works: *Irish Elegies*, 411; *Our Friend James Joyce*, 327n135, 331n151, 354n1, 410n45, 770n8
Comerford, John (artist), possibly painted Joyce family portraits, 47n11
communism, 829; in *Finnegans Wake*, 842
Confederates Club, the (Cumann na bPáirtíde), University College, Dublin, 261, 339
Conmee, Rev John, S.J. (rector of Clongowes), 96; in *Ulysses*, 616n49
Connolly, James, 208, 458, 460, 551; Easter Rising and, 309, 352–53, 827; Irish Socialist Republican Party and, 459; *Labour, Nationality and Religion*, 208
Conservative Party (colloquially 'Tories'), 18, 59–60, 62–69, 369, 551, 592; *Irish Times* and, 67, 67n70; Liberals and, 20–21, 62, 416, 417
Conway, Elizabeth Hearn ('Dante', governess to Joyce children, model for Dante Riordan in *Portrait*), 123, 171, 171n45, 330n147
Cork, county and city, 27, 71, 76, 165, 424, 687; and alleged connections with Fenians in, 58; Edmund Burke and, 378n58; by-election 1891 in, 90, 214; and campaigns in Parnellite interest in, 85, 91; George Clancy's connections in, 337; endures in Joyce's accent, 393n98; John Stanislaus Joyce educated in, 50–51; John Stanislaus Joyce has urban property in, 55, 72, 94, 95, 96, 781; Joyce family origins in, 46–50; Joyce visits with Triestine businessmen, 720
Il Corriere della Sera (newspaper), 713
Il Corriere Israelitico (newspaper), 791
Cosgrave, Vincent, 465; allegations about Nora Barnacle, 351, 628, 715–16, 719, 764; introduces Joyce to Gogarty, 408n31; as model for Robert Hand, 331–32
Costello, Peter (biographer of John Stanislaus Joyce), 30–31, 47, 330n147
Countess Cathleen, The (play by Yeats), 623, 625, 649; press reports and, 276–81, 325; University College, Dublin and denunciation of, 273, 276–82, 303–4, 325, 627
Cousins, James, describes Joyce as 'a lost angel of a ruined paradise', 414
Cranly, Thomas (Archbishop of Dublin), 348
Creagh, John (Redemptorist priest), incites Limerick Boycott, 784–85
Crimes Act (1882), 689, 695
Crispi, Francesco, 225n88, 227
Crispi, Luca (Joyce scholar), xii, xiii, xxvi, xxvii, 137n88, 467n218
Croce, Benedetto, 529; Joyce's indifference to, 811, 811n6
Croke, Thomas (Archbishop of Armagh), 198, 200–202, 206–7, 212, 236n116, 246n136
Cromwell, Oliver, 180n61, 246, 383, 608, 669, 808
Cullen, Paul (Cardinal), 58, 205n36, 210, 257n3, 265

Cumann na nGaedheal, 287n1, 598

Curran, Constantine P. ('Con'), 48, 170, 226, 257n3, 259n15, *260*, 581, 750; on Giordano Bruno, 225n88; on Catholic Church and Gaelic League, 290–91; on Arthur Clery, 359n9, 382; *Countess Cathleen* letter and, 279; on death of Mary Joyce, 412; Easter Rising and, 833; interview with May Monaghan, 101–2, 753n154; Irish Supreme Court and, 259; on John Stanislaus Joyce, 89, 106, 106n182, 107, 111n209; Joyce and, xviii, 32, 111n209, 256, 267, 270–72, 346, 402n5, 404n17, 415, 442–43, 461, 465, 469, 485–86; on Kettle, 324–25; letter from Joyce, 292n18; on *Lyceum*, 225, 230; *A Portrait* and, 485–86; on Sheehy-Skeffington, 289, 290, 292, 293, 306–7, 308; *Stephen Hero* and, 483, 485–86; University College, and, 260–61, 362. See also *James Joyce Remembered*; *Under the Receding Wave*

Curran, John Philpot, 48

Cusack, Michael (founder of GAA), 113–14, 338, 360, 494; as model for the Citizen in 'Cyclops' (*Ulysses*), 114, 338; in *Stephen Hero*, 114

Cuzzi, Emma (student of Joyce), possible model for 'lady of letters' in *Giacomo Joyce*, 641

Cuzzi, Paolo, student of Joyce, 634

'Cyclops' episode, *Ulysses*, 126n49, 665n14, 682; anti-Semitism and, 783–84, 789–91; Barney Kiernan's pub in, 397, 708, 784, 785, 789; the Citizen in, 114, 304n60, 338, 393, 555n40, 789–91; Jews and, 786, 794

Daedalus, Stephen. *See Stephen Hero*

Daily Chronicle (newspaper), 238n123, 281n76

Daily Express (Irish newspaper), 60n45, 471n238, 577n96, 716; book reviews, 382; John Clancy in, 136–37; 'The Dead' and, 389, 436, 442n137, 443; on Dublin election 1880, 61, 65; editors, 404, 436, 441–42; *Finnegans Wake* and, 443; Gerald Fitzgibbon's speech and, 367n38; 'An Irish Rural Library' list and, 433; John Stanislaus Joyce and lawsuit in, 99n152; Joyce as reviewer for, 177n54, 404, 428–31, 433, 436–43, 485, 832; on John Kelly, 120; letters to, 204n34; on Maamtrasna murders, 693–95; on national tribute raised for Parnell, 76; *Playboy* riots and, 627–28; on Taylor's King's Inns speech, 367; Taylor-Kinahan debate in, 381n64; on William Butler Yeats, 280–81

Daily Mail (British newspaper), 594, 716; Joyce reads in Rome, 617–22

Daily Nation (Irish newspaper), 222, 276, 278–79

Daly, John (cousin of John Stanislaus Joyce, member of Parliament in Cork City), 49, 76

Dana (journal), 444n146, 446n159, 525; editors, 35, 273, 444, 449, 527, 596; Joyce's essay 'A Portrait of the Artist' in, 400, 444, 450, 451–61; politics of, 443–50

D'Annunzio, Gabriele, 281, 281n75, 540, 816, 829, 829n68

Dante Alighieri, 156, 270, 660, 818

Davis, Eugene, Fenian, 139–42, 145

Davis, Thomas, 277n58, 369, 428–29, 501, 845

Davitt, Michael, 150, 156, 212, 382, 470, 690, 701n128; on Patrick Casey, 140–41; condemns attack on Jews of Limerick, 785; elections and, 166, 497n47; 'Gas from a Burner', quoted in, 179; Land League and, 141n103, 142n107, 143n109, 253–54; National Monuments Committee and, 129; O'Shea divorce crisis and, 236; Pigott and, 143–44; Sheehy-Skeffington, and, 180n61, 292–95, 298, 301n49; Stead and, 297; works: *Fall of Feudalism in Ireland*, 140–41, 150, 470; *Labour World*, 86, 232, 239

Dawson, William (journalist), 276, 276n56, 279n70, 325, 381
'Dead, The' (story, *Dubliners*), 440n135, 558, 560n57, 569n78, 636; *Daily Express* and, 389, 436, 442n137, 443; exile from Ireland influencing, 631; *Finnegans Wake* and, 583n105; Gabriel Conroy in, 389, 442n137, 443, 585–89; Gretta Conroy in, 588; influence of Anatole France on, 560–61; Michael Furey in, 560, 747; Miss Ivors in, 436, 442n137, 443, 585, 587; Morkan family in, 584n108, 585, 587–88; political resonance of, xviii; spectral subtext of, 434, 560, 583; writing of, 542, 566, 582–89, 626, 633. *See also* 'Destruction of Dá Derga's Hostel, The'
Deane, Seamus (literary critic), 40, 554; 'Dead Ends', 554n39
Dedalus, Simon (fictional character), 121n29; anticlericalism of, 81–82; Parnellism of, 84, 167–69, 182, 210; paternity of, 50; in *A Portrait*, 55, 124; in *Ulysses*, 55, 125n47, 388. *See also* Joyce, John Stanislaus
Dedalus, Stephen (fictional character), 42, 446, 589; aphorisms of, 450; Leopold Bloom and, 774–75, 808; blushing, 390; at Clongowes, 162–66, 168; Davin and, 340–42; 'enigma of a manner', 271; flight of, 334; Joyce's anticipation of, 827; as misleading guide to Joyce, 400; Buck Mulligan and, 442; Parnellism of, xv, 37, 166, 657–58; passing into silence, xxvii, 831–32; in *Portrait of the Artist as a Young Man* and, xv, xvi, xxvii, 14, 37, 42, 55, 84, 124, 161–70, 269, 333, 340, 400, 433, 589, 657–58, 822, 831–32; preoccupations of, 433; rhetoric and, 390, 393; stream of consciousness of, 389; in *Ulysses*, 148, 168n39, 720, 766, 793; understanding of politics, 162, 169
Defoe, Daniel, 663n3; Joyce's lecture on, 727–29
Delany, William, S.J. (president of University College, Dublin), 265, 284, 362, 465
'Destruction of Dá Derga's Hostel, The' ('Togail Bruidhne Dá Derga'), 434–35, 583–85. *See also* 'Dead, The'
De Tuoni, Dario (Joyce's friend in Trieste), 638–39, 761–62, 810; *Ricordo di Joyce*, 638n38, 646n72, 761n180, 811n7
De Valera, Eamon, 287n1, 344, 397
Devereux, Robert (Earl of Essex), 574–79
Devlin, Joseph, 298
Devoy, John (Fenian), 18, 351
Dickens, Charles, 726, 727n67, 790
Dickinson, Emily Monroe (sister of Charles Stewart Parnell, author of *A Patriot's Mistake*), 560
Dilke, Charles (Sir), 22, 235, 248, 699
Dillon, John, 90, 137, 181n67, 189, 257n5, 288, 416, 718; escape to France, 128–29; L&H and, 258; letter to *Freeman's Journal*, 205n35; politics and, 205n35, 421, 608; the Split and, 216
Dillon, Matthew (cousin of John Dillon), 137
Dillon, Valentine Blake (cousin of John Dillon), 70, 137
Dinneen, Patrick, *Creideamh agus Gorta*, 282; *Irish-English Dictionary*, 364, 470
Disraeli, Benjamin, 29–30, 61, 685, 740
Dixon, Henry (solicitor's clerk), and destruction of *Dubliners*, 754–55
Dlugacz, Moses (rabbi and student of Joyce), 791–93, 800; gives name to character in *Ulysses*, 792
Dodd, Reuben J. (solicitor), 94; gives name to character in *Ulysses*, 781, 783
Dowden, Edward, 377
Doyle, Arthur Conan, 633
Dreyfus, Alfred, xiv, 560n57
Drumont, Edouard (anti-Semitic journalist), *La France Juive*, 149; mentioned in *Ulysses*, 149, 766–67

Dublin, as centre of paralysis, 462, 581, 717; as city of ghosts, 388; royal visits to, 131, 419–21, 665–66; working class of, 130, 779. *See also main entries for Dubliners*; Easter Rising; Joyce, James; Joyce, John Stanislaus; University College, Dublin
Dublin Corporation, 70, 95, 146, 419, 422, 545, 551
Dubliners, 462, 531, 540, 594, 786, 835; Colum's introduction to, 559; destruction of first edition of, xxvii, 284–85, 475, 751n146, 755–56, 758–60; Joyce's letter to press concerning, 725; Ezra Pound on, 821; publishing history of, xviii, 4, 321, 332, 475, 478, 505, 530, 542, 565, 566n70, 571–72, 587, 596, 625n72, 628, 632, 634, 712–13, 715–16, 725, 726n60, 727, 745–46, 749–56, 820, 832; quadripartite schema for, 566; reviews of, 633; Vigilance Committee and, 750–51
Dubliners, stories: 'An Encounter', 542, 567, 746, 750, 752, 758; 'Grace', 136n84, 251, 542, 556, 566, 570, 621; 'A Little Cloud', 64, 542, 572; 'A Mother', 191, 492n30, 542, 566, 567–70, 676; 'A Painful Case', 458–59, 801; 'The Sisters,' 400, 461–62, 636, 806. *See also* 'Dead, The'; 'Ivy Day in the Committee Room'; 'Two Gallants, The'
Dublin Evening Mail (Irish newspaper), 62, 66
Dublin Metropolitan Police, 121, 127, 130
Dublin White Cross Vigilance Association, 751
Dublin Woollen Company, 602, 721
Dubois, L. Paul, Kettle provides introduction to his *Contemporary Ireland*, 314
Duffy, Charles Gavan, 672
Dujardin, Edouard, 444
Dunne, Finley Peter, 825

Easter, 487, 539, 636–37
Easter Rising (1916), xxvii, 288, 309, 312, 344, 417, 828; Joyce, and silence on, 833; leaders executed, 352–53, 643n58, 827
Eblana Literary and Debating Society, 423
Edalji, George, 705
Edward VII (British monarch), 222, 304n60, 421, 426, 558n52; in 'Ivy Day in the Committee Room', 545, 548–49, 560, 725; Nicholas II and, 304n60, 305
Egan Kenny, Henry (pseud. 'Sean-Ghall', journalist, friend of Griffith), 573–77, 579–80
Eglinton, John (nom de plume of W. K. Magee), 408n30; *Dana* and, 273, 449; Joyce jokes about, 445n152, 446; in *Ulysses*, 446; works: *Anglo-Irish Essays*, 446n159; *Bards and Saints*, 446; 'The Beginnings of Joyce', 446n158; 'De-Davization of Irish Literature, The', 446, 446n159; *Irish Literary Portraits*, 402n7, 413n59, 444n146, 446, 447. *See also* Magee, William Kirkpatrick
Egoist (magazine), 183, 566n69, 820, 821, 829
Egoist Press, 822, 829
Egypt, 384, 684, 772; 'Aeolus' episode and, 390; Egyptian Book of the Dead, 849; Jews revolt against, 801; in Joyce's lecture 'L'Irlanda: Isola dei santi e dei savi', 668, 704; Taylor's speech and, 366, 371, 381, 398
Eliot, T. S., 111, 153n2
Elkin Mathews Ltd (publishers), 403, 632
Ellmann, Richard, 51n30, 90, 353, 631, 638n40, 648; on Joseph Casey, 139; on Christmas dinner scene, 38n15, 171n45; on John Clancy, 126n49; on *Countess Cathleen* letter, 279n69; on 'The Holy Office', 159; Louis Hyman and, 792, 800; on influence of Anatole France on Joyce, 560; on Irish Free State, 836; on John Stanislaus Joyce, 54, 54n36, 89, 90; Stanislaus Joyce and, 353, 786; on Joyce's childhood poem to Parnell, 158n12, 159; on Joyce's deer imagery, 276n31; on Joyce's nationalism, 8–9; on Joyce's Parnellism, 38–40, 41n25, 89, 93; on Lady Gregory, 413n59; on *Language of the*

Outlaw pamphlet, 365; on Leinster Hall meeting, 85–87; misattributes Joyce's authorship of of 'Politics and Cattle Disease', 749n139; on *My Brother's Keeper*, 80n107, 153n3; Margot Norris's criticism of, 42–43, 43n29, 305n62; on Parnell, 54, 152n1; Pelaschiar's criticism of, 676n54; on prototype of Leopold Bloom, 648, 792, 799; on protype of Robert Hand, 331; on Sheehy-Skeffington, 303, 305n62, 448n164; on Taylor's speech, 364, 365

Emmet, Robert, 350, 407, 679

Engels, Friedrich, 826

Ennis, Edward, 698

Epstein, Edmund L. (critic), 14, 342; computes Christmas holidays in *Portrait*, 165n30

'Eumaeus' episode, *Ulysses*, xvii, 19, 27, 125n48, 235n114, 785–86, 807–8; Leopold Bloom in, 125, 135, 563, 564, 681; Mr John Casey in, 125; Parnell in, 563, 564

Evening Herald (Irish newspaper), 121, 121n33, 786

Evening Press (Irish newspaper), 221

Evening Telegraph (Irish newspaper), 179n59, 280n72, 387n79, 786n54; in 'Aeolus' episode, 177, 177n54, 387, 396; *Freeman's Journal* and, 97, 717; William Ewart Gladstone and, 683; Joyce and, 717, 718, 720; letter from Blackwood Price, 748; on politics, 60–61; *Ulysses* and, 718

Exiles (play by Joyce), 305n62, 319, 327–32, 330nn146–47, 331n151, 712n1; Robert Hand in, 319, 327–32; Beatrice Justice in, 328–30, 330n147; Jack Justice in, 330

Fabian Society, 538, 691

Falconer, John (printer), 285, 751, 754–57

Falkiner, Frederick (Sir), 781–84, 782n37; in *Ulysses*, 781, 783

Fallon, William G., 257, 258, 310, 602–3; on John Francis Byrne, 348; *Countess Cathleen* letter and, 279; on Joyce, 269, 270, 274; rugby football and, 274, 274n53

Fascio Rivoluzionario di Azione Internazionalista (1914), 518

fascism, xxvii, 634, 642, 829; *Finnegans Wake* and, 843; Joyce disdains, 838, 842–46

Faure, Felix, 149, 767

Fawkes, Guy, 774

Feilbogen, Siegmund (professor), 824, 825

Fenians, Fenianism, 31, 87, 210n48, 254, 294, 317, 341, 426, 430, 459–60, 604, 702, 763n190; anticlericalism and, xiv, 81, 83, 495–96; George Clancy and, 254, 341; John Clancy and, 126, 127, 128, 130–31, 135; Irish American Fenian movement, 139, 140; in 'Ivy Day in the Committee Room', 550; John Stanislaus Joyce and, 57–58, 70, 114; Joyce and, 150–51, 190, 192, 544, 604, 607, 617, 679–82, 679n71; John Kelly and, 119, 123n38; Parnell and, 18, 128, 129, 130, 192, 212, 254, 460, 551, 554, 607; Sheehy-Skeffington and, 294; violence and, 138–39, 150, 430, 666

Ferguson, Samuel, *Conary and Lays of the Western Gael*, 586

Ferrero, Guglielmo, 529, 670, 795, 802; burning of books by Fascists, 534; influence of, 528–35, 539, 572, 579; on Parnell, 533–34; positivism and, 528–30, 534; works: *L'Europa giovane*, 528, 531–32, 533, 795, 802; *Grandezza e decadenza di Roma*, 528, 531–32; *Il militarismo*, 528, 530, 572

Ferri, Enrico (socialist, professor of penal law in Rome), 516–17, 520–22

Fianna Éireann, 344

Field, William, 258, 748

Le Figaro (newspaper), 591–92

Finlay, Peter, S.J. (probable author of *Lyceum* articles), 225–30

Finlay, T. A., S.J. (founder of *Lyceum*, brother of Peter Finlay), 225, 225n86, 779–81; 'The Jew Amongst Us', 779; 'The Jew in Ireland', 779–80

Finnegans Wake, xx–xxi, 14–15, 44, 160n19, 217, 308, 669; *Daily Express* and, 443; 'The Dead' and, 583n105; Dublin city election in, 68–69; Earwicker in, 79–80; English language and, 839; fall and redemption in, xiv, 31, 840; Festy King in, 707; *Gaelic Lexicon* and, 363–64, 584n107; 'get my price', 26; gossip of washerwomen, 393n98; 'Instoppressible' in, 178–79; Irish independence in, 840; Irish language in, 364; Irish myths and, 538; Irish statehood and, 828, 837; John Stanislaus Joyce and, 54, 106–7; Stanislaus Joyce and, 80n107; Joyce newspaper reading and, 178, 180; Kettle and, 333; Mazzini and, 763; Hyacinth O'Donnell B. A. in, 735; Parnell and, xxiii, 37, 57, 119, 567, 745; parody of Joyce's juvenile poetry in, 158n12; patriarchal authority in, 539; Phoenix Park in, 79–80, 80n104; Pigott forgery, 21; Anna Livia Plurabelle, 107n190, 630, 849; political vision of, 841–43; Protestants and, 671n36; publishing of, 837, 851; recordings of, 393n98; Shem the Penman in, 12, 431n111, 450, 613, 639, 650, 710, 815, 822; Slataper and, 646n72; *Stephen Hero* and, 509; Tim Finnegan, 839; Trieste and, 762, 764; *triestino* dialect and, 765; as 'Work in Progress', 837

First World War (Great War), xxvi, 15–16, 23n3, 344, 565, 768, 838; Austria-Hungary and, 810, 811, 816–17; Home Rule and, 312n84; Italy and, 518, 641–42, 656, 811–13, 815–17; Joyce and, 762, 763; Zurich in, 814–19

FitzGerald, Desmond (government minister of Irish Free State), 656

FitzGerald, Edward (Lord), 669

FitzGerald, James (Duke of Leinster), 580–81

Fitzgerald, P. N. (Fenian), 129

Fitzgerald, T. A. (Franciscan), 326; 'Is It Not Enough to Be Anglicised without Becoming European?', 326n133

FitzGerald, Thomas (Earl of Kildare), 'Silken Thomas', 773, 774

Fitzgibbon, Gerald, 191, 367n38, 569n78; Christmas party of, 368n39; J. F. Taylor and, 364, 367–68, 367n38, 371–75, 380–81

Fitzgibbon, John, 117

Fitzharris, James, in *Ulysses*, 19–20

Flaubert, Gustave, 234n111, 573

Flood, William Henry Grattan, *History of Irish Music*, 573n88; *The Story of the Harp*, 572–73, 573n88, 577, 579–80

Ford, Ford Maddox, 820

Forster, William Edward (chief secretary), 115, 128

Fortnightly Review (newspaper), 214n57, 256, 269, 456n187

Fournier D'Albe, Edmund E. (lexicographer), 364

Fox, Charles James, 377

France, 15, 128, 145, 148, 227, 527; in First World War, 816; *laïcité* and, 213, 798, 844; military, 57–58, 147. *See also* Paris

France, Anatole, 514; as influence on 'Ivy Day' and 'The Dead', 560–61, 636

Francini Bruni, Alessandro, 634, 637, 648, 674, 761n180, 767n4; on Joyce's politics, 537; on Joyce's Triestine articles, 709; 'Joyce Stripped Naked in the Piazza' ('Joyce intimo spogliato in piazza'), 638n38, 658, 659; letter from Joyce, 634n19

Franck, Nino, 177

Franco, Francisco (General), 838

Franco-Prussian War (1870–71), 57–58, 139

Franz Ferdinand (Archduke), 810

Franz Joseph I (Emperor of Austria-Hungary), 543, 766

Freeman's Journal (Irish newspaper), cartoon of Parnell in, 302; on John Clancy, 128–29, 132n71, 133, 134; Dublin election 1880 and, 60–61, 64–67; editorials, 132n71, 202–3, 203n27, 211n52, 708n150; editors, 97, 121, 205n35, 463, 651n97, 717, 717n30; *Evening Telegraph*, as sister paper of, 97, 717; *Exiles* and, 328–29; on Gladstone's death, 683; 'Historicus' [Barry O'Brien] in, 206–7, 383; Home Rule and, 261; on Irish Parliamentary Party, 342–43; John Stanislaus Joyce and lawsuit in, 98, 99n152; Joyce's pastiche of style of, 328; John Kelly in, 115; Kettle's review of *Chamber Music* in, 325, 329, 632, 633; letter on *The Countess Cathleen* and, 278; letters from John O'Leary and, 186–90; on Maamtrasna murders, 693, 697–98, 703; misattributed Joyce article 'Politics and Cattle Disease' in, 708n150, 748–49; on national tribute raised for Parnell, 74–75, 76; on Parnell, 24, 74–76, 128n54, 184, 239, 243, 244, 421n90, 470, 786; on Parnell-O'Shea marriage, 83; *Playboy*, denounces, 621; *Playboy* riots and, 623, 625, 627; *Portrait of the Artist*, anonymous review of, 633; on the Split, 184, 202–3, 204n33; Taylor's article 'The Irish Revival' in, 374–77; Taylor's obituary, 383; Taylor's speech and, 364–65, 367; in *Ulysses*, 177, 223, 367, 387, 463, 546n7; on United Liberal Club, 59, 67; on University College degree conferring, 283; Archbishop Walsh criticizes, 202–3, 211n51

Freemasons, 202, 227, 648, 783

French, Percy, 470

French Revolution, 228, 490, 767

Freud, Sigmund, 634, 643

Freund, Gisèle, 109

Furlan, Boris (Joyce's friend in Trieste), 634–35, 649–50, 811

Gaelic Athletic Association, 338, 360

Gaelic League, 282n78, 359–60, 367, 375–76, 379, 407n29, 432; apolitical claims of, 261, 355–57, 427; Catholic Church and, 290–91, 496; George Clancy and, 338, 339, 341, 344–45; Irish Parliamentary Party and, 313, 318, 356, 357; Joyce and, 335, 354, 362–63, 396–97, 410, 586, 667; Kettle on, 313, 315, 318; nationalism and, 315, 354, 567; Skeffington opposes, 277, 290–91, 298n37, 307, 309; in *Stephen Hero*, 361, 363; University College and, 261–62, 277, 290, 338–39, 341, 355, 396

Gallaher, Ignatius, 64, 389, 463

Geiringer, Eugenio (architect), 761, 762

George III (British monarch), 206

George V (British monarch), 222, 725, 726

Germany, 309n72, 373, 455–56, 532, 826; in First World War, 810, 811; Nazis, 793, 838–39, 843–44, 846–47

Gerrards Brothers, 103

ghosts (spectres), 700n123, 748; 'The Dead' spectral subtext, 434, 560, 583; Parnell as spectral figure, xvii, 36, 37, 183, 196, 299, 480, 553, 560–61, 731, 741, 850–51; stories, 183, 560, 584n108; 'To a Shade,' 480, 850–51; in *Ulysses*, 37, 278n63, 383, 388, 391

Gibbon, Edward, 488

Gilbert, Stuart, 386–87, 454n183

Gill, T. P., 132–33, 280

Gillet, Louis, 45, 50, 105; *Claybook for James Joyce*, 45n8, 50n25, 105n178, 152n1; on John Stanislaus Joyce, 112; on Joyce and Parnell, 152n1, 542

Giolitti, Giovanni (Italian prime minister), 456, 516, 517

Gladstone, William Ewart (British prime minister), xix, 18, 185, 228, 493, 569n78, 577, 683, 811n6; administration, 23n3, 130; antifeminism and, 297; Home Rule and, 20, 418, 576, 579, 684–85, 729, 740–41; legacy, 682; letters from W. T. Stead, 237–38, 241; Liberals and, 20, 21, 22, 34, 740; Maamtrasna murders and, 698–99; Morley and, 741, 742; Parnell and, 21, 23, 30, 61–62, 156–57, 188, 195, 197, 204, 233n108, 563, 569, 739–40, 844; ultramontanism and, 228n97; 'union of hearts' and, 187. *See also* Liberals

Goethe, Johann Wolfgang von, 267n31, 326
Gogarty, Oliver St John, 290, 314, 597, 603, 611, 757n167; on 'Gas from a Burner', 285, 285n89, 757; *It Isn't That Time of Year at All*, 285, 285n89, 757n167; Joyce and, 321, 331n151, 408, 408n31, 410, 410n40, 413–15, 415n71, 445, 454n183, 462, 465, 468–69, 494, 519–20, 715, 806; limericks by, 322, 322n121; Martello Tower and, 468–69; mother (Margaret Gogarty) and, 415; on sexual morality in British army, 609–10, 614–15, 670, 672; *Sinn Féin* articles and, 608–17
Gonne, Maud, 131, 149, 367, 421, 666n20, 767; Arthur Griffith and, 435; Joyce and, 592; letter to W. B. Yeats, 380
Gorman, Herbert, 8, 147, 279, 402, 512n5, 814, 833; on book burning, 751n146; *James Joyce*, 160n19, 180n62, 512n5, 756n163; on John Stanislaus Joyce, 57, 59, 82; Joyce and, 402n6, 478, 511, 602, 633, 756n163, 758–59, 762–63, 813, 827; on Joyce and Kettle, 321–22; on Joyce's poem on death of Parnell, 160; on Parnell, 180n62
Gosse, Edmund, 823
Grant Richards (publisher), 462, 507; *Dubliners* and, 505, 566n70, 725, 726n60, 746, 756, 820; 'The Two Gallants' and, 530, 542, 571–72
Grattan, Henry, 212, 377, 377n55, 407, 573
Greece, 370, 392, 726n65; ancient, 239, 385, 392–93, 672n41, 801; Greek Orthodox Church, 636–37, 795, 806; Greeks, 373, 646, 823; 'Jewgreek is Greekjew', 801–9
Gregory, Augusta (Lady), 435, 608, 625; Joyce and, 56, 358n8, 404, 405–7, 409–10, 412–13, 436, 439–42, 453, 486n14, 627; letter from Synge, 405–6; W. B. Yeats and, 358n8, 404, 407, 411, 586, 622, 627; works: *Cuchulain of Muirthemne*, 435; *Gods and Fighting Men*, 586; *Poets and Dreamers*, 412–13, 436, 439–42
Griffith, Arthur, xx, 37, 139, 148, 361, 419, 425, 426n96; belief in incompatibility of nationalism and socialism, 536–37; biography of, 423–27; Leopold Bloom and, 786; on British military, 614–15; Celtic Literary Society and, 338; George Clancy and, 338; John Clancy and, 131; James Connolly, endorsement of, 551; Michael Cusack and, 494; economic programme of, 599–608, 680, 709; as founder, editor of *United Irishman* and *Sinn Féin*, 177, 426–27; as founder of Sinn Féin, 316, 426–27, 592, 596; Oliver St John Gogarty and, 608, 614; Maud Gonne and, 666n20; Hungarian policy, 655; Irish revivalism and, 355, 372; Joyce compares to Labriola, 521, 522, 524, 612; Joyce deploys arguments of in Triestine articles and lectures, 682, 684, 737; Joyce's affinity with, 39, 478, 508, 591, 595–96, 599, 603–7, 612; Joyce's meeting with, 478, 662, 754; Joyce's review of Rooney offends, 432, 726n61; Egan Kenny and, 573; William Magee and, 444; National Council, founder of, 558; nationalism and, 606, 711; parliamentarianism and, 522, 604, 683–84, 739n99; Parnell and, 423–24, 480, 690, 730–31, 733–34; parodies 'Dialogues of the Day', 592–93; John Redmond, and, 690, 731n78, 733; *Resurrection of Hungary*, 314, 426, 435, 617; William Rooney and, 382–83, 423, 428, 434; Sheehy-Skeffington and, 605–6; in *Stephen Hero*, 494–95; James Stephens on, 424–26; J. F. Taylor and, 369, 372, 379, 382, 383, 384, 384n72. *See also Sinn Féin*; Sinn Féin; *United Irishman*
Guinness, Sir Arthur Edward (Lord Ardilaun), 60, 63–65, 67–68, 107n190; brother Lord Iveagh and, 68
Gwynn, Stephen, 311n83, 436–38, 442, 608, 625

Hackett, Francis (reviewer), 483
Hague, The, 299, 303, 303n53
Halévy, Daniel, 519
Harcourt, William (Sir), 700, 700n122
Hardiman, Adrian, xii–xiii, 691; *Joyce in Court*, xii–xiii, xiiin4
Hardiman, James, *History of the Town and County of Galway*, 747
Harmsworth, Alfred (Lord Northcliffe), 618
Harrington, Timothy, 90, 98–99, 115, 126, 137, 258, 421; Irish National League and, 236; Maamtrasna murders and, 693, 698, 700, 702; Parnellism and, 70, 424; on the Split, 202, 205n35
Harris, Ernest Wormser (president of Dublin Hebrew Congregation), 782
Hauptmann, Gerhart (German dramatist), 514
Hayes, John Patrick, and Pigott forgery, 145
Healy, James (Reverend), 569n78
Healy, John (Archbishop of Tuam), 664–65; *Insula Sanctorum et Doctorum; or, Ireland's Ancient Schools and Scholars*, 665n14
Healy, Maurice (brother of T. M. Healy), 76
Healy, Michael (uncle of Nora Barnacle), 466–67, 719
Healy, Timothy Michael, xii, xv, 25, 76, 735n85; in 'A Mother', 191, 568–70; anti-Semitism, raises issue in House of Commons, 782; attends L&H, 258; author of *Why Ireland Is Not Free*, 181n67; clerical support of, 199–200, 222, 718; in Committee Room 15, 24; criticized by *United Ireland*, 213; detestation of J. F. Taylor, 382; feminising of, 191, 224, 492n30; in *Finnegans Wake*, 180, 186, 567, 849–50; as Governor-General, 567, 837; *Insuppressible* and, 178–79, 184, 186, 202; John Stanislaus Joyce and, 88; Joyce's childhood poem and, 157–59, 160n19, 550; as Judas Iscariot, 742; Leinster Hall meeting and, 22, 85–88, 569–70; Maamtrasna murders and, 698; maligns Kettle, 334; newspaper war of the Split and, 183–86; Parnell, rhetoric against, 186, 254, 395, 669, 734–35, 769; Parnellite loathing of, 24, 87; Parnell's principal adversary in the Split, xxiii, 22, 24, 27, 217, 219; in *Stephen Hero*, 493; in *Ulysses*, 191
Hebrew language, 363, 794
Hegel, G.W.F., 319, 322, 322n121
Heine, Heinrich, 802
Hellenism, 801, 802
Henry II (King of England), 207, 209, 671
Henry VIII (King of England), 773
Herring, Phillip F. (Joyce scholar), 12–13, 29n11, 40
Herzl, Theodor, 776n28; *Der Judenstaat*, 792
Hibernia (ship), 471
Hishon, D. J. (friend of John Stanislaus Joyce), 98–99, 104, 105n176, 120, 135
Hishon, Nora (manager of Eblana hotel), 104
Hitler, Adolf, 838, 839, 846
Hogan, Edmund, S.J., teaches Celtic Studies University College, 338
Hohenlohe-Schillingsfür, Konrad (Prince), Joyce teaches his wife and children, 649; recommends Joyce, 811–12
Holloway, Joseph (theatre critic), 277, 720, 752; *Joseph Holloway's Abbey Theatre*, 277n58
Holocaust, 793, 838–39
Homer, 30, 740, 806–7, 817–19
Home Rule, xi, 12, 59, 69, 216; George Clancy and, 344; Conservatives and, 369, 416, 579; crisis (1912–14), xviii, 476, 565, 591, 663, 832; Dublin election of 1880 and, 61–62, 66–67; *Exiles* and, 329–32; first Bill of (1886), 20, 26, 418, 426, 579, 683–84, 729, 740–41, 743; First World War and, 312n84; Griffith and, 426, 602, 605, 675, 683–84, 690, 730–33; 'Ivy Day in the Committee Room' and, 553; Joyce's 'two masters' critique and, 252; Joyce's view

Home Rule (*continued*)
of, 263, 422, 455, 479, 675, 677, 709; Kettle and, 314–16, 332; Liberals and, 22, 23, 26, 232, 260, 476, 577; *Lyceum* and, 225, 231; O'Shea divorce and, 22–23, 83; second Bill of (1893), 29, 426, 683–84, 744; the Split and, 26–29, 83, 211–14, 234; W. T. Stead and, 235–42, 246n136; third Bill of (1912), 309, 312n84, 329, 476, 591, 729–30, 744. *See also* Joyce, James, works, articles, essays, and pamphlets: 'La Cometa dell "Home Rule"', 'Home Rule maggiorenne'
Home Rule party. *See* Irish Parliamentary Party
Hone, Joseph (of Maunsel & Company), 746, 750
Hooper, John (editor of *Freeman's Journal*, friend of John Stanislaus Joyce), 97
Horgan, J. J. (Parnell's election agent in Cork), 741
Horse Show, the (Dublin), 716, 717
Houston, Edward Caulfield (secretary of Irish Loyal and Patriotic Union), 143; Pigott forgery and, 144n114, 236
Howes, Marjorie, 41–42, 554n39
Huddy, Joseph, murdered in Galway, 701
Huebsch, B. W. (Joyce's American publisher), 157, 279n69, 822
Hughes, Hugh Price (founder of *Methodist Times*), 232–33, 238, 244, 247
Humphreys, Susan L., on Ferrero, 532, 572
Hunter, Alfred H., possible model for 'Mr Hunter' in Joyce's unwritten short story and for Leopold Bloom, 531, 649n84, 729, 786–87
Huxley, T. H., 486
Hyde, Douglas, 440; *Casadh an tSúgáin* (*The Twisting of the Rope*), 281; and speech 'The Necessity for De-Anglicising Ireland', 261, 357–58, 358n8
Hyman, Louis (historian), 800; *Jews of Ireland from Earliest Times to the Year 1910, The*, 776nn28–29, 782n37, 786n54, 792
Ibsen, Henrik, 331, 616, 618–19, 620, 626, 643; Joyce as disciple of, 32, 269, 270, 281n76, 306n68, 399; Joyce's correspondence with, 252; Joyce's praise of, 306, 514, 541, 613; Joyce's review of, 269; Yeats and, 280; works: *A Doll's House*, 620; *Peer Gynt*, 270, 729n75; 'Til min Ven Revolutions-Taleren', 541
imperialism, 431, 612, 642, 688; in 'Aeolus', 389–92; anti-imperialism, Joyce and, xx, 40–41; *Callista* and, 384–86; in *Il Piccolo della Sera*, 674; W. T. Stead as imperialist, 235, 295–96; Taylor-Fitzgibbon King's Inns debate and, 370, 373–74. *See also* Austria-Hungary; Britain; 'two masters' thesis
India, 375, 592, 609, 609n35, 615, 620, 684
L'Indipendente (newspaper), 645, 800n92
Insuppressible (Irish newspaper), 117, 178–79, 186, 202
Invincibles, the, 19, 139–40, 680, 700, 702
Irish Catholic (newspaper), 203n29, 204n34, 217–24, 225n86; aligns with non-conformist conscience, 219, 242–43; Christmas dinner scene and, 223; W. F. Dennehy, as editor of, 217–18; Joyce's reading of in Rome, 594, 597–98; Joyce's 'two masters' thesis and, 217–24, 249; on Parnellism, 219–20, 249; Parnell's death, editorial response to, 221; on socialism, 222; the Split and, 202–3, 223–24; Archbishop Walsh and, 211n51, 222
Irish Council Bill (1907), 682, 683–84
Irish Daily Independent (Irish newspaper), 115, 120, 121n33, 367, 470, 470n234
Irish Free State, 41, 186, 258, 372, 387n79, 667, 836–37, 849
Irish Homestead (magazine), 400, 461
Irish independence, xiii, 340, 827; Joyce and, 833–37
Irish Independent (Irish newspaper), 426, 593–94, 620, 786; George Clancy in, 345; John Clancy in, 132; death of Ibsen,

620n58; editor, 222; Taylor-Kinahan debate in, 381n64
Irish Independent League, 131
Irish language, in *Finnegans Wake*, 364, 584n107; Griffith on commercial value of, 601; Hebrew and, 794; Joyce identifies it with Phoenician, 806–7; Joyce's knowledge of, 361–64, 407n29, 434, 586, 612; in *A Portrait of the Artist*, 341, 354, 362, 363; Synge and, 407n29. *See also* Gaelic League; Irish Revival
Irish Literary Revival, 400, 410n30, 582, 587–89, 678; Eglinton dissenting voice in, 408n30; Joyce and, 404, 407, 422, 835; Joyce's lecture on, 677–68; with Maunsel & Company, 715
Irish Literary Theatre, 281–82, 281n76
Irishman (newspaper), 61
Irish National Federation (anti-Parnellite party formed March 1891), 199
Irish National Land League, 18
Irish National League, 76, 195, 202, 225, 236; John Clancy's involvement with, 128–29; John Kelly's involvement with, 115, 119; Redmond speech and, 210–11, 213; the Split and, 210–13
Irish Parliamentary Party (IPP), xxiii, 16, 68, 416, 709, 729, 743; debate in Committee Room 15 and, 24–26, 81, 173, 178, 184, 188, 196, 199, 239–40, 249, 544, 563, 685; Gaelic League and, 313, 318, 356, 357; Joyce and, 458, 544, 607–8; leaders of, 313, 342–43, 357, 543; Liberals and, 22, 24; Parnell and, xi, 18, 20, 85, 317–18; reunification, 26, 29, 543–45, 557; Sinn Féin and, xix, 316, 324, 344, 591, 596, 616; the Split and, xii, xiii, 225–31; 'union of hearts' and, 20, 21, 187, 238, 251, 418, 187; United Irish League, 131, 309, 312–14, 313n89, 342–43, 460, 682, 684, 691n96. *See also* Home Rule
Irish People (Irish newspaper), 208
Irish Republican Army (IRA), 345, 836
Irish Republican Brotherhood (IRB), 119, 126n50, 129; leadership, 18, 138, 187; membership, 18, 410, 427, 604, 681
Irish Revival, 354–61; in 'Aeolus', 354, 387, 395; Catholic Church and, 355, 495–96; George Clancy and, 335–37; Douglas Hyde and, 261, 357–58; Irish Party and, 356; 'Ivy Day in the Committee Room' and, 567; Joyce's lecture 'L'Irlanda: Isola dei santi e dei savi' and, 668; Joyce's skepticism towards, 337, 358–60, 434, 441, 478, 612–13, 668, 793; 'A Mother' and, 567–68; William Rooney and, 424, 427; *Stephen Hero* and, 360–61, 435, 493–96, 498; J. F. Taylor's King's Inns speech and, 364–81, 393; at University College, 261–62, 355–60; Zionism, comparison with, 792–93. *See also* Gaelic League; Irish language
Irish Socialist Republican Party, 459, 460; Joyce attends meetings of, 458–59; in 'A Painful Case', 458
Irish Times (newspaper), 37, 51n30, 111n209, 259n11, 367, 387n79, 716; John Clancy at, 127; Conservatives and, 67, 67n70; on Dublin election 1880, 63, 66–67; John Stanislaus Joyce and lawsuit in, 99n152; Joyce and, 177n54; on Maamtrasna murders, 692–93; on Parnell, 560; Skeffington's letter to, 626
Irish Transvaal Committee, 418, 605
Irish Vigilance Association, 751
Irish Volunteers, 344
'L'Irlanda alla sbarra' ('Ireland at the Bar', Joyce's article in *Il Piccolo della Sera*, 16 Sept. 1907), 378, 398, 657, 691, 706–7
'L'Irlanda: Isola dei santi e dei savi' ('Ireland: Island of saints and sages', Joyce's lecture in Trieste, 27 April 1907), 10, 14, 398, 419, 526, 533, 586n116, 663–76, 796; criticism of Catholic Church and, 208–9; *Finnegans Wake* and, 840; on Irish language, 806–7; on Parnell, 673–74; on Queen Victoria's visit to Dublin, 420; the Split and, 711

irredentism (*Italia irredenta*), xvii, 642n57, 661, 791, 812; *L'Indipendente* and, 645, 800n92; Joyce and, 642–56, 659, 674; Università Popolare and, 641, 646, 653, 662, 675, 727

Italy, 227, 456, 489; First World War and, 810–13; Joyce, sick of, 593; Joyce's awareness of politics of, 489; Joyce's relationship to, 658, 659, 660–61, 727; language of, 361, 456n186, 761n180, 765; military of, 521–22, 642, 646, 816–17; Trieste becomes part of, 762. *See also* irredentism; revolutionary syndicalism; Rome; socialism

Ivy Day (annual commemorative day for Parnell), 152, 543, 544, 565

'Ivy Day in the Committee Room' (short story, *Dubliners*), 152, 302, 481, 542, 543–67, 587, 620, 713n7, 788, 789n62; Edward VII's visit to Ireland and, 421–22; Anatole France's influence on, 560–61; as ghost story, 560; issue with publication of, 183; objections to sections of, 432, 725–26, 746, 753; Parnell and, 534, 543, 544, 565, 570, 580; Parnell myth and, 36–37, 480, 508, 559–60, 564; poem by Joe Hynes, 'Death of Parnell, 6th October 1891', 549–54; publication of *Portrait* and, 566n69; *Sinn Féin* publishes Joyce's letter on, 432; socialism and, 550–51, 558, 570; spectral absence of Parnell in, 36

Jackson, John Wyse (biographer of John Stanislaus Joyce), 30–31, 47

James Joyce Remembered (Curran), 89, 101, 259, 271n45, 271n48, 273, 449–50, 463; limericks and, 322n121; Meehan as consultant for, 98n150, 113

Jesuits, 96, 333n155, 488, 507, 520, 528, 774; 'Ad Maiorem Dei Gloriam', 333n155; *Fathers of the Society of Jesus*, 225n86, 284n86, 287, 292n18, 339n175, 362n17; Irish Revival and, 355–56; Joyce and, 152; nationalism and, 257; in *Portrait*, xv, 303; the Split and, 225–31; in *Stephen Hero*, 386

Jewish Chronicle (newspaper), 771, 776, 776n28, 778

Jewish Literary and Social Club, 786

Jews, Judaism, 27, 523, 532, 648, 655, 806–7; Catholic Church and, 784–85, 795–96; Egyptians and, 801; of Europe, 763, 772, 787, 795; immigration, 771, 779, 787, 808; of Ireland, 769, 770–79, 785–87, 795, 808, 819; the Irish and, 387, 768–69, 794; 'Jewgreek is Greekjew', 801–9; *Der Judenstaat*, 792; of Lithuania, 771, 776n28, 779; River Liffey and, 773, 773n19, 775; of Trieste, 768, 791–800; *Ulysses* and, 533, 535, 655n108, 671n36, 768–69, 773, 776, 778, 785–87, 794, 798. *See also* anti-Semitism

Jolas, Eugene, 284n86, 292n18

Jolas, Maria, 47n13, 51n30, 107n190

Joyce, Charles (Joyce's brother), 100, 102–3, 594, 745, 749n139; *Dubliners* and, 756; letter to Stanislaus Joyce, 749, 754–55

Joyce, Eileen (Joyce's sister). *See* Schaurek, Eileen Joyce

Joyce, Eva (Joyce's sister), 97, 97n147, 103, 105n176, 333, 719–20, 722–24

Joyce, Florence Elizabeth (Joyce's sister), 95

Joyce, Georgie (Joyce's brother), 99–100, 102, 277

Joyce, Giorgio (Joyce's son), 5, 102, 109n199, 724, 811, 836; early years, 475, 484, 631n4, 632, 715, 761; Italian language and, 761n180; letter from Joyce, 71; in Rome, 593; in Trieste, 676, 723; trip to Ireland in 1909, 715, 719, 720; in 1912, 746

Joyce, Helen (Joyce's daughter-in-law), 71

Joyce, James, paternal ancestry and background, 46–47; ancestor Seán Mór Seoighe, 46, 47; grandfather James Augustine Joyce and, 46–50, 57; grandmother Ellen O'Connell Joyce and, 47–49, 51, 57–58, 71–72; great-grandfather

James Joyce 'the elder' and, 46, 47, 49, 57; great-grandfather John O'Connell and, 47–50; great-grandmother Anne Joyce and, 47; great-great-grandfather George Joyce and, 46; 'The Joycead', 44, 47, 49, 50n23, 50n26, 93n135; Joyce family coat of arms, 77, 78; Joyce family portraits, as household gods, 44, 45, 47, 77; portraits sent to Trieste, 109. *For parents, siblings, and children, see main entries*

Joyce, James, biographical:

—birth (Rathgar, Dublin, 1882), 72

—education: at Belvedere College, 96, 152, 288; at O'Connell's Christian Brothers School, 95–96 (*see also main entries* Clongowes; University College, Dublin)

—exile: leaves Ireland, 470–71; first return visit to Ireland, 715–20; second return visit, 720–22; third return visit, 745–56; moves to Zurick, 814; moves to Paris, 831

—finances, 404–5, 445–46, 470, 514, 522n30, 632, 640, 676, 714, 721, 722, 811–12, 813, 822–23, 828–29, 837

—health: drinking, 50, 413–14, 464, 484, 511, 638–39, 658, 714; eyesight, 28, 180, 633, 636, 638, 714, 837; rheumatic fever, 633

—jobs/business activities: as bank-clerk in Rome, 531, 593, 597; as cinema facilitator (Volta) in Dublin, 720; as teacher of English, 633–35, 640, 658, 674, 724–26, 761, 812, 819, 822; as tweed and wool agent in Trieste, 602, 720–21

—languages, knowledge of: ancient Greek, 806; Hebrew, 363, 794; Italian, 361, 456n186, 761n180, 765; Norwegian, 362, 363; *triestino* dialect, 638, 650, 764–65;

—marriage (London, 1931), 837

—music: interest in, 97, 101, 277, 411, 655, 714, 814; takes singing lessons, 714

—personality: aloofness, 256, 264, 265, 267, 268, 270, 272, 279, 350, 403, 410; 'enigma of a manner', 263–71, 443, 452, 453, 464; humour, 45, 753n154

Joyce, James, influences, principal intellectual and artistic. *See main entries for* Aquinas, Thomas; Bruno, Giordano; Cattaneo, Carlo; D'Annunzio, Gabriele; Dante Alighieri; Defoe, Daniel; Ferrero, Guglielmo; France, Anatole; Griffith, Arthur; Ibsen, Henrik; Labriola, Arturo; Lombroso, Cesare; Mangan, James Clarence; Marx, Karl; Mazzini, Giuseppe; Newman, John Henry; Nicholas of Cusa; Nietzsche, Friedrich; Parnell, Charles Stewart; Renan, Ernest; Shakespeare, William; Synge, John Millington; Taylor, John Francis; Tucker, Benjamin; Yeats, William Butler

Joyce, James, opinions, political, economic, social, and religious. *See main entries for* altruism; anarchism; anticlericalism; anti-Semitism; Catholic Church (*see also* 'two masters' thesis); Celtic Twilight; fascism; Fenians, Fenianism; Gaelic League; Home Rule; imperialism; Irish independence; Irish Revival; irredentism; Liberals (*sub-entry* 'nonconformist conscience'); Marxism; nationalism, of Joyce; Parnell, Charles Stewart, Joyce's identification with; positivism; revolutionary syndicalism; Sinn Féin; Slavs; social democracy; socialism; the Split; Zionism

Joyce, James, works, articles, essays, and pamphlets: alphabetical notebook (unpublished), 149, 569n79; 'City of the Tribes, The', 747; 'La Cometa dell "Home Rule"' ('The Home Rule Comet'), 679, 686, 687, 729, 744; 'Day of the Rabblement, The', 103, 275, 279, 280–82, 305, 403, 453, 488, 501, 598; 'Il Fenianismo: L'ultimo Feniano' ('Fenianism: The Last Fenian'), 190, 190n84, 679; *Giacomo Joyce*, 640, 641–42, 655, 767; 'Home Rule

Joyce, James (*continued*)
maggiorenne' ('Home Rule Comes of Age'), 537, 537n6, 679–91; 'Irish Literary Renaissance, The', 677, 678; 'Mirage of the Fisherman of Aran, The', 747–48; 'Oscar Wilde', 284n141, 727; review of Stephen Gwynn's *Today and Tomorrow in Ireland*, 436; review of Ibsen's *When We Dead Awaken*, 269; review of Lady Gregory's *Poets and Dreamers: Studies and Translations from the Irish*, 439–41; review of William Rooney's *Poems and Ballads*, 428–33; review of T. B. Russell's *Borlase and Son*, 442. *See main entries* 'L'Irlanda alla sbarra'; 'L'ombra di Parnell'; 'Portrait of the Artist, A'

Joyce, James, works, fiction: 'At Bay', unwritten short story, 563. *For principal novels, stories and play, see main entries*

Joyce, James, works, lectures: 'Drama and Life' (1900, L&H), 264; 'Hamlet', missing Trieste lectures on (1912–13), 760; 'Irish Literary Renaissance, The', 677, 678; 'James Clarence Mangan' (1902, L&H), 258, 282, 324, 348, 362, 403, 430 ; 'James Clarence Mangan' (undelivered lecture in Trieste), 676, 677. *See also main entry* 'L'Irlanda: Isola dei santi e dei savi'

Joyce, James, works, poetry and polemics: *Chamber Music*, 325, 329, 400, 632; 'Dooleysprudence' (1916), 825–26; 'Et tu, Healy' (attributed title of missing juvenile poem on death of Parnell), 152–53, 157–62, 169–70, 550; 'Gas from a Burner' (1912), 33, 179, 198, 282–86, 756, 756n163, 757, 758, 759; 'The Holy Office' (1904), 16, 159, 266, 445, 463–66, 485

Joyce, John Augustine (Joyce's older brother), dies after birth, 72

Joyce, John Stanislaus (Joyce's father), 73, *110*, 44–112, 750; anticlericalism of, 57, 81, 83, 89; Nora Barnacle and, 102, 105, 471; Joseph Theobald Casey and, 114, 123n38, 137; Patrick Casey and, 114, 123n38, 137, 148; Christmas dinner and, xiv, 81–82, 171n45, 172, 176; John Clancy and, 114, 126, 133, 335; death of, 45, 107, 111; death of daughter Mabel, 103–4; death of son Georgie, 99; death of wife, 100; drinking of, 50, 53n34, 65–66, 74, 99; Dublin election of 1880 and, 60, 63–68; Fenianism and, 57–58, 70; financial troubles of, 54, 54n36, 69–81, 94–99, 169, 756n163, 781; *Finnegans Wake* and, 54–55, 57, 79–80, 106–7; grave of, 121n33; Healy and, 85–88; Jolas interview with, 47n13, 51n30, 107–8; James Joyce and, 45, 49, 100, 105–8, 107n190, 111–12, 470–71, 504n64, 715, 721, 745, 753–54; Mary Jane Murray Joyce and, 71–72, 172, 412; Stanislaus Joyce on, 48n18, 50, 51, 52, 53n34, 55, 90–92, 99, 154, 408–9; John Kelly and, 38n15, 53, 83, 85, 113, 119, 121, 122, 171n45, 172, 176; Thomas Michael Kettle and, 333; lawsuit and, 98–99, 137; Leinster Hall meeting and, 85–88; letter from Eva Joyce, 105n176; letter from James Joyce, 104; letters to James Joyce, 100, 102, 104–5, 111; as medical student, 50, 57; on Daniel O'Connell, 47; Office of the Collector-General and, 72, 77, 78–79, 95; origins of, 46–51; Parnellism of, xiv, 30–31, 53–57, 53n34, 70, 74, 82–93, 154; the Parnell Split and, 54, 81–94; in *Portrait*, as model for Simon Dedalus, 50, 55, 81–82, 84, 121n29, 124, 167–69, 182, 210; portrait by Tuohy, 46; in *Stephen Hero*, as model for Simon Daedalus, 50, 55, 71, 93–94, 269, 361, 504–5; in *Ulysses*, as model for Simon Dedalus, 55, 125n47, 388

Joyce, Lucia (Joyce's daughter), 724, 761n180, 836, 837; early years, 5, 475, 633, 638, 723, 745, 761; letter from Joyce, 569n78

Joyce, Mabel (Joyce's sister), 96, 100, 105n176, 333, 451, 719; death, 102, 103–5, 412n53; Stanislaus Joyce on, 105

Joyce, Margaret 'Poppie' (Joyce's sister), 99, 103, 412, 594, 715, 719

Joyce, Mary Jane 'May', née Murray (Joyce's mother), 73, 74; as devout Catholic, 172; illness and death, 100, 101, 321, 400, 411–13, 457, 464; James Joyce and, 147, 177n54, 289, 404, 441, 569n78; marriage to John Stanislaus Joyce, 71–72

Joyce, Mary Kathleen 'May'. *See* Monaghan, Mary Kathleen 'May'

Joyce, Myles (convicted of Maamtrasna murders), 691, 694–95, *696*, 697–99, 702–4, 706; James Joyce and, 378, 398, 702–4, 706, 707n149. *See also* 'L'Irlanda alla sbarra'; Maamtrasna murders

Joyce, Nora. *See* Barnacle, Nora

Joyce, P. W. (author), *English as We Speak It in Ireland*, 780n32; *Old Celtic Romances*, 435; *A Short History of Ireland*, 667n25

Joyce, Stanislaus (Joyce's brother), 9–10, 48, 105, 459, 468, 565, 591; bails brother out financially, 714, 722, 724, 830; on brother in University College, 335, 348; on brother's Catholicism, 250; on brother's drinking, 413–14; on brother's meeting with Synge, 405–7; on brother's personality, 100–101, 256, 307, 399, 409, 430, 457, 471; on brother's socialism, 457–59, 511–15, 520; on John Francis Byrne, 347–49, 353; on Patrick Casey, 146, 150n136; Christmas dinner scene and, 155–56, 171–72; on George Clancy, 335, 363; on John Clancy, 133–34; on Padraic Colum, 409; death, 101, 153n2; on *Dubliners*, 564–65, 752; education, 95–96; in *Finnegans Wake*, 639; on *Finnegans Wake*, 80n107; on Gladstone, 156; Gogarty and, 408–9, 414; on irredentism, 652, 656; on 'Ivy Day', 458–59, 564; on John Stanislaus Joyce, 48n18, 50–52, 53n34, 55, 70, 90–92, 99, 154, 408–9; on John Kelly, 122–23, 171; on Kettle, 319, 321, 752; leaves Ireland, 476; letter from Charles Joyce, 749, 754–55; letter to Constantine Curran, 348–49; on mother's death, 411–12; on 'Portrait of the Artist' essay, 451; as prisoner of war, 812, 830; on Sheehy-Skeffington, 289, 292; on sister Mabel's death, 105; *Stephen Hero* and, 268, 496; strained relations with brother, 632, 656, 722, 830; in Trieste, 515, 632–39, 649, 656n111, 676, 765, 795–96; on *Ulysses*, 729n75

Joyce, Stanislaus, letters from James Joyce, 172, 283, 306, 438, 445–46, 448, 476, 484, 505, 510, 513–15, 519–23, 522n30, 526n35, 527–28, 531, 541, 580, 582–83, 583n103, 590, 593–99, 603–4, 608, 610–17, 610n36, 611n39, 611n41, 619–23, 623nn68–69, 625–26, 628, 637, 647, 656, 670–71, 709, 712–13, 720, 722, 723, 726–27, 753–54, 786, 795, 802, 813, 833

Joyce, Stanislaus, works:

—*The Complete Dublin Diary of Stanislaus Joyce*, 48n14, 146, 156, 333, 457, 510–11, 513

—*My Brother's Keeper*, 48n17, 80n107, 91n131, 282n77; Christmas scene absent from, 171; Ellmann on, 153n3; T. S. Eliot on, 153n2; May Joyce Monaghan offended by, 101; on the Split, 155n9, 274n52; on Joyce's Parnellism, 153–57, 274; on Joyce's childhood poem on death of Parnell, 158–60, 162, 169

—*Recollections of James Joyce*, 58n42, 273n51, 414n69, 451n171, 451n173, 559n53, 560n56; Joyce's exilic treatment of Ireland in, 412n52; Joyce's poem on Parnell in, 159n13; Joyce's socialism in, 515–16; last meeting with Joyce, 411n50; refuses copy of *Finnegans Wake*, 80n107

—'Triestine Book of Days 1907–09' (unpublished), 617n51, 632n8, 676n54

Joyce, Stephen (Joyce's grandson), 109n199

Joyce Country, Galway-Mayo, 46, 47n12, 692, 694

Judas Iscariot (biblical figure), 26, 551, 685, 742

Kane, Robert, S.J., discourse against socialism, 208
Kearney, Colbert (Joyce scholar), 'The Joycead', 44, 47, 49, 50n23, 50n26, 93n135
Keating, Geoffrey, *Annals of the Four Masters*, 433; *Eochairsgiath an Aifrinn* (*Defence of the Mass*), 345; Joyce's reading of *History of Ireland*, 433
Keegan, John (poet), 'Caoch the Piper', 125
Kelleher, John V., *Finnegans Wake* and, 583n105; 'Irish History and Mythology in James Joyce's "The Dead"', 434, 560, 583–88
Kelly, John 'of Tralee', 114–25; Christmas dinner scene and, 38n15, 171n45, 172, 176; John Clancy and, 126, 134, 135; incarceration of, 115–16, 119n21; death of, 115, 120–22; John Stanislaus Joyce, friendship with, 38n15, 53, 70, 83, 85, 114, 122, 182, 191; Stanislaus Joyce on, 122–23, 171; as model for 'Mr Casey' in *Portrait*, 84, 123, and in *Stephen Hero*, 124, and in *Ulysses*, 125; as Parnellite, 5, 85, 116–19, 121, 736
Kennedy, Hugh (first attorney general of Irish Free State), 258; in University College, 279, 292, 362, 419
Kenny, Timothy, S.J., 181
Keogh, William, 205
Kerrigan, Sarsfield, in University College, 343–44
Kettle, Andrew (father of T. M. Kettle), 28, 121, 204–5, 212, 310, 310n76, 333–34
Kettle, Mary, née Sheehy (wife of T. M. Kettle), 288, 310, 320–22, 347, 719
Kettle, Thomas Michael, 28, 303–4, 310–34, *311*; alcoholism of, 311n83, 312; aphorisms of, 328; Catholic Church and, 16, 319, 322–23, 327n136; *Chamber Music*, review of, 325, 329, 632, 633; Arthur Clery on, 287; Padraic Colum on, 310, 312, 321, 327n135, 334; *Countess Cathleen* letter and, 279, 325; William Dawson on, 325; death, 312, 321, 326–27, 815; depressive condition of, 312; 'An Encounter', view of, 752, 758; Europeanism of, 16, 327nn135–136; in *Exiles* (model for Robert Hand), 319, 327–32; family, 276n56, 310n76; in *Finnegans Wake*, 333; First World War and, 311–12; Margaret Gogarty, letter from, 415n71; Herbert Gorman on, 321–22; Hegel, influence of, 319, 322, 322n12; Home Rule and, 737; John Stanislaus Joyce and, 333; Stanislaus Joyce on, 752; Joyce on, 320–21, 525, 595, 716, 719; member of Parliament for Tyrone East, 311, 592; *Nationist* and, 314–16, 315n95, 323, 592, 594–95; Parnellism and, xix, 32, 276, 318–20, 322, 323n123; *Sinn Féin*, letter to, 730; Skeffington and, 288, 295n30, 309–11, 312n84, 323, 346; in University College, 310, 312, 324; wedding of, 719; Yeats and, 626–27; the 'Yibs' and, 312–14
Kettle, Thomas Michael, works: 'The Celtic Revival', 324; *The Day's Burden*, 320n111, 326–27, 331n148; *Home Rule Finance*, 320n111; 'Note on Sinn Féin in Ireland', 317–18, 317n100; 'On Saying Goodbye', 331; *The Open Secret of Ireland*, 323; *The Philosophy of Politics*, 598; 'Religion and Politics in Ireland', 322–23; *The Ways of War*, 321n117; 'Would the "Hungarian Policy" Work?', 316
Kickham, Charles, 208
Kilmainham Jail, 19, 128, 695, 698, 744
Kinahan, Robert (auditor of L&H), as model for Moynihan in *Stephen Hero*, 264; Taylor replies to his inaugural address, 381
Kipling, Rudyard, 829n68; *Plain Tales from the Hills*, 620
Kirn, Maria (maid in Joyce household in Trieste), 723
Kitchener, Herbert (Lord), 296, 311n83, 419, 672
Knox, Major (proprietor of *Irish Times*), 127

Koss, Stephen (historian), 419; analysis of New Journalism, 234n111

Labour World (newspaper), 86, 232, 239
Labriola, Arturo (socialist politician), 516–24, 611–12
Lake Wannsee conference (1942), 793, 838–39
L&H. *See* Literary and Historical Society
Land League, 187, 225, 492n30, 497, 556, 702, 846; agrarian violence and, 143, 701; as anarchistic organization, 513n7; John Clancy and, 127–28; Davitt and, 253–54; John Kelly and, 115, 119, 121; Ladies Land League, 695n110; of Mayo, 18
Land War, 18, 317, 395
Lane, Hugh (art collector), 480, 622
Larbaud, Valéry (critic), 667; delivers lecture on Joyce in Shakespeare and Company, 834–36
Lassalle, Ferdinand (German socialist), 513, 525, 532
Laurier, Wilfrid (Sir) (Canadian Prime Minister), 437
Il Lavoratore (newspaper), 647
Lawless, Emily (author), *History of Ireland*, 576; *With Essex in Ireland*, 576–79
Leader (Irish newspaper), 303n53, 317, 379, 623; D. P. Moran and, 185, 261–62, 289–90, 314, 359–60, 379, 603; on nationalism, 261–62; 'The Sect of the Gael', 359; on Sheehy-Skeffington, 289–90; University College in, 283–84
Leamy, Edmund (Irish politician and writer), 212–13
Le Caron, Henri (English spy), 145
Legion of Mary, 751
Leinster Literary Society, 423, 424
Lenin, Vladimir, 517, 823
Lennon, Michael, in *Stephen Hero*, 465
Léon, Paul, 47n11, 506
Leonard, Hugh (playwright), *Stephen D.: A Play in Two Acts*, 101
Leone, Enrico, 517, 519
Leventhal, A. J. (lecturer, Trinity College Dublin), 772n15; 'What It Means to Be a Jew', 776n28, 778
Lewis, Wyndham, 519
Liberal Registration Association, 59
Liberals, 22, 24, 27–28, 66, 369, 592, 740; Conservatives and, 20–21, 62, 416, 417; Home Rule and, 23, 26, 476, 577; nationalists and, 21, 83, 219, 239, 318–19, 418, 579; newspapers and, 60, 219, 232, 276; 'nonconformist conscience' and, 34, 219, 232, 234–35, 238–39, 241, 251, 844; United Liberal Club, 59–60, 65, 67–69, 68n73, 76. *See also* Split, the
Libya, 518, 656
Lidwell, George (solicitor), 99, 105, 750, 753
Liffey (Dublin river), 92, 411, 584n108, 587, 594; in *Finnegans Wake*, 393n98; Joyce and, 411, 467, 520; Anna Livia Plurabelle and, 107n190, 630, 849; topography of Dublin Jewry and, 773, 775
Limerick Leader (newspaper), 345
limericks, 322, 445
Linati, Carlo, 751, 751n146, 770
Lipsett, Edward Raphael ('Halitvack'), 771; 'Jews in Ireland', 776–78
Literary and Historical Society (L&H) (debating society of University College, Dublin), 274, 279, 282, 324, 334; auditors, 258, 264, 285, 289, 292, 310; Arthur Clery and, 285, 382; debates, 258, 285, 362n17; 'Gas from a Burner' and, 757, 758; Joyce and, 258, 348, 453, 677; Kennedy and, 258, 292; Skeffington and, 289, 626; Taylor and, 259, 381; 'Yibs' and, 313
Lloyd George, David (British Prime Minister), 297, 687
Logue, Michael (Archbishop of Armagh), 167, 203, 278, 367, 718

Lombroso, Cesare (Italian criminologist), 516, 530–32, 802; *La donna delinquente, la prostituta e la donna normale*, 530
Longworth, E. V. (editor), 404, 436, 439, 441–42
Lukács, György, 540
Lyceum (Irish newspaper), 225–31, 281n75, 779. *See also* Finlay, Peter, S.J.; Finlay, T. A., S.J.
Lyons, F.S.L. (historian), xxiv, 40, 193, 205n35, 224
Lyons, Robert Spencer Dyer (member of Parliament for Dublin city), 18, 60–65, 67–68

Maamtrasna murders (1882), 691–95, 697–704, 706–7; Big John Casey of Bunacrick, 702; Patrick Casey, convicted of, 695, 697; Thomas Casey, accuser of Myles Joyce, 695, 698; Anthony and John Joyce, accusers, 694; John Joyce, victim, 693–94, 700, 702; Margaret Joyce, victim, 701; Martin Joyce, convicted of, 693; Michael Joyce, victim, 698; Patrick 'John' Joyce, convicted of, 693, 695, 697; Patsy Joyce, survivor of, 698; Thomas 'Pat' Joyce, convicted of, 693; Anthony Philbin, 'approver', 695, 698. *See also* 'L'Irlanda alla sbarra'; Joyce, Myles
Macaulay, Thomas Babington (historian), 488
MacBride, John (revolutionary), 418, 592
MacCarthy, Denis Florence (poet and translator), 430
MacCurtain, Thomas (Lord Mayor of Cork), 345–46
MacDonagh, Thomas (poet and revolutionary), 334, 827
MacDonnell, Antony (Sir), 592–93
MacGeoghegan, James (Abbé), *The History of Ireland, Ancient and Modern*, 664
MacGreevy, Thomas (poet and critic), 86–89, 109
MacManus, Terence Bellew, 210, 265
MacMurrough, Dermott, 733
MacNally, Leonard (informer), 613
MacNeill, Eoin, 259, 338, 367, 387n79, 432, 449
MacNeill, Hugh, model for professor MacHugh in *Ulysses*, 387n79
Magalaner, Marvin (Joyce scholar), 54n36; Joyce's Parnellism and, 92, 786n53
Magee, William Kirkpatrick (critic and essayist, pseud. John Eglinton), *Dana* and, 273, 444, 446n159, 449–50, 460, 525, 596; Joyce and, 407–8, 413, 414, 445–52, 469; Joyce meets on return visit to Ireland, 715; Joyce's repudiation of, 596; National Library and, 408n30, 447, 451, 469; Yeats and, 402, 445, 446. *See also* Eglinton, John
Magennis, William (professor), 225n86, 269
Maginn, William (writer and humorist), 414
Maguire, Thomas (professor), 143
Mahaffy, John Pentland (Provost of Trinity), 376, 377
Mallon, John (Chief Superintendent of Dublin Metropolitan Police), 126n50, 127, 129–31
Maloney, William J., 597
Manchester Guardian (newspaper), 243–44, 257n5, 365–67, 365n28, 369
'Manchester Martyrs,' 138, 680
Mangan, James Clarence, xxvi; death of, 398, 688, 414n64; Joyce's comparison of modern writers to, 437; Joyce's implicit comparison of Yeats to, 282n78; Joyce's lecture on, 258, 282, 324, 348, 362, 403, 430
Manganiello, Dominic (Joyce scholar), 572; *Joyce's Politics*, xii, 3, 43
Manning, Henry Edward (Cardinal), 228–29
Martello Tower, 278, 400, 468–69
Martyn, Edward, 281n76, 603, 604

Marx, Karl, 525, 532, 802, 826; *Das Kapital*, 512
Marxism, 517, 525, 540, 588, 647; Joyce mistrusts, 460, 538; in *Stephen Hero*, 498, 502
Mason, Ellsworth (Joyce scholar), 708, 748–49; *Critical Writings of James Joyce, The* (with Ellmann), 705n140, 708, 748–49, 825n53 (abbreviated *CW*)
Mass, Catholic, 155, 163, 361, 447, 723, 806; Greek Orthodox, 636, 806
Il Mattino (newspaper), 713
Maunsel & Company (publishers), *Dubliners* and, 628, 712–13, 715–16, 725, 745–46, 750, 753–54, 832; 'Gas from a Burner' and, 284–85, 285n89, 756–57, 756n163; Joyce's letter to press regarding, 725–26
Mayer, Teodoro (owner of *Il Piccolo della Sera*), 648, 649n84, 791, 800n92
Mazzini, Giuseppe (Italian revolutionary), 14, 642, 644, 763–64, 763n190
McCann, Philip (Joyce's godfather), 497n47
McCarthy, Justin, 188, 294, 357
McCormack, John (tenor), 107, 107n190, 313n89
McCormack, W. J. (literary critic), 664
McCormick, Harold (Mrs) (Edith Rockefeller), 829
McDermott, 'Red Jim', 141
McGarvey, Cathal (owner of An Stad, tobacconist), 313n89, 360, 435, 494; as model for the Citizen, 338
McGee, Thomas D'Arcy, 430
McGrath, John, 116, 117
McHugh, Michael (curate of Clonbur), 695
McSwiney, Peter Paul (Lord Mayor of Dublin 1864–65 and 1875–76), 49, 58–59
Mead, Patrick J. (editor of *Freeman's Journal*), inspires Myles Crawford in *Ulysses*, 717
Medcalf, Mary (takes John Stanislaus Joyce as lodger), 107
Meehan, Patrick, recalls John Stanislaus Joyce, 98n150, 113
Meenan, James (professor), 312n87
Melchiori, Giorgio (Joyce scholar), 572n86, 618n52, 663
Menton, J. H. (solicitor), 121
Methodist Times (newspaper), 232, 233
Michelangelo, 168n39, 390
Millevoye, Lucien (reactionary French journalist), 767n2; mentioned in *Ulysses*, 149
Mitchel, John (journalist and nationalist), 664, 737; *A Continuation of the History of Abbé MacGeoghegan from the Treaty of Limerick to the Year 1868*, 664
Monaghan, Mary Kathleen 'May' (sister of Joyce), 89, 101–4, 404n17, 412n53, 753n154
Montgomery, Niall (architect and Joyce scholar), 111n209
Moore, George (novelist), 275, 281, 407, 444, 448
Moore, Thomas (poet), 340, 571, 573, 576n94, 582
Moran, D. P., 305, 334, 605; *Leader* and, 185, 186, 261–62, 289–90, 314, 359–60, 603, 605; revivalism of Irish language and, 359–60, 379
Morley, John (Chief Secretary of Ireland), 22–23, 130, 233–35, 418, 741–42
Morning Advertiser (newspaper), 143
Mosconi, Antonio (Italian civil commissioner), 829
Moses (biblical figure), Michelangelo and, 168n39, 390, 390n39; Parnell and, xviii, 27, 204, 391–92, 562, 569, 738; J. F. Taylor on, 366–67, 371, 377
Muldoon, Paul (poet and literary critic), 434; *To Ireland, I*, 560n56, 584–86, 588
Mulqueeny, George (putative author of the 'Black Pamphlet'), 141–42

Mulvey, Will, romance with Nora Barnacle, 467
murders, 337, 340, 430, 700, 736, 771, 774, 810; Childs trial, 389; of George Clancy, 345–46; of Huddy, 701; Limerick City curfew, 339n175, 340, 342n187; of Thomas MacCurtain, 345–46; of Sheehy-Skeffington, 312, 353, 815. *See also* Maamtrasna murders
Murphy, Gregory (barrister), family memories of Parnell, 170n44
Murphy, Nicholas Dan (politician), 67
Murphy, William Martin, 217, 218; owner of *Daily Nation*, 276; owner of *Irish Independent*, 222
Murray, John (Joyce's maternal grandfather), 71, 73
Murray, John, Jr. (Joyce's uncle), 411
Murray, Josephine (Joyce's aunt), 107n190, 470; confidant to Joyce, 412; letters from Joyce, 484, 661, 762, 831; sends Joyce newspapers from Ireland, 283, 594–95, 597, 623
Murray, Margaret Theresa Flynn (Joyce's maternal grandmother), 71
Murray, William (Joyce's uncle), 100, 412
Mussolini, Benito, 642, 648, 838, 846

Nation (Irish newspaper), 62, 217
Nation (London newspaper), 632
National Club (41 Rutland Square, Dublin), 119–20; 'Fenian haunt' taken over by Parnellites, 129–30, 557
National Council (precursor of Sinn Féin), 422, 558n52; co-founded by Griffith, 599–601, 603–4, 608, 616; formed in opposition to visit of Edward VII, 426–27
National Democrat (magazine), 448n164
nationalism, xiv, 125, 187, 162, 222, 263, 294, 341, 371–72, 416; anti-Semitism and, 789; John Francis Byrne and, 349–50; Catholic Church and, 207, 209, 211, 219, 223, 224, 486, 491, 607, 721; Celtic Twilight and, 441; George Clancy and, 322, 341; cultural nationalism, 313–14, 344, 358, 379, 397, 432, 450, 454, 460, 469, 544, 607, 710; Gaelic League, 315, 354, 567; Griffith and, 316, 356, 421–22, 596, 599, 606, 609, 652, 711; Irish language and, 261–62, 342, 362n17, 372, 427; Irish Party and, 316; with Italian socialism, 519, 522, 536–37; Jesuits and, 257; Jews and, 795, 798; Stanislaus Joyce and, 812; Kettle and, 315–16; Liberals and, 21, 83, 219, 239, 318–19, 418, 579; nationalist voters, 67, 185, 252; Parnell and, 5, 18, 22, 29, 369, 711; William Rooney and, 427; Sinn Féin and, 10, 416, 460; George Sorel and, 518; Unionists and, 216, 369; *United Irishman* and, 410; University College and, 354–56; Zionism and, 14n14, 769, 792
nationalism, of Joyce: xix–xx, xxiv, xxv, 7–16, 476; critics' view of, 41–2; Con Curran's understanding of, 273; as dissentient, 675; as European, 15, 845; with Fenian strain, 31, 262; in *Finnegans Wake*, 332–33; and identifying contradictions within, 437; and incommensurate with socialism, 535–36; irredentism and, 654, 659; Stanislaus Joyce's understanding of, 254; as Parnellite, 31–33, 155–56, 192, 252–53, 358, 666, 678; pluralistic conception of, 652; refusal to avow, 9, 12, 508–9; revivalism and, 494; Ettore Schmitz's understanding of, 658n115; as separate from Magee and Ryan's nationalism, 447–49; *Stephen Hero* and, 12, 170, 486, 491, 493, 499–505, 508; suspicions of cultural nationalism and, 450, 460, 544, 710; sympathy with Griffith's nationalism and, 596, 599, 606, 609, 613, 631
Nationalist Party, Italy, 518
National Liberal Party, Italy, 645
National Library of Ireland (NLI), 176, 181, 348, 354n1, 823n47; W. K. Magee and,

408n30, 447, 451, 469; Yeats and, 400–401
National Literary Society, 261n17, 280, 357, 357n6
National Monuments Committee, 129
National Press (newspaper), 119, 741; in 'Aeolus', 223; editorials, 179, 180, 186, 200; founding of, 222; Joyce and, 186; National Federation and, 199; on Parnell, 211, 249; the Split and, 184–86, 224
National Review (newspaper), 687
National Student (newspaper), 287n1
National Theatre Society, 414
National Volunteers, 344
Nationist (newspaper), 314–16, 315n95, 323, 592, 594–95, 597
Le Navire d'argent (literary review), 107n190
Nazis, 793, 838–39, 843–44, 846–47
Nebuchadnezzar (Babylonian king), 826
Neue Zürcher Zeitung (newspaper), 177, 828
New Age (newspaper), 821
New Ireland Review (literary review), 225n86, 314, 360, 598
Newman, John Henry (Cardinal), 257; *Callista*, 384–87, 488, 489n22
New York Herald (newspaper), 139, 147
New York Nationalist (newspaper), 145
New Zealand, 103, 374, 719
Nicholas II (Tsar of Russia), and petition of in *Portrait* and *Stephen Hero*, 298–305, 309n72
Nicholas of Cusa, 840; coincidence of opposites and, 251n146
Nietzsche, Friedrich, 316, 511, 547n12, 635, 801–2
Nolan, Emer (Joyce scholar), *James Joyce and Nationalism*, 40n23, 41
Nolan, John Wyse, mentioned in *Ulysses*, 655n108, 786
Nordio, Mario (student of Joyce in Trieste), 634, 638–39
Norris, Margot (Joyce scholar), on art of Stephen Dedalus, 169n42; on Mr Henchy, 554–55; on Joyce and politics, 43, 333, 631; *Joyce's Web*, 42–43, 333n158, 506n67; on modernist aestheticism, 42; on Skeffington, 305n62; on *Stephen Hero* and *A Portrait*, 506n67
North American Review (newspaper), 317–18, 317n100, 318n102
Northern Whig (newspaper), 367n38, 726
Norwegian language, 362, 363

Oberdan, Guglielmo (irredentist martyr), 643, 646n72
Oblath, Elody, 646
O'Brien, Conor Cruise, xxiv, 198n10, 309n73, 378n58
O'Brien, Flann, 286; 'Cruiskeen Lawn' (as Myles na gCopaleen), 51n30; 'Irishman's Diary', 51n30
O'Brien, Francis Cruise (journalist), 312–13, 317, 624
O'Brien, Kathleen Sheehy (wife of Francis Cruise O'Brien), 317. *See also main entries for Sheehy family members*
O'Brien, Richard Barry (pseud. 'Historicus'), 27, 37, 75, 75n92, 116, 181, 187; on Captain Moonlight, 701n126; Gladstone and, 739n100; as influence on Joyce's lecture, 735; letter to *Freeman's Journal*, 206–7; *Life of Charles Stewart Parnell*, 27n9, 563, 669n32, 735, 736; on Parnell, 117n15, 134–35, 201
O'Brien, William, 90, 128–29, 205n35, 687–89
O'Callaghan, Margaret, xxvi, xxvii, 115n6; on Thomas Kettle, 310n76, 312n84, 327n136
O'Callaghan, Michael (mayor of Limerick), 345

O'Connell, Daniel ('the Liberator'), 218; centenary of, 58; Dublin municipal politics and, 61; family connection to Joyce, 47, 48, 49, 58, 59, 107n190; Fitzgibbon's lecture and, 373; opposed by bishops, 206; rivalry in myth with Parnell, 58–59; William Rooney, loathed by, 427; in *Ulysses*, 392
O'Connor, Arthur, 188
O'Connor, Frank (writer), 547, 554; *The Mirror in the Roadway*, 554n37
O'Connor, John (member of Parliament, IPP), 121
O'Connor, T. P. (journalist and politician), *Charles Stewart Parnell: A Memory*, 669n32; on execution of Myles Joyce, 697, 699; on Kettle, 311n83; on W. T. Stead, 234n111, 235
O'Curry, Eugene (Gaelic scholar), 376
O'Donnell, Frank Hugh, 276, 738; adopts Healy's rhetoric against Parnell, 734–35; *History of the Irish Parliamentary Party*, 734–35; as Hyacinth O'Donnell B. A. in *Finnegans Wake*, 735
O'Donoghue, D. J., 720
O'Donoghue, Joseph, 345
O'Donovan, John (scholar and translator), 376, 665n14
Odysseus/Ulysses, as Homer's fictional character, Joyce's views on, 817–19
O'Leary, John (Fenian), 129, 208, 430–31, 689; death, 190, 679; letters to *Freeman's Journal*, 186–90; Parnellism of, 186–92, 410; *Recollections of Fenians and Fenianism*, 208
O'Mahony, Eoin, 47n13
'L'ombra di Parnell' ('The Shade of Parnell', article by Joyce in *Il Piccolo della Sera*), xxiii, xxvii, 23, 156, 424, 553, 679, 729–45, 850; cartoon in *Sinn Féin* and, 733; compares Parnell to Disraeli and Gladstone, 30; deer/hunting imagery in, 267, 453, 553, 741; influence of Griffith on, 591, 730–34; Irish betrayal of Parnell and, 88, 178, 741–42; on national tribute to Parnell, 75; Ettore Schmitz on, 657, 743; on the Split, 195–96, 741
O'Neill, Hugh (Earl of Tyrone), 574
O'Neill, Owen Roe, 206
O'Neill, Shane, 731, 734
Ó Raifteari, Antoine. *See* Raftery
O'Shea, Katharine, affair with Parnell, xi, 21, 142, 185, 211, 214; divorce crisis, 21–22, 27, 34, 116, 144, 187, 198n10, 231, 369, 730, 743; divorce crisis in *Finnegans Wake*, 707; marriage to Parnell, 28, 83, 173, 219; memoir of, 736; *Portrait* and, 163, 167, 224; W. T. Stead and, 236–41
O'Shea, William Henry (Captain), 21–22, 87, 236, 743; as putative author of 'Black Pamphlet', 141–42
Osservatore Romano (newspaper), 177
O'Sullivan, John Marcus, 597, 598–99
O'Sullivan, Seamus (pen name of James Starkey), 277n60, 610
O'Sullivan Burke, Ricard (Irish nationalist), 138–39, 150

Pall Mall Gazette (newspaper), 179–81, 179n59, 232, 236–37, 239, 699n121, 735n85
Paris, 14n14, 111, 304n60; Joseph and Patrick Casey in, 114, 138–44, 146–48, 150–51; Joyce living in, 109, 177, 274, 320, 327n135, 364, 387, 400, 404, 476, 767, 834, 846; Joyce publishes 'Work in Progress' in, 837; Joyce's departure from Trieste to, 475, 762, 831; Joyce sends book reviews from, 428, 436, 439, 441; Joyce with Silvio Benco in, 661; Joyce with Francini Bruni in, 761n180; Joyce with J. F Byrne in, 353; Joyce with Louis Gillet in, 45, 105, 152n1; Joyce with W. K. Magee in, 447; Joyce with Ettore Schmitz in, 635; Joyce with James Stephens in, 424, 827, 833; Joyce

with Synge in, 404–7, 434, 582, 625; Joyce writes to Stanislaus from, 656; John O'Leary's return from, 187, 190; James Stephens's (Fenian) return from, 130, 146

Parnell, Charles Stewart, biographical: character of, 21, 30, 159, 273, 561, 739, 740; death of, 5, 27, 180, 196; family background of, 17; funeral of, 27, 146; health of, 117–18, 733, 734, 741; marriage, 28, 83, 173, 219; portrait, *19*. *See also* O'Shea, Katharine

Parnell, Charles Stewart, commemoration and myth, 183, 192–94, 564; comparison with Christ, 552, 742; Ivy Day (annual commemoration) and, 152, 543, 544, 565; monument to, 318, 470, 729, 733; as Moses, xviii, 27, 204, 391–92, 562, 569, 738; 'Mourn and Then Onwards,' 161; quotations of in *Words of the Dead Chief*, 433; as spectral figure, xvii, 36, 37, 183, 196, 299, 480, 553, 560–61, 731, 741, 850–51; 'To a Shade', 480, 850–51; Yeats and, 29, 194, 267n31, 481–82, 562

Parnell, Charles Stewart, Joyce's identification with, 29–38, 479–82, 673–74, 711, 714, 739, 753, 849; in 'Aeolus', 391–92, 395–96, 718; childhood poem on death of, 152–53, 157–62, 550; childhood support for, 5, 84–85, 152–55, 170–74; Padraic Colum on, 410n45; and comparison of Parnell to Christ, 26, 39, 552, 685, 742; critics' treatment of, 38–43; deer/hunting imagery and, 267, 452–53, 465–66, 563; in 'Eumaeus' (*Ulysses*), 563, 564; father's Parnellism and, 54, 83, 87–89, 90–91; in *Finnegans Wake*, xxiii, 31, 37, 57, 119, 567, 745; in 'Ivy Day in the Committee Room', 543–67, 589; Stanislaus Joyce on, 153–57, 274; Joyce's 'enigma of manner' and, 267; Joyce's support for Sinn Féin and, 591–92; in *A Portrait*, 83–84, 157, 164–66, 169–71, 173, 182–83, 224, 254, 756n163; Ettore Schmitz on, 658; in *Stephen Hero*, 157, 169–70; in *Ulysses*, 37, 39, 392, 682, 734; in University College, 272–76. *See also* 'L'ombra di Parnell'; 'two masters' thesis

Parnell, Charles Stewart, political life, 18–29; Catholic Church and, 200, 213–14, 219, 221, 231; John Clancy and, 117–18, 126, 128, 130, 134–35; Dublin election 1880 and, 61–62; Fenians and, 18, 31–32, 87, 186, 189–90, 192, 254; Gladstone and, 21, 23, 30, 61–62, 100, 156–57, 188, 195, 204, 233, 563, 569, 739–40, 844; Griffith and, 423–24, 690, 711, 730–31, 733–34; Healy and, xxiii, 22, 24, 27, 86–88, 180, 184–85, 191, 199–200, 219, 254, 567, 568–70, 669, 734–35, 735n85, 849–50; Irish Parliamentary Party and, xi, 18, 20, 85, 317–18; John Kelly and, 5, 116–19, 121, 736; Andrew Kettle and, 28, 121, 204, 323n123, 333–34; T. M. Kettle and, 318–19; in Kilmainham Jail, 19, 128, 744; Leinster Hall meeting and, 22, 85–88, 569–70; Maamtrasna murders and, 698, 701; manifesto 'To the People of Ireland', 23, 26, 234, 563, 742; National Club and, 129; national tribute raised for, 74–76, 74n88, 75n92, 76n95; Daniel O'Connell and, 58–59; John O'Leary's support for, 186–92; O'Shea divorce crisis and, 21–22, 27, 34, 116, 144, 187, 198n10, 231, 369, 730, 743; Parnell Leadership Committee and, 130, 189; Phoenix Park murders and, 20, 21; Pigott and, 143–44; Prince of Wales's visit, response to, 421; as Protestant, 21, 27, 201, 211–12, 738, 769; Rotunda banquet 1883 and, 74–76; Rotunda speech 1890 and, 26–27, 86, 135, 163, 391–92, 673–74; Special Commission and, 731, 744; W. T. Stead and, 237–41; as 'uncrowned king', 20, 27, 30, 741–42. *See also* Home Rule; Irish Parliamentary Party; Split, the

Parnell, John Howard (brother of C. S. Parnell), 17, 288, 350–51, 419–20

Parnell, Sir John (grandfather of C. S. Parnell), 18
La Patrie (newspaper), 149, 767, 767n2
Pearse, Patrick (Pádraig), 334, 338, 344, 367, 449; Easter Rising and death of, 827; Joyce attends classes of, 362–63; L&H and, 259; lectures in University College, 284n86, 339
Peep o' Day Boys (agrarian Protestant association), referenced in *Ulysses*, 149
PEN Club, London, 534
Perry's Weekly (newspaper), 95
Petitti di Roreto, Carlo (General), 817
Phoenicians, 806–7
Phoenix Park murders, 19–21, 140, 142–43, 145, 389, 680–81, 693–95, 697–703, 706
Pigott, Richard (forger), 21, 82, 141n103, 142–46, 144n114, 236–37
Pigott and Company, advertises *Familiar Irish Songs*, 470
Pitt, William (British statesman), 377, 377n55
Il Piccolo (newspaper), 641, 648, 662; offices burnt down, 813
Il Piccolo della Sera (evening paper of *Il Piccolo*), 674, 754; Francini Bruni works for, 709; Ferrero and, 528; Joyce writes for, 177n54, 659, 661, 662, 663, 716, 727, 755, 760, 800, 832; Robert Prezioso as editor of, 332, 648, 661–62, 679, 760. *See also* Joyce, James, works, articles, essays, and pamphlets
Pittoni, Valentino (Triestine politician), 647
Playboy of the Western World, The, 406n27, 582; Joyce's reaction to riots over, 627–29; riots over, 280, 406n23, 448, 583, 594, 621–29, 713; Yeats and, 480, 621–25, 627
Plunkett, David (Irish parliamentarian), 63, 743
Plunkett, Horace (senator and agricultural reformer), 431
Popper, Amalia (student of Joyce, daughter of Leopoldo Popper), 640–41
'Portrait of the Artist, A' (essay by Joyce in *Dana*), xviii, 265, 400, 444, 450, 451–61, 485; 'the enigma of a manner' and, 266; socialism and, 512, 515; *Stephen Hero* and, 266, 268, 451, 483
Portrait of the Artist as a Young Man, A (novel), 33, 152–83, 835; historical actuality of, 170–74; Irish language in, 341, 354, 362, 363; 'Ivy Day in the Committee Room' and, 566n69; Jesuits in, 303; Joyce attempts to burn manuscript of, 723; newspapers mentioned in, 174–76; passing into silence and, 831–32, 843; Ezra Pound on, 820, 822; publication of, 183, 566n69, 820, 829; review (anonymous) of, 633; the Split in, 161–70, 223–24, 298; *Stephen Hero* and, 505–8; tsar's petition for peace in, 299–302; writing of, 712–13, 760
Portrait of the Artist as a Young Man, A, Christmas dinner scene: Dante Conway and, 171n45; Fenian anticlericalism and, 496; Irish Catholicism and, 209–10, 224; John Stanislaus Joyce and, xiv, 38n15, 81–82, 171n45, 172, 176; Stanislaus Joyce and, 155–56, 171–72; John Kelly and, 38n15, 171n45, 172, 176; misreading of, 119n21; newspapers and, 175–76; the Split and, xiv, 30, 166, 170–71, 173–76, 183, 223–24, 254
Portrait of the Artist as a Young Man, A, fictional characters: Mr [John] Casey, 84, 119n21, 121n29, 123–24, 125n48, 162, 167–69, 182, 191, 209–10, 224, 390n88; Cranly, 55, 300–301, 304n59, 347, 349, 831; Davin, 334–35, 337, 339–42, 342n185, 346, 362, 503; MacCann, 298–99, 299n39, 301n46, 491–93, 504–5; Dante Riordan, 119n21, 166–69, 172, 182, 209, 224. *See also* Dedalus, Simon; Dedalus, Stephen
positivism, 528–30, 533n53, 534; Joyce and, 378, 530
Pound, Ezra, 106, 819–23, 830–31

Power, Arthur (artist and friend of Joyce), 75n92, 108
Power, Jennie Wyse, *Words of the Dead Chief*, 433, 786n55
Power, John Wyse, 121; gives lecture on the Jews in Ireland, 786
Prezioso, Roberto (editor of *Il Piccolo della Sera*), 331, 332, 641, 648, 661–62, 679, 760
Proust, Marcel, xiv, 847

Raftery (Antoine Ó Raifteari) (poet), 439–40
Ralli, Ambrogio di Stefano (Baron), 806, 813, 814n17
Reclus, Élisée (French anarchist), 511, 513
Redmond, John, 131, 357; deprecates attack on Jews of Limerick, 785; Griffith and, 730–31, 733; inaugural meeting of 'Yibs' and, 313; Irish Council Bill, rejection of, 682; Irish enlistment and, 309; Irish National League speech and, 210–11, 213; Joyce and, 686–87, 689–90; as leader of Irish Parliamentary Party, 313, 342–43, 543; 'The Lesson of South Meath', 214n57; Parnell and, 24–26, 90, 166, 729, 733; welcomes Queen Victoria to Dublin, 419–20; wins Waterford by-election December 1891, 214
Reform Act (1867), 62
Renan, Ernest, 560n57, 616, 654, 670
Renner, Karl (Austrian politician), 647
Renoche, Margherita de (Joyce's examiner, University of Padua), 726, 727n67
Renunciation Act (1783), 426
Repeal of the Union Conspiracy, The ('Black Pamphlet'), anonymous, 141–42
Review of Reviews (newspaper), 225n86, 234n109; on Parnell, 237–42; Skeffington devout reader of, 295, 296–97; W. T. Stead establishes, 237; in *Stephen Hero*, 299–300
revolutionary syndicalism (Italian), 518, 524; Joyce and, 231, 477–78, 515–25, 528, 531, 538, 653, 691, 798, 802, 807
Revue Celtique (journal), 585, 585n115
Revue Française (newspaper), 202
Reynolds, Thomas (informer), 613
Ribbonism, 701
Richards, Grant (publisher), 462, 505, 507, 530, 542, 571–72
Risorgimento, 533n53, 642, 672, 815, 835
Roberts, Frederick (Lord), 419, 672
Roberts, George (publisher), 285, 321, 715–16, 725, 745–46, 749–58, 755n161
Robespierre, Maximilien, 349
Rockefeller, Edith. *See* McCormick, Harold (Mrs)
Rolleston, Thomas William Hazen (translator), 383–84, 386, 430–31
Rome, 617–21, 618n52, 622; 'Aeolus', mentioned in, 389–90; Giordano Bruno procession in, 526; Joyce living in, 475, 519, 521, 590, 592–617, 593; Joyce's reading of newspapers in, 608–17; Ministry of Education of, 726, 727; Newman's *Callista* and, 385–86; papacy in, 489–90
Rooney, William, 261, 427n101, 573, 726n61, 754, 846; Celtic Literary Society and, 338; Gaelic League and, 432; Griffith and, 382–83, 423, 428; as Irish language revivalist, 424, 427; Joyce's review of his *Poems and Ballads*, 382, 428–33, 436, 494, 726n61, 754; *United Irishman* and, 426–28; works: 'Gaelicism in Practice', 427; *Prose Writing*, 427n101; 'Recent Irish Literature, A', 427, 427n101
Rosebery (Lord), 311, 688
Ross, Robert, 713, 714n9
Roth, Joseph (writer), 645, 766
Royal Exchange Ward, 67n70, 545
Royal Hibernian Academy, 109
Royal Irish Constabulary (RIC), 80n106, 115n6, 141n103, 467, 689
Royal University of Ireland, 63, 257, 283, 284n87
rugby football, 266, 274
Russell, Charles (Sir), 21, 144

Russell, George (Æ), 141n103, 322n121, 409, 410, 444n146, 461, 623; Joyce and, 400, 402, 453, 464, 715
Russell, T. Baron, 442
Russia, 615, 769, 771, 779
Russian Orthodox Church, 301
Russian Revolution (1917), 540, 648, 826
Ryan, Frederick (journalist), 295n30, 536, 623; *Dana* and, 273, 444, 449, 450, 460, 525, 527, 596; Joyce and, 413, 448–50, 448n164, 596

Sadleir, John (politician), 205, 205n36
Sainati, Alfredo (actor-manager), 713
Salisbury, Marquess of (leader of Conservatives), 21, 579, 688, 700
Samhain (magazine), Yeats's contributions and Joyce's response to, 281, 282
Samuel, Stuart (politician), 782
Saturday Review of Literature (magazine), 249, 256, 408n31
Schaurek, Eileen Joyce (Joyce's sister), 105, 170n103, 637; arrival in Trieste, 722–24; dissolution of marriage, 830; letters from Nora Barnacle to, 745–46, 749; marriage of, 812–13
Schleimer, Anna Maria 'Annie' (possible model for 'lady of letters' in *Giacomo Joyce*), 641
Schmitz, Ettore (Italo Svevo), 630, 637, 638n39, 662, 712; death of, 661, 804; English lessons from Joyce, 635–36; hopes Joyce will write about Trieste, 767; Joyce employed by father-in-law of, 811; Joyce's politics and, 657–59; letter from Joyce, 640; as model for Leopold Bloom, 648, 799; witnesses Trieste celebrations of end Austrian rule, 817
Schmitz, Livia Veneziani (wife of Ettore Schmitz), 640, 645, 649
Scholes, Robert (Joyce scholar), on *Dubliners*, 530–31; on politics of Joyce, 9, 42–43, 452
Schopenhauer, Arthur, 635, 799
Scotland, 62, 232, 242, 622, 667, 728, 774
Scotland Yard, 143, 145
Scully, Vincent (candidate in North Kilkenny election), 116, 117n15
Scuola Commerciale di Perfezionamento, Joyce appointed to teach at, 722
Scuola Superiore di Commercio, 'Revoltella,' closing of, 813; Joyce appointed to, 760–61; Joyce resumes position at, 830; Joyce suspended without pay from, 811
Sebag Montefiore, Joseph (Sir), 782
Second World War, xxvii, 534, 778; completion of *Finnegans Wake* after, 15; Joyce's reception after, 6, 822
Sexton, Thomas (politician), 68n73, 718
'Shade of Parnell, The.' *See* 'L'ombra di Parnell'
Shakespeare, William, 264, 818; Joyce lectures on *Hamlet*, 760; reference to *Henry V* in *Ulysses*, 148; Shylock (*Merchant of Venice*), 781, 782; theory on Hamlet in *Ulysses*, 446
Shaw, George Bernard, 290, 716, 717, 718; 'The Impossibilities of Anarchism', 538n64; *The Shewing-Up of Blanco Posnet*, 716
Shaw, William (politician), 68, 205
Shawe-Taylor, John (Captain), 608
Sheehan, Daniel T. (medical student, University College), defends *Playboy*, 624–25
Sheehan, Stephen (solicitor), 63
Sheehy, David (nationalist member of Parliament), 288, 492n30, 612; family as model for the Daniels in *Stephen Hero*, 491; wife Elizabeth 'Bessie', 288. *See also entries for daughters:* Kettle, Mary, née Sheehy; O'Brien, Kathleen Sheehy; Skeffington, Hanna Sheehy-
Sheehy, Eugene (nationalist priest, brother of David Sheehy), suggested model for Fr Healy in *Stephen Hero*, 492n30

Sheehy, Eugene (son of David Sheehy), 56, 264n20, 651n97; description of George Clancy, 335; *May It Please the Court*, 268n34, 651n97; physical description of Joyce, 267–68; recalls Joyce wearing ivy leaf to school, 152; recalls Kettle and Skeffington, 288, 292

Sheehy, Richard (son of David Sheehy), 267, 288, 625; recalls condemnation of *Countess Cathleen*, 624; signs letter of protest against *Countess Cathleen*, 279

Sheridan, Niall (architect and Joyce scholar), 87–88, 87n120

Sherlock, Lorcan (Lord Mayor of Dublin), 132

Silvestri, Tullio, 811

Simpkin Marshall (publisher), 746

Sinclair, William and Harry (Jewish friends of Joyce in Dublin), 770n8

Sinn Féin (newspaper), 619; anti-Semitism in, 611; cartoon 'The Shade of Parnell' in, 732; Gogarty's articles in, 608–11; Griffith as founder editor of, 177, 426, 731; Griffith's editorial on twenty-first anniversary of First Home Rule Bill, 683; Home Rule and, 479, 683, 686; Joyce meets Griffith at offices of, 432–33; Joyce's reading of, 177, 523, 592, 593–95, 599, 613, 684; Kettle and, 730; Parnell and, 37, 730–31, 733–34; *Playboy of the Western World* and, 623; publishes Joyce's open letter, 432, 726; reviews in, 180n61; sanctimony of, 609n35, 613–16; as successor to *United Irishman*, 592n2

Sinn Féin (political movement founded by Griffith in 1905), 345, 416, 454, 730, 786; Bloom and, 786; Catholic Church and, 607; George Clancy and, 344–45, 346; Con Curran and, 485; economic programme of, 600–606, 652; emergence of, 596, 603, 616–17, 619; in *Finnegans Wake*, 80n106; founding of, 427; Gaelic League and, 355–56; Griffith as founder of, 316, 360, 426, 599–600; Home Rule and, 332; Irish language and, 372, 613; Stanislaus Joyce, hostility to, 459, 591, 812; Joyce's interest in, 9–10, 15, 190, 356, 424, 458, 478, 508; Joyce's interest in from Rome and Trieste, 519, 535, 536–37, 558, 591, 612–13, 675, 680; Joyce's movement away from, 737; Kettle and, 316–17, 323–24; National Council as precursor of, 422, 426; origins of, 416, 418, 421, 422, 604; Parnell and, 39, 711; Parnellism and, 551; precursors, 454, 599; socialism and, 460, 478, 524. *See also* Griffith, Arthur

Skeffington, Francis Sheehy-, 289–309, *291*, 334, 651; anti-Parnellism of, xix, 273, 293, 319, 320; John Francis Byrne and, 351–52, 353, 465; as contemporary of Joyce in University College, 35, 234, 284n86, 287, 292, 598, 612; *Countess Cathleen* and, 279, 280, 280n72, 623–24; on Davitt, 180n61, 292–95, 292n19, 294n27, 295n30, 298; death of, 309, 309n72, 312, 353, 815, 827; Gaelic League, against, 277, 290–91, 298n37, 309; Griffith and, 605–6; hyphenates name on marriage, 290; Irish Parliamentary Party and, 32; Kettle and, 288, 295n30, 309–11, 309n73, 312n84, 320, 323, 334, 460, 525, 591; marriage of, 290; as model for MacCann in *Portrait*, 298, 300, 337; as model for McCann in *Stephen Hero*, 298, 299n39, 491–93, 504–5; *Nationist* and, 314–16, 594–95; opposes influence of Catholic Church, 292, 294; organizes signatures for Tsar's petition, 303–4; physical description, 289, 290, 361; *Playboy of the Western World* and, 448, 626; politics in contrast to Joyce's, 272–73, 293, 298, 305, 307–9, 596, 615, 651; politics of, 33, 294, 346, 536, 582; publishes article alongside Joyce, 281; records Joyce's novel in diary, 465; refuses loan to Joyce, 306; W. T. Stead and, 295–98; supports rights of women,

Skeffington, Francis Sheehy (*continued*) 305, 582; visits United States, 351; works: 'Dialogues of the Day', 592, 595, 597, 599, 609n35; *Forgotten Aspect of the University Question, A*, 305, 598; 'Irish Playwrights and the Irish Public', 280n72, 625n71; *Michael Davitt*, 292n19, 293, 294n27, 295n30; 'Michael Davitt's Unfinished Campaign', 292, 292n19; 'Stray Thoughts about the Modern Dramatic Movement in Ireland', 626
Skeffington, Hanna Sheehy- (wife of Francis Sheehy-Skeffington), 288, 289, 290, 291
Skrivanich, Alois (student of Joyce in Trieste), 650
Slataper, Scipio (writer and irredentist), 646n72, 654; description of Trieste, 643–44; enlists in Italian army, 645–46; *Il mio Carso*, 646
Slavs, 655, 829; cultural tension, 642; irridentist sympathy with and fear of, 644–47; Joyce compares Celts to, 675–76; Joyce's engagement with, 650, 652–53
Smith, Elder & Company (publishers), 576
Smith, F. E. (Conservative politician), 687
Smith O'Brien, William (Irish nationalist member of Parliament), 621
social democracy, Austrian Social Democrats, 646–47; German, 455–56; German Social Democrats, 826; Joyce's sympathy with, 515–16; revolutionary socialism and, 805
socialism, xvi; anarchism and, xx, 524–25, 538, 539; anticlericalism and, 526, 528; British socialism, 737; Catholic Church and, 208, 222, 264, 381, 490, 526; *Dubliners* and, 540; *Finnegans Wake* and, 477–78, 842; Germany and, 532; Ibsen and, 541; Irish, 35, 460; Irish Nationalism and, 519, 536; Italian, 516–18, 521–23, 525, 617; Stanislaus Joyce and, 459; Joyce's disillusion with, 659; Joyce's identification with, 510–16; Joyce's interest in, 227, 300, 457, 477–79; Joyce's loss of interest in, 535–36, 588, 844–45; Joyce's reading of Ferrero, 528–29; Joyce's study of, 476–78, 524, 685; 'Painful Case, A' and, 458; Parnellism and, 558; 'Portrait of the Artist' essay and, 453–54, 456; Ryan and, 273; Sinn Féin and, 612; *Stephen Hero* and, 499, 501; Triestine socialism, 646–47, 648; 'Two Gallants' and, 570; Wilde and, 456–57, 478, 713
Società di Minerva, 649
Solemn League and Covenant, signed in resistance to Home Rule, 476, 832
Solomons, Maurice (consul for Austro-Hungarian Empire), 786
Sonne, Isaiah (rabbi), Joyce discusses Greek-Hebrew cognates with, 807
Sordina, Francesco (Count), 806; Joyce's permission to leave Trieste secured by, 813, 814n17
Sorel, George, 518–19; *Réflexions sur la violence*, 519
South Africa, Boer War, 418; Griffith in, 426, 605; South African War, 431
Spain, 239, 489, 490, 670; expulsion of Jews from, 808; Spanish Civil War, 838
Special Commission [on Parnellism and Crime], 75n92; *Finnegans Wake* and, 707; Healy and, 87; Joyce's engagement with, 744; Parnell and, 82, 731; Pigott and, 21, 144; prelude to, 143; Stead's attendance at, 237; *The Times'* report on, 141n103
Spencer, Herbert (English philosopher), 512, 670
Spencer, John (Lord) (Viceroy), 75; with Lady Spencer, 699; Maamtrasna and, 697–700
Split, the, anti-Parnellites in, 83, 141, 185, 188, 216–17, 219, 223, 228, 272–73, 293–94, 319, 320, 395, 492n30, 549, 557n59; Catholic Church and, 36, 198–217, 552; Christmas dinner scene and, xiv, 30, 81–82, 166–70,

171–74, 183; John Clancy and, 126, 130; Committee Room debates as source of, 24, 26; cultural destitution after, 395; Davitt and, 180; effect on Joyce of, 5, 29, 32, 152; effect on Parnell's health of, 28; *Finnegans Wake* and, 37; Griffith's support for Parnell during, 423, 591; T. M. Healy and, 183–86, 567, 837; Hyde exploits disillusionment over, 357; 'Ivy Day in the Committee Room' and, 543; John Stanislaus Joyce and, 52–57, 82–83, 88–89; Joyce adopts Parnell's perspective of, 190, 195–96; Joyce's conception of Irish politics inflected by, 153; Joyce's critique of, 33, 193; Joyce's opposition to Kettle in attitudes towards, 319; Joyce's 'two masters' thesis and, 33–36, 197, 250–53, 758; John Kelly and, 116, 118, 119, 121; 'long Split', 90, 192, 194, 544; newspapers of, 174–76; newspaper wars of, 183–86; O'Leary, John and, 186–87, 192; *A Portrait* and, 161–65, 223–24, 298; relation of Ireland to England during, 242–49; as repudiation of the modern, 253–55; reunion of Parnell's party after, 194. *See also* Healy, Timothy Michael; Irish Parliamentary Party; Parnell, Charles Stewart, political life

Staley, Thomas (Joyce scholar), 723

La Stampa (newspaper), 713

Star (newspaper), 238n123

Starkie, Walter (writer), 621

Stead, W. T. (editor of *Review of Reviews*), 195, 225n86; on Catholic Church, 246; death of, 296; as exponent of nonconformist conscience, 301; influence on Skeffington, 290, 293, 295, 298; journalism of, 234, 238, 247–48; Joyce's view of, 249; letters to Gladstone, 237–38, 241; moralism of, 235, 241; O'Shea divorce crisis and, 236; *Pall Mall Gazette* and, 232, 237; visit to Ireland, 236. See also *Review of Reviews*

Stead, W. T., works: *Discrowned King of Ireland, The*, 238–41, 240n126; 'Maiden Tribute of Modern Babylon, The', 235; 'North Kilkenny and Its Moral', 244–48; *War against War*, 299

Steed, Henry Wickham (journalist and historian), 804–5

Stephen Hero (unfinished novel by Joyce), artistic egoism of, 540; as bildungsroman, xx, 486, 507; Catholic Church and, 487–91, 495, 503, 526; Christmas party in, 172; difficulty of writing, 466, 505, 508; *Finnegans Wake* and, 509, 822; Griffith in, 435, 654–55; as impasse, 506–9; Irish language in, 354, 363, 589; lost chapters of, 483, 485, 497; manuscript of, 415; nationalism and, 12, 499–505; as origin of *Portrait*, 450, 505; Parnell in, 493; 'the patriots' in, 360–61, 491–96; poem about Parnell in, 157, 169–70; politics of, 476–77, 483–86; recasting of early essay as, 451; socialism in, 512, 515; the Split in, 298; Stead in, 299–300; tentativeness of, 461

Stephen Hero, fictional characters: Mr [John] Casey, 124–25; Emma Clery, 361, 492; Cranly, 264–65, 271, 299, 347, 487; Daniels family, 491–93, 492n30, 495, 569n78; Simon Daedalus, 55, 71, 93–94, 269; Stephen Daedalus, 495–96, as author 'Art and Life,' 124, 500n58, 501, and 'enigma of a manner', 263–66, as literary artist, 7n3, 263, 268, 269n39, 499–501, 513, and nationalism, 491, 499–505, 508, and paralysis, 463; Fr Healy, 492–93, 569n78; Madden, 334, 361, 374n48, 435, 491, 501–2, 503, 463n205; McCann, 298–99, 301n46, 491–93, 504–5; Moynihan, 264

Stephens, James (Fenian leader), 138; Patrick and Joseph Casey and, 139; escape of, 149–50; at Parnell's funeral, 189, and grave, 120; return from Paris, 130, 146; in *Ulysses*, 150

Stephens, James (writer), befriends Joyce in Paris, 346, 424; informs Joyce on Easter Rising, 827, 833; introduces Patrick Tuohy to Joyce, 108
Stirling, James (Conservative candidate), 60, 60n45, 65, 67–68, 67n70
Stirner, Max (German philosopher), Joyce's reading of, 511, 512
St Mary's Abbey Synagogue (Dublin), 771–75
Stokes, Whitley (lawyer and Celtic scholar), 585–86, 585nn115–116
Strauss, Richard (German composer), 643, 713
St Stephen's Review (college magazine), conferring ceremony and, 283; 'The Day of the Rabblement' vetoed from, 281; Joyce offers 'The Holy Office' to, 463; Joyce's aloofness noted in, 264, 381; Joyce's future considered in, 282; Joyce's refusal to sign *Countess Cathleen* letter noted in, 279; Skeffington satirised in, 303
Stubbs' Gazette (newspaper), John Stanislaus Joyce's name appears in, 95
Sturli, Adriano (pupil of Joyce in Trieste), 635
Sullivan, A. M. (barrister and parliamentarian), 328n138
Sullivan, John (Irish opera singer), 88n123, 101, 107, 109
Sullivan, T. D. (Irish nationalist and politician), 430
Suppressed United Ireland (Irish newspaper), anti-Parnellism of, 135, 184
Svevo, Italo. *See* Schmitz, Ettore
Sweetman, John (anti-Parnellite member of Parliament), 603, 604
Swift, Jonathan, 107n190, 329
Sykes, Claud (stage actor and director), 828
Symons, Arthur, Joyce's engagement with, 256; reviews *Chamber Music*, 632
Synge, John Millington, criticism of Irish language revival, 407; death, 713; 'Gas from a Burner' references to, 756–57; Griffith's misjudgment of, 432; Joyce meets in Paris, 404–6, 434; Lady Gregory, letter to, 405–6; *Playboy* riots, reaction to, 621; Pound discusses, 821; published by George Roberts, 756; *Riders to the Sea*, 406, 621, 625–26, 649, and Joyce's translation of, 713; Skeffington and, 626; in *Ulysses*, 405; Yeats and, 405n20, 624n70, 627. *See also Playboy of the Western World, The*

Tamaro, Attilio (secretary of Università Popolare), as anti-Slav, 675–76; author pamphlet *L'Adriatico—golfo d'Italia*, 646; invites Joyce to contribute articles, 641, 662; as irredentist and historian, 646, 655
Taxil, Léo (French journalist), 149n130; recalled in *Ulysses*, 148
Taylor, John Francis, 195; in 'Aeolus', 355, 365, 367, 387–94; article in *Freeman's Journal*, 374; attends L&H, 258–59, 264; *Callista* and, 384–87; Davitt and, 382; death of, 365; Edward Dowden and, 377; Griffith and, 369, 372, 379, 382, 383, 384, 384n72; Irish language revivalism and, 371, 375, 378, 379; Joyce's knowledge of, 381–83; King's Inns speech and, 364, 371, 394–98; 'Mr. Rolleston's Recantation', 383, 384, 431; John O'Leary and, 430–31; oratory compared to Joyce's, 264; Parnell and, 243–44; Yeats and, 368–69, 380–81, 397n102
Le Temps (newspaper), Joyce's reading of, 177
Times, The (newspaper), attempts to establish Parnell's complicity in terrorism, 145; Joyce's reading of, 177; 'nonconformist conscience' in, 231–32; publishes letters from Parnell, 21; Special Commission and, 141n103, 143; Stead

attempts to discredit case of, 237; Steed and, 236, 804, 805; Tolstoy's extended letter to, 515
Tito, Josip Broz (Yugoslavian politician), 635
Tolstoy, Leo, 515; Joyce engages with anarchism of, 538–39; Joyce's praise of, 829n68; political influence on Joyce, 299n38
trade unions, 550n27; revolutionary syndicalists and, 517, Joyce's description of, 521
Transatlantic Review (literary magazine), first extract from 'Work in Progress' published in, 837; Stanislaus Joyce receives copy of, 80n107
transition (journal), publishes instalments of 'Work in Progress', 837
Treaty of London (1915), 810–11
Trench, Samuel Chevenix (model for Haines in *Ulysses*), 469
Trieste, xi, xviii, 543, 761; brothels of, 639; climate of, 748; economy of, 640, 652, 806, 830; *Finnegans Wake* and, 762, 764; irredentism in, 649–55, 674; *italianità* of, 643, 644, 646, 656, 662, 764; Jews of, 768, 791–800, 803; Stanislaus Joyce and, 153–54, 476, 617, 632–33, 656n111, 676, 722, 795–96; Joyce living in (1910–1912), 722–29, and (1919), 829–31; Joyce's drinking in, 638; Joyce's lectures in, 662–76; Joyce's letters to Stanislaus from, 590, 591, 619, 723; Joyce unsentimental about, 764; landscape of, 630; politics of, 641–48; pupils of Joyce in, 633, 634–41, 649–50, 723, 792, 800, 811, 828; Socialist Party of, 648, 659, 829; *triestinità* of, 642, 764; *triestino* dialect, 635, 638, 650, 764–65; in *Ulysses*, 767
Trinity College Dublin, 143, 191, 284, 377, 418, 467, 592; as electoral constituency, 60; Irish language and, in J. F. Taylor's speech, 376–77; A. J. Leventhal, lectures in, 778; *Playboy* riots and, 622; University of Bonn and, 598
Tripcovich, Mario (Count) (student of Joyce in Trieste), 649
Triple Alliance, 810, 811n5, 815
Tristan and Isolde ('Tristram and Iseult'), 233n108, 574; Diarmaid and Grainne and, 586
Tucker, Benjamin (anarchist writer), Joyce's reading of, 512–13, 513n7
Tuohy, Patrick, 46, 237; death of, 111; paints Joyce, 109–10; portrait of John Stanislaus Joyce and, 107n190, 108–10
Turati, Filippo (Italian socialist politician), 516
'Two Gallants, The' (story in *Dubliners*), 510n1; added to *Dubliners*, 542; English printers refuse to print, 530; Ferrero's influence on, 571–72; harp image in, 572–74, 579, 581; relation of Myles Joyce to, 706; 'Song of Fionnuala' ('Silent, O'Moyle') in, 570, 571, 582
'two masters' thesis (of Joyce), 250, 252, 488; British Empire and Catholic Church, 196–213; 'coincidence of opposites' and, 198, 242–49, 251, 689; destruction of *Dubliners* and, 758; *Irish Catholic* and, 217–24; Stanislaus Joyce's account of, 750; *Lyceum* and, 225–31; origins of, 195–98; in *Portrait*, 300–301; Skeffington's 'twin tyrannies' equated to, 292; the Split and, 33–36, 253–55; in *Ulysses*, 196, 252–53, 490–91
Tymoczko, Maria (Joyce scholar), 584
Tynan, Katharine (writer), 319, 669n32, 695n110; John O'Leary and, 187, 188; poem in response to Parnell's death, 221; the Split and, 395, 562
typhoid, John Stanislaus Joyce possibly suffering from, 50n26; Joyce's brother Georgie dies of, 277; Joyce's grandfather dies of, 50; Joyce's sister Mabel dies of, 103, 412n53

ultramontanism, of First Vatican Council (1869–70), 228, 228nn96–97, 490

Ulysses, 630, 831; anti-Semitism in, 784, 787–91, 796, 805; County Cork and, 47n13; Ferrero and, 531; foot-and-mouth disease in, 748, 749n139; formal and temporal constraints of, 837, 840; ghosts in, 278n63, 388; Ivy Day (annual commemoration) in, 565; 'Jewgreek is Greekjew' in, 807; Jews and, 533, 535, 655n108, 671n36, 768–69, 773, 776, 778, 785–87, 794, 798; John Stanislaus Joyce, influence on, 45, 55, 74, 113; Joyce records reading of, 394; left-wing critical arguments about, 540; miscegenation in, 671n36; 'Parable of the Plums', 393; Parnell in, xvii, xviii, 37, 39, 392, 734; piracy of, 534; political violence in, 681; reception of, 833; short story as genesis of, 531, 649n84, 729; sparse reference to Irish Party in, 608; 'Tinahely twelve' in, 349; Triestine experiences referenced in, 653, 765, 767; 'un libro di Zois' as, 634n19; writing of, 808, 813, 817, 831, 834

Ulysses, episodes of: 'Calypso', 792, 793–94; 'Circe', 197, 235n114, 278, 304, 446, 827n58; 'Ithaca', 351, 363, 396, 720, 774–75, 794; 'Lestrygonians', 783; 'Lotus Eaters', 546n7; 'Nestor', 431, 803n108; 'Proteus', 267, 766; 'Scylla and Charybdis', 819, 837; 'Sirens', 471; 'Telemachus', 33, 196–98, 252–53, 490–91; 'Wandering Rocks', 135–36, 350–51, 616n49, 691, 773–74. *See also main entries for* 'Aeolus' episode, *Ulysses*; 'Cyclops' episode, *Ulysses*; 'Eumeus' episode, *Ulysses*

Ulysses, fictional characters: Marian ('Molly') Bloom, 74, 137–38, 467–68, 471; Rudolph Bloom, 804, 809; O'Madden Burke, 393, 774; Mr [John] Casey, 125; Dr Punch Costello, 803; Myles Crawford, 191, 389, 463, 717; Martin Cunningham, 136n84, 790; Garrett Deasy, 749n139, 805; Mat Dillon, 137, 137n88; Kevin Egan, 148–51, 766–67; 'Long John' Fanning, 126, 134, 136, 136n84; Geraghty, 784; Haines, 196–97, 469, 618–19; Moses Herzog, 784; Ned Lambert, 773n21, 774, 784; Hugh C. Love, 774; Bantam Lyons, 396–97; professor MacHugh, 355, 366, 387–94, 387n79, 396; Buck Mulligan, 351, 405, 442, 778; J. J. O'Molloy, 168n39, 191, 366, 388–92, 396, 774; Dante Riordan, 171n45, 172. *See also* Bloom, Leopold; Dedalus, Simon; Dedalus, Stephen

Under the Receding Wave (Curran), 170n44, 225n87 and n88, 259, 279n70, 304n59; Hegel and Kettle in, 322n121; on Joyce and prophecy, 308n71; on politics of Joyce, 32n13, 272–73; on politics of Sheehy-Skeffington, 272–73

Unionists, 42, 52, 146, 369, 417, 545; *Daily Express*, as newspaper of, 61, 65, 76n95, 136; Garrett Deasy as, 805; Dublin election 1880 and, 60; in *Dubliners*, 545, 550; in *Finnegans Wake*, 397; Home Rule and, 252, 416, 577, 579, 832; *Irish Times* and, 367; Parnell as target of, 20; the Split and, 369

United Ireland (newspaper), 216–17; Mathias McDonnell Bodkin, as editor of, 134; cartoons in, 302; John Clancy and, 117, 134, 135; critique of Catholic Church, 205n36, 206n38; extravagant prose of, 75; 'historic fracas' of in *Ulysses*, 27; John Kelly in, 116; Maamtrasna and, 702; William O'Brien as editor of, 128; Parnell and, 37, 178–79, 184, 421n90; Parnell ousts anti-Parnellites from office of, 27; Parnell, visual images in, 302; response to *Irish Catholic*, 221; response to Parnellite defeat in 1892 election, 215–16; verses on death of Parnell in, 159

United Irish League, George Clancy's involvement in, 342; convention of, 682, 684; establishment of, 131; Grange

Branch of, 343; Griffith and, 691n96; Skeffington's resignation from, 309; Young Ireland Branch (Yibs) of, 312–13, 316, 460
United Irishman (newspaper), 314; account of Queen's visit in, 420–21; as basis for Joyce's Paris-Pola Commonplace Book, 433; ceases publication April 1906, 592n2; James Connolly, candidacy endorsed in, 551; *The Countess Cathleen* and, 325; John Creagh, defense in, 785; 'The Destruction of Da Dearga's Hostel' published in, 435; founding of, 605; Maud Gonne and, 592; Griffith, as editor of, 177, 314, 423, 426–28, 551; Griffith's *Resurrection of Hungary* origin as articles in, 426, 617; hostility to the Abbey, 622; Joyce defends, 595–96; Joyce's reading of, 423–35, 460, 592, 596, 617; Kettle and, 320, 325; *Language of the Outlaw* pamphlet printed in, 365; W. K. Magee and, 446; review of *Story of the Harp* in, 572–79; William Rooney and, 426–28; succeeded by *Sinn Féin*, 592n2; J. F. Taylor as contributor to, 369, 383; J. F. Taylor, obituary in, 383, 384n72; Yeats's reviews in, 445. *See also* Griffith, Arthur
United Liberal Club, 68, 68n73; *Freeman's Journal* on, 67; John Stanislaus Joyce, as secretary of, 59–60, 65, 76; as pro-Home Rule, 69
United States, 128, 145, 825; Byrne emigrates to, 351; Connolly returns from, 459; intellectuals in, 477; Irish Party emissaries in, 239; Irish Republican Brotherhood in, 18; piracy of *Ulysses* in, 534; Skeffington visits, 351; in *Stephen Hero*, 492
Università Popolare, 641, 646, 662; Joyce delivers lectures in, 208, 420, 653, 675, 727, 760
University College, Dublin, 258; Thomas Arnold teaches at, 801; J. F. Byrne at, 347–50; George Clancy at, 337–39, 342; *Countess Cathleen* denounced in, 272–73, 276–82, 303–4, 325, 627; Con Curran and, 485; degree conferring, 282–83; establishing of, 257, 283; Gaelic League and, 335, 338, 362; 'Gas from a Burner' and, 282–85; graduation class 1902 photo, *260*; Irish Revival and, 261–62, 355–60; Joyce at, 56, 256–86, 324, 433, 452, 514, 815; Joyce's veiled Parnellism in, 272–76, 832; T. M. Kettle as student, 310–12, 324, and lecturer, 311; L&H debates at, 285, 757; Padraig Pearse and, 284n86, 338, 362–63; reconstituted, 257, 716; Skeffington at, 289, 292, 612; *Stephen Hero* and, 260–61, 362, 484; women and the 'university question', 305, 597

Vallencey, Charles (English antiquarian), 807
Vance, Eileen (Joyce's childhood friend), Ellmann's interview with, 171n45
Vanhomrigh, Esther (lover and correspondent of Swift), 107n190
Vatican, 489, 685; First Vatican Council, 621; Index of Prohibited Books, 281; Library of, 160n18
Vaughan, Bernard, S.J, 615–16; in *Ulysses*, 616n49
Venezian, Felice (leading irredentist), 645, 648, 791, 799
Veneziani, Gioacchino (father of Livia Veneziani Schmitz), 635; Joyce works for, 812
Vico, Giambattista (Italian philosopher and historian), 634, 840
Victoria (British monarch), 142, 605; Dublin visit, 131, 419–21, 665–66; in 'Ivy Day in the Committee Room', 725; in *Portrait*, 123; in *Ulysses*, 149, 766–67

Vidacovich, Nicolò (pupil and friend of Joyce in Trieste), 649; collaborates with Joyce on Synge translation, 406, 713, 713n7
Vidan, Ivo (Joyce scholar), on Joyce's engagement with Slav culture, 650

Wagner, Richard, 643, 726n65; *Die Meistersinger* in *Ulysses*, 714, 714n14
Waldron, L. A. (member of Parliament), John Stanislaus Joyce sues, 98–99, 137
Walsh, William (Archbishop of Dublin), attends Taylor debate, 367; letters by, 202, 204n34, 211n51, 718; in the Split, 198, 202–4, 222
War of Independence, Irish, 288; Joyce reads about from Paris, 834; violence of, 340
Weaver, Harriet Shaw, 157, 160, 279n69, 821, 837; as benefactor to Joyce, 828–29; Egoist Press and, 239, 821; Joyce provides autobiography to, 361; letters from Joyce, 45, 68, 107n190, 110, 113, 157n11, 804, 806
Weekly News (newspaper), 218
Weininger, Otto, Joyce's reading of, 802, 803; Stephen Dedalus and, 803n108
Weiss, Ottocaro (friend of Joyce), 794–95, 802
Wells, H. G., suggests Joyce move to England, 820
Whitman, Walt, mentioned by Joyce in review, 440
Wilde, Oscar, 107n190, 464, 747; Catholic Church and, 401; fall of, 248n141; Gogarty emulates, 408; influence on *Exiles*, 330–31; influence on Joyce's politics, 515, 538; Joyce's essay on, 713, 717n28; Joyce's view of, 672, 744, 745; in *Stephen Hero*, 500n57; trial of in *Finnegans Wake*, 707; works: *De Profundis*, 464; *Importance of Being Earnest*, 828; *Soul of Man under Socialism*, 456–57, 478, 500n57, 713, 714n9
Wilfan, Josip (member of Italian parliament and student of Joyce), 649–50
working class, 423, 647, 826; of Dublin, 779; influence of socialism on, 522; Joyce aligns to politics of in Trieste, 652–53; Joyce drinks with in Trieste, 638; Labriola discusses, 518; in the Split, 130; in Trieste, 645, 648
Wyndham, George (chief secretary for Ireland), 372
Wyndham Land Act (1903), 416, 688

Yeats, Jack Butler (artist), recalls seeing John Stanislaus Joyce at Parnellite rally, 86
Yeats, John Butler (artist), 405n20; dines with Joyce, 404
Yeats, William Butler, 310, 393, 399, 413, 577; Abbey Theatre and, 622, 629; Padraic Colum and, 409; *Dana* and, 444; Gaelic League and, 282n78; Griffith misjudges, 432; Ibsen and, 280; Joyce and, 451, 627, 678–79, 822–23, 845; Joyce, meetings with, 400–404, 411, 587, 746; Joyce's view of, 279, 325, 437, 439, 501, 582, 613–14, 627; T. M. Kettle and, 626–27; Lady Gregory and, 358n8, 404, 407, 411, 586, 622, 627; Magee and, 445, 446; John O'Leary and, 187, 430–31; Parnell and, 480–81, 850–51; Parnell myth and, 29, 194, 480, 562; *Playboy* and, 480, 621–22, 623, 625; Pound and, 819–21; Queen Victoria's visit, condemns, 419; reviews Fr Patrick Dineen, 282; the Revival and, 407; Skeffington and, 280; the Split and, 29, 191, 194, 395, 482, 562; on Synge, 406, 626; Tailteann Games and, 759; J. F. Taylor and, 368–69, 380–81, 397n102; as true addressee of 'The Holy Office', 464–65, 466; in *Ulysses*, 442; Wilde and, 672n41
Yeats, William Butler, works: 'Adoration of the Magi, The' (short story, also anthologized in *'Tables of the Law' and*

the 'Adoration of the Magi'), 282, 403, 403n10; *Autobiographies*, 267n31, 381n63; *The Celtic Twilight*, 439; 'Come Gather Round Me, Parnellites', 217; *Explorations*, 445n150; *Ideas of Good and Evil*, 401; 'Modern Ireland' lecture, 177, 402–3; 'Mourn and Then Onwards', 161–62; *Reveries over Childhood and Youth*, 380; 'September 1913', 480; 'To a Shade', 850–51; *Trembling of the Veil*, 368–69, 380–81, 402; 'Who Goes with Fergus', 278; *Wind among the Reeds*, 282. See also *Countess Cathleen, The*

Yibs. *See* United Irish League

Young Ireland League, Yeats and O'Leary collaborate to establish, 191

Young Ireland movement, 429, 678, 845; Joyce describes, 678, 679; Thomas D'Arcy McGee and, 430; Terence Bellew McManus and, 265

Yugoslavia, 635, 829

Zionism, 14n14; Irish nationalism and, 769; Joyce and, 769, 794, 795; limited support for among Triestine Jews, 791; revival of Irish language and, 792; Steed's support for, 805

Zola, Émile, 234n111, 625, 768

Zürcher Post (newspaper), 828

Zurich, Switzerland, death of Joyce in, 534; during First World War, 814–19; Joyce lives in, 822–30